AUTOMOTIVE CHASSIS SYSTEMS

FIFTH EDITION

James D. Halderman

Prentice Hall
Boston   Columbus   Indianapolis   New York   San Francisco   Upper Saddle River
Amsterdam   Cape Town   Dubai   London   Madrid   Milan   Munich   Paris   Montreal
Toronto   Delhi   Mexico City   Sao Paulo   Sydney   Hong Kong   Seoul   Singapore   Taipei   Tokyo

Editor in Chief: Vernon Anthony
Acquisitions Editor: Wyatt Morris
Editorial Assistant: Christopher Reed
Director of Marketing: David Gesell
Marketing Manager: Kara Clark
Senior Marketing Coordinator: Alicia
Wozniak
Marketing Assistant: Les Roberts
Senior Managing Editor: JoEllen Gohr
Project Manager: Jessica H. Sykes
Senior Operations Supervisor: Pat
Tonneman
Operations Specialist: Laura Weaver

Senior Art Director: Diane Ernsberger
Text and Cover Designer: Anne DeMarinis
Cover Art: Shutterstock
Media Editor: Michelle Churma
Lead Media Project Manager: Karen Bretz
Full-Service Project Management: Kelli Jauron
Composition: S4Carlisle Publishing Services
Printer/Binder: Webcrafters, Inc.
Cover Printer: Lehigh-Phoenix Color/Hagerstown
Text Font: Helvetica Neue

10 9 8 7 6 5 4 3 2 1

Prentice Hall
is an imprint of

PEARSON

www.pearsonhighered.com

ISBN 10:   0-13-508503-9
ISBN 13: 978-0-13-508503-5

PREFACE

PROFESSIONAL TECHNICIAN SERIES Part of Pearson Automotive's Professional Technician Series, the fifth edition of *Automotive Chassis Systems* represents the future of automotive textbooks. The series is a full-color, media-integrated solution for today's students and instructors. The series includes textbooks that cover all 8 areas of ASE certification, plus additional titles covering common courses.

Current revisions are written by a team of very experienced writers and teachers. The series is also peer reviewed for technical accuracy.

UPDATES TO THE FIFTH EDITION

- All content is correlated to the latest NATEF and ASE tasks.

- A dramatic, new full-color design enhances the subject material.

- One entirely new chapter has been added on **Electronic Stability Control Systems** (Chapter 20). This important new chapter covers the purpose, function, parts, and operation of the electronic stability control system that uses the antilock brake system components to control vehicle stability.

- Over 40 new color photos and line drawings have been added to this edition.

- Content has been streamlined for easier reading and comprehension.

- This text is fully integrated with MyAutomotiveKit, an online supplement for homework, quizzing, testing, multimedia activities, and videos.

- Unlike other textbooks, this book is written so that the theory, construction, diagnosis, and service of a particular component or system is presented in one location. There is no need to search through the entire book for other references to the same topic.

ASE AND NATEF CORRELATED NATEF certified programs need to demonstrate that they use course material that covers NATEF and ASE tasks. All Professional Technician textbooks have been correlated to the appropriate ASE and NATEF task lists. These correlations can be found in two locations:

- As an appendix to each book.
- At the beginning of each chapter in the Annotated Instructor's Guide.

A COMPLETE INSTRUCTOR AND STUDENT SUPPLEMENTS PACKAGE All Professional Technician textbooks are accompanied by a full set of instructor and student supplements. Please see page vi for a detailed list of supplements.

A FOCUS ON DIAGNOSIS AND PROBLEM SOLVING The Professional Technician Series has been developed to satisfy the need for a greater emphasis on problem diagnosis. Automotive instructors and service managers agree that students and beginning technicians need more training in diagnostic procedures and skill development. To meet this need and demonstrate how real-world problems are solved, "Real World Fix" features are included throughout and highlight how real-life problems are diagnosed and repaired.

The following pages highlight the unique core features that set the Professional Technician Series book apart from other automotive textbooks.

SAFETY TIP

Shop Cloth Disposal

Always dispose of oily shop cloths in an enclosed container to prevent a fire. ● **SEE FIGURE 1–69.** Whenever oily cloths are thrown together on the floor or workbench, a chemical reaction can occur, which can ignite the cloth even without an open flame. This process of ignition without an open flame is called **spontaneous combustion.**

SAFETY TIPS alert students to possible hazards on the job and how to avoid them.

OBJECTIVES AND KEY TERMS appear at the beginning of each chapter to help students and instructors focus on the most important material in each chapter. The chapter objectives are based on specific ASE and NATEF tasks.

REAL WORLD FIX

Three Brake Jobs in 40,000 Miles

A service technician was asked to replace the front disc brake pads on a Pontiac Grand Am because the sensors were touching the rotors and making a squealing sound. This was the third time that the front brakes needed to be replaced. Previous brake repairs had been limited to replacement of the front disc brake pads only.

When the caliper was removed and the pads inspected, it was discovered that a part of one pad had broken and a piece of the lining was missing. ● **SEE FIGURE 13–15.**

REAL WORLD FIXES present students with actual automotive scenarios and shows how these common (and sometimes uncommon) problems were diagnosed and repaired.

TECH TIP

It Just Takes a Second

Whenever removing any automotive component, it is wise to screw the bolts back into the holes a couple of threads by hand. This ensures that the right bolt will be used in its original location when the component or part is put back on the vehicle.

TECH TIPS feature real-world advice and "tricks of the trade" from ASE-certified master technicians.

 ### FREQUENTLY ASKED QUESTION

How Many Types of Screw Heads Are Used in Automotive Applications?

There are many, including Torx, hex (also called Allen), plus many others used in custom vans and motor homes. ● **SEE FIGURE 1–9.**

FREQUENTLY ASKED QUESTIONS are based on the author's own experience and provide answers to many of the most common questions asked by students and beginning service technicians.

NOTE: Most of these "locking nuts" are grouped together and are commonly referred to as *prevailing torque nuts*. This means that the nut will hold its tightness or torque and not loosen with movement or vibration.

NOTES provide students with additional technical information to give them a greater understanding of a specific task or procedure.

CAUTION: *Never* use hardware store (nongraded) bolts, studs, or nuts on any vehicle steering, suspension, or brake component. Always use the exact size and grade of hardware that is specified and used by the vehicle manufacturer.

CAUTIONS alert students about potential damage to the vehicle that can occur during a specific task or service procedure.

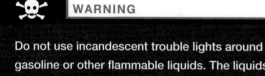

☠ **WARNING**

Do not use incandescent trouble lights around gasoline or other flammable liquids. The liquids can cause the bulb to break and the hot filament can ignite the flammable liquid which can cause personal injury or even death.

WARNINGS alert students to potential dangers to themselves during a specific task or service procedure.

THE SUMMARY, REVIEW QUESTIONS, AND CHAPTER QUIZ at the end of each chapter help students review the material presented in the chapter and test themselves to see how much they've learned.

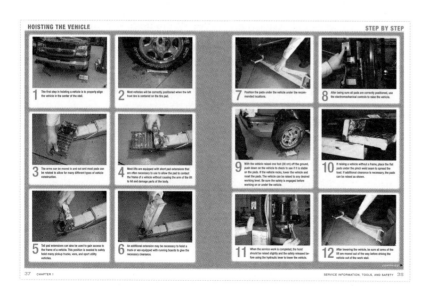

STEP-BY-STEP photo sequences show in detail the steps involved in performing a specific task or service procedure.

SUPPLEMENTS

INSTRUCTOR SUPPLEMENTS The instructor supplement package has been completely revamped to reflect the needs of today's instructors. The all new **Annotated Instructor's Guide (ISBN 0-13-509346-5)** is the cornerstone of the package and includes:

- Chapter openers that list
  - NATEF/ASE tasks covered in the chapter
  - all key terms
  - all Chapter Objectives
- The entire text (matching page numbers with student edition) with margin notes. These notes include:
  - Tips for in-class demonstrations
  - Suggested hands-on activities
  - Cross-curricular activities
  - Internet search tips
  - Assessments
  - Safety tips
  - Classroom discussion questions
- A guide to using MyAutomotiveKit in the course

Also, in every Professional Technician Series Annotated Instructor's Guide there is an **Instructor's CD** that contains:

- PowerPoint presentations*
- Image Library containing every image in the book for use in class or customized PowerPoints*
- Test Generator software and test bank*
- Chapter Quizzes
- Chapter Review Questions
- English and Spanish Glossary*
- NATEF Correlated task Sheets* (also available as a printed supplement [ISBN: 0-13-509377-5])
- NATEF/ASE Correlation Charts

* All of these are available for download from www.pearson-highered.com

MYAUTOMOTIVEKIT An offshoot of the extremely popular MyAutomotiveLab, these online kits can be used with all Professional Technician Series textbooks for quizzing, testing, homework, and multimedia activities. All assignments are automatically graded and entered into a gradebook for the course. In addition to assessment materials, MyAutomotiveKit includes:

- **Interactive Animations**
- Two- to five-minute **video clips** showing procedures
- A **3D virtual garage** that simulates the shop experience in the real world by focusing on customer complaints, conducting tests to determine the problem with the vehicle, and submitting a written work order to the instructor.
- All materials are broken down by chapter for easy navigation and use.

To get instructor access to MyAutomotiveKit, please visit

www.myautomotivekit.com

STUDENT SUPPLEMENTS   NO MORE CDs!!
As a result of extensive student input, Pearson is no longer binding CDs into automotive students' textbooks. Today's student has more access to the Internet than ever, so all supplemental materials are downloadable at the following site for no additional charge:

www.pearsoned.com/autostudent

On the site, students will find:

- PowerPoint presentations
- Chapter review questions and quizzes
- English and Spanish Glossary
- A full Spanish translation of the text
- Links to MyAutomotiveKit

MYAUTOMOTIVEKIT FOR THE STUDENT   For the student, **MyAutomotiveKit** is a one-stop shop for homework, quizzes, tests, and a new way of learning. Key concepts are reinforced through media. Students will find part identification activities, word search games, interactive animations, and a 3D virtual garage for help with diagnosis.

ACKNOWLEDGMENTS

A large number of people and organizations have cooperated in providing the reference material and technical information used in this text. The author wishes to express sincere thanks to the following organizations for their special contributions:

ASE
Automotion, Inc.
Automotive Parts Rebuilders Association (APRA)
Bendix
British Petroleum (BP)
Cooper Automotive Company
CR Services
Dana Corporation
Fluke Corporation
FMC Corporation
Ford Motor Company
Hennessy Industries
Hunter Engineering Company
Lee Manufacturing Company
MOOG Automotive Inc.
Perfect Hofmann-USA
SKF USA, Inc.
Society of Automotive Engineers (SAE)
Specialty Products Company
Tire and Rim Association, Inc.
Toyota Motor Sales, USA, Inc.
TRW Inc.
Wurth USA, Inc.

TECHNICAL AND CONTENT REVIEWERS The following people reviewed the manuscript before production and checked it for technical accuracy and clarity of presentation. Their suggestions and recommendations were included in the final draft of the manuscript. Their input helped make this textbook clear and technically accurate while maintaining the easy-to-read style that has made other books from the same author so popular.

Jim Anderson
Greenville High School

Victor Bridges
Umpqua Community College

Dr. Roger Donovan
Illinois Central College

A. C. Durdin
Moraine Park Technical College

Herbert Ellinger
Western Michigan University

Al Engledahl
College of Dupage

Larry Hagelberger
Upper Valley Joint Vocational School

Oldrick Hajzler
Red River College

Betsy Hoffman
Vermont Technical College

Steven T. Lee
Lincoln Technical Institute

Carlton H. Mabe, Sr.
Virginia Western Community College

Roy Marks
Owens Community College

Tony Martin
University of Alaska Southeast

Kerry Meier
San Juan College

Fritz Peacock
Indiana Vocational Technical College

Dennis Peter
NAIT (Canada)

Kenneth Redick
Hudson Valley Community College

Mitchell Walker
St. Louis Community College at Forest Park

Jennifer Wise
Sinclair Community College

Special thanks to instructional designer **Alexis I. Skriloff James.**

PHOTO SEQUENCES The author wishes to thank Blaine Heeter, Mike Garblik, and Chuck Taylor of Sinclair Community College in Dayton, Ohio, and James (Mike) Watson who helped with many of the photos.

Most of all, I wish to thank Michelle Halderman for her assistance in all phases of manuscript preparation.

—James D. Halderman

ABOUT THE AUTHOR

JIM HALDERMAN brings a world of experience, knowledge, and talent to his work. His automotive service experience includes working as a flat-rate technician, a business owner, and a professor of automotive technology at a leading U.S. community college for more than 20 years.

He has a Bachelor of Science Degree from Ohio Northern University and a Masters Degree in Education from Miami University in Oxford, Ohio. Jim also holds a U.S. Patent for an electronic transmission control device. He is an ASE certified Master Automotive Technician and Advanced Engine Performance (L1) ASE certified.

Jim is the author of many automotive textbooks all published by Prentice Hall.

Jim has presented numerous technical seminars to national audiences including the California Automotive Teachers (CAT) and the Illinois College Automotive Instructor Association (ICAIA). He is also a member and presenter at the North American Council of Automotive Teachers (NACAT). Jim was also named Regional Teacher of the Year by General Motors Corporation and an outstanding alumnus of Ohio Northern University.

Jim and his wife, Michelle, live in Dayton, Ohio. They have two children. You can reach Jim at

jim@jameshalderman.com

BRIEF CONTENTS

CONTENTS

chapter 16
POWER BRAKE UNIT OPERATION, DIAGNOSIS, AND SERVICE   291

chapter 17
REGENERATIVE BRAKING SYSTEMS   308

chapter 18
ABS COMPONENTS AND OPERATION   321

chapter 19
ABS DIAGNOSIS AND SERVICE   338

chapter 1

SERVICE INFORMATION, TOOLS, AND SAFETY

OBJECTIVES

After studying Chapter 1, the reader will be able to:

1. Understand the ASE knowledge content for vehicle identification and the proper use of tools and shop equipment.
2. Retrieve vehicle service information.
3. Identify the strength ratings of threaded fasteners.
4. Describe how to safely hoist a vehicle.
5. Discuss how to safely use hand tools.
6. Identify the personal protective equipment (PPE) that all service technicians should wear.
7. Describe what tool is the best to use for each job.
8. Explain the difference between the brand name (trade name) and the proper name for tools.
9. Explain how to maintain hand tools.
10. Identify the precautions that should be followed when working on hybrid electric vehicles.

KEY TERMS

Bench grinder 25
Bolts 5
Breaker bar 11
Bump cap 25
Calibration codes 3
Campaign 4
Casting number 3
Cheater bar 13
Chisels 19
Drive sizes 11
Extensions 11
Eye wash station 34
Files 17
Fire blanket 33
Fire extinguisher classes 32
GAWR 3
Grade 6
GVWR 3
Hacksaws 19
Hammers 14
HEV 35
LED 23
Metric bolts 6
Nuts 8

PPE 25
Pinch weld seam 28
Pitch 5
Pliers 15
Punches 18
Ratchet 11
Recall 4
Screwdrivers 13
Snips 18
Socket 11
Socket adapter 13
Spontaneous combustion 28
SST 22
Stud 5
Tensile strength 6
Trouble light 23
TSB 4
UNC 5
UNF 5
Universal joint 11
VECI 3
VIN 2
Washers 8
Wrenches 9

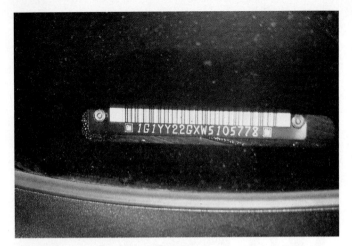

FIGURE 1–1 Typical vehicle identification number (VIN) as viewed through the windshield.

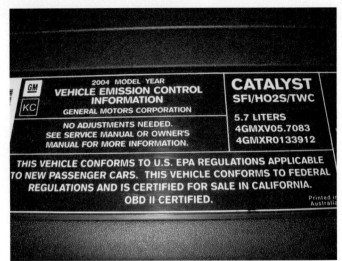

FIGURE 1–2 The vehicle emissions control information (VECI) sticker is placed under the hood.

VEHICLE IDENTIFICATION

MAKE, MODEL, AND YEAR   All service work requires that the vehicle and its components be properly identified. The most common identification is the make, model, and year of the vehicle.

Make: e.g., Chevrolet

Model: e.g., Impala

Year: e.g., 2008

VEHICLE IDENTIFICATION NUMBER   The year of the vehicle is often difficult to determine exactly. A model may be introduced as the next year's model as soon as January of the previous year. Typically, a new model year starts in September or October of the year prior to the actual new year, but not always. This is why the **vehicle identification number**, usually abbreviated **VIN**, is so important. ● **SEE FIGURE 1–1.**

Since 1981, all vehicle manufacturers have used a VIN that is 17 characters long. Although every vehicle manufacturer assigns various letters or numbers within these 17 characters, there are some constants, including:

- The first number or letter designates the country of origin. ● **SEE CHART 1–1.**
- The fourth or fifth character is the car line/series.
- The sixth character is the body style.
- The seventh character is the restraint system.
- The eighth character is often the engine code. (Some engines cannot be determined by the VIN number.)
- The tenth character represents the year on all vehicles. ● **SEE CHART 1–2.**

1 = United States	J = Japan	W = Germany
2 = Canada	K = Korea	X = Russia
3 = Mexico	L = China	Y = Sweden
4 = United States	R = Taiwan	Z = Italy
5 = United States	S = England	
6 = Australia	T = Czechoslovakia	
8 = Argentina	U = Romania	
9 = Brazil	V = France	

CHART 1–1

The first number or letter in the VIN identifies the country where the vehicle was made.

A = 1980/2010	L = 1990/2020	Y = 2000/2030
B = 1981/2011	M = 1991/2021	1 = 2001/2031
C = 1982/2012	N = 1992/2022	2 = 2002/2032
D = 1983/2013	P = 1993/2023	3 = 2003/2033
E = 1984/2014	R = 1994/2024	4 = 2004/2034
F = 1985/2015	S = 1995/2025	5 = 2005/2035
G = 1986/2016	T = 1996/2026	6 = 2006/2036
H = 1987/2017	V = 1997/2027	7 = 2007/2037
J = 1988/2018	W = 1998/2028	8 = 2008/2038
K = 1989/2019	X = 1999/2029	9 = 2009/2039

CHART 1–2

The pattern repeats every 30 years for the year of manufacture.

FIGURE 1–3 A typical calibration code sticker on the case of a controller. The information on the sticker is often needed when ordering parts or a replacement controller.

FIGURE 1–4 Casting numbers on major components can be either cast or stamped.

VEHICLE SAFETY CERTIFICATION LABEL A vehicle safety certification label is attached to the left side pillar post on the rearward-facing section of the left front door. This label indicates the month and year of manufacture as well as the **gross vehicle weight rating (GVWR)**, the **gross axle weight rating (GAWR)**, and the vehicle identification number (VIN).

VECI LABEL The **vehicle emissions control information (VECI)** label under the hood of the vehicle shows informative settings and emission hose routing information. ● **SEE FIGURE 1–2**.

The VECI label (sticker) can be located on the bottom side of the hood, the radiator fan shroud, the radiator core support, or on the strut towers. The VECI label usually includes the following information:

- Engine identification
- Emissions standard that the vehicle meets
- Vacuum hose routing diagram
- Base ignition timing (if adjustable)
- Spark plug type and gap
- Valve lash
- Emission calibration code

CALIBRATION CODES **Calibration codes** are usually located on Powertrain Control Modules (PCMs) or other controllers. Whenever diagnosing an engine operating fault, it is often necessary to use the calibration code to be sure that the vehicle is the subject of a technical service bulletin or other service procedure. ● **SEE FIGURE 1–3**.

CASTING NUMBERS When an engine part such as a block is cast, a number is put into the mold to identify the casting. ● **SEE FIGURE 1–4**. These **casting numbers** can be used to identify the part and check dimensions such as the cubic inch displacement and other information, such as the year of manufacture. Sometimes changes are made to the mold, yet the casting number is not changed. Most often the casting number is the best piece of identifying information that the service technician can use for identifying an engine.

FIGURE 1–5 Electronic service information is available from aftermarket sources such as All-Data and Mitchell-on-Demand, as well as on websites hosted by vehicle manufacturers.

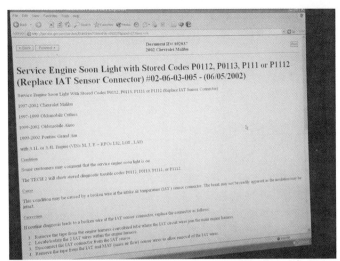

FIGURE 1–6 Technical service bulletins (TSB) are issued by vehicle manufacturers when a fault occurs that affects many vehicles with the same problem. The TSB then provides the fix for the problem including any parts needed and detailed instructions.

SERVICE INFORMATION

SERVICE MANUALS Service information is used by the service technician to determine specifications and service procedures, and any needed special tools.

Factory and aftermarket service manuals contain specifications and service procedures. While factory service manuals cover just one year and one or more models of the same vehicle, most aftermarket service manufacturers cover multiple years and/or models in one manual. Included in most service manuals are the following:

- Capacities and recommended specifications for all fluids
- Specifications including engine and routine maintenance items
- Testing procedures
- Service procedures including the use of special tools when needed

ELECTRONIC SERVICE INFORMATION Electronic service information is available mostly by subscription and provides access to an Internet site where service manual-type information is available. ● **SEE FIGURE 1–5**. Most vehicle manufacturers also offer electronic service information to their dealers and to most schools and colleges that offer corporate training programs.

TECHNICAL SERVICE BULLETINS **Technical service bulletins**, often abbreviated **TSB**, sometimes called *technical service information bulletins (TSIB)* are issued by the vehicle

manufacturer to notify service technicians of a problem and include the necessary corrective action. Technical service bulletins are designed for dealership technicians but are republished by aftermarket companies and made available along with other service information to shops and vehicle repair facilities. ● **SEE FIGURE 1–6**.

INTERNET The Internet has opened the field for information exchange and access to technical advice. One of the most useful websites is the International Automotive Technician's Network at **www.iatn.net**. This is a free site but service technicians must register to join. If a small monthly sponsor fee is paid, the shop or service technician can gain access to the archives, which include thousands of successful repairs in the searchable database.

RECALLS AND CAMPAIGNS A **recall** or **campaign** is issued by a vehicle manufacturer and a notice is sent to all owners in the event of a safety-related fault or concern. While these faults may be repaired by shops, it is generally handled by a local dealer. Items that have created recalls in the past have included potential fuel system leakage problems, exhaust leakage, or electrical malfunctions that could cause a possible fire or the engine to stall. Unlike technical service bulletins whose cost is only covered when the vehicle is within the warranty period, a recall or campaign is always done at no cost to the vehicle owner.

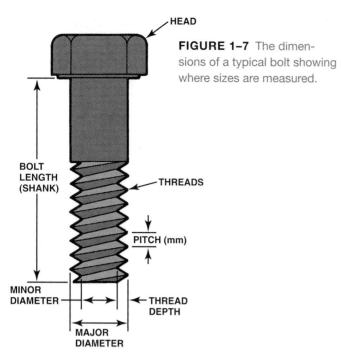

HEAD

FIGURE 1–7 The dimensions of a typical bolt showing where sizes are measured.

BOLT LENGTH (SHANK)

THREADS

PITCH (mm)

MINOR DIAMETER

THREAD DEPTH

MAJOR DIAMETER

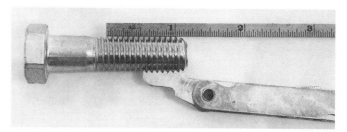

FIGURE 1–8 Thread pitch gauge used to measure the pitch of the thread. This bolt has 13 threads to the inch.

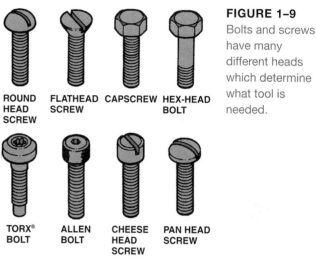

FIGURE 1–9 Bolts and screws have many different heads which determine what tool is needed.

ROUND HEAD SCREW   FLATHEAD SCREW   CAPSCREW   HEX-HEAD BOLT

TORX® BOLT   ALLEN BOLT   CHEESE HEAD SCREW   PAN HEAD SCREW

FREQUENTLY ASKED QUESTION

What Should Be Included on a Work Order?

A work order is a legal document that should include the following information:

1. Customer information
2. Identification of the vehicle including the VIN
3. Related service history information
4. The "three Cs":
   • Customer concern (complaint)
   • Cause of the concern
   • Correction or repairs that were required to return the vehicle to proper operation.

THREADED FASTENERS

BOLTS AND THREADS Most of the threaded fasteners used on vehicles are **bolts**. Bolts are called *cap screws* when they are threaded into a casting. Automotive service technicians usually refer to these fasteners as *bolts*, regardless of how they are used. In this chapter, they are called bolts. Sometimes, studs are used for threaded fasteners. A **stud** is a short rod with threads on both ends. Often, a stud will have coarse threads on one end and fine threads on the other end. The end of the stud with coarse threads is screwed into the casting. A nut is used on the opposite end to hold the parts together.

The fastener threads *must* match the threads in the casting or nut. The threads may be measured either in fractions of an inch (called fractional) or in metric units. The size is measured across the outside of the threads, called the *crest* of the thread. ● **SEE FIGURE 1–7.**

FRACTIONAL BOLTS Fractional threads are either coarse or fine. The coarse threads are called **unified national coarse (UNC)**, and the fine threads are called **unified national fine (UNF)**. Standard combinations of sizes and number of threads per inch (called **pitch**) are used. Pitch can be measured with a thread pitch gauge as shown in ● **FIGURE 1–8.** Bolts are identified by their diameter and length as measured from below the head, and not by the size of the head or the size of the wrench used to remove or install the bolt.

Fractional thread sizes are specified by the diameter in fractions of an inch and the number of threads per inch. Typical UNC thread sizes would be 5/16-18 and 1/2-13. Similar UNF thread sizes would be 5/16-24 and 1/2-20. ● **SEE CHART 1–3.**

FREQUENTLY ASKED QUESTION

How Many Types of Screw Heads Are Used in Automotive Applications?

There are many, including Torx, hex (also called Allen), plus many others used in custom vans and motor homes. ● **SEE FIGURE 1–9.**

SIZE	THREADS PER INCH NC UNC	NF UNF	OUTSIDE DIAMETER INCHES
0	..	80	0.0600
1	64	..	0.0730
1	..	72	0.0730
2	56	..	0.0860
2	..	64	0.0860
3	48	..	0.0990
3	..	56	0.0990
4	40	..	0.1120
4	..	48	0.1120
5	40	..	0.1250
5	..	44	0.1250
6	32	..	0.1380
6	..	40	0.1380
8	32	..	0.1640
8	..	36	0.1640
10	24	..	0.1900
10	..	32	0.1900
12	24	..	0.2160
12	..	28	0.2160
1/4	20	..	0.2500
1/4	..	28	0.2500
5/16	18	..	0.3125
5/16	..	24	0.3125
3/8	16	..	0.3750
3/8	..	24	0.3750
7/16	14	..	0.4375
7/16	..	20	0.4375
1/2	13	..	0.5000
1/2	..	20	0.5000
9/16	12	..	0.5625
9/16	..	18	0.5625
5/8	11	..	0.6250
5/8	..	18	0.6250
3/4	10	..	0.7500
3/4	..	16	0.7500
7/8	9	..	0.8750
7/8	..	14	0.8750
1	8	..	1.0000
1	..	12	1.0000
1 1/8	7	..	1.1250
1 1/8	..	12	1.1250
1 1/4	7	..	1.2500
1 1/4	..	12	1.2500
1 3/8	6	..	1.3750
1 3/8	..	12	1.3750
1 1/2	6	..	1.5000
1 1/2	..	12	1.5000
1 3/4	5	..	1.7500
2	4 1/2	..	2.0000
2 1/4	4 1/2	..	2.2500
2 1/2	4	..	2.5000
2 3/4	4	..	2.7500
3	4	..	3.0000
3 1/4	4	..	3.2500
3 1/2	4	..	3.5000
3 3/4	4	..	3.7500
4	4	..	4.0000

CHART 1–3

American standard is one method of sizing fasteners.

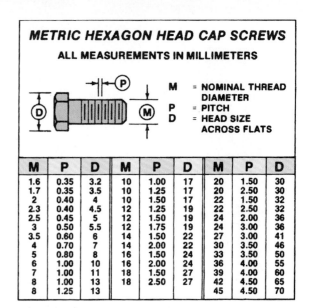

FIGURE 1–10 The metric system specifies fasteners by diameter, length, and pitch.

THREADED FASTENERS (CONTINUED)

METRIC BOLTS The size of a **metric bolt** is specified by the letter *M* followed by the diameter in millimeters (mm) across the outside (crest) of the threads. Typical metric sizes would be M8 and M12. Fine metric threads are specified by the thread diameter followed by X and the distance between the threads measured in millimeters (M8 X 1.5). ● **SEE FIGURE 1–10**.

GRADES OF BOLTS Bolts are made from many different types of steel, and for this reason some are stronger than others. The strength or classification of a bolt is called the **grade**. The bolt heads are marked to indicate their grade strength.

The actual grade of bolts is two more than the number of lines on the bolt head. Metric bolts have a decimal number to indicate the grade. More lines or a higher grade number indicate a stronger bolt. In some cases, nuts and machine screws have similar grade markings. Higher grade bolts usually have threads that are rolled rather than cut, which also makes them stronger. ● **SEE FIGURE 1–11**.

CAUTION: *Never* use hardware store (nongraded) bolts, studs, or nuts on any vehicle steering, suspension, or brake component. Always use the exact size and grade of hardware that is specified and used by the vehicle manufacturer.

TENSILE STRENGTH OF FASTENERS Graded fasteners have a higher tensile strength than nongraded fasteners. **Tensile strength** is the maximum stress used under tension

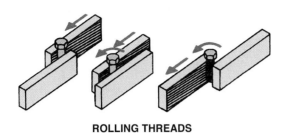

ROLLING THREADS

FIGURE 1–11 Stronger threads are created by cold-rolling a heat-treated bolt blank instead of cutting the threads, using a die.

4.6	8.8	9.8	10.9	**METRIC CLASS**
60,000	120,000	130,000	150,000	**APPROXIMATE MAXIMUM POUND FORCE PER SQUARE INCH**

FIGURE 1–12 Metric bolt (cap screw) grade markings and approximate tensile strength.

SAE BOLT DESIGNATIONS

SAE GRADE NO.	SIZE RANGE	TENSILE STRENGTH, PSI	MATERIAL	HEAD MARKING
1	1/4 through 1 1/2	60,000	Low or medium carbon steel	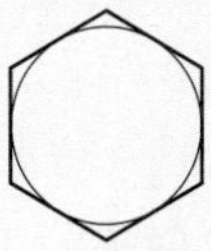
2	1/4 through 3/4	74,000		
	7/8 through 1 1/2	60,000		
5	1/4 through 1	120,000	Medium carbon steel, quenched and tempered	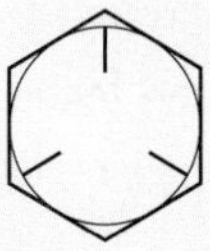
	1-1/8 through 1 1/2	105,000		
5.2	1/4 through 1	120,000	Low carbon martensite steel,* quenched and tempered	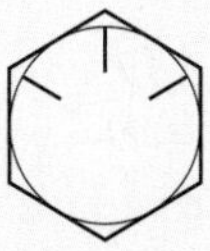
7	1/4 through 1 1/2	133,000	Medium carbon alloy steel, quenched and tempered	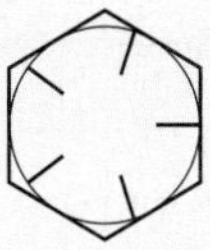
8	1/4 through 1 1/2	150,000	Medium carbon alloy steel, quenched and tempered	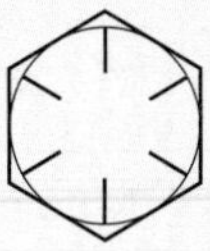
8.2	1/4 through 1	150,000	Low carbon martensite steel,* quenched and tempered	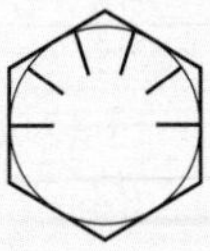

CHART 1–4

The tensile strength rating system as specified by the Society of Automotive Engineers (SAE).

(lengthwise force) without causing failure of the fastener. Tensile strength is specified in pounds per square inch (psi).

The strength and type of steel used in a bolt is supposed to be indicated by a raised mark on the head of the bolt. The type of mark depends on the standard to which the bolt was manufactured. Most often, bolts used in machinery are made to

SAE Standard J429. ● **SEE CHART 1–4** that shows the grade and specified tensile strength.

Metric bolt tensile strength property class is shown on the head of the bolt as a number, such as 4.6, 8.8, 9.8, and 10.9; the higher the number, the stronger the bolt. ● **SEE FIGURE 1–12.**

HEX NUT | JAM NUT | NYLON LOCK NUT | CASTLE NUT | ACORN NUT

FIGURE 1–13 Nuts come in a variety of styles, including locking (prevailing torque) types, such as the distorted thread and nylon insert type.

FLAT WASHER | LOCK WASHER | STAR WASHER | STAR WASHER

FIGURE 1–14 Washers come in a variety of styles, including flat and serrated used to help prevent a fastener from loosening.

THREADED FASTENERS (CONTINUED)

 TECH TIP

A 1/2-Inch Wrench Does Not Fit a 1/2-Inch Bolt

A common mistake made by persons new to the automotive field is to think that the size of a bolt or nut is the size of the head. The size of the bolt or nut (outside diameter of the threads) is usually smaller than the size of the wrench or socket that fits the head of the bolt or nut. Examples are given in the following table:

Wrench Size	Thread Size
7/16 in.	1/4 in.
1/2 in.	5/16 in.
9/16 in.	3/8 in.
5/8 in.	7/16 in.
3/4 in.	1/2 in.
10 mm	6 mm
12 mm or 13 mm*	8 mm
14 mm or 17 mm*	10 mm

* European (Système International d'Unités-SI) metric.

NUTS Nuts are the female part of a threaded fastener. Most nuts used on cap screws have the same hex size as the cap screw head. Some inexpensive nuts use a hex size larger than the cap screw head. Metric nuts are often marked with dimples to show their strength. More dimples indicate stronger nuts. Some nuts and cap screws use interference fit threads to keep them from accidentally loosening. This means that the shape of the nut is slightly distorted or that a section of the threads is deformed. Nuts can also be kept from loosening with a nylon washer fastened in the nut or with a nylon patch or strip on the threads. ● **SEE FIGURE 1–13.**

 **TECH TIP**

It Just Takes a Second

Whenever removing any automotive component, it is wise to screw the bolts back into the holes a couple of threads by hand. This ensures that the right bolt will be used in its original location when the component or part is put back on the vehicle. Often, the same diameter of fastener is used on a component, but the length of the bolt may vary. Spending just a couple of seconds to put the bolts and nuts back where they belong when the part is removed can save a lot of time when the part is being reinstalled. Besides making certain that the right fastener is being installed in the right place, this method helps prevent bolts and nuts from getting lost or kicked away. How much time have you wasted looking for that lost bolt or nut?

NOTE: Most of these "locking nuts" are grouped together and are commonly referred to as *prevailing torque nuts*. This means that the nut will hold its tightness or torque and not loosen with movement or vibration. Most prevailing torque nuts should be replaced whenever removed to ensure that the nut will not loosen during service. Always follow the manufacturer's recommendations. Anaerobic sealers, such as Loctite, are used on the threads where the nut or cap screw must be both locked and sealed.

WASHERS Washers are often used under cap screw heads and under nuts. ● **SEE FIGURE 1–14.** Plain flat washers are used to provide an even clamping load around the fastener. Lock washers are added to prevent accidental loosening. In some accessories, the washers are locked onto the nut to provide easy assembly.

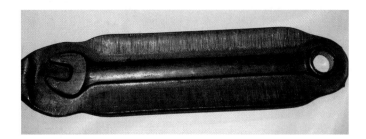

FIGURE 1–15 A forged wrench after it has been forged but before the flashing, extra material around the wrench, has been removed.

15° 1/2 9/16 15°

FIGURE 1–16 A typical open-end wrench. The size is different on each end and notice that the head is angled 15 degrees at the end.

HAND TOOLS

WRENCHES   Wrenches are the most used hand tool by service technicians. **Wrenches** are used to grasp and rotate threaded fasteners. Most wrenches are constructed of forged alloy steel, usually chrome-vanadium steel. ● **SEE FIGURE 1–15**.

After the wrench is formed, the wrench is hardened, and then tempered to reduce brittleness, and then chrome plated. There are several types of wrenches.

OPEN-END WRENCH.   An open-end wrench is usually used to loosen or tighten bolts or nuts that do not require a lot of torque. Because of the *open* end, this type of wrench can be easily placed on a bolt or nut with an angle of 15 degrees, which allows the wrench to be flipped over and used again to continue to rotate the fastener. The major disadvantage of an open-end wrench is the lack of torque that can be applied due to the fact that the open jaws of the wrench only contact two flat surfaces of the fastener. An open-end wrench has two different sizes; one at each end. ● **SEE FIGURE 1–16**.

BOX-END WRENCH.   A *box-end wrench*, also called a *closed-end wrench*, is placed over the top of the fastener and grips the points of the fastener. A box-end wrench is angled 15 degrees to allow it to clear nearby objects.

Therefore, a box-end wrench should be used to loosen or to tighten fasteners because it grasps around the entire head of the fastener. A box-end wrench has two different sizes; one at each end. ● **SEE FIGURE 1–17**.

Most service technicians purchase *combination wrenches*, which have the open end at one end and the same size box end on the other end. ● **SEE FIGURE 1–18**.

A combination wrench allows the technician to loosen or tighten a fastener using the box end of the wrench, turn it around, and use the open end to increase the speed of rotating the fastener.

ADJUSTABLE WRENCH.   An *adjustable wrench* is often used where the exact size wrench is not available or when a large nut, such as a wheel spindle nut, needs to be rotated but not tightened. An adjustable wrench should not be used to loosen or tighten fasteners because the torque applied to the wrench can cause the movable jaws to loosen their grip on the fastener, causing it to become rounded. ● **SEE FIGURE 1–19**.

LINE WRENCHES.   Line wrenches are also called *flare-nut wrenches*, *fitting wrenches,* or *tube-nut wrenches* and are designed to grip almost all the way around a nut used to retain a

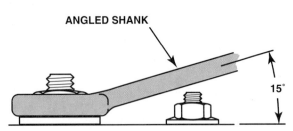

FIGURE 1–17 The end of a box-end wrench is angled 15 degrees to allow clearance for nearby objects or other fasteners.

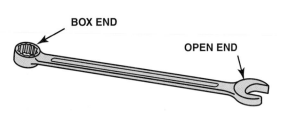

FIGURE 1–18 A combination wrench has an open end at one end and a box end at the other end.

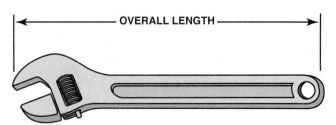

FIGURE 1–19 An adjustable wrench. Adjustable wrenches are sized by the overall length of the wrench and not by how far the jaws open. Common sizes of adjustable wrenches include 8, 10, and 12 inch.

FIGURE 1–20 The end of a typical line wrench, which shows that it is capable of grasping most of the head of the fitting.

HAND TOOLS (CONTINUED)

TECH TIP

Hide Those from the Boss

An apprentice technician started working for a dealership and put his top tool box on a workbench. Another technician observed that, along with a complete set of good-quality tools, the box contained several adjustable wrenches. The more experienced technician said, "Hide those from the boss." The boss does not want any service technician to use adjustable wrenches. If any adjustable wrench is used on a bolt or nut, the movable jaw often moves or loosens and starts to round the head of the fastener. If the head of the bolt or nut becomes rounded, it becomes that much more difficult to remove.

fuel or refrigerant line, and yet, be able to be installed over the line. ● **SEE FIGURE 1–20.**

SAFE USE OF WRENCHES Wrenches should be inspected before use to be sure they are not cracked, bent, or damaged. All wrenches should be cleaned after use before being returned to the tool box. Always use the correct size of wrench for the fastener being loosened or tightened to help prevent the rounding of the flats of the fastener. When attempting to loosen a fastener, pull a wrench—do not push a wrench. If a wrench is pushed, your knuckles can be hurt when forced into another object if the fastener breaks loose or if the wrench slips. Always keep wrenches and all hand tools clean to help prevent rust and to allow for a better, firmer grip. Never expose any tool to excessive heat. High temperatures can reduce the strength ("draw the temper") of metal tools.

Never use a hammer on any wrench unless you are using a special "staking face" wrench designed to be used with a hammer. Replace any tools that are damaged or worn.

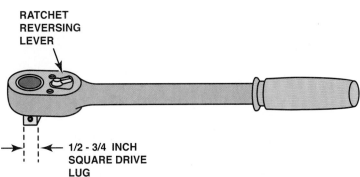

FIGURE 1–21 A typical ratchet used to rotate a socket. A ratchet makes a ratcheting noise when it is being rotated in the opposite direction from loosening or tightening. A knob or lever on the ratchet allows the user to switch directions.

FIGURE 1–22 A typical flex handle used to rotate a socket, also called a breaker bar because it usually has a longer handle than a ratchet and therefore, can be used to apply more torque to a fastener than a ratchet.

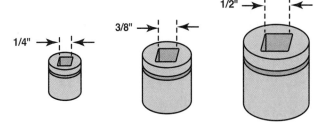

FIGURE 1–23 The most commonly used socket drive sizes include 1/4-inch, 3/8-inch, and 1/2-inch drive.

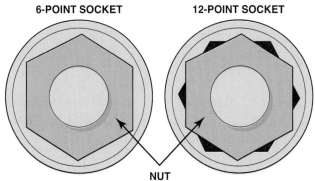

FIGURE 1–24 A 6-point socket fits the head of a bolt or nut on all sides. A 12-point socket can round off the head of a bolt or nut if a lot of force is applied.

RATCHETS, SOCKETS, AND EXTENSIONS

A **socket** fits over the fastener and grips the points and/or flats of the bolt or nut. The socket is rotated (driven) using either a long bar called a **breaker bar** (flex handle) or a ratchet. ● SEE FIGURES 1–21 and 1–22.

A **ratchet** is a tool that turns the socket in only one direction and allows the rotating of the ratchet handle back and forth in a narrow space. Socket **extensions** and **universal joints** are also used with sockets to allow access to fasteners in restricted locations.

DRIVE SIZE. Sockets are available in various **drive sizes**, including 1/4 inch, 3/8 inch, and 1/2 inch sizes for most automotive use. ● SEE FIGURES 1–23 and 1–24.

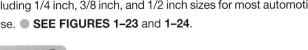

TECH TIP

Right to Tighten

It is sometimes confusing which way to rotate a wrench or screwdriver, especially when the head of the fastener is pointing away from you. To help visualize while looking at the fastener, say "righty tighty, lefty loosey."

Many heavy-duty truck and/or industrial applications use 3/4 in. and 1 in. sizes. The drive size is the distance of each side of the square drive. Sockets and ratchets of the same size are designed to work together.

REGULAR AND DEEP WELL. Sockets are available in regular length for use in most applications or in a deep well design that allows for access to a fastener that uses a long stud or other similar conditions. ● SEE FIGURE 1–25.

TORQUE WRENCHES

Torque wrenches are socket turning handles that are designed to apply a known amount of force to the fastener. There are two basic types of torque wrenches including:

1. **Clicker type.** This type of torque wrench is first set to the specified torque and then it "clicks" when the set torque value has been reached. When force is removed from the torque wrench handle, another click is heard. The setting on a clicker-type torque wrench should be set back to zero after use and checked for proper calibration regularly. ● SEE FIGURE 1–26.

2. **Beam-type.** This type of torque wrench is used to measure torque, but instead of presenting the value, the actual torque is displayed on the dial of the wrench as the fastener is being

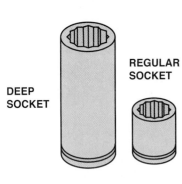

DEEP SOCKET

REGULAR SOCKET

FIGURE 1–25 Allows access to the nut that has a stud plus other locations needing great depth, such as spark plugs.

FIGURE 1–26 Using a clicker-type torque wrench to tighten connecting rod nuts on an engine.

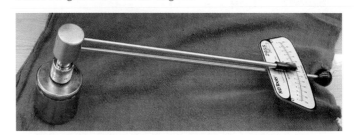

FIGURE 1–27 A beam-type torque wrench that displays the torque reading on the face of the dial. The beam display is read as the beam deflects, which is in proportion to the amount of torque applied to the fastener.

HAND TOOLS (CONTINUED)

tightened. Beam-type torque wrenches are available in 1/4 in., 3/8 in., and 1/2 in. drives and both English and metric units. ● **SEE FIGURE 1–27.**

SAFE USE OF SOCKETS AND RATCHETS Always use the proper size socket that correctly fits the bolt or nut. All sockets and ratchets should be cleaned after use before being placed back into the tool box. Sockets are available in short and deep well designs. Never expose any tool to excessive heat. High temperatures can reduce the strength ("draw the temper") of metal tools.

Never use a hammer on a socket handle unless you are using a special "staking face" wrench designed to be used with a hammer. Replace any tools that are damaged or worn.

Also select the appropriate drive size. For example, for small work, such as on the dash, select a 1/4-in. drive. For most general service work, use a 3/8-in. drive and for suspension and steering and other large fasteners, select a 1/2-in. drive. When loosening a fastener, always pull the ratchet toward you rather than push it outward.

 **TECH TIP**

Check Torque Wrench Calibration Regularly

Torque wrenches should be checked regularly. For example, Honda has a torque wrench calibration setup at each of their training centers. It is expected that a torque wrench be checked for accuracy before every use. Most experts recommend that torque wrenches be checked and adjusted as needed at least every year and more often if possible. ● **SEE FIGURE 1–28.**

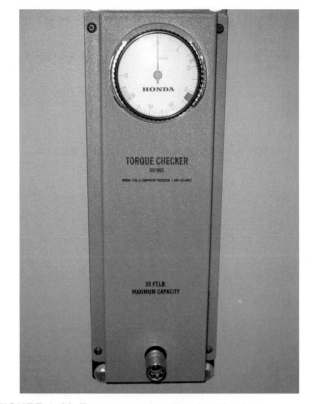

FIGURE 1–28 Torque wrench calibration checker.

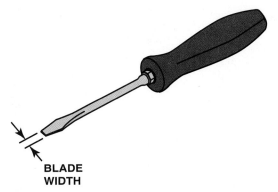

BLADE WIDTH

FIGURE 1-29 A flat-tip (straight-blade) screwdriver. The width of the blade should match the width of the slot in the fastener being loosened or tightened.

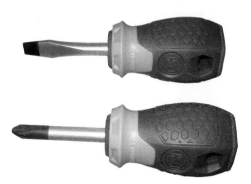

FIGURE 1-30 Two stubby screwdrivers that are used to access screws that have limited space above. A straight blade is on top and a #2 Phillips screwdriver is on the bottom.

TECH TIP

Use Socket Adapters with Caution

A **socket adapter** allows the use of one size of socket and another drive size ratchet or breaker bar. Socket adapters are available and can be used for different drive size sockets on a ratchet. Combinations include:

- 1/4-in. drive—3/8-in. sockets
- 3/8-in. drive—1/4-in. sockets
- 3/8-in. drive—1/2-in. sockets
- 1/2-in. drive—3/8-in. sockets

Using a larger drive ratchet or breaker bar on a smaller size socket can cause the application of too much force to the socket, which could crack or shatter. Using a smaller size drive tool on a larger socket will usually not cause any harm, but would greatly reduce the amount of torque that can be applied to the bolt or nut.

SCREWDRIVERS

STRAIGHT-BLADE SCREWDRIVER. Many smaller fasteners are removed and installed by using a **screwdriver**. Screwdrivers are available in many sizes and tip shapes. The most commonly used screwdriver is called a *straight blade* or *flat tip*.

Flat-tip screwdrivers are sized by the width of the blade and this width should match the width of the slot in the screw. ● **SEE FIGURE 1–29.**

TECH TIP

Avoid Using "Cheater Bars"

Whenever a fastener is difficult to remove, some technicians will insert the handle of a ratchet or a breaker bar into a length of steel pipe sometimes called a **cheater bar.** The extra length of the pipe allows the technician to exert more torque than can be applied using the drive handle alone. However, the extra torque can easily overload the socket and ratchet, causing them to break or shatter, which could cause personal injury.

CAUTION: Do not use a screwdriver as a pry tool or as a chisel. Screwdrivers are hardened steel only at the tip and are not designed to be pounded on or used for prying because they could bend easily. Always use the proper tool for each application.

PHILLIPS SCREWDRIVER. Another type of commonly used screwdriver is called a Phillips screwdriver, named for Henry F. Phillips, who invented the crosshead screw in 1934. Due to the shape of the crosshead screw and screwdriver, a Phillips screw can be driven with more torque than can be achieved with a slotted screw.

A Phillips head screwdriver is specified by the length of the handle and the size of the point at the tip. A #1 tip has a sharp point, a #2 tip is the most commonly used, and a #3 tip is blunt and is only used for larger sizes of Phillips head fasteners. For example, a #2 × 3 in. Phillips screwdriver would typically measure 6 in. from the tip of the blade to the end of the handle (3 in. long handle and 3 in. long blade) with a #2 tip.

Both straight-blade and Phillips screwdrivers are available with a short blade and handle for access to fasteners with limited room. ● **SEE FIGURE 1–30.**

FIGURE 1–31 An offset screwdriver is used to install or remove fasteners that do not have enough space above to use a conventional screwdriver.

FIGURE 1–32 An impact screwdriver used to remove slotted or Phillips head fasteners that cannot be broken loose using a standard screwdriver.

HAND TOOLS (CONTINUED)

OFFSET SCREWDRIVERS. Offset screwdrivers are used in places where a conventional screwdriver cannot fit. An offset screwdriver is bent at the ends and is used similar to a wrench. Most offset screwdrivers have a straight blade at one end and a Phillips end at the opposite end. **SEE FIGURE 1–31.**

IMPACT SCREWDRIVER. An *impact screwdriver* is used to break loose or tighten a screw. A hammer is used to strike the end after the screwdriver holder is placed in the head of the screw and rotated in the desired direction. The force from the hammer blow does two things: It applies a force downward holding the tip of the screwdriver in the slot and then applies a twisting force to loosen (or tighten) the screw. ● **SEE FIGURE 1–32.**

SAFE USE OF SCREWDRIVERS
Always use the proper type and size screwdriver that matches the fastener. Try to avoid pressing down on a screwdriver because if it slips, the screwdriver tip could go into your hand, causing serious personal injury. All screwdrivers should be cleaned after use. Do not use a screwdriver as a prybar; always use the correct tool for the job.

HAMMERS AND MALLETS
Hammers and mallets are used to force objects together or apart. The shape of the back part of the hammer head (called the *peen*) usually determines the name. For example, a ball-peen hammer has a rounded end like a ball and it is used to straighten oil pans and valve covers, using the hammer head, and for shaping metal, using the ball peen. ● **SEE FIGURE 1–33.**

NOTE: A claw hammer has a claw used to remove nails and is not used for automotive service.

A hammer is usually sized by the weight of the head of the hammer and the length of the handle. For example, a commonly used ball-peen hammer has an 8-ounce head with an 11-inch handle.

? **FREQUENTLY ASKED QUESTION**

What Is a Robertson Screwdriver?

A Canadian named P. L. Robertson invented the Robertson screw and screwdriver in 1908, which uses a square-shaped tip with a slight taper. The Robertson screwdriver uses color-coded handles because different size screws required different tip sizes. The color and sizes include:

- Orange (#00)—Number 1 and 2 screws
- Yellow (#0)—Number 3 and 4 screws
- Green (#1)—Number 5, 6, and 7 screws
- Red (#2)—Number 8, 9, and 10 screws
- Black (#3)—Number 12 and larger screws

The Robertson screws are rarely found in the United States but are common in Canada.

FIGURE 1–33 A typical ball-peen hammer.

FIGURE 1–34 A rubber mallet used to deliver a force to an object without harming the surface.

FIGURE 1–35 A dead-blow hammer that was left outside in freezing weather. The plastic covering was damaged, which destroyed this hammer. The lead shot is encased in the metal housing and then covered.

MALLETS. *Mallets* are a type of hammer with a large striking surface, which allows the technician to exert force over a larger area than a hammer, so as not to harm the part or component. Mallets are made from a variety of materials including rubber, plastic, or wood. ● **SEE FIGURE 1–34.**

DEAD-BLOW HAMMER. A shot-filled plastic hammer is called a *dead-blow hammer*. The small lead balls (shot) inside a plastic head prevent the hammer from bouncing off of the object when struck. ● **SEE FIGURE 1–35.**

SAFE USE OF HAMMERS AND MALLETS
All mallets and hammers should be cleaned after use and not exposed to extreme temperatures. Never use a hammer or mallet that is damaged in any way and always use caution to avoid doing damage to the components and the surrounding area. Always follow the hammer manufacturer's recommended procedures and practices.

PLIERS

SLIP-JOINT PLIERS. A **pliers** is capable of holding, twisting, bending, and cutting objects and is an extremely useful classification of tools. The common household type of pliers is called the *slip-joint pliers.* There are two different positions where the junction of the handles meets to achieve a wide range of sizes of objects that can be gripped. ● **SEE FIGURE 1–36.**

MULTIGROOVE ADJUSTABLE PLIERS. For gripping larger objects, a set of *multigroove adjustable pliers* is a commonly used

---

🔧 **TECH TIP**

Pound with Something Softer

If you must pound on something, be sure to use a tool that is softer than what you are about to pound on to avoid damage. Examples are given in the following table.

The Material Being Pounded	What to Pound with
Steel or cast iron	Brass or aluminum hammer or punch
Aluminum	Plastic or rawhide mallet or plastic-covered dead-blow hammer
Plastic	Rawhide mallet or plastic dead-blow hammer

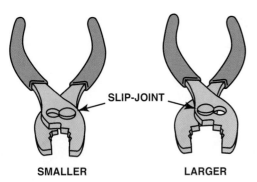

FIGURE 1–36 Typical slip-joint pliers is a common household pliers. The slip joint allows the jaws to be opened to two different settings.

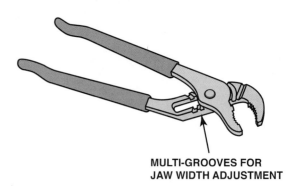

FIGURE 1–37 Multigroove adjustable pliers is known by many names, including the trade name "Channel Locks.®"

FIGURE 1–38 Linesman's pliers are very useful because it can help perform many automotive service jobs.

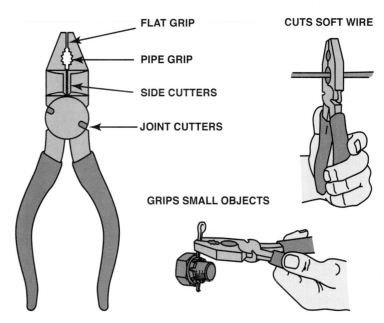

HAND TOOLS (CONTINUED)

tool of choice by many service technicians. Originally designed to remove the various size nuts holding rope seals used in water pumps, the name *water pump pliers* is also used. These types of pliers are commonly called by their trade name *Channel Locks®*. ● **SEE FIGURE 1–37**.

LINESMAN'S PLIERS. *Linesman's pliers* is a hand tool specifically designed for cutting, bending, and twisting wire. While commonly used by construction workers and electricians, linesman's pliers is a very useful tool for the service technician who deals with wiring. The center parts of the jaws are designed to grasp round objects such as pipe or tubing without slipping. ● **SEE FIGURE 1–38**.

DIAGONAL PLIERS. *Diagonal pliers* is designed to cut only. The cutting jaws are set at an angle to make it easier to cut wires. Diagonal pliers are also called *side cuts* or *dikes*. These pliers are constructed of hardened steel and they are used mostly for cutting wire. ● **SEE FIGURE 1–39**.

NEEDLE-NOSE PLIERS. *Needle-nose pliers* are designed to grip small objects or objects in tight locations. Needle-nose pliers have long, pointed jaws, which allow the tips to reach into narrow openings or groups of small objects. ● **SEE FIGURE 1–40**.

Most needle-nose pliers have a wire cutter located at the base of the jaws near the pivot. There are several variations of needle nose pliers, including right angle jaws or slightly angled to allow access to certain cramped areas.

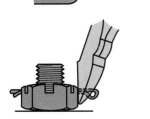

CUTTING WIRES CLOSE TO TERMINALS

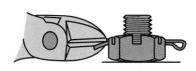

PULLING OUT AND SPREADING COTTER PIN

FIGURE 1–39 Diagonal-cut pliers is another common tool that has many names.

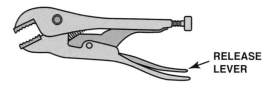

RELEASE LEVER

FIGURE 1–41 Locking pliers are best known by their trade name Vise Grips.®

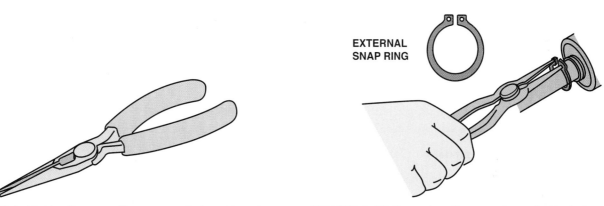

INTERNAL SNAP RING

EXTERNAL SNAP RING

FIGURE 1–40 Needle-nose pliers are used where there is limited access to a wire or pin that needs to be installed or removed.

FIGURE 1–42 Snap-ring pliers are also called lock ring pliers and most are designed to remove internal and external snap rings (lock rings).

LOCKING PLIERS. *Locking pliers* are adjustable pliers that can be locked to hold objects from moving. Most locking pliers also have wire cutters built into the jaws near the pivot point. Locking pliers come in a variety of styles and sizes and are commonly referred to by the trade name *Vise Grips*®. The size is the length of the pliers, not how far the jaws open. ● **SEE FIGURE 1–41**.

SNAP-RING PLIERS. *Snap-ring pliers* is used to remove and install snap-rings. Many snap-ring pliers are designed to be able to remove and install both inward, as well as outward, expanding snap rings. Some snap-ring pliers can be equipped with serrated-tipped jaws for grasping the opening in the snap ring, while others are equipped with points, which are inserted into the holes in the snap ring. ● **SEE FIGURE 1–42**.

SAFE USE OF PLIERS Pliers should not be used to remove any bolt or other fastener. Pliers should only be used when specified for use by the vehicle manufacturer.

FILES Files are used to smooth metal and are constructed of hardened steel with diagonal rows of teeth. Files are available with a single row of teeth called a *single cut file*, as well as two rows of teeth cut at an opposite angle called a *double cut file*. Files are available in a variety of shapes and sizes from small flat files, half-round files, and triangular files. ● **SEE FIGURE 1–43**.

SAFE USE OF FILES Always use a file with a handle. Because files only cut when moved forward, a handle must be attached to prevent possible personal injury. After making a

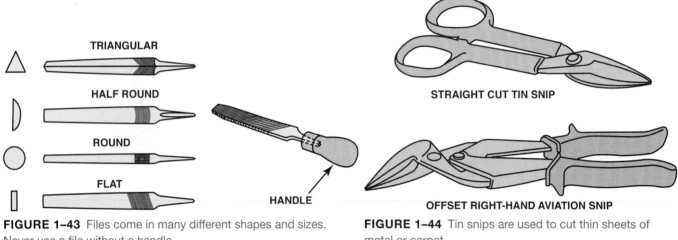

FIGURE 1–43 Files come in many different shapes and sizes. Never use a file without a handle.

FIGURE 1–44 Tin snips are used to cut thin sheets of metal or carpet.

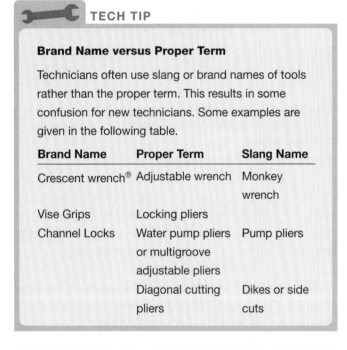

TECH TIP

Brand Name versus Proper Term

Technicians often use slang or brand names of tools rather than the proper term. This results in some confusion for new technicians. Some examples are given in the following table.

Brand Name	Proper Term	Slang Name
Crescent wrench®	Adjustable wrench	Monkey wrench
Vise Grips	Locking pliers	
Channel Locks	Water pump pliers or multigroove adjustable pliers	Pump pliers
	Diagonal cutting pliers	Dikes or side cuts

forward strike, lift the file and return the file to the starting position; avoid dragging the file backward.

SNIPS   Service technicians are often asked to fabricate sheet metal brackets or heat shields and need to use one or more types of cutters available called **snips**. *Tin snips* are the simplest and are designed to make straight cuts in a variety of materials, such as sheet steel, aluminum, or even fabric. A variation of the tin snips is called *aviation tin snips*. There are three designs of aviation snips including one designed to cut straight (called a *straight cut aviation snip*), one designed to cut left (called an *offset left aviation snip*), and one designed to cut right (called an *offset right aviation snip*). ● **SEE FIGURE 1–44.**

UTILITY KNIFE   A *utility knife* uses a replaceable blade and is used to cut a variety of materials such as carpet, plastic, wood, and paper products, such as cardboard. ● **SEE FIGURE 1–45.**

SAFE USE OF CUTTERS   Whenever using cutters, always wear eye protection or a face shield to guard against the possibility of metal pieces being ejected during the cut. Always follow recommended procedures.

PUNCHES   A **punch** is a small diameter steel rod that has a smaller diameter ground at one end. A punch is used to drive a pin out that is used to retain two components. Punches come in a variety of sizes, which are measured across the diameter of the machined end. Sizes include 1/16″, 1/8″, 3/16″, and 1/4″. ● **SEE FIGURE 1–46.**

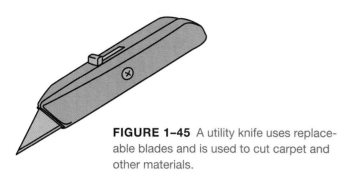

FIGURE 1–45 A utility knife uses replaceable blades and is used to cut carpet and other materials.

FIGURE 1–47 Warning stamped on the side of a punch warning that goggles should be worn when using this tool. Always follow safety warnings.

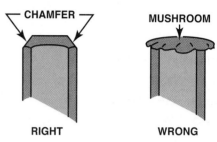

FIGURE 1–48 Use a grinder or a file to remove the mushroom material on the end of a punch or chisel.

FIGURE 1–46 A punch used to drive pins from assembled components. This type of punch is also called a pin punch.

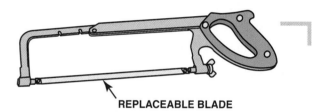

FIGURE 1–49 A typical hacksaw that is used to cut metal. If cutting sheet metal or thin objects, a blade with more teeth should be used.

CHISELS   A **chisel** has a straight, sharp cutting end that is used for cutting off rivets or to separate two pieces of an assembly. The most common design of chisel used for automotive service work is called a *cold chisel*.

SAFE USE OF PUNCHES AND CHISELS   Always wear eye protection when using a punch or a chisel because the hardened steel is brittle and parts of the punch could fly off and cause serious personal injury. See the warning stamped on the side of this automotive punch in ● **FIGURE 1–47**.

The tops of punches and chisels can become rounded off from use, which is called "mushroomed." This material must be ground off to help avoid the possibility of the overhanging material being loosened and becoming airborne during use. ● **SEE FIGURE 1–48.**

HACKSAWS   A **hacksaw** is used to cut metals, such as steel, aluminum, brass, or copper. The cutting blade of a hacksaw is replaceable and the sharpness and number of teeth can be varied to meet the needs of the job. Use 14 or 18 teeth per inch (TPI) for cutting plaster or soft metals, such as aluminum and copper. Use 24 or 32 teeth per inch for steel or pipe. Hacksaw blades should be installed with the teeth pointing away from the handle. This means that a hacksaw only cuts while the blade is pushed in the forward direction. ● **SEE FIGURE 1–49.**

SAFE USE OF HACKSAWS   Check that the hacksaw is equipped with the correct blade for the job and that the teeth are pointed away from the handle. When using a hacksaw, move the hacksaw slowly away from you, then lift slightly and return for another cut.

BASIC HAND TOOL LIST

The following is a typical list of hand tools every automotive technician should possess. Specialty tools are not included.

Safety glasses

Tool chest

1/4-in. drive socket set (1/4 in. to 9/16 in. standard and deep sockets; 6 mm to 15 mm standard and deep sockets)

1/4-in. drive ratchet

1/4-in. drive 2-in. extension

1/4-in. drive 6-in. extension

1/4-in. drive handle

3/8-in. drive socket set (3/8 in. to 7/8 in. standard and deep sockets; 10 mm to 19 mm standard and deep sockets)

3/8-in. drive Torx set (T40, T45, T50, and T55)

3/8-in. drive 13/16-in. plug socket

3/8-in. drive 5/8-in. plug socket

3/8-in. drive ratchet

3/8-in. drive 1 1/2-in. extension

3/8-in. drive 3-in. extension

3/8-in. drive 6-in. extension

3/8-in. drive 18-in. extension

3/8-in. drive universal

1/2-in. drive socket set (1/2 in. to 1 in. standard and deep sockets)

1/2-in. drive ratchet

1/2-in. drive breaker bar

1/2-in. drive 5-in. extension

1/2-in. drive 10-in. extension

3/8-in. to 1/4-in. adapter

1/2-in. to 3/8-in. adapter

3/8-in. to 1/2-in. adapter

Crowfoot set (fractional in.)

Crowfoot set (metric)

3/8- through 1-in. combination wrench set

10 mm through 19 mm combination wrench set

1/16-in. through 1/4-in. hex wrench set

2 mm through 12 mm hex wrench set

3/8-in. hex socket

13 mm to 14 mm flare-nut wrench

15 mm to 17 mm flare-nut wrench

5/16-in. to 3/8-in. flare-nut wrench

7/16-in. to 1/2-in. flare-nut wrench

1/2-in. to 9/16-in. flare-nut wrench

Diagonal pliers

Needle pliers

Adjustable-jaw pliers

Locking pliers

Snap-ring pliers

Stripping or crimping pliers

Ball-peen hammer

Rubber hammer

Dead-blow hammer

Five-piece standard screwdriver set

Four-piece Phillips screwdriver set

#15 Torx screwdriver

#20 Torx screwdriver

Center punch

Pin punches (assorted sizes)

Chisel

Utility knife

Valve core tool

Filter wrench (large filters)

Filter wrench (smaller filters)

Test light

Feeler gauge

Scraper

Pinch bar

Magnet

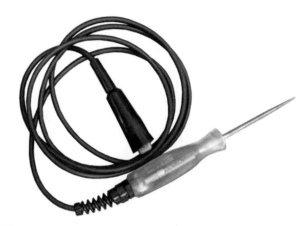

FIGURE 1–51 A typical large tool box, showing just one of many drawers.

FIGURE 1–50 A typical beginning technician tool set that includes the basic tools to get started.

TOOL SETS AND ACCESSORIES

A beginning service technician may wish to start with a small set of tools before purchasing an expensive tool set. ● **SEE FIGURES 1–50** and **1–51**.

🔧 TECH TIP

Need to Borrow a Tool More Than Twice? Buy It!

Most service technicians agree that it is okay for a beginning technician to borrow a tool occasionally. However, if a tool has to be borrowed more than twice, then be sure to purchase it as soon as possible. Also, whenever a tool is borrowed, be sure that you clean the tool and let the technician you borrowed the tool from know that you are returning the tool. These actions will help in any future dealings with other technicians.

FIGURE 1–52 A typical 12-volt test light.

ELECTRICAL HAND TOOLS

TEST LIGHT A test light is used to test for electricity. A typical automotive test light consists of a clear plastic screwdriver-like handle that contains a lightbulb. A wire is attached to one terminal of the bulb, which the technician connects to a clean metal part of the vehicle. The other end of the bulb is attached to a point that can be used to test for electricity at a connector or wire. When there is power at the point and a good connection at the other end, the lightbulb lights. ● **SEE FIGURE 1–52.**

SOLDERING GUNS

ELECTRIC SOLDERING GUN. This type of soldering gun is usually powered by 110-volt AC and often has two power settings expressed in watts. A typical electric soldering gun will produce from 85 to 300 watts of heat at the tip, which is more than adequate for soldering.

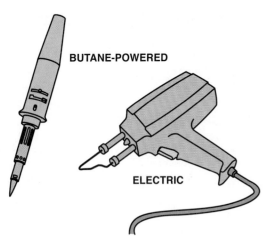

FIGURE 1–53 An electric and butane-powered soldering guns used to make electrical repairs. Soldering guns are sold by the wattage rating. The higher the wattage, the greater amount of heat created. Most solder guns used for automotive electrical work usually fall within the 60- to 160-watt range.

ELECTRICAL HAND TOOLS (CONTINUED)

ELECTRIC SOLDERING PENCIL. This type of soldering iron is less expensive and creates less heat than an electric soldering gun. A typical electric soldering pencil (iron) creates 30 to 60 watts of heat and is suitable for soldering smaller wires and connections.

BUTANE-POWERED SOLDERING IRON. A butane-powered soldering iron is portable and very useful for automotive service work because an electrical cord is not needed. Most butane-powered soldering irons produce about 60 watts of heat, which is enough for most automotive soldering. ● **SEE FIGURE 1–53.**

ELECTRICAL WORK HAND TOOLS In addition to a soldering iron, most service technicians who do electrical-related work should have the following:

- Wire cutters
- Wire strippers
- Wire crimpers
- Heat gun for heat shrink tubing

DIGITAL METER A digital meter is a necessary tool for any electrical diagnosis and troubleshooting. A digital multimeter, abbreviated DMM, is usually capable of measuring the following units of electricity:

- DC volts
- AC volts
- Ohms
- Amperes

HAND TOOL MAINTENANCE

Most hand tools are constructed of rust-resistant metals but they can still rust or corrode if not properly maintained. For best results and long tool life, the following steps should be taken:

- Clean each tool before placing it back into the tool box.
- Keep tools separated. Moisture on metal tools will start to rust more readily if the tools are in contact with another metal tool.
- Line the drawers of the tool box with a material that will prevent the tools from moving as the drawers are opened and closed. This helps to quickly locate the proper tool and size.
- Release the tension on all "clicker-type" torque wrenches.
- Keep the tool box secure.

? FREQUENTLY ASKED QUESTION

What Is an "SST"?

Vehicle manufacturers often specify a **special service tool (SST)** to properly disassemble and assemble components, such as transmissions and other components. These tools are also called special tools and are available from the vehicle manufacturer or their tool supplier, such as Kent-Moore and Miller tools. Many service technicians do not have access to special service tools so they use generic versions that are available from aftermarket sources.

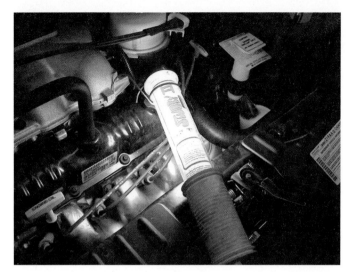

FIGURE 1–54 A fluorescent trouble light operates cooler and is safer to use in the shop because it is protected against accidental breakage where gasoline or other flammable liquids would happen to come in contact with the light.

FIGURE 1–55 A typical 1/2-in. drive air impact wrench. The direction of rotation can be changed to loosen or tighten a fastener.

FIGURE 1–56 A typical battery-powered 3/8-in. drive impact wrench.

TROUBLE LIGHTS

INCANDESCENT *Incandescent lights* use a filament that produces light when electric current flows through the bulb. This was the standard **trouble light**, also called a *work light* for many years until safety issues caused most shops to switch to safer fluorescent or LED lights. If incandescent lightbulbs are used, try to locate bulbs that are rated "rough service," which is designed to withstand shock and vibration more than conventional lightbulbs.

☠ **WARNING**

Do not use incandescent trouble lights around gasoline or other flammable liquids. The liquids can cause the bulb to break and the hot filament can ignite the flammable liquid which can cause personal injury or even death.

FLUORESCENT A trouble light is an essential piece of shop equipment, and for safety, should be fluorescent rather than incandescent. Incandescent lightbulbs can scatter or break if gasoline were to be splashed onto the bulb creating a serious fire hazard. Fluorescent light tubes are not as likely to be broken and are usually protected by a clear plastic enclosure. Trouble lights are usually attached to a retractor, which can hold 20 to 50 feet of electrical cord. ● **SEE FIGURE 1–54**.

LED TROUBLE LIGHT **Light-emitting diode (LED)** trouble lights are excellent to use because they are shock resistant, long lasting, and do not represent a fire hazard. Some trouble lights are battery powered and therefore can be used in places where an attached electrical cord could present problems.

AIR AND ELECTRICALLY OPERATED TOOLS

IMPACT WRENCH An impact wrench, either air or electrically powered, is a tool that is used to remove and install fasteners. The air-operated 1/2-in. drive impact wrench is the most commonly used unit. ● **SEE FIGURE 1–55**.

Electrically powered impact wrenches commonly include:

- Battery-powered units. ● **SEE FIGURE 1–56**.
- 110-volt AC-powered units. This type of impact is very useful, especially if compressed air is not readily available.

FIGURE 1–57 A black impact socket. Always use an impact-type socket whenever using an impact wrench to avoid the possibility of shattering the socket which could cause personal injury.

AIR AND ELECTRICITY OPERATED TOOLS (CONTINUED)

FIGURE 1–58 An air ratchet is a very useful tool that allows fast removal and installation of fasteners, especially in areas that are difficult to reach or do not have room enough to move a hand ratchet or wrench.

FIGURE 1–59 This typical die grinder surface preparation kit includes the air-operated die grinder as well as a variety of sanding disks for smoothing surfaces or removing rust.

> **☠ WARNING**
>
> Always use impact sockets with impact wrenches, and always wear eye protection in case the socket or fastener shatters. Impact sockets are thicker walled and constructed with premium alloy steel. They are hardened with a black oxide finish to help prevent corrosion and distinguish them from regular sockets. ● SEE FIGURE 1–57.

AIR RATCHET   An air ratchet is used to remove and install fasteners that would normally be removed or installed using a ratchet and a socket. ● **SEE FIGURE 1–58**.

DIE GRINDER   A die grinder is a commonly used air-powered tool which can also be used to sand or remove gaskets and rust. ● **SEE FIGURE 1–59**.

BENCH- OR PEDESTAL-MOUNTED GRINDER   These high-powered grinders can be equipped with a wire brush wheel and/or a stone wheel.

- **Wire brush wheel**—This type is used to clean threads of bolts as well as to remove gaskets from sheet metal engine parts.
- **Stone wheel**—This type is used to grind metal or to remove the mushroom from the top of punches or chisels. ● **SEE FIGURE 1–60**.

FIGURE 1–60 A typical pedestal grinder with a wire wheel on the left side and a stone wheel on the right side. Even though this machine is equipped with guards, safety glasses or a face shield should always be worn whenever using a grinder or wire wheel.

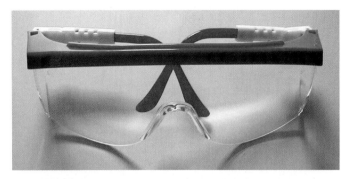

FIGURE 1–61 Safety glasses should be worn at all times when working on or around any vehicle or servicing any components.

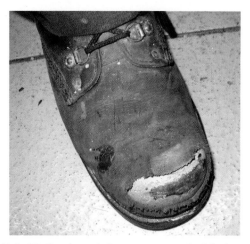

FIGURE 1–62 Steel-toed shoes are a worthwhile investment to help prevent foot injury due to falling objects. Even these well-worn shoes can protect the feet of this service technician.

Air and Electrically Operated Tools (CONTINUED)

> ☠ **WARNING**
>
> Always wear a face shield when using a wire wheel or a grinder.

Most **bench grinders** are equipped with a grinder wheel (stone) on one end and a wire brush wheel on the other end. A bench grinder is a very useful piece of shop equipment and the wire wheel end can be used for the following:

- Cleaning threads of bolts
- Cleaning gaskets from sheet metal parts, such as steel valve covers

CAUTION: Only use a steel wire brush on steel or iron components. If a steel wire brush is used on aluminum or copper-based metal parts, it can remove metal from the part.

The grinding stone end of the bench grinder can be used for the following:

- Sharpening blades and drill bits
- Grinding off the heads of rivets or parts
- Sharpening sheet metal parts for custom fitting

PERSONAL PROTECTIVE EQUIPMENT

Service technicians should wear **personal protective equipment (PPE)** to prevent personal injury. The personal protection devices include the following:

SAFETY GLASSES Wear safety glasses at all times while servicing any vehicle and be sure that they meet standard ANSI Z87.1. ● **SEE FIGURE 1–61.**

STEEL-TOED SAFETY SHOES ● **SEE FIGURE 1–62.** If steel-toed safety shoes are not available, then leather-topped shoes offer more protection than canvas or cloth.

BUMP CAP Service technicians working under a vehicle should wear a **bump cap** to protect the head against under-vehicle objects and the pads of the lift. ● **SEE FIGURE 1–63.**

HEARING PROTECTION Hearing protection should be worn if the sound around you requires that you raise your voice (sound level higher than 90 dB). For example, a typical lawn-mower produces noise at a level of about 110 dB. This means that everyone who uses a lawnmower or other lawn or garden equipment should wear ear protection.

GLOVES Many technicians wear gloves not only to help keep their hands clean but also to help protect their skin from the effects of dirty engine oil and other possibly hazardous materials.

FIGURE 1–63 One version of a bump cap is a molded plastic insert that is worn inside a regular cloth cap.

FIGURE 1–64 Protective gloves are available in several sizes and materials.

Personal Protective Equipment (CONTINUED)

Several types of gloves and their characteristics include:

- **Latex surgical gloves.** These gloves are relatively inexpensive, but tend to stretch, swell, and weaken when exposed to gas, oil, or solvents.

- **Vinyl gloves.** These gloves are also inexpensive and are not affected by gas, oil, or solvents.

- **Polyurethane gloves.** These gloves are more expensive, yet very strong. Even though these gloves are also not affected by gas, oil, or solvents, they do tend to be slippery.

- **Nitrile gloves.** These gloves are exactly like latex gloves, but are not affected by gas, oil, or solvents, yet they tend to be expensive.

- **Mechanic's gloves.** These gloves are usually made of synthetic leather and spandex and provide thermo protection, as well as protection from dirt and grime.
- ● **SEE FIGURE 1–64.**

SAFETY PRECAUTIONS

Besides wearing personal safety equipment, there are also many actions that should be performed to keep safe in the shop. These actions include:

- Remove jewelry that may get caught on something or act as a conductor to an exposed electrical circuit. ● **SEE FIGURE 1–65.**

- Take care of your hands. Keep your hands clean by washing with soap and hot water that is at least 110°F (43°C).

- Avoid loose or dangling clothing.

- When lifting any object, get a secure grip with solid footing. Keep the load close to your body to minimize the strain. Lift with your legs and arms, not your back.

- Do not twist your body when carrying a load. Instead, pivot your feet to help prevent strain on the spine.

- Ask for help when moving or lifting heavy objects.

- Push a heavy object rather than pull it. (This is opposite to the way you should work with tools—never push a wrench! If you do and a bolt or nut loosens, your entire weight is used to propel your hand(s) forward. This usually results in cuts, bruises, or other painful injury.)

- Always connect an exhaust hose to the tailpipe of any running vehicle to help prevent the buildup of carbon monoxide inside a closed garage space. ● **SEE FIGURE 1–66.**

- When standing, keep objects, parts, and tools with which you are working between chest height and waist height. If seated, work at tasks that are at elbow height.

- Always be sure the hood is securely held open.

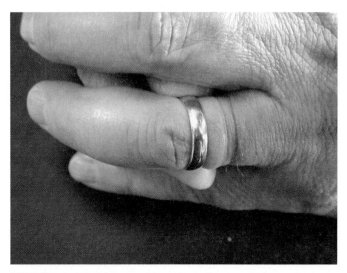

FIGURE 1–65 Remove all jewelry before performing service work on any vehicle.

FIGURE 1–66 Always connect an exhaust hose to the tailpipe of a vehicle to be run inside a building.

FIGURE 1–67 A binder clip being used to keep a fender cover from falling off.

FIGURE 1–68 Covering the interior as soon as the vehicle comes in for service helps improve customer satisfaction.

VEHICLE PROTECTION

FENDER COVERS Whenever working under the hood of any vehicle be sure to use fender covers. They not only help protect the vehicle from possible damage but they also provide a clean surface to place parts and tools. The major problem with using fender covers is that they tend to move and often fall off the vehicle. To help prevent the fender covers from falling off secure them to a lip of the fender using a *binder clip* available at most office supply stores. ● **SEE FIGURE 1–67**.

INTERIOR PROTECTION Always protect the interior of the vehicle from accidental damage or dirt and grease by covering the seat, steering wheel, and floor with a protective covering. ● **SEE FIGURE 1–68**.

SAFETY TIP

Shop Cloth Disposal

Always dispose of oily shop cloths in an enclosed container to prevent a fire. ● **SEE FIGURE 1–69.** Whenever oily cloths are thrown together on the floor or workbench, a chemical reaction can occur, which can ignite the cloth even without an open flame. This process of ignition without an open flame is called **spontaneous combustion.**

FIGURE 1–69 All oily shop cloths should be stored in a metal container equipped with a lid to help prevent spontaneous combustion.

SAFETY LIFTING (HOISTING) A VEHICLE

Many chassis and underbody service procedures require that the vehicle be hoisted or lifted off the ground. The simplest methods involve the use of drive-on ramps or a floor jack and safety (jack) stands, whereas in-ground or surface-mounted lifts provide greater access.

Setting the pads is a critical part of this hoisting procedure. All vehicle service information including service, shop and owner's manuals, include recommended locations to be used when hoisting (lifting) a vehicle. Newer vehicles have a triangle decal on the driver's door indicating the recommended lift points. The recommended standards for the lift points and lifting procedures are found in SAE Standard JRP-2184. ● **SEE FIGURE 1–70.**

These recommendations typically include the following points:

1. The vehicle should be centered on the lift or hoist so as not to overload one side or put too much force either forward or rearward. ● **SEE FIGURE 1–71.**

2. The pads of the lift should be spread as far apart as possible to provide a stable platform.

3. Each pad should be placed under a portion of the vehicle that is strong and capable of supporting the weight of the vehicle.

   a. Pinch welds at the bottom edge of the body are generally considered to be strong.

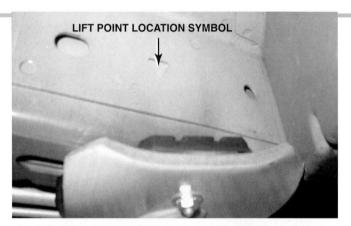

FIGURE 1–70 Most newer vehicles have a triangle symbol indicating the recommended hoisting lift location.

CAUTION: Even though pinch weld seams are the recommended location for hoisting many vehicles with unitized bodies (unit-body), care should be taken not to place the pad(s) too far forward or rearward. Incorrect placement of the vehicle on the lift could cause the vehicle to be imbalanced, and the vehicle could fall. This is exactly what happened to the vehicle in ● FIGURE 1–72.

   b. Boxed areas of the body are the best places to position the pads on a vehicle without a frame. Be careful to note whether the arms of the lift might come into contact with other parts of the vehicle before the pad

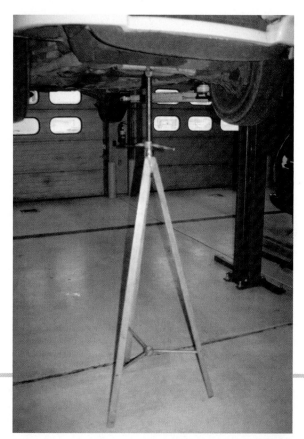

(a)

(b)

FIGURE 1–71 (a) Tall safety stands can be used to provide additional support for the vehicle while on the hoist.
(b) A block of wood should be used to avoid the possibility of doing damage to components supported by the stand.

touches the intended location. Commonly damaged areas include the following:

(1) Rocker panel moldings

(2) Exhaust system (including catalytic converter)

(3) Tires or body panels (● **SEE FIGURES 1–73** and **1–74.**)

FIGURE 1–72 This training vehicle fell from the hoist because the pads were not set correctly. No one was hurt but the vehicle was damaged.

4. The vehicle should be raised about a foot (30 centimeters [cm]) off the floor, then stopped and shaken to check for stability. If the vehicle seems to be stable when checked at a short distance from the floor, continue raising the vehicle and continue to view the vehicle until it has reached the desired height. The hoist should be lowered onto the mechanical locks, and then raised off of the locks before lowering.

CAUTION: Do not look away from the vehicle while it is being raised (or lowered) on a hoist. Often one side or one end of the hoist can stop or fail, resulting in the vehicle being slanted enough to slip or fall, creating physical damage not only to the vehicle and/or hoist but also to the technician or others who may be nearby.

HINT: Most hoists can be safely placed at any desired height. For ease while working, the area in which you are working should be at chest level. When working on brakes or suspension components, it is not necessary to work on them down near the floor or over your head. Raise the hoist so that the components are at chest level.

5. Before lowering the hoist, the safety latch(es) must be released and the direction of the controls reversed. The speed downward is often adjusted to be as slow as possible for additional safety.

(a)

(b)

FIGURE 1–73 (a) An assortment of hoist pad adapters that are often needed to safely hoist many pickup trucks, vans, and sport utility vehicles (SUVs). (b) A view from underneath a Chevrolet pickup truck showing how the pad extensions are used to attach the hoist lifting pad to contact the frame.

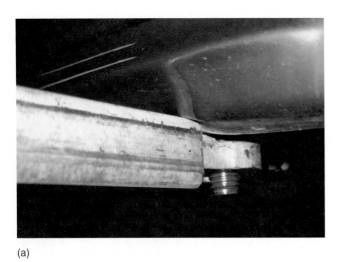
(a)

(b)

FIGURE 1–74 (a) The pad arm is just contacting the rocker panel of the vehicle. (b) The pad arm has dented the rocker panel on this vehicle because the pad was set too far inward underneath the vehicle.

JACKS AND SAFETY STANDS

Floor jacks properly rated for the weight of the vehicle being raised are a common vehicle lifting tool. Floor jacks are portable and relatively inexpensive and must be used with safety (jack) stands. The floor jack is used to raise the vehicle off the ground and safety stands should be placed under the frame on the body of the vehicle. The weight of the vehicle should never be kept on the hydraulic floor jack because a failure of the jack could cause the vehicle to fall. ● **SEE FIGURE 1–75**. The jack is then slowly released to allow the vehicle weight to be supported on the safety stands. If the front or rear of the vehicle is being raised, the opposite end of the vehicle must be blocked.

CAUTION: Safety stands should be rated higher than the weight they support.

(a)

(b)

FIGURE 1–75 (a) A typical 3-ton (6,000-pound) capacity hydraulic jack. (b) Whenever a vehicle is raised off the ground, a safety stand should be placed under the frame, axle, or body to support the weight of the vehicle.

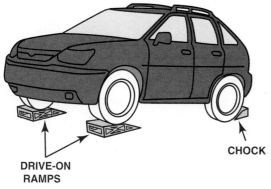

DRIVE-ON
RAMPS

CHOCK

FIGURE 1–76 Drive-on-type ramps are dangerous to use. The wheels on the ground level must be chocked (blocked) to prevent accidental movement down the ramp.

DRIVE-ON RAMPS

Ramps are an inexpensive way to raise the front or rear of a vehicle. ● **SEE FIGURE 1–76.** Ramps are easy to store, but they can be dangerous because they can "kick out" when driving the vehicle onto the ramps.

CAUTION: Professional repair shops do not use ramps because they are dangerous to use. Use only with extreme care.

ELECTRICAL CORD SAFETY

Use correctly grounded three-prong sockets and extension cords to operate power tools. Some tools use only two-prong plugs. Make sure these are double insulated and repair or replace any electrical cords that are cut or damaged to prevent the possibility of an electrical shock. When not in use, keep electrical cords off the floor to prevent tripping over them. Tape the cords down if they are placed in high foot traffic areas.

JUMP STARTING AND BATTERY SAFETY

To jump start another vehicle with a dead battery, connect good-quality copper jumper cables as indicated in ● **FIGURE 1–77** or a jump box. The last connection made should always be on the engine block or an engine bracket as far from the battery as possible. It is normal for a spark to be created when the jumper cables finally complete the jumping circuit, and this spark could cause an explosion of the gases around the battery. Many newer vehicles have special ground connections built away from the

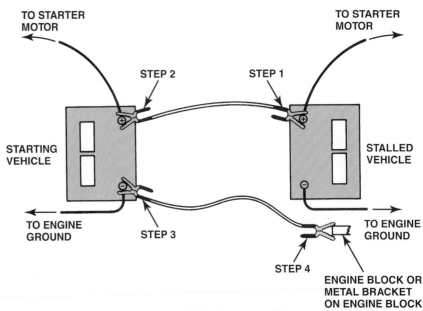

FIGURE 1–77 Jumper cable usage guide. Follow the same connections if using a portable jump box.

TO STARTER MOTOR

TO STARTER MOTOR

STEP 2

STEP 1

STARTING VEHICLE

STALLED VEHICLE

TO ENGINE GROUND

STEP 3

TO ENGINE GROUND

STEP 4

ENGINE BLOCK OR METAL BRACKET ON ENGINE BLOCK

JUMP STARTING AND BATTERY SAFETY (CONTINUED)

battery just for the purpose of jump starting. Check the owner's manual or service information for the exact location.

Batteries contain acid and should be handled with care to avoid tipping them greater than a 45-degree angle. Always remove jewelry when working around a battery to avoid the possibility of electrical shock or burns, which can occur when the metal comes in contact with a 12-volt circuit and ground, such as the body of the vehicle.

 **SAFETY TIP**

Air Hose Safety

Improper use of an air nozzle can cause blindness or deafness. Compressed air must be reduced to less than 30 psi (206 kPa). ● **SEE FIGURE 1–78.** If an air nozzle is used to dry and clean parts, make sure the airstream is directed away from anyone else in the immediate area. Coil and store air hoses when they are not in use.

FIGURE 1–78 The air pressure going to the nozzle should be reduced to 30 psi or less to help prevent personal injury.

FIRE EXTINGUISHERS

There are four **fire extinguisher classes**. Each class should be used on specific fires only:

- **Class A** is designed for use on general combustibles, such as cloth, paper, and wood.
- **Class B** is designed for use on flammable liquids and greases, including gasoline, oil, thinners, and solvents.
- **Class C** is used only on electrical fires.
- **Class D** is effective only on combustible metals such as powdered aluminum, sodium, or magnesium.

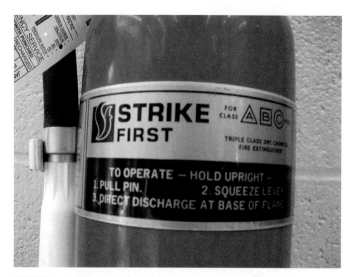

FIGURE 1–79 A typical fire extinguisher designed to be used on type A, B, or C fires.

FIGURE 1–80 A CO_2 fire extinguisher being used on a fire set in an open drum during a demonstration at a fire training center.

The class rating is clearly marked on the side of every fire extinguisher. Many extinguishers are good for multiple types of fires. ● **SEE FIGURE 1–79.**

When using a fire extinguisher, remember the word "PASS."

P = Pull the safety pin.

A = Aim the nozzle of the extinguisher at the base of the fire.

S = Squeeze the lever to actuate the extinguisher.

S = Sweep the nozzle from side-to-side.

● **SEE FIGURE 1–80.**

TYPES OF FIRE EXTINGUISHERS Types of fire extinguishers include the following.

- **Water.** A water fire extinguisher, usually in a pressurized container, is good to use on Class A fires by reducing the temperature to the point where a fire cannot be sustained.

- **Carbon dioxide (CO_2).** A carbon dioxide fire extinguisher is good for almost any type of fire, especially Class B or Class C materials. A CO_2 fire extinguisher works by removing the oxygen from the fire and the cold CO_2 also helps reduce the temperature of the fire.

- **Dry chemical (yellow).** A dry chemical fire extinguisher is good for Class A, B, or C fires by coating the flammable materials, which eliminates the oxygen from the fire. A dry chemical fire extinguisher tends to be very corrosive and will cause damage to electronic devices.

FIGURE 1–81 A treated wool blanket is kept in an easy-to-open wall-mounted holder and should be placed in a central location in the shop.

FIRE BLANKETS

Fire blankets are required to be available in the shop areas. If a person is on fire, a fire blanket should be removed from its storage bag and thrown over and around the victim to smother the fire. ● **SEE FIGURE 1–81** showing a typical fire blanket.

FIGURE 1–82 A first aid box should be centrally located in the shop and kept stocked with the recommended supplies.

FIGURE 1–83 A typical eye wash station. Often a thorough flushing of the eyes with water is the first and often the best treatment in the event of eye contamination.

FIRST AID AND EYE WASH STATIONS

All shop areas must be equipped with a first aid kit and an eye wash station centrally located and kept stocked with emergency supplies. ● **SEE FIGURE 1–82.**

FIRST AID KIT A first aid kit should include:

- Bandages (variety)
- Gauze pads
- Roll gauze
- Iodine swab sticks
- Antibiotic ointment
- Hydrocortisone cream
- Burn gel packets
- Eye wash solution
- Scissors
- Tweezers
- Gloves
- First aid guide

Every shop should have a person trained in first aid. If there is an accident, call for help immediately.

EYE WASH STATION An **eye wash station** should be centrally located and used whenever any liquid or chemical gets into the eyes. If such an emergency does occur, keep eyes in a constant stream of water and call for professional assistance. ● **SEE FIGURE 1–83.**

 **SAFETY TIP**

Infection Control Precautions

Working on a vehicle can result in personal injury including the possibility of being cut or hurt enough to cause bleeding. Some infections such as hepatitis B, HIV (which can cause acquired immunodeficiency syndrome, or AIDS), hepatitis C virus, and others are transmitted in the blood. These infections are commonly called blood-borne pathogens. Report any injury that involves blood to your supervisor and take the necessary precautions to avoid coming in contact with blood from another person.

FIGURE 1–84 A warning label on a Honda hybrid warns that a person can be killed due to the high-voltage circuits under the cover.

FIGURE 1–85 The high-voltage disconnect switch is in the trunk area on a Toyota Prius. Insulated rubber lineman's gloves should be worn when removing this plug. (Courtesy of Tony Martin)

HYBRID ELECTRIC VEHICLE SAFETY ISSUES

Hybrid electric vehicles (HEVs) use a high-voltage battery pack and an electric motor(s) to help propel the vehicle. ● **SEE FIGURE 1–84** for an example of a typical warning label on a hybrid electric vehicle. The gasoline or diesel engine also is equipped with a generator or a combination starter and an integrated starter generator (ISG) or integrated starter alternator (ISA). To safely work around a hybrid electric vehicle, the high-voltage (HV) battery and circuits should be shut off following these steps:

STEP 1 Turn off the ignition key (if equipped) and remove the key from the ignition switch. (This will shut off all high-voltage circuits if the relay[s] is [are] working correctly.)

STEP 2 Disconnect the high-voltage circuits.

> ☠ **WARNING**
>
> Some vehicle manufacturers specify that insulated rubber *lineman's gloves* be used whenever working around the high-voltage circuits to prevent the danger of electrical shock.

TOYOTA PRIUS The cutoff switch is located in the trunk. To gain access, remove three clips holding the upper left portion of the trunk side cover. To disconnect the high-voltage system, pull the orange handled plug while wearing insulated rubber lineman's gloves. ● **SEE FIGURE 1–85**.

FORD ESCAPE/MERCURY MARINER Ford and Mercury specify that the following steps should be included when working with the high-voltage (HV) systems of a hybrid vehicle:

- Four orange cones are to be placed at the four corners of the vehicle to create a buffer zone.

- High-voltage insulated gloves are to be worn with an outer leather glove to protect the inner rubber glove from possible damage.

- The service technician should also wear a face shield and a fiberglass hook should be in the area and used to move a technician in the event of electrocution.

The high-voltage shut-off switch is located in the rear of the vehicle under the right side carpet. ● **SEE FIGURE 1–86**. Rotate the handle to the "service shipping" position, lift it out to

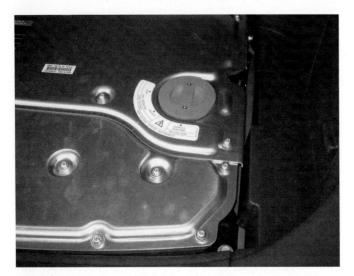

FIGURE 1–86 The high-voltage shut-off switch on a Ford Escape hybrid. The switch is located under the carpet at the rear of the vehicle.

FIGURE 1–87 The shut-off switch on a GM parallel hybrid truck is green because this system uses 42 volts instead of higher, and possibly fatal, voltages used in other hybrid vehicles.

JUMP STARTING AND BATTERY SAFETY (CONTINUED)

disable the high-voltage circuit, and wait 5 minutes before removing high-voltage cables.

HONDA CIVIC   To totally disable the high-voltage system on a Honda Civic, remove the main fuse (labeled number 1) from the driver's side underhood fuse panel. This should be all that is necessary to shut off the high-voltage circuit. If this is not possible, then remove the rear seat cushion and seat back. Remove the metal switch cover labeled "up" and remove the red locking cover. Move the "battery module switch" down to disable the high-voltage system.

CHEVROLET SILVERADO/GMC SIERRA PICKUP TRUCK   The high-voltage shut-off switch is located under the rear passenger seat. Remove the cover marked "energy storage box" and turn the green service disconnect switch to the horizontal position to turn off the high-voltage circuits. ● **SEE FIGURE 1–87.**

   **WARNING**

Do not touch any orange wiring or component without following the vehicle manufacturer's procedures and wearing the specified personal protective equipment.

1 The first step in hoisting a vehicle is to properly align the vehicle in the center of the stall.

2 Most vehicles will be correctly positioned when the left front tire is centered on the tire pad.

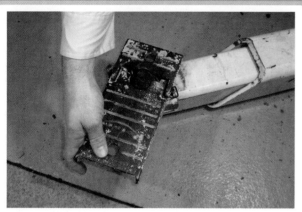

3 The arms can be moved in and out and most pads can be rotated to allow for many different types of vehicle construction.

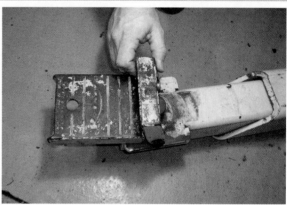

4 Most lifts are equipped with short pad extensions that are often necessary to use to allow the pad to contact the frame of a vehicle without causing the arm of the lift to hit and damage parts of the body.

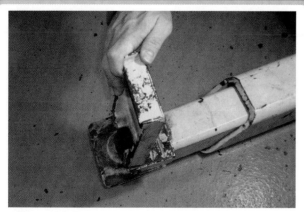

5 Tall pad extensions can also be used to gain access to the frame of a vehicle. This position is needed to safely hoist many pickup trucks, vans, and sport utility vehicles.

6 An additional extension may be necessary to hoist a truck or van equipped with running boards to give the necessary clearance.

CONTINUED ▶

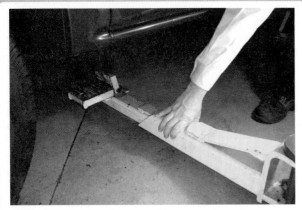

7 Position the pads under the vehicle under the recommended locations.

8 After being sure all pads are correctly positioned, use the electromechanical controls to raise the vehicle.

9 With the vehicle raised one foot (30 cm) off the ground, push down on the vehicle to check to see if it is stable on the pads. If the vehicle rocks, lower the vehicle and reset the pads. The vehicle can be raised to any desired working level. Be sure the safety is engaged before working on or under the vehicle.

10 If raising a vehicle without a frame, place the flat pads under the pinch weld seam to spread the load. If additional clearance is necessary, the pads can be raised as shown.

11 When the service work is completed, the hoist should be raised slightly and the safety released before using the hydraulic lever to lower the vehicle.

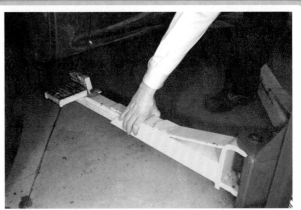

12 After lowering the vehicle, be sure all arms of the lift are moved out of the way before driving the vehicle out of the work stall.

SUMMARY

1. Bolts, studs, and nuts are commonly used as fasteners in the chassis. The sizes for fractional and metric threads are different and are not interchangeable. The grade is the rating of the strength of a fastener.

2. Whenever a vehicle is raised above the ground, it must be supported at a substantial section of the body or frame.

3. Wrenches are available in open end, box end, and combination open and box end.

4. An adjustable wrench should only be used where the proper size is not available.

5. Line wrenches are also called flare-nut wrenches, fitting wrenches, or tube-nut wrenches and are used to remove fuel or refrigerant lines.

6. Sockets are rotated by a ratchet or breaker bar, also called a flex handle.

7. Torque wrenches measure the amount of torque applied to a fastener.

8. Screwdriver types include straight blade (flat tip) and Phillips.

9. Hammers and mallets come in a variety of sizes and weights.

10. Pliers are a useful tool and are available in many different types, including slip-joint, multigroove, linesman's, diagonal, needle-nose, and locking pliers.

11. Other common hand tools include snap-ring pliers, files, cutters, punches, chisels, and hacksaws.

12. Hybrid electric vehicles should be de-powered if any of the high-voltage components are going to be serviced.

REVIEW QUESTIONS

1. List three precautions that must be taken whenever hoisting (lifting) a vehicle.

2. Describe how to determine the grade of a fastener, including how the markings differ between fractional and metric bolts.

3. List four items that are personal protective equipment (PPE).

4. List the types of fire extinguishers and their usage.

5. Why are wrenches offset 15 degrees?

6. What are the other names for a line wrench?

7. What are the standard automotive drive sizes for sockets?

8. Which type of screwdriver requires the use of a hammer or mallet?

9. What is inside a dead-blow hammer?

10. What type of cutter is available in left and right cutters?

CHAPTER QUIZ

1. The correct location for the pads when hoisting or jacking the vehicle can often be found in the _____.
   a. Service manual
   b. Shop manual
   c. Owner's manual
   d. All of the above

2. For the best working position, the work should be _____.
   a. At neck or head level
   b. At knee or ankle level
   c. Overhead by about 1 foot
   d. At chest or elbow level

3. A high-strength bolt is identified by _____.
   a. A UNC symbol
   b. Lines on the head
   c. Strength letter codes
   d. The coarse threads

4. A fastener that uses threads on both ends is called a _____.
   a. Cap screw
   b. Stud
   c. Machine screw
   d. Crest fastener

5. When working with hand tools, always _____.
   a. Push the wrench—don't pull toward you
   b. Pull a wrench—don't push a wrench away from you

6. The proper term for Channel Locks is _____.
   a. Vise Grips
   b. Crescent wrench
   c. Locking pliers
   d. Multigroove adjustable pliers

7. The proper term for Vise Grips is _____.
   a. Locking pliers
   b. Slip-joint pliers
   c. Side cuts
   d. Multigroove adjustable pliers

8. Two technicians are discussing torque wrenches. Technician A says that a torque wrench is capable of tightening a fastener with more torque than a conventional breaker bar or ratchet. Technician B says that a torque wrench should be calibrated regularly for the most accurate results. Which technician is correct?
   a. Technician A only
   b. Technician B only
   c. Both Technicians A and B
   d. Neither Technician A nor B

9. What type of screwdriver should be used if there is very limited space above the head of the fastener?
   a. Offset screwdriver
   b. Stubby screwdriver
   c. Impact screwdriver
   d. Robertson screwdriver

10. What type of hammer is plastic coated, has a metal casing inside, and is filled with small lead balls?
    a. Dead-blow hammer
    b. Soft-blow hammer
    c. Sledgehammer
    d. Plastic hammer

ENVIRONMENTAL AND HAZARDOUS MATERIALS

OBJECTIVES

After studying Chapter 2, the reader will be able to:

1. Prepare for the ASE assumed knowledge content required by all service technicians to adhere to environmentally appropriate actions and behavior.
2. Define the Occupational Safety and Health Act (OSHA).
3. Explain the term material safety data sheet (MSDS).
4. Identify hazardous waste materials in accordance with state and federal regulations and follow proper safety precautions while handling hazardous waste materials.
5. Define the steps required to safely handle and store automotive chemicals and waste.

KEY TERMS

Aboveground storage tank (AGST) 45
Asbestosis 43
BCI 48
CAA 42
CFR 41
EPA 41
Hazardous waste material 41
HEPA vacuum 43
Mercury 50
MSDS 42
OSHA 41
RCRA 42
Right-to-know laws 41
Solvent 43
Underground storage tank (UST) 45
Used oil 44
WHMIS 42

HAZARDOUS WASTE

DEFINITION OF HAZARDOUS WASTE **Hazardous waste materials** are chemicals, or components, that the shop no longer needs that pose a danger to the environment and people if they are disposed of in ordinary garbage cans or sewers. However, no material is considered hazardous waste until the shop has finished using it and is ready to dispose of it.

PERSONAL PROTECTIVE EQUIPMENT (PPE) When handling hazardous waste material, one must always wear the proper protective clothing and equipment detailed in the right-to-know laws. This includes respirator equipment. All recommended procedures must be followed accurately. Personal injury may result from improper clothing, equipment, and procedures when handling hazardous materials.

FEDERAL AND STATE LAWS

OCCUPATIONAL SAFETY AND HEALTH ACT The United States Congress passed the **Occupational Safety and Health Act (OSHA)** in 1970. This legislation was designed to assist and encourage the citizens of the United States in their efforts to assure:

- Safe and healthful working conditions by providing research, information, education, and training in the field of occupational safety and health.

- Safe and healthful working conditions for working men and women by authorizing enforcement of the standards developed under the Act.

Because about 25% of workers are exposed to health and safety hazards on the job, the OSHA standards are necessary to monitor, control, and educate workers regarding health and safety in the workplace.

EPA The **Environmental Protection Agency (EPA)** publishes a list of hazardous materials that is included in the **Code of Federal Regulations (CFR)**. The EPA considers waste hazardous if it is included on the EPA list of hazardous materials, or it has one or more of the following characteristics:

- **Reactive**—Any material that reacts violently with water or other chemicals is considered hazardous.

- **Corrosive**—If a material burns the skin, or dissolves metals and other materials, a technician should consider it hazardous. A pH scale is used, with the number 7 indicating neutral. Pure water has a pH of 7. Lower numbers indicate an acidic solution and higher numbers indicate a caustic solution. If a material releases cyanide gas, hydrogen sulfide gas, or similar gases when exposed to low pH acid solutions, it is considered hazardous.

- **Toxic**—Materials are hazardous if they leak one or more of eight different heavy metals in concentrations greater than 100 times the primary drinking water standard.

- **Ignitable**—A liquid is hazardous if it has a flash point below 140°F (60°C), and a solid is hazardous if it ignites spontaneously.

- **Radioactive**—Any substance that emits measurable levels of radiation is radioactive. When individuals bring containers of a highly radioactive substance into the shop environment, qualified personnel with the appropriate equipment must test them.

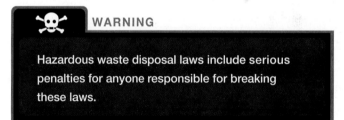

☠ **WARNING**

Hazardous waste disposal laws include serious penalties for anyone responsible for breaking these laws.

RIGHT-TO-KNOW LAWS The **right-to-know laws** state that employees have a right to know when the materials they use at work are hazardous. The right-to-know laws started with the Hazard Communication Standard published by the Occupational Safety and Health Administration (OSHA) in 1983. Originally, this document was intended for chemical companies and manufacturers that required employees to handle hazardous materials in their work situation but the federal courts have decided to apply these laws to all companies, including automotive service shops. Under the right-to-know laws, the employer has responsibilities regarding the handling of hazardous materials by their employees. All employees must be trained about the types of hazardous materials they will

FIGURE 2–1 Material safety data sheets (MSDS) should be readily available for use by anyone in the area who may come into contact with hazardous materials.

FEDERAL AND STATE LAWS (CONTINUED)

encounter in the workplace. The employees must be informed about their rights under legislation regarding the handling of hazardous materials.

MATERIAL SAFETY DATA SHEETS (MSDS). All hazardous materials must be properly labeled, and information about each hazardous material must be posted on **material safety data sheets (MSDS)** available from the manufacturer. In Canada, MSDS information is called **Workplace Hazardous Materials Information Systems (WHMIS)**.

The employer has a responsibility to place MSDS information where they are easily accessible by all employees. The MSDS information provide the following information about the hazardous material: chemical name, physical characteristics, protective handling equipment, explosion/fire hazards, incompatible materials, health hazards, medical conditions aggravated by exposure, emergency and first-aid procedures, safe handling, and spill/leak procedures.

The employer also has a responsibility to make sure that all hazardous materials are properly labeled. The label information must include health, fire, and reactivity hazards posed by the material, as well as the protective equipment necessary to handle the material. The manufacturer must supply all warning and precautionary information about hazardous materials. This information must be read and understood by the employee before handling the material. ● **SEE FIGURE 2–1.**

RESOURCE CONSERVATION AND RECOVERY ACT (RCRA)
Federal and state laws control the disposal of hazardous waste materials and every shop employee must be familiar with these laws. Hazardous waste disposal laws include the **Resource Conservation and Recovery Act (RCRA)**. This

law states that hazardous material users are responsible for hazardous materials from the time they become a waste until the proper waste disposal is completed. Many shops hire an independent hazardous waste hauler to dispose of hazardous waste material. The shop owner, or manager, should have a written contract with the hazardous waste hauler. Rather than have hazardous waste material hauled to an approved hazardous waste disposal site, a shop may choose to recycle the material in the shop. Therefore, the user must store hazardous waste material properly and safely, and be responsible for the transportation of this material until it arrives at an approved hazardous waste disposal site, where it can be processed according to the law. The RCRA controls the following types of automotive waste:

- Paint and body repair products waste
- Solvents for parts and equipment cleaning
- Batteries and battery acid
- Mild acids used for metal cleaning and preparation
- Waste oil, and engine coolants or antifreeze
- Air-conditioning refrigerants and oils
- Engine oil filters

CLEAN AIR ACT Air-conditioning (A/C) systems and refrigerant are regulated by the **Clean Air Act (CAA)**, Title VI, Section 609. Technician certification and service equipment is also regulated. Any technician working on automotive A/C systems must be certified. A/C refrigerants must not be released or vented into the atmosphere, and used refrigerants must be recovered.

ASBESTOS HAZARDS

Friction materials such as brake and clutch linings often contain asbestos. While asbestos has been eliminated from most original equipment friction materials, the automotive service technician cannot know whether or not the vehicle being serviced is or is not equipped with friction materials containing asbestos. It is important that all friction materials be handled as if they do contain asbestos.

Asbestos exposure can cause scar tissue to form in the lungs. This condition is called **asbestosis**. It gradually causes increasing shortness of breath, and the scarring to the lungs is permanent.

Even low exposures to asbestos can cause *mesothelioma*, a type of fatal cancer of the lining of the chest or abdominal cavity. Asbestos exposure can also increase the risk of *lung cancer* as well as cancer of the voice box, stomach, and large intestine. It usually takes 15 to 30 years or more for cancer or asbestos lung scarring to show up after exposure. Scientists call this the *latency period*.

Government agencies recommend that asbestos exposure should be eliminated or controlled to the lowest level possible. These agencies have developed recommendations and standards that the automotive service technician and equipment manufacturer should follow. These U.S. federal agencies include the National Institute for Occupational Safety and Health (NIOSH), Occupational Safety and Health Administration (OSHA), and Environmental Protection Agency (EPA).

ASBESTOS OSHA STANDARDS

The Occupational Safety and Health Administration (OSHA) has established three levels of asbestos exposure. Any vehicle service establishment that does either brake or clutch work must limit employee exposure to asbestos to less than 0.2 fibers per cubic centimeter (cc) as determined by an air sample.

If the level of exposure to employees is greater than specified, corrective measures must be performed and a large fine may be imposed.

NOTE: Research has found that worn asbestos fibers such as those from automotive brakes or clutches may not be as hazardous as first believed. Worn asbestos fibers do not have sharp flared ends that can latch onto tissue, but rather are worn down to a dust form that resembles talc. Grinding or sawing operations on unworn brake shoes or clutch discs *will* contain *harmful* asbestos fibers. To limit health damage, always use proper handling procedures while working around any component that may contain asbestos.

ASBESTOS EPA REGULATIONS

The federal Environmental Protection Agency (EPA) has established procedures for the removal and disposal of asbestos. The EPA procedures require that products containing asbestos be "wetted" to prevent the asbestos fibers from becoming airborne. According to the EPA, asbestos-containing materials can be disposed of as regular waste. Only when asbestos becomes airborne is it considered to be hazardous.

ASBESTOS HANDLING GUIDELINES

The air in the shop area can be tested by a testing laboratory, but this can be expensive. Tests have determined that asbestos levels can easily be kept below the recommended levels by using a liquid, like water, or a special vacuum.

NOTE: Even though asbestos is being removed from brake and clutch lining materials, the service technician cannot tell whether or not the old brake pads, shoes, or clutch discs contain asbestos. Therefore, to be safe, the technician should assume that all brake pads, shoes, or clutch discs contain asbestos.

HEPA VACUUM. A special **high-efficiency particulate air (HEPA) vacuum** system has been proven to be effective in keeping asbestos exposure levels below 0.1 fibers per cubic centimeter.

SOLVENT SPRAY. Many technicians use an aerosol can of brake cleaning solvent to wet the brake dust and prevent it from becoming airborne. A **solvent** is a liquid that is used to dissolve dirt, grime, or solid particles. Commercial brake cleaners are available that use a concentrated cleaner that is mixed with water. ● **SEE FIGURE 2–2.** The waste liquid is filtered, and when dry, the filter can be disposed of as solid waste.

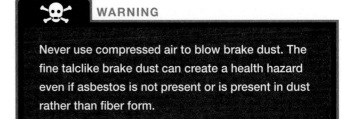

☠ **WARNING**

Never use compressed air to blow brake dust. The fine talclike brake dust can create a health hazard even if asbestos is not present or is present in dust rather than fiber form.

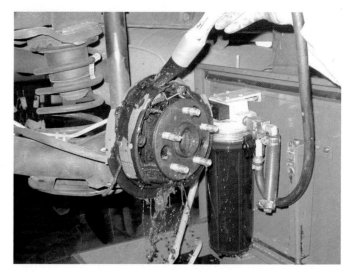

FIGURE 2–2 All brakes should be moistened with water or solvent to help prevent brake dust from becoming airborne.

DISPOSAL OF BRAKE DUST AND BRAKE SHOES. The hazard of asbestos occurs when asbestos fibers are airborne. Once the asbestos has been wetted down, it is then considered to be solid waste, rather than hazardous waste. Old brake shoes and pads should be enclosed, preferably in a plastic bag, to help prevent any of the brake material from becoming airborne. *Always follow current federal and local laws concerning disposal of all waste.*

USED BRAKE FLUID

Most brake fluid is made from polyglycol, is water soluble, and can be considered hazardous if it has absorbed metals from the brake system.

STORAGE AND DISPOSAL OF BRAKE FLUID

- Collect brake fluid in a container clearly marked to indicate that it is designated for that purpose.
- If the waste brake fluid is hazardous, be sure to manage it appropriately and use only an authorized waste receiver for its disposal.
- If the waste brake fluid is nonhazardous (such as old, but unused), determine from your local solid waste collection provider what should be done for its proper disposal.
- Do not mix brake fluid with used engine oil.
- Do not pour brake fluid down drains or onto the ground.
- Recycle brake fluid through a registered recycler.

USED OIL

Used oil is any petroleum-based or synthetic oil that has been used. During normal use, impurities such as dirt, metal scrapings, water, or chemicals can get mixed in with the oil. Eventually, this used oil must be replaced with virgin or re-refined oil. The EPA's used oil management standards include a three-pronged approach to determine if a substance meets the definition of *used oil*. To meet the EPA's definition of used oil, a substance must meet each of the following three criteria.

- **Origin.** The first criterion for identifying used oil is based on the oil's origin. Used oil must have been refined from crude oil or made from synthetic materials. Animal and vegetable oils are excluded from the EPA's definition of used oil.
- **Use.** The second criterion is based on whether and how the oil is used. Oils used as lubricants, hydraulic fluids, heat transfer fluids, and for other similar purposes are considered used oil. The EPA's definition also excludes products used as cleaning agents, as well as certain petroleum-derived products like antifreeze and kerosene.
- **Contaminants.** The third criterion is based on whether or not the oil is contaminated with either physical or chemical impurities. In other words, to meet the EPA's definition, used oil must become contaminated as a result of being used. This aspect of the EPA's definition includes residues and contaminants generated from handling, storing, and processing used oil.

FIGURE 2–3 A typical above-ground oil storage tank.

NOTE: The release of only one gallon of used oil (a typical oil change) can make a million gallons of fresh water undrinkable.

If used oil is dumped down the drain and enters a sewage treatment plant, concentrations as small as 50 to 100 PPM (parts per million) in the waste water can foul sewage treatment processes. Never mix a listed hazardous waste, gasoline, waste water, halogenated solvent, antifreeze, or an unknown waste material with used oil. Adding any of these substances will cause the used oil to become contaminated, which classifies it as hazardous waste.

STORAGE AND DISPOSAL OF USED OIL   Once oil has been used, it can be collected, recycled, and used over and over again. An estimated 380 million gallons of used oil are recycled each year. Recycled used oil can sometimes be used again for the same job or can take on a completely different task. For example, used engine oil can be re-refined and sold at the store as engine oil or processed for furnace fuel oil. After collecting used oil in an appropriate container such as a 55-gallon steel drum. The material must be disposed of in one of two ways:

- Shipped offsite for recycling
- Burned in an onsite or offsite EPA-approved heater for energy recovery

Used oil must be stored in compliance with an existing **underground storage tank (UST)** or an **aboveground storage tank (AGST)** standard, or kept in separate containers. ● **SEE**

FIGURE 2–3. Containers are portable receptacles, such as a 55-gallon steel drum.

KEEP USED OIL STORAGE DRUMS IN GOOD CONDITION. This means that they should be covered, secured from vandals, properly labeled, and maintained in compliance with local fire codes. Frequent inspections for leaks, corrosion, and spillage are an essential part of container maintenance.

NEVER STORE USED OIL IN ANYTHING OTHER THAN TANKS AND STORAGE CONTAINERS. Used oil may also be stored in units that are permitted to store regulated hazardous waste.

USED OIL FILTER DISPOSAL REGULATIONS. Used oil filters contain used engine oil that may be hazardous. Before an oil filter is placed into the trash or sent to be recycled, it must be drained using one of the following hot-draining methods approved by the EPA.

- Puncture the filter antidrainback valve or filter dome end and hot-drain for at least 12 hours
- Hot-drain and crushing
- Dismantling and hot draining
- Any other hot-draining method, which will remove all the used oil from the filter

After the oil has been drained from the oil filter, the filter housing can be disposed of in any of the following ways:

- Sent for recycling
- Picked up by a service contract company
- Disposed of in regular trash

FIGURE 2–4 Washing hands and removing jewelry are two important safety habits all service technicians should practice.

FIGURE 2–5 Typical fireproof flammable storage cabinet.

SOLVENTS

The major sources of chemical danger are liquid and aerosol brake cleaning fluids that contain chlorinated hydrocarbon solvents. Several other chemicals that do not deplete the ozone, such as heptane, hexane, and xylene, are now being used in nonchlorinated brake cleaning solvents. Some manufacturers are also producing solvents they describe as environmentally responsible, which are biodegradable and noncarcinogenic (non-cancer-causing).

There is no specific standard for physical contact with chlorinated hydrocarbon solvents or the chemicals replacing them. All contact should be avoided whenever possible. The law requires an employer to provide appropriate protective equipment and ensure proper work practices by an employee handling these chemicals.

EFFECTS OF CHEMICAL POISONING The effects of exposure to chlorinated hydrocarbon and other types of solvents can take many forms. Short-term exposure at low levels can cause symptoms such as:

- Headache
- Nausea
- Drowsiness
- Dizziness
- Lack of coordination
- Unconsciousness

It may also cause irritation of the eyes, nose, and throat, and flushing of the face and neck. Short-term exposure to higher concentrations can cause liver damage with symptoms

such as yellow jaundice or dark urine. Liver damage may not become evident until several weeks after the exposure.

HAZARDOUS SOLVENTS AND REGULATORY STATUS

Most solvents are classified as hazardous wastes. Other characteristics of solvents include the following:

- Solvents with flash points below 60°C are considered flammable and, like gasoline, are federally regulated by the Department of Transportation (DOT).
- Solvents and oils with flash points above 60°C are considered combustible and, like engine oil, are also regulated by the DOT. All flammable items must be stored in a fireproof container. ● **SEE FIGURE 2–5.**

It is the responsibility of the repair shop to determine if its spent solvent is hazardous waste. Solvent reclaimers are available that clean and restore the solvent so it lasts indefinitely.

FIGURE 2–6 Using a water-based cleaning system helps reduce the hazards from using strong chemicals.

FIGURE 2–7 Used antifreeze coolant should be kept separate and stored in a leakproof container until it can be recycled or disposed of according to federal, state, and local laws. Note that the storage barrel is placed inside another container to catch any coolant that may spill out of the inside barrel.

 FREQUENTLY ASKED QUESTION

How can you tell if a solvent is hazardous?

If a solvent or any of the ingredients of a product contains "fluor" or "chlor" then it is likely to be hazardous. Check the instructions on the label for proper use and disposal procedures.

USED SOLVENTS Used or spent solvents are liquid materials that have been generated as waste and may contain xylene, methanol, ethyl ether, and methyl isobutyl ketone (MIBK). These materials must be stored in OSHA-approved safety containers with the lids or caps closed tightly. Additional requirements include the following:

- Containers should be clearly labeled "Hazardous Waste" and the date the material was first placed into the storage receptacle should be noted.
- Labeling is not required for solvents being used in a parts washer.
- Used solvents will not be counted toward a facility's monthly output of hazardous waste if the vendor under contract removes the material.
- Used solvents may be disposed of by recycling with a local vendor, such as SafetyKleen®, to have the used solvent removed according to specific terms in the vendor agreement.
- Use aqueous-based (nonsolvent) cleaning systems to help avoid the problems associated with chemical solvents. ● **SEE FIGURE 2–6.**

COOLANT DISPOSAL

Coolant is a mixture of antifreeze and water. New antifreeze is not considered to be hazardous even though it can cause death if ingested. Used antifreeze may be hazardous due to dissolved metals from the engine and other components of the cooling system. These metals can include iron, steel, aluminum, copper, brass, and lead (from older radiators and heater cores). Coolant should be disposed of in one of the following ways:

- Coolant should be recycled either onsite or offsite.
- Used coolant should be stored in a sealed and labeled container. ● **SEE FIGURE 2–7.**
- Used coolant can often be disposed of into municipal sewers with a permit. Check with local authorities and obtain a permit before discharging used coolant into sanitary sewers.

p

q

r

s

t

u

v

w

x

y

z

aa

LEAD-ACID BATTERY WASTE

About 70 million spent lead–acid batteries are generated each year in the United States alone. Lead is classified as a toxic metal and the acid used in lead–acid batteries is highly corrosive. The vast majority (95% to 98%) of these batteries are recycled through lead reclamation operations and secondary lead smelters for use in the manufacture of new batteries.

BATTERY DISPOSAL Used lead–acid batteries must be reclaimed or recycled in order to be exempt from hazardous waste regulations. Leaking batteries must be stored and transported as hazardous waste. Some states have more strict regulations, which require special handling procedures and transportation. According to the **Battery Council International (BCI)**, battery laws usually include the following rules:

1. Lead–acid battery disposal is prohibited in landfills or incinerators. Batteries are required to be delivered to a battery retailer, wholesaler, recycling center, or lead smelter.

2. All retailers of automotive batteries are required to post a sign that displays the universal recycling symbol and indicates the retailer's specific requirements for accepting used batteries.

3. Battery electrolyte contains sulfuric acid, which is a very corrosive substance capable of causing serious personal injury, such as skin burns and eye damage. In addition, the battery plates contain lead, which is highly poisonous. For this reason, disposing of batteries improperly can cause environmental contamination and lead to severe health problems.

BATTERY HANDLING AND STORAGE Batteries, whether new or used, should be kept indoors if possible. The storage location should be an area specifically designated for battery storage and must be well ventilated (to the outside). If outdoor storage is the only alternative, a sheltered and secured area with acid-resistant secondary containment is strongly recommended. It is also advisable that acid-resistant secondary containment be used for indoor storage. In addition, batteries should be placed on acid-resistant pallets and never stacked.

FUEL SAFETY AND STORAGE

Gasoline is a very explosive liquid. The expanding vapors that come from gasoline are extremely dangerous. These vapors are present even in cold temperatures. Vapors formed in gasoline tanks on many vehicles are controlled, but vapors from gasoline storage may escape from the can, resulting in a hazardous situation. Therefore, place gasoline storage containers in a well-ventilated space. Although diesel fuel is not as volatile as gasoline, the same basic rules apply to diesel fuel and gasoline storage. These rules include the following:

1. Use storage cans that have a flash-arresting screen at the outlet. These screens prevent external ignition sources from igniting the gasoline within the can when someone pours the gasoline or diesel fuel.

2. Use only a red approved gasoline container to allow for proper hazardous substance identification. ● **SEE FIGURE 2–8.**

3. Do not fill gasoline containers completely full. Always leave the level of gasoline at least one inch from the top of the container. This action allows expansion of the gasoline at higher temperatures. If gasoline containers are completely full, the gasoline will expand when the temperature increases. This expansion forces gasoline from the can and creates a dangerous spill. If gasoline or diesel fuel containers must be stored, place them in a designated storage locker or facility.

4. Never leave gasoline containers open, except while filling or pouring gasoline from the container.

5. Never use gasoline as a cleaning agent.

6. Always connect a ground strap to containers when filling or transferring fuel or other flammable products from one container to another to prevent static electricity that could result in explosion and fire. These ground wires prevent the buildup of a static electric charge, which could result in a spark and disastrous explosion.

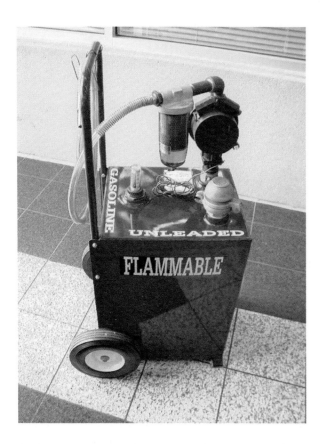

FIGURE 2–8 This red gasoline container holds about 30 gallons of gasoline and is used to fill vehicles used for training.

AIRBAG HANDLING

Airbag modules are pyrotechnic devices that can be ignited if exposed to an electrical charge or if the body of the vehicle is subjected to a shock. Airbag safety should include the following precautions:

1. Disarm the airbag(s) if you will be working in the area where a discharged bag could make contact with any part of your body. Consult service information for the exact procedure to follow for the vehicle being serviced. The usual procedure is to deploy the airbag using a 12-volt power supply, such as a jump start box, using long wires to connect to the module to ensure a safe deployment.

2. Do not expose an airbag to extreme heat or fire.

3. Always carry an airbag pointing away from your body.

4. Place an airbag module facing upward.

5. Always follow the manufacturer's recommended procedure for airbag disposal or recycling, including the proper packaging to use during shipment.

6. Wear protective gloves if handling a deployed airbag.

7. Always wash your hands or body well if exposed to a deployed airbag. The chemicals involved can cause skin irritation and possible rash development.

USED TIRE DISPOSAL

Used tires are an environmental concern because of several reasons, including the following:

1. In a landfill, they tend to "float" up through the other trash and rise to the surface.

2. The inside of tires traps and holds rainwater, which is a breeding ground for mosquitoes. Mosquito-borne diseases include encephalitis and dengue fever.

3. Used tires present a fire hazard and, when burned, create a large amount of black smoke that contaminates the air.

Used tires should be disposed of in one of the following ways:

1. Used tires can be reused until the end of their useful life.

2. Tires can be retreaded.

3. Tires can be recycled or shredded for use in asphalt.

4. Derimmed tires can be sent to a landfill (most landfill operators will shred the tires because it is illegal in many states to landfill whole tires).

5. Tires can be burned in cement kilns or other power plants where the smoke can be controlled.

6. A registered scrap tire handler should be used to transport tires for disposal or recycling.

FIGURE 2–9 Air-conditioning refrigerant oil must be kept separated from other oils because it contains traces of refrigerant and must be treated as hazardous waste.

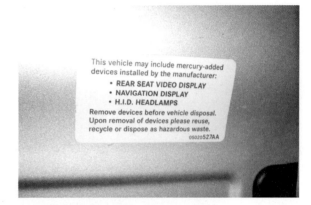

FIGURE 2–10 Placard near driver's door, including what devices in the vehicle contain mercury.

AIR-CONDITIONING REFRIGERANT OIL DISPOSAL

Air-conditioning refrigerant oil contains dissolved refrigerant and is therefore considered to be hazardous waste. This oil must be kept separated from other waste oil or the entire amount of oil must be treated as hazardous. Used refrigerant oil must be sent to a licensed hazardous waste disposal company for recycling or disposal. ● **SEE FIGURE 2–9.**

WASTE CHART All automotive service facilities create some waste and while most of it is handled properly, it is important that all hazardous and nonhazardous waste be accounted for and properly disposed. ● **SEE CHART 2–1** for a list of typical wastes generated at automotive shops, plus a checklist for keeping track of how these wastes are handled.

 **TECH TIP**

Remove Components that Contain Mercury

Some vehicles have a placard near the driver's side door that lists the components that contain the heavy metal, mercury. **Mercury** can be absorbed through the skin and is a heavy metal that once absorbed by the body does not leave. ● **SEE FIGURE 2–10.**

These components should be removed from the vehicle before the rest of the body is sent to be recycled to help prevent releasing mercury into the environment.

 **TECH TIP**

What Every Technician Should Know

The Hazardous Materials Identification Guide (HMIG) is the standard labeling for all materials. The service technician should be aware of the meaning of the label. ● **SEE FIGURE 2–11.**

WASTE STREAM	TYPICAL CATEGORY IF NOT MIXED WITH OTHER HAZARDOUS WASTE	IF DISPOSED IN LANDFILL AND NOT MIXED WITH A HAZARDOUS WASTE	IF RECYCLED
Used oil	Used oil	Hazardous waste	Used oil
Used oil filters	Nonhazardous solid waste, if completely drained	Nonhazardous solid waste, if completely drained	Used oil, if not drained
Used transmission fluid	Used oil	Hazardous waste	Used oil
Used brake fluid	Used oil	Hazardous waste	Used oil
Used antifreeze	Depends on characterization	Depends on characterization	Depends on characterization
Used solvents	Hazardous waste	Hazardous waste	Hazardous waste
Used citric solvents	Nonhazardous solid waste	Nonhazardous solid waste	Hazardous waste
Lead–acid automotive batteries	Not a solid waste if returned to supplier	Hazardous waste	Hazardous waste
Shop rags used for oil	Used oil	Depends on used oil characterization	Used oil
Shop rags used for solvent or gasoline spills	Hazardous waste	Hazardous waste	Hazardous waste
Oil spill absorbent material	Used oil	Depends on used oil characterization	Used oil
Spill material for solvent and gasoline	Hazardous waste	Hazardous waste	Hazardous waste
Catalytic converter	Not a solid waste if returned to supplier	Nonhazardous solid waste	Nonhazardous solid waste
Spilled or unused fuels	Hazardous waste	Hazardous waste	Hazardous waste
Spilled or unusable paints and thinners	Hazardous waste	Hazardous waste	Hazardous waste
Used tires	Nonhazardous solid waste	Nonhazardous solid waste	Nonhazardous solid waste

CHART 2–1

Typical Wastes Generated at Auto Repair Shops and Typical Category (Hazardous or Nonhazardous) by Disposal Method

FIGURE 2–11 The Environmental Protection Agency (EPA) Hazardous Materials Identification Guide is a standardized listing of the hazards and the protective equipment needed.

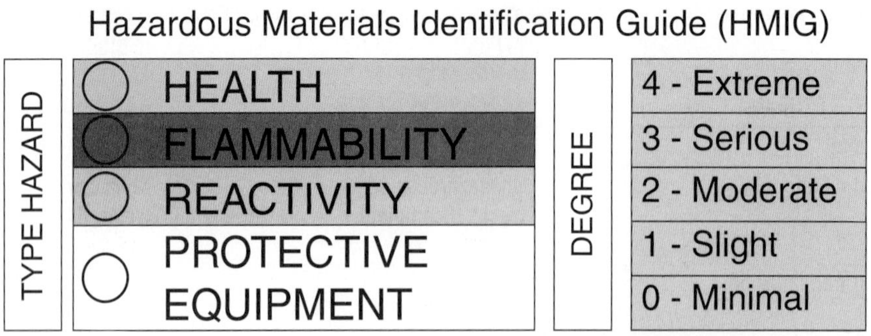

Hazardous Materials Identification Guide (HMIG)

TYPE HAZARD		DEGREE	
○	HEALTH	4 - Extreme	
○	FLAMMABILITY	3 - Serious	
○	REACTIVITY	2 - Moderate	
○	PROTECTIVE EQUIPMENT	1 - Slight	
		0 - Minimal	

HAZARD RATING AND PROTECTIVE EQUIPMENT

	Health		Flammable		Reactive
	Type of Possible Injury		Susceptibility of materials to burn		Susceptibility of materials to release energy
4	Highly Toxic. May be fatal on short-term exposure. Special protective equipment required.	4	Extremely flammable gas or liquid. Flash Point below 73°F.	4	Extreme. Explosive at room temperature.
3	Toxic. Avoid inhalation or skin contact.	3	Flammable. Flash Point 73°F to 100°F.	3	Serious. May explode if shocked, heated under confinement or mixed w/ water.
2	Moderately Toxic. May be harmful if inhaled or absorbed.	2	Combustible. Requires moderate heating to ignite. Flash Point 100°F to 200°F.	2	Moderate. Unstable, may react with water.
1	Slightly Toxic. May cause slight irritation.	1	Slightly Combustible. Requires strong heating to ignite.	1	Slight. May react if heated or mixed with water.
0	Minimal. All chemicals have a slight degree of toxicity.	0	Minimal. Will not burn under normal conditions.	0	Minimal. Normally stable, does not react with water.

Protective Equipment

A	Safety Glasses	E	Safety Glasses + Gloves + Dust Respirator	I	Safety Glasses + Gloves + Combination Dust & Vapor Respirator
B	Safety Glasses + Gloves	F	Safety Glasses + Gloves + Apron + Dust Respirator	J	Chemical Goggles + Gloves + Apron + Combination Dust & Vapor Respirator
C	Safety Glasses + Gloves + Apron	G	Safety Glasses + Gloves + Vapor Respirator	K	Apron + Gloves + Full Protection Suit + Boots
D	Faceshield + Gloves + Apron	H	Chemical Goggles + Gloves + Apron + Vapor Respirator	X	Ask your supervisor for guidance.

1. Hazardous materials include common automotive chemicals, liquids, and lubricants, especially those whose ingredients contain *chlor* or *fluor* in their name.

2. Right-to-know laws require that all workers have access to material safety data sheets (MSDS).

3. Asbestos fibers should be avoided and removed according to current laws and regulations.

4. Used engine oil contains metals worn from parts and should be handled and disposed of properly.

5. Solvents represent a serious health risk and should be avoided as much as possible.

6. Coolant should be disposed of properly or recycled.

7. Batteries are considered to be hazardous waste and should be discarded to a recycling facility.

REVIEW QUESTIONS

1. List five common automotive chemicals or products that may be considered hazardous materials.

2. List five precautions to which every technician should adhere when working with automotive products and chemicals.

CHAPTER QUIZ

1. Hazardous materials include all of the following *except* _____.
   - **a.** Engine oil
   - **b.** Asbestos
   - **c.** Water
   - **d.** Brake cleaner

2. To determine if a product or substance being used is hazardous, consult _____.
   - **a.** A dictionary
   - **b.** An MSDS
   - **c.** SAE standards
   - **d.** EPA guidelines

3. Exposure to asbestos dust can cause what condition?
   - **a.** Asbestosis
   - **b.** Mesothelioma
   - **c.** Lung cancer
   - **d.** All of the above are possible

4. Wetted asbestos dust is considered to be _____.
   - **a.** Solid waste
   - **b.** Hazardous waste
   - **c.** Toxic
   - **d.** Poisonous

5. An oil filter should be hot drained for how long before disposing of the filter?
   - **a.** 30 to 60 minutes
   - **b.** 4 hours
   - **c.** 8 hours
   - **d.** 12 hours

6. Used engine oil should be disposed of by all *except* the following methods.
   - **a.** Disposed of in regular trash
   - **b.** Shipped offsite for recycling
   - **c.** Burned onsite in a waste oil-approved heater
   - **d.** Burned offsite in a waste oil-approved heater

7. All of the following are the proper ways to dispose of a drained oil filter *except* _____.
   - **a.** Sent for recycling
   - **b.** Picked up by a service contract company
   - **c.** Disposed of in regular trash
   - **d.** Considered to be hazardous waste and disposed of accordingly

8. Which act or organization regulates air-conditioning refrigerant?
   - **a.** Clean Air Act (CAA)
   - **b.** MSDS
   - **c.** WHMIS
   - **d.** Code of Federal Regulations (CFR)

9. Gasoline should be stored in approved containers that include what color(s)?
   - **a.** A red container with yellow lettering
   - **b.** A red container
   - **c.** A yellow container
   - **d.** A yellow container with red lettering

10. What automotive devices may contain mercury?
    - **a.** Rear seat video displays
    - **b.** Navigation displays
    - **c.** HID headlights
    - **d.** All of the above

BRAKING SYSTEM COMPONENTS AND PERFORMANCE STANDARDS

OBJECTIVES

After studying Chapter 3, the reader will be able to:

1. Prepare for the Brakes (A5) ASE certification test.
2. List the parts and terms for disc and drum brakes.
3. Describe brake design requirements.
4. List the six brake system categories.
5. Discuss federal braking and stopping standards.

KEY TERMS

Adjustable pedals 58
Antilock braking system (ABS) 59
Apply system 57
Base brakes 55
Boost system 57
Brake balance control system 58
Brake pedal 57
Brake warning lights 58
Disc brakes 56
DOT 60

Drum brakes 55
EAP 58
FMVSS 60
Foundation brakes 55
GVWR 60
Hydraulic system 57
LLVW 60
Parking brake 57
Red brake warning lamp 58
Service brakes 55
Wheel brakes 58

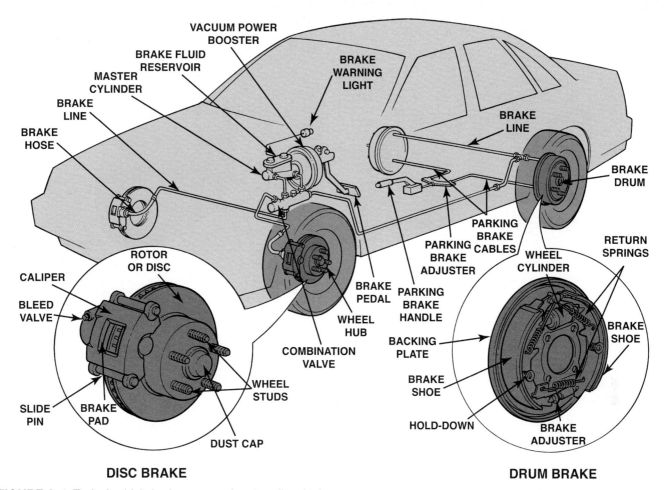

FIGURE 3–1 Typical vehicle brake system showing all typical components.

FUNDAMENTALS OF BRAKE SYSTEMS

Brakes are by far the most important mechanism on any vehicle because the safety and lives of those riding in the vehicle depend on proper operation of the braking system. It has been estimated that the brakes on the average vehicle are applied 50,000 times a year!

Brakes are an energy-absorbing mechanism that converts vehicle movement into heat while stopping the rotation of the wheels. All braking systems are designed to reduce the speed and stop a moving vehicle and to keep it from moving if the vehicle is stationary. **Service brakes** are the main driver-operated brakes of the vehicle. Service brakes are also called **base brakes** or **foundation brakes**. ● SEE FIGURE 3–1.

BRAKE SYSTEM PARTS
Most vehicles built since the late 1920s use a brake on each wheel. To stop a wheel, the driver exerts a force on a brake pedal. The force on the brake pedal pressurizes brake fluid in a master cylinder. This hydraulic force (liquid under pressure) is transferred through steel lines and flexible brake lines to a wheel cylinder or caliper at each wheel. Hydraulic pressure to each wheel cylinder or caliper is used to force friction materials against the brake drum or rotor. The friction between the stationary friction material and the rotating drum or rotor (disc) causes the rotating part to slow and eventually stop. Since the wheels are attached to the drums or rotors, the wheels of the vehicles also stop.

The heavier the vehicle and the higher the speed, the more heat the brakes have to be able to absorb. Long, steep hills can cause the brakes to overheat, reducing the friction necessary to slow and stop a vehicle.

DRUM BRAKES.
Drum brakes are used on the rear of many rear-wheel-drive, front-wheel-drive, and four-wheel-drive vehicles. When drum brakes are applied, brake shoes are moved outward against a rotating brake drum. The wheel studs for the wheels are attached to the drum. When the drum slows and stops, the wheels also slow and stop.

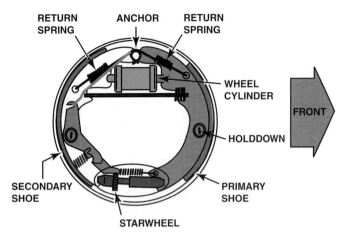

FIGURE 3–2 Typical drum brake assembly.

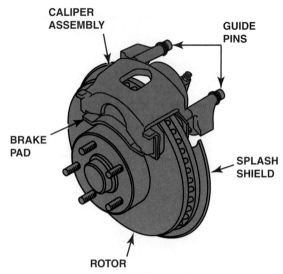

FIGURE 3–3 Typical disc brake assembly.

FUNDAMENTALS OF BRAKE SYSTEMS (CONTINUED)

Drum brakes are economical to manufacture, service, and repair. Parts for drum brakes are generally readily available and reasonably priced. On some vehicles, an additional drum brake is used as a parking brake on vehicles equipped with rear disc brakes. ● **SEE FIGURE 3–2.**

DISC BRAKES. Disc brakes are used on the front of most vehicles built since the early 1970s and on the rear wheels of many vehicles. A disc brake operates by squeezing brake pads on both sides of a rotor or disc that is attached to the wheel. ● **SEE FIGURE 3–3.**

Type of Brake	Rotating Part	Friction Part
Drum brakes	Brake drum	Brake shoes
Disc brakes	Rotor or disc	Brake pads

Due to the friction between the road surface and the tires, the vehicle stops. To summarize, the sequence of events necessary to stop a vehicle include the following:

1. The driver presses on the brake pedal.

2. The brake pedal force is transferred hydraulically to a wheel cylinder or caliper at each wheel.

3. Hydraulic pressure inside the wheel cylinder or caliper presses friction materials (brake shoes or pads) against rotating brake drums or rotors.

4. The friction slows and stops the drum or rotor. Since the drum or rotor is bolted to the wheel of the vehicle, the wheel also stops.

5. When the wheels of the vehicle slow and stop, the tires must have friction (traction) with the road surface to stop the vehicle.

BRAKE DESIGN REQUIREMENTS

All braking forces must provide for the following:

■ Equal forces must be applied to both the left and right sides of the vehicle to assure straight stops.

■ Hydraulic systems must be properly engineered and serviced to provide for changes as vehicle weight shifts forward during braking. Hydraulic valves must be used in the hydraulic system to permit the maximum possible braking forces but still prevent undesirable wheel lockup. Antilock braking systems (ABS) are specifically designed to prevent wheel lockup under all driving conditions, including wet or icy road conditions.

■ The hydraulic system must use a fluid that will not evaporate or freeze. The fluid has to withstand extreme temperatures without boiling and must not damage rubber or metal parts of the braking system.

■ The friction material (brake lining or brake pads) must be designed to provide adequate friction between the stationary shoes or pads and the rotating drum or rotor. The friction material should be environmentally safe. Nonasbestos lining is generally considered to be safe for the environment and the technician.

■ The design of the braking system should secure the brake lining solidly to prevent the movement of the friction material during braking. It is this movement of the friction material that causes brake noise (squeal).

■ Most braking systems incorporate a power assist unit that reduces the driver's effort but does not reduce stopping distance. The most commonly used brake booster is vacuum operated.

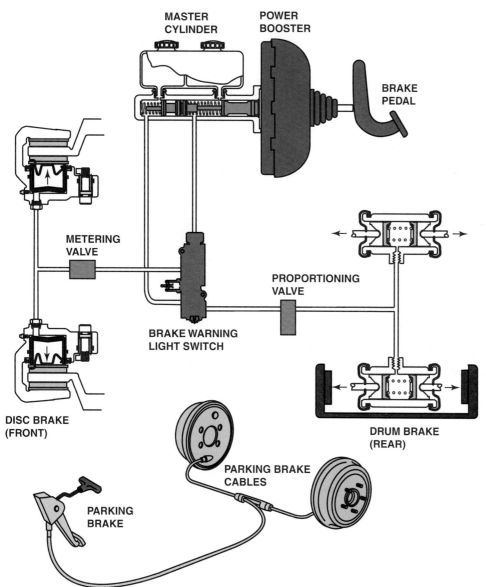

FIGURE 3–4 Typical brake system components.

MASTER CYLINDER

POWER BOOSTER

BRAKE PEDAL

METERING VALVE

PROPORTIONING VALVE

BRAKE WARNING LIGHT SWITCH

DISC BRAKE (FRONT)

DRUM BRAKE (REAR)

PARKING BRAKE CABLES

PARKING BRAKE

BRAKE SYSTEM CATEGORIES

Brake system components can be classified and placed into six subsystem categories, depending on their function. ● **SEE FIGURE 3–4** for an overall view of the entire braking system.

1. **Apply System.** The driver starts the operation of the braking system by pressing on the **brake pedal** or applying the **parking brake**. The apply system includes all the levers, pedals, or linkage needed to activate a braking force.

2. **Boost System.** The boost (power brake) system is used on most vehicles to reduce the force that the driver must exert on the brake pedal.

3. **Hydraulic System.** The brake pedal force is transferred to the hydraulic system, where the force is directed through lines and hoses to the wheel brakes.

4. **Wheel Brakes.** Hydraulic pressure from the hydraulic system moves a piston, in either a disc or drum brake system, which uses friction to press material against a rotating drum or rotor. The resulting friction slows the rotation of the wheels.

FIGURE 3–5 The red brake warning light will remain on after a bulb test if there is a fault with the hydraulic part of the brake system.

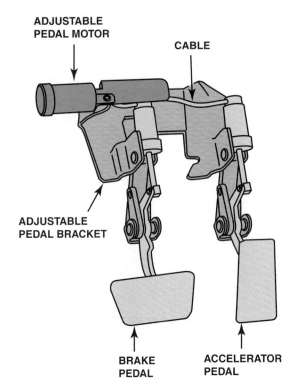

FIGURE 3–6 A typical adjustable pedal assembly. Both the accelerator and the brake pedal can be moved forward and rearward by using the adjustable pedal position switch.

BRAKE SYSTEM CATEGORIES (CONTINUED)

5. **Brake Balance Control System.** Mechanical, electrical, and hydraulic components are used to ensure that brakes are applied quickly and with balanced pressure for safe operation. Components in this category include metering valves, proportioning valves, and antilock braking system components.

6. **Brake warning lights.** There are two brake system-related warning lights.

   ■ The **red brake warning lamp (RBWL)** lights whenever a hydraulic system failure occurs. The red brake warning lamp lights when the ignition is turned on as a bulb check then goes out unless a hydraulic fault has been detected. ● **SEE FIGURE 3–5.**

   CAUTION: Do not test-drive a vehicle if the red brake warning light is on.

   ■ The amber ABS warning lamp or dim red brake light indicates an ABS self-test and/or a possible problem in the ABS system. This warning light will usually flash several times during a self-test when the engine is first started and then go out unless a fault with the antilock braking system was detected.

? **FREQUENTLY ASKED QUESTION**

How Do Adjustable Pedals Work?

Adjustable pedals, also called **electric adjustable pedals (EAP),** place the brake pedal and the accelerator pedal on movable brackets that are motor operated. A typical adjustable pedal system includes the following components:

• **Adjustable pedal position switch,** which allows the driver to position the pedals.
• **Adjustable pedal assembly,** which includes the motor, threaded adjustment rods, and a pedal position sensor. ● **SEE FIGURE 3–6.**

The position of the pedals, as well as the position of the seat system, is usually included as part of the memory seat function and can be set for two or more drivers.

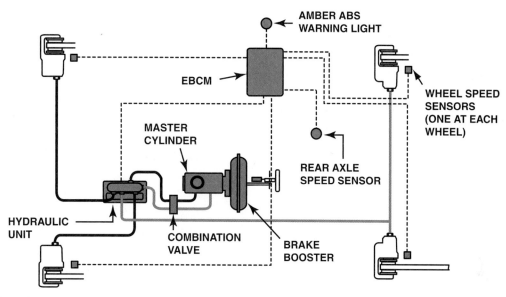

FIGURE 3–7 Typical components of an antilock braking system (ABS) used on a rear-wheel-drive vehicle.

ANTILOCK BRAKE SYSTEM OVERVIEW

The purpose of an **antilock braking system (ABS)** is to prevent the wheels from locking during braking, especially on low-friction surfaces such as wet, icy, or snowy roads. Remember, it is the friction between the tire tread and the road that does the actual stopping of the vehicle. Therefore, ABS does not mean that a vehicle can stop quickly on all road surfaces. ABS uses sensors at the wheels to measure the wheel speed. If a wheel is rotating slower than the others, indicating possible lockup (for example, on an icy spot), the ABS computer will control the brake fluid pressure to that wheel for a fraction of a second. *A locked wheel has less traction to the road surface than a rotating wheel.*

The ABS computer can reapply the pressure from the master cylinder to the wheel a fraction of a second later. Therefore, if a wheel starts to lock up, the purpose of the ABS system is to pulse the brakes on and off to maintain directional stability with maximum braking force. Many ABS units will cause the brake pedal to pulse if the unit is working in the ABS mode. The pulsating brake pedal is a cause for concern for some drivers. However, the pulsing brake pedal informs the driver that the ABS is being activated. Some ABS units use an isolator valve in

the ABS unit to prevent brake pedal pulsations during ABS operation. With these types of systems, it is often difficult for the driver to know if and when the ABS unit is working to control a locking wheel. ● **SEE FIGURE 3–7** for an overview of a typical ABS on a rear-wheel-drive vehicle.

Another symptom of normal ABS unit operation is the activation of the hydraulic pressure pump used by many ABS units. In some ABS units, the hydraulic pump is run every time the vehicle is started and moved. Other types of units operate randomly or whenever the pressure in the system calls for the pump to operate.

FEDERAL BRAKE STANDARDS

The statutes pertaining to automotive brake systems are part of the **Federal Motor Vehicle Safety Standards (FMVSS)** established by the United States **Department of Transportation (DOT).** Several standards apply to specific components within the brake system. The overall service and parking brake systems are dealt with in standard 135.

FMVSS 135 was first mandated on September 1, 2000, for passenger vehicles, and September 1, 2002, for multipurpose vehicles, trucks, and buses with a gross vehicle weight rating (GVWR) of 7,716 pounds (3,500 kilograms). Its purpose is to "ensure safe braking performance under normal and emergency conditions." FMVSS 135 applies to "passenger vehicles, multipurpose passenger vehicles, trucks, and buses."

FMVSS 135 deals with brake system safety by establishing specific brake performance requirements. It does not dictate the *design* of the system, although some requirements may make older technologies impractical or obsolete. Only four parts of the brake system are specifically regulated:

- Fluid reservoir and labeling
- Dashboard warning lights
- A method of automatic adjustment
- A mechanically engaging, friction-type parking brake system

The FMVSS 135 tests are used by manufacturers to certify the braking performance of all new vehicles available for public purchase.

FMVSS 135 BRAKE TEST

The overall FMVSS 135 brake test procedure consists of up to 24 steps, depending on the vehicle's configuration and braking system. The actual performance tests are made with the vehicle loaded to both the manufacturer's specified **gross vehicle weight rating (GVWR)** and the **lightly loaded vehicle weight (LLVW),** with certain applied brake forces. There are precise instructions for every step of the test, including the number of times the tests must be repeated, the sequence of the testing, and the allowable stopping distance for the particular type of vehicle. Some highlights of the testing procedure include:

- **Burnish Procedure.** The brakes are burnished by making 200 stops from 50 mph (80 km/h) at a fixed rate of deceleration with a controlled cool-down period after each stop. This procedure conditions the friction material.
- **Adhesion Utilization (torque wheel method).** For vehicles not equipped with ABS, this test is to determine

if the brake system will make adequate use of the road surface in stopping the vehicle.

- **Cold Effectiveness.** This test is performed to determine if the vehicle will have sufficient stopping power when the brake lining materials are not preheated by previous stops.
- **High Speed Effectiveness.** This test is performed to determine if the brake system will provide adequate stopping power for all loading conditions. The allowable stopping distance is calculated from the maximum speed the vehicle can attain.
- **Stops With the Engine Off.** This test is for vehicles equipped with brake power assist units. The vehicle, loaded to GVWR, must stop within 230 ft (70 m), from a speed of 62 mph (100 km/h). This test must be repeated six times.
- **Antilock Functional Failure.** This test ensures that service brakes will function correctly in the event of an antilock functional failure, and the brake system warning indicator is activated when an ABS electrical function failure occurs.
- **Variable Brake Proportioning System.** This test is performed on vehicles equipped with either a mechanical or an electrical variable proportioning system. It ensures that, in the event of a failure, the vehicle can still come to a stop in an acceptable distance.
- **Hydraulic Circuit Failure.** This test is performed to ensure that the driver will be alerted via the brake warning system indicator that a failure has occurred, and that the vehicle can still be stopped in an acceptable distance.
- **Brake Power Assist Unit Inoperative.** This test makes sure the service brake can stop the vehicle in an acceptable distance with the brake power assist unit in an inoperative state. It is performed on vehicles with brake power assist units turned off or inoperative.
- **Parking Brake.** The parking brake alone will hold the vehicle stationary in either the forward or reverse direction on a 20% grade for a period of at least 5 minutes.
- **Brake Heat Test.** This procedure heats the brake system by making a series of 15 stops from a high speed. The vehicle is loaded to GVWR, with rapid acceleration between each stop to minimize cooling the brakes.
- **Hot Performance.** After the brake system has been heated by a series of heating snubs, the hot performance test is immediately performed. The vehicle is loaded to

GVWR and two stops are made. The stopping distance must be within acceptable limits as specified in the test. This test ensures that the brake system on the vehicle will not fade following a series of high-speed stops at GVWR.

Although these tests may seem extreme, these tests are only a minimum standard of performance. Any brake repair work should also leave the brake system capable of meeting FMVSS 135.

 FREQUENTLY ASKED QUESTION

Do the FMVSS 135 Standards Apply to Replacement Brake Part Performance?

No. The Federal Motor Vehicle Safety Standard 135 applies to new vehicles. Replacement parts used during a brake repair or replacement may or may not permit the vehicle to achieve the same standards as when new.

To help ensure like-new braking performance, the service technician should always use quality brake parts from a known manufacturer.

BRAKE REPAIR AND THE LAW

Once an automobile leaves the factory, the responsibility for maintaining the designed-in level of braking performance falls on the owner of the vehicle. Owners look to trained automotive technicians to service their brake systems. Many states have laws that regulate brake work to help ensure safe repairs. These laws vary from one area to another, but they may require special licensing for brake technicians, or special business practices when selling brake work. In some cases, the laws provide the consumer with specific warranties and the right to outside arbitration in cases of defective or substandard repairs.

Regardless of whether there are specific laws governing brake repair, a technician is always liable for damage or injuries resulting from repairs performed in an unprofessional or unworkman-like manner. Considering the lives and property that depend on good brakes, there is only one acceptable goal when making brake system repairs: to restore the system and its component parts so they perform to original specifications. In other words, *the purpose of any repair is to restore like-new performance.*

SUMMARY

1. Drum brakes are used on the rear of most vehicles.
2. Disc brakes are used on the front of most vehicles.
3. The six brake subsystems include: apply system, boost system, hydraulic system, wheel brakes, brake balance control system (which includes ABS), and brake panel warning lights.
4. An antilock braking system (ABS) pulses the hydraulic force to the wheels to prevent the tires from locking up. A locked tire has lower friction than a rolling tire.
5. The federal brake standards regulate specific brake performance requirements, but not the actual design of the braking system.

REVIEW QUESTIONS

1. List the differences between drum brakes and disc brakes.
2. List the six brake subsystem categories.
3. Explain how ABS units prevent wheel lockup.
4. List ten of the brake tests performed under the Federal Motor Vehicle Safety Standard (FMVSS) 135.

1. Disc brakes use replaceable friction material called _____.
   a. Linings
   b. Pads
   c. Core
   d. Web

2. Drum brakes use replaceable friction material called _____.
   a. Shoes
   b. Pads
   c. Core
   d. Web

3. Technician A says that a power-assisted brake reduces stopping distances compared with a nonpower-assisted brake system. Technician B says that the power-assisted brake system reduces the force that the driver must exert on the brake pedal. Which technician is correct?
   a. Technician A only
   b. Technician B only
   c. Both Technicians A and B
   d. Neither Technician A nor B

4. A locked wheel _____ to the road surface than a rolling wheel.
   a. Has less traction
   b. Has greater traction

5. Technician A says that all vehicles equipped with ABS will experience a pulsating brake pedal even during normal braking. Technician B says that ABS will result in quicker stops on all road surfaces. Which technician is correct?
   a. Technician A only
   b. Technician B only
   c. Both Technicians A and B
   d. Neither Technician A nor B

6. The FMVSS 135 standards determine _____.
   a. The design of the braking system
   b. The performance of the braking system
   c. The materials used in the braking system
   d. All of the above

7. An owner of a vehicle equipped with ABS brakes complained that whenever he tried to stop on icy or slippery roads, the brake pedal would pulse up and down rapidly. Technician A says that this is normal for many ABS units. Technician B says that the ABS unit is malfunctioning. Which technician is correct?
   a. Technician A only
   b. Technician B only
   c. Both Technicians A and B
   d. Neither Technician A nor B

8. Electric adjustable pedals operate _____.
   a. Parking brake only
   b. Accelerator pedal only
   c. Brake pedal only
   d. Both the accelerator and brake pedal

9. All of the following are specified by the FMVSS 135 except:
   a. Brake burnish procedure
   b. Variable brake proportioning system
   c. Brake noise levels
   d. Cold effectiveness

10. What is the purpose of any brake repair?
    a. Reduce noise during braking
    b. Replace pads and linings
    c. Restore proper brake pedal height
    d. Restore like-new performance

BRAKING SYSTEM PRINCIPLES

OBJECTIVES

After studying Chapter 4, the reader will be able to:

1. Prepare for the Brakes (A5) ASE certification test.
2. Explain kinetic energy and why it is so important to brake design.
3. Discuss mechanical advantage and how it relates to the braking system.
4. Explain the coefficient of friction.
5. Describe how brakes can fade due to excessive heat.

KEY TERMS

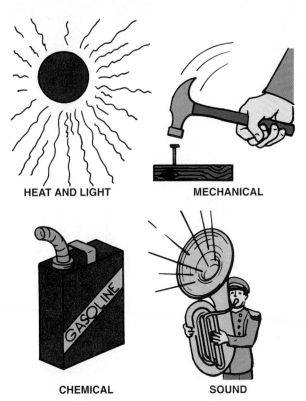

FIGURE 4–1 Energy which is the ability to perform work exists in many forms.

HEAT AND LIGHT

MECHANICAL

CHEMICAL

SOUND

ENERGY PRINCIPLES

Energy is the ability to do work. There are many forms of energy, but chemical, mechanical, and electrical energy are the most familiar kinds involved in the operation of an automobile.
● **SEE FIGURE 4–1**.

For example, when the ignition key is turned to the "Start" position, chemical energy in the battery is converted into electrical energy to operate the starter motor. The starter motor then converts the electrical energy into mechanical energy that is used to crank the engine.

In the example above, energy is being used to perform work. **Work** is the transfer of energy from one physical system to another—especially the transfer of energy to an object through the application of force. This is precisely what occurs when a vehicle's brakes are applied: The *force* of the actuating system *transfers* the energy of the vehicle's motion to the brake drums or rotors where friction *converts* it into heat energy and stops the vehicle.

KINETIC ENERGY **Kinetic energy** is a fundamental form of mechanical energy. It is the energy of mass in motion. Every moving object possesses kinetic energy, and the amount of that energy is determined by the object's mass and speed. The greater the mass of an object and the faster it moves, the more kinetic energy it possesses. Even at low speeds, a moving vehicle has enough kinetic energy to cause serious injury and damage. The job of the brake system is to dispose of that energy in a safe and controlled manner.

Engineers calculate kinetic energy using the following formula:

$$\frac{mv^2}{29.9} = E_k$$

where:

m = **mass or weight of the vehicle in pounds (lb)**

v = **velocity of the vehicle in miles per hour**

E_k = **kinetic energy in foot-pounds (ft-lb)**

Another way to express this equation is as follows.

$$\frac{\text{weight} \times \text{speed}^2}{29.9} = \text{kinetic energy}$$

If a 3,000-lb vehicle traveling at 30 mph is compared with a 6,000-lb vehicle also traveling at 30 mph as shown in

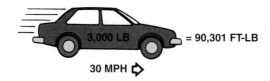

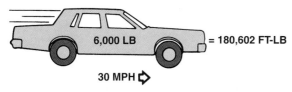

FIGURE 4–2 Kinetic energy increases in direct proportion to the weight of the vehicle.

FIGURE 4–3 Kinetic energy increases as the square of any increase in vehicle speed.

● **FIGURE 4–2**, the equations for computing their respective kinetic energies look like this:

$$\frac{3{,}000 \text{ lb} \times 30^2 \text{ mph}}{29.9} = 90{,}301 \text{ ft-lb}$$

$$\frac{6{,}000 \text{ lb} \times 30^2 \text{ mph}}{29.9} = 180{,}602 \text{ ft-lb}$$

The results show that when the weight of a vehicle is doubled from 3,000 to 6,000 lb, its kinetic energy is also doubled from 90,301 ft-lb to 180,602 ft-lb. In mathematical terms, kinetic energy increases *proportionally* as weight increases. In other words, if the weight of a moving object doubles, its kinetic energy also doubles. If the weight quadruples, the kinetic energy becomes four times as great.

If a 3,000-lb vehicle traveling at 30 mph is compared with the same vehicle traveling at 60 mph (● **FIGURE 4–3**), the equations for computing their respective kinetic energies look like this:

$$\frac{3{,}000 \text{ lb} \times 30^2 \text{ mph}}{29.9} = 90{,}301 \text{ ft-lb}$$

$$\frac{3{,}000 \text{ lb} \times 60^2 \text{ mph}}{29.9} = 361{,}204 \text{ ft-lb}$$

The results show that the vehicle traveling at 30 mph has over 90,000 ft-lb of kinetic energy, but at 60 mph the figure increases to over 350,000 ft-lb. In fact, at twice the speed, the vehicle has exactly four times as much kinetic energy. If the speed were doubled again to 120 mph, the amount of kinetic energy would grow to almost 1,500,000 ft-lb! In mathematical terms, kinetic energy increases as the *square of its speed*. In other words, if the speed of a moving object doubles (2), the kinetic energy becomes four times as great ($2^2 = 4$). And if the speed quadruples (4), say from 15 to 60 mph, the kinetic energy becomes 16 times as great ($4^2 = 16$). This is the reason speed has such an impact on kinetic energy.

KINETIC ENERGY AND BRAKE DESIGN   The relationships between weight, speed, and kinetic energy have significant practical consequences for the brake system engineer. If vehicle A weighs twice as much as vehicle B, it needs a brake system that is twice as powerful. But if vehicle C has twice the speed potential of vehicle D, it needs brakes that are, not twice, but four times more powerful.

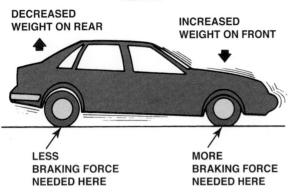

FIGURE 4–4 Inertia creates weight transfer that requires the front brakes to provide most of the braking force.

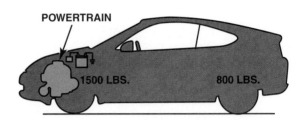

FIGURE 4–5 Front wheel drive vehicles have most of their weight over the front wheels.

INERTIA

Although brake engineers take both weight and speed capability into account when designing a brake system, these are not the only factors involved. Another physical property, inertia, also affects the braking process and the selection of brake components. **Inertia** is defined by Isaac Newton's first law of motion, which states that a body at rest tends to remain at rest, and a body in motion tends to remain in motion in a straight line unless acted upon by an outside force.

WEIGHT TRANSFER AND BIAS   Inertia, in the form of **weight transfer**, plays a major part in a vehicle's braking performance. Newton's first law of motion dictates that a moving vehicle will remain in motion unless acted upon by an outside force. The vehicle brakes provide that outside force, but when the brakes are applied at the wheel friction assemblies, only the wheels and tires begin to slow immediately. The rest of the vehicle, all of the weight carried by the suspension, attempts to remain in forward motion. The result is that the front suspension compresses, the rear suspension extends, and the weight is transferred toward the front of the vehicle. ● **SEE FIGURE 4–4.**

The total weight of the vehicle does not change, only the amount supported by each axle. To compound the problem of weight transfer, most vehicles also have a forward **weight bias**, which means that even when stopped, more than 50% of their weight is supported by the front wheels. This occurs because

the engine, transmission, and most other heavy parts are located toward the front of the vehicle. ● **SEE FIGURE 4–5.**

Front-wheel-drive (FWD) vehicles, in particular, have a forward weight bias. Whenever the brakes are applied, weight transfer and weight bias greatly increase the load on the front wheels, while the load on the rear wheels is substantially reduced. This requires the front brakes to provide 80% to 90% of the total braking force. To deal with the extra load, the front brakes are much more powerful than the rear brakes. They are able to convert more kinetic energy into heat energy.

TECH TIP

Brakes Cannot Overcome the Laws of Physics

No vehicle can stop on a dime. The energy required to slow or stop a vehicle must be absorbed by the braking system. All drivers should be aware of this fact and drive at a reasonable speed for the road and traffic conditions.

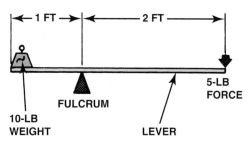

FIGURE 4–6 A first-class lever increases force and changes the direction of the force.

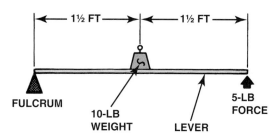

FIGURE 4–7 A second class lever increases the force in the same direction as the applied force.

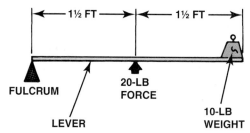

FIGURE 4–8 A third-class lever reduces force but increases the speed and travel of the resulting work.

MECHANICAL PRINCIPLES

LEVERS The primary mechanical principle used to increase application force in every brake system is **leverage**. In the science of mechanics, a lever is a simple machine that consists of a rigid object, typically a metal bar that pivots about a fixed point called a **fulcrum**. There are three basic types of levers, but the job of all three is to change a quantity of energy into a more useful form.

FIRST-CLASS LEVERS. A **first-class lever** increases the force applied to it and also changes the direction of the force. ● **SEE FIGURE 4–6**.

With a first-class lever, the weight is placed at one end while the lifting force is applied to the other. The fulcrum is positioned at some point in between. If the fulcrum is placed twice as far from the long end of the lever as from the short end, a 10-lb weight on the short end can be lifted by only a 5-lb force at the long end. However, the short end of the lever will travel only half as far as the long end. Moving the fulcrum closer to the weight will further reduce the force required to lift it, but it will also decrease the distance the weight is moved.

SECOND-CLASS LEVERS. A **second-class lever** increases the force applied to it and passes it along in the same direction. ● **SEE FIGURE 4–7**.

With a second-class lever, the fulcrum is located at one end while the lifting force is applied at the other. The weight is positioned at some point in between. If a 10-lb weight is placed at the center of the lever, it can be lifted by only a 5-lb force at the end of the lever. However, the weight will only travel half the distance the end of the lever does. As the weight is moved closer to the fulcrum, the force required to lift it, and the distance it travels, are both reduced.

THIRD-CLASS LEVERS. A **third-class lever** actually reduces the force applied to it, but the resulting force moves farther and faster. ● **SEE FIGURE 4–8**.

With a third-class lever, the fulcrum is located at one end and the weight is placed at the other. The lifting force is applied at some point in between. If a 10-lb weight is placed at the end of the lever, it can be lifted by a 20-lb force applied at the middle of the lever. Although the force required to move the weight has doubled, the weight is moved twice as far and twice as fast as the point on the lever where the force was applied. The closer to the fulcrum the lifting force is applied, the greater the force required by the weight and the farther and faster the weight will move.

LEVERS IN BRAKING SYSTEMS The levers in brake systems are used to increase force, so they are either first- or second-class. Second-class levers are the most common, and the service brake pedal is a good example. In a typical suspended brake pedal, the pedal arm is the lever, the pivot point

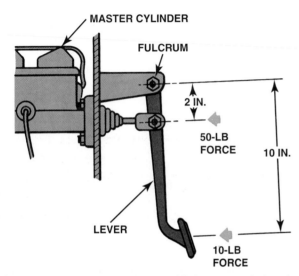

FIGURE 4–9 A brake pedal assembly is a second-class lever design that provides a 5 to 1 mechanical advantage.

MECHANICAL PRINCIPLES (CONTINUED)

is the fulcrum, and the force is applied at the foot pedal pad. ● **SEE FIGURE 4–9**.

The force applied to the master cylinder by the pedal pushrod attached to the pivot is much greater than the force applied at the pedal pad, but the pushrod does not travel nearly as far.

MECHANICAL ADVANTAGE Leverage creates a **mechanical advantage** that, at the brake pedal, is called the **pedal ratio**. For example, a pedal ratio of 5 to 1 is common for manual brakes, which means that a force of 10 lb at the brake pedal will result in a force of 50 lb at the pedal pushrod. In practice, leverage is used at many points in both the service and parking brake systems to increase braking force while making it easier for the driver to control the amount of force applied.

FRICTION PRINCIPLES

The wheel brakes use friction to convert kinetic energy into heat energy. **Friction** is the resistance to movement between two surfaces in contact with one another. Brake performance is improved by increasing friction (at least to a point), and brakes that apply enough friction to use all the grip the tires have to offer will always have the potential to stop a vehicle faster than brakes with less ability to apply friction.

COEFFICIENT OF FRICTION The amount of friction between two objects or surfaces is commonly expressed as a value called the **coefficient of friction** and is represented by the Greek letter mu (μ). The coefficient of friction, also referred to as the friction coefficient, is determined by dividing tensile force by weight force. The tensile force is the pulling force required to slide one of the surfaces across the other. The weight force is the force pushing down on the object being pulled. The equation for calculating the coefficient of friction is as follows.

$$\frac{F_t}{G} = \mu$$

where:

F_t = **tensile force in pounds**
G = **weight force in pounds**
μ = **coefficient of friction**

Another way to express the equation is as follows.

$$\frac{\text{Tensile force}}{\text{Weight force}} = \text{Coefficient of friction}$$

This equation can be used to show the effect different variables have on the coefficient of friction. At any given weight (application) force there are three factors that affect the friction coefficient of vehicle brakes:

- Surface finish
- Friction material
- Heat

For reasons that will be explained later, the friction coefficient of the wheel friction assemblies of vehicle brake systems is always less than one.

SURFACE FINISH EFFECTS The effect of surface finish on the friction coefficient can be seen in ● **FIGURE 4–10**.

In this case, 100 lb of tensile force is required to pull a 200-lb block of wood across a concrete floor. The equation for computing the coefficient of friction is as follows.

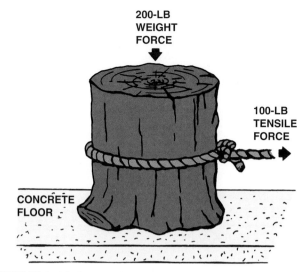

FIGURE 4–10 The coefficient of friction in this example is 0.5.

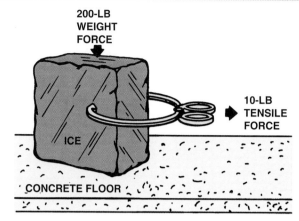

FIGURE 4–11 The type of friction material affects the coefficient of friction which is just 0.05 in this example.

$$\frac{100\ lb}{200\ lb} = 0.5$$

The friction coefficient in this instance is 0.5. Now take the same example, except assume that the block of wood has been sanded smooth, which improves its surface finish and reduces the force required to move it to only 50 lb. In this case the equation reads as follows.

$$\frac{50\ lb}{200\ lb} = 0.25$$

The friction coefficient drops by half, and it would decrease even further if the surface finish of the floor were changed from rough concrete to smooth marble.

It is obvious that the *surface finish* of two connecting surfaces has a major effect on their coefficient of friction.

FRICTION MATERIAL EFFECTS

Taking the example above one step further, consider the effect if a 200-lb block of ice, a totally different type of material, is substituted for the wood block. In this case, it requires only a 10-lb force to pull the block across the concrete. ● **SEE FIGURE 4–11.**

The equation reads as follows.

$$\frac{10\ lb}{200\ lb} = 0.05$$

The coefficient of friction in this example decreases dramatically to only 0.05, and once again, even further reductions would be seen if the floor surface were changed to polished marble or some other similar smooth surface.

It is obvious that the *type* of materials being rubbed together have a very significant effect on the coefficient of friction. The choice of materials for brake drums and rotors is limited. Iron and steel are used most often because they are relatively inexpensive and can stand up under the extreme friction brake drums and rotors must endure.

The brake lining material, however, can be replaced relatively quickly and inexpensively, and therefore does not need to have as long a service life. Brake shoe and pad friction materials play a major part in determining coefficient of friction. There are several fundamentally different materials to choose from, and each has its own unique friction coefficient and performance characteristics.

FRICTION CONTACT AREA

For *sliding* surfaces, such as those in wheel friction assemblies, the amount of contact area has no effect on the amount of friction generated. This fact is related to the earlier statement that brake friction materials always have a friction coefficient of less than 1.0. To have a friction coefficient of 1.0 or more, material must be *transferred* between the two friction surfaces. The amount of contact area does not affect the coefficient of friction, but it does have significant effects on lining life and the dissipation of heat that can lead to brake fade.

Tires are an example where contact area makes a difference. All other things being equal, a wide tire with a large contact area on the road has a higher coefficient of friction than a narrow tire with less contact area. This occurs because the tire and road *do not* have a sliding relationship. A tire conforms to and engages the road surface, and during a hard stop, a portion of the breaking force comes from shearing or tearing away the tire tread rubber. The rubber's tensile strength, its internal resistance to being pulled apart, adds to the braking efforts of friction. A racing tire making a hard stop on dry pavement, for example, has a friction coefficient of 1.0 or better. The transfer of material between the two surfaces can be seen as skid marks on the pavement.

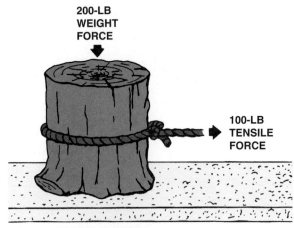

200-LB WEIGHT FORCE

100-LB TENSILE FORCE

BLOCK AT REST

STATIC AND KINETIC FRICTION   There are actually two measurements of the coefficient of friction, the **static friction** coefficient and the **kinetic friction** coefficient. The static value is the coefficient of friction with the two friction surfaces at rest. The kinetic value is the coefficient of friction while the two surfaces are sliding against one another.

The coefficient of static friction is always higher than that of kinetic friction, which explains why it is harder to *start* an object moving than to *keep* it moving. In the example shown in ● **FIGURE 4–12**, it takes 100 lb of tensile force to start the wooden block sliding, but once in motion, it takes only 50 lb to keep it sliding.

The relatively high static friction is harder to overcome than the somewhat lower kinetic friction. The static and kinetic friction coefficients for several combinations of materials are shown in ● **CHART 4–1**.

The difference between static and kinetic friction explains why parking brakes, although much less powerful than service brakes, are still able to hold a vehicle in position on a hill. The job of the parking brakes is relatively easy because the stationary vehicle has no kinetic energy, and the brake lining and drum or disc are not moving when they are applied. To start the vehicle moving, enough force would have to be applied to overcome the relatively high static friction of the parking brakes. The service brakes, however, have a much more difficult job. The moving vehicle has a great deal of kinetic energy, and the fact that the brake friction surfaces are in relative motion means that kinetic friction makes them less efficient.

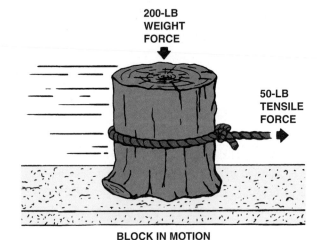

200-LB WEIGHT FORCE

50-LB TENSILE FORCE

BLOCK IN MOTION

FIGURE 4–12 The static coefficient of friction of an object at rest is higher than the kinetic (dynamic) friction coefficient once in motion.

	COEFFICIENT OF FRICTION	
CONTACTING SURFACES	**STATIC**	**KINETIC**
STEEL ON STEEL (DRY)	0.6	0.4
STEEL ON STEEL (GREASY)	0.1	0.05
TEFLON ON STEEL	0.04	0.04
BRASS ON STEEL (DRY)	0.5	0.4
BRAKE LINING ON CAST IRON	0.4	0.3
RUBBER TIRES		
ON SMOOTH PAVEMENT (DRY)	0.9	0.8
METAL ON ICE	–	0.02

CHART 4–1

Every combination of materials has different static and kinetic friction coefficients

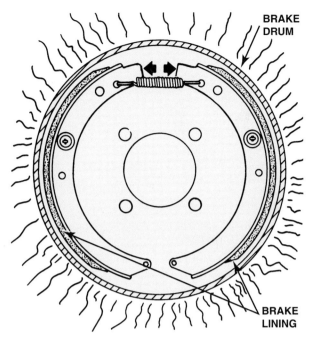

FIGURE 4–13 Mechanical fade occurs when the brake drums become so hot that they expand away from the brake lining.

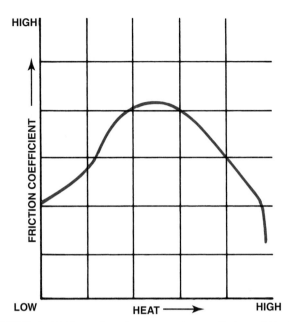

FIGURE 4–14 Some heat increases the coefficient of friction but too much heat can cause it to drop off sharply.

FRICTION AND HEAT

The function of the brake system is to convert kinetic energy into heat energy through friction.

It is the *change* in kinetic energy that determines the amount of temperature increase, and kinetic energy increases proportionately with increases in weight, and as the square of any increase in speed. If the weight of the vehicle is doubled to 6,000 lb, the change in kinetic energy required to bring it to a full stop will be 180,602 ft-lb.

The thicker and heavier the brake rotors and drums, the more heat they can absorb. Some of the heat is absorbed by the brake drums and rotors, some goes into the shoes and pads, and some is conducted into the wheel cylinders, calipers, and brake fluid. In addition, the front brakes provide 60% to 80% of the total braking force and they receive a similar percentage of the average temperature increase. The increase at each axle is divided evenly between the two wheel friction assemblies unless there is unequal traction from one side to the other, or there is a problem within the brake system itself.

BRAKE FADE

The temperature of a brake drum or rotor may rise more than 100°F (55°C) in only seconds during a hard stop, but it could take 30 seconds or more for the rotor to cool to the temperature that existed before the stop. If repeated hard stops are performed, the brake system components can overheat and lose effectiveness, or possibly fail altogether. This loss of braking power is called **brake fade**.

The point at which brakes overheat and fade is determined by a number of factors including the brake design, its cooling ability, and the type of friction material being used. There are four primary types of brake fade including:

- **Mechanical fade** occurs when a brake drum overheats and expands away from the brake lining. ● **SEE FIGURE 4–13**. To maintain braking power, the brake shoes must move farther outward, which requires additional brake pedal travel. When the drum expands to a point where there is not enough pedal travel to keep the lining in contact with the drum, brake fade occurs. Mechanical fade is not a problem with disc brakes because as a brake rotor heats up it expands *toward* the brake pads rather than away from them.

- **Lining fade** affects both drum and disc brakes, and occurs when the friction material overheats to the point where its coefficient of friction drops off. ● **SEE FIGURE 4–14**. When lining fade occurs on drum brakes, partial braking power can sometimes be restored by increasing pressure

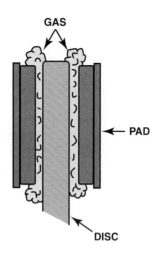

FIGURE 4–15 One cause of brake fade occurs when the phenolic resin, a part of the friction material, gets so hot that it vaporizes. The vaporized gas from the disc brake pads gets between the rotor (disc) and the friction pad. Because the friction pad is no longer in contact with the rotor, no additional braking force is possible.

GAS

PAD

DISC

BRAKE FADE (CONTINUED)

on the brake pedal, although this may only make matters worse since the extra pressure increases the amount of heat and fade. With disc brakes, lining fade is possible, but less of a problem because of disc brakes' superior ability to dissipate heat. The rotor friction surfaces are exposed to the passing air, and most rotors have internal ventilation passages that further aid in cooling.

- **Gas fade** is a relatively rare type of brake fade that occurs under very hard braking when a thin layer of hot gases and dust particles builds up between the brake drum or rotor and linings. The gas layer acts as a lubricant and reduces friction. ● SEE FIGURE 4–15.

As with lining fade, greater application force at the brake pedal is required to maintain a constant level of stopping power. Gas fade becomes more of a problem as the size of the brake lining increases because gases and particles have a harder time escaping from under a drum brake shoe than a disc brake pad. Some high-performance brake shoes and pads have slotted linings to provide paths for gas and particles to escape.

In most cases brake fade is a temporary condition. The brakes will return to normal once they have all been allowed to cool.

- **Water fade.** If a vehicle is driven through deep water or during a severe rainstorm, water can get between the brake drum and the linings. When this occurs, no stopping power is possible until the water is pushed out and normal friction is restored. While water fade is most likely to occur with drum brakes, it can also occur on disc brakes. After driving through deep water, the wise driver should lightly apply the brakes to check the operation and to help remove any water trapped between the friction material and the rotor or drum.

TECH TIP

How to Reduce Possible Brake Fade

To help prevent possible brake fade while descending long hills, place the gear selector into a lower drive range such as "2" or even "1" if going slowly enough. This action allows for additional engine braking and takes the load off of the wheel brakes.

DECELERATION RATES

Deceleration rates are measured in units of "feet per second per second" (No, this is not a misprint). What it means is that the vehicle will change in velocity during a certain time interval divided by the time interval. Deceleration is abbreviated "ft/sec^2" (pronounced "feet per second per second" or "feet per second squared") or meters per sec^2 (m/sec^2) in the metric system. Typical deceleration rates include the following.

- Comfortable deceleration is about 8.5 ft/sec^2 (3 m/sec^2).
- Loose items in the vehicle will "fly" above 11 ft/sec^2 (3.5 m/sec^2).
- Maximum deceleration rates for most vehicles and light trucks range from 16 to 32 ft/sec^2 (5 to 10 m/sec^2).

An average deceleration rate of 15 ft/sec^2 (3 m/sec^2) can stop a vehicle traveling at 55 mph (88 km/h) in about 200 ft (61 m) in less than 4 seconds. During a standard brake system test, a vehicle is braked at this rate 15 times. Temperatures at the front brake pads can reach 1,300°F (700°C) or higher, sometimes reaching as high as 1,800°F (980°C). Brake fluid and rubber components may reach 300°F (150°C) or higher.

SUMMARY

1. Energy is the ability to do work. A vehicle in motion represents kinetic energy, which must be absorbed by the braking system during a stop.

2. The front brakes must provide a higher percentage of the braking force due to weight bias and weight transfer.

3. The brake pedal uses mechanical advantage to increase the force applied by the driver to the master cylinder.

4. Coefficient of friction represents the amount of friction between two surfaces.

5. Friction creates heat during a stop and the braking system must be able to absorb and dissipate this heat.

6. Brake fade results when the heat generated by the brakes causes changes in the friction materials that reduce the braking force or by water that can get between the brake drum and the linings.

7. Deceleration rates are expressed in feet per second per second or ft/sec^2.

REVIEW QUESTIONS

1. What is kinetic energy?

2. How is mechanical advantage used in the braking system?

3. What is the coefficient of friction?

4. Why do brakes fade due to excessive heat or water?

CHAPTER QUIZ

1. All of the following are correct statements about braking except:
   a. Kinetic energy must be absorbed by the braking system.
   b. Kinetic energy of a vehicle doubles when the speed doubles.
   c. The heavier the vehicle, the greater the kinetic energy when moving.
   d. If the vehicle weight is doubled, the kinetic energy of a moving vehicle is doubled.

2. Technician A says that the front brakes do most of the braking because the front brakes are larger. Technician B says that due to weight transfer, most of the braking force needs to be done by the front brakes. Which technician is correct?
   a. Technician A only
   b. Technician B only
   c. Both Technicians A and B
   d. Neither Technician A nor B

3. The brake pedal assembly uses a mechanical lever to _____.
   a. Increase the driver's force on the brake pedal applied to the master cylinder
   b. Increase the distance the brake pedal needs to be depressed by the driver
   c. Decrease the driver's force on the brake pedal applied to the master cylinder
   d. Allow for clearance between the brake pedal and the floor when the brakes are applied

4. The friction between two surfaces is affected by all except _____.
   a. Speed difference between the two surfaces
   b. Surface finish
   c. Frictional material
   d. Heat

5. Technician A says that the thicker or heavier the disc brake rotor, the more heat can be absorbed. Technician B says that the faster the vehicle is traveling when the brakes are applied, the greater the amount of heat created in the brake system. Which technician is correct?
   a. Technician A only
   b. Technician B only
   c. Both Technicians A and B
   d. Neither Technician A nor B

6. All of the following are types of brake fade except _____.
   a. Mechanical fade
   b. Lining fade
   c. Gas fade
   d. Rotor fade

7. Brake fade caused by water can occur _____.
   a. Only if the vehicle is driven in water above the centerline of the axle
   b. Whenever it rains and the roads are wet or damp
   c. Due to moisture in the air on a humid day
   d. Whenever driving through water puddles or during a severe rainstorm

8. What can the driver do to reduce the possibility of brake fade caused by heat?
   a. Ride the brakes to keep the shoes and pads against the drum or rotor
   b. Pump the brake pedal while descending a steep hill
   c. Select a lower transmission gear
   d. Shift the transmission into neutral and allow the vehicle to coast down long or steep hills

9. Maximum deceleration rates for a typical passenger car or light truck range from _____.
   a. 1 to 3 ft/sec
   b. 5 to 10 ft/sec
   c. 16 to 32 ft/sec^2
   d. 200 to 250 ft/sec^2

10. Disc brake pads can reach temperatures as high as _____.
    a. 300°F (150°C)
    b. 1,000°F (540°C)
    c. 1,300°F (700°C)
    d. 2,000°F (1093°C)

chapter 5
BRAKE HYDRAULIC SYSTEMS

OBJECTIVES

After studying Chapter 5, the reader will be able to:

1. Prepare for the Brakes (A5) ASE certification test content area "A" (Hydraulic System Diagnosis and Repair).
2. State Pascal's law.
3. Describe the function, purpose, and operation of the master cylinder.
4. Explain how hydraulic force can be used to supply high pressures to each individual wheel brake.
5. Describe the process of troubleshooting master cylinders and related brake hydraulic components.
6. Explain how a quick take-up master cylinder works.

KEY TERMS

FIGURE 5–1 Hydraulic brake lines transfer the brake effort to each brake assembly attached to all four wheels.

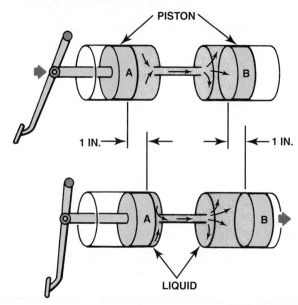

FIGURE 5–2 Because liquids cannot be compressed, they are able to transmit motion in a closed system.

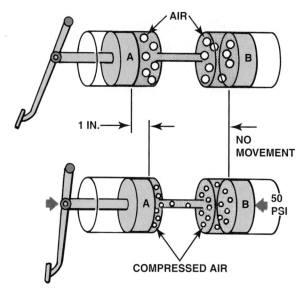

FIGURE 5–3 Hydraulic system must be free of air to operate properly. If air is in the system, the air is compressed when the brake pedal is depressed and the brake fluid does not transmit the force to the wheel brakes.

HYDRAULIC PRINCIPLES

In addition to the mechanical advantage provided by leverage, all vehicles use hydraulic pressure to help increase brake application force.

All braking systems require that a driver's force is transmitted to the drum or rotor attached to each wheel. ● **SEE FIGURE 5–1**.

The force that can be exerted on the brake pedal varies due to the strength and size of the driver. Engineers design braking systems to require less than 150 lb of force (68 kg) from the driver, yet provide the force necessary to stop a heavy vehicle from high speed.

NONCOMPRESSIBILITY OF LIQUIDS   Hydraulic systems use liquids to transmit motion. For all practical purposes, a liquid cannot be compressed. No matter how much pressure or force is placed on a quantity of liquid, its volume will remain the same. This fact enables liquids in a closed system to transmit motion. ● **SEE FIGURE 5–2**.

If piston A is moved a distance of 1 in., the liquid will be displaced ahead of it and piston B will move 1 in. as well.

Liquids cannot be compressed, but any air trapped in the system can be compressed. The simple hydraulic system has been contaminated with air. ● **SEE FIGURE 5–3**.

Even though piston A is moved a distance of 1 in., piston B will not move if the load on it is greater than the pressure of the air in the system. For example, if the load on piston B is 50 pounds per square inch (PSI), the movement of piston A must compress the air in the system to that same pressure before piston B will begin to move. A brake hydraulic system must be air free or the brakes will not operate correctly and the driver will feel a spongy brake pedal that is also often lower than normal.

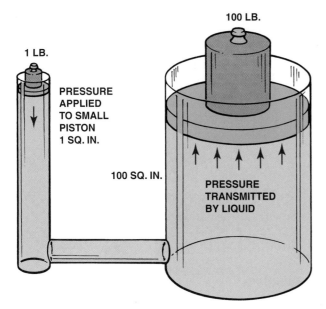

FIGURE 5–4 A one-pound force exerted on a small piston in a sealed system transfers the pressure to each square inch throughout the system. In this example, the 1-lb force is able to lift a 100-lb weight because it is supported by a piston that is 100 times larger in area than the small piston.

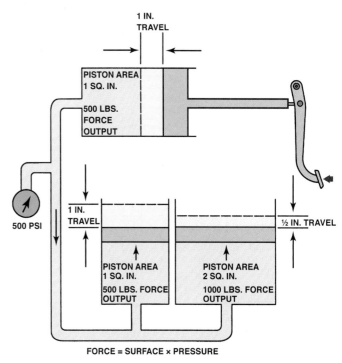

FORCE = SURFACE × PRESSURE

FIGURE 5–5 The amount of force (F) on the piston is the result of pressure (P) multiplied by the surface area (A).

PASCAL'S LAW

The hydraulic principles that permit a brake system to function were discovered by a French physicist, Blaise Pascal (1632–1662). **Pascal's law** states that "when force is applied to a liquid confined in a container or an enclosure, the pressure is transmitted equal and undiminished in every direction." To help understand this principle, assume that a force of 10 lb is exerted on a piston with a surface area of 1 square inch (sq. in.). Since this *force* measured in lb or Newtons (N) is applied to a piston with an area measured in square inches (sq. in.), the *pressure* is the force divided by the area or "10 pounds per square inch (PSI)." It is this "pressure" that is transmitted, without loss, throughout the entire hydraulic system. ● **SEE FIGURE 5–4**.

If two out of the three factors are known, then the other one can be calculated by using this formula.

> **F = P × A (force is equal to the pressure multiplied by the area)**
>
> **P = F ÷ A (pressure is equal to the force divided by the area)**
>
> **A = F ÷ P (area is equal to the force divided by the pressure)**
>
> where the capital letters mean:
>
> **F** = force (lb) (Newtons)
>
> **P** = pressure in lb per sq. in. (kilo Pascals [kPa])
>
> **A** = area in sq. in. (cm²)

A practical example involves a master cylinder with a piston area of 1 sq. in., and one wheel cylinder with an area of 1 sq. in., and one wheel cylinder with a piston area of 2 sq. in. ● **SEE FIGURE 5–5**.

The real "magic" of a hydraulic brake system is the fact that different forces can be created at different wheel cylinders. More force is necessary for front brakes than for rear brakes because, as the brakes are applied, the weight of the vehicle moves forward.

Larger (area) pistons are used in brake calipers on the front wheels to increase the force used to apply the front brakes.

Not only can hydraulics act as a "force machine" (by varying piston size), but the hydraulic system also can be varied to change piston stroke distances.

On a typical vehicle, a driver-input force of 150 lb (660 Newtons) is boosted both mechanically (through the brake pedal linkage) and by the power booster to a fluid pressure of about 1,700 PSI (11,700 kPa). With a drum brake, the wheel cylinder expands and pushes the brake shoes against a brake drum. *The distance the shoes move is only about 0.005–0.012 in. (5 to 12 thousandths of an inch) (0.015–0.30 mm).* ● **SEE FIGURE 5–6**.

With a disc brake, brake fluid pressure pushes on the piston in the caliper a small amount and causes a clamping of

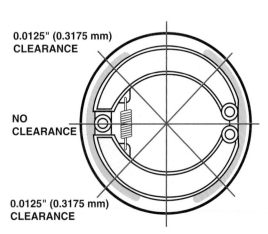

FIGURE 5–6 Drum brake illustrating the typical clearance between the brake shoes (friction material) and the rotating brake drum represented as the outermost black circle.

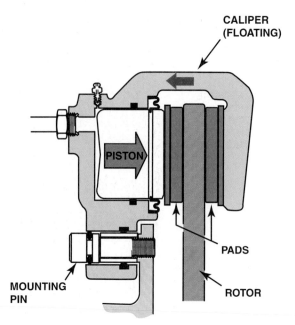

FIGURE 5–7 The brake pad (friction material) is pressed on both sides of the rotating rotor by the hydraulic pressure of the caliper.

PASCAL'S LAW (CONTINUED)

? FREQUENTLY ASKED QUESTION

How Much Brake Fluid Is Moved When the Brake Pedal Is Depressed?

During a typical brake application, only about *1 teaspoon (5 ml or cc) of brake fluid* actually is moved from the master cylinder and into the hydraulic system to cause the pressure buildup to occur.

the disc brake pads against both sides of a rotor (disc).
● **SEE FIGURE 5–7**. *The typical distance the pads move is only about 0.001–0.003 in. (1 to 3 thousandths of an inch) (0.025–0.076 mm).*

HYDRAULIC PRESSURE AND PISTON SIZE If a mechanical force of 100 lb is exerted by the brake pedal pushrod onto a master cylinder piston with 1 sq. in. of surface area, the equation reads as follows.

$$\frac{100\ lb}{1\ sq.\ in.} = 100\ PSI$$

The result in this case is 100 PSI of brake system hydraulic pressure. ● **SEE FIGURE 5–8**. However, if the same 100-lb force is

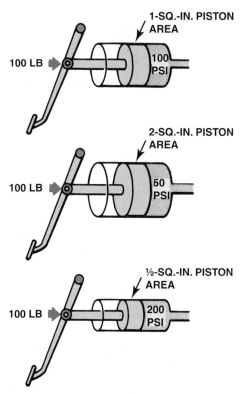

FIGURE 5–8 Mechanical force and the master cylinder piston area determine the hydraulic pressure in the brake system.

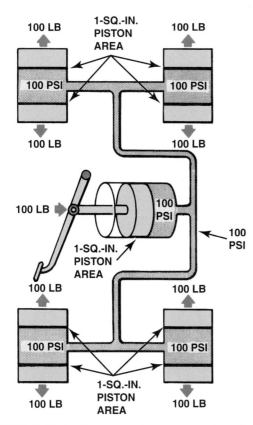

FIGURE 5–9 Hydraulic pressure is the same throughout a closed system and acts with equal force on equal areas.

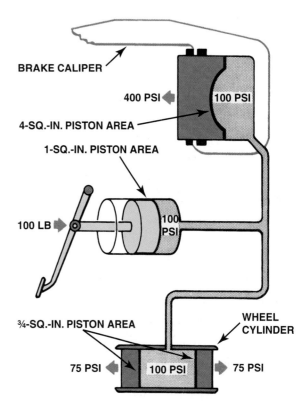

FIGURE 5–10 Differences in brake caliper and wheel cylinder piston area have a major effect on brake application force.

applied to a master cylinder piston with twice the area (2 sq. in.) the equation will read as follows.

$$\frac{100\ lb}{2\ sq.\ in.} = 50\ PSI$$

Doubling the area of the master cylinder piston cuts the hydraulic system pressure in half. Conversely, if the same 100-lb force is applied to a master cylinder piston with only half the area (0.5 or 1/2 sq. in.), the equation will show that the system pressure is doubled:

$$\frac{100\ lb}{0.5\ sq.\ in.} = 200\ PSI$$

APPLICATION FORCE AND PISTON SIZE While the size of the master cylinder piston affects the hydraulic pressure of the entire brake system, weight shift and bias require that the heavily loaded front brakes receive much higher application force than the lightly loaded rear brakes. These differences in force are obtained by using different-sized pistons in the wheel cylinders and brake calipers. Pascal's law states that a pressurized liquid in a confined space acts with equal pressure on equal *areas* and as long as the pistons in a hydraulic system have the same area, 100 PSI from the master cylinder will result in 100 PSI of braking force. ● **SEE FIGURE 5–9**. However, when

equal pressure acts on *unequal* areas, as with different-sized pistons, the brake application force will differ as well.

The mechanical *force(f)* at the brake pedal pushrod is applied to the master cylinder piston *area(a)* and converted into brake system hydraulic *pressure(p)*. Brake calipers and wheel cylinders perform exactly the opposite. Hydraulic *pressure* applied to the wheel cylinder or brake caliper piston *area* is converted back into mechanical *force* that is used to apply the wheel friction assemblies. Because the variables are identical, the same equation can be rewritten to explain how changes in piston size affect brake application force.

$$P \times A = F$$

It is piston surface *area*, not diameter, that affects force.

In the simple brake system, the pedal and linkage apply a 100-lb force on a master cylinder piston with an area of 1 sq. in. ● **SEE FIGURE 5–10**. This results in a pressure of 100 PSI throughout the hydraulic system. At the front wheels, the 100 PSI is applied to a brake caliper piston that has an area of 4 sq. in. The equation for this example is as follows.

100 PSI × 4 sq. in. = 400 lb

In this case the difference in piston areas (1 sq. in. compared to 4 sq. in.) results in the 100-PSI brake pedal pushrod force being

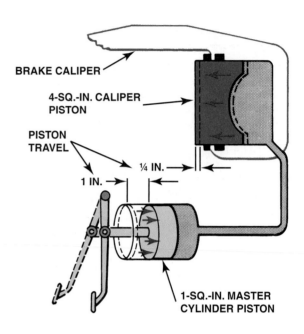

FIGURE 5–11 The increase in application force created by the large brake caliper piston is off-set by a decrease in piston travel.

BRAKE CALIPER

4-SQ.-IN. CALIPER PISTON

PISTON TRAVEL

¼ IN.

1 IN.

1-SQ.-IN. MASTER CYLINDER PISTON

PASCAL'S LAW (CONTINUED)

increased for 400 lb of application force at the wheel friction assembly. The hydraulic pressure is still 100 PSI at all points within the system and the increase in application pressure is solely the result of 100 PSI acting on a 4-sq.-in. piston. The 400 lb is a mechanical force, not hydraulic pressure.

The drum brakes at the rear wheels of the same brake system use wheel cylinders whose pistons have three-quarters (3/4 or 0.75) of an inch of surface area. If the hydraulic system pressure remains 100 PSI, the equation for this example is as follows.

$$100 \text{ PSI} \times 0.75 \text{ sq. in.} = 75 \text{ lb}$$

Just as larger pistons increase application force, this example shows that smaller pistons decrease it. The system hydraulic pressure remains 100 PSI at all points, but the smaller piston is unable to transmit all of the available pressure. As a result, the mechanical application force is reduced to only 75 lb.

PISTON SIZE VERSUS PISTON TRAVEL   In disc brakes, the mechanical force available to apply the brakes is four times greater because of the size difference between the master cylinder and caliper pistons. Some of the hydraulic

energy is converted into *increased* mechanical force. The trade-off is that the larger caliper piston with the greater force will not move as far as the smaller master cylinder piston. The amount of hydraulic energy converted into mechanical motion is *decreased*. For example in a typical disc brake system, if the master cylinder piston stroke is 1 In., the caliper piston will move only 1/4 inch. ● **SEE FIGURE 5–11.**

HYDRAULIC PRINCIPLES AND BRAKE DESIGN   When a brake system is designed, the hydraulic relationships play a major part in determining the sizes of the many pistons within the system. The piston sizes selected must move enough fluid to operate the wheel cylinder and brake caliper pistons through a wide range of travel, while at the same time they must create enough application force to lock the wheel brakes. The piston sizes chosen should also provide the driver with good brake pedal "feel" so the brakes are easy to apply in a controlled manner.

Most vehicles with disc brakes have large master cylinder pistons to move the required volume of fluid, and a power booster to reduce the required brake pedal force.

Bigger Is Not Better

A vehicle owner wanted better braking performance from his off-road race vehicle. Thinking that a larger master cylinder would help, a technician replaced the original 1-in.-bore-diameter master cylinder with a larger master cylinder with a 1 1/8-in.-bore-diameter master cylinder.

After bleeding the system, the technician was anxious to test-drive the "new" brake system. During the test-drive the technician noticed that the brake pedal "grabbed" much higher than with the original master cylinder. This delighted the technician. The owner of the vehicle was also delighted until he tried to stop from highway speed. *The driver had to use both feet to stop!*

The technician realized, after the complaint, that the larger master cylinder was able to move more brake fluid, but with *less* pressure to the wheel cylinders. The new master cylinder gave the impression of better brakes because the fluid was moved into the wheel cylinders (and calipers) quickly, and the pads and shoes contacted the rotor and drums sooner because of the greater volume of brake fluid moved by the larger pistons in the master cylinder.

To calculate the difference in pressure between the original (stock) master cylinder and the larger replacement, the technician used Pascal's law with the following results:

Original Master Cylinder (1 in. bore)	Replacement Master Cylinder (1 1/8 in. bore)
$\text{Pressure} = \dfrac{\text{Force}}{\text{Area}}$	$\text{Pressure} = \dfrac{\text{Force}}{\text{Area}}$
$\text{PSI} = \dfrac{450 \text{ lb}}{\text{Area}}$ (typical)	$\text{PSI} = \dfrac{450 \text{ lb}}{\text{Area}}$ (typical)
$\text{Area} = \pi r^2 = 3.14 \times .5^2$ (1/2 of 1 in.)	$\text{Area} = \pi r^2 = 3.14 \times .5625^2$ (1/2 of 1 1/8 in.)
$\text{Area} = 3.14 \times .25$	$\text{Area} = 3.14 \times .316$
$\text{Area} = .785$ sq. in.	$\text{Area} = .992$ sq. in.
$\text{Pressure} = \dfrac{450}{.785} = 573 \text{ PSI}$	$\text{Pressure} = \dfrac{450}{.992} = 454 \text{ PSI}$

The difference in pressure is 119 PSI less with the larger master cylinder (573 − 454 = 119).

The stopping power of the brakes was reduced because the larger diameter master cylinder piston produced lower pressure (the same force was spread over a larger area and this means that the pressure [PSI] is less).

All master cylinders are sized correctly from the factory for the correct braking effort, pressure, pedal travel, and stopping ability. *A technician should never change the sizing of any hydraulic brake component on any vehicle!*

MASTER CYLINDERS

The **master cylinder** is the heart of the entire braking system. No braking occurs until the driver depresses the brake pedal. The brake pedal linkage is used to apply the force of the driver's foot into a closed hydraulic system that begins with the master cylinder.

MASTER CYLINDER RESERVOIRS Most vehicles built since the early 1980s are equipped with see-through master cylinder reservoirs, which permit owners and service technicians to check the brake fluid level without having to remove the top of the reservoir. Some countries have laws that require this type of reservoir. ● **SEE FIGURE 5–12**.

The reservoir capacity is great enough to allow for the brakes to become completely worn out and still have enough reserve for safe operation. The typical capacity of the entire braking system is usually 2 to 3 pints (1 to 1.5 liters). Vehicles equipped with four-wheel disc brakes usually hold 4 pints (2 liters) or more.

MASTER CYLINDER RESERVOIR DIAPHRAGM The entire brake system is filled with brake fluid up to the "full" level of the master cylinder reservoir.

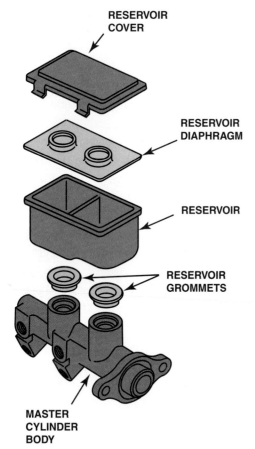

FIGURE 5–12 Typical master cylinder showing the reservoir and associated parts. The reservoir diaphragm lays directly on top of the brake fluid, which helps keep air from the surface of the brake fluid because brake fluid easily absorbs moisture from the air.

MASTER CYLINDERS (CONTINUED)

CAUTION: The master cylinder should never be filled higher than the recommended full mark to allow for brake fluid expansion that occurs normally when the brake fluid gets hot due to the heat generated by the brakes.

The reservoir is vented to the atmosphere so the fluid can expand and contract without difficulty as would be the case if the reservoir were sealed.

Being open to the atmosphere allows the moisture in the air to come in contact with the brake fluid. This moisture in the air is absorbed into the brake fluid because brake fluid has an affinity (attraction) to moisture (water).

To help reduce the moisture from getting in contact with the brake fluid, master cylinders use a rubber diaphragm or floating disc to help seal outside air from direct contact with brake fluid. This seal still allows the brake fluid to expand and contract as the fluid heats up and cools down during normal brake system

FIGURE 5–13 Master cylinder with brake fluid level at the "max" (maximum) line.

 TECH TIP

Don't Fill the Master Cylinder Without Seeing Me!

The boss explained to the beginning technician that there are two reasons why the customer should be told not to fill the master cylinder reservoir when the brake fluid is down to the "minimum" mark, as shown in ● FIGURE 5–13.

1. If the master cylinder reservoir is low, there may be a leak that should be repaired.
2. As the brakes wear, the disc brake piston moves outward to maintain the same distance between friction materials and the rotor. Therefore, as the disc brake pads wear, the brake fluid level goes down to compensate.

Therefore if the brake fluid is low, the vehicle should be serviced—either for new brakes or to repair a leak.

operation. This rubber diaphragm is vented between the steel cap and diaphragm. As the brake fluid level drops due to normal disc brake pad wear, the rubber diaphragm also lowers to remain like a second skin on top of the brake fluid.

Whenever adding brake fluid, push the rubber diaphragm back up into the cover. Normal atmospheric pressure will allow the diaphragm to return to its normal position on top of the brake fluid. Whenever servicing a brake system, be sure to check that the vent hole is clear on the cover to allow air to get between the cover and the diaphragm.

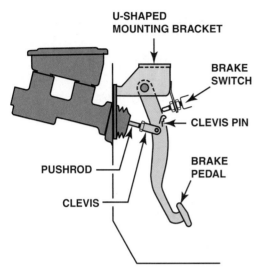

FIGURE 5–14 The typical brake pedal is supported by a mount and attached to the pushrod by a U-shaped bracket. The pin used to retain the clevis to the brake pedal is usually called a clevis pin.

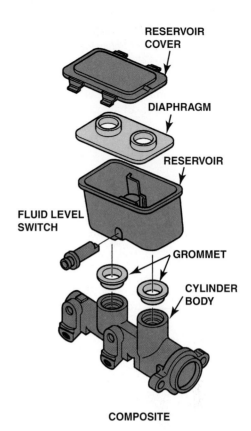

COMPOSITE

FIGURE 5–15 The composite master cylinder is made from two different materials—aluminum for the body and plastic materials for the reservoir and reservoir cover. This type of reservoir feeds both primary and secondary chambers, and therefore uses a fluid level switch that activates the red dash warning lamp if the brake fluid level drops.

MASTER CYLINDER OPERATION The master cylinder is the heart of any hydraulic braking system. Brake pedal movement and force are transferred to the brake fluid and directed to wheel cylinders or calipers. ● **SEE FIGURE 5–14.** The master cylinder is also separated into two pressure-building chambers (or circuits) to provide braking force to one-half of the brake in the event of a leak or damage to one circuit. ● **SEE FIGURE 5–15.**

Both pressure-building sections of the master cylinder contain two holes from the reservoir. The Society of Automotive Engineers' (SAE) term for the forward (tapered) hole is the **vent port**, and the rearward straight drilled hole is called the **replenishing port**. ● **SEE FIGURE 5–16.**

Various vehicle and brake component manufacturers call these ports by various names. For example, the vent port is the high-pressure port. This tapered forward hole is also called the **compensating port**.

The replenishing port is the low-pressure rearward, larger diameter hole. The inlet port is also called the **bypass port**, **filler port**, or **breather port**.

The function of the master cylinder can be explained from the at-rest, applied, and released positions.

AT-REST POSITION. The primary sealing cups are between the compensating port hole and the inlet port hole. In this position, the brake fluid is free to expand and move from the calipers, wheel cylinders, and brake lines up into the reservoir through the vent port (compensation port) if the temperature rises and the fluid expands. If the fluid was trapped, the pressure of the brake fluid would increase with temperature, causing the brakes to **self-apply**. ● **SEE FIGURE 5–17.** The pistons (primary and secondary) are retained by a clip at the pushrod end and held in position by return springs.

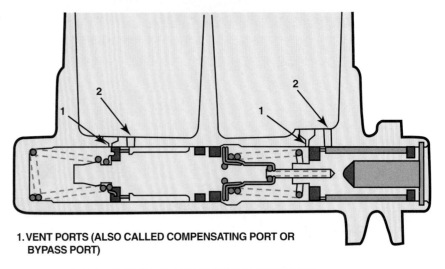

FIGURE 5–16 Note the various names for the vent port (front port) and the replenishing port (rear port). Names vary by vehicle and brake component manufacturer. The names vent port and replenishing port are the terms recommended by the Society of Automotive Engineers (SAE).

1. VENT PORTS (ALSO CALLED COMPENSATING PORT OR BYPASS PORT)

2. REPLENISHING PORTS (ALSO CALLED INLET PORT, BYPASS PORT, FILLER PORT, OR BREATHER PORT)

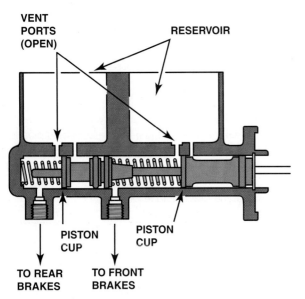

FIGURE 5–17 The vent ports must remain open to allow brake fluid to expand when heated by the friction material and transferred to the caliper and/or wheel cylinder. As the brake fluid increases in temperature, it expands causing the brakes to self-apply which is prevented by the open vent ports.

TECH TIP

Too Much Is Bad

Some vehicle owners or inexperienced service people may fill the master cylinder to the top. Master cylinders should only be filled to the "maximum" level line or about 1/4 in. (6 mm) from the top to allow room for expansion when the brake fluid gets hot during normal operation. If the master cylinder is filled to the top, the expanding brake fluid has no place to expand and the pressure increases. This increased pressure can cause the brakes to "self-apply," shortening brake friction material life and increasing fuel consumption. Overheated brakes can result and the brake fluid may boil, causing a total loss of braking.

MASTER CYLINDERS (CONTINUED)

APPLIED POSITION. When the brake pedal is depressed, the pedal linkage forces the pushrod and primary piston down the bore of the master cylinder. ● SEE FIGURE 5–18. As the piston moves forward, the primary sealing cup covers and blocks off the vent port (compensating port). Hydraulic pressure builds in front of the primary seal as the pushrod moves forward. The back of the piston is kept filled through the replenishing port. ● SEE FIGURE 5–19. This stops any suction (vacuum) from forming behind the piston. The secondary piston is moved

forward as pressure is exerted by the primary piston. If, for any reason, such as a leak, the primary piston cannot build pressure, a mechanical link on the front of the primary piston will touch the secondary piston and move it forward, as the primary piston is pushed forward by the pushrod and brake pedal.

RELEASED POSITION. Releasing the brake pedal removes the pressure on the pushrod and master cylinder pistons. A spring on the brake pedal linkage returns the brake pedal to its normal at-rest (up) position. The spring in front of the master cylinder

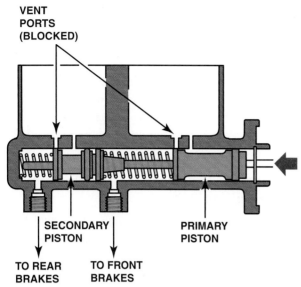

VENT PORTS (BLOCKED)

SECONDARY PISTON

PRIMARY PISTON

TO REAR BRAKES

TO FRONT BRAKES

FIGURE 5–18 As the brake pedal is depressed, the pushrod moves the primary piston forward, closing off the vent port. As soon as the port is blocked, pressure builds in front of the primary sealing cup, which pushes on the secondary piston. The secondary piston also moves forward, blocking the secondary vent port and building pressure in front of the primary sealing cup.

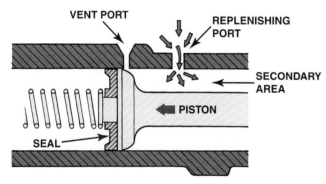

VENT PORT

REPLENISHING PORT

SECONDARY AREA

PISTON

SEAL

FIGURE 5–19 The purpose of the replenishing port is to keep the volume behind the primary piston filled with brake fluid from the reservoir as the piston moves forward during a brake application.

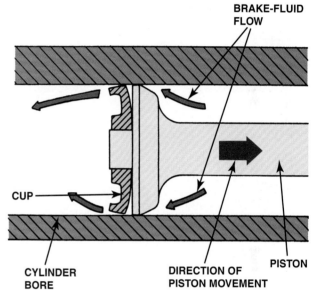

BRAKE-FLUID FLOW

CUP

CYLINDER BORE

DIRECTION OF PISTON MOVEMENT

PISTON

FIGURE 5–20 When the brake pedal is released, the master cylinder piston moves rearward. Some of the brake fluid is pushed back up through the replenishing port, but most of the fluid flows past the sealing cup. Therefore, when the driver pumps the brake pedal, the additional fluid in front of the pressure-building sealing cup is available quickly.

piston expands, pushing the pistons rearward. At the same time, pressure is released from the entire braking system and the released brake fluid pressure is exerted on the master cylinder pistons, forcing them rearward. As the piston is pushed back, the lips of the seal fold forward allowing fluid to quickly move past the piston, as shown in ● **FIGURE 5–20**. Some pistons have small holes that allow the fluid to move more quickly. Once the primary seal passes the vent port, the remaining hydraulic pressure forces any excess fluid into the reservoir.

DUAL SPLIT MASTER CYLINDERS **Dual split master cylinders** use two separate pressure-building sections. One section operates the front brakes and the other section operates the rear brakes on vehicles equipped with a front/rear-split system. ● **SEE FIGURE 5–21**. The *nose end* of the master cylinder is the closed end toward the front of the vehicle. The open end is often called the *pushrod end* of the master cylinder. ● **SEE FIGURE 5–22**. Some manufacturers operate the front brakes (which do the most braking) from the "nose end" section

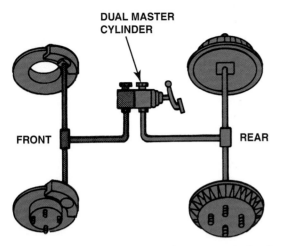

FIGURE 5–21 Rear-wheel-drive vehicles use a dual split master cylinder.

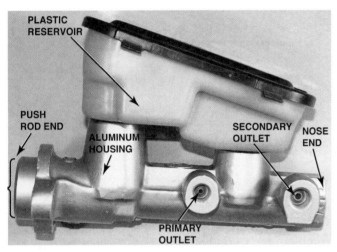

FIGURE 5–22 The primary outlet is the outlet closest to the pushrod end of the master cylinder and the secondary outlet is closest to the nose end of the master cylinder.

MASTER CYLINDERS (CONTINUED)

(secondary piston end) of the master cylinder. The secondary piston has only one pressure-building seal. The primary piston (pushrod end) requires two seals to build pressure. Therefore, the nose end of the master cylinder is considered the more reliable of the two master cylinder pressure-building sections.

NOTE: On vehicles equipped with front and rear split master cylinders, the front brakes may or may *not* be operated from the front chamber. General Motors typically uses the front (nose end) chamber for the front brakes and the rear (pushrod end) for the rear brakes. Many other makes and models of vehicles use the rear chamber for the front brakes. If in doubt, consult the factory service information for the exact vehicle being serviced.

 **TECH TIP**

Always Check for Venting (Compensation)

Whenever diagnosing any braking problem, start the diagnosis at the master cylinder—the heart of any braking system. Remove the reservoir cover and observe the brake fluid for spurting while an assistant depresses the brake pedal.

Normal operation (movement of fluid observed in the reservoir)

There should be a squirt or movement of brake fluid out of the vent port of both the primary and secondary chambers. This indicates that the vent port is open and that the sealing cup is capable of moving fluid upward through the port before the cup seals off the port as it moves forward to pressurize the fluid.

No movement of fluid observed in the reservoir in the primary piston

This indicates that brake fluid is not being moved as the brake pedal is depressed. This can be caused by the following:

a. Incorrect brake pedal height—brake pedal or pushrod adjustment could be allowing the primary piston to be too far forward, causing the seal cup to be forward of the vent port. Adjust the brake pedal height to a higher level and check for a too-long pushrod length.

b. A defective or swollen rubber sealing cup on the primary piston could cause the cup itself to block the vent port.

NOTE: If the vent port is blocked for any reason, the brakes of the vehicle may *self-apply* when the brake fluid heats up during normal braking. Since the vent port is blocked, the expanded hotter brake fluid has no place to expand and instead increases the pressure in the brake lines. The increase in pressure causes the brakes to apply. Loosening the bleeder valves and releasing the built-up pressure is a check that the brakes are self-applying. Then check the master cylinder to see if it is "venting."

FIGURE 5-27 Some seepage is normal when a trace of fluid appears on the vacuum booster shell. Excessive leakage, however, indicates a leaking secondary (end) seal.

DIAGNOSING AND TROUBLESHOOTING MASTER CYLINDERS

A thorough visual inspection is important when inspecting any master cylinder. The visual inspection should include checking the following items:

1. Check the brake fluid for proper level and condition. (Brake fluid should not be rusty, thick, or contaminated.)

2. Check that the vent holes in the reservoir cover are open and clean.

3. Check that the reservoir cover diaphragm is not torn or enlarged.

   NOTE: If the cover diaphragm is enlarged, this is an indication that a mineral oil, such as automatic transmission fluid or engine oil, has been used in or near the brake system, because rubber that is brake fluid resistant expands when exposed to mineral oil.

4. Check for any external leaks at the lines or at the pushrod area. ● **SEE FIGURE 5-27.**

After a thorough visual inspection, check for proper operation of **pedal height**, **pedal free play**, and **pedal reserve distance**. ● **SEE FIGURES 5-28 AND 5-29.**

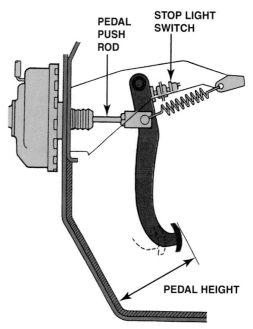

FIGURE 5-28 Pedal height is usually measured from the floor to the top of the brake pedal. Some vehicle manufacturers recommend removing the carpet and measuring from the asphalt matting on the floor for an accurate measurement. Always follow the manufacturer's recommended procedures and measurements. *(Courtesy of Toyota Motor Sales, U.S.A., Inc.)*

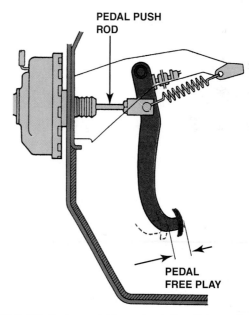

FIGURE 5-29 Brake pedal free play is the distance between the brake pedal fully released and the position of the brake pedal when braking resistance is felt. *(Courtesy of Toyota Motor Sales, U.S.A., Inc.)*

Proper brake pedal height is important for the proper operation of the stop (brake) light switch. If the pedal is not correct, the pushrod may be in too far forward, preventing the master cylinder cups from uncovering the vent port. If the pedal is too high, the free play will be excessive. Pedal reserve height is

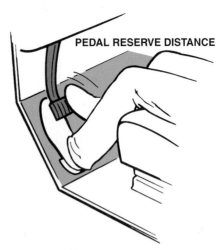

easily checked by depressing the brake pedal with the right foot and attempting to slide your left foot under the brake pedal.

● **SEE FIGURE 5–30.** Free play is the distance the brake pedal travels before the primary piston in the master cylinder moves. *Most vehicles require brake pedal free play between 1/8 to 1 1/2 in. (3 to 38 mm).* Too little or too much free play can cause braking problems that can be mistakenly contributed to a defective master cylinder, such as the following:

■ **Spongy brake pedal.** A spongy pedal with a larger than normal travel indicates air in the lines. Check for leaks and bleed the air from the system as discussed later in this chapter.

■ **Lower-than-normal brake pedal.** A brake pedal that travels downward more than normal and then gets firm is an indication that one circuit of the dual-circuit hydraulic system is probably not working. Check for leaks in the system and repair as necessary. Another possible reason is an out-of-adjustment drum brake allowing too much pedal travel before the shoes touch the brake drum.

NOTE: A lower-than-normal brake pedal may also be an indication of air in the hydraulic system.

■ **Sinking brake pedal.** If the brake pedal sinks all the way to the floor especially when the vehicle is not moving, suspect a defective master cylinder that is leaking internally. This internal leakage is often called **bypassing** because the brake fluid is leaking past the sealing cup.

FIGURE 5–30 Brake pedal reserve is usually specified as the measurement from the floor to the top of the brake pedal with the brakes applied. A quick-and-easy test of pedal reserve is to try to place your left toe underneath the brake pedal while the brake pedal is depressed with your right foot. If your toe will *not* fit, then pedal reserve *may* not be sufficient.

MASTER CYLINDER SERVICE

Many master cylinders can be disassembled, cleaned, and restored to service.

NOTE: Check the vehicle manufacturer's recommendation before attempting to overhaul or service a master cylinder. Many manufacturers recommend replacing the master cylinder as an assembly.

STEP 1 Remove the master cylinder from the vehicle, being careful to avoid dripping or spilling brake fluid onto painted surfaces of the vehicle. Dispose of all old brake fluid and clean the outside of the master cylinder.

STEP 2 Remove the reservoir, if possible, as shown in ● **FIGURE 5–31**.

STEP 3 Remove the retaining bolt that holds the secondary piston assembly in the bore.

STEP 4 Depress the primary piston with a *blunt* tool such as a Phillips screwdriver, a rounded wooden dowel, or an engine pushrod. Use of a straight-blade screwdriver or other nonrounded tool can damage and distort the aluminum piston.

CAUTION: If holding the master cylinder in a vise, use the flange area. Never clamp the body of the master cylinder.

TECH TIP

Check for Bypassing

If a master cylinder is leaking internally, brake fluid can be pumped from the rear chamber into the front chamber of the master cylinder. This internal leakage is called *bypassing*. When the fluid bypasses, the front chamber can overflow while emptying the rear chamber. Therefore, whenever checking the level of brake fluid, do not think that a low rear reservoir is always due to an external leak. Also, a master cylinder that is bypassing (leaking internally) will usually cause a lower-than-normal brake pedal.

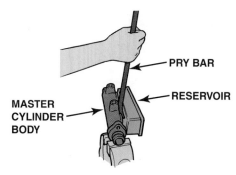

FIGURE 5–31 Using a prybar to carefully remove the reservoir from the master cylinder.

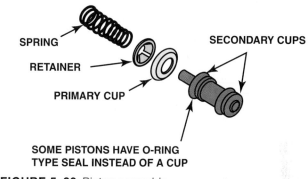

SOME PISTONS HAVE O-RING TYPE SEAL INSTEAD OF A CUP

FIGURE 5–33 Piston assembly.

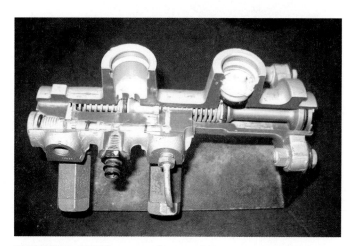

FIGURE 5–32 Whenever disassembling a master cylinder, note the exact order of parts as they are removed. Master cylinder overhaul kits (when available) often include entire piston assemblies rather than the individual seals.

STEP 5 Remove the snap ring and slowly release the pressure on the depressing tool. Spring pressure should push the primary piston out of the cylinder bore. ● **SEE FIGURE 5–32**.

STEP 6 Remove the master cylinder from the vise and tap the open end of the bore against the top of a workbench to force the secondary piston out of the bore. If necessary, use compressed air in the outlet to force the piston out.

 WARNING

Use extreme care when using compressed air. The piston can be shot out of the master cylinder with a great force, which could cause personal injury.

INSPECTION AND REASSEMBLY OF THE MASTER CYLINDER
Inspect the master cylinder bore for pitting, corrosion, or wear. Most cast-iron master cylinders cannot be honed because of the special bearingized surface finish that is applied to the bore during manufacturing. Slight corrosion or surface flaws can usually be removed with a hone or crocus cloth. Otherwise, the master cylinder should be replaced as an assembly. Always follow the recommended procedures for the vehicle being serviced.

Aluminum master cylinders cannot be honed. Aluminum master cylinders have an anodized surface coating applied that is hard and wear resistant. Honing would remove this protective coating. Thoroughly clean the master cylinder and any other parts to be reused (except for rubber components) in clean denatured alcohol. If the bore is okay, replacement **piston assemblies** can be installed into the master cylinder after dipping them into clean brake fluid.

NOTE: While most master cylinder overhaul kits include the entire piston assemblies, some kits just contain the sealing cups and/or O-rings. Always follow the installation instructions that accompany the kit and always use the installation tool that is included to prevent damage to the replacement seals.

STEP 1 Install the secondary (smaller) piston assembly into the bore, spring end first. ● **SEE FIGURE 5–33**.

STEP 2 Install the primary piston assembly, spring end first.

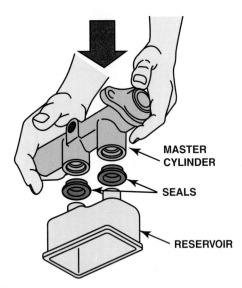

FIGURE 5–34 To reinstall the reservoir onto a master cylinder, place the reservoir on a clean flat surface and push the housing down onto the reservoir after coating the rubber seals with brake fluid.

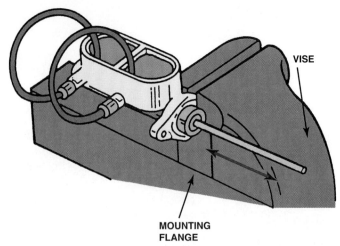

FIGURE 5–35 Bleeding a master cylinder before installing it on the vehicle. The master cylinder is clamped into a bench vise while using a rounded end of a dowel rod to push on the pushrod end with bleeder tubes down into the brake fluid. Master cylinders should be clamped on the mounting flange as shown to prevent distorting the master cylinder bore.

MASTER CYLINDER SERVICE (CONTINUED)

STEP 3 Depress the primary piston and install the snap ring.

STEP 4 Install the retaining bolt.

STEP 5 Reinstall the plastic reservoir, if equipped, as shown in ● **FIGURE 5–34**.

STEP 6 Bench bleed the master cylinder. This step is very important. ● **SEE FIGURE 5–35**.

INSTALLING THE MASTER CYLINDER
After the master cylinder has been bench bled, it can be installed in the vehicle.

NOTE: Brake fluid can drip from the outlet of the master cylinder and could drip onto the vehicle. Brake fluid is very corrosive and can remove paint. Use fender covers and avoid letting brake fluid touch any component of the vehicle.

Tighten the fasteners to factory specifications. ● **SEE FIGURE 5–36**. Bleed the system as needed.

FIGURE 5–36 Installing a master cylinder. Always tighten the retaining fastener and brake lines to factory specifications.

1. During a typical brake application, only about 1 teaspoon (5 ml or cc) of brake fluid actually is moved from the master cylinder and into the hydraulic system.

2. Pascal's law states that: "When a force is applied to a liquid confined in a container or enclosure, the pressure is transmitted equally and undiminished in every direction."

3. Master cylinder reservoirs are large enough for the brakes to be worn completely down and still have a small reserve.

4. The front port of the master cylinder is called the compensating port and the rear port is called the inlet port.

5. Brake system diagnosis should always start with checking for venting (compensation).

6. Dual split master cylinders that separate the front brakes from the rear brakes are used on rear-wheel-drive vehicles.

7. Diagonal split master cylinders that separate right front and left rear from the left front and right rear brakes are used on front-wheel-drive vehicles.

8. Some master cylinders can be rebuilt, but the cylinder bore should not be honed unless recommended by the manufacturer.

REVIEW QUESTIONS

1. Explain Pascal's law.

2. Describe how a master cylinder works.

3. Discuss the difference between a dual split and a diagonal split master cylinder.

4. What is the difference between checking for venting (compensation) and bypassing?

CHAPTER QUIZ

1. Two technicians are discussing master cylinders. Technician A says that it is normal to see fluid movement in the reservoir when the brake pedal is depressed. Technician B says a defective master cylinder can cause the brake pedal to slowly sink to the floor when depressed. Which technician is correct?
   a. Technician A only
   b. Technician B only
   c. Both Technicians A and B
   d. Neither Technician A nor B

2. If the brake pedal linkage is not adjusted correctly, brake fluid may not be able to expand back into the reservoir through the _____ port of the master cylinder when the brakes get hot.
   a. Vent port (forward hole)
   b. Replenishing port (rearward hole)

3. The primary brake circuit fails due to a leak in the lines, leaving the rear section of a dual split master cylinder. Technician A says that the driver will notice a lower than normal brake pedal and some reduced braking power. Technician B says that the brake pedal will "grab" higher than normal. Which technician is correct?
   a. Technician A only
   b. Technician B only
   c. Both Technicians A and B
   d. Neither Technician A nor B

4. Two technicians are discussing a problem where the brake pedal travels too far before the vehicle starts to slow. Technician A says that the brakes may be out of adjustment. Technician B says that one circuit from the master cylinder may be leaking or defective. Which technician is correct?
   a. Technician A only
   b. Technician B only
   c. Both Technicians A and B
   d. Neither Technician A nor B

5. Air in the lines will cause what type of problem?
   a. Vibration in the brake pedal during stops
   b. Low spongy brake pedal
   c. Brake noise
   d. Hard brake pedal

6. The master cylinder is able to move about how much brake fluid during each brake application?
   a. One tablespoon
   b. One teaspoon
   c. One cu. in.
   d. 50 ml

7. Brake fluid pressure is measured in what unit?
   a. Sq. in.
   b. Pounds
   c. Inches
   d. PSI

8. How much brake fluid is in a typical master cylinder reservoir?
   a. One gallon
   b. Enough to allow all brakes to become completely worn
   c. 15 to 20 liters
   d. One pint

9. What part in the master cylinder helps keep air from contacting the brake fluid yet allows the fluid level to drop as the disc brakes wear?
   a. Vent valve
   b. Compensating valve
   c. Residual valve
   d. Rubber diaphragm or floating disc

10. The brakes on a vehicle work okay for a while, then the vehicle slows because the brakes self-applied. Technician A says that an overfilled master cylinder could be the cause. Technician B says that a blocked vent port (compensating port) could be the cause. Which technician is correct?
   a. Technician A only
   b. Technician B only
   c. Both Technicians A and B
   d. Neither Technician A nor B

chapter 6

HYDRAULIC VALVES AND SWITCHES

OBJECTIVES

After studying Chapter 6, the reader will be able to:

1. Prepare for the Brakes (A5) ASE certification test content area "A" (Hydraulic System Diagnosis and Repair).
2. Describe the operation of a residual check valve.
3. Explain how a proportioning valve works.
4. Discuss the need and use of a metering valve.
5. List testing procedures used to test hydraulic valves.
6. Describe how the brake fluid level and brake light switches work.

KEY TERMS

Brake fluid level sensor 97
Brake light switch 105
Combination valve 104
Electronic brake proportioning 102
Expander 95
Height-sensing proportioning valve 100
Metering valve 102
Pressure-differential switch 95
Proportioning valve 98
Residual check valve 95
Slope 98
Split point 98

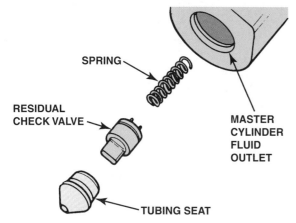

FIGURE 6–1 Most residual check valves are located under the tubing seals in the master cylinder outlet ports.

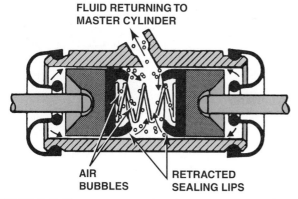

FIGURE 6–2 The momentary drop in pressure created when the brakes are released can draw air into the hydraulic system.

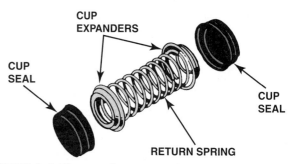

FIGURE 6–3 The use of cup expanders is the main reason why residual check valves are not used in most braking systems today.

FIGURE 6–4 A red brake warning lamp.

RESIDUAL CHECK VALVE

A **residual check valve** has been used on some drum brake systems to keep a slight amount of pressure on the entire hydraulic system for drum brakes (5 to 12 PSI). ● **SEE FIGURE 6–1**.

This residual check valve is located in the master cylinder at the outlet for the drum brakes. The check ball and spring in the residual check valve permit all the brake fluid to return to the master cylinder until the designated pressure is reached.

This slight pressure prevents air leaks from entering into the hydraulic system in the event of a small hole or leak. With a low pressure kept on the hydraulic system, any small hole will cause fluid to leak out rather than permit air to enter the system. This slight pressure also keeps the wheel cylinder sealing cups tight against the inside wall of the wheel cylinder. ● **SEE FIGURE 6–2**.

Residual check valves are often *not* used on late-model vehicles equipped with front disc/rear drum brakes. The residual check valve has been eliminated by equipping the wheel cylinder internal spring with a sealing cup **expander** to prevent sealing cup lip collapse. ● **SEE FIGURE 6–3**.

PRESSURE-DIFFERENTIAL SWITCH (BRAKE WARNING SWITCH)

PURPOSE AND FUNCTION A **pressure-differential switch** is used on all vehicles built after 1967 with dual master cylinders to warn the driver of a loss of pressure in one of the two separate systems by lighting the dashboard red brake warning indicator lamp. ● **SEE FIGURES 6–4 AND 6–5**.

The brake lines from both the front and the rear sections of the master cylinder are sent to this switch, which lights the brake warning indicator lamp in the event of a "difference in pressure" between the two sections. ● **SEE FIGURE 6–6**.

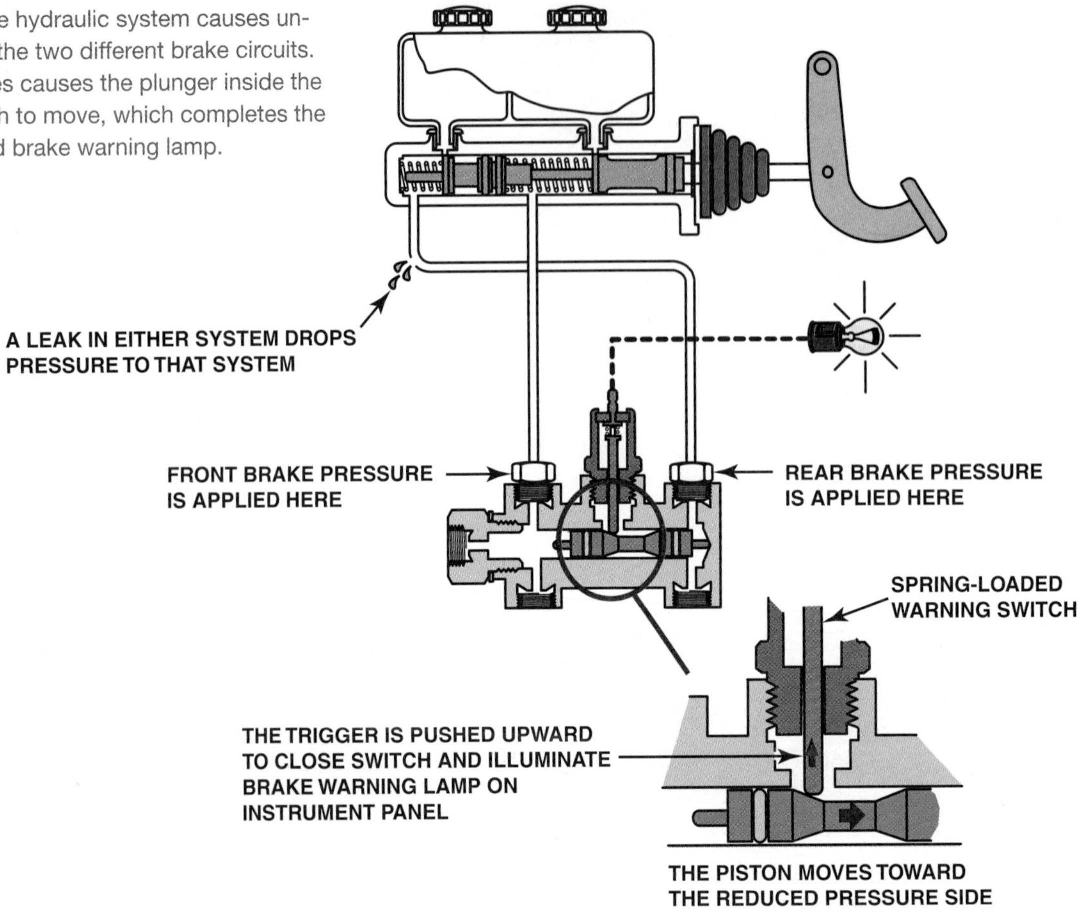

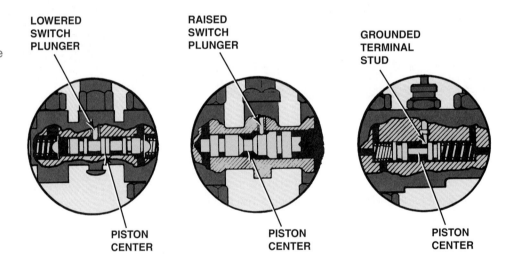

FIGURE 6–5 A leak in the hydraulic system causes unequal pressures between the two different brake circuits. This difference in pressures causes the plunger inside the pressure-differential switch to move, which completes the electrical circuit for the red brake warning lamp.

A LEAK IN EITHER SYSTEM DROPS PRESSURE TO THAT SYSTEM

FRONT BRAKE PRESSURE IS APPLIED HERE

REAR BRAKE PRESSURE IS APPLIED HERE

SPRING-LOADED WARNING SWITCH

THE TRIGGER IS PUSHED UPWARD TO CLOSE SWITCH AND ILLUMINATE BRAKE WARNING LAMP ON INSTRUMENT PANEL

THE PISTON MOVES TOWARD THE REDUCED PRESSURE SIDE

FIGURE 6–6 The pressure-differential switch piston is used to provide the electrical ground for the red brake warning light circuit.

LOWERED SWITCH PLUNGER

RAISED SWITCH PLUNGER

GROUNDED TERMINAL STUD

PISTON CENTER

PISTON CENTER

PISTON CENTER

PRESSURE-DIFFERENTIAL SWITCH (BRAKE WARNING SWITCH) (CONTINUED)

A failure in one part of the brake system does not result in a failure of the entire hydraulic system. After the hydraulic system has been repaired and bled, moderate pressure on the brake pedal will center the piston in the switch and turn off the warning lamp.

If the lamp remains on, it may be necessary to do the following.

1. Apply light pressure to the brake pedal.
2. Momentarily open the bleeder valve on the side that did not have the failure.

This procedure should center the pressure-differential switch valve in those vehicles that are not equipped with self-centering springs.

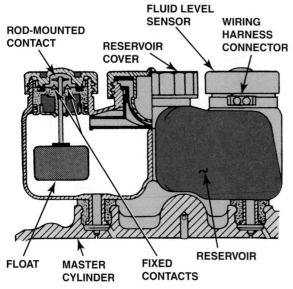

FIGURE 6–7 A movable contact brake fluid level switch.

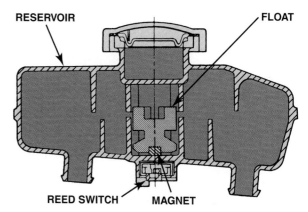

FIGURE 6–8 A magnetic brake fluid level switch.

BRAKE FLUID LEVEL SENSOR SWITCH

Many master cylinders, especially systems that are a diagonal split, usually use a **brake fluid level sensor** or switch in the master cylinder reservoir. This sensor will light the red brake warning lamp on the dash if low brake fluid level is detected. A float-type sensor or a magnetic reed switch are commonly used and provide a complete electrical circuit when the brake fluid level is low. After refilling the master cylinder reservoir to the correct level, the red "brake" warning lamp should go out. ● SEE FIGURES 6–7 AND 6–8.

DIAGNOSING A RED "BRAKE" DASH WARNING LAMP
Activation of the red brake dash warning lamp can be for any one of several reasons:

1. **Parking Brake "On."** The same dash warning lamp is used to warn the driver that the parking brake is on.

2. **Low Brake Fluid.** This lights the red dash warning lamp on vehicles equipped with a master cylinder reservoir brake fluid level switch.

3. **Unequal Brake Pressure.** The pressure-differential switch is used on most vehicles with a front/rear brake split system to warn the driver whenever there is low brake pressure to either the front or rear brakes.

NOTE: Brake systems use *either* a pressure-differential switch *or* a low brake fluid switch to light the dash red "brake" lamp, but not both.

The most likely cause of the red "brake" warning lamp being on is low brake fluid caused by a leaking brake line, wheel cylinder, or caliper. Therefore, the first step in diagnosis is to determine the cause of the lamp being on, then to repair the problem.

STEP 1 **Check the Level of the Brake Fluid.** If low, carefully inspect the entire hydraulic brake system for leaks and repair as necessary.

STEP 2 **Disconnect the Wire from the Pressure-Differential Switch.** If the lamp is still "on," the problem is due to the parking brake lever switch being "on" or grounded, or the wire going to the switch is shorted to ground. If the red brake warning lamp is "off" after being disconnected from the pressure-differential switch, then the problem is due to a hydraulic failure (a low pressure in either the front or the rear system that creates a difference in pressure of at least 150 PSI).

NOTE: Some older Japanese vehicles energize the relay that turns off the red "brake" warning lamp from the output terminal of the alternator. If a quick inspection of the brake system seems to indicate that everything is okay, check for correct charging voltage before continuing a more detailed brake system inspection.

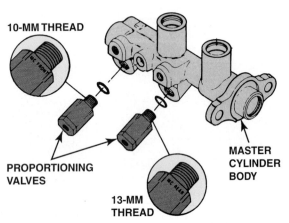

FIGURE 6–9 Many proportioning valves are mounted directly to the master cylinder in the outlet to the rear brakes.

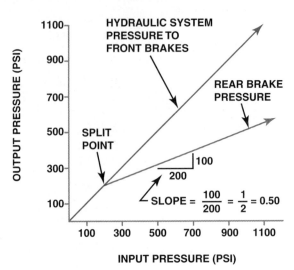

FIGURE 6–10 Typical proportioning valve pressure relationship. Note that, at low pressures, the pressure is the same to the rear brakes as is applied to the front brakes. After the split point, only a percentage (called the slope) of the master cylinder pressure is applied to the rear brakes.

PROPORTIONING VALVE

PURPOSE AND FUNCTION A **proportioning valve** improves brake balance during hard stops by limiting hydraulic pressure to the rear brakes. ● **SEE FIGURE 6–9.**

A proportioning valve is necessary because inertia creates weight shift toward the front of the vehicle during braking. The weight shift unloads the rear axle, which reduces traction between the tires and the road, and limits the amount of stopping power that can be delivered. Unless application pressure to the rear wheels is limited, the brakes will lock, making the vehicle unstable and likely to spin. The best overall braking performance is achieved when the front brakes lock just before the rear brakes.

Vehicles with front disc and rear drum brakes require a proportioning valve for two reasons.

1. Disc brakes require higher hydraulic pressure for a given stop than do drum brakes. In a disc/drum system, the front brakes always need more pressure than the rear brakes.

2. Once braking has begun, drum brakes require less pressure to *maintain* a fixed level of stopping power than they did to *establish* that level. In a disc/drum system, the rear brakes will always need less pressure than the front brakes.

A proportioning valve is used to compensate for these differences because it is easier to reduce pressure to the rear brakes than to increase pressure to the front brakes.

The proportioning valve does not work at all times. During light or moderate braking, there is insufficient weight transfer to make rear wheel locking a problem. Before proportioning action will begin, brake system hydraulic pressure must reach a minimum level called the **split point**. Below the split point full system pressure is supplied to the rear brakes. ● **SEE FIGURE 6–10.**

Above the split point, the proportioning valve allows only a portion of the pressure through to the rear brakes.

The proportioning valve gets its name from the fact that it regulates pressure to the rear brakes *in proportion* to the pressure applied to the front brakes. Once system hydraulic pressure exceeds the split point, the rear brakes receive a fixed percentage of any further increase in pressure. Brake engineers refer to the ratio of front to rear brake pressure proportioning as the **slope**. Full system pressure to the rear brakes equals a slope of 1, but if only half the pressure is allowed to reach the rear brakes, the proportioning valve is said to have a slope of 0.50. The proportioning valves on most vehicles have a slope between 0.25 and 0.50. ● **SEE FIGURES 6–11 AND 6–12.**

PROPORTIONING VALVE OPERATION A simple proportioning valve consists of a spring-loaded piston that slides in a stepped bore. ● **SEE FIGURE 6–13.** The piston is exposed to pressure on both sides. The smaller end of the piston is acted on by pressure from the master cylinder, while the larger end reacts to pressure in the rear brake circuit. The actual proportioning valve is located in the center of the piston and is opened or closed depending on the position of the piston in the stepped bore.

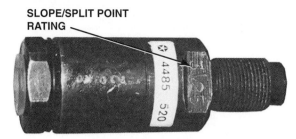

FIGURE 6–11 A Chrysler proportioning valve. Note that slope and split point are stamped on the housing.

FIGURE 6–12 These two proportioning valves are found under the vehicle on this Dodge minivan.

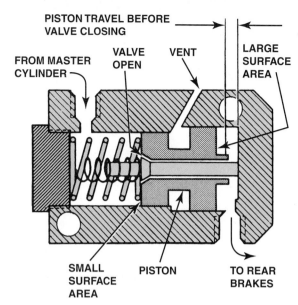

FIGURE 6–13 The proportioning valve piston can travel within the range shown without reducing pressure to the rear brakes.

When the brakes are first applied, hydraulic pressure passes through the proportioning valve to the rear brakes. Hydraulic pressure is the same on both sides of the piston, but because the side facing the rear brakes has more surface area than the side facing the master cylinder, greater force is developed and the piston moves to the left against the spring tension. At pressures below the split point, the proportioning valve is open, and pressure to both the front and rear brakes is the same.

As the vehicle is braked harder, increased system pressure forces the piston so far to the left that the proportioning valve is closed. ● SEE FIGURE 6–14. This seals off the brake line and prevents any additional pressure from reaching the rear brakes. The pressure at the moment the proportioning valve first closes is the split point of the valve. From this point on, the rear brakes receive only a portion of the pressure supplied to the front brakes.

As system pressure (the pressure to the front brakes) increases, enough force is developed on the master cylinder side of the piston to overcome the pressure trapped in the rear brake circuit. This forces the piston back to the right and opens the proportioning valve. Some of the higher pressure enters the rear brake circuit, but before pressure in the two circuits can equalize, the force developed on the larger piston area in

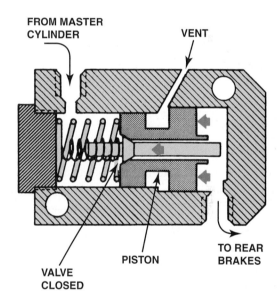

FIGURE 6–14 At the split point, the proportioning valve piston closes the fluid passage through the valve.

the rear circuit moves the piston back to the left and closes the valve. The difference in surface area between the two ends of the piston determines the slope of the valve, and thus the percentage of system pressure allowed to reach the rear brakes.

As long as system pressure continues to increase, the piston will repeatedly cycle back and forth, opening and closing the proportioning valve, and maintaining a fixed proportion of full system pressure to the rear brakes. When the brakes are released, the spring returns the piston all the way to the right, which opens the valve and allows fluid to pass in both directions.

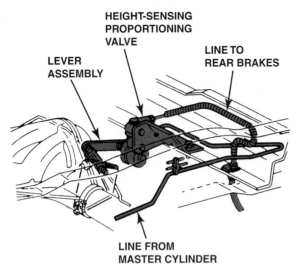

FIGURE 6–15 A height-sensing proportioning valve provides the vehicle with variable brake balance. The valve allows higher pressure to be applied to the rear brakes when the vehicle is heavily loaded and less pressure when the vehicle is lightly loaded.

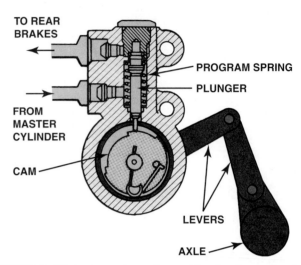

FIGURE 6–16 A stepped cam is used to alter the split point of this height-sensing proportioning valve.

PROPORTIONING VALVE (CONTINUED)

TECH TIP

Always Inspect Both Front and Rear Brakes

If a vehicle tends to lock up the rear brakes during a stop, many technicians may try to repair the problem by replacing the proportioning valve or servicing the rear brakes. Proportioning valves are simple spring-loaded devices that are usually trouble free. If the rear brakes lock up during braking, carefully inspect the rear brakes looking for contaminated linings or other problems that can cause the rear brakes to grab. Do not stop there—always inspect the front brakes, too. If the front brakes are rusted or corroded, they cannot operate efficiently and greater force must be exerted by the driver to stop the vehicle. Even if the proportioning valve is functioning correctly, the higher brake pedal pressure by the driver could easily cause the rear brakes to lock up.

A locked wheel has less traction with the road than a rotating wheel. As a result, if the rear wheels become locked, the rear of the vehicle often "comes around" or "fishtails," causing the vehicle to skid. Careful inspection of the *entire* braking system is required to be assured of a safe vehicle.

HEIGHT-SENSING PROPORTIONING VALVES Many vehicles use a proportioning valve that varies the amount of pressure that can be sent to the rear brakes depending on the height of the rear suspension. This type of valve is called a **height-sensing proportioning valve.** If the vehicle is lightly loaded, the rear suspension is high, especially during braking. In this case, the amount of pressure allowed to the rear brakes is reduced. This *helps* prevent rear-wheel lockup and possible skidding. Besides, a lightly loaded vehicle requires less braking force to stop than a heavily loaded vehicle.

When the vehicle is loaded, the rear suspension is forced downward. The lever on the proportioning valve moves and allows a greater pressure to be sent to the rear brakes. ● **SEE FIGURES 6–15 AND 6–16.** This greater pressure allows the rear brakes to achieve more braking force, helping to slow a heavier vehicle. When a vehicle is heavily loaded in the rear, the chances of rear-wheel lockup are reduced.

CAUTION: Some vehicle manufacturers warn that service technicians should never install replacement air lift shock absorbers or springs that may result in a vehicle height different than specified by the vehicle manufacturer. If the ride height is increased, the front to rear brake proportional relationship will be changed and could reduce stopping distances.

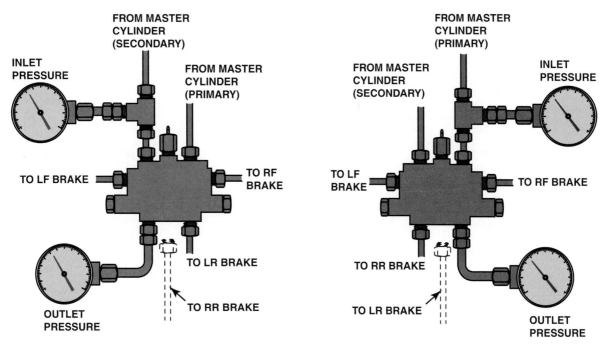

FIGURE 6–17 A proportioning valve pressure test can be performed using two pressure gauges—one to register the pressure from the master cylinder and the other gauge to read the pressure being applied to the rear brakes. This test has to be repeated in order to read the pressure to each rear wheel.

PROPORTIONING VALVE ADJUSTMENT. Height-sensing proportioning valves should be adjusted when replaced. The proper adjustment ensures that the proper pressure is applied to the rear brakes in relation to the loading of the vehicle.

Procedures vary from one vehicle to another. Always consult the factory service information for the exact procedure. Some trucks require the use of special plastic gauges available from the dealer.

PROPORTIONING VALVE DIAGNOSIS AND TESTING

A defective proportioning valve usually allows rear brake pressure to increase too rapidly, causing the rear wheels to lock up during hard braking. When the rear brakes become locked, the traction with the road surface decreases and the vehicle often skids. Whenever rear brakes tend to lock during braking, the proportioning valve should be checked for proper operation.

If the proportioning valve is height sensing, verify the proper vehicle ride (trim) height and adjustment of the operating lever.
● **SEE FIGURE 6–17.**

Pressure gauges can also be used to check for proper operation. Install one gauge into the brake line from the master cylinder and the second gauge to the rear brake outlet of the proportioning valve. While an assistant depresses the brake pedal, observe the two gauges. Both gauges should register an increasing pressure as the brake pedal is depressed until the split point. After the split point, the gauge connected to the proportioning valve (rear brakes) should increase at a slower rate than the reading on the gauge connected to the master cylinder.

If the pressures do not react as described, the proportioning valve should be *replaced*. The same procedure can be performed on a diagonal split-type system as used on most front-wheel-drive vehicles.

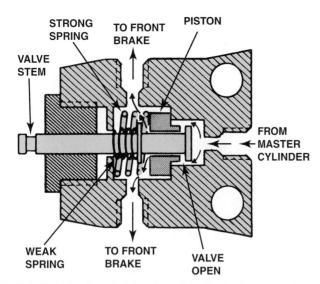

FIGURE 6–18 A metering valve when the brakes are not applied. Notice the brake fluid can flow through the metering valve to compensate for brake fluid expansion and contraction that occurs with changes in temperature.

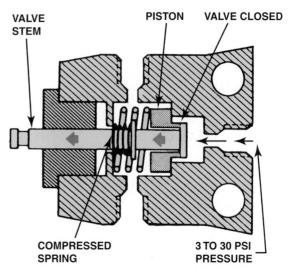

FIGURE 6–19 A metering valve under light brake pedal application.

ELECTRONIC BRAKE PROPORTIONING

Many newer antilock braking systems eliminate the need for a conventional brake proportioning valve. A proportioning valve is usually necessary to reduce pressure to the rear brakes to keep them from locking up. This is because there is less weight over the rear wheels, and weight shifts forward when braking. Proportioning is needed most when a vehicle is lightly loaded or braking from a high speed. Most proportioning valves are calibrated to reduce pressure to the rear brakes by a fixed amount, which may increase the risk of rear-wheel lockup if the vehicle is loaded differently or is braking on a wet or slick surface. Dynamic rear proportioning is overcome by adjusting brake balance to match the need of the vehicle to changing road and load conditions.

Electronic brake proportioning (EBP) in the antilock braking system is accomplished by monitoring front- and rear-wheel speeds, and reducing pressure to the rear brakes as needed using the ABS solenoids when there is a difference in wheel deceleration rates. The controller energizes the inlet valve solenoids for both rear brakes to hold pressure in the lines, and then energizes both rear outlet valve solenoids to release pressure as needed.

The dynamic rear proportioning function is enabled at all times unless there is a failure of the antilock brake controller or two wheel speed sensors on the same axle both fail at the same time. But as long as there is at least one functional speed sensor on the front and rear axles, the antilock brake controller can compare the relative speeds of the front and rear wheels.

METERING VALVE (HOLD-OFF) OPERATION

PURPOSE AND FUNCTION   A **metering valve** is used on all front-disc, rear-drum-brake-equipped vehicles. The metering valve prevents the full operation of (holds off) the disc brakes until between 75 to 125 PSI is sent to the rear drum brakes to overcome rear-brake return spring pressure. This allows the front and rear brakes to apply at the same time for even stopping. Most metering valves also allow for the pressure to the front brakes to be gradually blended up to the metering valve pressure to prevent front brake locking under light pedal pressures on icy surfaces.

PARTS AND OPERATION   A metering valve consists of a piston controlled by a strong spring and a valve stem controlled by a weak spring. ● SEE FIGURE 6–18. When the brakes are not applied, the strong spring seats the piston and prevents fluid flow around it. At the same time, the weak spring holds the valve stem to the right and opens a passage through the center of the piston. Brake fluid is free to flow through this passage to compensate for changes in system fluid volume.

When the brakes are applied and pressure in the front brake line reaches 3 to 30 PSI (20 to 200 kPa), the tension of the weak spring is overcome and the metering valve stem moves to the left, which closes the passage through the piston and prevents fluid flow to the front brakes. ● SEE FIGURE 6–19.

The small amount of pressure applied to the calipers before the metering valve closes is enough to take up any clearance, but not enough to generate braking force.

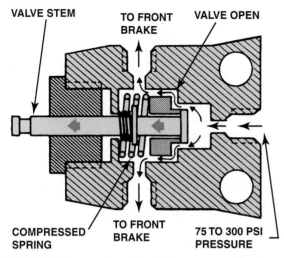

FIGURE 6–20 A metering valve during a normal brake application.

While the fluid flow to the front calipers is shut off, the rear brake shoes move into contact with the drums, braking begins, and hydraulic pressure throughout the brake system increases. When the pressure at the metering valve reaches 75 to 300 PSI, the tension of the strong spring is overcome and the valve stem and piston move farther to the left. ● **SEE FIGURE 6–20**. This opens a passage around the outside of the piston and allows fluid to flow through the valve to the front brake calipers.

When the brakes are released, the strong spring seats the piston and prevents fluid flow around it. At the same time, the weak spring opens the fluid passage through the center of the piston. Excess fluid returns to the master cylinder through this passage and the valve is ready for another brake application.

SYSTEMS WITHOUT METERING VALVES Braking systems that are diagonal split, such as those found on most front-wheel-drive vehicles, do *not* use a metering valve. A metering valve is only used on front/rear split braking systems such as those found on most rear-wheel-drive vehicles.

There are three reasons why front-wheel-drive vehicles do not use metering valves.

1. Front-wheel-drive vehicles usually have a diagonally split dual braking system that would require a separate metering valve for each hydraulic circuit. This would make the brake system more costly and complicated.

2. Front-wheel-drive vehicles have a forward weight bias that requires the front brakes to supply up to 80% of the total braking power. Since the front brakes do most of the work, it is desirable to apply them as soon as possible when the brake pedal is depressed. A metering valve would create a slight delay.

3. Until all the clearance in the brake system is taken up, there will not be enough pressure in the brake hydraulic system for the front disc brakes to overcome the engine torque applied to the driven front wheels.

Engine torque and a heavy front weight bias help prevent front-wheel lockup from being a problem during light braking or when the brakes are first applied.

Most rear-wheel-drive vehicles without metering valves are equipped with four-wheel disc brakes. Because the clearance between the pads and rotors is approximately the same at all four wheels, there is no need to delay front brake actuation. Some of these vehicles also have antilock brake systems that prevent the wheels from locking at any time.

METERING VALVE DIAGNOSIS AND TESTING A defective metering valve can leak brake fluid and/or cause the front brakes to apply before the rear brakes. This is most commonly noticed on slippery surfaces such as on snow or ice or on rain-slick roads. If the front brakes lock up during these

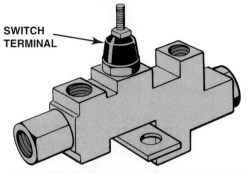

PROPORTIONING—PRESSURE DIFFERENTIAL

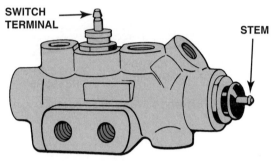

METERING—PRESSURE DIFFERENTIAL

FIGURE 6–21 Typical two-function combination valves.

TECH TIP

Push-In or Pull-Out Metering Valve?

Whenever bleeding the air out of the hydraulic brake system, the metering valve should be bypassed. The metering valve stops the passage of brake fluid to the front wheels until pressure exceeds about 125 PSI (860 kPa). It is important not to push the brake pedal down with a great force so as to keep from dispersing any trapped air into small and hard-to-bleed bubbles. To bypass the metering valve, the service technician has to push or pull a small button located on the metering valve. An easy way to remember whether to push in or to pull out is to inspect the button itself. *If the button is rubber coated, then you push in. If the button is steel, then pull out.*

Special tools allow the metering valve to be held in the bypass position. Failure to remove the tool after bleeding the brakes can result in premature application of the front brakes before the rear drum brakes have enough pressure to operate.

conditions, the front wheels cannot be steered. Inspect the metering valve for these two conditions:

1. Look around the bottom of the metering valve for brake fluid leakage. (Ignore slight dampness.) Replace the metering valve assembly if it is leaking.

2. As the pressure builds to the front brakes, the metering valve stem should move. If it does not, replace the valve.

More accurate testing of the metering valve can be accomplished using pressure gauges. Install two gauges, one in the pressure line coming from the master cylinder and the other in the outlet line leading to the front brakes. When depressing the brake pedal, both gauges should read the same until about 3 to 30 PSI (20 to 200 kPa) when the metering valve shuts, thereby delaying the operation of the front brakes. The master cylinder outlet gauge should show an increase in pressure as the brake pedal is depressed further.

Once 75 to 300 PSI is reached, the gauge showing pressure to the front brakes should match the pressure from the master cylinder. If the pressures do not match these ranges, the metering valve assembly should be replaced.

COMBINATION VALVE

Most vehicle manufacturers combine the function of a proportioning valve with one or more other valves into one unit called a **combination valve**. ● SEE FIGURES 6–21 AND 6–22.

On a typical rear-wheel-drive vehicle, a typical combination valve consists of the following components all in one replaceable unit:

- Metering valve
- Proportioning valve
- Pressure-differential switch

Some combination valves have only two functions and contain the pressure-differential and the metering valve, while others combine the pressure-differential with the proportioning valve.

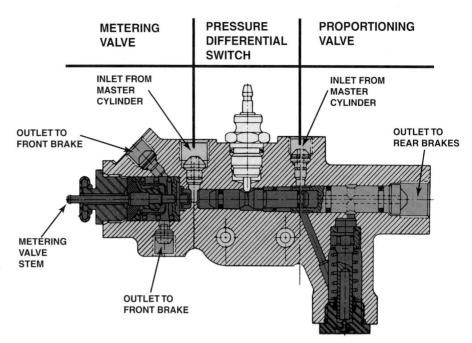

METERING VALVE | **PRESSURE DIFFERENTIAL SWITCH** | **PROPORTIONING VALVE**

INLET FROM MASTER CYLINDER

INLET FROM MASTER CYLINDER

OUTLET TO FRONT BRAKE

OUTLET TO REAR BRAKES

METERING VALVE STEM

OUTLET TO FRONT BRAKE

FIGURE 6–22 Combination valve containing metering, pressure-differential (warning switch), and proportioning valves all in one unit. This style is often called a "pistol grip" design because the proportioning valve section resembles the grip section of a handgun.

FIGURE 6–23 Typical brake light switches.

TECH TIP

No Valves Can Cause a Pull

When diagnosing a pull to one side during braking, some technicians tend to blame the metering valve, proportional valve, the pressure-differential switch, or the master cylinder itself.

Just remember that if a vehicle pulls during braking that the problem *has* to be due to an individual wheel brake or brake line. The master cylinder and all the valves control front or rear brakes together or diagonal brakes and cannot cause a pull if not functioning correctly.

BRAKE LIGHT SWITCH

The job of the **brake light switch** is to turn on the brake lights at the back of the vehicle when the brakes are applied. A properly adjusted light switch will activate the brake lights as soon as the brake pedal is applied and before braking action actually begins at the wheels.

Mechanical switches that operate directly off the brake pedal arm are most often used. ● **SEE FIGURE 6–23.**

Brake light switches are normally open. When the brakes are applied, the switch closes, which completes the brake light circuit. Most newer vehicles use the brake switch as an input to the body computer for many functions including:

- Brake lights
- Antilock brake system (ABS) input signal
- Traction control is disabled when the brake pedal is depressed
- Electronic stability control (ESC) system input signal

1. Residual check valves are used in older vehicles to keep a slight amount of pressure on the system to help prevent air from entering the system when the brake pedal is released.

2. A pressure-differential switch is used to turn on the red brake warning lamp in the event of a hydraulic pressure failure.

3. Brake fluid level sensors are used in many vehicles to warn the driver that the brake fluid level is low.

4. Proportioning valves are used to limit the maximum fluid pressure sent to the rear wheel brakes during heavy braking to help prevent rear-wheel lockup.

5. Metering valves are used on some vehicles to keep the front disc brakes from locking up on slippery surfaces.

6. Combination valves include two or more hydraulic valves in one assembly.

REVIEW QUESTIONS

1. Why are residual check valves not used in most vehicles?

2. List the three possible reasons that could cause the red brake warning lamp to come on during driving.

3. Explain why metering valves are not used on all vehicles.

4. Explain the split point and the slope of a proportioning valve.

CHAPTER QUIZ

1. Technician A says a pull to the right during braking could be caused by a defective metering valve. Technician B says a pull to the left could be caused by a defective proportioning valve. Which technician is correct?
   a. Technician A only
   b. Technician B only
   c. Both Technicians A and B
   d. Neither Technician A nor B

2. The rear brakes lock up during a regular brake application. Technician A says the metering valve could be the cause. Technician B says that stuck front disc brake calipers could be the cause. Which technician is correct?
   a. Technician A only
   b. Technician B only
   c. Both Technicians A and B
   d. Neither Technician A nor B

3. The rear wheels lock up during hard braking. Technician A says that a defective metering valve could be the cause. Technician B says that a defective proportioning valve could be the cause. Which technician is correct?
   a. Technician A only
   b. Technician B only
   c. Both Technicians A and B
   d. Neither Technician A nor B

4. A combination valve could include _____.
   a. Metering and proportioning valves
   b. Proportioning and pressure-differential valves
   c. Proportioning, metering, and pressure-differential valves
   d. Any of the above depending on the make and model of the vehicle

5. A residual check valve is used to _____.
   a. Maintain a slight pressure on the hydraulic system
   b. Prevent front-wheel lockup during hard braking
   c. Prevent rear-wheel lockup during hard braking
   d. Speed brake release to reduce brake wear

6. Technician A says that the red brake warning light can be turned on if a difference in pressure is detected by the pressure-differential switch. Technician B says that the red brake warning light can be turned on if the brake fluid level sensor detected low brake fluid level. Which technician is correct?
   a. Technician A only   c. Both Technicians A and B
   b. Technician B only   d. Neither Technician A nor B

7. Which type of vehicles most often do not use metering valves?
   a. Rear-wheel drive   c. Front-wheel drive
   b. Four-wheel drive   d. All-wheel drive

8. Technician A says that some proportioning valves are one part and used to control both rear brakes. Technician B says that some proportioning valves are two parts; one for each rear wheel brake.
   a. Technician A only   c. Both Technicians A and B
   b. Technician B only   d. Neither Technician A nor B

9. The button on the _____ valve should be held when pressure bleeding the brakes.
   a. Metering   c. Pressure-differential
   b. Proportioning   d. Residual check

10. A typical brake light is electrically _____.
    a. Normally open   b. Normally closed

BRAKE FLUID AND LINES

OBJECTIVES

After studying Chapter 7, the reader will be able to:

1. Prepare for the Brakes (A5) ASE certification test.
2. List the types of brake fluids.
3. Describe where armored brake line is used.
4. Discuss the differences between double-flare and ISO flare.
5. Explain how flexible brake lines should be handled during service.
6. List the precautions necessary when handling or disposing of brake fluid.
7. Discuss the types of rubber that are used in brake system components.

KEY TERMS

Armored brake line 118
Brake fluid 108
Brake lines 114
Brake pipes 114
Brake tubing 114
DOT 3 108
DOT 4 109
DOT 5 109
DOT 5.1 109
Double flare 114

Elastomers 113
Flexible brake hoses 118
Hydraulic system mineral oil (HSMO) 110
Hygroscopic 108
ISO 114
Nonhygroscopic 109
Polyglycol 108
Silicone brake fluid 109

PURPOSE AND FUNCTION **Brake fluid** is designed to function in the hydraulic brake system under all operating conditions. Brake fluid boiling point is one of the most critical aspects and ratings for brake fluid. As brake fluid ages, it absorbs moisture, which lowers its boiling point and causes increased corrosion of the brake system components.

All automotive experts agree that brake fluid should be changed regularly as part of normal routine service. Even through the driver may not notice an immediate improvement, the reduced corrosion will eventually result in less money being spent for brake system component replacement in the future. Getting the old low-boiling-point brake fluid out of the system could prevent a total loss of brakes due to brake fluid boiling.

All brake fluids must be able to pass tests for the following:

1. Fluidity at low temperatures
2. Controlled percentage loss due to evaporation at high temperatures (tested at 212°F [100°C])
3. Compatibility with other brake fluids
4. Resistance to oxidation
5. Specific effects on rubber, including:
   a. No disintegration
   b. No increase in hardness of the rubber tested
   c. Limited amount of decrease in hardness of the rubber

PHYSICAL PROPERTIES Brake fluid is made from a combination of various types of glycol, a non-petroleum-based fluid. Brake fluid is a polyalkylene–glycol–ether mixture called **polyglycol** for short. All *polyglycol brake fluid is clear to amber in color.* Brake fluid has to have the following characteristics:

- A high boiling point
- A low freezing point
- No ability to damage rubber parts in the brake system

BRAKE FLUID SPECIFICATIONS All automotive brake fluid must meet Federal Motor Vehicle Safety Standard (FMVSS) 116. The Society of Automotive Engineers (SAE) and the Department of Transportation (DOT) have established brake fluid specification standards as shown in the following chart.

FIGURE 7–1 Brake fluid can absorb moisture from the air even through plastic, so many experts recommend that brake fluid be purchased in metal containers, if possible.

	DOT 3	DOT 4	DOT 5.1	DOT 5
Dry boiling point				
°F	401	446	500	500
°C	205	230	260	260
Wet boiling point				
°F	284	311	356	356
°C	140	155	180	180

The wet boiling point is often referred to as "equilibrium reflux boiling point" (ERBP). ERBP refers to the method in the specification (SAE J1703) by which the fluid is exposed to moisture and tested.

DOT 3. **DOT 3** brake fluid is the type most often used. However DOT 3 brake fluid has some important characteristics including:

1. DOT 3 absorbs moisture. According to the Society of Automotive Engineers (SAE), DOT 3 can absorb 2% of its volume in water per year. Moisture is absorbed by the brake fluid through microscopic seams in the brake system and around seals. Over time, the water will corrode the system and thicken the brake fluid. The moisture can also cause a spongy brake pedal, due to reduced vapor-lock temperature. ● **SEE FIGURES 7–1 AND 7–2.**

2. DOT 3 must be used from a sealed (capped) container. If allowed to remain open for any length of time, DOT 3 will absorb moisture from the surrounding air, which is called **hygroscopic**.

3. Always check the brake fluid recommendations on the top of the master cylinders of imported vehicles before adding DOT 3.

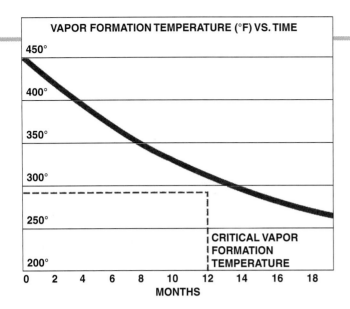

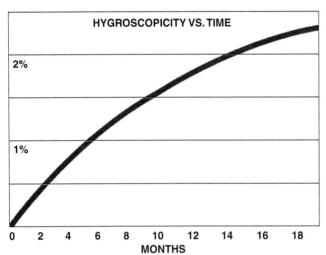

FIGURE 7–2 Brake fluid absorbs moisture from the air at the rate of about 2% per year. As the brake fluid absorbs water, its boiling temperature decreases.

 FREQUENTLY ASKED QUESTION

What Is Blue Brake Fluid?

Some brake fluid vendors market a high-performance DOT 4 brake fluid that is dyed blue and is called super blue while others market a super DOT 4 that is yellow. These brake fluids are designed to be sold in Europe. The advertising states that the bright color of the brake fluid makes it easy to see when all of the old fluid has been purged from the system during a brake fluid replacement procedure.

CAUTION: DOT 3 brake fluid is a very strong solvent and can remove paint! Care is required when working with DOT 3 brake fluid to avoid contact with the vehicle's painted surfaces. It also takes the color out of leather shoes.

DOT 4. DOT 4 brake fluid is formulated for use by all vehicles, imported or domestic. DOT 4 is polyglycol based but has borate esters added to provide an extra buffer for the fluid against acids that can form in the moisture that has been absorbed in the fluid when it is heated. DOT 4 is approximately double the cost of DOT 3. DOT 4 can often be used where DOT 3 is used and even though the two types of brake fluid are compatible and miscible (able to be mixed), some vehicle manufacturers recommend that DOT 3 and DOT 4 not be mixed. If DOT 4 is to be used, the system should be purged of all of the old DOT 3 and replaced with DOT 4.

NOTE: Because brake fluid absorbs moisture over time, many vehicle manufacturers recommend changing the brake fluid as part of the standard services to be performed routinely. The typical recommended brake fluid change interval is every two years or every 30,000 miles (48,000 km), whichever comes first. This is particularly important for vehicles equipped with an antilock braking system (ABS) because of the problem of expensive brake component wear or corrosion caused by contaminated brake fluid.

DOT 5.1. DOT 5.1 brake fluid is a non-silicone-based polyglycol fluid and is clear to amber in color. This severe duty fluid has a boiling point of over 500°F equal to the boiling point of silicone-based DOT 5 fluid. Unlike DOT 5, DOT 5.1 can be mixed with either DOT 3 or DOT 4 according to brake fluid manufacturers' recommendations.

CAUTION: Some vehicle manufacturers such as Chrysler do not recommend the use of or the mixing of other types of polyglycol brake fluid and specify the use of DOT 3 brake fluid only. Always follow the vehicle manufacturer's recommendation.

DOT 5. DOT 5 brake fluid is commonly called **silicone brake fluid** and is made from polydimethylsiloxanes. DOT 5 brake fluid is purple (violet) in color to distinguish it from DOT 3 or DOT 4 brake fluid. It does not absorb any water, and is therefore called **nonhygroscopic.** Even though DOT 5 does not normally absorb water, it is still tested using standardized SAE procedures in a humidity chamber. After a fixed amount of time, the brake fluid is measured for boiling point. Since it has had a chance to absorb moisture, the boiling point after this sequence is called the minimum wet boiling point.

Silicones have about three times the amount of dissolved air as glycol fluids (about 15% of dissolved air versus only about 5% for standard glycol brake fluid). It is this characteristic of silicone brake fluid that causes the most concern about its use.

1. Silicone brake fluid has an affinity for air; therefore, it is more difficult to bleed the hydraulic system of trapped air.

2. The trapped air expands with increasing temperature. This causes the brake pedal to feel "mushy" because the pressure exerted on the hydraulic system simply compresses the air in the system and does not transfer the force to the wheel cylinders and calipers as it should.

NOTE: The characteristic of DOT 5 silicone brake fluid to absorb air is one of the major reasons why it is not recommended for use with an antilock braking system (ABS). In an ABS, valves and pumps are used which can aerate the brake fluid. Brake fluid filled with air bubbles cannot properly lubricate the ABS components and will cause a low, soft brake pedal.

3. The air trapped in the silicone brake fluid can also "off-gas" at high altitudes, causing a mushy brake pedal and reduced braking performance. DOT 5 brake fluid has been known to create a braking problem during high-altitude (over 5,000 ft [1,500 m]) and high-temperature driving. The high altitude tends to vaporize (off-gassing) some parts of the liquid, creating bubbles in the brake system, similar to having air in the brake system.

4. DOT 5 brake fluid should not be mixed with any other type of brake fluid. Therefore, the entire braking system must be completely flushed and refilled with DOT 5.

5. DOT 5 does not affect rubber parts and will not cause corrosion.

6. DOT 5 is expensive. It is approximately four times the cost of DOT 3 brake fluid. ● **SEE FIGURE 7–3.**

BRAKE FLUID INSPECTION AND TESTING
The brake fluid should be inspected regularly, including the following items:

1. **Proper Level.** The brake fluid level should be above the minimum level (labeled MIN) and below the maximum (labeled MAX) on the side of the master cylinder reservoir. Do not add brake fluid unless the entire brake system is carefully inspected for worn brake pads and shoes and for signs of any external leakage.

FIGURE 7–3 DOT 5 brake fluid is used mostly in motorcycles because if spilled, it will not hurt painted surfaces.

? FREQUENTLY ASKED QUESTION

What Is Hydraulic Brake System Mineral Oil?

Some French-built Citroen and British-designed Rolls-Royce vehicles use **hydraulic system mineral oil (HSMO)** as part of their hydraulic control systems. The systems in these vehicles use a hydraulic pump to pressurize hydraulic oil for use in the suspension leveling and braking systems.

CAUTION: Mineral hydraulic oil should never be used in a braking system that requires DOT 3 or DOT 4 polyglycol-based brake fluid. If any mineral oil, such as engine oil, transmission oil, or automatic transmission fluid (ATF), gets into a braking system that requires glycol brake fluid, every rubber part in the entire braking system must be replaced. Mineral oil causes the rubber compounds that are used in glycol brake fluid systems to swell (● SEE FIGURE 7–4).

To help prevent hydraulic system mineral oil from being mixed with glycol brake fluid, *hydraulic mineral oils are green.*

FIGURE 7–4 Both rubber sealing cups were exactly the same size. The cup on the left was exposed to mineral oil. Notice how the seal greatly expanded.

FIGURE 7–5 If the brake fluid is black in color, it should be replaced.

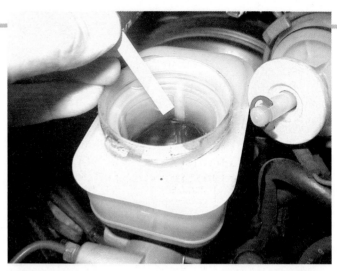

(a)

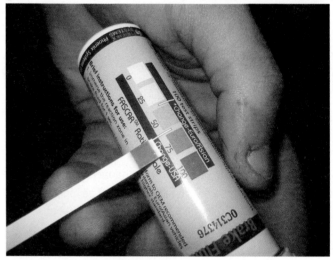

(b)

FIGURE 7–6 (a) A brake fluid test strip is being used to test the condition of the brake fluid. (b) The color of the test strip is then compared with a chart on the package, which indicates the condition and if the fluid should be replaced.

2. **Color/Condition.** New brake fluid is clear or amber in color. If the brake fluid is black or discolored like black coffee or coffee with cream, the fluid should be changed. ● **SEE FIGURE 7–5**.

3. **Tested Using a Tester or Test Strips.** Often, brake fluid does not look as if it is bad but has absorbed moisture enough to reduce its effectiveness. Test strips can be used to measure copper ions that increase as the brake fluid becomes deteriorated. The copper comes from sealing washers and other brass or copper brake system components. ● **SEE FIGURE 7–6**.

4. **Boiling Point tester.** An electronic tester can be used to measure the actual boiling temperature of the brake fluid. The tester probe is inserted into the brake fluid and then a button is pushed and the boiling temperature is displayed. ● **SEE FIGURE 7–7**.

5. **Brake Fluid Contamination Test.** If brake fluid is mixed with any mineral oil, such as engine oil, power steering fluid, or automatic transmission fluid, rubber components will swell and cause brake system failure. To check for possible contamination, remove the reservoir cover from the master cylinder. If the rubber diaphragm is swelled or distorted, brake fluid contamination is likely. To check the brake fluid, use a Styrofoam cup filled with water.

- Place a teaspoon (1 ml) of brake fluid from the master cylinder into the water.
- Pure brake fluid will completely dissolve in the water. Petroleum or mineral oil fluids will float on the surface

FIGURE 7–7 An electronic tester that measures the boiling temperature of the brake fluid is useful to help determine if the brake fluid needs to be replaced.

BRAKE FLUID (CONTINUED)

 REAL WORLD FIX

The Sinking Brake Pedal

This author has experienced what happens when brake fluid is not changed regularly. Just as many technicians will tell you, we do not always do what we know should be done to our own vehicles.

While driving a four-year-old vehicle on vacation in very hot weather in mountainous country, the brake pedal sank to the floor. When the vehicle was cold, the brakes were fine. But after several brake applications, the pedal became soft and spongy and sank slowly to the floor if pressure was maintained on the brake pedal. Because the brakes were okay when cold, I knew it had to be boiling brake fluid. Old brake fluid (four years old) often has a boiling point under 300°F (150°C). With the air temperature near 100°F (38°C), it does not take much more heat to start boiling the brake fluid. After bleeding over a quart (1 liter) of new brake fluid through the system, the brakes worked normally. I'll never again forget to replace the brake fluid as recommended by the vehicle manufacturer.

of the water and retain their color. Petroleum fluids will also dissolve the Styrofoam cup at the waterline.

- If the brake fluid is contaminated, the entire braking system must be drained and flushed and all rubber components replaced.

BRAKE FLUID SERVICE PROCEDURES AND PRECAUTIONS

1. Store brake fluid only in its original container.
   - To help prevent possible contamination with moisture, air, or other products, purchase brake fluid in small containers.
   - Keep all brake fluid containers tightly closed to prevent air (containing moisture) from being absorbed.
2. Before opening a brake fluid container, remove any dirt, moisture, or other contamination from the top and outside of the container.
3. When a brake fluid container is empty, it should be discarded—the container should never be used for anything except brake fluid.
4. Do not transfer brake fluid to any other container that may have contained oil, kerosene, gasoline, antifreeze, water, cleaners, or any other liquids or chemicals.
5. Do not reuse brake fluid that has been siphoned from another vehicle or drawn out during a brake bleeding operation. (Brake bleeding means to open special bleeder valves in the hydraulic system to rid the system of any trapped air.)
6. Use only fresh, new brake fluid for flushing the hydraulic brake system.

CAUTION: Alcohol or flushing fluids should not be used because they cannot be totally removed and will contaminate the system. Disassembled parts, however, can and should be cleaned with denatured alcohol or spray brake cleaner where the parts can be visually inspected to be free of cleaning solutions.

BRAKE FLUID HANDLING AND DISPOSAL Polyglycol brake fluid presents little toxicity hazard, but for some individuals, brake fluid may produce moderate eye and skin irritation. For good safety practice, protective clothing and safety glasses or goggles should be worn.

Brake fluid becomes a hazardous waste if spilled onto open ground, where it can seep into groundwater. The disposal requirements for brake fluid spilled onto open ground vary with the exact amount spilled and other factors. Refer to local EPA guidelines and requirements for the exact rules and regulations in your area.

REAL WORLD FIX

The Pike's Peak Brake Inspection

All vehicles must stop about halfway down Pike's Peak Mountain in Colorado (14,110 ft [4,300 m]) for a "brake inspection." When this author stopped at the inspection station, a uniformed inspector simply looked at the right front wheel and waved us on. I pulled over and asked the inspector what he was checking. He said that when linings and drums/rotors get hot, the vehicle loses brake effectiveness. But if the brake fluid boils, the vehicle loses its brakes entirely. The inspector was listening for boiling brake fluid at the front wheel and feeling for heat about 1 ft (30 cm) from the wheel. The inspector used an infrared pyrometer to measure the front wheel brakes and if the brakes were too hot to continue, you would be instructed to pull over and wait for the brakes to cool. The inspector recommended placing the transmission into a lower gear, which uses the engine to slow the vehicle during the descent without having to rely entirely on the brakes.

RUBBER TYPES

Vehicles use a wide variety of rubber in the braking system, suspension system, steering system, and engine. Rubber products are called **elastomers**. Some are oil- and grease-resistant elastomers and can be harmed by brake fluid, while others are brake-fluid resistant and can swell or expand if they come in contact with oil or grease. ● **SEE CHART 7–1** for types and compatible fluids.

● **SEE FIGURES 7–8 THROUGH 7–10** for examples of where rubber is used in the braking system.

Brake fluid (DOT 3 or DOT 4 glycol brake fluid) affects all elastomers and causes a slight swelling effect (about 5%). This swelling action is necessary for the seals to withstand high hydraulic pressures. Silicone (DOT 5) brake fluid does not cause rubber to swell; therefore, a rubber swell additive is used in silicone brake fluid. While these additives work well for EPDM rubber, it can cause SBR rubber to swell too much. Although most seals today use EPDM, many drum brakes still use SBR seals. This is a major reason that DOT 5 brake fluid is not recommended by many vehicle manufacturers.

RUBBER COMPATIBILITY CHART

NAME	ABBREVIATIONS	OK	NOT OK	USES
Ethylene propylene diene (developed in 1963)	EPM, EPDM, EPR	Brake fluid, silicone fluids	Petroleum fluids	Most brake system seals and parts
Styrene, butadiene (developed in 1920s)	SBR, BUNA S, GRS	Brake fluid, silicone fluids, alcohols	Petroleum fluids	Some drum brake seals, O-rings
Nitrile (nitrile butadiene rubber)	NBR, BUNA N	Petroleum fluids, ethylene glycol (antifreeze)	Brake fluid	Engine seals, O-rings
Neoprene (polychloroprene)	CR	Refrigerants (Freons: R-12 and R-134a), petroleum fluids	Brake fluids	Refrigerant, O-rings
Polyacrylate	ACM	Petroleum fluids, automatic transmission fluids	Brake fluids	Automatic transmission and engine seals
Viton (fluorocarbon)	FKM	Petroleum fluids	Brake fluid, 134a refrigerant	Engine seals, fuel system parts
Natural rubber	NR	Water, brake fluid	Petroleum fluids	Tires

CHART 7–1

Notice that if a rubber is OK to use for brake fluid it is not OK to use for oil or grease.

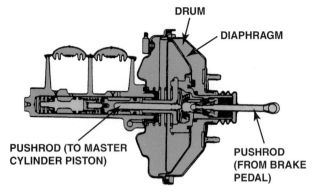

FIGURE 7–8 The master cylinder piston seals are usually constructed from EPDM rubber, and the diaphragm of the vacuum power brake booster is usually made from SBR.

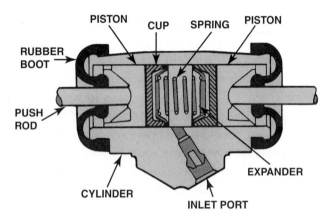

FIGURE 7–9 Cross-sectional view of a typical drum brake wheel cylinder. Most wheel cylinder boots and cups are either SBR or EPDM rubber.

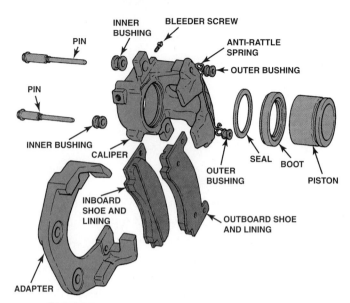

FIGURE 7–10 Exploded view of a typical disc brake caliper. Both the caliper seal and dust boot are constructed of EPDM rubber.

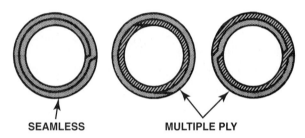

FIGURE 7–11 Steel brake tubing is double-walled for strength and plated for corrosion resistance.

BRAKE LINES

High-pressure double-walled steel brake lines or high-strength flexible lines are used to connect the master cylinder to each wheel. The steel **brake lines** are also called **brake pipes** or **brake tubing**. Brake lines carry brake fluid from the master cylinder to the wheel cylinder and brake calipers. The brake lines contain and direct the pressure of the brake hydraulic system.

Most of the total length of the brake line consists of rigid tubing. For maximum strength and durability, all brake systems use double-walled brake tubing made from plated steel sheet. There are two types of double-walled tubing:

- Seamless
- Multiple ply
  - ● **SEE FIGURE 7–11.**

All double-walled brake tubing is plated with tin, zinc, or other similar substances for protection against rust and corrosion.

The Society of Automotive Engineers (SAE) has guidelines for brake tubing. SAE Standard J1047 specifies that a sample section of brake line must be able to withstand 8,000 PSI (55,000 kPa) plus other standards for resistance to fatigue, heat, rust, and corrosion.

CAUTION: Copper tubing should *never* be used for brake lines. Copper tends to burst at a lower pressure than steel.

All steel brake lines have one of two basic types of ends:

- **Double Flare**. ● **SEE FIGURE 7–12.**
- **ISO**, which means **International Standards Organization** (also called a *ball flare* or *bubble flare*).
  - ● **SEE FIGURE 7–13.**

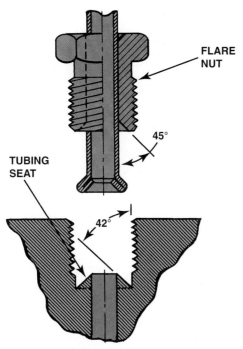

FIGURE 7–12 Because of the slight difference in flare angle, double-flare fitting seals cause a wedging action.

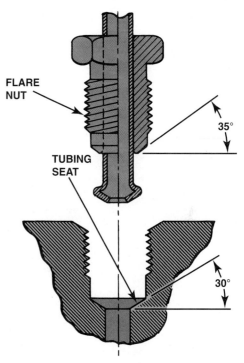

FIGURE 7–13 An ISO fitting.

When replacing steel brake line, new steel tubing should be used and a double lap flare or an ISO flare completed at each end using a special flaring tool. ● **SEE FIGURES 7–14 AND 7–15.**

Brake line can also be purchased in selected lengths already correctly flared. They are available in different diameters, the most commonly used being 3/16 in. (4.8 mm), 1/4 in. (6.4 mm), and 5/16 in. (7.9 mm) outside diameter (O.D.).

CAUTION: According to vehicle manufacturers' recommended procedures, compression fittings should never be used to join two pieces of steel brake line. Only use double-flare ends and connections, if necessary, when replacing damaged steel brake lines.

Brake line diameter is also very important and replacement lines should be the same as the original. Many vehicle manufacturers use larger diameter brake lines for the rear brakes because the larger line decreases brake response time. *Response time is the amount of time between the pressure increase at the master cylinder and the pressure increase at the brakes.* On most vehicles, the brake lines to the front wheels are shorter. To help assure that the rear brakes apply at the same time as the front brakes, the diameter of the brake lines is increased to the rear brakes. Brake engineers size each line to keep the time lag to less than 0.2 second (200 milliseconds). Fast response time is critical for the proper operation of the antilock braking system (ABS). Also, as brake fluid ages, its viscosity (resistance to flow) increases, resulting in longer response time.

(a)

(b)

(c)

(d)

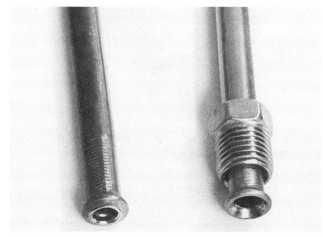

(e)

FIGURE 7–14 Double flaring the end of a brake line.
(a) Clamp the line at the correct height above the surface of
the clamping tool using the shoulder of the insert as a gauge.
(b) The insert is pressed into the end of the tubing. This
creates the first bend. (c) Remove the insert and use the
pointed tool to complete the overlap double flare. (d) The
completed operation as it appears while still in the clamp.
(e) The end of the line as it appears after the first operation
on the left and the completed double flare on the right.

(a)

(b)

FIGURE 7–15 Making an ISO flare requires a special tool. (a) Position the brake line into the two-part tool at the correct height using the gauge end of the tool. (b) Assemble the two blocks of the tool together and clamp in a vise. Turn the tool around and thread it into the tool block. The end of the threaded part of the tool forms the "bubble" or ISO flare.

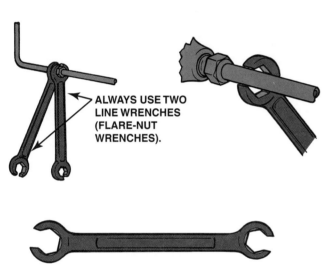

ALWAYS USE TWO LINE WRENCHES (FLARE-NUT WRENCHES).

FIGURE 7–16 Whenever disconnecting or tightening a brake line, always use the correct size flare-nut wrench. A flare-nut wrench is also called a tube-nut wrench or a line wrench.

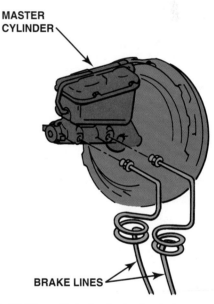

MASTER CYLINDER

BRAKE LINES

FIGURE 7–17 The coils in the brake line help prevent cracks caused by vibration.

BRAKE LINES (CONTINUED)

CAUTION: The exhaust system near brake lines should be carefully inspected for leaks when diagnosing a "lack of brakes" complaint. Exhaust gases can hit the brake line going to the rear brakes, causing the brake fluid to boil. Since brake fluid vapors are no longer liquid, they can be compressed, resulting in a total loss of brakes. After the vehicle is stopped and allowed to cool, the brakes often return to normal.

Always use two line wrenches when disconnecting or reattaching brake lines. ● **SEE FIGURE 7–16.**

COILED BRAKE LINE Steel brake line is often coiled, as shown on a race car in ● **FIGURE 7–17.** The purpose of the coils is to allow movement between the brake components without stress that could lead to metal fatigue and brake line breakage. The typical master cylinder attaches to the bulkhead of the vehicle and the combination valve is often attached to the frame. Because the body and frame are usually insulated from each other using rubber isolators, some movement occurs while driving.

ARMORED BRAKE LINE   In many areas of the brake system, the steel brake line is covered with a wire coil wrap, as shown in ● **FIGURE 7–18**. This type of brake line is called **armored brake line**. This armor is designed to prevent damage from stones and other debris that could dent or damage the brake line. If a section of armored brake line is to be replaced, armored replacement line should be installed.

FLEXIBLE BRAKE HOSE   **Flexible brake hoses** are used on each front wheel to allow for steering and suspension

TECH TIP

Bend It Right the First Time

Replacing rusted or damaged brake line can be a difficult job. It is important that the replacement brake line be located in the same location as the original to prevent possible damage from road debris or heat from the exhaust. Often this means bending the brake line with many angles and turns. To make the job a lot easier, use a stiff length of wire and bend the wire into the exact shape necessary. Then use the wire as a pattern to bend the brake line. Always use a tubing bender to avoid kinking the brake line. A kink not only restricts the flow of brake fluid, but also weakens the line. To bend brake line without a tubing bender tool, use an old V-belt pulley. Clamp the pulley in a vise, lay the tubing in the groove, and smoothly bend the tubing. Different diameter pulleys will create various radius bends. ● **SEE FIGURE 7–19**.

NOTE: Always use a tubing cutter instead of a hacksaw when cutting brake line. A hacksaw will leave a rough and uneven end that will not flare properly except when forming an ISO flare. A hacksaw is used to provide a rough surface to allow the flaring tool to grip the line during the procedure. Always check the instructions that came with the flaring tool for the exact procedure to follow.

FIGURE 7–18 Armored brake line is usually used in the location where the line may be exposed to rock or road debris damage. Even armored brake line can leak and a visual inspection is an important part of any brake service.

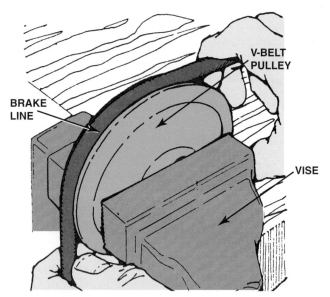

FIGURE 7–19 If a tubing bender is not available, then using a V-belt pulley in a vise to bend brake line will get the job done without kinking the brake line.

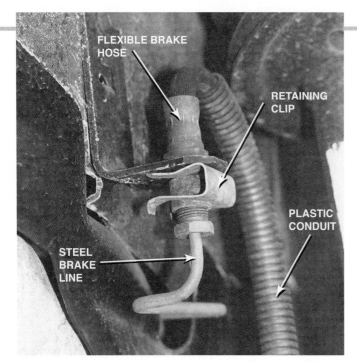

FLEXIBLE BRAKE
HOSE

RETAINING
CLIP

PLASTIC
CONDUIT

STEEL
BRAKE
LINE

FIGURE 7–20 Flexible brake hoses are used between the frame or body of the vehicle and the wheel brakes. Because of suspension and/or steering movement, these flexible brake lines must be strong enough to handle high brake fluid pressures, yet remain flexible. Note that this flexible brake hose is further protected against road debris with a plastic conduit covering.

FIGURE 7–22 Brake hose fabric being woven at the factory.

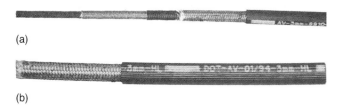

(a)

(b)

FIGURE 7–21 (a) Typical flexible brake hose showing the multiple layers of rubber and fabric. (b) The inside diameter (ID) is printed on the hose (3 mm).

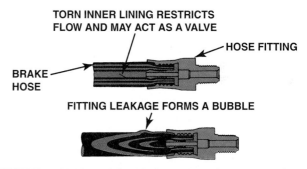

TORN INNER LINING RESTRICTS
FLOW AND MAY ACT AS A VALVE

HOSE FITTING

BRAKE
HOSE

FITTING LEAKAGE FORMS A BUBBLE

FIGURE 7–23 Typical flexible brake hose faults. Many faults cannot be seen, yet can cause the brakes to remain applied after the brake pedal is released.

movement and at the rear to allow for rear suspension travel. ● **SEE FIGURE 7–20**. These rubber high-strength hoses can crack, blister, or leak, and should be inspected at least every six months. ● **SEE FIGURE 7–21**.

Flexible brake hose is made from synthetic yarn (poly vinyl alcohol, abbreviated PVA) that is braided into position from multi-end yarn spindles. By braiding the yarn, all of the strands operate in tension and, therefore, have great strength to withstand braking system pressure over 1,000 PSI (6,900 kPa). ● **SEE FIGURE 7–22**.

A typical brake hose has an inner tube for conveying the brake fluid and a cushion liner that is between the braided layers

to prevent the braids from chafing. All three layers use ethylene-propylene-diene-monomer (EPDM)-type thermosetting polymers, which help prevent the hose from absorbing moisture from the outside air. An outside jacket is made from rubber and protects the reinforcement fabric from moisture and abrasion. The outside covering is also ribbed as part of the manufacturing process to hide surface blemishes. These ribs also make it easy for the technician to see if the hose is twisted. It is not unusual for flexible brake lines to become turned around and twisted when the disc brake caliper is removed and then replaced during a brake pad change. ● **SEE FIGURE 7–23**.

A constricted brake hose can cause the brakes to remain applied, thereby causing excessive brake pad wear and unequal braking. A constricted flexible brake line can also cause the vehicle to pull to one side. ● **SEE FIGURE 7–24**.

CAUTION: Never allow a disc brake caliper to hang by the flexible brake hose. Damage to the line can result. Always use a wire to support the weight of the caliper.

FIGURE 7–24 Flexible brake hose should be carefully inspected for cuts or other damage, especially near sections where the brake hose is attached to the vehicle. Notice the crack and cut hose next to the mounting bracket.

SUMMARY

1. Most brake fluid is amber in color and polyglycol based.
2. DOT 3 is the type of brake fluid most often recommended for use.
3. DOT 3, 4 and 5.1 brake fluid absorbs moisture over time and can remove paint.
4. DOT 4 and DOT 5.1 are also polyglycol-based fluids, whereas DOT 5 is silicone based.
5. Brake fluid should be checked for proper level and color and tested for condition or for contamination.
6. Brake fluid should be disposed of according to local and state guidelines.
7. Most brake systems use EPR- or SBR-type rubber that is compatible with brake fluid but they can swell in size if exposed to mineral oil such as power steering fluid, engine oil, or automatic transmission fluid.
8. Brake lines are double-walled steel with a rust prevention coating with either a double lap flare or an ISO flare end.
9. Flexible brake hose is constructed of braided synthetic yarn and EPDM rubber.

REVIEW QUESTIONS

1. What is the difference between DOT 3, DOT 4, DOT 5.1, and DOT 5 brake fluid?
2. List four things that should be done during a thorough inspection of the brake fluid.
3. List four precautions that should be followed when handling brake fluid.
4. What are the two types of flares used on brake lines?
5. Why are some brake lines coiled?

CHAPTER QUIZ

1. The type of brake fluid most often recommended by vehicle manufacturers is _____.
   a. DOT 3
   b. DOT 4
   c. DOT 5
   d. DOT 5.1

2. Which of the following is *not* a characteristic of conventional brake fluid?
   a. Absorbs moisture from the air
   b. Removes paint if spilled on vehicle surfaces
   c. Lasts the life of the vehicle unless there is a leak
   d. Is clear or amber in color

3. Technician A says that DOT 5 brake fluid can be added to DOT 3 brake fluid. Technician B says that it is wise to purchase brake fluid that is in metal rather than plastic containers. Which technician is correct?
   a. Technician A only
   b. Technician B only
   c. Both Technicians A and B
   d. Neither Technician A nor B

4. As brake fluid ages, what happens?
   a. The boiling temperature decreases
   b. The boiling temperature increases
   c. The viscosity (thickness) decreases
   d. The color changes to purple

5. Technician A says that glycol-based brake fluid causes the seals to swell slightly. Technician B says the DOT 5 (silicone-based) brake fluid causes rubber seals to swell slightly. Which technician is correct?
   a. Technician A only
   b. Technician B only
   c. Both Technicians A and B
   d. Neither Technician A nor B

6. The two types of flares used on brake lines are _____.
   a. SAE and DOT
   b. Double flare and ISO
   c. Ball flare and bubble flare
   d. SAE and double flare

7. Two technicians are discussing why the brake lines are coiled near the master cylinder on many vehicles. Technician A says that these coils help prevent moisture from flowing from the master cylinder to the calipers. Technician B says that they help prevent cracks that could be caused by vibrations. Which technician is correct?
   a. Technician A only
   b. Technician B only
   c. Both Technicians A and B
   d. Neither Technician A nor B

8. Flexible brake hose should be inspected for all of the following *except:*
   a. Cracks
   b. Leakage
   c. Twisted
   d. Worn outer ribs

9. Why should brake calipers be supported by a wire during brake service and not allowed to hang by the flexible brake hose?
   a. To keep air from getting into the system
   b. To help prevent damage to the brake hose
   c. To hold the caliper higher than the master cylinder to prevent fluid loss
   d. To prevent bending the hose support bracket

10. Used brake fluid should be _____.
    a. Mixed with and recycled with used oil
    b. Poured down the drain
    c. Dispose of properly according to State and local laws
    d. Poured onto open ground to reduce dust

BRAKE BLEEDING METHODS AND PROCEDURES

OBJECTIVES

After studying Chapter 8, the reader will be able to:

1. Prepare to take the Brakes (A5) ASE certification test content area "A" (Hydraulic System Diagnosis and Repair).

2. Explain how to bench bleed a master cylinder.

3. Describe the proper brake bleeding sequence.

4. Describe the single stroke manual brake bleeding procedure.

5. Discuss how to gravity bleed the hydraulic brake system.

6. List the steps needed to perform a pressure bleed procedure.

7. Discuss how to vacuum bleed an hydraulic brake system.

KEY TERMS

Bleeder valve 123
Brake bleeding 123
Gravity bleeding 128
Power bleeding 129

Pressure bleeding 129
Single stroke bleeding method 126
Vacuum bleeding 127

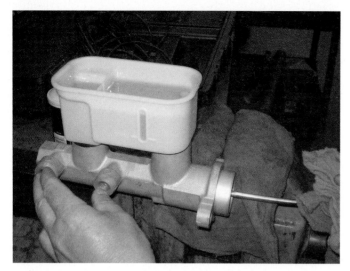

FIGURE 8–1 Bench bleeding a master cylinder. Always clamp a master cylinder in a vise by the mounting flange to prevent distortion of the cylinder bore. Bench bleeding tubes can also be used that route the fluid back into the reservoir.

BRAKE BLEEDING

THE NEED FOR BRAKE BLEEDING **Brake bleeding** is removing any trapped air from the hydraulic system. If air is the brake hydraulic system, the brake pedal will often feel "spongy". The brake pedal will also travel farther (lower than normal brake pedal) before the brakes start to apply. Air can get into the hydraulic system whenever any hydraulic brake line or unit is opened. Air can also be drawn into the hydraulic system through small holes or loose brake line connections during the release of the brake pedal. A common source of air in the brake system of this type can occur through very small holes in rubber flexible brake lines. Another source of air in the braking system is through the absorption of moisture by the brake fluid. When moisture is absorbed, the boiling point of the brake fluid is reduced. During severe braking, the heat generated can cause the brake fluid to boil and create air bubbles in the hydraulic brake system. Air eventually travels to the highest part of the brake system, if not restricted by pressure control valves.

BLEEDING THE MASTER CYLINDER Whenever the master cylinder is replaced or the hydraulic system has been left opened for several hours, the air may have to be bled from the master cylinder. The master cylinder is located in the highest section of the hydraulic braking system. Some master cylinders are equipped with bleeder valves. If the master cylinder is not equipped with bleeder valves, it can be bled by loosening the brake line fittings at the master cylinder. Bleed the master cylinder "on the bench" before installing it on the vehicle. ● **SEE FIGURE 8–1**.

Bench bleeding the master cylinder includes the following steps:

STEP 1 Fill the master cylinder with clean brake fluid from a sealed container up to the recommended "full" level.

STEP 2 Have an assistant slowly depress the brake pedal as you "crack open" the master cylinder bleed screw starting with the section closest to the brake pedal. It is very important that the primary section of the master cylinder be bled before attempting to bleed the air out of the secondary section of the master cylinder. Before the brake pedal reaches the floor, close the bleeder valve.

NOTE: A proper manual bleeding of the hydraulic system requires that accurate communications occur between the person depressing the brake pedal and the person opening and closing the bleeder valve(s). The bleeder valve (also called a *bleed valve*) should be open only when the brake pedal is being depressed. The valve *must* be closed when the brake pedal is released to prevent air from being drawn into the system.

STEP 3 Repeat the procedure several times until a solid flow of brake fluid is observed leaving the bleeder valve. If the master cylinder is not equipped with bleeder valves, the outlet tube nuts can be loosened instead.

BRAKE BLEEDER VALVE LOOSENING METHODS

Attempting to loosen a bleeder valve often results in breaking (shearing off) the bleeder valve. Several of these service procedures can be tried that help prevent the *possibility* of breaking a bleeder valve. Bleeder valves are tapered and become wedged in the caliper on the wheel cylinder housing. ● SEE FIGURES 8–2 AND 8–3. All of these methods use shock to "break the taper" and to loosen the stuck valve.

HIT AND TAP METHOD

STEP 1 Tap on the end of the bleeder valve with a steel hammer. This shock often "breaks the taper" at the base of the bleeder valve. The shock also breaks loose any rust or corrosion on the threads.

STEP 2 Using a 6-point wrench or socket, *tap* the bleeder valve in the clockwise direction (tighten).

STEP 3 Using the same 6-point socket or wrench, *tap* the bleeder valve counter-clockwise to loosen and remove the bleeder valve.

> **NOTE: It is the *shock* of the tap on the wrench that breaks loose the bleeder valve. Simply pulling on the wrench often results in breaking off the bleeder.**

STEP 4 If the valve is still stuck (frozen), repeat Step 1 through Step 3.

AIR PUNCH METHOD

Use an air punch near the bleeder valve while attempting to loosen the bleeder valve at the same time. ● SEE FIGURE 8–4.

The air punch creates a shock motion that often loosens the taper and threads of the bleeder valve from the caliper or wheel cylinder. It is also helpful to first attempt to turn the bleeder valve in the clockwise (tightening) direction, then turn the bleeder in the counter-clockwise direction to loosen and remove the bleeder valve.

HEAT AND TAP METHOD

Heat the area around the bleeder valve with a torch. The heat expands the size of the hole and usually allows the bleeder to be loosened and removed.

CAUTION: The heat from a torch will damage the rubber seals inside the caliper or wheel cylinder. Using heat to free a stuck bleeder valve will *require* that all internal rubber parts be replaced.

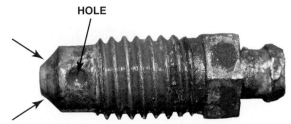

FIGURE 8–2 Typical bleeder valve from a disc brake caliper. The arrows point to the taper section that does the actual sealing. It is this taper that requires a shock to loosen. If the bleeder is simply turned with a wrench, the bleeder usually breaks off because the tapered part at the bottom remains adhered to the caliper or wheel cylinder. Once loosened, brake fluid flows around the taper and out through the hole in the side of the bleeder valve. The hole is clogged in this example and needs to be cleaned out.

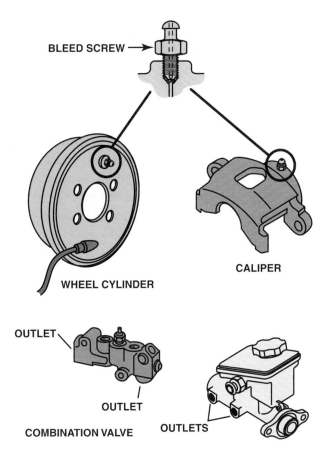

FIGURE 8–3 Typical bleeder locations. Note that the combination valve and master cylinder shown do not have bleeder valves; therefore, bleeding is accomplished by loosening the brake line at the outlet ports.

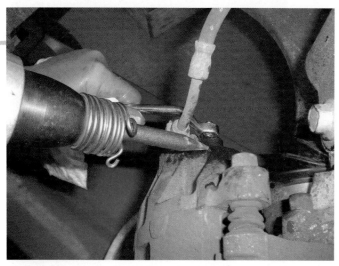

FIGURE 8–4 Using an air punch next to the bleeder valve to help "break the taper" on the bleeder valve.

FIGURE 8–5 Most vehicle manufacturers recommend starting the brake bleeding process at the rear wheel farthest from the master cylinder.

WAX METHOD

STEP 1 Heat the bleeder valve itself with a torch. The heat causes the valve itself to expand.

STEP 2 Remove the heat from the bleeder valve. As the valve is cooling, touch paraffin wax or candle wax to the hot valve. The wax will melt and run down around the threads of the bleeder valve.

STEP 3 Allow the bleeder valve to cool until it can be safely touched with your hand. This assures that the temperature is low enough for the wax to return to a solid and provide the lubricating properties necessary for the easy removal of the bleeder valve. Again, turn the bleeder valve clockwise before turning the valve counterclockwise to remove.

BLEEDING SEQUENCE

After bleeding the master cylinder, the combination valve should be bled if equipped. Check the level in the master cylinder frequently being careful not to allow the master cylinder to run dry and keep it filled with clean brake fluid throughout the brake bleeding procedure.

For most rear-wheel-drive vehicles equipped with a front/rear split system, start the bleeding with the wheel farthest from the master cylinder and work toward the closest. ● **SEE FIGURE 8–5**.

For most vehicles, this sequence is as follows:

1. Right rear
2. Left rear
3. Right front
4. Left front

NOTE: If the vehicle has two wheel cylinders on one brake, bleed the upper wheel cylinder first.

For vehicles equipped with a diagonal split section or equipped with ABS, follow the brake bleeding procedure recommended in the service information for the vehicle.

FIGURE 8–6 Bleeding brakes using clear plastic tubing makes it easy to see air bubbles. Submerging the hose in a container of clean brake fluid helps ensure that all of the air will be purged by the system.

MANUAL BLEEDING

Manual bleeding is the most commonly used method and uses hydraulic pressure created by the master cylinder to pump fresh fluid through the brake system. This method is also called the **single stroke bleeding method**.

ADVANTAGES OF MANUAL BLEEDING The manual method of brake bleeding is the most common. Manual bleeding requires the following:

- An assistant to apply and release the brake pedal
- A bleeder screw wrench
- Approximately 2 feet of clear, plastic hose with an inside diameter small enough to fit snugly over the bleeder screws
- A clear jar partially filled with clean brake fluid

MANUAL BLEEDING PROCEDURE To manually bleed the brake system, follow these steps:

STEP 1 Discharge the vacuum or hydraulic power booster (if equipped) by pumping the brake pedal with the ignition OFF until the pedal feels hard.

STEP 2 Fill the master cylinder reservoir with new brake fluid and make sure it remains at least half full throughout the bleeding procedure.

STEP 3 Attach the plastic hose over the bleeder screw of the first wheel cylinder or caliper in the bleeding sequence, and submerge the end of the tube in the jar of brake fluid. ● **SEE FIGURE 8–6**.

STEP 4 Loosen the bleeder screw approximately one-half turn, and have an assistant slowly depress the brake pedal. It is extremely important when manually bleeding a brake system that the pedal be applied and released slowly and gently. Rapid pedal pumping can churn up the fluid and reduce the size of trapped air bubbles, making them more difficult to bleed from the system. Air bubbles leaving the bleeder screw will be visible in the hose to the jar.

STEP 5 Tighten the bleeder screw, then have your assistant slowly release the brake pedal.

Tiny Bubbles

Do not use excessive brake pedal force while bleeding and never bleed the brake with the engine running! The extra assist from the power brake unit greatly increases the force exerted on the brake fluid in the master cylinder. The trapped air bubbles may be dispersed into tiny bubbles that often cling to the inside surface of the brake lines. These tiny air bubbles may not be able to be bled from the hydraulic system until enough time has allowed the bubbles to re-form. To help prevent excessive force, do *not* start the engine. Without power assistance, the brake pedal force can be kept from becoming excessive. If the dispersal of the air into tiny bubbles is suspected, try tapping the calipers or wheel cylinders with a plastic hammer. After this tapping, simply waiting for a period of time will cause the bubbles to re-form into larger and easier-to-bleed air pockets. Most brake experts recommend waiting *15 seconds or longer* between attempts to bleed each wheel. This waiting period is critical and allows time for the air bubbles to form.

NOTE: To help prevent depressing the brake pedal down too far, some experts recommend placing a 2 × 4 in. board under the brake pedal. This helps prevent the seals inside the master cylinder from traveling over unused sections inside the bore that may be corroded or rusty.

STEP 6 Wait at least 15 seconds to allow time for any small bubbles to form into larger bubbles. See the Tech Tip called, "Tiny Bubbles."

STEP 7 Repeat steps 4 and 5 until no more air bubbles emerge from the bleeder.

STEP 8 Transfer the plastic hose to the bleeder screw of the next wheel cylinder or caliper in the bleeding sequence, and repeat steps 4 through 7. Continue around the vehicle in the specified order until the brakes at all four wheels have been bled.

FIGURE 8–7 Using a compressed air-powered vacuum bleeder.

VACUUM BLEEDING

Vacuum bleeding uses a special suction pump that attaches to the bleeder screw. The pump creates a low-pressure area at the bleeder screw, which allows atmospheric pressure to force brake fluid through the system when the bleeder screw is opened.

ADVANTAGES OF VACUUM BLEEDING Vacuum bleeding requires only one technician. It is easy and the equipment needed can be low cost.

DISADVANTAGES OF VACUUM BLEEDING The disadvantage of using a vacuum bleeding method is that a vacuum tool must be used and often air can be drawn into the line between the bleeder valve and the hose creating some bubbles that can be interpreted by the technician as air in the system.

VACUUM BLEEDING PROCEDURE To vacuum bleed a brake system, use the following steps:

STEP 1 Fill the master cylinder reservoir with new brake fluid and make sure it remains at least half full throughout the bleeding procedure.

STEP 2 Attach the plastic tube from the vacuum bleeder to the bleeder screw of the first wheel cylinder or caliper in the bleeding sequence. ● **SEE FIGURES 8–7 AND 8–8**. If necessary, use one of the adapters provided with the vacuum in the catch bottle.

STEP 3 Operate the pump handle to create a partial vacuum in the catch bottle.

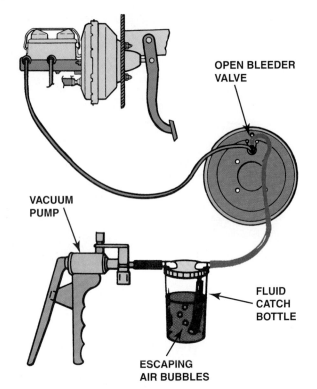

OPEN BLEEDER VALVE

VACUUM PUMP

FLUID CATCH BOTTLE

ESCAPING AIR BUBBLES

FIGURE 8–8 Vacuum bleeding uses atmospheric pressure to force brake fluid through the hydraulic system.

VACUUM BLEEDING (CONTINUED)

STEP 4 Loosen the bleeder screw approximately one-half turn. Brake fluid and air bubbles will flow into the bottle. When the fluid flow stops, tighten the bleeder screw.

STEP 5 Repeat steps 3 and 4 until no more air bubbles emerge from the bleeder.

STEP 6 Transfer the vacuum bleeder to the bleeder screw of the next wheel cylinder or caliper in the bleeding sequence, and repeat steps 3 and 4. Continue around the vehicle in the specified order until the brakes at all four wheels have been bled.

GRAVITY BLEEDING

Gravity bleeding is a slow, but effective, method that will work on many vehicles to rid the hydraulic system of air. The procedure involves simply opening the bleeder valve and waiting until brake fluid flows from the open valve. Any air trapped in the part being bled will rise and escape from the port when the valve is opened. It may take several minutes before brake fluid escapes. Gravity bleeding works because any liquid tends to seek its own level. This means that the brake fluid in the master cylinder tends to flow downward toward the wheel cylinders or calipers. As long as the brake fluid level in the master cylinder is higher than the bleeder valve, the brake fluid will flow downward and out the open bleeder valve, as shown in ● **SEE FIGURE 8–9**.

This flow of brake fluid can even get past the metering valve and proportioning valve. The proportioning valve is normally open to the rear brakes until the pressure reaches a predetermined level when it starts to limit increasing pressure to the rear brakes. The metering valve used to control or delay the operation of the front brakes is open to the front wheels until the pressure exceeds 10 to 15 PSI (70 to 100 kPa). Therefore, as long as no one is pushing on the brake pedal, the metering valve remains open to the front wheels and the brake fluid from the master cylinder can easily flow downward through the valve and out the open bleeder valve.

Since no pressure is exerted on the brake fluid, the large air bubbles remain large air bubbles and are not separated into smaller, harder-to-bleed air bubbles that can occur with manual bleeding.

ADVANTAGES OF GRAVITY BLEEDING All four wheel brakes can be bled at one time using the gravity method. In this process, the bleeder screws at all four wheels are opened at the same time, and the system is allowed to drain naturally until the fluid coming out of the bleeders is free of air. Gravity bleeding can be done by a single technician, who is freed to attend to other jobs while the brakes bleed.

DISADVANTAGES OF GRAVITY BLEEDING Gravity bleeding is a slow process that can take an hour or more. In addition, this procedure cannot be used on brake systems with residual pressure check valves because the valves restrict the fluid flow. When other bleeding procedures fail, gravity bleeding can sometimes be effective on brake systems that trap small pockets of air.

FIGURE 8–9 Gravity bleeding is simply opening the bleeder valve and allowing gravity to force the brake fluid out of the bleeder valve. Because air is lighter than brake fluid all of the air escapes before the brake fluid runs out.

GRAVITY BLEEDING PROCEDURE

Gravity bleeding requires:

- A bleeder wrench
- Four lengths of plastic hose that fit snugly over the bleeder screws
- Four jars to catch the dripping fluid—one for each wheel brake

Unless a plastic hose is used to "start a siphon" at each bleeder screw, it is possible that air may enter the system rather than be bled from it. This can occur because the total open area of the four bleeder screws is somewhat larger than that of the two compensating ports through which the fluid must enter the system. To gravity bleed the brake system, follow these steps:

STEP 1 Fill the master cylinder reservoir with new brake fluid. During the bleeding process, check the fluid level periodically to ensure that the reservoir remains at least half full.

STEP 2 Attach a length of plastic tubing to each bleeder screw, and place the ends of the tubes in jars to catch the drainage. Open each bleeder screw approximately one full turn and make sure that fluid begins to drain. Allow the system to drain until the fluid flowing from the bleeder screws is free of air bubbles. If no brake fluid comes out, remove the bleeder valve entirely—it may be clogged. Nothing but air and brake fluid will be *slowly* coming out of the wheel cylinder or caliper when the bleeder valve is removed. *Do not press on the brake pedal with the bleeder valve out while gravity bleeding.*

STEP 3 Close the bleeder screws and top up the fluid level in the master cylinder reservoir.

 **TECH TIP**

The Master Cylinder One-Drip-Per-Second Test

Excessive brake wear is often caused by misadjusted brake linkage or brake light switches keeping the brake pedal from fully releasing. If the brake pedal is not fully released, the primary piston sealing cup blocks the compensating port from the brake fluid reservoir. To test if this is the problem, loosen both lines from the master cylinder. Brake fluid should drip out of both lines about one drip per second. This is why this test is also called the "Master Cylinder Drip Test." If the master cylinder does not drip, the brake pedal may not be allowing the master cylinder to fully release. Have an assistant pull up on the brake pedal. If the dripping starts, the problem is due to a misadjusted brake light or speed (cruise) control switch or pedal stop. If the master cylinder still does not drip, loosen the master cylinder from the power booster. If the master cylinder now starts to drip, the pushrod adjustment is too long.

If the master cylinder still does not drip, the problem is in the master cylinder itself. Check for brake fluid contamination. If mineral oil, such as engine oil, power steering fluid, or automatic transmission fluid (ATF), has been used in the system, the rubber sealing cups swell and can block off the compensating port. If contamination is discovered, *every* brake component that contains rubber *must* be replaced.

PRESSURE BLEEDING

Pressure bleeding, sometimes called **power bleeding,** is a common method used to bleed the brake hydraulic system. In this process, a pressure bleeder attached to the master cylinder forces brake fluid through the system under pressure to purge any trapped air. Once the hydraulic system is pressurized, the technician simply opens the bleeder screws in the prescribed order and allows fluid to flow until it is free of air bubbles.

The tools required for pressure bleeding include a plastic hose and fluid catch jar as used in manual bleeding, as well as a pressure bleeder, a source of air pressure to charge the bleeder, and an adapter to attach the pressure bleeder to the master cylinder fluid reservoir. Cast-metal cylinders with integral reservoirs commonly use a flat, plate-type adapter that seals against the same surface as the reservoir cover. ● **SEE FIGURE 8–10.**

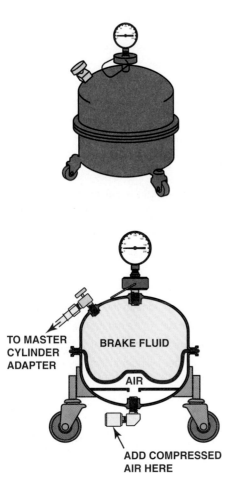

FIGURE 8–10 A typical pressure bleeder. The brake fluid inside is pressurized with air pressure in the air chamber. This air pressure is applied to the brake fluid in the upper section. A rubber diaphragm separates the air from the brake fluid.

TO MASTER CYLINDER ADAPTER

BRAKE FLUID

AIR

ADD COMPRESSED AIR HERE

FIGURE 8–11 Brake fluid under pressure from the power bleeder is applied to the top of the master cylinder. It is very important that the proper adapter be used for the master cylinder. Failure to use the correct adapter or failure to release the pressure on the brake fluid before removing the adapter can cause fluid to escape under pressure.

PRESSURE BLEEDING (CONTINUED)

Some plastic master cylinder reservoirs also use plate-type adapters, but others require adapters that seal against the bottom of the reservoir. ● SEE FIGURE 8–11. Pressure bleeder manufacturers offer many adapters to fit specific applications.

METERING VALVE OVERRIDE TOOLS   In addition to the tools previously described, a metering valve override tool is required when pressure bleeding the front brakes of certain vehicles. The override tool is used to deactivate the metering valve because the operating pressure of power bleeders is within the range where the metering valve blocks fluid flow to the front brakes. Metering valves that require an override tool have a stem or button on one end that is either pushed in or pulled out to hold the valve open. The override tool performs this service.

To install the override tool used on General Motors vehicles, loosen the combination valve mounting bolt and slip the slot in the tool under the bolt head.

Push the end of the tool toward the valve body until it depresses the valve plunger, then tighten the mounting bolt to hold the tool in place.

Some full-size Ford vehicles have a metering valve with a stem that must be pushed in to bleed the front brakes, but Ford does not offer a special tool for this purpose. An assistant is needed to override the valve when the front brakes are being bled.

To install the override tool used on older Chrysler and Ford vehicles, slip one fork of the tool under the rubber boot, and the other fork under the valve stem head. ● SEE FIGURE 8–12.

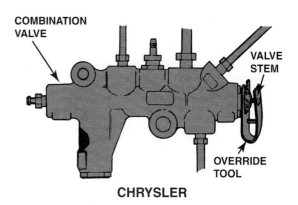

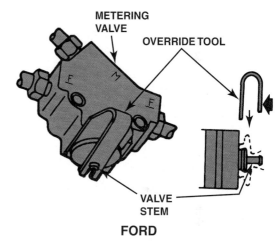

FIGURE 8-13 Pull-out-type metering valves being held out using a special override tool.

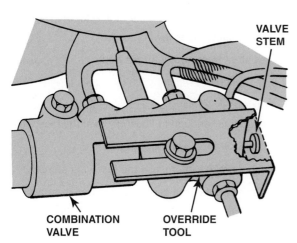

FIGURE 8-12 Metering valve override tool on a General Motors vehicle.

The spring tension of the tool holds the valve open, but allows the valve stem to move slightly when the system is pressurized. If the valve is held rigidly open, internal damage will result.

PRESSURE BLEEDING PROCEDURE Just as in manual bleeding, it is important to follow the proper sequence when pressure bleeding a brake system. Some manufacturers recommend one sequence for manual bleeding and another for pressure bleeding. To pressure bleed a brake system, follow these steps:

STEP 1 If it has not already been done, consult the equipment manufacturer's instructions and fill the pressure bleeder with the proper type of brake fluid.

STEP 2 Make sure the bleeder is properly sealed and the fluid supply valve is closed, then use compressed air to pressurize the bleeder until approximately 30 PSI (207 kPa) is indicated on the bleeder gauge.

STEP 3 If the vehicle is equipped with a metering valve, override it with the appropriate tool. ● **SEE FIGURE 8-13**.

STEP 4 Clean the top of the master cylinder, then remove the master cylinder cover and clean around the gasket surface. Be careful not to allow any dirt to fall into the reservoir.

STEP 5 Fill the reservoir about half full with new brake fluid, then install the proper pressure bleeder adapter on the master cylinder.

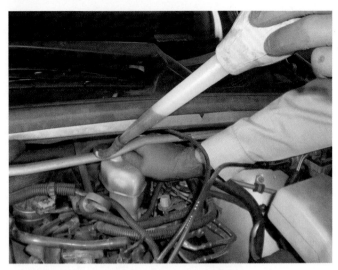

FIGURE 8–14 A turkey baster can be used to remove the old brake fluid from the master cylinder reservoir. A rubber hose was attached to the end of the turkey baster to get access to the brake fluid.

PRESSURE BLEEDING (CONTINUED)

STEP 6 Connect the pressure bleeder fluid supply hose to the adapter, making sure the hose fitting is securely engaged.

STEP 7 Open the fluid supply valve on the pressure bleeder to allow pressurized brake fluid to enter the system. Check carefully for fluid leaks that can damage the vehicle finish.

STEP 8 Slip the plastic hose over the bleeder screw of the first wheel cylinder or caliper to be bled, and submerge the end of the tube in the jar of brake fluid.

STEP 9 Open the bleeder screw approximately one-half turn, and let the fluid run until air bubbles no longer emerge from the tube. Close the bleeder screw.

STEP 10 Transfer the plastic hose to the bleeder screw of the next wheel cylinder or caliper in the bleeding sequence, and repeat steps 8 and 9. Continue around the vehicle in the specified order until the brakes at all four wheels have been bled.

STEP 11 Remove the metering valve override tool.

STEP 12 Close the fluid supply valve on the pressure bleeder.

STEP 13 Wrap the end of the fluid supply hose in a shop towel, and disconnect it from the master cylinder adapter. Be careful to avoid spilling brake fluid.

STEP 14 Remove the master cylinder adapter, adjust the fluid level to the full point, and install the fluid reservoir cover.

BRAKE FLUID REPLACEMENT/FLUSHING

Brake fluid flushing is a procedure where the old brake fluid is removed and new brake fluid is added to the hydraulic system.

FLUSHING PROCEDURE The brake fluid flushing procedure usually requires the following:

- An assistant to pump the brake pedal
- A bleeder screw wrench
- Approximately 2 feet of clear, plastic hose with an inside diameter small enough to fit snugly over the bleeder screw
- A jar partially filled with clean brake fluid

To flush a brake system, use the following steps:

STEP 1 Using a turkey baster or similar tool, remove the old brake fluid from the master cylinder reservoir. ● **SEE FIGURE 8–14.**

STEP 2 Fill the master cylinder reservoir with new brake fluid from a sealed container.

STEP 3 Slip the plastic hose over the bleeder screw of the wheel cylinder or caliper to be bled and submerge the end of the tube in the jar of brake fluid.

STEP 4 Open the bleeder screw approximately one-half turn.

STEP 5 With the bleeder screw *open*, have your assistant slowly depress the brake pedal.

STEP 6 While your assistant holds the brake pedal to the floor, close the bleeder screw.

STEP 7 Continue to bleed at each wheel until the fluid that emerges from the bleeder screw is free of any discoloration and contamination.

STEP 8 Repeat steps 4 through 7 at each bleeder screw in the recommended order.

STEP 9 Check the brakes for proper operation and re-bleed the system if needed.

SUMMARY

1. Bleeding the brakes means to remove all of the air from the brake hydraulic system.

2. A new or replacement master cylinder should be bench bled before installing it in the vehicle.

3. Bleeder valves are located on all disc brake calipers and drum brake wheel cylinders.

4. The most commonly used method of brake bleeding is the single stroke manual bleeding method.

5. Vacuum bleeding is used to draw the old fluid and any trapped air from the hydraulic system through the bleeder valve.

6. Gravity bleeding is an excellent but slow method.

7. Pressure bleeding requires adapters and special equipment, plus the metering valve must be held open to allow fluid to flow to the front brakes.

REVIEW QUESTIONS

1. Describe how to bench bleed a master cylinder.

2. List the steps necessary to manually bleed a brake hydraulic system.

3. Discuss the equipment and the procedures needed to pressure bleed a brake hydraulic system.

4. Explain how to gravity bleed a brake hydraulic system.

5. Describe how to vacuum bleed a brake hydraulic system.

CHAPTER QUIZ

1. The button on the _____ valve should be held when pressure bleeding the brakes.
   - **a.** Metering
   - **b.** Proportioning
   - **c.** Pressure-differential
   - **d.** Residual check

2. The brake bleeding procedure usually specified for a rear-wheel vehicle with a dual split master cylinder is _____.
   - **a.** RR, LR, RF, LF
   - **b.** LF, RF, LR, RR
   - **c.** RF, LR, LF, RR
   - **d.** LR, RR, LF, RF

3. Two technicians are discussing bench bleeding a master cylinder. Technician A says that the front (nose end) of the master cylinder should be bled first. Technician B says that the rear (brake pedal end) should be bled first. Which technician is correct?
   - **a.** Technician A only
   - **b.** Technician B only
   - **c.** Both Technicians A and B
   - **d.** Neither Technician A nor B

4. Two technicians are discussing how to loosen bleeder valves. Technician A says that a shock is usually necessary to break the taper at the base of the valve. Technician B says to apply steady, loosening torque to the bleeder valve using a 6-point wrench. Which technician is correct?
   - **a.** Technician A only
   - **b.** Technician B only
   - **c.** Both Technicians A and B
   - **d.** Neither Technician A nor B

5. Technician A says that the brake pedal should be depressed with as much force as possible during the normal bleeding procedure. Technician B says that the brake pedal should be pumped rapidly during this manual bleeding procedure to force the air down toward the bleeder valve(s). Which technician is correct?
   - **a.** Technician A only
   - **b.** Technician B only
   - **c.** Both Technicians A and B
   - **d.** Neither Technician A nor B

6. Vacuum is applied where during vacuum bleeding?
   - **a.** At each wheel brake bleeder valve
   - **b.** At the master cylinder reservoir
   - **c.** At the vacuum booster check valve
   - **d.** At the metering valve end of the combination valve

7. The bleeder is opened at a caliper and no brake fluid flows out. Technician A says that this is normal and that brake fluid should not flow or drip out of an open bleeder valve. Technician B says that the vent port in the master cylinder may be blocked. Which technician is correct?
   - **a.** Technician A only
   - **b.** Technician B only
   - **c.** Both Technicians A and B
   - **d.** Neither Technician A nor B

8. The usual maximum pressure that should be used when pressure bleeding a brake system is _____.
   - **a.** 20 PSI
   - **b.** 30 PSI
   - **c.** 50 PSI
   - **d.** 70 PSI

9. How does a bleeder valve seal?
   - **a.** O-ring
   - **b.** By the threads
   - **c.** Lip seal
   - **d.** Tapered end

10. Air in the brake hydraulic system can cause all *except* _____.
    - **a.** Spongy brake pedal
    - **b.** Hard brake pedal
    - **c.** Lower than normal brake pedal
    - **d.** May require the driver to "pump up" the brakes before they will stop the vehicle

FIGURE 9–1 Rolling contact bearings include (left to right) ball, roller, needle, and tapered roller.

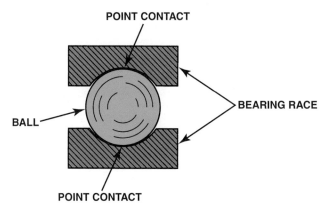

FIGURE 9–2 Ball bearing point contact.

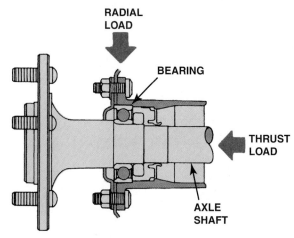

FIGURE 9–3 Radial load is the vehicle weight pressing on the wheels. The thrust load occurs as the chassis components exert a side force during cornering.

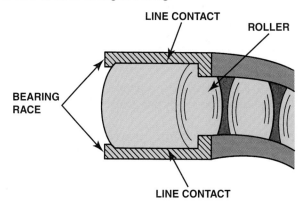

FIGURE 9–4 Roller bearing line contact.

ANTIFRICTION BEARINGS

PURPOSE AND FUNCTION Bearings allow the wheels of a vehicle to rotate and still support the weight of the entire vehicle. **Antifriction bearings** use rolling parts inside the bearing to reduce friction. Four styles of rolling contact bearings include ball, roller, needle, and tapered roller bearings, as shown in ● **FIGURE 9–1**. All four styles convert sliding friction into rolling motion. All of the weight of a vehicle or load on the bearing is transferred through the rolling part. In a ball bearing, the entire load is concentrated into small spots where the ball contacts the *inner and outer race (rings).* ● **SEE FIGURE 9–2**.

BALL BEARINGS **Ball bearings** use hardened steel balls between the inner and outer race to reduce friction. While ball bearings cannot support the same weight as roller bearings, there is less friction in ball bearings and they generally operate at higher speeds. Ball bearings can control thrust movement of

an axle shaft because the balls ride in grooves on the inner and outer races. The groove walls resist lateral movement of the wheel on the spindle. The most frequent use of ball bearings is at the rear wheels of a rear-wheel-drive vehicle with a solid rear axle. These bearings are installed into the axle housing and are often press fitted to the axle shaft. Many front-wheel-drive vehicles use sealed double-row ball bearings as a complete sealed unit and are nonserviceable except as an assembly. ● **SEE FIGURE 9–3**.

ROLLER BEARINGS **Roller bearings** use rollers between the inner and outer race to reduce friction. A roller bearing having a greater (longer) contact area can support heavier loads than a ball bearing. ● **SEE FIGURE 9–4**.

A needle bearing is a type of roller bearing that uses smaller rollers called **needle rollers.** The clearance between the diameter

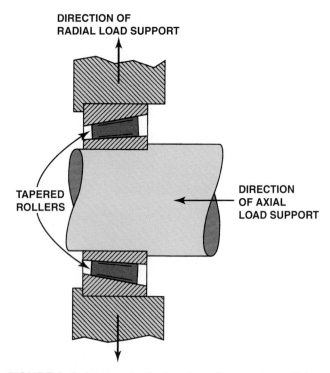

DIRECTION OF
RADIAL LOAD SUPPORT

TAPERED
ROLLERS

DIRECTION
OF AXIAL
LOAD SUPPORT

FIGURE 9–5 A tapered roller bearing will support a radial load and an axial load in only one direction.

FIGURE 9–6 Many tapered roller bearings use a plastic cage to retain the rollers.

ANTIFRICTION BEARINGS (CONTINUED)

of the straight roller is manufactured into the bearing to provide the proper *radial clearance* and is *not adjustable*.

TAPERED ROLLER BEARINGS The most commonly used automotive wheel bearing is the **tapered roller bearing.** Not only is the bearing itself tapered, but the rollers are also tapered. By design, this type of bearing can withstand **radial loads** (up and down) as well as **axial loads** (thrust) in one direction. ● **SEE FIGURE 9–5.**

Many non-drive-wheel bearings use tapered roller bearings. The taper allows more weight to be handled by the friction-reducing bearings because the weight is directed over the entire length of each roller rather than concentrated on a small spot, as with ball bearings. The rollers are held in place by a **cage** between the inner race (also called the **inner ring** or **cone**) and the outer race (also called the **outer ring** or **cup**). Tapered roller bearings must be loose in the cage to allow for heat expansion. Tapered roller bearings should always be adjusted for a certain amount of free play to allow for heat expansion. On non-drive-axle vehicle wheels, the cup is tightly fitted to the wheel hub and the cone is loosely fitted to the wheel spindle. New bearings come packaged with the rollers, cage, and inner race assembled

together with the outer race wrapped with moisture-resistant paper. ● **SEE FIGURE 9–6.**

INNER AND OUTER WHEEL BEARINGS Many rear-wheel-drive vehicles use an inner and an outer wheel bearing on the front wheels. The inner wheel bearing is always the larger bearing because it is designed to carry most of the vehicle weight and transmit the weight to the suspension through to the spindle. Between the inner wheel bearing and the spindle, there is a grease seal, which prevents grease from getting onto the braking surface and prevents dirt and moisture from entering the bearing. ● **SEE FIGURE 9–7.**

STANDARD BEARING SIZES Bearings use standard dimensions for inside diameter, width, and outside diameter. The standardization of bearing sizes helps interchangeability. The dimensions that are standardized include bearing bore size (inside diameter), bearing series (light to heavy usage), and external dimensions. When replacing a wheel bearing, note the original bearing brand name and number. Replacement bearing catalogs usually have cross-over charts from one brand to another. The bearing number is usually the same because of the

FIGURE 9–7 Non-drive-wheel hub with inner and outer tapered roller bearings. By angling the inner and outer in opposite directions, axial (thrust) loads are supported in both directions.

interchangeability and standardization within the wheel bearing industry.

SEALED FRONT-WHEEL-DRIVE BEARINGS

Most front-wheel-drive (FWD) vehicles use a sealed nonadjustable front wheel bearing. This type of bearing can include either two preloaded tapered roller bearings or a double-row ball bearing. This type of sealed bearing is also used on the rear of many front-wheel-drive vehicles and are usually called *hub assemblies*.

Double-row ball bearings are often used because of their reduced friction and greater seize resistance. ● SEE FIGURES 9–8 AND 9–9.

BALL-BEARING ASSEMBLY

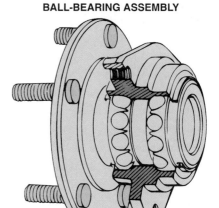

TAPERED ROLLER BEARING ASSEMBLY

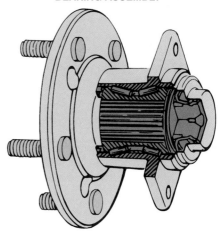

FIGURE 9–8 Sealed bearing and hub assemblies are used on the front and rear wheels of many vehicles.

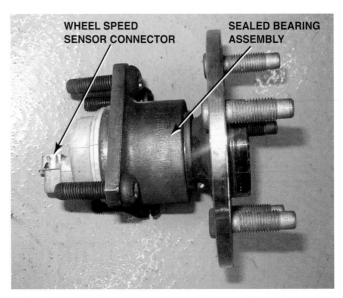

FIGURE 9–9 Sealed bearing and hub assemblies are serviced as a complete unit as shown. This assembly includes the wheel speed sensor.

BEARING GREASES

DEFINITION OF GREASE Vehicle manufacturers specify the type and consistency of grease for each application. The technician should know what these specifications mean. **Grease** is oil with a thickening agent to allow it to be installed in places where a liquid lubricant would not stay. Greases are named for their thickening agent, such as aluminum, barium, calcium, lithium, or sodium.

GREASE ADDITIVES Commonly used additives in grease include the following:

- Antioxidants
- Antiwear agents
- Rust inhibitors
- Extreme pressure (EP) additives such as sulfurized fatty oil or chlorine

Grease also contains a dye to not only provide product identification but also to give the grease a consistent color.

The grease contains a solid such as graphite or molybdenum disulfide (moly), which acts as an antiseize additive.

FREQUENTLY ASKED QUESTION

What Do Different Grease Colors Mean?

Nothing. According to grease manufacturers, grease is colored for identification, marketing, and for consistency of color reasons.

- **Identification.** The color is often used to distinguish one type of grease from another within the same company. The blue grease from one company may be totally different from the blue grease produced or marketed by another company.
- **Marketing.** According to grease manufacturers, customers tend to be attracted to a particular color of grease and associate that color with quality.
- **Consistency of color.** All greases are produced in batches, and the color of the finished product often varies in color from one batch to another. By adding color to the grease, the color can be made consistent.

Always use the grease recommended for the service being performed.

NLGI CLASSIFICATION The **National Lubricating Grease Institute (NLGI)** uses the penetration test as a guide to assign the grease a number. Low numbers are very fluid and higher numbers are more firm or hard. Number 2 grease is the most commonly used. See the chart.

NATIONAL LUBRICATING GREASE INSTITUTE (NLGI) NUMBERS	
NLGI NUMBER	**RELATIVE CONSISTENCY**
000	Very fluid
00	Fluid
0	Semi-fluid
1	Very soft
2	Soft (typically used for wheel bearings)
3	Semi-firm
4	Firm
5	Very firm
6	Hard

Grease is also classified according to quality. Wheel bearing classifications include the following:

- GA—mild duty
- GB—moderate duty
- GC—severe duty, high temperature (frequent stop-and-go service)

GC indicates the highest quality. Chassis grease, such as is used to lubricate steering and suspension components, includes the following classifications:

- LA—mild duty (frequent relubrication)
- LB—high loads (infrequent relubrication)

LB indicates the highest quality. Most multipurpose greases are labeled with both wheel bearing and chassis grease classifications such as **GC-LB.**

More rolling bearings are destroyed by overlubrication than by underlubrication because the heat generated in the bearings cannot be transferred easily to the air through the excessive grease. Bearings should never be filled beyond one-third to one-half of their grease capacity by volume.

FIGURE 9–10 Typical lip seal with a garter spring.

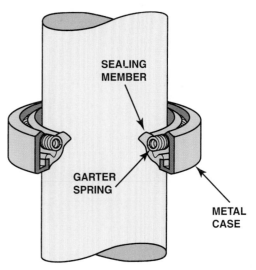

FIGURE 9–11 A garter spring helps hold the sharp lip edge of the seal tight against the shaft.

SAFETY TIP

Smoking Can Kill You

Some greases contain polymers such as Teflon® that turn to a deadly gas when burned. Always wash your hands thoroughly after handling grease that contains these ingredients before smoking. If some of the grease is on the cigarette paper and is burned, these polymers turn into nitrofluoric acid—a deadly toxin.

SEALS

PURPOSE AND FUNCTION   Seals are used in all vehicles to keep lubricant, such as grease, from leaking out and to prevent dirt, dust, or water from getting into the bearing or lubricant.

TYPES OF SEALS   Two general applications of seals are static and dynamic.

- **Static seals** are used between two surfaces that do not move.
- **Dynamic seals** are used to seal between two surfaces that move.

Wheel bearing seals are dynamic-type seals that must seal between rotating axle hubs and the stationary spindles or axle housing. Most dynamic seals use a synthetic rubber lip seal encased in metal. The lip is often held in contact with the moving part with the aid of a **garter spring,** as seen in ● **FIGURE 9–10.** The sealing lip should be installed toward the grease or fluid being contained. ● **SEE FIGURE 9–11.**

BEARING DIAGNOSIS

SYMPTOMS OF A DEFECTIVE BEARING   Wheel bearings control the positioning and reduce the rolling resistance of vehicle wheels. Whenever a bearing fails, the wheel may not be kept in position and noise is usually heard. Symptoms of defective wheel bearings include the following:

1. A hum, rumbling, or growling noise that increases with vehicle speed
2. Roughness felt in the steering wheel that changes with the vehicle speed or cornering
3. Looseness or excessive play in the steering wheel especially while driving over rough road surfaces
4. A loud grinding noise in severe cases, indicating a defective front wheel bearing
5. Pulling during braking

DETERMINING BEARING NOISE FROM TIRE NOISE
A defective wheel bearing is often difficult to diagnose because the noise is similar to a noisy winter tire or a severely cupped tire. Customers often request that tires be replaced as a result of the noise when the real problem is a bad wheel bearing. To help determine if the noise is caused by a wheel bearing or a tire, try these tests:

Test #1   Drive the vehicle over a variety of road surfaces. If the noise changes with a change in road surface, then the

FIGURE 9–12 Removing the grease cap with grease cap pliers.

WHEEL BEARING SERVICE

The steps in a non-drive-wheel bearing inspection include the following:

1. Hoist the vehicle safely.

2. Remove the wheel.

3. Remove the brake caliper assembly and support it with a coat hanger or other suitable hook to avoid allowing the caliper to hang by the brake hose.

4. Remove the grease cap (dust cap). ● **SEE FIGURE 9–12**.

5. Remove the old cotter key and discard.

   NOTE: The term *cotter*, **as in cotter key or cotter pin, is derived from the Old English verb meaning "to close or fasten."**

6. Remove the spindle nut (castle nut).

7. Remove the washer and the outer wheel bearing. ● **SEE FIGURE 9–13**. Remove the bearing hub from the spindle. The inner bearing will remain in the hub and may be removed (simply lifted out) after the grease seal is pried out.

8. Most vehicle and bearing manufacturers recommend cleaning the bearing thoroughly in solvent or acetone. ● **SEE FIGURE 9–14**. If there is no acetone, clean the solvent off the bearings with denatured alcohol or brake cleaner to make certain that the thin solvent layer is

Easy Wheel Bearing Looseness Test

Looseness in a front wheel bearing can allow the rotor to move whenever the front wheel hits a bump, forcing the caliper piston in, which causes the brake pedal to kick back and creates the feeling that the brakes are locking up. Loose wheel bearings are easily diagnosed by removing the cover of the master cylinder reservoir and watching the brake fluid as the front wheels are turned left and right with the steering wheel. If the brake fluid moves while the front wheels are being turned, caliper piston(s) are moving in and out, caused by loose wheel bearing(s). If everything is OK, the brake fluid should not move. Loose wheel bearings can also cause the brake pedal to sink due to movement of the rotor, causing the caliper piston to move. This sinking brake pedal is usually caused by a defective master cylinder. Before replacing a master cylinder, check the wheel bearings.

BEARING DIAGNOSIS (CONTINUED)

noise is caused by a tire(s). If the noise remains the same, then the cause is a defective wheel bearing.

Test #2   Try temporarily overinflating the tires. If the noise changes, then the tires are the cause. If the noise is the same, then defective wheel bearings are the cause.

TESTING A WHEEL BEARING   With the vehicle off the ground, rotate the wheel by hand, listening and feeling carefully for bearing roughness. Grasp the wheel at the top and bottom and wiggle it back and forth, checking for bearing looseness.

FIGURE 9–13 Using a seal puller to remove the grease seal.

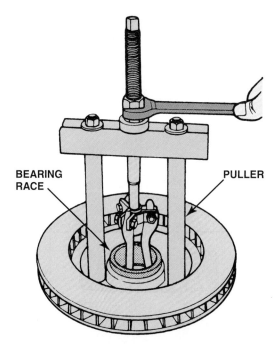

FIGURE 9–15 A wheel bearing race puller.

FIGURE 9–14 Cleaning a wheel bearing with a parts brush and solvent.

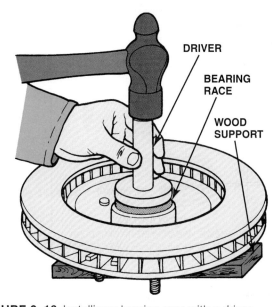

FIGURE 9–16 Installing a bearing race with a driver.

completely washed off and dry. *All solvent must be removed or allowed to dry from the bearing because the new grease will not stick to a layer of solvent.*

9. Carefully inspect the bearings and the races for the following:

   a. The outer race for lines, scratches, or pits.

   b. The cage should be round. If the round cage has straight sections, this is an indication of an overtightened adjustment or a dropped cage. ● **SEE CHART 9–1.**

If either of the above is observed, then the bearing, including the outer race, must be replaced. Failure to replace the outer race (which is included when purchasing a bearing) could lead to rapid failure of the new bearing. ● **SEE FIGURES 9–15 AND 9–16.** Pack the cleaned or new bearing thoroughly with clean, new, approved wheel bearing grease. Always clean out all of the old grease before applying the recommended type of new grease. *Because of compatibility problems, it is not recommended that*

BENT CAGE

CAGE DAMAGE CAUSED BY IMPROPER HANDLING OR TOOL USE

GALLING

METAL SMEARS OR ROLLER ENDS CAUSED BY OVERHEATING, OVERLOADING, OR INADEQUATE LUBRICATION

STEP WEAR

NOTCHED WEAR PATTERN ON ROLLER ENDS CAUSED BY ABRASIVES IN THE LUBRICANT

ETCHING AND CORROSION

EATEN AWAY BEARING SURFACE WITH GRAY OR GRAY-BLACK COLOR CAUSED BY MOISTURE CONTAMINATION OF THE LUBRICANT

PITTING AND BRUISING

PITS, DEPRESSIONS, AND GROOVES IN THE BEARING SURFACES CAUSED BY PARTICULATE CONTAMINATION OF THE LUBRICANT

SPALLING

FLAKING AWAY OF THE BEARING SURFACE METAL CAUSED BY FATIGUE

MISALIGNMENT

SKEWED WEAR PATTERN CAUSED BY BENT SPINDLE OR IMPROPER BEARING INSTALLATION

HEAT DISCOLORATION

FAINT YELLOW TO DARK BLUE DISCOLORATION FROM OVERHEATING CAUSED BY OVERLOADING OR INADEQUATE LUBRICATION

BRINELLING

INDENTATIONS IN THE RACES CAUSED BY IMPACT LOADS OR VIBRATION WHEN THE BEARING IS NOT TURNING

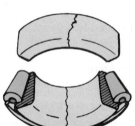

CRACKED RACE

CRACKING OF THE RACE CAUSED BY EXCESSIVE PRESS FIT, IMPROPER INSTALLATION OR DAMAGED BEARING SEATS

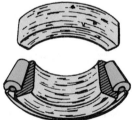

SMEARING

SMEARED METAL FROM SLIPPAGE CAUSED BY POOR FIT, POOR LUBRICATION, OVERLOADING, OVERHEATING, OR HANDLING DAMAGE

FRETTAGE

ETCHING OR CORROSION CAUSED BY SMALL RELATIVE MOVEMENTS BETWEEN PARTS WITH NO LUBRICATION

CHART 9–1

Wheel bearing inspection chart. Replace the bearing if it has any of the faults shown.

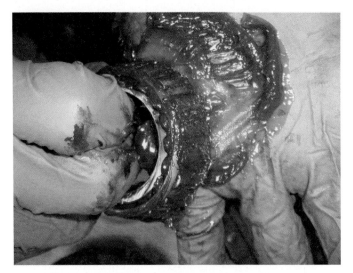

FIGURE 9–17 Notice the new blue grease has been forced through the bearing.

FIGURE 9–18 A commonly used hand-operated bearing packer.

WHEEL BEARING SERVICE (CONTINUED)

greases be mixed. There are several different ways to pack wheel bearings including:

- **By hand.** Place some grease in the palm of the hand and then force the grease through the bearing until grease can be seen out the other side. ● **SEE FIGURE 9–17**.

- **By hand-operated bearing packer.** A hand-operated bearing packer is faster to use and produces excellent results. ● **SEE FIGURE 9–18**.

- **Grease gun-type bearing packer.** This type of bearing packer uses a grease gun to fill the bearing with grease. The grease gun can be hand-operated or powered by electric or air. ● **SEE FIGURE 9–19**.

10. Place a thin layer of grease on the outer race.

11. Apply a thin layer of grease to the spindle, being sure to cover the outer bearing seat, inner bearing seat, and shoulder at the grease seal seat.

12. Install a new **grease seal** (also called a *grease retainer*) flush with the hub using a seal driver.

13. Place approximately 3 tablespoons of grease into the grease cavity of the wheel hub. Excessive grease could cause the inner grease seal to fail, with the possibility of grease getting on the brakes. Place the rotor with the inner bearing and seal in place over the spindle until the grease seal rests on the grease seal shoulder.

14. Install the outer bearing and the bearing washer.

15. Install the spindle nut and, while rotating the tire assembly, tighten to about 12 to 30 lb-ft with a wrench to "seat" the

FIGURE 9–19 The wheel bearing is placed between two nylon cones and then a grease gun is used to inject grease into the center of the bearing.

bearing correctly in the race (cup) and on the spindle. ● **SEE FIGURE 9–20**.

16. While still rotating the tire assembly, loosen the nut approximately one-half turn and then *hand tighten only* (about 5 lb-in.).

NOTE: If the wheel bearing is properly adjusted, the wheel will still have about 0.001 to 0.005 in. (0.03 to 0.13 mm) end play. This looseness is necessary to allow the tapered roller bearing to expand when hot and not bind or cause the wheel to lock up.

17. Install a new cotter key. (An old cotter key could break a part off where it was bent and lodge in the bearing, causing major damage.)

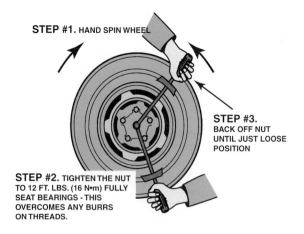

STEP #1. HAND SPIN WHEEL

STEP #3.
BACK OFF NUT
UNTIL JUST LOOSE
POSITION

STEP #2. TIGHTEN THE NUT
TO 12 FT. LBS. (16 N•m) FULLY
SEAT BEARINGS - THIS
OVERCOMES ANY BURRS
ON THREADS.

STEP #5. LOOSEN NUT UNTIL EITHER
HOLE IN THE SPINDLE LINES UP WITH
A SLOT IN THE NUT – THEN INSERT
COTTER PIN.

STEP #4.
HAND "SNUG-UP"
THE NUT

NOTICE: BEND ENDS OF COTTER
PIN AGAINST NUT, CUT OFF EXTRA
LENGTH TO PREVENT
INTERFERENCE WITH DUST CAP.

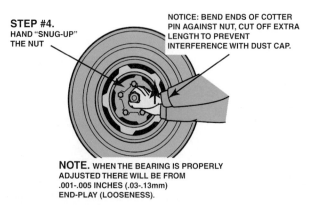

NOTE. WHEN THE BEARING IS PROPERLY
ADJUSTED THERE WILL BE FROM
.001-.005 INCHES (.03-.13mm)
END-PLAY (LOOSENESS).

FIGURE 9–20 The wheel bearing adjustment procedure as specified for rear-wheel-drive vehicles. Always check service information for the exact specified procedure for the vehicle being serviced.

WHEEL BEARING SERVICE (CONTINUED)

NOTE: Most vehicles use a cotter key that is 1/8 in. in diameter by 1 1/2 in. long.

18. If the cotter key does not line up with the hole in the spindle, loosen slightly (no more than 1/16 in. of a turn) until the hole lines up. Never tighten more than hand tight.

19. Bend the cotter key ends up and around the nut, not over the end of the spindle where the end of the cotter key could rub on the grease cap, causing noise. ● **SEE FIGURE 9–21**.

20. Install the grease cap (dust cap) with a rubber mallet or soft-faced hammer to help prevent denting or distorting the grease cap. Install the wheel cover or hub cap.

21. Clean grease off the disc brake rotors or drums after servicing the wheel bearings. Use a brake cleaner and a shop cloth. Even a slight amount of grease on the friction surfaces of the brakes can harm the friction lining and/or cause brake noise.

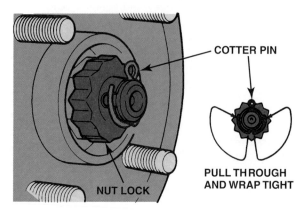

COTTER PIN

PULL THROUGH
AND WRAP TIGHT

NUT LOCK

FIGURE 9–21 A properly secured wheel bearing adjust nut.

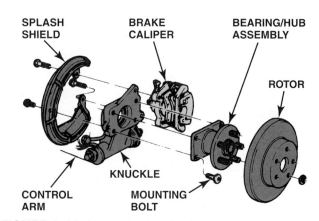

SPLASH
SHIELD

BRAKE
CALIPER

BEARING/HUB
ASSEMBLY

ROTOR

KNUCKLE

CONTROL
ARM

MOUNTING
BOLT

FIGURE 9–22 A rear wheel sealed bearing hub assembly.

SEALED BEARING REPLACEMENT

Diagnosing a defective front bearing on a front-wheel-drive vehicle is sometimes confusing. A defective wheel bearing is usually noisy while driving straight, and the noise increases with vehicle speed (wheel speed). A drive axle shaft U-joint (CV joint) can also be the cause of noise on a front-wheel-drive vehicle, but usually makes *more noise* while turning and accelerating. Most front-wheel-drive vehicles use a sealed bearing assembly that is bolted to the steering knuckle and supports the drive axle or the rear, as shown in ● **FIGURE 9–22**.

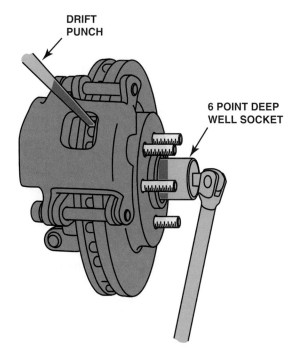

FIGURE 9–23 Removing the drive axle shaft hub nut. This nut is usually very tight and the drift (tapered) punch wedged into the cooling fins of the brake rotor keeps the hub from revolving when the nut is loosened. Never use an impact to remove or install a drive axle shaft hub nut because the hammering action can damage the bearing.

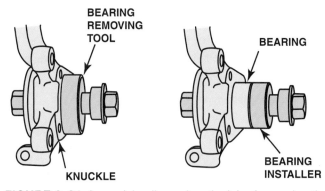

FIGURE 9–24 A special puller makes the job of removing the hub bearing from the knuckle easy without damaging any component.

Many front-wheel-drive vehicles use a bearing that must be pressed off the steering knuckle. Special aftermarket tools are also available to remove many of the bearings without removing the knuckle from the vehicle. Check the service information for the exact procedures to follow for the vehicle being serviced. ● SEE FIGURES 9–23 AND 9–24.

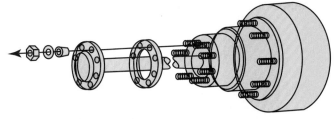

FIGURE 9–25 A typical full-floating rear axle assembly.

REAR DRIVE AXLE CLASSIFICATIONS

There are three rear drive axle classifications:

- Full-floating
- Three-quarter-floating
- Semi-floating

These classifications indicate whether the axle shafts or the axle housing supports the wheel. The category of a rear drive axle is determined by how the wheel and wheel bearing mount to the axle or housing.

FULL-FLOATING AXLE On a full-floating axle, the bearings are mounted and retained in the hub of the brake drum or rotor. The hub and bearing mount onto the axle housing, and are held in place by a bearing retainer or adjustment nuts and safety locks. The flanged end of the drive axle is attached to the hub by bolts or nuts. The inner end of the axle splines into the differential side gears. The wheel mounts onto the hub, and lug bolts or nuts retain it. In this design, the axle shafts "float" in the axle housing and drive the wheels without supporting their weight. Because the axle shafts do not retain the wheel, the axle shafts can usually be removed from the vehicle while it is standing on the wheels. Many three-quarter-ton pickups, all heavy-duty truck tractors, and trailers use full-floating axles. ● SEE FIGURE 9–25.

THREE-QUARTER-FLOATING AXLE The bearings in a three-quarter-floating axle are mounted and retained in the brake drum or rotor hub, which mounts onto the axle housing. The outer extension of the hub fits onto the end of the axle, which is usually splined and tapered, and a nut and cotter pin secure the hub to the axle. The axle shaft splines to the side gears inside the differential. The wheels are mounted on the hub and retained by lug bolts or nuts. As in the full-floating axle, the axle housing and bearings in the hub support the weight in a three-quarter-floating axle. Because of the construction of a

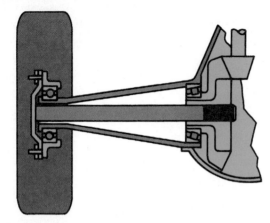

THREE-QUARTER-FLOATING

FIGURE 9–26 A three-quarter-floating rear axle.

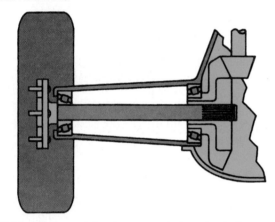

SEMI-FLOATING

FIGURE 9–27 A semi-floating rear axle housing is the most commonly used in light rear-wheel-drive vehicles.

REAR DRIVE AXLE CLASSIFICATIONS (CONTINUED)

three-quarter-floating axle, the wheel must be removed before removing the axle shaft from the vehicle. ● **SEE FIGURE 9–26.**

SEMI-FLOATING AXLE The wheel bearings in a semi-floating axle either press onto the axle shaft or are installed in the outer end of the axle housing. A retainer plate at the outer end of the axle shaft or a C-clip inside the differential at the other end keeps the axle shaft in the housing. The brake drum or rotor fits onto the end of the axle, and lug bolts or nuts fasten the wheel to the drum or rotor and to the axle. These axles are called "semi-floating" because only the inboard ends of the axle shaft "float" in the housing. The outboard end of the shaft retains the wheel and transmits the weight of the wheel to the housing. Most solid-axle rear-wheel-drive cars and light trucks use a semi-floating type of axle. ● **SEE FIGURE 9–27.**

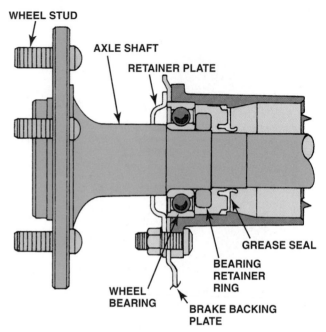

FIGURE 9–28 A retainer plate-type rear axle bearing. Access to the fasteners is through a hole in the axle flange.

REAR AXLE BEARING AND SEAL REPLACEMENT

The rear bearings used on rear-wheel-drive vehicles are constructed and serviced differently from other types of wheel bearings. Rear axle bearings are either sealed or lubricated by the rear-end lubricant. The rear axle must be removed from the vehicle to replace the rear axle bearing. There are two basic types of axle retaining methods:

- **Retainer plate-type**
- **C-lock**

RETAINER PLATE-TYPE REAR AXLES The retainer plate-type rear axle uses four fasteners that retain the axle in the axle housing. To remove the axle shaft and the rear axle bearing and seal, the retainer bolts or nuts must be removed.

NOTE: If the axle flange has an access hole, then a retainer plate-type axle is used.

The hole or holes in the wheel flange permit a socket wrench access to the fasteners. After the fasteners have been removed, the axle shaft must be removed from the rear axle housing. With the retainer plate-type rear axle, the bearing and the retaining ring are press fit onto the axle and the bearing cup (outer race) is also tightly fitted into the axle housing tube. ● **SEE FIGURE 9–28.** ● **SEE FIGURE 9–29** for one way to remove the axle shaft using a rear axle puller.

FIGURE 9–29 A slide hammer-type axle puller can also be used.

 TECH TIP

The Brake Drum Slide Hammer Trick

To remove the axle from a vehicle equipped with a retainer plate-type rear axle, simply use the brake drum as a slide hammer to remove the axle from the axle housing. ● **SEE FIGURE 9–30**. If the brake drum does not provide enough force, a slide hammer can also be used to remove the axle shaft.

C-LOCK-TYPE AXLES Vehicles that use C-locks (clips) use a straight roller bearing supporting a semi-floating axle shaft inside the axle housing. The straight rollers do not have an inner race. The rollers ride on the axle itself. If a bearing fails, both the axle and the bearing usually need to be replaced. The outer bearing race holding the rollers is pressed into the rear axle housing. The axle bearing is usually lubricated by the rear-end lubricant and a grease seal is located on the outside of the bearing.

NOTE: Some replacement bearings are available that are designed to ride on a fresh, unworn section of the old axle. These bearings allow the use of the original axle, saving the cost of a replacement axle.

The C-lock-type rear axle retaining method requires that the differential cover plate be removed. After removal of the cover, the differential pinion shaft has to be removed before the C-lock that retains the axle can be removed. ● **SEE FIGURES 9–31 AND 9–32**.

FIGURE 9–30 To remove the axle from this vehicle equipped with a retainer-plate rear axle, the brake drum was placed back onto the axle studs backward so that the drum itself can be used as a slide hammer to pull the axle out of the axle housing. A couple of pulls and the rear axle is pulled out of the axle housing.

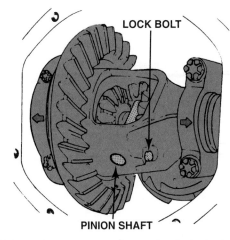

FIGURE 9–31 To remove the C-lock (clip), the lock bolt has to be moved before the pinion shaft.

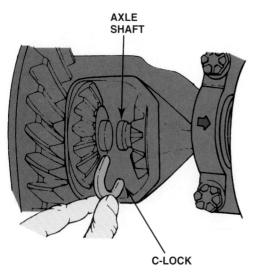

FIGURE 9–32 The axle must be pushed inward slightly to allow the C-lock to be removed. After the C-lock has been removed, the axle can be easily pulled out of the axle housing.

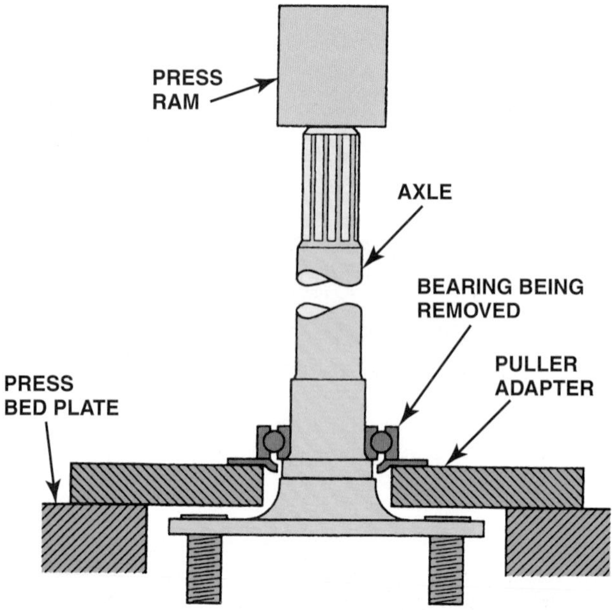

FIGURE 9–33 Using a hydraulic press to press an axle bearing from the axle. When pressing a new bearing back onto the axle, pressure should only be on the inner bearing race to prevent damaging the bearing.

REAR AXLE BEARING AND SEAL REPLACEMENT (CONTINUED)

NOTE: When removing the differential cover, rear axle lubricant will flow from between the housing and the cover. Be sure to dispose of the old rear axle lubricant in the environmentally approved way, and refill with the proper type and viscosity (thickness) of rear-end lubricant. Check the vehicle specifications for the recommended grade.

Once the C-lock has been removed, the axle simply is pulled out of the axle tube. Axle bearings with inner races are pressed onto the axle shaft and must be pressed off using a hydraulic press. A bearing retaining collar should be chiseled or drilled into to expand the collar, allowing it to be removed. ● SEE FIGURE 9–33.

Always follow the manufacturer's recommended bearing removal and replacement procedures. Always replace the rear axle seal whenever replacing a rear axle bearing. ● SEE FIGURE 9–34 for an example of seal removal.

Always check the differential vent to make sure it is clear. A clogged vent can cause excessive pressure to build up inside the differential and cause the rear axle seals to leak. If rear-end lubricant gets on the brake linings, the brakes will not have the proper friction and the linings themselves are ruined and must be replaced.

FIGURE 9–34 Removing an axle seal using the axle shaft as the tool.

FIGURE 9–35 This is a normally worn bearing. If it does not have too much play, it can be reused. *(Courtesy SKF USA Inc.)*

(a)

(b)

FIGURE 9–36 (a) When corrosion etches into the surface of a roller or race, the bearing should be discarded. (b) If light corrosion stains can be removed with an oil-soaked cloth, the bearing can be reused. *(Courtesy SKF USA Inc.)*

(a)

(b)

FIGURE 9–37 (a) When just the end of a roller is scored, it is because of excessive preload. Discard the bearing. (b) This is a more advanced case of pitting. Under load, it will rapidly lead to spalling. *(Courtesy SKF USA Inc.)*

BEARING FAILURE ANALYSIS

Whenever a bearing is replaced, the old bearing must be inspected and the cause of the failure eliminated. ● **SEE FIGURES 9–35 THROUGH 9–41** for examples of normal and abnormal bearing wear.

A wheel bearing may also fail for reasons that include the following.

METAL FATIGUE Long vehicle usage, even under normal driving conditions, causes metal to fatigue. Cracks often appear, and eventually these cracks expand downward into the metal from the surface. The metal between the cracks can break out into small chips, slabs, or scales of metal. This process of breaking up is called **spalling.** ● **SEE FIGURE 9–42.**

ELECTRICAL ARCING Bearings can be damaged caused by poor ground wires or improper welding on the vehicle.

SHOCK LOADING Dents can be formed in the race of a bearing, which eventually leads to bearing failure. ● **SEE FIGURE 9–43.**

(a)

(b)

FIGURE 9-38 (a) Always check for faint grooves in the race. This bearing should not be reused. (b) Grooves like this are often matched by grooves in the race (above). Discard the bearing. *(Courtesy SKF USA Inc.)*

(a)

(b)

FIGURE 9-39 (a) Regular patterns of etching in the race are from corrosion. This bearing should be replaced. (b) Light pitting comes from contaminants being pressed into the race. Discard the bearing. *(Courtesy SKF USA Inc.)*

(a)

(b)

FIGURE 9-40 (a) This bearing is worn unevenly. Notice the stripes. It should not be reused. (b) Any damage that causes low spots in the metal renders the bearing useless. *(Courtesy SKF USA Inc.)*

(a)

(b)

FIGURE 9–41 (a) In this more advanced case of pitting, you can see how the race has been damaged. (b) Discoloration is a result of overheating. Even a lightly burned bearing should be replaced. *(Courtesy SKF USA Inc.)*

(a)

(b)

FIGURE 9–42 (a) Pitting eventually leads to spalling, a condition where the metal falls away in large chunks. (b) In this spalled roller, the metal has actually begun to flake away from the surface. *(Courtesy SKF USA Inc.)*

FIGURE 9–43 These dents resulted from the rollers "hammering" against the race, a condition called brinelling. *(Courtesy SKF USA Inc.)*

TECH TIP

"Bearing Overload"

It is not uncommon for vehicles to be overloaded. This is particularly common with pickup trucks and vans. Whenever there is a heavy load, the axle bearings must support the entire weight of the vehicle, including its cargo. If a bump is hit while driving with a heavy load, the balls of a ball bearing or the rollers of a roller bearing can make an indent in the race of the bearing. This dent or imprint is called **brinelling,** named after Johann A. Brinell, a Swedish engineer who developed a process of testing for surface hardness by pressing a hard ball with a standard force into a sample material to be tested.

Once this imprint is made, the bearing will make noise whenever the roller or ball rolls over the indent. Continued use causes wear to occur on all of the balls or rollers and eventual failure. While this may take months to fail, the *cause* of the bearing failure is often overloading of the vehicle. Avoid shock loads and overloading for safety and for longer vehicle life.

1 After safely hoisting the vehicle, remove the rear wheels and brake drums.

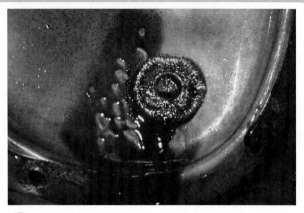

2 Remove the rear differential cover and inspect the magnet for metal particles that would indicate serious wear or damage.

3 Remove the retaining bolt and allow the pinion shaft to be removed.

4 Push the axle inward toward the center of the vehicle to free the axle clip.

5 After removing the clip, the axle can then be removed. Note that the backing plate is wet, indicating that the axle seal has been leaking.

6 A seal removal tool being used to remove the axle seal.

7 If a retainer-type axle is being serviced, the bearing and seal need to be pressed off of the axle.

8 After installing a new bearing and seal, insert the axle and install the clip, then the pinion shaft.

9 Clean the differential housing before installing the cover gasket and cover. Refill the differential with the specified fluid.

1. Wheel bearings support the entire weight of a vehicle and are used to reduce rolling friction. Ball and straight roller-type bearings are nonadjustable while tapered roller-type bearings must be adjusted for proper clearance.

2. Most front-wheel-drive vehicles use sealed bearings, either two preloaded tapered roller bearings or double-row ball bearings.

3. Most wheel bearings are standardized sizes.

4. A defective bearing can be caused by metal fatigue that leads to spalling, shock loads that cause brinelling, or damage from electrical arcing due to poor body ground wires or improper electrical welding on the vehicle.

5. Bearing grease is an oil with a thickener. The higher the NLGI number of the grease, the thicker or harder the grease consistency.

6. Tapered wheel bearings must be adjusted by hand tightening the spindle nut after properly seating the bearings. A new cotter key must always be used.

7. Defective wheel bearings usually make more noise while turning because more weight is applied to the bearing as the vehicle turns.

8. All bearings must be serviced, replaced, and/or adjusted using the vehicle manufacturer's recommended procedures as stated in the service manual.

REVIEW QUESTIONS

1. List three common types of automotive antifriction bearings.

2. Explain the adjustment procedure for a typical tapered roller wheel bearing.

3. List four symptoms of a defective wheel bearing.

4. Describe how the rear axle is removed from a C-lock-type axle.

CHAPTER QUIZ

1. Which type of automotive bearing can withstand radial and thrust loads, yet must be adjusted for proper clearance?
   a. Roller bearing
   b. Tapered roller bearing
   c. Ball bearings
   d. Needle roller bearing

2. Most sealed bearings used on the front wheels of front-wheel-drive vehicles are usually which type?
   a. Roller bearing
   b. Single tapered roller bearing
   c. Double-row ball bearing
   d. Needle roller bearing

3. On a bearing that has been shock loaded, the race (cup) of the bearing can be dented. This type of bearing failure is called _____.
   a. Spalling
   b. Arcing
   c. Brinelling
   d. Fluting

4. The bearing grease most often specified is rated NLGI _____.
   a. #00
   b. #0
   c. #1
   d. #2

5. A non-drive-wheel bearing adjustment procedure includes a final spindle nut tightening torque of _____.
   a. Finger tight
   b. 5 lb-in.
   c. 12 to 30 lb-ft
   d. 12 to 15 lb-ft plus 1/16 in. turn

6. After a non-drive-wheel bearing has been properly adjusted, the wheel should have how much end play?
   a. Zero
   b. 0.001 to 0.005 in.
   c. 0.10 to 0.30 in.
   d. 1/16 to 3/32 in.

7. The differential cover must be removed before removing the rear axle on which type of axle?
   a. Retainer plate
   b. C-lock
   c. Press fit
   d. Welded tube

8. What part(s) should be replaced when servicing a wheel bearing on a non-drive wheel?
   a. The bearing cup
   b. The grease seal
   c. The cotter key
   d. Both the grease seal and the cotter key

9. Technician A says that a defective wheel or axle bearing often makes a growling or rumbling noise. Technician B says that a defective wheel or axle bearing often makes a noise similar to a tire with an aggressive mud or snow design. Which technician is correct?
   a. Technician A only
   b. Technician B only
   c. Both Technicians A and B
   d. Neither Technician A nor B

10. Two technicians are discussing differentials. Technician A says all differentials are vented. Technician B says that a clogged vent can cause the rear axle seal to leak. Which technician is correct?
    a. Technician A only
    b. Technician B only
    c. Both Technicians A and B
    d. Neither Technician A nor B

DRUM BRAKES

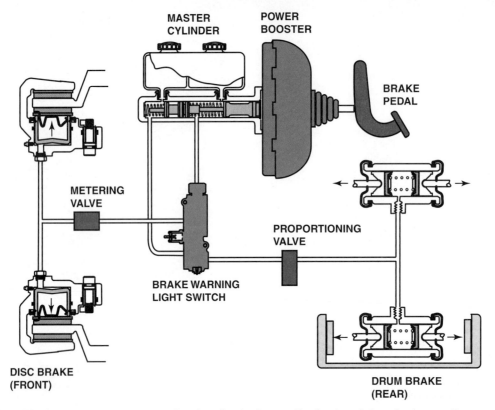

MASTER CYLINDER

POWER BOOSTER

BRAKE PEDAL

METERING VALVE

PROPORTIONING VALVE

BRAKE WARNING LIGHT SWITCH

DISC BRAKE (FRONT)

DRUM BRAKE (REAR)

FIGURE 10–1 Typical brake system components showing disc brakes on the front and drum brakes on the rear.

DRUM BRAKE ADVANTAGES

Drum brakes were the first type of brakes used on motor vehicles. Even today, over 100 years after the first "horseless carriages," drum brakes are still used on the rear of most vehicles, as shown in ● **FIGURE 10–1**. The drum brake has been more widely used than any other automotive brake design. ● **SEE FIGURE 10–2**.

Although the disc brake has proven its superiority in extreme braking conditions, and has replaced the drum brake on the front axle of vehicles, the drum brake continues to have a number of advantages that contribute to its widespread use on the rear axle of most automobiles.

SELF-ENERGIZING AND SERVO ACTION The primary advantage of drum brakes is that they can apply more stopping power for a given amount of force applied to the brake pedal than can disc brakes. This is possible because the drum brake design offers a self-energizing action that helps force the brake linings tightly against the drum. In addition, some drum

brake designs use an effect called servo action that enables one brake shoe to help apply the other for increased stopping power. Both self-energizing and servo action are explained in detail later in the chapter.

PARKING BRAKE One advantage of drum brakes is that they make excellent parking brakes. A simple linkage fitted to the brake assembly allows relatively low effort from the driver to hold a heavy vehicle in place when parked. Disc brakes, which do not benefit from self-energizing or servo action, require a complex set of extra parts to provide enough force to work well as parking brakes.

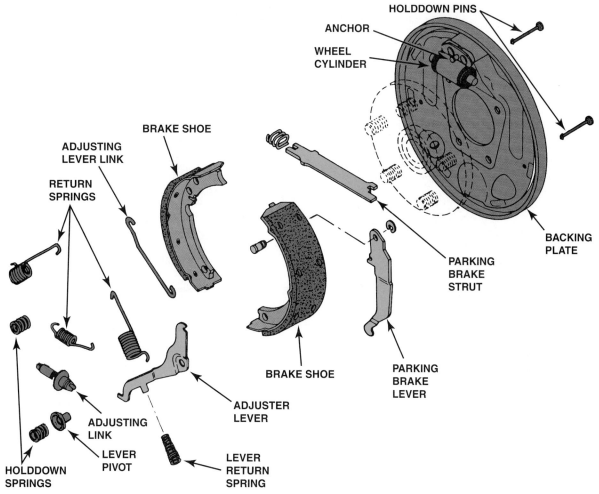

FIGURE 10–2 An exploded view of a typical drum brake assembly.

DRUM BRAKE DISADVANTAGES

BRAKE FADE Drum brakes are not very efficient at dissipating heat. The brake drum covers the linings, and most of the heat produced during braking must pass through the drum, from the inside out into the air.

The greatest drawback of drum brakes is that they are susceptible to fade. **Brake fade** is the loss of stopping power that occurs when excessive heat reduces the friction between the brake shoe linings and the drum. The four types of brake fade include:

1. **Mechanical Fade. Mechanical fade** occurs when the brake drum gets so hot it expands away from the brake linings. The brake shoes then move outward to maintain contact with the drum, causing the brake pedal to drop toward the floor as additional brake fluid moves into the hydraulic system.

2. **Lining Fade. Lining fade** occurs when the friction coefficient of the brake lining material drops off sharply because intense heat makes it "slippery." Unlike mechanical fade, brake pedal travel does not increase when lining fade occurs. Instead, the pedal becomes hard and there is a noticeable loss of braking power.

3. **Gas Fade. Gas fade** occurs under extended hard braking from high speeds, a thin layer of hot gases and dust particles can build up between the brake shoe linings and drum. The gas layer acts as a lubricant and reduces friction. As with the lining fade, the brake pedal becomes hard, and greater application force is required to maintain a constant level of stopping power.

4. **Water Fade. Water fade** occurs when moisture is trapped between the shoes and drum, where it acts as a lubricant. This lowers braking efficiency until friction creates enough heat to evaporate the water.

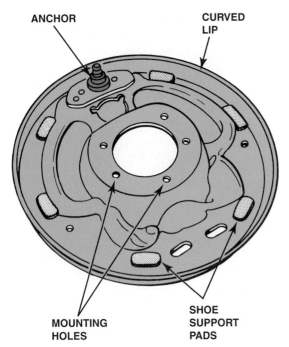

ANCHOR   CURVED LIP

MOUNTING HOLES

SHOE SUPPORT PADS

FIGURE 10–3 The backing plate is the foundation of every drum brake. There are normally six pads where the brake shoes contact the backing plate.

DRUM BRAKE DISADVANTAGES (CONTINUED)

BRAKE ADJUSTMENT Another disadvantage of the drum brake design is its need for an adjusting mechanism. As the brake shoe lining material wears, the clearance between the linings and drum increases, resulting in longer brake pedal travel. To maintain a high brake pedal, a mechanism must be included in the brake assembly for adjustment of the clearance between the brake shoe and drum. Most vehicles have automatic adjusters that maintain the proper clearance between the brake linings and the drum.

BRAKE PULL Brake pull occurs when the friction assemblies on opposite sides of the vehicle have different amounts of stopping power. These differences can be caused by brake fade or mis-adjustment of the clearance between the brake linings and drum.

 **TECH TIP**

Quick-and-Easy Drum Brake Adjustment Check

Tap the brake drum lightly with a hammer or wrench. If the brake shoes are not contacting the drum, the drum will ring like a bell. If the shoes are contacting the drum, the sound will be muffled.

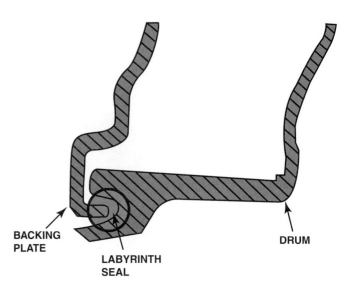

BACKING PLATE

LABYRINTH SEAL

DRUM

FIGURE 10–4 A labyrinth seal is created between the lip of the backing plate and the groove in the brake drum.

DRUM BRAKE PARTS

BACKING PLATE The foundation of every drum brake is the backing plate that mounts to the steering knuckle on the front brakes, or to the suspension or axle housing on the rear brakes. ● **SEE FIGURE 10–3**.

The backing plate serves as the mounting surface for all the other friction assembly parts. The backing plate also functions as a dust and water shield to keep contaminants out of the brake assembly. The edge of the backing plate curves outward to form a lip that strengthens the backing plate and fits inside the brake drum to help prevent water entry. The lip fits into a machined groove in the open edge of the brake drum to provide an even better water barrier or seal. This type of seal is called a **labyrinth seal**. ● **SEE FIGURE 10–4**.

In addition to mounting holes for the various brake parts, the backing plate may also have openings that are used to inspect the wear of the brake linings, or adjust the lining-to-drum clearance. These openings are sometimes sealed with metal plugs that must be punched out the first time inspection or adjustment is needed. Rubber plugs are available to seal the holes and prevent water entry once the metal plugs have been removed.

SHOE ANCHORS Shoe anchors prevent the brake shoes from rotating with the drum when the brakes are applied. The majority of drum brakes have a single anchor, but some drum brake designs use two or more.

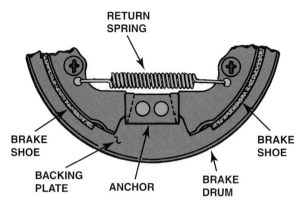

FIGURE 10–5 A keystone anchor allows the brake shoes to self-center in the drum.

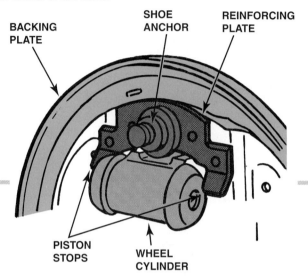

FIGURE 10–6 Piston stops prevent the wheel cylinder from coming apart.

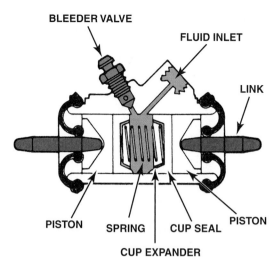

FIGURE 10–7 Cross-section of a wheel cylinder that shows all of its internal parts. The brake line attaches to the fluid inlet. The cup extender prevents the cup seal lip from collapsing when the brakes are released.

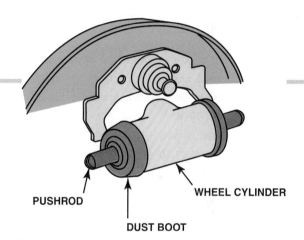

FIGURE 10–8 The pushrods are held in place by the rubber dust boots. As the wheel cylinder pistons move outward, the pushrods transfer the movement to the brake shoes.

Many anchors are a simple round post that is permanently mounted on the backing plate. The brake shoes have semicircular cutouts where they contact the anchor, and the anchor positively locates the shoe on the backing plate. Another type of anchor is the self-centering or keystone anchor. ● SEE FIGURE 10–5. It is called a keystone anchor because of the angled shape similar to a keystone used on the top center of a stone arch.

PISTON STOPS
Some backing plates incorporate **piston stops** that prevent the wheel cylinder pistons from coming out of their bores when the friction assembly is disassembled for servicing. The stops may be part of a reinforcing plate positioned under the anchor or they can be stamped directly into the shape of the backing plate itself. ● SEE FIGURE 10–6.

When piston stops are used, the wheel cylinder must be removed from the backing plate before it can be taken apart for servicing.

SHOE SUPPORT PADS
The **shoe support pads** are stamped into the backing plate and contact the edges of the brake shoes to keep the linings properly aligned with the center of the friction surface inside the brake drum. These pads are also called **ledges** or **shoe contact areas**. The support pads are slightly coated with special high-temperature silicone brake grease to minimize wear, prevent rust, and eliminate squeaking that can occur when the shoes move slightly on the pads during a stop.

WHEEL CYLINDERS
Hydraulic pressure is transferred from the master cylinder to each wheel cylinder through brake fluid. The force exerted on the brake fluid by the driver forces the piston inside the wheel cylinder to move outward. ● SEE FIGURE 10–7. Through pushrods or links, this movement acts on the brake shoes, forcing them outward against the brake drum. ● SEE FIGURE 10–8.

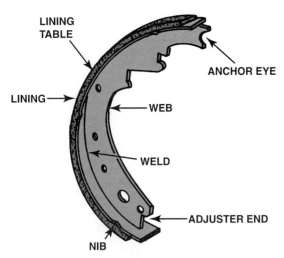

FIGURE 10–9 Steelbrake shoes are made from two stampings welded together—the web and the lining table.

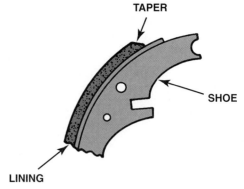

FIGURE 10–10 Tapered ends on the linings help to reduce brake noise.

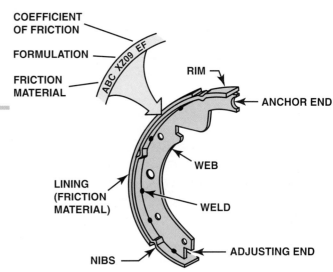

FIGURE 10–11 Typical drum brake shoe and the names of the parts.

DRUM BRAKE SHOES

The linings of drum brakes are attached to curved metal assemblies called **brake shoes**. Most shoes are made of two pieces of sheet steel welded together in a T-shaped cross section. ● **SEE FIGURE 10–9.**

The outer edge is lined with a friction material that contacts the brake drum to generate the actual stopping power. The ends of the linings on most brake shoes are tapered to prevent vibration and brake noise as shown in ● **FIGURE 10–10.**

The curved metal piece on the outer portion of the shoe is called the **lining table**, the **shoe rim** or **platform**. The lining table supports the block of friction material that makes up the brake lining. On some shoes, the edge of the lining table contains small V- or U-shaped notches called **nibs**. The nibs rest against the shoe support pads on the backing plate when the shoe is installed.

The metal piece of the shoe positioned under the lining table and welded to it is called the **shoe web**. All of the application force that actuates the shoe is transferred through the web to the lining table. The web usually contains a number of holes in various shapes and sizes for the shoe return springs, hold-down hardware, parking brake linkage, and self-adjusting mechanism.

One end of the web usually has a notch where the wheel cylinder touches the shoe, while the other end commonly has a flat or curved surface where the shoe meets an anchor or adjusting link. The upper ends of the webs on dual-servo brake shoes have semicircular cutouts called **anchor eyes**. ● **SEE FIGURE 10–11.**

Brake shoes are parts that can be relined and reused many times if the web and lining table are not damaged. Brake shoes for any given application are usually available in both "new" and "relined" versions from suppliers. Relined brake shoes are usually sold on an exchange basis. At the time of purchase, a **core charge** is added to the cost of the relined parts. This charge is refunded when the old shoes are returned in rebuildable condition.

PRIMARY AND SECONDARY BRAKE SHOES In a dual-servo drum brake system, the shoes in a dual-servo brake perform different jobs. The primary shoe (forward facing shoe) is self-energized by drum rotation to create a servo action that forces the secondary shoe more firmly against the drum. Because of this, the two shoes have physical differences and cannot be interchanged.

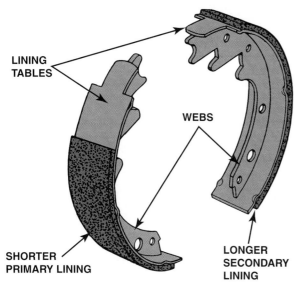

FIGURE 10–12 The primary (forward facing) brake shoe often has a shorter lining than the secondary shoe (rearward facing).

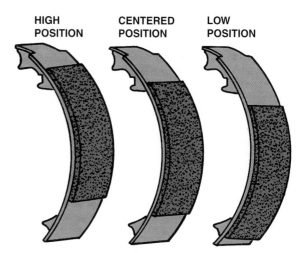

FIGURE 10–13 Primary shoe lining may vary depending on the application.

To help deal with the added friction, heat, and wear it undergoes, the lining of the secondary shoe extends nearly the full length of the shoe lining table. ● SEE FIGURE 10–12. The secondary shoe lining material also has a high coefficient of friction to provide good stopping power. The primary shoe undergoes far less stress than the secondary shoe, and its lining is often shorter—sometimes less than half the length of the lining table. In addition, the lining material usually has a lower coefficient of friction. This prevents the shoe from engaging the drum too quickly or harshly, which could cause the brakes to grab or lock.

On most dual-servo brake primary shoes, the lining is positioned near the center of the lining table. However, in some cases, the lining may be positioned above or below the lining table centerline. Higher or lower lining positions provide better braking action, or prevent noise, in some vehicles. ● SEE FIGURE 10–13.

LINING ASSEMBLY METHODS There are two main methods used to mount brake linings to the brake shoe.

RIVETING. The brake lining is attached to the lining table or backing plate with copper or aluminum rivets. ● SEE FIGURE 10–14. Riveting has the following advantages:

- The major advantage of riveting is that it allows a small amount of flex between the brake block and lining table or backing plate. This play enables the assembly to absorb vibration, and the result is that **riveted linings** operate more quietly than bonded linings.

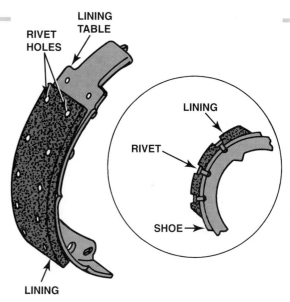

FIGURE 10–14 Riveted brake linings are quiet and reliable at high temperatures.

- Rivets are also very reliable and will not loosen at high temperatures.

Riveting has the following disadvantages:

- Rivet holes however do create stress points in the lining where cracks are likely to occur.
- Riveted lining has a reduced service life because the linings must be replaced before the rivet head contacts the brake drum.
- The rivet can cause deep grooves to be cut into the drum often requiring replacement if the worn brakes are not detected early enough to prevent damage.

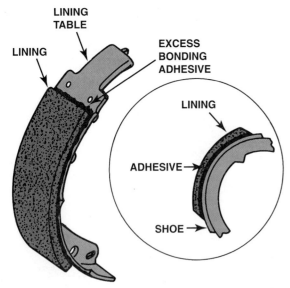

FIGURE 10-15 Many brake linings are bonded.

Code C	0.00 to 0.15
Code D	0.15 to 0.25
Code E	0.25 to 0.35
Code F	0.35 to 0.45
Code G	0.45 to 0.55
Code H	0.55 and above
Code Z	ungraded

CHART 10-1 Edge code letters represent a range of coefficient of friction of the linings.

DRUM BRAKE SHOES (CONTINUED)

BONDING. **Bonded linings** use high-temperature adhesive to glue the brake block directly to the shoe lining table or pad backing plate as shown in ● **FIGURE 10–15**. Heat and pressure are then applied to cure the assembly. Bonding is a common form of shoe and pad assembly, and is most often used to mount organic friction materials.

Bonding has several advantages including:

- Without rivets, bonded linings can wear closer to the lining table or backing plate and provide a longer service life. If the linings wear too far, bonding adhesive is not as destructive to drums or rotors as rivets.

- Bonded linings also have fewer problems with cracking because they have no rivet holes to weaken the brake block.

Bonded linings have the following disadvantages:

- If a bonded lining gets too hot, the bonding adhesive will fail and allow the brake block to separate from the lining table or backing plate.

- Bonded linings are also more prone to be noisy because they do not allow any vibration absorbing flex between the brake block and lining table or backing plate.

EDGE CODES
Starting in 1964, brake linings have been using a standardized way to identify the brake lining materials. The edge codes follow the Society of Automotive Engineers (SAE) Standard J866a. The **edge codes** contain three groups of letters and numbers:

- The first group is a series of letters that identify the manufacturer of the lining.

- The second group is a series of numbers, letters, or both that identify the lining compound or formula. This code is usually known to the manufacturer of the lining material and helps identify the lining after manufacture.

- The third group is two letters that identify the coefficient of friction.

The coefficient of friction is a pure number that indicates the amount of friction between two surfaces. A coefficient of friction will always be less than 1; the higher the number, the greater the amount of friction between two surfaces. (For example, a material with 0.55 coefficient of friction has more friction than a material with a coefficient of friction of 0.39.)

These codes include letters that represent a range of coefficient of friction. ● **SEE CHART 10–1**.

There are always two letters used side by side and the first letter indicates its coefficient of friction when brakes are cold (250°F/121°C), and the second letter indicates the coefficient of friction of the brake lining when the brakes are hot (600°F/316°C).

For example, FF indicates that the brake lining material has a coefficient of friction between 0.35 and 0.45 when both cold and hot. ● **SEE FIGURE 10–16**.

These letters do not mean the relative quality of the lining material. Lining wear, fade resistance, tensile strength, heat

FIGURE 10–16 Typical drum brake lining edge codes, showing the coefficient of friction codes for cold and hot circled.

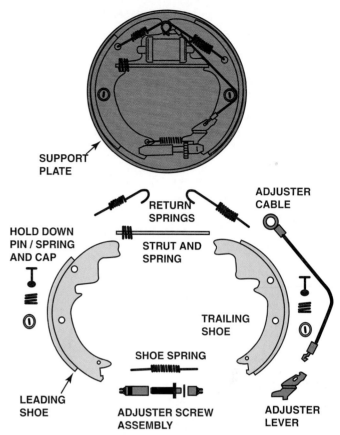

FIGURE 10–17 A typical drum brake assembly showing the support plate (backing plate), anchor pin, and springs.

recovery rate, wet friction, noise, and coefficient of friction must be considered when purchasing high-quality linings. Unfortunately, there are no standards that a purchaser can check regarding all of these other considerations. For best brake performance, always purchase the best-quality name-brand linings that you can afford.

 **TECH TIP**

Purchase Quality Brake Linings for Best Performance

While many brands of replacement brake lining provide acceptable stopping power and long life, purchasing factory brake lining from a dealer is usually the best opportunity to get lining material that meets all vehicle requirements. Aftermarket linings are not required by federal law to meet performance or wear standards that are required of original factory brake linings.

DRUM BRAKE PARTS

RETURN SPRINGS The **brake shoe return springs** retract the shoes to their unapplied positions when the brake pedal is released. This helps prevent brake drag, and aids the return of brake fluid to the master cylinder reservoir. Most brakes use closed-coil return springs to retract the brake shoes. ● **SEE FIGURE 10–17**.

The coils on these springs are very tightly wound and contact one another when the spring is relaxed. Some vehicles have a single, large, horseshoe-shaped return spring. ● **SEE FIGURE 10–18**.

The type, location, and number of return springs vary from one brake design to the next. All springs are installed in one of two ways. Some connect directly from shoe to shoe, while others connect from one shoe to the anchor post.

BRAKE SHOE HOLDDOWNS While the return springs retract the brake shoes to their unapplied positions, the **brake shoe holddowns** keep the shoes securely against the support pads on the backing plate. The holddowns prevent noise, vibration, and wear, but still allow the shoes to move out and back as the brakes are applied and released. The holddowns

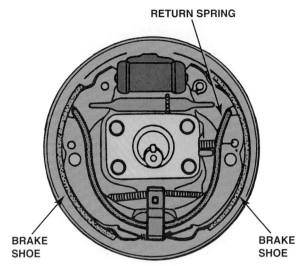

FIGURE 10–18 A single spring-steel spring is used on some drum brakes.

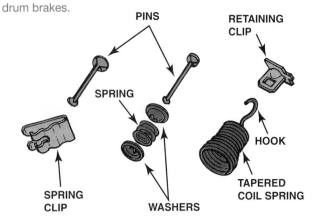

FIGURE 10–19 Various types and styles of hold-down springs. The hold down pins are commonly called *nails.*

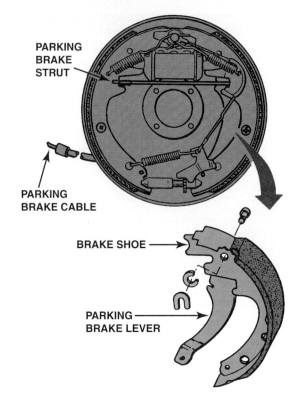

FIGURE 10–20 A mechanical brake linkage is part of most drum brake assemblies.

FIGURE 10–21 An aluminum brake drum with a cast iron friction surface. The cooling fins around the outside help dissipate the heat from the friction surface to the outside air.

DRUM BRAKE PARTS (CONTINUED)

also provide enough freedom of movement to allow adjustments of the shoes outward as the linings wear. Shoe hold-downs take many forms, as shown in ● FIGURE 10–19.

The most common design is a steel pin installed through a hole in the backing plate and a corresponding hole in the brake shoe web. A spring fits over the end of the pin against the shoe web, and a special washer compresses the spring and locks onto the flattened end of the pin.

Another type of holddown is a taper-wound coil spring with a hook formed on its end. Because of its shape, this part is sometimes called a **beehive holddown**. The hook end of the spring is installed through a hole in the brake shoe web and attached into a retaining clip that fits into a corresponding hole in the backing plate.

PARKING BRAKE LINKAGE
Most rear drum brake friction assemblies include a parking brake linkage. The linkage commonly consists of a cable, lever, and strut system that spread the brake shoes apart to apply the brake mechanically.

The parking brake strut plays a large part in many of the automatic brake adjusters. ● SEE FIGURE 10–20.

BRAKE DRUMS
The brake drum is not connected to the backing plate, but turns with the wheel. The drum mounts on the hub or axle, and covers the rest of the brake assembly. Brake drums are made of cast iron or cast aluminum with a cast-iron liner. Many of these drum types may have ribs or fins on their outer edge to help dissipate heat. ● SEE FIGURE 10–21.

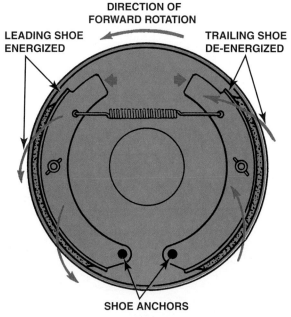

FIGURE 10–22 Self-energizing action can increase or decrease the stopping power of a brake shoe.

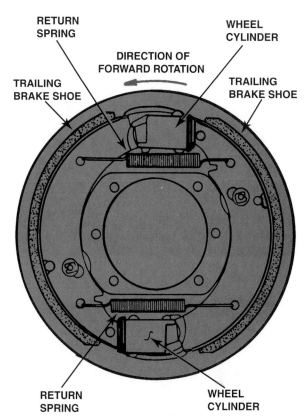

FIGURE 10–23 A double-trailing non-servo drum brake.

NON-SERVO BRAKE DESIGN

PURPOSE AND FUNCTION A **non-servo brake** feature is that each brake shoe is applied individually. The action of one shoe has no effect on the action of the other. Many non-servo drum brakes use **self-energizing action** to improve their braking performance.

PARTS AND OPERATION Self-energizing action occurs when the forward or **leading shoe** contacts the drum and the drum attempts to rotate the shoe along with it. However, the shoe cannot rotate because its far end (relative to drum rotation) is fixed in place by an anchor. As a result, drum rotation *energizes* the shoe by forcing it outward and wedging it tightly against the brake drum.

The drum also attempts to rotate the reverse or **trailing shoe** as it contacts the drum. However, in this case, the far end of the shoe (relative to drum rotation) is not solidly anchored. As a result, drum rotation *de-energizes* the shoe by forcing it inward away from the brake drum.

When this type of brake is applied with the vehicle backing up, the roles of the forward and reverse shoes are switched. The reverse shoe becomes the leading shoe, which is self-energized by drum rotation, while the forward shoe becomes the trailing shoe, which is de-energized. *A leading shoe is always energized by drum rotation. A trailing shoe is always de-energized by drum rotation.* The simple drum brake assembly shown in ● **FIGURE 10–22** shows how the self-energizing process works.

To identify the leading shoe on a non-servo brake with only one wheel cylinder, the first shoe from the wheel cylinder in the direction of drum rotation is the leading shoe. If the piston of a wheel cylinder moves in the same direction as drum rotation when the brakes are applied, the shoe it actuates is a leading shoe. If the piston moves opposite the direction of drum rotation, the shoe actuated is the trailing shoe.

Leading shoes generally wear at a faster rate than trailing shoes because they are applied with greater force. Where a brake uses one leading and one trailing shoe, the leading shoe will sometimes have a thicker lining or one with a larger surface area than that of the trailing shoe. The thicker or larger lining balances the wear between the two shoes so that they will both need replacement at about the same time.

DOUBLE-TRAILING BRAKE The least powerful non-servo drum brake is the **double-trailing brake**. ● **SEE FIGURE 10–23**. This design has two trailing shoes and does not use any self-energization. Both shoes have the same size and shaped linings

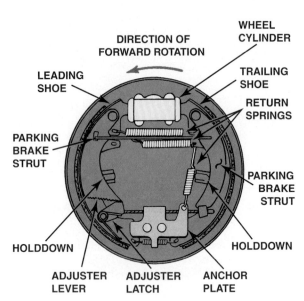

FIGURE 10–24 A leading-trailing non-servo brake.

FIGURE 10–25 A typical dual-servo drum brake.

NON-SERVO BRAKE DESIGN (CONTINUED)

that are applied with equal force by a pair of single-piston wheel cylinders. Each shoe is anchored at the end opposite the wheel cylinder that applies it. In many double-trailing brakes, the backside of one wheel cylinder serves as the anchor for the brake shoe actuated by the other wheel cylinder.

LEADING-TRAILING BRAKE DESIGN The non-servo **leading-trailing brake** has one leading shoe and one trailing shoe. ● **SEE FIGURE 10–24.** Typically, a single, two-piston wheel cylinder is mounted at the top of the backing plate and the two brake shoes are anchored at the bottom of the backing plate.

The brake design has one energized and one de-energized shoe regardless of whether it is applied while the vehicle is traveling forward or in reverse. This allows the leading-trailing brake to work equally well in either direction. The leading shoe usually wears more than the trailing shoe.

Leading-trailing brakes are popular on the rear wheels of many small and front-wheel-drive vehicles because, although they are not as powerful as a servo brake, they are less prone to lockup. They have the further benefit of making a good parking brake in both directions.

DUAL-SERVO BRAKE DESIGN

PURPOSE AND FUNCTION The **dual-servo brake** is the most common drum brake design. The name "servo" comes from the fact that one shoe "serves" the other to increase application force. All servo brakes used on automobiles are of the dual-servo design that works with equal force in both directions.

The primary advantage of the dual-servo brake is that it is more powerful than any of the non-servo designs. Another advantage of the dual-servo brake is that it makes a good parking brake. Dual-servo action not only makes the brake very powerful, it allows the brake to hold equally well in both directions.

Dual-servo brakes are more susceptible to pull than other brake designs, and their greater application force can lead to faster fade under extreme braking conditions.

NOTE: Dual-servo brakes are also called Duo-Servo, which is a brand name of the Bendix Corporation.

DUAL-SERVO BRAKE CONSTRUCTION The basic dual-servo brake uses one anchor and a single two-piston wheel cylinder. ● **SEE FIGURE 10–25.** The anchor is usually mounted at the top of the backing plate with the wheel cylinder directly beneath it. The tops of the brake shoes are held against

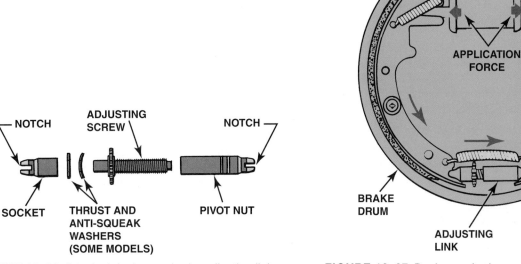

FIGURE 10–26 A typical dual-servo brake adjusting link assembly commonly called a *starwheel adjuster*.

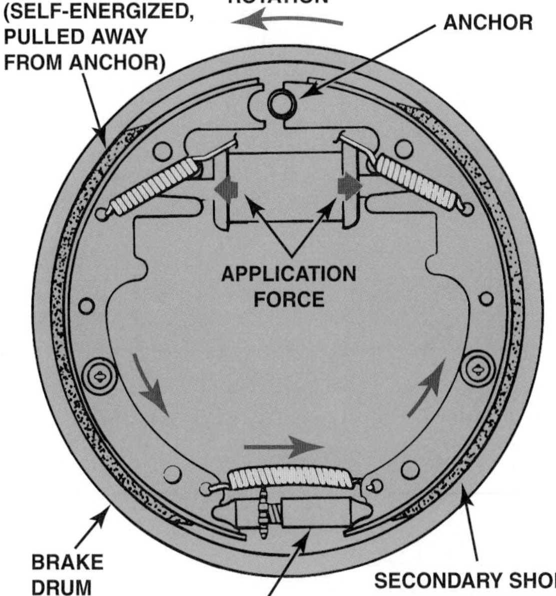

FIGURE 10–27 Dual-servo brake operation. The primary shoe on the left exerts a force on the secondary shoe on the right.

the anchor by individual return springs. The bottoms of the shoes are spaced apart by an adjusting link held in position by a third return spring that connects the two shoes.

ADJUSTING LINK. The adjusting link consists of a starwheel that is part of an adjusting screw, a pivot nut that one end of the adjusting screw threads into, and a socket that rotates freely on the opposite end of the adjusting screw. ● **SEE FIGURE 10–26.** The outer ends of the pivot nut and socket are notched to fit over the brake shoe webs. Some adjusting links have a steel thrust washer and/or spring washer installed between the socket and the starwheel. These washers allow easier rotation of the starwheel and help reduce brake squeal.

NOTE: Adjusting links generally have specific left- or right-hand threads, and must be installed on the correct side of the vehicle.

PRIMARY AND SECONDARY BRAKE SHOES. Although dual-servo brakes make use of self-energizing action to help provide servo action, the two brake shoes are not called leading and trailing parts as in non-servo brakes. Instead, they are identified as the **primary shoe** and the **secondary shoe**. To identify the primary shoe on a

dual-servo brake with a single two-piston wheel cylinder, point to the wheel cylinder, and then move your finger in the direction of drum rotation. The first shoe reached is the primary shoe (always facing to the front of the vehicle) and the other shoe is the secondary shoe (always facing toward the rear of the vehicle).

The secondary brake shoe provides approximately 70% of the total braking power in a dual-servo brake. For this reason, the lining is usually somewhat larger than that of the primary shoe. In addition, some manufacturers use different types of friction materials on the primary and secondary shoes to help equalize wear.

DUAL-SERVO BRAKE OPERATION When a dual-servo brake is applied, the wheel cylinder attempts to force the tops of both brake shoes outward against the drum. ● **SEE FIGURE 10–27.** As the primary shoe makes contact it rotates with the drum because its far end (relative to the direction of drum rotation) is not directly anchored to the backing plate. As the primary shoe rotates, it forces the adjusting link and the secondary shoe to also rotate until the secondary shoe seats firmly against the anchor.

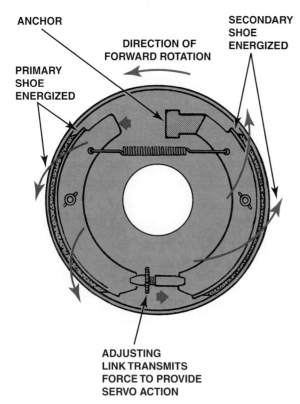

ANCHOR

DIRECTION OF
FORWARD ROTATION

SECONDARY
SHOE
ENERGIZED

PRIMARY
SHOE
ENERGIZED

ADJUSTING
LINK TRANSMITS
FORCE TO PROVIDE
SERVO ACTION

FIGURE 10–28 Dual servo action greatly increases the application force on the secondary shoe.

DUAL-SERVO BRAKE DESIGN (CONTINUED)

Although the wheel cylinder attempts to push the top of the secondary shoe outward, the rotational force developed by friction between the brake shoes and drum is much greater than the force developed by hydraulic pressure in the wheel cylinder. As a result, the secondary shoe is held against the anchor. In effect, only one-half of the wheel cylinder is used to apply the brakes.

SERVO ACTION Once all clearance is taken up between the brake shoes, adjusting link, and anchor, both brake shoes become self-energized like the leading shoes in a non-servo brake. The anchor pin prevents the secondary shoe from rotating, and the adjusting link (held in position by the secondary shoe) serves as the anchor for the primary shoe. Servo action then occurs as a part of the braking force generated by the primary shoe is transferred through the adjusting link to help apply the secondary shoe. ● **SEE FIGURE 10–28**.

When a dual-servo brake is applied with the vehicle moving in reverse, the primary and secondary shoes switch roles. The primary shoe is forced against the anchor while the secondary shoe moves outward and rotates with the drum to apply the primary shoe with a greater force.

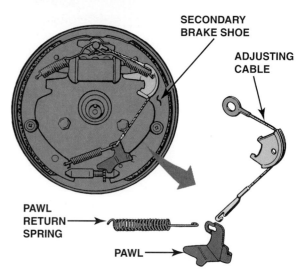

SECONDARY
BRAKE SHOE

ADJUSTING
CABLE

PAWL
RETURN
SPRING

PAWL

FIGURE 10–29 A cable-actuated starwheel adjuster. This type of adjuster makes the adjustment when the vehicle is being driven in reverse and the brakes are released.

🔧 **TECH TIP**

Rear Wheel Lockup? Check the Adjustment

Servo action enables a drum brake to provide increased stopping power, but it can also cause the brakes to grab and lock if they get too far out of adjustment. As clearance between the shoes and drum increases, the primary brake shoe is allowed a greater range of movement. The farther the shoe moves, the more speed it picks up from the rotating brake drum. At the moment the slack is taken up between the brake shoes, adjusting link, and anchor, the speed of the primary shoe is converted into application force by servo action. If the primary shoe is moving too quickly, it will apply the secondary shoe very hard and fast, causing the brakes to grab and possibly lock the wheels.

AUTOMATIC BRAKE ADJUSTERS

SERVO BRAKE STARWHEEL AUTOMATIC ADJUSTERS

Servo brakes use three styles of starwheel adjusters:

- **Cable.** ● **SEE FIGURE 10–29**.
- **Lever.** ● **SEE FIGURE 10–30**.
- **Link.** ● **SEE FIGURE 10–31**.

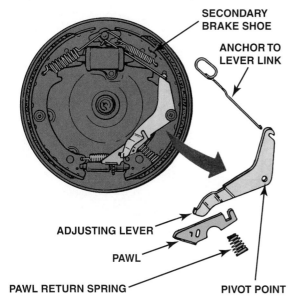

FIGURE 10–30 A lever-actuated starwheel automatic adjuster. This type of adjuster makes the adjustment when the vehicle is being driven in reverse and the brakes are applied.

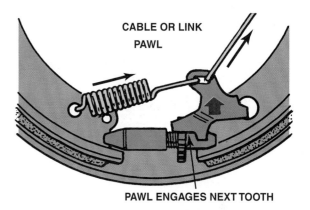

BRAKES APPLIED

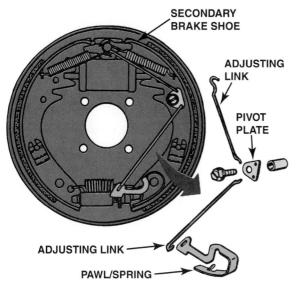

FIGURE 10–31 A link-actuated starwheel adjuster. This type of adjuster makes the adjustment when the brakes are released.

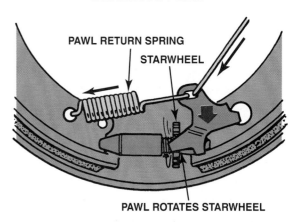

BRAKES RELEASED

FIGURE 10–32 The operation of a typical self-adjuster. Notice that the adjuster actually moves the starwheel.

All three adjusters mount on the secondary brake shoe and adjust only when the brakes are applied while the vehicle is moving in reverse.

As the brakes are applied on a vehicle with a cable or link automatic adjuster, the wheel cylinder and drum rotation combine to move the secondary shoe away from the anchor. Movement of the shoe causes the cable or linkage to pull up on the adjuster **pawl**. ● **SEE FIGURE 10–32.** If the brake lining has worn far enough, the pawl engages the next tooth on the starwheel. When the brakes are released, the pawl return spring pulls the pawl down, rotating the starwheel and moving the brake shoes apart to reduce the lining-to-drum clearance.

Some servo brakes with cable-actuated starwheel automatic adjusters have an **over-travel spring** assembly on the end

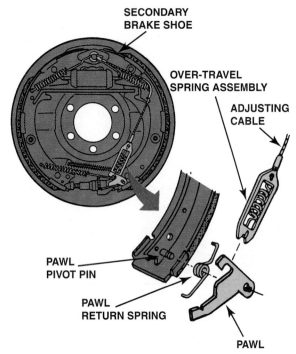

FIGURE 10–33 A cable-actuated starwheel adjuster with an over-travel spring.

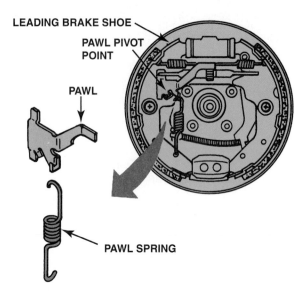

FIGURE 10–34 A non-servo brake with a lever-actuated starwheel automatic adjuster on a leading shoe. This type of adjuster makes an adjustment as the brakes are applied.

AUTOMATIC BRAKE ADJUSTERS (CONTINUED)

of the cable. ● **SEE FIGURE 10–33**. In this design, the adjuster pawl is mounted *under* the starwheel, and adjustment is made as the brakes are applied rather than released. The over-travel spring dampens the movements of the adjuster mechanism, and prevents overadjustment if the brakes are applied very hard and fast. It also prevents damage to the adjusting mechanism if the starwheel seizes or is otherwise unable to rotate.

The lever starwheel adjuster makes the adjustment as the brakes are applied rather than released. The operation includes the following actions:

- As the secondary shoe moves away from the anchor, the solid link between the anchor and the top of the adjuster lever forces the lever to rotate around the pivot point where it attaches to the brake shoe.

- This moves the bottom half of the lever downward, which causes the pawl to rotate the starwheel and make the adjustment.

- The separate pawl piece is free to pivot on the lever to prevent damage if the starwheel will not rotate.

- When the brakes are released, the return springs lift the lever. If the brakes have worn enough, the end of the lever engages the next tooth on the starwheel and additional adjustment will be made the next time the brakes are applied.

NON-SERVO STARWHEEL AUTOMATIC ADJUSTERS

OPERATION. The starwheel automatic adjusters used on non-servo brakes may be mounted on either the leading or trailing shoe. These types of adjusters work whenever the brakes are applied—in either the forward or reverse direction. A leading-shoe design is shown in ● **FIGURE 10–34**.

When the brakes are not applied, the adjuster pawl is held in position by the parking brake strut. When the brakes are applied and the primary shoe moves out toward the brake drum (away from the parking brake strut), the pawl spring pivots the pawl downward where it mounts on the brake shoe and rotates the starwheel to adjust the brake. When the brakes are released, the return springs retract the shoes and the pawl is levered back into its resting position by the parking brake strut. If the linings have worn far enough, the lever engages the next tooth on the starwheel and further adjustment will occur the next time the brakes are applied.

The trailing-shoe non-servo starwheel adjuster shown in ● **FIGURE 10–35** works somewhat like the leading-shoe design, but it makes the adjustment as the brakes are released rather than applied. The upper shoe return spring in this design returns the brake shoes and operates the automatic adjuster, as follows:

- When the brakes are not applied, spring tension holds the trailing shoe and the adjuster pawl tightly against the parking brake strut.

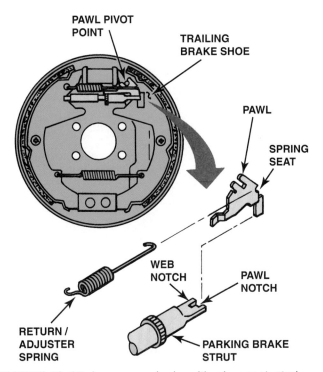

FIGURE 10–35 A non-servo brake with a lever-actuated starwheel automatic adjuster on the trailing shoe. This type of adjuster makes the adjustment as the brakes are released.

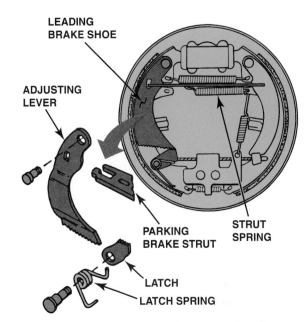

FIGURE 10–36 A lever-latch ratchet automatic adjuster.

■ When the brakes are applied, the trailing shoe moves out toward the drum and away from the parking brake strut. This allows the adjuster pawl, which is restrained by the return spring, to pivot where it attaches to the brake shoe, causing the adjuster arm to move upward.

■ If the brakes have worn far enough, the arm will engage the next tooth of the starwheel.

■ When the brakes are released, the return spring pulls the brake shoes back together and the parking brake strut levers the adjuster pawl downward to rotate the starwheel and adjust the brakes.

RATCHET-TYPE AUTOMATIC ADJUSTERS Most ratchet automatic adjusters use movement of the brake shoes to adjust the lining-to-drum clearance. The adjustment of a ratchet adjuster is carried out by two parts that have small interlocking teeth. As the adjustment is made, the two toothed elements ratchet across one another. Once adjustment is complete, the teeth lock together to hold the brake shoes in their new positions.

LEVER-LATCH RATCHET AUTOMATIC ADJUSTER. The lever-latch automatic adjuster installs on the leading shoe of a non-servo brake and operates whenever the brakes are applied. ● **SEE FIGURE 10–36.** This design consists of a large lever and a smaller latch with interlocking teeth. A spring on the latch piece

TECH TIP

Cool the Brakes before Backing

Self-adjusters can overadjust the rear drum brakes if the brake drums are hot and have increased in diameter due to the heat. For example, if a pickup truck towing a boat had to brake while backing down a long, steep grade to the boat ramp, the rear brake drums could become larger in diameter due to the heat created during braking. The brakes could overadjust if the driver repeatedly depresses and releases the brake pedal while backing the trailer down the boat ramp. Then, after the boat has been removed from the trailer and the rear brakes have cooled, the drums will shrink and keep the rear brakes from releasing, preventing the truck from moving up the ramp.

NOTE: Some drum brakes are equipped with a bimetallic heat sensor that prevents the self-adjusters from working if the brakes are hot.

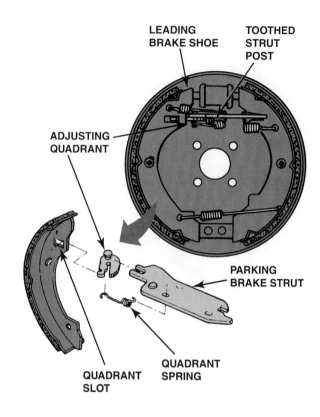

FIGURE 10–37 A strut-quadrant ratchet automatic adjuster.

LEADING BRAKE SHOE

TOOTHED STRUT POST

ADJUSTING QUADRANT

PARKING BRAKE STRUT

QUADRANT SLOT

QUADRANT SPRING

AUTOMATIC BRAKE ADJUSTERS (CONTINUED)

keeps it in contact with the lever to maintain the adjustment. One end of the parking brake strut hooks into an opening in the lever and the other end is held against the trailing brake shoe by a strong spring. As the brakes are applied and the shoes move outward toward the drum, the parking brake strut pulls on the adjuster lever and forces it to pivot inward from where it attaches to the top of the leading shoe. If the brakes are sufficiently worn, the bottom of the lever will ratchet one or more teeth on the latch. When the brakes are released, the parking brake strut, which bottoms against the lever, will hold the shoes farther apart to reduce the lining-to-drum clearance.

STRUT-QUADRANT RATCHET AUTOMATIC ADJUSTER. The strut-quadrant automatic adjuster is used on some non-servo brakes. ● **SEE FIGURE 10–37.** The strut-quadrant adjuster consists of three basic parts:

1. The parking brake strut
2. Adjusting quadrant
3. A quadrant spring

The strut has a toothed post solidly mounted on its underside. The adjuster quadrant pivots on a pin that slips into a notch in the end of the strut, and the backside of the quadrant has a toothed, cam-shaped surface that interlocks with the toothed post on the strut. The quadrant also has an arm that extends through an opening in

the web of the leading brake shoe. The outer side of this arm serves as the brake shoe stop when the brakes are released. The quadrant spring holds the quadrant in contact with the post to maintain the adjustment.

STEP 1 When the brakes are applied, the leading shoe moves out toward the brake drum.

STEP 2 If there is sufficient wear of the brake lining, the edge of the slot in the shoe web contacts the inner side of the adjuster quadrant arm and pulls it outward.

STEP 3 When this happens, the toothed section of the quadrant is lifted away from the post on the parking brake strut.

STEP 4 The quadrant spring then rotates the quadrant until its pivot pin is bottomed in the slot in the parking brake strut.

STEP 5 When the brakes are released, the quadrant returns inward with the leading shoe.

STEP 6 The toothed section of the quadrant then engages the teeth on the strut post, causing the quadrant arm to remain in its new extended position that holds the shoes farther apart and reduces the lining-to-drum clearance.

SUMMARY

1. Drum brake shoes include the lining table and shoe web plus holes for the springs to attach and semicircular anchor eyes.

2. Brake linings can be attached using rivets or bonding.

3. Lining edge codes identify the manufacturer and include two letters at the end, which identify the coefficient of friction of the material. The first letter indicates the coefficient when the lining is cold and the second indicates the coefficient when the lining is hot.

4. Brake shoes are forced outward against a brake drum by hydraulic action working on the brake shoes by the piston of a wheel cylinder.

5. The curved arch of the brake shoe causes a wedging action between the brake shoe and the rotating drum. This wedging action increases the amount of force applied to the drum.

6. Dual-servo brakes use primary and secondary brake shoes that are connected at one end. The wedge action on the front (primary) shoe forces the rear (secondary) shoe into the drum with even greater force. This action is called servo self-energizing.

7. Leading-trailing brakes use two brake shoes that are not connected. Leading-trailing brakes operate on a more linear basis and are therefore more suited than dual-servo for ABS.

8. Most self-adjusting mechanisms usually operate from the secondary or rearward facing brake shoe and adjust the brakes as the brakes are released.

9. Some self-adjusters operate on the primary shoe and adjust the brakes as they are being applied.

REVIEW QUESTIONS

1. Describe the difference between a dual-servo and a leading–trailing drum brake system.

2. List all the parts of a typical drum brake.

3. Explain how a self-adjusting brake mechanism works.

4. What do the last two letters of the lining or pad edge code identify?

CHAPTER QUIZ

1. Two technicians are discussing drum brake shoes. Technician A says that forward and rearward facing shoes are the same and can be installed in either position on any drum brake system. Technician B says that the darker color lining should always be placed toward the front of the vehicle. Which technician is correct?
   a. Technician A only
   b. Technician B only
   c. Both Technicians A and B
   d. Neither Technician A nor B

2. Two technicians are discussing brake lining edge codes. Technician A says that the code can identify the manufacturer. Technician B says that all friction material from the same manufacturer will have the same edge codes. Which technician is correct?
   a. Technician A only
   b. Technician B only
   c. Both Technicians A and B
   d. Neither Technician A nor B

3. Technician A says that starwheel adjusters use different threads (left- and right-handed) for the left and right sides of the vehicle. Technician B says that a pawl controls the teeth of the starwheel adjuster. Which technician is correct?
   a. Technician A only
   b. Technician B only
   c. Both Technicians A and B
   d. Neither Technician A nor B

4. Technician A says that drum brakes can fail to slow the vehicle if driven through deep water. Technician B says that when drum brakes get hot, the brake pedal will drop because the drum expands away from the shoes. Which technician is correct?
   a. Technician A only
   b. Technician B only
   c. Both Technicians A and B
   d. Neither Technician A nor B

5. Technician A says that self-adjusters used on most drum brakes work when the brakes are applied, then release while traveling in reverse. Technician B says that some adjusters can overadjust if the brake drums are hot. Which technician is correct?
   a. Technician A only
   b. Technician B only
   c. Both Technicians A and B
   d. Neither Technician A nor B

6. Drum brake shoes _____.
   a. Can have riveted linings
   b. Can have bonded linings
   c. Can have one shoe that is longer than the other on the same wheel brake
   d. All of the above are possible

7. Which lining does most of the braking on a dual-servo brake?
   a. Front (forward facing)
   b. Rear (rearward facing)
   c. Both contribute equally
   d. Depends on the speed of the vehicle

8. Which lining does most of the braking on a leading-trailing brake?
   a. Leading (forward facing)
   b. Trailing (rearward facing)
   c. Both contribute equally
   d. Depends on the speed of the vehicle

9. Two technicians are discussing drum brake self-adjusters. Technician A says that a frozen starwheel adjuster can cause the brakes to lock up due to the adjusting lever being unable to move the adjuster causing the linkage to bind. Technician B says that some brakes self-adjust when the brakes are applied rather than when released. Which technician is correct?
   a. Technician A only
   b. Technician B only
   c. Both Technicians A and B
   d. Neither Technician A nor B

10. A typical drum brake backing plate has how many shoe support pads (also called ledges)?
   a. 3   c. 6
   b. 4   d. 8

DRUM BRAKE DIAGNOSIS AND SERVICE

OBJECTIVES

After studying Chapter 11, the reader will be able to:

1. Prepare for the Brakes (A5) ASE certification test content area "B" (Drum Brake Diagnosis and Repair).
2. Discuss the procedure recommended for brake drum removal.
3. Discuss the inspection and lubrication points of the backing plate.
4. Explain the importance of the proper drum brake hardware.
5. Disassemble and reassemble a drum brake assembly.

KEY TERMS

Bearingized 181	Speed nuts 176
Brake hardware kits 183	Tinnerman nuts 176

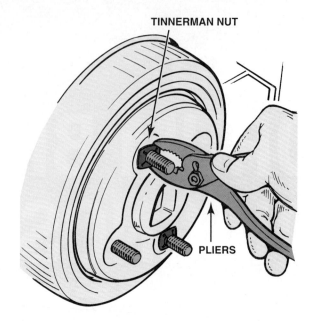

FIGURE 11–1 Tinnerman nuts are used at the assembly plant to prevent the brake drum from falling off until the wheels are installed.

TINNERMAN NUT

PLIERS

DRUM BRAKE DIAGNOSIS

Diagnosing brake concerns includes the following steps:

STEP 1 Verify the customer complaint (concern). For example, common drum brake concerns include:

- Low brake pedal
- Parking brake does not hold the vehicle on a hill
- Noise while braking
- Noise when the vehicle is moving, but the brakes are not applied

STEP 2 Perform a visual inspection of the brakes and related parts, such as the wheels, tires, and suspension system.

STEP 3 Determine the root cause. For example, this could include determining that the parking brake is corroded causing the brake shoes to wear. Replacing just the brake shoes will not correct the root cause.

STEP 4 Restore the brake system to like-new operation, which is the purpose of any repair.

STEP 5 Test-drive the vehicle to verify that the service has corrected the customer's complaint.

Drum brake service usually involves the following steps:

STEP 1 Remove the brake drums.

STEP 2 Inspect the brake drums for damage and measure the inside diameter and compare to specifications.

STEP 3 Inspect brake linings and hardware for wear or damage.

STEP 4 Inspect the wheel cylinder and brake lines for leakage.

STEP 5 Check the backing plate for excessive rust or wear.

BRAKE DRUM REMOVAL

The drum has to be removed before inspection or repair of a drum brake can begin. There are two basic types of drums, and the removal procedure depends on which type is being serviced. With either type it is usually recommended that the drums be marked with an "L" for left or an "R" for right so that they can be replaced in the same location.

HUB OR FIXED DRUMS   A fixed or hub-mounted drum is often used on the rear of front-wheel-drive vehicles. The drum has a hub for inner and outer bearings and is retained by a spindle nut. To remove the brake drum, remove the dust cap and cotter key that is used to retain the spindle nut. Remove the spindle nut and washer and then the brake drum can be carefully pulled off the spindle.

HUBLESS OR FLOATING DRUMS   Floating or hubless drums are usually used on the rear of a rear-wheel-drive vehicle. The drums are secured to the axle flange by the wheel and lug nuts. New vehicles have **tinnerman nuts** (clips), also called **speed nuts,** on the stud when the vehicle is being assembled. These thin sheet-metal nuts keep the brake drum from falling off during shipping and handling prior to installation of the rear wheels. ● **SEE FIGURE 11–1.**

The tinnerman nuts can be discarded because they are not needed after the vehicle leaves the assembly plant. After removing the wheels, the drum *should* move freely on the hub and slip off over the brake shoes. Some drum brakes have

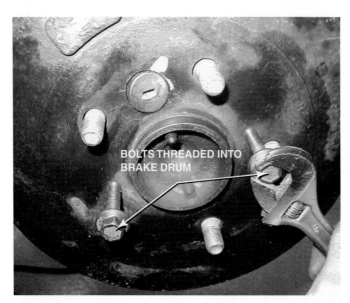

FIGURE 11–2 Turning the bolts that are threaded into the brake drum forces the drum off of the hub.

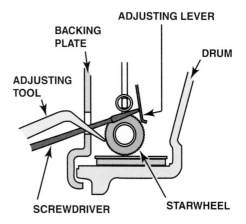

ACCESS THROUGH BACKING PLATE

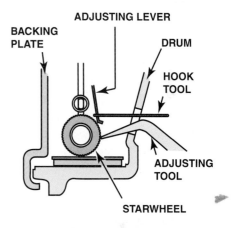

ACCESS THROUGH DRUM

FIGURE 11–3 If the brake shoes have worn into the drum, the adjuster can be backed in after removing the access plug. After removing the plug, use a wire or a screwdriver to move the adjusting lever away from the starwheel, then turn the starwheel with a brake adjusting tool, often called a "brake spoon."

two threaded holes in the drum that allow bolts to be installed.
● **SEE FIGURE 11–2.**

By tightening the bolts, the drum is forced off of the hub. Two situations that can prevent the drum from being removed include the following:

1. **The Drum Is Rusted to the Hub.** The fit between the drum and the hub is very close because it is this center pilot hole in the drum that centers the drum on the axle. Rust and corrosion often causes the drum to seize to the hub. Striking the area inside the wheel studs will usually break the drum loose from the hub. Sometimes a torch has to be used to expand the pilot hole.

   NOTE: Use of an air hammer with a flat-headed driver against the hub also works well to break the drum loose from the hub.

   CAUTION: Overheating or not allowing the drum to cool slowly can cause the brake drum to distort. Using a puller can also damage a drum.

2. **The Brake Shoes Are Worn into the Drum.** Even if the center hole is loose, many brake drums cannot be removed because the inner edge of the brake drum catches on the lining. Pulling outward on the drum often bends the backing plate or breaks some of the mounting hardware. To prevent damage, remove the adjuster plug from the backing plate or drum and back off the adjuster. ● **SEE FIGURE 11–3.**

NOTE: Be sure to reinstall the adjuster opening plugs. These plugs help keep water and debris out of the brakes.

After removing the brake drums, they should be cleaned, inspected, measured, and possibly machined before being returned to service.

TECH TIP

Cutting the Nails Trick

Many times a brake drum cannot be removed because the linings have worn a groove into the drum. Attempting to adjust the brakes inward is often a frustrating and time-consuming operation. The easy solution is to use a pair of diagonal side-cut pliers and cut the heads off the hold-down pins (nails) at the backing plate. This releases the brake shoes from the backing plate and allows enough movement of the shoes to permit removal of the brake drum without bending the backing plate.

The hold-down pins (nails) must obviously be replaced, but they are included in most drum brake hardware kits. Since most brake experts recommend replacing all drum brake hardware anyway, this solution does not cost any more than normal, may save the backing plate from damage, and saves the service technician lots of time. ● **SEE FIGURE 11–4.**

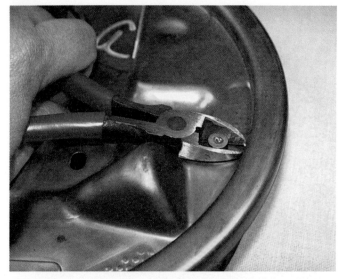

FIGURE 11–4 Using side-cut pliers to cut the heads off of the hold-down pins (nails) from the backing plate to release the drum from the shoes.

FIGURE 11–5 A liquid soaking solvent, such as brake cleaner, should be used to wet the linings. The purpose of wetting the lining material while the drum is still on the vehicle is to prevent the possibility of asbestos from the lining becoming airborne. Asbestos is only hazardous when asbestos dust is airborne and is breathed in during brake system service.

DRUM BRAKE DISASSEMBLY

After removal of the brake drum, the brake shoes and other brake hardware should be wetted down with a solvent or enclosed in an approved evacuation system to prevent possible asbestos release into the air. Precautions should be taken to prevent any asbestos that may be present in the brake system from becoming airborne. Removal of the brake drum should occur inside a sealed vacuum enclosure equipped with a HEPA filter or washed with water or solvent. ● **SEE FIGURE 11–5.**

Usually, the first step in the disassembly of a drum brake system is removal of the return (retracting) springs. ● **SEE FIGURE 11–6.**

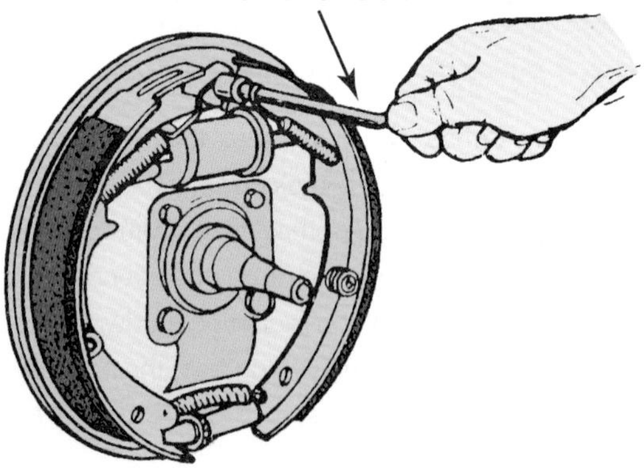

After the return springs have been removed, the hold-down springs and other brake hardware can be removed. ● **SEE FIGURE 11–7.**

NOTE: There are generally no "exact" disassembly or reassembly procedures specified by the manufacturer. The order in which the parts are disassembled or reinstalled is based on experience and the personal preference of the technician.

BRAKE SPRING TOOL

FIGURE 11–6 Using a brake spring tool to release a return (retracting) spring from the anchor pin.

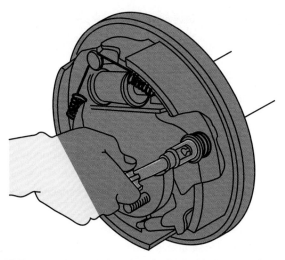

FIGURE 11-7 A special tool, called a hold-down spring tool, being used to depress and rotate the retainer.

RUSTY BACKING PLATE SHOE PAD

FIGURE 11-8 A typical rusting backing plate shoe pad. This can cause the brakes to squeak when the shoes move outward during a brake application and again when the brake pedal is released.

INSPECTING THE BACKING PLATE

The backing plate supports the parts of the drum brake and helps to keep water from getting onto the brake shoes. The backing plate bolts to the rear axle or spindle and is made from stamped steel. Backing plates are plated (usually with cadmium) or painted to prevent rusting. To inspect the backing plate, follow these steps:

STEP 1 When brakes are serviced, the six raised contact surfaces, called pads, ledges, or shoe contact areas, of the backing plate should be inspected because they rub against the sides of the shoes. If the pads are worn more than 1/16 in. (1.5 mm), the backing plate should be replaced. ● **SEE FIGURE 11-8.**

STEP 2 The backing plate must be inspected for looseness or bending.

STEP 3 Backing plates should also be inspected to ensure that they are parallel with the axle flange.

STEP 4 The raised pads should be cleaned and lubricated. Lithium high-temperature brake grease, synthetic brake grease, silicone grease, or antiseize should be used to lubricate drum brake parts. ● **SEE FIGURE 11-9.**

FIGURE 11-9 Applying lithium grease to the raised pads on the backing plate.

FIGURE 11–10 A rule of thumb is that the lining should be at least the thickness of a nickel. This applies to both drum brake shoes and disc brake pads.

FIGURE 11–11 Cracked brake lining must be replaced.

DRUM BRAKE LINING INSPECTION

Both primary (front facing) and secondary (rear facing) lining material must be thicker than 0.060 in. (1.5 mm). To inspect the drum brake lining, follow these steps:

STEP 1 Some vehicles are equipped with holes in the backing plate that allow for a visual inspection of the thickness of the lining. Most vehicle and brake lining manufacturers recommend replacing worn brake lining when the thickness of the riveted lining reaches 0.060 in. or less. An American nickel is about 0.060 in. thick, so simply remember that you must always have at least "a nickel's worth of lining." ● **SEE FIGURE 11–10.**

STEP 2 Most experts agree that the best possible inspection involves removing the brake drum and making a thorough visual inspection of the entire brake instead of just looking at the thickness of the remaining lining. If a riveted brake lining is cracked between rivets, the lining should be replaced. The lining must be replaced if cracked, as shown in ● **FIGURE 11–11.**

BRAKE SPRING INSPECTION

RETURN SPRINGS Each lining has a return spring (retracting spring) that returns the brake shoes back from the drums whenever the brakes are released. The springs are called primary and secondary return springs. The primary return spring attaches to the primary brake shoe and the secondary return spring attaches to the secondary brake shoe. These springs should be tested prior to a brake overhaul, especially when uneven lining wear is discovered.

Some drum brakes use a spring that connects the primary and secondary shoes and is commonly called a shoe-to-shoe spring. Return springs can get weak due to heat and time and can cause the linings to stay in contact with the drum when the brakes are released.

HOLD-DOWN SPRINGS Hold-down springs (one on each shoe) are springs used with a retainer and a hold-down spring pin (or nail) to keep the linings on the backing plate. Other types of hold-down springs include U-shape, flat spring steel type, and the combination return-and-hold spring. These springs still allow the freedom of movement necessary for proper braking operation.

CONNECTING SPRING (ADJUSTING SCREW SPRING)
The connecting spring attaches to the lower portion and connects the two shoes together. Check or replace at every brake lining change for best results.

 **TECH TIP**

The Drop Test

Brake return (retracting) springs can be tested by dropping them to the floor. A good spring should "thud" when the spring hits the ground. This noise indicates that the spring has not stretched and that all coils of the springs are touching each other. If the spring "rings" when dropped, the spring should be replaced because the coils are not touching each other. ● **SEE FIGURE 11–12.**

Although this drop test is often used, many experts recommend replacing all brake springs every time the brake linings are replaced. Heat generated by the brake system often weakens springs enough to affect their ability to retract brake shoes, especially when hot, yet not "ring" when dropped.

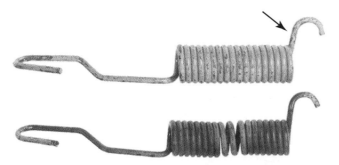

FIGURE 11-12 The top spring is a good-looking spring because all coils of the spring are touching each other. The bottom spring is stretched and should be discarded. The arrow points to the back side of the spring, which goes into a hole in the brake shoe. The open loop of the spring is not strong enough to keep from straightening out during use. Using the back side of the hook provides a strong, long-lasting hold in the brake shoe.

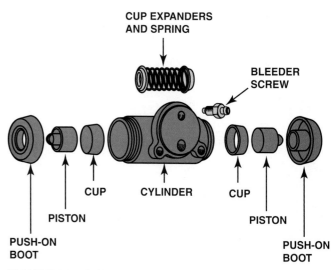

FIGURE 11-13 Exploded view of a typical wheel cylinder. Note how the flat part of the cups touches the flat part of the piston. The cup expander and spring go between the cups.

WHEEL CYLINDER INSPECTION

Drum brake wheel cylinders are cast iron with a bore (hole) drilled and finished to provide a smooth finish for the wheel cylinder seals and pistons. This special finish is called **bearingized.** The final step in manufacture of the wheel cylinder is to force a hardened steel ball through the bore to bend over the "grain" of the metal and to smooth the inner surface. This process provides a smooth porous-free surface for the sealing caps to travel over. It is this bearingized surface finish on the inside of the wheel cylinder that is often destroyed when a wheel cylinder is honed.

CAUTION: It is because of this bearingized surface finish that most vehicle manufacturers do not recommend that wheel cylinders be honed. Be sure to follow the vehicle manufacturer's recommended procedures. Some manufacturers state that the wheel cylinders can be overhauled using new (replacement) sealing cups and dust shields after cleaning the cylinder bore only.

Outside each wheel cylinder piston are dust boots installed to keep dirt out of the cylinder bore. Between both piston seals, there is a spring with piston seal expanders to keep the seals from collapsing toward each other and to keep pressure exerted on the lips of both seals to ensure proper sealing. ● **SEE FIGURE 11-13.**

On the back of each wheel cylinder there is a threaded hole for the brake line and a bleeder valve that can be loosened to remove (bleed) air from the hydraulic system. The wheel cylinder is bolted or clipped to the backing plate. ● **SEE FIGURES 11-14 AND 11-15.**

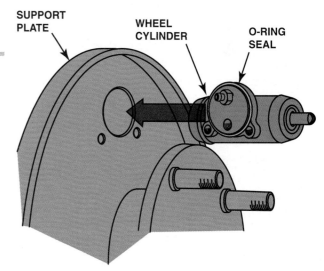

FIGURE 11-14 Many wheel cylinders are bolted to the support plate (backing plate). The O-ring seal helps keep water and dirt out of the drum brake.

 TECH TIP

Wet Is OK—Dripping Is Not OK

When inspecting a wheel cylinder, use a blunt nose tool and pry up the dust boot. If the inside of the seal is wet, this means that some seepage has occurred, which is normal. If, however, brake fluid drips from the dust seal, this indicates that the wheel cylinder sealing cups have failed and the wheel cylinder should be replaced. Also check to see if the internal pistons can move easily by pushing on the pushrods. Replace the wheel cylinder if a piston does not move.

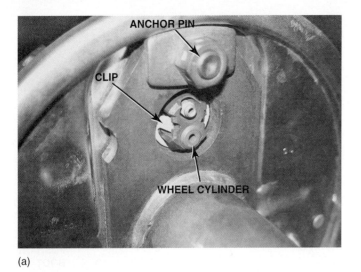

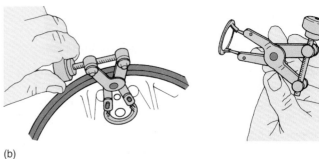

(a)   (b)

FIGURE 11–15 (a) Some wheel cylinders are simply clipped to the backing plate. (b) This special tool makes it a lot easier to remove the wheel cylinder clip. A socket (1 1/8 in., 12 point) can be used to push the clip back onto the wheel cylinder.

WHEEL CYLINDER INSPECTION (CONTINUED)

OVERHAUL OF THE WHEEL CYLINDERS If defective or leaking, wheel cylinders can be overhauled if recommended by the vehicle manufacturer. The following steps and procedures should be followed:

STEP 1 Loosen the bleeder valve. If unable to loosen the bleeder valve without having it break off, a new replacement wheel cylinder is required. To help prevent broken bleeder valves, attempt to tighten the bleeder valve while tapping on the valve to loosen the rust before loosening the valve.

STEP 2 To remove the wheel cylinder, the brake line must first be removed from the wheel cylinder. Unbolt or remove the wheel cylinder retainer clip. Be careful not to twist the brake line when removing the line from the wheel cylinder or the brake line will also require replacement.

STEP 3 If the bleeder valve can be removed, remove all internal parts of the wheel cylinder.

> **NOTE: With some vehicles, the wheel cylinder must be unbolted from the backing plate to enable removal of the seals and piston.**

STEP 4 Clean and/or hone a wheel cylinder as specified by the manufacturer to remove any rust and corrosion.
● **SEE FIGURE 11–16.**

STEP 5 Install the pistons (usually not included in a wheel cylinder overhaul kit), seals, spring, and dust boots. Install on the vehicle and bleed the system.

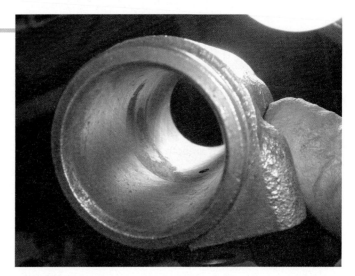

FIGURE 11–16 The rust inside this wheel cylinder will not affect the operation as it is located inside the working area of the sealing cups.

NOTE: Even though the wheel cylinder is not leaking, some brake experts recommend replacing or rebuilding the wheel cylinder every time new replacement linings are installed. Any sludge buildup in the wheel cylinder can cause the wheel cylinder to start to leak shortly after a brake job. When the new, thicker replacement linings are installed, the wheel cylinder piston may be pushed inward enough to cause the cup seals to ride on a pitted or corroded section of the wheel cylinder. As the cup seal moves over this rough area, the seal can lose its ability to maintain brake fluid pressure and an external brake fluid leak can occur. ● **SEE FIGURE 11–17.**

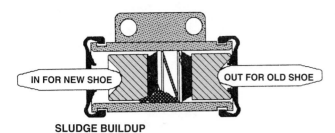

SLUDGE BUILDUP

IN FOR NEW SHOE OUT FOR OLD SHOE

FIGURE 11–17 When new, thicker brake linings are installed, the pistons and cups are forced back into the wheel cylinder and pushed through the sludge that is present in every cylinder.

FIGURE 11–18 This starwheel adjuster is damaged and must be replaced. A lack of proper lubrication can cause the starwheel to become frozen in one place and not adjust properly.

DRUM BRAKE HARDWARE KIT

If any spring is found to be defective, it is possible to purchase most parts individually or in pairs. However, for best results, many brake suppliers sell drum **brake hardware kits.** These kits usually include the items listed below for two drum brakes (axle set):

1. Primary and secondary return springs
2. Connecting spring
3. Hold-down springs
4. Hold-down spring retainers
5. Hold-down spring pins (nails)

Self-adjuster kits are available if needed. Other brake parts such as adjusters are available separately or as part of a self-adjuster kit. ● **SEE FIGURE 11–18.**

INSPECTING THE DRUM BRAKE SHOES

Carefully inspect the replacement brake shoes. Check all of the following:

1. Check that the replacements are exactly the same size (width and diameter) as the original. Hold the replacement shoes up against the old shoes to make the comparison.
2. Check for sound rivets (if rivet type). The friction material should also be snug against the metal brake shoe backing.

After checking that the replacement brake lining is okay, place the old shoes into the new linings' box. This helps ensure proper credit for the old shoes (called the core) as well as protection against asbestos contamination exposure.

BRAKE PARTS CLEANING

Whenever cleaning brake parts or components always use the following guidelines:

- Denatured alcohol or "brake clean" should only be used to clean brake parts that are disassembled. When individual parts are cleaned, they should be allowed to dry before being assembled.

- Never clean or flush assembled brake components with denatured alcohol or brake clean. Often, the alcohol cannot evaporate entirely from an assembled component. The trapped alcohol will evaporate inside the brake system, causing contamination. The trapped alcohol vapors also act like trapped air in the braking system and can cause a spongy brake pedal.

REASSEMBLING THE DRUM BRAKE

Reassembling the drum brake includes the following steps:

STEP 1 Carefully clean the backing plate.

STEP 2 Check the anchor pin for looseness.

STEP 3 Lubricate the shoe contact surfaces (shoe pads) with antiseize, brake grease, or synthetic grease.

STEP 4 Reassemble the primary and secondary shoes and brake strut, along with all springs.

STEP 5 Finish assembling the drum brake, being careful to note the correct location of all springs and parts.

NOTE: Many technicians preassemble the primary and secondary shoes with the connecting (lower retracting) spring as a unit before installing them onto the backing plate. ● SEE FIGURES 11–19 AND 11–20.

Most self-adjusters operate off the rear (secondary) shoe and should therefore be assembled toward the rear of the vehicle. Be sure that the star wheel adjuster is used on the correct side of the vehicle as the threads are different. ● SEE FIGURE 11–21.

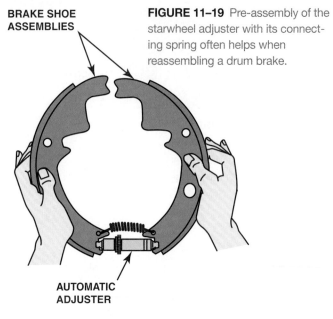

BRAKE SHOE ASSEMBLIES

AUTOMATIC ADJUSTER

FIGURE 11–19 Pre-assembly of the starwheel adjuster with its connecting spring often helps when reassembling a drum brake.

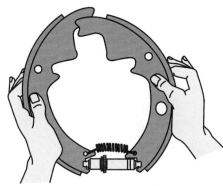

FIGURE 11–20 Sometimes it is necessary to cross the shoes when pre-assembling the starwheel adjuster and connecting spring.

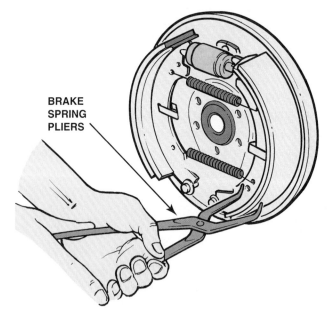

BRAKE SPRING PLIERS

FIGURE 11–21 Brake spring pliers being used to install the connecting spring.

FIGURE 11-22 Notice that the brake shoe is not contacting the anchor pin. This often occurs when the parking brake cable is stuck or not adjusted properly.

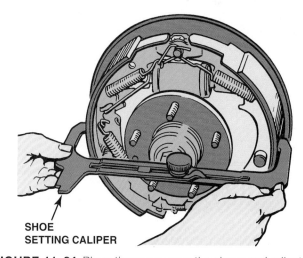

FIGURE 11-23 The first step in using a brake shoe clearance gauge is to adjust it to the drum inside diameter and tighten the lock screw.

ADJUSTING DRUM BRAKES

Most drum brakes are adjusted by rotating a starwheel or rotary adjuster. As the adjuster is moved, the brake shoes move toward the drum. If the brakes have been assembled correctly and with the parking brake fully released, both brake shoes should make contact with the anchor pin at the top. ● SEE FIGURE 11-22 for an example where one shoe does not make contact with the anchor pin.

If the clearance between the brake shoes and the brake drum is excessive, a low brake pedal results. The wheel cylinder travel may not be adequate to cause the lining to contact the drums. Often, the driver has to pump the brakes to force enough brake fluid into the wheel cylinder to move it enough for braking action to occur.

Many technicians use a brake shoe clearance gauge to adjust the brake shoes before installing the drum. ● SEE FIGURES 11-23 AND 11-24.

CAUTION: Before installing the brake drum, be sure to clean any grease off the brake lining. Some experts warn not to use sandpaper on the lining to remove grease. The sandpaper may release asbestos fiber into the air. Grease on the linings can cause the brakes to grab.

FIGURE 11-24 Place the gauge over the shoes and adjust the brakes until they contact the inside of the gauge.

TECH TIP

The Masking Tape Trick

Some technicians cover the friction material with masking tape to prevent contaminating the linings with dirt or grease during installation. After everything has been installed and double-checked, the masking tape is removed and the brake drums are installed. ● SEE FIGURE 11-25.

FIGURE 11–25 To prevent getting grease on the lining, the wise service technician covers the friction material with masking tape. The tape is removed after the brake shoes have been installed.

LUBRICATION CHECKLIST

For proper operation, the following points should be lubricated with approved brake lubricant:

1. The starwheel adjuster threads and under end caps
2. The backing plate contact areas (pads or ledges)
3. Anchor pins

CAUTION: Do not use wheel bearing or chassis grease on a braking system. Use only approved brake lubricant such as molybdenum disulfide (moly) grease, synthetic grease, lithium-based brake grease, or anti-seize compound.

Also, be sure to check and lubricate the parking brake cable, if necessary.

DRUM BRAKE SYMPTOM-BASED TROUBLESHOOTING GUIDE

LOW PEDAL OR THE PEDAL GOES TO THE FLOOR

Possible causes for low pedal include the following:

1. Excessive clearance between the linings and drum
2. Automatic adjusters not working
3. Leaking wheel cylinder
4. Air in the system

SPRINGY, SPONGY PEDAL
Possible causes for springy, spongy pedal include the following:

1. Drums worn below specifications
2. Air in the system

EXCESSIVE PEDAL PRESSURE REQUIRED TO STOP THE VEHICLE
Possible causes for excessive pedal pressure include the following:

1. Grease or fluid-soaked linings
2. Frozen wheel cylinder pistons
3. Linings installed on wrong shoes

LIGHT PEDAL PRESSURE—BRAKES TOO SENSITIVE

Possible causes for light pedal pressure include the following:

1. Brake adjustment not correct
2. Loose backing plate
3. Lining loose on the shoe
4. Excessive dust and dirt in the drums
5. Scored, bell-mouthed, or barrel-shaped drum
6. Improper lining contact pattern

BRAKE PEDAL TRAVEL DECREASING
Possible causes for brake pedal travel decreasing include the following:

1. Weak shoe retracting springs
2. Wheel cylinder pistons sticking

PULSATING BRAKE PEDAL (PARKING BRAKE APPLY PULSATES ALSO)
Possible cause for pulsating brake pedal include the following:

1. Drums out-of-round

BRAKES FADE (TEMPORARY LOSS OF BRAKE EFFECTIVENESS WHEN HOT)
Possible causes for brake fade include the following:

1. Poor lining contact
2. Drums worn below the discard dimension
3. Charred or glazed linings

SHOE CLICK NOISE
Possible causes for shoe click noise include the following:

1. Shoes lift off the backing plate and snap back
2. Hold-down springs weak
3. Shoe bent
4. Grooves in the backing plate pads

THUMPING NOISE WHEN BRAKES ARE APPLIED
Possible causes for thumping noise include the following:

1. Cracked drum; hard spots in the drum
2. Retractor springs unequal—weak

GRINDING NOISE
Possible causes for grinding noise include the following:

1. Shoe hits the drum
2. Bent shoe web
3. Brake improperly assembled

ONE WHEEL DRAGS
Possible causes for one wheel dragging include the following:

1. Weak or broken shoe retracting springs
2. Brake-shoe-to-drum clearance too tight—brake shoes not adjusted properly
3. Brake assembled improperly
4. Wheel cylinder piston cups swollen and distorted
5. Pistons sticking in the wheel cylinder
6. Drum out-of-round
7. Loose anchor pin/plate
8. Parking brake cable not free
9. Parking brake not adjusted properly

VEHICLE PULLS TO ONE SIDE
Possible causes for vehicle pulling to one side include the following:

1. Brake adjustment not correct
2. Loose backing plate
3. Linings not of specified kind; primary and secondary shoes reversed or not replaced in pairs
4. Water, mud, or other material in brakes
5. Wheel cylinder sticking
6. Weak or broken shoe retracting springs
7. Drums out-of-round
8. Wheel cylinder size different on opposite sides
9. Scored drum

WET WEATHER: BRAKES GRAB OR WILL NOT HOLD
Possible causes for brakes grabbing or not holding include the following:

1. Bent backing plate flange
2. Incorrect or abused shoe and linings

BRAKES SQUEAK
Possible causes for brakes squeaking include the following:

1. Backing plate is bent or shoes twisted
2. Shoes scraping on backing plate pads
3. Weak or broken hold-down springs
4. Loose backing plate, anchor, or wheel cylinder
5. Glazed linings
6. Dry shoe pads and hold-down pin surfaces

BRAKES CHATTER
Possible causes for brake chattering include the following:

1. Incorrect lining-to-drum clearance
2. Loose backing plate
3. Weak or broken retractor spring
4. Drums out-of-round
5. Tapered or barrel-shaped drums
6. Improper lining contact pattern

DRUM BRAKE SERVICE

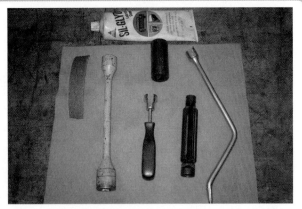

1 Tools needed to service a drum brake assembly include brake tools, silicone grease, wheel lug nut sockets, and torque limiting adapters or a torque wrench.

2 After safely hoisting the vehicle to chest height, remove the brake drum.

3 Remove the primary (forward facing) shoe return spring, using a brake tool. Then, remove the secondary return spring.

4 Remove the parking brake strut along with the antirattle spring.

5 Use a brake tool to depress the hold-down spring, and then rotate it until the slot in the retainer lines up with the flattened part of the hold-down pin.

6 Removing the primary brake shoe plus the starwheel adjuster and connecting spring.

7 When the secondary lining hold-down spring is removed, the adjusting lever and pawl return spring can be removed.

8 The parking brake lever can now be disconnected from the secondary brake shoe.

9 Check the wheel cylinder for leakage. Check the pistons can move too during the inspection. This wheel cylinder is relatively new and not leaking.

10 Clean all six brake shoe ledges. Lubricate the ledges with silicone brake grease.

11 Many technicians prefer to assemble the connecting spring and starwheel adjuster to both shoes to help in the reinstallation.

12 Attaching the parking brake lines to the secondary shoe. The assembled parts at the bottom help keep everything together.

CONTINUED ▶

DRUM BRAKE SERVICE (CONTINUED)

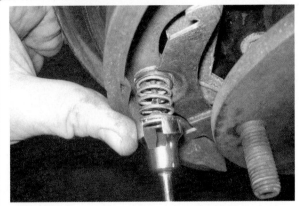

13 Installing the secondary shoe hold-down spring.

14 Installing the secondary shoe return spring. Note that the primary return spring has already been installed.

15 After installing the brake shoes and springs, use a drum/shoe clearance gauge and set it to the inside diameter of the drum.

16 Adjust the starwheel adjuster until the linings contact the drum brake shoe clearance gauge.

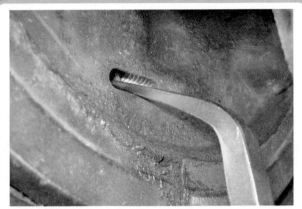

17 After installing the drum, it may be necessary to make the final adjustment using a brake adjusting tool (spoon).

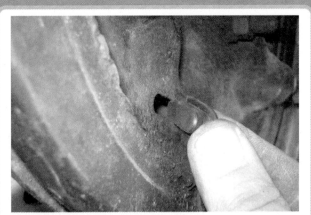

18 After completing the brake service, be sure to cover the brake adjustment opening to prevent water from getting into the brake.

1. Care should be exercised when removing a brake drum so as not to damage the drum, backing plate, or other vehicle components.

2. After disassembly of the drum brake component, the backing plate should be inspected and cleaned.

3. Most experts recommend replacing the wheel cylinder as well as all brake springs as part of a thorough drum brake overhaul.

4. Measure the brake drum and adjust the brake shoes to fit the drum.

5. Use care to prevent getting grease on brake linings. It can cause the brake to grab.

REVIEW QUESTIONS

1. Explain how to remove a brake drum.

2. List all items that should be lubricated on a drum brake.

3. List the steps necessary to follow when replacing drum brake linings.

4. Explain why many vehicle manufacturers do not recommend the wheel cylinder be honed.

CHAPTER QUIZ

1. Technician A says that the tinnerman nuts are used to hold the brake drum on and should be reinstalled when the drum is replaced. Technician B says that a drum should be removed inside a sealed vacuum enclosure or washed with water or solvent to prevent possible asbestos dust from being released into the air. Which technician is correct?
   a. Technician A only
   b. Technician B only
   c. Both Technicians A and B
   d. Neither Technician A nor B

2. The backing plate should be replaced if the shoe contact areas (pads or ledges) are worn more than _____.
   a. 1/2 in. (13 mm)
   b. 1/4 in. (7 mm)
   c. 1/8 in. (4 mm)
   d. 1/16 in. (1.5 mm)

3. Technician A says that silicone brake grease can be used to lubricate the shoe contact ledges. Technician B says that synthetic brake grease, lithium brake grease, or anti-seize compound can be used as a brake lubricant. Which technician is correct?
   a. Technician A only
   b. Technician B only
   c. Both Technicians A and B
   d. Neither Technician A nor B

4. Most brake experts and vehicle manufacturers recommend replacing brake lining when the lining thickness is _____.
   a. 0.030 in. (0.8 mm)
   b. 0.040 in. (1.0 mm)
   c. 0.050 in. (1.3 mm)
   d. 0.060 in. (1.5 mm)

5. Technician A says that starwheel adjusters use different threads (left- and right-handed) for the left and right sides of the vehicle. Technician B says that the threads and end caps of the adjusters should be lubricated with brake grease before being installed. Which technician is correct?
   a. Technician A only
   b. Technician B only
   c. Both Technicians A and B
   d. Neither Technician A nor B

6. Technician A says that many vehicle manufacturers recommend that wheel cylinders not be honed because of the special surface finish inside the bore. Technician B says that some experts recommend that the wheel cylinders be replaced every time the brake linings are replaced. Which technician is correct?
   a. Technician A only
   b. Technician B only
   c. Both Technicians A and B
   d. Neither Technician A nor B

7. Most manufacturers recommend that brake parts should be cleaned with _____.
   a. Clean water only
   b. Denatured alcohol
   c. Stoddard solvent
   d. Detergent and water

8. Old brake shoes are often returned to the manufacturer when new friction material is installed. These old shoes are usually called the _____.
   a. Core
   b. Web
   c. Rim
   d. Nib

9. After assembling a drum brake, it is discovered that the brake drum will not fit over the new brake shoes. Technician A says that the parking brake cable may not have been fully released. Technician B says to check to see if both shoes are contacting the anchor pin. Which technician is correct?
   a. Technician A only
   b. Technician B only
   c. Both Technicians A and B
   d. Neither Technician A nor B

10. Technician A says to use masking tape temporarily over the lining material to help prevent getting grease on the lining. Technician B says that grease on the brake lining can cause the brakes to grab. Which technician is correct?
    a. Technician A only
    b. Technician B only
    c. Both Technicians A and B
    d. Neither Technician A nor B

DISC BRAKES

OBJECTIVES

After studying Chapter 12, the reader will be able to:

1. Prepare for the Brakes (A5) ASE certification test content area "C" (Disc Brake Diagnosis and Repair).
2. Describe how disc brakes function.
3. Name the parts of a typical disc brake system.
4. Describe the construction of disc brake pads.
5. Describe the difference between fixed caliper and floating or sliding caliper.
6. Explain the difference between a standard caliper and a low-drag caliper.

KEY TERMS

Anchor plate 204	Mold bonded lining 201
Antirattle clips 197	NAO 202
Aramid fiber 202	NAS 202
Bonded linings 201	Natural frequency 197
Brake block 201	Nonasbestos 202
Brake pad 199	Pad wear indicators 200
CFRC 202	Pin-slider caliper 206
Fixed brake caliper 203	Riveted linings 200
Floating caliper 206	Semimets 202
Gas fade 195	Sintered metal 202
Integrally molded 201	Sintering 202
Kevlar 202	Sliding caliper 207
Lining fade 194	Swept area 194
Low-drag caliper 207	Water fade 195
Mechanical fade 194	Ways 207

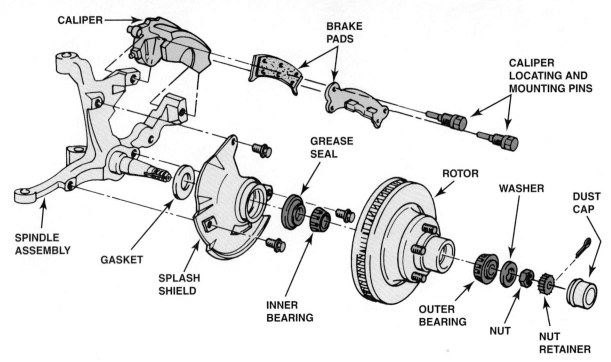

FIGURE 12–1 An exploded view of a typical disc brake assembly.

DISC BRAKES

PARTS AND OPERATION Disc brakes use a piston(s) to squeeze friction material (pads) on both sides of a rotating disc (rotor). Disc may be spelled *disk* by some manufacturers, but *disc* is the SAE (Society of Automotive Engineers) term and the most commonly used spelling in the industry. The rotor is attached to and stops the wheel.

Disc brakes are used on the front wheels of late-model vehicles, and on the rear wheels of an increasing number of automobiles. Disc brakes were adopted primarily because they can supply greater stopping power than drum brakes with less likelihood of fade. This makes disc brakes especially well suited for use as front brakes, which must provide 60% to 80% of the vehicle's total stopping power.

DISC BRAKE ADVANTAGES Although increased federal brake performance standards hastened the switch to disc brakes, the front drum brakes would eventually have been eliminated anyway because disc brakes are superior in almost every respect. The disc brake friction assembly has several significant strong points, and only a few relatively minor weak points. ● **SEE FIGURE 12–1**.

The main advantages of the disc brake include the following.

FADE RESISTANCE. The main design features that help disc brakes avoid heat-induced fade is their cooling ability because

all of the major parts of a disc brake are exposed to the air flowing over the friction assembly. Many brake rotors also have cooling passages cast into them to further reduce operating temperatures and have greater fade resistance than drum brakes because they have greater swept area. **Swept area** is the amount of brake drum or rotor friction surface that moves past the brake linings every time the drum or rotor completes a rotation. Disc brakes are resistant to all kinds of fade, including the following:

■ **Mechanical fade** is not a problem with disc brakes because, unlike a brake drum, the disc brake rotor expands *toward* the brake linings as it heats up rather than *away* from them. This fundamental design difference makes it physically impossible for heat to cause the rotor to expand out of contact with the brake linings. Because of this, there is never the need to move the brake linings out to keep them in contact with the rotor, so brake pedal travel does not increase. If the brake pedal on a vehicle with disc brakes drops toward the floor, it is almost always a sign of vapor lock, a fluid leak, fluid bypassing the seals in the master cylinder, or mechanical fade of the rear *drum* brakes.

■ **Lining fade** can and does occur if the brakes become overheated. A little bit of heat brings the brake pads to

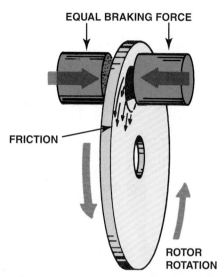

FIGURE 12–2 Braking force is applied equally to both sides of the brake rotor.

FIGURE 12–3 Disc brakes can absorb and dissipate a great deal of heat. During this demonstration, the brakes were gently applied as the engine drove the front wheels until the rotor became cherry red. During normal braking, the rotor temperature can exceed 350°F (180°C), and about 1,500°F (800°C) on a race vehicle.

their operating temperature and actually increases the friction coefficient of the lining material. A warm brake performs better than a cold brake. However, when too much heat is generated by braking, the lining material overheats. Its friction coefficient drops, and lining fade occurs.

The primary symptom of lining fade is a hard brake pedal that requires the driver to apply greater force to maintain stopping power. Unlike the similar situation in a drum brake, however, increased application force will not distort the brake rotor because the caliper applies equal force to both sides. ● **SEE FIGURE 12–2**.

Increased pressure will, however, create even more heat, and if brake lining temperatures continue to increase, gas fade and vapor lock of the hydraulic system can occur. If the pads are overheated to the point where the lining material is physically damaged, the brakes will not recover their full stopping power until the pads are replaced. ● **SEE FIGURE 12–3**.

■ **Gas fade** is a problem only under severe braking conditions when hot gases and dust particles from the linings are trapped between the brake linings and rotor, where they act as lubricants. The symptoms of gas fade are the same as those for lining fade. The pedal becomes

hard and increased force is required to maintain stopping power.

Even though disc brakes operate at higher temperatures than drum brakes, they have fewer problems with gas fade for a number of reasons.

1. Disc brakes do not have a drum to contain gases and particles in the area around the brake linings.

2. The constant flow of air over the brake carries away contaminants that might otherwise build up.

3. The surface area of the brake lining material in a disc brake is smaller than that of a comparable drum brake and this allows gases and particles to escape more easily.

To help prevent gas fade, many brake pads have slots cut in the lining material. These slots allow gases and dust particles to escape. ● **SEE FIGURE 12–4**. The holes required in riveted linings also perform this function. For even greater protection against gas fade, high-performance vehicles and motorcycles sometimes have holes or slots cut into the rotor. These openings allow gases and water to escape, and their sharp edges continually wipe loose particles off the linings.

■ **Water fade** is not a big problem with disc brakes because centrifugal force created by the spinning rotor

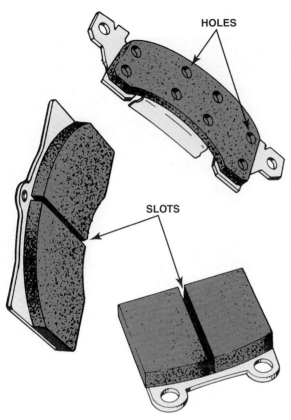

FIGURE 12–4 Slots and holes in the brake linings help prevent gas and water fade.

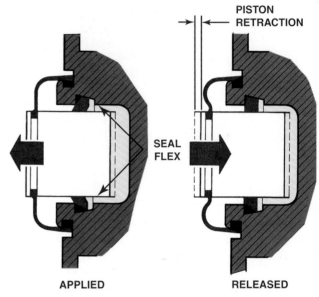

FIGURE 12–5 The square-cut O-ring not only seals hydraulic brake fluid, but also retracts the caliper piston when the brake pedal is released.

DISC BRAKES (CONTINUED)

throws off most moisture, and the brake pads positioned only a few thousandths of an inch away from the rotor continuously wipe it clean. When the brakes are applied, the leading edge of the brake pad lining material wipes the last bit of water from the disc. Once good lining-to-rotor contact is established, water is unable to enter the space between the linings and rotor until the brakes are released.

Although far more resistant to water fade than drum brakes, disc brakes are not entirely free from its effects. Splash shields and the vehicle's wheels help keep water off of the rotor, and the brake lining materials specified for most vehicles minimize the effects of water fade.

SELF-ADJUSTING ABILITY. Disc brakes are self-adjusting because any wear of the linings is automatically compensated for by the action of the brake caliper.

When the brakes are applied, the caliper pistons move out as far as needed to force the brake pads into contact with the rotor. When the brakes are released, the piston retracts only the small distance dictated by rotor runout and piston seal flex. ● **SEE FIGURE 12–5.** The surface finish on the piston must be

clean to allow the piston to slide past this seal. Excessive friction between the caliper piston and the caliper bore can prevent the piston from retracting. If the force of the caliper seal is not strong enough, the piston stays in the applied position. Because the brake pads are still in contact with the rotor, one or both pads will show excessive wear.

FREEDOM FROM PULL. A disc brake will stop straighter under a wider range of conditions than will a drum brake. A disc brake is self-cleaning, will throw off most water, and is less likely to pull.

Disc brakes do not have self-energizing or servo action. Because disc brakes are not self-energizing to increase their braking power, the effects of a loss of friction on one side of the vehicle are far less pronounced than with drum brakes.

DISC BRAKE DISADVANTAGES
The most notable fact about the disadvantages of disc brakes is that there are so few. The weaknesses of disc brakes include the following.

- **No Self-Energizing or Servo Action**—The disc brake's lack of self-energizing or servo action is a disadvantage for two reasons.

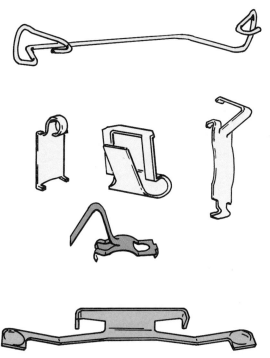

FIGURE 12–6 Antirattle clips reduce brake pad movement and vibration.

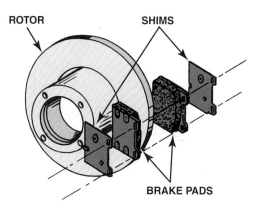

FIGURE 12–7 Antivibration shims are used behind the pads on many disc brake caliper designs.

1. It contributes to poor parking brake performance and requires the driver to push harder on the brake pedal for a given stop. However, the problem of high pedal pressures has been eliminated through the use of brake power boosters.

2. It is easier to control the brakes for the exact amount of stopping power desired.

■ **Brake Noise**—Probably the biggest complaint about disc brakes is that they sometimes make various squeaks and squeals during a brake application. As long as the brake linings are not worn down to the backing plate, these noises are usually caused by high-frequency rattling or vibration of the brake pads. Several methods are used to quiet noisy disc brakes. Manufacturers use specific lining materials that damp vibrations, and most calipers have **antirattle clips** or springs that hold the pads in the caliper under tension to help prevent vibration. ● SEE FIGURE 12–6.

Some calipers use special shims between the brake pad backing plate and the caliper piston to damp vibrations. ● SEE FIGURE 12–7. These shims may be made of metal or fiber. Antinoise sprays and brush-on liquids are available and provide a cushion layer between the pad and the caliper piston. The bond lowers the **natural frequency** of the pad, and the cushion layer damps any vibration that may still occur.

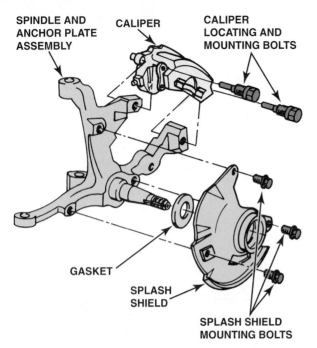

FIGURE 12-8 This brake caliper attaches to the front spindle.

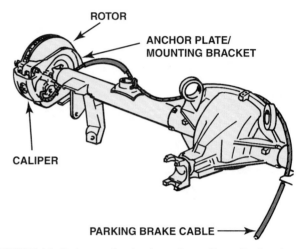

FIGURE 12-9 A rear disc brake caliper often attaches to a mounting bracket on the rear axle housing.

DISC BRAKES (CONTINUED)

BRAKE DUST. Because the lining is exposed on a disc brake, rather than being enclosed as on a drum brake, some brake dust can accumulate on the wheels. This brake dust is often dark brown or black and can stain wheels if not cleaned often or protected from the dust.

POOR PARKING BRAKE PERFORMANCE. The lack of self-energizing and servo action plays a large part in poor disc brake parking brake performance. The lining-to-rotor contact area of a disc brake is somewhat smaller than the lining-to-drum contact area of a drum brake. This causes the disc brake to have a lower static coefficient of friction, and therefore less holding power when the vehicle is stopped.

 **TECH TIP**

Wax the Wheels

Brake dust from semimetallic brake pads often discolors the front wheels. Customers often complain to service technicians about this problem, but it is normal for the front wheels to become dirty because the iron and other metallic and nonmetallic components wear off the front disc brake pads and adhere to the wheel covers. A coat of wax on the wheels or wheel covers helps prevent damage and makes it easier to wash off the brake dust.

DISC BRAKE CONSTRUCTION

A disc brake is relatively simple compared with a drum brake. The major disc brake friction assembly components include the following.

CALIPER With the exception of the rotor, the caliper is the largest part of a disc brake friction assembly. The brake caliper uses hydraulic pressure to create the mechanical force required to move the brake pads into contact with the brake rotor. At the front axle, the caliper mounts to the spindle or steering knuckle. ● **SEE FIGURE 12-8.** Rear disc brake calipers mount to a support bracket on the axle flange or suspension. ● **SEE FIGURE 12-9.**

SPLASH SHIELD The splash shield bolts to the front spindle or steering knuckle, or in rear disc brake applications, to the axle flange or a suspension adapter plate. The job of the splash shield is to protect the inner side of the brake rotor from water and other contaminants, whereas the outer side of the rotor is protected by the wheel. Most splash shields are made of stamped steel or plastic.

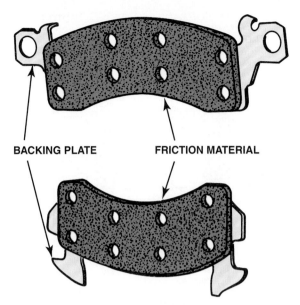

FIGURE 12–10 A typical disc brake pad.

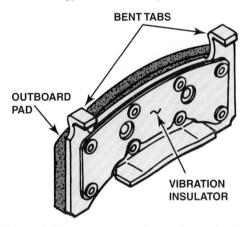

FIGURE 12–11 To prevent noise, bent tabs on the backing plate hold some brake pads to the caliper housing.

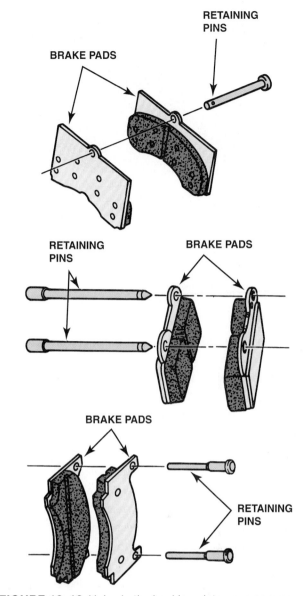

FIGURE 12–12 Holes in the backing plate are a common method of locating a pad in the caliper.

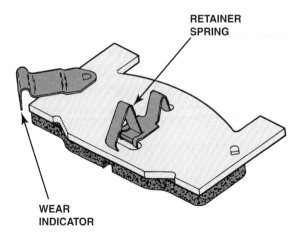

FIGURE 12–13 Retainer springs lock the pad to the caliper piston to prevent brake noise.

DISC BRAKE PADS

The lining of a disc brake is part of an assembly called the **brake pad**. ● **SEE FIGURE 12–10**. Compared to a brake shoe, a brake pad is a relatively simple part that consists of a block of friction material attached to a stamped steel backing plate. Some pad backing plates have tabs that bend over the caliper to hold the pad tightly in place and help prevent brake noise. ● **SEE FIGURE 12–11**.

Other pad backing plates have tabs with holes in them as shown in ● **FIGURE 12–12**. A pin slips through the holes and fastens to the caliper body to hold the pads in position. Still other pad backing plates have a retainer spring attached that locates the pad in the caliper by locking it to the caliper piston. ● **SEE FIGURE 12–13**.

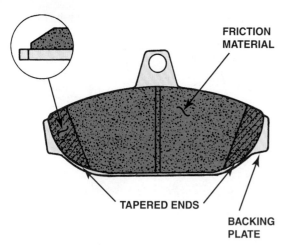

FIGURE 12–14 The lining edges of some brake pads are tapered to help prevent vibration.

DISC BRAKE PADS (CONTINUED)

As with brake shoes, the lining material of a disc pad can be any one of a number of products that can be fastened to the backing plate in several ways. The edges of the lining material on a brake pad are usually perpendicular to the rotor surface, although a few larger pads do have tapered edges to help combat vibration and noise. ● **SEE FIGURE 12–14.**

PAD WEAR INDICATORS Although not required by law, a growing number of vehicle manufacturers are fitting **pad wear indicators** to their brakes for safety reasons. Pad wear indicators are either mechanical or electrical, and signal the driver when the lining material has worn to the point where pad replacement is necessary.

A mechanical wear indicator is a small spring-steel tab riveted to the pad backing plate. When the friction material wears to a predetermined thickness, the tab contacts the rotor and makes a squealing or chirping noise (when the brakes are not applied) that alerts the driver to the need for service. ● **SEE FIGURE 12–15.**

Electrical wear indicators, such as those shown in ● **FIGURE 12–16,** use a coated electrode embedded in the lining material to generate the warning signal. The electrode is wired to a warning light in the instrument panel and when the lining wears sufficiently, the electrode grounds against the rotor to complete the circuit and turn on the warning light.

PAD ASSEMBLY METHODS As mentioned previously, there are several methods that are used to mount brake linings, including:

- **Riveted linings** take advantage of the oldest method of lining attachment still in use. In this system, the brake block is attached to the backing plate with copper or aluminum rivets.

FIGURE 12–15 Typical pad wear sensor operation. It is very important that the disc brake pads are installed on the correct side of the vehicle to be assured that the wear sensor will make a noise when the pads are worn. If the pads with a sensor are installed on the opposite side of the vehicle, the sensor tab is turned so that the rotor touches it going the opposite direction. Usually the correct direction is where the rotor contacts the sensor before contacting the pads when the wheels are being rotated in the forward direction.

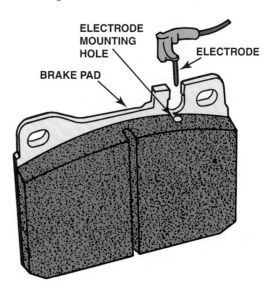

FIGURE 12–16 Electrical wear indicators ground a warning light circuit when the pads need replacement.

The major advantage of riveting is that it allows a small amount of flex between the brake block backing plate. This play enables the assembly to absorb vibration, and the result is that riveted linings operate more quietly than bonded linings. However the rivet holes create stress points in the lining where cracks are likely to develop.

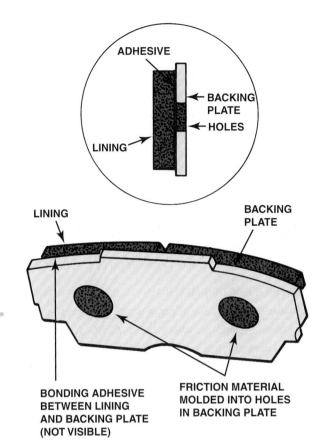

FIGURE 12–17 Mold-bonded linings are commonly used in many applications.

INGREDIENT	TYPICAL FORMULA RANGE
Phenolic resin (binder)	9–15%
Asbestos fiber	30–50%
Organic friction modifiers (rubber scrap)	8–19%
Inorganic friction modifiers (barites, talc, whiting)	12–26%
Abrasive particles (alumina)	4–20%
Carbon	4–20%

CHART 12–1

Typical compositions for asbestos (organic) lining.

■ **Bonded linings** use high-temperature adhesive to glue the brake block directly to the shoe pad backing plate. Heat and pressure are then applied to cure the assembly. Bonding is a common form of shoe and pad assembly, and is most often used to mount organic friction materials.

Bonding offers several advantages. Without rivets, bonded linings can wear closer to the backing plate and provide a longer service life. If the linings wear too far, bonding adhesive is not as destructive to rotors as rivets. Bonded linings also have fewer problems with cracking because they have no rivet holes to weaken the brake block. The primary disadvantage of bonded linings is a limited ability to withstand high temperatures. If a bonded lining gets too hot, the bonding adhesive will fail and allow the brake block to separate from the backing plate. Bonded linings are also more prone to be noisy because they do not allow any vibration absorbing flex between the brake block and backing plate.

■ **Mold-bonded linings** are found on some disc brake pads. Mold bonding is a manufacturing process that combines the advantages of bonding with some of the mechanical strength of riveting. Instead of riveting and/or

bonding a cured brake block to a separate backing plate, the friction material in a mold-bonded pad is cured on the backing plate during manufacture. This process is also called **integrally molded**. Most high-performance disc brake pads are made in this way.

To make a mold-bonded pad, one or more holes are punched in the pad backing plate, and a high-temperature adhesive is applied to it. The backing plate is then installed in a molding machine where uncured friction material is formed onto the plate and forced into the holes. ● **SEE FIGURE 12–17**. Once the pad is cured under heat and pressure, the bonding adhesive combines with the portions of the lining that extend into the backing plate holes to solidly lock the brake block in place.

BRAKE LINING COMPOSITION Shoes and pads operate under the most extreme conditions in the entire brake system and are subject to a great deal of wear. The replacement of worn brake shoes and pads is a common part of brake service.

Friction materials such as disc brake pads or drum brake shoes contain a mixture of ingredients. These materials include a binder such as a thermosetting resin, fibers for reinforcement, and friction modifiers to obtain a desired coefficient of friction (abbreviated μ— Greek letter mu).

The various ingredients in brake lining are mixed and molded into the shape of the finished product. The fibers in the material are the only thing holding this mixture together. A large press is used to force the ingredients together to form a **brake block**, which eventually becomes the brake lining. ● **SEE CHART 12–1**.

INGREDIENT	FORMULA RANGE
Phenolic resin	15–40%
Graphite or carbon particles	15–40%
Steel fibers	0–25%
Ceramic powders	2–10%
Steel, copper, brass metal powders	15–40%
Other modifiers (rubber scrap)	0–20%

CHART 12-2

Typical compositions for semimetallic disc brake pads

TECH TIP

Competitively Priced Brakes

The term *competitively priced* means lower cost. Most brake manufacturers offer "premium" as well as lower-price linings, to remain competitive with other manufacturers or with importers of brake lining material produced overseas by U.S. or foreign companies. Organic asbestos brake lining is inexpensive to manufacture. In fact, according to warehouse distributors and importers, the box often costs more than the brake lining inside.

Professional brake service technicians should only install brake linings and pads that will give braking performance equal to that of the original factory brakes. For best results, always purchase high-quality brake parts from a known brand-name manufacturer.

SEMIMETALLIC FRICTION MATERIAL. The term *semimetallic* refers to brake lining material that uses metal rather than asbestos in its formulation. It still uses resins and binders and is, therefore, not 100% metal, but rather, semimetallic. Semimetallics are commonly called **semimets**. The metal in most metallic linings is made from metal particles that have been fused together without melting. This process is called **sintering** and the result is called **sintered metal** linings. ● **SEE CHART 12-2.**

Most semimetallic linings do not contain asbestos. Semimetallic linings require a very smooth finish on the rotor because the metal in the lining does not conform to the surface of the rotor, as does asbestos lining.

NOTE: If a magnet sticks the lining material, it is semimetallic.

NONASBESTOS FRICTION MATERIAL. Brake pads and linings that use synthetic material such as aramid fibers instead of steel are usually referred to as **nonasbestos**, **nonasbestos organic (NAO)**, or **nonasbestos synthetic (NAS)**. Linings are called *synthetic* because synthetic (man-made) fibers are used. These linings use **aramid fiber** instead of metal as the base material. Aramid is the generic name for aromatic polyamide fibers. **Kevlar** is the Dupont brand name of aramid and a registered trademark of E.I. Dupont de Nemours and Company. Nonasbestos linings are often quieter than semimetallics and do not cause as much wear to brake rotors as do semimetallic pads.

CARBON FIBER FRICTION MATERIAL. Carbon fiber brake lining is the newest and most expensive of the lining materials. Carbon fiber material is often called **CFRC (carbon fiber-reinforced carbon)**. It is composed of a carbon mix into which reinforcing carbon fibers are embedded. CFRC is commonly used in the brakes of jet aircraft and racing cars. CFRC brakes provide constant friction coefficient whether cold or hot, low wear rates, and low noise development.

CERAMIC FRICTION MATERIAL. Some vehicle manufacturers use friction materials that contain ceramic fibers. These ceramic fibers are usually potassium titanite. Some vehicle manufacturers do not recommend the use of ceramic friction material because they tend to wear the rotors more than NAO or semimetallic friction materials.

FREQUENTLY ASKED QUESTION

What Does "D³EA" Mean?

Original equipment brake pads and shoes are required to comply with the Federal Motor Vehicle Safety Standard (FMVSS) 135, which specifies maximum stopping distances. There is also a requirement for fade resistance, but no standard for noise or wear. Aftermarket (replacement) brake pads and shoes are not required to meet the FMVSS standard. However, several manufacturers of replacement brake pads and shoes are using a standardized test that closely matches the FMVSS standard and is called the "Dual Dynamometer Differential Effectiveness Analysis" or D³EA. This test is currently voluntary and linings that pass the test can have a "D³EA certified" seal placed on the product package.

Code C	0.00 to 0.15
Code D	0.15 to 0.25
Code E	0.25 to 0.35
Code F	0.35 to 0.45
Code G	0.45 to 0.55
Code H	0.55 and above
Code Z	ungraded

CHART 12–3

The SAE brake pad edge codes are used to indicate the coefficient of friction of the pad material.

EDGE CODES As explained previously, the lining edge codes help identify the coefficient of friction. These codes were established by the SAE (Society of Automotive Engineers) and published as Standard J886a. ● **SEE CHART 12–3**.

The first letter, which is printed on the side of most linings, indicates its coefficient of friction when brakes are cold, and the second letter indicates the coefficient of friction of the brake lining when the brakes are hot. For example, FF indicates that the brake lining material has a coefficient of friction between 0.35 and 0.45 when both cold and hot.

BRAKE ROTORS

The brake rotor provides the friction surfaces for the brake pads to rub against. The rotor, the largest and heaviest part of a disc brake, is usually made of cast iron because that metal has excellent friction and wear properties. There are two basic types of rotors:

- **Solid**—Solid rotors are most often used on the rear of vehicles equipped with four-wheel disc brakes.
- **Vented**—Vented rotors have radial cooling passages cast between the friction surfaces. ● **SEE FIGURE 12–18**.

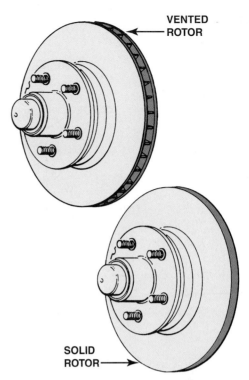

FIGURE 12–18 Disc brake rotors can be either solid or vented.

DISC BRAKE DESIGNS

There are basically three types of calipers: fixed, floating, and sliding designs.

FIXED CALIPER DESIGN The **fixed brake caliper** is the earliest design. ● **SEE FIGURE 12–19**. The fixed caliper has a body manufactured in two halves, and uses two, four, or six pistons to apply the brake pads. The fixed caliper gets its name from the fact that the caliper is rigidly mounted to the suspension. When the brakes are applied, the pistons extend from the caliper bores and apply the brake pads with equal force from both sides of the rotor. No part of the caliper body moves when the brakes are applied.

FIXED CALIPER ADVANTAGES. Fixed calipers are relatively large and heavy, which enables them to absorb and dissipate great amounts of heat. This allows the brake rotor and pads to run cooler, and reduce the amount of heat transferred to the brake fluid. Compared with other caliper designs, a fixed caliper is able to withstand a greater number of repeated hard stops without heat-induced fade or vapor lock of the hydraulic system.

The size and rigid mounting of a fixed caliper also means it does not flex as much as other designs. A caliper that is flexing is usually felt by the driver as a spongy brake pedal. Fixed calipers are very strong and provide a firm and linear brake pedal feel.

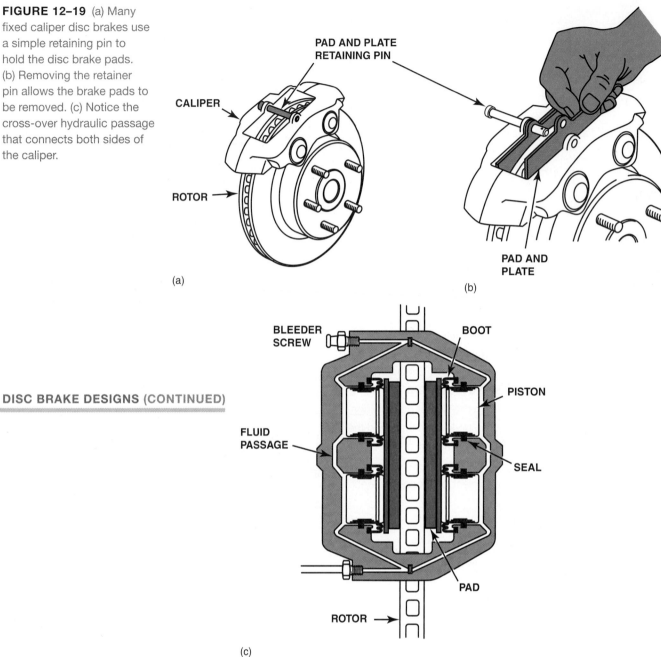

FIGURE 12–19 (a) Many fixed caliper disc brakes use a simple retaining pin to hold the disc brake pads. (b) Removing the retainer pin allows the brake pads to be removed. (c) Notice the cross-over hydraulic passage that connects both sides of the caliper.

PAD AND PLATE RETAINING PIN

CALIPER

ROTOR

(a)

PAD AND PLATE

(b)

BLEEDER SCREW

BOOT

PISTON

FLUID PASSAGE

SEAL

PAD

ROTOR

(c)

DISC BRAKE DESIGNS (CONTINUED)

The strength and heat-dissipating abilities of fixed calipers make them best suited for heavy-duty use such as in most race vehicles.

FIXED CALIPER DISADVANTAGES. The size and weight of fixed calipers are advantages in heavy-duty use, but they add weight to the vehicle.

Another disadvantage of fixed calipers is that, with multiple pistons and split bodies, service is more difficult and allows greater opportunity for leaks. The drilled passages that route fluid through the inside of the caliper body also contribute to cracking as miles accumulate and the caliper goes through hundreds of thousands of heating and cooling cycles.

FLOATING AND SLIDING CALIPER DESIGN The front brakes of most vehicles are fitted with either floating or sliding calipers, which are *not* rigidly mounted. The caliper is free to move within a limited range on an **anchor plate** that *is* solidly mounted to the vehicle suspension. The anchor plate may be cast into a suspension member (often the front spindle) or it can be a separate piece that bolts to the suspension. ● **SEE FIGURE 12–20.**

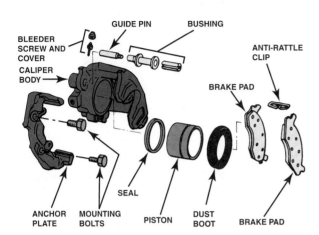

FIGURE 12-20 This floating caliper mounts on a separate anchor plate that bolts to the vehicle suspension.

Labels for Figure 12-20:
GUIDE PIN
BUSHING
BLEEDER SCREW AND COVER
CALIPER BODY
ANTI-RATTLE CLIP
BRAKE PAD
ANCHOR PLATE
MOUNTING BOLTS
SEAL
PISTON
DUST BOOT
BRAKE PAD

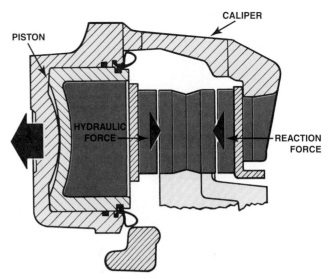

Labels for Figure 12-21:
CALIPER
PISTON
HYDRAULIC FORCE
REACTION FORCE

FIGURE 12-21 Hydraulic force on the piston (left) is applied to the inboard pad and the caliper housing itself. The reaction of the piston pushing against the rotor causes the entire caliper to move toward the inside of the vehicle (large arrow). Since the outboard pad is retained by the caliper, the reaction of the moving caliper applies the force of the outboard pad against the outboard surface of the rotor.

When the brakes are applied, the caliper piston moves out of its bore and applies the inner brake pad. At the same time, the caliper body moves in the opposite direction on the anchor plate and applies the outer brake pad. With a floating or sliding caliper, the caliper body moves every time the brakes are applied. ● SEE FIGURE 12-21.

NORMAL CALIPER OPERATION. The piston moves just enough to distort the caliper seal and returns to the original position when the brake pedal is released.

WEAR COMPENSATION. The piston moves more than the caliper seal can distort. The piston moves through the seal until the pad contacts the rotor. The caliper piston returns to the released position by the seal distortion, the same as during normal operation, except now in a different, more applied position.

As the wear occurs and the piston moves, additional brake fluid is needed behind the piston. This additional brake fluid comes from the master cylinder and the brake fluid level drops as the disc brake pads wear.

FLOATING AND SLIDING CALIPER ADVANTAGES. The biggest advantages of floating and sliding calipers are lower cost, simple construction, and compact size. Most floating and sliding calipers are single-piston designs. Because they have fewer pieces, floating and sliding calipers are cheaper to build and service, and have fewer places where leaks can develop.

The smaller size of floating and sliding calipers also allows better packaging of the caliper on the vehicle. A single-piston caliper with the piston located on the inboard side of the brake rotor fits easily within the diameter of a small wheel. The inboard position of the caliper piston also contributes to better cooling because the bulk of the caliper body is exposed to the passing airflow.

Like any disc brake, floating and sliding calipers have poor parking brake performance. Unlike a fixed caliper, a floating or sliding caliper can be mechanically actuated by applying the single piston with a cable and lever mechanism.

FLOATING AND SLIDING CALIPER DISADVANTAGES. The movable caliper body allows a certain degree of flex, which can contribute to a spongy brake pedal. Caliper flex also allows the caliper body to twist slightly when the brakes are applied, causing tapered wear of the brake pad lining material. ● SEE FIGURE 12-22.

Although the inboard piston location of floating and sliding calipers provides good cooling, these designs can never absorb as much heat (and therefore have the fade resistance) as a fixed caliper with similar stopping power. Floating and sliding calipers simply do not have the mass of fixed calipers, and their flexible mounting systems slow the transfer of heat from the caliper body to the anchor plate and other suspension components that aid in the cooling process.

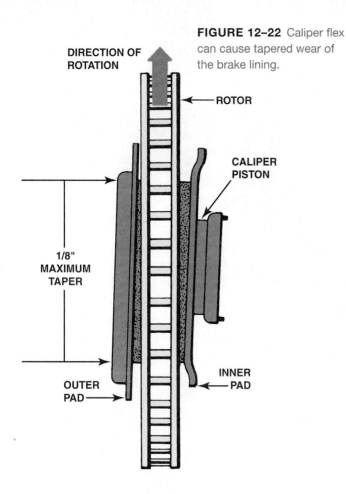

FIGURE 12–22 Caliper flex can cause tapered wear of the brake lining.

DIRECTION OF ROTATION

ROTOR

CALIPER PISTON

1/8" MAXIMUM TAPER

OUTER PAD

INNER PAD

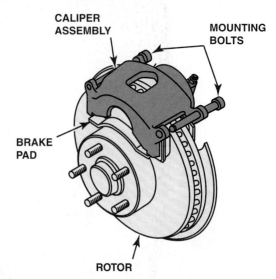

CALIPER ASSEMBLY

MOUNTING BOLTS

BRAKE PAD

ROTOR

FIGURE 12–23 A typical single-piston floating caliper. In this type of design, the entire caliper moves when the single piston is pushed out of the caliper during a brake application. When the caliper moves, the outboard pad is pushed against the rotor.

DISC BRAKE DESIGNS (CONTINUED)

FLOATING CALIPER OPERATION The body of a **floating caliper** does not make direct metal-to-metal contact with the anchor plate. ● **SEE FIGURE 12–23**. Instead, the caliper body is supported by bushings and/or O-rings that allow it to "float" or slide on metal guide pins or locating sleeves attached to the anchor plate. For this reason, some automakers call the floating caliper a **pin-slider caliper**.

The bushings that support floating calipers are made from a number of materials including rubber, Teflon, and nylon. The O-rings are generally made from high-temperature synthetic rubber. ● **SEE FIGURE 12–24**. The guide pins and sleeves are made of steel and come in a variety of shapes and sizes for different caliper designs. ● **SEE FIGURE 12–25**.

Floating calipers depend on proper lubrication of their pins, sleeves, bushings, and O-rings for smooth operation. If these parts become rusted or corroded, the caliper will bind and stick, causing loss of braking power that is usually accompanied by rapid and unusual wear of brake pads. Special high-temperature brake grease must be used to lubricate these parts any time the caliper is disassembled. Many manufacturers recommend that floating caliper pins, sleeves, bushings, and

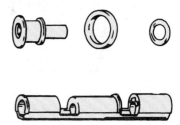

FIGURE 12–24 Floating calipers are supported by rubber O-rings or plastic bushings.

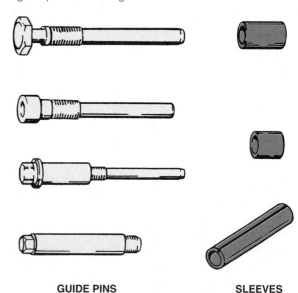

GUIDE PINS

SLEEVES

FIGURE 12–25 Metal guide pins and sleeves are used to retain and locate floating calipers.

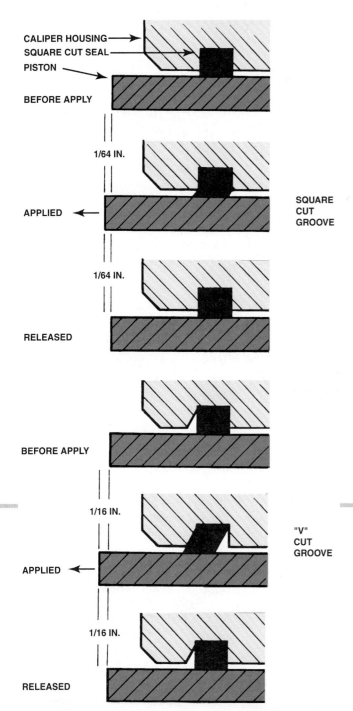

FIGURE 12–26 In a standard disc brake caliper, the square-cut O-ring deforms when the brakes are applied and returns the piston to its original (released) position due to the elastic properties of the rubber seal. In a low-drag caliper design, the groove for the square-cut O-ring is V-shaped, allowing for more retraction. When the brake pedal is released, the piston is moved away from the rotor further, resulting in less friction between the disc brake pads and the rotor when the brakes are released.

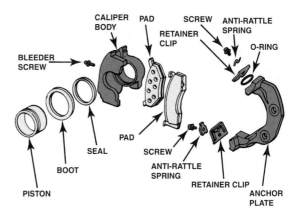

FIGURE 12–27 Exploded view of a typical sliding brake caliper.

O-rings be replaced whenever the caliper is serviced. These parts come in a "small parts kit" available from brake part suppliers.

SLIDING CALIPERS Unlike a floating caliper, the body of a **sliding caliper** mounts in direct metal-to-metal contact with the anchor plate. ● SEE FIGURE 12–27.

Instead of pins and bushings, sliding calipers move on **ways** cast and machined into the caliper body and anchor plate. ● SEE FIGURE 12–28. Retaining clips and the design of the caliper prevent the body from coming out of the ways once the caliper is assembled. On some calipers, the ways may have to be filed for proper clearance between the caliper body and anchor plate if the caliper is replaced.

Like floating calipers, sliding calipers depend on good lubrication of their ways for proper operation. If not properly coated with high-temperature brake grease, the ways can rust or corrode, causing the caliper to drag or seize.

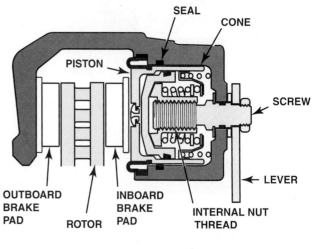

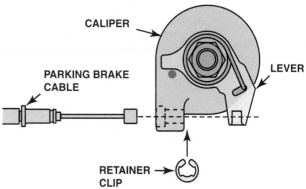

FIGURE 12–29 Exploded view of a typical rear disc brake with an integral parking brake. The parking brake lever mechanically pushes the caliper piston against the rotor.

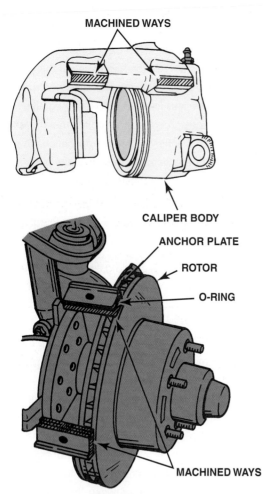

FIGURE 12–28 Sliding calipers move on machined ways.

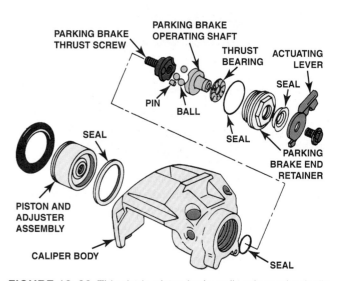

FIGURE 12–30 This single-piston brake caliper is mechanically actuated to serve as a parking brake.

REAR DISC BRAKES

In recent years, four-wheel disc brake systems have become more common. In most rear-wheel applications, drum brakes are adequate to provide the relatively small portion of a vehicle's total braking power required of them. Because rear drum brakes are lightly loaded, fade is a problem only in extreme conditions when the front brakes fade and force the rear brakes to take on a larger part of the braking load. The automatic adjusting ability of disc brakes is also less of an advantage in slow-wearing rear brakes.

REAR DISC PARKING BRAKES   There are two methods of providing parking brakes when rear discs are installed on a vehicle.

1. Adapt the disc brake to also function as the parking brake. This is done by installing a series of cables, levers, and internal parts to mechanically actuate the brake caliper. ● **SEE FIGURES 12–29 AND 12–30**.

2. Use mechanically actuated drum brakes inside the rear rotors. ● **SEE FIGURE 12–31**.

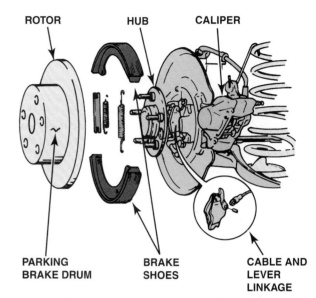

ROTOR   HUB   CALIPER

PARKING BRAKE DRUM   BRAKE SHOES   CABLE AND LEVER LINKAGE

FIGURE 12–31 Drum parking brakes are fitted inside the rotors on this vehicle equipped with rear disc brakes.

SUMMARY

1. Disc brakes are superior to drum brakes because they are fade-resistant, self-adjusting, and are less likely to pull during braking.

2. Disc brakes, however, lack self-energization requiring greater force be applied to the brake pedal compared with the drum brakes.

3. Disc brakes are more prone to noise than drum brakes.

4. A typical disc brake assembly includes the caliper assembly, splash shield, brake pads, and brake rotor.

5. The three basic types of disc brake calipers include fixed, floating, and sliding designs.

6. A low-drag caliper requires the use of a quick-take-up master cylinder.

7. Some disc brakes are equipped with integral parking brakes.

8. Brake pads can be attached using rivets, bonding, or integrally molded.

9. Typical semimetallic brake linings contain phenolic resin, graphite or carbon particles, steel fibers, ceramic and metal powders, plus other modifiers such as rubber scraps.

10. Other types of friction material include nonasbestos organic (NAO), nonasbestos synthetic (NAS), and carbon fiber-reinforced carbon (CFRC).

11. Lining edge codes identify the manufacturer and include two letters at the end, which identify the coefficient of friction of the material. The first letter indicates the coefficient when the lining is cold and the second indicates the coefficient when the lining is hot.

REVIEW QUESTIONS

1. What are the advantages and disadvantages of disc brakes?

2. What parts are included in a typical disc brake?

3. How does a low-drag caliper work?

4. What mechanism is used to apply the parking brake on a vehicle equipped with rear disc brakes?

5. What do the abbreviations NAO, NAS, and CFRC mean?

1. What part causes the disc brake caliper piston to retract when the brakes are released?
   a. Return (retracting) spring
   b. The rotating rotor (disc) that pushes the piston back
   c. The square-cut O-ring
   d. The caliper bushings

2. Two technicians are discussing the reason that the brake fluid level in the master cylinder drops. Technician A says that it may be normal due to the wear of the disc brake pads. Technician B says that a low brake fluid level may indicate a hydraulic leak somewhere in the system. Which technician is correct?
   a. Technician A only
   b. Technician B only
   c. Both Technicians A and B
   d. Neither Technician A nor B

3. Two technicians are discussing a floating-type disc brake caliper. Technician A says that if the caliper slides are corroded, one pad may wear more than the other pad on the same wheel brake. Technician B says that if a caliper slide is corroded, reduced braking may occur. Which technician is correct?
   a. Technician A only
   b. Technician B only
   c. Both Technicians A and B
   d. Neither Technician A nor B

4. Technician A says that disc brakes are self-adjusting and the brake pedal height should not become lower as the disc brake pads wear. Technician B says that as the disc brake pads wear, the level of brake fluid in the master cylinder reservoir drops. Which technician is correct?
   a. Technician A only
   b. Technician B only
   c. Both Technicians A and B
   d. Neither Technician A nor B

5. Which type of disc brake caliper may leak brake fluid more often?
   a. Sliding   c. Floating
   b. Fixed   d. Single-piston

6. A quick-take-up master cylinder is required when what type of caliper design is used on a vehicle?
   a. Fixed   c. Sliding
   b. Two-piston   d. Low-drag

7. Technician A says that all vehicles equipped with rear disc brakes use a parking brake that is integrated in the caliper. Technician B says that all vehicles equipped with rear disc brakes use a small drum brake inside the rear rotor for a parking brake. Which technician is correct?
   a. Technician A only
   b. Technician B only
   c. Both Technicians A and B
   d. Neither Technician A nor B

8. The brake pad edge code letters "FF" mean _____.
   a. Brand name
   b. Coefficient of friction rating
   c. Quality factor
   d. Noise level rating

9. Semimetallic brake pads are made by a process called _____.
   a. Sintering   c. Grating
   b. Melting   d. Composition

10. Technician A says that riveted disc brake pads are often quieter than bonded disc brake pads. Technician B says integrally molded disc brake pads are molded into holes in the steel backing of the pads. Which technician is correct?
    a. Technician A only
    b. Technician B only
    c. Both Technicians A and B
    d. Neither Technician A nor B

chapter 13
DISC BRAKE DIAGNOSIS AND SERVICE

DISC BRAKE DIAGNOSTIC PROCEDURES

When diagnosing disc brake concerns, perform the following steps:

STEP 1 The first step is to verify the customer complaint. This step usually includes test driving the vehicle to see if the complaint can be duplicated. If the problem cannot be duplicated, then the repair or service cannot be verified.

> **CAUTION: Do not test drive the vehicle on public roads if the red brake warning light is on. Perform a visual inspection to determine the reason for the warning light being on and correct before test driving the vehicle.**

STEP 2 Check the brake pedal height and verify proper operation. If the brake pedal is low, count the number of "clicks" it takes to apply the parking brake. There should be 3 to 7 clicks. If there are over 10 clicks, check the rear brakes.

STEP 3 Safely hoist the vehicle and remove the wheels. Visually check the following:
- Flexible brake hoses for wear or damage
- Disc brake rotors for excessive rust or scoring
- Disc brake calipers for leakage or damage

STEP 4 Remove disc brake calipers and check the disc brake pads for proper lining thickness and check for cracks or other damage.

STEP 5 Replace all components that do not meet factory specifications.

STEP 6 Test drive the vehicle to verify that the repairs did correct the customer concern.

TECH TIP

Let the Owner Drive

When verifying the customer complaint, ask the owner or driver of the vehicle to drive. Often, the problem is best discovered if the vehicle is being driven exactly the same way as when the complaint first occurred. For example, the technician may brake harder or softer than the driver so the problem may not be detected.

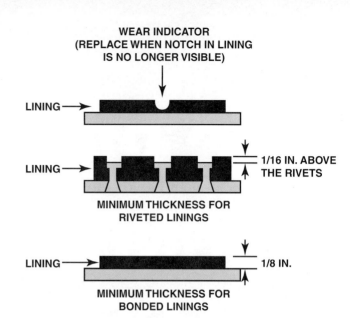

FIGURE 13–1 Minimum thickness for various types of disc brake pads. Pad wear sensors often make a "chirping" sound when the vehicle is moving if the pads are worn. Do not confuse that noise for a defective wheel bearing or other fault.

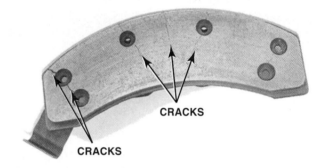

FIGURE 13–2 This cracked disc brake pad must be replaced even though it is thicker than the minimum allowed by the vehicle manufacturer.

VISUAL INSPECTION

Even with operating wear-indicating sensors, a thorough visual inspection is very important. ● **SEE FIGURE 13–1.** A lining thickness check alone should not be the only inspection performed on a disc brake. *A thorough visual inspection can only be accomplished by removing the friction pads.* ● **SEE FIGURE 13–2** for an example of a disc brake pad that shows usable lining thickness, but is severely cracked and *must* be replaced.

NOTE: Some disc brake pads use a heat barrier (thermo) layer between the steel backing plate and the friction material. The purpose of the heat barrier is to prevent heat from transferring into the caliper piston where it may cause the brake fluid to boil. Do not confuse

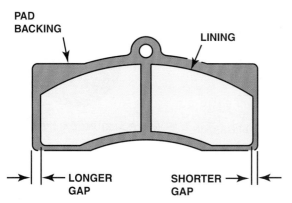

PAD BACKING

LINING

← LONGER GAP → ← SHORTER GAP →

FIGURE 13–3 Be careful to observe the direction in which replacement linings are facing. Some vehicle manufacturers offset the friction material on the steel backing to help prevent or minimize tapered pad wear. Check service information for details as to which direction the pads should be installed.

 **TECH TIP**

The Bleed and Squirt Test

If you suspect a brake is not being fully released, simply loosen the bleeder valve. If brake fluid squirts out under pressure, then the brake is being kept applied. Look for a defective flexible brake hose.

If the vehicle is off the ground, the wheels should be able to be rotated with the brakes off. If a wheel is difficult or hard to turn by hand and is easy to turn after opening the bleeder valve, then there is a brake fluid restriction between the master cylinder and the brake.

BRAKE INSPECTION OPENING

FIGURE 13–4 Most disc brake calipers have a brake inspection opening. For a thorough inspection, however, the caliper should be removed and the entire braking system thoroughly inspected.

the thickness of the barrier as part of the thickness of the friction lining material. The barrier material is usually a different color and usually can be distinguished from the lining material.

Some disc brake pads may show more wear on the end of the pad that first contacts the rotor as compared to the trailing end of the pad. This uneven wear is caused by the force between the pad and the abutment (slide area). In designs that place the caliper piston exactly in the center of the leading edge of the pad that first contacts the rotor as it is revolving through

the caliper, pressures are often one-third higher than the average pressure exerted on the entire pad. The result of this higher pressure is greater wear.

Brake engineers design brakes to minimize or eliminate tapered pad wear by offsetting the piston more toward the trailing edge of the shoe or by other caliper/pad mounting designs.

One method used to help reduce tapered pad wear is the design that offsets the friction material off center. Be certain to position the pads correctly or severe tapered pad wear will occur. ● **SEE FIGURES 13–3 AND 13–4.**

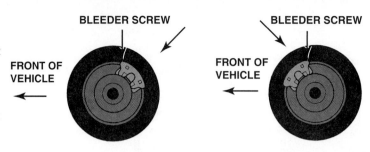

FIGURE 13–5 Both rear- and forward-mounted calipers have the bleeder valve at the top. Some calipers will fit on the wrong side of the vehicle, yet not be able to be bled correctly because the bleeder valve would point down, allowing trapped air to remain inside the caliper bore. If both calipers are being removed at the same time, mark them "left" and "right."

BLEEDER SCREW   BLEEDER SCREW

FRONT OF VEHICLE   FRONT OF VEHICLE

REAR-MOUNT CALIPER POSITION   FORWARD-MOUNT CALIPER POSITION

FIGURE 13–6 Many manufacturers recommend removing one-half of the brake fluid from the master cylinder before servicing disc brakes. Use a squeeze bulb and dispose of the used brake fluid properly.

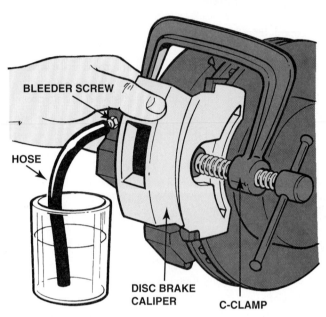

BLEEDER SCREW

HOSE

DISC BRAKE CALIPER   C-CLAMP

FIGURE 13–7 Most manufacturers recommend that the bleeder valve be opened and the brake fluid forced into a container rather than back into the master cylinder reservoir. This helps prevent contaminated brake fluid from being forced into the master cylinder where the dirt and contamination could cause problems.

DISC BRAKE CALIPER SERVICE

REMOVAL Hoist the vehicle and remove the wheel(s). Note the caliper mount position as shown in ● **FIGURE 13–5** before removing the caliper. Knowing whether the caliper is "rear-mount" position or "forward-mount" position is often needed when purchasing replacement calipers. Remove the caliper following the steps shown in ● **FIGURES 13–6 THROUGH 13–10.**

INSPECTION AND DISASSEMBLY Check for brake fluid in and around the piston boot area. If the boot is damaged or a fluid leak is visible, then a caliper assembly repair or replacement is required. ● **SEE FIGURES 13–11 AND 13–12.**

PHENOLIC CALIPER PISTONS. **Phenolic caliper pistons** are made from a phenol-formaldehyde resin combined with various

reinforcing fibers. When phenolic brake caliper pistons were first used, the results were not good and the problem was blamed on "those *darn* plastic pistons." What was happening was that the pistons were becoming stuck in the caliper, which caused the brake pads to remain applied. This caused the brake pads to wear out very rapidly. The problem occurred because the phenolic pistons absorbed moisture and swelled in size.

NOTE: Uneven disc brake pad wear (inside pad compared to the outside pad) can be caused by a stuck caliper piston or if the caliper is unable to "float."

Phenolic caliper pistons are natural thermal insulators and help keep heat generated by the disc brake pads from transferring

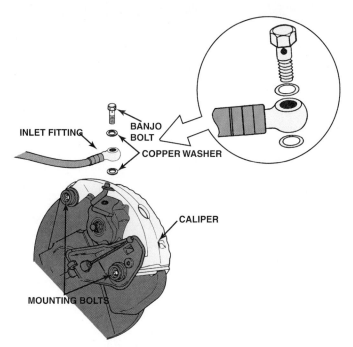

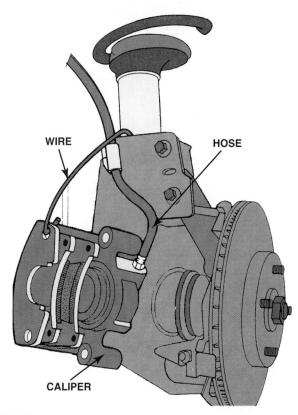

FIGURE 13–8 Many calipers use a hollow "banjo bolt" to retain the flexible brake line to the caliper housing. The fitting is usually round like a banjo. The copper washers should always be replaced and not reused.

FIGURE 13–10 If the caliper is not being removed, it must be supported properly so that the weight of the caliper is not pulling on the flexible rubber brake line. A suitable piece of wire, such as a coat hanger, may be used.

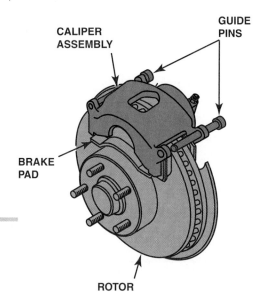

FIGURE 13–9 Caliper retaining bolts are often called guide pins. These guide pins are used to retain the caliper to the steering knuckle. These pins also slide through metal bushings and rubber O-rings.

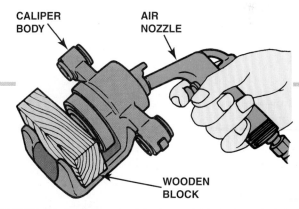

FIGURE 13–11 A wooden block or a folded shop cloth helps prevent damage when caliper pistons are removed.

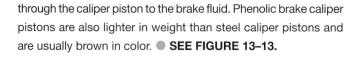

through the caliper piston to the brake fluid. Phenolic brake caliper pistons are also lighter in weight than steel caliper pistons and are usually brown in color. ● **SEE FIGURE 13–13.**

STEEL CALIPER PISTONS. Many manufacturers still use steel pistons. The stamped steel pistons are plated first with nickel,

then chrome to achieve the desired surface finish. ● **SEE FIGURE 13–14.** Unlike phenolic caliper pistons, steel pistons can transfer heat from the brake pads to the brake fluid. The surface finish on a steel piston is critical. Steel can rust and corrode. Any surface pitting can cause the piston to stick.

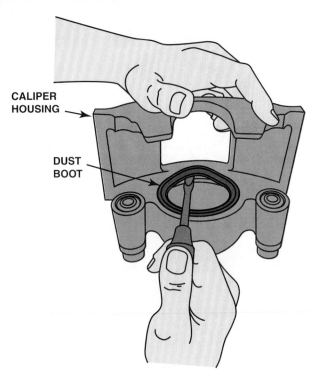

FIGURE 13–12 After the piston is removed from the caliper housing, the dust boot can often be removed using a straight-blade screwdriver.

CALIPER HOUSING

DUST BOOT

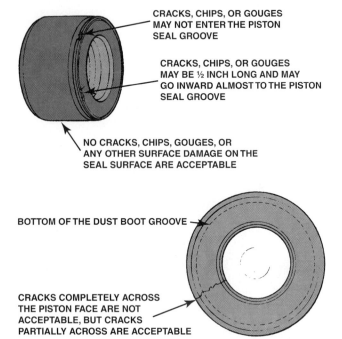

CRACKS, CHIPS, OR GOUGES MAY NOT ENTER THE PISTON SEAL GROOVE

CRACKS, CHIPS, OR GOUGES MAY BE ½ INCH LONG AND MAY GO INWARD ALMOST TO THE PISTON SEAL GROOVE

NO CRACKS, CHIPS, GOUGES, OR ANY OTHER SURFACE DAMAGE ON THE SEAL SURFACE ARE ACCEPTABLE

BOTTOM OF THE DUST BOOT GROOVE

CRACKS COMPLETELY ACROSS THE PISTON FACE ARE NOT ACCEPTABLE, BUT CRACKS PARTIALLY ACROSS ARE ACCEPTABLE

FIGURE 13–13 Phenolic (plastic) pistons should be carefully inspected.

FIGURE 13–14 If there are any surface flaws such as rust pits on the piston, it should be replaced.

DISC BRAKE CALIPER SERVICE (CONTINUED)

NOTE: Care should be taken when cleaning steel pistons. Use crocus cloth to remove any surface staining. Do not use sandpaper, emery cloth, or any other substance that may remove or damage the chrome surface finish.

REAL WORLD FIX

Three Brake Jobs in 40,000 Miles

A service technician was asked to replace the front disc brake pads on a Pontiac Grand Am because the sensors were touching the rotors and making a squealing sound. This was the third time that the front brakes needed to be replaced. Previous brake repairs had been limited to replacement of the front disc brake pads only.

When the caliper was removed and the pads inspected, it was discovered that a part of one pad had broken and a piece of the lining was missing.

● SEE FIGURE 13–15.

Then the technician spotted something at the rear of the vehicle that told the whole story—a trailer hitch.

The owner confirmed that a heavy jet ski was towed in hilly terrain. The technician recommended overhauling the front disc brake calipers to prevent the possibility of the front pads dragging. The technician also recommended an inspection of the rear brakes. The rear brakes were glazed and out-of-adjustment. The technician received permission to replace the rear brakes, overhaul both front calipers, and install quality disc brake pads. When the customer returned, the technician advised the customer to use the transmission on long downhill roads to help keep the brakes from overheating and failing prematurely.

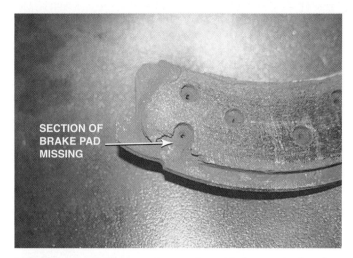

FIGURE 13–15 These pads were found to be cracked and a section was missing from a part of one pad.

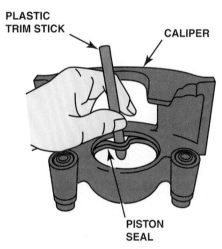

FIGURE 13–16 Removing the square-cut O-ring seal from the caliper bore. Use a wooden or plastic tool to prevent damage to the seal groove.

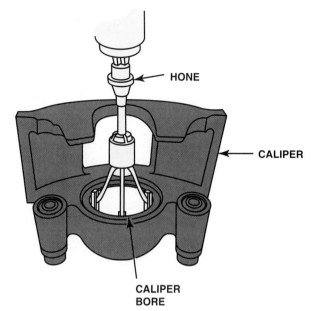

FIGURE 13–17 Some manufacturers recommend cleaning the inside of the caliper bore using a honing tool as shown. Even though the caliper piston does not contact the inside of this bore, removing any surface rust or corrosion is important to prevent future problems. If the honing process cannot remove any pits or scored areas, the caliper should be replaced.

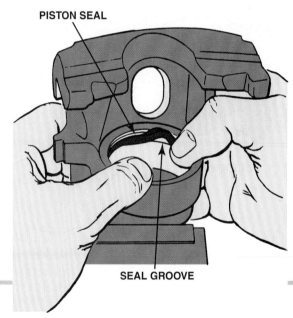

FIGURE 13–18 Installing a new piston seal. Never reuse old rubber parts. A caliper overhaul kit includes just two items: the square-cut piston seal O-ring and dust boot.

SERVICING DISC BRAKE CALIPERS

INSPECTION After removing the caliper piston then remove the square-cut O-ring. ● **SEE FIGURE 13–16.** Then the caliper should be thoroughly cleaned in denatured alcohol and closely examined. If the caliper bore is rusted or pitted, some manufacturers recommend that a special hone be used, as shown in ● **FIGURE 13–17.**

Some manufacturers do *not* recommend honing the caliper bore because the actual sealing surface in the caliper is between the piston seal and the piston itself. This is the reason why the surface condition of the piston is so important.

CALIPER ASSEMBLY To assemble the disc brake caliper, perform the following steps:

STEP 1 Carefully clean the caliper bore with clean brake fluid from a sealed container. Coat a new piston seal with clean brake fluid and install it in the groove inside the caliper bore, as shown in ● **FIGURE 13–18.**

FIGURE 13–19 Brake assembly fluid or clean brake fluid from a sealed container can be used to lubricate the caliper seal and caliper pistons before assembly.

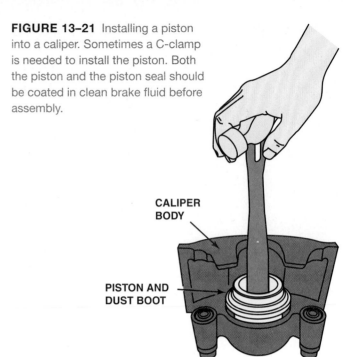

FIGURE 13–21 Installing a piston into a caliper. Sometimes a C-clamp is needed to install the piston. Both the piston and the piston seal should be coated in clean brake fluid before assembly.

CALIPER BODY

PISTON AND DUST BOOT

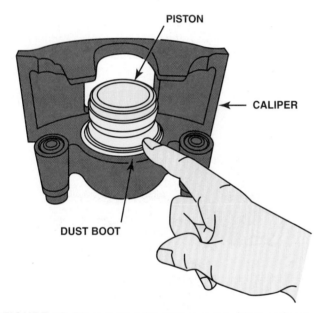

PISTON

CALIPER

DUST BOOT

FIGURE 13–20 Installing the caliper piston. Many calipers require that the dust boot be installed in the groove of the piston and/or caliper before installing the piston.

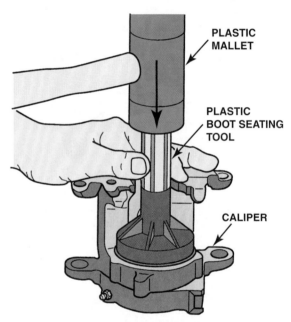

PLASTIC MALLET

PLASTIC BOOT SEATING TOOL

CALIPER

FIGURE 13–22 Seating the dust boot into the caliper housing using a special plastic seating tool.

SERVICING DISC BRAKE CALIPERS (CONTINUED)

STEP 2 Check the piston-to-caliper bore clearance. Typical piston-to-caliper bore clearance is as follows.

- steel piston   0.002–0.005 in. clearance (0.05–0.13 mm)
- phenolic piston   0.005–0.010 in. clearance (0.13–0.25 mm)

STEP 3 Coat a new piston boot with brake fluid or **brake assembly fluid.** ● **SEE FIGURE 13–19.** Brake

assembly fluid is similar to brake fluid but has antiwear additives.

STEP 4 Install the piston into the caliper piston, as shown in ● **FIGURES 13–20 AND 13–21.**

STEP 5 Some caliper boots require a special boot-seating tool, as shown in ● **FIGURE 13–22.**

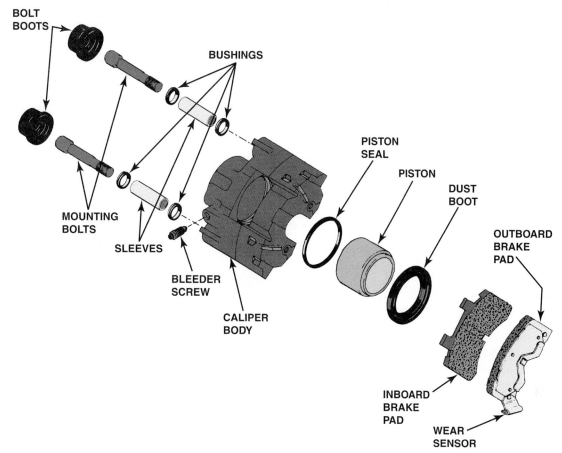

FIGURE 13–23 All rubber bushings should be lubricated with silicone brake grease for proper operation.

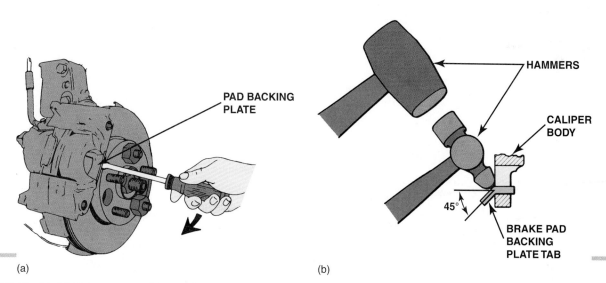

(a)   (b)

FIGURE 13–24 (a) Using a screwdriver to force the outboard pad into proper position before bending the retaining tabs. (b) Use two hammers to bend the tab where it extends through the hole in the caliper body.

STEP 6 Always lubricate caliper bushings, shims, and other brake hardware as instructed by the manufacturer. ● **SEE FIGURE 13–23.**

STEP 7 The pads should also be securely attached to the caliper as shown in ● **FIGURES 13–24 AND 13–25.**

CAUTION: Installing disc brake pads on the wrong side of the vehicle (left versus right) will often prevent the sensor from making noise when the pads are worn down.

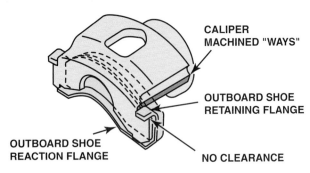

CALIPER MACHINED "WAYS"

OUTBOARD SHOE RETAINING FLANGE

OUTBOARD SHOE REACTION FLANGE

NO CLEARANCE

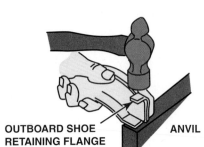

OUTBOARD SHOE RETAINING FLANGE

ANVIL

FIGURE 13–25 Often, a hammer is necessary to bend the retainer flange to make certain that the pads fit tightly to the caliper. If the pads are loose, a "click" may be heard every time the brakes are depressed. This click occurs when the pad(s) move and then hit the caliper or caliper mount. If the pads are loose, a clicking noise may be heard while driving over rough road surfaces.

SERVICING DISC BRAKE CALIPERS (CONTINUED)

 **TECH TIP**

Using "Loaded Calipers" Saves Time

Many technicians find that disassembly, cleaning, and rebuilding calipers can take a lot of time. Often the bleeder valve breaks off or the caliper piston is too corroded to reuse. This means that the technician has to get a replacement piston, caliper overhaul kit (piston seal and boot), plus the replacement friction pads and hardware kit.

To save time (and sometimes money), many technicians are simply replacing the old used calipers with "loaded calipers." **Loaded calipers** are remanufactured calipers that include (come loaded with) the correct replacement friction pads and all the necessary hardware. ● **SEE FIGURE 13–26.**

Therefore, only one part number is needed for each side of the vehicle for a complete disc brake overhaul.

FIGURE 13–26 A loaded caliper includes all hardware and shims with the correct pads all in one convenient package, ready to install on the vehicle.

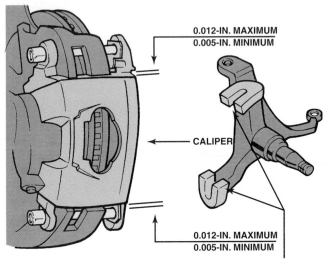

0.012-IN. MAXIMUM
0.005-IN. MINIMUM

CALIPER

0.012-IN. MAXIMUM
0.005-IN. MINIMUM

FILE ABUTMENTS (REACTION PADS) IF NECESSARY TO OBTAIN CLEARANCE

FIGURE 13–27 Floating calipers must be able to slide during normal operation. Therefore, there must be clearance between the caliper and the caliper mounting pads (abutments). Too little clearance will prevent the caliper from sliding and too much clearance will cause the caliper to make a clunking noise when the brakes are applied.

CALIPER MOUNT SERVICE When the hydraulic force from the master cylinder applies pressure to the disc brake pads, the entire caliper tends to be forced in the direction of rotation of the rotor. All calipers are mounted to the steering knuckle or axle housing. ● **SEE FIGURE 13–27.**

All braking force is transferred through the caliper to the mount. The places where the caliper contacts the caliper mount are called the **abutments, reaction pads,** or **ways.** The sliding surfaces of the caliper support should be cleaned with a wire brush and coated with a synthetic grease or antiseize compound according to manufacturers' recommendations. ● **SEE FIGURE 13–28.**

As the vehicle ages and the brakes are used thousands of times, these abutments (pads) can wear, causing too much clearance between the caliper and the mounting. When this occurs, the caliper often rotates against the abutment when the brakes are first applied, making a loud "knocking" noise. If

FIGURE 13–28 Using an air-powered sanding disc to clean the caliper mount pads.

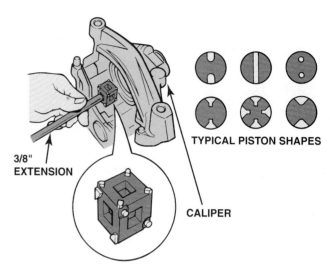

TYPICAL PISTON SHAPES

3/8"
EXTENSION

CALIPER

FIGURE 13–29 Determine which face of the special tool best fits the holes or slots in the piston. Sometimes needle-nose pliers can be used to rotate the piston back into the caliper bore.

this occurs, the service technician can repair this type of wear two ways:

METHOD 1 Replace the entire steering knuckle or caliper mount. This is the recommended method and also the most expensive. Replacement caliper mounts or knuckles may also be difficult to locate.

METHOD 2 Some aftermarket brake supply companies offer "abutment repair kits" that include oversize slides.

ROTATING PISTONS BACK INTO THE CALIPER

Many disc brake calipers used on the rear wheels require that the piston be rotated to reseat the pistons. When the parking brake is applied, the actuating screw moves the piston outward, forcing the pads against the disc brake rotor. The piston is kept from rotating because of an antirotation device or notches on the inboard pad and piston.

When the disc brake pads are being replaced, use a special tool to rotate the piston back into the brake calipers. Insert the tip of the tool in the holes or slots in the piston. Exert inward pressure while turning the piston. Make sure that the piston is retracting into the caliper and continue to turn the piston until it bottoms out.

NOTE: Some pistons are activated with left-handed threads.

After replacing the pads back into the caliper, check that the clearance does not exceed 1/16 in. (1.5 mm) from the rotor. Clearance greater than 1/16 in. may allow the adjuster to be pulled out of the piston when the service brake is applied. If the clearance is greater than 1/16 in., readjust by rotating the piston outward to reduce the clearance. ● **SEE FIGURE 13–29.**

TECH TIP

Always Double-Check Your Work

Whenever reassembling brakes, it is easy to twist the flexible brake hose as shown in ● **FIGURE 13–30.** To prevent possible brake hose failure and possibly an accident, always double-check that the ribs on the brake hose are straight. The ribs allow the service technician to easily spot if the hose has been twisted.

FIGURE 13–30 Note the twisted flexible brake line. This was caught by an automotive instructor before the brake work on the vehicle was completed. The twisted brake line can cause brake hose failure if not corrected.

SERVICING DISC BRAKE CALIPERS (CONTINUED)

TEST DRIVE AFTER BRAKE REPLACEMENT
After installing replacement disc brake pads or any other brake work, depress the brake pedal several times before driving the vehicle. This is a very important step! New brake pads are installed with the caliper piston pushed all the way into the caliper. The first few brake pedal applications usually result in the brake pedal going all the way to the floor. The brake pedal must be depressed ("pumped") several times before enough brake fluid can be moved from the master cylinder into the calipers to move the piston tight against the pads and the pads against the rotors.

CAUTION: Never allow a customer to be the first to test drive the vehicle after brake work has been performed.

BEDDING-IN REPLACEMENT BRAKE PADS
Some manufacturers recommend that their replacement brake pads be **bedded-in** or **burnished** before returning the vehicle to the owner. This break-in process varies with the manufacturer, but usually involves stopping the vehicle from 30 mph (48 km/h) up to 30 times, allowing the brakes to cool 2 to 3 minutes between stops. This break-in procedure helps the replacement pads to conform to the rotor and helps cure the resins used in the manufacture of the pads. Failure to properly break in new pads according to the manufacturer's recommended procedure could result in a hard brake pedal complaint from the driver and/or reduced braking effectiveness.

Even if the brake pad manufacturer does not recommend a break-in procedure, high-speed stops and overheating of the brakes should be avoided as much as possible during the first 50 to 100 stops.

DISC BRAKE SQUEAL CORRECTION

CAUSES OF BRAKE SQUEAL
Disc brakes tend to create brake noise (squeal). The cause and correction of brake noise is a major concern for both the vehicle manufacturers and the service technicians. The greatest customer complaint about brake work involves brake noise. Noise is caused by moving air, which is a result of moving brake components.

TECH TIP

Increasing Pad Life

Many vehicles seem to wear out front disc brakes more often than normal. Stop-and-go city-type driving is often the cause. Driving style, such as rapid stops, also causes a lot of wear to occur.

The service technician can take some actions to increase brake pad life that are easier than having to cure the driver's habits. These steps include the following.

1. Make sure the rear brakes are properly adjusted and working correctly. If the rear brakes are not functioning, all of the braking is accomplished by the front brakes alone.

   NOTE: Remind the driver to apply the parking brake regularly to help maintain proper rear brake clearance on the rear brakes.

2. Use factory brake pads or premium brake pads from a known manufacturer. Tests performed by vehicle manufacturers show that many aftermarket replacement brake pads fail to deliver original equipment brake pad life.

CORRECTING DISC BRAKE SQUEAL
Brake squeal can best be *prevented* by careful attention to details whenever servicing any disc brake. Some of these precautions include the following:

- **Keep the Disc Brake Pads Clean.** Grease on brake lining material causes the friction surface to be uneven. When the brakes are applied, this uneven brake surface causes the brake components to move.

FIGURE 13–31 For best braking performance, purchase replacement disc brake pads that include all clips and shims specified by the vehicle manufacturer. Some pads even come with a package of the specified grease to use on the shims to reduce the possibility of brake noise.

FACTOR	INCREASE NOISE	REDUCE NOISE
Brake pad thickness	Thinner (worn) pads	Thicker (new) pads
Rotor (disc) thickness	Thinner (worn) rotor	Thicker (new) rotor
Brake pad material	Harder	Softer
Lubrication of parts	Dry—not lubricated	Properly lubricated
Dampening	No dampening	Dampening material behind the pads
Pad mounting	Pad tabs not bent over	Pad tabs securely crimped
Antirattle clips	Worn, defective, or not lubricated	New and properly lubricated

CHART 13–1

The causes of brake noise can have many reasons and corrections.

■ **Use Factory-Type Clips and Anti-squeal Shims.** The vehicle manufacturer has designed the braking system to be as quiet as possible. To assure that the brakes are restored to like-new performance, all of the original hardware should be used. Many original equipment brake pads use **constrained layer shims (CLS)** on the back of the brake pads. These shims are constructed with dampening material between two layers of steel.
● **SEE FIGURE 13–31.**

NOTE: Many aftermarket disc brake pads do *not* include replacement hardware that usually includes noise-reducing shims and clips. One of the advantages of purchasing original equipment (OE) disc brake pads is that they usually come equipped with all necessary shims and often with special grease that is recommended to be used on metal shims.

■ **Lubricate All Caliper Slide Points as per Manufacturer's Recommendation.** Lubrication of moving or sliding components prevents noise from being generated as the parts move over each other. Many vehicle manufacturers recommend one or more of the following greases:

1. **Lithium-based brake grease**

2. **Silicone grease**

3. **Molybdenum disulfide (MOS$_2$) grease** ("Molykote") often referred to as "moly" grease

4. **Synthetic grease** (usually **polyalphaolefin [PAO]**) sometimes mixed with graphite, Teflon, and/or MOS$_2$

5. **Antiseize compound**

The grease should be applied on both sides of shims used between the pad and the caliper piston.

CAUTION: Grease should only be applied to the nonfriction (steel) side of the disc brake pads.

■ **Machine the Brake Rotor as Little as Possible and with the Correct Surface Finish.** Machining the brake rotor reduces its thickness. A thinner rotor will vibrate at a different frequency than a thicker rotor. For factors that can help or hurt brake squeal, ● **SEE CHART 13–1.**

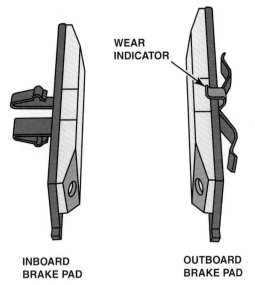

WEAR INDICATOR

INBOARD BRAKE PAD

OUTBOARD BRAKE PAD

FIGURE 13–32 Notice the beveled pads. The shape of the pad helps reduce brake noise.

DISC BRAKE SQUEAL CORRECTION (CONTINUED)

Vehicle manufacturers also change brake pad (lining) composition and the shape of the pads to help eliminate brake noise. The change of shape changes the frequency of the sound. Noise is vibration, but much of the vibration generated is not heard because the noise is beyond the normal frequency to be heard. Most people can hear from 20 to 20,000 cycles per second (called hertz). To stop brake noise, the manufacturer can change the frequency of the vibration to above or below the hertz range that can be heard. ● **SEE FIGURE 13–32.**

NOTE: All metal-to-metal contacts *must* be lubricated to help prevent brake noise.

 **TECH TIP**

The Screwdriver Trick

A low brake pedal on GM vehicles equipped with rear disc brakes is a common customer complaint. Often the reason is a lack of self-adjustment that *should* occur whenever the brake pedal (or parking brake) is released. During brake release, the pressure is removed from the caliper piston and the spring inside the caliper piston is free to adjust. Often this self-adjustment does not occur and a low brake pedal results.

A common trick that is used on the vehicle assembly line is to use a screwdriver to hold the piston against the rotor while an assistant releases the brake pedal. ● **SEE FIGURE 13–33.**

As the brake pedal is released, the adjusting screw inside the caliper piston is free to move. Sometimes, it may be necessary to tap on the caliper itself with a dead-blow hammer to free the adjusting screw. Repeat the process as necessary until the proper brake pedal height returns.

If this method does not work, replace the caliper assembly.

In summary, recall these steps.

STEP 1   Have an assistant depress the brake pedal.

STEP 2   Using a screwdriver through the hole in the top of the caliper, hold the piston against the rotor.

NOTE: Be careful not to damage the dust boot.

STEP 3   While still holding the piston against the rotor, have the assistant release the brake pedal. The adjusting screw adjusts when the brake pedal is *released* and a slight vibration or sound will be noticed as the brake is released. This vibration or sound is created by the self-adjusting mechanism inside the caliper piston taking up the excess clearance.

STEP 4   Repeat as necessary until normal brake pedal height is achieved.

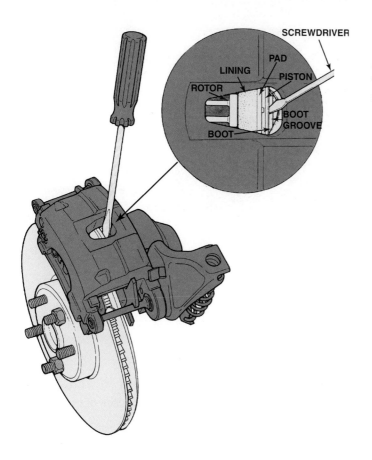

FIGURE 13–33 The screwdriver blade is used to keep the piston applied to allow self-adjustment to occur when the brake pedal is released.

Labels in figure: SCREWDRIVER, PAD, LINING, PISTON, ROTOR, BOOT GROOVE, BOOT

DISC BRAKE SYMPTOM GUIDE

PULLS TO ONE SIDE DURING BRAKING   Possible causes of this include the following:

1. Incorrect or unequal tire pressures
2. Front end out of alignment
3. Unmatched tires on the same axle
4. Restricted brake lines or hoses
5. Stuck or seized caliper or caliper piston
6. Defective or damaged shoe and lining (grease or brake fluid on the lining, or a bent shoe)
7. Malfunctioning rear brakes
8. Loose suspension parts
9. Loose calipers

BRAKE ROUGHNESS OR CHATTER (PEDAL PUL-SATES)   Possible causes of this include the following:

1. Excessive lateral runout of rotor
2. Parallelism of the rotor not within specifications
3. Wheel bearings not adjusted correctly

4. Rear drums out-of-round
5. Brake pads worn to metal backing plate

EXCESSIVE PEDAL EFFORT   Possible causes of this include the following:

1. Binding or seized caliper mounting
2. Binding brake pedal mechanism
3. Improper rotor surface finish
4. Malfunctioning power brake
5. Partial system failure
6. Excessively worn shoe and lining
7. Piston in the caliper stuck or sluggish
8. Fading brakes due to incorrect lining

EXCESSIVE PEDAL TRAVEL   Possible causes of this include the following:

1. Partial brake system failure
2. Insufficient fluid in the master cylinder

(a)

(b)

FIGURE 13–34 (a) A brake pressure tester. (b) The small "pads" can be placed between the caliper piston and the rotor to check for applied pressure and inserted between the caliper and the rotor on the outside of the rotor to test the pressure—the pressure should be the same if the caliper is able to slide on its pins or slides.

DISC BRAKE SYMPTOM GUIDE (CONTINUED)

3. Air trapped in the system
4. Bent shoe and lining
5. Excessive pedal effort
6. Excessive parking brake travel (four-wheel disc brakes, except Corvette)

DRAGGING BRAKES
Possible causes of this include the following:

1. Pressure trapped in the brake lines (to diagnose, momentarily open the caliper bleeder valve to relieve the pressure)
2. Restricted brake tubes or hoses
3. Improperly lubricated caliper mounting system
4. Improper clearance between the caliper and torque abutment surfaces
5. Check valve installed in the outlet of the master cylinder to the disc brakes

FRONT DISC BRAKES VERY SENSITIVE TO LIGHT BRAKE APPLICATIONS
Possible causes of this include the following:

1. Metering valve not holding off the front brake application
2. Incorrect lining material
3. Improper rotor surface finish
4. Check other causes listed under "PULLS"

REAR DRUM BRAKES SKIDDING UNDER HARD BRAKE APPLICATIONS
Possible causes of this include the following:

1. Proportioning valve
2. Contaminated rear brake lining
3. Caliper or caliper piston stuck or corroded

 TECH TIP

Pressure Testing Can Help Find Problems

A stuck caliper or caliper slide is often difficult to see or diagnose as a problem because the movement of the broken pads is so little. Using a pressure gauge between the caliper piston and the rotor (inboard) or between the rotor and the caliper (outboard) can tell the service technician if there is a difference between the left and the right side brakes. ● **SEE FIGURE 13–34.**

DISC BRAKE SERVICE

1 After properly setting the hoist pads under the vehicle, raise the vehicle to chest level and remove the lug nuts.

2 Remove the wheel/tire assembly and place it where it will not get in the way or be damaged.

3 It is recommended that the entire brake assembly be washed using a commercially available cleaner to avoid the possibility of allowing brake dust from becoming airborne.

4 If a commercial brake cleaning unit is not available, use brake cleaner from an aerosol or pressurized container.

5 To service the front disc brake pads on this vehicle, loosen the upper caliper retainer bolt and remove the lower bolt.

6 After the lower caliper bolt has been removed, the caliper assembly can be lifted upward by pivoting on the upper retaining bolt.

CONTINUED ▶

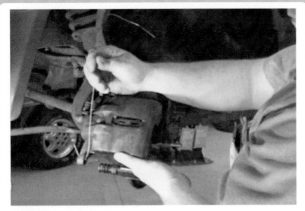

7 Use mechanic's wire to hold the caliper in the raised position to allow access to the disc brake pads.

8 Notice that both the inboard and outboard pad remain attached to the steering knuckle. The pads and shims can be lifted off.

9 A C-clamp can be used to push the piston into the caliper, but be sure to open the bleeder valve first.

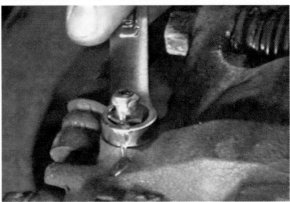

10 The bleeder valve should be opened to allow the old brake fluid to flow out of the caliper and not be forced up into the ABS hydraulic unit or master cylinder.

11 Often factory replacement disc brake pads include noise-dampening shims, antirattle clips, and special "moly" disc brake grease that is to be used on the shims.

12 All hardware, including this anchor shim, should be replaced.

13 Install new shims after thoroughly cleaning the steering knuckle area of any rust using a wire brush or other suitable tool.

14 The replacement disc brake pads are installed next to the rotor and held in place by the tension of the anchor shims.

15 After double-checking that all shims, clips, and spacers are correctly installed, lower the calipers and install this lower attaching bolt.

16 Torque the retaining bolts to factory specifications. Repeat the process on the other side and bleed the hydraulic system.

17 Reinstall the wheel/tire assembly.

18 Torque the lug nuts to factory specifications or use a torque-limiting adapter. Test drive the vehicle before returning it to the customer.

CONTINUED ▶

1. Caliper pistons are either chrome-plated steel or plastic (phenolic). Any damaged piston must be replaced. Both the square-cut O-ring and the dust boot must be replaced when the caliper is disassembled.

2. All metal-to-metal contact points of the disc brake assembly should be coated with an approved brake lubricant such as synthetic grease, "moly" (molybdenum disulfide) grease, or antiseize compound.

3. After a brake overhaul, the brake pedal should be depressed several times until a normal brake pedal is achieved before performing a thorough test drive.

4. Many rear disc brake systems use an integral parking brake. Regular use of the parking brake helps maintain proper rear brake clearance.

REVIEW QUESTIONS

1. List what parts are included in a typical overhaul kit for a single-piston floating caliper.

2. Describe how to remove caliper pistons and perform a caliper overhaul.

3. Explain what causes disc brake squeal and list what a technician can do to reduce or eliminate the noise.

CHAPTER QUIZ

1. Uneven disc brake pad wear is being discussed. Technician A says the caliper piston may be stuck. Technician B says the caliper may be stuck on the slides and unable to "float." Which technician is correct?
   a. Technician A only
   b. Technician B only
   c. Both Technicians A and B
   d. Neither Technician A nor B

2. A "chirping" noise is heard while the vehicle is moving forward, but stops when the brakes are applied. Technician A says that the noise is likely caused by the disc brake pad wear sensors. Technician B says the noise is likely a wheel bearing because the noise stops when the brakes are applied. Which technician is correct?
   a. Technician A only
   b. Technician B only
   c. Both Technicians A and B
   d. Neither Technician A nor B

3. Technician A says that disc brake pads should be replaced when worn to minimum allowable thickness. Technician B says the pads should be removed and inspected whenever there is a brake performance complaint. Which technician is correct?
   a. Technician A only
   b. Technician B only
   c. Both Technicians A and B
   d. Neither Technician A nor B

4. A typical disc brake caliper overhaul (OH) kit usually includes what parts?
   a. Square-cut O-ring seal and dust boot
   b. Replacement caliper piston and dust boot
   c. Dust boot, return spring, and caliper seal
   d. Disc brake pad clips, dust boot, and caliper piston assembly

5. Technician A says that a lack of lubrication on the back of the disc brake pads can cause brake noise. Technician B says that pads that are not correctly crimped to the caliper housing can cause brake noise. Which technician is correct?
   a. Technician A only
   b. Technician B only
   c. Both Technicians A and B
   d. Neither Technician A nor B

6. Two technicians are discussing ways of removing a caliper piston. Technician A says to use compressed air. Technician B says to use large pliers. Which technician is correct?
   a. Technician A only
   b. Technician B only
   c. Both Technicians A and B
   d. Neither Technician A nor B

7. Which is *not* a recommended type of grease to use on brake parts?
   a. Silicone grease
   b. Wheel bearing (chassis) grease
   c. Synthetic grease
   d. Antiseize compound

8. Technician A says that a loaded caliper includes an overhauled caliper assembly but no brake pads or hardware. Technician B says that a loaded caliper includes the pads and all needed hardware. Which technicain is correct?
   a. Technician A only
   b. Technician B only
   c. Both Technicians A and B
   d. Neither Technician A nor B

9. A vehicle is hoisted during routine service and the service technician discovers that the left front wheel does not turn when force is applied. Technician A says that the hoist (lift) pads could be against the left front tire. Technician B says that there could be a brake fluid restriction between the master cylinder and the brake. Which technician is correct?
   a. Technician A only
   b. Technician B only
   c. Both Technicians A and B
   d. Neither Technician A nor B

10. Technician A says that a steel piston should be cleaned with sandpaper to remove rust. Technician B says that the brake assembly fluid or clean brake fluid should be used to lubricate the caliper pistons before installing in the caliper. Which technician is correct?
    a. Technician A only
    b. Technician B only
    c. Both Technicians A and B
    d. Neither Technician A nor B

PARKING BRAKE OPERATION, DIAGNOSIS, AND SERVICE

OBJECTIVES

After studying Chapter 14, the reader will be able to:

1. Prepare for the Brakes (A5) ASE certification test content area "E" (Miscellaneous Systems Diagnosis and Repair).
2. Describe what is required of a parking brake.
3. Describe the parts and operation of the parking brake as used on a rear drum brake system.
4. Describe how a parking brake functions when the vehicle is equipped with rear disc brakes.
5. Explain how to adjust a parking brake properly.

KEY TERMS

Application cables 236
Control cables 236
Electric parking brake (EPB) 246
Equalizer 237

Intermediate lever 237
Red brake warning lamp 236
Transfer cable 236
Vacuum servo 235

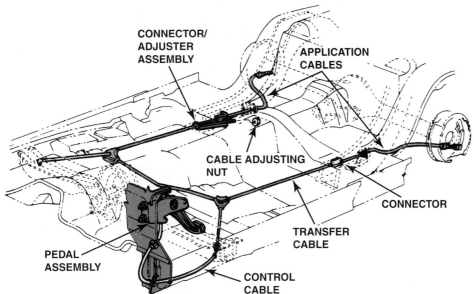

FIGURE 14–1 Typical parking brake cable system showing the foot-operated parking brake lever and cable routing.

CONNECTOR/ ADJUSTER ASSEMBLY

APPLICATION CABLES

CABLE ADJUSTING NUT

CONNECTOR

TRANSFER CABLE

PEDAL ASSEMBLY

CONTROL CABLE

PARKING BRAKE STANDARDS

BACKGROUND Before 1967, most vehicles had only a single master cylinder operating all four brakes. If the fluid leaked at just one wheel, the operation of all brakes was lost. This required the use of a separate method to stop the vehicle in case of an emergency. This alternative method required that a separate mechanical method be used to stop the vehicle using two of the four wheel brakes. After 1967, federal regulations required the use of dual or tandem master cylinders where half of the braking system has its own separate hydraulic system. In case one-half of the system fails, a dash brake warning lamp lets the driver know that a failure has occurred. The term *parking brake* has replaced the term *emergency brake* since the change to dual master cylinder design.

FMVSS 135 According to Federal Motor Vehicle Safety Standard (FMVSS) 135, the parking brake must hold a fully loaded (laden) vehicle stationary on a slope of 20% up or down grade. The hand force required cannot exceed 80 lb (18 N) or a foot force greater than 100 lb (22 N). ● **SEE FIGURE 14–1** for a typical parking brake system.

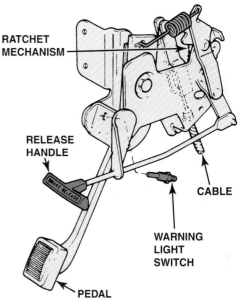

RATCHET MECHANISM

RELEASE HANDLE

CABLE

WARNING LIGHT SWITCH

PEDAL

FIGURE 14–2 A typical parking brake pedal assembly.

PEDALS, LEVERS, AND HANDLES

Parking brakes are applied by a pedal, a lever, or a handle from inside the vehicle. Foot pedals and floor-mounted levers are the most common means of applying parking brakes. ● **SEE FIGURES 14–2 AND 14–3.** All parking brake controls incorporate a *ratchet* mechanism to lock the brake in the applied position. ● **SEE FIGURE 14–4.**

When service brake friction assemblies are used as the parking brakes, the service brake pedal should be depressed while the parking brake control is set. Applying the service brake increases parking brake holding power because the

FIGURE 14–3 Typical hand-operated parking brake. Note that the adjustment for the cable is underneath the vehicle at the equalizer.

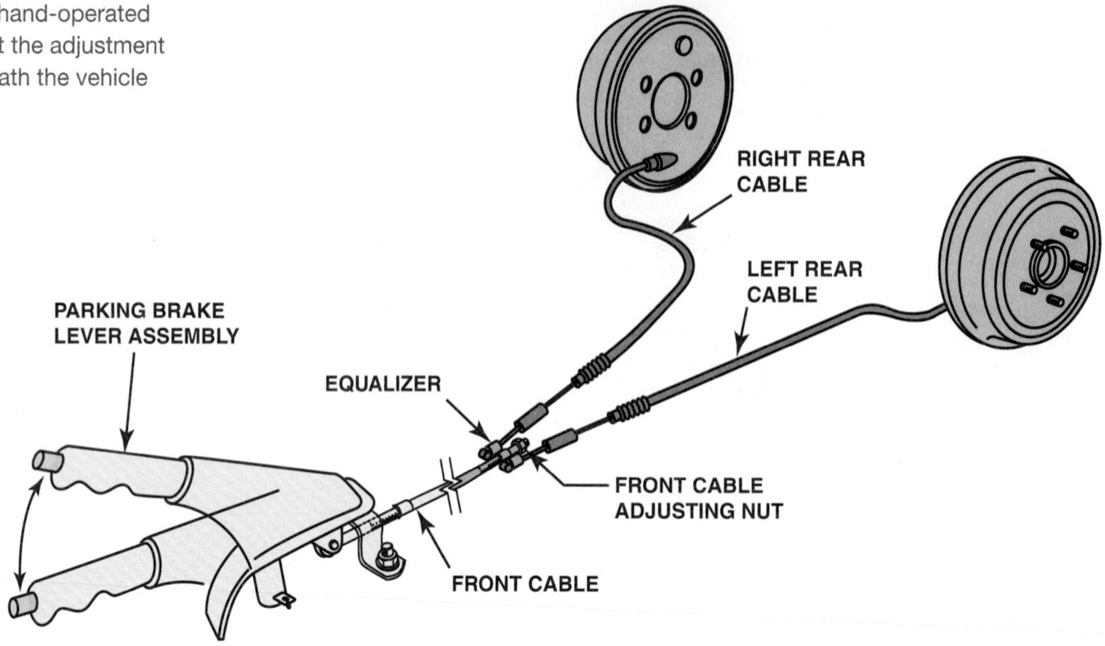

RIGHT REAR CABLE

LEFT REAR CABLE

PARKING BRAKE LEVER ASSEMBLY

EQUALIZER

FRONT CABLE ADJUSTING NUT

FRONT CABLE

FIGURE 14–4 A ratchet mechanism is used to lock parking brakes in the applied position.

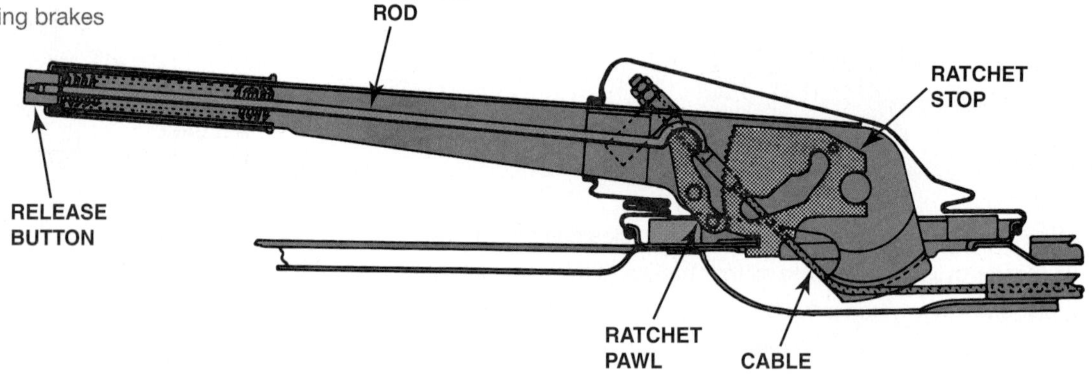

RELEASE ROD

RATCHET STOP

RELEASE BUTTON

RATCHET PAWL

CABLE

PEDALS, LEVERS, AND HANDLES (CONTINUED)

brake hydraulic system provides the actual application force, which is far greater than the force that can be developed mechanically. The parking brake mechanism simply locks the brakes in position. If the parking brake is operated only by the pedal, lever, or handle, holding power will be reduced, and the cables in the linkage will tend to stretch.

All parking brakes are applied manually and the release procedure varies with the design of the parking brake control.

PARKING BRAKE PEDALS A parking brake pedal is applied by depressing it with a foot. The ratchet engages automatically and the pedal remains in the depressed position. The pedal is released by a pull or a small T-handle or lever under the dash. This disengages the ratchet mechanism, and allows a return spring to move the pedal to the unapplied position. On some vehicles, the release lever is integrated into the underside

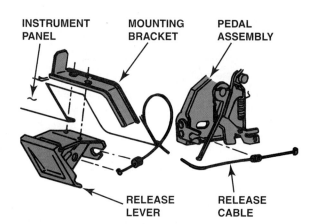

INSTRUMENT PANEL

MOUNTING BRACKET

PEDAL ASSEMBLY

RELEASE LEVER

RELEASE CABLE

FIGURE 14–5 A remote-mounted parking brake release lever.

of the dash and connects to the release mechanism through a rod or cable. ● **SEE FIGURE 14–5.**

Some vehicles were equipped with a special pedal design that enabled them to meet federal regulations on parking brake

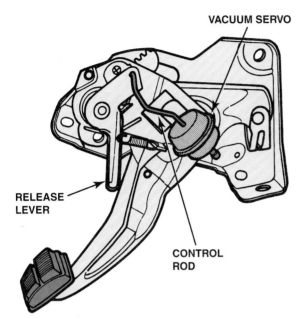

FIGURE 14–6 Automatic parking brake release mechanisms usually use a vacuum servo to operate the release lever.

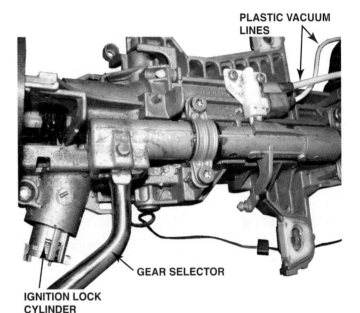

FIGURE 14–7 The two plastic vacuum tubes on the steering column are used to release the parking brake when the gear selector is moved from park into a drive gear.

 REAL WORLD FIX

Pump to Release?

A customer called and asked a dealer for help because the parking brake could not be released. The service technician discovered that the customer was attempting to release the parking brake by depressing the parking brake pedal, as was done on the customer's previous vehicle. The service technician simply pulled on the release lever and the parking brake was released.

holding power while keeping maximum pedal application force within legal limits. This type of pedal had a high leverage ratio and a special ratchet mechanism that locked the brake pedal in the applied position, but allowed the pedal to return after it had been depressed. Two full pedal strokes, or several partial strokes, were required to fully apply the parking brake. The brake was released by a single pull on a T-handle or release lever.

Some vehicles were equipped with a system that required the driver to depress the parking brake pedal to release the

parking brake once it was set. The rubber pad on the parking brake pedal usually states "push to release."

AUTOMATIC PARKING BRAKE RELEASE Some vehicles with pedal-operated parking brakes have an automatic release mechanism that disengages the parking brake using a **vacuum servo** controlled by an electrical solenoid. ● **SEE FIGURE 14–6**.

A metal rod connects the vacuum servo to the upper end of the parking brake release lever. When the engine is running (to provide vacuum) and the shifter is placed in gear, an electrical contact closes to energize the solenoid and route vacuum to the servo. The servo diaphragm then retracts the rod, which releases the parking brake. ● **SEE FIGURE 14–7**.

PARKING BRAKE WARNING LAMP

A **red brake warning lamp** lights on the dash if any of the following events occur.

- On most vehicles, this is the same lamp that lights when there is a hydraulic or brake fluid level problem.

- The warning lamp for the parking brake warns the driver that the parking brake is applied or partially applied. This warning helps prevent damage or overheating to the brake drums and linings that could occur if the vehicle was driven with the parking brake applied.

If the red BRAKE warning lamp is on, check the parking brake to see if it is fully released. If the BRAKE lamp is still on, the parking brake switch may be defective, out of adjustment, or there may be a hydraulic problem.

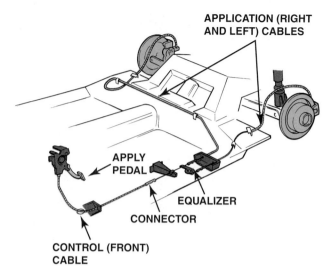

FIGURE 14–8 The cable from the activating lever to the equalizer is commonly called the control cable. From the equalizer, the individual brake cables are often called application cables. These individual cables can usually be purchased separately.

PARKING BRAKE LINKAGES

Parking brake linkages transmit force from the pedal, lever, or handle inside the vehicle to the brake friction assemblies.

LINKAGE RODS   Parking brake linkage rods made from solid steel are commonly used with floor-mounted actuating levers to span the short distance to an intermediate lever or an equalizer.

LINKAGE CABLES   The typical parking brake cable is made of woven-steel wire encased in a reinforced rubber or plastic housing. The housing is fixed in position at both ends, and is routed under the vehicle through mounting brackets that hold the cable in position, yet allow a small amount of movement. The cable slides back and forth inside the housing to transmit application force, and depending on the linkage design, the outer housing may play a part in parking brake application as well.

Parking brake linkages use control cables, transfer cables, and application cables.

- **Control cables** attach to the parking brake pedal, lever, or handle inside the vehicle.

- A **transfer cable** transmits force to an intermediate lever or equalizer to the application cables.

- The **application cables** use the force passed through the linkage to apply the rear wheel brake assembly. ● **SEE FIGURE 14–8.**

FIGURE 14–9 Notice how rust inside the covering of this parking brake cable has caused the cable to swell.

   TECH TIP

Look for Swollen Parking Brake Cables

Always inspect parking brake cables for proper operation. A cable that is larger in diameter in one section indicates that it is rusting inside and has swollen.
● **SEE FIGURE 14–9.**

A rusting parking brake cable can keep the rear brake applied even though the parking brake lever has been released. This can cause dragging brakes, reduced fuel economy, and possible vehicle damage due to overheated brakes.

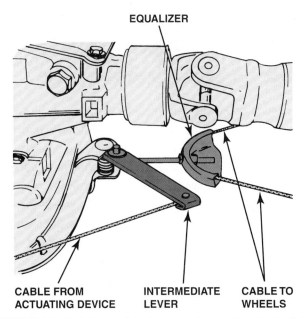

FIGURE 14–10 Intermediate levers in the parking brake linkage increase the application force.

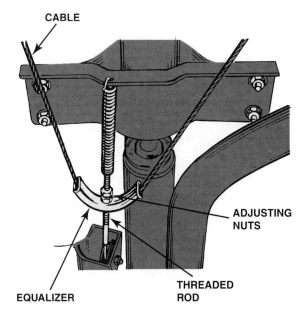

FIGURE 14–11 A cable guide is a common type of parking brake linkage equalizer.

Parking brake cables are subject to damage from water, dirt, and other debris thrown up under the vehicle by the tires. Most parking brake cables do not require lubrication because they are lined with nylon or Teflon, and any cable housing ends located under the vehicle are protected by rubber or nylon seals.

LINKAGE LEVERS Unfortunately, the amount of physical force a driver can apply to the parking brake control is often not enough to apply the parking brake. For this reason, all parking brake linkages contain one or more levers that increase application force.

The parking brake pedals, floor-mounted levers, and pivoting under dash handles described earlier are all types of levers used to increase parking brake application force. A lever in the parking brake linkage under the vehicle is called an **intermediate lever**. ● SEE FIGURE 14–10.

To further increase parking brake application force, intermediate levers provide leverage in addition to that supplied by the parking brake control.

LINKAGE EQUALIZERS In some parking brake linkages, the rods or cables to the two friction assemblies are adjusted separately. If the adjustments are unequal, one brake will apply before the other, preventing full lining-to-drum contact at the opposite wheel and greatly reducing the holding power of the

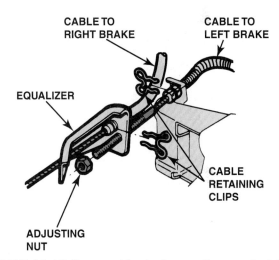

FIGURE 14–12 Some parking brake equalizers are installed in the brake cable.

parking brake. To prevent unequal application, most parking brake linkages use an **equalizer** to balance the force from the parking brake control, and transmit an equal amount to each friction assembly.

Equalizers come in many shapes and sizes, but the simplest is the cable guide attached to a threaded rod. ● SEE FIGURE 14–11. This type of equalizer pivots or allows the inner cable to slide back and forth to even out application force.

Another type of equalizer installs in a long application cable that runs from the linkage at the front of the vehicle to one rear brake. ● SEE FIGURE 14–12.

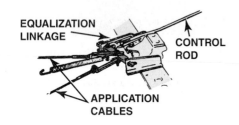

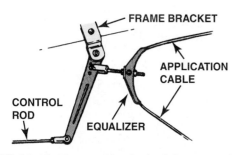

FIGURE 14–13 Many parking brake linkages use both an intermediate lever and an equalizer.

PARKING BRAKE LINKAGES (CONTINUED)

LINKAGE DESIGN   The number of different parking brake linkage designs is almost as great as the number of vehicle models on the road. Most linkages combine intermediate levers and equalizers in various ways and use from one to four cables to actuate the friction assemblies. ● **SEE FIGURE 14–13**.

The parking brake standard requires that the vehicle be held stationary on a 20% grade facing either uphill or downhill. Many drum parking brake systems attach the parking brake lever on the secondary (rearward) shoe and push the primary (forward facing) brake shoe against the drum. The parking brake cable enters the backing plate from the front of the vehicle (front entry). Because the primary shoe is attached to the secondary shoe on dual-servo brakes, any forward motion of the vehicle tends to wedge the primary shoe into the brake drum *and* force the rear secondary lining also against the drum.

Applying only the forward brake shoe tends to hold the vehicle best when the vehicle is being held on a hill with the front pointing downward. To help provide the same holding power for a vehicle being held from backing up, some vehicles reverse the parking brake arrangement for the right side. Instead of having the parking brake cable enter the backing plate from the front, this style has the cable entering from the rear (rear entry). In this case, the right rear brake has the parking brake lever installed on the *primary* shoe. This creates a reverse servo action when the vehicle is parked with the rear facing downward.

NOTE: An easy way to remember how to reassemble a drum brake is to realize that the parking brake lever is usually attached to the secondary (rearward) brake shoe. The parking brake strut attaches between the shoes with the spring toward the front of the vehicle (remember, "spring forward").

DRUM PARKING BRAKES

Drum parking brakes are the most common types on vehicles and light trucks. Drum brakes make excellent parking brakes because they have a high static coefficient of friction combined with self-energizing action and, in the case of dual-servo brakes, servo action that increases their application force.

INTEGRAL DRUM PARKING BRAKES   Integral drum parking brakes mechanically apply the rear drum service brakes to serve as the parking brakes. ● **SEE FIGURE 14–14**.

Integral drum parking brakes are the most common type not only because of their natural superiority in this application, but because it is simple and inexpensive to design a parking brake linkage into a drum brake.

The typical integral drum parking brake has a pivoting lever mounted on one brake shoe, and a strut placed between the

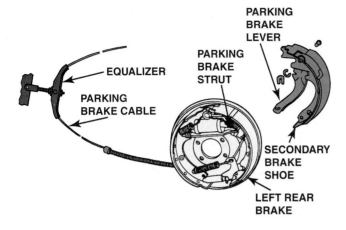

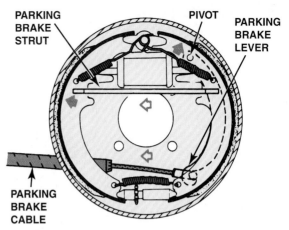

FIGURE 14–15 The parking brake cable pulls on the parking brake lever, which in turn forces the brake shoe against the drum.

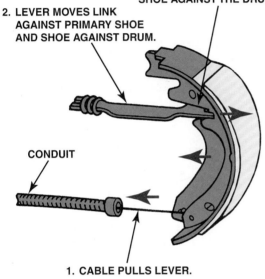

2. LEVER MOVES LINK AGAINST PRIMARY SHOE AND SHOE AGAINST DRUM.

3. LEVER WORKS AGAINST LINK, AND PIVOT FORCES SECONDARY SHOE AGAINST THE DRUM.

CONDUIT

1. CABLE PULLS LEVER.

FIGURE 14–14 Notice the spring at the end of the parking brake strut. This antirattle spring keeps tension on the strut. The parking brake lever is usually attached with a pin and spring (wavy) washer and retained by a horseshoe clip.

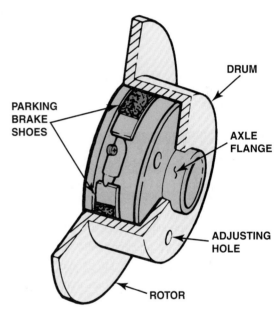

FIGURE 14–16 The inside "hat" of the disc brake rotor is the friction surface for the parking brake shoes.

lever and the other shoe. The strut may be fitted with a spring that takes up slack to prevent noise when the parking brake is not applied. The end of the lever opposite the pivot is moved by the parking brake cable, which enters through an opening in the backing plate. All integral drum parking brakes operate in essentially the same manner. ● **SEE FIGURE 14–15.**

When the parking brake control is operated, the cable pulls the end of the lever away from the shoe it is attached to. The lever pivots at the attaching point and moves the strut to apply the forward shoe. Once the forward brake shoe lining contacts the drum, the strut can travel no farther. The lever then pivots on the strut and forces the lining of the reverse shoe against the drum.

REAR DISC AUXILIARY DRUM PARKING BRAKES

Rear disc service brakes with fixed calipers commonly have a

parking brake drum formed into the hub of the brake rotor. ● **SEE FIGURE 14–16.** Inside the drum is a small dual-servo drum brake friction assembly that serves as the parking brake. The rotor splash shield, or a special mounting bracket, provides the backing plate for the friction assembly. Rear disc auxiliary drum parking brakes use the dual-servo friction assembly design because it provides the most holding power, and does so equally in both forward and reverse directions. Dual-servo parking brake friction assemblies operate in essentially the same manner as service brakes except that the wheel cylinder is eliminated and the friction assembly is actuated mechanically. ● **SEE FIGURE 14–17.**

All rear disc auxiliary drum parking brakes are adjusted manually using a starwheel adjuster, which is reached through an opening in the outside of the drum.

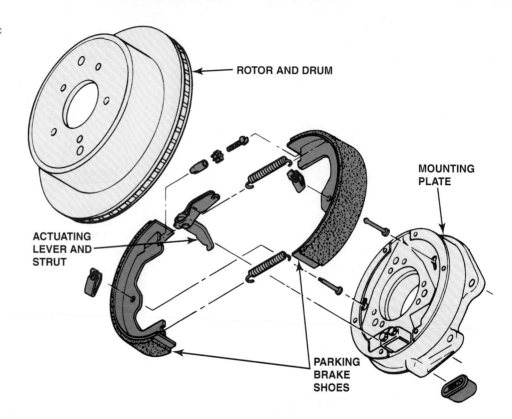

FIGURE 14–17 A typical rear disc brake auxiliary drum brake friction assembly.

ROTOR AND DRUM

MOUNTING PLATE

ACTUATING LEVER AND STRUT

PARKING BRAKE SHOES

CALIPER-ACTUATED DISC PARKING BRAKES

Caliper-actuated disc parking brakes are used on vehicles whose rear disc brakes are equipped with floating or sliding brake calipers. The single-piston construction of these calipers makes them easier to mechanically actuate than multiple-piston fixed calipers. In this design, a special mechanism in the caliper applies the caliper piston mechanically. The mechanism is operated by a parking brake cable attached to a lever that protrudes from the inboard side of the caliper.

BALL AND RAMP ACTUATION The ball and ramp actuating system found in Ford rear brake calipers has three steel balls located in ramp-shaped detents between two plates. ● **SEE FIGURE 14–18.** One plate has a thrust screw attached that is threaded into an adjuster mechanism in the caliper piston. The other plate is part of the operating shaft that extends out of the caliper. The actuating lever is mounted to the end of this shaft.

As the parking brake cable moves the lever and rotates the operating shaft, the balls ride up the ramps and force the two plates apart. The operating shaft plate cannot move because it butts against the caliper body. The thrust screw plate, which is pinned to the caliper body to prevent it from rotating, is driven away from the operating shaft and toward the rotor where the

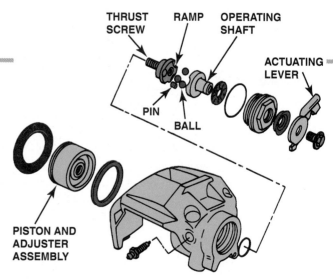

THRUST SCREW **RAMP** **OPERATING SHAFT**

ACTUATING LEVER

PIN **BALL**

PISTON AND ADJUSTER ASSEMBLY

FIGURE 14–18 A Ford rear brake caliper ball and ramp-type apply mechanism.

thrust screw moves the caliper piston to apply the brake. ● **SEE FIGURE 14–19.**

Adjustment of the ball and ramp linkage within the caliper is automatic, and takes place during service brake application. When the caliper piston moves away from the thrust screw, an adjuster nut inside the piston rotates on the thrust screw to take up any slack created by wear. ● **SEE FIGURE 14–20.** A drive ring on the nut prevents it from rotating in the opposite direction when the parking brake is applied.

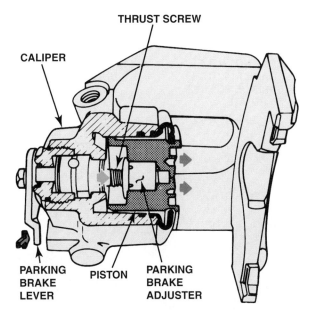

FIGURE 14–19 Operation of a ball and ramp-type rear disc brake caliper parking brake.

CALIPER

THRUST SCREW

PARKING BRAKE LEVER

PISTON

PARKING BRAKE ADJUSTER

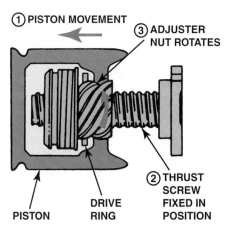

① PISTON MOVEMENT

③ ADJUSTER NUT ROTATES

② THRUST SCREW FIXED IN POSITION

PISTON

DRIVE RING

FIGURE 14–20 Automatic adjustment of a ball and ramp-type rear disc brake parking brake occurs when the service brakes are applied.

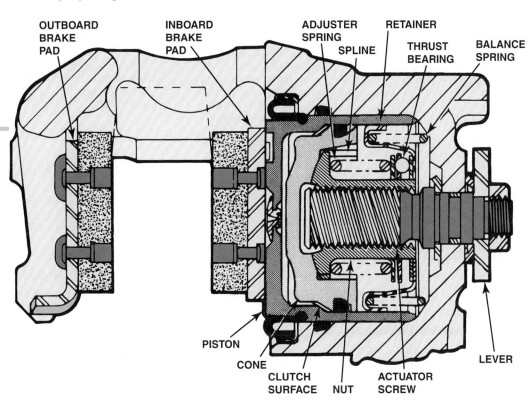

OUTBOARD BRAKE PAD

INBOARD BRAKE PAD

ADJUSTER SPRING

SPLINE

RETAINER

THRUST BEARING

BALANCE SPRING

PISTON

CONE

CLUTCH SURFACE

NUT

ACTUATOR SCREW

LEVER

FIGURE 14–21 A typical General Motors rear disc brake with an integral parking brake. This type uses a screw, nut, and cone mechanism to apply the caliper piston.

SCREW, NUT, AND CONE ACTUATION

General Motors' rear disc parking brake uses a screw, nut, and cone mechanism to apply the caliper piston. ● **SEE FIGURE 14–21**.

In this design, the actuator screw with the parking brake lever attached to it extends through the caliper body. The caliper piston contains a specially shaped nut that threads onto the actuator screw when the piston is installed in the bore. The nut butts against the backside of the cone, and is splined to the

cone so that it cannot rotate unless the cone does so as well. The cone is a slip fit in the piston, and is free to rotate unless it is held tightly against a clutch surface located near the outer end of the piston bore.

When the parking brake is applied, the cable moves the lever and rotates the actuator screw. ● **SEE FIGURE 14–22**. The nut then unthreads along the screw, and jams the cone against the clutch surface of the caliper piston. This prevents the cone

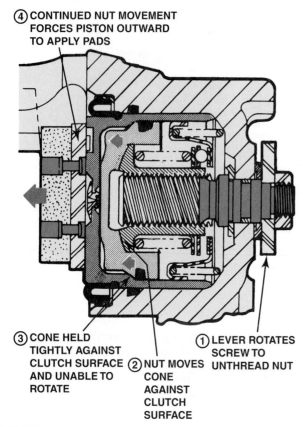

④ CONTINUED NUT MOVEMENT FORCES PISTON OUTWARD TO APPLY PADS

③ CONE HELD TIGHTLY AGAINST CLUTCH SURFACE AND UNABLE TO ROTATE

② NUT MOVES CONE AGAINST CLUTCH SURFACE

① LEVER ROTATES SCREW TO UNTHREAD NUT

FIGURE 14–22 Parking brake application of a General Motors rear drive brake caliper.

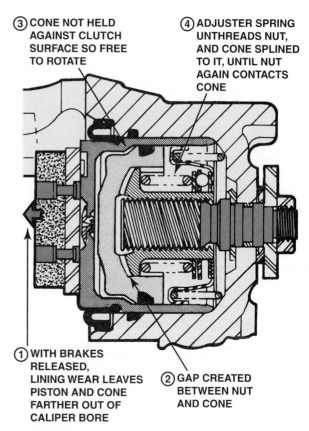

③ CONE NOT HELD AGAINST CLUTCH SURFACE SO FREE TO ROTATE

④ ADJUSTER SPRING UNTHREADS NUT, AND CONE SPLINED TO IT, UNTIL NUT AGAIN CONTACTS CONE

① WITH BRAKES RELEASED, LINING WEAR LEAVES PISTON AND CONE FARTHER OUT OF CALIPER BORE

② GAP CREATED BETWEEN NUT AND CONE

FIGURE 14–23 Automatic adjustment of a General Motors rear disc brake caliper.

CALIPER-ACTUATED DISC PARKING BRAKES (CONTINUED)

from rotating because the caliper piston is keyed to the brake pad, which is fixed in the caliper. Because the cone cannot rotate, movement of the nut along the actuator thread forces the cone and piston outward against the inboard pad to apply the brake.

Adjustment of the screw, nut, and cone mechanism occurs automatically during normal operation as the service brakes are released. ● **SEE FIGURE 14–23.** When the service brakes are applied, the cone and piston move outward in the bore under hydraulic pressure. The nut, however, remains fixed because the actuator screw does not rotate. As long as there is brake application pressure, the cone is held tightly against the clutch surface of the piston, which prevents the cone, and the nut splined to it, from rotating.

The result of the above actions is that a gap develops between the outer end of the nut and the backside of the cone when the brakes are applied. If sufficient brake lining wear has occurred, a gap remains after seal deflection retracts the piston and cone when the brakes are released. Once the brakes are

released, the cone is no longer held against the clutch surface, and becomes free to rotate in the piston. At this point, the adjuster spring, which exerts strong axial pressure on the nut, causes the nut and cone to unthread along the actuator screw and take up any clearance between the cone and piston.

The balance spring between the piston and the caliper bore has two purposes.

1. It prevents excessive piston retraction when the brakes are released.

2. It counterbalances the pressure of the adjuster spring.

Note that the outer end of the nut is in constant contact with the cone whenever the service brakes are not applied. If the automatic adjusting system fails, the tension of the adjuster spring against the thrust bearing at the back of the piston will retract the cone and piston from the rotor until the cone does contact the nut, resulting in a low brake pedal. ● **SEE FIGURES 14–24 THROUGH 14–31.**

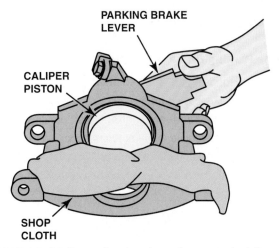

FIGURE 14–24 Removing the piston from a typical General Motors rear disc brake caliper.

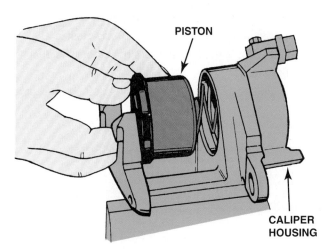

FIGURE 14–25 Installing the piston into a General Motors rear disc brake caliper.

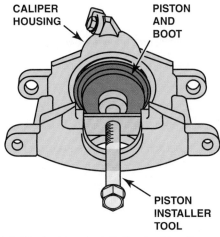

FIGURE 14–26 A piston installation tool is often needed to complete the installation of the piston in a General Motors rear disc brake.

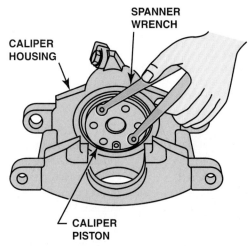

FIGURE 14–27 A spanner wrench (or needle-nose pliers) can be used to rotate the caliper piston prior to installing the disc brake pads. A notch on the piston must line up with a tab on the back of the brake pad to keep the piston from rotating when the parking brake is applied.

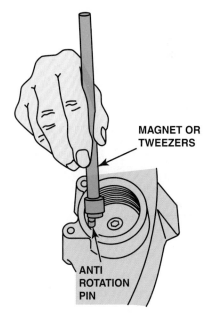

FIGURE 14–28 After removing the parking brake lever and thrust bearing, remove the antirotation pin.

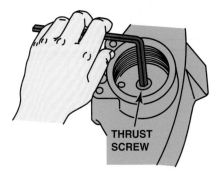

FIGURE 14–29 Unscrew the thrust screw from the piston with an Allen (hex) wrench. After removing the thrust screw, push the piston out of the caliper bore.

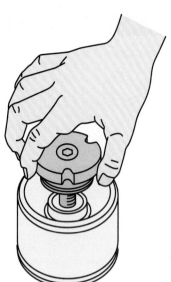

FIGURE 14–30 To test the piston adjuster, thread the thrust screw into the piston. Hold the piston and pull the thrust screw outward 1/4 in. (6 mm). The adjuster nut should not turn when the thrust screw retracts. Replace the piston assembly if not functioning correctly.

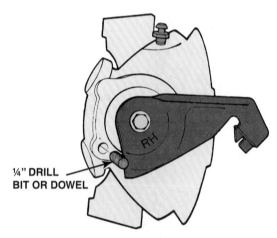

¼" DRILL
BIT OR DOWEL

FIGURE 14–31 To adjust the parking brake cable on a Ford vehicle equipped with rear disc brakes, start by loosening the cable adjustment until the cables to the calipers are slack. Tighten until the caliper lever moves. Position a 1/4-in. drill bit or dowel into the caliper alignment hole. Adjustment is correct if the parking brake lever does not hit the 1/4-in. dowel.

 TECH TIP

The Parking Brake "Click" Test

When diagnosing any brake problem, apply the parking brake and count the "clicks." This method works for both hand- and foot-operated parking brakes. Most vehicle manufacturers specify a maximum of 10 clicks. If the parking brake travel exceeds this amount, the rear brakes may be worn or out of adjustment.

CAUTION: Do not adjust the parking brake cable until the rear brakes have been thoroughly inspected and adjusted.

If the rear brake lining is usable, check for the proper operation of the self-adjustment mechanism. If the rear brakes are out of adjustment, the service brake pedal will also be low. This 10-click test is a fast and easy way to determine if the problem is due to rear brakes.

PARKING BRAKE CABLE ADJUSTMENT

Most manufacturers specify a minimum of 3 or 4, and a maximum of 8 to 10, clicks when applying the parking brake. Check service information for the vehicle being serviced for the exact specifications and adjustment procedures. Most vehicle manufacturers specify that the rear brakes be inspected and adjusted correctly before attempting to adjust the parking brake cable. Always follow the manufacturer's recommended procedure exactly.

Below is a general procedure for parking brake adjustment.

1. Make certain that the rear service brakes are adjusted correctly and the lining is serviceable.

2. With the drums installed, apply the parking brake 3 or 4 clicks. There should be a slight drag on both rear wheels.

3. Adjust the cable at the equalizer (equalizes one cable's force to both rear brakes) if necessary until there is a slight drag on both rear brakes. ● **SEE FIGURES 14–32 AND 14–33.**

4. Release the parking brake. Both rear brakes should be free and not dragging. Repair or replace rusted cables or readjust as necessary to ensure that the brakes are not dragging.

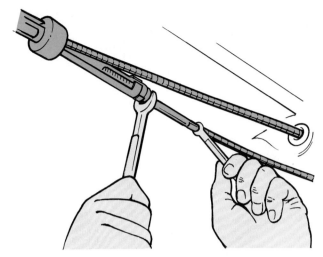

FIGURE 14–32 After checking that the rear brakes are okay and properly adjusted, the parking brake cable can be adjusted. Always follow the manufacturer's recommended procedure.

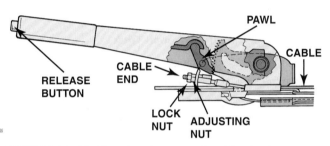

FIGURE 14–33 Many hand-operated parking brakes are adjusted inside the vehicle.

NOTE: The rear parking brake adjustment should always be checked whenever replacing the rear brake linings. It may be necessary to loosen the parking brake cable adjustment to allow clearance to get the drum over the new linings. This could happen because someone may have adjusted the parking brake cable during the life of the rear linings. ● SEE FIGURE 14–34.

With new thicker linings, the parking brake adjustment can keep the brake shoes pushed outward toward the drum.

To prevent possible parking brake cable adjustment problems when installing new rear brakes, always observe the following:

1. Both brake shoes should make contact with the anchor pin at the top. If not, check the parking brake cable for improper adjustment or improper installation of the brake shoes.

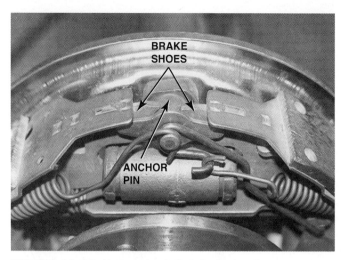

FIGURE 14–34 Always check that the brake shoes contact the anchor pin.

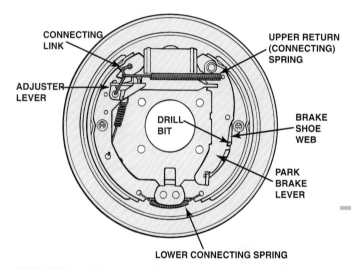

FIGURE 14–35 A 1/8-in. (3-mm) drill bit is placed through an access hole in the backing plate to adjust this General Motors leading-trailing rear parking brake. Adjust the parking brake cable until the drill can just fit between the shoe web and the parking brake lever.

2. Feel the tension of the parking brake cable underneath the vehicle. It should be slightly loose (with the parking brake "off").

3. Lubricate the parking brake cable to ensure that water or ice will not cause rust or freezing of the cable. This is necessary because even though the parking brake lever is released inside the vehicle, a stuck parking brake cable could cause the linings to remain out against the drums.

4. If the parking brake needs to be adjusted (will not hold on a hill or requires excessive lever movement), always check and adjust the rear brake adjustment before adjusting the parking brake cable. ● SEE FIGURE 14–35.

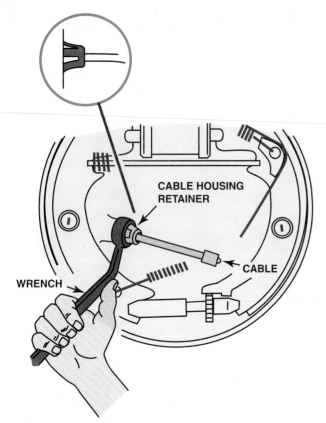

FIGURE 14–36 Many parking brake cables can be removed easily from the backing plate using a 1/2-in. (13-mm) box-end wrench. The wrench fits over the retainer finger on the end of the parking brake cable.

PARKING BRAKE
CABLE ADJUSTMENT (CONTINUED)

NOTE: Some vehicles are equipped with an automatic adjusting parking brake lever/cable. Simply cycling the parking brake on/off/on three times is often all that is required to adjust the parking brake cable.

5. Replace any stuck, corroded, or broken parking brake cable.

FIGURE 14–37 An electric parking brake button on the center console of a Jaguar.

🔧 **TECH TIP**

The Hose Clamp or Wrench Trick

It is often difficult to remove a parking brake cable from the backing plate due to the design of the retainer. The many fingers used to hold the cable to the backing plate can be squeezed all at once if a hose clamp is used to compress the fingers. A wrench as shown in ● **FIGURE 14–36** can also be used.

ELECTRIC PARKING BRAKE

Electric parking brake (EPB) systems are available using two different designs including:

1. A cable-pulling type that uses an electric motor to pull the parking brake cable rather than a mechanical handle or foot pedal.

2. A more advanced unit uses a computer-controlled motor attached to the brake caliper to activate it.

Some vehicles already use an electric parking brake (EPB) that can be activated when the vehicle stops and then goes off as soon as the gas pedal is pressed, preventing the vehicle from moving while stopped. ● **SEE FIGURE 14–37.**

SUMMARY

1. Government regulation requires that the parking brake be able to hold a fully loaded vehicle on a 20% grade.

2. The typical parking brake uses either a hand-operated lever or a foot-operated pedal to activate the parking brake.

3. On a typical drum brake system, the parking brake cable moves a parking brake lever attached to the secondary brake shoe. The primary shoe is applied through force being transferred through the strut.

4. All parking brake cables should move freely. The rear brakes should be adjusted properly before the parking brake is adjusted.

REVIEW QUESTIONS

1. Describe how a typical parking brake functions on a vehicle equipped with rear drum brakes.

2. Describe how a typical parking brake functions on a vehicle equipped with an integral rear disc brake system.

3. Explain how to adjust a parking brake cable properly.

CHAPTER QUIZ

1. Technician A says that the parking brake cable should be adjusted at each wheel. Technician B says that the parking brake cable adjustment is usually done after adjusting the rear brakes. Which technician is correct?
   a. Technician A only
   b. Technician B only
   c. Both Technicians A and B
   d. Neither Technician A nor B

2. Technician A says that the parking brake hand lever can turn on the red brake warning lamp. Technician B says that a foot-operated parking brake can turn on the red brake warning lamp. Which technician is correct?
   a. Technician A only
   b. Technician B only
   c. Both Technicians A and B
   d. Neither Technician A nor B

3. Technician A says that if the parking brake cable is adjusted too tight, the rear brakes may drag and overheat. Technician B says that the parking brake is adjusted properly if the cable is tight when in the released position. Which technician is correct?
   a. Technician A only
   b. Technician B only
   c. Both Technicians A and B
   d. Neither Technician A nor B

4. On most drum brake systems, the parking brake lever and strut transfer the pulling force of the parking brake cable against the _____.
   a. Primary shoe
   b. Secondary shoe

5. On most vehicles, the antirattle spring (strut spring) should be installed on the parking brake strut toward the _____ of the vehicle.
   a. Front
   b. Rear

6. In a typical integral rear disc brake caliper, the parking brake cable moves the _____.
   a. Caliper
   b. Actuator screw
   c. Auxiliary piston
   d. Rotor

7. The rear brakes should be inspected, and adjusted if necessary, if the parking brake requires more than _____.
   a. 5 clicks
   b. 10 clicks
   c. 15 clicks
   d. 20 clicks

8. A rear drum brake is being inspected. The primary shoe is not contacting the anchor pin at the top. Technician A says that this is normal. Technician B says that the parking brake cable may be adjusted too tight or is stuck. Which technician is correct?
   a. Technician A only
   b. Technician B only
   c. Both Technicians A and B
   d. Neither Technician A nor B

9. Technician A says that a hose clamp can be used to compress the retainer fingers of a parking brake cable in order to remove it from the backing plate. Technician B says a box-end wrench can be used instead of a hose clamp. Which technician is correct?
   a. Technician A only
   b. Technician B only
   c. Both Technicians A and B
   d. Neither Technician A nor B

10. Technician A says that an electric parking brake (EPB) uses an electric motor to pull on the parking brake cable. Technician B says that some electric parking brake systems use a computer-controlled motor attached to the caliper. Which technician is correct?
    a. Technician A only
    b. Technician B only
    c. Both Technicians A and B
    d. Neither Technician A nor B

chapter 15

MACHINING BRAKE DRUMS AND ROTORS

OBJECTIVES

After studying Chapter 15, the reader will be able to:

1. Prepare for the Brakes (A5) ASE certification test content area "E" (Miscellaneous Systems Diagnosis and Repair).

2. Discuss the construction of brake drums and rotors.

3. Explain the formation of hard spots in drums and rotors.

4. Describe how to measure and inspect drums and rotors before machining.

5. Discuss how surface finish is measured and its importance to satisfactory brake service.

6. Demonstrate how to machine a brake drum and rotor correctly.

KEY TERMS

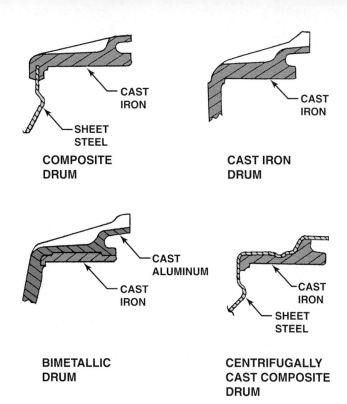

FIGURE 15–1 Types of brake drums. Regardless of the design, all types use cast iron as a friction surface.

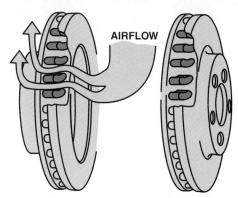

FIGURE 15–2 The airflow through cooling vents helps brakes from overheating.

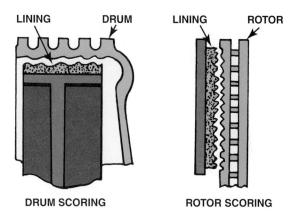

FIGURE 15–3 Scored drums and rotors often result in metal-to-metal contact.

BRAKE DRUMS

CAST-IRON DRUMS Brake drums are constructed of cast iron where the lining contacts the drum, with mild steel centers. The drum is drilled for the lug studs. Cast iron contains approximately 3% carbon, which makes the drum hard, yet brittle. For this reason it is recommended that any pounding needed to remove drums be done on the center mild steel portion, which, due to its material characteristics, can take this force without damage. This 3% carbon content of the cast iron also acts as a lubricant, which prevents noise during braking. Also, the rubbing surface can be machined without the need of a coolant (as would be required if constructed of mild steel). Because of these properties, cast iron is used on the friction surface of all drums. ● **SEE FIGURE 15–1.**

ALUMINUM DRUMS Even aluminum brake drums use cast iron for the friction surface area. Besides saving weight, aluminum brake drums transfer heat to the surrounding air faster than cast iron or steel.

Brake drums and rotors are the major energy-absorbing parts of the braking system. Friction between the friction material and the drum or rotor creates heat. This heat is absorbed by the drum or rotor and travels from the friction surface to the remainder of the drum or rotor by heat **convection.** As energy continues to be absorbed, the drum or rotor increases in temperature. Airflow across the drum or rotor helps to dissipate the heat and keep the temperature rise under control. ● **SEE FIGURE 15–2.**

BRAKE DRUM AND ROTOR DAMAGE

Besides wear, drums and rotors often experience damage to their friction surfaces. Because drum and rotor damage is caused by extremes of operation, it is most commonly found on front brakes, which experience more severe use than rear brakes.

SCORING **Scoring** is an extreme form of drum and rotor wear consisting of scratches, deep grooves, and a generally rough finish on the friction surface. ● **SEE FIGURE 15–3.**

There are a number of causes for scoring including:

1. The most common is brake linings that have worn to the point where a rivet, lining table, or pad backing plate contacts the drum or rotor.

2. Certain friction materials are more likely to score drums and rotors than others, and glazed linings that have hardened from exposure to extreme heat can also cause scoring.

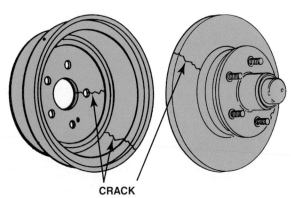

CRACK

FIGURE 15–4 Cracked drums or rotors must be replaced.

FIGURE 15–5 A heat-checked surface of a disc brake rotor.

BRAKE DRUM AND ROTOR DAMAGE (CONTINUED)

3. Drum brakes are more likely to become scored than disc brakes because their closed construction holds dirt, sand, and abrasive dust inside the friction assembly. This allows the contaminants to be scrubbed repeatedly between the linings and drum.

4. Severe drum scoring often results when metal parts of the friction assembly fatigue, break loose, and are trapped between the linings and drum.

A scored drum or rotor will cause very rapid lining wear, often accompanied by a growling or grinding noise, particularly if there is metal-to-metal contact between the shoe and drum or pad and rotor. Scoring can be machined out of a drum or rotor so long as the amount of metal removed is within the allowable limits.

CRACKING   Cracks in a brake drum or rotor are caused by the stress of severe braking or an impact during an accident. ● **SEE FIGURE 15–4**. Generally, drums and rotors that have been previously machined are more susceptible to cracking than new parts. Cracks can appear anywhere on a drum or rotor, although on drums they are most often found near the bolt circle on the web, or at the open edge of the friction surface. Rotors generally crack first at the edge of their friction surfaces.

HEAT CHECKING   A lesser form of drum and rotor cracking is called **heat checking,** which consists of many small, interlaced

TECH TIP

The Tap Test
Using a steel hammer, lightly tap a brake drum or rotor. It should ring if it is not cracked. If a dull thud is heard, the drum or rotor is likely cracked and should be replaced.

cracks on the friction surface. ● **SEE FIGURE 15–5**. These cracks typically penetrate only a few thousandths of an inch into the metal and seldom pass through the structure of the drum or rotor. Heat checking is usually caused by a driver who leaves one foot on the brake pedal while applying the accelerator with the other. Heat checking can also be caused by repeated heavy braking or numerous panic stops made in rapid succession.

Light heat checking can often be machined away. In more severe cases the drum or rotor must be replaced.

HARD OR CHILL SPOTS   Earlier it was stated that cast-iron drums and rotors are durable because the friction, heat, and pressure of braking cause a tough "skin" to form on their friction surfaces. However, if brake temperatures become too great, localized impurities in the metal can be burned away, altering the structure of the metal and causing **hard spots,** also called

FIGURE 15-6 These dark hard spots are created by heat that actually changes the metallurgy of the cast-iron drum. Most experts recommend replacement of any brake drum that has these hard spots.

hot spots, to appear. Hard spots are roughly circular, bluish gold, glassy-appearing areas on the friction surface. ● **SEE FIGURE 15–6**.

Hard spots create a number of problems including the following:

- They are harder than surrounding areas of the friction surface, and do not wear at the same rate. Once the spots begin to stand out from the rest of the friction surface, they cause rapid brake lining wear.

- The friction coefficient of hard spots is less than that of surrounding areas so braking power is reduced or becomes uneven. This can cause the brakes to chatter, or result in a hard or pulsating brake pedal.

- A drum or rotor is more likely to crack in the area of hard spots than elsewhere.

Most vehicle manufacturers recommend that the drum or rotor should be replaced if hard spots are found.

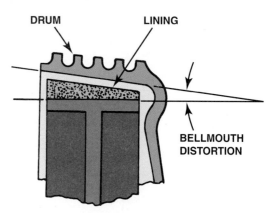

FIGURE 15–7 Bellmouth brake drum distortion.

BRAKE DRUM DISTORTION

To ensure smooth brake application without pedal pulsation or other problems, brake drum friction surfaces must remain a fixed position in relation to the shoes. In some cases, a position variation of less than a thousandth of an inch will create braking problems. Distortion puts the drum friction surfaces out of proper alignment with the shoes.

DRUM DISTORTION The friction surface of a brake drum in perfect condition is parallel to the axis of the axle, and rotates in a precise circle centered on the axle or hub. All brake drums suffer from distortion during brake operation, but they usually return to their original shape once the brakes are released. When the friction surface does not return to its proper shape, is no longer parallel to the axle, or does not rotate in a precise circle around the axle, the drum is distorted.

BELLMOUTH DRUMS When an open edge of a brake drum friction surface has a larger diameter than the closed edge, the drum is suffering from **bellmouth** distortion. ● **SEE FIGURE 15–7**. Bellmouth distortion is caused by poor drum rigidity combined with high heat and brake application force.

 **TECH TIP**

Storing Drums and Rotors

A common cause of distortion in new brake drums and rotors is improper storage. Drums and rotors should always be stored lying flat; they should never be stood on edge. Distortion of new drums and rotors is common, so they should be routinely checked before installation.

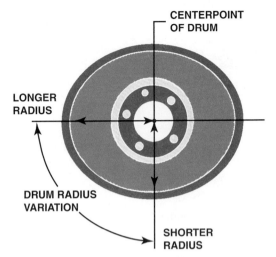

FIGURE 15–8 Out-of-round brake drum distortion.

BRAKE DRUM DISTORTION (CONTINUED)

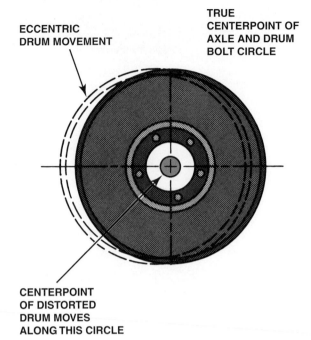

FIGURE 15–9 Eccentric brake drum distortion.

Bellmouth distortion occurs when a drum suffers mechanical fade and its open edge, unsupported by the drum web, expands more than its closed edge. When the brakes are applied harder to compensate for the fade, the shoes distort the open edge of the drum so far outward that the **elastic limit** of its metal is exceeded. Once this happens, the drum will not return to its original shape after it cools. Repeated occurrences of this process eventually cause the drum to take on a bellmouth shape.

Bellmouth distortion is especially common on wide drums and commonly occurs when a drum has had too much metal machined from it. If new shoes are installed in a bellmouthed drum, brake fade and unusual lining wear will result.

OUT-OF-ROUND DRUMS Uneven heat distribution can sometimes cause **out-of-round** distortion in which the drum radius varies when measured at different points around its circumference. ● SEE FIGURE 15–8. Out-of-round distortion can take place when a vehicle drives through a puddle after a series of hard stops and cold water splashed on the brakes causes rapid and uneven cooling of the drums. It can also result if the parking brake is firmly applied after a series of hard stops before the drums have had a chance to cool. In this case, the shoes extend out against the heat-expanded drum and prevent it from contracting to its original circular shape as it cools. Instead, the extended shoes force the drum into an out-of-round shape.

The most common symptom of an out-of-round drum is a pulsating brake pedal when the brakes are applied at all speeds. Out-of-round drums can also cause a vibration or brake chatter at speeds above approximately 40 mph (60 km/h). In more extreme cases, an out-of-round drum can result in erratic braking action, and possibly cause the brakes to grab with every revolution of the wheel.

 **TECH TIP**

The Parking Brake Trick

Whenever attempting to diagnose a brake pedal pulsation, drive to a deserted area or parking lot and try stopping the vehicle using the parking brake. If a vibration occurs, the problem is due to a fault with the rear brakes. If a vibration does not occur except when using the service brakes, the problem is most likely due to a fault with the front brakes.

ECCENTRIC DRUMS **Eccentric distortion** exists when the geometric center of the circle described by the brake drum friction surface is other than the center of the axle or the bolt circle of the drum web. ● SEE FIGURE 15–9. This type of distortion causes the drum to rotate with a camlike motion. An eccentric drum will result in a pulsating brake pedal similar to that caused by an out-of-round drum.

Eccentric distortion is often caused by overtightened or unevenly tightened lug nuts or bolts. Not only will this cause an immediate problem, but it can lead to additional problems later. If a vehicle is driven for an extended time with an eccentric drum, the linings may slowly wear the friction surface "round" again. However, as soon as tension on the lug nuts or bolts is released, the drum will relax back to its original shape creating an out-of-round condition that was not apparent before the wheel was removed.

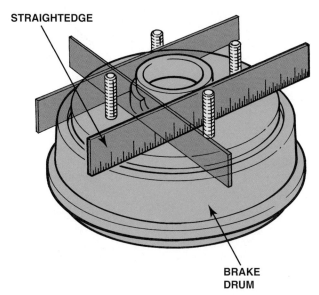

STRAIGHTEDGE

BRAKE DRUM

FIGURE 15–10 A straightedge can be used to check for brake drum warpage.

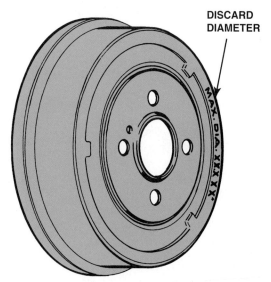

DISCARD DIAMETER

FIGURE 15–11 Discard diameter and maximum diameter are brake drum machining and wear limits.

REMOVING DRUMS

Metal clips called **tinnerman nuts** are installed at the factory to keep the brake drums from falling off during vehicle assembly. These clips can be removed and do not need to be reinstalled since the wheel lug nuts hold onto the brake drum.

The first inspection step after removing a brake drum is to check it for warpage using a straightedge, as shown in **● FIGURE 15–10**.

A warped drum is often a source of vibration. A brake drum that is out-of-round can cause a brake pedal pulsation during braking.

NOTE: To help diagnose if the front brakes or rear brakes are the cause of the vibration, try slowing the vehicle using the parking brake. If vibration occurs, the problem is due to the rear brakes.

🔧 **TECH TIP**

Mark It to Be Sure

Most experts recommend that brake rotors, as well as drums and wheels, be marked before removing them for service. Many disc brake rotors are directional and will function correctly only if replaced in the original location. A quick-and-easy method is to use correction fluid. This alcohol-based liquid comes in small bottles with a small brush inside, making it easy to mark rotors with an "L" for left and an "R" for right. Correction fluid (also called "white-out" or "liquid paper") can also be used to make marks on wheel studs, wheels, and brake drums to help ensure reinstallation in the same location.

"MACHINE TO" VERSUS "DISCARD"

Brake drums can usually be machined a maximum of 0.060 in. (1.5 mm) oversize (for example, a 9.500-in. drum could wear or be machined to a maximum inside diameter of 9.560 in.) unless otherwise stamped on the drum. Most brake experts recommend that both drums on the same axle be within 0.010 in. (0.25 mm) of each other. *The maximum specified inside diameter (ID) means the maximum wear inside diameter.* **● SEE FIGURE 15–11.**

Always leave at least 0.015 in. (0.4 mm) after machining (resurfacing) for wear. Many manufacturers recommend that 0.030 in. (0.8 mm) be left for wear.

REASONS FOR EQUAL DRUM INSIDE DIAMETER
There are several reasons why the service technician should check and make sure that both brake drums on the same axle are close to the same inside diameter (ID).

FIGURE 15–12 Most brake drums have a chamfer around the edge. If the chamfer is no longer visible, the drum is usually worn (or machined) to its maximum allowable ID.

"MACHINE TO" VERSUS "DISCARD" (CONTINUED)

- **Reason 1.** Since heat is generated by braking, if there is less material (larger ID), the drum will tend to expand more rapidly than a drum with more material (smaller ID).
- **Reason 2.** If one drum expands more than the drum on the other side of the vehicle, unequal braking forces result.
- **Reason 3.** The drum that is larger in ID will expand away from the brake linings more than the other side.

For example:

Left Drum	Right Drum
9.500 in.	9.560 in.

In this example, when the drums get hot (heavy braking), the vehicle will tend to pull to the left.

 TECH TIP

Brake Drum Chamfer

Look at the chamfer on the outer edge of most brake drums. When the chamfer is no longer visible, the brake drum is usually at or past its maximum ID. ● **SEE FIGURE 15–12.** Although this chamfer is not an accurate gauge of the ID of the brake drum, it still is a helpful indicator to the technician.

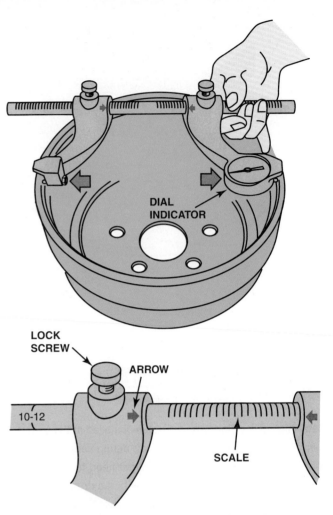

FIGURE 15–13 Typical needle-dial brake drum micrometer. The left movable arm is set to the approximate drum diameter and the right arm to the more exact drum diameter. The dial indicator (gauge) reads in thousandths of an inch.

MACHINING BRAKE DRUMS

MEASURING A DRUM Before measuring a brake drum, be sure it is not cracked by tapping it with a steel hammer. The brake drum should ring like a bell. If the brake drum makes a dull thud sound, discard the drum. Brake drums are usually measured using a micrometer especially designed for brake drums. ● **SEE FIGURE 15–13.**

Compare the micrometer reading to the discard diameter. Both drums should be measured whenever they are removed for any brake service or inspection.

MACHINING A DRUM PROCEDURE Always start any machining operation by making certain that the brake drum is

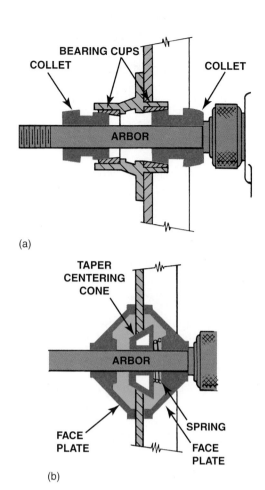

(a)

(b)

FIGURE 15–14 (a) A rotor or brake drum with a bearing hub should be installed on a brake lathe using the appropriate size collet that fit the bearing cups (races). (b) A hubless rotor or brake drum requires a spring and a tapered centering cone. A faceplate should be used on both sides of the rotor or drum to provide support. Always follow the operating instructions for the specified setup for the brake lathe being used.

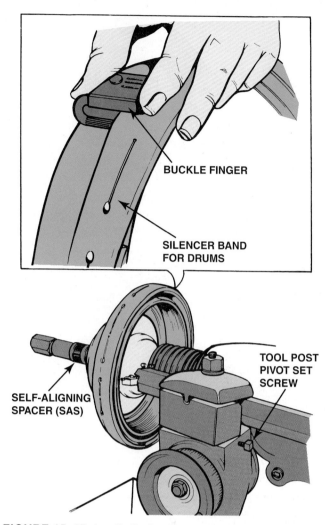

FIGURE 15–15 A self-aligning spacer (SAS) should always be used between the drum or rotor and the spindle retaining nut to help ensure an even clamping force and to prevent the adapters and cone from getting into a bind. A silence band should always be installed to prevent turning-tool chatter and to ensure a smooth surface finish. *(Courtesy of Ammco Tools, Inc.)*

clean and that excess grease is removed from the hub. If the drum has a hub with bearings, check the outer bearing races (cups) for wear and replace as necessary before placing the drum on the brake lathe. Also, carefully inspect and clean the lathe spindle shaft and cones before use. Use a **self-aligning spacer (SAS)** to be assured of even force being applied to the drum by the spindle nut. Always follow the instructions for the lathe you are using.

Hubless drums use a hole in the center of the brake drum for centering. Always check that the center hole is clean and

free of burrs or nicks. Typical drum brake machining steps include the following:

STEP 1 Mount the drum on the lathe and install the silencer band as shown in ● **FIGURES 15–14 AND 15–15**.

STEP 2 Turn the drum by hand before turning on the lathe to be sure everything is clean. Advance the tool bit manually until it just contacts the drum. This is called a **scratch cut**. ● **SEE FIGURE 15–16**.

FIGURE 15–16 After installing a brake drum on the lathe, turn the cutting tool outward until the tool just touches the drum. This is called a scratch cut. *(Courtesy of Ammco Tools, Inc.)*

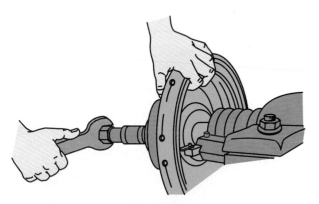

FIGURE 15–17 After making a scratch cut, loosen the retaining nut, rotate the drum on the lathe, and make another scratch cut. If both cuts are in the same location, the drum is installed correctly on the lathe and drum machining can begin. *(Courtesy of Ammco Tools, Inc.)*

MACHINING BRAKE DRUMS (CONTINUED)

STEP 3 Stop the lathe and back off the tool bit. Loosen the arbor nut, rotate the drum one-half turn (180°) on the arbor, and retighten the arbor nut. ● **SEE FIGURE 15–17**.

Turn the lathe on and make a second scratch cut.
  a. If the scratch cuts are side-by-side, the lathe is okay and machining can begin.
  b. If the scratch cuts are opposite, remove the drum and check for nicks, burrs, or chips on the mounting surfaces.

STEP 4 Start the lathe and set the depth of the cut. ● **SEE FIGURES 15–18 AND 15–19**.

The maximum rough cut depends on the lathe type. The minimum cut is usually specified as no less than 0.002 in. (0.05 mm). A shallower cut usually causes the tool bit to slide over the surface of the metal rather than cut into the metal.

● **SEE FIGURE 15–20** for an example of a drum machined without properly positioning the antichatter (vibration) strap.

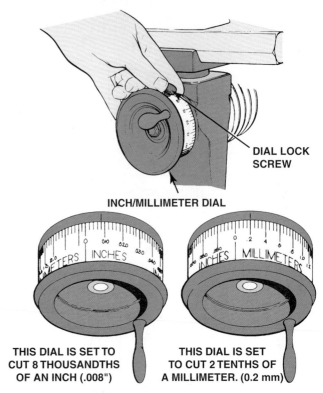

INCH/MILLIMETER DIAL

THIS DIAL IS SET TO CUT 8 THOUSANDTHS OF AN INCH (.008")

THIS DIAL IS SET TO CUT 2 TENTHS OF A MILLIMETER. (0.2 mm)

FIGURE 15–18 Set the depth of the cut indicator to zero just as the turning tool touches the drum. *(Courtesy of Ammco Tools, Inc.)*

FIGURE 15–19 This lathe has a dial that is "diameter graduated". This means that a reading of 0.030 in. indicates a 0.015 in. cut that increases the inside diameter of the brake drum by 0.030 in.

FIGURE 15–20 Notice the chatter marks at the edge of the friction-area surface of the brake drum. These marks were caused by vibration of the drum because the technician failed to wrap the dampening strap (silencer band) over the friction-surface portion of the brake drum.

DISC BRAKE ROTORS

Disc brake rotors use cast gray iron at the area that contacts the friction pad. Rotors, also called **discs** or **disks,** have mass (weight) that absorbs heat. The heavier the rotor, the more heat can be absorbed. Vehicle downsizing has resulted in the use of thinner- and lighter-weight rotors. As the weight of the rotor decreases, the less heat the rotor can "store" or absorb, resulting in the rotor getting hotter. As the rotor gets hotter, the rotor expands and "grows" larger where it is the hottest. If the rotor is allowed to cool gradually, the rotor simply returns to its original shape. If, however, the rotor is exposed to water, it may cool rapidly, causing the rotor to distort.

STYLES OR ROTORS Rotors are made in several styles, including the following:

1. **Solid.** These are used on the rear of many vehicles equipped with rear disc brakes and on the front of some small and midsize vehicles. Solid rotors are usually used on the rear where only 20% to 40% of the braking occurs. Solid rotors are much thinner than vented rotors. ● **SEE FIGURE 15–21** for an example of an excessively worn solid rotor.

2. **Vented.** These are used on the front of most vehicles. The internal vanes allow air to circulate between the two friction surfaces of the rotor. Rotors can either be straight vane design, as shown in ● **FIGURE 15–22**, or directional vane design, as shown in ● **FIGURE 15–23**.

FIGURE 15–21 This excessively worn (thin) rotor was removed from the vehicle in this condition. It is amazing that the vehicle was able to stop with such a thin rotor.

FIGURE 15–22 Severely worn vented disc brake rotor. The braking surface has been entirely worn away exposing the cooling fins. The owner brought the vehicle to a repair shop because of a "little noise in the front." Notice the straight vane design.

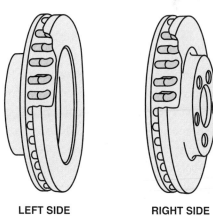

LEFT SIDE   RIGHT SIDE

FIGURE 15–23 Directional vane vented disc brake rotors. Note that the fins angle toward the rear of the vehicle. It is important that this type of rotor be reinstalled on the correct side of the vehicle.

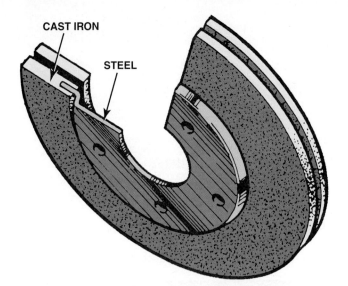

CAST IRON

STEEL

FIGURE 15–24 Typical composite rotor that uses cast iron friction surfaces and a steel center section.

DISC BRAKE ROTORS (CONTINUED)

COMPOSITE ROTORS Composite rotors use a steel center section with a cast iron wear surface. These composite rotors are lighter in weight than conventional cast-iron rotors. ● SEE FIGURE 15–24.

The light weight of composite rotors makes them popular with vehicle manufacturers. However, technicians should be aware that full-contact adapters that simulate the actual wheel being bolted to the rotor must be used when machining composite rotors. If composite rotors are machined incorrectly, they must usually be replaced.

ALUMINUM METAL MATRIX COMPOSITE ROTORS Some disc brake rotors are manufactured from an aluminum metal matrix composite alloy reinforced with 20% silicon carbide particulate. Aluminum composites combine the light weight and thermal conductivity of aluminum with the stiffness and wear resistance of a ceramic to create a disc brake rotor with excellent heat dissipation and service life.

These rotors can be distinguished from conventional cast-iron rotors in several ways. At first glance the rotors are silver gray with a dark gray or black transfer layer (from the brake pad) on the rubbing surface. Unlike cast iron, these rotors will show no signs of rust and are nonmagnetic. When removed from the vehicle, the aluminum composite rotors can be further distinguished by their light weight, usually under 6 lb (2.7 kg) versus over 12 lb (5.4 kg) for cast-iron rotors on the typical passenger vehicle.

 FREQUENTLY ASKED QUESTION

What Does "Cross-Drilled" and "Slotted" Mean?

The expression "cross-drilled" and "slotted" refers to two separate processes. The first procedure involves drilling rows of holes through the friction surfaces of the rotor. The second procedure refers to milling a series of specially machined grooves from the center of the disc toward the edge. When the friction surfaces of a rotor are smooth and flat, there is no means of escape for the gases and dust, which build up between pad and rotor. This is not a huge problem in normal driving, but is an important consideration in street performance applications.

The drill holes (which are sometimes called "gas relief openings") provide an exit route for the dust and gas. The holes are also commonly labeled "cooling holes" because of the improvements they make in this area. Better cooling means less fade during repeated heavy brake application. They also help dissipate water when driving in poor weather. ● SEE FIGURE 15–25.

Slotting increases the bite of the pads and is even more effective than cross-drilling in combating the problem known as "out-gassing." This is when, at very high braking temperatures, the bonding agents used in some brake pads produce a gas. Under extreme conditions, this gas can create a gas cushion between pad and rotor, giving a driver a normal pedal feel but reducing the amount of friction being generated. The slots pump away gas and restore full contact. The "micro-shaving" effect of the slots also serves to deglaze the pads and this is why the edges of the slots are not chamfered or "radiused." It also tends to even out the wear across the brake pad faces, increasing the effective contact area.

Servicing these rotors is slightly different from cast-iron rotors. The dark transfer layer on the rubbing surface does not harm rotor performance and should not be removed unless the rotor needs to be machined due to being warped. Carbide tools can be used to machine a single set of aluminum composite rotors. If a shop receives these rotors on a regular basis, a polycrystalline diamond (PCD)-tipped tool is a good investment. Although more expensive initially, the PCD tool can last 100 times longer than a carbide tool.

FIGURE 15–25 This Porsche is equipped with high-performance brakes including cross-drilled brake rotors.

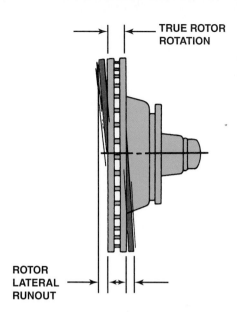

FIGURE 15–26 Brake rotor lateral-runout distortion.

DISC BRAKE ROTOR DISTORTION

CAUSES OF ROTOR DISTORTION The friction surfaces of a rotor in perfect condition are perpendicular to the axle centerline, and have no side-to-side movement. Unlike brake drums, rotors do not suffer distortion as a routine part of brake operation. However, distortion can occur during braking if there is a problem with the friction assembly, such as a frozen caliper piston that creates unequal application force on the two sides of the rotor.

Friction surface distortion is much more significant in a disc brake rotor than in a brake drum because the design of the friction assembly magnifies the effect of any wear. The hydraulic principles dictate that small movements of the large pistons in the brake calipers are converted into large movements of the small pistons in the master cylinder. Even very small amounts of distortion in a disc brake rotor can cause large amounts of pedal pulsation.

ROTOR LATERAL RUNOUT **Lateral runout,** often abbreviated **LRO** or **T.I.R.** for **total indicator runout,** is side-to-side wobble of the rotor as it rotates on the spindle. ● **SEE FIGURE 15–26.**

A small amount of runout provides caliper piston knockback that reduces drag when the brakes are not applied. However, if the amount of runout is too great, excessive brake pedal travel and front-end vibration, felt in the steering wheel, will result. In cases of severe runout, a pulsating brake pedal may also be present.

Lateral runout can be caused by several factors. Overtightened or unevenly tightened lug nuts or bolts are a common source of runout on newer vehicles with downsized brake rotors. Extreme heat or rapid temperature variations also cause runout. Inaccurate machining at the factory or in the field is also a common cause of this distortion. Most maximum values range

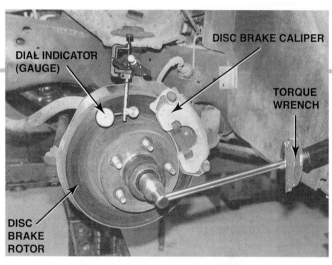

FIGURE 15–27 Before measuring lateral runout with a dial indicator (gauge), remove any wheel bearing end play by tightening the spindle nut to 10 to 20 ft-lb with a torque wrench. This step helps prevent an inaccurate reading. If the vehicle is to be returned to service, be sure to loosen the spindle nut and retighten to specifications (usually, finger tight) to restore proper bearing clearance.

between 0.002 and 0.008 in. (0.05 and 0.20 mm). ● **SEE FIGURES 15–27 AND 15–28.**

ROTOR LACK OF PARALLELISM Lack of **parallelism,** also called **thickness variation (TV),** is a variation in the thickness of the rotor when it is measured at several places around its circumference. ● **SEE FIGURE 15–29.**

A rotor with friction surfaces that are not parallel is the most common disc brake cause of a pulsating brake pedal. A lack of rotor parallelism will cause a pedal pulsation when the brakes are applied at all speeds, and can also cause front-end vibration during braking. ● **SEE FIGURE 15–30.**

Lack of parallelism can be caused by a soft spot in the rotor casting that wears more rapidly than surrounding areas, but the

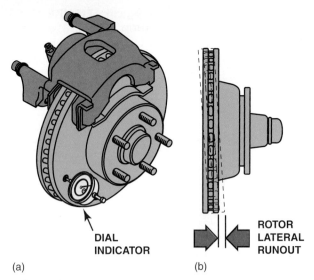

DIAL
INDICATOR

ROTOR
LATERAL
RUNOUT

(a)

(b)

FIGURE 15–28 (a) Rotate the disc brake rotor one complete revolution while observing the dial indicator (gauge). (b) Most vehicle manufacturers specify a maximum runout of about 0.003 in. (0.08 mm).

DISC BRAKE ROTOR DISTORTION (CONTINUED)

TECH TIP

Braking Vibration Could Be Due to the Tires

A vibrating condition (roughness) during braking is usually caused by disc brake rotor thickness variation or an out-of-round brake drum. Both conditions should be investigated. However, the tires and/or road conditions can also cause the same vibrations.

Tests performed by vehicle and tire-manufacturing engineers have shown that tires, and tires alone, could be the cause. If no other problem can be isolated, install a different brand of tire on the vehicle and retest. The cause of the tire vibration seems to be due to distortion or movement of the tire tread. A different brand of tires would have a different tread rubber compound, carcass body ply angles, or other factor that can contribute to a vibration during braking.

most common cause is rust buildup on the rotor when the vehicle is not driven for an extended period. The part of the friction surface protected by the brake pads does not rust as much as the rest of the rotor, and because the rusted areas wear faster, this results in a thickness variation when the vehicle is driven again.

Because parallelism variation is much more likely to cause a problem than lateral runout, the maximum amount allowed is much smaller than for runout. Most manufacturers specify that the two friction surfaces of a rotor must be parallel within half a thousandth of an inch, 0.0005 in. (0.013 mm), or less.

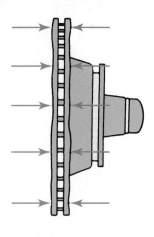

FIGURE 15–29 Brake rotor lack-of-parallelism distortion.

THICKNESS VARIATION
AT DIFFERENT POINTS
AROUND THE ROTOR

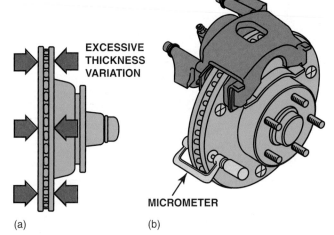

EXCESSIVE
THICKNESS
VARIATION

MICROMETER

(a)

(b)

FIGURE 15–30 (a) Disc brake rotor thickness variation (parallelism). (b) The rotor should be measured with a micrometer at four or more equally spaced locations around the rotor.

TECH TIP

Think of a Human Hair

Measurements and specifications do not seem to mean much unless you can visualize the size compared to something with which you are familiar. The diameter of a human hair is from 0.002 to 0.004 in. (2 to 4 thousandths of an inch).

The maximum lateral runout of a rotor is usually within this same dimension. The reason a dial indicator has to be used to measure runout, and a micrometer to measure parallelism, is that the dimensions involved are less than the diameter of a human hair. ● **SEE FIGURE 15–31.**

0.968" =

FIGURE 15–31 Sample micrometer readings. Each larger line on the barrel between the numbers represents 0.025″. The number on the thimble is then added to the number showing and the number of lines times 0.025″.

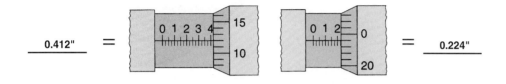

0.335" =

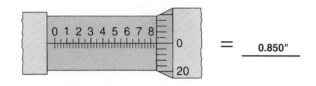

0.412" =   = 0.224"

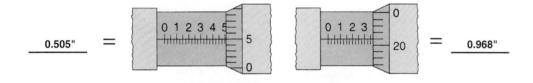

= 0.850"

0.505" =   = 0.968"

0.687 =

DISC BRAKE ROTOR THICKNESS

Most rotors have a minimum thickness cast or stamped into the rotor. This thickness is minimum wear thickness. At least 0.015 in. (0.4 mm) must remain after machining to allow for wear. Some vehicle manufacturers, such as General Motors,

specify that 0.030 in. [0.8 mm] be left for wear. ● **SEE FIGURE 15–32**.

Whenever machining (resurfacing) a rotor, an equal amount of material must be removed from each side.

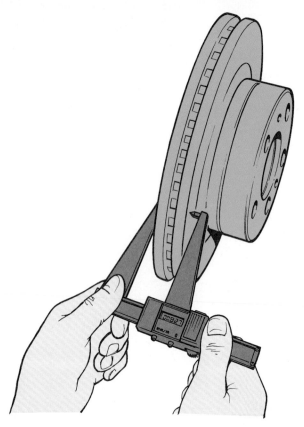

FIGURE 15–32 A digital readout rotor micrometer is an accurate tool to use when measuring a rotor. Both fractional inches and metric millimeters are generally available.

WHEN THE ROTORS SHOULD BE MACHINED

According to brake design engineers, a worn rotor has a very smooth friction surface that is ideal for replacement (new) disc brake pads. Often when the rotors are machined, the surface finish is not as smooth as specified. Therefore, a rotor should be machined only if one of the following conditions exists:

1. Deep grooves deeper than 0.060 in. (1.5 mm). This is the approximate thickness of a nickel! ● **SEE FIGURE 15–33**.

2. Thickness variation exceeding specifications and a brake pedal pulsation complaint.

3. Heavy rust that has corroded the friction surface of the rotor. ● **SEE FIGURES 15–34 AND 15–35**.

Therefore, if there is no complaint of a pulsating brake pedal during braking and the rotor is not deeply grooved or rusted, it should not be machined. New disc brake pads perform best against a smooth surface, and a used disc brake rotor is often smoother than a new rotor.

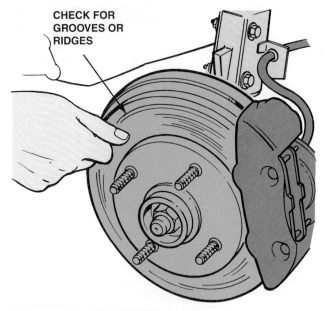

FIGURE 15–33 If a fingernail catches on a groove in the rotor, the rotor should be machined.

FIGURE 15–34 This rusted rotor should be machined.

FIGURE 15–35 Rotors that have deep rust pockets usually cannot be machined.

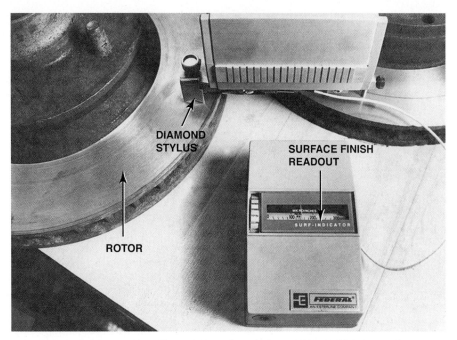

FIGURE 15–36 Electronic surface finish machine. The reading shows about 140 μin. This is much too rough for use but is typical for a rough cut surface.

ROTOR FINISH

The smoothness of the rotor is called rotor finish or surface finish. Surface finish is measured in units called **microinches,** abbreviated **μin.,** where the symbol in front of "in." is the Greek lowercase letter μ (mu). One microinch equals 0.000001 in. (0.025 micrometer [μm]). The finish classification of microinch means the distance between the highest peaks and the deepest valley. The usual method of expressing surface finish is the arithmetic average roughness height, abbreviated **Ra,** which is the average of all peaks and valleys from the mean (average) line. This surface finish is measured using a machine with a diamond stylus, as shown in ● **FIGURE 15–36**.

Another classification of surface finish that is becoming obsolete is the *root mean square (RMS)*. The RMS method gives a slightly higher number and can be obtained by multiplying Ra × 1.11 = RMS.

Often, a machined rotor will not be as smooth as a new rotor, resulting in a hard-stopping complaint after new brakes have been installed. A rough rotor has less surface area touching the new brake pads, resulting in a hard brake pedal and reduced braking effectiveness. Most new rotors have a surface finish of 45 to 60 μin. Ra.

- The higher the Ra of a rotor, the rougher the surface finish.
- The lower the Ra number, the smoother the surface finish

 **TECH TIP**

The Ballpoint Pen Test

A smooth friction surface on a drum or rotor is necessary for proper brake operation. To quickly determine if the friction surface of a brake drum or rotor is not smooth enough, draw a ballpoint pen across the surface. If the surface is smooth enough, a solid ink line will be observed. If the line drawn by the pen is not solid, then the surface is not smooth enough.

MACHINING A DISC BRAKE ROTOR

Before machining a rotor, be sure that it can be machined by comparing the minimum thickness specification and the measured thickness of the rotor. Many lathes are capable of removing a large amount of material in one pass, thereby reducing the time necessary to refinish a rotor. These lathes usually use a positive rake tool bit angle. ● **SEE FIGURE 15–37**.

Other lathes that use six-sided reversible tool bits usually use a negative rake tool bit angle. Ammco is an example of a negative rake lathe, whereas Perfect-Hofmann and Accu-turn are examples of positive rake lathes.

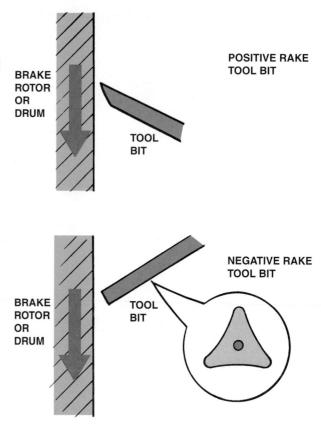

FIGURE 15–37 Most positive rake brake lathes can cut any depth in one pass, thereby saving time. A typical negative rake lathe uses a three-sided turning tool that can be flipped over, thereby giving six cutting edges.

POSITIVE RAKE TOOL BIT

BRAKE ROTOR OR DRUM

TOOL BIT

NEGATIVE RAKE TOOL BIT

BRAKE ROTOR OR DRUM

TOOL BIT

MACHINING A DISC BRAKE ROTOR (CONTINUED)

CAUTION: Some original equipment and replacement disc brake rotors are close to the minimum allowable thickness when new. Often, these rotors cannot be safely machined at all!

Following is an example of the steps necessary to machine a disc brake rotor. Always follow the instructions for the equipment you are using.

STEP 1 Mount the disc brake rotor to the spindle of the lathe using the cones and adapters recommended. ● **SEE FIGURES 15–38 AND 15–39.**

STEP 2 Install a rotor damper and position the cutting tools close to the rotor surface as shown in ● **FIGURE 15–40.**

NOTE: Failure to install the damper causes vibrations to occur during machining that create a rough surface finish.

STEP 3 Make a scratch cut on the rotor face, as shown in ● **FIGURE 15–41.**

STEP 4 To check that the rotor is mounted correctly, loosen the retaining nut, turn the rotor one-half turn (180°), and retighten the nut. Make another scratch cut.

a. The second scratch cut should be side-by-side with the first scratch cut if the rotor is properly installed, as shown in ● **FIGURE 15–42.**

b. If the second scratch cut is on the opposite side (180°) from the first scratch cut, the rotor may not be installed on the lathe correctly.

NOTE: The runout as measured with a dial indicator on the brake lathe should be the same as the runout measured on the vehicle. If the runout is not the same, the rotor is not installed on the brake lathe correctly.

STEP 5 After proper installation of the disc brake rotor on the brake lathe, proceed with machining the rotors. For best results do not machine any more material from the rotor than is absolutely necessary. Always follow the recommendations and guidelines as specified by the vehicle manufacturer.

ROUGH CUT A rough cut on a lathe involves cutting 0.005 in. per side with a feed of 0.008 in. per revolution and 150 RPM spindle speed. This usually results in a very coarse surface finish of about 150 μin. Ra.

FINISH CUT A finish cut means removing 0.002 in. per side with a feed of 0.002 in. per revolution and 150 RPM spindle speed. Although this cut usually looks smooth, the surface finish is about 90 to 100 μin. Ra. Even a typical finish cut is still not nearly as smooth as a new rotor.

TYPICAL ROTOR MOUNTING CONFIGURATIONS

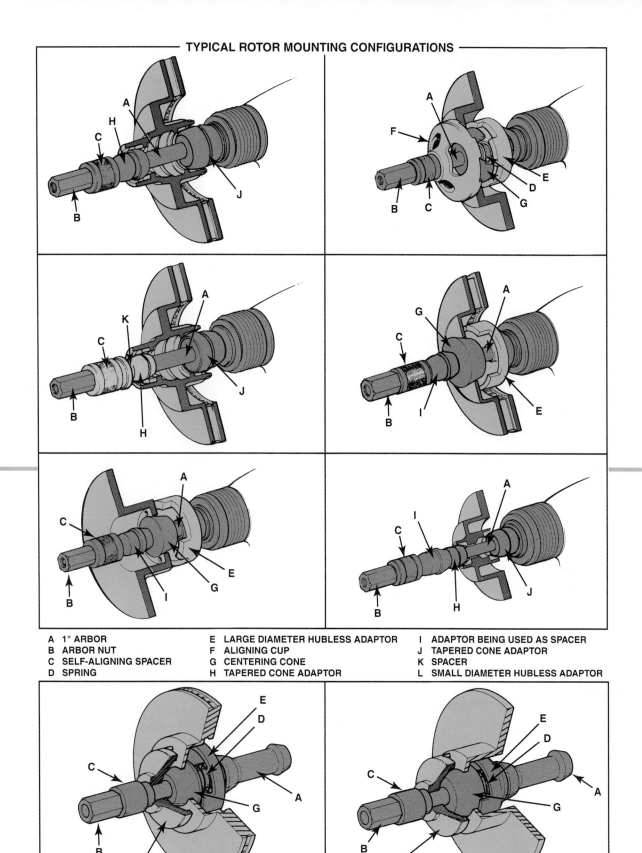

A 1" ARBOR
B ARBOR NUT
C SELF-ALIGNING SPACER
D SPRING

E LARGE DIAMETER HUBLESS ADAPTOR
F ALIGNING CUP
G CENTERING CONE
H TAPERED CONE ADAPTOR

I ADAPTOR BEING USED AS SPACER
J TAPERED CONE ADAPTOR
K SPACER
L SMALL DIAMETER HUBLESS ADAPTOR

FIGURE 15–38 Recommended adapters and location for machining hubbed and hubless rotors. *(Courtesy of Ammco Tools, Inc.)*

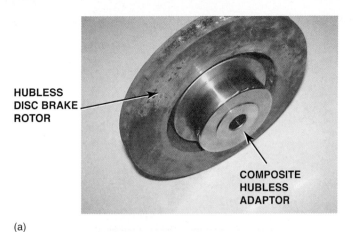

HUBLESS DISC BRAKE ROTOR

COMPOSITE HUBLESS ADAPTOR

(a)

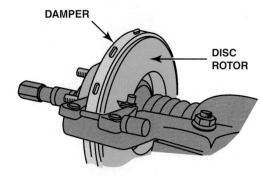

DAMPER

DISC ROTOR

FIGURE 15–40 A damper is necessary to reduce cutting-tool vibrations that can cause a rough surface finish.

SPINDLE NUT

SELF-ALIGNING SPACER

(b)

FIGURE 15–39 (a) Composite adapter fitted to a rotor. (b) Composite rotor properly mounted on a lathe.

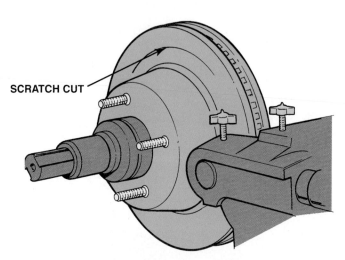

SCRATCH CUT

FIGURE 15–41 After installing the rotor on the brake lathe, turn the cutting tool in just enough to make a scratch cut.

MATCHING A DISC BRAKE ROTOR (CONTINUED)

NOTE: Measure the thickness of the rotor after the finish cut and compare with manufacturers' specifications. Be sure to allow for wear. ● SEE CHART 15–1 for a metric/fractional measurement chart.

NONDIRECTIONAL FINISH Most vehicle and brake component manufacturers recommend a nondirectional finish to help prevent the grooves machined into the rotor from acting like record grooves that can force the pads to move outward while the rotor rotates.

CAUTION: Some nondirectional finish tools such as those that use Scotch Brite (a registered trademark) plastic pads often do not make the rotor as smooth as new, even though the finish has been swirled. ● SEE FIGURE 15–43.

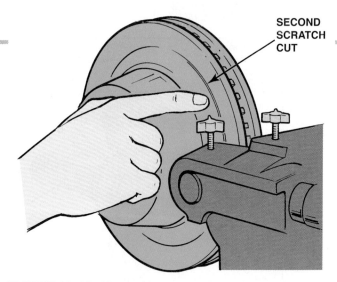

SECOND SCRATCH CUT

FIGURE 15–42 After making a scratch cut, loosen the retaining nut and rotate the rotor on the spindle of the lathe one-half turn. Tighten the nut and make a second scratch cut. The second scratch cut should be side-by-side with the first scratch if the rotor is installed correctly on the brake lathe.

(a)

(b)

FIGURE 15-43 (a) This technician uses two sanding blocks each equipped with 150-grit aluminum-oxide sandpaper. (b) With the lathe turned on, the technician presses the two sanding blocks against the surface of the rotor after the rotor has been machined, to achieve a smooth microinch surface finish.

INCH	DECIMAL INCH	MILLIMETER	INCH	DECIMAL INCH	MILLIMETER
1/64	0.015625	0.396785	33/64	0.515625	13.096875
1/32	0.03125	0.79375	17/32	0.53125	13.49375
3/64	0.046875	1.190625	35/64	0.546875	13.890625
1/16	0.0625	1.5875	9/16	0.5625	14.2875
5/64	0.078125	1.984375	37/64	0.578125	14.684375
3/32	0.09375	2.38125	19/32	0.59375	15.08125
7/64	0.109375	2.778125	39/64	0.609375	15.478125
1/8	0.125	3.175	5/8	0.625	15.875
9/64	0.140625	3.571875	41/64	0.640625	16.271875
5/32	0.15625	3.96875	21/32	0.65625	16.66875
11/64	0.171875	4.365625	43/64	0.671875	17.065625
3/16	0.1875	4.7625	11/16	0.6875	17.4625
13/64	0.203125	5.159375	45/64	0.703125	17.859375
7/32	0.21875	5.55625	23/32	0.71875	18.25625
15/64	0.234375	5.953125	47/64	0.734375	18.653125
1/4	0.25	6.35001	3/4	0.75	19.05
17/64	0.265625	6.746875	49/64	0.765625	19.446875
9/32	0.28125	7.14375	25/32	0.78125	19.84375
19/64	0.296875	7.540625	51/64	0.796875	20.240625
5/16	0.3125	7.9375	13/16	0.8125	20.6375
21/64	0.328125	8.334375	53/64	0.828125	21.034375
11/32	0.34375	8.73125	27/32	0.84375	21.43125
23/64	0.359375	9.128125	55/64	0.859375	21.828125
3/8	0.375	9.525	7/8	0.875	22.225
25/64	0.390625	9.921875	57/64	0.890625	22.621875
13/32	0.40625	10.31875	29/32	0.90625	23.01875
27/64	0.421875	10.715625	59/64	0.921875	23.415625
7/16	0.4375	11.1125	15/16	0.9375	23.8125
29/64	0.453125	11.509375	61/64	0.953125	24.209375
15/32	0.46875	11.90625	31/32	0.96875	24.60625
31/64	0.484375	12.303125	63/64	0.984375	25.003125
1/2	0.50	12.7	1	1.00000	25.4

CHART 15-1

Metric/fractional chart.

(a)

(b)

FIGURE 15–44 (a) After machining and sanding the rotor, it should be cleaned. In this case brake cleaner from an air pressurized spray can is used. (b) With the lathe turning, the technician stands back away from the rotor and sprays both sides of the rotor to clean it of any remaining grit from the sanding process. This last step ensures a clean, smooth surface for the disc brake pads and a quality brake repair. Sanding each side of the rotor surface for one minute using a sanding block and 150-grit aluminum-oxide sandpaper after a finish cut gives the rotor the proper smoothness and finish.

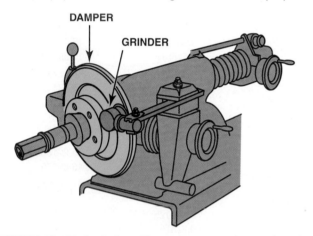

FIGURE 15–45 A grinder with sandpaper can be used to give a smooth nondirectional surface finish to the disc brake rotor.

MATCHING A DISC BRAKE ROTOR (CONTINUED)

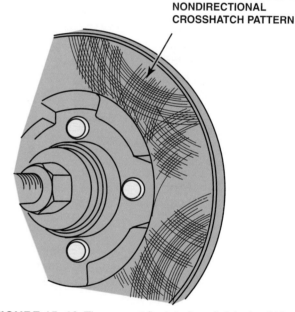

FIGURE 15–46 The correct final surface finish should be smooth and nondirectional.

SURFACE FINISHING THE ROTOR The goal of any brake repair or service should be to restore the braking effectiveness to match new vehicle brakes. This means that the rotor finish should be as smooth or smoother than a new rotor for maximum brake pad contact. Research conducted at Delphi has shown that like-new rotor finish can easily be accomplished by using a block and sandpaper. After completing the finish cut, place 150-grit aluminum-oxide sandpaper on a block and apply steady pressure against the rotor surface for 60 seconds on each side of the rotor. ● **SEE FIGURE 15–44.**

The aluminum oxide is hard enough to remove the highest ridges left by the lathe cutting tool. This results in a surface finish ranging from 20 to 80 μin. and usually less than 40 μin., which is smoother than a new rotor. ● **SEE FIGURE 15–45.**

NOTE: Many commercial rotor-finish products may also give as smooth a surface finish. ● **SEE FIGURES 15–46 AND 15–47.**

Always compare rotor finish to the rotor finish of a new rotor. Microinch finish is often hard to distinguish unless you have a new rotor with which to compare.

FIGURE 15–47 Rust should always be cleaned from both the rotor and the hub whenever the rotors are machined or replaced. An air-powered die grinder with a sanding disc makes quick work of cleaning this hub.

FIGURE 15–48 A typical hub-mount on-the-vehicle lathe. This particular lathe oscillates while machining the rotor, thereby providing a smooth and nondirectional finish at the same time.

 TECH TIP

Turn or Machine?

When asked about what was done to their vehicle, a common response of customers is "They rotated my rotors." Many customers do not understand the terms that are commonly used in the vehicle service industry. Try to use terms that are technically correct and avoid slang when talking to customers. For example, the expression *machined the rotors* indicates an operation, whereas the expression *turned the rotors* may be misinterpreted by some customers as simply meaning using your hand and moving (rotating) the rotor. *Resurfacing*, *refinishing*, and *reconditioning* are other terms that could be used to describe a drum or rotor machining operation.

ON-THE-VEHICLE ROTOR MACHINING

Many vehicle manufacturers recommend on-the-vehicle machining for rotors if the disc brake rotor must be machined due to deep scoring or pulsating brake pedal complaint. This is especially true of composite rotors or for vehicles such as many Honda vehicles that require major disassembly to remove the rotors.

Caliper-mount, on-the-vehicle lathes require that the disc brake caliper be removed. The cutter attaches to the steering knuckle or caliper support in the same location as the caliper. ● **SEE FIGURE 15–48.** Hub-mount, on-the-vehicle lathes attach to the hub using the lug nuts of the vehicle. To achieve a proper cut, the hub mount must be calibrated for any runout caused by the hub bearings and the outside surface face of the rotor.

NOTE: All on-the-vehicle lathes require that the wheel be removed. For best results, always use a torque wrench when tightening lug nuts or lathe adapters. Unequal torque on the bolts causes stress and distortion that can cause warped rotors and a pulsating brake pedal.

Always Check the Wheel Studs

Before installing the wheel after brake service, check the condition of the wheel studs and lug nuts. Check for stripped threads, rust, or cracks. If necessary, replace the stud. Most studs are replaced by driving them out using a large hammer and then using washers and a lug nut to draw the serrated shoulder of the lug stud into the rotor stud hole. ● **SEE FIGURE 15–49**. Always use a torque wrench when installing lug nuts to ensure proper and even torque on all lug nuts. This helps to prevent rotor distortion, which can lead to vibration in the steering and/or pedal pulsation during braking.

FIGURE 15–49 A wheel stud was replaced on the rotor hub assembly when it was discovered to be stripped.

DRUM MACHINING

1 Before starting to machine a brake drum, check the drum for any obvious damage such as heat cracks or hard spots.

2 Lightly tap the drum. It should ring like a bell. If a dull thud is heard, the drum may be cracked and should be discarded.

3 Use a drum micrometer to measure the inside diameter of the drum and compare this measurement to specifications to be sure that the drum can be safely machined.

4 Most brake drums have the maximum inside diameter cast into the drum as shown. Allow 0.030 inch for wear after the machining has been performed.

5 Thoroughly clean the outside and inside of the drum.

6 Be sure the center hole in the drum is clean and free from any burrs that could prevent the drum from being properly centered on the shaft of the brake lathe.

CONTINUED ▶

7 A typical brake lathe used to machine drums.

8 Locate a tapered, centering cone that best fits inside the hole of the brake drum.

9 Slide the large face plate over the shaft of the brake lathe.

10 Slide the tapered centering cone onto the shaft with the spring between the face plate and the centering cone.

11 Slide the other face plate onto the shaft.

12 Install a bearing collet used as a spacer, then the self-aligning spacer (SAS) and left-hand-thread spindle nut.

13 Tighten the spindle nut.

14 Loosen the turning bar retainer.

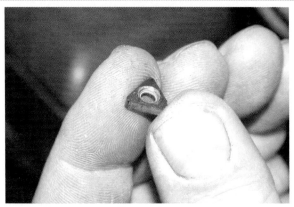

15 Carefully check the cutting bits and either rotate the bit to a new cutting point or replace it with a new part as necessary.

16 Turn the spindle control knob until the spindle is as short as possible (i.e., the drum as close to the machine as possible) to help reduce vibration as much as possible.

17 Position the cutting bar so that the cutting bit is located at the back surface of the drum.

18 Install the silencer band (vibration dampener strap).

CONTINUED ▶

19 Be sure the tool bit and clothing are away from the drum and turn the brake lathe on.

20 Center the bit in the center of the brake surface of the drum and rotate the control knob that moves the bit into contact with the drum friction surface. This should produce a light scratch cut.

21 Turn the lathe off.

22 Observe the scratch cut.

23 Loosen the spindle nut.

24 Rotate the drum 180° (one-half turn) on the spindle.

25 Tighten the spindle nut.

26 Turn the lathe on, rotate the control knob, and run the cutter into the drum for another scratch cut.

27 Observe the scratch cut. If the second scratch cut is in the same place as the first scratch cut or extends all the way around the drum, the drum is correctly mounted on the lathe.

28 Adjust the depth gauge to zero when the cutter just touches the drum.

29 Run the cutter all the way to the back surface of the drum.

30 Adjust the depth of the cut and lock it in position by turning the lock knob. Most vehicle manufacturers recommend a rough cut depth should be 0.005–0.010 in. and a finish cut of 0.002 in.

CONTINUED ▶

DRUM MACHINING (CONTINUED)

31 Select a fast-feed rate if performing a rough cut (0.006–0.016 in. per revolution) or 0.002 in. per revolution for a finish cut.

32 Turn the lock knob to keep the feed adjustment from changing.

33 Engage the automatic feed.

34 The drum will automatically move as the tool remains stationary to make the cut.

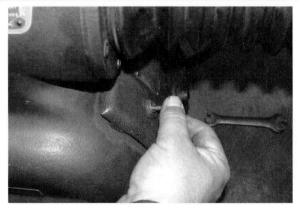

35 Turn the lathe off.

36 If additional material must be removed, proceed with the finish cut. Clean thoroughly before installing on a vehicle.

ROTOR MACHINING

1 Before machining any rotor, use a micrometer and measure the thickness of the rotor.

2 Check the specifications for the minimum allowable thickness.

‣ Brakes and Traction Control ➔ Disc Brake System ➔ Brake Rotor/Disc

Specifications

Nominal Thickness	1.03 in
Minimum Refinish Thickness	0.972 in
Thickness Variation (Parallelism)	0.0005 in
Lateral Run-out (T.I.R.)	0.003 in
Finish	10-80 micro-in

3 Visually check the rotor for evidence of heat cracks or hard spots that would require replacement (rather than machining) of the rotor.

4 After removing the grease seal and bearings, remove the grease from the bearing races.

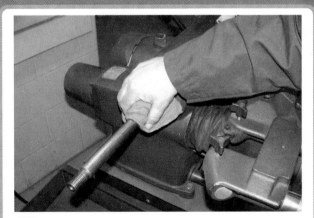

5 Clean and inspect the brake lathe spindle for damage or burrs that could affect its accuracy.

6 Select a tapered cone adapter that fits the inner bearing race.

CONTINUED ▶

7 Slide the cone adapter onto the brake lathe spindle.

8 Select the proper size cone adapter for the smaller outer wheel bearing race.

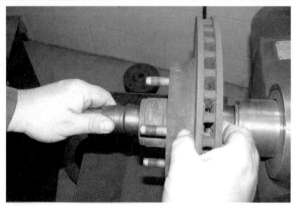

9 Place the rotor onto the large cone adapter and then slide the small cone adapter into the outer wheel bearing race.

10 Install the self-aligning spacer (SAS) and spindle nut.

11 Tighten the spindle nut (usually left-hand threads).

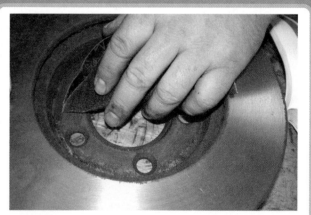

12 If a hubless rotor is being machined, be sure to thoroughly clean the inside surface.

13 Also remove all rust from the other side of the hubless rotor.

14 Select the proper centering cone for the hole in the center of the hub.

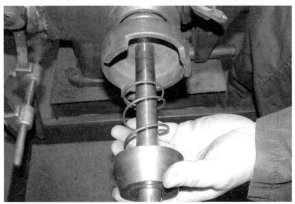

15 Select the proper size cone-shaped hubless adapter and the tapered centering cone with a spring in between.

16 After sliding the rotor over the centering cone, install the matching hubless adapter.

17 Install the self-aligning spacer (SAS) and spindle nut.

18 After the rotor has been secured to the brake lathe spindle, install the noise silencer band (dampener).

CONTINUED ▶

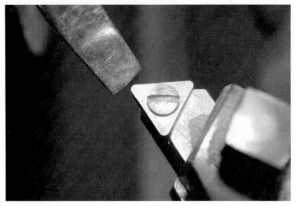

19 Carefully inspect the cutting bits and replace, if necessary.

20 Loosen the tool holder arm.

21 Adjust the twin cutter arm until the rotor is centered between the two cutting bits.

22 Turn the lathe on.

23 Move the cutter arm toward the center of the rotor, placing the cutting bits in about the center of the friction surface.

24 Turn one cutting bit into the surface of the rotor to make a scratch cut. This step checks the lathe setup for accuracy.

25 Turn the lathe off.

26 Observe the first scratch cut.

27 Loosen the spindle retaining nut.

28 Rotate the rotor 180° (one-half turn) on the spindle of the brake lathe.

29 Tighten the spindle nut.

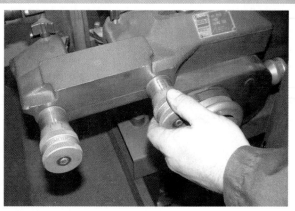

30 Turn the lathe back on and turn the cutting bit slightly into the rotor until a second scratch cut is made.

CONTINUED ▶

31 If the second scratch cut is in the same location as the first scratch cut or extends all around the surface of the rotor, then the rotor is properly installed on the lathe.

32 Start the machining process by moving the twin cutters to about the center of the rotor friction surface.

33 Turn the cutting bits inward until they touch the rotor and zero the depth adjustment.

34 Adjust the twin cutters, then dial in the amount of depth (0.005–0.010 in. per side for a rough cut or 0.002 in. for a finish cut) and lock the adjustment so that vibration will not change the setting.

35 Turn the feed control knob until the desired feed rate is achieved for the first or rough cut (0.006–0.010 in. per revolution) or finish cut (0.002 in. per revolution).

36 Engage the automatic feed.

37 Observe the machining operation.

38 After the cutting bits have cleared the edge of the rotor, turn the lathe off and measure the thickness of the rotor.

39 Readjust the feed control to a slow rate (0.002 in. per revolution or less) for the finish cut.

40 Reposition the cutting bits for the finish cut.

41 Loosen the adjustment locks.

42 Turn the depth of the cut for the finish cut (0.002 in. maximum).

CONTINUED ▶

43 Lock the adjustment.

44 Engage the automatic feed.

45 Use 150-grit aluminum-oxide sandpaper on a block of wood for 60 seconds per side or a grinder to give a nondirectional and smooth surface to both sides of the rotor.

46 After the sanding or grinding operation, thoroughly clean the machined surface of the rotor to remove any and all particles of grit that could affect the operation and life of the disc brake pads.

47 Remove the silencer band.

48 Loosen the spindle retaining nut and remove the rotor.

1 Prepare to machine a disc brake rotor using an on-the-vehicle lathe by properly positioning the vehicle in the stall and hoisting the vehicle to a good working height.

2 Remove the wheels and place them out of the way.

3 Remove the disc brake caliper and use a wire to support the caliper out of the way of the rotor.

4 Measure the rotor thickness and compare it with factory specifications before machining. If a discard thickness is specified, be sure to allow an additional 0.015 in. for wear.

5 Install the hub adapter onto the hub and secure it using the wheel lug nuts. Never use an impact wrench to install the lug nuts.

6 Engage the drive unit by aligning the hole in the drive plate with the raised button on the adapter.

CONTINUED ▶

7 Use the thumb wheel to tighten the drive unit to the adapter.

8 Attach a dial indicator to a secure part on the vehicle and position the dial indicator on a flat portion of the lathe to measure the lathe runout.

9 Rotate the wheel or turn the lathe motor on and measure the amount of runout. Newer models are self-adjusting.

10 Use a wrench to adjust the runout using the four numbers stamped on the edge of the drive flange as a guide.

11 After the hub runout is adjusted to 0.005 in. or less, remove the dial indicator from the vehicle.

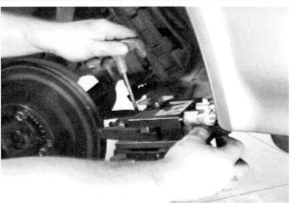

12 Using a T-handle Allen wrench, adjust the cutter arms until they are centered on the disc brake rotor.

13 Move the cutters to the center of the rotor.

14 Adjust the cutter depth until each cutter barely touches the rotor.

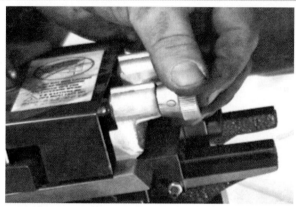

15 Position the cutters to the inside edge of the rotor surface and adjust the cutters to the desired depth of cut.

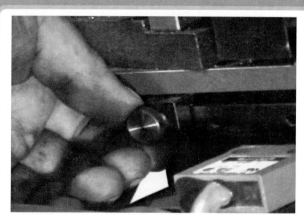

16 Adjust the automatic shut-off so the lathe will turn itself off at the end of the cut.

17 Turn the lathe on by depressing the start button.

18 Monitor the machining operations as the lathe automatically moves the cutters from the center toward the outside edge of the rotor.

CONTINUED ▶

19 After the lathe reaches the outside edge of the rotor, the drive motor should stop.

20 Measure the thickness of the rotor after machining to be certain that the rotor thickness is within service limits.

21 The technician is using 150-grit aluminum-oxide sandpaper and a wood block for 60 seconds on each side of the rotor to provide a smooth surface finish.

22 After completing the machining and resurfacing of the rotor unclamp the drive unit from the hub adapter and clean the rotor.

23 After the drive unit has been removed, remove the lug nuts holding the adapter to the rotor hub.

24 After removing the hub adapter, the caliper can be reinstalled.

25 Be sure to torque the caliper retaining bolts to factory specifications.

26 Install the wheel and wheel cover. On this vehicle, the wheel cover must be installed before the lug nuts because the lug nuts hold the wheel cover on the wheel.

27 Always use a torque wrench or a torque-limiting adapter with an air impact wrench as shown here when tightening lug nuts.

28 Be sure to clean the wheel covers of any grease or fingerprints before returning the vehicle to the customer.

29 Pump the brake pedal several times to restore proper brake pedal height. Check and add brake fluid as necessary before moving the vehicle.

30 Carefully back out of the stall and test-drive the vehicle to be assured of proper brake operation before returning the vehicle to the customer.

SUMMARY

1. Brake drums and rotors must absorb the heat generated by the friction of slowing and stopping a vehicle.

2. All rotors should be marked before removing them from the vehicle to assure that they will be reinstalled in the same position and on the same side of the vehicle.

3. All brake drums should be machined only enough to restore proper braking action. Brake drums should be the same size on the same axle to help prevent unequal braking.

4. Disc brake rotors should be machined and allow up to 0.030 in. (0.8 mm) for wear.

5. To assure proper braking, all rotors should be machined to a very smooth surface of less than 60 µin. finish.

REVIEW QUESTIONS

1. Explain the difference between "machine to" specifications and "discard."

2. List the steps for machining a brake drum.

3. Describe how to measure a disc brake rotor for lateral runout and thickness variation.

4. List the steps for machining a disc brake rotor.

5. Describe what is necessary to achieve "like-new" disc brake rotor finish.

CHAPTER QUIZ

1. Technician A says that aluminum brake drums use cast iron friction surfaces. Technician B says that up to 0.030 in. (0.8 mm) should be left after machining a drum to allow for wear. Which technician is correct?
   a. Technician A only
   b. Technician B only
   c. Both Technicians A and B
   d. Neither Technician A nor B

2. Technician A says that hard spots in a brake drum should be removed using a carbide-tip machining tool. Technician B says that the drum should be replaced if hard spots are discovered. Which technician is correct?
   a. Technician A only
   b. Technician B only
   c. Both Technicians A and B
   d. Neither Technician A nor B

3. Technician A says that brake drums on the same axle should be close to the same inside diameter for best brake balance. Technician B says that a brake drum may be cracked if it rings like a bell when tapped with a light steel hammer. Which technician is correct?
   a. Technician A only
   b. Technician B only
   c. Both Technicians A and B
   d. Neither Technician A nor B

4. A hubless brake drum cannot be machined because it cannot be held in a lathe.
   a. True
   b. False

5. The major reason for brake pedal pulsation during braking is due to excessive rotor thickness variation.
   a. True
   b. False

6. Rotor finish is measured in _____.
   a. Millimeters
   b. Inches
   c. Microinches
   d. Centimeters

7. The lower the Ra of a rotor, the _____ the surface.
   a. Smoother
   b. Rougher
   c. Higher
   d. Lower

8. A disc brake rotor is being installed on a lathe for machining. During the setup a scratch test is performed. The scratch extended all the way around the rotor. Technician A says that the rotor should be loosened, rotated 180°, and retightened. Technician B says that the rotor is not warped. Which technician is correct?
   a. Technician A only
   b. Technician B only
   c. Both Technicians A and B
   d. Neither Technician A nor B

9. Typical maximum rotor runout specifications are _____.
   a. 0.0003 to 0.0005 in. (0.008 to 0.013 mm)
   b. 0.003 to 0.005 in. (0.08 to 0.13 mm)
   c. 0.030 to 0.050 in. (0.8 to 1.3 mm)
   d. 0.300 to 0.500 in. (8.0 to 13 mm)

10. Typical maximum rotor thickness variation (parallelism) specifications are _____.
    a. 0.0003 to 0.0005 in. (0.008 to 0.013 mm)
    b. 0.003 to 0.005 in. (0.08 to 0.13 mm)
    c. 0.030 to 0.050 in (0.8 to 1.3 mm)
    d. 0.300 to 0.500 in. (8.0 to 13 mm)

POWER BRAKE UNIT OPERATION, DIAGNOSIS, AND SERVICE

After studying Chapter 16, the reader will be able to:

1. Prepare for the Brakes (A5) ASE certification test content area "D" (Power Assist Units Diagnosis and Repair).
2. List the parts of a vacuum brake booster.
3. Describe how a vacuum brake booster operates.
4. Explain how to test a vacuum brake booster.
5. Describe how a hydraulic brake booster operates.

Atmospheric pressure 293

Brake assist system (BAS) 298

Dual-diaphragm vacuum booster 298

in. Hg (inches of mercury) 293

mm Hg (millimeters of mercury) 293

Power chamber 294

Pressure differential 293

Supplemental brake assist (SBA) 301

Tandem-diaphragm vacuum booster 298

Vacuum 293

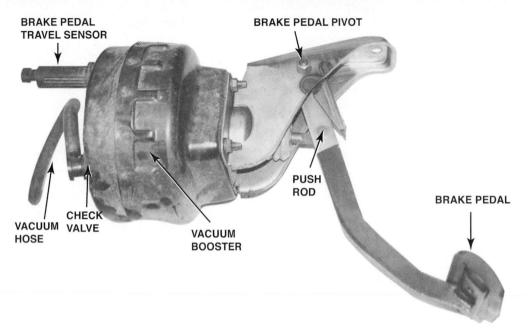

FIGURE 16–1 Typical vacuum brake booster assembly. The vacuum hose attaches to the intake manifold of the engine. The brake pedal travel sensor is an input sensor for the antilock braking system.

THE NEED FOR POWER BRAKE ASSIST

To double the stopping power of a disc brake, the driver must double the force on the brake pedal. This is the reason that most vehicles equipped with disc brakes are power assisted, even on small, lightweight vehicles. The use of semimetallic brake pads also requires greater force. The most commonly used power-assisted units are vacuum operated.

When a power booster is fitted, the brake pedal ratio is decreased and the master cylinder bore size is increased. The combined effect of these changes is to reduce pedal effort, while greatly increasing pedal reserve. ● SEE FIGURE 16–1.

Power boosters do not alter the hydraulic system and they still allow braking even if the booster fails or its power supply is cut off. All boosters have a power reserve that provides assist for at least one hard stop, and sometimes several light brake applications, even after power is lost. However, because power brake systems are designed with the added force of the booster taken into account, the amount of brake pedal pressure required to slow or stop a vehicle is much higher than in a non-boosted system once the reserve is used up. For this reason, some vehicles with power brakes have a brake pedal that is wide enough to allow two-foot braking should the booster fail. ● SEE FIGURE 16–2.

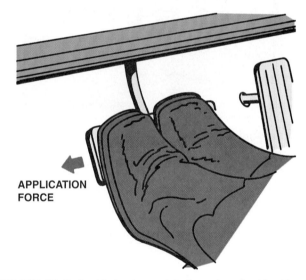

FIGURE 16–2 A wide brake pedal allows two-foot braking if power assist is lost.

PRINCIPLES OF VACUUM

Most vacuum-powered brake boosters get their vacuum supply from the engine intake manifold. An engine is essentially a big air pump because the pistons move up and down in the cylinders to pump in air and fuel, and pump out exhaust. They do this by creating differences in air pressure.

As a piston moves downward on an intake stroke with the intake valve open, it creates a larger area inside the cylinder for air to fill. This lowers the air pressure within the cylinder, and the higher-pressure air outside the engine flows in through the intake manifold in an attempt to fill the low-pressure area. Although it may seem as though the low pressure is pulling air into the engine, it is really the higher pressure outside that forces air in. The difference in pressure between two areas is called a **pressure differential.**

Because throttle valves and manifold shape restrict intake airflow, high-pressure air from outside the engine is almost never able to move into the cylinders fast enough to fill the space created. As a result, gasoline-powered internal-combustion engines normally operate with a low-pressure area, or partial vacuum, in the intake manifold. The term **vacuum** is used to refer to any pressure lower than **atmospheric pressure.** Atmospheric pressure varies with altitude, but is approximately 14.7 pounds per square inch (PSI) at sea level. ● **SEE FIGURE 16–3.**

MEASURING VACUUM　Vacuum is measured in **inches of mercury (in. Hg)** or in **millimeters of mercury (mm Hg),** a figure that indicates how far a column of mercury in a tube will rise when a vacuum is applied at one end, and atmospheric pressure at the other. Vacuum is a measurement of the pressure differential between the lower pressure inside the tube, and the higher pressure outside it.

A perfect vacuum is about 30 in. Hg (762 mm Hg). However, a perfect vacuum occurs only in space, and is never achieved in an engine's intake manifold. Manifold vacuum varies with throttle position. The lowest manifold vacuum (highest pressure) occurs when the throttle is wide open with the engine under load. The highest manifold vacuum (lowest pressure) may be as much as 24 in. Hg (610 mm Hg) when the vehicle is rolling rapidly downhill in gear with the throttle closed. Manifold vacuum at idle typically falls between 15 and 20 in. Hg (381 and 508 mm Hg), and most vacuum brake boosters are designed to operate with vacuum levels in this range.

BOOSTER VACUUM SUPPLY　Vacuum boosters get their vacuum supply from the engine intake manifold. Diesel engines, however, run unthrottled (engine speed is controlled strictly by

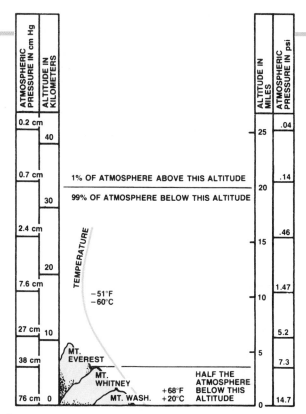

FIGURE 16–3 Atmospheric pressure varies with altitude.

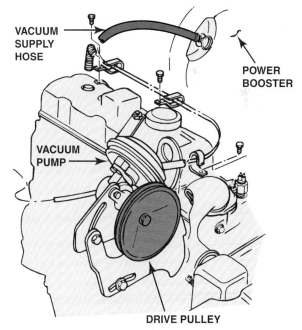

FIGURE 16–4 A belt-driven auxiliary vacuum pump.

the amount of fuel injected) and have little or no intake manifold vacuum. If a vehicle with a diesel engine is equipped with a vacuum-powered brake booster, it must also be fitted with an auxiliary vacuum pump.

Some small gasoline-powered and diesel engines use a belt-driven add-on pump. ● **SEE FIGURE 16–4.**

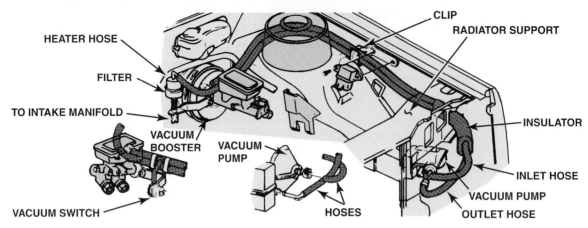

FIGURE 16–5 An electrically powered vacuum pump.

PRINCIPLES OF VACUUM (CONTINUED)

An electrically powered vacuum pump is turned on and off by a pressure switch on the booster. This means they operate only when needed, and thus reduce power drain on the engine. ● **SEE FIGURE 16–5.**

VACUUM BOOSTER THEORY

Vacuum boosters use the principle of pressure differential to increase brake application force. The typical vacuum booster has a **power chamber** separated into two smaller chambers by a flexible diaphragm. When air pressure is greater on one side of the diaphragm than the other, a pressure differential is created. In an attempt to equalize pressure in the two chambers, the higher pressure exerts a force that moves the diaphragm toward the lower-pressure area. Rods attached to the diaphragm transmit this force, plus the force the driver exerts on the brake pedal, to the master cylinder.

The amount of force created in this manner is proportional to the difference in pressure between the two sides. In other words, the greater the pressure differential, the greater the force. To calculate the force, the pressure differential is multiplied by the diaphragm surface area. For example, if a power booster diaphragm has atmospheric pressure (14.7 PSI) on one side, and a typical intake manifold vacuum of 20 in. Hg (10 PSI of absolute pressure), the pressure differential acting on the diaphragm would be as follows.

14.7 PSI − 10 PSI = 4.7 PSI

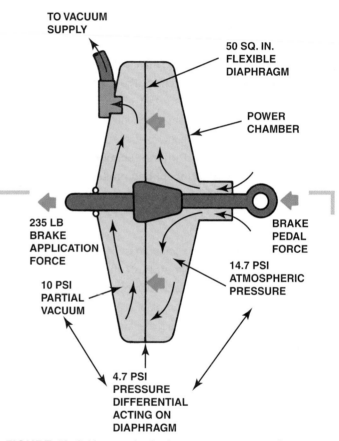

FIGURE 16–6 Vacuum brake boosters operate on the principle of pressure differential.

If we once again multiply this times the area of the diaphragm, the result is as follows.

4.7 PSI × 50 sq. in. = 235 pounds of force

Vacuum booster diaphragms are sized to fit specific applications and provide the necessary application force. Most vacuum boosters are capable of providing hundreds of pounds of application force. ● **SEE FIGURE 16–6.**

Check the Vacuum, Then the Brakes

A customer complained of a very rough idle and an occasional pulsating brake pedal. The customer was certain that the engine required serious work since there were over 100,000 miles on the vehicle. During the troubleshooting procedure, a spray cleaner was used to find any vacuum (air) leaks. A large hole was found melted through a large vacuum hose next to the vacuum hose feeding the vacuum-operated power brake booster.

After repairing the vacuum leak, the vehicle was test driven again to help diagnose the cause of the pulsating brake pedal. The engine idled very smoothly after the vacuum leak was repaired and the brake pulsation was also cured. The vacuum leak resulted in lower-than-normal vacuum being applied to the vacuum booster. During braking, when engine vacuum is normally higher (deceleration), the vacuum booster would assist, then not assist when the vacuum was lost. This on-and-off supply of vacuum to the vacuum booster was noticed by the driver as a brake pulsation. Always check the vacuum at the booster whenever diagnosing any brake problems. Most vehicle manufacturers specify a minimum of 15 in. Hg of vacuum at the booster. The booster should be able to provide at least two or three stops even with no vacuum. The booster should also be checked to see if it can hold a vacuum after several hours. A good vacuum booster, for example, should be able to provide a power assist after sitting all night without starting the engine.

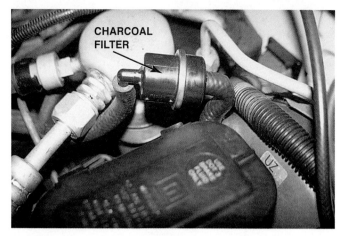

FIGURE 16–7 The charcoal filter traps gasoline vapors that are present in the intake manifold and prevents them from getting into the vacuum chamber of the booster.

VACUUM CHECK VALVE

All vacuum boosters use a one-way vacuum check valve. This valve allows air to flow in only one direction—from the booster toward the engine. This valve prevents loss of vacuum when the engine stops. Without this check valve, the vacuum stored in the vacuum booster would simply be lost through the hose and intake manifold of the engine. ● **SEE FIGURES 16–8 AND 16–9.**

CAUTION: Sometimes an engine backfire can destroy or blow the vacuum check valve out of the booster housing. If this occurs, all power assist will be lost and a much greater-than-normal force must be exerted on the brake pedal to stop the vehicle. Be sure to repair the cause of the backfire before replacing the damaged or missing check valve. Normal causes of backfire include an excessively lean air–fuel ratio or incorrect firing order or ignition timing.

CHARCOAL FILTER

The vacuum hose leading from the engine to the power booster should run downward without any low places in the hose. If a dip or sag occurs in the vacuum hose, condensed fuel vapors and/or moisture can accumulate that can block or restrict the vacuum to the booster. Many manufacturers use a small charcoal filter in the vacuum line between the engine and booster, as shown in ● **FIGURE 16–7.**

The charcoal filter attracts and holds gasoline vapors and keeps fumes from entering the vacuum booster. Without this filter, gasoline fumes can enter the vacuum booster, where they can deteriorate the rubber diaphragm and other rubber components of the booster.

VACUUM BRAKE BOOSTER OPERATION

A vacuum power-brake booster contains a rubber diaphragm(s) connected to the brake pedal at one end and to the master cylinder at the other end. When the brakes are off or released, there is equal vacuum on both sides of the diaphragm.

The vacuum power unit contains the power-piston assembly, which houses the control valve and reaction mechanism, and the power-piston return spring. The control valve is composed of the air valve (valve plunger), the floating control-valve assembly,

(a)

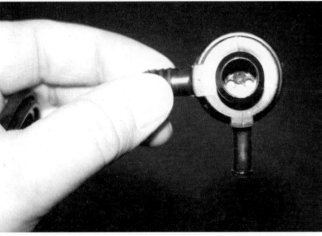

(b)

FIGURE 16–8 (a) Many vacuum brake booster check valves are located where the vacuum hose from the engine (vacuum source) attaches to the vacuum booster. (b) This one-way valve prevents the loss of vacuum when the engine is off. The diaphragm inside allows air to flow in one direction only.

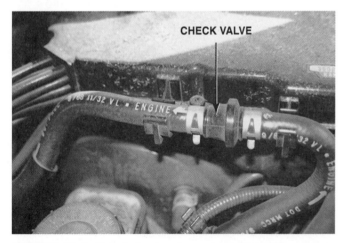

FIGURE 16–9 Not all check valves are located at the vacuum line to the booster housing connection. This vehicle uses an inline check valve located between the intake manifold of the engine and the vacuum brake booster.

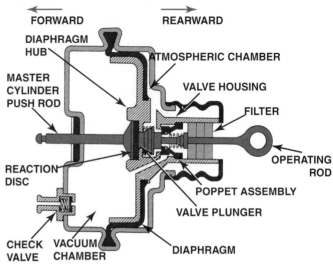

FIGURE 16–10 Cross-sectional view of a typical vacuum brake booster assembly.

VACUUM BRAKE BOOSTER OPERATION (CONTINUED)

and the pushrod. The reaction mechanism consists of a hydraulic piston reaction plate and a series of reaction levers. An air filter, air silencer, and filter retainer are assembled around the valve operating rod, filling the cavity inside the hub of the power piston. The pushrod that operates the air valve projects out of the end. ● **SEE FIGURE 16–10.**

RELEASED-POSITION OPERATION At the released position (brake pedal up), the air valve is seated on the floating control valve, which shuts off the air. The floating control valve is held away from the valve seat In the power-piston insert. Vacuum from the engine is present in the space on both sides of the power piston. Any air in the system is drawn through a small passage in the power piston, over the seat in the power-piston insert, and through a passage in the power-piston insert. There is a vacuum on both sides of the power piston, and it is held against the rear of the housing by the power-piston return spring. At rest, the hydraulic reaction plate is held against the reaction retainer. The air-valve spring holds the reaction lever against the hydraulic reaction plate and holds the air valve against its stop in the tube of the power piston. The floating control-valve assembly is held against the air-valve seat by the floating control-valve spring. ● **SEE FIGURE 16–11.**

APPLIED-POSITION OPERATION As the brake pedal is depressed, the floating control valve is moved toward its seat in the power piston, away from the rear of the booster. The smaller air valve spring causes the air valve to stretch out toward the retreating floating control valve until it bottoms out on the lip of

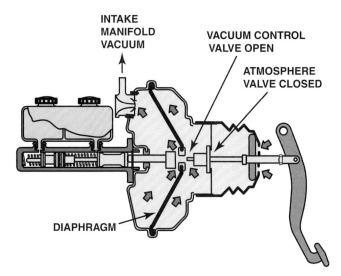

FIGURE 16–11 In the release position (brake pedal up), the vacuum is directed to both sides of the diaphragm.

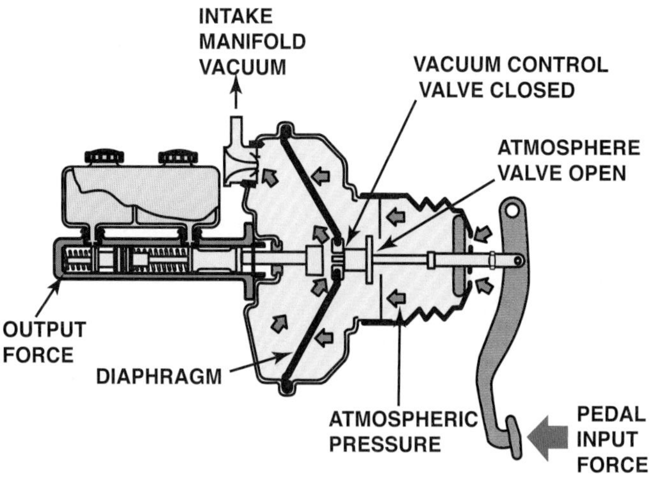

FIGURE 16–12 Simplified diagram of a vacuum brake booster in the apply position. Notice that the atmospheric valve is open and air pressure is being applied to the diaphragm.

the power piston's vacuum passage. This closes off the vacuum supply to the rear section of the housing. Since the floating control valve travels farther than the sealing end of the air valve, atmospheric air is allowed to enter between the air valve and the floating control valve pressurizing the rear section of the housing. At this point, the rear section of the housing is pressurized and the front section is under vacuum. Atmospheric pressure can then force the power piston forward.

NOTE: This movement of air into the rear chamber of the brake booster may be heard inside the vehicle as a hissing noise. The loudness of this airflow varies from vehicle to vehicle and should be considered normal.

As the power piston travels forward, the pushrod pushes against the hydraulic reaction plate in the master cylinder, pushing the master cylinder primary and secondary pistons forward. As back-pressure builds up on the end of the master cylinder piston, the floating control valve is pushed back off of its seat in the power piston, applying back-pressure to the brake pedal. The power piston return spring also generates some brake pedal force. All in all, approximately 30% of the brake load is applied back to the brake pedal. This gives the driver a feel that is proportional to the degree of brake application. ● **SEE FIGURE 16–12.**

HOLD-POSITION OPERATION
When the desired brake pedal force is reached and there is balance between the opposing forces of the brake pedal and the master cylinder, the power piston moves forward "around" the floating control valve and reaction disc until the air valve sealing end "catches up" with the floating

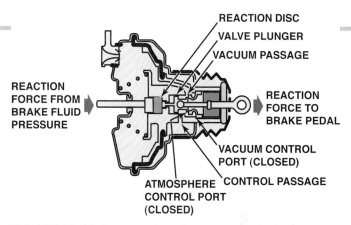

FIGURE 16–13 Cross section of a vacuum brake booster in the hold position with both vacuum and atmospheric valves closed. Note that the reaction force from the brake fluid pressure is transferred back to the driver as a reaction force to the brake pedal.

control valve. At this point, the air valve is once again sealed against the floating control valve and is no longer blocking the vacuum passage in the power piston. The floating control valve is again held away from its seat. Vacuum once again is present on both sides of the diaphragm and power piston. The status of the booster is almost exactly as it was in the released state except that the positions of the power piston and subsequently the master cylinder pistons are farther forward. Brake pedal force is keeping the power piston in its position. If additional braking is required (brake pedal pushed farther), the floating control valve moves away from the air valve permitting the power of atmospheric pressure to push the power piston and master cylinder pistons forward. If the pedal is released, since vacuum is then present on both sides of the diaphragm, the power piston return spring moves the power piston to its released state. ● **SEE FIGURE 16–13.**

DUAL- (TANDEM-) DIAPHRAGM VACUUM BOOSTERS

To provide power assist, air pressure must work against a rubber diaphragm. The larger the area of the diaphragm, the more force can be exerted. The usual method of increasing the area of the vacuum diaphragm was to increase the diameter of the vacuum booster. However, a larger vacuum booster took up too much room under the hood of many vehicles. Instead of increasing the diameter, vacuum booster manufacturers used two smaller-diameter diaphragms and placed one in front of the other. These designs increased the total area without increasing the physical diameter of the booster. This style is called a **dual-diaphragm** or **tandem-diaphragm** vacuum booster. ● SEE FIGURE 16–14.

BRAKE ASSIST SYSTEM

Some vehicles are equipped with a **brake assist system (BAS)** that applies the brakes with maximum force if the system detects that the driver is making a panic stop. Tests performed by brake engineers have indicated that it is normal for a person to first apply the brakes rapidly during a panic situation. However, it was also found that the driver would tend to reduce the force applied to the brake pedal. As a result, the vehicle did not brake with the maximum effort.

OPERATION The brake assist system opens an air valve on the rear part of the vacuum booster assembly. As a result, more air at atmospheric pressure can flow into the rear chamber of the vacuum booster, thereby increasing the force applied to the master cylinder. The BAS function works with the electronic stability control (ESC) system to ensure maximum braking efficiency during evasive or emergency situations.

If the speed of the brake pedal application exceeds a predetermined limit as determined by the brake pedal travel sensor, the ABS controller energizes the BAS solenoid valve. When the solenoid valve opens, additional air at atmospheric pressure enters the driver's side of the booster. The additional pressure applies the brakes faster and with more force. The BAS solenoid is deenergized when the brake pedal is released and normal braking returns. ● SEE FIGURES 16–15 AND 16–16.

VACUUM BRAKE BOOSTER OPERATION (CONTINUED)

TECH TIP

A Low, Soft Brake Pedal Is Not a Power Booster Problem

Some service technicians tend to blame the power brake booster if the vehicle has a low, soft brake pedal. A defective power brake booster causes a hard brake pedal, not a soft brake pedal. A soft or spongy brake pedal is usually caused by air being trapped somewhere in the hydraulic system.

Many times, the technician has bled the system and, therefore, thinks that the system is free of any trapped air. According to remanufacturers of master cylinders and power brake boosters, most of the returned parts under warranty are not defective. Incorrect or improper bleeding procedures account for much of the problem.

VACUUM-FAILURE MODE In case of vacuum source interruption, the brake operates as a standard brake as follows. As the pedal is pushed down, the operating rod forces the floating control valve against the power piston and reaction disc. This force is then applied to the pushrod and subsequently the hydraulic reaction plate fastened to the master cylinder piston rod, which applies pressure in the master cylinder. For safety in the event of a stalled engine and a loss of vacuum, a power brake booster should have adequate storage of vacuum for several power-assisted stops.

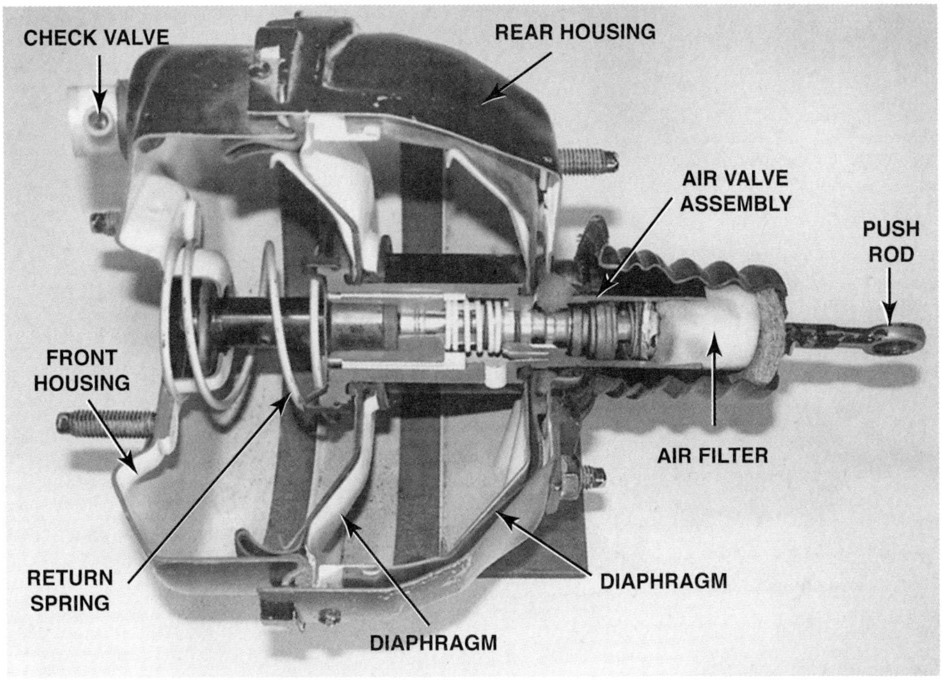

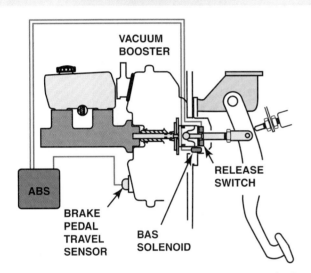

FIGURE 16–14 Cutaway showing a dual-diaphragm (tandem) vacuum brake booster.

CHECK VALVE

REAR HOUSING

AIR VALVE ASSEMBLY

PUSH ROD

FRONT HOUSING

AIR FILTER

RETURN SPRING

DIAPHRAGM

DIAPHRAGM

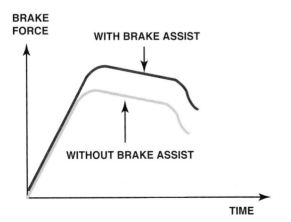

VACUUM BOOSTER

ABS

RELEASE SWITCH

BRAKE PEDAL TRAVEL SENSOR

BAS SOLENOID

FIGURE 16–15 A typical brake assist system uses a brake pedal travel sensor and a BAS solenoid to apply the brakes during a panic condition.

BRAKE FORCE

WITH BRAKE ASSIST

WITHOUT BRAKE ASSIST

TIME

FIGURE 16–16 When the brake assist function operates, the brake force is much higher than normal.

VACUUM BOOSTER OPERATION TEST

With the engine "off," apply the brakes several times to deplete the vacuum. With your foot on the brake pedal, start the engine. The brake pedal *should* drop. If the brake pedal does *not* drop, check for proper vacuum source to the booster. There should be at least 15 in. Hg of vacuum at the booster for proper operation. If there is proper vacuum, repair or replacement of the power booster is required.

VACUUM BOOSTER LEAK TEST

To test if the vacuum booster can hold a vacuum perform the following steps:

STEP 1 Operate the engine to build up a vacuum in the booster, then turn the engine off.

STEP 2 Wait one minute.

STEP 3 Depress the brake pedal several times. There should be two or more power-assisted brake applications.

If applications are not power assisted, either the vacuum check valve or the booster is leaking. To test the check valve, remove the valve from the booster and blow through the check valve. If air passes through, the valve is defective and must be replaced. If the check valve is okay, the vacuum booster is leaking and should be repaired or replaced based on the manufacturer's recommendations.

HYDRAULIC SYSTEM LEAK TEST

An internal or external hydraulic leak can also cause a brake system problem. To test if the hydraulic system (and not the booster) is leaking, depress and release the brake pedal (service brakes) several times. This should deplete any residual power assist. On some ABS units, this may require depressing the brake pedal 20 or more times!

After depleting the power-assist unit, depress and then hold the brake pedal depressed with medium force (20 to 35 lb or 88 to 154 N). The brake pedal should *not* fall away. If the pedal falls, the hydraulic brake system is leaking. Check for external leakage at wheel cylinders, calipers, hydraulic lines, and hoses. If there is no external leak, there may be an internal leak inside the master cylinder. Repair or replace components as needed to correct the leakage.

PUSHROD CLEARANCE ADJUSTMENT

Whenever the vacuum brake booster or the master cylinder is replaced, the pushrod length should be checked. The length of the pushrod must match correctly with the master cylinder.
● SEE FIGURE 16–17.

If the pushrod is too long and the master cylinder is installed, the rod may be applying a force on the primary piston of the master cylinder even though the brake pedal is not applied. This can cause the brakes to overheat, causing the brake fluid to boil. If the brake fluid boils, a total loss of braking force can occur. Obviously, this pushrod clearance check and adjustment is very important. A gauge is often used to measure the position of the master cylinder piston, and then the other end of the gauge is used to determine the proper pushrod clearance.
● SEE FIGURE 16–18.

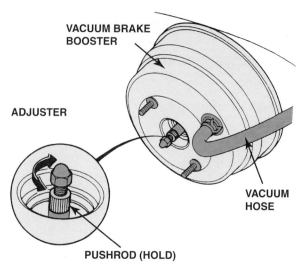

FIGURE 16–17 Typical adjustable pushrod. This adjustment is critical for the proper operation of the braking system. If the pushrod is too long, the brakes may be partially applied during driving. If the rod is too short, the brake pedal may have to be depressed farther down before the brakes start to work.

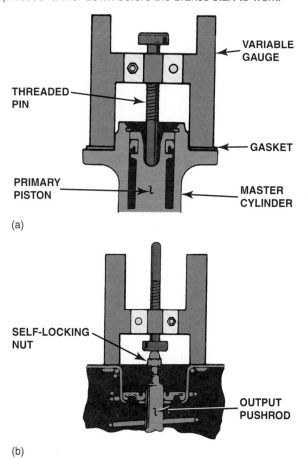

(a)

(b)

FIGURE 16–18 Typical vacuum brake booster pushrod gauging tool. (a) The tool is first placed against the mounting flange of the master cylinder and the depth of the piston determined. (b) The gauge is then turned upside down and used to gauge the pushrod length. Some vacuum brake boosters do not use adjustable pushrods. If found to be the incorrect length, a replacement pushrod of the correct length should be installed.

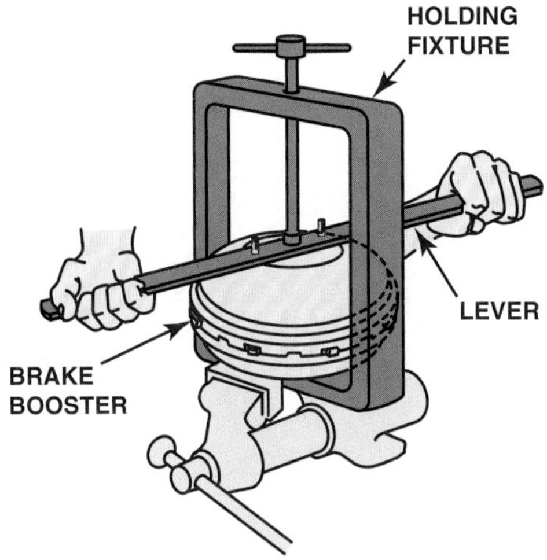

FIGURE 16–19 A holding fixture and a long tool being used to rotate the two halves of a typical vacuum brake booster.

? **FREQUENTLY ASKED QUESTION**

What Is Supplemental Brake Assist?

Supplemental brake assist, SBA, is a motor-driven vacuum pump that can supplement engine vacuum to the vacuum brake booster. This unit is used on some General Motors vehicles. When a vehicle is driven under a heavy load, engine vacuum is low. To meet the brake standards, some vehicles are equipped with the brake assist system that consists of the following components:

- A pressure sensor that is used to measure the vacuum in the vacuum booster.
- An intake manifold check valve that is used to prevent vacuum from escaping the vacuum boost.
- A motor-driven vacuum pump.

The vacuum pump motor will start and run if the pressure sensor detects the vacuum in the booster is below 7 in. Hg and will shut off after the vacuum level increases to 9 in. Hg.

VACUUM BOOSTER DISASSEMBLY AND SERVICE

Some vehicle manufacturers recommend that the vacuum brake booster be disassembled and overhauled if defective. A special holding fixture should be used before rotating (unlocking) the front and rear housing because the return spring is strong. ● **SEE FIGURE 16–19.**

CAUTION: Some vehicle manufacturers recommend that the vacuum brake booster be replaced as an assembly if tested to be leaking or defective. Always follow the manufacturer's recommendations.

Disassemble the vacuum brake booster according to the manufacturer's recommended procedures for the specific unit being serviced. ● **SEE FIGURE 16–20.**

A rebuilding kit is available that includes all necessary parts and the proper silicone grease. The manufacturer warns that all parts included in the kit be replaced.

HYDRO-BOOST HYDRAULIC BRAKE BOOSTER

Hydro-Boost is a hydraulically operated power-assist unit built by Bendix. The Hydro-Boost system uses the pressurized hydraulic fluid from the vehicle's power steering pump as a power source rather than using engine vacuum as is used with vacuum boosters. ● **SEE FIGURES 16–21 AND 16–22.**

The Hydro-Boost unit is used on vehicles that lack enough engine vacuum, such as turbocharged or diesel engine vehicles. During operation, diesel engines do not produce vacuum in the intake manifold. As a result, diesel engines must use accessory engine-driven vacuum pumps to operate vacuum accessories. Turbocharged and supercharged engines do not create engine vacuum during periods of acceleration. Even though vacuum is available when the engine is decelerating, some vehicle manufacturers elect to install a Hydro-Boost system rather than equip the vehicle with an accessory engine-driven vacuum pump.

OPERATION Fluid pressure from the power steering pump enters the unit and is directed by a spool valve. ● **SEE FIGURE 16–23.** When the brake pedal is depressed, the lever and primary valve are moved. The valve closes off the return port, causing pressure to build in the boost pressure chamber. The hydraulic pressure pushes on the power piston, which then

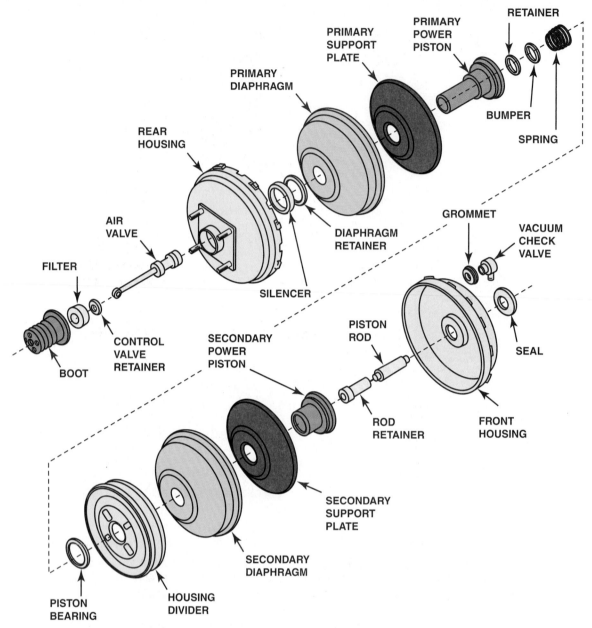

FIGURE 16–20 Exploded view of a typical dual-diaphragm vacuum brake booster assembly.

FIGURE 16–21 Hydro-Boost unit attaches between the bulkhead and the master cylinder and is powered by the power steering pump.

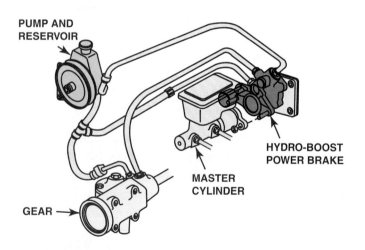

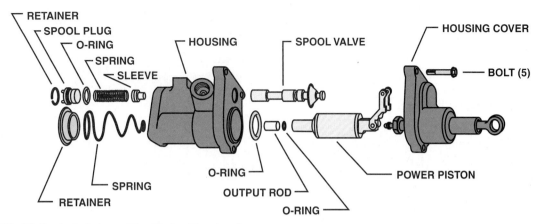

FIGURE 16–22 Exploded view of the Hydro-Boost unit.

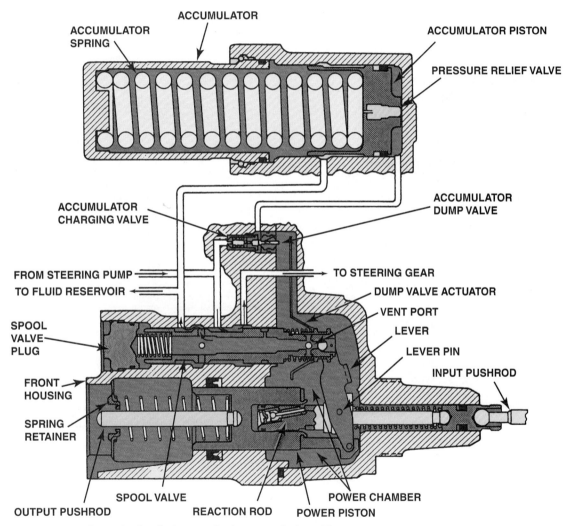

FIGURE 16–23 A Hydro-Boost hydraulic booster in the unapplied position.

HYDRO-BOOST HYDRAULIC BRAKE BOOSTER (CONTINUED)

applies force to the output rod that connects to the master cylinder piston. In the event of a power steering pump failure, power assist is still available for several brake applications. ● **SEE FIGURE 16–24.**

During operation, hydraulic fluid under pressure from the power steering pump pressurizes an accumulator. ● **SEE FIGURE 16–25.** While some units use a spring inside the accumulator, most Hydro-Boost units use nitrogen gas. The fluid

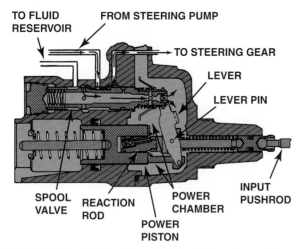

FIGURE 16–24 A Hydro-Boost hydraulic booster as the brakes are applied.

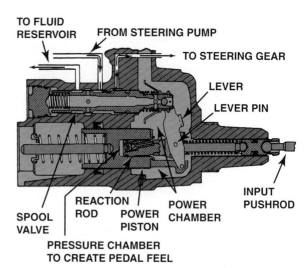

FIGURE 16–25 A Hydro-Boost hydraulic booster in the holding position.

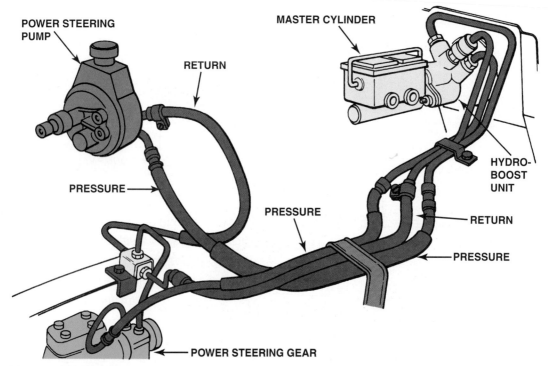

FIGURE 16–26 A typical Hydro-Boost hydraulic line arrangement showing the pump, steering gear, and brake booster assembly.

HYDRO-BOOST HYDRAULIC BRAKE BOOSTER (CONTINUED)

trapped in the accumulator under pressure is used to provide power-assisted stops in the event of a hydraulic system failure.

DIAGNOSIS The power source for Hydro-Boost units comes from the power steering pump. The first step of troubleshooting is to perform a thorough visual inspection, including the following:

1. Checking for proper power steering fluid level
2. Checking for leaks from the unit or power steering pump

3. Checking the condition and tightness of the power steering drive belt
4. Checking for proper operation of the base brake system

After checking all of the visual components, check for proper pressure and volume from the power steering pump using a power steering pump tester, as shown in ● **FIGURES 16–26 AND 16–27.**

The pump should be capable of producing a minimum of 2 gallons (7.5 liters) with a maximum pressure of 150 PSI

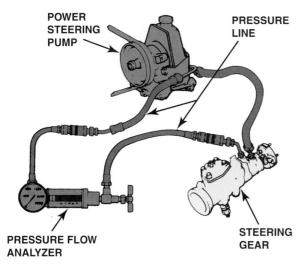

FIGURE 16–27 Pressure and flow analyzer installation to check the power steering pump output.

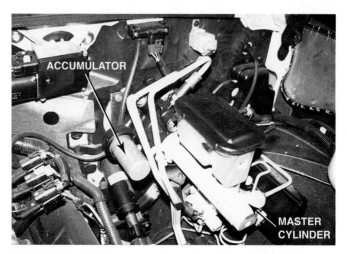

FIGURE 16–28 The accumulator should be able to hold pressure and feel tight when hand force is used to try to move it.

(1,000 kPa) with the steering in the straight-ahead position. With the engine "off," the accumulator should be able to supply a minimum of two power-assisted brake applications.

HYDRO-BOOST FUNCTION TEST With the engine off, apply the brake pedal several times until the accumulator is depleted completely. Depress the service brake pedal and start the engine. The pedal should fall and then push back against the driver's foot.

HYDRO-BOOST SYMPTOM-BASED GUIDE

EXCESSIVE BRAKE PEDAL EFFORT Possible causes for this include the following:

1. Loose or broken power steering pump belt
2. No fluid in the power steering reservoir
3. Leaks in the power steering, booster, or accumulator hoses
4. Leaks at tube fittings, power steering, booster, or accumulator connections
5. External leakage at the accumulator
6. Faulty booster piston seal, causing leakage at the booster flange vent
7. Faulty booster cover seal with leakage between the housing and cover
8. Faulty booster spool plug seal

SLOW BRAKE PEDAL RETURN Possible causes for this include the following:

1. Excessive seal friction in the booster
2. Faulty spool action
3. Broken piston return spring
4. Restriction in the return line from the booster to the pump reservoir
5. Broken spool return spring

GRABBY BRAKES Possible causes for this include the following:

1. Broken spool return spring
2. Faulty spool action caused by contamination in the system

BOOSTER CHATTERS—PEDAL VIBRATES Possible causes for this include the following:

1. Power steering pump belt slipping
2. Low fluid level in the power steering pump reservoir
3. Faulty spool operation caused by contamination in the system

SUMMARY

1. Vacuum brake boosters use air pressure acting on a diaphragm to assist the driver's force on the brake master cylinder.
2. At rest, there is vacuum on both sides of the vacuum booster diaphragm. When the brake pedal is depressed, atmospheric air pressure is exerted on the back side of the diaphragm.
3. The use of two diaphragms in tandem allows a smaller-diameter booster with the same area. The larger the area of the booster diaphragm, the more air pressure force can be applied to the master cylinder.
4. Hydraulic-operated brake boosters use the engine-driven power steering pump.
5. When replacing a vacuum brake booster, always check for proper pushrod clearance.
6. To be assured of power-assisted brake application in the event of failure, hydraulic power-assisted brake systems use an accumulator to provide pressure to the system.

REVIEW QUESTIONS

1. Describe the purpose and function of the one-way check valve used on vacuum brake booster units.
2. Explain how vacuum is used to assist in applying the brakes.
3. Describe how to perform a vacuum booster leak test and hydraulic system leak test.
4. Explain how a Hydro-Boost system functions.

CHAPTER QUIZ

1. Two technicians are discussing vacuum brake boosters. Technician A says that a low, soft brake pedal is an indication of a defective booster. Technician B says that there should be at least two power-assisted brake applications after the engine stops running. Which technician is correct?
   a. Technician A only
   b. Technician B only
   c. Both Technicians A and B
   d. Neither Technician A nor B

2. Technician A says that to check the operation of a vacuum brake booster, the brake pedal should be depressed until the assist is depleted and then start the engine. Technician B says that the brake pedal should drop when the engine starts, if the booster is okay. Which technician is correct?
   a. Technician A only
   b. Technician B only
   c. Both Technicians A and B
   d. Neither Technician A nor B

3. Brake pedal feedback to the driver is provided by the _____.
   a. Vacuum check-valve operation
   b. Reaction system
   c. Charcoal filter unit
   d. Vacuum diaphragm

4. The proper operation of a vacuum brake booster requires that the engine be capable of supplying at least _____.
   a. 15 in. Hg vacuum
   b. 17 in. Hg vacuum
   c. 19 in. Hg vacuum
   d. 21 in. Hg vacuum

5. The purpose of the charcoal filter in the vacuum hose between the engine and the vacuum brake booster is to _____.
   a. Filter the air entering the engine
   b. Trap gasoline vapors to keep them from entering the booster
   c. Act as a one-way check valve to help keep a vacuum reserve in the booster
   d. Direct the vacuum

6. A defective vacuum brake booster will cause a _____.
   a. Hard brake pedal
   b. Soft (spongy) brake pedal
   c. Low brake pedal
   d. Slight hiss noise when the brake pedal is depressed

7. An accumulator such as that used on hydraulic brake boosters _____.
   a. Reduces brake pedal noise
   b. Provides higher force being fed back to the driver's foot
   c. Provides a reserve in the event of a failure
   d. Works against engine vacuum

8. The first step in diagnosing a Hydro-Boost problem is _____.
   a. A pressure test of the pump
   b. A volume test of the pump
   c. To tighten the power steering drive belt
   d. A thorough visual inspection

9. A brake pedal feels spongy when depressed. Technician A says that a defective hydraulic brake booster could be the cause. Technician B says that a defective vacuum brake booster could be the cause. Which technician is correct?
   a. Technician A only
   b. Technician B only
   c. Both Technicians A and B
   d. Neither Technician A nor B

10. If the engine stops running, the Hydro-Boost will not be able to provide any power assist for the brakes.
    a. True
    b. False

chapter 17
REGENERATIVE BRAKING SYSTEMS

OBJECTIVES

After studying Chapter 17, the reader will be able to:

1. Describe how regenerative braking works.
2. Explain the principles involved in regenerative braking.
3. Discuss the parts and components involved in regenerative braking systems.
4. Describe the servicing precautions involved with regenerative brakes.

KEY TERMS

Base brakes 309
Brake pedal position (BPP) 313
Electrohydraulic brake (EHB) 311
F = ma 309
Force 309
G = 317
Inertia 309
Kinetic energy 309
Mass 309
Regen 310
Regeneration 310
Torque 309

INTRODUCTION

When test driving a hybrid vehicle the driver may notice that there is a slight surge or pulsation that occurs at lower speeds usually about 5 to 20 mph (8 to 32 km/h). The brakes may also be touchy and seem to be very sensitive to the brake force applied to the brake pedal. This is where the regenerative braking system stops regenerating electricity for charging the batteries and where the mechanical (friction) brakes take over. This chapter describes how this system works and how the various components of a hybrid electric vehicle (HEV) work together to achieve the highest possible efficiency.

 FREQUENTLY ASKED QUESTION

What Is the Difference Between Mass and Weight?

Mass is the amount of matter in an object. One of the properties of mass is inertia. Inertia is the resistance of an object to being put in motion and the tendency to remain in motion once it is set in motion. The weight of an object is the force of gravity on the object and may be defined as the mass times the acceleration of gravity.

Therefore, mass means the property of an object and weight is a force.

PRINCIPLES OF REGENERATIVE BRAKING

INERTIA, FORCE, AND MASS If a moving object has a mass, it has **inertia**. Inertia is the resistance of an object to change its state of motion. In other words, an object in motion tends to stay in motion and an object at rest tends to stay at rest unless acted on by an outside force.

A hybrid electric vehicle reclaims energy by converting the energy of a moving object, called **kinetic energy,** into electric energy. According to basic physics:

A **force** applied to move an object results in the equation:

$$F = ma$$

where:
F = force
m = mass
a = acceleration

The faster an object is accelerated, the more force that has to be applied. Energy from the battery (watts) is applied to the coil windings in the motor. These windings then produce a magnetic force on the rotor of the motor, which produces torque on the output shaft. This torque is then applied to the wheels of the vehicle by use of a coupling of gears and shafts. When the wheel turns, it applies a force to the ground, which due to friction between the wheel and the ground, causes the vehicle to move along the surface.

All vehicles generate **torque** to move the wheels to drive the vehicle down the road. During this time, it is generating friction and losses. When standard brakes are applied, it is just another friction device that has specially designed material to handle the heat from friction, which is applied to the drums and rotors that stop the wheel from turning. The friction between the wheel and the ground actually stops the vehicle. However, the energy absorbed by the braking system is lost in the form of heat and cannot be recovered or stored for use later to help propel the vehicle.

RECLAIMING ENERGY IN A HYBRID On a hybrid vehicle that has regenerative brakes, the kinetic energy of a moving vehicle can be reclaimed that would normally be lost due to braking. Using the inertia of the vehicle is the key. Inertia is the kinetic energy that is present in any moving object. The heavier the object, and the faster it is traveling, the greater the amount of energy and therefore, the higher the inertia. It is basically what makes something difficult to start moving and what makes something hard to stop moving. Inertia is the reason energy is required to change the direction and speed of the moving object.

TRANSFERRING TORQUE BACK TO THE MOTOR Inertia is the fundamental property of physics that is used to reclaim energy from the vehicle. Instead of using 100% friction brakes (**base brakes**), the braking torque is transferred from the wheels back into the motor shaft. One of the unique things about most electric motors is that electrical energy can be converted into mechanical energy and also mechanical energy can be converted back into electrical energy. In both cases, this can be done very efficiently.

Through the use of the motor and motor controller, the force at the wheels transfers torque to the electric motor shaft. The magnets on the shaft of the motor (called the rotor—the moving part of the motor) move past the electric coils on the

FIGURE 17–1 This Honda Insight hybrid electric vehicle is constructed mostly of aluminum to save weight.

FIGURE 17–2 A Toyota Prius hybrid electric vehicle. This sedan weighs more and therefore has greater kinetic energy than a smaller, lighter vehicle.

PRINCIPLES OF REGENERATIVE BRAKING (CONTINUED)

stator (the stationary part of the motor), passing the magnetic fields of the magnets through the coils, producing electricity. Simply stated, the electric motor(s) becomes a generator to recharge the batteries during braking. This process is called **regeneration, regen,** or simply "reclaiming energy."

PRINCIPLES INVOLVED Brakes slow and stop a vehicle by converting kinetic energy, the energy of motion, into heat energy, which is then dissipated to the air. Fuel is burned in the internal combustion engine to make heat, which is then converted to mechanical energy and finally this is used to create kinetic energy in the moving vehicle. The goal of regenerative braking is to recover some of that energy, store it, and then use it to put the vehicle into motion again. It is estimated that regenerative braking can eventually be developed to recover about half the energy wasted as braking heat. Depending on the type of vehicle, this would reduce fuel consumption by 10% to 25% below current levels.

Regenerative braking can be extremely powerful and can recover about 20% of the energy normally wasted as brake heat. Regenerative braking has the following advantages:

- Reduces the drawdown of the battery charge
- Extends the overall life of the battery pack
- Reduces fuel consumption

All production hybrid electric vehicles use regenerative braking as a method to improve vehicle efficiency, and this feature alone provides the most fuel economy savings. How much energy is reclaimed depends on many factors, including weight of the vehicle, speed, and the rate of deceleration. ● **SEE FIGURE 17–1.**

The amount of kinetic energy in a moving vehicle increases with the square of the speed. This means that at 60 mph, the kinetic energy is four times the energy of 30 mph. The speed is doubled (times 2) and the kinetic energy is squared (2 times 2 equals 4). ● **SEE FIGURE 17–2.**

The efficiency of the regenerative braking is about 80%, which means that only about 20% of the inertia energy is wasted to heat. There are losses when mechanical energy is converted to electrical energy by the motor/generator(s) and then some energy is lost when it is converted into chemical energy in the high-voltage batteries.

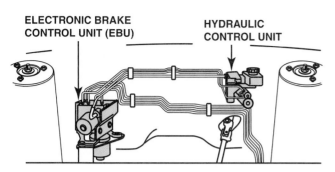

FIGURE 17–3 The electronic brake control unit (EBU) is shown on the left (passenger side) and the brake hydraulic unit is shown on the right (driver's side) on this Ford Escape system.

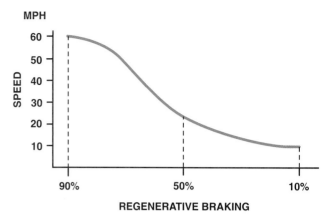

FIGURE 17–4 A typical brake curve showing the speed on the left and the percentage of regenerative braking along the bottom. Notice that the base brakes are being used more when the vehicle speed is low.

TYPES OF REGENERATIVE BRAKING SYSTEMS

Two different regeneration designs include:

- **Series regeneration.** In series regenerative braking systems, the amount of regeneration is proportional to the brake pedal position. As the brake pedal is depressed further, the controller used to regulate the regenerative braking system computes the torque needed to slow the vehicle as would occur in normal braking. As the brake pedal is depressed even further, the service brakes are blended into the regenerative braking to achieve the desired braking performance based on brake pedal force and travel. Series regenerative braking requires active brake management to achieve total braking to all four wheels. This braking is more difficult to achieve if the hybrid electric vehicle uses just the front or rear wheels to power the vehicle. This means that the other axle must use the base brakes alone, whereas the drive wheels can be slowed and stopped using a combination of regenerative braking and base brake action. All series regenerative braking systems use an **electrohydraulic brake (EHB)** system, which includes the hydraulic control unit that manages the brake cylinder pressures, as well as the front-rear axle brake balance. Most hybrid vehicles use this type of regenerative braking system.
  ● SEE FIGURE 17–3.

    The regenerative braking system mainly uses the regenerative capability, especially at higher vehicle speeds, and then gradually increases the amount of the base braking force at low vehicle speeds.

- **Parallel regeneration.** A parallel regenerative braking system is less complex because the base (friction) brakes are used along with energy recovery by the motors becoming generators. The controller for the regenerative braking system determines the amount of regeneration that can be achieved based on the vehicle speed. Front and rear brake balance is retained because the base brakes are in use during the entire braking event. The amount of energy captured by a parallel regenerative braking system is less than from a series system. As a result, the fuel economy gains are less.

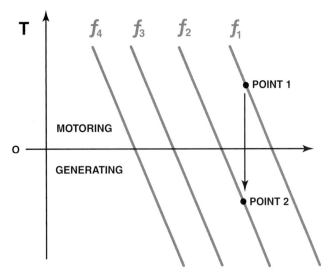

FIGURE 17–5 The frequency ("f") applied to the stator windings of an AC synchronous motor can be varied to create either forward torque ("T") or regenerative braking. If the frequency is changed from point 1 to point 2 as shown on the chart, the torque is changed from motoring (powering the vehicle) to generating and this change can be made almost instantly by the controller.

 FREQUENTLY ASKED QUESTION

How Does the Computer Change a Motor to a Generator So Quickly?

The controller of the drive motors uses a varying frequency to control power and speed. The controller can quickly change the frequency, and can therefore change the operation of a typical AC synchronous motor from propelling the vehicle (called motoring) to a generator. ● **SEE FIGURE 17–5.**

 FREQUENTLY ASKED QUESTION

Do Regenerative Brake Systems Still Use a Parking Brake?

Yes. Regenerative braking systems work while the vehicle is moving and supplements but does not replace the conventional brake system including the parking brake system.

BATTERY CHARGING DURING REGENERATION

BACKGROUND   Kinetic energy can be converted into electrical energy with a generator and it can be returned to the high-voltage batteries and stored for later use. Electric regenerative braking has its roots in the "dynamic brakes" used on electric trolley cars in the early Twentieth Century.

In the early electric trolley cars, the driver's control handle had a position that cut power to the electric motors and supplied a small, finely controlled excitation current to the motors' field windings. This turned the motors into generators that were driven by the motion of the trolley car. Increasing the magnetic field current increased the generating load, which slowed the trolley car, and the current being generated was routed to a set of huge resistors. These resistors converted the current to heat, which was dissipated through cooling fins. By the 1920s, techniques had been developed for returning that current to the power grid, making it available to all the other trolley cars in the system, reducing the load on the streetcar system's main generator by as much as 20%.

Regenerative braking systems are still being used in cities around the world. It is relatively easy to feed the current generated from braking into an on-board high-voltage battery system. The challenge was to make those components small enough to be practical, but still have enough storage capacity to be useful. A big breakthrough came with the development of the electronically controlled permanent-magnet motors.

PARTS AND OPERATION   Motors work by activating electromagnets in just the right position and sequence. A conventional DC motor has groups of wire windings on the armature that act as electromagnets. The current flows through each winding on the armature only when the brushes touch its contacts located on the commutator. Surround the armature with a magnetic field and apply current to just the windings that are in the right position, and the resulting magnetic attraction causes the armature to rotate. The brushes lose contact with that set of windings just as the next set comes into the right position. Together, the brushes and rotation of the armature act like a mechanical switch to turn on each electromagnet at just the right position.

Another way to make a motor, instead of using electromagnets on the armature, is to use permanent magnets. Because it is impossible to switch the polarity of permanent magnets, the polarity of the field windings surrounding them needs to be switched. This is a brushless, permanent-magnet motor and the switching is only possible with the help of electronic controls that can switch the current in the field windings

? FREQUENTLY ASKED QUESTION

What Do Regenerative Brakes Look Like?

Regenerative brakes use the rotation of the wheels applied to the electric traction (drive) motor to create electricity. Therefore the brakes themselves look the same as conventional brakes because the hydraulic brakes are still in place and work the same as conventional brakes. The major difference is that the standard wheel brakes work mostly at low vehicle speeds whereas conventional brakes work at all speeds. As a result, the brakes on a hybrid electric vehicle should last many times longer than the brakes on a conventional vehicle.

fast enough. The computer-controlled, brushless, permanent-magnet motor is ideal for use in electric vehicles. When connected to nickel-metal hydride (NiMH) batteries that can charge and discharge very quickly, the package is complete.

LIMITATIONS OF REGENERATIVE BRAKES
There are some limitations that will always affect even the best regenerative braking systems including:

- It only acts on the driven wheels.
- The system has to be designed to allow for proper use of the antilock braking system.
- The batteries are commanded to be kept at a maximum of about 60%, plus or minus 20%, which is best for long battery life and to allow for energy to be stored in the batteries during regenerative braking. If the batteries were allowed to be fully charged, then there would be no place for the electrical current to be stored and the conventional friction brakes alone have to be used to slow and stop the vehicle. Charging the batteries over 80% would also overheat the batteries.

So far its use is limited to electric or hybrid electric vehicles, where its contribution is to extend the life of the battery pack, as well as to save fuel.

DASH DISPLAY The Toyota Prius is equipped with a center dash LCD that shows how many watt-hours of regeneration have occurred every 5 minutes. These are indicated by small "suns" that appear on the display and each sun indicates 50 watt-hours. When a sun appears, enough power has been put back into the battery to run a 50-watt lightbulb for an hour. Depending on the driver and the traffic conditions, some drivers may not be seeing many suns on the display, which indicates that the regeneration is not contributing much energy back to the batteries. The battery level also gives an indication of how much regeneration is occurring. The battery state-of-charge (SOC) is also displayed.

REGENERATIVE BRAKE COMPONENTS It is the ABS ECU that handles regenerative braking, as well as ABS functions, sending a signal to the hybrid ECU as to how much regeneration to impose. But how does the ABS ECU know what to do?

Rather than measuring brake pedal travel, which could vary with pad wear, the system uses pressure measuring sensors to detect master cylinder pressure. Some systems use a **brake pedal position (BPP)** sensor as an input signal to the brake ECU. The higher the master cylinder pressure, the harder the driver is pushing on the brake pedal.

If the driver is pushing only gently, the master cylinder piston displacement will be small and the hydraulic brakes will be only gently applied. In this situation, the ECU knows that the driver wants only gentle deceleration and instructs the hybrid ECU to apply only a small amount of regeneration. However, as master cylinder pressure increases, so does the amount of regeneration that can automatically be applied.

There are four pressure sensors in the braking system and two pressure switches. However, it is the master cylinder pressure sensor that is most important. ● **SEE FIGURES 17–6 AND 17–7.**

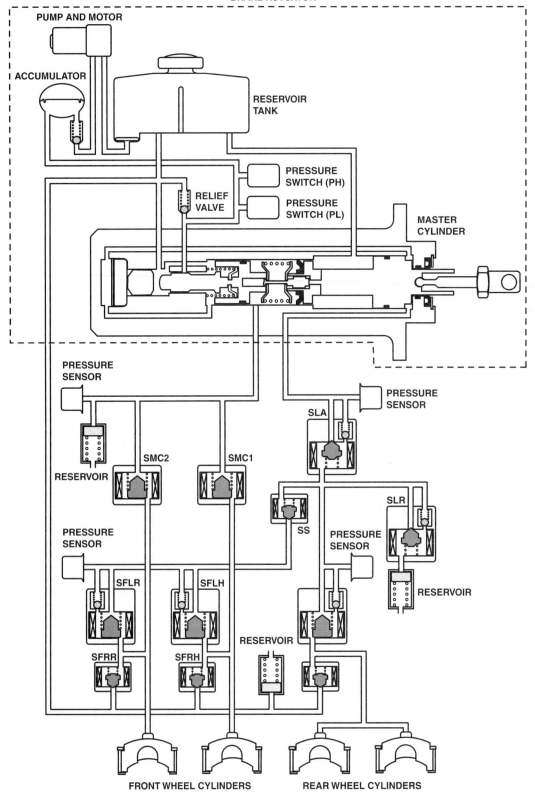

FIGURE 17–6 The Toyota Prius regenerative braking system component showing the master cylinder and pressure switches.

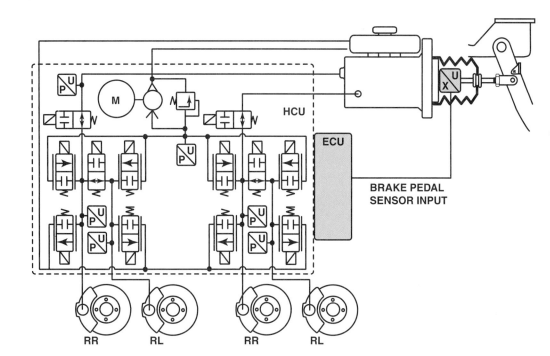

FIGURE 17–7 The Ford Escape regenerative braking system, showing all of the components. Notice the brake pedal position sensor is an input to the ECU, which controls both the brake and traction control systems.

BRAKE PEDAL SENSOR INPUT

 TECH TIP

"B" Means Braking

All Toyota hybrid vehicles have a position on the gear selector marked "B." This position is to be used when descending steep grades and the regenerative braking is optimized. This position allows the safe and controlled descent without having the driver use the base brakes. Having to use the base brakes only wastes energy that could be captured and returned to the batteries. It can also cause the brakes to over-heat. ● **SEE FIGURE 17–8.**

FIGURE 17–8 The "B" position on the shift display on this Lexus RX 400h means braking. This shifter position can be selected when descending long hills or grades. The regenerative braking system will be used to help keep the vehicle from increasing in speed down the hill without the use of the base brakes.

HOW THE REGENERATION SYSTEM WORKS

To keep the hybrid electric vehicles feeling as much like other vehicles as possible, the hybrids from Toyota and Honda have both the regeneration and conventional brakes controlled by the one brake pedal. In the first part of its travel, the brake pedal operates the regenerative brakes alone, and then as further pressure is placed on the pedal, the friction brakes come into play as well. The current Honda Civic Hybrid mixes the two brake modes together imperceptibly, whereas the first model Toyota Prius, for example, has more of a two-stage pedal.

Regeneration also occurs only when the throttle has been fully lifted. In the Hybrid Civic, it is like decelerating in fourth gear (in a five- or six-speed transaxle), while in the Prius models it feels less strong.

The wear of the hydraulic brakes and pads will also be reduced. The base brakes are still used when descending long hills, though as the battery becomes more fully charged, regeneration progressively reduces its braking action and the hydraulic brakes then do more and more of the work. Regeneration switches off at low speeds, so the disc brake pads and rotors stay clean and fully functional.

NOTE: One of the major concerns with hybrid vehicles is rust and corrosion on the brake rotors and drums. This occurs on hybrids because the base brakes are usually only used at low vehicle speeds.

The amount of regeneration that occurs is largely dictated by the output of the master cylinder pressure sensor. The ECU looks at the brake pressure signal from the sensor when the brake pedal switch is not triggered and uses this as the starting value. When the brake pedal is pushed, it then checks the difference between the starting value and the "brake pedal on" value and sets the regeneration value, according to this difference.

The voltage output of the pressure sensor ranges from about 0.4 to 3.0 volts, rising with increasing pressure. Service information states that a fault will be detected if the voltage from the sensor is outside of the range of 0.14V to 4.4V, or if the voltage output of the sensor is outside a certain ratio to its nominally 5V supply voltage. ● **SEE FIGURE 17–9.**

ELECTRIC MOTOR BECOMES A GENERATOR
When a motor is used for regenerative braking, it acts as a generator and produces an alternating current (AC). The AC current needs to be rectified (converted) to DC current to go into the batteries. Each of the three main power wires coming out of the motor needs two large diodes. The two large diodes on each main wire do the job of converting the AC into DC.

Regenerative braking is variable. In the same way as the accelerator pedal is used to adjust the speed, the braking is varied by reducing the speed.

There are deceleration programs within the Powertrain Control Module (PCM), which varies the maximum deceleration rates according to vehicle speed and battery state-of-charge (SOC).

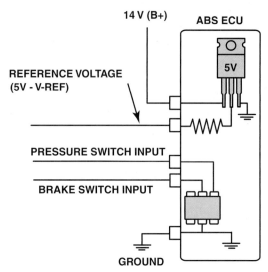

FIGURE 17–9 The ABS ECU on a Toyota Prius uses the brake switch and pressure sensor inputs to control the regenerative braking system. The circuit includes a voltage signal from the sensor, the regulated 5V supply to it, the input from the brake light switch (12V when the brakes are on), and the ground connection.

? FREQUENTLY ASKED QUESTION

Can an On-Vehicle Brake Lathe Be Used on a Hybrid Electric Vehicle?

Yes. When a brake rotor needs to be machined on a hybrid electric vehicle, the rotor is being rotated. On most hybrids, the front wheels are also connected to the traction motor that can propel the vehicle and generate electricity during deceleration and braking. When the drive wheels are being rotated, the motor/generator is producing electricity. However, unless the high-voltage circuit wiring has been disconnected, no harm will occur.

DECELERATION RATES

Deceleration rates are measured in units of "feet per second per second." What it means is that the vehicle will change in velocity during a certain time interval divided by the time interval. Deceleration is abbreviated "ft/sec²" (pronounced "feet per second, per second" or "feet per second squared") or meters per sec² (m/s²) in the metric system. Typical deceleration rates include the following.

- Comfortable deceleration is about 8.5 ft/sec² (3 m/s²).

- Loose items in the vehicle will "fly" above 11 ft/sec² (3.5 m/s²).

- Maximum deceleration rates for most vehicles and light trucks range from 16 to 32 ft/sec² (5 to 10 m/s²).

An average deceleration rate of 15 ft/sec² (FPSPS) (3 m/s²) can stop a vehicle traveling at 55 mph (88 km/h) in about 200 ft (61 m) and in less than 4 seconds. Deceleration is also expressed in units called a **g.** One g is the acceleration of gravity, which is 32 feet per second per second.

With a conventional hydraulic braking system, the driver can brake extremely gently, thereby only imperceptibly slowing the vehicle. A typical hybrid using regenerative braking will normally indicate a 0.1 g (about 3 ft/sec²) deceleration rate when the throttle is released and the brake pedal has not been applied. This rate is what a driver would normally expect to occur when the accelerator pedal is released. This slight deceleration feels comfortable to the driver, as well as the passengers, because this is what occurs in a nonhybrid vehicle that does not incorporate regenerative braking. When the brake pedal is pressed, the deceleration increases to a greater value than 0.1 g, which gives the driver the same feeling of deceleration that would occur in a conventional vehicle. Maximum deceleration rates are usually greater than 0.8 g and could exceed 1 g in most vehicles. ● **SEE FIGURE 17–10.**

ENGINE DESIGN CHANGES RELATED TO REGENERATIVE BRAKING

Some hybrid vehicles, such as the second-generation Honda Civic and Accord, use a variation of the VTEC valve actuation system to close all of the valves in three cylinders in both the V-6 and the inline four cylinder engines during deceleration. This traps some exhaust in the cylinders and because no air enters

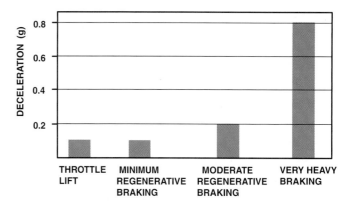

FIGURE 17–10 This graph compares the figures: at the far left a throttle lift typically giving about 0.1 g deceleration; second from the left a minimum regenerative braking of about 0.1 g; second from the right, a moderate regenerative braking is about 0.2 g; and on the far right a hard emergency stop resulting in braking of (at least) 0.8 g, which uses both the regenerative braking system, as well as the base hydraulic brake system.

FIGURE 17–11 This Honda valve train photo shows the small spring used to absorb the motion of the rocker arm when the cam is switched to a lobe that has zero lift. This action causes the valves to remain closed thereby reducing engine braking, which increases the amount of energy that can be captured by the regenerative braking system when the vehicle is slowing. The powertrain control module controls this valve action through a solenoid valve in response to inputs from the throttle position (TP) sensor and vehicle speed information.

the pistons, the cylinders do not have anything to compress. As a result, the engine does not cause any engine braking and therefore allows more of the inertia of the moving vehicle to be converted to electrical energy due to regenerative braking. ● **SEE FIGURE 17–11.**

FIGURE 17–12 A master cylinder from a Toyota Highlander hybrid electric vehicle.

FIGURE 17–13 When working on the brakes on a Ford Escape or Mercury Mariner hybrid vehicle, disconnect the black electrical connector on the ABS hydraulic control unit located on the passenger side under the hood.

SERVICING REGENERATIVE BRAKING SYSTEMS

ROUTINE BRAKE SERVICE Routine brake service such as replacing the brake pads and shoes is the same on an HEV equipped with regenerative brakes as it is on a conventional vehicle.

UNIQUE MASTER CYLINDERS Most hybrid electric vehicles use unique master cylinders that do not look like conventional master cylinders. Some use more than one brake fluid reservoir and others contain sensors and other components, which are often not serviced separately. ● **SEE FIGURE 17–12.**

FORD ESCAPE PRECAUTIONS On the Ford Escape hybrid system, the regenerative braking system checks the integrity of the brake system as a self-test. After a certain amount of time, the brake controller will energize the hydraulic control unit and check that pressure can be developed in the system.

- This is performed when a door is opened as part of the wake-up feature of the system.
- The ignition key does not have to be in the ignition for this self-test to be performed.
- This is done by developing brake pressure for short periods of time.

 FREQUENTLY ASKED QUESTION

When Does Regenerative Braking Not Work?

There is one unusual situation where regenerative braking will not occur. What happens if, for example, the vehicle is at the top of a long hill and the battery charge level is high? In this situation, the controller can only overcharge the batteries. Overcharging is not good for the batteries, so the controller will disable regenerative braking and use the base brakes only. This is one reason why the SOC of the batteries is kept below 80% so regenerative braking can occur.

CAUTION: To prevent physical harm or causing damage to the vehicle when serving the braking system, the technician should do the following:

1. In order to change the brake pads, it is necessary to enter the "Pad Service Mode" on a scan tool and disable the self-test. This will prevent brake pressure from being applied.
2. Disconnect the wiring harness at the hydraulic control unit. ● **SEE FIGURE 17–13.**
3. Check service information regarding how to cycle the ignition switch to enter the Pad Service Mode.

1. All moving objects that have mass (weight) have kinetic energy.

2. The regenerative braking system captures most of the kinetic energy from the moving vehicle and returns this energy to high-voltage batteries to be used later to help propel the vehicle.

3. The two types of regenerative braking include parallel and series.

4. Brushless DC and AC induction motors are used in hybrid electric vehicles to help propel the vehicle and to generate electrical energy back to the batteries during braking.

5. Most hybrid electric vehicles use an electrohydraulic braking system that includes pressure sensors to detect the pressures in the system.

6. The controller is used to control the motors and turn them into a generator as needed to provide regenerative braking.

REVIEW QUESTIONS

1. What is inertia?

2. What is the difference between series and parallel regenerative braking systems?

3. What happens in the regenerative braking system when the high-voltage batteries are fully charged?

4. Describe what occurs when the driver starts to brake on a hybrid electric vehicle equipped with regenerative braking.

CHAPTER QUIZ

1. Which type of regenerative braking system uses an electrohydraulic system?
   - a. Series
   - b. Parallel
   - c. Both series and parallel
   - d. Neither series nor parallel

2. Kinetic energy is _____.
   - a. The energy that the driver exerts on the brake pedal
   - b. The energy needed from the batteries to propel a vehicle
   - c. The energy in any moving object
   - d. The energy that the motor produces to propel the vehicle

3. Inertia is _____.
   - a. The energy of any moving object that has mass (weight)
   - b. The force that the driver exerts on the brake pedal during a stop
   - c. The electric motor force that is applied to the drive wheels
   - d. The force that the internal combustion engine and the electric motor together apply to the drive wheels during rapid acceleration

4. Technician A says that the Powertrain Control Module (PCM) or controller can control the voltage to the motor(s) in a hybrid electric vehicle. Technician B says that the PCM or controller can control the electric motors by varying the frequency of the applied current. Which technician is correct?
   - a. Technician A only
   - b. Technician B only
   - c. Both Technicians A and B
   - d. Neither Technician A nor B

5. During braking on a hybrid electric vehicle equipped with regenerative braking system, what occurs when the driver depresses the brake pedal?
   - a. The friction brakes are only used as a backup and not used during normal braking.
   - b. The motors become generators.
   - c. The driver needs to apply a braking lever instead of depressing the brake pedal to energize the regenerative braking system.
   - d. The batteries are charged to 100% SOC.

6. Technician A says that a front-wheel-drive hybrid electric vehicle can only generate electricity during braking from the front wheel motor(s). Technician B says that the antilock braking (ABS) is not possible with a vehicle equipped with a regenerative braking system. Which technician is correct?
   a. Technician A only
   b. Technician B only
   c. Both Technicians A and B
   d. Neither Technician A nor B

7. In a regenerative braking system, which part of the electric motor is being controlled by the computer?
   a. The rotor
   b. The stator
   c. Both the rotor and the stator
   d. Neither the rotor nor the stator

8. In a Toyota Prius regenerative braking system, how many pressure *sensors* are used?
   a. One
   b. Two
   c. Three
   d. Four

9. In a Toyota Prius regenerative braking system, how many pressure *switches* are used?
   a. One
   b. Two
   c. Three
   d. Four

10. Two technicians are discussing deceleration rates. Technician A says that a one "g" stop is a gentle slowing of the vehicle. Technician B says that a stopping rate of 8 ft/sec^2 is a severe stop. Which technician is correct?
    a. Technician A only
    b. Technician B only
    c. Both Technicians A and B
    d. Neither Technician A nor B

ABS COMPONENTS AND OPERATION

OBJECTIVES

After studying Chapter 18, the reader will be able to:

1. Prepare for the Brakes (A5) ASE certification test content area "F" (Antilock Brake System Diagnosis and Repair).
2. Explain the reason for ABS.
3. Describe the purpose and function of the ABS components, such as wheel speed sensors, electrohydraulic unit, and electronic controller.
4. Discuss how the ABS components control wheel slippage.

KEY TERMS

Accumulator 330
Active sensor 328
Air gap 328
Antilock braking systems (ABS) 322
Channel 325
Control module 324
Flash codes 329
Integral ABS 325
Isolation solenoid 330
Nonintegral ABS 325
Pressure decay stage 330
Pressure dump stage 330
Pressure holding stage 330
Pressure increase stage 330

Pressure reduction stage 330
Pressure release stage 330
Rear Antilock Braking System (RABS) 325
Rear Wheel Antilock (RWAL) 325
Release solenoid 330
Select low principle 325
Solenoid valves 324
Tire pressure monitoring system (TPMS) 333
Tire slip 322
Tone ring 327
Traction 322
Wheel speed sensors (WSS) 327

ANTILOCK BRAKING SYSTEM

OVERVIEW **Antilock braking systems (ABS)** help prevent the wheels from locking during sudden braking, especially on slippery surfaces. This helps the driver maintain control.

Antilock brakes increase safety because they eliminate lockup and minimize the danger of skidding, allowing the vehicle to stop in a straight line. ABS also allows the driver to maintain steering control during heavy braking so the vehicle can be steered to avoid an obstacle or another vehicle.

ABS can improve braking when road conditions are less than ideal, as when making a sudden panic stop or when braking on a wet or slick road. ABS does this by monitoring the relative speed of the wheels to one another. It uses this information to modulate brake pressure as needed to control slippage and maintain traction when the brakes are applied.

ABS AND TIRE TRACTION Preventing brake lockup is important because of the adverse effect a locked wheel has on tire **traction**. The brakes slow the rotation of the wheels, but it is friction between the tire and road that stops the vehicle and allows it to be steered. If tire traction is reduced, stopping distances increase, and the directional stability of the vehicle suffers.

Traction is defined in terms of **tire slip,** which is the difference between the actual speed and the rate at which the tire tread moves across the road. A free-rolling wheel has nearly zero tire slip, while a locked wheel has 100% tire slip. ● **SEE FIGURE 18–1.**

When the brakes are applied, the rotational speed of the wheel drops, and tire slip increases because the tread moves across the road slower than the actual vehicle speed. This slip creates friction that converts kinetic energy into braking and cornering force.

TIRE SLIP AND BRAKING DISTANCE On dry or wet pavement, maximum braking traction occurs when tire slip is held between approximately 15% and 30%. ● **SEE FIGURE 18–2.**

On snow- or ice-covered pavement, the optimum slip range is 20% to 50%. In each case, if tire slip increases beyond these levels, the amount of traction decreases. A skidding tire with 100% slip provides 20% to 30% less braking traction on dry pavement, and this is generally true on slippery roads as well. In nearly all cases, the shortest stopping distances are obtained when the brakes are applied with just enough force to keep the tire slip in the range where traction is greatest.

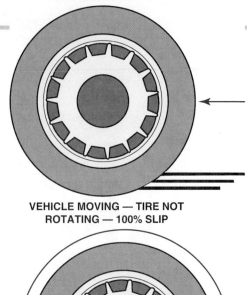

VEHICLE MOVING — TIRE NOT ROTATING — 100% SLIP

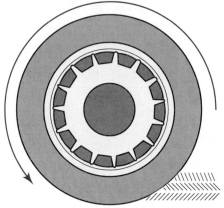

TIRE ROTATING — 0% SLIP

FIGURE 18–1 Maximum braking traction occurs when tire slip is between 10% and 20%. A rotating tire has 0% slip and a locked-up wheel has 100% slip.

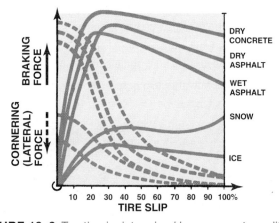

FIGURE 18–2 Traction is determined by pavement conditions and tire slip.

NOTE: All antilock braking systems stop controlling the wheel brakes when the vehicle speed drops to about 5 MPH (8 km/h). The wheel speed sensors are often not accurate that these low speeds and loss of vehicle control at this low speed is unlikely.

TIRE SLIP AND VEHICLE STABILITY A tire's contact
patch with the road can provide only a certain amount of traction.
When a vehicle is stopped in a straight line, nearly all of the available traction can be used to provide braking force. Only a small
amount of traction is required to generate lateral force that keeps
the vehicle traveling in a straight line. However, if a vehicle has to
stop and turn at the same time, the available traction must be
divided to provide both cornering (lateral) and braking force.

No tire can provide full cornering power and full braking
power at the same time. When a brake is locked and the tire has
100% slip, all of the available traction is used for braking, and
none is left for steering. As a result, a skidding tire follows the
path of least resistance. This means that if the rear brakes lock,
the back end of the vehicle will tend to swing around toward the
front causing a spin. If the front brakes lock, steering control will
be lost and the vehicle will slide forward in a straight line until the
brakes are released to again make traction available for steering.

ABS AND BASE BRAKES An antilock braking system is
only an "add-on" to the existing base brake system. ABS only
comes into play when traction conditions are marginal or during
sudden panic stops when the tires lose traction and begin to
slip excessively. The rest of the time ABS has no effect on normal driving, handling, or braking.

ABS also makes no difference in the maintenance, inspection, service, or repair of conventional brake system components. A vehicle with ABS brakes uses the same brake linings,
calipers, wheel cylinders, and other system components as a
vehicle without ABS brakes. The only exception being the
master cylinder on certain applications.

All ABS systems are also designed to be as "fail-safe" as
possible. Should a failure occur that affects the operation of the
ABS system, the system will deactivate itself and the vehicle will
revert to normal braking. Therefore, an ABS failure will not prevent the vehicle from stopping.

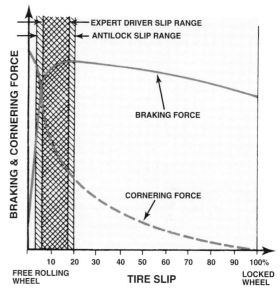

FIGURE 18–3 A good driver can control tire slip more
accurately than an ABS if the vehicle is traveling on a smooth,
dry road surface.

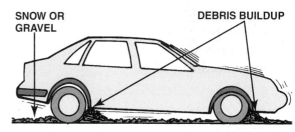

FIGURE 18–4 A wedge of gravel or snow in the front of a locked
wheel can help stop a vehicle faster than would occur if the wheel
brakes were pulsed on and off by an antilock braking system.

ABS LIMITATIONS There are two situations in which an
antilock brake system will *not* provide the shortest stopping
distances. The first involves straight stops made on smooth, dry
pavement by an *expert* driver. Under these conditions, a skilled
driver can hold the tires consistently closer to the ideal slip rate
than the ABS can. ● **SEE FIGURE 18–3.**

This is possible because current antilock braking systems
may allow the amount of tire slip to drop as low as 5%, which is
somewhat below the point where maximum tire traction is
achieved. However, for the average driver, or under less than
ideal conditions, antilock brakes will almost always stop the vehicle in a shorter distance.

The other situation in which antilock brakes will not provide
the shortest stops is when braking on loose gravel or dirt, or in
deep, fluffy snow. Under these conditions, a locked wheel will
stop the vehicle faster because loose debris builds up and
forms a wedge in front of the tire that helps stop the vehicle.
● **SEE FIGURE 18–4.**

FIGURE 18–5 Being able to steer and control the vehicle during rapid braking is one major advantage of an antilock braking system.

ANTILOCK BRAKING SYSTEM (CONTINUED)

An antilock braking system will prevent this wedge from forming, so some vehicles with antilock brakes have a switch on the instrument panel that allows the system to be deactivated when driving on these kinds of road surfaces.

ABS AND THE LAWS OF PHYSICS
No ABS can overcome the laws of physics. The weight and speed of a moving vehicle give it a great deal of kinetic energy, and only so much of that energy can be converted into braking or cornering force at any given time. The limiting factor in this conversion is the traction between the tires and road.

Although a vehicle with four-wheel antilock brakes will stop in very nearly the shortest possible distance, this will still not prevent an accident if the brakes are applied too late to bring the vehicle to a complete stop before impact. However, because steering control is retained with four-wheel antilock brakes, it may be possible to drive the vehicle around a potential accident while in the process of braking.

Another situation where antilock brakes cannot defy the laws of physics occurs when a vehicle enters a corner traveling faster than it is physically possible to negotiate the turn. In this situation, antilock brakes will not prevent the vehicle from leaving the road. However, they will allow the vehicle to be slowed and steered in the process, thus lessening the severity of the eventual impact. ● **SEE FIGURE 18–5.**

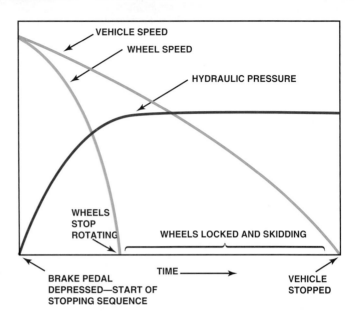

FIGURE 18–6 A typical stop on a slippery road surface without antilock brakes. Notice that the wheels stopped rotating and skidded until the vehicle finally came to a stop.

ABS OPERATION

WHEEL SPEED SENSOR INPUT
All ABS systems control tire slip by monitoring the relative deceleration rates of the wheels during braking. Wheel speed is monitored by one or more wheel speed sensors. If one wheel starts to slow at a faster rate than the others, or at a faster rate than that which is programmed in the antilock **control module,** it indicates a wheel is starting to slip and is in danger of losing traction and locking. The ABS responds by momentarily reducing hydraulic pressure to the brake on the affected wheel or wheels. This allows the wheel to speed up momentarily so it can regain traction. As traction is regained, brake pressure is reapplied to again slow the wheel. The cycle is repeated over and over until the vehicle stops or until the driver eases pressure on the brake pedal.

CONTROL VALVES
Electrically operated **solenoid valves** (or motor-driven valves in the case of Delphi ABS-VI applications) are used to hold, release, and reapply hydraulic pressure to the brakes. This produces a pulsating effect, which can be felt in the brake pedal during hard braking. The rapid modulation of brake pressure in a given brake circuit reduces the braking load on the affected wheel and allows it to regain traction to prevent lockup. The effect is much the same as pumping the brakes, except that the ABS system does it automatically for each brake circuit, and at speeds that would be humanly impossible—up to 20 times per second depending on the system (some cycle faster than others). ● **SEE FIGURE 18–6.**

Once the rate of deceleration for the affected wheel catches up with the others, normal braking function and pressure resume, and antilock reverts to a passive mode.

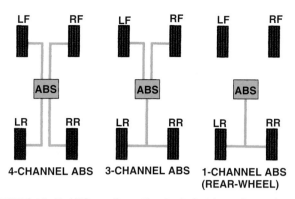

FIGURE 18–7 ABS configuration includes four-channel, three-channel, and single-channel.

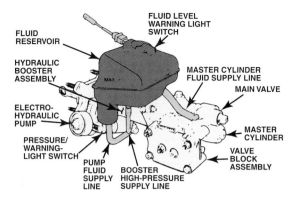

FIGURE 18–8 A typical integral ABS unit that combines the function of the master cylinder, brake booster, and antilock braking system in one assembly.

SYSTEM CONFIGURATIONS

All ABS systems keep track of wheel deceleration rates with wheel speed sensors. The various ABS systems use a different number of sensors, depending on how the system is configured. These include four-channel, three-channel, and single-channel systems. ● **SEE FIGURE 18–7.**

FOUR-CHANNEL ABS SYSTEMS On some applications, each wheel is equipped with its own speed sensor. This type of arrangement is called a "four-wheel, four-channel" system since each wheel speed sensor provides input for a separate hydraulic control circuit or "channel."

The term **channel** always refers to the number of separate or individually controlled ABS hydraulic circuits in an ABS system, not the number of wheel speed sensor electrical circuits.

NOTE: For vehicle stability systems to function, there has to be four wheel speed sensors and four channels so the hydraulic control unit can pulse individual wheel brakes to help achieve vehicle stability.

THREE-CHANNEL ABS SYSTEMS Some four-wheel ABS systems have a separate wheel speed sensor for each front wheel but use a common speed sensor for both rear wheels. These are called "three-channel" systems. The rear wheel speed sensor is mounted in either the differential or the transmission. The sensor reads the combined or average speed of both rear wheels. This type of setup saves the cost for an additional sensor and reduces the complexity of the system by allowing both rear wheels to be controlled simultaneously. This is known as the **select low principle.** Three-channel systems are

the most common type of ABS setup used on rear-wheel-drive applications.

SINGLE-CHANNEL ABS SYSTEMS The single-channel rear-wheel-only ABS system is used on many rear-wheel-drive pickups and vans. Ford's version is called **Rear Antilock Braking System (RABS),** while General Motors and Chrysler call theirs **Rear Wheel Antilock (RWAL).** The front wheels have no speed sensors, and only a single speed sensor mounted in the differential or transmission is used for both rear wheels. Rear-wheel antilock systems are typically used on applications where vehicle loading can affect rear wheel traction, which is why it is used on pickup trucks and vans. Because the rear-wheel antilock systems have only a single channel, they are much less complex and costly than their multichannel, four-wheel counterparts.

INTEGRAL AND NONINTEGRAL Another distinction between ABS systems is whether they are **integral** or **nonintegral ABS.** Integral systems combine the brake master cylinder and ABS hydraulic modulator, pump, and accumulator into one assembly. ● **SEE FIGURE 18–8.**

Integral systems do not have a vacuum booster for power assist and rely instead on pressure generated by the electric pump for this purpose. Most of the older ABS applications are integral systems. Integral ABS systems include the Bendix 10 and Bendix 9 (Jeep) ABS systems, Bosch 3, Delco Moraine Powermaster III, and Teves Mark 2.

Nonintegral ABS systems, which are sometimes referred to as "add-on" systems, have become the most common type of

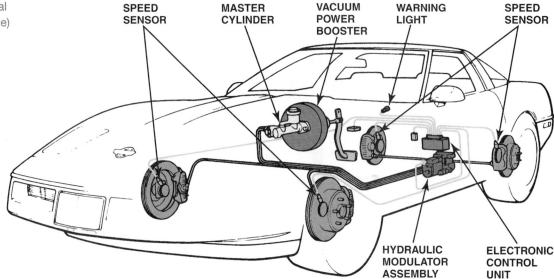

FIGURE 18–9 A typical nonintegral-type (remote) ABS.

SPEED SENSOR

MASTER CYLINDER

VACUUM POWER BOOSTER

WARNING LIGHT

SPEED SENSOR

HYDRAULIC MODULATOR ASSEMBLY

ELECTRONIC CONTROL UNIT

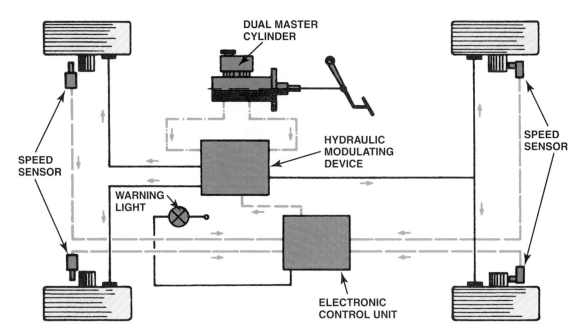

FIGURE 18–10 A schematic drawing of a typical antilock braking system.

DUAL MASTER CYLINDER

HYDRAULIC MODULATING DEVICE

SPEED SENSOR

SPEED SENSOR

WARNING LIGHT

ELECTRONIC CONTROL UNIT

SYSTEM CONFIGURATIONS (CONTINUED)

ABS system because of their lower cost and simplicity. ● **SEE FIGURE 18–9.**

Nonintegral ABS systems have a conventional brake master cylinder and vacuum power booster with a separate hydraulic modulator unit. Some also have an electric pump for ABS braking (to reapply pressure during the ABS hold-release-reapply cycle), but do not use the pumps for normal power assist.

Nonintegral (add-on) systems include Bendix 3, Bendix 6, Bendix ABX-4, Bendix Mecatronic, Bosch 2, Bosch 2S Micro, Bosch 2U, Bosch 2E, Bosch 5, Delco Moraine ABS-VI, Kelsey-Hayes RABS/RWAL, 4WAL, EBC-5 and EBC-10, Sumitomo ABS, Teves Mark 4 ABS and MK20, and Toyota rear-wheel ABS.

ABS COMPONENTS

Basic components that are common to all antilock brake systems include the following.

- Wheel speed sensors
- Electronic control unit
- ABS warning lamp
- Hydraulic modulator assembly with electrically operated solenoid valves (or motor-driven valves in the case of Delphi ABS-VI)

Some systems also have an electric pump and accumulator to generate hydraulic pressure for power assist as well as ABS braking. ● **SEE FIGURE 18–10.**

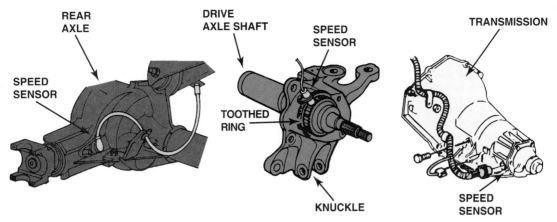

FIGURE 18–11 Wheel speed sensors for the rear wheels may be located on the rear axle, on the transmission, or on the individual wheel knuckle.

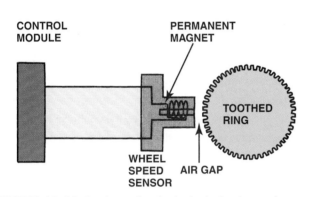

FIGURE 18–12 A schematic of a typical wheel speed sensor.

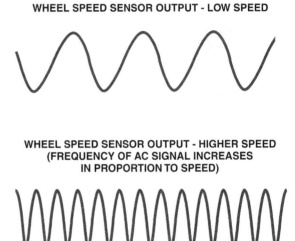

FIGURE 18–13 Wheel speed sensors produce an alternating current (AC) signal with a frequency that varies in proportion to wheel speed.

WHEEL SPEED SENSORS The **wheel speed sensors,** abbreviated **WSS,** consist of a magnetic pickup and a toothed sensor ring (usually called a **tone ring**). The sensor may be mounted in the steering knuckle, wheel hub, brake backing plate, transmission tailshaft, or differential housing. ● **SEE FIGURE 18–11.**

On some applications, the sensor is an integral part of the wheel bearing and hub assembly. The sensor rings may be mounted on the axle hub behind the brake rotors, on the brake rotors or drums, on the outside of the outboard constant velocity joints on a front-wheel-drive vehicle, on the transmission tailshaft, or inside the differential on the pinion gear shaft.

SENSOR OPERATION. The sensor pickup has a magnetic core surrounded by coil windings. ● **SEE FIGURE 18–12.**

As the wheel turns, teeth on the sensor ring move through the pickup's magnetic field. This reverses the polarity of the magnetic field and induces an alternating current (AC) voltage in the sensor windings. The number of voltage pulses per second induced in the pickup changes frequency. ● **SEE FIGURE 18–13.**

The frequency of the signal is therefore proportional to wheel speed. The higher the frequency, the faster the wheel is turning.

The signals are sent to the ABS control module (or an intermediate module in some General Motors rear-wheel ABS

FIGURE 18–14 A digital wheel speed sensor produces a square wave output signal.

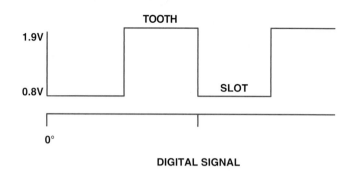

ABS COMPONENTS (CONTINUED)

applications), where the AC signal is converted into a digital signal for processing. The control module then monitors wheel speed by counting the pulses from each of the wheel speed sensors. If the frequency signal from one wheel starts to change abruptly with respect to the others, it tells the module that wheel is starting to lose traction. The module then applies antilock braking if needed to maintain traction.

SENSOR AIR GAP. The distance or **air gap** between the end of the sensor and its ring is critical. A close gap is necessary to produce a strong, reliable signal. But metal-to-metal contact between the sensor and its ring must be avoided since this would damage both. The air gap must not be too wide or a weak or erratic signal (or no signal) may result. The air gap on some wheel speed sensors is adjustable, and is specified by the vehicle manufacturer.

SENSOR APPLICATIONS AND PRECAUTIONS. Wheel speed sensor readings are affected by the size of the wheels and tires on the vehicle. A tire with a larger overall diameter will give a slower speed reading than one with a smaller diameter. Because the ABS system is calibrated to a specific tire size, vehicle manufacturers warn against changing tire sizes. A different tire size or aspect ratio could have an effect on the operation of the ABS system.

Wheel speed sensors are also magnetic, which means they can attract metallic particles. These particles can accumulate on the end of the sensor and reduce its ability to produce an accurate signal. Removing the sensor and cleaning the tip may be necessary if the sensor is producing a poor signal.

DIGITAL WHEEL SPEED SENSORS. A conventional wheel speed sensor uses a permanent magnet with a surrounding coil of wire to produce an AC voltage signal that is proportional to wheel speed. The major problem with this type of sensor is that the voltage output and frequency are very low at slow speeds and therefore, cannot produce accurate wheel speed for ABS and traction control.

A digital wheel speed sensor, also called an **active sensor,** uses either a Hall-effect or a variable-reluctance circuit to produce a square waveform where the frequency is proportional to the wheel speed. A digital wheel speed sensor can also detect direction and can therefore be used by the controller for hill holding. The accuracy of these digital sensors also makes correlation to global positioning used in navigational systems more accurate, especially when the vehicle is being driven at slow speeds.

NOTE: While all GPS navigation systems use satellites for global positioning, the vehicle uses other sensors to keep track of minor changes in speed and vehicle direction.

The typical digital wheel speed sensor uses two wires:

- A 12-volt supply
- A DC signal from the sensor

The sensor voltage toggles between about 0.8V and 1.9V.
● **SEE FIGURE 18–14.**

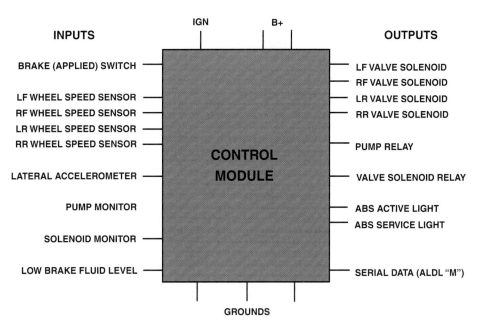

INPUTS

IGN   B+

BRAKE (APPLIED) SWITCH

LF WHEEL SPEED SENSOR
RF WHEEL SPEED SENSOR
LR WHEEL SPEED SENSOR
RR WHEEL SPEED SENSOR

LATERAL ACCELEROMETER

PUMP MONITOR

SOLENOID MONITOR

LOW BRAKE FLUID LEVEL

CONTROL
MODULE

GROUNDS

OUTPUTS

LF VALVE SOLENOID
RF VALVE SOLENOID
LR VALVE SOLENOID
RR VALVE SOLENOID

PUMP RELAY

VALVE SOLENOID RELAY

ABS ACTIVE LIGHT
ABS SERVICE LIGHT

SERIAL DATA (ALDL "M")

FIGURE 18–15 Typical inputs and outputs for brake control modules.

ABS CONTROL MODULE

CONTROL MODULE TERMS   The ABS electronic control module, which may be referred to as an "electronic brake control module" (EBCM), "electronic brake module" (EBM), or "controller antilock brakes" (CAB) module, is a digital microprocessor that uses inputs from its various sensors to regulate hydraulic pressure during braking to prevent wheel lockup. The module may be located on the hydraulic modulator assembly (as it is on many of the newer compact ABS systems), or it may be located elsewhere in the vehicle, such as the trunk, passenger compartment, or under the hood.

MODULE INPUTS   The key inputs for the ABS control module come from the wheel speed sensors and the brake pedal switch. ● **SEE FIGURE 18–15.**

The brake pedal switch signals the control module when the brakes are being applied, which causes it to go from a "standby" mode to an active mode. At the same time, the wheel speed sensors provide information about what is happening to the wheels while the brakes are being applied.

NOTE: A fault with the brake switch will not prevent ABS operation. The brake switch allows the controller to react faster to an ABS event.

MODULE OPERATION   If the control module detects a difference in the deceleration rate between one or more wheels

when braking, or if the overall rate of deceleration is too fast and exceeds the limits programmed into the control module, it triggers the ABS control module to momentarily take over. The control module cycles the solenoid valves in the modulator assembly to pulsate hydraulic pressure in the affected brake circuit (or circuits) until sensor information indicates that the deceleration rates have returned to normal and braking is under control. Normal braking resumes. When the brake pedal is released or when the vehicle comes to a stop, the control module returns to a standby mode until it is again needed.

ABS WARNING LAMP   Every ABS system has an amber indicator lamp on the instrument panel that warns the driver when a problem occurs within the ABS system. The lamp comes on when the ignition is turned on for a bulb check, then goes out after the engine starts. If the warning light remains on or comes on while driving, it usually indicates a fault in the ABS system that will require further diagnosis. On most applications, the ABS system disables if the ABS warning light comes on and remains on. This should have no effect on normal braking, unless the red brake warning lamp is also on. The ABS warning light is also used for diagnostic purposes when retrieving **flash codes** (trouble codes) from the ABS module.

FIGURE 18–16 An ABS three-way solenoid can increase, maintain, or decrease brake pressure to a given brake circuit.

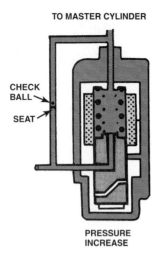
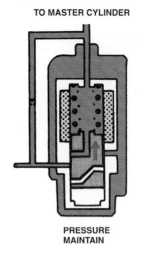
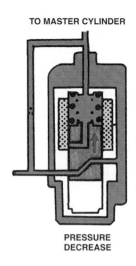

TO MASTER CYLINDER TO MASTER CYLINDER TO MASTER CYLINDER

CHECK BALL

SEAT

PRESSURE INCREASE PRESSURE MAINTAIN PRESSURE DECREASE

HYDRAULIC MODULATOR ASSEMBLY

PURPOSE AND FUNCTION The modulator valve body is part of the master cylinder assembly in nonintegral antilock systems but separate in nonintegral systems. It contains solenoid valves for each brake unit (in Delphi ABS-VI applications, however, motor-driven valves are used instead of solenoids). The exact number of valves per circuit depends on the ABS system and the application. Some use a pair of on-off solenoid valves for each brake circuit while others use a single valve that can operate in more than one position.

ABS SOLENOID A solenoid consists of a wire coil with a movable core and a return spring. When current from the ABS control module energizes the coil, it pulls on the movable core. Depending on how the solenoid is constructed, this may open or close a valve that is attached to the movable core. When the control current is shut off, the solenoid snaps back to its normal or rest position.

Some solenoids are designed to do more than just switch on or off to open or close a valve. Some pull a valve to an intermediate position when a certain level of current is applied to the coil, then pull the valve to a third position when additional current is provided. ● **SEE FIGURE 18–16.**

This design allows a single solenoid to perform the same functions as two or even three single-position solenoids.

The solenoids in the hydraulic modulator assembly are used to open and close passageways between the master cylinder and the individual brake circuits. By opening or closing the modulator valves to which they're attached, brake pressure within any given circuit can be held, released, and reapplied to prevent lockup during hard braking.

ABS CONTROL PRESSURE STAGES The standard ABS control strategy that is used is a three-step cycle:

- The first step is to hold or isolate the pressure in a given brake circuit by closing an **isolation solenoid** in the modulator assembly. This solenoid is normally electrically and hydraulically opened. ● **SEE FIGURE 18–17.** When the solenoid is electrically closed, it becomes hydraulically closed, which blocks off the line and prevents any further pressure from the master cylinder reaching the brake. This is called the **pressure holding stage.**

- If the wheel speed sensor continues to indicate the wheel is slowing too quickly and is starting to lock, the same solenoid or a second **release solenoid** is energized to open a vent port that releases pressure from the brake circuit. ● **SEE FIGURE 18–18.** The fluid is usually routed into a spring-loaded or pressurized storage reservoir (called an **accumulator**) so it can be reused as needed. Releasing pressure in the brake circuit allows the brake to loosen its grip so the wheel can speed up and regain traction. This is called **pressure reduction, pressure release, pressure decay,** or **pressure dump stage.** The pressure reduction solenoid is normally hydraulically closed and electrically opened.

- The release and/or isolation solenoid(s) are then closed and/or the additional solenoid energized so pressure can be reapplied to the brake from the master cylinder or accumulator to reapply the brake. ● **SEE FIGURE 18–19.** This is called the **pressure increase stage.** During the pressure increase stages, the isolation solenoid is electrically and hydraulically opened. The pressure reduction solenoid is electrically opened and hydraulically closed.

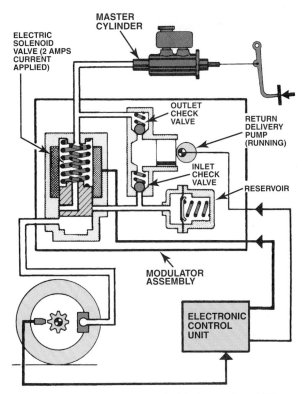

FIGURE 18–17 The isolation or hold phase of an ABS on a Bosch 2 system.

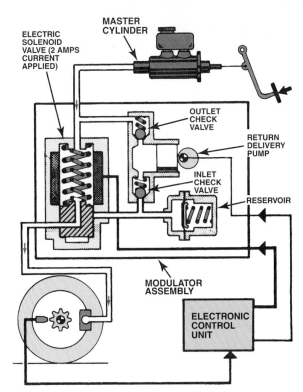

FIGURE 18–19 The control module reapplies pressure to the affected brake circuit once the tire achieves traction so that normal braking can continue.

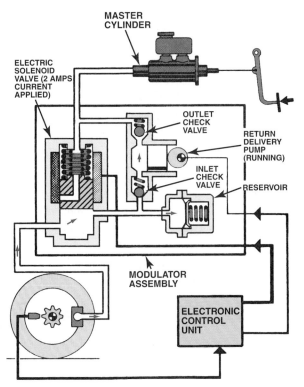

FIGURE 18–18 During the pressure reduction stage, pressure is vented from the brake circuit so the tire can speed up and regain traction.

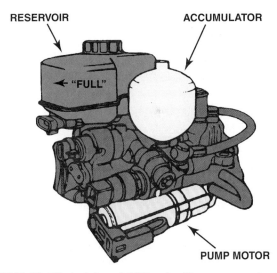

FIGURE 18–20 An integral ABS unit with a pump motor to provide power assist during all phases of braking and brake pressure during ABS stops.

The hold-release-reapply cycle repeats as many times as needed until the vehicle either comes to a halt or the driver releases the brake pedal. The speed at which this occurs depends on the particular ABS system that is on the vehicle, but can range from a few times per second up to dozens of times per second.

PUMP MOTOR AND ACCUMULATOR A high-pressure electric pump is used in some ABS systems to generate power assist for normal braking as well as the reapplication of brake pressure during ABS braking. ● **SEE FIGURE 18–20.** In some systems, it is used only for the reapplication of pressure during ABS braking.

The pump motor is energized by a relay, which is switched on and off by the ABS control module. The fluid pressure generated by the pump is stored in the accumulator. Some ABS systems have more than one accumulator. The accumulator on ABS systems, where the hydraulic modulator is part of the master cylinder assembly, consists of a pressure storage chamber filled with nitrogen gas. A thick rubber diaphragm forms a barrier between the nitrogen gas and brake fluid. As fluid is pumped into the accumulator, it compresses the gas and stores pressure. When the brake pedal is depressed, pressure from the accumulator flows to the master cylinder to provide power assist.

A pair of pressure switches mounted in the accumulator circuit signals the ABS control module to energize the pump when pressure falls below a preset minimum, then to shut the pump off once pressure is built back up.

Should the pump fail (a warning lamp comes on when reserve pressure drops too low), there is usually enough reserve pressure in the accumulator for 10 to 20 power-assisted stops. After that, there is no power assist. The brakes still work, but with greatly increased effort.

On ABS systems that have a conventional master cylinder and vacuum booster for power assist, a small accumulator or pair of accumulators may be used as temporary storage reservoirs for brake fluid during the hold-release-reapply cycle. This type of accumulator typically uses a spring-loaded diaphragm rather than a nitrogen-charged chamber to store pressure.

ACCUMULATOR PRECAUTIONS
A fully charged accumulator in an integral ABS system can store up to 2,700 PSI (19,000 kPa) of pressure for power-assist braking and for reapplying the brakes during the hold-release-reapply cycle for antilock braking. This stored pressure represents a potential hazard for a brake technician who is servicing the brakes, so the accumulator should be depressurized prior to doing any type of brake service work by pumping the brake pedal 25 to 40 times with the ignition key off.

In nonintegral ABS systems where an accumulator is used to temporarily hold fluid during the release phase of the hold-release-reapply ABS cycle, the accumulator consists of a spring-loaded diaphragm. This type of accumulator does not have to be depressurized prior to performing brake service.

BRAKE PEDAL FEEDBACK

Many ABS units force brake fluid back into the master cylinder under pressure during an ABS stop. This pulsing brake fluid return causes the brake pedal to pulsate. Some vehicle manufacturers use the pulsation of the brake pedal to inform the driver that the wheels are tending toward lockup and that the ABS is pulsing the brakes.

NOTE: A pulsating brake pedal may be normal only during an ABS stop. It is not normal for a vehicle with ABS to have a pulsating pedal during normal braking. If the brake pedal is pulsating during a non-ABS stop, the brake drums or rotor may be warped.

Some manufacturers use an isolation valve that prevents brake pedal pulsation even during an ABS stop.

 **TECH TIP**

Best to Keep Stock Tire Diameter

Vehicles equipped with antilock brakes are "programmed" to pulse the brakes at just the right rate for maximum braking effectiveness. A larger tire rotates at a slower speed and a smaller-than-normal tire rotates at a faster speed. Therefore, tire size affects the speed and rate of change in speed of the wheels as measured by the wheel speed sensors.

While changing tire size will not prevent ABS operation, it will cause less effective braking during hard braking with the ABS activated. Using the smaller spare tire can create such a difference in wheel speed compared with the other wheels that a false wheel speed sensor code may be set and an amber ABS warning lamp on the dash may light. However, most ABS systems will still function with the spare tire installed, but the braking performance will not be as effective. For best overall performance, always replace tires with the same size and type as specified by the vehicle manufacturer.

BRAKE PEDAL TRAVEL SWITCH (SENSOR)

Some ABS systems, such as the Teves Mark IV system, use a brake pedal travel switch (sensor). The purpose of the switch is to turn on the hydraulic pump when the brake pedal has been depressed to 40% of its travel. The pump runs and pumps brake fluid back into the master cylinder, which raises the brake pedal until the switch closes again, turning off the pump.

NOTE: Some early ABS systems did not use a brake switch. The problem occurred when the ABS could be activated while driving over rough roads. The brake switch can be the same as the brake light switch or a separate switch.

The brake pedal switch is an input for the electronic controller. When the brakes are applied, the electronic controller "gets ready" to act if ABS needs to "initialize" the starting sequence of events.

CAUTION: If the driver pumps the brakes during an ABS event, the controller will reset and reinitialization starts over again. This resetting process can disrupt normal ABS operation. The driver need only depress and hold the brake pedal down during a stop for best operation.

TIRE PRESSURE MONITORING SYSTEM (TPMS)

Tire pressure monitoring systems (TPMS) are required on all new vehicles. The type often used before the 2008 model year was an *indirect* system that used the wheel speed sensors. A tire that is underinflated will have a slightly smaller rolling radius than one that is properly inflated. This will create a difference in the wheel speed sensor reading if the difference in inflation pressure is 12 PSI or more. The ABS controller will then turn on the *low tire pressure* warning lamp to warn the driver that tires need attention. To help compensate for speed variation during cornering, an indirect tire pressure monitoring system checks the rotating speeds of diagonally opposed wheels. The system adds the speeds of the right front and left rear and then subtracts that value from the sum of the left front and right rear tires. If the total is less than or equal to a threshold value, no warning is given. However, if the total is greater than a predetermined value, the TPMS warning light is illuminated. The warning lamp will stay on until air is added to the tire and the ignition is cycled off and on.

NOTE: This system cannot detect if all of the tires are underinflated, only if one tire is underinflated.

1 A tone ring and a wheel speed sensor on the rear of a Dodge Caravan.

2 The wiring from the wheel speed sensor should be inspected for damage.

3 To test a wheel speed sensor, disconnect the sensor connector to gain access to the terminals.

4 Pulling down the rubber seal reveals the connector.

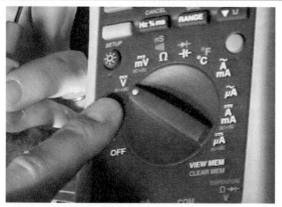

5 The ABS controller (computer) on this vehicle supplies a 2.5-volt reference signal to the wheel speed sensors.

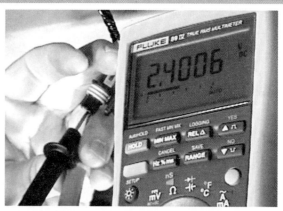

6 The meter reads about 2.4 volts, indicating that the ABS controller is supplying the voltage to the wheel speed sensor.

7 The test probes are touched to the terminals leading to the wheel speed sensor and the resistance is 1.1032 k ohms or 1,103.2 ohms.

8 The meter should (and does) read "OL," indicating that the wheel speed sensor and pigtail wiring is not shorted to ground.

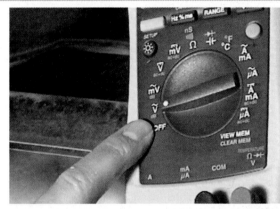

9 To measure the output of the wheel speed sensor, select AC volts on the digital multimeter.

10 Rotate the wheel and tire assembly by hand while observing the AC voltage output on the digital multimeter.

11 A good wheel speed sensor should be able to produce at least 100 mV (0.1 V) when the wheel is spun by hand.

12 After testing, carefully reinstall the wiring connector into the body and under the rubber grommet.

1. Antilock braking systems are designed to limit the amount of tire slip by pulsing the wheel brake on and off up to 20 times per second.

2. Steering control is possible during an ABS stop if the tires maintain traction with the road surface.

3. The three stages of ABS operation are pressure increase, pressure holding, and pressure reduction.

4. The heart of an antilock braking system is the electronic controller (computer). Wheel speed sensors produce an electrical frequency that is proportional to the speed of the wheel. If a wheel is slowing down too fast, the controller controls the pressure of the wheel brake through an electrohydraulic unit.

5. Both integral and nonintegral antilock braking systems control the rear wheels only, both front wheels individually and the rear as one unit (three-channel), or all four wheel brakes independently (four-channel).

REVIEW QUESTIONS

1. Describe how an antilock braking system (ABS) works.

2. List the three stages of ABS operation.

3. Explain how wheel speed sensors work.

4. Describe the difference between a three- and a four-channel system.

CHAPTER QUIZ

1. Technician A says that the ABS system may not result in shorter stopping distance compared to brakes without ABS. Technician B says that a pulsating brake pedal during normal braking is a characteristic feature of most ABS-equipped vehicles. Which technician is correct?
   a. Technician A only
   b. Technician B only
   c. Both Technicians A and B
   d. Neither Technician A nor B

2. The maximum traction between a tire and the road occurs when the tire is _____.
   a. Locked and skidding
   b. Rotating freely
   c. Slipping 10% to 20%
   d. Slipping 80% to 90%

3. Technician A says that ABS-equipped vehicles can stop quickly and without skidding on all road surfaces even if covered with ice. Technician B says that steering is possible during an ABS stop. Which technician is correct?
   a. Technician A only
   b. Technician B only
   c. Both Technicians A and B
   d. Neither Technician A nor B

4. A customer wanted the ABS checked because of tire chirp noise during hard braking. Technician A says that the speed sensors may be defective. Technician B says that tire chirp is normal during an ABS stop on dry pavement. Which technician is correct?
   a. Technician A only
   b. Technician B only
   c. Both Technicians A and B
   d. Neither Technician A nor B

5. Two technicians are discussing ABS wheel speed sensors. Technician A says that some ABS systems use a sensor located in the rear-axle pinion gear area. Technician B says that all ABS systems use a wheel speed sensor at each wheel. Which technician is correct?
   a. Technician A only
   b. Technician B only
   c. Both Technicians A and B
   d. Neither Technician A nor B

6. Technician A says that most ABS units are non-integral. Technician B says that the ABS is disabled (does not function) below about 5 mph (8 km/h). Which technician is correct?
   a. Technician A only
   b. Technician B only
   c. Both Technicians A and B
   d. Neither Technician A nor B

7. Which type of antilock braking system (ABS) requires the use of four wheel speed sensors?
   a. one channel
   b. two channel
   c. three channel
   d. four channel

8. Technician A says that ABS brakes are designed to allow the front wheel to be steered during heavy braking. Technician B says that the ABS dash warning lamp is amber. Which technician is correct?
   a. Technician A only
   b. Technician B only
   c. Both Technicians A and B
   d. Neither Technician A nor B

9. The faster a wheel rotates, the higher the frequency produced by a wheel speed sensor.
   a. True
   b. False

10. Technician A says that some wheel speed sensors are enclosed in a wheel bearing assembly. Technician B says that some wheel speed sensors are exposed to possible damage from road debris. Which technician is correct?
    a. Technician A only
    b. Technician B only
    c. Both Technicians A and B
    d. Neither Technician A nor B

After studying Chapter 19, the reader will be able to:

1. Prepare for Brakes (A5) ASE certification test content area "F" (Antilock Brake System Diagnosis and Repair).
2. Describe normal ABS dash lamp operation.
3. Discuss visual inspection of the various types and brands of ABS.
4. Explain how to retrieve trouble codes.
5. List the methods used to clear trouble codes.
6. Explain the various methods for bleeding ABS systems.
7. Discuss methods and tools needed to diagnose an ABS-equipped vehicle.

Amber ABS warning lamp 339

Breakout box (BOB) 348

Red brake warning lamp (RBWL) 339

ABS DIAGNOSTIC PROCEDURE

Customer concerns about a fault with the antilock braking system can be best handled by performing the following:

STEP 1 **Verify the customer concern.** This step is very important because often a problem with the base brakes is thought by the customer to be a fault with the antilock braking system. It is helpful for the owner to drive the vehicle with a service technician if the problem is not readily apparent.

STEP 2 **Perform a visual inspection.** If both the red and the amber brake warning lights are on, look for a fault in the hydraulic system, including leaks or faults at the following locations:
- Master cylinder
- Electrohydraulic control unit
- Flexible brake hoses
- Brake lines and fittings
- Calipers and/or wheel cylinders

STEP 3 **Check for stored diagnostic trouble codes (DTCs).** Use a scan tool or other necessary methods to retrieve diagnostic trouble codes. If found, follow the specified factory procedures to isolate and determine the cause.

STEP 4 **Complete the repair.** This step may involve replacing a hydraulic component. If so, then the hydraulic system should be bled using the factory-specified procedure. Clear all diagnostic trouble codes.

STEP 5 **Verify the repair.** Always test drive the vehicle under the same conditions that were needed to verify the problem to be sure that the cause has been corrected.

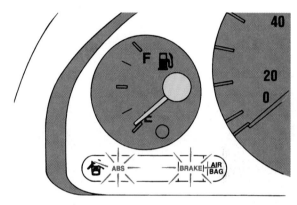

FIGURE 19–1 On most vehicles equipped with ABS, the ABS and the BRAKE warning lamp should come on as a bulb check when the ignition is first switched on.

BRAKE WARNING LAMP OPERATION

The first step in the visual diagnosis of an antilock braking system problem is to check the status of the brake warning lamps. ● **SEE FIGURE 19–1.**

RED BRAKE WARNING LAMP A **red brake warning lamp (RBWL)** warns of a possible dangerous failure in the base brakes, such as low brake fluid level or low pressure in half of the hydraulic system. The red brake warning lamp will also light if the parking brake is applied and may light due to an ABS failure, such as low brake pressure on an integral system.

AMBER ABS WARNING LAMP The **amber ABS warning lamp** usually comes on after a start during the initialization or start-up self-test sequence. The exact time the amber lamp remains on after the ignition is turned on varies with the vehicle and the ABS design.

FIGURE 19–2 A thorough visual inspection should include carefully inspecting around the electrohydraulic unit for signs of obvious problems or the installation of aftermarket devices such as alarm systems.

THOROUGH VISUAL INSPECTION

Many ABS-related problems can be diagnosed quickly if all the basics are carefully inspected. ● **SEE FIGURE 19–2**.

A thorough visual inspection should include the following items:

Brake fluid level	Check the conditions and level in the reservoir.
Brake fluid leaks	Check for cracks in flexible lines or other physical damage.
Fuses and fusible links	Check all ABS-related fuses.
Wiring and connections	Check all wiring, especially wheel speed sensor leads, for damage.
Wheel speed sensors	Check that the sensor ring teeth are not damaged. Clean debris from the sensor if possible.

NOTE: Most wheel speed sensors are magnetic and therefore can attract and hold metallic particles. Be sure to remove any metallic debris from around the magnetic wheel speed sensor.

Base brake components	All base brake components, such as disc brake calipers, drum brake wheel cylinders, and related components, must be in proper working condition.
Parking brake	Check that the parking brake is correctly adjusted and fully released.
Wheel bearings	All wheel bearings must be free of defects and adjusted properly.
Wheels and tires	Check for correct size, proper inflation, and legal tread depth.

 TECH TIP

Quick and Easy Wheel Speed Sensor Diagnosis

A fault in a wheel speed sensor (WSS) is a common ABS problem. A quick and easy test that works on most Bosch ABS systems (and perhaps others) involves the following steps:

STEP 1 Hoist the vehicle safely.

STEP 2 Turn the ignition on (engine off).

STEP 3 Spin a tire by hand as fast as possible.

STEP 4 The ABS amber warning light should come on, indicating that a speed was detected but not by all the wheel speed sensors.

STEP 5 Turn the ignition off to reset the ABS warning light.

STEP 6 Repeat the test on each of the remaining wheels.

If any wheel fails to turn on the ABS light, carefully inspect the wheel speed sensor for proper resistance and the tone ring and wiring. If the ABS light is on all the time and does not reset when the ignition is turned off, the problem is not caused by a wheel speed sensor.

A test drive is a very important diagnostic procedure. Many ABS systems and diagnostic trouble codes (DTCs) will not set unless the vehicle is moving. Often, the driver has noticed something like the self-test while driving and believed it to be a fault in the system.

NOTE: Some ABS units, such as the Delphi VI, will cause the brake pedal to move up and down slightly during cycling of the valves during the self-test. Each system has unique features. The service technician will have to learn to avoid attempting to repair a problem that is not a fault of the system.

Before driving, start the engine and observe the red and amber brake warning lamps. If the red brake warning lamp is on, the base brakes may not be functioning correctly. Do not drive the vehicle until the base brakes are restored to proper operation.

?   FREQUENTLY ASKED QUESTION

What's That Noise and Vibration?

Many vehicle owners and service technicians have been disturbed to hear and feel an occasional groaning noise. It is usually heard and felt through the vehicle after first being started and driven. Because it occurs when first being driven in forward or reverse, many technicians have blamed the transmission or related driveline components. This is commonly heard on many ABS vehicles as part of a system check. As soon as the ABS controller senses speed from the wheel speed sensors after an ignition cycles on, the controller will run the pump either every time or whenever the accumulator pressure is below a certain level. This can occur while the vehicle is being backed out of a driveway or being driven forward because wheel sensors can only detect speed—not direction. Before serious and major repairs are attempted to "cure" a noise, make sure that it is not the normal ABS self-test activation sequence of events.

General Motors ABS Summary Guide

Type of ABS System	Code Clearing Procedure	Scan Tool* Code Retrieval
Teves IV Nonintegral	Yes	Yes
Bosch 2U Nonintegral	Yes	Yes
Delphi (Delco) VI	Yes	Yes
Bosch 2S	Yes	Yes
Delco Powermaster III	Yes	Yes
Kelsey-Hayes RWAL	Yes or disconnect the ABS fuse	Yes or flash codes
Kelsey-Hayes 4WAL	Yes	Yes

*A jumper key can be used for some systems. Not all scan tools can perform all functions.

Ford ABS Summary Guide

Type of ABS System	Code Clearing Procedure	Scan Tool* Code Retrieval
Teves IV Nonintegral	Drive the vehicle after the repair.	Yes
Kelsey-Hayes RABS	Drive the vehicle after the repair.	Flash codes
Teves 4WABS	Drive the vehicle after the repair.	Yes

*A jumper wire can be used on some systems. Not all scan tools can perform all functions.

NOTE: Some systems are diagnosed by "antilock" and "brake" warning lamps, vehicle symptoms, and the use of a breakout box.

Chrysler ABS Summary Guide

Type of ABS System	Code Clearing Procedure	Scan Tool* Code Retrieval
Bendix 6 Nonintegral	Yes or disconnect the battery	Yes
Bosch MMC	Yes	Yes
Bosch 2U Nonintegral	No codes available on this system	No codes available on this system
Teves Mark IV	Yes	Yes
Kelsey-Hayes RWAL	Disconnect the battery	Flash codes
Kelsey-Hayes 4WAL	Yes	Yes

*A jumper wire can be used on some systems. Not all scan tools can perform all functions.

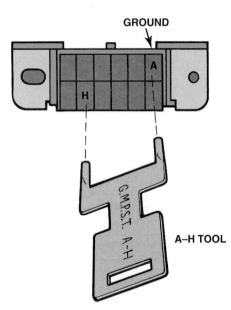

FIGURE 19–3 General Motors diagnostic connector. Flash codes are available by using a jumper wire to ground (terminal A) to terminal H. This connector is located under the dash near the steering column on most General Motors vehicles.

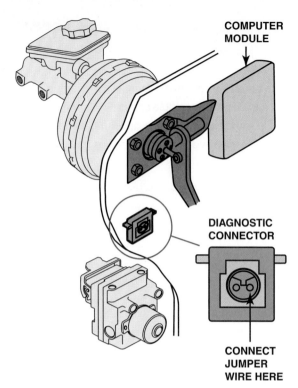

FIGURE 19–4 Connecting a jumper wire from the diagnostic connector to ground. The exact location of this diagnostic connector varies with the exact vehicle model and year.

RETRIEVING DIAGNOSTIC TROUBLE CODES

After performing a thorough visual inspection and after verifying the customer's complaint, retrieve any stored ABS-related diagnostic trouble codes (DTCs). The exact procedure varies with the type of ABS and with the make, model, and year of the vehicle.

Always consult factory service information for the vehicle being diagnosed. Some systems can only display flash codes (flashing ABS or brake lamp in sequence), whereas other systems can perform self-diagnosis and give all information to the technician through a scan tool.

NOTE: With some early antilock braking systems, the diagnostic trouble code is lost if the ignition is turned "off" before grounding the diagnostic connector.

KELSEY-HAYES ANTILOCK (NONINTEGRAL)

The Kelsey-Hayes rear-wheel antilock uses two solenoids and valves to control the rear-wheel brakes. Kelsey-Hayes four-wheel antilock uses the computer to pulse the valves rather than turning them on or off. The pulsing is called pulse-width modulated (PWM) and the valve is called a PWM valve.

RETRIEVING DIAGNOSTIC TROUBLE CODES GM trucks' (RWAL) DTCs are retrieved by flash codes or scan data through the use of a scan tool or connect H to A at the data link connector (DLC). ● **SEE FIGURE 19–3**.

NOTE: Be sure that the brake warning lamp is on before trying to retrieve DTCs. If the lamp is not on, a false code 9 could be set.

Ford RABS DTCs are retrieved by jumper lead flash codes only. ● **SEE FIGURE 19–4**.

Dodge light truck DTCs are retrieved by ground diagnostic connections. ● **SEE FIGURE 19–5**.

NOTE: If the ignition is turned off, the failure code will be lost unless it is a hard code that will be present when the ignition is turned back on.

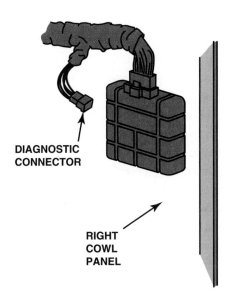

**DIAGNOSTIC
CONNECTOR**

**RIGHT
COWL
PANEL**

FIGURE 19–5 Chrysler diagnostic connector location varies with the model and year.

Kelsey-Hayes RWAL ABS Diagnostic Trouble Codes

Code	Description
2	Open isolation valve solenoid circuit or malfunctioning EBCM/VCM
3	Open dump valve solenoid circuit or malfunctioning EBCM/VCM
4	Grounded valve reset switch circuit
5	Excessive actuations of dump valve during antilock braking
6	Erratic speed signal
7	Shorted isolation valve circuit or faulty EBCM/VCM
8	Shorted dump valve circuit or faulty EBCM/VCM
9	Open or grounded circuit to vehicle speed sensor
10	Brake switch circuit
12 to 17	Computer malfunction

NOTE: A scan tool may or may not be able to retrieve or display diagnostic trouble codes. Check with the technical literature for the specific vehicle being scanned.

 REAL WORLD FIX

RWAL Diagnosis

The owner of an S-10 pickup truck complained that the red brake warning lamp on the dash remained on even when the parking brake was released. The problem could be one of the following:

1. A serious hydraulic problem
2. Low brake fluid
3. A stuck or defective parking brake switch
4. If the brake lamp is dim, RWAL trouble is indicated.

The technician found that the brake lamp was on dimly, indicating that an antilock braking problem was detected. The first step in diagnosing an antilock braking problem with a dash lamp on is to check for stored trouble codes. The technician used a jumper between terminals A and H on the DLC (ALCL), and four flashes of the brake lamp indicated a code 4.

Checking a service manual, code 4 was found to be a grounded switch inside the hydraulic control unit. The hardest part about the repair was getting access to, and the replacement of, the defective (electrically grounded) switch. After bleeding the system and a thorough test drive, the lamp sequence and RWAL functioned correctly.

Kelsey-Hayes 4WAL Diagnostic Trouble Codes

Code	Description
12	System normal (2WD applications)
13	System normal—brake applied (2WD applications)
14	System normal (4WD/AWD applications)
15	System normal—brake applied (4WD/AWD applications)
21 RF	Speed sensor circuit open
25 LF	
31 RR	
35 LR	
35	VSS circuit open
22 RF	Missing speed sensor signal
26 LF	
32 RR	
36 LR	
36	Missing VSS signal
23 RF	Erratic speed sensor signal
27 LF	
33 RR	
37 LR	
37	Erratic VSS signal
28	Simultaneous dropout of front-wheel speed sensors
29	Simultaneous dropout of all speed sensors
35	Vehicle speed sensor circuit open
36	Missing LR or vehicle speed sensor signal
37	Erratic LR or vehicle speed sensor signal
38	Wheel speed error
41 to 66	Malfunctioning BPMV/EHCU
67	Open motor circuit or shorted EBCM output
68	Locked motor or shorted motor circuit
71 to 74	Memory failure
81	Open or shorted brake switch circuit
86	Shorted ABS warning lamp
88	Shorted red brake warning lamp (RBWL)

BOSCH 2 ABS (NONINTEGRAL)

The Bosch 2U/2S ABS is used on many domestic and imported brands of vehicles.

RETRIEVING DIAGNOSTIC TROUBLE CODES
On General Motors vehicles, DTCs can be retrieved by connecting A to H at the data link connector (DLC). On most Bosch 2 systems, a scan tool can and should be used if available to retrieve DTC.

REAL WORLD FIX

The Nervous Taurus

A customer complained that, sometimes during normal braking, the ABS would be activated just before coming to a stop. However, the ABS light would not come on. The service technician was able to duplicate the condition and there were no DTCs stored. Using a scan tool to monitor the wheel speed sensors, the technician discovered that the left front wheel speed was slightly different than the others. A thorough visual inspection revealed that the tone wheel (sensor ring) was cracked. This crack created a different wheel speed signal to the ABS controller than the other wheels and the controller activated the ABS as it would normally—that was why there were no DTCs.

Other things that could have caused this problem, which is often called "false modulation," include a bent wheel, mismatched tire sizes, or metal debris around the sensor.

Bosch 2U/2S ABS Diagnostic Trouble Codes

Code	Description
12	Diagnostic system operational
21 RF	Wheel speed sensor fault
25 LF	
32 RR	
35 LR	
35	Rear-axle speed sensor fault
22 RF	Toothed wheel frequency error
26 LF	
32 RR	
36 LR	
36	Rear-axle toothed wheel frequency error
41 RF	Valve solenoid fault
45 LF	
55	Rear valve solenoid fault
61	Pump motor or motor relay fault
63	Solenoid valve relay fault
71	Electronic brake control module (EBCM) fault
72	Serial data link fault
74	Low voltage
75	Lateral acceleration sensor fault
76	Lateral acceleration sensor fault

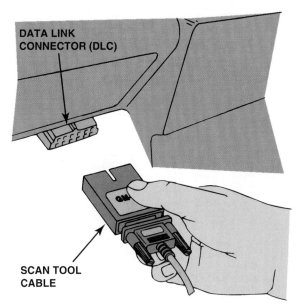

DATA LINK
CONNECTOR (DLC)

SCAN TOOL
CABLE

FIGURE 19–6 A scan tool is the recommended method to use to access General Motors Teves Mark IV systems.

TEVES MARK IV

The Teves Mark IV is a nonintegral (remote) ABS system.

RETRIEVING DIAGNOSTIC TROUBLE CODES Trouble codes are accessed only by a bidirectional scan tool connected to the data link connector (DLC). ● **SEE FIGURE 19–6.**

CLEARING DIAGNOSTIC TROUBLE CODES A scan tool is required to clear DTCs on some vehicles. Driving the vehicle over 20 mph (32 km/h) will clear the codes on some vehicles. Disconnecting the battery will also clear the codes but will cause other "keep-alive" functions of the vehicle to be lost.

DELPHI (DELCO) ABS-VI (NONINTEGRAL)

The Delphi (Delco) ABS-VI is unique from all other antilock systems because it uses motor-driven ball screws and pistons for brake pressure to reduce, hold, and apply. ● **SEE FIGURE 19–7.**

RETRIEVING DIAGNOSTIC CODES The Delphi (Delco) VI antilock braking system has extensive self-diagnostic capability. Access to this vast amount of information requires the use of a scan tool designed to interface (work) with the Delphi VI system.

Teves Mark IV ABS Diagnostic Trouble Codes

Code	Description
21	RF speed sensor circuit open
22	RF speed sensor signal erratic
23	RF wheel speed is 0 mph
25	LF speed sensor circuit open
26	LF speed sensor signal erratic
27	LF wheel speed is 0 mph
31	RR speed sensor circuit open
32	RR speed sensor signal erratic
33	RR wheel speed is 0 mph
35	LR speed sensor circuit open
36	LR speed sensor signal erratic
37	LR wheel speed is 0 mph
41	RF inlet valve circuit
42	RF outlet valve circuit
43	RF speed sensor noisy
45	LF inlet valve circuit
46	LF outlet valve circuit
47	LF speed sensor noisy
51	RR inlet valve circuit
52	RR outlet valve circuit
53	RR speed sensor noisy
55	LR inlet valve circuit
56	LR outlet valve circuit
57	LR speed sensor noisy
61	Pump motor test fault
62	Pump motor fault in ABS stop
71	EBCM check sum error
72	TCC/antilock braking switch circuit
73	Fluid level switch circuit

Delphi (Delco) ABS-VI Diagnostic Trouble Codes

Code	Description
11	ABS lamp open or shorted to ground
13	ABS lamp circuit shorted to battery
14	Enable relay contacts open, fuse open
15	Enable relay contacts shorted to battery
16	Enable relay coil circuit open
17	Enable relay coil shorted to ground
18	Enable relay coil shorted to B1 or 0 ohms
21	Left-front wheel speed
23	Left-rear wheel speed
24	Right-rear wheel speed
25	Excessive left-front wheel acceleration

(continued)

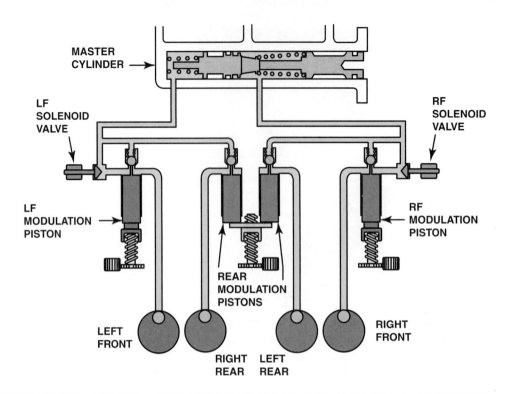

FIGURE 19–7 The Delphi (Delco) VI attaches to the side of the master cylinder and connects hydraulically through transfer tube assemblies.

MASTER CYLINDER

LF SOLENOID VALVE

RF SOLENOID VALVE

LF MODULATION PISTON

RF MODULATION PISTON

REAR MODULATION PISTONS

LEFT FRONT

RIGHT REAR

LEFT REAR

RIGHT FRONT

Code	Description
26	Excessive right-front wheel acceleration
27	Excessive left-rear wheel acceleration
28	Excessive right-rear wheel acceleration
31	Two-wheel speed sensors open
36	System voltage is low
37	System voltage is high
38	Left-front EMB will not hold motor
41	Right-front EMB will not hold motor
42	Rear-axle ESB will not hold motor
44	Left-front EMB will not release motor, gears frozen
45	Right-front EMB will not release motor, gears frozen
46	Rear-axle ESB will not release motor, gears frozen
47	Left-front nut failure (motor free-spins)
48	Right-front nut failure (motor free-spins)
51	Rear-axle nut failure (motor free-spins)
52	Left-front channel in release too long
53	Right-front channel in release too long
54	Rear axle in release too long
55	Motor driver interface (MDI) fault detected
56	Left-front motor circuit open
57	Left-front motor circuit shorted to ground
58	Left-front motor circuit shorted to battery
61	Right-front motor circuit open
62	Right-front motor circuit shorted to ground
63	Right-front motor circuit shorted to battery
64	Rear-axle motor circuit open
65	Rear-axle motor circuit shorted to ground

Code	Description
66	Rear-axle motor circuit shorted to battery
67	Left-front EMB release circuit open or shorted to ground
68	Left-front EMB release circuit shorted to battery or driver open
71	Right-front EMB release circuit open or shorted to ground
72	Right-front EMB release circuit shorted to battery or driver open
76	Left-front solenoid circuit open or shorted to battery
77	Left-front solenoid circuit shorted to ground or driver open
78	Right-front solenoid circuit open or shorted to battery
81	Right-front solenoid circuit shorted to battery or driver open
82	Calibration memory failure
86	ABS controller turned "on"; red brake telltale circuit fault
87	Red brake telltale circuit open
88	Red brake telltale circuit shorted to battery or driver open
91	Open brake switch contacts (deceleration detected)
92	Open brake switch contacts
93	Test 91 or 92 failed last or current ignition cycle
94	Brake switch contacts shorted
95	Brake switch circuit open
96	Brake lamps open, brake lamp ground open, center high-mounted stop lamp open during four-way flasher operations

The Mystery ABS Amber Warning Light

The owner of an Acura Legend complained to a service technician that the ABS warning light would come on but only while driving down from a parking garage. When the driver turned off the ignition and restarted the engine, the ABS amber light was not on and did not come on again until the vehicle was again driven down the spiral parking garage ramp. The service technician used a scan tool and found that no DTCs had been stored.

NOTE: Some ABS systems will not retain a DTC unless the problem is currently present and the ABS amber warning light is on.

All of the brakes were in excellent condition, but the brake fluid level was down a little. After topping off the master cylinder with clean DOT 3 brake fluid, the vehicle was returned to the customer with the following information:

- The ABS amber warning light may have been triggered by the brake fluid level switch. While driving down the steep parking garage ramp, the brake fluid moved away from the fluid level sensor.

  NOTE: While the brake fluid level sensor normally would turn on the red brake warning light, in some systems it turns on the amber ABS light if the brake fluid falls below a certain level in the ABS reservoir.

- The difference in wheel speed between the outboard and the inboard wheels could have triggered a fault code for a wheel speed sensor during the drive down the spiral parking garage ramp.

Sometimes It Pays to Look at the Entire Vehicle

There are often strange electrical problems that can occur including false DTCs or intermittent operation of electrical sensors, ABS, accessories, or gauges. Sometimes the root of these problems is due to rust and corrosion after a vehicle is involved in a flood. Here are some telltale signs that a vehicle may have been in a flood or in deep water.

- Mud, silt, or caked dust under the dash and inside the doors
- Corroded electrical connectors at the computer, fuse box, or ABS controller (computer)
- Visible water line in the doors or behind panels
- Rust in abnormal places such as seat springs or brackets behind the dash
- Moisture in lenses
- Musty smell and/or strong air freshener smell
- Powdery corrosion on aluminum parts such as intake manifold and inside the throttle bore
- Rust or moisture inside electrical switches or relays
- Areas that are normally dusty such as an ashtray or glove box are very clean

FIGURE 19–8 A breakout box is being used to diagnose an ABS problem. The controller (computer) is located in the trunk of this vehicle, and a digital multimeter is being used to measure resistance and voltage at various points in the system, following the service manual procedure.

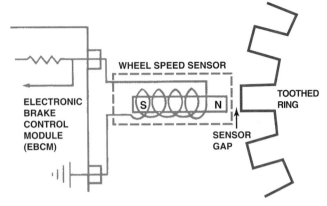

FIGURE 19–9 Typical wheel speed sensor. When a tooth on the sensor ring is close to the sensor, the strength of the magnetic field is stronger because the metal of the tooth conducts magnetic lines of force better than air. When the tooth moves away, the magnetic field strength is reduced. It is this changing magnetic field strength that produces the changing voltage. Frequency of the signal is determined by the speed of the rotating sensor.

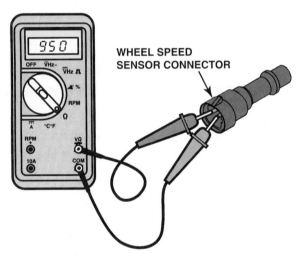

FIGURE 19–10 Measuring the resistance of a wheel speed sensor.

WHEEL SPEED SENSOR DIAGNOSIS

Wheel speed sensor (WSS) circuits are often the cause of many ABS problems. ● **SEE FIGURE 19–8**. These components may suffer from physical damage, buildup of metallic debris on the sensor tip, corrosion, poor electrical connections, and damaged wiring.

Test a WSS by measuring its output voltage and circuit continuity. A **breakout box (BOB)** cable connects to the ABS harness near the ABS module. All WSS resistance checks, including the wiring to the sensors, can be measured at one location. ● **SEE FIGURE 19–9**.

Follow the equipment manufacturer's instructions for connecting the breakout box to the vehicle, and for probing the appropriate pins on the breakout box.

RESISTANCE MEASUREMENT The resistors of most WSS range from 800 Ω to 1,400 Ω. Therefore, a reading of about 1,000 ohms or 1 KΩ would indicate proper sensor coil resistance. ● **SEE FIGURE 19–10**.

CHECKING FOR SHORT-TO-GROUND Connect either lead of the ohmmeter to one of the WSS wires and the other to a good, clean chassis ground. The resistance should be infinity (OL). If a low resistance reading is obtained, the sensor or sensor wiring is shorted-to-ground and must be replaced.

AC VOLTAGE CHECK Connect a digital meter to the WSS terminals or input to the controller in the breakout box and set the meter to read AC volts. Rotate the wheel by hand at a rate of one revolution per second. A good WSS should produce voltage of at least 0.1 volt (100 mV). A sensor voltage of lower than 0.1 volt (100 mV) may be caused by three things.

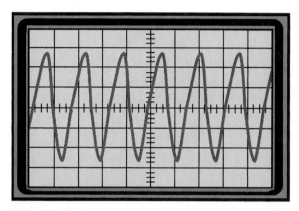

FIGURE 19–11 A scope can be used to check for proper operation of a wheel speed sensor.

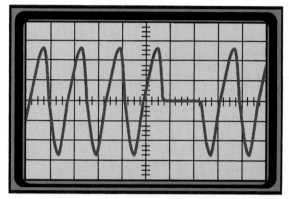

FIGURE 19–12 A broken tooth on a wheel speed sensor tone ring shows on the scope trace as a missing wave.

1. Excessive clearance between the sensor and the tone ring.

2. Buildup of debris on the end of the sensor. Most wheel speed sensors are magnetic and can attract metallic particles, which can affect the operation of the sensor.

3. Excessive resistance in the sensor or sensor wiring, which can also cause a weak signal to be produced by the WSS.

SCOPE TESTING   Attach the scope leads to the sensor terminals or to the input connector on the breakout box. Rotate the wheel by hand or by using engine power with the vehicle safely hoisted with all four wheels off the ground.

- A good WSS should produce an alternating current (AC) sine wave signal that increases in frequency and amplitude with increasing wheel speed. ● **SEE FIGURE 19–11**.

- Damaged or missing teeth on the tone ring will cause flat spots or gaps in the sine wave pattern. ● **SEE FIGURE 19–12**.

- A bent axle or hub will produce a wavelike pattern that fluctuates as the strength of the sensor signal changes with each revolution.

SCAN TOOL TESTING   A scan tool can be used to check for the proper operation of the WSS. As an assistant drives the vehicle, connect the scan tool and monitor the speed of all of the sensors. All of the sensors should indicate the same speed. If a sensor shows a slower or faster speed than the others, carefully check the tone ring for damage such as a crack.

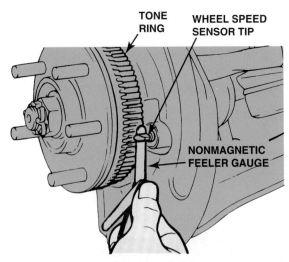

FIGURE 19–13 Use a nonmagnetic brass or plastic feeler gauge to check wheel speed sensor gap. A steel gauge would be attracted by the magnet in the sensor and would produce a drag on the gauge as it is moved between the sensor and the tone ring. This drag could be interpreted as a correct clearance reading.

WHEEL SPEED SENSOR ADJUSTMENT

Some ABS applications use adjustable wheel speed sensors. Most sensors adjust by first loosening a set screw, then inserting a nonmagnetic brass or plastic feeler gauge between the tip of the sensor and a high point on the tone ring. ● **SEE FIGURE 19–13**.

Adjust the position of the sensor so there is a slight drag on the feeler gauge, and then tighten the setscrew to lock the sensor in place.

When installing new sensors, look for a piece of paper or plastic on the tip end of the unit. This is more than a protective covering and must be left in place during installation. The paper or plastic is the precise thickness to guarantee a correct air gap between the tip of the sensor and the tone ring. Adjust the sensor so the tip just touches the tone ring and you can slip the paper or plastic out without ripping it. Tighten the setscrew and the air gap is properly set. ● **SEE FIGURE 19–14**.

Some manufacturers recommend leaving a paper covering in place. The motion of the tone ring removes it after the vehicle is driven for several miles.

DIGITAL WHEEL SPEED SENSOR DIAGNOSIS Test a digital WSS by first checking that battery voltage is available at the sensor with the key on, engine off. If the sensor does not

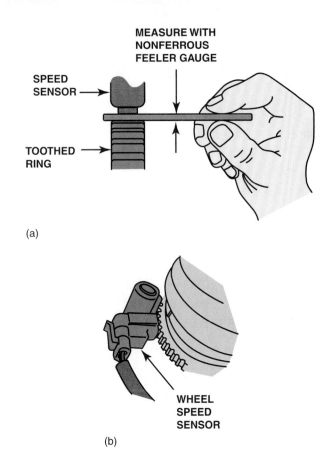

(a)

(b)

FIGURE 19–14 (a) Always use a nonferrous (brass or plastic) feeler (thickness) gauge when measuring the gap between the toothed ring and the wheel speed sensor. (b) Sometimes a sensor is equipped with a paper spacer that is the exact thickness of the spacing required between the toothed ring and the sensor. If equipped, the sensor is simply installed with the paper touching the toothed wheel. A typical gap ranges from 0.020 to 0.050 in. (0.5 to 1.3 mm).

have 12 volts, then the problem is most likely in the ABS controller or the wiring between the controller and the sensor.

If there are 12 volts at the sensor, measure the signal voltage. The voltage should switch from about 0.8V to about 1.9V as the wheel is rotated by hand.

 **TECH TIP**

Space Saver Spare Tire May Trigger Wheel Speed Fault Code

If a vehicle has been using a small space saver-type spare tire, then the difference in outside diameter may trigger a wheel speed sensor diagnostic trouble code (DTC) and turn on the amber ABS warning lamp. Try to find out from the customer if they had driven on a spare tire before replacing a wheel speed sensor based on a stored DTC.

HYDRAULIC ABS SERVICE

CHECK SERVICE INFORMATION Before doing any brake work on a vehicle equipped with antilock brakes, always consult the appropriate service information for the exact vehicle being serviced. For example, some manufacturers recommend discharging the hydraulic accumulator by depressing the brake pedal many times before opening bleeder valves. Many service checks require that a pressure gauge be installed in the system.

BLEEDING THE ELECTRONIC-HYDRAULIC ASSEMBLY

Air can easily get trapped in the ABS electronic-hydraulic (E-H) assembly whenever the hydraulic system is opened. Even though the master cylinder and all four wheel cylinders/calipers have been bled, sometimes the brake pedal will still feel spongy. Some E-H units can be bled through the use of a scan tool where the valves are pulsed in sequence by the electronic brake controller (computer). Some units are equipped with bleeder valves while others must be bled by loosening the brake lines. Bleeding the E-H unit also purges out the older brake fluid, which can cause rust and corrosion damage. Only DOT 3 brake fluid is specified for use in an antilock braking system. Always check the label on the brake fluid reservoir and/or service manual or owner's manual.

CAUTION: Some ABS units require that the brake pedal be depressed as many as 40 times to discharge brake fluid fully from the accumulator. Failure to discharge the accumulator fully can show that the brake fluid level is too low. If additional brake fluid is added, the fluid could overflow the reservoir during an ABS stop when the accumulator discharges brake fluid back into the reservoir.

MANUALLY BLEEDING ABS WHEEL BRAKES During routine brake service, attempt to keep the air from entering the hydraulic system by doing the following:

1. Do not allow the brake system to run dry. Use a brake pedal depressor or plug any open brake line to keep brake fluid from flowing out of the brake master cylinder reservoir.

2. Do not allow the master cylinder to run dry during the bleeding operation. Check the master cylinder reservoir often and keep it filled with fresh brake fluid from a sealed container.

3. Always bench bleed a replacement master cylinder to help prevent against introducing air into the hydraulic system.

FIGURE 19–15 Special bleed valve tools are often required when bleeding some ABS units such as the Kelsey-Hayes 4WAL system.

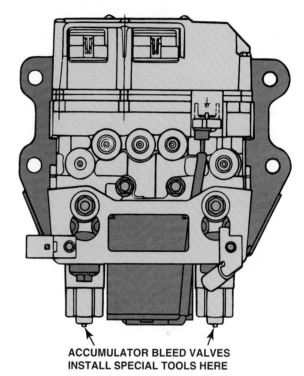

**ACCUMULATOR BLEED VALVES
INSTALL SPECIAL TOOLS HERE**

FIGURE 19–16 Two bleed valve tools are needed to bleed the Kelsey-Hayes 4WAL system, which attaches to the bleeder valves on the accumulator.

After depressing the unit as per manufacturer's recommended procedures, the brakes can be bled using the same procedure as for a vehicle without ABS. Air trapped in the ABS hydraulic unit may require that a scan tool be used to cycle the valves. ● **SEE FIGURES 19–15 AND 19–16.**

The bleeding procedure for vehicles equipped with antilock brakes is often different than vehicles without ABS. Consult the service information for the specified bleeding procedure and sequence.

SCAN TOOL BLEEDING To bleed the system using a scan tool use the following steps:

STEP 1 Check service information and determine the specified procedure to follow. This usually involves manually bleeding the wheel brakes before using a scan tool.

FIGURE 19–17 To perform an automated brake bleed procedure on an antilock braking system, first connect a factory or enhanced scan tool to the data link connector (DLC) located under the dash on this vehicle.

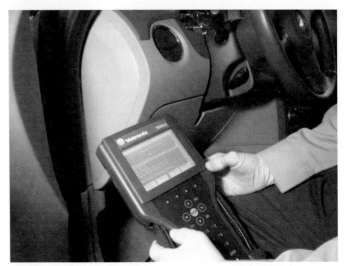

FIGURE 19–18 Access the menu that includes antilock brake system (ABS) functions.

HYDRAULIC ABS SERVICE (CONTINUED)

STEP 2   Use a factory scan tool or one that is capable of performing an automated bleed procedure.

STEP 3   Connect the scan tool to the data link connector (DLC). This connector can be located under the dash or in the center console or even covered by a panel. Check service information for the exact location of the DLC for the vehicle being serviced. ● **SEE FIGURE 19–17**.

STEP 4   Enter vehicle information as shown on the display of the scan tool and locate the antilock brake system (ABS) function area. ● **SEE FIGURE 19–18**.

STEP 5   Select ABS automated bleed from the ABS menu. The instructions on the scan tool could include several steps including manually bleeding the system, then allowing the scan tool to cycle the hydraulic ABS solenoid valves and then bleeding again. ● **SEE FIGURE 19–19**.

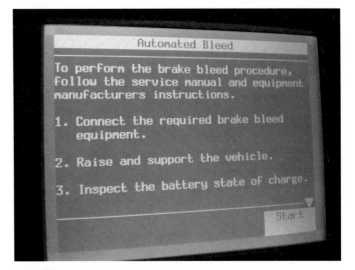

FIGURE 19–19 Scroll through the menus and select automated bleed procedure and follow the on-screen instructions.

 **TECH TIP**

ABS Bleeding Made Easy

To avoid having to bleed the hydraulic unit, use a brake pedal depressor during brake service to avoid losing brake fluid. This simple precaution keeps air from getting into the hard-to-bleed passages of the hydraulic unit.

ABS SAFETY PRECAUTIONS

1. Avoid mounting the antenna for the transmitting device near the ABS control unit. Transmitting devices include cellular (cell) telephones, citizen-band radios, and so on.

2. Avoid mounting tires of different diameter than that of the original tires. Different size tires generate different wheel speed sensor frequencies, which may not be usable by the ABS controller.

3. Never open a bleeder valve or loosen a hydraulic line while the ABS is pressurized. The accumulator must be depressurized according to the manufacturer's recommended procedures.

4. If arc welding on a vehicle, disconnect all computers (electronic control modules) to avoid possible damage due to voltage spikes.

5. Do not pry against or hit the wheel speed sensor ring.

SUMMARY

1. ABS diagnosis starts with checking the status of both the red brake warning lamp and the amber ABS warning lamp.

2. The second step in diagnosis of an ABS problem is to perform a thorough visual inspection.

3. The third step in diagnosis of an ABS problem is to test drive the vehicle and verify the fault.

4. Always consult the factory service information for the specific vehicle being serviced for the proper procedure to use to retrieve and clear diagnostic trouble codes (DTCs).

5. A breakout box is used with a digital multimeter to diagnose electrical ABS components.

6. Hydraulic service on most integral ABS units requires that the brake pedal be depressed as many as 40 times with the ignition key "off" to depressurize the hydraulic system.

REVIEW QUESTIONS

1. Describe the proper operation of the red and amber brake warning lamps.

2. List the items that should be checked as part of a thorough visual inspection.

3. Explain how to retrieve a diagnostic trouble code from a General Motors vehicle equipped with Kelsey-Hayes RWAL ABS.

4. Describe how to use a breakout box to check for proper wheel speed sensor operation.

CHAPTER QUIZ

1. The red brake warning lamp is on and the amber ABS lamp is off. Technician A says that a fault is possible in the base brake system. Technician B says that the red brake warning lamp can be turned on by a low brake fluid level in the master cylinder. Which technician is correct?
   a. Technician A only
   b. Technician B only
   c. Both Technicians A and B
   d. Neither Technician A nor B

2. Two technicians are discussing magneto-type wheel speed sensors. Technician A says that wheel speed sensors are magnetic. Technician B says that the toothed sensor ring is magnetic. Which technician is correct?
   a. Technician A only
   b. Technician B only
   c. Both Technicians A and B
   d. Neither Technician A nor B

3. Technician A says that using the space-saving small spare tire may trigger an ABS amber warning lamp. Technician B says the use of the small spare tire may trigger the red brake warning lamp. Which technician is correct?
   a. Technician A only
   b. Technician B only
   c. Both Technicians A and B
   d. Neither Technician A nor B

4. Technician A says that, with some antilock braking systems, the diagnostic trouble code may be lost if the ignition is turned off before retrieving the code. Technician B says that some antilock braking systems require that a terminal be grounded to cause the amber ABS warning lamp to flash diagnostic trouble codes. Which technician is correct?
   a. Technician A only
   b. Technician B only
   c. Both Technicians A and B
   d. Neither Technician A nor B

5. Technician A says that a scan tool may be required to retrieve data and diagnostic trouble codes from some antilock braking systems. Technician B says that a jumper wire can be used to retrieve diagnostic trouble codes on some antilock braking systems. Which technician is correct?
   a. Technician A only
   b. Technician B only
   c. Both Technicians A and B
   d. Neither Technician A nor B

6. Technician A says that a breakout box is sometimes required to diagnose an antilock braking system. Technician B says that a breakout box requires the use of a digital multimeter. Which technician is correct?
   a. Technician A only
   b. Technician B only
   c. Both Technicians A and B
   d. Neither Technician A nor B

7. Technician A says that a noise or vibration may be sensed by the driver when the ABS performs a self test. Technician B says that the ABS fuse may have to be removed to erase some ABS diagnostic codes if a scan tool is not used. Which technician is correct?
   a. Technician A only
   b. Technician B only
   c. Both Technicians A and B
   d. Neither Technician A nor B

8. The ABS computer uses what signal characteristic from a wheel speed sensor?
   a. Voltage
   b. Frequency
   c. Resistance
   d. Electromagnetic

9. Most wheel speed sensors should measure how much resistance?
   a. 800 to 1,400 ohms
   b. 100 to 300 ohms
   c. 1 to 3 ohms
   d. 0.1 to 1 ohm

10. Technician A says that the ABS electrohydraulic unit can be bled using bleeder screws and the manual method. Technician B says that a scan tool is often required to bleed the ABS electrohydraulic unit. Which technician is correct?
    a. Technician A only
    b. Technician B only
    c. Both Technicians A and B
    d. Neither Technician A nor B

chapter 20

ELECTRONIC STABILITY CONTROL SYSTEMS

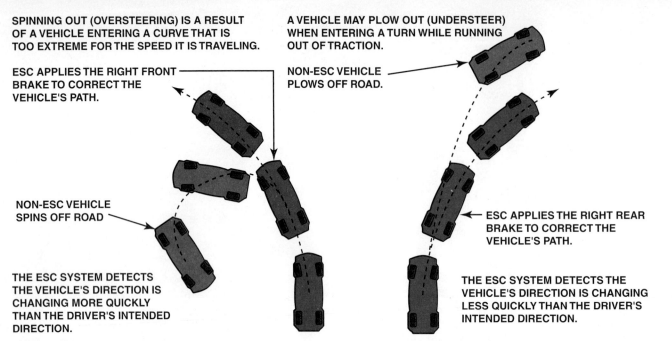

SPINNING OUT (OVERSTEERING) IS A RESULT OF A VEHICLE ENTERING A CURVE THAT IS TOO EXTREME FOR THE SPEED IT IS TRAVELING.

A VEHICLE MAY PLOW OUT (UNDERSTEER) WHEN ENTERING A TURN WHILE RUNNING OUT OF TRACTION.

ESC APPLIES THE RIGHT FRONT BRAKE TO CORRECT THE VEHICLE'S PATH.

NON-ESC VEHICLE PLOWS OFF ROAD.

NON-ESC VEHICLE SPINS OFF ROAD

ESC APPLIES THE RIGHT REAR BRAKE TO CORRECT THE VEHICLE'S PATH.

THE ESC SYSTEM DETECTS THE VEHICLE'S DIRECTION IS CHANGING MORE QUICKLY THAN THE DRIVER'S INTENDED DIRECTION.

THE ESC SYSTEM DETECTS THE VEHICLE'S DIRECTION IS CHANGING LESS QUICKLY THAN THE DRIVER'S INTENDED DIRECTION.

FIGURE 20–1 The electronic stability control (ESC) system applies individual wheel brakes to keep the vehicle under control of the driver.

THE NEED FOR ELECTRONIC STABILITY CONTROL

PURPOSE AND FUNCTION Electronic stability control **(ESC)** is a system designed to help drivers to maintain control of their vehicles in situations where the vehicle is beginning to lose control. Keeping the vehicle on the road prevents run-off-road crashes, which are the conditions that lead to most single-vehicle accidents and rollovers.

SYSTEM REQUIREMENTS The ESC is defined as a system that has all of the following features:

1. Helps vehicle directional stability by applying and adjusting individual wheel brakes to help bring the vehicle back to the intended direction.

2. Uses sensors to determine when the vehicle is not under control.

3. Uses a steering wheel position sensor to determine the intended direction of the driver.

4. Operates at all vehicle speeds, except at low speeds where loss of control is unlikely.

The electronic stability control (ESC) system applies individual wheel brakes to bring the vehicle under control if either of the following conditions occur:

■ **Oversteering**—In this condition, the rear of the vehicle tends to move outward or breaks loose, resulting in the vehicle spinning out of control. This condition is also called *loose*. If the condition is detected during a left turn,

the ESC system would apply the right front brake to bring the vehicle back under control.

■ **Understeering**—In this condition, the front of the vehicle tends to continue straight ahead when turning, a condition that is also called *plowing* or *tight*. If this condition is detected during a right turn, the ESC system would apply the right rear wheel brake to bring the vehicle back under control. ● **SEE FIGURE 20–1.**

NOTE: When the brakes are applied during these corrections, a thumping sound and vibration may be sensed.

TELLTALE LAMP. The ESC lamp, called a **telltale light,** is required to remain on for as long as the malfunction exists, whenever the ignition is in "On" ("Run") position. The ESC malfunction telltale will flash to indicate when the ESC system is operating to help restore vehicle stability.

ESC SWITCH. Some, but not all, vehicle manufacturers install a switch to temporarily disable or limit the ESC functions. This allows the driver to disengage ESC or limit the operation when the full ESC might not be needed such as:

■ When a vehicle is stuck in sand/gravel

■ When the vehicle is being operated on a racetrack for maximum performance

The electronic stability control system is turned back on when the ignition is turned off and then back on and is in the default position.

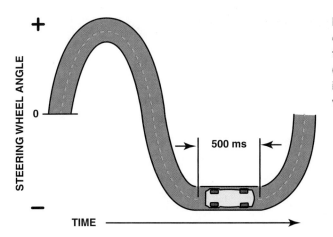

FIGURE 20–2 The sine with dwell test is designed to test the electronic stability control (ESC) system to determine if the system can keep the vehicle under control.

FEDERAL MOTOR VEHICLE SAFETY STANDARD (FMVSS) NO. 126

Federal Motor Vehicle Safety Standard (FMVSS) No. 126 (June 26, 2008), Electronic Stability Control Systems, requires that all passenger cars, multipurpose passenger vehicles, trucks, and buses that have a gross vehicle weight rating (GVWR) of 10,000 pounds (4,536 kg) or less to be equipped with an electronic stability control (ESC) system by September 1, 2011 (2012 model year vehicles).

The ESC system must meet the following requirements:

1. The ESC system must be able to apply all four brakes individually. This means that the vehicle must be equipped with a four-channel antilock braking system (ABS) which uses a wheel speed sensor at each wheel.

2. The ESC must be programmed to work during all phases of driving including acceleration, coasting, and deceleration (including braking).

3. The ESC system must work when the antilock brake system (ABS) or Traction Control is activated.

SINE WITH DWELL TEST

The standardized test used to determine if an electronic stability control system functions okay is called the **sine with dwell (SWD) test.** A vehicle is driven at 50 mph (80 km/h) and driven on a curved course that looks like a sine wave or the letter "S" on its side. Then the vehicle is held in a straight-ahead position for 0.5 second (500 milliseconds) and before being steered back onto the curved section of the test. ● SEE FIGURE 20–2.

The quick changes involved in this test are designed to upset the chassis of the vehicle and cause the electronic stability control system to act to keep the vehicle under control during the entire test.

 FREQUENTLY ASKED QUESTION

Can a Vehicle with a Modified Suspension Pass the Test?

Yes, if the system is properly engineered. To be sure, check with the company offering a suspension test to verify that the vehicle will still be able to pass the sine with dwell (SWD) test. This ensures that any changes are within the range where the ESC system can control the vehicle during emergency maneuvers. ● SEE FIGURE 20–3.

FIGURE 20–3 Using a simulator is the most cost-effective way for vehicle and aftermarket suspension manufacturers to check that the vehicle is able to perform within the FMVSS No. 126 standard for vehicle stability.

NAMES OF VARIOUS ESC SYSTEMS

Stability control systems are offered under the following names:

- **Acura:** Vehicle Stability Assist (VSA)
- **Audi:** Electronic Stabilization Program (ESP)
- **BMW:** Dynamic Stability Control (DSC), including Dynamic Traction Control
- **Chrysler:** Electronic Stability Program (ESP)
- **Dodge:** Electronic Stability Program (ESP)
- **Ferrari:** Controllo Stabilita (CST)
- **Ford:** AdvanceTrac and Interactive Vehicle Dynamics (IVD)
- **General Motors:** StabiliTrak (except Corvette—Active Handling)
- **Hyundai:** Electronic Stability Program (ESP)
- **Honda:** Electronic Stability Control (ESC), Vehicle Stability Assist (VSA), and Electronic Stability Program (ESP)
- **Infiniti:** Vehicle Dynamic Control (VDC)
- **Jaguar:** Dynamic Stability Control (DSC)
- **Jeep:** Electronic Stability Program (ESP)
- **Kia:** Electronic Stability Program (ESP)
- **Land Rover:** Dynamic Stability Control (DSC)
- **Lexus:** Vehicle Dynamics Integrated Management (VDIM) with Vehicle Stability Control (VSC) and Traction Control (TRAC) systems
- **Lincoln:** Advance Trak
- **Maserati:** Maserati Stability Program (MSP)
- **Mazda:** Dynamic Stability Control (DSC)
- **Mercedes:** Electronic Stability Program (ESP)
- **Mercury:** AdvanceTrak
- **Mini Cooper:** Dynamic Stability Control (DSC)
- **Mitsubishi:** Active Skid and Traction Control MULTIMODE
- **Nissan:** Vehicle Dynamic Control (VDC)
- **Porsche:** Porsche Stability Management (PSM)
- **Rover:** Dynamic Stability Control (DSC)
- **Saab:** Electronic Stability Program (ESP)
- **Saturn:** StabiliTrak
- **Subaru:** Vehicle Dynamics Control Systems (VDCS)
- **Suzuki:** Electronic Stability Program (ESP)
- **Toyota:** Vehicle Dynamics Integrated Management (VDIM) with Vehicle Stability Control (VSC)
- **Volvo:** Dynamic Stability and Traction Control (DSTC)
- **VW:** Electronic Stability Program (ESP)

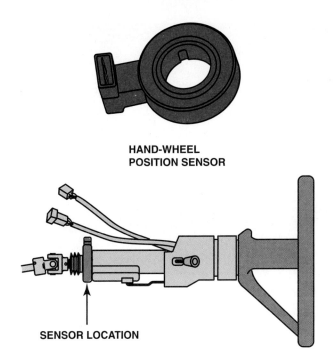

HAND-WHEEL
POSITION SENSOR

SENSOR LOCATION

FIGURE 20–4 The hand-wheel position sensor is usually located at the base of the steering column.

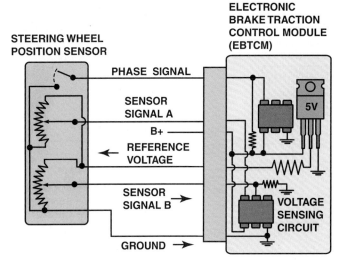

FIGURE 20–5 Hand-wheel (steering wheel) position sensor schematic.

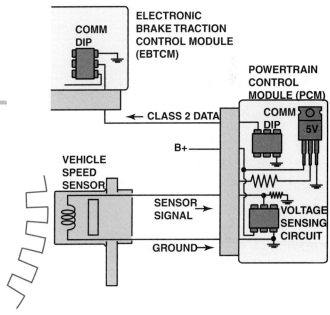

FIGURE 20–6 The VS sensor information is transmitted to the EBCM by Class 2 serial data.

ESC SENSORS

STEERING WHEEL POSITION SENSOR Depending on the vehicle, the **steering wheel position sensor** may also be called a **hand-wheel position sensor**. The function of this sensor is to provide the driver's intended direction with signals relating to steering wheel position, speed, and direction. ● **SEE FIGURES 20–4 AND 20–5.**

VEHICLE SPEED SENSOR The **vehicle speed (VS) sensor** is used by the **Electronic Brake Control Module (EBCM)** to help control the suspension system. The vehicle speed sensor is a magnetic sensor and generates an analog signal whose frequency increases as the speed increases. ● **SEE FIGURE 20–6.**

LATERAL ACCELERATION SENSOR The function of the **lateral acceleration sensor** is to provide the suspension control module with feedback regarding vehicle cornering forces. This type of sensor is also called a G-sensor, with the letter "G" representing the force of gravity. For example, when a vehicle enters a turn, the sensor provides information as to how hard the vehicle is cornering. This information is processed by the suspension control module to provide appropriate damping on the inboard and outboard dampers during cornering events.

This sensor can be either a stand-alone unit or combined with the yaw rate sensor.

Typically, the sensor is mounted in the passenger compartment:

- under a front seat
- in the center console
- on the package shelf

● **SEE FIGURE 20–7.**

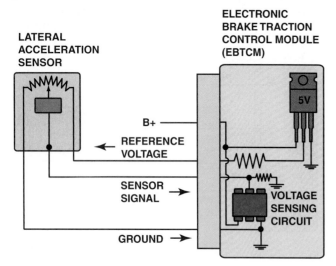

FIGURE 20–7 A schematic showing the lateral acceleration sensor and EBCM.

FIGURE 20–8 The lateral accelerometer sensor (G-sensor) is usually located under the center console.

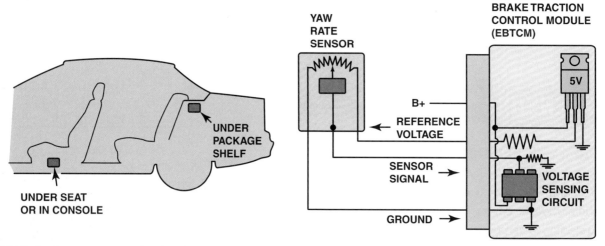

FIGURE 20–9 Yaw rate sensor showing the typical location and schematic.

ESC SENSORS (CONTINUED)

 TECH TIP

Quick and Easy Lateral Acceleration Sensor Test

Most factory scan tools will display the value of sensors, including the lateral acceleration sensor. However, the sensor value will read zero unless the vehicle is cornering. A quick and easy test of the sensor is to simply unbolt the sensor and rotate it 90 degrees with the key on engine off. ● SEE FIGURE 20–8. Now the sensor is measuring the force of gravity and should display 1.0 G on the scan tool. If the sensor does not read close to 1.0 G or reads zero all of the time, the sensor or the wiring is defective.

YAW RATE SENSOR The **yaw rate sensor** provides information to the suspension control module and the EBCM. This information is used to determine how far the vehicle has deviated from the driver's intended direction.

This sensor can be either a stand-alone unit or combined with the lateral acceleration sensor. Typically, the sensor is mounted in the passenger compartment under the front seat, in the center console, or on the rear package shelf.

This sensor does set DTC codes. These codes can be found in service information. ● SEE FIGURE 20–9.

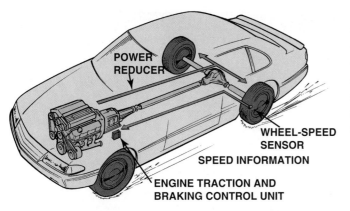

FIGURE 20–10 Typical traction control system that uses wheel speed sensor information and the engine controller (PCM) to apply the brakes at lower speeds and also reduce engine power applied to the drive wheels.

POWER REDUCER

WHEEL-SPEED SENSOR

SPEED INFORMATION

ENGINE TRACTION AND BRAKING CONTROL UNIT

TRACTION CONTROL

PURPOSE AND FUNCTION
Traction control (TC) can be separate or used as part of the electronic stability control (ESC) system. Traction control allows an ABS system to control wheel spin during acceleration. When tires lose traction during acceleration, it is called **positive slip.**

Low-speed traction control uses the braking system to limit positive slip up to a vehicle speed of about 30 mph (48 km/h). Traction control is usually a part of the electronic stability control system. ● **SEE FIGURE 20–10.**

Traction control uses the same wheel speed sensors as ABS, but requires additional programming in the control module so the system monitors wheel speed continuously, not just when braking. Traction control also requires:

- Additional solenoids in the hydraulic modulator so the brake circuits to the drive wheels can be isolated from the non-drive wheels when braking is needed to control wheel spin.

- Use of a pump and accumulator to generate and store pressure for traction control braking. If a wheel speed sensor detects wheel spin in one of the drive wheels during acceleration, the control module energizes a solenoid that allows stored fluid pressure from the accumulator to apply the brakes on the wheel that is spinning. This slows the wheel that is spinning and redirects engine torque through the differential to the opposite drive wheel to restore traction.

Traction control works just as well on front-wheel-drive vehicles as it does on rear-wheel-drive vehicles.

SYSTEM COMPONENTS
The main controller for the traction can include one of the following, depending on make, model, and year of vehicle:

1. The body control module (BCM)
2. The powertrain control module (PCM)
3. The antilock brake system controller

The controller uses inputs from several sensors to determine if a loss of traction is occurring. The input signals used for traction control include:

- **Throttle position (TP) sensor**—This indicates the position of the throttle, which is the driver command for power.

- **Wheel speed sensor (WSS)**—The controller monitors all four wheel speed sensors. If one wheel is rotating faster than the other, this indicates that the tire is slipping or has lost traction.

- **Engine speed (RPM)**—This information is supplied from the engine controller powertrain control module (PCM) and indicates the speed of the engine.

- **Transmission range switch**—Determines which gear the driver has selected so that the PCM can take corrective action.

TRACTION CONTROL OPERATION
The outputs of the traction control system can include one or more of the following:

- Retard ignition timing to reduce engine torque.

- Decrease the fuel injector pulse-width to reduce fuel delivery to the cylinder to reduce engine torque.

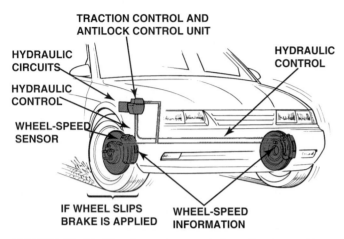

FIGURE 20–11 Wheel speed sensor information is used to monitor if a drive wheel is starting to spin.

FIGURE 20–12 A traction control or low traction light on the dash is confusing to many drivers. When the lamp is on or flashing, it indicates that a low traction condition has been determined and the traction control system is working to restore traction. A flashing traction dash light does not indicate a fault.

TRACTION CONTROL (CONTINUED)

- Reduce the amount of intake air if the engine is equipped with an electronic throttle control (ETC). Reduced airflow will reduce engine torque.

- Upshift the automatic transmission/transaxle. If the transmission is shifted into a higher gear, the torque applied to the drive wheels is reduced.

Most traction control systems are capable of reducing positive wheel slip at all vehicle speeds. Most speed traction control systems use accelerator reduction and engine power reduction to limit slip before applying the brakes to the wheel that is spinning. This action helps reduce the possibility of overheating the brakes if the vehicle were being driven on an icy or snow-covered road. ● **SEE FIGURE 20–11.**

Therefore the controller usually performs actions to restore traction in the following order:

1. Reduces engine torque to the drive wheels. This can include some or all of the following:
   - Retard spark timing
   - Reduce injector on-time (pulse-width)
   - Close or reduce the throttle opening
   - Shift the automatic transmission to a higher gear

2. Applying individual wheel brakes to slow or stop the wheel from spinning. The ABS controller supplies to the wheel brake only the pressure that is required to prevent tire slipping during acceleration. The amount of pressure varies according to the condition of the road surface and the amount of engine power being delivered to the drive wheels. A program inside the controller will disable traction control if brake system overheating is likely to occur.

3. Lights a low traction or traction control warning light on the dash.

   ● **SEE FIGURE 20–12.**

TRACTION ACTIVE LAMP On most applications, a "TRAC CNTL" indicator light or "TRACTION CONTROL ACTIVE" message flashes on the instrumentation when the system is engaging traction control. This helps alert the driver that the wheels are losing traction. In most applications, the message does not mean there is anything wrong with the system—unless the ABS warning lamp also comes on, or the traction control light remains on continuously.

TRACTION DEACTIVATION SWITCH Many vehicles with traction control have a dash-mounted switch that allows the driver to deactivate the system when desired (as when driving in deep snow). An indicator light shows when the system is on or off, and may also signal the driver when the traction control system is actively engaged during acceleration.

Does Traction Control Engage Additional Drive Wheels?

When the term *traction control* is used, many people think of four-wheel-drive or all-wheel-drive vehicles and powertrains. Instead of sending engine torque to other drive wheels, it is the purpose and function of the traction control system to prevent the drive wheel(s) from slipping during acceleration. A slipping tire has less traction than a nonslipping tire—therefore, if the tire can be kept from slipping (spinning), more traction will be available to propel the vehicle. Traction control works with the engine computer to reduce torque delivery from the engine, as well as the controller to apply the brakes to the spinning wheel if necessary to regain traction.

FIGURE 20–13 The use of a factory scan tool is often needed to diagnose the ESC system.

ESC/TC DIAGNOSIS

Because the electronic stability control (ESC) and traction control (TC) systems use some of the same sensors and controllers, the diagnosis for them is about the same. To diagnose faults with either system, follow the recommended procedures found in service information. The usual procedure involves the following steps.

STEP 1 **Verify the customer concern (complaint).** This step includes trying to duplicate what the customer or driver is concerned about the system. If the traction control or ESC light is flashing, this indicates that it is trying to bring the vehicle under control. This may be normal operation if the following conditions exist:
- Icy or slippery road conditions
- Worn tires that lack traction

STEP 2 **Perform a thorough visual inspection** including:
- Check that all tires are the same size and tread depth.

NOTE: **Using a spare tire on the drive wheel could cause the traction control and/or ESC amber warning light to flash because the controller is seeing that the smaller tire is rotating faster than the other side.**

STEP 3 **Check service information** for the specified procedure to follow to retrieve diagnostic trouble codes. Most vehicles require the use of a factory-brand scan tool. ● **SEE FIGURE 20–13.**

STEP 4 **Follow the troubleshooting procedure** as specified to fix the root cause of the problem. This means following the instructions displayed on the scan tool or service information. The steps usually include all or many of the following:
- Brake fluid level
- Wheel speed sensor resistance
- Fault with the base brake system, such as air in the lines that could prevent the traction control controller from applying the wheel brakes

STEP 5 **Repair the fault.**

STEP 6 **Road test the vehicle** under the same conditions that were performed to verify the fault to be sure that the fault has been repaired.

1. The purpose and function of the electronic stability control (ESC) system is to help maintain directional stability under all driving conditions by applying individual wheel brakes as needed to restore control.

2. The Federal Motor Vehicle Safety Standard (FMVSS) number 126 requires that all vehicles with a gross vehicle weight of less than 10,000 pounds be equipped with ESC by September 1, 2011.

3. The ESC can be switched off but will default to on when the ignition is turned back on.

4. The sine with dwell test (SWD) is the standard test used to test electronic stability control systems.

5. Electronic stability control sensors include steering wheel position sensor, vehicle speed sensor, lateral acceleration sensor, and yaw rate sensor.

6. Traction control (TC) systems use a variety of actions to help achieve traction of the drive wheels during acceleration, including retarding ignition timing, upshifting the transmission, and applying individual wheel brakes.

7. Diagnosis of the ESC or TC system involves the following steps:
   a. Verify the customer concern.
   b. Perform a thorough visual inspection.
   c. Check service information for specified test procedures.
   d. Follow specified testing procedures.
   e. Repair the fault.
   f. Perform a roadtest to verify the repair.

REVIEW QUESTIONS

1. What is the difference between oversteering and understeering?

2. What is the "sine with dwell" test?

3. What are some of the other names used to identify an electronic stability control (ESC) system?

4. What sensors are used in the electronic stability control system?

5. What action does the traction control system perform to help the drive wheels maintain traction during acceleration?

6. What is the typical diagnostic procedure to follow when troubleshooting a fault with the electronic stability control or traction control system?

CHAPTER QUIZ

1. The electronic stability control (ESC) system requires that the vehicle be equipped with what type of brake system?
   a. Four-wheel disc brakes
   b. Four-channel ABS
   c. Three-channel ABS
   d. Front disc with rear drum brakes

2. Which Federal Motor Safety Standard requires electronic stability control to be on all vehicles by 2011?
   a. 126
   b. 113
   c. 109
   d. 101

3. What is the name of the standard test that is performed to verify ESC operation?
   a. ESC plus
   b. Vehicle stability enhancement test
   c. Sine with dwell
   d. Anti-skid test

4. What other name is used to describe an electronic stability control (ESC) system?
   a. Vehicle Stability Assist (VSA)
   b. Electronic Stability Program (ESP)
   c. Vehicle Dynamic Control (VDC)
   d. Any of the above

5. Which sensor is used by the ESC controller to determine the driver's intended direction?
   a. Yaw sensor
   b. Steering wheel (hand-wheel) position sensor
   c. Vehicle speed (VS) sensor
   d. Lateral acceleration sensor

6. A diagnostic trouble code (DTC) has been set for a fault with lateral acceleration sensor or circuit. What test could be performed to check if the sensor is working?
   a. Unplug it and see if the scan tool reads 1.0G
   b. Disconnect the sensor and hold it sideways to see if a scan tool reads 0.0G
   c. Disconnect the sensor and hold it sideways to see if a scan tool reads 1.0G
   d. Drive the vehicle in a circle to see if the scan tool reads 0.0G

7. A lateral acceleration sensor is usually located where in the vehicle?
   a. Under the front seat
   b. In the center console
   c. On the package shelf
   d. Any of the above locations

8. If a vehicle tends to continue straight ahead while cornering, this condition is called _____.
   a. Understeer
   b. Plowing
   c. Tight
   d. All of the above

9. Traction control uses the antilock braking system and other devices to limit _____ of the drive wheels during acceleration.
   a. Positive slip
   b. Negative slip

10. A traction control system can often control all *except* _____.
   a. Limit engine torque delivered to the drive wheel
   b. Engage four-wheel drive
   c. Upshift the automatic transmission
   d. Apply the wheel brake to the wheel that is losing traction

chapter 21
TIRES AND WHEELS

INTRODUCTION TO TIRES

The friction (traction) between the tire and the road determines the handling characteristics of any vehicle. Think about this statement for a second. The compounding, construction, and condition of tires are some of the most important aspects of the steering, suspension, alignment, and braking systems of any vehicle. A vehicle that handles poorly or that pulls, darts, jumps, or steers "funny" may be suffering from defective or worn tires. Understanding the construction of a tire is important for the technician to be able to identify tire failure or vehicle handling problems.

Tires are mounted on wheels that are bolted to the vehicle to provide the following:

1. Shock absorber action when driving over rough surfaces

2. Friction (traction) between the wheels and the road

All tires are assembled by hand from many different component parts consisting of various rubber compounds, steel, and various types of fabric material. Tires are also available in many different designs and sizes.

PARTS OF A TIRE

TREAD **Tread** refers to the part of the tire that contacts the ground. *Tread rubber* is chemically different from other rubber parts of a tire, and is compounded for a combination of traction and tire wear. *Tread depth* is usually 11/32 in. deep on new tires (this could vary, depending on manufacturer, from 9/32 to 15/32 in.). ● **FIGURE 21–1** shows a tread depth gauge.

NOTE: A tread depth is always expressed in 1/32s of an inch, even if the fraction can be reduced to 1/16s or 1/8s.

Wear indicators are also called **wear bars**. When tread depth is down to the legal limit of 2/32 in., bald strips appear across the tread. ● **SEE FIGURE 21–2.**

Tie bars are molded into the tread of most all-season-rated tires. These rubber reinforcement bars are placed between tread blocks on the outer tread rows to prevent unusual wear and to reduce tread noise. As the tire wears normally, the tie bars will gradually appear. This should not be mistaken for an indication of excess outer edge wear. A tire tread with what appears to be a solid band across the entire width of the tread is what the service technician should consider the wear bar indicator.

Grooves are large, deep recesses molded in the tread and separating the tread blocks. These grooves are called *circumferential grooves* or *kerfs.* Grooves running sideways across the tread of a tire are called *lateral grooves.* ● **SEE FIGURE 21–3.**

(a)

(b)

FIGURE 21–1 (a) A typical tire tread depth gauge. The center movable plunger is pushed down into the groove of the tire. (b) The tread depth is read at the top edge of the sleeve. In this example, the tread depth is 6/32 in.

FIGURE 21–2 Wear indicators (wear bars) are strips of bald tread that show when the tread depth is down to 2/32 in., the legal limit in many states.

TIRE TREAD

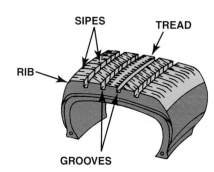

FIGURE 21–3 The tire tread runs around the circumference of the tire, and its pattern helps maintain traction. The ribs provide grip, while the grooves direct any water on the road away from the surface. The sipes help the tire grip the road.

PARTS OF A TIRE (CONTINUED)

Grooves in both directions are necessary for wet traction. The trapped water can actually cause the tires to ride up on a layer of water and lose contact with the ground, as shown in ● FIGURE 21–4. This is called **hydroplaning**. With worn tires, hydroplaning can occur at speeds as low as 30 mph on wet roads. Stopping and cornering is impossible when hydroplaning occurs. *Sipes* are small slits in the tread area to increase wet and dry traction.

SIDEWALL The **sidewall** is that part of the tire between the tread and the wheel. The sidewall contains all the size and construction details of the tire.

Some tires turn brown on the sidewalls after a short time. This is due to ozone (atmosphere) damage that actually causes the rubber to oxidize. Premium-quality tires contain an anti-oxidizing chemical additive blended with the sidewall rubber to prevent this discoloration.

WHITE SIDEWALL/LETTERED When pneumatic tires were first constructed in the early 1900s, only natural rubber was used. The entire tire was white. When it was discovered that carbon

black greatly increased the toughness of a tire, it was used. The public did not like the change from white tires to black, so tire manufacturers put the carbon black (lamp black) only in the rubber that was to be used for the tread portion of the tire. This tire lasted a lot longer because the black rubber tread that touched the ground was stronger and tougher; it sold well because the sidewalls were white.

White sidewall or white lettered tires actually contain a strip of white rubber under the black sidewall. This is ground off at the factory to reveal the white rubber. Only whitewalls or white letter lines contain this expensive white rubber. Various widths of whitewalls are made possible simply by changing the width of the grinding wheel.

BEAD The **bead** is the foundation of the tire and is located where the tire grips the inside of the wheel rim.

1. The bead is constructed of many turns of copper- or bronze-coated steel wire.

2. The main body plies (layers of material) are wrapped around the bead.

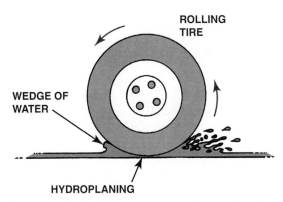

FIGURE 21–4 Hydroplaning can occur at speeds as low as 30 mph (48 km/h). If the water is deep enough and the tire tread cannot evacuate water through its grooves fast enough, the tire can be lifted off the road surface by a layer of water. Hydroplaning occurs at lower speeds as the tire becomes worn.

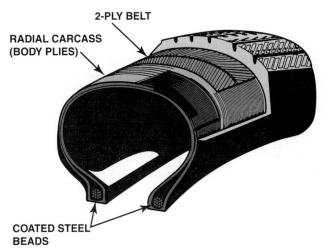

FIGURE 21–5 Typical construction of a radial tire. Some tires have only one body ply, and some tires use more than two belt plies.

CAUTION: If the bead of a tire is cut or damaged, the tire must be replaced!

3. Most radial-ply tires and all truck tires wrap the bead with additional material to add strength.

BODY PLY A tire gets its strength from the layers of material wrapped around both beads under the tread and sidewall rubber. This creates the main framework, or "carcass," of the tire; these **body plies** are often called **carcass plies**. A 4-ply tire has four separate layers of material. If the body plies overlap at an angle (bias), the tire is called a *bias-ply* tire. If only one or two body plies are used and they do not cross at an angle, but lie directly from bead to bead, then the tire is called *radial ply*. ● **SEE FIGURE 21–5**.

1. Rayon is a body ply material used in many tires because it provides a very smooth ride. A major disadvantage of rayon is that it rots if exposed to moisture.

2. Nylon is a strong body ply material. Though it is still used in some tires, it tends to "flat-spot" after sitting overnight.

3. Aramid is the generic name for aromatic polyamide fibers developed in 1972. Aramid is several times stronger than steel (pound for pound), and is used in high-performance-tire construction. Kevlar is the DuPont brand name for aramid and a registered trademark of E.I. Dupont de Nemours and Co.

4. Polyester is the most commonly used tire material because it provides the smooth ride characteristics of rayon with the rot resistance and strength of nylon.

BELT A tire **belt** is two or more layers of material applied over the body plies and under the tread area only, to stabilize the tread and increase tread life and handling.

1. Belt material can consist of the following:
   a. Steel mesh
   b. Nylon
   c. Rayon
   d. Fiberglass
   e. Aramid

2. **All radial tires are belted.**

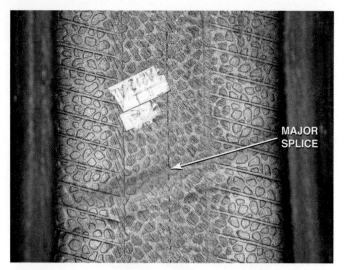

FIGURE 21–6 The major splice of a tire can often be seen and felt on the inside of the tire. The person who assembles (builds) the tire usually places a sticker near the major splice as a means of identification for quality control.

PARTS OF A TIRE (CONTINUED)

NOTE: Most tires rated for high speed use a nylon "overlay" or "cap belt" between the 2-ply belt and the tread of the tire. This overlay helps stabilize the belt package and helps hold the tire together at high speeds, when centrifugal force acts to tear a tire apart.

INNER LINER The **inner liner** is the soft rubber lining (usually a butyl rubber compound) on the inside of the tire that protects the body plies and helps provide for self-sealing of small punctures.

MAJOR SPLICE When the tire is assembled by a craftsperson on a tire-building machine, the body plies, belts, and tread rubber are spliced together. The fabric is overlapped approximately five threads. The point where the majority of these overlaps occur is called the **major splice**, which represents the stiffest part of the tire. This major splice is visible on most tires on the inside, as shown in ● **FIGURE 21–6**.

NOTE: On most new vehicles and/or new tires, the tire manufacturer paints a dot on the sidewall near the bead, indicating the largest diameter of the tire. The largest diameter of the tire usually is near the major splice. The wheel manufacturer either marks the wheel or drills the valve core hole at the smallest diameter of the wheel. Therefore, the dot should be aligned with the valve core or marked for best balance and minimum radial runout.

FIGURE 21–7 Tire construction is performed by assembling the many parts of a tire together on a tire-building machine.

TIRE MOLDING

After the tire has been assembled by the tire builder, it is called a **green tire**. ● **SEE FIGURE 21–7**. At this stage in construction, the rubber can be returned and reused because it has not been changed chemically. The completed green tire is then placed in a mold where its shape, tread design, and all sidewall markings are formed. ● **SEE FIGURE 21–8**.

While in the mold, a steam bladder fills the inside of the tire and forces the tire against the outside of the mold. After approximately 30 minutes at 300°F (150°C), the heat changes the chemistry of the rubber. The tire is no longer called a green tire but a *cured tire,* and after inspection and cleaning, it is ready for shipment.

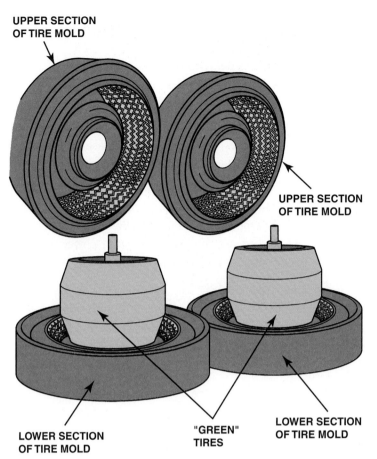

UPPER SECTION OF TIRE MOLD

UPPER SECTION OF TIRE MOLD

LOWER SECTION OF TIRE MOLD

"GREEN" TIRES

LOWER SECTION OF TIRE MOLD

FIGURE 21–8 After the entire tire has been assembled into a completed "green" tire, it is placed into a tire-molding machine where the tire is molded into shape and the rubber is changed chemically by the heat. This nonreversible chemical reaction is called vulcanization.

METRIC DESIGNATION

European and Japanese tires use metric designations. For example, 185SR × 14 denotes the following:

185	the tire is 185 millimeters (mm) wide (cross-sectional width)
S	the speed rating
R	radial design
14	fits a 14-in.-diameter wheel

The European size indicates the exact physical size (width) of the tire and the speed ratings. Because of the lack of speed limits in many countries, this information is important. Because of tire design changes needed for H- and V-rated tires, their cost is usually much higher. European sizes also include the tire's aspect ratio, for example, 185/70SR × 14. If the aspect ratio of a European-sized tire is not indicated, it is generally 83% for most radials.

? FREQUENTLY ASKED QUESTION

Why Do I Get Shocked by Static Electricity When I Drive a Certain Vehicle?

Static electricity builds up in insulators due to friction of the tires with the road. Newer tires use silica and contain less carbon black in the rubber, which makes the tires electrically conductive. Because the tires cannot conduct the static electricity to the ground, static electricity builds up inside the vehicle and is discharged through the body of the driver and/or passenger whenever the metal door handle is touched.

NOTE: Toll booth operators report being shocked by many drivers as money is being passed between the driver and the toll booth operator.

Newer tire sidewall designs that use silica usually incorporate carbon sections that are used to discharge the static electricity to ground. To help reduce the static charge buildup, spray the upholstery with an antistatic spray available at discount and grocery stores.

AMERICAN METRIC TIRE SIZE DESIGNATIONS

After 1980, American tires were also designated using the metric system. For example, P205/75R × 14 denotes the following:

P	passenger vehicle
205	205-mm cross-sectional width
75	75% aspect ratio. The height of the tire (from the wheel to the tread) is 75% as great as its cross-sectional width (the width measured across its widest part). This percentage ratio of height to width is called the **aspect ratio**. (A 60 series tire is 60% as high as it is wide.)
R	radial
14	14-in.-diameter wheel

If a tire is constructed as a bias-ply tire only, then its size designation uses the letter D to indicate *diagonal:* P205/75D × 14.

NOTE: Many "temporary use only" spare tires are constructed with diagonal (bias) plies; the size designation is *T* for *temporary*.

If a tire is constructed as a bias ply with a belt of additional material under the tread area, its size designation uses the letter B to indicate belted: P205/75B × 14. Some tires use letters at the end of the tire size (suffixes) to indicate special applications, including the following:

LT	light truck
ML	mining and logging
MH	mobile home
ST	special trailer
TR	truck

FREQUENTLY ASKED QUESTION

How Much Does Tire Pressure Change with a Change in Temperature?

As the temperature of a tire increases, the pressure inside the tire also increases. The general amount of pressure gain (when temperatures increase) or loss (when temperatures decrease) is as follows:

10°F increase causes 1 PSI increase

10°F decrease causes 1 PSI decrease

For example, if a tire is correctly inflated to 35 PSI when cold and then driven on a highway, the tire pressure may increase 5 PSI or more.

CAUTION: DO NOT LET AIR OUT OF A HOT TIRE! If air is released from a hot tire to bring the pressure down to specifications, the tire will be *underinflated* when the tire has cooled. The tire pressure specification is for a cold tire.

Always check the tire pressures on a vehicle that has been driven fewer than 2 miles (3.2 km).

Air pressure in the tires also affects fuel economy. If all four tires are underinflated (low on air pressure), fuel economy is reduced about **0.1 mile per gallon (mpg) for each 1 PSI low.** For example, if all four tires were inflated to 25 PSI instead of 35 PSI, not only is tire life affected but fuel economy is reduced by about 1 mile per gallon (10 × 0.1 = 1 mpg).

How Much Bigger Can I Go?

Many owners think they can improve their vehicle by upgrading the tire size over the size that comes from the factory to make their vehicle look sportier and ride and handle better. When changing tire size, there are many factors to consider:

1. The tire should be the same outside diameter as the original to maintain the proper suspension, steering, and ride height specifications.

2. Tire size affects vehicle speed sensor values, ABS brake wheel sensor values that can change automatic transmission operation, and ABS operation.

3. The tire should not be so wide as to contact the inner wheel well or suspension components.

4. Generally, a tire that is 10 mm wider is acceptable. For example, an original equipment tire size 205/75 × 15 (outside diameter = 27.1 in.) can be changed to 215/75 × 15 (outside diameter = 27.6 in.). This much change is less than 1/2 in. in width and increases the outside diameter by 1/2 in.

NOTE: Outside diameter is calculated by adding the wheel diameter to the cross-sectional height of the tire, multiplied by 2.
● **SEE FIGURE 21–9.**

5. Whenever changing tires, make sure that the load capacity is the same or greater than that of the original tires.

6. If wider tires are desired, a lower aspect ratio is required to maintain the same, or close to the same, overall outside diameter of the tire.

Old	New
P205/75 × 15	P215/70 × 15
$205 \times 0.75 = 154$ mm	$215 \times 0.70 = 151$ mm

Notice that the overall sidewall height is generally maintained.

If even larger tires are needed, then 225/60 × 15s may be OK—let's check the math:

$$225 \times 0.60 = 135 \text{ mm}$$

Notice that this is much too short a sidewall height when compared with the original tire (see no. 6).

7. Use the "plus 1" or "plus 2" concept. When specifying wider tires, the sidewall height must be reduced to maintain the same, or close to the same, original equipment specifications. The "plus 1" concept involves replacing the wheels with wheels 1 in. larger in diameter to compensate for the lower aspect of wider tires.

Original	Plus 1
205/75 × 15	225/60 × 16

The overall difference in outside diameter is only 0.5 in., even though the tire width has increased from 205 mm to 225 mm and the wheel diameter has increased by 1 in. If money is no object and all-out performance is the goal, a "plus 2" concept can also be used (use a P245/50 × 17 tire and change to 17-in.-diameter wheels).

Here the overall diameter is within 1/20″ of the original tire/wheel combination, yet the tire width is 1.6 inches (40 mm) wider than the original tire. Refer to the section entitled "Wheels" later in this chapter for proper wheel back spacing and offset when purchasing replacement wheels.

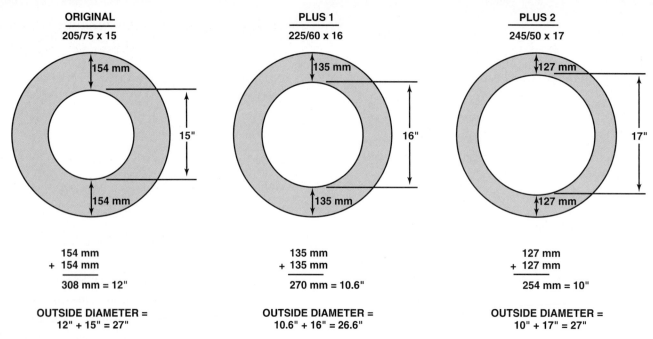

ORIGINAL	PLUS 1	PLUS 2
205/75 x 15	225/60 x 16	245/50 x 17

ORIGINAL
154 mm
15"
154 mm

154 mm
+ 154 mm
308 mm = 12"

OUTSIDE DIAMETER =
12" + 15" = 27"

PLUS 1
135 mm
16"
135 mm

135 mm
+ 135 mm
270 mm = 10.6"

OUTSIDE DIAMETER =
10.6" + 16" = 26.6"

PLUS 2
127 mm
17"
127 mm

127 mm
+ 127 mm
254 mm = 10"

OUTSIDE DIAMETER =
10" + 17" = 27"

FIGURE 21–9 Notice that the overall outside diameter of the tire remains almost the same and at the same time the aspect ratio is decreased and the rim diameter is increased.

SERVICE DESCRIPTION

Tires built after 1990 use a "service description" method of sidewall information in accordance with ISO 4000 (International Standards Organization) that includes size, load, and speed rating together in one easy-to-read format. ● **SEE FIGURE 21–10.**

P-Metric Designation	Service Description
P205/75HR × 15	205/75R × 15 92H
P passenger vehicle	205 cross-sectional width in mm
205 cross-sectional width in mm	75 aspect ratio
75 aspect ratio	R radial construction
H speed rating (130 mph/210 km/h)	15 rim diameter in inches
R radial construction	92 load index
15 rim diameter in inches	H speed rating (130 mph/210 km/h)

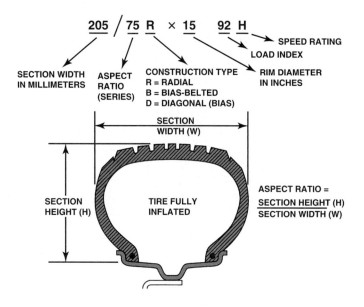

205 / 75 R × 15 92 H

SPEED RATING
LOAD INDEX
SECTION WIDTH IN MILLIMETERS
ASPECT RATIO (SERIES)
CONSTRUCTION TYPE
R = RADIAL
B = BIAS-BELTED
D = DIAGONAL (BIAS)
RIM DIAMETER IN INCHES

SECTION WIDTH (W)
SECTION HEIGHT (H)
TIRE FULLY INFLATED
$$\text{ASPECT RATIO} = \frac{\text{SECTION HEIGHT (H)}}{\text{SECTION WIDTH (W)}}$$

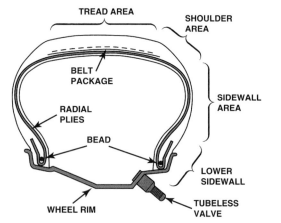

TREAD AREA
SHOULDER AREA
BELT PACKAGE
RADIAL PLIES
BEAD
SIDEWALL AREA
WHEEL RIM
LOWER SIDEWALL
TUBELESS VALVE

FIGURE 21–10 Cross-sectional view of a typical tire showing the terminology.

What Effect Does Tire Size Have on Overall Gear Ratio?

Customers often ask what effect changing tire size has on fuel economy and speedometer readings. If larger (or smaller) tires are installed on a vehicle, many other factors also will change. These include the following:

1. **Speedometer reading. If larger-diameter tires are used, the speedometer will read slower** than you are actually traveling. This can result in speeding tickets!

2. **Odometer reading.** Even though larger tires are said to give better fuel economy, just the opposite can be calculated! Since a larger-diameter tire travels farther than a smaller-diameter tire, the larger tire will cause the odometer to read a shorter distance than the vehicle actually travels. For example, if the odometer reads 100 miles traveled on tires that are 10% oversized in circumference, the actual distance traveled is 110 miles.

3. **Fuel economy.** If fuel economy is calculated on miles traveled, the result will be *lower* fuel economy than for the same vehicle with the original tires.

$$\text{Calculation: mph} = \frac{\text{RPM} \times \text{diameter} \times 3.14}{\text{gear ratio}}$$

$$\text{RPM} = \frac{\text{mph} \times \text{gear ratio}}{\text{diameter} \times 3.14}$$

$$\text{gear ratio} = \frac{\text{RPM} \times \text{diameter} \times 3.14}{\text{mph}}$$

HIGH-FLOTATION TIRE SIZES

High-flotation tires for light trucks are designed to give improved off-road performance on sand, mud, and soft soil and still provide acceptable hard-road surface performance. These tires are usually larger than conventional tires and usually require a wider-than-normal wheel width. High-flotation tires have a size designation such as 33 × 12.50R × 15LT:

33	approximate overall tire diameter in inches
12.50	approximate cross-sectional width in inches
R	radial-type construction
15	rim diameter in inches
LT	light-truck designation

If I Have an Older Vehicle, What Size Tires Should I Use?

Newer radial tires can be used on older-model vehicles if the size of the tires is selected that best matches the original tires. See the following cross-reference chart.

Cross-Reference Chart
(This Chart Does Not Imply Complete Interchangeability.)

Pre-1964	1965 to 1972	80 Series Metric	Alpha Numeric 78 Series	P-Metric 75 Series Radial	P-Metric 70 Series Radial
590-13	600-13	165-13	A78-13	P165/75R13	P175/70R13
640-13	650-13	175-13	B78-13	P175/75R13	P185/70R13
725-13	700-13	185-13	D78-13	P185/75R13	P205/70R13
590-14	645-14	155-14	B78-14	P175/75R14	P185/70R14
650-14	695-14	175-14	C78-14	P185/75R14	P195/70R14
700-14	735-14	185-14	E78-14	P195/75R14	P205/70R14
750-14	775-14	195-14	F78-14	P205/75R14	P215/70R14
800-14	825-14	205-14	G78-14	P215/75R14	P225/70R14
850-14	855-14	215-14	H78-14	P225/75R14	P235/70R14
590-15	600-15	165-15	A78-15	P165/75R15	P175/70R15
650-15	685-15	175-15	C78-15	P175/75R15	P185/70R15
640-15	735-15	185-15	E78-15	P195/75R15	P205/70R15
670-15	775-15	195-15	F78-15	P205/75R15	P215/70R15
710-15	815-15	205-15	G78-15	P215/75R15	P225/70R15
760-15	855-15	215-15	H78-15	P225/75R15	P235/70R15
800-15	885-15	230-15	J78-15	P225/75R15	P235/70R15
820-15	900-15	235-15	L78-15	P235/75R15	P255/70R15

NOTE: Vehicles designed for older bias-ply tires may drive differently when equipped with radial tires.

LOAD INDEX AND EQUIVALENT LOADS

The **load index**, as shown in ● **FIGURE 21–11**, is an abbreviated method to indicate the load-carrying capabilities of a tire. The weights listed in the chart represent the weight that *each tire* can safely support. Multiply this amount by 4 to get the maximum that the vehicle should weigh fully loaded with cargo and passengers.

SPEED RATINGS

Tires are rated according to the maximum *sustained* speed. A vehicle should never be driven faster than the **speed rating** of the tires. See **Chart 21-1.**

CAUTION: A high speed rating does not guarantee that the tires will not fail, even at speeds much lower than the rating. Tire condition, inflation, and vehicle loading also affect tire performance.

As the speed rating of a tire increases, fewer compromises exist for driver comfort and low noise level. The higher speed rating does not mean a better tire. To survive, a high-speed tire

FIGURE 21–17 Typical "Uniform Tire Quality Grading System" (UTQGS) ratings imprinted on the tire sidewall.

? **FREQUENTLY ASKED QUESTION**

Is There a Rule-of-Thumb for Rim Size?

According to the Tire and Rim Association, Inc., the answer is no. Each tire size has a designated rim width on which it is designed to be mounted so as to provide the best performance and wear. The width of the specified rim also varies with rim diameter. A 235/45 × 17 tire may require a 7.5-in. rim but a 235/45 × 19 tire may require an 8.0-in. rim. A rule-of-thumb that has been used is to multiply the width of the rim by 33.55 to determine the approximate tire size for the rim. For example, consider the following.

Rim width 5.0 in. × 33.55 = 167.85 (165 mm) tire

Rim width 5.5 in. × 33.55 = 184.50 (185 mm) tire

Rim width 6.0 in. × 33.55 = 201.30 (195 mm) tire

Rim width 6.5 in. × 33.55 = 218.00 (215 mm) tire

Rim width 7.0 in. × 33.55 = 234.90 (235 mm) tire

Rim width 7.5 in. × 33.55 = 252.00 (245 mm) tire

Rim width 8.0 in. × 33.55 = 268.00 (265 mm) tire

Rim width 8.5 in. × 33.55 = 285.00 (285 mm) tire

Rim width 9.0 in. × 33.55 = 302.00 (305 mm) tire

Rim width 10.0 in. × 33.55 = 335.60 (335 mm) tire

　　Always check with the tire manufacturer as to the specified tire rim width that should be used.

UNIFORM TIRE QUALITY GRADING SYSTEM

The U.S. Department of Transportation (DOT) and the National Highway Traffic Safety Administration (NHTSA) developed a system of tire grading, the **Uniform Tire Quality Grading System (UTQGS)**, to help customers better judge the relative performance of tires. The three areas of tire performance are tread wear, traction, and temperature resistance, as shown in ● **FIGURE 21–17**.

NOTE: All tires sold in the United States must have UTQGS ratings molded into the sidewall.

TREAD WEAR　The tread wear grade is a comparison rating based on the wear rate of a standardized tire, tested under carefully controlled conditions, which is assigned a value of 100. A tire rated 200 should have a useful life twice as long as the standard tire's.

NOTE: The standard tire has a rating for tread wear of 100. This value has generally been accepted to mean a useful life of 20,000 miles of normal driving. Therefore, a tire rated at 200 could be expected to last 40,000 miles.

Installing a tire on too narrow a wheel will cause the tire to wear excessively in the center of the tread. Installing a tire on too wide a wheel will cause excessive tire wear on both edges.

　　See a tire store representative for recommended tire sizes that can be safely installed on your rims.

Tread Wear Rating Number	Approximate Number of mi/km
100	20,000/32,000
150	30,000/48,000
200	40,000/64,000
250	50,000/80,000
300	60,000/96,000
400	80,000/129,000
500	100,000/161,000

UNIFORM TIRE QUALITY GRADING SYSTEM (CONTINUED)

The tread wear life of any tire is affected by driving habits (fast stops, starts, and cornering will decrease tread life), tire rotation (or lack of tire rotation), inflation, wheel alignment, road surfaces, and climate conditions.

TRACTION Traction performance is rated by the letters AA, A, B, and C, with AA being the highest.

NOTE: The traction rating is for wet braking distance only! It does not include cornering traction or dry braking performance.

The traction rating is only one of many other factors that affect wet braking traction, including air inflation, tread depth, vehicle speed, and brake performance.

TEMPERATURE RESISTANCE Temperature resistance is rated by the letters A, B, and C, with A being the highest rating. Tires generate heat while rotating and flexing during normal driving conditions. A certain amount of heat buildup is desirable because tires produce their highest coefficient of traction at normal operating temperatures. For example, race car drivers frequently swerve their cars left and right during the pace laps, causing increased friction between the tire and the road surface, which warms their tires to operating temperature. However, if temperatures rise too much, a tire can start to come apart—the oils and rubber in the tire start to become a liquid! Grade C is the minimum level that all tires must be able to pass under the current Federal Motor Vehicle Safety Standard No. 109.

ALL-SEASON TIRE DESIGNATION

Most all-season tires are rated and labeled as *M & S*, *MS*, or *M + S*, and therefore must adhere to general design features as specified by the Rubber Manufacturers Association (RMA).

Tires labeled M & S are constructed with an aggressive tread design as well as tread compounds and internal construction that are designed for mud and snow. One design feature is that the tire has at least 25% void area. This means that the tread blocks have enough open space around them to allow the blocks to grab and clean themselves of snow and mud. Block angles, dimensional requirements, and minimum cross-sectional width are also a requirement for the M & S designation.

The tread rubber used to make all-season tires is also more flexible at low temperatures. This rubber compound is low-bounce (called high-hysteresis) and is more likely to remain in contact with the road surface. The rubber compound is also called *hydrophilic*, meaning that the rubber has an affinity for water (rather than being *hydrophobic* rubber, which repels water).

NOTE: Most vehicle manufacturers recommend that the same *type* of tire be used on all four wheels even though the size of the tire may vary between front and rear on some high-performance vehicles. Therefore, if all-season replacement tires are purchased, a complete set of four should be used to be assured of proper handling and uniform traction characteristics. While *tire* manufacturers have been recommending this for years—since the late 1980s—most *vehicle* manufacturers are also recommending that all four tires be of the same construction and tread type to help ensure proper vehicle handling.

DOT TIRE CODE

All tires sold in the United States must be approved by the U.S. Federal Department of Transportation (DOT). The **DOT tire code** requirements include resistance to tire damage that could be caused by curbs, chuckholes, and other common occurrences for a tire used on public roads.

NOTE: Most race tires are *not* DOT-approved and must never be used on public streets or highways.

Each tire that is DOT-approved has a DOT number molded into the sidewall of the tire. This number is usually imprinted on only one side of the tire and is usually on the side *opposite the*

Load Index	Load (kg)	Load (lb)
75	387	853
76	400	882
77	412	908
78	425	937
79	437	963
80	450	992
81	462	1,019
82	475	1,047
83	487	1,074
84	500	1,102
85	515	1,135
86	530	1,168
87	545	1,201
88	560	1,235
89	580	1,279
90	600	1,323
91	615	1,356
92	630	1,389
93	650	1,433
94	670	1,477
95	690	1,521
96	710	1,565
97	730	1,609
98	750	1,653
99	775	1,709
100	800	1,764
101	825	1,819
102	850	1,874
103	875	1,929
104	900	1,934
105	925	2,039
106	950	2,094
107	975	2,149
108	1,000	2,205
109	1,030	2,271
110	1,060	2,337
111	1,090	2,403
112	1,120	2,469
113	1,150	2,535
114	1,180	2,601
115	1,215	2,679

FIGURE 21–11 Typical sidewall markings for load index and speed rating following the tire size.

must be built with stiff tread compounds, reinforced body (carcass) construction, and fabric angles that favor high speed and high performance over other considerations. For example, a V-rated tire often has less tread depth than a similar tire with an H-speed rating, and therefore will often not give as long of a service life. Since the speed ratings were first developed in Europe, the letters correspond to metric speed in kilometers per hour, with a conversion to miles per hour as noted.

Letter	Maximum Rated Speed
L	120 km/h (75 mph)
M	130 km/h (81 mph)
N	140 km/h (87 mph)
P	150 km/h (93 mph)
Q	160 km/h (99 mph)
R	170 km/h (106 mph)
S	180 km/h (112 mph)
T	190 km/h (118 mph)
U	200 km/h (124 mph)
H	210 km/h (130 mph)
V	240 km/h (149 mph)
W	270 km/h (168 mph)
Y	300 km/h (186 mph)
Z	open-ended*

CHART 21–1

Speed ratings are based on continuous operation at the speed rating speed.

*The exact speed rating for a particular Z-rated tire is determined by the tire manufacturer and may vary according to size. For example, not all Brand X Z-rated tires are rated at 170 mph, even though one size may be capable of these speeds.

FIGURE 21-12 The E.C.E. symbol on a sidewall of a tire. Notice the small -s at the end, indicating that the tire meets the "pass-by" noise limits.

? **FREQUENTLY ASKED QUESTION**

What Does the Little "e" Mean on the Sidewall?

Most countries have government agencies that regulate standards for motor vehicles sold and/or driven within their jurisdiction. In the United States, the U.S. Department of Transportation and National Highway Traffic Safety Administration are responsible for developing many of the nationwide standards for vehicles. Tires that are certified by their manufacturers to meet U.S. standards are branded with "DOT" (Department of Transportation) preceding the Tire Identification Code on their sidewall.

In Europe, because so much personal and commercial travel extends beyond the borders of any one country, the Economic Commission for Europe (E.C.E.) helps develop uniform motor vehicle standards for its member countries to regulate and standardize passenger and commercial vehicle components.

While sound is a by-product of modern society, it's one thing that most Europeans would enjoy less of. Excessive noise is considered a form of environmental pollution readily apparent to humans. People who express being disturbed by noise during the day and/or night cite truck, motorcycle, and automobile traffic as the most universal sources.

Besides physical specifications, the E.C.E. standards now require tire "pass-by" noise to meet specific limits. These standards were phased-in starting in 2004. The tires must pass noise emission testing, and the standards will continue to expand in scope until 2009, when the standards will be applied to all tires sold in Europe.

The E.C.E. symbol on a tire's sidewall identifies that the manufacturer certifies that the tire meets all regulations, including the load index and speed symbol that appear in its service description. In order to be E.C.E. branded, tires must receive laboratory approval, pass confirmation testing, and have their manufacturing plant pass quality control inspections.

The letter "e" and number code combination (positioned in a circle or rectangle) identify the country originally granting approval, followed by two digits indicating the Regulation Series under which the tire was approved. Tires that have also been tested and meet the "pass-by" noise limits can have a second E.C.E. branding followed by an "-s" (for *sound*). ● SEE FIGURE 21-12.

The following list indicates selected E.C.E. codes and the countries they represent:

Code	Country	Code	Country
E1	Germany	E14	Switzerland
E2	France	E15	Norway
E3	Italy	E16	Finland
E4	Netherlands	E17	Denmark
E5	Sweden	E18	Romania
E6	Belgium	E19	Poland
E7	Hungary	E20	Portugal
E8	Czech Republic	E21	Russian Federation
E9	Spain	E22	Greece
E10	Yugoslavia	E23	Ireland
E11	United Kingdom	E24	Croatia
E12	Austria	E25	Slovenia
E13	Luxembourg	E26	Slovakia

Tire Date Code Information Saved Me Money!

This author was looking at a three-year-old vehicle when I noticed that the right rear tire had a build date code newer than the vehicle. I asked the owner, "How badly was this vehicle hit?" The owner stumbled and stuttered a little, then said, "How did you know that an accident occurred?" I told the owner that the right rear tire, while the exact same tire as the others, had a date code indicating that it was only one year old, whereas the original tires were the same age as the vehicle. The last three numbers of the DOT code on the sidewall indicate the week of manufacture (the first two numbers of the three-digit date code) followed by the last number of the year.

The owner immediately admitted that the vehicle slid on ice and hit a curb, damaging the right rear tire and wheel. Both the tire and wheel were replaced and the alignment checked. The owner then dropped the price of the vehicle $500! Knowing the date code helps assure that fresh tires are purchased and can also help the technician determine if the tires have been replaced. For example, if new tires are found on a vehicle with 20,000 miles, then the technician should check to see if the vehicle may have been involved in an accident or may have more miles than indicated on the odometer.

FIGURE 21–18 Typical DOT date code. This tire was built the sixth week of 2005.

SPARE TIRES

Most vehicles today come equipped with space-saver spare tires that are smaller than the wheels and tires that are on the vehicle. The reason for the small size is to reduce the size and weight of the entire vehicle and to increase fuel economy by having the entire vehicle weigh less by not carrying a heavy spare tire and wheel around. The style and type of these spare tires have changed a great deal over the last several years, and different makes and types of vehicles use various types of spare tires.

CAUTION: Before using a spare tire, always read the warning label (if so equipped) and understand all use restrictions. For example, some spare tires are not designed to exceed 50 mph (80 km/h) or be driven more than 500 miles (800 km).

Many small, space-saving spare tires use a higher-than-normal air inflation pressure, usually 60 PSI (414 kPa). Even though the tire often differs in construction, size, diameter, and width from the vehicle's original tires, it is amazing that the vehicle usually handles the same during normal driving. Obviously, these tires are not constructed with the same durability as a full-size tire and should be removed from service as soon as possible.

NOTE: When was the last time you checked the tire pressure in your spare tire? The spare tire pressure should be checked regularly.

whitewall. The DOT code includes letters and numbers, such as MJP2CBDX264. See appendix 2 for a list of where tires are built.

The first two letters identify the manufacturer and location. For this example, the first two letters (MJ) mean that the tire was made by the Goodyear Tire and Rubber Company in Topeka, Kansas. The last three numbers are the build date code. The last of these three numbers is the year (1994), and the 26 means that it was built during the 26th week of 1994. Starting with tires manufactured after January 1, 2000, the tire build date includes four digits rather than three digits. A new code such as "3406" means the 34th week of 2006 ("3406"). ● **SEE FIGURE 21–18**.

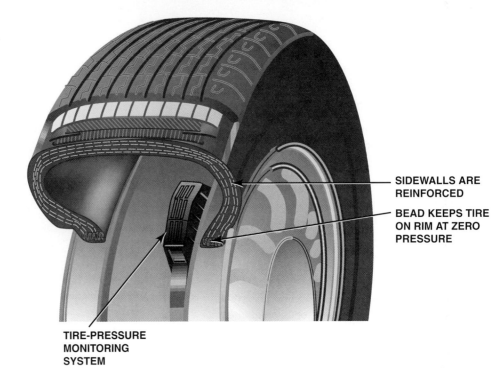

FIGURE 21–19 Cutaway of a run-flat tire showing the reinforced side-walls and the required pressure sensor.

SIDEWALLS ARE REINFORCED

BEAD KEEPS TIRE ON RIM AT ZERO PRESSURE

TIRE-PRESSURE MONITORING SYSTEM

RUN-FLAT TIRES

Run-flat tires (abbreviated RFT) are designed to operate without any air for a limited distance (usually 50 miles at 55 mph). This feature allows vehicle manufacturers to build vehicles without the extra room and weight of a spare tire and jack assembly.

A typical run-flat tire (also called *extended mobility tire* [EMT] or *zero pressure* [ZP] *tire*) requires the use of an air pressure sensor/transmitter and a dash-mounted receiver to warn the driver that a tire has lost pressure. Because of the reinforced sidewalls, the vehicle handles almost the same with or without air pressure. ● **SEE FIGURES 21–19 AND 21–20.**

CAUTION: Tire engineers warn that rapid cornering should be avoided if a run-flat tire has zero air pressure. The handling during quick maneuvers is often unpredictable and could be dangerous.

PAX RUN-FLAT TIRES Michelin developed a run-flat tire that has three unique components:

- A special wheel that has two bead seats that are of different diameters. The outside bead seat is 10 mm smaller in diameter than the inside bead seat. This means that a conventional tire cannot be installed on a PAX-style wheel.

- A urethane support ring that is designed to support the weight of the vehicle in the event of a flat tire.

- A special tire that is designed to operate without air. ● **SEE FIGURE 21–21.**

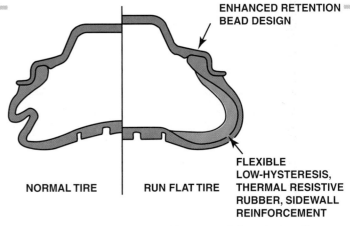

ENHANCED RETENTION BEAD DESIGN

FLEXIBLE LOW-HYSTERESIS, THERMAL RESISTIVE RUBBER, SIDEWALL REINFORCEMENT

NORMAL TIRE   RUN FLAT TIRE

FIGURE 21–20 A conventional tire on the left and a run-flat tire on the right, showing what happens when there is no air in the tire.

The PAX tire design has a unique sizing, such as:

P245/680R 460A 102V

P	= passenger
245	= the cross-section width in millimeters (mm)
680	= the tire diameter in mm (26.77 inches)
R	= radial ply construction
460	= the wheel, diameter in mm (18.1 inches)
A	= asymmetric wheel, meaning that one bead is smaller than the other bead by 10 mm (0.040 in.)
102	= the load index
V	= the speed rating

FIGURE 21-21 The PAX run-flat tire system is composed of three unique components—a special asymmetrical wheel, a urethane support ring, and special tire.

FIGURE 21-22 The Tire Performance Criteria (TPC) specification number is imprinted on the sidewall of all tires used on General Motors vehicles from the factory.

 **TECH TIP**

PAX Replacement Tip

In most cases, the fastest and easiest approach to follow if a PAX tire requires replacement is to purchase a replacement tire/wheel assembly. While more expensive than replacing just the tire, this approach is often used to help the vehicle owner get back on the road faster without any concerns as to whether the replacement tire was properly installed.

SERVICING A PAX WHEEL/TIRE ASSEMBLY If a flat tire occurs or when a PAX tire becomes worn and requires replacement, special care should be taken to properly remove the tire from the wheel. Because the urethane support ring prevents the tire bead from entering the dropped center section of the wheel, the outside bead should be broken from the wheel, and then the support ring removed before the tire can be removed from the wheel.

GENERAL MOTORS TPC RATING

All General Motors original equipment (OE) tires have a rating that identifies the size as well as the tread design, wear, traction, and heat resistance factors. All of these factors are combined in a set of numbers and letters that is imprinted in the tire mold. This is referred to as the **Tire Performance Criteria (TPC)** rating of the tire. If a customer wants to have the same tire performance in a replacement tire, then replace the tire with any brand of tire that has the same TPC identification.
● **SEE FIGURE 21-22.**

What Is a Low-Rolling-Resistance Tire?

Low-rolling-resistance (LRR) tires reduce rolling resistance, which is the power-robbing friction between the tire and crown. The **E-metric tire**, designated for use on electric or hybrid vehicles, operates at higher inflation pressures, reduced load percentages, and lower rolling resistance. These tires were first used on the GM EV1 electric vehicle.

To soften the ride of tires pumped with additional air, a new tire profile was developed. Narrower rim width and rounder sidewalls make the tire more shock absorbent.

To make the tires roll more freely, low-rolling-resistant tread compounds are molded into smaller tread elements that flex easily and with less friction when they touch the road. LRR tires are available from most major tire manufacturers, including Michelin the Energy MXV4 Plus and Goodyear VIVA 2. According to tire engineers, the basic tradeoff of low rolling resistance is poor wet traction performance. To improve wet road performance and traction requires the use of more silica in the tread, which increases the cost of the tire. Neither a technician nor a vehicle owner can determine the relative rolling resistance unless the tires are compared using a coast-down test from highway speed to zero or a laboratory testing machine.

TIRE SELECTION CONSIDERATIONS

Selecting the proper tire is very important for the proper handling and safety of any vehicle. Do not select a tire by styling or looks alone. For best value and highest satisfaction, follow these guidelines:

Purchasing Suggestions	Reason Why
1. Purchase the same type of tire that came on your vehicle when new.	1. Chassis and tire engineers spend hundreds of hours testing and evaluating the best tire to use for each vehicle.
2. Purchase the same size as the original tire. The width of the tire should be within 10 mm of the width of the original tire. For example, a stock 195/75 × 14 tire's acceptable replacement *could be* 185/75 × 14 or 205/75 × 14.	2. The size of the tire is critical to the handling of any vehicle. Tire width, size, and aspect ratio affect the following: a. Braking effectiveness b. Headlight aiming c. Vehicle height d. Acceleration potential e. Speedometer calibration
3. Purchase tires with the same speed rating as the original.	3. When any vehicle is manufactured, it is optimized for its designed use. High-performance tires are generally stiffer and have a speed rating as well. If you purchase non-high-performance tires, the carcass is not as stiff and the suspension is not designed to work with softer tires. Therefore, the cornering and handling, especially fast evasive maneuvers, could be dangerous. The vehicle may be capable of far more speed than the tires are designed to handle.
4. Purchase four of the same type of tire. Most vehicle manufacturers recommend against installing snow tires or all-season tires on just the drive wheels.	4. Every vehicle is designed to function best with four tires of the same size, construction, and tread design, unless the vehicle is specifically designed for different sizes of tires at the front and rear. Different tire styles and tread compounds have different slip angles. It is these different slip angles that can cause a vehicle to handle "funny" or cause the vehicle to get out of control in the event of a sudden maneuver.

5. Purchase the same *brand* of tire for both front and/or both rear wheels.

5. The sizes of tires are nominal and vary according to exact size (and shape) of the mold as well as tire design and construction. The same size of tire from two different manufacturers can often differ in diameter and width. While the differences should be slight, many vehicles are extremely sensitive to these small differences, and poor vehicle handling, torque steer, and pulling could result if different brands of tires are used.

6. Purchase fresh tires. Tires that are older may have been stored in a hot warehouse, where oxygen can attack rubber and cause deterioration.

6. Look at the tire build date code (the last three numbers of the DOT code). TRY to purchase four tires with the same or similar date codes.

CAUTION: If changing tire sizes or styles beyond the recommendations as stated here, consult a knowledgeable tire store representative for help in matching wheel and tire combinations to your vehicle.

NOTE: Some tires may be five or more years old when purchased. Always check the date code!

WHEELS

The concept of a wheel has not changed in the last 5,000 years, but the style and materials used have changed a lot. Early automotive wheels were constructed from wood with a steel band as the tire.

Today's wheels are constructed of steel or aluminum alloy. The center section of the wheel that attaches to the hub is called the **center section** or **spider** because early wheels used wooden spokes that resembled a spider's web. The rubber tire attaches to the rim of the wheel. The rim has two *bead flanges* where the bead of the tire is held against the wheel when the tire is inflated. The shape of this flange is very important and is designated by Tire and Rim Association letters. For example, a wheel designated 14 × 6JJ means that the diameter of the wheel is 14 in. and the wheel is 6 in. wide measured from inside to inside of the flanges. The letters JJ indicate the *exact* shape

FIGURE 21–23 The size of the wheel is usually cast or stamped into the wheel. This wheel is 7 inches wide. The letter "J" refers to the contour of the bead seat area of the wheel.

WHEEL RIM CONTOUR

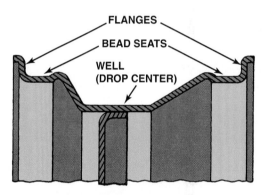

FIGURE 21–24 The wheel rim well provides a space for the tire to fit during mounting; the bead seat provides a tire-to-wheel sealing surface; the flange holds the beads in place.

of the flange area. ● **SEE FIGURE 21–23.** This flange area shape and the angle that the rim drops down from the flange are important because of the following:

- They permit a good seal between the rim and the tire.
- They help retain the tire on the rim in the event of loss of air. This is the reason why modern wheels are called "safety rim wheels." ● **SEE FIGURE 21–24.**
- Run-flat tires (tires that are designed to operate without air for a limited distance without damage) often require a specific wheel rim shape.

WHEEL OFFSET **Offset** is a very important variable in wheel design. If the center section (spider) is centered on the outer rim, the offset is zero. Wheel offset is often referred

FIGURE 21–25 A cross section of a wheel showing part designations.

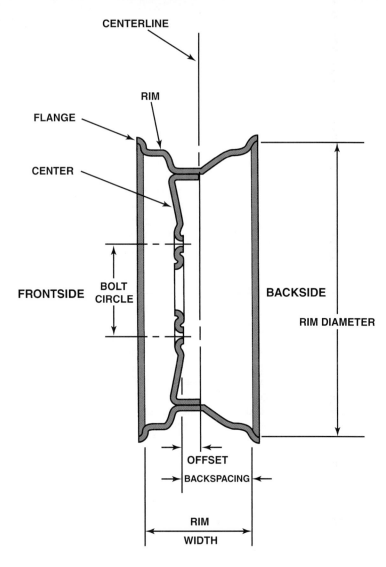

CENTERLINE

RIM

FLANGE

CENTER

FRONTSIDE

BOLT CIRCLE

BACKSIDE

RIM DIAMETER

OFFSET

BACKSPACING

RIM WIDTH

WHEELS (CONTINUED)

to as ET, which stands for *Einpress Tieffe* in German. ● **SEE FIGURE 21–25.**

POSITIVE OFFSET The wheel has a positive offset if the center section is outward from the wheel centerline. Front-wheel-drive vehicles commonly use positive-offset wheels to improve the loading on the front wheels and to help provide for a favorable scrub radius.

NEGATIVE OFFSET The wheel has a negative offset if the center section is inboard (or "dished") from the wheel centerline. ● **SEE FIGURE 21–26.** Avoid using replacement wheels that differ from the original offset.

BACK SPACING **Back spacing,** also called *rear spacing* or *backside setting,* is the distance between the back rim edge and

the wheel center section mounting pad. **This is not the same as offset.** Back spacing can be measured directly with a ruler, as shown in ● **FIGURE 21–27.**

DETERMINING BOLT CIRCLE On four-lug axles and wheels, the **bolt circle** measurement is simply taken from center to center on opposite studs or holes, as shown in ● **FIGURE 21–28.**

On five-lug axles and wheels, it is a little harder to determine bolt circle. One method is to measure from the far edge of one bolt hole to the center of the hole two over from the first, as shown in ● **FIGURE 21–29.** Another method for a five-lug wheel is to measure from center to center between two adjacent studs and convert this measurement into bolt circle diameter, as in the following chart. ● **SEE FIGURE 21–30.**

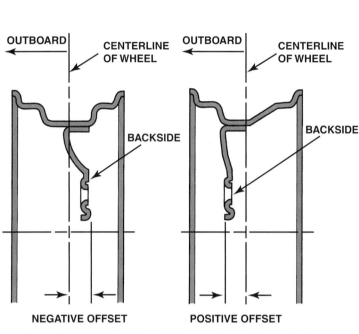

FIGURE 21–26 Offset is the distance between the centerline of the wheel and the wheel mounting surface.

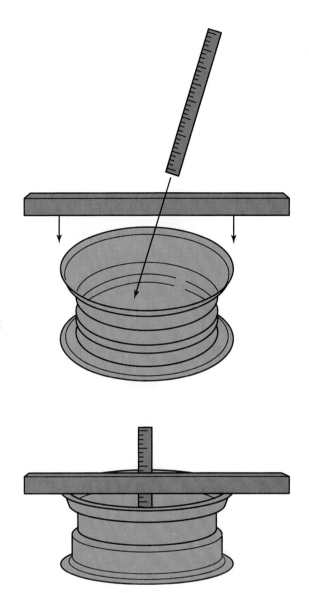

FIGURE 21–27 Back spacing (rear spacing) is the distance from the mounting pad to the edge of the rim. Most custom wheels use this measurement method to indicate the location of the mounting pad in relation to the rim.

Center-to-Center Distance	Bolt Circle Diameter
2.645 in.	4 1/2-in. bolt circle
2.792 in.	4 3/4-in. bolt circle
2.939 in.	5-in. bolt circle
3.233 in.	5 1/2-in. bolt circle

STEEL WHEELS Steel is the traditional wheel material. A steel wheel is very strong due to its designed shape and the fact that it is *work hardened* during manufacturing. In fact, most of the strength of a steel wheel is due to its work hardening. Painting and baking cycles also increase the strength of a steel wheel. Steel wheels are formed from welded hoops that are flared and joined to stamped spiders.

ALUMINUM WHEELS Forged and cast aluminum wheels are commonly used on cars and trucks. *Forged* means that the aluminum is hammered or forged under pressure into shape. A forged aluminum wheel is much stronger than a *cast* aluminum wheel.

A cast aluminum wheel is constructed by pouring liquid (molten) aluminum into a mold. After the aluminum has cooled, the cast aluminum wheel is removed from the mold and machined. Aluminum wheels are usually thicker than steel wheels and require special wheel weights when balancing. Coated or covered wheel weights should be used when balancing aluminum wheels to prevent galvanic corrosion damage to the wheel. Most aluminum wheels use an alloy of aluminum. Aluminum can be combined (alloyed) with copper, manganese, silicon, or other elements to achieve the physical strength and characteristics for the exact product. Aluminum ally wheels are often called alloy wheels.

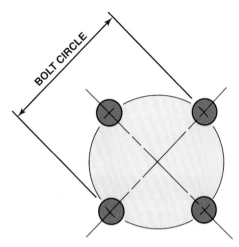

FIGURE 21–28 Bolt circle is the diameter of a circle that can be drawn through the center of each lug hole or stud. The bolt circle is sometimes referred to as PCD for pitch circle diameter.

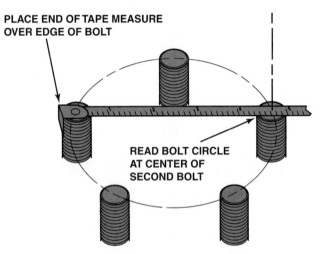

FIGURE 21–29 Measuring the bolt circle on a five lug wheel is difficult, but a quick and easy way includes measuring as shown to determine the approximate bolt circle of a five-lug wheel.

WHEELS (CONTINUED)

Some racing wheels are made from a lighter-weight metal called magnesium. These wheels are called *mag* wheels (an abbreviation for *magnesium*). True magnesium wheels are not practical for production wheels because their cost and corrosion are excessive compared with steel or aluminum alloy wheels. The term *mag wheel*, however, is still heard when referring to alloy (aluminum) wheels.

NOTE: If purchasing replacement aftermarket wheels, check that they are certified by the SFI. SFI is the Specialty Equipment Manufacturers Association (SEMA) Foundation, Incorporated. SEMA and SFI are nongovernment agencies that were formed by the manufacturers themselves to establish standards for safety.

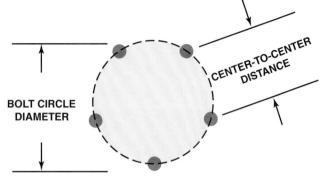

FIGURE 21–30 Measure center-to-center distance and compare the distance to the figures in the chart in the text to determine the diameter for a five-lug bolt circle.

FREQUENTLY ASKED QUESTION

What Does This Mark in a Wheel Mean?

The symbol **JWL,** for the Japan Wheel Light Metal Standard Mark, means that the wheel meets the technical standards for passenger-car light-alloy disk wheels. See the mark in ● **FIGURE 21–31**.

The manufacturer is responsible for conducting the inspections set forth in the technical standard, and the JWL mark is displayed on those products that pass the inspection.

TIRE VALVES

All tires use a tire valve, called a **Schrader valve**, to hold air in the tire. The Schrader valve was invented in New York in 1844 by August Schrader for the Goodyear Brothers: Charles, Henry, and Nelson. Today, Schrader valves are used not only as valves in tires but on fuel-injection systems, air-conditioning systems, and air shock (ride control) systems. Most tire experts agree that the valve stem (which includes the Schrader valve) should be replaced whenever tires are replaced—tires can last four or more years, and in that time the valve stem can become brittle and crack. A defective or leaking valve stem is a major cause of air loss. Low tire pressure can cause the tire to become overheated. Replacement valve stems are therefore a wise investment whenever purchasing new tires. Aluminum (alloy) wheels often require special metal valve stems that use a rubber washer and are actually bolted to the wheel. ● **SEE FIGURE 21–32.**

FIGURE 21–31 A typical JWL symbol for the Japan Wheel Light Metal standard mark.

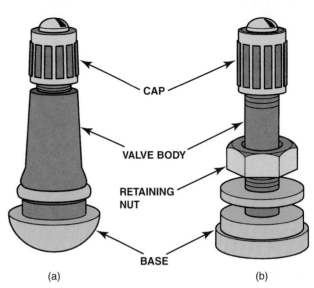

(a)   (b)

FIGURE 21–32 (a) A rubber snap-in style tire valve assembly. (b) A metal clamp-type tire valve assembly used on most high-pressure (over 60 PSI) tire applications such as is found on many trucks, RVs, and trailers. The internal Schrader valve threads into the valve itself and can be replaced individually, but most experts recommend replacing the entire valve assembly every time the tires are replaced to help prevent air loss.

UNSPRUNG WEIGHT

The lighter the wheel and tire assembly, the faster it can react to bumps and dips in the road surface and thus the better the ride. The chassis and the body of any vehicle are supported by some sort of spring suspension system. It is the purpose of the suspension system to isolate the body of the vehicle from the road surface. Also, for best handling, all four tires must remain in contact with the road. After all, a tire cannot grip the road if it leaves the ground after hitting a bump. The wheel and tire are **unsprung weight** because they are not supported by the vehicle's springs. If heavy wheels or tires are used, every time the vehicle hits a bump, the wheel is forced upward. The heavy mass of the wheel and tire would transmit this force through the spring of the vehicle and eventually to the driver and passengers. Obviously, a much lighter wheel

and tire assembly reacts faster to bumps and dips in the road surface. The end result is a smoother-riding vehicle with greater control.

An aluminum wheel is *generally* lighter than the same-size stamped steel wheel. This is not always the case, however, so before purchasing aluminum wheels, check their weight!

NOTE: Putting oversized tires on an off-road-type vehicle is extremely dangerous. The increased unsprung weight can cause the entire vehicle to leave the ground after hitting a bump in the road. The increased body height necessary to clear the larger tires seriously affects driveshaft angles and wheel alignment angles, making the vehicle very difficult to control.

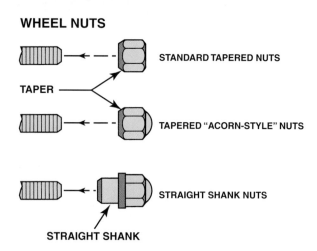

WHEEL NUTS

TAPER → STANDARD TAPERED NUTS

TAPER → TAPERED "ACORN-STYLE" NUTS

STRAIGHT SHANK NUTS

STRAIGHT SHANK

FIGURE 21–33 Various styles of lug nuts.

LUG NUTS

Lug nuts are used to hold a wheel to the brake disc, brake drum, or wheel bearing assembly. Most manufacturers use a stud in the brake or bearing assembly with a lug nut to hold the wheel. Some models of VW, Audi, and Mazda use a lug *bolt* that is threaded into a hole in the brake drum or bearing assembly.

NOTE: Some aftermarket manufacturers offer a stud conversion kit to replace the lug bolt with a conventional stud and lug nut.

Typical lug nuts are tapered so that the wheel stud will center the wheel onto the vehicle. Another advantage of the taper of the lug nut and wheel is to provide a suitable surface to prevent the nuts from loosening. The taper, usually 60 degrees, forms a wedge that helps ensure that the lug nut will not loosen. Steel wheels are deformed slightly when the lug nut is torqued down against the wheel mounting flange; be certain that the taper is *toward* the vehicle.

Many alloy wheels use a *shank-nut*-type lug nut that has straight sides without a taper. This style of nut must be used with wheels designed for this nut type. If replacement wheels are used on any vehicle, check with the wheel manufacturer as to the proper type and style of lug nut. ● **FIGURE 21–33** shows several of the many styles of lug nuts that are available.

SIZE   Lug nuts are sized to the thread size of the stud onto which they screw. The diameter and the number of threads per inch are commonly stated. Since some vehicles use left-hand threads, RH and LH are commonly stated, indicating "right-hand" and "left-hand" threads. A typical size is 7/16-20RH, where the 7/16 indicates the diameter of the wheel stud and 20 indicates that there are 20 threads per inch. Another common fractional size is 1/2 × 20. Metric sizes such as M12 × 1.5 use a different sizing method.

M	metric
12	12-mm diameter of stud
1.5	1.5-mm distance from one thread peak to another

Other commonly used metric lug sizes include M12 × 1.25 and M14 × 1.5. Obviously, metric wheel studs require metric lug nuts.

LUG STUDS   Lug studs are usually installed in hubs or drums using a press fit. Serrations on the shoulder of the stud provide support. Most studs are replaceable and should be replaced if the treads are damaged.

1 Check the tire information placard, usually located on the driver's door or door jamb, for the specified tire size and inflation pressure.

2 Visually check the tires for abnormal wear or damage.

3 Remove the tire valve cap and visually check the condition of the valve stem.

4 Check inflation pressure by pushing the tire pressure gauge straight onto the end of the tire valve. If a "hissing" sound is heard, then the reading will not be accurate.

5 Read the pressure and compare to specifications. Use an analog or digital gauge if possible which have been proven to be more accurate than a mechanical pencil-type gauge.

6 A typical tire tread depth gauge.

CONTINUED ▶

7 The blade of the tire tread depth gauge is pushed down into the groove of the tire at the lowest part.

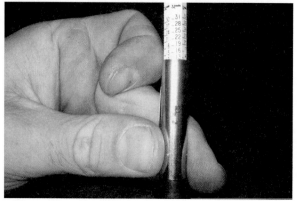

8 Remove the gauge from the tire and read the tread depth at the metal housing. Tread depth is usually measured in 1/32's of an inch.

9 If the top of Lincoln's head is visible, then the tread depth is lower than 2/32 in., the legal limit in many states.

1. New tires have between 9/32 in. and 15/32 in. tread depth. Wear bars (indicators) show up as a bald strip across the tread of the tire when the tread depth gets down to 2/32 in.

2. All tires are assembled by hand from many different materials and chemical compounds. After a green tire is assembled, it is placed into a mold under heat and pressure for about 30 minutes. Tread design and the tire shape are determined by the mold design.

3. A 205/75R × 14 92S tire is 205 mm wide at its widest section and is 75% as high as it is wide. The R stands for radial-type construction. The tire is designed for a 14-in.-diameter rim. The number 92 is the load index of the tire (the higher the number, the more weight the tire can safely support). The S is the speed rating of the tire (S × 112 mph maximum sustained).

4. The Uniform Tire Quality Grading System is a rating for tread wear (100, 150, etc.), traction (A, B, C), and temperature resistance (A, B, C).

5. For best overall handling and satisfaction, always select the same size and type of tire that came on the vehicle when new.

6. Replacement wheels should have the same offset as the factory wheels to prevent abnormal tire wear and/or handling problems.

7. All wheels must be secured with the proper size and style of lug nuts. If a wheel stud is broken, it should be replaced immediately to avoid possible wheel damage or loss of vehicle control.

REVIEW QUESTIONS

1. List the various parts of a tire and explain how a tire is constructed.

2. What is the aspect ratio?

3. List the factors that should be considered when purchasing tires.

4. Explain the three major areas of the Uniform Tire Quality Grading System.

5. How is the proper tire inflation pressure determined?

CHAPTER QUIZ

1. The part of the tire that is under just the tread of a radial tire is called the _____.
   a. Bead
   b. Body (carcass) ply
   c. Belt
   d. Inner liner

2. The aspect ratio of a tire means _____.
   a. Its width to diameter of a wheel ratio
   b. The ratio of height to width
   c. The ratio of width to height
   d. The ratio of rolling resistance

3. A tire is labeled 215/60R × 15 92T; the T indicates _____.
   a. Its speed rating
   b. Its tread wear rating
   c. Its load rating
   d. Its temperature resistance rating

4. The 92 in the tire designation in question 3 refers to the tire's _____.
   a. Speed rating
   b. Tread wear rating
   c. Load rating
   d. Temperature resistance rating

5. Radial tires can cause a vehicle to pull to one side while driving. This is called "radial tire pull" and is often due to _____.
   a. The angle of the body (carcass) plies
   b. Tire conicity
   c. Tread design
   d. Bead design

6. Tire inflation is very important to the safe and economical operation of any vehicle. Technician A says that the pressure should never exceed the maximum pressure imprinted on the sidewall of the tire. Technician B says to inflate the tires to the pressures recommended on the tire information decal or placard on the driver's door. Which technician is correct?
   a. Technician A only
   b. Technician B only
   c. Both Technicians A and B
   d. Neither Technician A nor B

7. When purchasing replacement tires, do not change tire width from the stock size by more than _____.
   a. 10 mm
   b. 15 mm
   c. 20 mm
   d. 25 mm

8. What do the letters JJ mean in a wheel designation size labeled 14 × 7JJ?
   a. The offset of the rim
   b. The bolt circle code
   c. The back spacing of the rim
   d. The shape of the flange area

9. Technician A says that a PAX run-flat tire uses a special wheel. Technician B says that a standard tire can be used to replace a PAX run-flat tire. Which technician is correct?
   a. Technician A only
   b. Technician B only
   c. Both Technicians A and B
   d. Neither Technician A nor B

10. Wheel back spacing is also called _____.
    a. Rear spacing
    b. Positive offset
    c. Negative offset
    d. Offset

chapter 22
TIRE PRESSURE MONITORING SYSTEMS

OBJECTIVES

After studying Chapter 22, the reader will be able to:

1. Explain why a tire-pressure monitoring system is used.
2. Discuss the TREAD Act.
3. List the two types of TPMS sensors.
4. Describe how to program or relearn TPMS sensors.
5. List the tools needed to service a tire-pressure monitoring system.

KEY TERMS

Active mode 402
Alert mode 402
Cold placard inflation pressure 398
Delta pressure method 405
Initialization 400

Relearn 400
Sleep mode 402
Storage mode 403
Tire-pressure monitoring system (TPMS) 398
Transmitter ID 405
TREAD Act 400

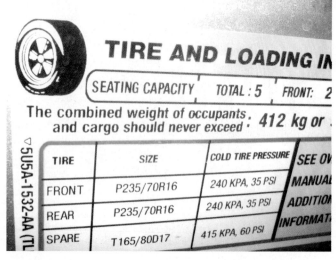

FIGURE 22-1 The tire pressure placard (sticker) on the driver's side door or door jamb indicates the specified tire pressure.

Temperature	Tire Pressure (PSI)	Change from Cold Placard Inflation Pressure
120°F (49°C)	37	+5
110°F (43°C)	36	+4
100°F (38°C)	35	+3
90°F (32°C)	34	+2
80°F (27°C)	33	+1
70°F (21°C)	32	0
60°F (16°C)	31	−1
50°F (10°C)	30	−2
40°F (4°C)	29	−3
30°F (−1°C)	28	−4
20°F (−7°C)	27	−5
10°F (−12°C)	26	−6
0°F (−18°C)	25	−7
−10°F (−23°C)	24	−8
−20°F (−29°C)	23	−9

CHART 22-1

The effects of outside temperature on tire inflation, assuming a placard pressure of 32 PSI.

NEED FOR TIRE PRESSURE MONITORING

BACKGROUND A **tire-pressure monitoring system (TPMS)** is a system that detects a tire that has low inflation pressure and warns the driver. A tire-pressure monitoring system was first used when run-flat tires were introduced in the 1990s. A driver was often not aware that a tire had gone flat after a puncture. Because a run-flat tire is designed to be driven a limited distance and at limited speed after it loses air pressure, a method of alerting the driver had to be found. There were two systems used, indirect and direct, until the 2008 model year when the use of direct-reading pressure systems was required by law.

LOW TIRE PRESSURE EFFECTS Low-tire inflation pressures have led to all of the following:

- Reduces fuel economy due to increased rolling resistance of the tires—3 PSI below specifications results in an increase of 1% in fuel consumption

- Reduces tire life—3 PSI below specifications results in a decrease of 10% of tire life

- Increases the number of roadside faults, which have been estimated to be 90% related to tire issues

- Reduces handling and braking efficiency

- Hundreds of deaths and thousands of personal injuries are due to problems associated with low-tire inflation pressure.

COLD PLACARD INFLATION PRESSURE The term **cold placard inflation pressure** is used in service information to indicate the specified tire inflation pressure. The "placard" is the driver's side door jamb sticker that shows the tire size and the specified tire inflation pressure. The pressure stated is measured when the tires are cold or at room temperature, which is about 70°F (21°C). ● **SEE FIGURE 22-1.**

The tires become warmer while the vehicle is being driven, so tires should be checked before the vehicle has been driven or allowed to cool after being driven. Tire inflation pressure changes 1 PSI for every 10 degrees. ● **SEE CHART 22-1.**

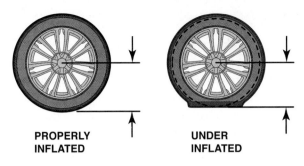

FIGURE 22–2 A tire with low inflation will have a shorter distance (radius) between the center of the wheel and the road and will therefore rotate faster than a tire that is properly inflated.

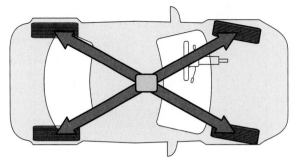

FIGURE 22–3 The speeds of the diagonally opposed wheels are added together and then compared to the other two wheels to check if one tire is rotating faster.

INDIRECT TPMS

PURPOSE AND FUNCTION Indirect tire-pressure monitoring systems do not measure the actual tire pressure. Instead, the system uses the wheel speed sensors to detect differences in the speed of the wheels. The indirect system uses the wheel speed sensors to check the rolling speed of each of the tires. If a tire is underinflated, the following occurs:

- A tire that is underinflated will have a smaller diameter than a properly inflated tire. ● **SEE FIGURE 22–2.**
- An underinflated tire will rotate faster than a properly inflated tire.

COMPENSATION FOR CORNERING When a vehicle turns a corner, the outside wheels rotate faster than the inside wheels. To compensate for this normal change in wheel rotation speed, the indirect tire-pressure monitoring system checks the diagonally opposed wheels. ● **SEE FIGURE 22–3.**

If the calculation of the diagonal wheel speed indicates that one of the wheels is rotating faster than the other, the TPMS warning light is illuminated.

ADVANTAGES Advantages for using the indirect system include:

- This system does not require additional components, such as tire-pressure sensors.
- This system is easily added to existing vehicles that were equipped with four-wheel speed sensors.
- It is low cost.

DISADVANTAGES Disadvantages for using the indirect system include:

- System cannot detect if all four tires are underinflated.
- Use of a space-saver spare tire may trigger the warning light.
- Cannot detect if more than one tire is low.
- Does not meet the Federal Highway Traffic Safety Standard (FMVSS) 138, which requires the system to be able to detect if any tire is underinflated by 25%.

DIAGNOSIS OF INDIRECT TPMS The diagnosis of an indirect tire-pressure monitoring system includes the following steps:

STEP 1 Verify the fault.
- If the TPMS warning light is on but not flashing, this indicates that the system has detected a tire with low inflation pressure.
- If the TPMS warning light flashes, this indicates that the system has detected a fault. Check service information for the specified steps to follow.

STEP 2 If the system has detected low tire pressure, check and adjust the tire pressure to that listed on the door pillar placard or factory specifications as stated in the owner's manual or service information.

STEP 3 Determine and correct the cause of the underinflated tire.

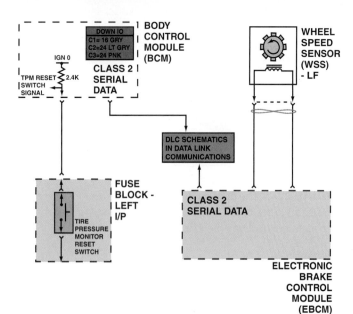

FIGURE 22–4 The indirect tire-pressure monitoring system has a reset switch that should be depressed after rotating or replacing tires.

INDIRECT TPMS (CONTINUED)

RELEARN (RESET) PROCEDURES After checking that all four tires are the same size and condition, the system may require resetting, also called **relearn** or **initialization**. Check service information for the exact steps to follow, which could include driving the vehicle over an extended period of time. The procedure usually includes the following:

- Inflate all four tires to the placard inflation pressure.
- Depress and hold the reset switch for 3 seconds. ● **SEE FIGURE 22–4.** The TPMS warning lamp should flash three times.
- Drive the vehicle so the ABS controller can learn the new "good" values. Typical driving times include:
  - Ford—20 minutes of driving
  - Toyota—30 to 60 minutes of driving
  - General Motors—60 minutes of driving

Check service information for the exact procedure to follow. Many service technicians ask the vehicle owner to drive the vehicle instead of taking the technician's time.

TREAD ACT

The **Transportation Recall Enhancement, Accountability and Documentation (TREAD) Act** requires that all vehicles be equipped with a tire-pressure monitoring system that will warn the driver in the event of an underinflated tire. This act was passed due to many accidents that were caused at least in part to underinflated tires. These accidents resulted in many deaths.

Congress passed the TREAD Act on November 1, 2000. The National Highway Traffic Safety Administration (NHTSA) requires the installation of tire-pressure monitoring systems (TPMSs) in passenger vehicles and light trucks manufactured after September 1, 2007 (2008 model year).

The NHTSA ruling is part one of a two-part final ruling.

- Part one establishes a new Federal Motor Vehicle Safety Standard (FMVSS) 138 that requires tire-pressure monitoring systems be installed in passenger vehicles and light trucks to warn the driver when a tire is 25% below the cold placard pressure.
- Part two includes the requirement to equip vehicles with a tire-pressure monitoring system that was phased-in starting in 2004. The phase-in included:
  - 20% from October 5, 2005 to August 31, 2006
  - 70% from September 1, 2006 to August 31, 2007
  - 100% from September 1, 2007 (2008 model year vehicles)

FMVSS 138 requires all cars, trucks, and vans with a gross vehicle weight rating (GVWR) of 10,000 pounds or less to illuminate a warning lamp within 10 minutes when the inflation pressure drops 25% or more from the vehicle manufacturer's specified cold tire inflation pressure as printed on the door placard.

WARNING LAMP The FMVSS 138 specifies that the driver must be warned of a low-tire inflation pressure by turning on an amber warning lamp. The warning lamp must also come on during a bulb check. The spare tire is not required to be monitored, but many vehicle manufacturers do equip full-size spare tires with a pressure sensor.

- If the TPMS warning lamp is on at start-up, the system has detected a tire with low inflation pressure.
- If the TPMS warning lamp is flashing for 60 to 90 seconds, a system fault has been detected.

TWENTY-FIVE PERCENT RULE The TREAD Act specifies that the driver be warned if any tire inflation pressure drops by 25% or more from the cold placard pressure. ● **SEE CHART 22–2.**

Cold Placard Inflation Pressure (PSI)	Warning Light Pressure (−25%)	PSI Low
40	30.0	10.0
39	29.3	9.7
38	28.5	9.5
37	27.8	9.2
36	27.0	9.0
35	26.3	8.7
34	25.5	8.5
33	24.8	8.2
32	24	8.0
31	23.3	7.7
30	22.5	7.5
29	21.8	7.2
28	21	7.0

CHART 22–2 Placard inflation pressure compared with the pressure when the TPMS triggers a warning light.

FIGURE 22–5 A clear plastic valve-stem tire-pressure monitoring sensor, showing the round battery on the right and the electronic sensor and transistor circuits on the left.

 **TECH TIP**

Check Tire Pressure and Do Not Rely on the Warning Light

Industry experts think that 25% is too low and that this generally means that a tire has to be lower by about 8 PSI to trigger a warning light. All experts agree that tire pressure should be checked at least every month and kept at the specified cold placard inflation pressure.

IDENTIFYING A VEHICLE WITH TPMS

All vehicles sold in the United States since the 2008 model year must be equipped with a tire-pressure sensor. If the tire/wheel assembly has a tire-pressure monitoring system (TPMS) valve-type sensor, it can usually be identified by the threaded portion of the valve stem. ● **SEE FIGURE 22–5.**

RUBBER TIRE VALVE STEMS Some TPMS sensors are black rubber like a conventional valve core but it uses a tapered brass section and a longer cap. ● **SEE FIGURE 22–6.** If the cap is short then it does not have a stem-mounted tire-pressure sensor. However, the wheel may be equipped with a

FIGURE 22–6 A conventional valve stem is on the right compared with a rubber TPMS sensor stem on the left. Notice the tapered and larger brass stem. The rubber TPMS sensor also uses a longer cap that makes it easy for a technician to spot that this is not a conventional rubber valve stem.

wheel-mounted sensor, so care should still be taken to avoid damaging the sensor during service.

ALUMINUM TIRE VALVE STEMS If the vehicle has an aluminum tire valve stem, it is equipped with a direct tire-pressure monitoring system. The valve stem itself is the antenna for the sensor.

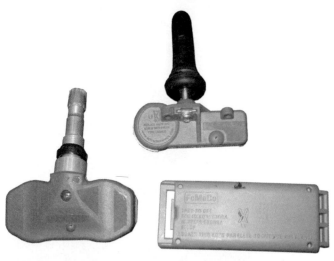

FIGURE 22-7 The three styles of TPMS sensors most commonly found include the two stem-mounted (rubber and aluminum, left and top), and the banded style (right).

TECH TIP

Use TPMS-Friendly Replacement Tires

Some replacement tires use steel body plies and could therefore block the low-level radio frequency signal sent from the tire-pressure sensor. Before installing replacement tires, check that the tires are safe and recommended for use on vehicles equipped with a direct-type tire-pressure monitoring system.

TPMS PRESSURE SENSORS

TYPES All direct TPMS sensors transmit tire inflation pressure to a module using a radio frequency (RF) signal. There are two basic designs used in direct pressure-sensing systems. These sensors are manufactured by a variety of manufacturers, including:

- Beru
- Lear
- Pacific
- Schrader
- Siemens
- TRW

Each sensor uses a 3-volt lithium ion battery that has a service life of 7 to 10 years.

1. **Valve stem-mounted sensor**—This type of sensor uses the valve stem as the transmitter. The correct (nickel plated) valve core *must* be used in the aluminum valve stem. If a conventional brass valve is used, moisture in the air will cause corrosion between the two different metals.

2. **Banded sensor**—Banded sensors are installed in the drop well of the wheel and banded or clamped to keep them secure. Early banded sensors, such as those used in Corvettes equipped with run-flat tires, were piezoelectric and did not require a battery. All newer banded sensors include a battery.

● **SEE FIGURE 22-7.**

MODES OF OPERATION Tire-pressure sensors operate in three modes of operation:

1. **Active mode**—When the sensor inside detects that the vehicle is traveling above 20 mph (32 km/h), the sensor transmits once every minute.

2. **Sleep mode**—When the vehicle is stopped, the sensor "goes to sleep" to help improve battery life. In this mode, the transmitter still will broadcast tire inflation information every hour or every 6 hours, depending on the sensor.

3. **Alert mode**—Alert mode is triggered if a rapid change in inflation pressure is detected. In alert (or rapid mode), the tire inflation pressure is sent about every second (every 800 milliseconds on some sensors).

TPMS SENSOR OPERATION

Depending on the type and manufacturer, tire-pressure monitoring sensors can be any of several different designs. The TREAD Act does not specify the type or operation of the pressure sensors, only that the system must be capable of measuring tire inflation pressure and light the TPMS warning lamp. The types of sensors include:

- **Continuous-wave-type sensor**—designed to signal a tester when exposed to 5 to 7 seconds of continuous 125 KHz wave signal.

FIGURE 22–8 A typical tire-pressure monitoring system tester. The unit should be held near the tire and opposite the valve stem if equipped with a wheel-mounted sensor, and near the valve stem if equipped with a valve-stem-type sensor.

FIGURE 22–9 Some vehicles display the actual measured tire pressure for each tire on a driver information display.

 TECH TIP

Check the TPMS Sensors Before and After Service

It is wise to check that all of the tire-pressure monitoring system sensors are working before beginning service work. For example, if the tires need to be rotated, the sensors will have to be reprogrammed for their new location. If a tire-pressure monitoring sensor is defective, the procedure cannot be performed. Use an aftermarket or original equipment tire-pressure monitoring sensor tester, as shown in ● **FIGURE 22–8.**

Then the tire-pressure sensors should be checked again after the service to make sure that they are working correctly before returning the vehicle to the customer.

? FREQUENTLY ASKED QUESTION

Does a TPMS Sensor Work before Being Installed?

No. New tire-pressure warning sensors (transmitters) are shipped in **storage mode**. This mode prevents the battery from becoming discharged while in storage. When the transmitter is installed in a wheel/tire assembly and the tire is inflated to more than 14 PSI (97 kPa), the transmitter automatically cancels storage mode. Once a transmitter has canceled storage mode, it cannot enter this mode again. Therefore, once a sensor has been installed and the tire inflated above 14 PSI, the clock is ticking on battery life.

- **Magnetically-triggered-type sensor**—designed to trigger a tester if exposed to a powerful magnetic force.
- **Pulse-width-modulated-type sensor**—designed to be triggered when exposed to modulated wave 125 KHz signal.

The sensor also can vary according to the frequency at which it transmits tire-pressure information to the receiver in the vehicle. The two most commonly used frequencies are:

- 315 MHz
- 433.92 MHz (commonly listed as 434 MHz)

TPMS RECEIVER

The wireless TPMS receiver is housed in one of the following locations, depending on the vehicle:

- Remote keyless entry (RKE) receiver
- Body control module (BCM)
- Door module
- Individual antennas near each wheel well. These individual antennas then transmit tire-pressure information to the driver information center. ● **SEE FIGURE 22–9.**

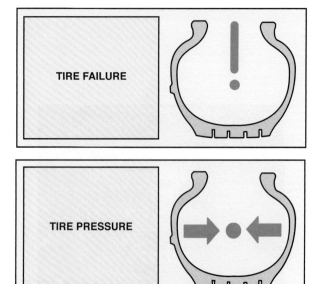

FIGURE 22–10 A tire-pressure warning light can vary depending on the vehicle, but includes a tire symbol.

 TECH TIP

Check the Spare Tire

Many vehicles equipped with a full-size spare tire also have a TPMS sensor. If the inflation pressure decreases enough, the system will trigger the TPMS warning light. This is confusing to many vehicle owners who have checked all four tires and found them to be properly inflated. This fault often occurs during cold weather when the tire inflation pressure drops due to the temperature change. Most 2008 and newer vehicles equipped with a full size spare tire will come equipped with a TPMS sensor in the spare.

DIRECT TPMS DIAGNOSIS

WARNING LIGHT ON If the TPMS warning light is on and not flashing, the system has detected a tire that has low inflation pressure. ● **SEE FIGURE 22–10.**

If the TPMS light is on, perform the following steps:

STEP 1 Check the door placard for the specified tire inflation pressure.

STEP 2 Check all tires using a known-accurate tire-pressure gauge.

STEP 3 Inflate all tires to the specified pressure.

NOTE: Some systems will trigger the TPMS warning light if a tire is overinflated. An overinflated tire is also a safety-related problem.

WARNING LIGHT FLASHING If the TPMS warning lamp is flashing on and off, the system has detected a fault in the system. Faults could include:

- Defective wheel sensors, such as a sensor with a dead battery.
- A fault in the receiver, such as in the remote keyless entry module.

Check service information for the exact procedure to follow if the TPMS warning lamp is flashing. Always follow the specified diagnostic and service procedures.

INSTALLING A NEW PRESSURE SENSOR

When installing a new pressure sensor either because it failed or was damaged, the new sensor has to be relearned. This process is usually done with either:

- A scan tool
- A TPMS tester

The identification number on each sensor must be recorded before being installed, so it can register to a specific location on the vehicle. All four sensor identification numbers usually have to be entered into the tool within 300 seconds (5 minutes). On some vehicles, all four sensors must be relearned even if only one sensor is replaced.

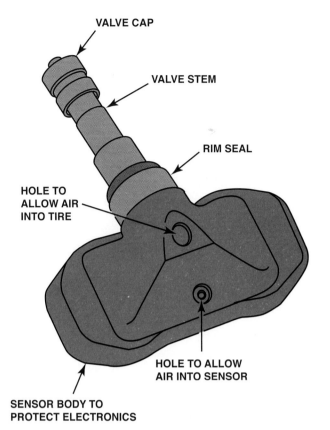

FIGURE 22–11 The parts of a typical stem-mounted TPMS sensor. Notice the small hole used to monitor the inflation pressure. The use of stop-leak can easily clog this small hole.

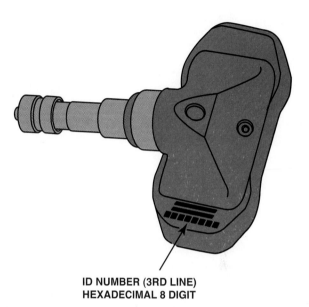

ID NUMBER (3RD LINE)
HEXADECIMAL 8 DIGIT

FIGURE 22–12 When replacing a TPMS sensor, be sure to record the sensor ID because this needs to be entered into the system through the use of a tester or scan tool.

TPMS DIAGNOSTIC TOOLS

SCAN TOOLS Scan tools can be used for TPMS service if the scan tool is an original equipment tool for the vehicle make or if an aftermarket scan tool has original equipment-compatible software to access the chassis or body functions of the vehicle. A scan tool is used to perform the following functions:

1. **Register TPMS sensors**—A replacement TPMS transmitter has an 8-digit number, called the **transmitter ID,** on each valve/transmitter assembly. ● **SEE FIGURE 22–11.**

2. **Perform initialization**—This step assigns a transmitter ID to the correct position on the vehicle, such as right front (RF). ● **SEE FIGURE 22–12.**

3. **Monitor sensor values**—TPMS transmitters send information to the controller including:
   ▪ Sensor identification
   ▪ Tire inflation pressure
   ▪ Tire air temperature (some sensors)
   ▪ Sensor battery voltage (some sensors)

TPMS SENSOR ACTIVATIONS

ACTIVATING THE SENSOR A tire-pressure monitoring system sensor needs to be activated to verify that the sensor actually works. This should be performed before any tire or wheel service is performed. There are three methods used to activate a TPMS sensor to cause it to send a signal that can be captured to verify proper operation. These activation methods include:

1. **Using a magnet** (aluminum wheels and stem-mounted sensors only) ● **SEE FIGURE 22–13.**

2. **Changing inflation pressure** (usually requires lowering the inflation pressure by 5 to 10 PSI) This method is called the **delta pressure method.** The term *delta* refers to a change and is named for the Greek letter delta (Δ).

3. **Triggered by a handheld TPMS tester** that transmits a signal to wake up the sensor. There are two formats used, depending on the sensor. They include:
   ▪ 125 KHz constant or continuous pulse
   ▪ 125 KHz pulse-width-modulated pulse

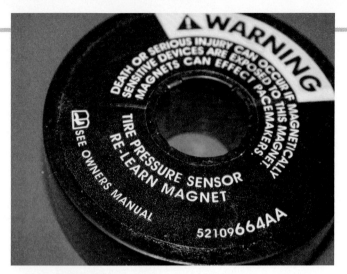

FIGURE 22–13 A magnet is placed around the valve stem to reprogram some stem-mounted tire-pressure sensors.

HANDHELD TESTERS Several manufacturers produce handheld testers to reset the sensors. These tools are used to perform the following functions:

- TPMS sensor activation
- TPMS sensor relearn
- To program a new TPMS sensor

Tools are available from the following companies:

- OTC (http://www.otctools.com)
- Bartec (http://www.bartecusa.com)
- Snap-on (http://www.snapon.com)

TPMS RELEARN PROCEDURE

The following procedure will allow the service technician to reprogram the TPMS after tire rotation on a General Motors vehicle without using a scan tool.

1. With KOEO (key on, engine off), the "lock" and "unlock" buttons on the key fob should be simultaneously pressed and held. The horn will chirp within 10 seconds, indicating the receiver is in programming mode. The programming procedure must now be completed within five minutes, with no more than one minute between programming.

   NOTE: If the horn does not chirp at the start of this procedure, the TPMS option has not been enabled. A scan tool is needed to enable the system.

2. At the left front wheel, the special magnet tool must be held over the valve stem to force the sensor to transmit its code. The horn will chirp once, indicating the system has recognized the sensor. The next sensor must be programmed within one minute.

3. The remaining sensors should be programmed in the following order: RF, RR, LR. The horn will chirp once when each sensor has been detected. It will chirp twice to indicate completion of the programming process.

TPMS SENSOR SERVICE TOOLS

ITEMS NEEDED Whenever servicing a tire/wheel assembly that has a direct TPMS system, certain items are needed. When a stem-mounted sensor is removed, the following items are needed:

1. **Information**—Check service information for the exact procedure to follow for the vehicle being serviced. Vehicles and sensors are different for different vehicles.

2. **Digital tire-pressure gauge**—Many mechanical tire-pressure gauges are not accurate. An old mechanical gauge may be used to ensure that all tires are inflated to the same pressure, but the pressure may not be accurate.
   ● **SEE FIGURE 22–14.**

3. **Tire valve core torque wrench**—This calibrated tool ensures that the valve core is tightened enough to prevent air loss, but not too tight to cause harm. The recommended torque is 3 to 5 inch-pounds (0.34 to 0.56 N.m).
   ● **SEE FIGURE 22–15.**

4. **Tire valve nut torque wrench**—Most are 11 or 12 mm in size and the torque ranges from 30 to 90 in.-lb (4.25 to 10.0 N.m).

5. **Sensor service kit**—If a pressure sensor is going to be reused, the following service parts must be replaced:
   - Cap
   - Valve core (nickel plated only)

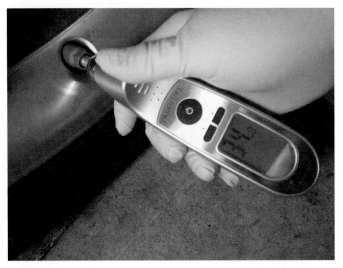

FIGURE 22–14 Always use an accurate, known-good tire-pressure gauge. Digital gauges are usually more accurate than mechanical gauges.

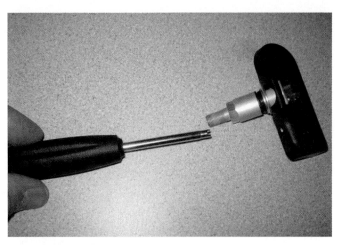

FIGURE 22–15 A clicker-type valve core tool ensures that the valve core is tightened to factory specifications.

TECH TIP

All TPMS Sensors Will Fail

All TPMS pressure sensors will fail because they contain a battery that has a service life of 7 to 10 years. What does this mean to the service technician? This means that if new tires are being installed on a 5- or 6-year-old vehicle equipped with tire-pressure sensors, then the customer should be notified that the TPMS sensors could fail almost anytime.

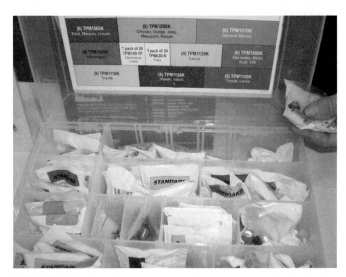

FIGURE 22–16 An assortment of service parts that include all of the parts needed to service a stem-mounted TPMS sensor being installed after removal for a tire replacement or repair.

- Nut
- Grommet

These parts are usually available individually or in an assortment package. Pressure sensor and kit information can be found at the following websites:

- http://www.schrader-bridgeport.com
- http://www.myerstiresupply.com
- http://www.rubber-inc.com
  ● SEE FIGURE 22–16.

FREQUENTLY ASKED QUESTION

Can TPMS sensors be switched to new wheels?

Maybe. It depends on the style of the new or replacement wheels as to whether the sensors will fit or not. Some vehicles are designed to allow for a second set of sensors such as for winter tires. Many Lexus vehicles can be programmed to use set #1 or set #2. It is best to check before purchasing new wheels. Another set of TPMS sensors could be a major added expense.

1. Low-tire inflation pressure can cause a decrease in fuel economy, reduced tire life, and increase the chance of tire failure.

2. The designated tire inflation pressure is stated on the driver's side door jamb placard.

3. Tire inflation pressure drops 1 PSI for every 10 degrees drop in temperature.

4. The indirect tire-pressure monitoring system uses the wheel speed sensors to detect a low tire.

5. The TREAD Act, also called the Federal Motor Vehicle Safety Standard 138, specifies that all cars, trucks, and vans under 10,000 pounds gross vehicle weight rating (GVWR) must be equipped with a direct pressure-sending tire-pressure monitoring system after September 1, 2007 (2008 model year vehicles).

6. The two basic types of TPMS sensors include:
   • Valve stem-mounted
   • Banded

7. After a tire rotation, the sensors need to be reset or re-learned.

8. Special tools are recommended to relearn, activate, or service a tire-pressure monitoring system.

REVIEW QUESTIONS

1. How does the use of wheel speed sensors detect a tire with low inflation pressure?

2. What is the difference between faults when the TPMS warning lamp is on compared with when it is flashing?

3. What is the percentage of vehicles that each vehicle manufacturer must equip with TPMS?

4. TPMS pressure sensors can be made by what manufacturer?

5. What are the three modes of sensor operation?

6. What information is sent to the TPMS controller from the sensor?

7. After removing a stem-type pressure sensor to replace a tire or perform a tire repair, what should be replaced?

CHAPTER QUIZ

1. A tire with lower than specified inflation pressure could lead to what condition?
   a. Reduced fuel economy
   b. Reduced tire life
   c. Increased chances of roadside faults or accidents
   d. All of the above

2. Which tire inflation information should be checked to determine the proper tire inflation pressure?
   a. Cold placard inflation pressure
   b. The maximum pressure as stated on the sidewall of the tire
   c. 32 PSI in all tires
   d. Any of the above

3. Two technicians are discussing tire pressure and temperature. Technician A says that tire pressure will drop 1 PSI for every 10 degrees drop in temperature. Technician B says that the tire pressure will increase as the vehicle is being driven. Which technician is correct?
   a. Technician A only
   b. Technician B only
   c. Both Technicians A and B
   d. Neither Technician A nor B

4. Two technicians are discussing the indirect tire-pressure monitoring system. Technician A says that it was used by some vehicle manufacturers on vehicles before the 2008 model year. Technician B says that it uses the speeds of the RF and LR tires and compares the rotating speeds of the LF and RR tires to detect a low tire. Which technician is correct?
   a. Technician A only
   b. Technician B only
   c. Both Technicians A and B
   d. Neither Technician A nor B

5. The FMVSS 138 law requires that the driver be notified if the tire inflation pressure drops how much?
   a. 30%
   b. 25%
   c. 20%
   d. 15%

6. The two basic types of direct TPMS sensors include _____.
   a. Rubber stem and aluminum stem
   b. Beru and Schrader
   c. Stem-mounted and banded
   d. Indirect and direct

7. What mode does a direct pressure sensor enter when the vehicle is stopped?
   a. Sleep mode
   b. Storage mode
   c. Alert mode
   d. Active mode

8. To activate or learn a direct pressure sensor, what does the service technician need to do?
   a. Enter learn mode and use a magnet
   b. Enter learn mode and decrease inflation pressure
   c. Use a handheld tester
   d. Any of the above depending on the vehicle and system

9. What does the "delta pressure method" mean?
   a. Change the inflation pressure
   b. Activate the sensor so it broadcasts the pressure to the scan tool
   c. Inflating the tire to the specified pressure
   d. Using a handheld tester to read the pressure as reported by the sensor

10. What type of valve core is used in stem-mounted sensors?
    a. Brass
    b. Nickel plated
    c. Steel
    d. Aluminum

TIRE AND WHEEL SERVICE

OBJECTIVES

After studying Chapter 23, the reader will be able to:

1. Prepare for ASE Suspension and Steering (A4) certification test content area "E" (Wheel and Tire Diagnosis and Repair).
2. Discuss proper tire mounting procedures.
3. Describe recommended tire rotation methods.
4. Discuss how to properly balance a tire.
5. Describe tire repair procedures.
6. Explain wheel and tire safety precautions.

KEY TERMS

Dynamic balance 421
Lateral runout 420
Match mounting 413
Modified X 417
Radial force variation 419
Radial runout 418

Shimmy 420
Static balance 421
Tire rotation 416
Tramp 418
Wheel mounting torque 415

7. What mode does a direct pressure sensor enter when the vehicle is stopped?
   a. Sleep mode
   b. Storage mode
   c. Alert mode
   d. Active mode

8. To activate or learn a direct pressure sensor, what does the service technician need to do?
   a. Enter learn mode and use a magnet
   b. Enter learn mode and decrease inflation pressure
   c. Use a handheld tester
   d. Any of the above depending on the vehicle and system

9. What does the "delta pressure method" mean?
   a. Change the inflation pressure
   b. Activate the sensor so it broadcasts the pressure to the scan tool
   c. Inflating the tire to the specified pressure
   d. Using a handheld tester to read the pressure as reported by the sensor

10. What type of valve core is used in stem-mounted sensors?
   a. Brass
   b. Nickel plated
   c. Steel
   d. Aluminum

TIRE AND
WHEEL SERVICE

OBJECTIVES

After studying Chapter 23, the reader will be able to:

1. Prepare for ASE Suspension and Steering (A4) certification test content area "E" (Wheel and Tire Diagnosis and Repair).

2. Discuss proper tire mounting procedures.

3. Describe recommended tire rotation methods.

4. Discuss how to properly balance a tire.

5. Describe tire repair procedures.

6. Explain wheel and tire safety precautions.

KEY TERMS

FIGURE 23–1 Using soapy water from a spray bottle is an easy method to find the location of an air leak from a tire.

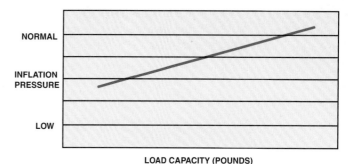

FIGURE 23–2 This chart shows the relationship between tire inflation pressure and load capacity of the tire.

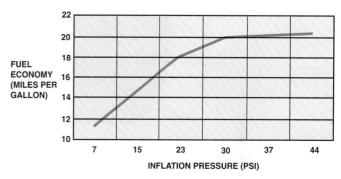

FIGURE 23–3 This chart shows that a drop in inflation pressure has a major effect on fuel economy.

Proper tire service is extremely important for the safe operation of any vehicle. Premature wear can often be avoided by checking and performing routine service, such as frequent rotation and monthly inflation checks. Avoid overloading the vehicle and have any leaks repaired as soon as possible. ● **SEE FIGURE 23–1.**

TIRE INFLATION

Tires should always be inflated to the pressure indicated on the driver's door or pillar sticker. Tires should be checked when cold, before the vehicle has been driven, because driving on tires increases the temperature and therefore the pressure of the tires. Proper tire inflation is important for the following reasons:

- **Inflation pressure carries the load of the vehicle.** If the pressure is low, the load capacity of the tire is decreased. ● **SEE FIGURE 23–2.**

- **Inflation pressure varies with temperature.** Tires lose 1 PSI for every 10-degree drop in temperature. This means that as the sensors change and the temperature changes, so does the inflation pressure inside the tires. For example, if tires were inflated to 35 PSI on the first day of summer (June 21) when the temperature was 90°F (32°C), then the following pressures would occur, assuming no air loss at all:

  Summer (June 21) 90°F—35 PSI

  Fall (September 21) 80°F—34 PSI

  Winter (December 21) 30°F—29 PSI

Therefore, it is very important to check and correct inflation pressures regularly.

- **Tire inflation affects fuel economy.** A drop in inflation pressure from 30 PSI to 23 PSI can result in a drop of fuel economy from 20 miles per gallon to 18 miles per gallon. ● **SEE FIGURE 23–3.**

- **Tire inflation affects tire life.** Even a slight drop in air pressure can have a major effect on the life of a tire. If, for example, the inflation pressure dropped 10 PSI, the life of the tire would be reduced by 40%. ● **SEE FIGURE 23–4.**

- **The TREAD Act specifies that the driver be notified if the inflation of a tire drops by 25%.** However, 25% represents a loss of air pressure of about 8 PSI. A drop of 8 PSI means an approximate 2-mpg decrease in fuel economy as well as about a 25% reduction in tread wear.

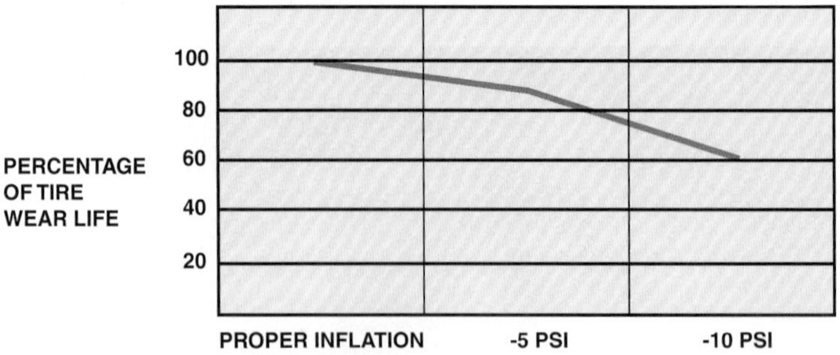

FIGURE 23–4 Notice that if a tire is underinflated by 10 PSI, the life expectancy is reduced by 40%.

PERCENTAGE OF TIRE WEAR LIFE

100
80
60
40
20

PROPER INFLATION   -5 PSI   -10 PSI

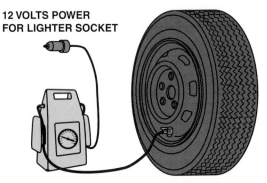

12 VOLTS POWER FOR LIGHTER SOCKET

FIGURE 23–5 A temporary inflation pump that uses 12 volts from the cigarette lighter to inflate the tire.

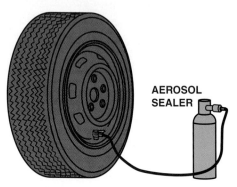

AEROSOL SEALER

FIGURE 23–6 Many vehicle manufacturers include an aerosol can of sealer on vehicles that are not equipped with a conventional spare tire.

? FREQUENTLY ASKED QUESTION

What Is a "Temporary Mobility Kit"?

A temporary mobility kit is a system to inflate a flat tire supplied by the vehicle manufacturer instead of a spare tire. A temporary mobility kit can include:

- A compressor powered by the cigarette lighter with stop leak. ● **SEE FIGURE 23–5.**
- An aerosol spray can that provides inflation and sealer. ● **SEE FIGURE 23–6.**

Either type can be found in many vehicles because such devices save weight, increase trunk space, and cost less than a conventional spare tire and jack. However, these kits are designed to be a temporary repair only because the cause of the low tire was never determined. If the tire appears to be fixed, many vehicle owners may think that the tire has been repaired. However, the tire should be carefully inspected inside and out for damage and properly repaired.

NITROGEN INFLATION

Some shops recommend and inflate tires using nitrogen instead of using compressed air. Compressed air contains about 78% nitrogen, 21% oxygen, and 1% other gases. If air already contains mostly nitrogen, why use pure nitrogen? There are several reasons, including:

- The nitrogen molecule is slightly larger than the oxygen molecule so the tire will lose pressure faster if air is used instead of nitrogen.
- Compressed nitrogen contains less moisture than compressed air. When the tire heats up, moisture in the tire vaporizes and expands, causing the pressure inside the tire to increase. Even small changes in tire pressure can noticeably affect the handling of the vehicle.
- Race teams use nitrogen because they already come to the track with a cylinder of nitrogen to power the air tools.
- Race teams also have more control over how much the pressure will increase when the tires heat up, because nitrogen has less tendency to change pressure with temperature change.
- Some oxygen in the tires could, over a long period of time, cause the oxidation of the inner liner of the tire and the corrosion of the wheel. ● **SEE FIGURE 23–7.**

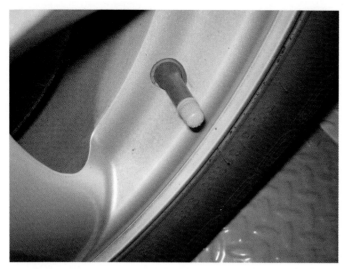

FIGURE 23-7 Most shops that use nitrogen inflation install a green tire value cap to let others know that nitrogen, rather than air has been used to inflate the tire.

TIRE MOUNTING RECOMMENDATIONS

1. When removing a wheel from a vehicle for service, mark the location of the wheel and lug stud to ensure that the wheel can be replaced in exactly the same location. This ensures that tire balance will be maintained if the tire/wheel assembly was balanced on the vehicle.

2. Make certain that the wheel has a good, clean metal-to-metal contact with the brake drum or rotor. Grease, oil, or dirt between these two surfaces could cause the wheel lug nuts to loosen while driving.

3. Always check the rim size. For example, simply by looking it is hard to distinguish a 16-in. wheel from a 16.5-in. wheel used on some trucks. ● SEE FIGURE 23-8. The rim size is marked on the sidewall of the tire, and the rim's diameter and width are stamped somewhere on the wheel.

4. Install the tire-pressure monitoring system (as shown in ● FIGURE 23-9).

5. Many tires have been marked with a paint dot or sticker, as shown in ● FIGURE 23-10. This mark represents the largest diameter (high point) and/or stiffest portion of the tire. This variation is due to the overlapping of carcass and belt fabric layers, as well as tread and sidewall rubber splices. The tire should be mounted to the rim with this mark lined up with the valve stem. The valve stem hole is typically drilled at the smallest diameter (low point) of the wheel. Mount the tires on the rim with the valve stem matched to (lined up next to) the mark on the tire. This is called **match mounting.**

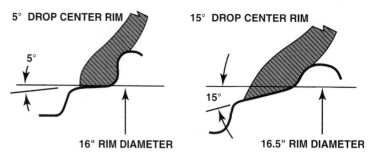

FIGURE 23-8 Note the difference in the shape of the rim contour of the 16-in. and 16 1/2-in. diameter wheels. While it is possible to mount a 16-in. tire on a 16 1/2-in. rim; it cannot be inflated enough to seat against the rim flange. If an attempt is made to seat the tire bead by overinflating (over 40 PSI), the tire bead can break, resulting in an explosive force that could cause serious injury or death.

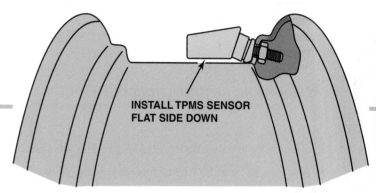

FIGURE 23-9 When installing a tire-pressure monitoring system sensor, be sure that the flat part of the sensor is parallel to the center section of the rim.

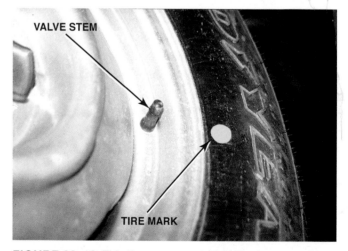

FIGURE 23-10 This tire on a new vehicle has been match mounted at the factory. The yellow sticker is placed at the largest diameter of the tire. The valve core hole in the wheel is usually drilled at the smallest diameter of the wheel. The best way to make sure the assembly is as round as possible and to reduce the number of wheel weights needed to balance the tire is to align the sticker with the valve core.

(a)

(b)

FIGURE 23–11 (a) Cleaning the bead area of an aluminum (alloy) wheel using a handheld wire brush. The technician is using the tire changer itself to rotate the wheel as the brush is used to remove any remnants of the old tire. (b) Using an electric or air-powered wire brush speeds the process, but care should be exercised not to remove any of the aluminum itself. (Remember, steel is harder than aluminum and a steel wire brush could cause recesses to be worn into the aluminum wheel, which would prevent the tire from proper seating in the bead area.) The bead seat area on steel wheels should also be cleaned to prevent air leaks at the rim.

TIRE MOUNTING RECOMMENDATIONS (CONTINUED)

6. Never use more than 40 PSI (275 kPa) to seat a tire bead.

7. Rim flanges must be free of rust, dirt, scale, or loose or flaked rubber build-up prior to mounting the tire. ● **SEE FIGURE 23–11.**

8. When mounting new tires, do *not* use silicone lubricant on the tire bead. Use special lubricant such as rendered (odorless) animal fat or rubber lubricant to help prevent tire rotation on the rim. This rubber lube is a water-based soap product that is slippery when wet (coefficient of friction when less than 0.3) and acts almost as an adhesive when dry (coefficient of friction when dry of over 0.5 for natural products and over 1.0 for synthetic products). ● **SEE FIGURE 23–12.** If the wrong lubricant is used, the rubber in the bead area of the tire can be softened or weakened. Also, most other lubricants do not increase in friction when they dry like rubber lubricant does. The result can be the rotation of the tire on the rim (wheel), especially during rapid acceleration or braking.

NOTE: **Many experts recommend that when a new tire is installed the vehicle should be driven at less than 50 mph (80 km/h) for the first 50 miles (80 km) to allow the tires to adhere to the rim. During this break-in period, the rubber lube used to mount the tire is drying and the tire is becoming fully seated on the rim. By avoiding high speeds, rapid acceleration, and fast braking, the driver is helping to prevent the tire from rotating on the rim.**

TECH TIP

Spin the Tires

When performing a vehicle inspection and the vehicle has been hoisted on a frame-type lift, check the tires by rotating them by hand. The tires on the nondrive wheels should spin freely.

- On front-wheel-drive vehicles, rear wheels should rotate easily.
- On rear-wheel-drive vehicles, front wheels should rotate easily.
- On all-wheel-drive vehicles, all four wheels may require effort to rotate.

What to Look For:

- When rotating the wheels, look at the tires from the front or rear and check that the tread of the tires does not change or look as if the tread is moving inward or outward. If the tread is moving, this indicates an internal fault with the tire and it should be replaced. This type of fault can cause a vibration even though the tire/wheel assembly has been correctly balanced.
- Look from the side of the vehicle as the wheel/tire assembly is being rotated. Look carefully at the tread of the tire and see if the tire is round. If the tire is out-of-round, the tread will appear to move up and down as the tire is being rotated.

FIGURE 23–12 Rendered (odorless) animal fat is recommended by some manufacturers of tire changing equipment for use as a rubber lubricant.

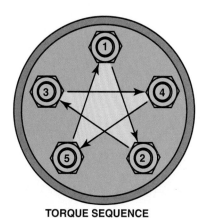

TORQUE SEQUENCE

FIGURE 23–13 Always tighten wheel lug nuts (or studs) in a star pattern to ensure even pressure on the axle flange, brake rotors or drums, and the wheel itself.

WHEEL MOUNTING TORQUE

For **wheel mounting torque,** make certain that the wheel studs are clean and dry, and torqued to the manufacturer's specifications.

CAUTION: Most manufacturers warn that the wheel studs should not be oiled or lubricated with grease; this can cause the wheel lug nuts to loosen while driving. Always follow the vehicle manufacturers' recommended service procedures.

Always tighten lug nuts gradually in the proper sequence—star pattern (tighten one nut, skip one, and tighten the next nut). This helps prevent warping the brake drums or rotors, or bending a wheel. ● **SEE FIGURE 23–13.**

If the exact torque value is not available, use the following chart as a guide for the usual value based on the size (diameter) of the lug studs.

Stud Diameter	Torque (lb-ft)
3/8 in.	35–45
7/16 in.	55–65
1/2 in.	75–85
9/16 in.	95–115
5/8 in. (usually only trucks)	125–150
12 mm	70–80
14 mm	85–95

 **TECH TIP**

Fine-Tune Handling with Tire-Pressure Changes

The handling of a vehicle can be changed by changing tire pressures between the front and rear tires.

Understeer—A term used to describe how a vehicle handles when cornering where additional steering input is needed to maintain the corner, or resisting turning into a corner. This is normal handling for most vehicles.

Oversteer—A term used to describe handling where correction while cornering is often necessary because the rear tires lose traction before the front tires.

Tire Pressure	To Decrease Understeer	To Decrease Oversteer
Front tire inflation pressure	Increase	Decrease
Rear tire inflation pressure	Decrease	Increase

CAUTION: Do not exceed the maximum inflation pressure as imprinted on the tire sidewall.

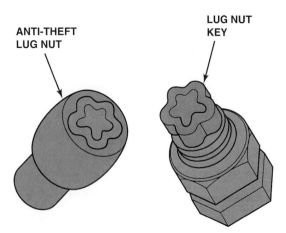

ANTI-THEFT
LUG NUT

LUG NUT
KEY

FIGURE 23–14 Most manufacturers recommend using hand tools rather than an air impact wrench to remove and install lock-type lug nuts to prevent damage. If either the key or the nut is damaged, the nut may be very difficult to remove.

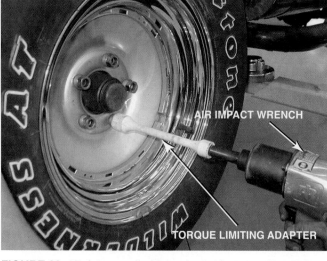

AIR IMPACT WRENCH

TORQUE LIMITING ADAPTER

FIGURE 23–15 A torque-limiting adapter for use with an air impact wrench still requires care to prevent overtightening. The air pressure to the air impact should be limited to 125 PSI (860 kPa) in most cases, and the proper adapter must be selected for the vehicle being serviced. The torque adapter absorbs any torque beyond its designed rating. Most adapters are color coded for easy identification as to the size of lug nut and torque value.

WHEEL MOUNTING TORQUE (CONTINUED)

Many factory-installed and aftermarket wheels use anti-theft wheel lug nuts, as shown in ● **FIGURE 23–14,** usually on only one wheel stud. When removing or installing a locked lug nut, be sure the key is held square to the lug nut to prevent damaging either the nut or the key.

Whenever you install a brand new set of aluminum wheels, re-torque the wheels after the first 25 miles. The soft aluminum often compresses slightly, loosening the torque on the wheels.

NOTE: The use of torque-absorbing adapters (torque-limiting shank sockets) on lug nuts with an air impact wrench properly set has proved to give satisfactory results. ● SEE FIGURE 23–15 for a photo of a torque-absorbing adapter.

TIRE ROTATION

To ensure long life and even tire wear, **tire rotation** is essential. It is important to rotate each tire to another location. Some rear-wheel-drive vehicles, for example, may show premature tire wear on the front tires. The wear usually starts on the outer tread row. This wear usually appears as a front-to-back (high and low) wear pattern on individual tread blocks. These *blocks of tread*

 REAL WORLD FIX

I Thought the Lug Nuts Were Tight!

Proper wheel nut torque is critical, as one technician discovered when a customer returned complaining of a lot of noise from the right rear wheel. ● **SEE FIGURE 23–16** for a photo of what the technician discovered. The lug (wheel) nuts had loosened and ruined the wheel.

CAUTION: Most vehicle manufacturers also specify that the wheel studs/nuts should not be lubricated with oil or grease. The use of a lubricant on the threads could cause the lug nuts to loosen.

FIGURE 23–16 This wheel was damaged because the lug nuts were not properly torqued.

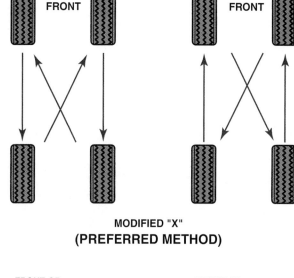

MODIFIED "X"
(PREFERRED METHOD)

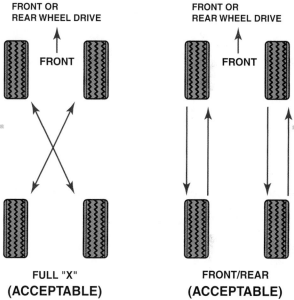

FULL "X"
(ACCEPTABLE)

FRONT/REAR
(ACCEPTABLE)

FIGURE 23–17 The method most often recommended is the modified X method. Using this method, each tire eventually is used at each of the four wheel locations. An easy way to remember the sequence, whether front wheel drive or rear wheel drive, is to say to yourself, "Drive wheels straight, cross the nondrive wheels."

TECH TIP

Tire Rotation

Tire rotation should be done at every *other* oil change. Most manufacturers recommend changing the engine oil every 3,000 miles (4,800 km) or every three months; tire rotation is recommended every 6,000 miles (9,600 km), or every six months.

rubber are deformed during cornering, stopping, and turning. This type of tread block wear can cause tire noise and/or tire roughness. While some shoulder wear on front tires is normal, it can be reduced by proper inflation, alignment, and tire rotation. For best results, tires should be rotated every 6,000 miles or every six months. ● **SEE FIGURE 23–17** for suggested methods of rotation, such as the **modified X.**

NOTE: Radial tires can cause a radial pull due to their construction. If wheel alignment is correct, attempt to correct a pull by rotating the tires front to rear or, if necessary, side to side.

Some tire manufacturers do not recommend rotating the tires on front-wheel-drive vehicles because the front tires often wear three times as fast as the rear. They recommend replacing just front tires, because the rear tires often last over 90,000 miles (145,000 km).

CAUTION: General Motors also warns that the wheels on many vehicles such as the Pontiac Trans Am and the newer Grand Prix cannot be rotated front to rear because the wheels and tires are different sizes. Always check service information as to the specified tire rotation procedure to follow on the vehicle being serviced.

FIGURE 23–18 Tire showing excessive shoulder wear resulting from underinflation and/or high-speed cornering.

FIGURE 23–19 Tire showing excessive wear in the center, indicating overinflation or heavy acceleration on a drive wheel.

TIRE INSPECTION

All tires should be carefully inspected for faults in the tire itself or for signs that something may be wrong with the steering or suspension systems of the vehicle. ● **SEE FIGURES 23–18 THROUGH 23–20** for examples of common problems.

WEAR ON OUTSIDE SHOULDER

FIGURE 23–20 Wear on the outside shoulder only is an indication of an alignment problem.

 **TECH TIP**

All-Wheel-Drive Tire Concerns

It is very important that all-wheel-drive vehicles be equipped with tires that are all the same outside diameter. If, for example, the vehicle has 20,000 miles and the tires are half worn, all of the tires should be replaced in the event of a problem requiring replacement of only one tire.

Most vehicle manufacturers specify that all tires must be within 2/32 in. of tread depth without causing a constant strain on the drive train.

RADIAL RUNOUT

Even though a tire has no visible faults, it can be the cause of vibration. If vibration is felt above 45 mph, regardless of the engine load, the cause is usually an out-of-balance or a defective out-of-round tire. Both of these problems cause a **tramp** or *up-and-down*-type vibration. If the vibration is seen in the hood of the vehicle or felt in the steering wheel, then the problem is usually the *front* tires. If the vibration is felt throughout the entire vehicle or in the seat of your pants, then the rear tires (or drive shaft, in rear-wheel-drive vehicles) are the problem. This can be checked by using a runout gauge and checking for **radial runout.** ● **SEE FIGURES 23–21 AND 23–22.** To check radial runout (checking for out-of-round) and lateral runout (checking for side-to-side movement), follow these steps:

1. Raise the vehicle so that the tires are off the ground approximately 2 in. (5 cm).

FIGURE 23–21 A tire runout gauge being used to measure the radial runout of a tire.

 FREQUENTLY ASKED QUESTION

I Thought Radial Tires Couldn't Be Rotated!

When radial tires were first introduced by American tire manufacturers in the 1970s, rotating tires side-to-side was *not* recommended because of concerns about belt or tread separation. Since the late 1980s, most tire manufacturers throughout the world, including the United States, have used tire-building equipment specifically designed for radial-ply tires. These newer radial tires are constructed so that the tires can now be rotated from one side of the vehicle to the other without fear of causing a separation by the resulting reversal of the direction of rotation.

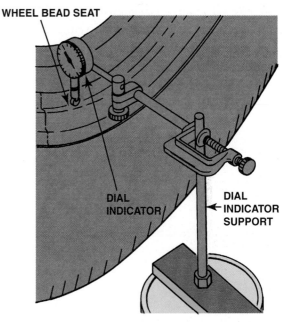

WHEEL BEAD SEAT

DIAL INDICATOR

DIAL INDICATOR SUPPORT

FIGURE 23–22 To check wheel radial runout, the dial indicator plunger tip rides on a horizontal surface of the wheel, such as the bead seat.

2. Place the runout gauge against the tread of the tire in the center of the tread and, while rotating the tire, observe the gauge reading.

3. Note that maximum radial runout should be less than 0.060 in. (1.5 mm). Little, if any, tramp will be noticed with less than 0.030 in. (0.8 mm) runout. If the reading is over 0.125 in. (3.2 mm), replacement of the tire is required.

4. Check all four tires.

CORRECTING RADIAL RUNOUT Excessive radial runout may be corrected by one of several methods:

1. Try relocating the wheel on the mounting studs. Mark one stud and remount the wheel two studs away from its original position. Excessive wheel hole and/or stud tolerance may be the cause. If the radial runout is now satisfactory, re-mark the stud and wheel to prevent a future occurrence of the problem.

2. Remount the tire on the wheel 180 degrees from its original location. This can solve a runout problem, especially if the tire was not match mounted to the wheel originally.

3. If runout is still excessive, remove the tire from the wheel and check the runout of the *wheel.* If the wheel is within 0.035 in. (0.9 mm), yet the runout of the tire/wheel assembly is excessive, the problem has to be a defective tire and it should be replaced.

Sometimes a problem within the tire itself can cause a vibration, and yet not show up as being out-of-round when tested for radial runout. A condition called **radial force variation** can cause a vibration even if correctly balanced.

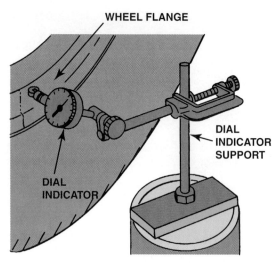
FIGURE 23–23 To check lateral runout, the dial indicator plunger tip rides on a vertical surface of the wheel, such as the wheel flange.

RADIAL RUNOUT (CONTINUED)

NOTE: Some tire balancers are equipped with a roller that is pressed against the tread of the tire to measure radial force variations. Follow the instructions as shown on the balancer display to correct for excessive radial force variations.

RADIAL RUNOUT

LATERAL RUNOUT

Another possible problem that tires can cause is a type of vibration called **shimmy**. This *rapid back-and-forth motion* can be transmitted through the steering linkage to the steering wheel. Excessive runout is usually noticeable by the driver of the vehicle as a side-to-side vibration, especially at low speeds between 5 and 45 mph (8 and 72 km/h). Shimmy can be caused by an internal defect of the tire or a bent wheel. This can be checked using a runout gauge on the side of the tire or wheel to check for **lateral runout.**

Place the runout gauge against the side of the tire and rotate the wheel. Observe the readings. The maximum allowable reading is 0.045 in. (1.1 mm). If close to or above 0.045 in. (1.1 mm), check on the edge of the wheel to see if the cause of the lateral runout is due to a bent wheel, as shown in ● **FIGURE 23–23.**

Most manufacturers specify a maximum lateral runout of 0.035 in. (0.9 mm) for alloy wheels and 0.045 in. (1.1 mm) for steel wheels. ● **SEE FIGURE 23–24.**

LATERAL RUNOUT

FIGURE 23–24 The most accurate method of measuring wheel runout is to dismantle the tire and take dial indicator readings on the inside of the wheel rim.

Proper tire balance is important for tire life, ride comfort, and safety. Tire balancing is needed because of the lack of uniform weight and stiffness (due to splices) and a combination of wheel runout and tire runout. Balancing a tire can compensate for most of these conditions. However, if a tire or wheel is excessively out of round or bent, then replacement of the wheel or tire is required.

STATIC BALANCE The term **static balance** means that the weight mass is evenly distributed around the axis of rotation.

1. For example, if a wheel is spun and stops at different places with each spin, then the tire is statically balanced.

2. **If the static balance is not correct, wheel tramp-type (vertical shake) vibration and uneven tire wear can result.**

3. Static balance can be tested with the tire stationary or while being spun to determine the heavy spot (sometimes called *kinetic balance*).

DYNAMIC BALANCE The term **dynamic balance** means that the centerline of weight mass is in the same plane as the centerline of the wheel. ● **SEE FIGURE 23–25.**

1. Dynamic balance must be checked while the tire and the wheel are rotated, to determine side-to-side as well as up-and-down out of balance.

2. **Incorrect dynamic balance causes shimmy.** Shimmy-type vibration causes the steering wheel to shake from side to side.

PREBALANCE CHECKS Before attempting to balance any tire, the following should be checked and corrected to ensure good tire balance:

1. Check the wheel bearing adjustment for looseness or wear.

2. Check the radial runout.

3. Check the lateral runout.

4. Remove stones from the tread.

5. Remove grease or dirt buildup on the inside of the wheel.

6. Check for dragging or misadjusted brakes.

7. Check for loose or backward lug nuts.

8. Check for proper tire pressures.

9. Remove all of the old weights.

10. Check for bent or damaged wheel covers.

 REAL WORLD FIX

The Greased Wheel Causes a Vibration

Shortly after an oil change and a chassis lubrication, a customer complained of a vibration at highway speed. The tires were checked for excessive radial runout to be certain the cause of the vibration was not due to a defective out-of-round tire. After removing the wheel assembly from the vehicle, excessive grease was found on the inside of the rim. Obviously, the technician who greased the lower ball joints had dropped grease on the rim. After cleaning the wheel, it was checked for proper balance on a dynamic computer balancer and found to be properly balanced. A test-drive confirmed that the problem was solved.

CORRECTING LATERAL RUNOUT Excessive lateral runout may be corrected by one of several methods:

1. Re-torque the wheel in the proper star pattern to the specified torque. Unequal or uneven wheel torque can cause excessive lateral runout.

2. Remove the wheel and inspect the wheel mounting flange for corrosion or any other reason that could prevent the wheel from seating flat against the brake rotor or drum surface.

3. Check the condition of the wheel or axle bearings. Looseness in the bearings can cause the wheel to wobble.

STATIC IMBALANCE

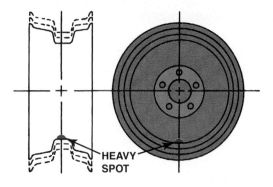

DYNAMIC IMBALANCE

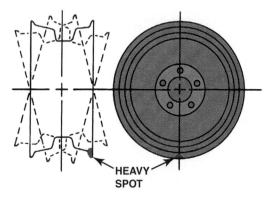

FIGURE 23–25 A wheel balancer detects heavy spots on the wheel and tire, and indicate where to place weight to offset both static and dynamic imbalance.

TIRE BALANCING (CONTINUED)

WHEEL WEIGHTS Wheel weights are available in a variety of styles and types, including the following:

1. Clip-on lead weights for standard steel rims.

2. Clip-on weights for alloy (aluminum) wheels. ● **SEE FIGURE 23–26**.

   a. Uncoated—generally *not* recommended by wheel or vehicle manufacturers because corrosion often occurs where the lead weight contacts the alloy wheel surface.

   b. Coated—lead weights that are painted or coated in a plastic material are usually the *recommended* type of weight to use on alloy wheels.

   Weights are usually coated with a nylon or polyester-type material that often matches the color of the aluminum wheels.

3. Steel wheel weights are being sold to replace weights made from lead. Some states have outlawed lead weights due to environmental concerns of lead on the ground from lost wheel weights.

FIGURE 23–26 An assortment of wheel weights designed to fit different shaped rims.

🚗 **REAL WORLD FIX**

The Vibrating Ford Van

A technician was asked to solve a vibration problem on a rear-wheel-drive Ford van. During a test-drive, the vibration was felt everywhere—the dash, the steering wheel, the front seat, the shoulder belts; everything was vibrating! The technician balanced all four tires on a computer balancer. Even though wheel weights were put on all four wheels and tires, the vibration was even worse than before. The technician rebalanced all four wheels time after time, but the vibration was still present. The shop supervisor then took over the job of solving the mystery of the vibrating van. The supervisor balanced one wheel/tire assembly and then tested it again after installing the weights. The balance was way off! The supervisor broke the tire down and found about 1 quart (1 liter) of liquid in the tire! Liquid was found in all four tires. No wonder the tires couldn't be balanced! Every time the tire stopped, the liquid would settle in another location.

The customer later admitted to using a tire stop-leak liquid in all four tires. Besides stop leak, another common source of liquid in tires is water that accumulates in the storage tank of air compressors, which often gets pumped into tires when air is being added. All air compressor storage tanks should be drained of water regularly to prevent this from happening. ● **SEE FIGURE 23–27**.

FIGURE 23–27 Liquid tire stop leak was found in all four tires. This liquid caused the tires to be out of balance.

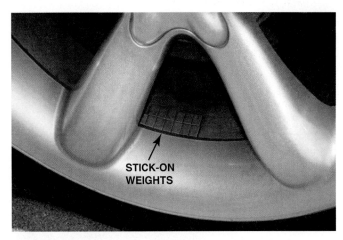

FIGURE 23–28 Stick-on weights are used from the factory to balance the alloy wheels of this Prowler.

FIGURE 23–29 Wheel weight pliers are specially designed to remove and install wheel weights.

TECH TIP

Stop Leak Can Damage TPMS Sensors

Stop leak should never be used in a tire that is equipped with the TPMS sensor because the sensor can be damaged.

? FREQUENTLY ASKED QUESTION

How Much Is Too Much Weight?

Whenever balancing a tire, it is wise to use as little amount of weight as possible. For most standard-size passenger vehicle tires, most experts recommend that no more than 5.5 oz of weight be added to correct an imbalance condition. If more than 5.5 oz is needed, remove the tire from the wheel (rim) and carefully inspect for damage to the tire or the wheel. If the tire still requires more than 5.5 oz and the wheel is not bent or damaged, replace the tire.

4. Adhesive (stick on) wheel weights are used on the inside of the rim where they do not show. Stick-on weights come with an adhesive backing that is most often used on alloy wheels. ● **SEE FIGURE 23–28.**

Most wheel weights come in 1/4 ounce (0.25-oz) increment (oz × 28 = grams).

0.25 oz = 7 gm	1.75 oz = 49 gm
0.50 oz = 14 gm	2.00 oz = 56 gm
0.75 oz = 21 gm	2.25 oz = 63 gm
1.00 oz = 28 gm	2.50 oz = 70 gm
1.25 oz = 35 gm	2.75 oz = 77 gm
1.50 oz = 42 gm	3.00 oz = 84 gm

Use a wheel weight pliers to help ensure proper installation and removal of wheel weights. ● **SEE FIGURE 23–29.**

BUBBLE BALANCER   This type of static balancer is commonly used and is accurate, if calibrated and used correctly. A bubble balancer is portable and can be easily stored away when not in use. It is also easy to use and is relatively inexpensive.

COMPUTER BALANCER   The most popular type of tire balancer is the computer dynamic balancer. Most computer balancers are designed to balance wheels and tires off the vehicle. Computer dynamic balancers spin the tire at a relatively slow speed (approximately 20 mph). Sensors attached to the spindle of the balancer determine the amount and location of

FIGURE 23–30 A tire balancer that can also detect radial and lateral force variation and instruct the operator where to rotate the tire to achieve the best ride, or indicate a bent wheel.

 FREQUENTLY ASKED QUESTION

Are the Brake Drums and Rotors Balanced?

Whenever an off-the-vehicle computer balancer is used, a question often asked by beginning technicians is, "What about the balance of the brake drums and rotors?" Brake drums and rotors are balanced at the factory, usually to within 0.5 oz-in. Imbalance measured in oz-in. means that any imbalance force is measured in ounces, then multiplied by the distance from the center measured in inches. This means that at a distance of 1 in. from the center of the drum or rotor, it is within 0.5 ounce of being perfectly balanced. Being within 0.5 ounce-inch also means that at 5 inches from the center, the imbalance is only 0.1 ounce.

What this means to the technician is that most drums and rotors are balanced well enough not to be a problem when using off-the-vehicle balancers. However, the smart technician should look for evidence that weights have been removed from brake drums to permit aluminum wheels to fit, or other cases where the factory balance of the drums and rotors has been changed.

TIRE BALANCING (CONTINUED)

weights necessary to balance the tire dynamically. All computer balancers must be programmed with the actual rim size and tire location for the electronic circuits to calibrate the required weight locations. Some computer balancers can perform loaded radial force and lateral force variation testing on the tire/wheel assembly and display corrective actions. ● **SEE FIGURE 23–30.**

Most computer balancers will be accurate to within 1/4 oz (0.25 oz), while some are accurate to within 1/8 oz (0.125 oz). (Most drivers can feel an out-of-balance of 1 oz or more, but few can feel a vibration caused by just 1/4 oz.) For sensitive drivers or vehicles used for high speeds, such as racing, most computer balancers can be programmed to balance within 1/8 oz (0.125 oz). Refer to the manufacturer's instructions for the exact capabilities and procedures for your computer balancer.

Most vehicle manufacturers specify that no more than 5.5 oz (150 gm) be used to balance any tire, with no more than 3.5 oz (100 gm) used per side of each wheel.

REPLACEMENT WHEELS

Whenever a replacement wheel is required, the same offset should be maintained. If wider or larger-diameter wheels are to be used, consult a knowledgeable wheel or tire salesperson to determine the correct wheel for your application.

CAUTION: Never remove the weights that are welded to the surface of the brake drum facing the wheel. ● SEE FIGURE 23–31. If replacement wheels do not fit without removing these weights, either replace the brake drum (one without a weight) or select another brand or style of wheel. Removing the weights from a brake drum can cause severe vibration at highway speeds.

FIGURE 23–31 Most brake drums do not have this much attached weight.

FIGURE 23–32 Notice that the rim touches the tie rod end.

REAL WORLD FIX

It Happened to Me—It Could Happen to You

During routine service, I rotated the tires on a Pontiac Trans Am. Everything went well and I even used a torque wrench to properly torque all of the lug nuts. Then, when I went to drive the car out of the service stall, I heard a horrible grinding sound. When I hoisted the car to investigate, I discovered that the front wheels were hitting the outer tie rod ends. ● **SEE FIGURE 23–32.** The 16-in. wheels had a different back spacing front and rear, and therefore these wheels could not be rotated. Always check replacement or aftermarket wheels for proper fit before driving the vehicle.

? FREQUENTLY ASKED QUESTION

What Are Hubcentric Wheels?

Most wheels are designed to fit over and be supported by the axle hub. Some wheels use an enlarged center hub section and rely on the wheel studs for support and to keep the wheel centered on the axle. Some aftermarket wheels may be designed to fit several different vehicles. As a result, the wheel manufacturers use plastic hubcentric adapter rings. ● **SEE FIGURE 23–33.**

TIRE REPAIR

Tread punctures, nail holes, or cuts up to 1/4 in. (2.6 mm) can be repaired. Repairs should be done from the inside of the tire using plugs or patches. The tire should be removed from the rim to make the repair. With the tire off the wheel, inspect the wheel and the tire for hidden damage. The proper steps to follow for a tire repair are as follows:

1. Mark the location of the tire on the wheel.

2. Dismount the tire; inspect and clean the punctured area with a prebuff cleaner. DO NOT USE GASOLINE!

3. Buff the cleaned area with sandpaper or a tire-buffing tool until the rubber surface has a smooth, velvet finish. ● **SEE FIGURE 23–34.**

4. Ream the puncture with a fine reamer from the inside. Cut and remove any loose wire material from the steel belts.

5. Fill the puncture with contour filling material, and cut or buff the material flush with the inner liner of the tire.

6. Apply chemical vulcanizing cement and allow to dry.

(a)

(b)

FIGURE 23–33 (a) A hubcentric plastic ring partially removed from an aftermarket wheel. (b) A hubcentric plastic ring left on the hub when removing a wheel.

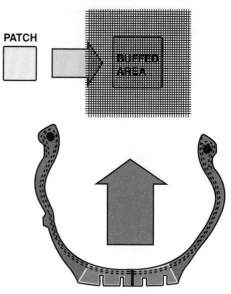

FIGURE 23–34 The area of the repair should be buffed slightly larger than the patch to be applied.

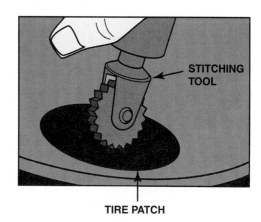

FIGURE 23–35 A stitching tool being used to force any trapped air out from under the patch.

TIRE REPAIR (CONTINUED)

7. Apply the patch and use a stitching tool from the center toward the outside of the patch to work any air out from between the patch and the tire. ● **SEE FIGURE 23–35.** Another excellent tire repair procedure uses a rubber plug. Pull the stem through the hole in the tire, as shown in ● **FIGURE 23–36.**

8. Remount the tire on the rim, aligning the marks made in step 1. Inflate to the recommended pressure and check for air leaks.

NOTE: Most vulcanizing (rubber) cement is highly flammable. Use out of the area of an open flame. Do not smoke when making a tire repair.

There are many tire repair products on the market. Always follow the installation and repair procedures exactly per the manufacturer's instructions.

Dispose of Old Tires Properly

Old tires cannot be thrown out in the trash. They must be disposed of properly. Tires cannot be buried because they tend to come to the surface. They also trap and hold water, which can be a breeding ground for mosquitoes. Used tires should be sent to a local or regional recycling center where the tires will be ground up and used in asphalt paving or other industrial uses. Because there is often a charge to dispose of old tires, it is best to warn the customer of the disposal fee.

FIGURE 23–36 A rubber plug being pulled through a hole in the tire. The stem is then cut off flush with the surface of the tire tread.

WARNING

Most experts agree that tire repairs should be done from the inside. Many technicians have been injured and a few killed when the tire they were repairing exploded as a steel reamer tool was inserted into the tire. The reamer can easily create a spark as it is pushed through the steel wires of a steel-belted tire. This spark can ignite a combustible mixture of gases inside the tire caused by using stop leak or inflator cans. Since there is no way a technician can know if a tire has been inflated with a product that uses a combustible gas, always treat a tire as if it could explode.

TECH TIP

Open-End Wrenches Make It Easier

Tire repair is made easier if two open-end wrenches are used to hold the beads of the tire apart. See step 4 in the tire repair photo sequence.

TIRE MOUNTING

1 A typical tire-changing machine showing the revolving table and movable arm used to remove a tire from the wheel.

2 The foot-pedal controls allow the service technician to break the tire bead, damp the wheel (rim) to the machine, rotate the tire/wheel assembly, and still have both hands free.

3 Using a tire valve removal tool, unscrew the valve core using extreme caution because the valve is under pressure and can be forced outward and cause personal injury.

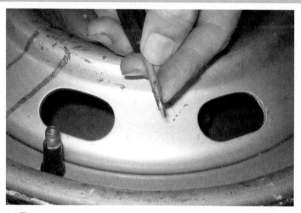

4 The valve core removed from the tire valve. Allow all of the air in the tire to escape.

5 A bead breaker is being used to separate the tire from the bead seat of the wheel. Repeat as needed to break the bead on both sides of the wheel.

6 After breaking the beads from both sides of the tire, install the wheel/tire assembly flat onto the machine and, using the foot-pedal control, lock the wheel to the changer.

7 To remove the tire from the wheel, position the arm of the changer against the rim of the wheel and lock in position.

8 The tire tool (flat bar) is placed between the bead of the tire and the wheel. Using tire lubricant can help prevent damage to the tire.

9 The foot pedal that causes the table to rotate is depressed and the tire is removed from the wheel.

10 Reposition the tire tool to remove the lower bead of the tire from the wheel.

11 As the table of the tire changer is rotated, the tire is released from the wheel and can be lifted off the wheel.

12 Before installing a tire, inspect and clean the bead seat.

CONTINUED ▶

13 Before installing a new tire, most experts recommend replacing the tire valve, being installed here, using a tool that pulls the valve through the hole in the wheel.

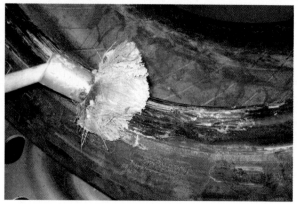

14 Apply tire soap or rubber lubricant to both beads of the tire.

15 Rotate the tire on the wheel and position the arm so that the tire will be guided onto the rim as the wheel is rotated.

16 Repeat for the upper bead.

17 Inflate the tire, being careful to not exceed 40 PSI. Experts suggest that a tire be in a cage during the initial bead seating inflation to help prevent personal injury if the wheel or tire fails.

18 Install the tire valve core and inflate the tire to specifications.

TIRE REPAIR

1 The source of the leak was detected by spraying soapy water on the inflated tire. Needle-nose pliers are being used to remove the object that caused the flat tire.

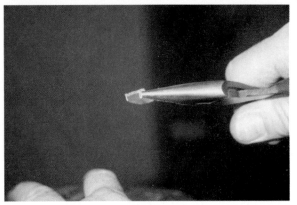

2 A part of a razor blade was found to be the cause of the flat tire.

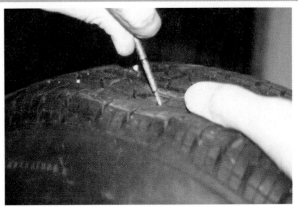

3 A reamer is being used to clean the puncture hole.

4 This technician is using two open-end wrenches to hold the tire beads apart if a tire bead spreader is not available.

5 The surrounding area is being buffed using an air-powered die grinder equipped with a special buffing tool specifically designed for this process.

6 After using a vacuum on all debris and rubber after buffing, apply rubber cement to the area.

CONTINUED ▶

7 The brush included with the rubber cement makes the job easy. Be sure to cover the entire area around the puncture.

8 Peel off the paper from the adhesive on the patch. Insert the tip of the patch through the puncture from the inside of the tire.

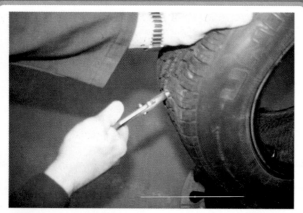

9 Use a pair of pliers to pull the plug of the patch through the puncture.

10 This view of the patch is from the inside of the tire.

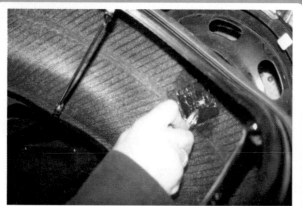

11 To be assured of an airtight patch, the adhesive of the patch should be "stitched" to the inside of the tire using a serrated roller called a stitching tool.

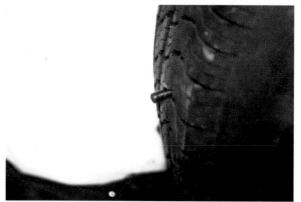

12 A view of the plug from the outside of the tire after metal covering used to pierce the puncture is removed from the patch plug. The plug can be trimmed to the level of the tread using side cutters or a knife.

SUMMARY

1. For safety and proper vehicle handling, all four tires of the vehicle should be of the same size, construction, and type, except where specified by the manufacturer, such as on some high-performance sports cars.

2. Wheels should always be tightened with a torque wrench to the proper torque in a star pattern.

3. Tires should be rotated every 5,000 to 7,000 miles (8,000 to 11,000 km), or at every other oil change.

4. Wheels should be cleaned around the rim area whenever tires are changed and carefully inspected for cracks or other defects such as excessive lateral or radial runout.

5. Properly balanced tires prolong tire life. Wheel tramp or an up-and-down type of vibration results if the tires are statically out of balance or if the tire is out-of-round.

6. Dynamic balance is necessary to prevent side-to-side vibration, commonly called shimmy.

7. Only coated or stick-on-type wheel weights should be used on alloy wheels to prevent corrosion damage.

REVIEW QUESTIONS

1. List the precautions and recommendations regarding tire selection and maintenance.

2. Determine the proper wheel mounting torque for your vehicle from the guidelines provided.

3. Describe how to check for lateral and radial runout of the wheels and tires.

4. Describe the difference between static and dynamic balance.

CHAPTER QUIZ

1. A tire is worn excessively on both edges. The most likely cause of this type of tire wear is _____.
   a. Overinflation
   b. Underinflation
   c. Excessive radial runout
   d. Excessive lateral runout

2. When seating a bead of a tire, never exceed _____ PSI.
   a. 30
   b. 40
   c. 50
   d. 60

3. For best tire life, most vehicle and tire manufacturers recommend tire rotation every _____.
   a. 3,000 miles
   b. 6,000 miles
   c. 9,000 miles
   d. 12,000 miles

4. What lubricant should be used when mounting a tire?
   a. Silicone spray
   b. Grease
   c. Water-based soap
   d. SAE 10W-30 engine oil

5. Using the modified X-method of tire rotation on a front-wheel-drive vehicle, where should be the left front wheel placed?
   a. Right front
   b. Right rear
   c. Left rear
   d. Kept at the left front

6. Which statement is *false?*
   a. Excessive radial runout can cause a tramp-type vibration.
   b. Excessive lateral runout can cause a tramp-type vibration.
   c. A tire out of balance dynamically can cause a shimmy-type vibration.
   d. A tire out of balance statically can cause a tramp-type vibration.

7. The recommended type of wheel weight to use on aluminum (alloy) wheels is _____.
   a. Lead with plated spring steel clips
   b. Coated (painted) or stick-on lead weights
   c. Lead weights with longer-than-normal clips
   d. Aluminum weights

8. Most vehicle and tire manufacturers recommend that no more than _____ ounces of balance weight be added to a wheel/tire assembly.
   a. 2.5
   b. 3.5
   c. 4.5
   d. 5.5

9. A vehicle vibrates at highway speed. Technician A says that water in the tire(s) could be the cause. Technician B says that an out-of-round tire could be the cause. Which technician is correct?
   a. Technician A only
   b. Technician B only
   c. Both Technicians A and B
   d. Neither Technician A nor B

10. Proper tire inflation pressure information is found _____.
    a. On the driver's door or post
    b. In the owner's manual
    c. On the sidewall of the tire
    d. Both a and b

After studying Chapter 24, the reader will be able to:

1. Prepare for ASE Suspension and Steering (A4) certification test content area "B" (Suspension System Diagnosis and Repair).
2. List various types of suspensions and their component parts.
3. Explain how coil, leaf, and torsion bar springs work.
4. Describe how suspension components function to allow wheel movement up and down and provide for turning.
5. Describe how shock absorbers control spring forces.

Air spring 456
Anti-dive 448
Anti-squat 448
Ball joints 450
Bulkhead 437
Bump stop 461
Center bolt 443
Coil springs 439
Composite leaf spring 444
Control arms 449
Cradle 435
Full frame 435
GVW 436
Hooke's Law 438
Independent suspension 437
Insulators 441
Kingpin 449
Ladder frame 435
Lateral links 447
Leaf springs 443
Load-carrying ball joint 450

Mono leaf 443
Non-load-carrying ball joint 450
Perimeter frame 435
Platforms 437
Rebound clips 443
Shackles 443
Shock absorbers 455
Space frame 436
Spring pocket 441
Spring rate 438
Springs 438
Sprung weight 437
Stabilizer bars 452
Steering knuckles 449
Stress riser 441
Strut rod 452
Struts 460
Stub-type frame 435
Torsion bar 445
Unit-body 435
Unsprung weight 437
Wheel rate 441

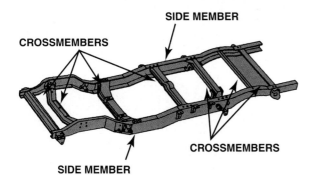

CROSSMEMBERS

SIDE MEMBER

CROSSMEMBERS

SIDE MEMBER

FIGURE 24–1 A typical truck frame is an excellent example of a ladder-type frame. The two side members are connected by a crossmember.

INTRODUCTION

Street-driven cars and trucks use a suspension system to keep the tires on the road and to provide acceptable riding comfort. A vehicle with a solid suspension, or no suspension, would bounce off the ground when the tires hit a bump. If the tires are off the ground, even for a fraction of a second, loss of control is possible. The purpose of the suspension is to provide the vehicle with the following:

1. A smooth ride
2. Accurate steering
3. Responsive handling
4. Support for the weight of the vehicle
5. Maintenance of acceptable tire wear

FRAME CONSTRUCTION

Frame construction usually consists of channel-shaped steel beams welded and/or fastened together. The frame of a vehicle supports all the "running gear" of the vehicle, including the engine, transmission, rear axle assembly (if rear-wheel drive), and all suspension components.

This frame construction, referred to as **full frame**, is so complete that most vehicles can usually be driven without the body. Most trucks and larger rear-wheel-drive cars use a full frame.

LADDER FRAME A **ladder frame** is a common name for a type of perimeter frame where the transverse (lateral) connecting members are straight across. ● SEE FIGURES 24–1 AND 24–2. When viewed with the body removed, the frame resembles a ladder. Most pickup trucks are constructed with a ladder-type frame.

PERIMETER FRAME A **perimeter frame** consists of welded or riveted frame members around the entire perimeter of

LADDER FRAME

TOP VIEW

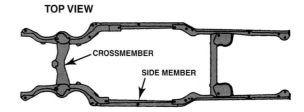

CROSSMEMBER

SIDE MEMBER

BODY BOLTS TO FRAME

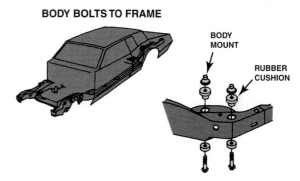

BODY MOUNT

RUBBER CUSHION

FIGURE 24–2 Rubber cushions used in body or frame construction isolate noise and vibration from traveling to the passenger compartment.

the body. This means that the frame members provide support underneath the sides as well as for the suspension and suspension components.

STUB-TYPE FRAMES A **stub-type frame** is a partial frame often used on unit-body vehicles to support the power train and suspension components. It is also called a **cradle** on many front-wheel-drive vehicles. ● SEE FIGURE 24–3.

UNIT-BODY CONSTRUCTION **Unit-body** construction (sometimes called *unibody*) is a design that combines the body with the structure of the frame. The body supports the engine and drive line components, as well as the suspension and steering components. The body is composed of many individual stamped-steel panels welded together.

The strength of this type of construction lies in the *shape* of the assembly. The typical vehicle uses 300 separate and

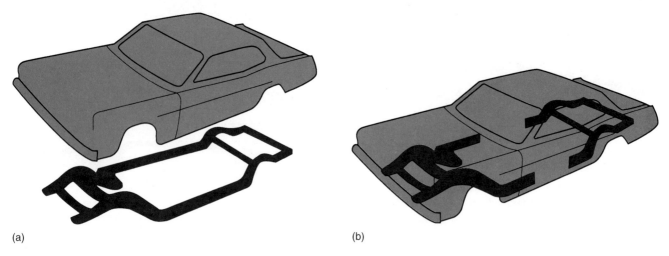

(a)   (b)

FIGURE 24–3 (a) Separate body and frame construction; (b) unitized construction: the small frame members are for support of the engine and suspension components. Many vehicles attach the suspension components directly to the reinforced sections of the body and do not require the rear frame section.

UNIT-BODY CONSTRUCTION

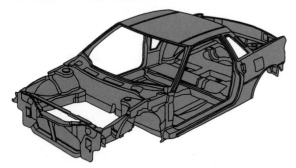

FIGURE 24–4 Welded metal sections create a platform that combines the body with the frame using unit-body construction.

FRAME CONSTRUCTION (CONTINUED)

different stamped steel panels that are spot-welded to form a vehicle's body. ● **SEE FIGURE 24–4.**

NOTE: A typical vehicle contains about 10,000 individual parts.

SPACE FRAME CONSTRUCTION **Space frame** construction consists of formed sheet steel used to construct a framework for the entire vehicle. The vehicle is drivable without the body, which uses plastic or steel panels to cover the steel framework.

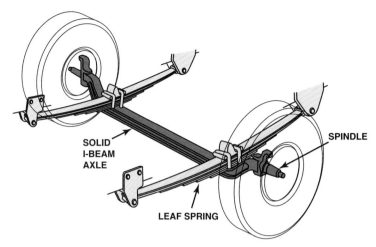

FIGURE 24–5 Solid I-beam axle with leaf springs.

PLATFORMS

The **platform** of any vehicle is its basic size and shape. Various vehicles of different makes can share the same platform, and therefore many of the same drive train (engine, transmission, and final drive components) and suspension and steering components.

A platform of a unit-body vehicle includes all major sheet-metal components that form the load-bearing structure of the vehicle, including the front suspension and engine-supporting sections. The area separating the engine compartment from the passenger compartment is called the **bulkhead.** The height and location of this bulkhead panel to a large degree determines the shape of the rest of the vehicle.

Other components of vehicle platform design that affect handling and ride are the track and wheelbase of the vehicle. *The track of a vehicle is the distance between the wheels, as viewed from the front or rear.* A wide-track vehicle is a vehicle with a wide wheel stance; this increases the stability of the vehicle, especially when cornering. *The wheelbase of a vehicle is the distance between the center of the front wheel and the center of the rear wheel, as viewed from the side.* A vehicle with a long wheelbase tends to ride smoother than a vehicle with a short one.

Examples of common platforms include the following:

1. Chevrolet Impala and Pontiac Grand Prix
2. Toyota Camry and Lexus ES 350
3. Buick Lucerne and Cadillac DTS

UNSPRUNG WEIGHT

A suspension system has to be designed to allow the wheels to move up and down quickly over bumps and dips without affecting the entire weight of the car or truck. In fact, the lighter the total weight of the components that move up and down, the better the handling and ride. This weight is called **unsprung weight.** The idea of very light weight resulted in magnesium wheels for racing cars, which are very light yet strong. Aftermarket wheels that resemble racing car wheels are often referred to as *mag* wheels. For best handling and ride, the unsprung weight should be kept as low as possible.

Sprung weight is the term used to identify the weight of the car or truck that does *not* move up and down and is supported or *sprung* by the suspension.

TYPES OF SUSPENSIONS

Early suspension systems on old horse wagons, buggies, and older vehicles used a solid axle for front and rear wheels. ● **SEE FIGURE 24–5.** If one wheel hit a bump, the other wheel was affected, as shown in ● **FIGURE 24–6.**

Most vehicles today use a separate control-arm-type of suspension for each front wheel, which allows for movement of one front wheel without affecting the other front wheel. This type of front suspension is called **independent suspension.** ● **SEE FIGURE 24–7.**

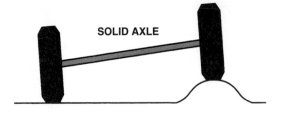

FIGURE 24–6 When one wheel hits a bump or drops into a hole, both left and right wheels are moved. Because both wheels are affected, the ride is often harsh and feels stiff.

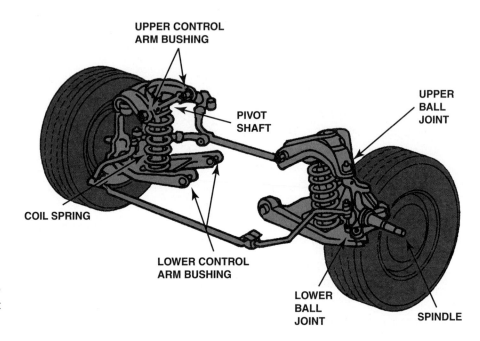

FIGURE 24–7 A typical independent front suspension used on a rear-wheel-drive vehicle. Each wheel can hit a bump or hole in the road independently without affecting the opposite wheel.

TYPES OF SUSPENSIONS (CONTINUED)

Many rear suspensions also use independent-type suspension systems. Regardless of the design type of suspension, all suspensions use springs in one form or another.

SPRINGS A suspension **spring** serves two purposes. First, it acts as a buffer between the suspension and frame to absorb vertical wheel and suspension movement without passing it on to the frame. Second, each spring transfers part of the vehicle weight to the suspension component it rests on, which transfers it to the wheels.

The basic method by which springs absorb road shocks varies according to the type of spring. Simply stated, leaf springs flatten, coil springs and air springs compress, and torsion bars twist. What all springs have in common is that they somehow give way to absorb the vertical force of the moving wheel during jounce, then release that force during rebound as they return to their original shape and position.

SPRING MATERIALS Most springs are made of a tempered steel alloy known as spring steel, usually chrome silicon or chrome-vanadium alloy. Tempering is a process of heating and cooling metal under controlled conditions, which increases the resilience

of the metal. Resilience is the ability of the metal to return to, or spring back to, its original shape after being twisted or compressed.

HOOKE'S LAW

Regardless of type, all suspensions use springs that share a common characteristic described by **Hooke's Law**. Robert Hooke (1635–1703), an English physicist, discovered the force characteristics of springs: *The deflection (movement or deformation) of a spring is directly proportional to the applied force.*

What this means is that when a coil spring (for example) is depressed 1 in., it pushes back with a certain force (in pounds), such as 400 pounds. If the spring is depressed another inch, the force exerted by the spring is increased by another 400 pounds. The **spring rate** or force constant for this spring is therefore "400 lb per inch," usually symbolized by the letter K. Since the force constant is the force per unit of displacement (movement), it is a measure of the stiffness of the spring. The higher the spring rate (K), the stiffer the spring. ● **SEE FIGURE 24–8.**

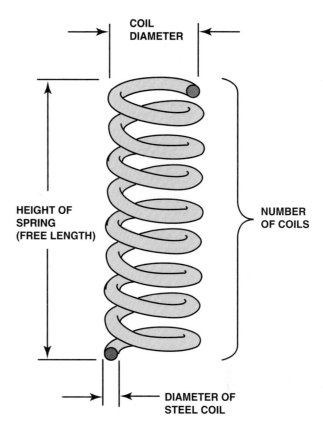

FIGURE 24–9 The spring rate of a coil spring is determined by the diameter of the spring and the diameter of the steel used in its construction plus the number of coils and the free length (height).

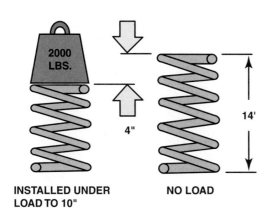

INSTALLED UNDER
LOAD TO 10"   NO LOAD

FIGURE 24–8 This spring was depressed 4 inches due to a weight of 2,000 lb. This means that this spring has a spring rate (K) of 500 lb per inch (2000 ÷ 4 in. = 500 lb./in.).

COIL SPRINGS

Coil springs are made of special round spring steel wrapped in a helix shape. The strength and handling characteristics of a coil spring depend on the following:

1. Coil diameter

2. Number of coils

3. Height of spring

4. Diameter of the steel coil that forms the spring. ● **SEE FIGURE 24–9**.

The spring rate (K) for coil springs is expressed by the formula:

$$K = \frac{Gd4}{8ND3}$$

where

G = 11,250,000 (constant for steel)

d = diameter of wire

N = number of coils

D = diameter of the coil

Coil springs are used in front and/or rear suspensions. The larger the diameter of the steel, the "stiffer" the spring. The shorter the height of the spring, the stiffer the spring. The fewer the coils, the stiffer the spring.

Springs are designed to provide desired ride and handling and come in a variety of spring ends, as shown in ● **FIGURE 24–10**.

CAUTION: The use of spacers between the coils of a coil spring is *not* recommended because the force exerted by the spacers on the springs can cause spring breakage. When a spacer is installed between the coils, the number of coils is reduced and the spring becomes stiffer. The force exerted on the coil spring at the contact points of the spacer can cause the spring to break.

SPRING RATE   Spring rate, also called *deflection rate*, is a value that reflects how much weight it takes to compress a spring a certain amount. Generally, spring rate is specified in

COIL SPRING ENDS

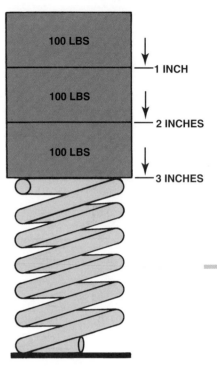

TAPERED END   TANGENTIAL END   PIG-TAIL

FIGURE 24–10 Coil spring ends are shaped to fit the needs of a variety of suspension designs.

COIL SPRINGS (CONTINUED)

pounds per inch, which is the weight in pounds it takes to compress the spring 1 inch. In other words, if a 100-pound weight causes a spring to compress 1 inch, the spring has a spring rate of 100 pounds.

A constant-rate spring continues to compress at the same rate throughout its complete range of deflection. For example, if a constant-rate spring compresses 1 inch under a 100-pound load, it will compress 2 inches under a 200-pound load, and so on. ● **SEE FIGURE 24–11.** Many automotive suspension springs, both coil and leaf, compress at a variable rate. That is, they become stiffer and exert more force the farther they compress. For example, a variable-rate spring may compress 1 inch under a 100-pound load, but only compress an additional 1/2 inch under a 200-pound load. Variable-rate springs offer a soft, comfortable ride under normal circumstances but will not bottom out as quickly when adverse road conditions compress them farther. ● **SEE FIGURE 24–12.**

Before a spring is installed on a vehicle or any load is placed on it, it is at its uncompressed length, or free length. Once installed, the weight of the corner of the vehicle resting on the spring is called its *static load*. The static load constantly compresses the spring. Therefore, the uncompressed length and the spring rate must be such that the spring has room to compress and keep the vehicle at the correct ride height *after* the static load is applied. ● **SEE FIGURE 24–13.**

Typical Front-Wheel-Drive Sedan Springs

	Force @ Height	Spring Rate
LF	1,343 lbs. @ 7.6 in.	256 lb. in.
RF	1,300 lbs. @ 7.6 in.	254 lb. in.
LR	638 lbs. @ 9.38 in.	200 lb. in.
RR	610 lbs. @ 9.38 in.	195 lb. in.

CONSTANT-RATE SPRING

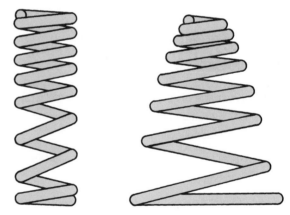

FIGURE 24–11 A constant-rate spring compresses at the same rate regardless of the amount of weight that is applied.

VARIABLE-RATE SPRINGS

FIGURE 24–12 Variable-rate springs come in a variety of shapes and compress more slowly as weight is applied.

Notice that each of the four coil springs used on this vehicle is unique. The higher spring rate on the left is used to help support the weight of the driver. Because each spring is designed for each location on the vehicle, they should be marked if they are removed from a vehicle during service.

SPRING FREQUENCY Spring frequency is a value that reflects the speed at which a spring oscillates, or bounces, after it is released from compression or extension. Frequency is

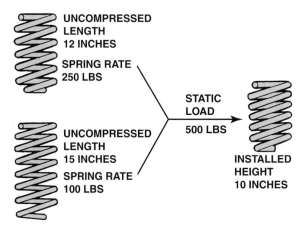

FIGURE 24–13 Two springs, each with a different spring rate and length, can provide the same ride height even though the higher-rate spring will give a stiffer ride.

? FREQUENTLY ASKED QUESTION

Does the Spring Rate Change as the Vehicle Gets Older?

No, the spring rate of a spring does not change, but the spring load can change due to fatigue. The spring rate is the amount of force it takes to compress the spring 1 inch. The spring load is the amount of weight that a spring can support at any given compressed height. When a spring fatigues, the spring's load capacity decreases and the vehicle will sag.

typically measured in cycles per second (CPS) or hertz (Hz). ● **SEE FIGURE 24–14.** There is a direct correlation between spring rate and spring frequency: the higher the spring rate, the higher the spring frequency. This means that stiffer springs bounce at a higher frequency, while softer springs bounce more slowly.

WHEEL RATE Depending on the suspension design, springs are installed a certain distance away from the wheel, which determines the ratio of wheel travel to spring travel, or **wheel rate.** ● **SEE FIGURE 24–15.** For example, if a coil spring is mounted on the midpoint of a control arm, or halfway between the center of the wheel and the arm pivot points, it compresses approximately 1 inch when the wheel travels vertically 2 inches. On a strut-type suspension, the coil spring has a more direct ratio because it is closer to the wheel, so when the wheel of a strut travels vertically 2 inches, the spring also compresses 2 inches. This means that a coil spring used on a strut-type suspension is less than half the spring rate of a coil spring used on suspensions that use control arms.

SPRING FREQUENCY

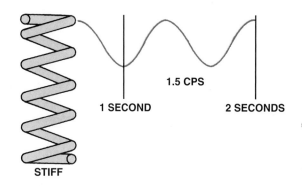

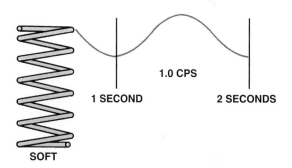

FIGURE 24–14 Stiffer springs bounce at a higher frequency than softer springs.

COIL SPRING MOUNTING Coil springs are usually installed in a **spring pocket** or spring seat. Hard rubber or plastic cushions or **insulators** are usually mounted between the coil spring and the spring seat. ● **SEE FIGURE 24–16** on page 443. The purpose of these insulators is to isolate and dampen road noise and vibration from the vehicle body. The type of end on the coil spring also varies and determines the style of the spring mount.

SPRING COATINGS All springs are painted or coated with epoxy to help prevent breakage. A scratch, nick, or pit caused by corrosion can cause a **stress riser** that can lead to spring failure. The service technician should be careful not to remove any of the protective coating. Whenever a service operation requires the spring to be compressed, always use a tool that will not scratch or nick the surface of the spring.

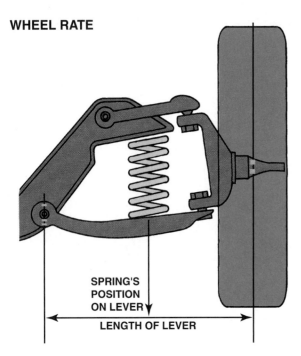

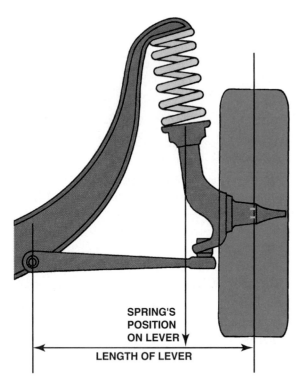

FIGURE 24–15 The wheel and arm act as a lever to compress the spring. The spring used on the top picture must be stiffer than the spring used on the strut-type suspension shown on the bottom because the length of the lever arm is shorter.

 **TECH TIP**

Don't Cut Those Coil Springs!

Chassis service technicians are often asked to lower a vehicle. One method is to remove the coil springs and cut off half or more coils from the spring. While this *will* lower the vehicle, this method is generally *not* recommended for the following reasons:

1. A coil spring could be damaged during the cutting-off procedure, especially if a torch is used to do the cutting.
2. The spring will get stiffer when shortened, often resulting in a very harsh ride.
3. The amount the vehicle is lowered is *less* than the amount cut off from the spring. This is because as the spring is shortened, it becomes stiffer. The stiffer spring will compress less than the original.

Instead of cutting springs to lower a vehicle, several preferable methods are available if the vehicle *must* be lowered:

1. There are replacement springs designed specifically to lower that model vehicle. A change in shock absorbers may be necessary because the shorter springs change the operating height of the stock (original) shock absorbers. Consult spring manufacturers for exact installation instructions and recommendations. ● **SEE FIGURE 24–17.**
2. There are replacement spindles designed to *raise* the location of the wheel spindle, thereby lowering the body in relation to the ground. Except for ground clearance problems, this is the method recommended by many chassis service technicians. Replacement spindles keep the same springs, shock absorbers, and ride, while lowering the vehicle without serious problems.

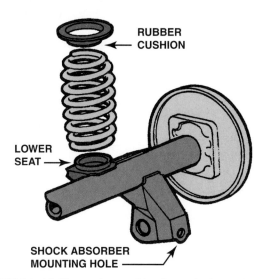

FIGURE 24–16 The spring cushion helps isolate noise and vibration from being transferred to the passenger compartment. *(Courtesy of Cooper Automotive Company)*

FIGURE 24–17 This replacement coil spring is coated to prevent rust and corrosion and colored to help identify the spring and/or spring manufacturer.

LEAF SPRINGS

Leaf springs are constructed of one or more strips of long, narrow spring steel. These metal strips, called leaves, are assembled with plastic or synthetic rubber insulators between the leaves, allowing for freedom of movement during spring operation. ● **SEE FIGURE 24–18.**

The ends of the spring are rolled or looped to form eyes. Rubber bushings are installed in the eyes of the spring and act as noise and vibration insulators. ● **SEE FIGURE 24–19.**

The leaves are held together by a **center bolt**, also called a *centering pin*. ● **SEE FIGURE 24–20.**

One end of a leaf spring is mounted to a hanger with a bolt and rubber bushings directly attached to the frame. The other end of the leaf spring is attached to the frame with movable mounting hangers called **shackles**. ● **SEE FIGURE 24–21.**

The shackles are necessary because as the spring hits a bump, the slightly curved spring (semi-elliptical) becomes longer and straighter, and the shackles allow for this rearward movement. **Rebound clips**, or spring alignment clips, help prevent the leaves from separating whenever the leaf spring is rebounding from hitting a bump or rise in the roadway. ● **SEE FIGURE 24–22** on page 445.

Single leaf steel springs, called **mono leaf**, are used on some vehicles. A single or mono leaf spring is usually tapered to produce a variable spring rate. Leaf springs are used for rear suspensions on cars and many light trucks. A variable rate can be accomplished with a leaf spring suspension by providing

FIGURE 24–18 A typical leaf spring used on the rear of a pickup truck showing the plastic insulator between the leaves, which allows the spring to move without creating wear or noise.

contacts on the mount that effectively shorten the spring once it is compressed to a certain point. This provides a smoother ride when the load is light and still provides a stiffer spring when the load is heavy. ● **SEE FIGURE 24–23** on page 445.

To provide additional load-carrying capacity, especially on trucks and vans, auxiliary or *helper* leaves are commonly used. This extra leaf becomes effective only when the vehicle is heavily loaded. ● **SEE FIGURE 24–24** on page 445.

Leaf springs are used on the front suspension of many four-wheel-drive trucks, especially medium and heavy trucks.

LEAF SPRING

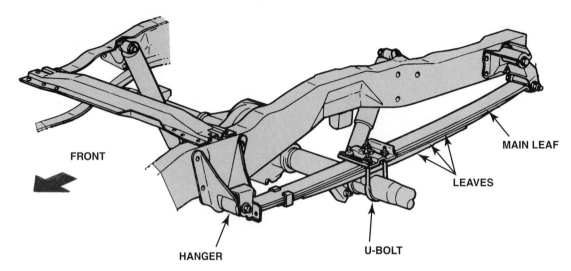

FRONT

MAIN LEAF

LEAVES

HANGER

U-BOLT

FIGURE 24–19 A typical leaf spring installation. The longest leaf, called the *main leaf*, attaches to the frame through a shackle and a hanger.

FIGURE 24–20 All multileaf springs use a center bolt to not only hold the leaves together but also help retain the leaf spring in the center of the spring perch.

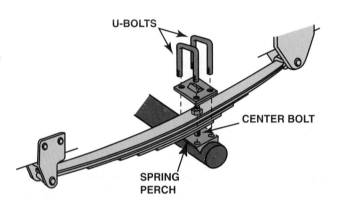

U-BOLTS

CENTER BOLT

SPRING PERCH

FIGURE 24–21 When a leaf spring is compressed, the spring flattens and becomes longer. The shackles allow for this lengthening. Rubber bushings are used in the ends of the spring and shackles to help isolate road noise from traveling into the passenger compartment.

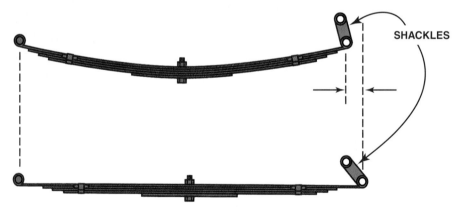

SHACKLES

LEAF SPRINGS (CONTINUED)

COMPOSITE LEAF SPRINGS Since the early 1980s, fiberglass-reinforced epoxy plastic **composite leaf springs** have been used on production vehicles. They save weight: An 8-pound spring can replace a conventional 40-pound steel leaf spring. The secret to making a strong plastic leaf spring is the glass fibers running continuously from one end of the spring to the other, and the use of 70% fiberglass with 30% epoxy composite. The single-leaf composite spring helps isolate road noise and vibrations. It is more efficient than a multileaf spring because it eliminates the interleaf friction of the steel leaves and requires less space. ● **SEE FIGURE 24–25** on page 446.

Leaf spring rate increases when the thickness increases, and decreases as the length increases.

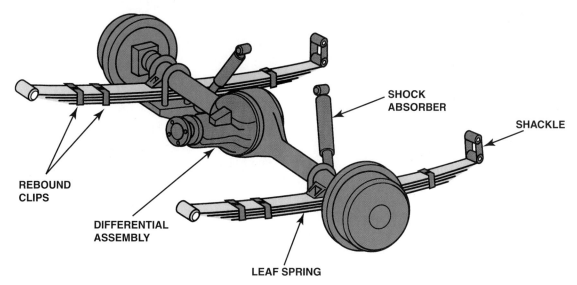

FIGURE 24–22 Typical rear leaf-spring suspension of a rear-wheel-drive vehicle.

SHOCK ABSORBER

SHACKLE

REBOUND CLIPS

DIFFERENTIAL ASSEMBLY

LEAF SPRING

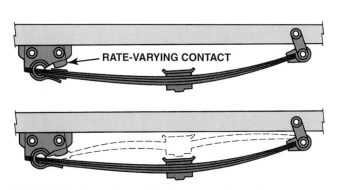

RATE-VARYING CONTACT

FIGURE 24–23 As the vehicle is loaded, the leaf spring contacts a section of the frame. This shortens the effective length of the spring, which makes it stiffer.

AUXILIARY LEAF

FIGURE 24–24 Many pickup trucks, vans, and sport utility vehicles (SUVs) use auxiliary leaf springs that contact the other leaves when the load is increased.

TORSION BARS

A **torsion bar** is a spring that is a long, *round,* hardened steel bar similar to a coil spring except that it is a *straight* bar. ● **SEE FIGURE 24–26** on page 446.

One end is attached to the lower control arm of a front suspension and the other end to the frame. When the wheels hit a bump, the bar twists and then untwists. General Motors pickup trucks use torsion-bar front suspension longitudinally. ● **SEE FIGURE 24–27** on page 446.

Many manufacturers of pickup trucks currently use torsion-bar-type suspensions, especially on their four-wheel-drive models. Torsion bars allow room for the front drive axle and constant velocity joint and still provide for strong suspension.

As with all automotive springs, spring action is controlled by the shock absorbers. Unlike other types of springs, torsion bars may be adjustable for correct ride height. ● **SEE FIGURE 24–28** on page 447.

Most torsion bars are labeled *left* or *right,* usually stamped into the end of the bars. The purpose of this designation is to make sure that the correct bar is installed on the original side of the vehicle. Torsion bars are manufactured without any built-in

FIGURE 24–25 (a) A fiberglass spring is composed of long fibers locked together in an epoxy (resin) matrix. (b) When the spring compresses, the bottom of the spring expands and the top compresses. Composite leaf springs are used and mounted transversely (side-to-side) on Chevrolet Corvettes and at the rear on some other General Motors vehicles.

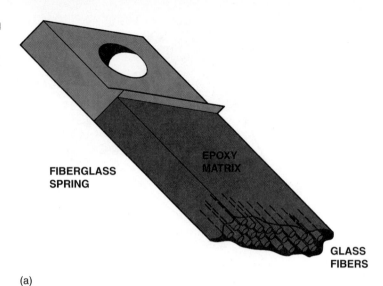

FIBERGLASS SPRING

EPOXY MATRIX

GLASS FIBERS

(a)

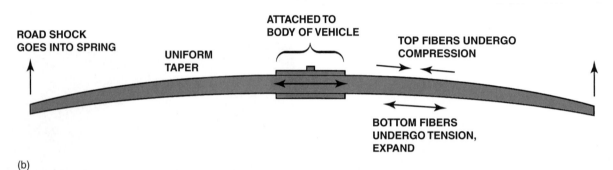

ROAD SHOCK GOES INTO SPRING

UNIFORM TAPER

ATTACHED TO BODY OF VEHICLE

TOP FIBERS UNDERGO COMPRESSION

BOTTOM FIBERS UNDERGO TENSION, EXPAND

(b)

FIGURE 24–26 A torsion bar resists twisting and is used as a spring on some cars and many four-wheel-drive pickup trucks and sport utility vehicles. The larger the diameter, or the shorter the torsion bar, the stiffer the bar. A torsion bar twists very little during normal operation and about a 1/16 of a revolution during a major suspension travel event.

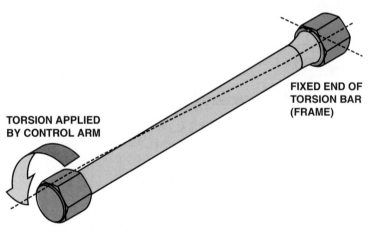

TORSION APPLIED BY CONTROL ARM

FIXED END OF TORSION BAR (FRAME)

FIGURE 24–27 Longitudinal torsion bars attach at the lower control arm at the front and at the frame at the rear of the bar.

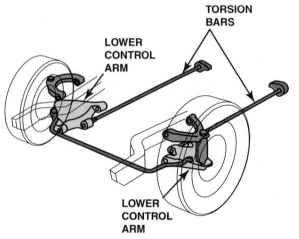

TORSION BARS

LOWER CONTROL ARM

LOWER CONTROL ARM

TORSION BAR

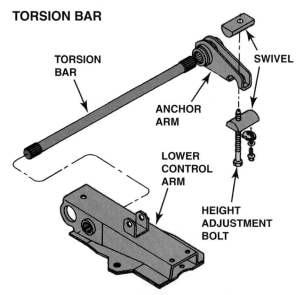

FIGURE 24–28 One end of the torsion bar attaches to the lower control arm and the other to an anchor arm that is adjustable.

TORSION BARS (CONTINUED)

direction or preload. However, after being in a vehicle, the bar takes a set; reversing the side the torsion bar is used on causes the bar to be twisted in the opposite direction. Even though the bars are usually interchangeable, proper ride height can be accomplished even if the bars were installed on the side opposite from the original. But because the bar is being "worked" in the opposite direction, it can weaken and break. If a torsion bar breaks, the entire suspension collapses; this can cause severe vehicle damage, as well as a serious accident.

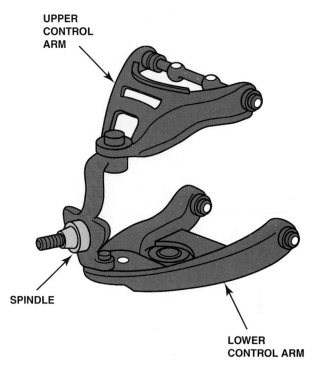

FIGURE 24–29 The spindle supports the wheels and attaches to the control arm with ball-and-socket joints called ball joints. The control arm attaches to the frame of the vehicle through rubber bushings to help isolate noise and vibration between the road and the body. *(Courtesy of Cooper Automotive Company)*

SUSPENSION PRINCIPLES

Suspensions use various links, arms, and joints to allow the wheels to move freely up and down; front suspensions also have to allow the front wheels to turn. All suspensions must provide for the following supports:

1. **Transverse (or side-to-side) wheel support.** As the wheels of the vehicle move up and down, the suspension must accommodate this movement and still keep the wheel from moving away from the vehicle or inward toward the center of the vehicle. ● SEE FIGURE 24–29. The control arm pivots on the vehicle frame. The wheels attach to a spindle that attaches to the ball joint at the end of the control arm. Transverse links are also called **lateral links**.

2. **Longitudinal (front-to-back) wheel support.** As the wheels of the vehicle move up and down, the suspension must allow for this movement and still keep the wheels from moving backward whenever a bump is hit. Note in ● **FIGURE 24–29** how the separation of the pivot points, where the control arm meets the frame, provides support to prevent front-to-back wheel movement.

At least two suspension links or arms are required in order to provide for freedom of movement up or down, and to *prevent* any in–out or forward–back movement. Some suspension designs use an additional member to control forward–back movement. ● SEE FIGURE 24–30.

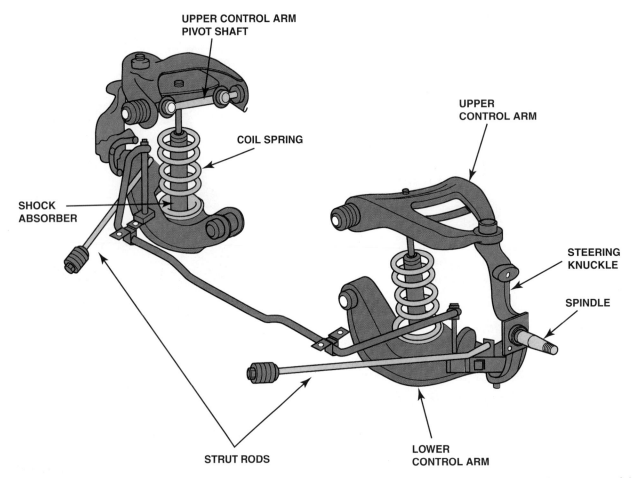

FIGURE 24–30 The strut rods provide longitudinal support to the suspension to prevent forward or rearward movement of the control arms.

SUSPENSION PRINCIPLES (CONTINUED)

The design of the suspension and the location of the suspension mounting points on the frame or body are critical to proper vehicle handling. Two very important design factors are called **anti-squat** and **anti-dive.**

1. **Anti-squat.** Anti-squat refers to the reaction of the body of a vehicle during acceleration. It is normal in most designs for the vehicle to squat down at the rear while accelerating. Most drivers feel comfortable feeling this reaction, even on front-wheel-drive vehicles. Anti-squat refers to the degree to which this normal force is neutralized. If 100% anti-squat were designed into the suspension system, the vehicle would remain level while accelerating.

2. **Anti-dive.** Anti-dive refers to the force that causes the front of the vehicle to drop down while braking. Some front-nose dive feels normal to most drivers. If 100% anti-dive

were designed into a vehicle, it would remain perfectly level while braking.

The service technician cannot, and should not, attempt to change anti-squat or anti-dive characteristics built into the design of the vehicle. However, if the customer notices more squat or dive than normal, then the technician should carefully inspect all suspension components, especially those mounting points to the frame or body.

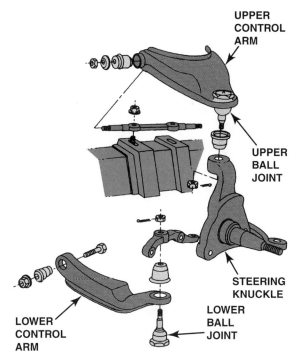

FIGURE 24–31 The steering knuckle used on a short/long-arm front suspension.

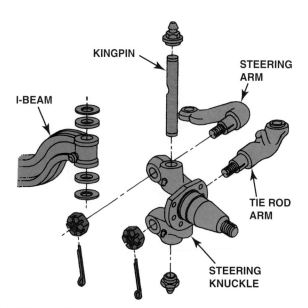

FIGURE 24–32 A kingpin is a steel shaft or pin that joins the steering knuckle to the suspension and allows the steering knuckle to pivot.

STEERING KNUCKLES

A **steering knuckle** is hard to classify either as part of the suspension or as part of the wheel. A knuckle serves two purposes:

- To join the suspension to the wheel
- Usually includes the spindle where the front wheel bearings are attached
- To provide pivot points between the suspension and wheel.

Knuckles are used with independent suspensions and at the wheels that steer the vehicle. ● **SEE FIGURE 24–31.**

The only knuckle that uses a **kingpin** is a steering knuckle on an I-beam or twin I-beam front suspension. ● **SEE FIGURE 24–32.** A kingpin steering knuckle keeps the wheel rigid in relation to the I-beam during up-and-down wheel movement, but rotates around the steering axis to turn the wheels left and right. The steering axis is the vertical center of the kingpin.

CONTROL ARMS

A **control arm** is a suspension link that connects a knuckle or wheel flange to the frame. One end of a control arm attaches to the knuckle or wheel flange, generally with either a ball joint or bushing. The opposite end of the arm, which attaches to a frame member, usually pivots on a bushing. ● **SEE FIGURE 24–33.** The end attached to the frame must pivot to allow the axle or knuckle to travel vertically.

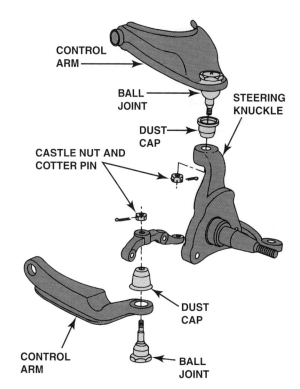

FIGURE 24–33 Control arms are used to connect the steering knuckle to the frame or body of the vehicle and provide the structural support for the suspension system.

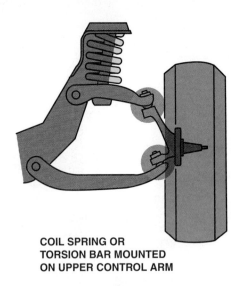

COIL SPRING OR
TORSION BAR MOUNTED
ON UPPER CONTROL ARM

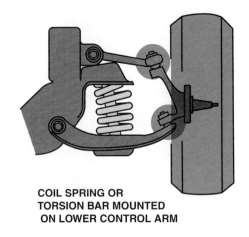

COIL SPRING OR
TORSION BAR MOUNTED
ON LOWER CONTROL ARM

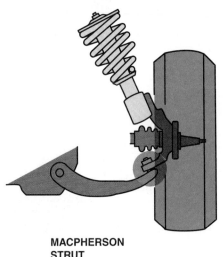

MACPHERSON
STRUT

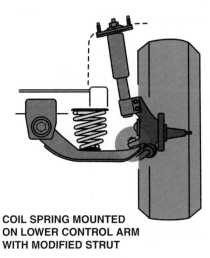

COIL SPRING MOUNTED
ON LOWER CONTROL ARM
WITH MODIFIED STRUT

FIGURE 24–34 Ball joints provide the freedom of movement necessary for steering and suspension movements.

BALL JOINTS

Ball joints are actually ball-and-socket joints, similar to the joints in a person's shoulder. Ball joints allow the front wheels to move up and down, as well as side to side (for steering).

A vehicle can be equipped with coil springs, mounted either above the upper control arm *or* on the lower control arm. ● SEE FIGURE 24–34.

If the coil spring is attached to the top of the upper control arm, then the upper ball joint is carrying the weight of the vehicle and is called the **load-carrying ball joint**. The lower ball joint is called the **non-load-carrying**, or *follower*, **ball joint**. ● SEE FIGURE 24–35.

If the coil spring is attached to the lower control arm, then the lower ball joint is the load-carrying ball joint and the upper joint is the follower ball joint. ● SEE FIGURE 24–36.

If a torsion-bar-type spring is used, the lower ball joint is a load-carrying joint because the torsion bar is attached to the lower control arm on most vehicles that use torsion bars.

BALL JOINT DESIGN There are two basic designs of ball joints: compression loaded and tension loaded. If the control arm rests on the steering knuckle, the ball joint is *compressed* into the control arm by the weight of the vehicle. If the knuckle rests on the control arm, the weight of the vehicle tends to pull the ball joint back into the control arm by *tension.* The type used is determined by the chassis design engineer, and the service technician cannot change the type of ball joint used for a particular application. ● SEE FIGURE 24–37 on page 452.

A specific amount of stud-turning resistance is built into each ball joint to stabilize steering. A ball joint that does not support the weight of the vehicle and acts as a suspension pivot is often called a follower ball joint or a friction ball joint. The load-carrying (weight-carrying) ball joint is subjected to the greatest amount of wear and is the most frequently replaced.

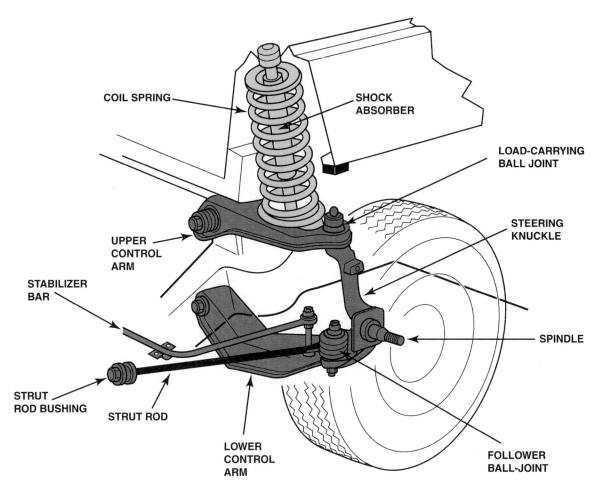

FIGURE 24–35 The upper ball joint is load carrying in this type of suspension because the weight of the vehicle is applied through the spring, upper control arm, and ball joint to the wheel. The lower control arm is a lateral link, and the lower ball joint is called a follower ball joint.

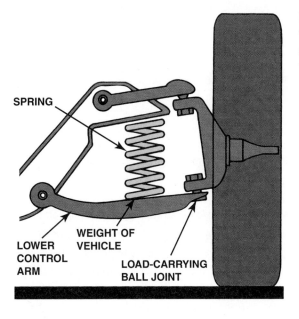

FIGURE 24–36 The lower ball joint is load carrying in this type of suspension because the weight of the vehicle is applied through the spring, lower control arm, and ball joint to the wheel.

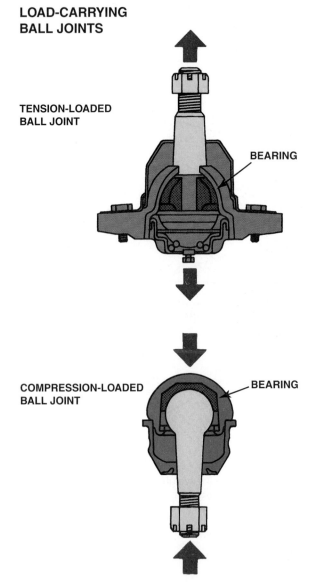

LOAD-CARRYING BALL JOINTS

TENSION-LOADED BALL JOINT

BEARING

COMPRESSION-LOADED BALL JOINT

BEARING

FIGURE 24–37 All ball joints, whether tension or compression loaded, have a bearing surface between the ball stud and socket.

STRUT RODS

Some vehicles are equipped with round steel rods that are attached between the lower control arm at one end and the frame of the vehicle with rubber bushings, called strut rod bushings, at the other end. The purpose of these **strut rods** is to provide forward/backward support to the control arms. Strut rods are used on vehicles equipped with MacPherson struts and many short/long-arm-type suspensions. The bushings are very important in maintaining proper wheel alignment while providing the necessary up-and-down movement of the control arms during suspension travel. Strut rods prevent lower control arm movement back and forth during braking. ● **SEE FIGURE 24–38.**

Strut rods are also called tension or compression rods or simply TC rods. Tension rods attach in *front* of the wheels to the body or frame where the rod is being pulled in tension. Compression rods attach to the body or frame *behind* the wheels where the rod is being pushed or compressed. Some vehicle manufacturers call the strut rod a drag rod because it is attached in front of the wheels, and therefore acts on the lower control arm as if to drag the wheels behind their attachment points.

The bushings are replaceable by removing a nut on the frame end of the strut rod. ● **SEE FIGURE 24–39.** If a strut rod has a nut on *both* sides of the bushings, then the strut rod is used to adjust *caster.*

STABILIZER BARS

Most cars and trucks are equipped with a **stabilizer bar** on the front suspension, which is a round, hardened steel bar (usually SAE 4560 or 4340 steel) attached to both lower control arms with bolts and rubber bushing washers called stabilizer bar bushings. ● **SEE FIGURE 24–40** on page 454.

A stabilizer bar is also called an anti-sway bar (sway bar) or anti-roll bar (roll bar). A stabilizer bar operates by *twisting* the

bar if one side of the vehicle moves up or down in relation to the other side, such as during cornering, hitting bumps, or driving over uneven road surfaces. ● **SEE FIGURE 24–41** on page 454.

The purpose of the stabilizer bar is to prevent excessive body roll while cornering and to add to stability while driving over rough road surfaces. The stabilizer bar is also used as a longitudinal (front/back) support to the lower control arm on

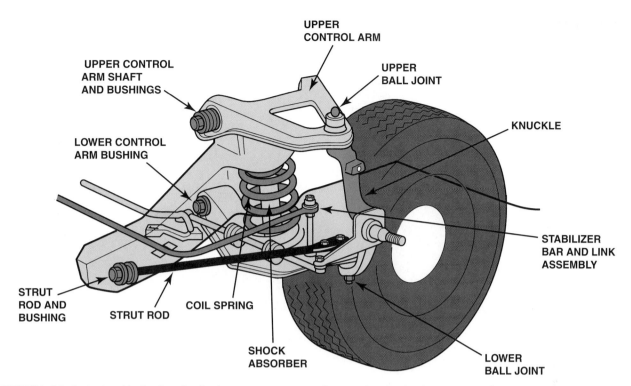

FIGURE 24–38 A strut rod is the longitudinal support to prevent front-to-back wheel movement. Struts rods are only used when there is only one lower control arm bushing and not used where there are two lower control arm bushings.

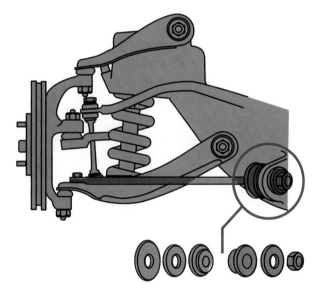

FIGURE 24–39 Strut rod bushings insulate the steel bar from the vehicle frame or body.

many vehicles equipped with MacPherson struts. The effective force of a stabilizer bar is increased with the diameter of the bar. Therefore, optional suspensions often include larger-diameter stabilizer bars and bushings.

Stabilizer links connect the ends of the stabilizer bar to the lower control arm. ● **SEE FIGURES 24–42 AND 24–43** on page 455. Careful inspection of the stabilizer bar links is important. Links are commonly found to be defective (cracked rubber washers or broken spacer bolts) because of the great amount of force that is transmitted through the links and the bushings. Defective links and/or bushings can cause unsafe vehicle handling and noise.

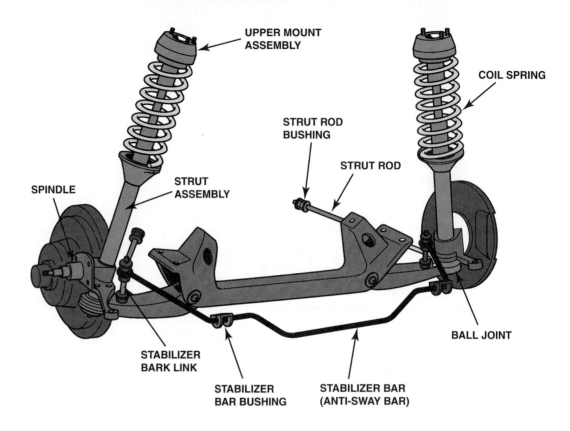

FIGURE 24–40 Typical stabilizer bar installation.

UPPER MOUNT ASSEMBLY

COIL SPRING

STRUT ROD BUSHING

STRUT ROD

SPINDLE

STRUT ASSEMBLY

BALL JOINT

STABILIZER BARK LINK

STABILIZER BAR BUSHING

STABILIZER BAR (ANTI-SWAY BAR)

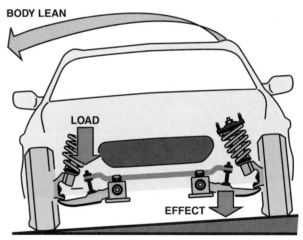

FIGURE 24–41 As the body of the vehicle leans, the stabilizer bar is twisted. The force exerted by the stabilizer bar counteracts the body lean.

BODY LEAN

LOAD

EFFECT

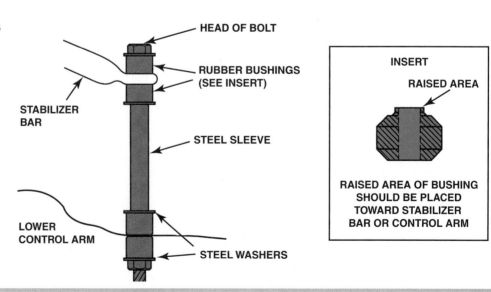

FIGURE 24–42 Stabilizer bar links are sold as a kit consisting of the long bolt with steel sleeve and rubber bushings. Steel washers are used on both sides of the rubber bushings as shown.

HEAD OF BOLT

RUBBER BUSHINGS (SEE INSERT)

STABILIZER BAR

STEEL SLEEVE

LOWER CONTROL ARM

STEEL WASHERS

INSERT

RAISED AREA

RAISED AREA OF BUSHING SHOULD BE PLACED TOWARD STABILIZER BAR OR CONTROL ARM

SHOCK ABSORBERS

Shock absorbers are used on all conventional suspension systems to dampen and control the motion of the vehicle's springs. Without shock absorbers (dampers), the vehicle would continue to bounce after hitting bumps. ● SEE FIGURE 24–44 on page 456.

The major purpose of any shock or strut is to control ride and handling. Standard shock absorbers *do not* support the weight of a vehicle. *The springs support the weight of the vehicle; the shock absorbers control the actions and reactions of the springs.* Shock absorbers are also called dampers.

Most shock absorbers are *direct acting* because they are connected directly between the vehicle frame or body and the axles. ● SEE FIGURE 24–45 on page 457.

As a wheel rolls over a bump, the wheel moves toward the body and compresses the spring(s) of the vehicle. As the spring compresses, it stores energy. The spring then releases this stored energy, causing the body of the vehicle to rise (rebound). ● SEE FIGURE 24–46 on page 457.

After the energy in the spring is used up, the body starts downward, causing the spring to compress. Without shock absorbers, the energy released from the spring would be very rapid and violent. The shock absorber helps dampen the rapid up-and-down movement of the vehicle springs by converting energy of movement into heat by forcing hydraulic fluid through small holes inside the shock absorber.

SHOCK ABSORBER OPERATION
The hydraulic shock absorber operates on the principle of fluid being forced through a small opening (orifice). ● SEE FIGURES 24–47 AND 24–48 on page 458. Besides small openings, pressure relief valves are built into most shock absorbers to control vehicle ride under all operating conditions. The greater the pressure drop of the fluid inside the shock and the greater the amount of fluid moved through the orifice, the greater the amount of dampening; therefore, larger shock absorbers can usually provide better dampening than smaller units.

GAS-CHARGED SHOCKS
Most shock absorbers on new vehicles are gas charged. Pressurizing the oil inside the shock absorber helps smooth the ride over rough roads. This pressure helps prevent air pockets from forming in the shock absorber oil

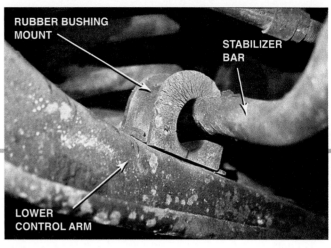

FIGURE 24–43 Notice how the stabilizer bar pulls down on the mounting bushing when the vehicle is hoisted off the ground, allowing the front suspension to drop down. These bushings are a common source of noise, especially when cold. Lubricating the bushings with paste silicone grease often cures the noise.

as it passes through the small passages in the shock. After the oil is forced through small passages, the pressure drops and the oil expands. As the oil expands, bubbles are created. The oil becomes foamy. This air-filled oil does not effectively provide dampening. The result of all of this aeration (air being mixed with the oil) is lack of dampening and a harsh ride.

The use of higher-pressure radial tires and lighter vehicle weight has created the need for more effective shock absorbers. To meet this need, shock absorber design engineers use a pressurized gas that does not react chemically with the oil in the shock. If a substance does not react with any other substances, it is called *inert.* The gas most often used is nitrogen, which is about 78% of our atmosphere. Typical gas-charged shocks are pressurized with 130 to 150 PSI (900 to 1,030 kPa) to aid in both handling and ride control. Some shocks use higher pressures, but the higher the pressure, the greater the possibility of leaks and the harsher the ride.

Some gas-charged shock absorbers use a single tube that contains two pistons that separate the high-pressure gas from the working fluid. Single-tube shocks are also called monotube or DeCarbon after the French inventor of the principle and manufacturer of suspension components. ● SEE FIGURE 24–49 on page 459.

AIR SHOCKS/STRUTS
Air-inflatable shock absorbers or struts are used in the rear of vehicles to provide proper vehicle ride height while carrying heavy loads. Many air shock/strut units are original equipment. They are often combined with a built-in air compressor and ride height sensor(s) to provide automatic ride height control.

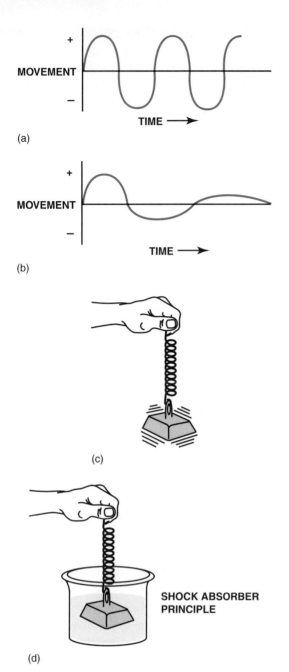

FIGURE 24–44 (a) Movement of the vehicle is supported by springs without a dampening device. (b) Spring action is dampened with a shock absorber. (c) The function of any shock absorber is to dampen the movement or action of a spring, similar to using a liquid to control the movement of a weight on a spring (d).

? **FREQUENTLY ASKED QUESTION**

What Are Remote Reservoir Shocks?

Remote reservoir shock absorbers are units designed for heavy-duty use that use a separate container for the working fluid. ● **SEE FIGURE 24–50** on page 459.

The purpose of the remote fluid reservoir is to keep the temperature of the fluid stable, which helps the shock absorber provide consistent dampening under all conditions.

SHOCK ABSORBERS (CONTINUED)

Air-inflatable shocks are standard shock absorbers with an air chamber with a rubber bag built into the dust cover (top) of the shock. ● **SEE FIGURE 24–51** on page 459.

Air pressure is used to inflate the bag, which raises the installed height of the shock. As the shock increases in height, the rear of the vehicle is raised. Typical maximum air pressure in air shocks ranges from 90 to 150 PSI (620 to 1,030 kPa). As the air pressure increases in the air-inflatable reservoir of the shock, the stiffness of the suspension increases. This additional stiffness is due to the shock taking weight from the spring, and therefore the air in the air shock becomes an air spring. Now, with two springs to support the vehicle, the spring rate increases and a harsher ride often results. *It is important that the load capacity of the vehicle not be exceeded or serious damage can occur to the vehicle's springs, axles, bearings, and shock support mounts.*

AIR SPRINGS Some electronically controlled suspension systems use air springs. A basic **air spring** consists of a rubber air chamber, generally closed at the bottom by a piston fitted into a control arm, or by a strut shock absorber. ● **SEE FIGURE 24–52** on page 460.

Electronically controlled suspension systems that use air springs as the only springs are available on some Hummer, and many Ford, Mercury, and Lincoln vehicles.

Some air springs are in effect auxiliary springs inside a coil-spring strut. In these designs, the coil spring supports the weight of the vehicle, while the air spring raises or lowers the body to adjust ride height according to load. ● **SEE FIGURE 24–53** on page 460.

COIL-OVER SHOCKS. A coil-over shock absorber uses the force of an external coil spring to boost the performance of the basic shock absorber. ● **SEE FIGURE 24–54** on page 461. The spring usually extends from the upper shock mount to a seat on the lower portion of the cylinder. The spring rate added to the hydraulic resistance makes the shock stiffer.

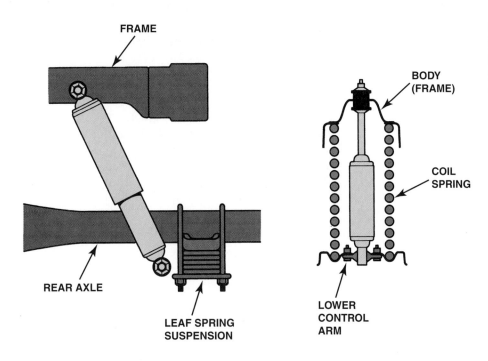

FRAME

REAR AXLE

LEAF SPRING
SUSPENSION

BODY
(FRAME)

COIL
SPRING

LOWER
CONTROL
ARM

FIGURE 24–45 Shock absorbers work best when mounted as close to the spring as possible. Shock absorbers that are mounted straight up and down offer the most dampening.

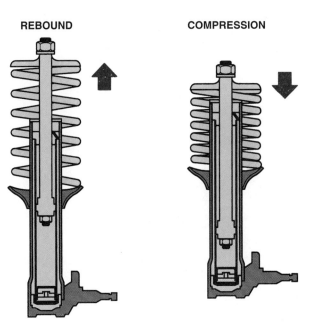

REBOUND

COMPRESSION

FIGURE 24–46 When a vehicle hits a bump in the road, the suspension moves upward. This is called compression or jounce. Rebound is when the spring (coil, torsion bar, or leaf) returns to its original position.

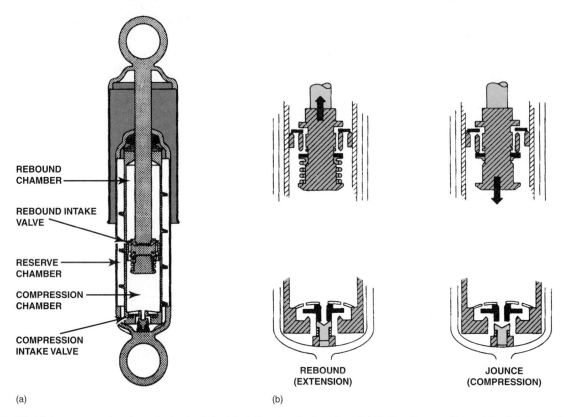

(a)   (b)

FIGURE 24–47 (a) A cutaway drawing of a typical double-tube shock absorber. (b) Notice the position of the intake and compression valve during rebound (extension) and compression.

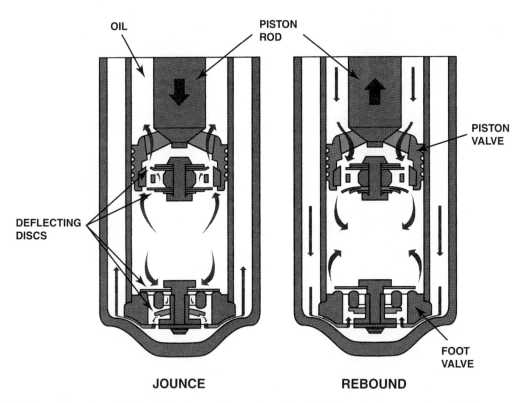

JOUNCE   REBOUND

FIGURE 24–48 Oil flow through a deflected disc-type piston valve. The deflecting disc can react rapidly to suspension movement. For example, if a large bump is hit at high speed, the disc can deflect completely and allow the suspension to reach its maximum jounce distance while maintaining a controlled rate of movement.

SINGLE (MONO) TUBE

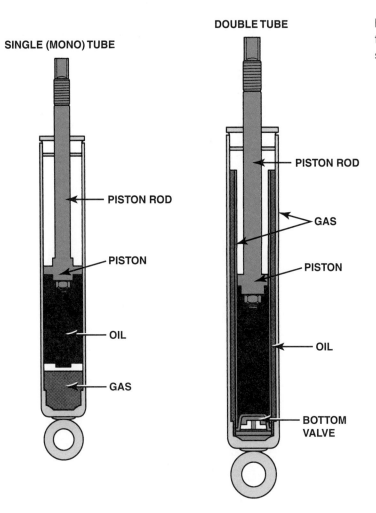

PISTON ROD

PISTON

OIL

GAS

DOUBLE TUBE

PISTON ROD

GAS

PISTON

OIL

BOTTOM VALVE

FIGURE 24–49 Gas-charged shock absorbers are manufactured with a double-tube design similar to conventional shock absorbers and with a single or monotube design.

FIGURE 24–50 The shock absorber is on the right and the fluid reservoir for the shock is on the left.

AIR SHOCK ABSORBER

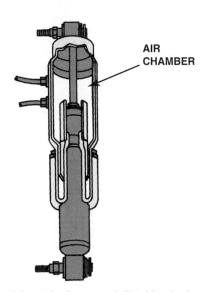

AIR CHAMBER

FIGURE 24–51 A rubber tube forms an inflatable air chamber at the top of an air shock. The higher the air pressure in the chamber, the stiffer the shock.

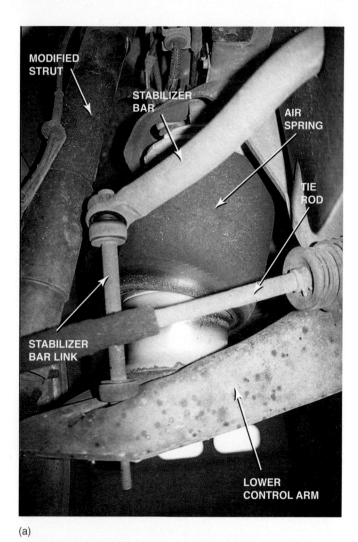

MODIFIED STRUT

STABILIZER BAR

AIR SPRING

TIE ROD

STABILIZER BAR LINK

LOWER CONTROL ARM

(a)

(b)

FIGURE 24–52 (a) The front suspension of a Lincoln with an air-spring suspension. (b) Always check in the trunk for the cutoff switch for a vehicle equipped with an air suspension before hoisting or towing the vehicle.

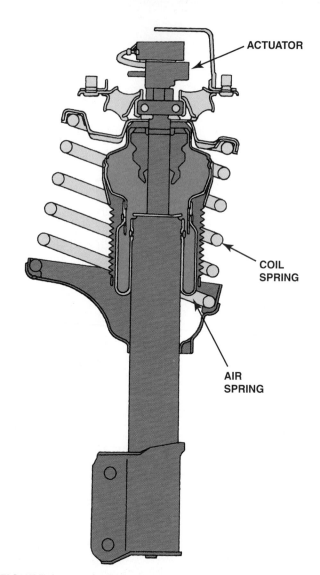

ACTUATOR

COIL SPRING

AIR SPRING

FIGURE 24–53 Some air springs are auxiliary units to the coil spring and are used to control ride height while the coil spring is the weight-bearing unit.

STRUTS

A **strut** is a sturdy shock absorber that is also a structural component of the suspension. A strut is a suspension link as well as a shock absorber. The casing of a strut must be strong and rigid to function as a suspension link. The shock absorber assembles inside the casing of a strut, and may be either a removable cartridge or an integral part of the strut.

MACPHERSON STRUTS   The MacPherson strut, which is named after Earle S. MacPherson, who developed the suspension design in the late 1940s and patented it in 1953, is the most commonly used type. A MacPherson strut includes the suspension spring—a coil spring that surrounds the strut casing—so that it transfers the weight of the body to the wheel. ● **SEE FIGURE 24–55.**

**COIL-OVER
SHOCK ABSORBER**

FIGURE 24–54 A coil-over shock is a standard hydraulic shock absorber with a coil spring wrapped around it to increase stiffness and/or take some of the carrying weight off of the springs.

MACPHERSON STRUT

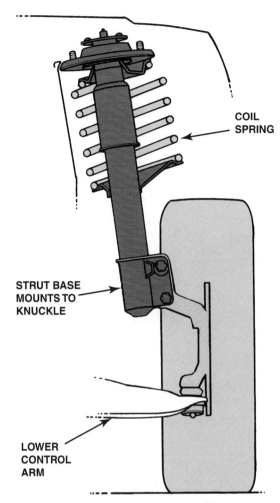

**COIL
SPRING**

**STRUT BASE
MOUNTS TO
KNUCKLE**

**LOWER
CONTROL
ARM**

FIGURE 24–55 A strut is a structural part of the suspension and includes the spring and shock absorber in one assembly.

A MacPherson strut typically incorporates an upper and a lower spring seat, a shock absorber mount and dust cap, a dust cover for the piston rod, and a bump stop. The upper mount secures the upper spring seat to the strut tower. A rubber bushing at the top of the strut absorbs vibrations. A bearing on a front-wheel strut allows it to rotate on the vertical steering axis without rubbing against the strut tower when the steering knuckle turns. The lower spring seat is attached to the strut casing.

MODIFIED STRUTS Unlike a MacPherson unit, a modified strut does not include a spring as part of the assembly and is used in the front on some vehicles and on the rear of others. ● **SEE FIGURE 24–56.** Most modified strut rear suspensions use coil springs mounted on the lower control arm.

BUMP STOPS

All suspension systems have a limit of travel. If the vehicle hits a large bump in the road, the wheels are forced upward toward the vehicle with tremendous force. This force is absorbed by the springs of the suspension system. If the bump is large enough, the suspension is compressed to its mechanical limit. Instead of allowing the metal components of the suspension to hit the frame or body of the vehicle, a rubber or foam bumper is used to absorb and isolate the suspension from the frame or body. ● **SEE FIGURE 24–57.**

These bumpers are called **bump stops,** suspension bumpers, strike-out bumpers, or jounce bumpers. *Jounce* means jolt, or to cause to bounce or move up and down. Bumpers are made from rubber or microcellular urethane.

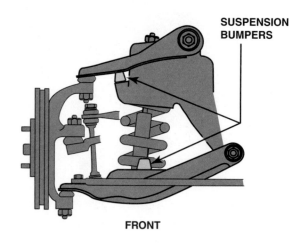

SUSPENSION BUMPERS

FRONT

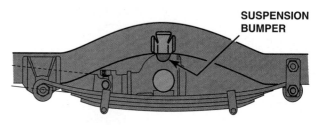

SUSPENSION BUMPER

REAR

FIGURE 24–57 Suspension bumpers are used on all suspension systems to prevent metal-to-metal contact between the suspension and the frame or body of the vehicle when the suspension "bottoms out" over large bumps or dips in the road.

MODIFIED STRUT

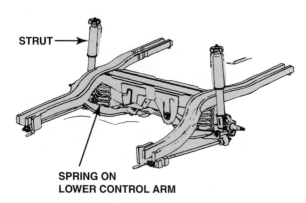

STRUT

SPRING ON LOWER CONTROL ARM

FIGURE 24–56 A modified strut used on the rear suspension; it is part of the structural part of the assembly.

BUMP STOPS (CONTINUED)

Urethane is a high-strength material with good resistance to wear and tear as well as good chemical resistance to most fluids. Forming urethane foam with small, regular air cells makes the material ideal for jounce bumpers.

Damaged suspension-limiting bump stops can be caused by the following:

1. Sagging springs that result in lower-than-normal ride (trim) height

2. Worn or defective shock absorbers

Most suspensions also use a rubber or foam stop to limit the downward travel of the suspension during rebound. The rebound stop also prevents metal-to-metal contact of the suspension on the frame when the vehicle is on a body-contact-type hoist and the wheels are allowed to hang or droop down. Some stops are built into the shock absorber or strut.

? FREQUENTLY ASKED QUESTION

What Is a Track Rod?

A track rod, also called a Panhard rod, is used in the rear of some suspension systems to keep the rear axle centered under the center of the vehicle. It is a straight rod or channel that connects to the frame on one end and the axle on the other end.

1. The lighter the wheel/tire combination, the lower the unsprung weight and the better the ride and handling of the vehicle.

2. All springs—including the coil, leaf, and torsion bar types—share Hooke's Law, which states that the force exerted by the spring is directly proportional to the amount the spring is deflected.

3. All springs are similar to torsion bars. As the torsion bar becomes longer or smaller in diameter, it becomes easier to twist. If a coil spring is cut, the remaining spring is shorter, yet stiffer.

4. Ball joints attach to control arms and allow the front wheels to move up and down, as well as turn.

5. Suspension designs include a straight or solid-axle, two-control-arm-type called an SLA or a MacPherson strut.

6. All shock absorbers dampen the motion of the suspension to control ride and handling.

REVIEW QUESTIONS

1. List the types of suspensions and name their component parts.

2. Explain Hooke's Law.

3. Describe the purpose and function of a stabilizer bar.

4. Explain the difference between a load-carrying and a friction ball joint.

CHAPTER QUIZ

1. The spring rate of a spring is measured in units of _____.
   a. lb per inch
   b. ft-lb
   c. PSI
   d. in.-lb

2. Two technicians are discussing torsion bars. Technician A says that many torsion bars are adjustable to allow for ride height adjustment. Technician B says that torsion bars are usually marked left and right and should not be switched side to side. Which technician is correct?
   a. Technician A only
   b. Technician B only
   c. Both Technicians A and B
   d. Neither Technician A nor B

3. What component(s) is considered to be unsprung weight?
   a. Frame
   b. Body
   c. Wheels and tires
   d. Both a and b

4. Two technicians are discussing MacPherson struts. Technician A says that in most applications the entire strut assembly rotates when the front wheels are turned. Technician B says a typical MacPherson strut suspension system uses only one control arm and one ball joint per side. Which technician is correct?
   a. Technician A only
   b. Technician B only
   c. Both Technicians A and B
   d. Neither Technician A nor B

5. Technician A says that regular replacement shock absorbers will raise the rear of a vehicle that is sagging down. Technician B says that replacement springs will be required to restore the proper ride height. Which technician is correct?
   a. Technician A only
   b. Technician B only
   c. Both Technicians A and B
   d. Neither Technician A nor B

6. What suspension component is used to counteract body lean during cornering?
   a. Torsion bar
   b. Strut rod
   c. Stabilizer bar
   d. Control arm

7. A center bolt is used in what type of spring?
   a. Coil
   b. Leaf
   c. Torsion bar
   d. All of the above

8. Two technicians are discussing air shocks. Technician A says that air is forced through small holes to dampen the ride. Technician B says that air shocks are conventional hydraulic shock absorbers with an airbag to control vehicle ride height. Which technician is correct?
   a. Technician A only
   b. Technician B only
   c. Both Technicians A and B
   d. Neither Technician A nor B

9. The owner of a pickup truck wants to cut the coil springs to lower the vehicle. Technician A says that the ride will be harsher than normal if the springs are cut. Technician B says that the springs could be damaged, especially if a cutting torch is used to cut the springs. Which technician is correct?
   a. Technician A only
   b. Technician B only
   c. Both Technicians A and B
   d. Neither Technician A nor B

10. A MacPherson strut is a structural part of the vehicle.
    a. True
    b. False

FRONT SUSPENSION AND SERVICE

After studying Chapter 25, the reader will be able to:

1. Prepare for ASE Suspension and Steering (A4) certification test content area "B" (Suspension System Diagnosis and Repair).

2. Explain how to perform a road test, a dry park test, a visual inspection, and a bounce test.

3. Discuss the procedures for testing load-carrying and follower-type ball joints.

4. Describe ball joint replacement procedures.

5. List the steps required to replace control arm and stabilizer bar bushings.

6. Explain routine service procedures of the suspension system.

A-arm 467	Pinch bolt 477
Cow catcher 484	Radius rod 466
Cuppy tire wear 481	SLA 467
Dry park test 472	Steering knuckle 466
Durometer 490	Strut suspension 469
Indicator ball joints 474	Twin I-beam 466
Kingpin 466	

FIGURE 25–1 Most early vehicles used single straight axles.

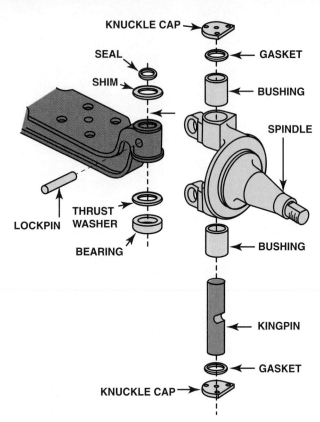

FIGURE 25–2 Typical kingpin used with a solid axle.

FRONT SUSPENSION TYPES

SOLID AXLES   Early cars and trucks used a solid (or *straight*) front axle to support the front wheels. ● **SEE FIGURE 25–1.**

A solid-axle front suspension is very strong and is still being used in the manufacture of medium and heavy trucks. The main disadvantage of solid-axle design is its lack of ride quality. When one wheel hits a bump or dip in the road, the forces are transferred through the axle to the opposite wheel. Solid axles are currently used in the rear of most vehicles.

KINGPINS   At the end of many solid I-beam or tube axles are **kingpins** that allow the front wheels to rotate for steering. Kingpins are hardened steel pins that attach the steering knuckle to the front axle, allowing the front wheels to move for steering. Kingpins usually have grease fittings to lubricate the kingpin bushings. Failure to keep these bushings lubricated with chassis grease can cause wear and freeplay or can cause

the pins to become galled (seized or frozen), resulting in hard steering and/or loud noise while turning. ● **SEE FIGURE 25–2.**

TWIN I-BEAMS   A **twin I-beam** front suspension was used for over 30 years on Ford pickup trucks and vans, beginning in the mid-1960s. Strong steel twin beams that cross provide independent front suspension operation with the strength of a solid front axle. Early versions of the twin I-beam systems used kingpins, while later models used ball joints to support the **steering knuckle** and spindle. Coil springs are usually used on twin I-beam suspensions, even though the original design and patent used leaf springs. ● **SEE FIGURE 25–3.**

To control longitudinal (front-to-back) support, a **radius rod** is attached to each beam and is anchored to the frame of the truck using rubber bushings. These bushings allow the front axle to move up and down while still insulating road noise and vibration from the frame and body.

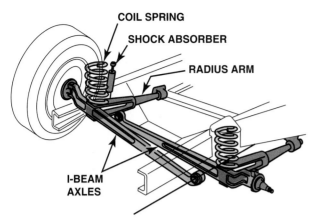

FIGURE 25–3 Twin I-beam front suspension. Rubber bushings are used to support the I-beams to the frame and help isolate road noise.

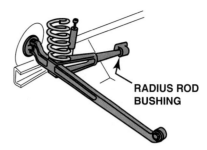

FIGURE 25–4 The rubber radius rod bushing absorbs road shocks and helps isolate road noise.

> **TECH TIP**
>
> **Radius Rod Bushing Noise**
>
> When the radius rod bushing on a Ford truck or van deteriorates, the most common complaint from the driver is noise. ● **SEE FIGURE 25–4.** Besides causing tire wear, worn or defective radius rod bushing deterioration can cause the following:
>
> 1. A clicking sound when braking (it sounds as if the brake caliper may be loose).
> 2. A clunking noise when hitting bumps.
>
> When the bushing deteriorates, the axles can move forward and backward with less control. Noise is the first sign that something is wrong. Without proper axle support, handling and cornering can also be affected.

SHORT/LONG-ARM (SLA) SUSPENSION

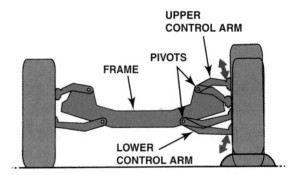

FIGURE 25–5 The upper control arm is shorter than the lower control arm on a short/long-arm (SLA) suspension.

SHORT/LONG-ARM SUSPENSIONS

The short/long-arm suspension uses a short upper control arm and a longer lower control arm and usually is referred to as the *SLA-type suspension.*

The two main links in a **short/long-arm (SLA)** suspension are the upper control arm and the lower control arm. The upper control arm is shorter than the lower one. ● **SEE FIGURE 25–5.** This type of suspension system goes by a variety of names, including unequal-arm suspension, double-wishbone suspension, or **A-arm** suspension. Unequal arm refers to the fact that the two arms are of different lengths, while double-wishbone and A-arm derive from the shape of the arms, which are frequently

triangular with one mounting point at the knuckle and two at the frame. When an SLA suspension uses a straight, two-point lower control arm, there is almost always a strut rod that braces the lower arm against the frame. The strut rod can attach to the frame at a point either forward or to the rear of the control arm.

A strut rod, also called a *reaction rod,* provides support to the axle during braking and acceleration forces.

Using a strut rod provides triangulation between the wheel and the frame. *Triangulation* means that the front suspension has a three-point brace that resists forces from every direction, while still allowing the wheels to pivot on the steering axis.

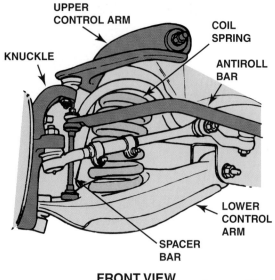

FRONT VIEW

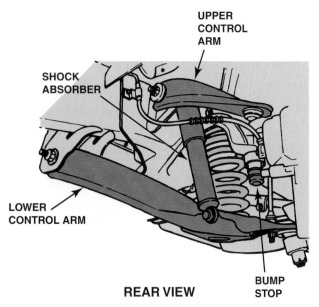

REAR VIEW

FIGURE 25–6 A typical SLA front suspension using coil springs.

SLA SUSPENSION - COIL SPRING ON UPPER ARM

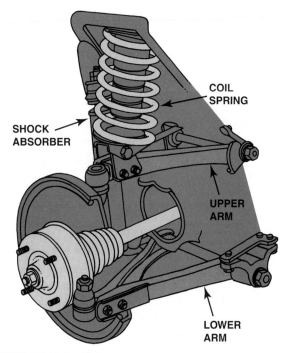

FIGURE 25–7 An SLA-type suspension with the coil spring placed on top of the upper control arm.

SHORT/LONG-ARM SUSPENSIONS (CONTINUED)

Locating the coil spring on the lower control arm is the most common SLA-type suspension configuration. ● **SEE FIGURE 25–6.**

The upper control arm is A-shaped, with two mounting points at the frame side member and one at the steering knuckle. The inboard ends of the arm attach to a pivot bar that is rigidly bolted to the frame, and the outboard end connects to the steering knuckle with a ball joint. Bushings between the inner arm mounts and the pivot bar allow the arm to swing vertically. The lower control arm is also A-shaped with two inboard pivot mounts and a ball joint connection at the knuckle. Bolts

attach the inboard ends of the lower arm to brackets that extend from the bottom of the frame crossmember. Bushings on the inboard mounts allow the arm to pivot vertically.

The coil springs seat between the lower control arm and a bracket below the frame side member. The shock absorber attaches to the lower control arm and the frame side member.

In a typical coil spring on the upper control arm design, a portion of the unit-body wheel well is reinforced to withstand spring force and act as the upper spring seats. ● **SEE FIGURE 25–7.** Short/long-arm suspensions use longitudinal torsion bars, especially in trucks.

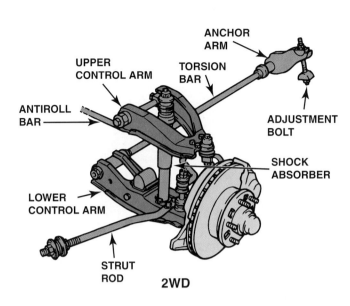

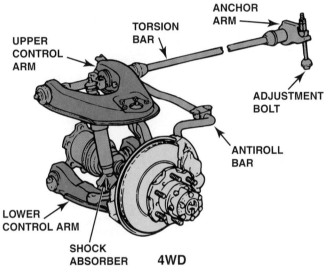

FIGURE 25–8 A torsion bar SLA suspension can use either the lower or the upper control arm.

SHORT/LONG-ARM SUSPENSIONS (CONTINUED)

The forward end of the torsion bar has external splines and shares the splined socket of the torque arm with the control arm through a bolt. Because the torque arm is rigidly bolted to the control arm, motion transfers to the torsion bar whenever the control arm pivots. The torsion bar extends rearward from the control arm and connects to an anchor arm that attaches to a frame crossmember. The torsion bar splines to the anchor arm and the anchor arm is secured to the frame by a bolt and adjusting nut. The adjusting nut varies the spring force of the torsion bar to establish the ride height of the vehicle. ● **SEE FIGURE 25–8.**

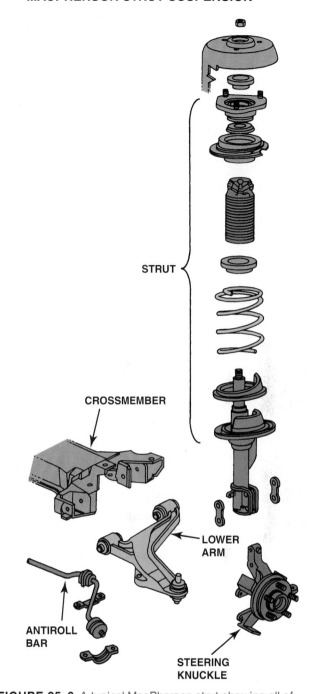

FIGURE 25–9 A typical MacPherson strut showing all of the components of the assembly. A strut includes the shock and the spring in one structural assembly.

STRUT SUSPENSION

Strut suspension can be of several types. A MacPherson strut includes the suspension spring that transfers the weight of the body to the wheel. A MacPherson strut is the main, load-carrying suspension spring. ● **SEE FIGURE 25–9.**

MODIFIED STRUT SUSPENSION

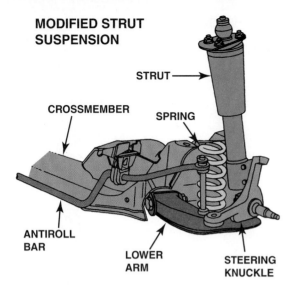

FIGURE 25–10 The modified strut front suspension is similar to a MacPherson strut suspension except that the coil spring is seated on the lower control arm and is not part of the strut assembly.

STRUT SUSPENSION (CONTINUED)

A MacPherson strut typically incorporates an upper and a lower spring seat, a shock absorber mount and dust cap, a dust cover for the piston rod, and a bump stop. The upper mount secures the upper spring seat to the strut tower. A rubber bushing at the top of the strut absorbs vibrations. In most applications, a bearing on the top of a front-wheel strut allows it to rotate on the vertical steering axis without rubbing against the strut tower when the steering knuckle turns. The lower spring seat is attached to the strut casing. The piston rod dust cover is similar to the dust cover on a conventional shock absorber, and a bump stop at the top of the piston rod keeps the strut from bottoming out during suspension jounce.

A modified strut does not include a spring as part of the assembly. ● **SEE FIGURE 25–10.** A modified strut is used on the rear of some GM vehicles. Except for the lack of a spring and spring seats, the construction and function of a modified strut are basically the same as those of a MacPherson strut. When used on the front suspension, a modified strut also rotates on the steering axis when the wheels turn.

A multilink front suspension uses two control arms as well as a structural strut assembly. This type of suspension is also called a strut/SLA or long spindle, short/long-arm suspension. ● **SEE FIGURE 25–11.**

STRUT/SLA SUSPENSION

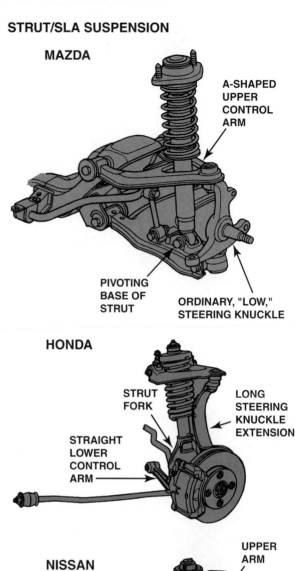

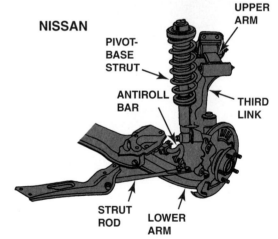

FIGURE 25–11 Multilink front suspension design varies depending on the vehicle manufacturer.

SERVICING THE SUSPENSION SYSTEM

Suspension systems are designed and manufactured to provide years of trouble-free service with a minimum amount of maintenance. In fact, the suspension system is often "invisible" or "transparent" to the driver because the vehicle rides and handles as expected. It is when the driver notices that the vehicle is not riding or handling as it did, or should, that a technician is asked to repair or align the vehicle and fix the problem.

The smart technician should always road test any vehicle before and after servicing (see Tech Tip for details). *The purpose of any diagnosis is to eliminate known good components.* (See the suspension problem symptom chart for a list of components that can cause the problem or customer complaint.)

SUSPENSION PROBLEM SYMPTOM CHART

Item or System to Check	CONCERN/PROBLEM					
	Noise	Instability/ Wander	Pull to One Side	Excessive Steering Play	Hard Steering	Shimmy
Tires/Wheels	Road/tire noise	Low/uneven air pressure	Low/uneven air pressure, mismatched tire sizes	Low/uneven air pressure	Low/uneven air pressure	Wheel out of balance/uneven tire wear/ overworn tires
Shock Absorbers (Struts)	Loose/worn mounts/ bushings	Loose/worn mounts/ bushings, worn/ damaged struts/shock absorbers	Loose/worn mounts/ bushings		Loose/worn mounts/ bushings on strut assemblies	Worn/damaged struts/shock absorbers
Strut Rods (If Equipped)	Loose/worn mounts/ bushings	Loose/worn mounts/ bushings	Loose/worn mounts/ bushings			Loose/worn mounts/ bushings
Springs	Brakes damaged	Brakes damaged	Brakes damaged, especially rear			
Control Arms	Steering knuckle contacting control arm stop, worn/damaged mounts/bushings	Worn/damaged mounts/ bushings	Worn/damaged mounts/ bushings		Worn/damaged mounts/ bushings	Worn/damaged mounts/ bushings
Steering System	Component wear/damage	Component wear/damage	Component wear/damage	Component wear/damage	Component wear/damage	Component wear/damage
Wheel Alignment		Front and rear, especially caster	Front, camber and caster	Front alignment	Front, especially caster	Front, especially caster
Wheel Bearings	Front-wheel bearings	Loose/worn (front and rear)	Loose/worn (front and rear)	Loose/worn (front and rear)		Loose/worn (front and rear)
Brake System			Stuck caliper/slide			
Other					Ball joint lubrication	Loose/worn friction ball joints

CAUTION: More than one factor may be the cause of a problem. Be sure to inspect all suspension components, and repair all parts that are worn or damaged. Failure to do so may allow the problem to reoccur and cause premature failure of other suspension components.

ROAD TEST DIAGNOSIS

If possible, perform a road test of the vehicle with the owner of the vehicle. It is also helpful to have the owner drive the vehicle. While driving, try to determine when and where the noise or problem occurs, such as the following:

1. In cold or warm weather
2. With cold or warm engine/vehicle
3. While turning, left only, right only

A proper road test for any suspension system problem should include the following:

1. **Drive beside parked vehicles.** Any noise generated by the vehicle suspension or tires is reflected off solid objects, such as a row of parked vehicles along a street. For best results, drive with the windows down and drive close to the parked vehicles or a retaining wall on the left side. Repeat the drive for the right side. Defective wheel bearings or power steering pumps usually make noise and can be heard during this test.

2. **Drive into driveways.** Suspension problems often occur when turning at the same time the suspension hits a bump. This action is best repeated by driving slowly into a driveway with a curb. The curb causes the suspension to compress while the wheels are turned (see the Real World Fix titled "The Rock-Hard Problem" for an example). Defective stabilizer bar bushings, control arm bushings, and ball joints will usually make noise during this test procedure.

3. **Drive in reverse while turning.** This technique is usually used to find possible defective outer CV joints used on the drive axle shaft of front-wheel-drive vehicles. This technique also forces the suspension system to work in reverse of normal. Any excessive clearances in the suspension system are reversed and often make noise or cause a vibration during the test. Besides defective CV joints, this test can often detect worn control arm bushings, ball joints, stabilizer bar bushings, or links. This test can also detect defective or worn steering system components such as an idler arm, tie rod end, or center link.

4. **Drive over a bumpy road.** Worn or defective suspension (and steering) components can cause the vehicle to bounce or dart side to side while traveling over bumps and dips in the road. Worn or defective ball joints, control arm bushings, stabilizer bar bushings, stabilizer bar links, or worn shock absorbers can be the cause.

Once the problem has been confirmed, then a further inspection can be performed in the service bay.

DRY PARK TEST (SUSPENSION)

A **dry park test** can also be used to help locate worn or defective suspension components. The dry park test is performed by having an assistant move the steering wheel side to side while feeling and observing for any freeplay in the steering or suspension. For best results, the vehicle should be on a level floor or on a drive-on-type hoist with the front wheels pointing straight ahead. In this suspension analysis using the dry park test, the technician should observe the following for any noticeable play or unusual noise:

1. **Front wheel bearings.** Loose or defective wheel bearings are often overlooked as a possible cause of poor handling or darting vehicle performance.

2. **Control arm bushing wear or movement.** Check for any abnormal movement in upper control arm bushings or lower control arm bushings.

3. **Ball joint movement.** Check for any noticeable play or noise from both load-carrying and follower-type ball joints on both sides of the vehicle.

NOTE: The dry park test (and many other chassis system tests) relies on the experience of the technician to be able to judge normal wear from abnormal wear. It is extremely important that all beginning technicians work closely with an experienced technician to gain this knowledge.

VISUAL INSPECTION

All suspension components should be carefully inspected for signs of wear or damage. A thorough visual inspection should include checking all of the following:

1. Shock absorbers. ● **SEE FIGURE 25–12.**
2. Springs. ● **SEE FIGURE 25–13.**
3. Stabilizer bar links
4. Stabilizer bar bushings
5. Upper and lower shock absorber mounting points
6. Bump stops
7. Body-to-chassis mounts
8. Engine and transmission (transaxle) mounts
9. Suspension arm bushings. ● **SEE FIGURE 25–14.**

Alignment equipment and procedures can often determine if a suspension component is bent or has been moved out of position. A careful *visual* inspection can often reveal suspected damaged components by observing scrape marks or rusty sections that could indicate contact with the road or another object.

While an assistant bounces the vehicle up and down, check to see if there is any freeplay in any of the suspension components.

FIGURE 25–12 A leaking strut. Either a cartridge insert or the entire strut will require replacement. If a light film of oil is seen, this is to be considered normal. If oil is dripping, then this means that the rod seal has failed.

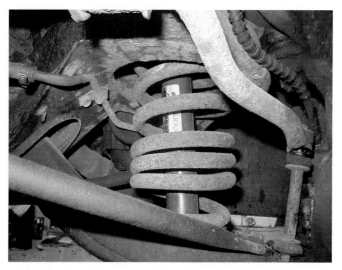

FIGURE 25–13 This front coil spring looks as if it has been heated with a torch in an attempt to lower the ride height of the vehicle. Both front springs will require replacement.

FIGURE 25–14 It is easy to see that this worn control arm bushing needed to be replaced. The new bushing is shown next to the original.

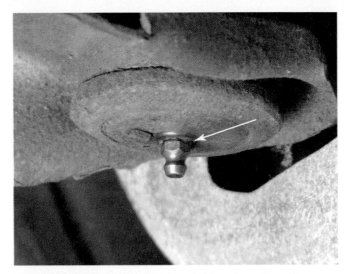

FIGURE 25–15 Grease fitting projecting down from the surrounding area of a ball joint. The ball joint should be replaced when the area around the grease fitting is flush or recessed.

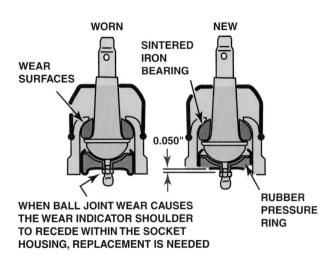

FIGURE 25–16 Indicator ball joints should be checked with the weight of the vehicle on the ground.

BALL JOINTS

DIAGNOSIS AND INSPECTION The life of ball joints depends on driving conditions, vehicle weight, and lubrication. Even with proper care and lubrication, the load-carrying (weight-carrying) ball joints wear more than the follower ball joints. Ball joints should be replaced in pairs, both lower or both upper, to ensure the best handling.

Defective or worn ball joints can cause looseness in the suspension and the following common driver complaints:

1. Loud popping or squeaking whenever driving over curbs, such as into a driveway
2. Shimmy-type vibration felt in the steering wheel
3. Vehicle wander or a tendency not to track straight
4. Excessive freeplay in the steering wheel

A ball joint inspection should also be performed when an alignment is performed or as part of any other comprehensive vehicle inspection.

Many load-carrying ball joints have wear indicators with a raised area around the grease fitting, called **indicator ball joints**. ● **SEE FIGURES 25–15 AND 25–16.**

Always check wear-indicator-type ball joints with the wheels of the vehicle on the ground. If the raised area around the grease fitting is flush or recessed with the surrounding area, the ball joint is worn more than 0.050 in. and must be replaced.

NOTE: Most ball joints must be replaced if the joint has more than 0.050 in. axial (up-and-down) movement. To help visualize this distance, consider that the thickness of an American nickel coin is about 0.060 in. It is helpful to know

that maximum wear should be less than the thickness of a nickel. There are dial indicators (gauges) available that screw into the grease-fitting hole of the ball joint that can accurately measure the wear. ● **SEE FIGURE 25–17.**

To perform a proper non-indicator-type ball joint inspection, the force of the vehicle's springs *must* be *unloaded* from the ball joint. If this force is not relieved, the force of the spring pushes the ball and socket joint tightly together and any wear due to movement will not be detected.

NOTE: The location of the load-carrying ball joint is closest to the seat of the spring or torsion bar.

If the coil spring or torsion bar is attached to the *lower* control arm, the *lower* ball joint is the load-carrying ball joint. ● **SEE FIGURE 25–18.** This includes vehicles equipped with modified MacPherson-strut-type suspension. ● **SEE FIGURE 25–19.**

1. Place the jack under the lower control arm as close to the ball joint as possible and raise the wheels approximately 1 to 2 in. (2.5 to 5 cm) off the ground to unload the lower ball joint.
2. Using a pry bar under the tire, lift the wheel up. If there is excessive vertical movement in the ball joint itself, it must be replaced. Most manufacturers specify a maximum vertical play of approximately 0.050 in. (1.3 mm), or the thickness of a nickel. Always check the manufacturer's specifications for exact maximum allowable movement. Vertical movement of a ball joint is often called axial play

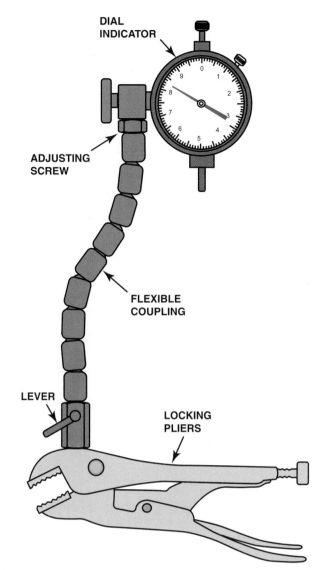

FIGURE 25–17 Typical dial indicator used to measure the suspension component movement. The locking pliers attach the gauge to a stationary part of the vehicle and the flexible coupling allows the dial indicator to be positioned at any angle.

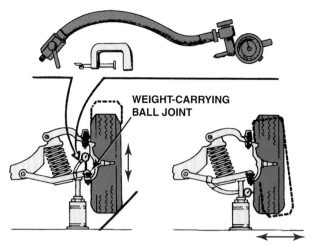

FIGURE 25–18 If the spring is attached to the lower control arm as in this SLA suspension, the jack should be placed under the lower control arm as shown. A dial indicator should be used to measure the amount of freeplay in the ball joints. Be sure that the looseness being measured is not due to normal wheel bearing endplay.

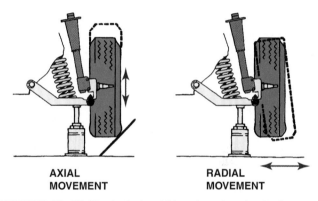

FIGURE 25–19 The jack should be placed under the lower control arm of this modified MacPherson-type suspension.

because the looseness is in the same axis as the ball joint stud. To check for *lateral* play, grip the tire at the top and bottom and move your hands in opposite directions.

NOTE: Be sure that the cause of any freeplay or looseness is not due to the wheel bearing. Closely observe the exact source of the freeplay movement.

If the coil spring is attached to the *upper* control arm, the *upper* ball joint is the load-carrying ball joint. ● **SEE FIGURE 25–20.**

1. Place a block of wood (2 × 4 in.) between the upper control arm and the frame, or use a special tool designed for this purpose. ● **SEE FIGURE 25–21.**

2. Place the jack under the vehicle's *frame* and raise the wheel approximately 1 in. to 2 in. off the ground. (The wood block or special tool keeps the weight of the vehicle off the upper ball joint.)

3. Using a pry bar under the tire, lift the wheel. If there is excessive vertical movement in the ball joint itself, it must be replaced. Always check the manufacturer's specifications for exact maximum allowable movement.

Follower ball joints (friction ball joints) should also be inspected while testing load-carrying ball joints. Grasp the tire at the top and the bottom and attempt to shake the wheel assembly while looking directly at the follower ball joint. Generally, there should be no lateral or axial movement at all in the follower

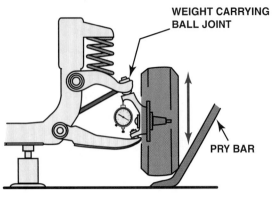

WEIGHT CARRYING
BALL JOINT

PRY BAR

AXIAL MOVEMENT

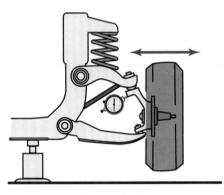

RADIAL MOVEMENT

FIGURE 25–20 If the spring is attached to the upper control arm, the jack should be placed under the frame to check for ball joint wear.

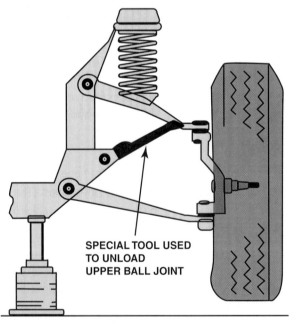

SPECIAL TOOL USED
TO UNLOAD
UPPER BALL JOINT

JACK PLACED UNDER THE FRAME

FIGURE 25–21 A special tool or a block of wood should be inserted between the frame and the upper control arm before lifting the vehicle off the ground. This tool stops the force of the spring against the upper ball joint so that a true test can be performed on the condition of the ball joint.

What Is the Difference Between a Low-Friction Ball Joint and a Steel-on-Steel Ball Joint?

Before the late 1980s, most ball joints were constructed with a steel ball that rubbed on a steel socket. This design created friction and provided for a tight high-friction joint until wear caused looseness in the joint.

Newer designs use a polished steel ball that is installed in a hard plastic polymer, resulting in a low-friction joint assembly. Because of the difference in friction characteristics, the vehicle may handle differently than originally designed if incorrect-style ball joints are installed. Most component manufacturers state that low-friction ball joints in a vehicle originally equipped with steel-on-steel high-friction ball joints are usually acceptable, but high-friction replacement ball joints should be avoided on a vehicle originally equipped with low-friction ball joints.

BALL JOINTS (CONTINUED)

ball joint. However, some manufacturers specify a maximum of 0.250 in. (1/4 in. or 0.6 cm) measured at the top of the tire. Always check the manufacturer's specifications before condemning a ball joint because of excessive play.

MacPherson-strut-equipped vehicles do not have a load-carrying ball joint. The weight of the vehicle is carried through the upper strut mount and bearing assembly. ● **SEE FIGURE 25–22.**

After checking axial play in a ball joint, grasp the tire from the side at the top and bottom and alternately push and pull. *Any lateral movement at the ball joint should generally be considered a good reason to replace the ball joints.* ● **SEE FIGURE 25–23.**

BALL JOINT REMOVAL Take care to avoid damaging grease seals when separating ball joints from their mounts. *The preferred method to separate tapered parts is to use a puller-type tool that applies pressure to the tapered joint as the bolt is tightened on the puller.* ● **SEE FIGURE 25–24.**

Sometimes the shock of a hammer can be used to separate the ball joint from the steering knuckle. For best results, another hammer should be used as a backup while striking the joint to be separated on the side with a heavy hammer.

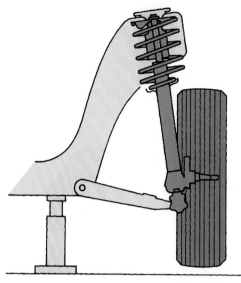

FIGURE 25–22 The jacking point is under the frame for checking the play of a lower ball joint used with a MacPherson strut.

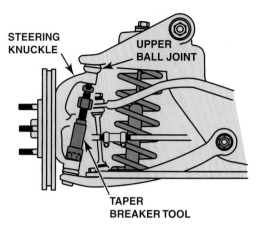

FIGURE 25–24 Taper breaker tool being used to separate the upper ball joint from the steering knuckle. This is especially important for vehicles equipped with aluminum alloy control arms.

FIGURE 25–23 This worn and rusty ball joint was found by moving the wheel and looking for movement in the joint.

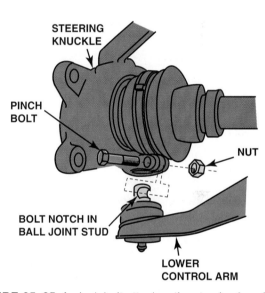

FIGURE 25–25 A pinch bolt attaches the steering knuckle to the ball joint. Remove the pinch bolt by turning the nut, not the bolt.

CAUTION: The use of tapered "pickle forks" should be avoided, unless the part is to be replaced, because they often damage the grease seal of the part being separated.

Some ball joint studs have a slot or groove where a **pinch bolt** is used to hold the ball joint to the steering knuckle. ● SEE FIGURE 25–25. Use penetrating oil in the steering knuckle groove and rotate the knuckle several times. Do not use a hammer on the pinch bolt because this can cause damage to the bolt and the ball joint. Do not widen the slot in the steering knuckle. Once

separated, check the shape of the steering knuckle. ● SEE FIGURE 25–26. If the pinch bolt has been deformed by overtightening, the steering knuckle should be replaced.

When removing ball joints that are riveted in place, always cut off or drill rivet heads before separating the ball joint from the spindle. This provides a more solid base to assist in removing rivets. *The preferred method to remove rivets from ball joints is to center punch and drill out the center of the rivet before using a drill or an air-powered chisel to remove the rivet heads.*

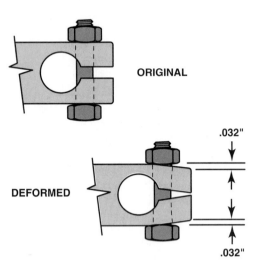

ORIGINAL

DEFORMED

.032"

.032"

FIGURE 25–26 If the pinch bolt is overtightened, the steering knuckle can be deformed. A deformed knuckle can cause the pinch bolt to break and the ball joint could become separated from the steering knuckle.

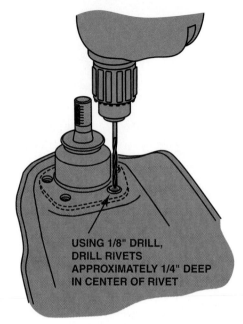

USING 1/8" DRILL, DRILL RIVETS APPROXIMATELY 1/4" DEEP IN CENTER OF RIVET

FIGURE 25–27 By drilling into the rivet, the holding force is released.

BALL JOINTS (CONTINUED)

Be careful not to drill or chisel into the control arms. ● **SEE FIGURES 25–27 THROUGH 25–29.**

Press-in-type ball joints are removed and installed using a special C-clamp-type tool. ● **SEE FIGURE 25–30.**

NOTE: Many replacement press-in-type ball joints are slightly larger in diameter—about 0.050 in. (1.3 mm)—than the original ball joint to provide the same press fit. If the ball joints have been replaced before, then the control arm must be replaced.

Avoid using heat to remove suspension or steering components. Many chassis parts use rubber and plastic that can be damaged if heated with a torch. *If heat is used to remove a part, it must be replaced.* For best results, try soaking with a penetrating oil and use the proper tools and procedures as specified by the manufacturer.

Many vehicles are equipped with nonreplaceable ball joints, and the entire control arm must be replaced if the ball joint is worn or defective.

CAUTION: Always follow manufacturers' recommended installation instructions whenever replacing any suspension or other chassis component part. Tie rod ends and ball joints use a taper to provide the attachment to other components. Whenever a nut is used to tighten a tapered part, it is important not to back off (loosen) the nut after

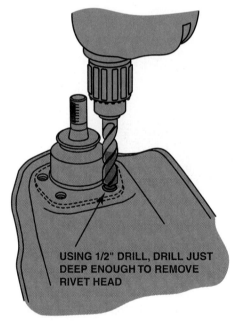

USING 1/2" DRILL, DRILL JUST DEEP ENOUGH TO REMOVE RIVET HEAD

FIGURE 25–28 The head of the rivet can be removed by using a larger-diameter drill bit as shown.

tightening. As the nut is being tightened, the taper is being pulled into the taper of the adjoining part. The specified torque on the nut ensures that the two pieces of the taper are properly joined. If the cotter key does not line up with the hole in the tapered stud when the nut has been properly torqued, tighten it more to line up a hole—never loosen the nut.

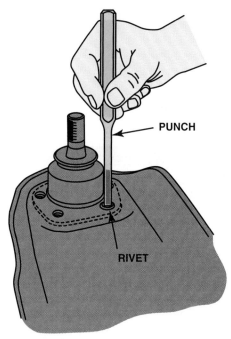

FIGURE 25–29 Using a punch and a hammer to remove the rivet after drilling down through the center and removing the head of the rivet.

FIGURE 25–30 Press-in ball joints are best removed using a large C-clamp press, as shown.

 REAL WORLD FIX

The Rattle Story

A customer complained that a rattle was heard every time the vehicle hit a bump. The noise sounded as if it came from the rear. All parts of the exhaust system and suspension system were checked. Everything seemed okay until the vehicle was raised with a frame-type hoist instead of a drive-on type. Then, whenever the right rear wheel was lifted, the noise occurred. The problem was a worn (elongated) shock absorber mounting hole. A washer with the proper-size hole was welded over the worn lower frame mount and the shock absorber was bolted back into place.

KINGPIN DIAGNOSIS AND SERVICE

Kingpins are usually used on trucks, sport utility vehicles, and other heavy-duty vehicles. ● **SEE FIGURE 25–31.**

Kingpins are designed to rotate inside kingpin bushings with a clearance between them of approximately 0.001 to 0.003 in. (0.025 to 0.075 mm). As wear occurs, this clearance distance increases and the kingpin becomes loose. Looseness in the kingpin causes looseness in the wheels and steering. *Kingpins can also gall or seize due to lack of lubrication, resulting in very hard steering.*

After supporting the vehicle safely off the ground, inspect for looseness by positioning a dial gauge (indicator) on the extreme inside bottom of the edge of the wheel and rock the tire. If the dial indicator registers more than 1/4 inch (6 mm), replace the kingpin and/or kingpin bushings.

To remove a typical kingpin, follow these basic steps:

STEP 1 Remove the tire, brake drum, and backing plate or caliper.

STEP 2 Remove the lockpin. The lockpin is usually tapered with a threaded end for the nut. Drive the lockpin out with a drift (punch).

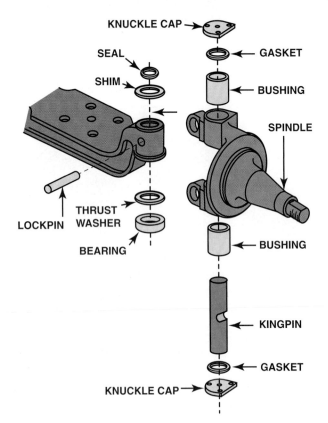

FIGURE 25–31 Typical kingpin assembly.

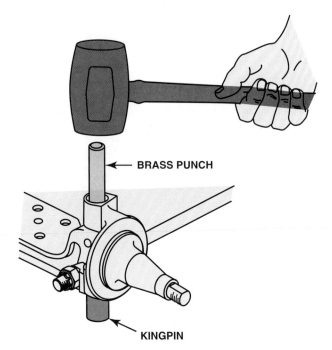

FIGURE 25–32 Driving a kingpin out with a hammer.

KINGPIN DIAGNOSIS AND SERVICE (CONTINUED)

STEP 3 Remove the grease caps and drive the kingpin from the steering knuckle and axle with a hammer and a brass punch or a hydraulic press, if necessary. ● **SEE FIGURE 25–32.**

To replace the kingpin bushings and/or kingpin, refer to the manufacturer's procedure and specifications. ● **SEE FIGURE 25–33.**

Some bronze bushings must be sized by reaming or honing to provide from 0.001 to 0.003 in. (0.025 to 0.075 mm) clearance between the kingpin and the bushing.

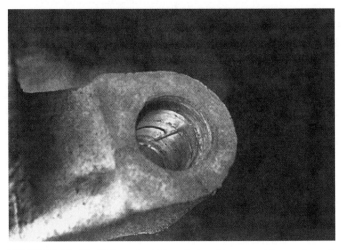

FIGURE 25–33 This galled kingpin bushing must be replaced.

SHOCK ABSORBERS AND STRUTS

DIAGNOSIS Shock absorber life depends on how and where the vehicle is driven. Original equipment (OE) shock absorbers are carefully matched to the vehicle springs and bushings to provide the best ride comfort and control. As the control arm bushings and ball joints age, the energy built up in the springs of the vehicle is controlled less by the friction of these joints and bushings, requiring more control from the shock absorbers. Shock absorber action is also reduced as the seals inside wear. Replacement shock absorbers may be required when any or all of the following symptoms appear:

1. **Ride harshness.** As the effectiveness of the shock absorber decreases, the rapid forces of the springs are not as dampened or controlled. Worn shocks can cause ride harshness and yet not cause the vehicle to bounce after hitting a bump.

2. **Frequent bottoming out on rough roads.** Shock absorbers provide a controlled movement of the axle whenever the vehicle hits a bump or dip in the road. As fluid is lost or wear occurs, the shock absorber becomes weaker and cannot resist the forces acting on the axle. The worn shock absorber can allow the spring to compress enough

so that the axle contacts the jounce bumper (bump stop) on the body or frame of the vehicle.

NOTE: Frequent bottoming out is also a symptom of reduced ride height due to sagging springs. Before replacing the shock absorbers, always check for proper ride height as specified in the vehicle service manual or any alignment specification booklet available from suppliers or companies of alignment or chassis parts and equipment.

3. **Extended vehicle movement after driving on dips or a rise in the road.** The most common shock absorber test is the bounce test. Push down on the body of the vehicle and let go; the vehicle should return to its normal ride height and stop. Worn shock absorbers can cause poor driver control due to excessive up-and-down suspension movements. If the vehicle continues to bounce two or three times, then the shocks or struts are worn and must be replaced.

4. **Cuppy-type tire wear.** Defective shock absorbers can cause **cuppy tire wear.** This type of tire wear is caused by the tire's bouncing up and down as it rotates.

5. **Leaking hydraulic oil.** When a shock or strut leaks oil externally, this indicates a defective seal. The shock absorber or strut cannot function correctly when low on oil inside.

6. **Springs and shock absorbers should be replaced in pairs.** Both front or both rear shocks should be replaced together to provide the best handling and control.

NOTE: Shock absorbers do not affect ride height except where special air shocks or coil overload carrying shocks are used. If a vehicle is sagging on one side or in the front or the rear, the springs should be checked and replaced if necessary.

Shock absorbers are filled with fluid and sealed during production. They are not refillable; if worn, damaged, or leaking, they must be replaced. A slight amount of fluid may bleed by the rod seal in cold weather and deposit a light film on the upper area of the shock absorber. This condition will not hurt the operation of the shock and should be considered normal. If noisy when driving, always check the tightness and condition of all shock absorber mounts.

Replacement shock absorbers and/or struts should match the original equipment unit in physical size.

 **TECH TIP**

The Shock Stud Trick

Front shock absorbers used on many rear-wheel-drive vehicles equipped with an SLA-type front suspension are often difficult to remove because the attaching nut is rusted to the upper shock stub. A common trick is to use a deep-well 9/16-in. socket and a long extension and simply bend the shock stud until it breaks off. At first you would think that this method causes harm, and it does ruin the shock absorber—but the shock absorber is not going to be reused and will be discarded anyway.

The usual procedure followed by many technicians is to simply take a minute or two to break off the upper shock stud, then hoist the vehicle to allow access to the lower two shock bolts, and then the shock can easily be removed. To install the replacement shock absorber, attach the lower bolts, lower the vehicle, and attach the upper rubber bushings and retaining nut.

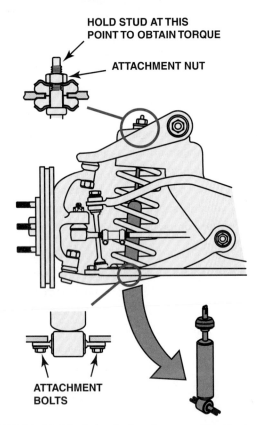

HOLD STUD AT THIS
POINT TO OBTAIN TORQUE

ATTACHMENT NUT

ATTACHMENT
BOLTS

FIGURE 25–34 Most shock absorbers used on the front suspension can be removed from underneath the vehicle after removing the attaching bolts or nuts.

SHOCK ABSORBERS AND STRUTS (CONTINUED)

FRONT SHOCK REPLACEMENT   Front shock absorbers provide ride control and are usually attached to the lower control arm by bolts and nuts. The upper portion of the shock usually extends through the spring housing and is attached to the frame of the vehicle with rubber grommets to help insulate noise, vibration, and harshness.

Most front shock absorbers can be replaced either with the vehicle still on the ground or while on a hoist. The front suspension of most vehicles allows the removal of the shocks without the need to support the downward travel of the lower control arm. The downward travel limit is stopped by a rubber stop or by the physical limit of the suspension arms.

Special sockets and other tools are available to remove the nut from the shocks that use a single mounting stem. The removal of the lower mounting of most front shock absorbers usually involves the removal of two bolts. After removal of the attaching hardware, the shock absorber is simply pulled through the front control arm. ● **SEE FIGURE 25–34.**

Reverse the removal procedure to install replacement shock absorbers. Always consult the manufacturer's recommended procedures and fastener tightening torque.

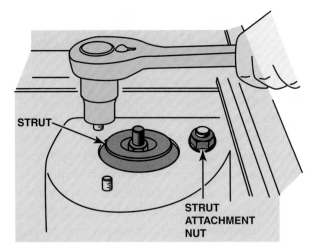

STRUT

STRUT
ATTACHMENT
NUT

FIGURE 25–35 Removing the upper strut mounting bolts. Some experts recommend leaving one of the upper strut mount nuts loosely attached to prevent the strut from falling when the lower attaching bolts are removed.

MACPHERSON STRUT REPLACEMENT

On most vehicles equipped with MacPherson strut suspensions, strut replacement involves the following steps.

CAUTION: Always follow the manufacturer's recommended methods and procedures whenever replacing a MacPherson strut assembly or component.

1. Hoist the vehicle, remove the wheels, and mark the attaching bolts/nuts.

2. Remove the upper strut mounting bolts except for one to hold the strut until ready to remove the strut assembly. ● **SEE FIGURE 25–35.**

3. Remove the brake caliper or brake hose from the strut housing. ● **SEE FIGURE 25–36.**

4. After removing all lower attaching bolts, remove the final upper strut bolt and remove the strut assembly from the vehicle. Place the strut assembly into a strut spring compressor fixture or use manual spring compressors as shown in ● **FIGURE 25–37.**

5. Compress the coil spring enough to relieve the tension on the strut rod nut. Remove the strut rod nut as shown in ● **FIGURE 25–38.**

6. After removing the strut rod nut, remove the upper strut bearing assembly and the spring. ● **SEE FIGURE 25–39.**

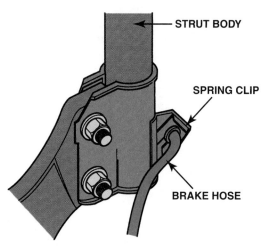

FIGURE 25–36 A brake hydraulic hose is often attached to the strut housing. Sometimes all that is required to separate the line from the strut is to remove a spring clip.

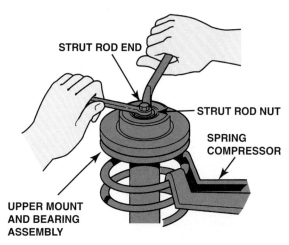

FIGURE 25–38 Removing the strut rod nut. The strut shaft is being helped with one wrench while the nut is being removed with the other wrench. Notice that the spring is compressed before the nut is removed.

FIGURE 25–37 Use a strut spring compressor fixture to compress the spring on a MacPherson strut before removing the strut retaining nut.

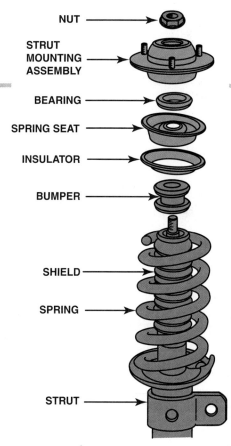

FIGURE 25–39 Typical MacPherson strut showing the various components.

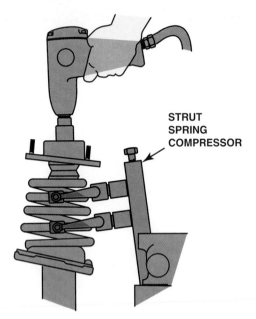

FIGURE 25–40 After installing the replacement strut cartridge, reinstall the spring and upper bearing assembly after compressing the spring. Notice that the strut is being held in a strut spring compressor fixture.

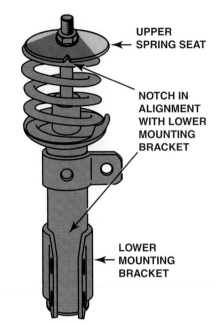

FIGURE 25–41 Before final assembly, make sure the marks you made are aligned. Some struts are manufactured with marks to ensure proper reassembly.

MACPHERSON STRUT REPLACEMENT (CONTINUED)

NOTE: The bearing assembly should be carefully inspected and replaced if necessary. Some automotive experts recommend replacing the bearing assembly whenever the strut is replaced.

7. Many MacPherson struts are replaced as an entire unit assembly. Other struts can have the cartridge inside the housing replaced. The cartridge is installed after removing the gland nut at the top of the strut tube and removing the original strut rod, valves, and hydraulic oil. Always replace the cartridge assembly per the manufacturer's recommended procedure. ● **SEE FIGURES 25–40, 25–41, AND 25–42.**

8. Reinstall the strut in the vehicle.

CAUTION: Many GM front-wheel-drive vehicles use a MacPherson strut with a large-diameter spring seat area. GM chassis engineers call this a **cow catcher** design. If the coil spring breaks, the extra-large cow catcher will prevent the end of the broken spring from moving outward where it could puncture a tire and possibly cause an accident. Always use a replacement strut that has this feature.

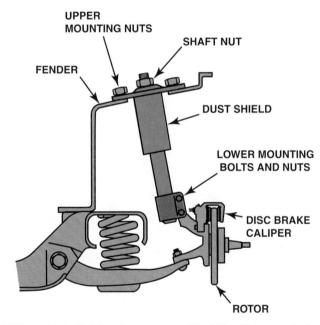

FIGURE 25–42 The strut on a modified MacPherson strut assembly can be replaced by removing the upper mounting nuts.

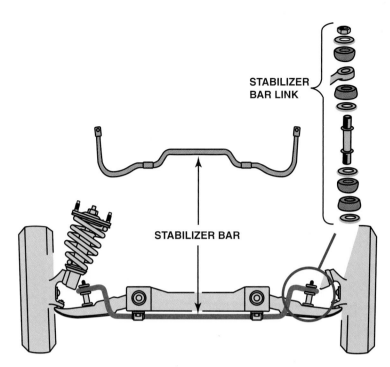

FIGURE 25–43 Stabilizer bar links should be replaced as a pair.

STABILIZER BAR LINK

STABILIZER BAR

STABILIZER BAR LINK AND BUSHINGS

DIAGNOSIS Stabilizer bars twist whenever a vehicle turns a corner or whenever one side of the vehicle rises or lowers. The more the body of the vehicle leans, the more the bar twists, and the more the bar counteracts the roll of the body. A great deal of force is transferred from the stabilizer bar to the body or frame of the vehicle through the stabilizer links at the control arm and the stabilizer bar mounting bushings on the body or frame. *The most common symptom of defective stabilizer bar links or bushings is noise while turning, especially over curbs.* When driving up and over a curb at an angle, one wheel is pushed upward. Since the stabilizer bar connects both wheels, the bar tends to resist this motion by twisting. If one or both links are broken, a loud knock or clanking sound is heard as the bar contacts the control arm. Any sound heard when driving should be investigated and the cause determined by a thorough visual inspection.

REPLACEMENT Stabilizer links are usually purchased as a kit consisting of replacement rubber bushings, retainers, a long bolt, and spacer with a nut and lock nut. General Motors recommends that stabilizer links be replaced in pairs and two kits purchased so that the links on both the left and the right can be replaced at the same time. ● **SEE FIGURE 25–43.**

Stabilizer links are replaced by simply unbolting the old parts and installing replacement parts. Special precautions are usually not necessary, but, as always, consult a service manual for the exact recommended procedure and fastener torque.

If the mounting bushings (also called isolator bushings) on the body or frame are worn or defective, a loud squeaking or knocking sound is usually heard.

Stabilizer bar bushings often fail because the rubber has deteriorated from engine oil or other fluid leaks. Before replacing defective bushings, make certain that all other fluid leaks are stopped. Stabilizer bar bushing replacement involves the removal (unbolting) of the bushing retainers that surround the bushing and attach to the vehicle body or frame. The bushings are usually split so that they can be easily removed and replaced on the stabilizer bar and can slide into proper position. Reinstall the bushing retainer bolts and tighten to the specified torque.

FIGURE 25–44 A strut rod as viewed from the front of the vehicle.

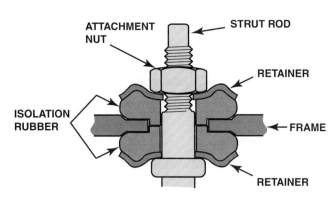

FIGURE 25–45 Typical strut rod bushing with rubber on both sides of the frame to help isolate noise, vibration, and harshness from being transferred to the passengers.

STRUT ROD BUSHINGS

DIAGNOSIS Strut rods are used on the front suspension of many front-wheel-drive and rear-wheel-drive vehicles. As with any rubber suspension component, strut rod bushings can deteriorate and crack. When strut rod bushings fail, the lower control arm can move forward and backward during braking or when hitting bumps in the road.

Since the lower control arm position is important to vehicle control, when the bushing fails, a pulling or drifting of the vehicle often occurs. *A common symptom of a defective strut rod bushing is noise and a pull toward one side while braking.*

REPLACEMENT To replace a strut rod bushing, the nut on the end of the strut rod has to be removed. ● **SEE FIGURE 25–44.** As the nut is being removed, the lower control arm is likely to move forward or backward, depending on the location of the strut rod frame mount. After removing the strut rod nut, remove the one or two fasteners that retain the strut rod to the lower control arm. The strut rod can now be removed from the vehicle and the replacement rubber bushings can be installed. Install the strut rod in the reverse order of installation. Most bushings use a serrated spacer to maintain the proper force on the rubber bushings; this prevents the technician from compressing the rubber bushing when the strut rod nut is tightened. ● **SEE FIGURE 25–45.**

CAUTION: Some suspension bushings are directional and must be installed according to the vehicle manufacturer's instructions. For example, on some vehicles, the bushings have a slit or void which must face the front of the vehicle. Always check service information when installing new bushings.

FRONT COIL SPRINGS

DIAGNOSIS Coil springs should be replaced in pairs if the vehicle ride height is lower than specifications. Sagging springs can cause the tires to slide laterally (side to side) across the pavement, causing excessive tire wear. ● **SEE FIGURE 25–46.** Sagging springs can also cause the vehicle to bottom out against the suspension bumpers when traveling over normal bumps and dips in the road.

If a vehicle is overloaded, the springs of the vehicle can *take a set* and not recover to the proper ride height. This commonly occurs with all types of vehicles whenever a heavy load is carried, even on a short trip.

It is normal for the rear of a vehicle to sag when a heavy load is carried, but it can permanently damage the spring by exceeding the yield point of the steel spring material.

REPLACEMENT The only solution recommended by the vehicle manufacturer is to replace the damaged springs in pairs (both front and both rear, or all four). Several aftermarket alternatives include the following:

- **Helper or auxiliary leaf springs.** These helper springs are usually designed to increase the load-carrying capacity of leaf springs or to restore the original ride height to sagging springs.

- **Spring inserts for coil springs.** Hard rubber or metal spacers are *not recommended* because they create concentrated pressure points on the coils that can cause the spring to break. Hard rubber stabilizers that bridge the gap between two coils without raising the ride height stiffen the

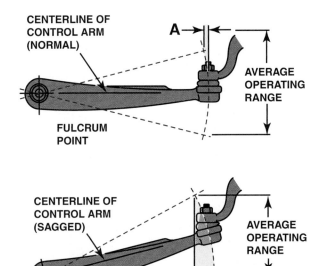

FIGURE 25–46 Notice that if the front coil springs are sagging, the resulting angle of the lower control arm causes the wheels to move from side to side as the suspension moves up and down. Note the difference between the distance at "A" with good springs and the distance at "B" with sagging springs.

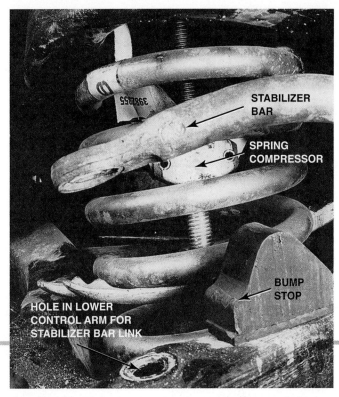

FIGURE 25–47 Spring compressing tool in place to hold the spring as the ball joint is separated. Note that the stabilizer bar links have been removed to allow the lower control arm to move downward enough to remove the coil spring.

ride by locking two coils together. With two coils connected, the spring rate increases and the spring becomes stiffer.

- **Air shocks or airbag devices.** Air shocks or airbags are generally used to restore or increase the load-carrying capacity to the rear of the vehicle. While these devices do allow the ride height to be maintained, the extra load is still being supported by the tires and rear axle bearings. Caution should be used not to overload the basic chassis or power train of the vehicle.

There are two designs for vehicles that use coil springs. The most commonly used design places the coil spring between the vehicle frame and the lower control arm.

Both front-suspension designs require that the front shock absorbers be removed in order to replace the coil springs. This first step in the coil spring removal procedure can be performed on the ground or on any type of hoist. After removing the shock absorber, use a coil spring compressor and install it through the center of the coil spring. ● **SEE FIGURE 25–47.** Hook the arms of the coil spring compressor over the rungs of the coil spring and rotate the adjusting nut on the spring compressor with a wrench to shorten the spring. Coil spring clips can also be used to retain the coil spring.

CAUTION: When compressed, all springs contain a great deal of stored energy. If a compressed spring were to become disconnected from its spring compressor or clips, it could be projected outward with enough force to cause injury or death.

After the coil spring is retained, the control arm can be separated from the steering knuckle and the coil spring can be removed as shown in ● **FIGURES 25–48 AND 25–49.**

Replacement springs should be compressed and installed using the reverse procedure.

NOTE: Many automotive experts recommend that new coil insulators be installed every time the coil springs are replaced.

Make sure that the spring is positioned correctly in the control arm and that the spring insulators are installed correctly. ● **SEE FIGURE 25–50.** Most control arms use two holes for the purpose of coil spring seating. The end of the spring should cover one hole completely and partially cover the second hole. ● **SEE FIGURE 25–51.**

FIGURE 25–48 The steering knuckle has been disconnected from the lower ball joint. The lower control arm and coil spring are being held up by a floor jack.

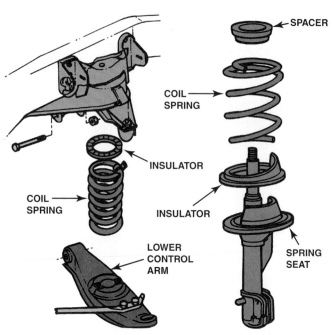

FIGURE 25–50 Spring insulators install between the spring seat and the coil spring to reduce noise.

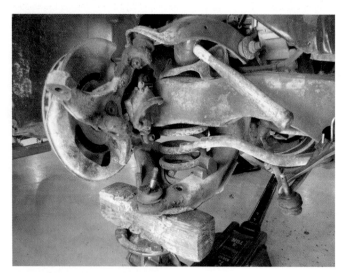

FIGURE 25–49 A rubber mallet is being used to support the upper control arm as the lower control is being lowered using a floor jack. After all of the tension has been removed from the coil spring it can be removed and the replacement installed.

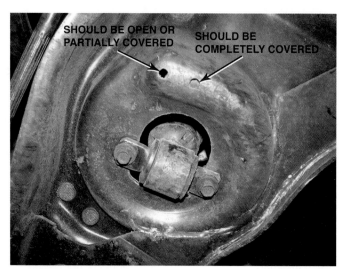

FIGURE 25–51 The holes in the lower arm are not only used to allow water to drain from the spring seat, but also are used as a gauge to show the service technician that the coil spring is correctly seated.

The Rock-Hard Problem

The owner of a six-month-old full-size pickup truck complained that occasionally when the truck was driven up into a driveway, a loud grinding sound was heard. Several service technicians worked on the truck, trying to find the cause for the noise. After the left front shock absorber was replaced, the noise did not occur for two weeks, and then started again. Finally, the service manager told the technician to replace anything and everything in the front suspension in an attempt to solve the customer's intermittent problem. Five minutes later, a technician handed the service manager a small, deformed rock. This technician had taken a few minutes to *carefully* inspect the entire front suspension. Around the bottom coil spring seat, the technician found the rock. Apparently, when the truck made a turn over a bump, the rock was forced between the coils of the coil spring, making a very loud grinding noise. But the rock did not always get between the coils. Therefore, the problem occurred only once in a while. The technician handed the rock to the very happy customer.

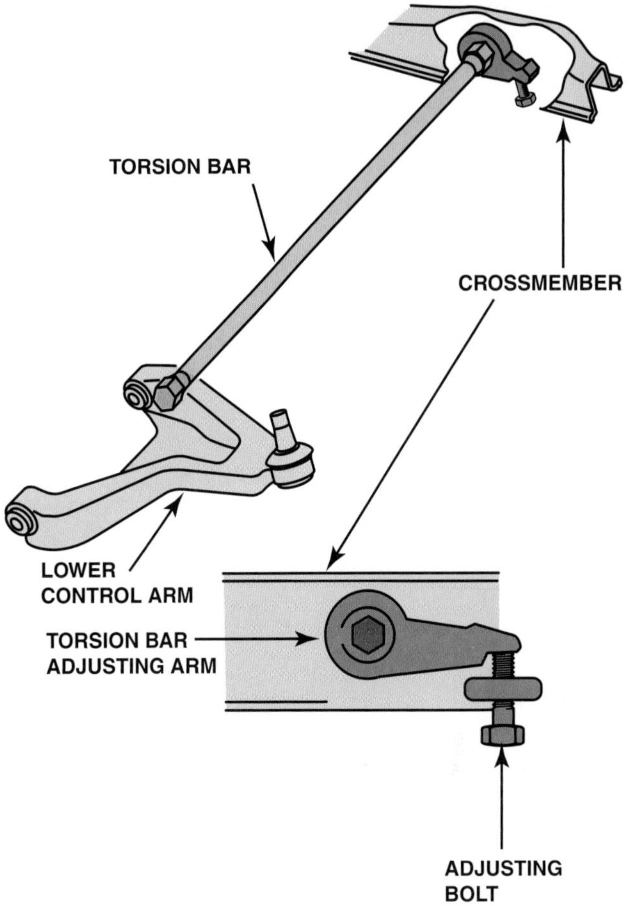

FIGURE 25–52 By rotating the adjusting bolt, the vehicle can be raised or lowered.

STEERING KNUCKLES

DIAGNOSIS Most steering knuckles are constructed of cast or forged cast iron. The steering knuckle usually incorporates the wheel spindle and steering arm. The steering knuckle/steering arm can become bent if the vehicle is in an accident or hits a curb sideways. Often this type of damage is not apparent until vehicle handling or excessive tire wear is noticed. Unless a thorough inspection is performed during a wheel alignment, a bent steering knuckle is often overlooked.

REPLACEMENT If the steering knuckle is bent or damaged, it must be replaced. It should *not* be bent back into shape or repaired. To replace the steering knuckle, both ball joints must be disconnected from the knuckle and the brake components removed. Be sure to support the control arm and spring properly during the procedure. See a factory service manual for the exact procedure and fastener torque for the vehicle you are servicing.

TORSION BARS

ADJUSTMENT Most torsion bar suspensions are designed with an adjustable bolt to permit the tension on the torsion bar to be increased or decreased to change the ride height. Unequal side-to-side ride height can be corrected by adjusting (turning) the torsion bar tension bolt. ● **SEE FIGURE 25–52.**

Torsion bar adjustment should be made if the difference in ride height from one side to another exceeds 1/8 in. (0.125 in. or 3.2 mm). If the ride height difference side to side is greater than 1/8 in., the vehicle will tend to wander or be unstable, with constant steering wheel movements required to maintain straight-ahead direction.

NOTE: Torsion bars should never be switched from one side of the vehicle to the other as they are twisted and work hardened in one direction and can break if installed on the opposite side of the vehicle.

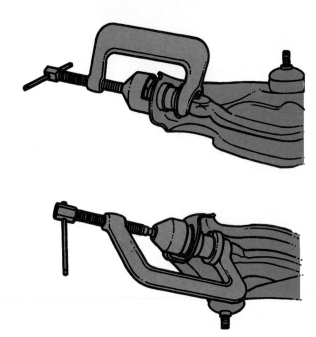

FIGURE 25–53 An adapter and a press or large clamp are used to remove the old bushing from the control arm and to install a new bushing.

CONTROL ARM BUSHINGS

DIAGNOSIS Defective control arm bushings are a common source of vehicle handling and suspension noise problems. Most suspension control arm bushings are constructed of three parts: an inner metal sleeve, the rubber bushing itself, and an outer steel sleeve. (Some vehicles use a two-piece bushing that does not use an outer sleeve.)

REPLACEMENT To remove an old bushing from a control arm, the control arm must first be separated from the suspension and/or frame of the vehicle. Several methods can be used to remove the bushing from the control arm, but all methods apply force to the *outer* sleeve. While an air chisel is frequently used to force the steel sleeve out of the suspension member, a puller tool is most often recommended by General Motors. ● **SEE FIGURE 25–53.** The puller can be used to remove the old bushing and install the replacement bushing without harming the control arm or the new bushing. All bushings should be tightened with the vehicle on the ground and the wheels in a straight-ahead position; this prevents the rubber bushing from exerting a pulling force on the suspension.

NOTE: Some replacement control arm bushings have a higher **durometer,** or hardness, rating than the original. Urethane bushings are often used in sporty or race-type

vehicles and deflect less than standard replacement bushings. These harder bushings also transfer more road noise, vibration, and harshness to the body.

The upper control arm bushings can be replaced in most vehicles that use a short/long-arm-type suspension by following just four easy steps:

STEP 1 Raise the vehicle and support the lower control arm with a safety stand or floor jack.

STEP 2 Disconnect the upper control arm from the frame by removing the frame-attaching nuts or bolts.

STEP 3 Using the upper ball joint as a pivot, rotate the upper control arm outward into the wheel well area. With the control arm accessible, it is much easier to remove and replace the upper control arm pivot shaft and rubber bushings.

STEP 4 After replacing the bushings, simply rotate the upper control arm back into location and reattach the upper control arm pivot shaft to the vehicle frame.

NOTE: An alignment should always be performed after making any suspension-related repairs.

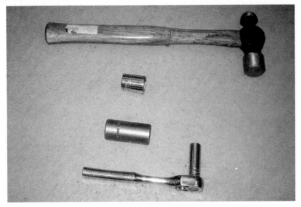

1 The tools needed to replace a front strut assembly include several sockets and a ball-peen hammer, plus a strut compressor.

2 After safely hoisting the vehicle to elbow height and removing the wheel covers, remove the front tire/wheel assembly.

3 Remove the two strut retaining nuts.

4 Before using a hammer to drive the retaining bolts from the steering knuckle, thread the nut into the bolt backwards to prevent causing damage to the threads.

5 Remove the retaining bolts and separate the strut from the steering knuckle.

6 Lower the vehicle and remove the upper strut retaining fasteners.

CONTINUED ▶

STRUT REPLACEMENT (CONTINUED)

7 Hold the strut while removing the last upper retaining nut and then remove the strut assembly.

8 After the strut has been removed from the vehicle, install the assembly into a strut compressor.

9 Position the jaws of the compressor under the bearing assembly as per the vehicle manufacturer's instructions.

10 Turn the compressor wheel until all tension of the spring has been relieved from the upper bearing assembly.

11 Remove the strut retaining nut.

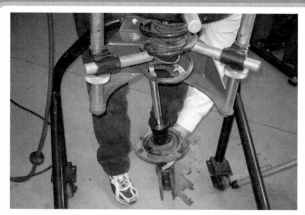

12 Remove the strut assembly.

13 Before installing the replacement strut, check the upper bearing by exerting a downward force on the bearing while rotating and check for roughness. Replace if necessary.

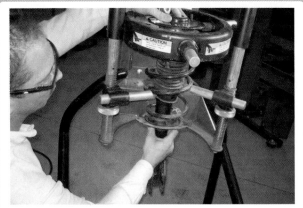

14 Install the strut from underneath the spring compressor fixture.

15 Install the strut retaining nut. Most vehicle manufacturers specify that the strut retaining nut be replaced and the old one discarded.

16 Before loosening the tension, check that the coil spring is correctly located at both the top and the bottom, then release the tension on the spring.

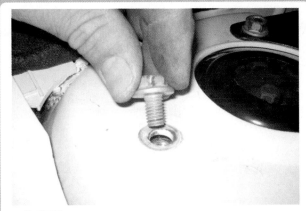

17 Remove the strut assembly from the compressor and back into the vehicle and install the upper fasteners. Do not torque to specifications until the lower fasteners have been installed.

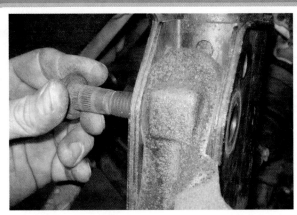

18 Attach the lower strut to the steering knuckle using the original hardened bolts and nuts.

CONTINUED ▶

19 Using a torque wrench, torque all fasteners to factory specifications.

20 Install the tire/wheel assembly, lower the vehicle, and torque the lug nuts to factory specifications. Align the vehicle before returning it to the customer.

SUMMARY

1. A thorough road test of a suspension problem should include driving beside parked vehicles and into driveways in an attempt to determine when and where the noise occurs.

2. A dry park test should be performed to help isolate defective or worn suspension components.

3. Ball joints must be unloaded before testing. The ball joints used on vehicles with a MacPherson strut suspension are *not* load carrying. Wear-indicator ball joints are observed with the wheels on the ground.

4. Always use a taper-breaker puller or two hammers to loosen tapered parts to remove them. Never use heat unless you are replacing the part; heat from a torch can damage rubber and plastic parts.

5. When installing a tapered part, always tighten the attaching nut to specifications. Never loosen the nut to install a cotter key. If the cotter key will not line up with a hole in the tapered part, tighten the nut more until the cotter key hole lines up with the nut and stud.

6. Defective shock absorbers can cause ride harshness as well as frequent bottoming out on rough roads.

7. Always follow manufacturers' recommended procedures whenever replacing springs or MacPherson struts. Never remove the strut end nut until the coil spring is compressed and the spring force is removed from the upper bearing assembly.

REVIEW QUESTIONS

1. Describe how to perform a proper road test for the diagnosis of suspension-related problems.

2. List four symptoms of worn or defective shock absorbers.

3. Explain the procedure for replacing front shock absorbers on an SLA-type suspension vehicle.

4. Describe the testing procedure for ball joints.

5. Describe the correct general procedure to remove and replace tapered suspension components.

CHAPTER QUIZ

1. Unusual noise during a test drive can be caused by _____.
   a. Defective wheel bearings or stabilizer bar links
   b. Defective or worn control arm bushings or ball joints
   c. Worn or defective CV joints
   d. All of the above

2. Two technicians are discussing non-indicator-type ball joint inspection. Technician A says that the vehicle should be on the ground with the ball joints *loaded,* then checked for freeplay. Technician B says that the ball joints should be *unloaded* before checking for freeplay. Which technician is correct?
   a. Technician A only
   b. Technician B only
   c. Both Technicians A and B
   d. Neither Technician A nor B

3. Most manufacturers specify a maximum axial play for ball joints of about _____.
   a. 0.003 in. (0.076 mm)
   b. 0.010 in. (0.25 mm)
   c. 0.030 in. (0.76 mm)
   d. 0.050 in. (1.27 mm)

4. The preferred method to separate tapered chassis parts is to use _____.
   a. A pickle fork tool
   b. A torch to heat the joint until it separates
   c. A puller tool or two hammers to shock and deform the taper
   d. A drill to drill out the tapered part

5. A light film of oil is observed on the upper area of a shock absorber. Technician A says that this condition should be considered normal. Technician B says that a rod seal may bleed fluid during cold weather, causing the oil film. Which technician is correct?
   a. Technician A only
   b. Technician B only
   c. Both Technicians A and B
   d. Neither Technician A nor B

6. Before the strut insert can be removed from a typical MacPherson strut assembly, which operation is necessary to prevent possible personal injury?
   a. The brake caliper and/or brake hose should be removed from the strut housing
   b. The coil spring should be compressed
   c. The upper strut mounting bolts should be removed
   d. The lower attaching bolts should be removed

7. What should the technician do when replacing stabilizer bar links?
   a. The stabilizer bar should be removed from the vehicle before replacing the links.
   b. The links can be replaced individually, yet the manufacturer often recommends that the links at both ends be replaced together.
   c. The stabilizer bar must be compressed using a special tool before removing or installing stabilizer bar links.
   d. Both b and c are correct.

8. A noise and a pull toward one side during braking is a common symptom of a worn or defective _____.
   a. Shock absorber
   b. Strut rod bushing
   c. Stabilizer bar link
   d. Track rod bushing

9. To help prevent vehicle wandering on a vehicle with torsion bars, the ride height (trim height) should be within _____ side to side.
   a. 0.003 in. (0.076 mm)
   b. 0.050 in. (1.27 mm)
   c. 0.100 in. (2.5 mm)
   d. 0.125 in. (3.2 mm)

10. Two technicians are discussing suspension bushings. Technician A says that replacing control arm bushings usually requires special tools. Technician B says using high-performance urethane bushings may cause excessive noise to be transferred to the passenger compartment. Which technician is correct?
    a. Technician A only
    b. Technician B only
    c. Both Technicians A and B
    d. Neither Technician A nor B

REAR SUSPENSION AND SERVICE

After studying Chapter 26, the reader will be able to:

1. Prepare for ASE Suspension and Steering (A4) certification test content area "B" (Suspension System Diagnosis and Repair).
2. Describe the various types and styles of rear suspension.
3. Explain the differences among the different types of rear axles.
4. List the steps necessary to replace rear shock absorbers.
5. Explain how to replace rear leaf and coil springs.

Axle windup 499
Chapman strut 502
Hotchkiss drive 499
IRS 501
Live axle 498
Panhard rod 500
Semi-independent suspension 503

Semi-trailing arm 501
Solid axle 498
Torque arm 500
Track rod 500
Trailing arm 500
Watts linkage 501

SOLID REAR AXLES

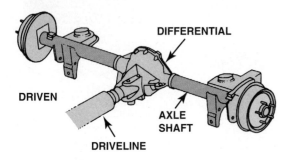

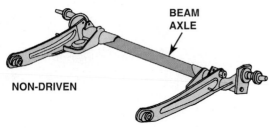

FIGURE 26–1 Solid axles are used on rear-wheel-drive vehicles as well as front-wheel-drive vehicles.

SOLID AXLES

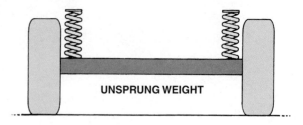

UNSPRUNG WEIGHT

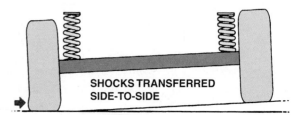

SHOCKS TRANSFERRED SIDE-TO-SIDE

FIGURE 26–2 A solid axle supports the springs, so the axle and suspension components are unsprung weight. When one wheel rides over a bump, the force of impact transfers through the solid axle to the opposite side, leading to unstable handling.

All suspensions have two basic jobs: keeping the tires on the ground and providing a smooth ride.

SOLID REAR AXLES

A **solid axle** can be used at the rear of either a rear-wheel-drive or front-wheel-drive vehicle. ● **SEE FIGURE 26–1.** On a rear-wheel-drive vehicle, a solid rear axle consists of the differential gears and axle shafts inside a solid housing. On a front-wheel-drive vehicle, a solid axle is usually a simple U-shaped or tubular beam that may contain a torsion bar, rod, or tube to allow some twisting action.

Certain characteristics apply to any solid rear axle, while other characteristics vary by the type of suspension used to attach the axle to the frame.

Solid axles have some handling characteristics that are inferior to those of an independent suspension. Disadvantages of a solid axle include the following:

- Increased proportion of unsprung weight
- Side-to-side road shock transference
- Poorer tire adhesion

Increasing the proportion of unsprung weight decreases ride quality. Transferring road shock from side-to-side causes wheel tramp and shimmy, and poor tire adhesion accelerates tire wear. ● **SEE FIGURE 26–2.**

The sprung weight of the frame and body must be heavy to oppose the unsprung weight of a solid axle, especially on a driven axle. Unsprung weight, wheel tramp, and shimmy all reduce tire adhesion. The effects of these problems are more noticeable in rear-wheel-drive vehicles due to the weight of the rear axle and differential assembly. On a typical front-wheel-drive vehicle, the simple axle beam is not heavy enough to decrease ride quality or cause extreme tire wear. In fact, the rear tires of a front-wheel-drive model always wear more slowly than the front tires because the rear axle is so much lighter than the power train.

If engine torque is applied to the rear axle to drive the vehicle, the axle is referred to as a **live axle**.

AXLE WINDUP

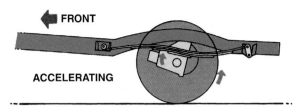

FIGURE 26–3 When the axle housing reacts against the force of axle shaft rotation, the front of the differential tilts upward, creating axle windup.

 FREQUENTLY ASKED QUESTION

What Is Axle Windup?

Axle windup is a product of the law of physics, which states that every action produces an equal and opposite reaction. As the axle shafts rotate in one direction to drive the wheels, the axle housing attempts to rotate in the opposite direction. The force of this reaction tends to lift the front end of the vehicle during acceleration. ● **SEE FIGURE 26–3.** Axle windup is a particular problem with a solid, driven rear axle because the axle housing concentrates the reacting force. Under extreme acceleration, the reacting force can actually tilt the drive shaft upward and lift the front wheels off the ground. Leaf springs, control arms, pinion snubbers, and torque arms all are means of controlling axle windup.

LEAF SPRING SUSPENSION - DRIVEN AXLE

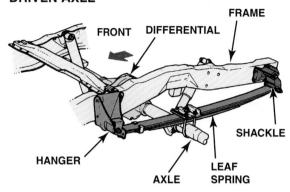

FIGURE 26–4 A typical rear-wheel-drive pickup truck rear suspension equipped with leaf springs. This type of arrangement is called a Hotchkiss drive and the drive train forces are controlled by the rear suspension components.

LEAF SPRING SUSPENSION - BEAM AXLE

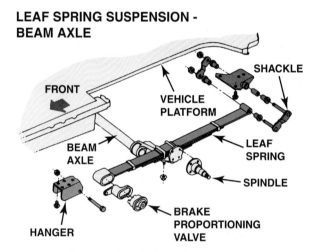

FIGURE 26–5 An exploded view of a beam axle with multi-leaf springs.

LEAF SPRING REAR SUSPENSIONS

A leaf spring suspension is a simple system because it does not require control arms to brace and position the axle. The leaf springs link the axle to the frame and effectively serve two purposes:

- Absorbing road shock
- Locating the axle under the vehicle

Most rear-wheel-drive trucks use a solid rear axle with leaf springs in an arrangement called a **Hotchkiss drive.** ● **SEE FIGURE 26–4.** Leaf springs on a driven axle control axle windup by transferring force from the axle housing to the frame. The front portion of the leaf spring, from the axle housing to the frame mount, acts like a trailing control arm. However, if the front section of the leaf spring is too flexible, it may not control axle windup as well. To compensate, some manufacturers make the front section of the spring shorter, and therefore less flexible, than the rear section.

Leaf springs are used on the rear of many light- and medium-duty trucks and vans. ● **SEE FIGURE 26–5.** The wheel spindles bolt to the flanges, the centers of the leaf springs rest on the seats, and U-bolts secure the springs to the axle. A shackle attaches the rear of each spring to the unit-body frame, while the front of each spring pivots through a bolt and bushing connected to a hanger that bolts to the body.

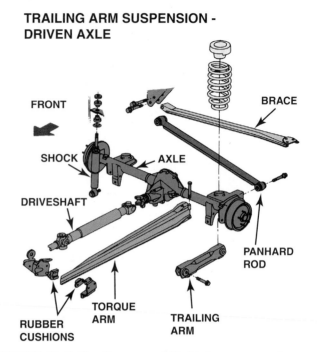

FIGURE 26–7 The Camaro and Firebird rear suspension systems use a torque arm to control axle windup. If the rubber torque arm bushings (cushions) are worn, a loud "bang" could be heard and felt when accelerating suddenly.

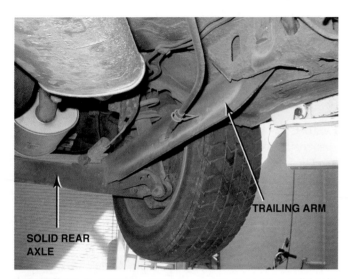

FIGURE 26–6 A trailing arm rear suspension with a solid axle used on a front-wheel-drive vehicle.

TRAILING ARM REAR SUSPENSIONS

A **trailing arm** extends from a frame crossmember located ahead of the rear axle back to the axle housing or a wheel knuckle. Trailing arms run parallel to the centerline of the chassis. ● SEE FIGURE 26–6. A trailing arm mounts to the frame with bushings, which allows the arm to pivot as the wheel rides over bumps. Some rear suspensions use two sets of trailing arms, one set positioned higher in the chassis than the other. Although the arms in this type of arrangement are commonly referred to as the *upper control arms* and *lower control arms*, they are usually called trailing arms. The word *trailing* applies to any link where the supported member trails the arm. Trailing arms may be used to brace either a driven or nondriven solid rear axle against front-to-rear forces, but they do not provide much resistance to side-to-side, or lateral, forces. The axle itself is one means of locating the wheels side-to-side, and solid rear suspensions frequently use another rod to provide additional support. Trailing arms transfer axle windup force to the frame and control front-to-rear axle movement. On a few models, especially those with a high-performance suspension, a **torque arm** provides additional resistance to axle windup. ● SEE FIGURE 26–7. The torque arm extends parallel to the drive shaft between the rear axle and the transmission. One end of the torque arm is rigidly bolted to the differential housing, while the other end attaches to the transmission through a cushioned bracket to allow some flex.

A trailing arm rear suspension on a nondriven solid axle virtually always includes a **track rod,** also called a **Panhard rod.** A track rod is a rod attached to the body or frame on one end and the rear axle on the other. The purpose of the track rod is to keep the rear axle centered under the vehicle. The suspension may use either coil springs or struts.

The rear axle is a U-shaped steel beam that is open on the bottom. ● SEE FIGURE 26–8. Flat metal axle end plates, to which the wheel spindles bolt, are attached to each end of the beam. A torsion tube or rod fits inside the beam and is welded to the axle end plates.

The trailing arms, which are welded to the outboard ends of the axle, extend forward and attach to the frame with pivot bushing mounts. A bracket on top of the beam axle locates the ring-type lower strut mount, and the upper strut mount attaches to a reinforced area of the wheel well.

TRAILING ARM SUSPENSION - BEAM AXLE

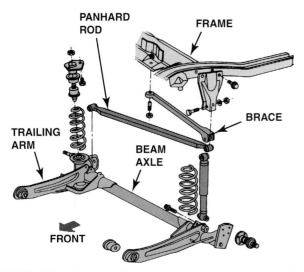

FIGURE 26–8 A typical beam axle rear suspension, which uses trailing arms and coil springs along with a track rod, also called a Panhard rod, to control side-to-side axle movement.

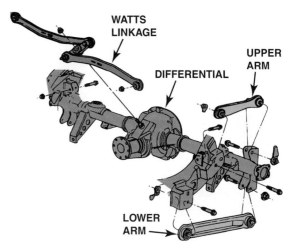

FIGURE 26–9 This Ford rear suspension uses upper and lower semi-trailing arms to mount the rear axle and a watts linkage to control side-to-side movement.

SEMI-TRAILING ARM REAR SUSPENSIONS

A **semi-trailing arm** is similar to a trailing arm in that it extends back from a frame member to the axle. However, a trailing arm is parallel to the vehicle centerline whereas a semi-trailing arm pivots at an angle to the vehicle centerline. Semi-trailing arms have an advantage over trailing arms because they control both side-to-side and front-to-rear motion. Typically, a semi-trailing arm suspension uses coil springs, air springs, or pivot-base struts.

A semi-trailing arm suspension may be used with either a solid axle or an independent suspension.

The Ford suspension uses two pairs, upper and lower, of semi-trailing arms and a center pivot arrangement to locate the driven rear axle. This axle centering pivot bracket and linkage is called a **watts linkage.** ● **SEE FIGURE 26–9.**

INDEPENDENT REAR SUSPENSIONS

The use of **independent rear suspension,** called **IRS,** has grown dramatically over the past several decades to the point where such systems are now fairly common, especially on front-wheel-drive vehicles and some rear-wheel-drive vehicles. Although rarely used on trucks, a number of rear-wheel-drive vehicles do feature an independent rear suspension.

The reduction in unsprung weight is particularly noticeable for driven axles, which are constructed to transfer the weight of the differential and axles to the frame. ● **SEE FIGURE 26–10.** A vehicle with an independent rear suspension rides and handles better than a similar vehicle equipped with a solid rear axle. An SLA-type of independent suspension may be used at the rear of a rear-wheel-drive vehicle. ● **SEE FIGURE 26–11.**

The differential carrier bolts to the rear subframe, which bears the weight of the axle. Equal-length axle shafts with constant-velocity (CV) joints at either end connect the differential to the rear wheels, and allow the wheels to move independently of each other.

INDEPENDENT SUSPENSION

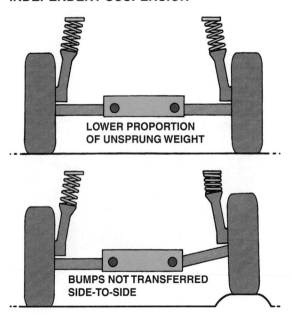

FIGURE 26–10 An independent rear suspension provides a better ride because less weight is unsprung and the suspension is able to react quickly to bumps in the road without affecting the opposite side.

SHORT-LONG-ARM (SLA) SUSPENSION

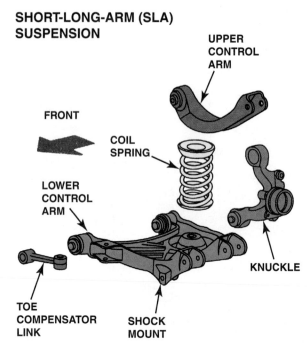

FIGURE 26–11 A typical short/long-arm independent rear suspension.

INDEPENDENT REAR SUSPENSIONS (CONTINUED)

The main benefit of an SLA suspension is that it reduces tire scrub and improves traction. The positioning of the control arms determines the suspension roll center location. In general, the lower the roll center, the less body roll.

Unit-body front-wheel-drive vehicles frequently use strut suspensions at the rear axle. Typically, the strut mounts to the knuckle and replaces the upper control arm. The first designer to put MacPherson-type struts in a rear suspension was an Englishman, Colin Chapman. For this reason, a rear strut suspension is often referred to as a **Chapman strut** suspension by European manufacturers and engineers.

The MacPherson strut system is the most popular independent rear suspension for late-model front-wheel-drive vehicles. ● **SEE FIGURE 26–12.** Modified strut rear suspensions are found on a variety of front-wheel-drive models from a number of different manufacturers. ● **SEE FIGURE 26–13.**

General Motors produced two different rear modified strut systems with transverse leaf springs. ● **SEE FIGURE 26–14.** A transverse leaf spring is also used on the Chevrolet Corvette and the Cadillac XLR.

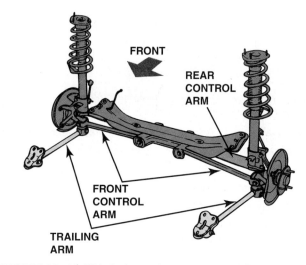

FIGURE 26–12 This independent rear suspension uses a MacPherson strut, two parallel lower transverse control arms, and a trailing arm.

MODIFIED STRUT SUSPENSION - COIL SPRING

REAR VIEW

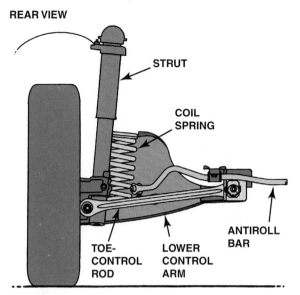

- STRUT
- COIL SPRING
- ANTIROLL BAR
- TOE-CONTROL ROD
- LOWER CONTROL ARM

FIGURE 26–13 The toe-control rod provides an extra brace to keep the rear wheels straight ahead during braking and acceleration on this modified-strut-type independent rear suspension.

SEMI-INDEPENDENT REAR SUSPENSIONS

A **semi-independent suspension** is used only at a nondriven rear axle. The semi-independent design is based on a cross-beam that is similar to the beam axle of a solid, nondriven rear suspension. However, on a semi-independent design the cross-beam is placed ahead, rather than at the centerline, of the wheels. ● **SEE FIGURE 26–15.** Trailing arms extend rearward from the crossbeam to the wheels. The name *semi-independent* indicates that although an axle does not directly link the wheels, the wheels are not completely independent of each other because they are indirectly connected through the crossbeam.

Some semi-independent rear suspensions use struts. ● **SEE FIGURE 26–16.**

MODIFIED STRUT SUSPENSION TRANSVERSE LEAF SPRING

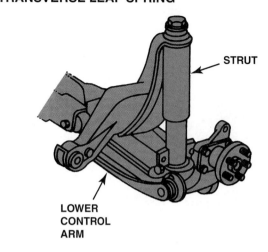

- STRUT
- LOWER CONTROL ARM

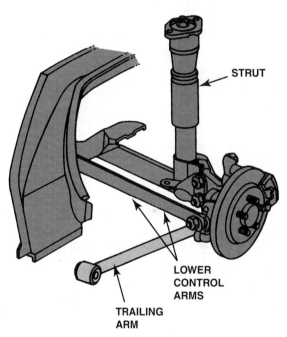

- STRUT
- LOWER CONTROL ARMS
- TRAILING ARM

FIGURE 26–14 The upper drawing shows a transverse-leaf-spring-type independent rear suspension that uses an "H"-shaped lower control arm. The lower drawing shows a transverse leaf spring suspension that uses two parallel lower links and a trailing arm.

SEMI-INDEPENDENT SUSPENSIONS

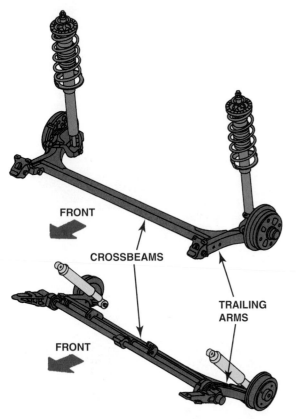

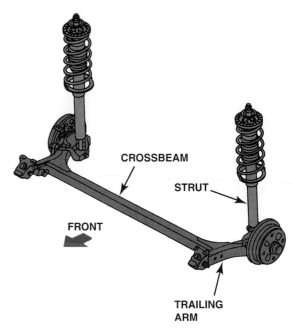

FIGURE 26-15 The crossbeam is placed toward the front of the vehicle rather than the centerline of the rear wheels on a semi-independent-type rear suspension.

SEMI-INDEPENDENT SUSPENSION-STRUT

FIGURE 26-16 A semi-independent rear suspension with MacPherson struts.

REAR SUSPENSION SERVICE

Rear suspension service starts with a thorough test drive, to observe any unusual noises or vibrations that may be caused by a fault with a rear suspension component.

After a test drive, safely hoist the vehicle and perform a thorough visual inspection. Use an appropriate prybar and move all of the bushings and joints, checking for deterioration or freeplay. ● SEE FIGURE 26-17.

Inspect the shock absorber or struts for leakage or damage. Inspect the bump stops for damage. ● SEE FIGURE 26-18. If the bump stops are damaged, this may indicate that the springs are fatigued and the vehicle is at lower-than-normal ride height, or that the shocks or studs are unable to control the springs. ● SEE FIGURE 26-19.

FIGURE 26-17 Check all rubber bushings for excessive cracking.

FIGURE 26–18 Carefully inspect the bump stops for damage during a thorough visual inspection.

REAR SHOCK REPLACEMENT

PRECAUTIONS Before removing the rear shock absorbers, the rear axle must be supported to prevent stretching of the rear brake flexible hose. Shocks are attached to the frame or body of the vehicle at the top and to a bracket on the rear axle housing at the bottom. Often, the top of the rear shock absorber is fastened *inside* the vehicle. Consult the vehicle manufacturer's service information for exact procedures and fastener torque values.

NOTE: Shock absorbers and/or struts should always be replaced as a pair.

AIR SHOCK INSTALLATION Air-adjustable shock absorbers are a popular replacement for conventional rear shock absorbers. Air shocks can be used to level the vehicle while towing a trailer or when heavily loaded. When the trailer or load is removed, air can be released from the air shocks to return the vehicle height to normal.

Most replacement air shocks are directional and are labeled *left* and *right*. This ensures that the plastic air hose line exits the shock absorber toward the center or rear of the vehicle and is kept away from the wheels.

The plastic air shock line attaches to the shock absorber with an O-ring or brass ferrule and nut. An air leak can result if this O-ring or ferrule is not installed according to the manufacturer's recommendations. Route the plastic air line along the body, keeping it away from the exhaust and any other body parts where the line could be damaged. Attach the line to both shocks to a junction at a convenient location for adding or releasing air.

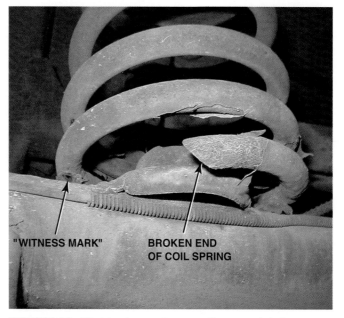

"WITNESS MARK"   BROKEN END OF COIL SPRING

FIGURE 26–19 A broken spring was discovered during a routine under-vehicle visual inspection. Notice the witness marks that show that the spring coils have been hitting each other.

REAR SPRING REPLACEMENT

REAR COIL SPRINGS

REPLACEMENT. Coil springs in the rear are easily replaced on both front-wheel-drive and rear-wheel-drive vehicles. The procedure includes the following steps:

1. Raise the vehicle safely on a hoist.
2. Remove both rear wheels.
3. Support the rear axle assembly with tall safety stands.
4. Remove the lower shock absorber mounting bolts/nuts and disconnect the shock absorber from the rear axle assembly.
5. Slowly lower the rear axle assembly by either lowering the height of the adjustable safety stands or raising the height of the vehicle on the hoist.
6. Lower the rear axle just enough to remove the coil springs. ● SEE FIGURE 26–20.

FIGURE 26–20 The shock absorber needs to be disconnected before removing the coil spring. Installation is the reverse of removal procedure.

FIGURE 26–21 The center bolt is used to hold the leaves of the leaf spring together. However, the hole for the center bolt also weakens the leaf spring. The crack shown is what a technician discovered when the leaf spring was removed during the diagnosis of a sagging rear suspension.

REAR SHOCK REPLACEMENT (CONTINUED)

CAUTION: The shock absorber is usually the only component that limits the downward movement of the rear axle to allow removal of the rear coil springs. Some vehicles may be equipped with rear suspension height sensors for the adjustable suspension system or an adjustable rear proportioning valve for the rear brakes. Some vehicles also require that the rear stabilizer bar or track rod be disconnected or removed before lowering the rear axle assembly. Always consult service information for the exact procedure and torque specifications for the vehicle being serviced.

REAR LEAF SPRINGS

REPLACEMENT. Rear leaf springs often need replacement due to one of the following common causes:

1. **Individual leaves of a leaf spring often crack, then break.** When a leaf spring breaks, the load-carrying capacity of the vehicle decreases and it often sags on the side with the broken spring. Metal fatigue, corrosion, and overloading are three of the most common causes of leaf spring breakage. ● **SEE FIGURE 26–21.**

NOTE: When one rear spring on one side sags, the opposite front end of the vehicle tends to *rise*. For example, if the right rear spring breaks or sags down, the left front of the vehicle tends to rise

higher than the right front. This unequal vehicle height can make the vehicle difficult to handle, especially around corners or curves.

2. **If the center bolt breaks,** the individual leaves can move and the rear axle is no longer held in the correct location. When one side of the rear axle is behind the other side, the vehicle will *dog track*. Dog tracking refers to the sideways angle of the vehicle while traveling straight. It is commonly caused by the rear axle steering the vehicle toward one side, while the driver controls the direction of the vehicle with the front wheels.

NOTE: Leaf springs should be replaced in pairs.

To replace leaf springs in the rear of a rear-wheel-drive vehicle, follow these steps:

1. Raise the vehicle safely on a hoist.

2. Support the rear axle with safety stands.

3. Remove the rear shackle bolts and forward mounting bolt or mounting bracket.

4. Remove the U-bolts.

5. Being careful of any nearby brake line, remove the spring.

6. Install the new spring, being careful to position the center bolt correctly into the hole on the axle pedestal.

1. Solid rear axles are commonly used on rear-wheel-drive and front-wheel-drive vehicles.
2. A Hotchkiss rear suspension uses the leaf springs to absorb axle windup.
3. Trailing arms run parallel to the centerline of the vehicle and are used to locate a solid rear axle.
4. A track rod (Panhard rod) or watts linkage is used to keep the rear axle centered under the vehicle.
5. Independent rear suspension (IRS) usually uses coil springs but can use a transversely mounted leaf spring.
6. The rear suspension should be supported whenever replacing the rear shock absorbers.

REVIEW QUESTIONS

1. What are the disadvantages of a solid rear axle?
2. What is the purpose of a torque arm?
3. What must be done to ensure safety when replacing the rear shock absorbers?

CHAPTER QUIZ

1. A vehicle equipped with a coil spring front suspension and a leaf spring rear suspension "dog tracks" while driving on a straight, level road. Technician A says that a broken center bolt could be the cause. Technician B says defective rear shock absorbers could be the cause. Which technician is correct?
   a. Technician A only
   b. Technician B only
   c. Both Technicians A and B
   d. Neither Technician A nor B

2. When axle windup is controlled by the rear-leaf spring during acceleration, this system is called _____.
   a. Trailing arm
   b. Semi-trailing arm
   c. Torque arm
   d. Hotchkiss drive

3. A loud "bang" is heard and felt every time the accelerator is depressed or released on a rear-wheel-drive vehicle. Technician A says that a leaking shock absorber could be the cause. Technician B says a broken torque arm could be the cause. Which technician is correct?
   a. Technician A only
   b. Technician B only
   c. Both Technicians A and B
   d. Neither Technician A nor B

4. Technician A says that leaf springs are mounted lengthwise on the rear of many vehicles. Technician B says that some vehicles use a transversely mounted leaf spring on the rear. Which technician is correct?
   a. Technician A only
   b. Technician B only
   c. Both Technicians A and B
   d. Neither Technician A nor B

5. A strut-type suspension is used _____.
   a. In the front only
   b. In the rear only
   c. In both the front and rear
   d. In rare vehicles no longer in production

6. Two technicians are discussing rear shock absorbers. Technician A says that if one shock is leaking, then both rear shock absorbers should be replaced. Technician B says that the rear axle should be supported before removing rear shock absorbers. Which technician is correct?
   a. Technician A only
   b. Technician B only
   c. Both Technicians A and B
   d. Neither Technician A nor B

7. A "witness mark" is a _____.
   a. Type of fastener
   b. Type of tool
   c. Mark where two parts have rubbed or touched
   d. Identification mark

8. The left front of the vehicle is higher than the right front and the right rear is lower than the left rear. What is the most likely cause of this problem?
   a. A weak right-rear shock absorber
   b. A broken track rod
   c. A broken left-front shock absorber
   d. A sagging right-rear spring

9. One rear leaf spring is broken. Technician A says that both rear leaf springs should be replaced. Technician B says that only the broken spring needs to be replaced. Which technician is correct?
   a. Technician A only
   b. Technician B only
   c. Both Technicians A and B
   d. Neither Technician A nor B

10. A track rod is also called a _____.
    a. Panhard rod
    b. Control rod
    c. Handing link
    d. Semi-independent rod

ELECTRONIC SUSPENSION SYSTEMS

OBJECTIVES

After studying Chapter 27, the reader will be able to:

1. Prepare for ASE Suspension and Steering (A4) certification test content area "B" (Suspension System Diagnosis and Repair).

2. Describe how suspension height sensors function.

3. Explain the use of the various sensors used for electronic suspension control.

4. Discuss the steering wheel position sensor.

5. Explain how solenoids and actuators are used to control the suspension.

KEY TERMS

Actuator 510
Air suspension 511
Armature 517
AS 519
Automatic level control (ALC) 519
CCVRTMR 526
Computer command ride (CCR) 515
Desiccant 525
Driver selector switch 515
EBCM 513
ECU 510
Electromagnet 516
Handwheel position sensor 512
Height sensor 510
Input 510
Lateral accelerometer sensor 514
LED 510
Magneto-rheological (MR) 526
Mode select switch 518
Motor 516

MRRTD 526
Output 510
Perform ride mode 521
Photocell 510
Phototransistor 510
Pulse width 516
Pulse-width modulation 516
Real-time dampening (RTD) 512
RPO 521
RSS 512
Selectable ride (SR) 515
Solenoid 516
Solenoid controlled damper 521
Stabilitrak 522
Steering wheel position sensor 512
Touring ride mode 521
Vehicle stability enhancement system (VSES) 514
VS sensor 513
Yaw rate sensor 514

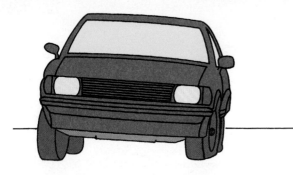 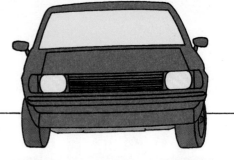

CONVENTIONAL SUSPENSION   ELECTRONICALLY CONTROLLED SUSPENSION

FIGURE 27–1 An electronically controlled suspension system can help reduce body roll and other reactions better than most conventional suspension systems.

THE NEED FOR ELECTRONIC SUSPENSIONS

Since the mid-1980s, many vehicle manufacturers have been introducing models with electronic suspension controls that provide a variable shock stiffness or spring rate. The main advantage of electronic controls is that the suspension can react to different conditions. The system provides a firm suspension feel for fast cornering and quick acceleration and braking, with a soft ride for cruising. ● **SEE FIGURE 27–1.**

ELECTRONIC SUSPENSION CONTROLS AND SENSORS

Sensors and switches provide **input** to the electronic control module (ECM), or system computer. The ECM, which may also be referred to as the **electronic control unit (ECU)**, is a small computer that receives input in the form of electrical signals from the sensors and switches and provides **output** electrical signals to the system actuators. ● **SEE FIGURE 27–2.** The electrical signal causes an **actuator** to perform some type of mechanical action.

HEIGHT SENSORS
Sensors, which are the input devices that transmit signals to the ECM, monitor operating conditions and component functions. A **height sensor** senses the vertical relationship between the suspension component and the body. Its signal indicates to the ECM how high the frame or body is, or how compressed the suspension is. A number of sensor designs are used to determine ride height, including a **photocell** type of sensor. ● **SEE FIGURE 27–3.**

Four height sensors, one at each wheel, deliver an input signal to the ECM. All four sensors are similar and use a control

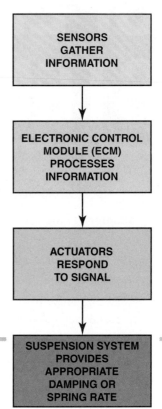

FIGURE 27–2 Input devices monitor conditions and provide information to the electronic control module, which processes the information and operates the actuators to control the movement of the suspension.

link, lever, slotted disc, and four photo interrupters to transmit a signal. Each photo interrupter consists of a **light-emitting diode (LED)** and a **phototransistor**, which reacts to the LED.

Inside the sensor, the LEDs and phototransistors are positioned opposite each other on each side of the slotted disc. ● **SEE FIGURE 27–4.** When the system is activated, the ECM applies voltage to the LEDs, which causes them to illuminate. Light from an LED shining on the phototransistor causes the transistor to generate a voltage signal. Signals generated by the phototransistors are delivered to the ECM as an input that reflects ride height.

As suspension movement rotates the disc, the slots or windows on the disc either allow light from the LEDs to shine on

HEIGHT SENSOR

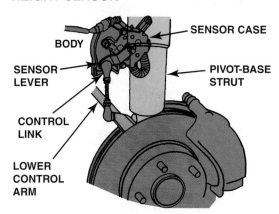

FIGURE 27–3 A typical electronic suspension height sensor, which bolts to the body and connects to the lower control arm through a control link and lever.

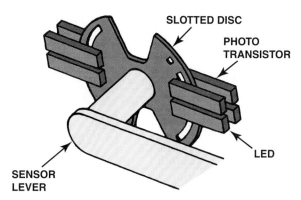

FIGURE 27–4 When suspension action moves the lever, it rotates the slotted disc and varies how much of the photo transistor is exposed to the LEDs, which vary the input signal.

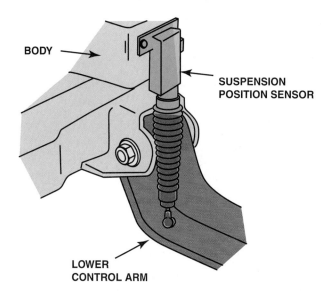

FIGURE 27–5 Typical suspension position sensor.

the phototransistors or prevent it. The windows are positioned in such a manner that, in combination with the four LEDs and transistors, the sensor is capable of generating 16 different levels of voltage. This variable voltage, which is transmitted to the ECM as an input signal, directly corresponds to 1 of 16 possible positions of the suspension. This input signal tells the ECM the position of the suspension in relation to the body. Whether the input voltage signal is increasing or decreasing allows the ECM to determine if the suspension is compressing or extending.

The ECM can also determine the relative position of the body to the suspension, or the attitude of the vehicle, from the four height sensors. Comparing front-wheel input signals to those of the rear wheels determines the amount of pitch caused by forces of acceleration or deceleration. A side-to-side comparison allows the ECM to determine the amount of body roll generated by cornering force.

GENERAL MOTORS ELECTRONIC SUSPENSION SENSORS

There are five different sensors found on electronic suspension systems, and GM vehicles can have between one and four of these sensors, depending on the system.

Depending on the vehicle, the *suspension position sensor* may be called by a different name. It can be called:

- An automatic level control sensor
- An electronic suspension position sensor
- A position sensor
- An air suspension sensor

The sensor provides the control module with information regarding the relative position and movement of suspension components. The common mounting location is between the vehicle body and the suspension control arm. ● **SEE FIGURE 27–5.**

The operation of the sensor is either an air suspension sensor two-wire type or a potentiometer three-wire type. The **air suspension** sensor is also known as a *linear Hall-effect* sensor.

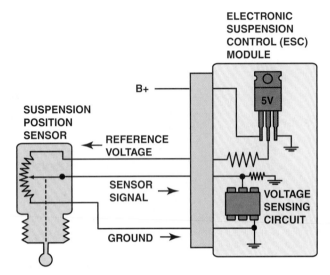

FIGURE 27–6 A three-wire suspension position sensor schematic.

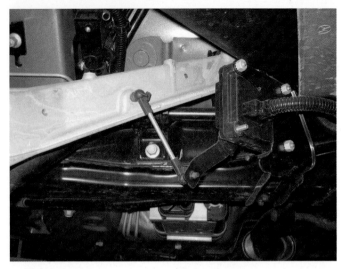

FIGURE 27–7 A suspension height sensor.

ELECTRONIC CONTROLS AND SENSORS (CONTINUED)

The air suspension sensor operation consists of a moveable iron core linked to the components. As the core moves, it varies the inductance of the internal sensor coil relative to suspension position.

The suspension control module energizes and de-energizes the coil approximately 20 times a second, thereby measuring sensor inductance as it relates to suspension position. The potentiometer three-wire sensor requires reference and ground voltage. Similar to the throttle position (TP) sensor, it produces a variable analog voltage signal. ● SEE FIGURE 27–6.

As the suspension moves up or down, an arm moves on the suspension position sensor through a ball-and-cup link. ● SEE FIGURE 27–7.

Suspension position sensor voltage changes relative to this movement. The sensor receives a 5-volt reference signal from the control module. The position sensor returns a voltage signal between 0 and 5 volts depending on suspension arm position.

NOTE: Some systems may require sensor learning or "reprogramming" after replacement. For instance, the sensor used on the Tahoe or Suburban needs to be programmed if replaced. Always check service information for the details and procedures to follow when replacing a sensor on the suspension.

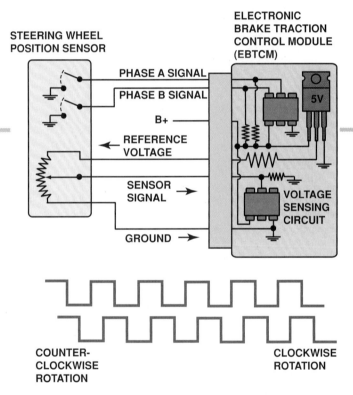

FIGURE 27–8 The steering wheel position (handwheel position) sensor wiring schematic and how the signal varies with the direction that the steering wheel is turned.

STEERING WHEEL POSITION SENSOR Depending on the vehicle, the **steering wheel position sensor** may also be called a **handwheel position sensor**. The function of this sensor is to provide the control module with signals relating to steering wheel position, the speed and direction of handwheel position.

The sensor is found on most **real-time dampening (RTD)** and **road-sensing suspension (RSS)** applications. The sensor

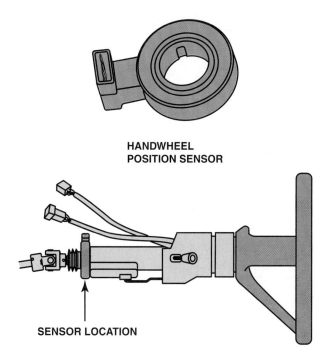

FIGURE 27–9 The handwheel position sensor is located at the base of the steering column.

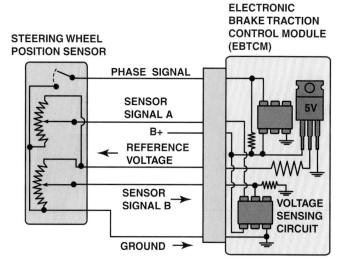

FIGURE 27–10 Steering wheel (handwheel) position sensor schematic.

is typically located at the base of the steering column. Always refer to service information for vehicle-specific information. ● **SEE FIGURES 27–8 AND 27–9.**

The handwheel sensor produces two digital signals, which are used by the **electronic brake control module (EBCM).** These signals are produced as the steering wheel is rotated. The sensor can also produce more than two signals. As an example, the Cadillac Escalade handwheel sensor produces one analog and three digital signals.

The sensor uses a 5-volt signal reference. Analog signal voltage values increase or decrease, between 0 and 5 volts, as the steering wheel is moved left and right of center. The digital signal is also a standard power-to-ground circuit as shown in the schematic.

There are three possible digital signals:

■ Phase A
■ Phase B
■ Index pulse

These signals provide the suspension control module with steering wheel speed and direction information. Digital signals are either high or low, 5 volts or 0 volts. ● **SEE FIGURE 27–10.**

The Tech 2 provides DTC faults for this sensor. If there is

an intermittent concern with a steering wheel position sensor, select Tech 2 snapshot and slowly turn the steering wheel lock to lock. After the snapshot is complete, plot the analog sensor voltage to see if the signal dropped out. Any dropout is an indication of an intermittent problem.

VEHICLE SPEED SENSOR The **vehicle speed (VS) sensor** is used by the EBCM to help control the suspension system. The vehicle speed sensor is a magnetic sensor and generates an analog signal whose frequency increases as the speed increases. The ride is made firmer at high speeds and during braking and acceleration and less firm at cruise speeds. ● **SEE FIGURE 27–11.**

PRESSURE SENSOR A pressure transducer (sensor) is typically mounted on the compressor assembly. This sensor is typically found on suspension systems that use a compressor assembly. The main function of the pressure sensor is to provide feedback to the suspension control module about the operation of the compressor. The sensor assures both that a minimum air pressure is maintained in the system and that a maximum value is not exceeded. A pressure transducer (sensor) is typically mounted on the compressor assembly. This

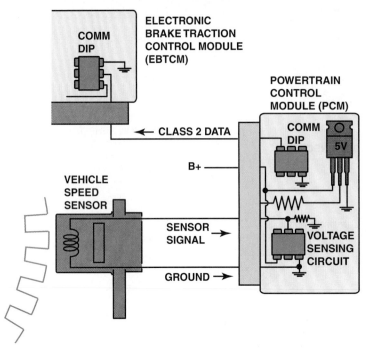

FIGURE 27–11 The VS sensor information is transmitted to the EBCM by Class 2 serial data.

ELECTRONIC CONTROLS AND SENSORS (CONTINUED)

sensor is typically found on systems such as air suspension, real-time damping, and road-sensing suspension that use a compressor assembly. ● **SEE FIGURE 27–12.**

The operation of the pressure sensor requires a 5-volt reference, a ground, and a signal wire to provide feedback to the control module. The voltage output on the signal wire will vary from 0 to 5 volts based upon pressure in the system. A high voltage indicates high pressure and low voltage indicates a low pressure.

LATERAL ACCELEROMETER SENSOR
The function of the **lateral accelerometer sensor** is to provide the suspension control module with feedback regarding vehicle cornering forces. This type of sensor is also called a G-sensor, with the letter "G" representing the force of gravity. For example, when a vehicle enters a turn, the sensor provides information as to how hard the vehicle is cornering. This information is processed by the suspension control module to provide appropriate damping on the inboard and outboard dampers during cornering events. The lateral accelerometer sensor is found on the more complex suspensions systems, such as RTD and RSS systems that incorporate the **vehicle stability enhancement system (VSES)**.

This sensor can be either a stand-alone unit or combined with the yaw rate sensor. Typically, the sensor is mounted in the passenger compartment under a front seat, center console, or package shelf.

The sensor produces a voltage signal of 0 to 5 volts as the vehicle maneuvers left or right through a curve. The signal is an input to the EBCM. If zero lateral acceleration, the sensor input is 2.5 volts. Check service information for specific codes that can be set.

If driving the vehicle and the voltage values increase or decrease during cornering events, this indicates proper operation. ● **SEE FIGURE 27–13.**

YAW RATE SENSOR
The **yaw rate sensor** provides information to the suspension control module and the EBCM. This

TECH TIP

Quick and Easy "G" Sensor Test

Most factory scan tools will display the value of sensors, including the lateral accelerometer sensor (G-sensor). However, the G-sensor value will read zero unless the vehicle is cornering. A quick and easy test of the sensor is to simply unbolt the sensor and rotate it 90 degrees with the key on engine off. ● **SEE FIGURE 27–14.** Now the sensor is measuring the force of gravity and should display 1.0 G on the scan tool. If the sensor does not read close to 1.0 G or reads zero all of the time, the sensor or the wiring is defective.

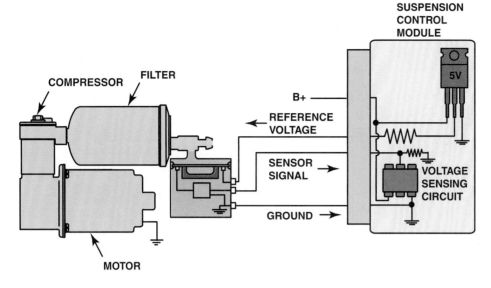

FIGURE 27-12 An air pressure sensor.

COMPRESSOR FILTER

MOTOR

SUSPENSION CONTROL MODULE

B+

REFERENCE VOLTAGE

SENSOR SIGNAL

GROUND

5V

VOLTAGE SENSING CIRCUIT

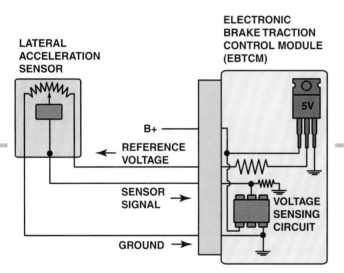

FIGURE 27-13 A schematic showing the lateral acceleration sensor and the EBCM.

FIGURE 27-14 The lateral accelerometer sensor (G-sensor) is usually located under the center console.

information is used to determine how far the vehicle has deviated from the driver's intended direction. The yaw sensor is used on vehicles equipped with Electronic Stability Control (ESC).

This sensor can be either a stand-alone unit or combined with the lateral accelerometer sensor. Typically, the sensor is mounted in the passenger compartment under the front seat, center console, or on the rear package shelf.

The sensor produces a voltage signal of 0 to 5 volts as the vehicle yaw rate changes. The voltage signal is an input to the EBCM. The yaw rate input to the EBCM indicates the number of degrees that the vehicle deviates from its intended direction.

For example, with a 0-degree yaw rate, the sensor output is 2.5 volts. During an emergency maneuver, the signal will vary above or below 2.5 volts. This sensor does set DTC codes. These codes can be found in service information. ● **SEE FIGURE 27-15.**

DRIVER SELECTOR SWITCH The **driver selector switch** is a two- or three-mode switch, usually located in the center console, and is an input to the suspension control module.

The switch that is used to select either touring (soft) or performance (firm) ride is found on the **Selectable Ride (SR)** and the **Computer Command Ride (CCR)** systems. The mode select switch status is generally displayed on a scan tool. The three-position switch is used on the Corvette RTD system, and allows the driver to select three modes of operation:

- Tour
- Sport
- Performance

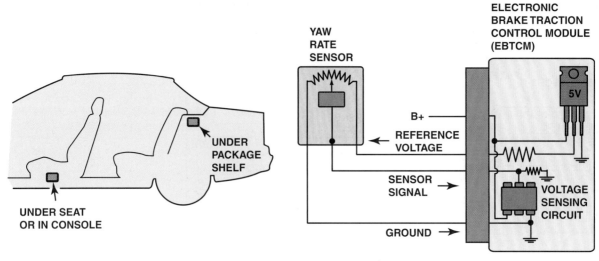

FIGURE 27-15 Yaw rate sensor showing the typical location and schematic.

ELECTRONIC SUSPENSION SYSTEM ACTUATORS

Each actuator in an electronically controlled suspension system receives output signals from the ECM and responds to these signals, or commands, by performing a mechanical action. Actuators are usually inductive devices that operate using an electromagnetic field. A simple **electromagnet** consists of a soft iron core with a coil of wire, usually copper, wrapped around it. ● **SEE FIGURE 27-16.**

Electrical current traveling through the coiled wire creates a magnetic field around the core. All magnets are polarized; that is, they have a north, or positive, and a south, or negative, pole. When the opposite poles of two magnets are placed near each other—positive-to-negative—the magnets attract each other. Place the same poles together, positive-to-positive or negative-to-negative, and the magnets repel each other. ● **SEE FIGURE 27-17.** Magnets also attract and are attracted to certain types of metals, especially iron and steel.

When an electromagnet has more than one coil, the stronger primary coil can induce voltage into the weaker secondary coil. This inductive transfer occurs even though there is no physical connection between the two coils.

SOLENOIDS In a **solenoid**, the core of the electromagnet also acts as a plunger to open and close a passage or to move a linkage. Solenoids are cylindrically shaped with a metal plate at one end and open at the other end to allow the plunger to move in and out. The electromagnetic coils are placed along the sides of the cylinder. A preload spring forces the plunger toward one end of the device when the solenoid is de-energized, or there is no current in the coil.

When the solenoid is energized, current passes through the coil and magnetizes the core. The magnetized core is attracted to the metal plate and the strength of the magnetic field overcomes spring force to pull the plunger inward. ● **SEE FIGURE 27-18.** When the electrical current switches off, the solenoid de-energizes and spring force returns the plunger to its rest position.

An airflow control valve is an example of a solenoid used in an electronically controlled suspension. ● **SEE FIGURE 27-19.** As the solenoid plunger extends and retracts, it opens and closes air passages between the system air-pressure tank and the air springs. The position of the plunger determines whether the springs receive more pressure or whether pressure bleeds out of them. Increasing the pressure in the air springs lifts the body higher, and decreasing the pressure by bleeding air from the springs lowers the body.

Solenoids are digital devices that are either on or off. However, the ECM can vary the amount a solenoid opens by pulsing the output signal to the coil. If the signal is rapidly switched on and off, spring and magnetic forces do not have enough time to react and effectively move the plunger between the signal changes. The amount of time the current is on compared to the amount of time it is off is called **pulse width**, and the control of a solenoid using this pulsing-on-and-off method is called **pulse-width modulation**.

ACTUATOR MOTORS If a current-carrying conductor is placed in a magnetic field, it tends to move from the stronger field area to the weaker field area. A **motor** uses this principle to convert electrical energy into mechanical movement. Electrical

ELECTROMAGNET

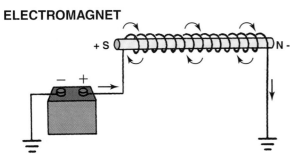

FIGURE 27–16 A magnetic field is created whenever an electrical current flows through a coil of wire wrapped around an iron core.

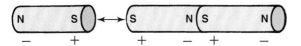

FIGURE 27–17 When magnets are near each other, like poles repel and opposite poles attract.

SOLENOID

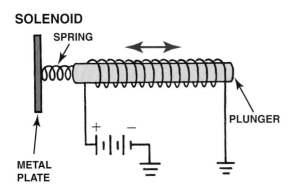

FIGURE 27–18 When electrical current magnetizes the plunger in a solenoid, the magnetic field moves the plunger against spring force. With no current, the spring pushes the plunger back to its original position.

SOLENOID OFF

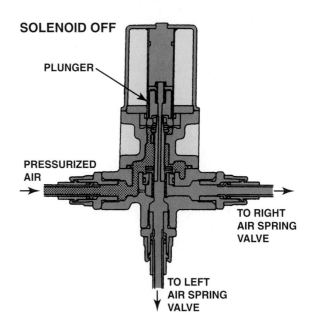

TO RIGHT AIR SPRING VALVE

TO LEFT AIR SPRING VALVE

SOLENOID ON

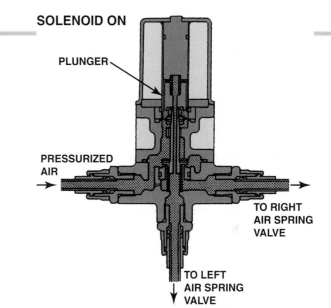

TO RIGHT AIR SPRING VALVE

TO LEFT AIR SPRING VALVE

FIGURE 27–19 This air supply solenoid blocks pressurized air from the air spring valves when off. The plunger pulls upward to allow airflow to the air spring valves when the solenoid is energized.

current is directed through the field coils on the motor frame to create a magnetic field within the frame. By applying an electrical current to the **armature**, which is inside the motor frame, the armature rotates from a strong field area to a weaker field area. Armature movement can in turn move another part, such as a gear, pulley, or shaft, attached to it.

Located at the top mount of the air spring variable shock assembly of each wheel, the suspension control actuator moves a control rod that regulates air pressure to the spring, which determines ride height. The actuator is an electromagnetic device consisting of four stator coils and a permanent magnet core. ● **SEE FIGURE 27–20.**

The ECM applies current to two stator coils at a time to create opposing magnetic fields around the core, which causes the core to rotate into a new position. Which coils are energized determines how far and in which direction the core

rotates. ● **SEE FIGURE 27–21.** By switching current from one pair of coils to the other, the ECM moves the core into a new position, and a third position is available by reversing the polarity of the coils.

A gear at the base of the permanent magnet connects to a rod that operates the air valve to the air spring. The gear also drives another gear, which operates the control rod of the variable shock absorber. Therefore, the three positions of the suspension control actuator motor provide three shock absorber stiffness settings in addition to a variable air spring.

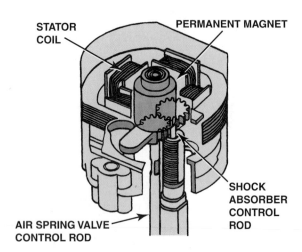

FIGURE 27-20 An actuator motor uses a permanent magnet and four stator coils to drive the air spring control rod.

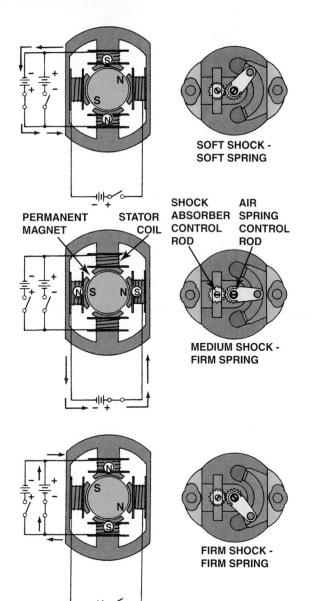

FIGURE 27-21 The stator coils of the actuator are energized in three ways to provide soft, medium, or firm ride from the air springs and shock absorbers.

TYPES OF ELECTRONIC SUSPENSION

The types of electronic suspension systems used on General Motors vehicles, as examples, include:

1. Selectable Ride

2. Automatic Level Control

3. Air Suspension

4. Computer Command Ride

5. Real-Time Dampening/Road-Sensing Suspension

6. Vehicle Stability Enhancement System

7. Magneto-Rheological Suspension (F55)

SELECTABLE RIDE (SR) The Selectable Ride (SR) system is the most basic of the electronic systems offered by General Motors. Selectable Ride (SR) allows the driver to choose between two distinct damping levels:

- Firm

- Normal

SR is found on Chevrolet and GMC full-size pickup trucks.
● SEE FIGURE 27-22.

A switch is used to control four electronically controlled gas-charged dampers. The **mode select switch** activates the

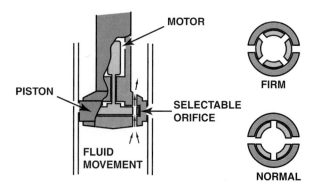

FIGURE 27-22 Selectable Ride as used on Chevrolet and GMC pickup trucks.

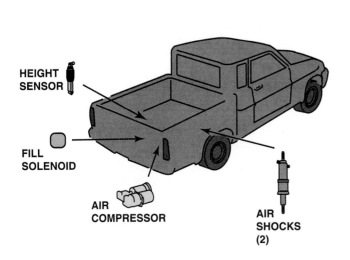

FIGURE 27–23 ALC maintains the same ride height either loaded or unloaded by increasing or decreasing the air pressure in the rear air shocks.

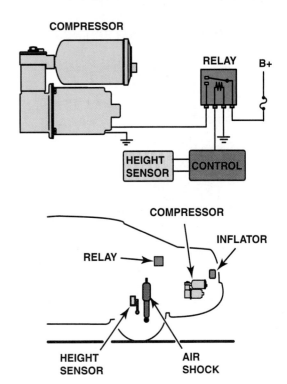

FIGURE 27–24 A typical schematic showing the air suspension compressor assembly and sensor.

bi-state (two settings) dampers at all four corners of the vehicle, allowing the driver to select vehicle ride characteristics. The system is either energizing or de-energizing the bi-state dampers to provide a firm or normal ride.

AUTOMATIC LEVEL CONTROL The **Automatic Level Control (ALC)** system automatically adjusts the rear height of the vehicle in response to changes in vehicle loading and unloading. Automatic Level Control is found on many General Motors vehicles. ALC controls rear leveling by monitoring the rear suspension position sensor and energizing the compressor to raise the vehicle or energizing the exhaust valve to lower the vehicle. ALC has several variations across the different platforms. ● **SEE FIGURE 27–23.**

AIR SUSPENSION (AS) **Air Suspension (AS)** is a system very similar to the ALC system. The purpose of the AS system includes:

1. Keep the vehicle visually level
2. Provide optimal headlight aiming
3. Maintain optimal ride height

The AS system includes the following components:

- An air suspension compressor assembly
- Rear air springs
- Air suspension sensors

The AS system is designed to maintain rear trim height within 3/16 inch (4 mm) in all loading conditions, and the leveling function will deactivate if the vehicle is overloaded.

The AS system also includes an accessory air inflator found in the rear cargo area. ● **SEE FIGURE 27–24.**

VARIABLE-RATE AIR SPRINGS In an air spring system with ordinary shock absorbers, the ECM uses the air springs to control trim height and is used on many Ford, Mercury, and Lincoln vehicles.

The three height sensors transmit a signal to the ECM that reflects trim height at each axle. ● **SEE FIGURE 27–25.** The ignition and brake light switches tell the ECM whether the ignition switch is on or off, and if the brake pedal is depressed. The dome light switch indicates whether any doors are open. The on/off switch disables the air spring system to avoid unexpected movement while towing or servicing the vehicle.

VARIABLE-RATE AIR SPRINGS

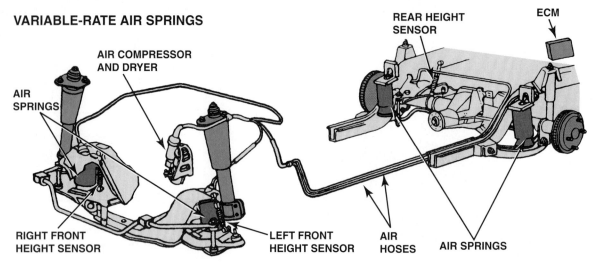

FIGURE 27–25 The typical variable-rate air spring system uses three height sensors, two in the front and one in the rear, to monitor trim height and to provide input signals to the ECM.

TYPES OF ELECTRONIC SUSPENSION (CONTINUED)

CAUTION: Failure to turn off the system will cause the air springs to be vented when the vehicle is hoisted. This will cause the vehicle to drop almost to the ground when the vehicle is lowered. This can cause damage to the air springs and/or to the vehicle. The shut-off switch is usually located in the trunk.

The ECM receives information from the height sensors indicating that the trim height is too high or too low, and it energizes the actuators to add or bleed air from the air springs. The system actuators can still operate for up to an hour after the ignition is switched off.

Any time the ignition is switched to the "run" position, the ECM raises the vehicle, if necessary, within the first 45 seconds. If trim height is too high and the vehicle must be lowered, the ECM delays doing so for 45 seconds after the ignition is switched on.

An air compressor with a regenerative dryer provides the air change required to inflate the air springs on the air suspension system, and a vent solenoid is used to relieve air pressure and deflate the springs. ● SEE FIGURE 27–26.

By energizing the compressor relay, the ECM directs current to turn on the compressor motor when trim height needs to be raised. The ECM command to lower the vehicle is an electrical signal that opens the vent solenoid to bleed air pressure out of the system. ● SEE FIGURE 27–27.

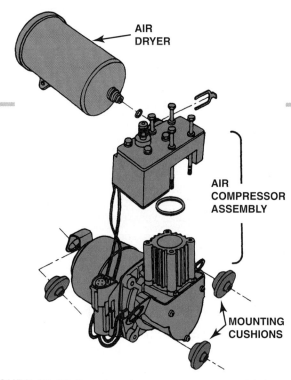

FIGURE 27–26 The air spring compressor assembly is usually mounted on rubber cushions to help isolate it from the body of the vehicle. All of the air entering or leaving the air springs flows through the regenerative air dryer.

GENERAL MOTORS COMPUTER COMMAND RIDE The

General Motors Computer Command Ride (CCR) system controls ride firmness by automatically controlling an actuator in each of the four struts to increase ride firmness as speed increases.

The three damping modes are:

- Comfort
- Normal
- Sport

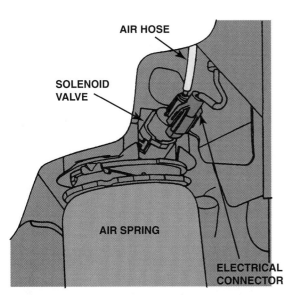

FIGURE 27–27 A solenoid valve at the top of each spring regulates airflow into and out of the air spring.

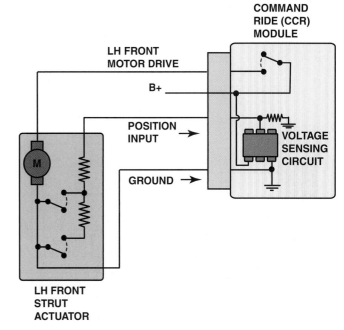

FIGURE 27–28 Schematic showing Computer Command Ride (CCR) system.

Damping mode selection is controlled by the CCR control module according to vehicle speed conditions, driver select switch position, and any error conditions that may exist.

In the **perform ride mode**, the system will place the damping level in the firm mode regardless of vehicle speed.

In the **touring ride mode**, the damping level depends on vehicle speed. ● **SEE FIGURE 27–28.**

REAL-TIME DAMPENING AND ROAD-SENSING SUSPENSION

Real-time dampening (RTD) independently controls a solenoid in each of the four shock absorbers in order to control the vehicle ride characteristics and is capable of making changes within milliseconds (0.001 second).

Road-sensing suspension (RSS), along with ALC, controls damping forces in the front struts and rear shock absorbers in response to various road and driving conditions.

RTD and RSS incorporate the following components:

- An electronic suspension control module,
- Front and rear suspension position sensors,
- Bi-state dampers,
- A ride select switch, and
- An air compressor is used on some models.

● **SEE FIGURES 27–29 AND 27–30.**

🔧 **TECH TIP**

Check the RPO Code

Whenever working on the suspension system check the **RPO (regular production option)** code for the type of suspension used. For example, the F55 RPO may be called by a different name depending on the make and model of vehicle. Also, service procedures will be different on the same vehicle depending on whether it is equipped with an F45 or an F55 system. The General Motors vehicle RPO codes are on a sticker on the spare tire cover in the trunk or in the glove compartment.

BI-STATE AND TRI-STATE DAMPERS

The bi-state damper is also known as a **solenoid controlled damper**. Bi-state dampers are found on the RTD, RSS, and SR systems. Each of the suspension dampers used in these systems have an integral solenoid. The solenoid valve provides various amounts of damping by directing hydraulic damping fluid in the suspension shock absorber or strut. ● **SEE FIGURE 27–31.**

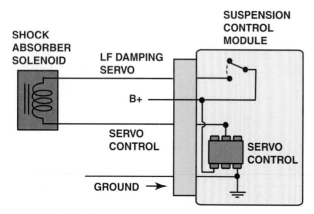

FIGURE 27–29 Schematic showing the shock control used in the RSS system.

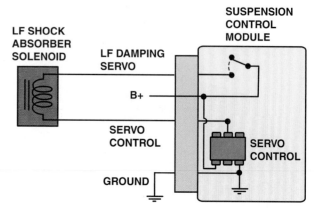

FIGURE 27–31 Solenoid valve controlled shock absorber circuit showing the left front (LF) shock as an example.

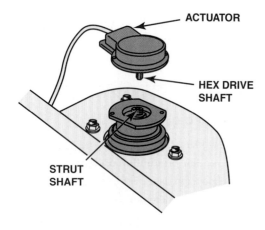

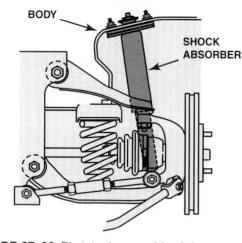

FIGURE 27–30 Bi-state dampers (shocks) use a solenoid to control fluid flow in the unit to control compression and rebound actions.

TYPES OF ELECTRONIC SUSPENSION (CONTINUED)

The General Motors version of ESC is called the vehicle stability enhancement system (VSES) and includes an additional level of vehicle control to the EBCM. VSES is also known as **Stabilitrak**.

The purpose of the vehicle stability enhancement system along with the antilock brake system (ABS) is to provide vehicle stability enhancement during oversteer or understeer conditions.

The pulse-width modulation (PWM) voltage signal from the suspension control module controls the amount of current flow through each of the damper solenoids. With a low PWM signal de-energized, more hydraulic damping fluid is allowed to bypass the main suspension damper passage, resulting in a softer damping mode.

As the PWM signal increases, or is energized, the damping mode becomes more firm. ● **SEE FIGURE 27–32.**

NOTE: If the suspension module does not control the shock absorber solenoid, a full soft damping mode results. In some system malfunctions, the module may command one or all of the damper solenoids to a full soft damping.

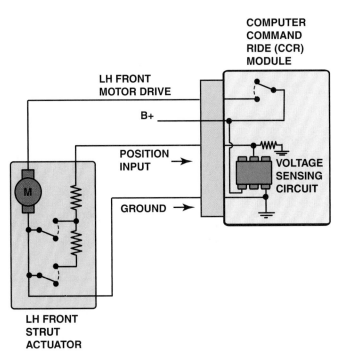

FIGURE 27–32 A typical CCR module schematic.

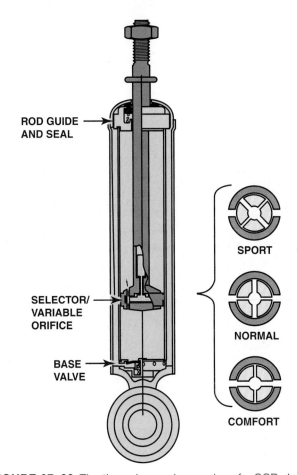

FIGURE 27–33 The three dampening modes of a CCR shock absorber.

The main difference between a tri-state damper and a bi-state damper is that the tri-state damper uses an electrical actuator, whereas the bi-state damper is solenoid controlled.

The three damping modes include:

- Comfort
- Normal
- Sport

A tri-state damper has an integral electrical strut actuator that rotates a selector valve to change the flow of hydraulic damping fluid. ● **SEE FIGURE 27–33.**

The CCR module controls the operation of the strut actuators to provide the three damping modes.

The strut position input provides feedback to the CCR module. The strut position input is compared to the commanded actuator position to monitor system operation. ● **SEE FIGURE 27–34.**

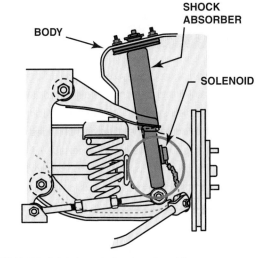

FIGURE 27–34 Integral shock solenoid.

FIGURE 27–35 A typical ZF Sachs self-leveling shock, as used on the rear of a Chrysler minivan.

AUTOMATIC LEVEL CONTROL (ALC)

Vehicles that have an air inflator system as part of the ALC system also have an air inflator switch. The air inflator switch is an input to the ALC and AS system. The inflator switch is used to control the air inflator system operation and provides a signal to the ALC or AS module to initiate compressor activation.

With the ignition on, the driver can turn the system to ON. The switch will command the compressor to run for up to 10 minutes, allowing time to inflate a tire or other items requiring air.

NOTE: There are no DTCs associated with compressor assembly.

INFLATOR OR COMPRESSOR RELAY The suspension control module energizes the relay to activate the compressor motor. This adjusts the rear trim height as needed. The suspension control module controls the compressor relay for normal operation or for the accessory air inflator.

What Are Self-Leveling Shocks?

A German company, ZF Sachs, supplies a self-leveling shock absorber to several vehicle manufacturers, such as Chrysler for use on the rear of minivans, plus BMW, Saab, and Volvo. The self-leveling shocks are entirely self-contained and do not require the use of height sensors or an external air pump.
● **SEE FIGURE 27–35.**

The shock looks like a conventional shock absorber but contains the following components:

• Two reservoirs in the outer tube
• An oil reservoir (low-pressure reservoir)
• A high-pressure chamber

Inside the piston rod is the pump chamber containing an inlet and an outlet valve. When a load is placed in the rear of the vehicle, it compresses the suspension and the shock absorber. When the vehicle starts to move, the internal pump is activated by the movement of the body. Extension of the piston rod causes oil to be drawn through the inlet valve into the pump. When the shock compresses, the oil is forced through the outlet valve into the high-pressure chamber. The pressure in the oil reserve decreases as the pressure in the high-pressure chamber increases. The increasing pressure is applied to the piston rod, which raises the height of the vehicle.

When the vehicle's normal height is reached, no oil is drawn into the chamber. Because the shock is mechanical, the vehicle needs to be moving before the pump starts to work. It requires about 2 miles of driving for the shock to reach the normal ride height. The vehicle also needs to be driven about 2 miles after a load has been removed from the vehicle for it to return to normal ride height.

To avoid compressor overheating, the timer within the suspension control module limits the compressor run time to 10 minutes. ● **SEE FIGURE 27–36.**

On RTD or RSS systems with a compressor, the scan tool may display DTCs associated with compressor relay operation. On some vehicle applications, the scan tool will display data relating to relay operation and can be used to command the relay to verify proper operation.

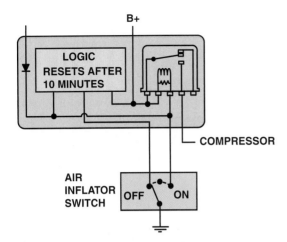

FIGURE 27–36 Schematic of the ALC system.

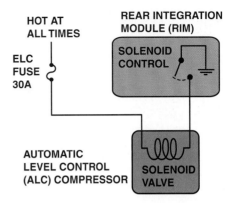

FIGURE 27–38 The exhaust solenoid is controlled by the rear integration module (RIM).

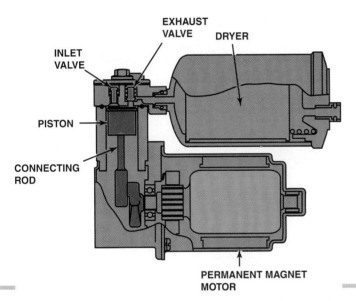

FIGURE 27–37 Air compressor assembly can be located at various locations depending on the vehicle.

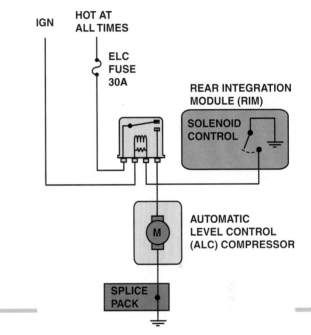

FIGURE 27–39 Schematic showing the rear integration module (RIM) and how it controls the ALC compressor.

COMPRESSOR The compressor is a positive-displacement air pump and can generate up to 150 lbs. of pressure per square inch (PSI). The compressor is found on the ALC, AS, RTD, and RSS systems. A 12-volt permanent magnet motor drives the compressor. The compressor supplies compressed air to the rear air shock absorbers or struts to raise the vehicle. ● **SEE FIGURE 27–37.**

AIR DRYER. Within the compressor is an air dryer. The air dryer is responsible for removing moisture from the compressor system. Improper air dryer operation can cause a premature failure in the system if an air line restriction occurs due to excessive moisture build-up. A dryer on the output side of the compressor contains silica gel **desiccant**, which removes moisture from the discharge air before it travels through the nylon air hoses to the air chamber of the rear shocks.

EXHAUST SOLENOID. The exhaust solenoid, which is located on the compressor, relieves pressure in the system. The ground-side switched exhaust solenoid has three main functions:

1. It releases compressed air from the shock absorbers or air springs to lower the vehicle body.

2. It relieves compressor head pressure. By exhausting air, it protects compressor start-up from high head pressure, which can possibly cause fuse failure.

3. The solenoid acts as a pressure relief valve, which limits overall system pressure.

The special functions on many scan tools can be used to command the solenoid and to verify its operation. ● **SEE FIGURES 27–38 AND 27–39.**

FIGURE 27–40 Vehicles that use magneto-rheological shock absorbers have a sensor located near each wheel, as shown on this C6 Corvette.

FIGURE 27–41 The controller for the magneto-rheological suspension system on a C6 Corvette is located behind the right front wheel.

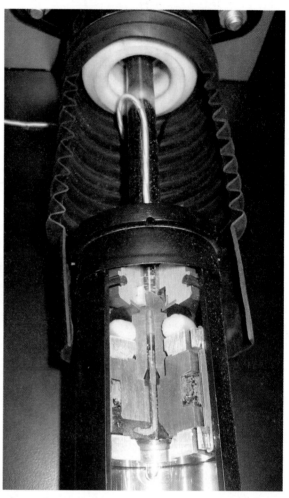

FIGURE 27–42 A cutaway of a magneto-rheological shock absorber as displayed at the Corvette Museum in Bowling Green, Kentucky.

MAGNETO-RHEOLOGICAL (MR) SUSPENSION

MR fluid shocks use a working fluid inside the shock that can change viscosity rapidly depending on electric current sent to an electromagnetic coil in each device. The fluid is called **magneto-rheological (MR)** and is used in monotube-type shock absorbers. This type of shock and suspension system is called the **magneto-rheological real-time damping (MRRTD)** or **chassis continuously variable real-time dampening magneto-rheological suspension (CCVRTMR)**.

Under normal operating conditions, the fluid flows easily through orifices in the shock and provides little dampening.

When a large or high-frequency bump is detected, a small electrical current is sent from the chassis controller to an electromagnetic coil in each shock and the iron particles in the fluid respond within 3 milliseconds (ms), aligning themselves in fiber-like strands. ● **SEE FIGURES 27–40 AND 27–41.**

This causes the MR fluid to become thick like peanut butter and increases the firmness of the shock. This type of shock absorber is used to control squat during acceleration and brake dive as well as to reduce body roll during cornering by the chassis controller. ● **SEE FIGURE 27–42.**

FREQUENTLY ASKED QUESTION

Can Computer-Controlled Shock Absorbers and Struts Be Replaced with Conventional Units?

Maybe. If the vehicle was manufactured with or without electronic or variable shock absorbers, it may be possible to replace the originals with the standard replacement units. The electrical connector must be disconnected, and this may cause the control system to store a diagnostic trouble code (DTC) and/or turn on a suspension fault warning light on the dash. Some service technicians have used a resistor equal in resistance value of the solenoid or motor across the terminals of the wiring connector to keep the controller from setting a DTC. All repairs to a suspension system should be done to restore the vehicle to like-new condition, so care should be exercised if replacing electronic shocks with nonelectronic versions.

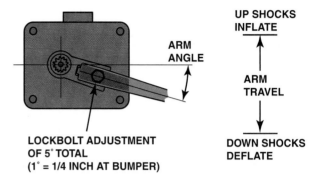

FIGURE 27–43 Most electronic level-control sensors can be adjusted, such as this General Motors unit.

TROUBLESHOOTING REAR ELECTRONIC LEVELING SYSTEMS

The first step with any troubleshooting procedure is to check for normal operation. Some leveling systems require that the ignition key be on (run), while other systems operate all the time. Begin troubleshooting by placing approximately 300 lb (135 kg) on the rear of the vehicle. If the compressor does not operate, check to see if the sensor is connected to a rear suspension member and that the electrical connections are not corroded.

Also check the condition of the compressor ground wire. It must be tight and free of rust and corrosion where it attaches to the vehicle body. If the compressor still does not run, check to see if 12 volts are available at the power lead to the compressor.

If necessary, use a fused jumper wire directly from the positive (+) of the battery to the power lead of the compressor. If the compressor does not operate, it must be replaced.

If the ride height compressor runs excessively, check the air compressor, the air lines, and the air shocks (or struts) with soapy water for air leaks. Most air shocks or air struts are not repairable and must be replaced. Most electronic leveling systems provide some adjustments of the rear ride height by adjusting the linkage between the height sensor and the rear suspension. ● **SEE FIGURE 27–43.**

SUMMARY

1. General Motors uses seven types of electronic suspension under many different names.
2. Suspension height sensors and steering wheel (handwheel) position sensors are used in many systems.
3. A vehicle speed sensor signal is used to control the suspension at various speeds.
4. Many electronic suspension systems use a lateral accelerometer sensor, which signals the suspension computer when the vehicle is rapidly accelerating, braking, or cornering.
5. Solenoids and motors are used to control the suspension movement by moving valves in the shock absorbers or air springs.
6. An air pump and air shocks are used to raise the rear of the vehicle to compensate for a heavy load.

1. What type of sensor is usually used on electronically controlled suspensions to sense the height of the vehicle?

2. Why is the vehicle speed sensor used as input for many electronic suspension systems?

3. What is a lateral accelerometer sensor and why is it used?

4. Why does the output side of the suspension air compressor contain a desiccant?

CHAPTER QUIZ

1. What type of sensor is used as a height sensor on vehicles equipped with an electronically controlled suspension?
   a. Hall-effect
   b. Photo cell
   c. Potentiometer
   d. All of the above

2. Which sensors do most vehicles use if equipped with electronic suspension?
   a. Height sensors
   b. Steering wheel position sensors
   c. Lateral accelerometer sensors
   d. All of the above

3. A lateral acceleration sensor is used to provide the suspension control module with feedback regarding _____ force.
   a. Cornering
   b. Acceleration
   c. Braking
   d. All of the above

4. A steering wheel position sensor is being discussed. Technician A says that the sensor is used to determine the direction the steering wheel is turned. Technician B says that the sensor detects how fast the steering wheel is turned. Which technician is correct?
   a. Technician A only
   b. Technician B only
   c. Both Technicians A and B
   d. Neither Technician A nor B

5. Technician A says that an electronic control module used in the suspension system is the same as that used for engine control. Technician B says that most electronically controlled suspension systems use a separate electronic control module. Which technician is correct?
   a. Technician A only
   b. Technician B only
   c. Both Technicians A and B
   d. Neither Technician A nor B

6. What type of actuator is used on electronically controlled suspensions?
   a. Solenoid
   b. Electric motor
   c. Either a or b
   d. Neither a nor b

7. Why is the typical rear load-leveling system connected to the ignition circuit?
   a. To keep the system active for a given time after the ignition is switched off
   b. To prevent the system from working unless the ignition key is on
   c. To keep the compressor from running for an extended period of time
   d. All of the above

8. Which sensor can be tested by unbolting the sensor and with the ignition on, engine off (KOEO), looking at the scan tool data?
   a. "G" sensor
   b. Wheel speed sensor
   c. Vehicle speed sensor
   d. Suspension sensor

9. The *firm* setting is usually selected by the electronic suspension control module whenever which of the following occurs?
   a. High speed
   b. Rapid braking
   c. Rapid acceleration
   d. All of the above

10. Which of the following is the *least likely* sensor to cause an electronic suspension fault?
    a. Yaw sensor
    b. Throttle position (TP) sensor
    c. Steering wheel position sensor
    d. Vehicle speed sensor

chapter 28
STEERING COLUMNS AND GEARS

OBJECTIVES

After studying Chapter 28, the reader will be able to:

1. Prepare for ASE Suspension and Steering (A4) certification test content area "A" (Steering System Diagnosis and Repair).
2. Discuss steering columns and intermediate shafts.
3. Explain how a recirculating ball-nut and worm gear steering gear system works.
4. Describe how a rack-and-pinion steering gear works.

KEY TERMS

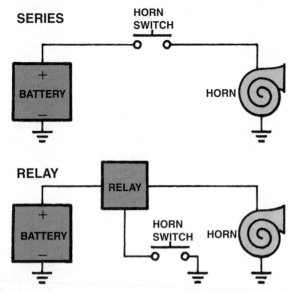

FIGURE 28–1 Most steering columns contain a horn switch. The horn button is a normally open (NO) switch. When the button is depressed, the switch closes, which allows electrical current to flow from the battery to sound the horn. Most horn circuits use a relay to conduct the horn current.

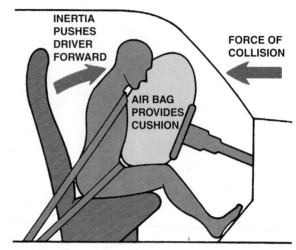

FIGURE 28–2 The airbag inflates at the same time the driver moves toward the steering wheel during a front-end collision and supplements the protection of the safety belt.

STEERING WHEELS

The steering wheel, which consists of a rigid rim and a number of spokes connecting the rim to a center hub, attaches to the top of the steering shaft at its center. Most steering wheel hubs have internal splines that fit over external splines on the steering shaft. A bolt or nut at the center of the hub secures the wheel to the shaft. The steering wheel may also contain controls for the cruise control and audio controls, as well as the driver's airbag.

HORN OPERATION The horn circuit is in a series circuit in which electricity has one path that it can follow when the circuit is complete. A normally open switch in an electrical circuit is inside the horn button. When the driver pushes the horn button, the contacts on the switch close, allowing electrical current through the circuit to operate the horn. ● **SEE FIGURE 28–1.** A relay circuit is a more common method of wiring the horn. In a relay, closing a switch in a low-current series circuit triggers the high-current circuit that powers the horn.

AIRBAGS An airbag is a device made of nylon cloth that is covered with neoprene. The airbag is folded and stored in the front center of the steering wheel. In a front-end collision, the airbag inflates in a fraction of a second to provide a cushion between the driver and the steering wheel and dashboard. ● **SEE FIGURE 28–2.** The part of the steering wheel where the airbag is stored is called the **inflator module.** The module also contains an igniter, a canister of flammable gas, and a number of sodium azide pellets. The sodium azide pellets burn quickly, and rapidly release nitrogen gas while they burn. The nitrogen gas fills the airbag. As it inflates, the airbag tears open the module cover and spreads out across the steering wheel, windshield, and dashboard. The entire process, from sensor reaction to full airbag deployment, takes 30 to 65 milliseconds. Within a second of inflating, the bag deflates partially as the nitrogen gas escapes through exhaust vents in the side of the airbag. Once deployed, an airbag cannot be reused.

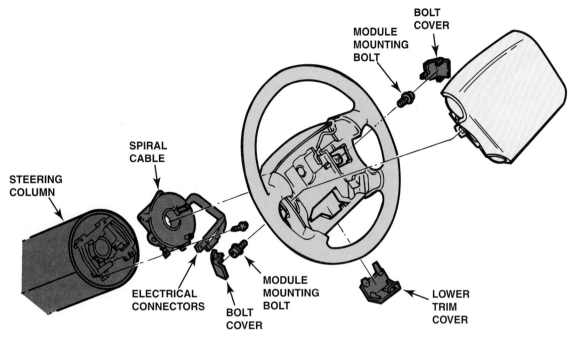

FIGURE 28–3 The airbag module attaches to the steering wheel and is removed as an assembly to service the steering wheel and column.

The module fits in front of the nut that secures the steering wheel to the steering shaft. Bolts at the back of the steering wheel fasten the airbag module to the steering wheel. Electrical current is provided to the airbag through the spiral cable, which is also known as a clockspring or coil. The spiral cable connects to the airbag module with two wire leads. The spiral cable is a tightly coiled metal strip that allows steering wheel rotation while maintaining electrical continuity. ● SEE FIGURE 28–3.

CAUTION: Whenever working on the steering column, consult service information for the recommended airbag disabling procedure.

STEERING COLUMNS

The steering shaft transmits rotary motion from the steering wheel to the steering gear, while the column jacket that encases it attaches to the vehicle body and offers a stationary mounting point for a number of switches and mechanisms. ● SEE FIGURE 28–4.

STEERING SHAFT The **steering shaft** extends from the steering wheel to the steering gear. A bolt or nut secures the shaft to the steering wheel, and a flexible coupling joins it to the steering gear input shaft. The coupling can be a simple rubber or fabric insert, a universal joint (U-joint), or a pot joint. In addition to allowing a directional change of the shaft, a pot joint permits a limited amount of plunging motion. ● SEE FIGURE 28–5.

UNIVERSAL JOINT A **universal joint,** or U-joint, consists of two yokes with a steel crosspiece joining them together. ● SEE FIGURE 28–6. Universal joints allow changes in the angle between two rotating shafts. In a steering shaft, U-joints allow rotary motion transfer between the steering wheel and the steering gear even though the steering shaft meets the steering gear input shaft at an angle. On some models the steering shaft itself is assembled in sections that are connected by U-joints.

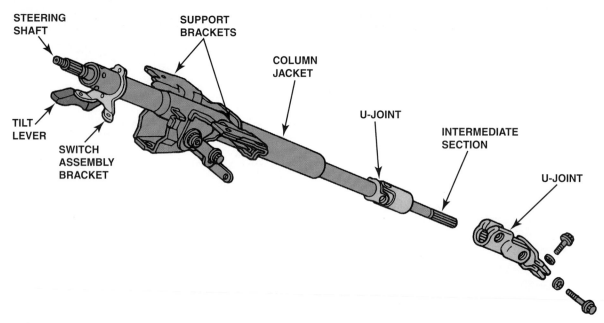

FIGURE 28–4 The steering shaft links the steering wheel to the steering gear while the column jacket, which surrounds part of the shaft, holds support brackets and switches. This steering shaft has a small intermediate section between the main section and the steering gear.

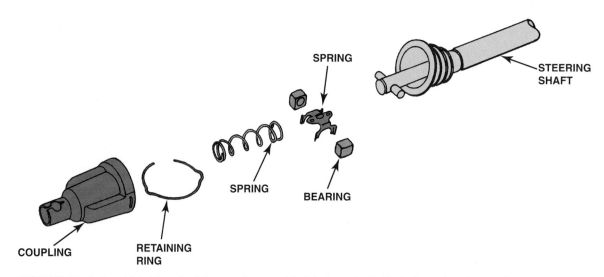

FIGURE 28–5 A pot joint is a flexible coupling used to join two shafts that allow plunging motion.

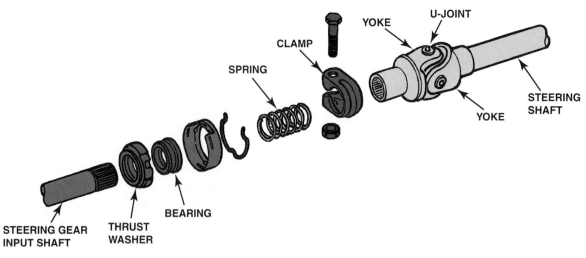

FIGURE 28–6 A typical intermediate steering shaft assembly showing a U-joint and related components.

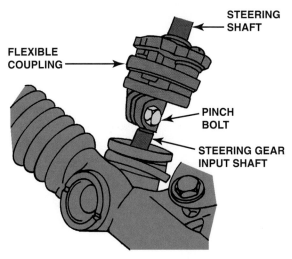

FIGURE 28-7 A flexible coupling is used to isolate road noise and vibration from the steering shaft.

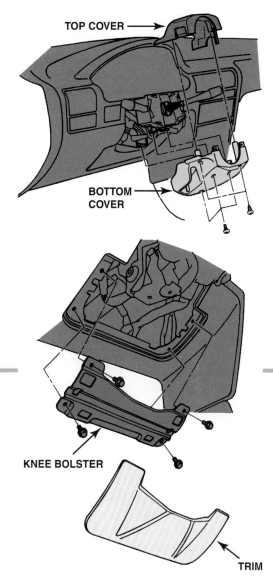

FIGURE 28-8 Steering column covers are often part of the interior trim.

STEERING COLUMNS (CONTINUED)

This permits the steering shaft to bend around obstacles between the steering wheel and the steering gear.

FLEXIBLE COUPLING A **flexible coupling** is a simple device made of rubber, or rubber reinforced with fabric, that is placed between two shafts to allow for a change in angle between them. ● **SEE FIGURE 28-7.** The rubber in a steering shaft flexible coupling absorbs vibrations and helps keep the steering wheel from shaking. A fail-safe connection between the steering shaft and the steering gear input shaft keeps the two shafts linked should the rubber coupling wear out or break. This allows the driver to maintain steering control, although the steering feels loose when this happens.

COLUMN COVER To keep the wiring from the jacket-mounted switches out of sight, the part of the steering column that extends into the passenger compartment is shrouded by the column cover. ● **SEE FIGURE 28-8.** The column cover is usually at least two separate pieces, top and bottom. A knee bolster that mounts under the steering column is a safety feature designed to keep the driver from sliding forward during a collision. Knee bolsters are part of the passive restraint system required to meet U.S. federal safety standards on certain vehicles.

COLLAPSIBLE COLUMN Federal law requires that all vehicles sold in the United States have steering columns and shafts that collapse, **collapsible columns,** during a head-on collision to absorb some of the energy of the crash and lessen the danger of injury to the driver. ● **SEE FIGURE 28-9.** One early method used a section of the steering column constructed out of mesh, which would collapse easily during a crash. Another method is to use a two-piece column. One section of the column has a smaller diameter so that it fits inside the other and rides on a roller bearing. During a collision, the smaller section slides down into the larger one to collapse like a telescope.

TILT MECHANISMS Many steering columns have tilt mechanisms, which allow the driver to adjust the angle of the steering wheel relative to the steering column. In a typical **tilt steering column,** the steering shaft has a short section at the top joined to the rest of the steering shaft either by a U-joint or gears. Most tilt mechanisms are some sort of ratchet device that

COLLAPSIBLE STEERING COLUMNS

MESH

BEARING

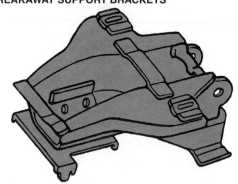

BREAKAWAY SUPPORT BRACKETS

FIGURE 28–9 Collapsible steering columns include a mesh design that crushes easily, a bearing design that allows one section of the column to slide into the other, and a breakaway device that separates the steering column from the body of the vehicle in the event of a front-end collision.

STEERING COLUMNS (CONTINUED)

TECH TIP

Do Not Pound on the Steering Column

Always use a steering wheel puller and/or the special tools recommended by the vehicle manufacturer when servicing the steering column. If a hammer is used on the steering shaft in an attempt to remove a steering wheel, the shaft could collapse, requiring the replacement of the entire steering column assembly.

enables the driver to lift the steering wheel and the top section of the shaft and place them in the desired position. ● **SEE FIGURE 28–10.** Usually, spring tension locks the steering wheel in place on the ratchet, and a release lever compresses the spring to allow tilt adjustment.

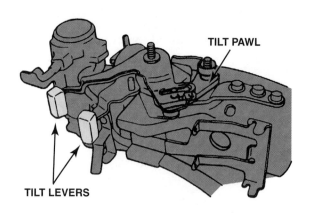

TILT PAWL

TILT LEVERS

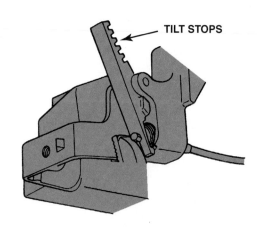

TILT STOPS

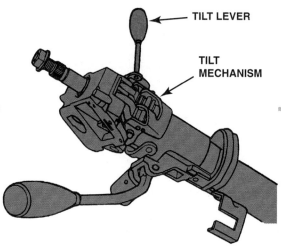

TILT LEVER

TILT MECHANISM

FIGURE 28–10 Tilt mechanisms vary by design and vehicle manufacturer, although most use a ratchet to position the top portion of the steering column.

TELESCOPING STEERING COLUMNS Some steering columns are designed to **telescope,** which means that the top of the steering shaft and jacket can be pulled out toward the driver or pushed in toward the dashboard, and then locked into the new position.

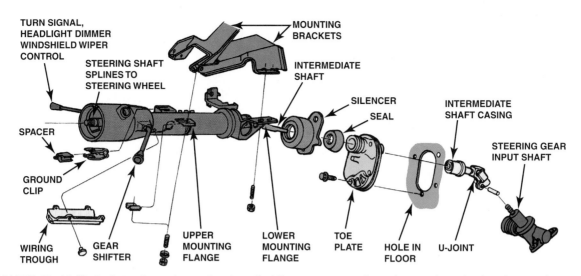

FIGURE 28–11 Typical steering column showing all of the components from the steering wheel to the steering gear.

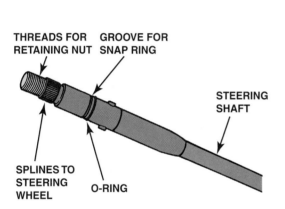

FIGURE 28–12 The steering shaft splines onto the steering wheel.

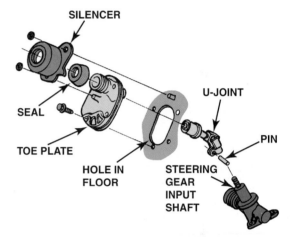

FIGURE 28–13 The toe plate seals the hole from the steering shaft and helps seal out noise and moisture.

STEERING COLUMN CONSTRUCTION The steering shaft is at the center of the steering column. ● **SEE FIGURES 28–11 AND 28–12.** The top end of the steering shaft splines to the center of the steering wheel, and a large nut fastens the steering wheel to the shaft. The lock housing, which contains the ignition lock cylinder, encases the top part of the steering shaft. The steering column jacket covers the shaft under the ignition lock housing, and the gear selector lever housing fits over a portion of the column jacket.

A U-joint connects the lower end of the steering shaft to a small intermediate shaft, often called a **stub shaft.** Because this steering column includes a gear selector lever, the lower end of the column also incorporates an attachment point that

connects the shift tube to the gear shift rod. The intermediate shaft extends through a hole in the floor where it is coupled to the steering gear input shaft by a U-joint.

A toe plate bolts to the floor of the passenger compartment to cover the shaft opening and to protect the interior from noise, drafts, and dirt. ● **SEE FIGURE 28–13.** The toe plate has a tube for the intermediate shaft, and a seal and silencer fit on top of the tube.

Two sections at the upper end of the steering column house the column-mounted controls. ● **SEE FIGURE 28–14.** The lock housing, seated on top of the column jacket, is the topmost piece and contains the turn signal lever, hazard light control, and ignition lock. The gear selector lever and its

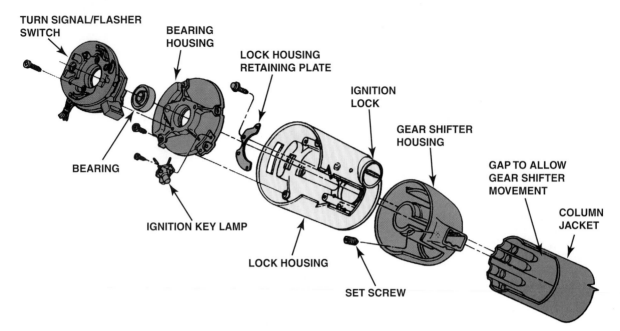

FIGURE 28–14 The upper section of the steering column includes the lock housing and switches.

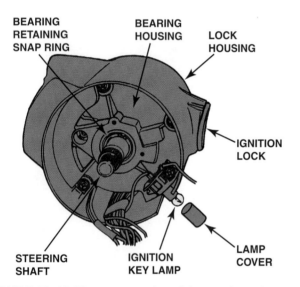

FIGURE 28–15 The upper section of the steering column contains the steering shaft bearing.

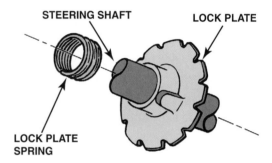

FIGURE 28–16 The lock plate engages an ignition lock pawl to keep the steering wheel in one position when the ignition is off.

STEERING COLUMNS (CONTINUED)

housing are just below the lock housing, and the housing encases the top of the steering column jacket.

The lock housing contains the ignition lock cylinder, several electrical switches, and a steering shaft bearing. Some of the switches have driver-operated controls on the outside of the lock housing.

A multifunction switch operates the turn signals, the windshield wiper and washer switch, and the dimmer switch.

Most steering shafts ride on at least two bearings, one near the top and one near the bottom of the shaft, to allow the shaft

to rotate freely without affecting other parts of the steering column. ● SEE FIGURE 28–15. A snap ring at the center of the bearing housing rests in a groove on the steering shaft to secure the bearing, and an O-ring on the steering shaft keeps lubricant in the bearing.

Underneath the bearing and housing is a **lock plate** and coil spring that lock the steering shaft into position when the driver removes the ignition key. ● SEE FIGURE 28–16. The ignition lock cylinder, which is under the lock plate, moves a bellcrank that in turn operates a spring and lever assembly linked to the ignition switch actuating rod.

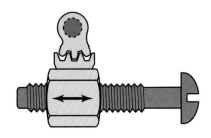

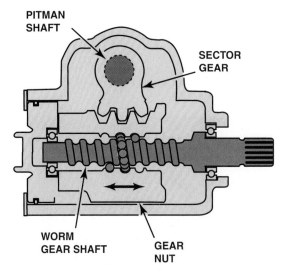

FIGURE 28–17 As the steering wheel is turned, the nut moves up or down on the threads, shown using a bolt to represent the worm gear and the nut representing the gear nut that meshes with the teeth of the sector gear.

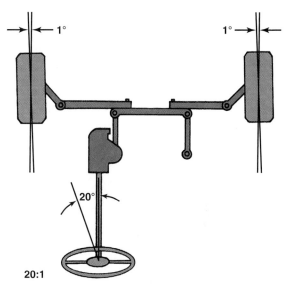

FIGURE 28–18 Steering gear ratio is the ratio between the number of degrees the steering wheel is rotated to the number of degrees the front wheel turns.

CONVENTIONAL STEERING GEARS

All steering gears have an input gear, which transmits rotary movement from the steering wheel into the steering gear, and an output gear, which causes the steering linkage to move laterally. The rotation of the steering wheel is transferred to the front wheels through a steering gear and linkage. The intermediate shaft is splined to a **worm gear** inside a conventional steering gear. Around the worm gear is a nut with gear teeth that meshes with the teeth on a section of a gear called a **sector gear.** The sector gear is part of a **pitman shaft,** also known as a **sector shaft,** as shown in ● **FIGURE 28–17.**

Ball, roller, or needle bearings support the sector shaft and the worm gear shaft, depending on the make and model of the gear assembly.

As the steering wheel is turned, the movement is transmitted through the steering gear to an arm attached to the bottom end of the pitman shaft. This arm is called the **pitman arm.** Whenever the steering wheel is turned, the pitman arm moves.

STEERING GEAR RATIO When the steering wheel is turned, the front wheels turn on their steering axis. If the steering wheel is rotated 20 degrees and results in the front wheels rotating 1 degree, then the steering gear ratio is 20:1 (read as "20 to 1"). ● **SEE FIGURE 28–18.** The front wheels usually are able to rotate through 60 to 80 degrees of rotation. The steering wheel, therefore, has to rotate 20 times the number of degrees that the wheels move.

20×60 degrees = 1,200 degrees, or about three full revolutions (360 degrees = 1 full turn) of the steering wheel

20×80 degrees = 1,600 degrees, or over four revolutions of the steering wheel

A vehicle that turns three complete revolutions from full left to full right is said to have three turns "lock to lock."

FIGURE 28–19 Constant-ratio steering gear sector shaft. Notice that all three gear teeth are the same size.

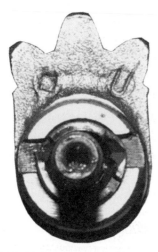

FIGURE 28–20 Variable-ratio steering gear sector shaft. Notice the larger center gear tooth.

FIGURE 28–21 The sector gear meshes with the gear teeth on the ball nut.

CONVENTIONAL STEERING GEARS (CONTINUED)

A high ratio, such as 22 to 1 (22:1), means that the steering wheel must be rotated 22 degrees to move the front wheels 1 degree. This high ratio means that the steering wheel is easier to turn than a steering wheel with a lower ratio such as 14:1. The 14:1 ratio is considered to be "faster" than the 22:1 ratio. This fast ratio allows the front wheels to be turned with less movement of the steering wheel, yet more force may be required to turn the wheel. This is considered by some to be more "sporty."

Most steering gears and some rack-and-pinion steering gears feature a **variable ratio.** This feature causes the steering ratio to decrease as the steering wheel is turned from the on-center position. The high on-center ratio (such as 16:1) provides good steering feel at highway speeds while the reduced off-center ratio (13:1) provides fewer steering wheel turns during turning and parking. The ratio is accomplished by changing the length of the gear teeth on the sector gear. ● **SEE FIGURE** 28–19 for an example of the teeth of a constant-ratio sector gear.

● **SEE FIGURE 28–20** for an example of the teeth on a variable-ratio sector gear.

The sector gear meshes with the ball nut inside the steering gear, as shown in ● **FIGURE 28–21.**

RECIRCULATING BALL STEERING GEAR

A recirculating ball steering gear is the most commonly used conventional steering gear. ● **SEE FIGURE 28–22.**

The end of the steering gear input shaft, or worm shaft, splines to the steering shaft U-joint and provides rotary input to the steering gear. An oil seal prevents fluid leakage where the input shaft enters the steering gear housing. At the top and the bottom of the worm gear are the upper and lower thrust bearings. The upper bearing cup seats in the housing, and the lower bearing cup seats in the adjuster plug. The thrust bearings reduce friction between the worm gear and the steering gear housing and control worm endplay.

The adjuster plug at the lower end of the worm gear holds the worm gear, shaft, and bearings inside the steering gear housing.

The ball nut, which has internal grooves that match the worm gear thread, fits over the worm gear. Steel balls roll through the tunnels formed by the ball nut grooves and the worm gear thread. Crescent-shaped ball-return guides link the ends of the ball-nut tunnels together, so the balls continuously circulate through the ball nut and worm gear, into the ball-return guides, and back again. A clamp secured by screws holds the return guides in place on one side of the ball nut. Gear teeth mesh with the teeth of the sector gear machined into the outside of the ball nut on the side opposite the ball-return guides.

The sector gear is an integral part of the sector shaft, which runs through the center of the sector gear, and forms the axis of the gear. One end of the sector shaft extends out of the steering gear housing and splines to the pitman arm. An oil seal prevents lubricant leakage where the sector shaft goes through the opening in the housing. To reduce friction, the sector shaft rides on two bushings. One bushing fits inside the housing and the other is part of the housing side cover. ● **SEE FIGURE 28–23.**

STEERING GEAR ADJUSTMENTS

For the steering gear to operate efficiently, the internal parts must be positioned correctly in relation to the housing and each other. As parts wear, clearances inside the housing and between parts increase, causing looseness and excessive play. The acceptable clearance between any two mechanical parts is called their tolerance. Insufficient tolerance causes binding between parts, increasing steering effort. Excessive tolerance causes delayed reaction to steering input and too much steering wheel freeplay.

Worm bearing preload, also referred to as worm endplay, is a measurement of how much force is required to turn the steering gear input shaft against the force, or **preload,** that the thrust bearings apply to the worm gear and shaft. Worm endplay, which is the distance the worm gear can move end-to-end between the thrust bearings, is directly related to preload. The higher the force the bearings push against the worm gear, the less endplay there is, and the more force it takes to turn the input shaft and worm gear. Worm bearing preload is adjusted by one of two methods: turning an adjustment nut or screw or installing selectively sized shims. Either adjustment method increases or decreases the worm endplay.

Worm endplay is a linear measurement, made in fractions of inches or millimeters, of how far the worm gear and shaft can slide axially. ● **SEE FIGURE 28–24.** Worm bearing preload is a measurement of how much force it takes to overcome bearing pressure in order to turn the input shaft. Preload is a torque, or turning force, measurement made in inch-pounds or Newton-meters. Because endplay and preload are related, one measurement affects the other. When measuring and adjusting the worm bearing preload, a technician measures preload and adjusts endplay. The endplay is correct when the preload measurement is correct. ● **SEE FIGURES 28–25 AND 28–26.**

Gear mesh preload is a measurement of how closely the teeth of the ball-nut gear and sector gear, or the worm gear and roller, fit together. Gear mesh preload is related to another measurement, called sector lash or **gear lash.**

Gear mesh preload is a measurement of how much turning force must be applied to the input shaft to overcome the resistance of the sector gear and move it. Gear mesh preload is usually measured in a 90-degree turn across the center of the input shaft movement. General Motors calls this adjustment the **overcenter adjustment.** Gear mesh preload (overcenter

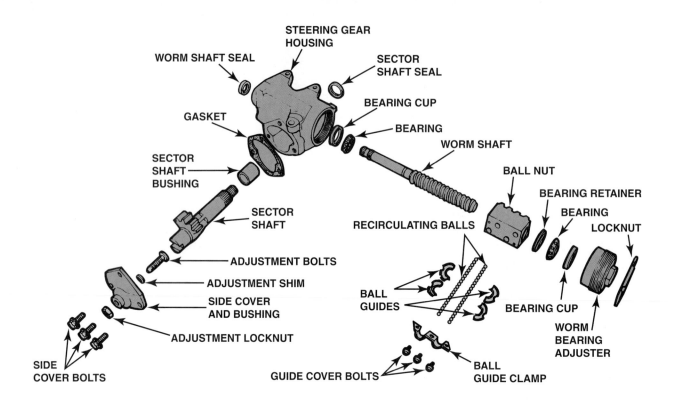

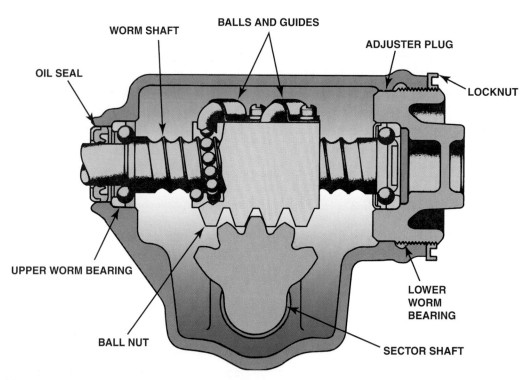

FIGURE 28–22 A typical manual recirculating ball steering gear.

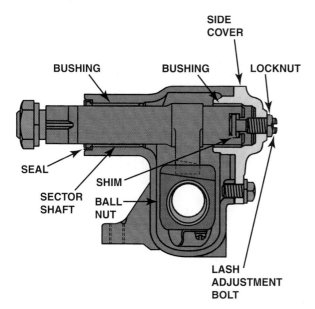

FIGURE 28-23 The sector shaft is supported by bushings, one in the housing and one in the side cover.

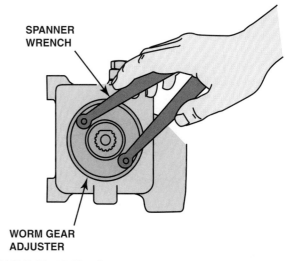

FIGURE 28-25 The first step to adjust worm gear freeplay is to bottom the worm gear nut, using a spanner wrench designed to fit into the two holes in the nut.

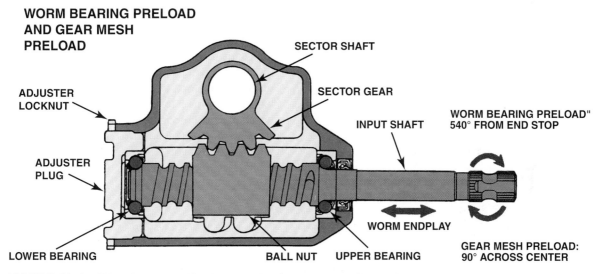

FIGURE 28-24 Worm bearing preload is a turning force measured in in.-lb or N-M, and worm endplay is axial movement measured in fractions of an inch or millimeters.

STEERING GEAR ADJUSTMENTS (CONTINUED)

adjustment) determines how sensitive the steering gear is to small steering wheel movements during straight-ahead driving. Insufficient preload contributes to steering wander.

If there is too much gear lash, the steering becomes unresponsive because the steering gear does not transmit small steering wheel movements to the linkage. Insufficient lash makes the gears bind, offering too much resistance to steering wheel movement. ● **SEE FIGURE 28-27.**

Sector shaft endplay is a measurement of how much room the sector shaft has to slide axially. ● **SEE FIGURE 28-28.** If provision is made to measure sector shaft endplay, the measurement is taken in fractions of inches or millimeters. Some steering gears provide an external adjusting method, but it is more common for sector shaft endplay to be adjusted by internal shims, if it is adjustable.

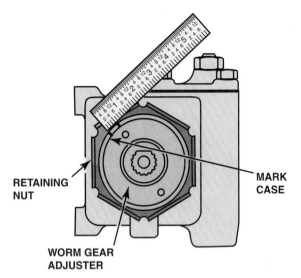

RETAINING
NUT

MARK
CASE

WORM GEAR
ADJUSTER

FIGURE 28–26 After the worm gear nut has been tightened, measure 1/2 inch (13 mm) and mark the case. Using the spanner wrench, rotate the worm gear nut counterclockwise 1/2 inch, align the marks, and then tighten the retaining nut. This procedure gives the proper worm gear endplay.

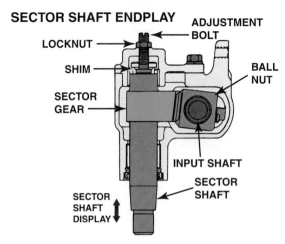

SECTOR SHAFT ENDPLAY

LOCKNUT

ADJUSTMENT
BOLT

SHIM

BALL
NUT

SECTOR
GEAR

INPUT SHAFT

SECTOR
SHAFT

SECTOR
SHAFT
DISPLAY

FIGURE 28–28 Sector shaft endplay is the measurement of how far the sector shaft can move axially and is measured in fractions of an inch or millimeters.

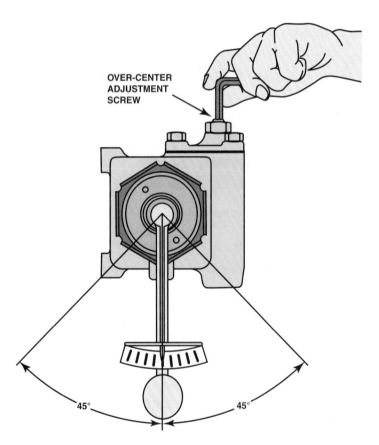

OVER-CENTER
ADJUSTMENT
SCREW

45°   45°

FIGURE 28–27 Performing an overcenter adjustment requires the use of a beam-type inch-lb torque wrench. After the worm bearing preload procedure has been completed, use the torque wrench to measure the rotating torque, which should be 6 to 15 lb-in. If the rotating torque is within the specified range, adjust the overcenter adjustment screw until you achieve 6 to 10 lb-in. more rotating torque and then tighten the retaining nut.

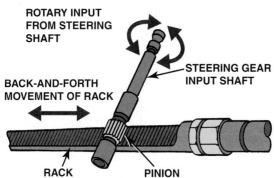

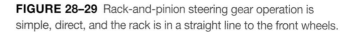

ROTARY INPUT
FROM STEERING
SHAFT

BACK-AND-FORTH
MOVEMENT OF RACK

STEERING GEAR
INPUT SHAFT

RACK   PINION

FIGURE 28–29 Rack-and-pinion steering gear operation is simple, direct, and the rack is in a straight line to the front wheels.

RACK-AND-PINION STEERING GEAR

PARTS AND OPERATION The term "rack and pinion" is simply a description of the basic design of this type of steering gear. The **rack-and-pinion** steering gear is widely used because it is light in weight and takes less space than a conventional steering gear. The input gear of a rack-and-pinion steering gear is a pinion gear that receives rotary input from the steering shaft. The rack is a rod with gear teeth machined into one side. The pinion gear teeth mesh with the teeth on the rack so that when the pinion gear turns, it pushes the rack from side to side. ● **SEE FIGURE 28–29.** The rack connects directly to the tie rod in the steering linkage to move the linkage back and forth in a straight line.

The steering gear input shaft is splined to the steering shaft U-joint. ● **SEE FIGURE 28–30.** At the end of the steering gear input shaft, which extends into the rack housing, is the pinion gear. Two ball bearings reduce friction between the shaft and the steering gear housing. The upper bearing is a press-fit on the input shaft, and the lower bearing installs inside the housing at the bottom of the pinion gear. A cover, which fits around the shaft and threads into the housing, seats on top of the upper ball bearing to preload it and close the top of the steering gear housing. An oil seal between the top cover and the input shaft keeps lubricant from leaking out of the housing. A lock nut holds the top cover in position.

The teeth of the pinion gear mesh with the teeth of the rack. The teeth are at one end of the rack and the pinion is offset at one side of the housing.

The rack is encased in the long, tubular steering gear housing with a mounting flange on the pinion end. Rubber bushings fit into the mounting flange bolt holes to absorb vibration and isolate the assembly from the frame.

A spring-loaded **rack support** and related hardware install through a hole at the back of the steering gear housing to position the rack. ● **SEE FIGURE 28–31.** The face of the rack support curves to match the back of the rack, which rests on it and

slides back and forth across it. A spring behind the rack support cushions the rack from vibration and shocks. While the rack support provides a sliding surface to reduce friction at the pinion end of the rack, the rack rides in a bushing pressed into the steering gear housing at the opposite end to reduce friction.

To adjust the rack-and-pinion gear preload, always check service information for the exact procedure to follow. The specified procedure usually includes these steps. ● **SEE FIGURE 28–32:**

1. Loosen the adjuster plug lock nut.

2. Turn the adjuster plug clockwise until the adjuster plug bottoms in the gear assembly.

3. Turn the adjuster plug back 50 degrees to 70 degrees (approximately one flat).

Most rack-and-pinion units use a small metal tube running along the outside of the housing to connect the two boots and transfer air from one to the other. ● **SEE FIGURE 28–33.** If there were no means for air displacement between the boots, they might collapse as they expanded or explode as they compressed.

Internal threads on each end of the rack allow attachment of the externally threaded tie rods.

A rubber boot at each side of the steering gear housing covers the end of the rack and the inner tie rod end to prevent dirt, water, and other contaminants from entering the assembly. Band clamps fasten the ends of the boots to the housing and tie rods. The tie rods move back and forth with the rack and connect it to the wheels through the steering linkage.

The housing generally bolts to either a flange on the firewall or to the subframe or engine cradle. ● **SEE FIGURE 28–34.** The mounting points have rubber cushions to isolate the steering gear from shock and vibration. If the driver can feel vibration and road shocks through the steering wheel, the condition is called **kickback.** Kickback is most noticeable when driving into a curbed driveway.

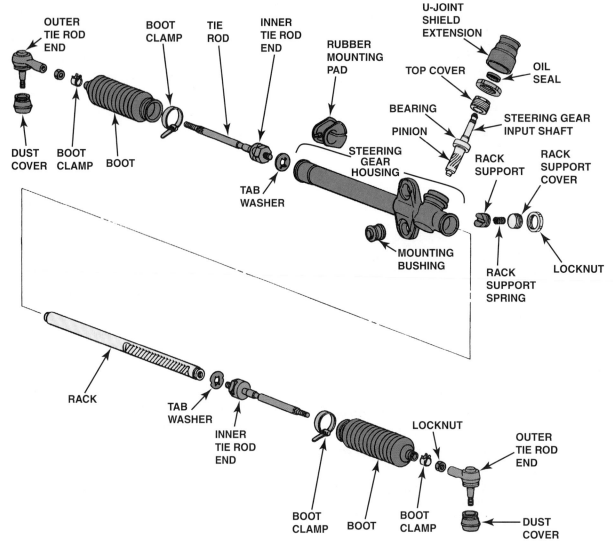

FIGURE 28–30 A typical manual rack-and-pinion steering gear used in a small front-wheel-drive vehicle.

FIGURE 28–31 The spring-loaded rack support positions the rack to keep it from rubbing against the housing and establishes the pinion torque.

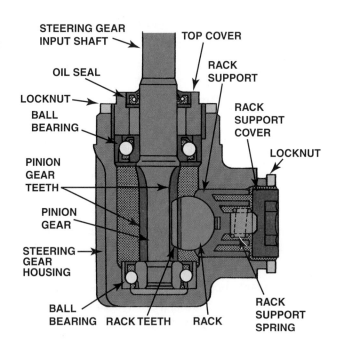

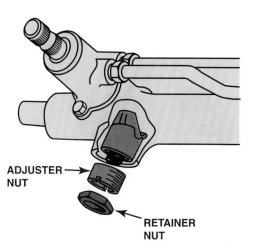

ADJUSTER
NUT

RETAINER
NUT

FIGURE 28-32 To adjust the rack-and-pinion gear preload, loosen the retaining nut and tighten the adjuster nut until it bottoms. Then loosen 60 degrees (one "flat" of the six-sided retainer). Tighten retaining nut.

AIR TUBE

RACK-AND-PINION
STEERING
GEAR ASSEMBLY

FIGURE 28-33 A small air tube is used to transfer air between the boots as they extend and compress during turns.

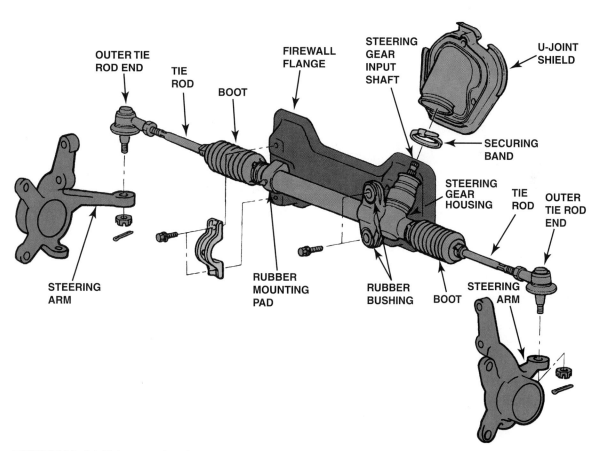

OUTER TIE
ROD END

TIE
ROD

BOOT

FIREWALL
FLANGE

STEERING
GEAR
INPUT
SHAFT

U-JOINT
SHIELD

SECURING
BAND

STEERING
GEAR
HOUSING

TIE
ROD

OUTER
TIE ROD
END

STEERING
ARM

RUBBER
MOUNTING
PAD

RUBBER
BUSHING

BOOT

STEERING
ARM

FIGURE 28-34 This manual rack-and-pinion steering gear mounts to the bulkhead (firewall), whereas others mount to the engine cradle or frame of the vehicle.

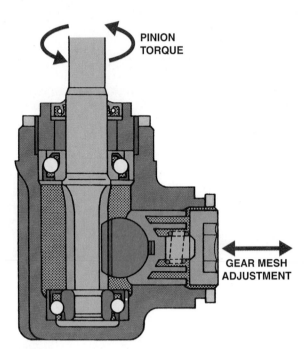

FIGURE 28–35 Pinion torque is a turning torque force measured in inch-pounds or Newton-meters. Tightening the rack support against the rack increases the pinion torque.

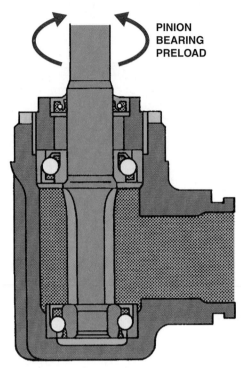

FIGURE 28–36 Pinion bearing preload is a measurement of the turning force required to overcome the resistance of the pinion shaft bearings.

RACK-AND-PINION ADJUSTMENTS

Some rack-and-pinion steering gears can be adjusted. **Pinion torque** is a measurement of how much turning force is needed at the input shaft for the pinion to overcome the resistance of the rack and move it. ● **SEE FIGURE 28–35.** The measurement gives an indication of how closely meshed the pinion teeth and the rack teeth are. Like gear mesh preload in a standard steering gear, pinion torque indicates steering system responsiveness. The adjustment method is to thread the rack support cover farther into the steering gear housing to reduce gear lash, or thread it out to increase gear lash. Manufacturers specify an acceptable range of pinion torque in inch-pounds or Newton-meters. Because the middle teeth on the rack wear before the teeth at either end, pinion torque should be checked across the whole stroke of the rack. Otherwise, reducing gear lash to a very close tolerance in the middle may cause binding as the pinion travels toward the end of the rack.

Pinion bearing preload in a rack-and-pinion steering gear is the same concept as worm bearing preload in a standard steering gear. That is, it is a measurement of how much force is required to turn the steering gear input shaft against the force, or preload, that the bearings apply to the pinion gear and shaft. ● **SEE FIGURE 28–36.** To provide adjustable pinion bearing preload, there may be a threaded adjustment mechanism or selectively sized shims that install behind a shim cover.

To set pinion bearing preload, the rack may need to be removed or loosened to prevent false readings caused by the resistance of the gears. Therefore, pinion bearing preload, when adjustable, must be set before pinion torque is measured and adjusted. Always check service information for the exact procedures to follow when servicing a rack and pinion steering gear assembly.

1. Most horn circuits use a relay. The horn button or contact on the steering wheel completes the control circuit of the relay, which then completes the power circuit to the horn(s).

2. The driver's side airbag uses a clockspring spiral cable in the steering column electronically connecting the airbag inflator module.

3. The steering column, which connects the steering wheel to the steering gear, includes the steering shaft universal joint and flexible coupling.

4. Conventional steering gears consist of an input gear and output gear, also called the sector gear.

5. Steering gear ratio is the number of degrees the steering wheel is rotated compared to the number of degrees the front wheels are rotated. Most steering gears provide a ratio of between 14:1 and 22:1.

6. A recirculating-ball-type steering gear is the most commonly used conventional steering gear.

7. A rack-and-pinion steering gear ties the two tie rods together in a straight line.

REVIEW QUESTIONS

1. What components are included in a typical steering column assembly?

2. When the driver turns the steering wheel, how is the motion transferred to the front wheels through a conventional steering gear?

3. Why are recirculating balls used in the recirculating ball steering gear?

4. What steering gear adjustments are possible on a conventional recirculating-ball-type steering gear?

5. What steering gear adjustments are possible on a typical rack-and-pinion steering gear?

CHAPTER QUIZ

1. The circuit to the airbag inflation module is connected from the steering column to the steering wheel through what component?
   a. Slip ring and carbon brushes
   b. Clockspring (coil)
   c. Magnetic field sensor
   d. Hall-effect switch

2. Which part in the steering column allows for changes in the angle between the upper and lower shafts?
   a. Flexible coupling
   b. Column cover
   c. Universal joint
   d. Collapsible section

3. The rotation of the steering wheel causes which part to move the actual steering linkage in a conventional steering gear?
   a. Sector shaft
   b. Pitman arm
   c. Worm gear
   d. Gear nut

4. The pitman shaft is also called the _____.
   a. Sector
   b. Input
   c. Worm
   d. Spline

5. The driver rotates the steering wheel one-half of one revolution (180 degrees) on a vehicle equipped with a steering gear with a 20:1 gear ratio. How many degrees will the front wheels be rotated?
   a. 9 degrees
   b. 0.1 degree
   c. 90 degrees
   d. 11.1 degrees

6. What causes a variable-ratio steering gear to be able to change the ratio as the steering wheel is turned?
   a. Using two or three different sector gears depending on design
   b. Using a variable-length pitman arm
   c. Changing the number of teeth on the worm gear
   d. Changing the length of the teeth on the sector gear

7. Recirculating steel balls are used in most conventional steering gears because they _____.
   a. Provide for a variable ratio
   b. Keep the steering wheel centered
   c. Reduce friction
   d. Help provide feedback to the driver regarding the road surface

8. Which conventional steering gear adjustment should be the first performed?
   a. Worm bearing preload
   b. Tolerance adjustment
   c. Gear mesh preload
   d. Sector shaft endplay

9. The two rack-and-pinion steering gear adjustments include _____.
   a. Worm bearing preload and tolerance adjustment
   b. Pinion bearing preload and rack support
   c. Sector shaft and stub shaft preload
   d. Stub shaft endplay and sector shaft preload

10. A driver of a vehicle equipped with a rack-and-pinion steering gear complains that the steering wheel jerks whenever the vehicle is being driven into a curbed driveway approach at an angle. Technician A says that the rack-and-pinion gears may have too little clearance between the teeth of the gears. Technician B says that a lack of lubrication of the rack-and-pinion is the most likely cause. Which technician is correct?
   a. Technician A only
   b. Technician B only
   c. Both Technicians A and B
   d. Neither Technician A nor B

STEERING LINKAGE AND SERVICE

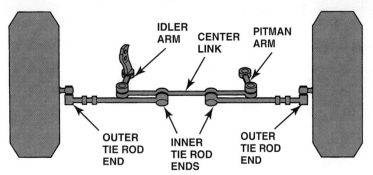

FIGURE 29–1 Steering movement is transferred from the pitman arm that is splined to the sector shaft (pitman shaft), through the center link and tie rods, to the steering knuckle at each front wheel. The idler arm supports the passenger side of the center link and keeps the steering linkage level with the road. This type of linkage is called a parallelogram-type design.

 FREQUENTLY ASKED QUESTION

Why Is a Grease Fitting Sometimes Called a Zerk Fitting?

In 1922 the *zerk* fitting was developed by Oscar U. Zerk, an employee of the Alemite Corporation, a manufacturer of pressure lubrication equipment. A zerk or grease fitting is also known as an *Alemite fitting*.

STEERING LINKAGE

The steering linkage relays steering forces from the steering gear to the front wheels. Most conventional steering linkages use the **parallelogram**-type design. A parallelogram is a geometric box shape where opposite sides are parallel and equal distance. A parallelogram-type linkage uses four **tie rods,** two inner and two outer (left and right), a **center link** (between the tie rods), and an idler arm on the passenger side and a **pitman arm** attached to the steering gear output shaft (pitman shaft). ● SEE FIGURE 29–1.

As the steering wheel is rotated, the pitman arm is moved. The pitman arm attaches to a center link. At either end of the center link are inboard (inner) tie rods, adjusting sleeves, and outboard (outer) tie rods connected to the steering arm, which moves the front wheels. The passenger side of all these parts is supported and held horizontal by an idler arm that is bolted to the frame. The center link may be known by several names, including the following:

- Center link
- Connecting link
- Connecting rod
- Relay rod
- Intermediate rod
- Drag link (usually a truck term only)

Other types of steering linkages often used on light trucks and vans include the **cross-steer linkage.** ● SEE FIGURE 29–2 for a comparison of parallelogram and cross-steer-type steering linkage arrangements.

NOTE: Many light trucks, vans, and some luxury cars use a steering dampener attached to the linkage. A steering dampener is similar to a shock absorber, and it absorbs and dampens sudden motions in the steering linkage. ● **SEE FIGURE 29–3.**

Connections between all steering component parts are constructed of small ball-and-socket joints. These joints allow side-to-side movement to provide steering of both front wheels, and allow the joints to move up and down, which is required for normal suspension travel.

It is important that all of these joints be lubricated with chassis grease through a **grease fitting,** also called a **zerk fitting,** at least every six months or per the vehicle manufacturer's specifications.

Some vehicles come equipped with sealed joints and do not require periodic servicing. Some vehicles come from the factory with plugs that need to be removed and replaced with grease fittings and then lubricated.

PARALLELOGRAM STEERING LINKAGE

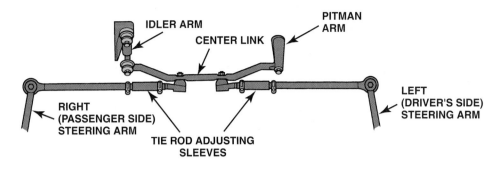

IDLER ARM

PITMAN ARM

CENTER LINK

RIGHT (PASSENGER SIDE) STEERING ARM

LEFT (DRIVER'S SIDE) STEERING ARM

TIE ROD ADJUSTING SLEEVES

CROSS-STEER LINKAGE

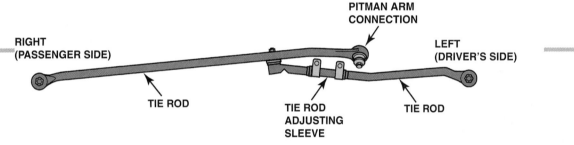

DRAG LINK

PITMAN ARM

RIGHT (PASSENGER SIDE) STEERING ARM

LEFT (DRIVER'S SIDE) STEERING ARM

TIE ROD

HALTENBERGER LINKAGE

RIGHT (PASSENGER SIDE)

PITMAN ARM CONNECTION

LEFT (DRIVER'S SIDE)

TIE ROD

TIE ROD ADJUSTING SLEEVE

TIE ROD

FIGURE 29–2 The most common type of steering is the parallelogram. The cross-steer and Haltenberger linkage designs are used on some trucks and vans.

FIGURE 29–3 Typical steering dampener used on a Hummer H2.

TIE ROD ENDS Tie rod ends connect the steering linkage to the steering knuckles and to other steering linkage components. Conventional tie rod ends use a hardened steel ball stud assembled into a hardened steel and thermoplastic bearing. An internal preload spring limits the ball stud endplay and helps compensate for ball-and-socket wear. ● **SEE FIGURE 29–4** for two designs of tie rod ends.

For many years, Ford Motor Company used tie rod ends that included a rubber-bonded steel ball stud. Because there is no sliding friction inside the tie rod end, no lubrication was needed. This type of tie rod end is called **RBS (rubber-bonded socket)**. ● **SEE FIGURE 29–5.**

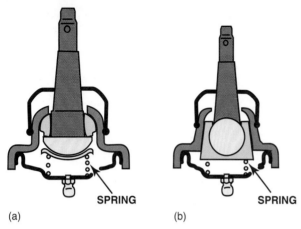

FIGURE 29–4 (a) A dual bearing design with a preload spring. The use of two bearing surfaces allows for one surface for rotation (for steering) and another surface for pivoting (to allow for suspension up-and-down movement). (b) The nylon wedge bearing type allows for extended lube intervals. Wear is automatically compensated for by the tapered design and spring-loaded bearing.

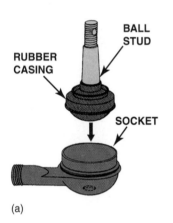

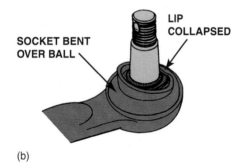

FIGURE 29–5 (a) A rubber-bonded socket is constructed of a rubber casing surrounding the ball stud, which is then inserted into the socket of the tie rod end. The hole in the socket allows air to escape as the ball stud is installed and there is not a place for a grease fitting. (b) The socket is crimped over the ball so that part of the socket lip retains the stud.

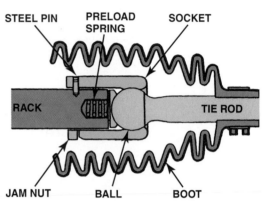

FIGURE 29–6 Rack-and-pinion steering systems use a ball-and-socket-type inner tie rod end.

RACK-AND-PINION INNER TIE ROD ENDS

Inner tie rod end assemblies used on rack-and-pinion steering units require special consideration and often special tools. The inner tie rod end is also called a **ball socket assembly.**

The inner tie rod assemblies are attached to the end of the steering rack by one of several methods. ● **SEE FIGURE 29–6.**

STAKED This method is common on Saginaw-style rack-and-pinion steering units found on General Motors vehicles.

The flange around the outer tie rod must be restaked to the flat on the end of the rack.

RIVETED OR PINNED This method is commonly found on Ford vehicles. Some roll pins require a special puller, or the pin can be drilled out. Many styles use an aluminum rivet. A special, very deep socket or a large open-end wrench can usually be used to shear the aluminum rivet by unscrewing the socket assembly from the end of the rack while the rack-and-pinion unit is still in the vehicle. ● **SEE FIGURE 29–7.**

CENTER TAKE-OFF RACKS For the **center take-off racks,** use bolts to secure the inner tie rods to the rack, as shown in ● **FIGURE 29–8.**

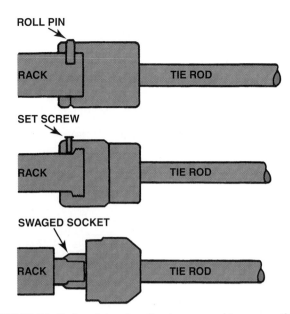

FIGURE 29–7 A variety of methods are used to secure the inner tie rod end socket assembly to the end of the rack.

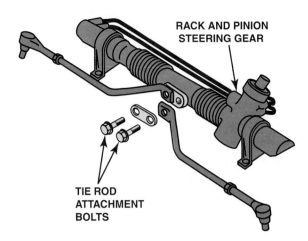

FIGURE 29–8 Exploded view of a center-take-off-style rack-and-pinion steering gear assembly.

FRONT STEER VERSUS REAR STEER

Front steer, also called *forward steer*, is the term used to describe a vehicle that has the steering gear in front of the front wheel centerline. Having the steering gear located in this position improves handling and directional stability, especially when the vehicle is heavily loaded.

Front-steer vehicles usually produce an understeer effect that makes the vehicle feel very stable while cornering. If the steering gear linkage is located behind the wheels, it is called **rear steer** and the cornering forces are imposed on the steering in the direction of the turn. This is an oversteer effect. It tends to make the steering easier and makes the vehicle feel less stable.

Most front-wheel-drive vehicles are rear steering, with the rack-and-pinion steering unit attached to the bulkhead or subframe behind the engine. ● **SEE FIGURE 29–9.**

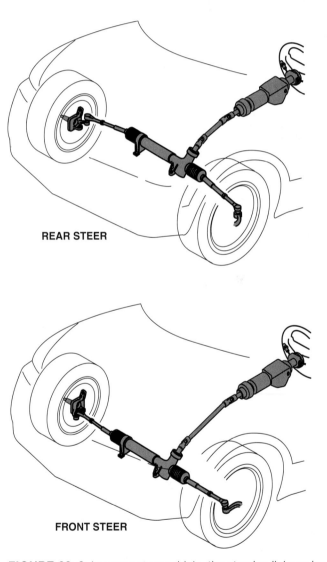

FIGURE 29–9 In a rear-steer vehicle, the steering linkage is behind the centerline of the front wheels, whereas the linkage is in front on a front-steer vehicle.

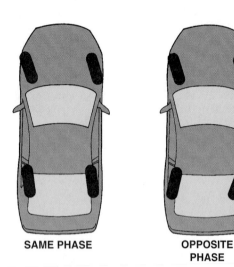

SAME PHASE **OPPOSITE PHASE**

FIGURE 29–10 Opposite-phase four-wheel steer is usually used only at low vehicle speed to help in parking maneuvers. Sample-phase steering helps at higher speeds and may not be noticeable by the average driver.

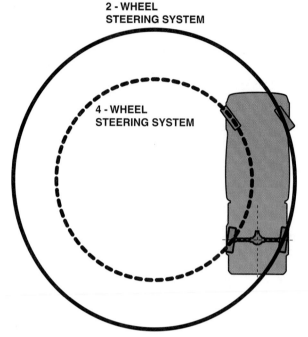

FIGURE 29–11 Being equipped with four-wheel steer allows a truck to make shorter turns than would otherwise be possible.

FOUR-WHEEL STEERING SYSTEMS

Some vehicles were equipped with a system that steers all four wheels. Two terms are commonly used when discussing four-wheel steering:

1. **Same-phase steering.** Same-phase steering means that the front and rear wheels are steered in the same direction. Same-phase steering improves steering response, especially during rapid-lane-change-type maneuvers.

2. **Opposite-phase steering.** Also called *negative-phase mode*, opposite-phase steering is when the front wheels and rear wheels are steered in the opposite direction. ● **SEE FIGURE 29–10.** Opposite-phase steering will quickly change the vehicle's direction, but may cause a feeling of oversteering.

Opposite-phase steering is best at low speeds; same-phase steering is best for higher-speed handling and lane-change maneuvers.

QUADRASTEER Quadrasteer™ is a four-wheel steering system that dramatically enhances low-speed maneuverability, high-speed stability, and towing capability. ● **SEE FIGURE 29–11.**

The system is an electrically powered rear wheel steering system comprised of the following components:

- A steerable, solid rear axle
- A heavy-duty wiring harness and fuse
- A programmable control module
- A power relay in the control module
- A rack-and-pinion-style steering actuator mounted on the rear differential cover
- An electric motor assembly on top of the rear steering actuator
- Three Hall-effect switches in the motor assembly
- A shorting relay in the motor assembly
- A rear wheel position sensor located under a cover on the bottom of the actuator, below the motor assembly
- A steering wheel position sensor located at the base of the steering column
- A mode select switch on the dash

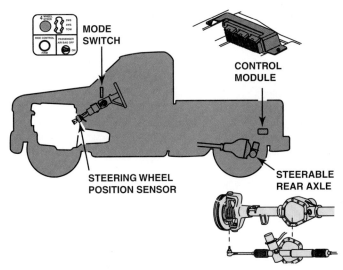

FIGURE 29-12 The Quadrasteer system includes many components that all work together.

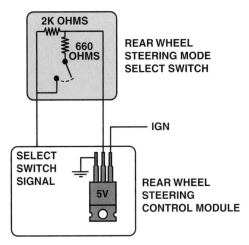

FIGURE 29-13 Rear steer select switch schematic.

● **SEE FIGURE 29–12** for an overall view of the components of the Quadrasteer system.

The rear wheel steering control module has the following inputs:

- Battery voltage
- Switched battery voltage
- Class 2 serial data
- Steering wheel position sensor analog signal, via class 2 message from the body control module (BCM)
- Steering wheel position sensor phase A
- Steering wheel position sensor phase B
- Steering wheel position sensor marker pulse
- Rear wheel position sensor position 1
- Rear wheel position sensor position 2
- Rear wheel steering motor Hall sensor A
- Rear wheel steering motor Hall sensor B
- Rear wheel steering motor Hall sensor C
- Vehicle speed signal from the instrument panel cluster (IPC)
- Rear wheel steering mode switch signal

● **SEE FIGURE 29–13.**

The system operates in three principal modes, as follows:

- **Two-wheel steer mode.** Normal steering operation—the rear wheels are held in a centered position and rear wheel steering is disabled while in this mode.

- **Four-wheel steer mode.** The four-wheel steering mode provides three principal phases of steering: negative phase, neutral phase, and positive phase. Negative phase occurs at low speeds and the rear wheels turn opposite of the front wheels. In the neutral phase, the rear wheels are centered and do not turn. Positive phase occurs at higher speeds and the rear wheels turn in the same direction as the front wheels.

- **Four-wheel steer tow mode.** The four-wheel steer tow mode provides more positive-phase steering than the normal four-wheel steering at high speed. During low-speed driving, the four-wheel steer tow mode provides similar negative-phase steering as it does in the normal four-wheel steering mode.

REAR WHEEL STEERING CONTROL MODULE The rear wheel steering control module controls all functions of the

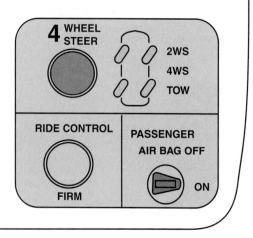

FIGURE 29–14 The dash-mounted select switch showing the three positions for the four-wheel steer system.

FOUR-WHEEL STEERING SYSTEMS (CONTINUED)

rear wheel steering system. The module has a dedicated power feed line from an underhood fuse holder, via a 125-amp mega fuse. The module is located in the rear of the vehicle on the underbody. The module uses the inputs listed earlier to determine when and how far to turn the rear wheels. The module uses the Hall switches in the motor assembly, a shorting relay, and a motor control relay to monitor and control the direction and speed of the motor. The module also controls the duty cycle of the phase leads to the motor. The motor control relay is part of the rear wheel steering control module and is not serviceable.

The control module allows the vehicle rear wheels to turn a maximum of 12 degrees left or right. When the vehicle is operated in reverse, the maximum rear wheel steering angle is 5 degrees left or right. When the vehicle is sitting still in the test mode, the system will move a maximum of 5 degrees left or right.

REAR WHEEL STEERING MODE SWITCH The mode switch located in the instrument panel allows the driver the option of selecting two-wheel steering, four-wheel steering, or four-wheel steering tow modes of operation. The mode switch has indicators that show which mode the rear wheel steering system is in. When all indicators are lit the rear wheel steering control module has lost its memory settings and the scan tool must be used to recalibrate the rear wheel steering control module. During a mode change, the indicator for the selected mode will flash until the mode change is complete. The rear wheel steering control module will wait for the steering wheel to pass the center position before entering the selected mode. The indicators on the mode switch are LEDs; the switch is also back lit. ● **SEE FIGURE 29–14.**

REAR WHEEL STEERING MOTOR ASSEMBLY. The rear wheel steering motor assembly is a three-phase, six-pole, brushless

DC motor. The motor assembly is located on the top of the rear steering actuator, and transmits its power through a planetary gearset inside the actuator. There are three Hall switches inside the assembly: Hall A, Hall B, and Hall C. The rear wheel steering control modules uses the Hall switch inputs to monitor the position, speed, and direction of the motor.

STEERING WHEEL POSITION SENSOR. The **steering wheel position sensor (SWPS)** provides one analog signal and three digital signals. The digital signals—Phase A, Phase B, and marker pulse—are direct inputs to the rear wheel steering control module. The analog signal is input to the body control module (BCM) and is sent via a class 2 message to the rear wheel steering control module. Battery voltage is supplied to the sensor from the cruise fuse to operate the digital portion of the sensor. A 12-volt reference is provided by the rear wheel steering control module to the Phase A, Phase B, and marker pulse circuits of the SWPS. The module monitors each circuit as it remains high or is pulled low by the SWPS. The scan tool displays the Phase A and Phase B data parameters as either high or low when the steering wheel is being rotated. Each change from high to low, or low to high, represents 1 degree of steering wheel rotation. When observing with the scan tool, the parameters for Phase A and Phase B will not always display the same value at the same time. The marker pulse is a digital pulse signal that is displayed as high by the scan tool with the steering wheel angle between +10 degrees and −10 degrees. At greater than 10 degrees steering wheel angle in either direction, the marker pulse data will be displayed as low. The BCM provides the 5-volt reference and low reference for the analog portion of the SWPS. The BCM reads the SWPS analog signal in voltage, which is typically 2.5 volts with the steering wheel on center. The

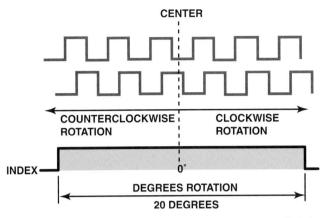

FIGURE 29–15 The output of the handwheel sensor digital signal.

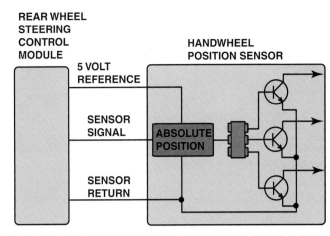

FIGURE 29–17 Handwheel position sensor analog signal to control module.

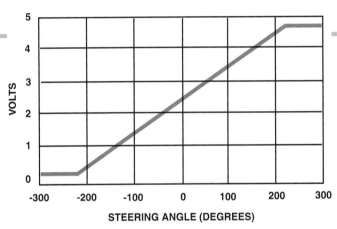

FIGURE 29–16 Handwheel analog signal.

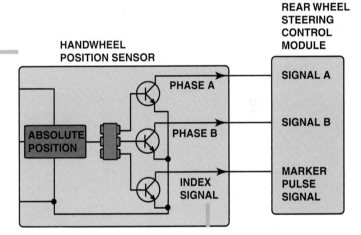

FIGURE 29–18 Handwheel position sensor digital signal to control module.

voltage ranges from 0.25 volts at approximately one full turn left to 4.75 volts at approximately one full turn right. The voltage will then remain at that level for the remainder of steering wheel travel. This voltage can be monitored in BCM data display on a scan tool. The sensor may also be utilized by other optional systems. ● SEE FIGURES 29–15 THROUGH 29–18.

REAR WHEEL POSITION SENSOR. The rear wheel position sensor has two signal circuits: position 1 and position 2. Position 1 is a linear measurement of voltage per degree. The voltage range for position 1 is from 0.25 to 4.75 volts, and the angular measurement range is from −620 degrees to +620 degrees. At 0.25 volts the steering wheel has been rotated −600 degrees past center. At 4.75 volts the steering wheel has been rotated +600 degrees past center. The position 2 circuit is a linear measurement of voltage per degree. The voltage for position 2 increases or decreases from 0.25 to 4.75 volts every 180 degrees. When the steering

wheel is 0 degrees center, the position 1 and position 2 output signals each measure 2.5 volts.

STEERABLE REAR AXLE. The steerable rear axle has a rack-and-pinion-style actuator mounted to the differential cover, specially designed axle shafts, and movable hub and bearing assemblies mounted by upper and lower ball joints. The actuator housing is part of the differential cover. In the event of a system malfunction, the actuator returns the rear wheels to the center position through internal springs. The actuator has specially designed inner and outer tie rod ends. There are inner tie rod boots to prevent contaminants from entering the actuator. The actuator has the rear wheel steering motor assembly attached to the upper housing. There are shields and a skid plate on the rear axle to protect the actuator. There are no internal adjustments to the actuator. ● SEE FIGURE 29–19.

FIGURE 29–19 A Quadrasteer system showing all of the components. The motor used to power the rear steering rack can draw close to 60 amperes during a hard turn and can be monitored using a Tech 2.

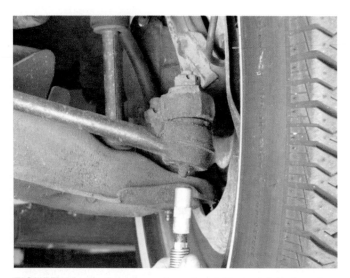

FIGURE 29–20 Greasing a tie rod end. Some joints do not have a hole for excessive grease to escape, and excessive grease can destroy the seal.

? FREQUENTLY ASKED QUESTION

What Is "Goofy Mode"?

Trucks that are equipped with the Quadrasteer system have a three-position switch on the dash:

1. 2WS
2. 4WS
3. Tow

The Quadrasteer module then determines the right amount of rear steer and in which direction based on vehicle speed and steering wheel angle. If trailer towing mode is selected and the truck is *not* towing a trailer, the computer will adjust the steering as if there is a trailer and will slightly delay the rear steering action when changing lanes and other maneuvers. As a result, when the steering wheel is turned the front wheels will of course turn in direct proportion to the input from the steering wheel; however, the rear wheels will be delayed in their action to allow the trailer to track properly. If, however, a trailer is not being towed, this delay feels "goofy" and could result in customer concerns about the proper operation of the Quadrasteer system. Be sure that the control switch is placed in the off or normal modes unless a trailer is in fact being towed.

STEERING LINKAGE LUBRICATION

Keeping all joints equipped with a grease fitting properly greased is necessary for long life and ease of steering. ● **SEE FIGURE 29–20.**

During a chassis lubrication, do not forget to put grease on the *steering stop,* if so equipped. **Steering stops** are the projections or built-up areas on the control arms of the front suspension designed to limit the steering movement at full lock. ● **SEE FIGURE 29–21.**

When the steering wheel is turned as far as it can go, the steering should *not* stop inside the steering gear! Forces exerted by the power steering system can do serious damage to the steering gear if absorbed by the steering gear rather than the steering stop.

NOTE: **Many rack-and-pinion steering units are designed with a rack-travel-limit internal stop and do not use an external stop on the steering knuckle or control arm.**

Most steering stops are designed so that the lower control arm hits a small section of the body or frame when the steering wheel is turned to the full "lock" position. Steering stops should be lubricated to prevent a loud grinding noise when turning while the vehicle is going over a bump. This noise is usually noticeable when turning into or out of a driveway.

FIGURE 29–21 Part of steering linkage lubrication is applying grease to the steering stops. If these stops are not lubricated, a grinding sound may be heard when the vehicle hits a bump when the wheels are turned all the way one direction or the other. This often occurs when driving into or out of a driveway that has a curb.

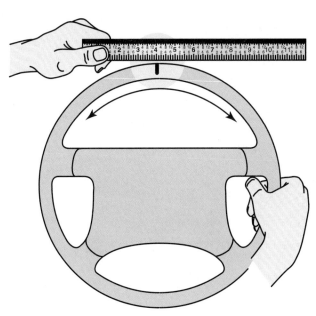

FIGURE 29–22 Checking for freeplay in the steering.

DRY PARK TEST

Since many steering (and suspension) components do *not* have exact specifications for replacement purposes, it is extremely important that the beginning service technician work closely with an experienced veteran technician. While most technicians can determine when a steering component such as a tie rod end is definitely in need of replacement, marginally worn parts are often hard to spot and can lead to handling problems. One of the most effective, yet easy to perform, steering component inspection methods is called the **dry park test.**

Excessive play in the steering wheel can be caused by worn or damaged steering components. Looseness in the steering components usually causes freeplay in the steering wheel. Freeplay refers to the amount of movement of the steering wheel required to cause movement of the front wheels. The exact cause of freeplay in the steering should be determined if the freeplay exceeds 2 in. (5 cm) for parallelogram-type steering linkages, or 3/8 in. (1 cm) for rack-and-pinion steering. ● SEE **FIGURE 29–22.**

This simple test is performed with the vehicle on the ground or on a drive-on ramp-type hoist, moving the steering wheel back and forth *slightly* while an assistant feels for movement at each section of the steering system. The technician can start checking for any looseness in the steering linkage starting

FREQUENTLY ASKED QUESTION

Why Do Only a Few Vehicles Use Grease Fittings?

Many years ago, all vehicles were equipped with grease fittings, while today very few vehicles are so equipped. The reasons for this, as given by engineers, include the following:

- It has been determined that the use of the wrong type of grease can cause more harm than good.
- If a grease fitting is used to allow grease to enter the suspension or steering joint, then water can also get inside the joint.
- Grease fittings are often ignored or the greasing of the joint is not performed by the service technician.
- Low-friction joints do not require routine service like the older metal-to-metal joints required.

either at the outer tie rod ends and working toward the steering column, or from the steering column toward the outer tie rod ends. It is important to check each and every joint and component of the steering system, including the following:

1. The intermediate shaft and flexible coupling.
2. All steering linkage joints, including the inner tie rod end ball socket. ● SEE **FIGURE 29–23.**
3. Steering gear mounting and rack-and-pinion mounting bushings.

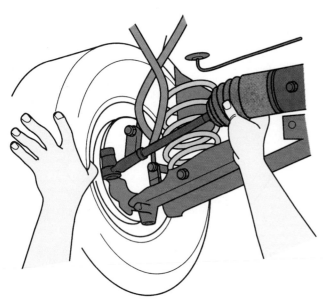

FIGURE 29–23 All joints should be felt during a dry park test. Even inner tie rod ends (ball socket assemblies) can be felt through the rubber bellows on many rack-and-pinion steering units.

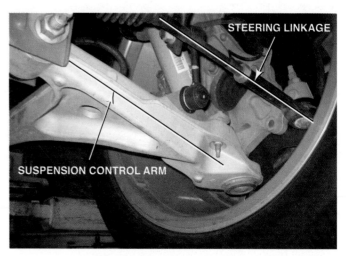

FIGURE 29–24 The steering and suspension arms must remain parallel to prevent the up-and-down motion of the suspension from causing the front wheels to turn inward or outward.

 TECH TIP

Jounce/Rebound Test

All steering linkage should be level and "work" at the same angle as the suspension arms, as shown in ● **FIGURE 29–24.** A simple test to check these items is performed as follows:

1. Park on a hard, level surface with the wheels straight ahead and the steering wheel in the *unlocked* position.
2. Bounce (jounce) the vehicle up and down at the front bumper while watching the steering wheel.

The steering wheel should *not* move during this test. If the steering wheel moves while the vehicle is being bounced, look for a possible bent steering linkage, suspension arm, or steering rack. ● **SEE FIGURE 29–25.**

PARALLELISM

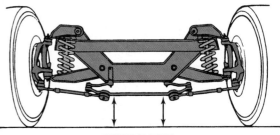

CENTER LINK
PARALLEL TO
LEVEL FLOOR

FIGURE 29–25 The center link should be parallel to the ground.

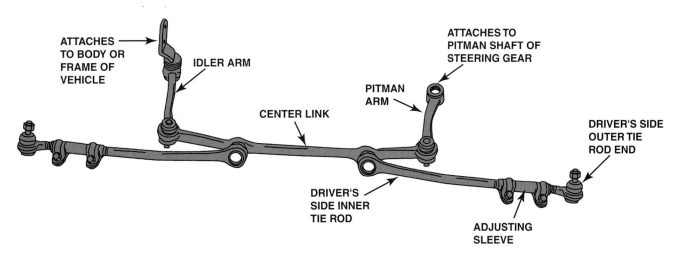

FIGURE 29–26 Typical parallelogram steering linkage. The center link can also be named the relay rod, drag link, or connecting link.

COMMON WEAR ITEMS

On a vehicle equipped with a conventional steering gear and parallelogram linkage, as shown in ● FIGURE 29–26, typical items that wear first, second, and so on include the following:

Steering Component	Estimated Mileage to Wear Out*
1. Idler arm	40,000–60,000 miles (60,000–100,000 km)
2. Outer tie rod ends (replaced in pairs only)	60,000–100,000 miles (100,000–160,000 km)
3. Inner tie rod ends	80,000–120,000 miles (130,000–190,000 km)
4. Center link	90,000–130,000 miles (140,000–180,000 km)
5. Pitman arm	100,000–150,000 miles (160,000–240,000 km)

*Mileage varies greatly due to different road conditions and levels of vehicle maintenance. This chart should be used as a guide only.

Note that there are overlapping mileage intervals for several components. Also note that the mileage interval for an idler arm is such that by the time other components are worn, the idler arm may need to be replaced a second time.

For vehicles that use rack-and-pinion-type steering systems, the list is shorter because there are fewer steering components and the forces exerted on a rack-and-pinion system are in a straight line. The first to wear is usually the outer tie rod ends (one or both) followed by the inner tie rod ball-and-socket joints, usually after 60,000 miles (100,000 km) or more. Intermediate shaft U-joints usually become worn and can cause steering looseness after 80,000 miles (130,000 km) or more.

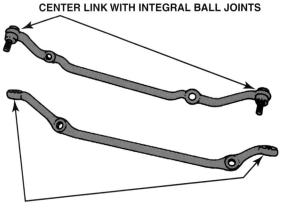

CENTER LINK WITH INTEGRAL BALL JOINTS

CENTER LINK WITHOUT INTEGRAL BALL JOINTS

FIGURE 29–27 Some center links have ball joints while others have tapered socket holes to accept ball joints on the pitman arm, idler arm, and inner tie rod ends.

TECH TIP

Wear and Nonwear Center Links

Some center links are equipped with ball-and-socket joints, which can wear. Other center links are manufactured with holes for ball joint studs only. ● SEE FIGURE 29–27. Generally, the center links that do not use joints are unlikely to need replacement unless a joint becomes loose and wears the tapered stud hole. Knowing which style of center link is used will help determine the most likely location to check for excessive steering linkage play.

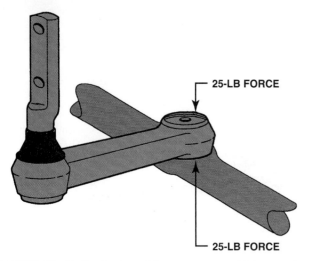

FIGURE 29–28 To check an idler arm, most vehicle manufacturers specify that 25 pounds of force be applied by hand up and down to the idler arm. The idler arm should be replaced if the total movement (up and down) exceeds 1/4 in. (6 mm).

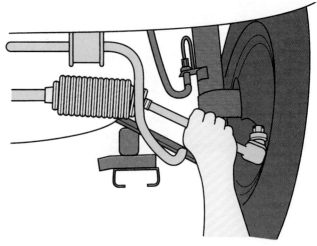

FIGURE 29–29 Steering system component(s) should be replaced if any noticeable looseness is detected when moved by hand.

NOTE: **Experienced front-end technicians can often guess the mileage of a vehicle simply by careful inspection of the steering linkage. For example, if the idler arm is a replacement part and again needs to be replaced, and the outer tie rods also need replacement, then the vehicle probably has at least 60,000 miles and usually more! When inspecting a used vehicle for possible purchase, perform a careful steering system inspection. This is one area of the vehicle where it is difficult to hide long or hard service.**

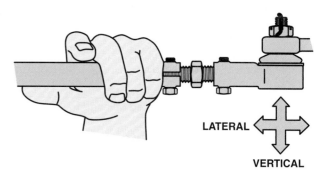

FIGURE 29–30 All joints should be checked by hand for any lateral or vertical play.

UNDER-VEHICLE INSPECTION

After checking the steering system components as part of a dry park test, hoist the vehicle and perform a thorough part-by-part inspection:

1. Inspect each part for damage due to an accident or bent parts due to the vehicle's hitting an object in the roadway.

   CAUTION: **Never straighten a bent steering linkage; always replace with new parts.**

2. Idler arm inspection is performed by using *hand* force of 25 lb (110 N-m) up and down on the arm. If the *total* movement exceeds 1/4 in. (6 mm), the idler arm should be replaced. ● **SEE FIGURE 29–28.**

3. All other steering linkage should be tested *by hand* for any vertical or side-to-side looseness. Tie rod ends use ball-and-socket joints to allow for freedom of movement for suspension travel and to transmit steering forces to the front wheels. It is therefore normal for tie rods to rotate in their sockets when the tie rod sleeve is rocked. **Endplay in any tie rod should be zero.** Many tie rods are spring loaded to help keep the ball-and-socket joint free of play as the joint wears. Eventually, the preloaded spring cannot compensate for the wear, and endplay occurs in the joint. ● **SEE FIGURES 29–29 AND 29–30.**

Bump Steer

Bump steer, or *orbital steer*, is used to describe what happens when the steering linkage is not level: The front tires turn inward or outward as the wheels and suspension move up and down. (Automotive chassis engineers call it *roll steer*.) The vehicle's direction is changed *without moving the steering wheel* whenever the tires move up and down over bumps, dips in the pavement, or even over gentle rises!

This author experienced bump steer once and will never forget the horrible feeling of not having control of the vehicle. After replacing an idler arm and aligning the front wheels, everything was OK until about 40 mph (65 km/h); then the vehicle started darting from one lane of the freeway to another. Because there were no "bumps" as such, bump steer was not considered as a cause. Even when holding the steering wheel perfectly still and straight ahead, the vehicle would go left, then right. Did a tie rod break? It certainly felt exactly like that's what happened. I slowed down to below 30 mph and returned to the shop.

After several hours of checking everything, including the alignment, I discovered that the idler arm was not level with the pitman arm. This caused a pull on the steering linkage whenever the suspension moved up and down. As the suspension compressed, the steering linkage pulled inward on the tie rod on that side of the vehicle. As the wheel moved inward (toed in), it created a pull just as if the wheel were turned by the driver.

This is why all steering linkages must be parallel with the lower control. The reason for the bump steer was that the idler arm was bolted to the frame, which was slotted vertically. I didn't pay any attention to the location of the original idler arm and simply bolted the replacement to the frame. After raising the idler arm back up where it belonged (about 1/2 in. [13 mm]), the steering problem was corrected.

Other common causes of bump steer are worn or deteriorated rack mounting bushings, a noncentered steering linkage, or a bent steering linkage. If the steering components are not level, any bump or dip in the road will cause the vehicle to steer one direction or the other. ● **SEE FIGURE 29–31.**

Always check the steering system carefully whenever a customer complains about any "weird" handling problem.

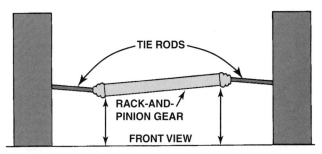

FIGURE 29–31 If a rack-and-pinion or any other steering linkage system is not level, the front tires will be moved inward and/or outward whenever the wheels of the vehicle move up or down.

 TECH TIP

The Killer Bs

The "three Bs" that can cause steering and suspension problems are bent, broken, or binding components. Always inspect each part under the vehicle for each of the killer Bs.

4. All steering components should be tested with the wheels in the straight-ahead position. If the wheels are turned, some apparent looseness may be noticed due to the angle of the steering linkage.

CAUTION: Do not turn the front wheels of the vehicle while suspended on a lift to check for looseness in the steering linkage. The extra leverage of the wheel and tire assembly can cause a much greater force to be applied to the steering components than can be exerted by hand alone. This extra force may cause some apparent movement in good components that may not need replacement.

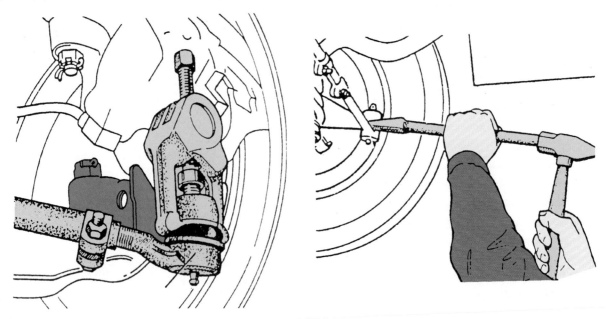

FIGURE 29–32 The preferred method for separating the tie rod end from the steering knuckle is to use a puller such as the one shown. A pickle-fork-type tool should only be used if the tie rod end is going to be replaced. A pickle-fork-type tool can damage or tear the rubber grease boot.

STEERING LINKAGE REPLACEMENT

PARALLELOGRAM TYPE When replacing any steering system component, it is best to replace all defective and marginally good components at the same time. Use the following guidelines.

Parts that can be replaced *individually* include the following:

Idler arm

Center link

Pitman arm

Intermediate shaft

Intermediate shaft U-joint

Parts that should be replaced in *pairs only* include the following:

Outer tie rod ends

Inner tie rod ends

Idler arm (if there are two on the same vehicle, such as GM's Astro van)

Replacing steering system components involves these steps:

STEP 1 Hoist the vehicle safely with the wheels in the straight-ahead position. Remove the front wheels, if necessary, to gain access to the components.

STEP 2 Loosen the retainer nut on tapered components, such as tie rod ends. Use a tie rod removal puller (also called a *taper breaker),* as shown in ● **FIGURE 29–32,** or use hammers to slightly deform the taper, as shown in ● **FIGURE 29–33.**

CAUTION: Vehicle manufacturers often warn not to use a tapered pickle-fork tool to separate tapered parts. The wedge tool can tear the grease seal and damage both the part being removed and the adjoining part.

Pitman arms require a larger puller to remove the pitman arm from the splines of the pitman shaft. ● **SEE FIGURES 29–34 AND 29–35.**

STEP 3 Replace the part using the hardware and fasteners supplied with the replacement part. *Do not reuse the precrimped torque prevailing nuts used at the factory as original equipment on many tie rod ends.*

CAUTION: Whenever tightening the nuts of tapered parts such as tie rods, *DO NOT* loosen after reaching the proper assembly torque to align the cotter key hole. If the cotter key does not fit, *tighten* the nut farther until the hole lines up for the cotter key. ● SEE FIGURE 29–36. Always use a new cotter key.

FIGURE 29-33 Two hammers being used to disconnect a tie rod end from the steering knuckle. One hammer is used as a backing for the second hammer. Notice that the attaching nut has been loosened, but not removed. This prevents the tie rod end from falling when the tapered connection is knocked loose.

FIGURE 29-35 Pitman arm and pitman shaft indexing splines.

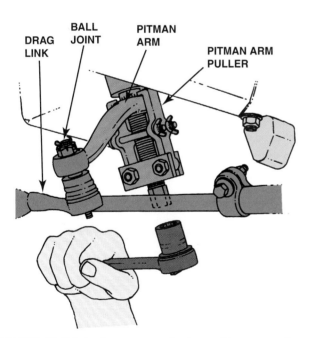

FIGURE 29-34 A pitman arm puller is used to remove the pitman arm from the pitman shaft.

FIGURE 29-36 Align the hole in the tie rod end with the slot in the retaining nut. If the holes do not line up, always tighten the nut farther (never loosen) until the hole lines up.

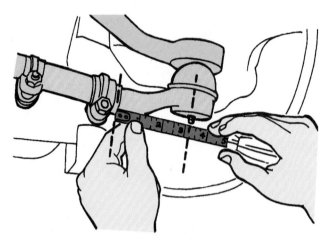

FIGURE 29–37 Replacement tie rods should be of the same overall length as the originals. Measure from the edge of the tie rod sleeve to the center of the grease fitting. When the new tie rod is threaded to this dimension, the toe setting will be close to the original.

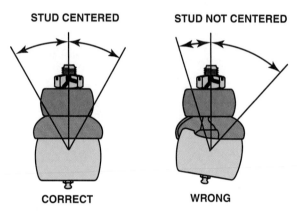

FIGURE 29–38 All tie rod ends should be installed so that the stud is in the center of its operating range, as shown.

STEERING LINKAGE REPLACEMENT (CONTINUED)

When replacing tie rod ends, use the adjusting sleeve to adjust the total length of the tie rod to the same position and length as the original. Measure the original length of the tie rods and assemble the replacement tie rod(s) to the same overall length. ● **SEE FIGURE 29–37.**

When positioning the tie rod end(s), check that the stud is centered in the socket, as shown in ● **FIGURE 29–38.** This permits maximum steering linkage movement without getting into a bind if the steering linkage is pivoted beyond the angle the tie rod end can move in the socket.

NOTE: To ensure proper wheel alignment, install the adjusting sleeve with an equal number of threads showing at each end of the sleeve. Some manufacturers also specify a _minimum_ of three threads showing at each end. If the sleeve itself is corroded or bent, it should be replaced along with either or both of the tie rod ends (inner and outer). ● SEE FIGURE 29–39.

SERVICE OF BALL SOCKET ASSEMBLIES Inner tie rod end assemblies used on rack-and-pinion steering units require special consideration and often special tools. The inner tie rod end, also called a ball socket assembly, should be replaced whenever there is any noticeable freeplay in the ball-and-socket joint. Another test of this joint is performed by disconnecting the outer tie rod end and measuring the effort required to move the tie rod in the socket, as shown in ● **FIGURE 29–40.** This is called the **articulation test.**

NOTE: The articulation test is to be used on metal-to-metal ball socket assemblies. Low-friction joints (polished ball and plastic liner-type joints) may require less effort to move and still be serviceable.

The inner tie rod assemblies are attached to the end of the steering rack by one of several methods.

Removing a ball socket assembly usually requires the use of two wrenches or a special tool. ● **SEE FIGURE 29–41.**

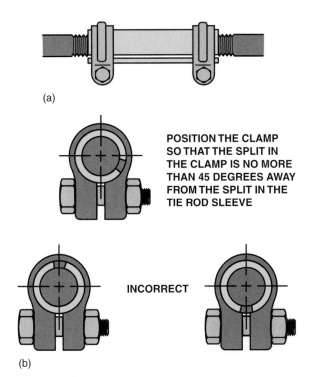

(a)

POSITION THE CLAMP
SO THAT THE SPLIT IN
THE CLAMP IS NO MORE
THAN 45 DEGREES AWAY
FROM THE SPLIT IN THE
TIE ROD SLEEVE

INCORRECT

(b)

FIGURE 29–39 (a) Tie rod adjusting sleeve. (b) Be sure to position the clamp correctly on the sleeve.

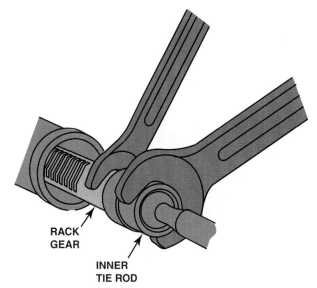

RACK
GEAR

INNER
TIE ROD

FIGURE 29–41 Removing a staked inner tie rod assembly requires two wrenches—one to hold the rack and the other to unscrew the joint from the end of the steering rack.

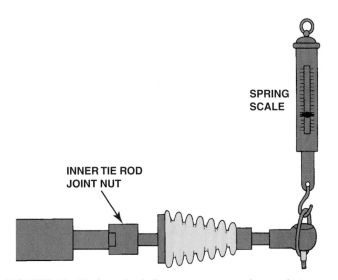

SPRING
SCALE

INNER TIE ROD
JOINT NUT

FIGURE 29–40 An articulation test uses a spring scale to measure the amount of force needed to move the tie rod in the ball socket assembly. Most manufacturers specify a minimum of 1 lb (4.4 N) of force and a maximum of 6 lb (26 N).

The flange around the outer tie rod must be restaked to the flat shoulder on the end of the rack, as shown in ● **FIGURE 29–42.**

Always follow the instructions that come with the replacement part(s). ● **SEE FIGURE 29–43.**

NOTE: **When replacing a rack-and-pinion assembly, specify an entire replacement rack and pinion assembly if possible. A short rack does not include the bellows (boots) or inner tie rod ends (ball socket assemblies). The labor and cost required to exchange or replace these parts usually make it easier and less expensive to replace the entire steering unit.**

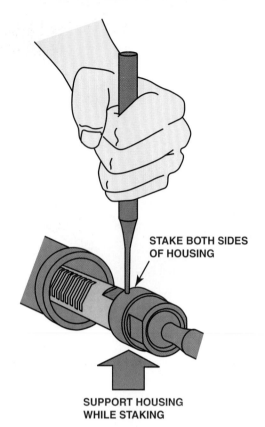

STAKE BOTH SIDES
OF HOUSING

SUPPORT HOUSING
WHILE STAKING

FIGURE 29–42 When the inner tie rod end is reassembled, both sides of the housing must be staked down onto the flat shoulder of the rack.

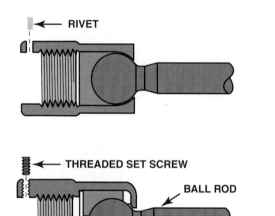

RIVET

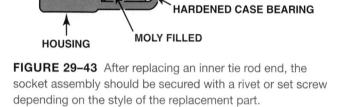

THREADED SET SCREW

BALL ROD

HARDENED CASE BEARING

HOUSING

MOLY FILLED

FIGURE 29–43 After replacing an inner tie rod end, the socket assembly should be secured with a rivet or set screw depending on the style of the replacement part.

1 Drive the vehicle onto a drive-on-type hoist and have an assistant gently rotate the steering wheel back and forth about 2 inches (50 mm).

2 Perform a visual inspection of the steering and suspension system, looking for damage from road debris or other faults.

3 As the assistant wiggles the steering wheel, grasp the joint at the outer tie rod end on the driver's side to check for any movement.

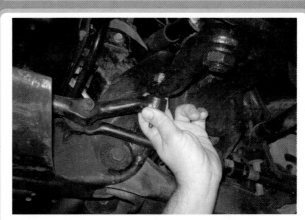

4 Next, check for any freeplay at the pitman arm.

CONTINUED ▶

5 Check the joint between the left inner tie rod end and the center link for play.

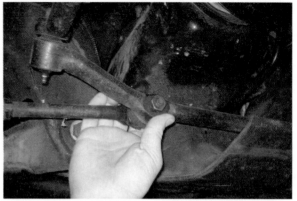

6 Move to the passenger side and check for any looseness at the joint between the center link and the right-side inner tie rod end.

7 Check for looseness at the idler arm connector to the center link and the idler arm at the frame mount.

8 Check for looseness at the passenger-side outer tie rod end. After the inspection, record the results on the work order.

SUMMARY

1. The dry park test is a very important test to detect worn or damaged steering parts. With the vehicle on the ground, have an assistant move the steering wheel back and forth while the technician feels for any looseness in each steering system part.

2. The steering system must be level side-to-side to prevent unwanted bump steer. Bump steer is when the vehicle's direction is changed when traveling over bumps or dips in the road.

3. The idler arm usually is the first steering system component to wear out in a conventional parallelogram-type steering system. Following the idler arm in wear are the tie rods, center link, and then the pitman arm.

4. Steering components should be checked for wear using hand force only.

5. All steering components should be installed and tightened with the front wheels in the straight-ahead position.

6. Always use a tie rod remover/puller or a taper breaker when separating tapered components, such as tie rods.

REVIEW QUESTIONS

1. Describe how to perform a dry park test.

2. List the steering parts that should be replaced in pairs.

3. What test procedure can be used to check that the steering linkage is straight and level?

4. What is the difference between a wear and nonwear center link?

CHAPTER QUIZ

1. A "dry park" test to determine the condition of the steering components and joints should be performed with the vehicle _____.
   a. On level ground on a drive-on lift
   b. On turn plates that allow the front wheels to move
   c. On a frame contact lift with the wheels off the ground
   d. Lifted off the ground about 2 in. (5 cm)

2. Two technicians are discussing bump steer. Technician A says that an unlevel steering linkage can be its cause. Technician B says that if the steering wheel moves when the vehicle is bounced up and down, the steering linkage may be bent. Which technician is correct?
   a. Technician A only
   b. Technician B only
   c. Both Technicians A and B
   d. Neither Technician A nor B

3. A vehicle has an excessive amount of freeplay in the steering wheel and it is difficult to keep it traveling straight on a straight and level road. Which is the *least likely* cause?
   a. Worn tie rod ends
   b. Excessive play in the ball socket assemblies
   c. Worn idler arms
   d. Loose pitman arm retaining nut

4. How are the inner tie rods attached to the rack on a center-take-off-type rack-and-pinion steering gear?
   a. Staked
   b. Bolted
   c. Riveted
   d. Pinned

5. What is the *most likely* cause of bump steer?
   a. Worn outer tie rod ends
   b. A worn center link
   c. Worn or oil-soaked rack bushings
   d. A lack of proper lubrication of all ball-and-socket joints

6. How much endplay is usually acceptable in tie rod ends?
   a. Zero
   b. 0.0010 to 0.030 in.
   c. 0.030 to 0.050 in.
   d. 0.050 to 0.100 in.

7. Technician A says that outer tie rod ends should be replaced in pairs, even if only one is worn. Technician B says that inner tie rod ends should be replaced in pairs, even if only one is worn. Which technician is correct?
   a. Technician A only
   b. Technician B only
   c. Both Technicians A and B
   d. Neither Technician A nor B

8. Which tool is *not* recommended to be used to separate tapered steering components because it can do harm?
   a. Taper breaker
   b. Pickle fork
   c. Tie rod removal puller
   d. Two hammers

9. Technician A says that torque prevailing nuts can be reused unless damaged. Technician B says that a new cotter key should always be used. Which technician is correct?
   a. Technician A only
   b. Technician B only
   c. Both Technicians A and B
   d. Neither Technician A nor B

10. New tie rods are being installed. Technician A says to tighten the retaining nuts to specification and then loosen, if needed, to align the cotter pin hole. Technician B says to tighten farther to align the cotter key hole. Which technician is correct?
    a. Technician A only
    b. Technician B only
    c. Both Technicians A and B
    d. Neither Technician A nor B

POWER-ASSISTED STEERING OPERATION AND SERVICE

OBJECTIVES

After studying Chapter 30, the reader will be able to:

1. Prepare for ASE Suspension and Steering (A4) certification test content area "A" (Steering Systems Diagnosis and Repairs).
2. Discuss the components and operation of power steering pumps.
3. List the components of a typical power-recirculating-ball-nut steering gear system.
4. Describe the operation of a power rack-and-pinion steering system.

KEY TERMS

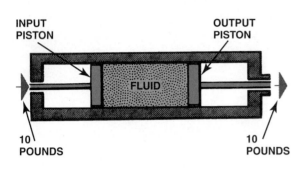

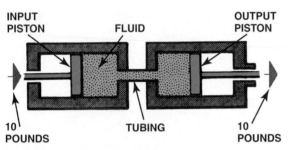

FIGURE 30–1 Hydraulic fluid transmits the same force whether it passes through a single chamber or two chambers connected by a narrow passage.

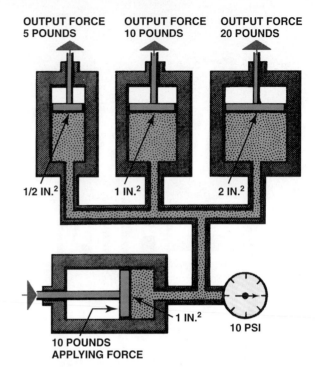

FIGURE 30–2 A fluid applies a force equal to the applied force on a surface that is equal in size to the applying surface. If the surface is half the size, then the fluid exerts half the force: if the surface is twice as large, the fluid exerts twice the force.

Power-assisted steering hydraulically boosts the mechanical steering gear operation so the driver can turn the steering wheel with less effort for the same response. Hydraulic power steering has been available since the 1950s, and many late-model systems are enhanced by electronic controls.

POWER STEERING HYDRAULIC SYSTEMS

Hydraulics is the study of liquids and their use to transmit force and motion. Hydraulic systems transmit force and motion through the use of fluid pressure. **Force** is a push or pull acting on an object and is usually measured in pounds or Newtons. **Pressure** is force applied to a specific area. Pressure is usually measured in force per unit of area, such as pounds per square inch (PSI), or kilopascals (kPa). One PSI is equal to 6.895 kPa.

The Pascal is a unit of measure named after the French scientist Blaise Pascal (1623–1662), who studied the behavior of fluids in closed systems. One of his discoveries, known as **Pascal's law**, was that pressure on a confined fluid is transmitted equally in all directions and acts with equal force on equal areas.

Hydraulic systems can transmit force and motion through liquids because, for all practical purposes, a liquid cannot be compressed. No matter how much pressure is placed on a liquid, its volume remains the same. This allows a liquid to transmit force much like a mechanical lever. ● **SEE FIGURE 30–1.**

The advantage of a liquid over a mechanical lever is that a liquid has volume but does not have a fixed shape. Because it assumes the shape of its container, a liquid can transfer force around obstacles or through pipes and passages of any shape. As explained by Pascal's law, a liquid can also decrease or increase the force it transmits depending on the area of the output surface to which the force is applied. ● **SEE FIGURE 30–2.**

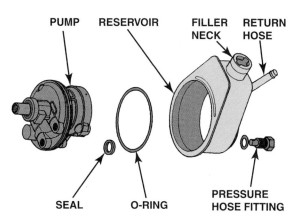

FIGURE 30–3 A typical integral power steering pump when the pump is mounted inside the reservoir.

PUMP RESERVOIR FILLER NECK RETURN HOSE

SEAL O-RING PRESSURE HOSE FITTING

FIGURE 30–4 Typical remote reservoir.

POWER STEERING PUMP AND RESERVOIR

The power steering pump draws fluid from the reservoir, pressurizes it, and delivers it to the power steering system. A power steering pump produces a high-pressure stream of fluid, typically in the 1,500-PSI (10,500 kPa) range. The fluid reservoir may be either integral to (built into) the pump or remotely mounted and connected to the pump by a hose. The power steering fluid reservoir is usually made of either plastic or stamped metal, and it includes the fluid filler neck, cap, and dipstick. It can be integral to or remote from the pump. An **integral reservoir** is part of the pump, and the pump itself operates submerged in power steering fluid. ● **SEE FIGURE 30–3.** Although once common, steering pumps with an integral reservoir have given way to those with a remote reservoir on many current-production vehicles. This is because the remote reservoir allows for a smaller, more compact pump assembly that is better suited to the cramped engine compartment of a modern vehicle.

A **remote reservoir** is a separate assembly from the pump and provides fluid to it through a suction hose. ● **SEE FIGURE 30–4.**

A typical power steering system requires only 2 to 3.5 lb (0.9 to 1.6 kg) of effort to turn the steering wheel.

Most power steering systems use an engine-driven hydraulic pump. Power steering hydraulic pumps are usually belt driven from the front crankshaft pulley of the engine. Pumps come in many sizes and styles. ● **SEE FIGURE 30–5.**

The power steering pump delivers a constant flow of hydraulic fluid to the power steering gear or rack. A typical power steering pump requires less than 1/2 horsepower, which is less than 1% of engine power while driving straight ahead. Even while parking at low speed, the power steering requires only about 3 horsepower while providing high hydraulic pressures. Typical pressures generated by a power steering system include the following.

Straight ahead	less than 150 PSI (1,400 kPa)
Cornering	about 450 PSI (3,100 kPa)
Parking (maximum)	750–1,400 PSI (5,200–10,000 kPa)

The power steering pump drive pulley is usually fitted to a chrome-plated shaft with a press fit. The shaft is applied to a rotor with vanes that rotate between a thrust plate and a pressure plate. ● **SEE FIGURE 30–6.**

Some power steering pumps are of the slipper or roller design instead of the vane type. When the engine starts, the drive belt rotates the power steering pump pulley and the rotor assembly inside the power steering pump.

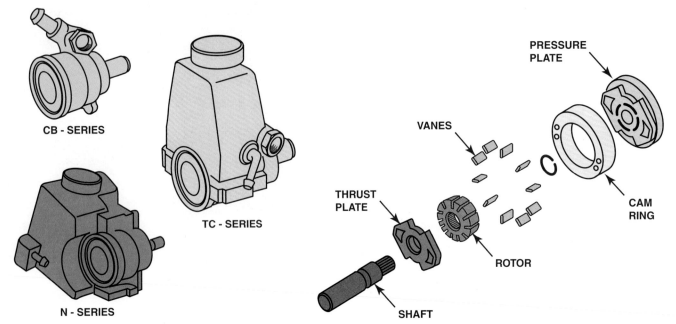

FIGURE 30–5 Typical power steering pump assemblies.

CB - SERIES

TC - SERIES

N - SERIES

FIGURE 30–6 General Motors vane-type pump.

PRESSURE PLATE

VANES

THRUST PLATE

CAM RING

ROTOR

SHAFT

POWER STEERING PUMP AND RESERVOIR (CONTINUED)

With a vane-type pump, centrifugal force and hydraulic pressure push the vanes of the rotor outward into contact with the pump ring. The shape of the pump ring causes a change in the volume of fluid between the vanes. As the volume increases, the pressure is decreased in the space between the vanes and draws in fluid from the pump reservoir. When the volume between the vanes decreases, the pressure is increased and flows out the pump discharge port. ● **SEE FIGURES 30–7, 30–8, AND 30–9.**

The pressure outlet hose connects to a fitting that threads into the outlet port of the pump body. A modulator valve, commonly called a **flow control valve**, installs in the same bore as the hose fitting. ● **SEE FIGURE 30–10.**

The modulator valve is a spring-loaded pressure-relief device that bleeds off excess pressure to prevent system damage. When pump output is more than the power steering system requires, the excess pressure overcomes spring force and moves the valve down in its bore. This uncovers an orifice through which the fluid can flow back into the inlet passages. An orifice is a small opening that regulates fluid pressure and flow. It can be a restriction in a fluid line or a hole between two fluid chambers. This particular opening is called a *variable orifice* because the size of the opening varies with the amount of pressure applied to the valve. When fluid pressure is not high, spring force

keeps the valve seated so that all of the pressurized fluid flows through the outlet port and into the pressure hose.

Because the engine drives the pump, the power steering pump places a load on the engine whenever the engine is running. Under certain conditions, such as when the steering wheel is turned to or near full stop for more than a few seconds, pressure builds in the system and the pump must work harder to keep up with the demand. As a result, the pump draws more power from the engine. If the engine is running at idle, the extra load can cause it to stall. A pressure switch, known as the **power steering pressure (PSP)** switch, transmits an electronic signal to the powertrain control module (PCM) when the pressure in the system is high enough to increase the load on the engine. In response to the PSP switch signal, the PCM increases the engine idle speed to prevent stalling.

The pressure increases when the steering wheel is turned to its full stop in either direction. To handle the excess pressure, a pressure-relief passage runs from a point near the pressure hose fitting to the spring end of the modulator valve. Inside the passage is a **pressure-relief valve**. The spring end of the modulator valve forms a seat for the pressure-relief check ball. Under normal circumstances, the check ball remains seated.

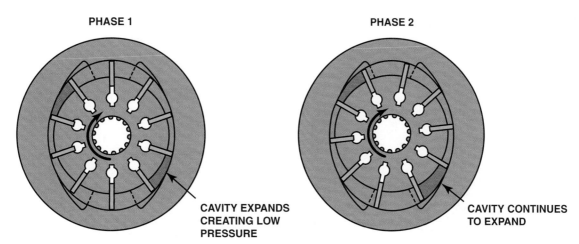

FIGURE 30–7 Vane pump operation. In phase 1, the rotor moves past the opposed suction ports, and the vanes move out to maintain contact with the ring. This creates a low-pressure area, drawing fluid into the cavities formed by the vanes. As the rotor continues to move during phase 2, the vanes follow the contour of the ring. The contour of the ring forms a larger cavity between the vanes. This increases the suction and draws more fluid into the pump.

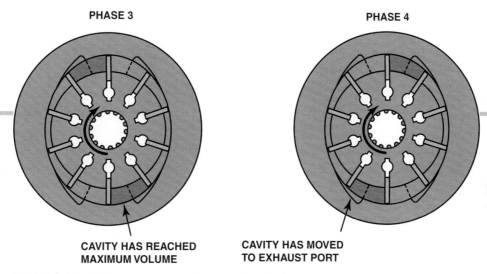

FIGURE 30–8 Vane pump operation—continued. At phase 3, the vanes are at the end of the intake port of the pump and the cavity has reached its maximum volume. In phase 4, the rotor moves into alignment with the opposed discharge ports.

The parts of the pressure-relief valve are the following:

- Spring
- Valve piston
- Check ball
- Seat

A shim installs on the check ball seat to adjust the pressure at which the check ball unseats to open the pressure-relief valve. Normally, the spring force holds the piston against the check ball to keep it in its seat. When pressure becomes excessive in the pressure-relief passage, the check ball raises off its seat to allow fluid to flow through the relief passage and out through an orifice in the modulator valve. ● **SEE FIGURE 30–11.** The pressure when this occurs varies from 750 to 1,400 PSI (5,200 to 10,000 kPa) depending on the calibration of the pressure-relief valve. When power steering systems are pushed to the limit, most will make a chattering or squealing noise until the pressure is reduced.

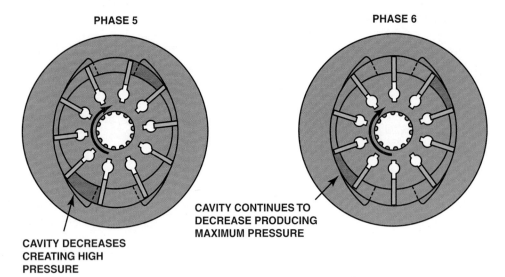

PHASE 5

PHASE 6

CAVITY DECREASES
CREATING HIGH
PRESSURE

CAVITY CONTINUES TO
DECREASE PRODUCING
MAXIMUM PRESSURE

FIGURE 30–9 Vane pump operation—continued. As the rotor continues to move during phase 5, the volume of the cavity decreases, which increases the discharge pressure. At phase 6, the last phase, the contour of the ring results in the minimum cavity volume, and the discharge of fluid is completed.

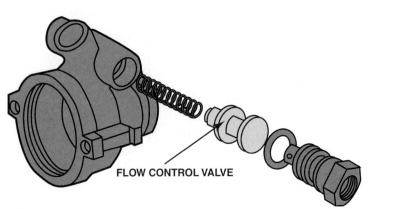

FLOW CONTROL VALVE

FIGURE 30–10 Flow control valve.

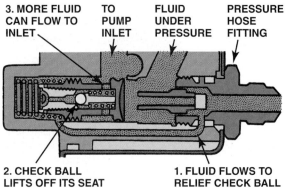

3. MORE FLUID
CAN FLOW TO
INLET

TO
PUMP
INLET

FLUID
UNDER
PRESSURE

PRESSURE
HOSE
FITTING

2. CHECK BALL
LIFTS OFF ITS SEAT

1. FLUID FLOWS TO
RELIEF CHECK BALL

FIGURE 30–11 The pressure-relief check ball unseats, allowing fluid to flow back into the pump inlet if the pressure rises above a certain limit.

POWER STEERING HOSES

Because the power steering pump and the steering gear are not part of the same assembly, the system requires two hoses to connect the power steering pump and gear assembly. The pressure hose is connected to the flow control/relief valve. This hose supplies pressurized fluid to the steering gear. The second hose is called the return hose and it returns the fluid from the steering gear back to the pump. Some vehicles will use a cooler in the return path to the pump. The cooler is used to reduce the temperature of the fluid before it enters the pump. ● **SEE FIGURE 30–12.**

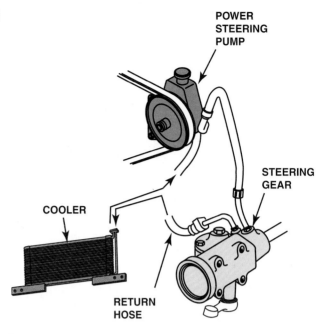

FIGURE 30–12 The power steering fluid cooler, if used, is located in the return hose. Often the "cooler" is simply a length of return metal line that is arranged in a loop and routed near the front of the vehicle. The airflow past the return line helps reduce the temperature of the fluid.

POWER STEERING PUMP

STEERING GEAR

COOLER

RETURN HOSE

INTEGRAL POWER STEERING

In an integral power steering system, the control valve and the power piston are incorporated into the steering gear construction. The control valve regulates the application of pressurized fluid against the power piston, and the power piston helps move the output member of the steering gear when pressure is applied to one side of it.

INTEGRAL STANDARD STEERING GEAR Most standard steering gears with power assist are the recirculating-ball type, and the ball nut functions as the power piston. Hydraulic pressure from the steering gear control valve is applied directly against the ball nut to help move it through the housing. The ball nut in this type of power steering gear is called the *power piston* because hydraulic pressure moves it as if it were a piston traveling in a cylinder. ● **SEE FIGURE 30–13.**

ROTARY CONTROL VALVE A **rotary control valve** is a two-piece assembly that operates by rotating an inner valve within an outer valve. A steering gear with a rotary control valve is also a *torsion bar steering* gear, because a small torsion bar is used to control valve movement.

The rotary control valve consists of two cylindrical elements: the inner valve element and outer valve element. The inner valve element is secured to the steering gear input shaft and the torsion bar. In the valve, the inner element and the input

shaft are one piece, and the torsion bar attaches to them. ● **SEE FIGURE 30–14.** The inner element assembly fits inside the outer valve element, and is also secured to the torsion bar by a pin. The outer valve element is also the steering worm gear. The torsion bar acts as a spring between the two elements to allow movement between them when the steering shaft turns. The spring force of the torsion bar tends to pull the elements back to their neutral positions when the steering wheel is released or returned to center. The strength of the torsion bar determines steering feel. A weak torsion bar moves easily and provides soft steering, while a strong bar resists movement and makes steering feel firm. Many high performance vehicles use a steering gear that has a thicker torsion bar to increase the firmness of the steering.

The facing surfaces of the inner and outer elements have grooves machined into them through which fluid can flow. Passages carry fluid from some of the inner-element grooves to the center of the element, where it travels through the return line to the pump reservoir. The outer element has three sets of fluid passages that connect the outside of the element to a groove at the inside. One set of passages carries fluid into the element from the pressure hose fitting, the second set carries fluid to and from the left-turn side of the power piston, and the third carries it to and from the right-turn side.

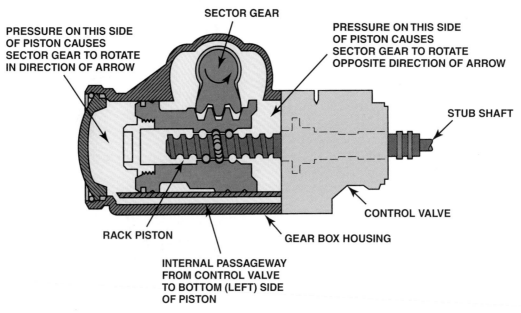

FIGURE 30–13 Forces acting on the rack piston of an integral power steering gear.

When the steering wheel is aimed straight ahead, the valve is in its neutral position. Fluid enters the valve and flows equally to both sides of the steering gear piston and to the return line. ● **SEE FIGURE 30–15.**

When the steering wheel and steering shaft turn to the left, the inner element twists on the torsion bar and repositions the valve ports. In this left-turn position, pressurized fluid flowing into the valve can only exit through the left-turn ports. ● **SEE FIGURE 30–16.** Meanwhile, the right-turn ports align with the return ports to bleed off residual pressure from the opposite side of the power piston. Pressurized fluid flowing through the left-turn ports is directed into the steering gear, where it applies force to the power piston and reduces the effort needed to turn the steering linkage to the left. ● **SEE FIGURE 30–17.** As the piston moves, it forces fluid out of the right-turn side, and that fluid returns through the control valve to the pump reservoir. Exactly the opposite flow occurs during a right-hand turn: The right-turn ports are opened and the left-turn ports exhaust to the return line. ● **SEE FIGURE 30–18.** Hydraulic pressure moves the piston up the housing bore during a right-hand turn. ● **SEE FIGURE 30–19.**

When the steering wheel is released, the spring force of the torsion bar returns the two elements to their natural positions. Fluid pressure equalizes throughout the steering gear and recenters the piston in the middle of the steering gear.

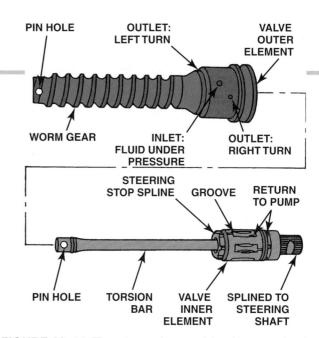

FIGURE 30–14 The rotary valve consists of inner and outer elements. The worm gear is part of the outer element and the torsion bar is part of the inner element. A pin attaches the worm gear to the bottom of the torsion bar to join the two elements together.

POWER RACK-AND-PINION STEERING The rotary control valve on a power rack-and-pinion steering gear is located between the steering gear input shaft and the pinion gear. ● **SEE FIGURE 30–20.**

Fluid discharged by the valve travels through external steel lines to either side of the power piston. A steel air-transfer tube

STRAIGHT-AHEAD

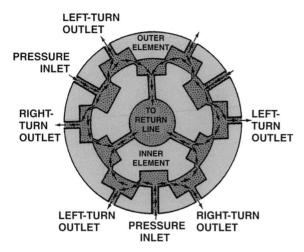

FIGURE 30–15 When the steering wheel is in the straight-ahead position, all of the ports in a rotary valve are open equally to the pressure and return circuits.

LEFT TURN

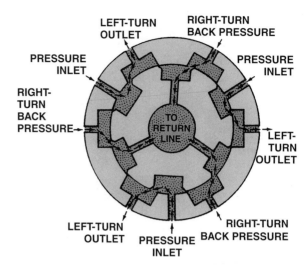

FIGURE 30–16 During a left turn, the inner element turns so that the left-turn circuits are open to pressure and the right-turn circuits are open to the return circuit.

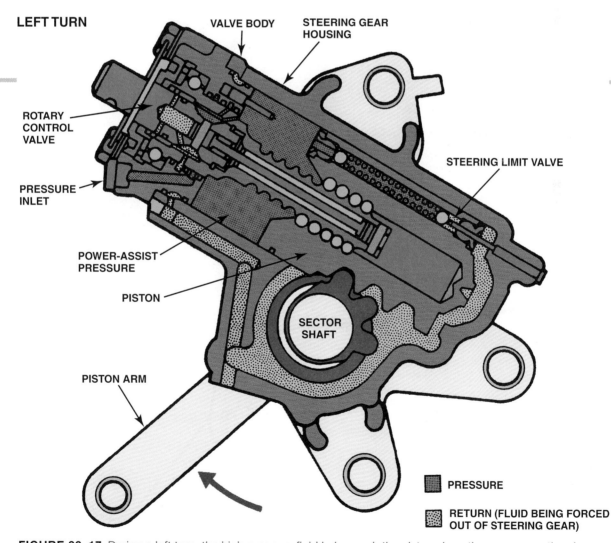

FIGURE 30–17 During a left turn, the high-pressure fluid helps push the piston along the worm gear, thereby reducing the steering effort from the driver.

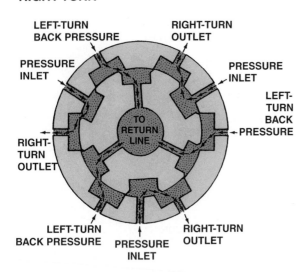

RIGHT TURN

LEFT-TURN BACK PRESSURE

RIGHT-TURN OUTLET

PRESSURE INLET

PRESSURE INLET

LEFT-TURN BACK PRESSURE

TO RETURN LINE

RIGHT-TURN OUTLET

LEFT-TURN BACK PRESSURE

PRESSURE INLET

RIGHT-TURN OUTLET

FIGURE 30–18 During a right turn, the inner element turns so that the right-turn outlets are open to pressure and the left-turn outlets are open to the return circuit.

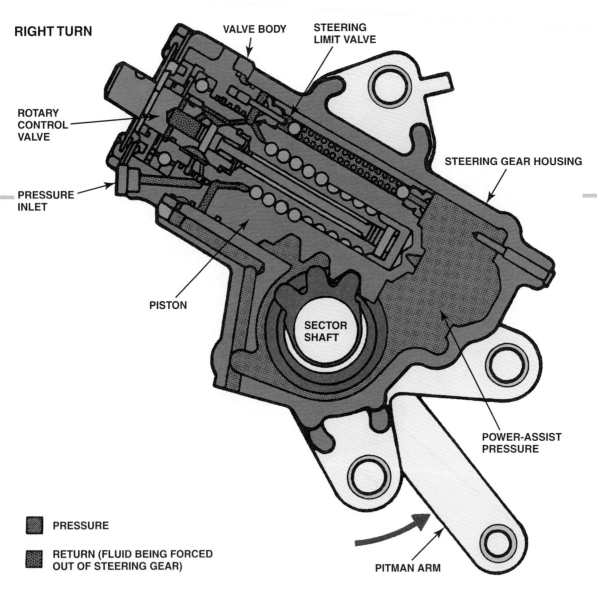

RIGHT TURN

VALVE BODY

STEERING LIMIT VALVE

ROTARY CONTROL VALVE

STEERING GEAR HOUSING

PRESSURE INLET

PISTON

SECTOR SHAFT

POWER-ASSIST PRESSURE

PITMAN ARM

◾ PRESSURE

◾ RETURN (FLUID BEING FORCED OUT OF STEERING GEAR)

FIGURE 30–19 During a right turn, high-pressure fluid pushes the piston up the worm gear, moving the sector shaft and pitman arm to provide assist during a right turn.

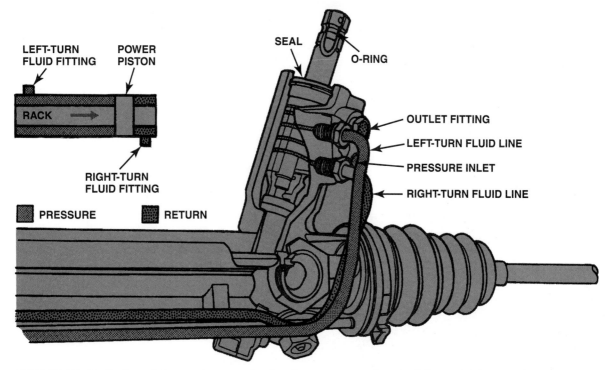

FIGURE 30–20 During a left turn, the control valve directs pressure into the left-turn fluid line and the rack moves left. (See inset.) Fluid pushed out of the right-turn fluid chamber travels back through the right-turn fluid line and control valve to the return circuit.

INTEGRAL POWER STEERING (CONTINUED)

allows air displacement between the boots as they compress and expand, since the power piston prevents air from passing through the rack housing. The rotary valve in a rack-and-pinion steering unit operates in the same manner as the one previously described for a standard steering gear. During a left-hand turn, the control valve directs fluid flow into the left-turn steel line, which routes it to the right-hand side of the power piston in order to move the rack to the left. As this happens, fluid on the opposite side of the power piston is forced out through the right-turn steel line and back to the control valve, where it is exhausted to the return circuit. When the steering wheel is turned to the right, fluid flow is reversed so the power piston moves to the right and fluid in the left-turn chamber is exhausted to the return circuit. ● **SEE FIGURE 30–21.**

FLOW CONTROL VALVE OPERATION
When the power steering pump begins operation, the fluid from the output of the pump flows into the control valve. The fluid then flows through the orifice, where a pressure differential is formed. The pressure differential results in a higher pressure on the pump side than on the system side. The fluid from the orifice flows into the power steering system and through a passage on the backside of the control valve. ● **SEE FIGURE 30–22.**

The fluid on the backside of the control valve is used to assist the spring force acting on the valve. At this point, the combination of the spring force and hydraulic pressure is higher than the output pressure of the pump. This causes the control valve to block the passage to the pump intake. When the output pressure is higher than the spring force, the pressure behind the valve forces the control valve to move. The movement of the valve opens the passage to the intake side of the pump. This allows some of the fluid to flow into the passage. As the pump speed continues to increase, the valve moves more to compensate for the higher pressure and flow. The pressure and flow in the power steering system must remain in the correct range or the steering system components can be damaged. Failure of the control valve to regulate the pressure in the power steering system can result in excessive pressure and temperature. As long as fluid can flow through the system, the control valve can regulate the pressure. ● **SEE FIGURE 30–23.**

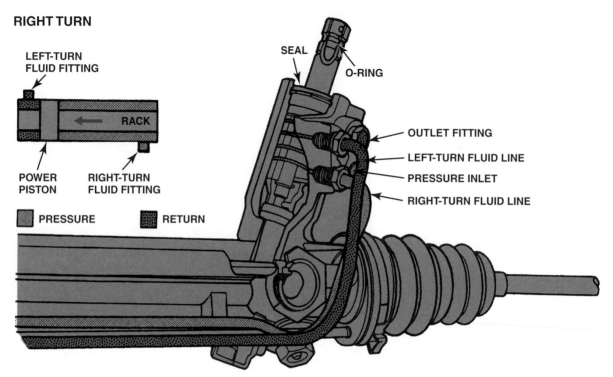

RIGHT TURN

LEFT-TURN FLUID FITTING

RACK

POWER PISTON

RIGHT-TURN FLUID FITTING

PRESSURE   RETURN

SEAL

O-RING

OUTLET FITTING

LEFT-TURN FLUID LINE

PRESSURE INLET

RIGHT-TURN FLUID LINE

FIGURE 30–21 The control valve routes high-pressure fluid to the left-hand side of the power piston, which pushes the piston and assists in moving the rack toward the right when the steering wheel is turned right.

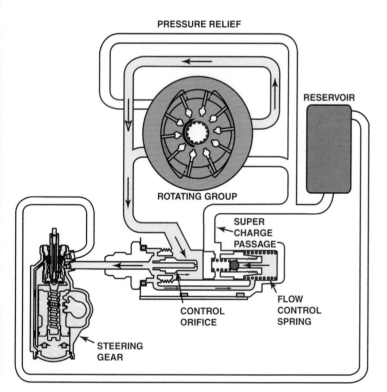

PRESSURE RELIEF

RESERVOIR

ROTATING GROUP

SUPER CHARGE PASSAGE

CONTROL ORIFICE

FLOW CONTROL SPRING

STEERING GEAR

FIGURE 30–22 Low-speed flow control.

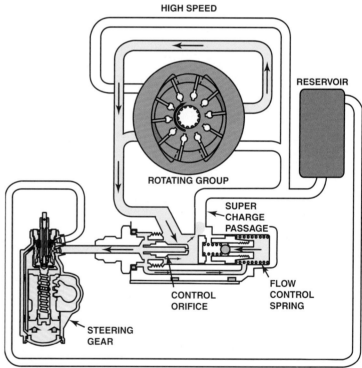

HIGH SPEED

RESERVOIR

ROTATING GROUP

SUPER CHARGE PASSAGE

CONTROL ORIFICE

FLOW CONTROL SPRING

STEERING GEAR

FIGURE 30–23 High-speed flow control operation.

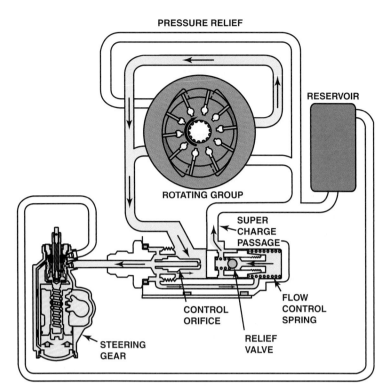

FIGURE 30–24 Pressure-relief mode. In this mode the steering gear has blocked the flow of fluid from the pump and the pressure rises, which unseats the pressure-relief valve. Now fluid flows back to the inlet through the pressure-relief orifice and passage.

INTEGRAL POWER STEERING (CONTINUED)

However, there are times during normal operation when the flow in the system will stop. Fluid flow can stop during parking maneuvers and when the steering wheel is turned to the extreme right and left positions.

When the fluid flow through the system stops, the pressure equalizes on both sides of the orifice. This creates equal pressure on both sides of the control valve. Because the backside of the valve has a spring, the combination of the hydraulic pressure and spring force positions the control valve to prevent flow into the pump intake passage. As the pump continues to operate, the pressure in the system builds. If the pressure is not relieved, the system can be damaged. To prevent this, the control valve has a check valve inside of it. At a specific pressure, the check valve opens to relieve the pressure on the backside of the control valve. This creates a pressure differential and allows the control valve to move. With the control valve moved, the high pressure is allowed into the pump intake passage. At this point, the check valve and control valve seat. ● SEE FIGURE 30–24.

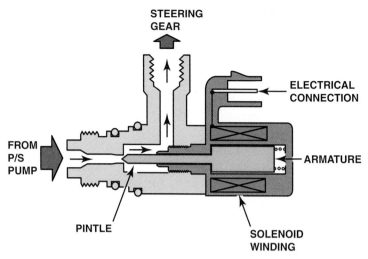

FIGURE 30–25 EVO actuator assembly.

VARIABLE-EFFORT STEERING

Variable-effort steering (VES) systems are designed to provide variable power-assisted steering. The amount of power assist increases at lower vehicle speeds to aid parking maneuvers and decreases at higher speeds for greater road feel.

As examples, General Motors uses four different variable-effort steering systems:

- **Electronic Variable Orifice (EVO)**
- **Two-Flow Electronic (TFE)**
- **Speed Sensitive Steering (SSS)**
- **Magnasteer**

The Electronic Variable Orifice (EVO) system provides a wide range of power-assisted steering based on the vehicle's operating conditions. ● **SEE FIGURE 30–25.**

The system uses vehicle speed and steering wheel speed to regulate the current to a solenoid that changes the orifice size of the flow control valve.

The size of the orifice controls the flow rate through the valve and the pressure in the hydraulic system. The desired amount is then directed to the steering gear for the power assist. The second type of power assist is the TFE system, which provides two rates of power assist:

- At low speeds, the TFE solenoid provides maximum power assist.
- At high speeds, the solenoid provides minimum power assist.

Another type of power assist is the Speed Sensitive Steering (SSS) system, which uses hydraulic pressure to resist movement in the steering gear as speed increases. This provides a firmer sense of control and stability in the steering gear at higher speeds.

ELECTRONIC VARIABLE ORIFICE (EVO) SYSTEM COMPONENTS

The main components of the EVO system are:

- Vehicle speed sensor
- Power steering control module
- Steering wheel speed sensor
- Power steering gear
- Power steering pump and solenoid actuator

The actuator is a solenoid-operated pintle valve. Electrical current flow through the solenoid controls the position of the pintle in relation to the orifice.

As the vehicle speed increases, the control module provides a higher current flow and the solenoid positions the pintle to change the size of the orifice.

This increased speed results in a reduced amount of hydraulic flow and provides less hydraulic pressure to the steering gear.

The control module uses the signal from the vehicle speed sensor to calculate the required amperage for the solenoid.

The amperage has a direct effect on steering effort and the flow rate to the gear. As the vehicle speed increases, the solenoid extends the pintle and reduces the size of the orifice. Hydraulic pressure is being reduced as the vehicle speed increases and less power assist is available.

The other sensor for the EVO system is the steering wheel speed sensor. This sensor is used to determine if the vehicle operator is performing an evasive steering maneuver.

In this situation, the controller increases the hydraulic pressure to assist the operator. The faster the driver turns the steering wheel, the stronger the signal generated by the sensor. The faster the steering wheel is rotated, the more the solenoid retracts the pintle and enlarges the size of the orifice. This increases hydraulic pressure to the steering gear and provides more power assist for the operator.

TWO-FLOW ELECTRONIC (TFE) SYSTEM

The main components of the TFE system are:

- Power steering pump and solenoid actuator
- Steering rack-and-pinion gear
- Powertrain Control Module (PCM)

The TFE actuator is a solenoid-operated pintle valve. The pintle valve only has two positions—maximum assist and reduced assist. When the solenoid is provided a ground from the chime module, the pintle extends out from the orifice and provides maximum assist. When the chime module opens the ground path, the pintle moves in to restrict the orifice and thus reduces steering assist.

The PCM provides the chime module with a vehicle speed signal. The logic circuits in the chime module determine when to energize the solenoid. The solenoid is energized whenever the vehicle speed is approximately 20 mph (32 km/h) or lower and the pintle is extended, causing the power steering pressure to increase. This provides maximum assist and the steering effort is low. When the vehicle speed is higher than 20 mph (32 km/h), the pintle is moved in and the steering pressure is low. This provides reduced assist and higher steering effort.

SSS SYSTEM

The major components of the SSS system are:

- Power steering pump
- SSS actuator
- Steering gear
- Road sensing suspension control module

The actuator is a solenoid-operated valve that controls the flow of fluid into the chambers of the steering gear valve. As more fluid flows into the chamber, pressure is built against the four pistons that are located around the spool shaft. As the pistons are loaded and pushed against the spool shaft, steering effort is increased.

Unlike the EVO and TFE systems, the SSS system uses hydraulic pressure to resist movement in the steering gear. The amount of fluid allowed into the chambers is based on the electrical current flow through the solenoid.

The Road Sensing Suspension (RSS) control module, using the signal from the vehicle speed sensor, calculates the required amperage for the solenoid.

The amperage has a direct effect on steering effort and the hydraulic flow rate into the chambers of the spool shaft. As the

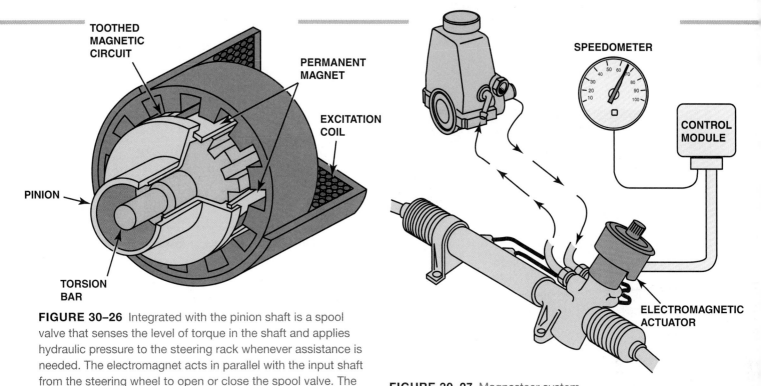

FIGURE 30–26 Integrated with the pinion shaft is a spool valve that senses the level of torque in the shaft and applies hydraulic pressure to the steering rack whenever assistance is needed. The electromagnet acts in parallel with the input shaft from the steering wheel to open or close the spool valve. The electromagnet generates variable torque, which can either increase or decrease the amount of steering torque that is needed to open the spool valve.

FIGURE 30–27 Magnasteer system.

vehicle's speed increases, more hydraulic pressure is built against the pistons and the steering effort is increased. The steering effort adjustment begins at a vehicle speed of 20 mph (32 km/h).

MAGNASTEER The fourth type of VES steering system used by General Motors is the Magnasteer system. This system uses a variable bi-directional magnetic rotary actuator built into the steering rack. The bi-directional magnetic rotary actuator has no effect on the hydraulic operation of the steering rack.

The main components in the system include:

- Power steering pump
- Magnasteer actuator assembly
- Steering gear
- Electronic brake control module (EBCM)

The Magnasteer system uses a conventional rack-and-pinion steering gear and an engine-driven hydraulic pump to provide power assist. The Magnasteer actuator consists of the following:

- A permanent magnet attached to the rotary input shaft
- A pole-piece assembly attached to the pinion
- An electromagnetic coil mounted in the steering gear housing

Integrated with the pinion shaft is a spool valve that senses the level of torque in the shaft and applies hydraulic pressure to the steering rack whenever assistance is needed. The electromagnet acts in parallel with the input shaft from the steering wheel to open or close the spool valve.

The electromagnet generates variable torque, which can either increase or diminish the amount of steering torque that is needed to open the spool valve. ● **SEE FIGURES 30–26 AND 30–27.**

To vary the amount of steering assist, the EBCM uses the signal from the wheel speed sensor to calculate the required amperage and direction of current flow to the Magnasteer actuator.

The amperage and direction of current flow have a direct effect on steering effort and the flow rate to the rack piston. When the vehicle is stationary, approximately 1.6 amps of current flow through the electromagnetic coil.

As the vehicle speed increases to approximately 45 mph, the current decreases to 0 amps. The EBCM then switches the direction of current flow. Current flow through the electromagnetic coil causes either a magnetic attraction or repelling in the Magnasteer actuator.

At low vehicle speeds below 45 mph, the direction of current flow creates a magnetic field that opposes the permanent

FIGURE 30–28 A Toyota Prius EPS assembly. *(Courtesy of Tony Martin)*

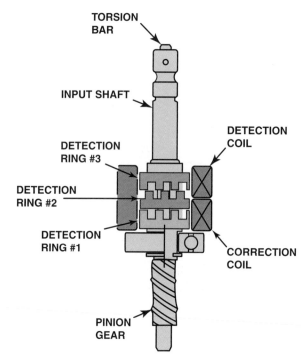

FIGURE 30–29 The torque sensor converts the torque the driver is applying to the steering wheel into a voltage signal.

VARIABLE-EFFORT STEERING (CONTINUED)

magnet. The repelling force of the magnetic field assists the spool valve in moving out of alignment with the valve body, and this increases the power assist.

With vehicle speeds below 45 mph, increased current provides increased steering assist. At vehicle speeds above 45 mph, the direction of current through the electromagnetic coil creates a magnetic field that attracts the permanent magnet.

- The magnet helps keep the spool valve aligned with the valve body, and this reduces the power assist and provides a greater road feel.
- As the vehicle speed increases, the amount of effort required to overcome the attracting force of the magnetic field increases.

With vehicle speeds above 45 mph, increased current flow provides decreased steering assist.

ELECTRIC POWER STEERING SYSTEM

Most electric power steering units use a DC electric motor. Some operate from 42 volts while others operate from 12 volts. The **electric power steering (EPS)** is also called electric power-assisted steering (EPAS).

The Toyota system on a Prius uses a DC motor, reduction gear, and torque sensor all mounted to the steering column. ● **SEE FIGURE 30–28.**

The electric power steering (EPS) is controlled by the EPS ECU, which calculates the amount of needed assist based on the input from the steering torque sensor. The steering torque sensor is a noncontact sensor that detects the movement and torque applied to the torsion bar. The torsion bar twists when the drive exerts torque to the steering wheel, and the more torque applied the farther the bar will twist. This generates a higher-voltage signal to the EPS ECU. ● **SEE FIGURE 30–29.**

The steering shaft torque sensor and the steering wheel position sensor are not serviced separately from each other or from the steering column assembly. The steering column assembly does not include the power steering motor and module

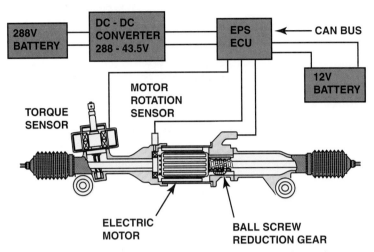

FIGURE 30–30 The electric power steering in Toyota/Lexus SUVs uses a brushless DC motor around the rack of the unit and operates on 42 volts.

FIGURE 30–31 Photo of the electric power steering gear on a Lexus RX 400h taken from underneath the vehicle.

assembly. The detection ring 1 and detection ring 2 are mounted on the input shaft and detection ring 3 is mounted on the output shaft. The input shaft and the output shaft are connected by a torsion bar. When the steering wheel is turned, the difference in relative motion between detection rings 2 and 3 is sensed by the detection coil and it sends two signals to the EPS ECU. These two signals are called Torque Sensor Signal 1 and Torque Signal 2. The EPS ECU uses these signals to control the amount of assist, and also uses the signals for diagnosis.

NOTE: If the steering wheel, steering column, or steering gear is removed or replaced, the zero point of the torque sensors must be reset.

The Toyota Highlander and Lexus RX 400h use a different electric power steering unit due to the larger size of the vehicles. This unit uses a brushless DC on the steering rack. ● SEE FIGURES 30–30 AND 30–31.

The Honda electric power steering uses an electric motor to provide steering assist and replaces the need for a hydraulic pump, hoses, and gear. A torque sensor is used to measure road resistance and the direction that the driver is turning the

steering wheel. The torque sensor input and the vehicle speed are used by the EPS controller to supply the EPS motor with the specified current to help assist the steering effort. ● SEE FIGURE 30–32.

The motor turns the pinion shaft using a worm gear. The worm gear is engaged with the worm wheel so that the motor turns the pinion shaft directly when providing steering assist. The steering rack is unique because the tie rods are mounted to the center of the rack rather than at the ends of the rack as in a conventional Honda power steering arrangement. ● SEE FIGURE 30–33.

If a major fault were to occur, the control module would first try to maintain power-assisted steering even if some sensors had failed. If the problem is serious, then the vehicle can be driven and steered manually. The EPS control unit will turn on the EPS dash warning light if a fault has been detected. A fault in the system will not cause the malfunction indicator light to come on because that light is reserved for emission-related faults only. Fault codes can be retrieved by using a scan tool and the codes will be displayed by the flashing of the EPS warning lamp.

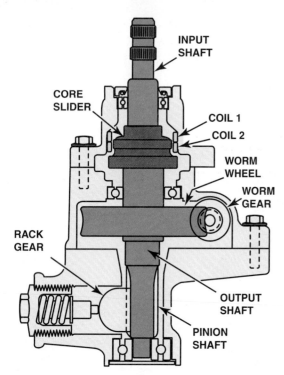

FIGURE 30–32 A cross-sectional view of a Honda electric power steering (EPS) gear.

FIGURE 30–33 Honda electric power steering unit cutaway.

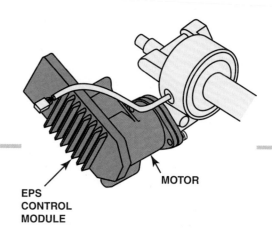

FIGURE 30–34 The Power Steering Control Module (PSCM) is attached to the motor of the electric power steering assembly.

ELECTRIC POWER STEERING SYSTEM (CONTINUED)

The EPS system includes the following components and inputs/outputs:

- Powertrain Control Module (PCM)
- Body control module (BCM)
- Power steering control module (PSCM)
- Battery voltage
- Steering shaft torque sensor
- Steering wheel position sensor
- Power steering motor
- Driver information center (DIC)
- Serial data circuit to perform the system functions

The **power steering control module (PSCM)** and the power steering motor are serviced as an assembly and are serviced separately from the steering column assembly. ● **SEE FIGURE 30–34.**

The steering shaft torque sensor and the steering wheel position sensor are not serviced separately from each other or from the steering column assembly. The steering column assembly does not include the power steering motor and module assembly.

STEERING SHAFT TORQUE SENSOR The PSCM uses the steering shaft torque sensor as a main input for determining steering direction and the amount of assist needed. The steer-

ing column has an input shaft, from the steering wheel to the torque sensor, and an output shaft, from the torque sensor to the steering shaft coupler. The input and output shafts are separated by a section of torsion bar, where the torque sensor is located. The sensor is a 5-volt dual-analog inverse signal device with a signal voltage range of 0.25 to 4.75 volts. The sensors are used to detect the direction the steering wheel is being rotated.

- When torque is applied to the steering column shaft during a right turn, the sensor signal 1 voltage increases, while the signal 2 voltage decreases.
- When torque is applied to the steering column shaft during a left turn, the sensor signal 1 voltage decreases, while the signal 2 voltage increases.

The PSCM recognizes this change in signal voltage as steering direction and steering column shaft torque.

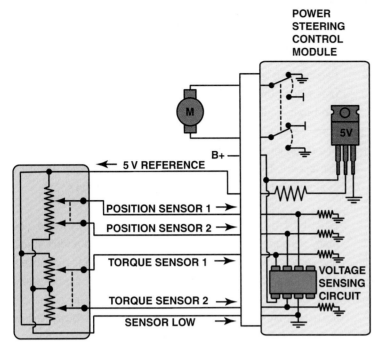

POWER
STEERING
CONTROL
MODULE

FIGURE 30–35 Schematic showing the electric power steering and the torque/position sensor.

STEERING WHEEL POSITION SENSOR

The PSCM uses the **steering position sensor (SPS)** to determine the steering system on-center position. Because the power steering motor provides a slight amount of return-to-center assist, the PSCM will command the power steering motor to the steering system center position and not beyond. The sensor is a 5-volt dual-analog signal device with a signal voltage range of 0 to 5 volts. The sensor's signal 1 and signal 2 voltage values will increase and decrease within 2.5 to 2.8 volts of each other as the steering wheel is turned. ● **SEE FIGURE 30–35.**

POWER STEERING MOTOR

The power steering motor is a 12-volt brushless DC reversible motor with a 65-amp rating. The motor assists steering through a worm gear and reduction gear located in the steering column housing.

POWER STEERING CONTROL MODULE (PSCM)

The PSCM uses a combination of steering shaft torque sensor input, vehicle speed, calculated system temperature, and steering tuning to determine the amount of steering assist. When the steering wheel is turned, the PSCM uses signal voltage from the steering shaft torque sensor to detect the amount of torque and steering direction being applied to the steering column shaft

and then commands the proper amount of current to the power steering motor. The PSCM receives a vehicle speed message from the PCM by way of the serial data circuit. At low speeds more assist is provided for easy turning during parking maneuvers, and at higher speeds, less assist is provided for improved road feel and directional stability.

NOTE: The PSCM and the power steering motor are not designed to handle 65 amps continuously. If the power steering system is exposed to excessive amounts of static steering conditions, the PSCM will go into a protection mode to avoid thermal damage to the power steering components. In this mode the PSCM will limit the amount of current commanded to the power steering motor, which reduces system temperature and steering assist levels. The PSCM has the ability to detect malfunctions within the power steering system. Any malfunction detected will cause the driver information center to display the *power steering* warning message and/or the *service vehicle soon* indicator.

The PSCM must also be set up with the correct steering tunings, which are different in relation to the vehicle's powertrain configuration, model type, tire and wheel size.

SELF-PARKING SYSTEM

Several vehicle manufacturers offer a **self-parking** feature that uses the electric power steering to steer the vehicle. The driver has control of the brakes. Most systems use the following sensors:

- Wheel speed sensor (WSS)
- Steering-angle sensor
- Ultrasonic sensors, which are used to plot a course into a parking space

Some systems, such as those manufactured by Valeo for Volkswagen, allow the driver to control the accelerator as well as the brakes, making it possible to add power to park uphill. The Toyota/Lexus system stops working if the accelerator is depressed during a self-parking event. The Toyota/Lexus system is camera based and uses the navigation system to display the parking spot with touch-screen controls. The system displays a green video box to indicate that the spot is large enough and a red box to indicate that the spot is too small. The driver positions a yellow flag on the video screen to mark the front corner of the parking spot and then the vehicle backs into the space at idle speed. The driver has to complete the parking event by straightening the vehicle and pulling forward in the spot.

DIAGNOSIS AND TESTING Self-parking systems use many sensors to achieve the parking event, and a fault in any one sensor will disable self-parking. Before trying to diagnose a self-parking fault, be sure that the driver is operating the system as designed. For example, the self-parking event is cancelled if the accelerator pedal is depressed on some units. Always follow the factory-recommended diagnostic and testing procedures.

ELECTROHYDRAULIC POWER STEERING

Electrohydraulic power steering is used on the Chevrolet Silverado hybrid truck.

The **electrohydraulic power steering (EHPS)** module controls the power steering motor, which has the function of providing hydraulic power to the brake booster and the steering gear.

A secondary function includes the ability to improve fuel economy by operating on a demand basis and the ability to provide speed-dependent variable-effort steering.

The EHPS module controls the EHPS powerpack, which is an integrated assembly consisting of the following components:

- Electric motor
- Hydraulic pump
- Fluid reservoir
- Reservoir cap
- Fluid level sensor
- Electronic controller
- Electrical connectors
  - **SEE FIGURE 30–36.**

EHPS MODULE The electrohydraulic power steering (EHPS) module is operated from the 36-volt (nominal) power supply. The EHPS module uses class 2 for serial communications. A 125-amp, 36-volt fuse is used to protect the EHPS module. If this fuse were to blow open, the EHPS system would not operate and communication codes would be set by the modules that communicate with the EHPS module. The Powertrain Control Module (PCM) is the gateway that translates controller area network (CAN) messages into class 2 messages when required for diagnostic purposes. The EHPS module receives the following messages from the CAN bus:

- Vehicle speed
- Service disconnect status
- PRNDL (shift lever) position
- Torque converter clutch (TCC)/Cruise Dump signal (gives zero-adjust brake switch position)

The EHPS module outputs the following messages to the CAN bus:

- Brake pedal rate, position, in-range rationality, and out-of-range diagnosis
- EHPS system status
- Diagnostic messages to driver information center (DIC) via hybrid control module (HCM)
- Diagnostic information requested by service technicians via Tech 2 link (class 2 via PCM)
- Steering wheel sensor diagnostic message (in-range, out-of-range failure)

The EHPS module is not attached to class 2 data and receives several signals through wiring. The signals received and used by the EHPS module include:

- The digital steering wheel speed signals from the steering wheel sensor mounted on the steering column. The

FIGURE 30–36 An electrohydraulic power steering assembly on a Chevrolet hybrid pickup truck.

steering wheel speed sensor output contains three digital signals that indicate the steering wheel position. The signals are accurate to within 1 degree. The index output references a steering wheel position of 0 degrees plus or minus 10 degrees (steering wheel centered) and is repeated every 360 degrees of steering wheel rotation.

- An analog brake pedal position signal from the brake-pedal-mounted **brake pedal position (BPP)** sensor. The BPP sensor outputs an analog signal, referenced to 5 volts, that increases or decreases with brake pedal depression. The electrical range of the BPP sensor motion is −55 degrees to +25 degrees. The mechanical range of the BPP sensor is −70 degrees to +40 degrees.

- The EHPS module also receives ignition key position signals. These signals are the ignition signal and the accessory signal. The EHPS module receives an input from the ignition 0 circuit indicating when the key is in the ACCY position. This input is used to provide an independent wake-up signal in the event of loss of the ignition input, and to activate the EHPS module when the key remains in the ACCY position.

EHPS system performance may be reduced with power steering fluid temperature change.

POWER STEERING DIAGNOSIS AND TROUBLESHOOTING

Power steering systems are generally very reliable, yet many problems, such as hard steering, are caused by not correcting simple service items such as the following:

1. **A loose, worn, or defective power steering pump drive belt.** This can cause jerky steering and belt noise, especially when turning. It is generally recommended that all belts, including the serpentine (poly V) belt, be replaced every four years.

   If the vehicle does not use a belt tensioner, then a belt tension gauge is needed to achieve the specified belt tension. Install the belt and operate the engine with all of the accessories turned on to "run-in" the belt for at least five minutes. Adjust the tension of the accessory drive belt to factory specifications or use the following table for an example of the proper tension based on the size of the belt.

Serpentine Belts

Number of Ribs Used	Tension Range (lbs.)
3	45–60
4	60–80
5	75–100
6	90–125
7	105–145

Replace any serpentine belt if more than three cracks appear in any one rib within a 3-inch span.

NOTE: Do not guess at the proper belt tension. Always use a belt tension gauge or observe the marks on the tensioner. ● SEE FIGURE 30–37.

2. **A bent or misaligned drive pulley** is usually caused by an accident or improper reassembly of the power steering pump after an engine repair procedure. This can cause a severe grinding noise whenever the engine is running and may sound like an engine problem.

3. **Low or contaminated power steering fluid** is usually caused by a slight leak at the high-pressure hose or defective inner rack seals on a power rack-and-pinion power steering system. This can cause a loud whine and a lack of normal power steering assist. See the Tech Tip, "The Visual Test."

4. **Broken or loose power steering pump mounting brackets.** In extreme cases, the pump mounting bolts can be broken. These problems can cause jerky steering. It is important to inspect the pump mounting brackets and

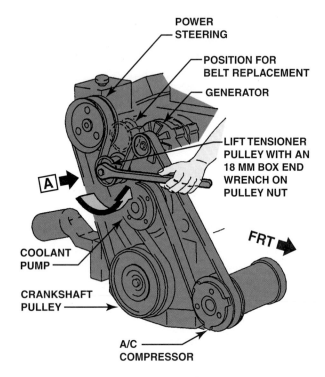

POWER STEERING

POSITION FOR BELT REPLACEMENT

GENERATOR

LIFT TENSIONER PULLEY WITH AN 18 MM BOX END WRENCH ON PULLEY NUT

FRT

A

COOLANT PUMP

CRANKSHAFT PULLEY

A/C COMPRESSOR

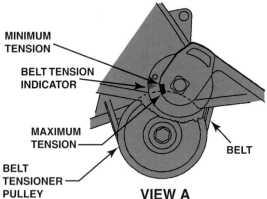

MINIMUM TENSION

BELT TENSION INDICATOR

MAXIMUM TENSION

BELT

BELT TENSIONER PULLEY

VIEW A

FIGURE 30–37 A typical service manual illustration showing the method to use to properly tension the accessory drive belt.

POWER STEERING DIAGNOSIS AND TROUBLESHOOTING (CONTINUED)

hardware carefully when diagnosing a steering-related problem. The brackets tend to crack at the adjustment points and pivot areas. Tighten all the hardware to ensure the belt will remain tight and not slip, which would cause noise or a power-assist problem.

5. **Underinflated tires.**

6. **Engine idle speed below specifications.**

7. **A defective power steering pressure switch.** If this switch fails, the computer will not increase engine idle speed while turning.

8. **Internal steering gear mechanical binding.**

As part of a complete steering system inspection and di-

FIGURE 30–38 A check of the power steering fluid should include inspecting not only the level but the condition and color of the fluid, which could indicate a possible problem with other components in the steering system.

🔧 **TECH TIP**

The Visual Test

Whenever diagnosing any power steering complaint, check the level *and* condition of the power steering fluid. Often this is best accomplished by putting your finger down into the power steering fluid reservoir and pulling it out to observe the texture and color of the fluid. ● **SEE FIGURE 30–38.**

A common problem with some power rack-and-pinion units is the wearing of grooves in the housing by the Teflon sealing rings of the spool (control) valve. When this wear occurs, aluminum particles become suspended in the power steering fluid, giving it a grayish color and thickening the fluid.

Normally clear power steering fluid that is found to be grayish in color and steering that is difficult when cold are clear indications as to what has occurred and why the steering is not functioning correctly.

agnosis, a steering wheel turning effort test should be performed. The power steering force, as measured by a spring scale during turning, should be less than 5 lb (2.3 kg).

NOTE: Some vehicles use power steering reservoir caps with *left-hand threads*. Always clean the top of the cap and observe all directions and cautions. Many power steering pump reservoirs and caps have been destroyed by technicians attempting to remove a cap in the wrong direction using large pliers.

FIGURE 30–39 Some power steering fluid is unique to the climate, such as this cold climate fluid recommended for use in General Motors vehicles when temperatures are low.

POWER STEERING FLUID The correct power steering fluid is *critical* to the operation and service life of the power steering system! The exact power steering fluid to use varies as to vehicle manufacturer. There are even differences within the same company because of various steering component suppliers.

NOTE: Remember, multiple-purpose power steering fluid does not mean *all*-purpose power steering fluid. Always consult the power steering reservoir cap, service manual, or owner's manual for the exact fluid to be used in the vehicle being serviced.

The main reason for using the specified power steering fluid is the compatibility of the fluid with the materials used in seals and hoses of the system. Using the wrong fluid (substituting ATF, for example) can lead to seal or hose deterioration and/or failure and fluid leaks.

NOTE: Always use the power steering fluid recommended by the manufacturer. The correct fluid to use is usually imprinted on or near the power steering reservoir fill cap. ● SEE FIGURE 30–39.

1. Check the power steering fluid level. Bleed the air from the system by turning the steering wheel lock-to-lock with the engine cranking.
2. Check the condition and tension of the drive belt. If in doubt, replace the belt.

3. Inspect the condition of all hoses, checking for any soft hose or places where the hose could touch another component.

4. Check the tightness of all mounting bolts of the pump and gear.

POWER STEERING FLUID FLUSHING PROCEDURE

Whenever there is any power steering service performed, such as replacement of a defective pump or steering gear or rack-and-pinion unit, the entire system should be flushed. If all of the old fluid is not flushed from the system, small pieces of a failed bearing or rotor could be circulated through the system. These metal particles can block paths in the control valve and cause failure of the new power steering pump or gear assembly.

NOTE: Besides flushing the old power steering fluid from the system and replacing it with new fluid, many technical experts recommend installing a filter in the low-pressure return line as an added precaution against serious damage from debris in the system. Power steering filters are commonly available through vehicle dealer parts departments, as well as aftermarket sources from local auto supply stores.

Always follow the vehicle manufacturer's recommended flushing procedure. Two people are needed to flush the system. Use the following steps:

STEP 1 Raise the front wheels off the ground.

STEP 2 Remove the low-pressure return hose from the pump and plug the line fitting on the pump.

STEP 3 Place the low-pressure return hose into an empty container.

STEP 4 Fill the pump reservoir with fresh fluid and start the engine.

STEP 5 As the old and dirty power steering fluid is being pumped into the container, keep the reservoir full of clean fluid while the assistant turns the steering wheel full lock one way to full lock the other way.

> **CAUTION: Never allow the pump reservoir to run dry of power steering fluid. Severe internal pump damage can result.**

STEP 6 When the fluid runs clean, stop the engine and reattach the low-pressure return hose to the pump reservoir.

STEP 7 Restart the engine and fill the reservoir to the full mark. Turn the steering wheel back and forth, avoiding the stops one or two times to bleed any trapped air in the system.

BLEEDING AIR OUT OF THE SYSTEM If the power steering fluid is tan, there may be air bubbles trapped in the fluid. Stop the engine and allow the air to burp out to the surface for several minutes. Lift the vehicle off the ground, then rotate the steering wheel. This method prevents the breakup of large air bubbles into thousands of smaller bubbles that are more difficult to bleed out of the system.

NOTE: To help rid the power steering system of unwanted trapped air, it is recommend that the engine be cranked and that the wheels be turned from stop to stop *with the tires off the ground*. Check service information for the specified procedure to follow to the disable ignition or fuel injection system to keep the engine from starting. Do not crank the engine for longer than 15 seconds to prevent starter damage due to overheating. Allow the starter to cool at least 30 seconds before cranking again.

Sometimes trapped air just cannot be bled out of the system using ordinary methods. This trapped air makes the pump extremely noisy and this noise sometimes convinces the technician that the pump itself is defective. If the power steering system has been opened for repairs and the system has been drained, trapped air may be the cause.

HOSE INSPECTION Both high-pressure and low-pressure return hoses should be inspected as part of any thorough vehicle inspection. While the low-pressure return hose generally feels softer than the high-pressure return hose, neither should feel *spongy*. A soft, spongy hose should always be replaced. ● **SEE FIGURE 30–40.**

When replacing any power steering hose, make certain that it is routed the same as the original and does not interfere with any accessory drive belt, pulley, or other movable component such as the intermediate steering shaft.

PRESSURE TESTING Use of a power steering pressure tester involves the following steps:

1. Disconnect the pressure hose at the pump.

2. Connect the hoses of the tester to the pump and the disconnected pressure line. ● **SEE FIGURE 30–41.**

3. Open the valve on the tester.

4. Start the engine. Allow the power steering system to reach operating temperatures.

5. The pressure gauge should register 80 to 125 PSI (550 to 860 kPa). If the pressure is greater than 150 PSI (1,400 kPa), check for restrictions in the system, including the

operation of the **poppet valve** located in the inlet of the steering gear.

6. Fully close the valve three times. (Do not leave the valve closed for more than five seconds!) All three readings should be within 50 PSI (345 kPa) of each other and the peak pressure should be higher than 1,000 PSI (6,900 kPa).

7. If the pressure readings are high enough *and* within 50 PSI (345 kPa) of each other, the pump is OK.

8. If the pressure readings are high enough, yet not within 50 PSI (345 kPa) of each other, the flow control valve is sticking.

9. If the pressure readings are less than 1,000 PSI (6,900 kPa), replace the flow control valve and recheck. If the pressures are still low, replace the rotor and vanes in the power steering pump.

10. If the pump is OK, turn the steering wheel to both stops. If the pressure at both stops is not the same as the maximum pressure, the steering gear (or rack and pinion) is leaking internally and should be repaired or replaced.

Many vehicle manufacturers recommend using a power steering analyzer that measures both pressure and volume, as shown in ● **FIGURE 30–42.**

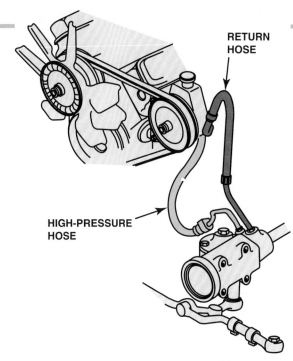

FIGURE 30–40 Inspect both high-pressure and return power steering hoses. Make sure the hoses are routed correctly and not touching sections of the body to prevent power steering noise from being transferred to the passenger compartment.

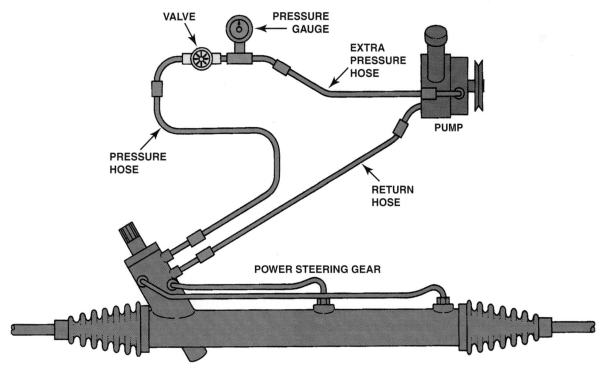

FIGURE 30–41 A drawing showing how to connect a power steering analyzer to the system.

FIGURE 30–42 A power steering analyzer that measures both pressure and volume. The shut-off valve is used to test the maximum pressure of the pump.

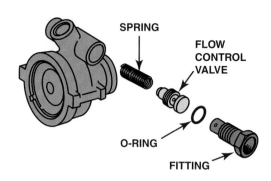

FIGURE 30–43 Typical power steering pump showing the order of assembly. The high-pressure (outlet) hose attaches to the fitting (#16). The flow control valve can be removed from the pump by removing the fitting.

POWER STEERING DIAGNOSIS AND TROUBLESHOOTING (CONTINUED)

Knowing the volume flow in the system provides information to the technician in addition to that of the pressure gauge. Many manufacturers' diagnostic procedures specify volume measurements and test results that can help pinpoint flow control or steering gear problems. Always follow the vehicle manufacturer's recommended testing procedures. Pressure and volume measurements specified by the manufacturer usually fall within the range noted in the following chart.

NOTE: Most replacement pumps are not equipped with a pulley. The old pulley must be removed and installed on the new pump. The old pulley should be carefully inspected for dents, cracks, or warpage. If the pulley is damaged, it must be replaced.

The pulley must be removed and installed with a pulley removal and installation tool. ● **SEE FIGURE 30–44.**

Typical Power Steering Pressures and Volume Specifications

Steering Action	Pressure, PSI (kPa)	Volume* (gal/min) (l/min)
Straight ahead, no steering	Less than 150 PSI (1,000 kPa)	2.0 to 3.3 gpm (10 to 15 lpm)
Slow cornering	300–450 PSI (2,000–3,000 kPa)	Within 1 gpm (4 lpm) of straight ahead
Full turn at stops	750–1,450 PSI** (5,200–10,000 kPa)	Less than 1 gpm (4 lpm)

*Volume is determined by orifice size in the outlet of the pump and is matched to the steering gear.
**Upper-limit pressure is determined by the calibration of the pressure-relief valve.

PUMP SERVICE Some power steering pump service can usually be performed without removing the pump, including the following:

1. Replacing the high-pressure and return hoses.
2. Removing and cleaning the flow control valve assembly. ● **SEE FIGURE 30–43.**

Most power steering pump service requires the removal of the pump from the engine mounting and/or removal of the drive pulley.

CAUTION: Do not hammer the pump shaft or pulley in an attempt to install the pulley. The shock blows will damage the internal components of the pump.

After removing the pump from the vehicle and removing the drive pulley, disassemble the pump according to the manufacturer's recommended procedure. ● **SEE FIGURES 30–45 THROUGH 30–49** for the disassembly and reassembly of a typical power steering pump.

Clean all parts in power steering fluid. Replace any worn or damaged parts and all seals.

FIGURE 30–44 Typical tools required to remove and install a drive pulley on a power steering pump. Often these tools can be purchased at a relatively low cost from automotive parts stores and will work on many different makes of vehicles.

SPECIAL TOOL C-4333

POWER STEERING PUMP PULLEY

REMOVE DRIVE PULLEY (TYPICAL)

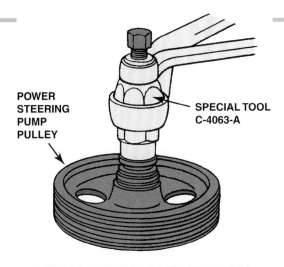

POWER STEERING PUMP PULLEY

SPECIAL TOOL C-4063-A

INSTALL DRIVE PULLEY (TYPICAL)

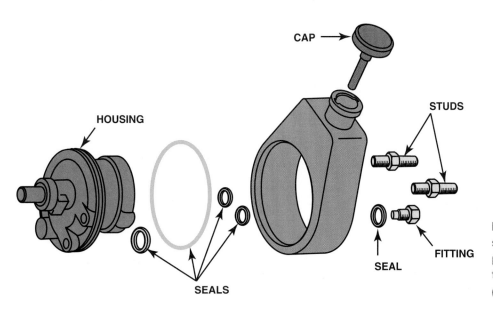

CAP

STUDS

HOUSING

SEALS

SEAL

FITTING

FIGURE 30–45 A typical submerged-type power steering pump. The pump is housed inside the fluid reservoir.
(Courtesy of Chrysler Corporation)

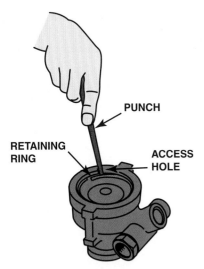

FIGURE 30–46 A punch is used to dislodge the retaining ring.

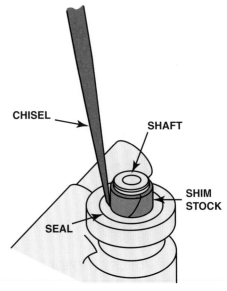

FIGURE 30–49 The shaft seal must be chiseled out. A thin metal shim stock should be used to protect the shaft from damage. Some technicians drill a small hole in the seal, then thread in a self-tapping sheet metal screw. Then pliers are used to pull out the old seal.

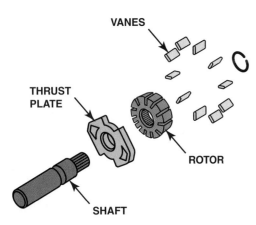

FIGURE 30–47 The driveshaft attaches to the drive pulley at one end and is splined to the pump rotor at the other end. The vanes are placed in the slots of the rotor.

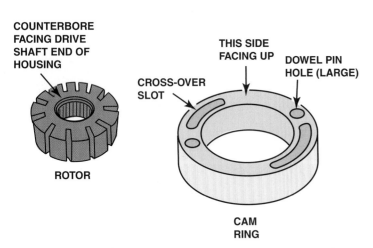

FIGURE 30–48 The pump ring *must* be installed correctly. If it is installed upside down, the internal passages will not line up and the pump will have no output.

TECH TIP

Pocket the Ignition Key to Be Safe

When replacing any steering gear such as a rack-and-pinion steering unit, be sure that no one accidentally turns the steering wheel! If the steering wheel is turned without being connected to the steering gear, the airbag wire coil (clock spring) can become off center. This can cause the wiring to break when the steering wheel is rotated after the steering gear has been replaced. To help prevent this from occurring, simply remove the ignition key from the ignition (make sure the steering wheel is locked) and put it in your pocket while servicing the steering gear.

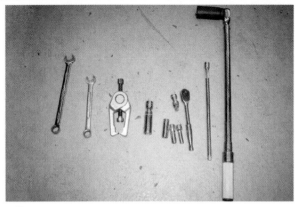

1 The tools required include a tie rod end puller and basic hand tools.

2 To help keep the steering wheel from rotating when the steering rack assembly is removed a steering wheel lock is being used.

3 After safely hoisting the vehicle and removing the front wheels, the outer tie rod end retaining nuts are removed.

4 Using a tie rod taper breaker to separate the outer tie rods from the steering knuckle without harming the rubber grease boots.

5 After moving the protective cover aside, the bolt used to retain the intermediate shaft to the steering gear stub shaft is removed.

6 The hydraulic lines attached to the steering rack to the power steering rack assembly are removed using a line wrench.

CONTINUED ▶

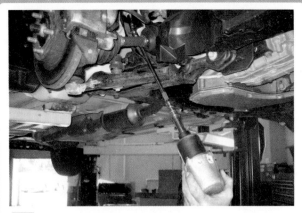

7 After supporting the engine cradle using a tall safety stand, an air impact wrench with a long extension is used to remove the engine cradle bolts.

8 Removing the lower engine cradle bolts. This will allow the cradle to be lowered to gain access to the steering rack assembly.

9 The screw jack on the tall safety stands is rotated allowing the engine cradle to be lowered.

10 Removing the steering rack attachment bolts.

11 The steering rack assembly can be lifted out of the support brackets.

12 On this General Motors vehicle, the steering rack assembly is removed from the driver's side.

13 Before reinstalling the steering gear assembly, note the notch on the stub shaft. This notch has to be aligned with the intermediate shaft retaining bolt when it is placed back into the vehicle.

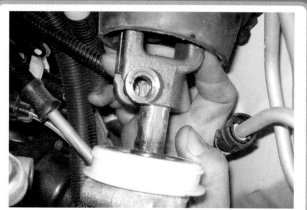

14 Installation is the reverse of removal. Be sure that the rack is centered and check that the through-bolt is properly aligned with the notch in the steering rack stub shaft.

15 While using a tall safety stand to support the engine cradle, the retaining bolts are installed.

16 A socket is being used to keep the tapered tie rod end from rotating while the retaining nut is tightened with a wrench.

17 After the hydraulic lines and retaining bolts have been installed, the power steering pump reservoir is filled using the specified fluid.

18 To bleed the trapped air out of the system, the steering wheel is rotated lock to lock with engine off and the wheels off the ground. Check for leaks then perform a test drive to verify a proper repair.

1. Always use a belt tension gauge when checking, replacing, or tightening a power steering drive belt. The proper power steering fluid should always be used to prevent possible seal or power steering hose failure.

2. Power steering troubles can usually be diagnosed using a power steering pressure gauge. Lower-than-normal pump pressure could be due to a weak (defective) power steering pump or internal leakage inside the steering gear itself.

If the pressure reaches normal when the shut-off valve on the gauge is closed, then the problem is isolated to being a defective gear.

3. Care should be taken when repairing or replacing any steering gear assembly to follow the vehicle manufacturer's recommended procedures exactly; do not substitute parts from one steering gear to another.

REVIEW QUESTIONS

1. List five possible causes for hard steering.

2. Explain the procedure for flushing a power steering system.

3. Describe how to pressure test a power steering system.

4. Briefly describe adjustment and service procedures for a power rack-and-pinion steering unit.

CHAPTER QUIZ

1. Two technicians are discussing the proper procedure for bleeding air from a power steering system. Technician A says that the front wheels of the vehicle should be lifted off the ground before bleeding. Technician B says that the steering wheel should be turned left and right with the engine off during the procedure. Which technician is correct?
   a. Technician A only
   b. Technician B only
   c. Both Technicians A and B
   d. Neither Technician A nor B

2. A power steering pressure test is being performed, and the pressure is higher than specifications with the engine running and the steering wheel stationary in the straight-ahead position. Technician A says that a restricted high-pressure line could be the cause. Technician B says that internal leakage inside the steering gear or rack-and-pinion unit could be the cause. Which technician is correct?
   a. Technician A only
   b. Technician B only
   c. Both Technicians A and B
   d. Neither Technician A nor B

3. When pressure testing an hydraulic assisted power steering system, the highest pressures were greater than 50 PSI of each other. This indicates a problem with the _____.
   a. Pump rotor
   b. Pump vanes
   c. Flow control valve
   d. Defective hose

4. Integral power steering gears use _____ for lubrication of the unit.
   a. SAE 80W-90 gear lube
   b. Chassis grease (NLGI #2)
   c. Power steering fluid in the system
   d. Molybdenum disulfide

5. What can cause hard steering on a vehicle equipped with hydraulic power assisted steering system?
   a. Low tire pressure
   b. Slipping P.S. pump drive belt
   c. Low or contaminated power steering fluid
   d. Any of the above

6. High-pressure hoses have to be used on the high-pressure side of the power steering system because pressures can reach as high as _____.
   a. 200 PSI   c. 1,500 PSI
   b. 750 PSI   d. 2,500 PSI

7. Some vehicles are equipped to signal the computer whenever the power steering pressures increase so that the idle speed can be increased to prevent stalling during turns at low speeds. What component signals the computer?
   a. Pressure-relief valve
   b. Power steering pressure switch
   c. Rotary valve
   d. Flow control valve

8. What type of motor is used in most electric power steering (EPS) systems?
   a. AC brush type
   b. DC brushless
   c. Stepper
   d. DC capacitor start

9. Electronically controlled variable-assist power steering systems vary the amount of boost by _____.
   a. Varying the pump output orifice size
   b. Speeding up or slowing down the power steering pump
   c. Changing the flow of fluid through the steering gear
   d. Bypassing some of the fluid back into the reservoir

10. Two technicians are discussing electric power steering (EPS) systems. Technician A says that some systems operate on 12 volts. Technician B says that some systems operate on 42 volts such as some hybrid electric vehicles. Which technician is correct?
    a. Technician A only
    b. Technician B only
    c. Both Technicians A and B
    d. Neither Technician A nor B

chapter 31

DRIVE AXLE SHAFTS AND CV JOINTS

OBJECTIVES

After studying Chapter 31, the reader will be able to:

1. Prepare for ASE Suspension and Steering (A4) certification test content area "C" (Related Suspension and Steering Service).
2. Name driveshaft and U-joint parts, and describe their function and operation.
3. Describe how CV joints work.
4. Explain how the working angles of the U-joints are determined.
5. List the various types of CV joints and their applications.

KEY TERMS

Cardan joints 609
Center support bearing 607
CV joint boot 614
CV joints 611
Double-Cardan joints 611
Drive axle shaft 613
Driveshaft 607
Fixed joint 612
Half shaft 613
Plunge joint 612
Propeller shaft 607
Rzeppa joint 611
Spider 609
Trunnions 609
Universal joints 609

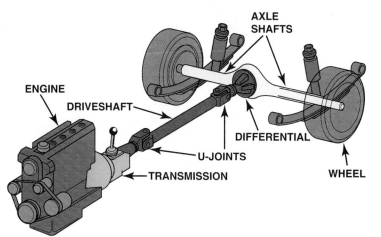

AXLE
SHAFTS

ENGINE

DRIVESHAFT

U-JOINTS

TRANSMISSION

DIFFERENTIAL

WHEEL

FIGURE 31–1 Typical rear-wheel-drive powertrain arrangement. The engine is mounted longitudinal (lengthwise).

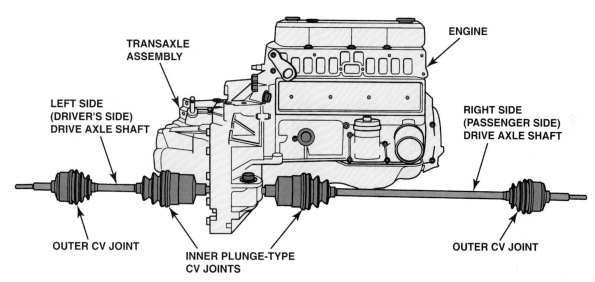

TRANSAXLE
ASSEMBLY

ENGINE

LEFT SIDE
(DRIVER'S SIDE)
DRIVE AXLE SHAFT

RIGHT SIDE
(PASSENGER SIDE)
DRIVE AXLE SHAFT

OUTER CV JOINT

INNER PLUNGE-TYPE
CV JOINTS

OUTER CV JOINT

FIGURE 31–2 Typical front-wheel-drive powertrain arrangement. The engine is usually mounted transversely (sideways).

A drive axle shaft transmits engine torque from the transmission or transaxle (if front wheel drive) to the rear axle assembly or drive wheels. ● **SEE FIGURES 31–1 AND 31–2.**

Driveshaft is the term used by the Society of Automotive Engineers (SAE) to describe the shaft between the transmission and the rear axle assembly on a rear-wheel-drive vehicle. General Motors and some other manufacturers use the term **propeller shaft** or *prop shaft* to describe this same part. The SAE term will be used throughout this textbook.

A typical driveshaft is a hollow steel tube. A splined end yoke is welded onto one end that slips over the splines of the output shaft of the transmission. ● **SEE FIGURE 31–3.** An end yoke is welded onto the other end of the driveshaft. Some driveshafts use a center support bearing.

DRIVESHAFT DESIGN

Most driveshafts are constructed of hollow steel tubing. *The forces are transmitted through the surface of the driveshaft tubing.* The surface is therefore in tension, and cracks can develop on the outside surface of the driveshaft due to metal fatigue. Driveshaft tubing can bend and, if dented, can collapse. A dented driveshaft should be replaced and no attempt should be made to repair the dent. ● **SEE FIGURE 31–4.**

Most rear-wheel-drive cars and light trucks use a one- or two-piece driveshaft. A steel tube driveshaft has a maximum *length of about 65 in. (165 cm).* Beyond this critical length, a **center support bearing** must be used, as shown in ● **FIGURE 31–5.** A center support bearing is also called a steady bearing or hanger bearing.

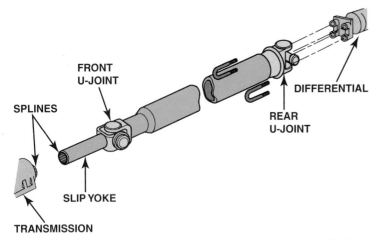

FIGURE 31–3 Typical driveshaft (also called a *propeller shaft*). The driveshaft transfers engine power from the transmission to the differential.

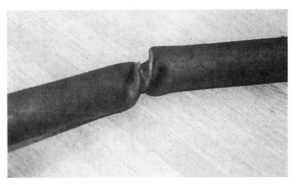

FIGURE 31–4 This driveshaft failed because it had a slight dent caused by a rock. When engine torque was applied, the driveshaft collapsed, twisted, and then broke.

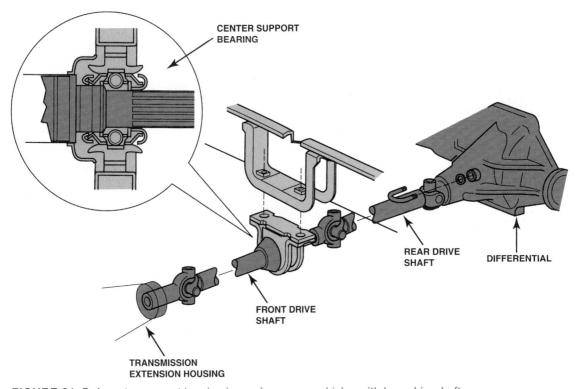

FIGURE 31–5 A center support bearing is used on many vehicles with long driveshafts.

DRIVESHAFT DESIGN (CONTINUED)

Some vehicle manufacturers use aluminum driveshafts; these can be as long as 90 in. (230 cm) with no problem. Many extended-cab pickup trucks and certain vans use aluminum driveshafts to eliminate the need (and expense) of a center support bearing. Composite-material driveshafts are also used in some vehicles. These carbon-fiber-plastic driveshafts are very strong yet lightweight, and can be made in extended lengths without the need for a center support bearing.

To dampen driveshaft noise, it is common to line the inside of the hollow driveshaft with cardboard or rubber. This helps eliminate the tinny sound whenever shifting between drive and reverse in a vehicle equipped with an automatic transmission. ● SEE FIGURE 31–6.

FIGURE 31-6 Some driveshafts use rubber between an inner and outer housing to absorb vibrations and shocks to the driveline.

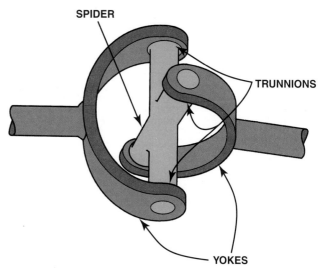

FIGURE 31-7 A simple universal joint (U-joint).

DRIVESHAFT BALANCE

All driveshafts are balanced. Generally, any driveshaft whose rotational speed is greater than 1000 RPM must be balanced. Driveshaft balance should be within 0.5% of the driveshaft weight. (This is one of the biggest reasons why aluminum or composite driveshafts can be longer because of their light weight.)

Driveshafts are often not available by make, model, and year of the vehicle. There are too many variations at the factory, such as transmission type, differential, or U-joint type. To get a replacement driveshaft, it is usually necessary to know the series of U-joints (type or style of U-joint) and the center-to-center distance between the U-joints.

U-JOINT DESIGN AND OPERATION

Universal joints (U-joints) are used at both ends of a driveshaft. U-joints allow the wheels and the rear axle to move up and down, remain flexible, and still transfer torque to the drive wheels. A simple universal joint can be made from two Y-shaped yokes connected by a crossmember called a cross or **spider**. The four arms of the cross are called **trunnions**. ● SEE FIGURE 31-7 for a line drawing of a simple U-joint with all part names identified. A similar design is the common U-joint used with a socket wrench set.

Most U-joints are called cross-yoke joints or **Cardan joints**. *Cardan* is named for a sixteenth-century Italian mathematician who worked with objects that moved freely in any direction. Torque from the engine is transferred through the U-joint. The engine drives the U-joint at a constant speed, but the output speed of the U-joint changes because of the angle of the joint. The speed changes twice per revolution. *The greater*

the angle, the greater the change in speed (velocity). ● SEE FIGURE 31-8.

If only one U-joint were used in a driveline, this change in speed of the driven side (output end) would generate vibrations in the driveline. To help reduce vibration, another U-joint is used at the other end of the driveshaft. If the angles of both joints are nearly equal, the acceleration and deceleration of one joint is offset by the alternate deceleration and acceleration of the second joint. *It is very important that both U-joints operate at about the same angle to prevent excessive driveline vibration.* ● SEE FIGURE 31-9.

ACCEPTABLE WORKING ANGLES Universal joints used in a typical driveshaft should have a *working angle* of 1/2 to 3 degrees. ● SEE FIGURE 31-10. The working angle is the angle between the driving end and the driven end of the joint. If the

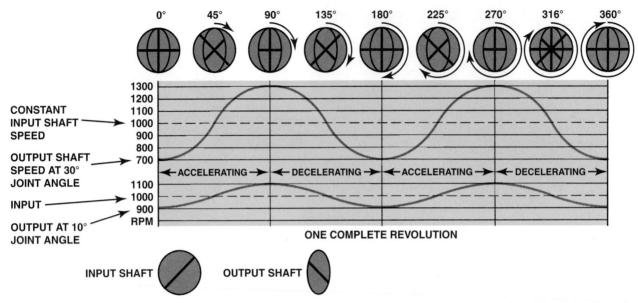

FIGURE 31–8 How the speed difference on the output of a typical U-joint varies with the speed and the angle of the U-joint. At the bottom of the chart, the input speed is a constant 1000 RPM, while the output speed varies from 900 RPM to 1100 RPM when the angle difference in the joint is only 10°. At the top part of the chart, the input speed is a constant 1000 RPM, yet the output speed varies from 700 to 1200 RPM when the angle difference in the joint is changed to 30°. *(Courtesy of Dana Corporation)*

U-JOINT DESIGN AND OPERATION (CONTINUED)

driveshaft is perfectly straight (0-degree working angle), then the needle bearings inside the bearing cap are not revolving because there is no force (no difference in angles) to cause the rotation of the needle bearings. If the needle bearings do not rotate, they can exert a constant pressure in one place and damage the bearing journal. If a two-piece driveshaft is used, one U-joint (usually the front) runs at a small working angle of about 1/2 degree, just enough to keep the needle bearings rotating. The other two U-joints (from the center support bearing and rear U-joint at the differential) operate at typical working angles of a single-piece driveshaft.

If the U-joint working angles differ by more than a 1/2 degree between the front and the rear joint, a vibration is usually produced that is *torque sensitive.* As the vehicle is first accelerated from a stop, engine torque can create unequal driveshaft angles by causing the differential to rotate on its suspension support arms. This vibration is most noticeable when the vehicle is heavily loaded and being accelerated at lower speeds. The vibration usually diminishes at higher speeds due to decrease in the torque being transmitted. If the driveshaft angles are excessive (over 3 degrees), a vibration is usually produced that increases as the speed of the vehicle (and driveshaft) increases.

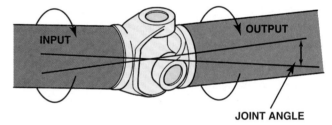

FIGURE 31–9 The joint angle is the difference between the angles of the joint. *(Courtesy of Dana Corporation)*

FIGURE 31–10 The angle of this rear Cardan U-joint is noticeable.

FIGURE 31–11 A double-Cardan U-joint.

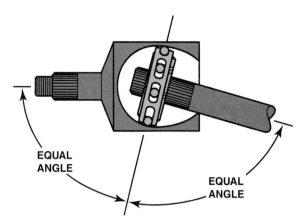

EQUAL ANGLE

EQUAL ANGLE

FIGURE 31–12 A constant velocity (CV) joint can operate at high angles without a change in velocity (speed) because the joint design results in equal angles between input and output.

CONSTANT VELOCITY JOINTS

Constant velocity joints, commonly called **CV joints**, are designed to rotate without changing speed. Regular U-joints are usually designed to work up to 12 degrees of angularity. If two Cardan-style U-joints are joined together, the angle at which this **double-Cardan joint** can function is about 18 to 20 degrees. ● SEE FIGURE 31–11.

Double-Cardan U-joints were first used on large rear-wheel-drive vehicles to help reduce drive-line-induced vibrations, especially when the rear of the vehicle was fully loaded and driveshaft angles were at their greatest. As long as a U-joint (either single or double Cardan) operates in a straight line, the driven shaft will rotate at the same constant speed (velocity) as the driving shaft. As the angle increases, the driven shaft speed or velocity varies during each revolution. This produces pulsations and a noticeable vibration or surge. The higher the shaft speed and the greater the angle of the joint, the greater the pulsations.

NOTE: **Many four-wheel-drive light trucks use standard Cardan-style U-joints in the front drive axles. If the front wheels are turned sharply and then accelerated, the entire truck often shakes due to the pulsations created by the speed variations through the U-joints. This vibration is normal and cannot be corrected. It is characteristic of this type of design and is usually not noticeable in normal driving.**

The first constant velocity joint was designed by Alfred H. Rzeppa (pronounced shep'pa) in the mid-1920s. The **Rzeppa joint** transfers torque through six round balls that are held in position midway between the two shafts. This design causes

the angle between the shafts to be equally split regardless of the angle. ● SEE FIGURE 31–12. Because the angle is always split equally, torque is transferred equally without the change in speed (velocity) that occurs in Cardan-style U-joints. This style

 FREQUENTLY ASKED QUESTION

What Is a 1350-Series U-Joint?

Most universal joints are available in sizes to best match the torque that they transmit. The larger the U-joint, the higher the amount of torque. Most U-joints are sized and rated by series numbers. See the accompanying chart for series numbers and sizes.

Series Number	Cap Diameter (inches)	Overall Length (inches)	Trunnion Diameter (inches)
1000	15/16	2 5/64	1/2
1100	15/16	2 13/64	1/2
1260/1270	1 1/16	2 31/32	19/32
1280	1 1/16	2 31/32	39/64
1310	1 1/16	2 31/32	21/32
1330	1 1/16	3 3/8	21/32
1350	1 3/16	3 3/8	49/64
1410	1 3/16	3 15/16	49/64
1480	1 3/8	3 7/8	57/64

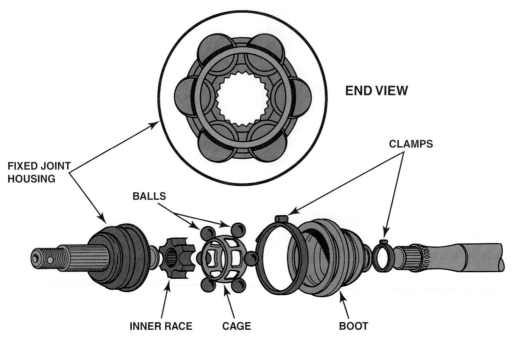

END VIEW

CLAMPS

FIXED JOINT
HOUSING

BALLS

INNER RACE   CAGE   BOOT

FIGURE 31–13 A Rzeppa fixed joint. This type of CV joint is commonly used at the wheel side of the drive axle shaft. This joint can operate at high angles to compensate for suspension travel and steering angle changes. *(Courtesy of Dana Corporation)*

CONSTANT VELOCITY JOINTS (CONTINUED)

of joint results in a constant velocity between driving and driven shafts. It can also function at angles greater than simple U-joints can, up to 40 degrees.

NOTE: CV joints are also called LOBRÖ joints, the brand name of an original equipment manufacturer.

While commonly used today in all front-wheel-drive vehicles and many four-wheel-drive vehicles, its first use was on the front-wheel-drive 1929 Cord. Built in Auburn, Indiana, the Cord was the first front-wheel-drive car to use a CV-type drive axle joint.

OUTER CV JOINTS
The Rzeppa-type CV joint is most commonly used as an outer joint on most front-wheel-drive vehicles. ● **SEE FIGURE 31–13.** The outer joint must do the following:

1. Allow up to 40 degrees or more of movement to allow the front wheels to turn

2. Allow the front wheels to move up and down through normal suspension travel in order to provide a smooth ride over rough surfaces

3. Be able to transmit engine torque to drive the front wheels

Outer CV joints are called **fixed joints**. The outer joints are also attached to the front wheels. They are more likely to suffer from road hazards that often can cut through the protective outer flexible boot. ● **SEE FIGURE 31–14.** Once this boot has

been split open, the special high-quality grease is thrown out and contaminants such as dirt and water can enter. Some joints cannot be replaced individually if worn. ● **SEE FIGURE 31–15.**

NOTE: Research has shown that in as few as eight hours of driving time, a CV joint can be destroyed by dirt, moisture, and a lack of lubrication if the boot is torn. The technician should warn the owner as to the possible cost involved in replacing the CV joint itself whenever a torn CV boot is found.

INNER CV JOINTS
Inner CV joints attach the output of the transaxle to the drive axle shaft. Inner CV joints are therefore inboard, or toward the center of the vehicle. ● **SEE FIGURE 31–16.**

Inner CV joints have to be able to perform two very important movements:

1. Allow the drive axle shaft to move up and down as the wheels travel over bumps.

2. Allow the drive axle shaft to change length as required during vehicle suspension travel movements (lengthening and shortening as the vehicle moves up and down; same as the slip yoke on a conventional RWD driveshaft). CV joints are also called **plunge joints**.

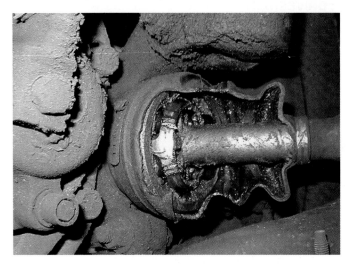

FIGURE 31–14 The protective CV joint boot has been torn away on this vehicle and all of the grease has been thrown outward onto the brake and suspension parts. The driver of this vehicle noticed a "clicking" noise, especially when turning.

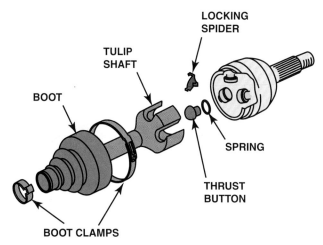

FIGURE 31–15 A tripod fixed joint. This type of joint is found on some Japanese vehicles. If the joint wears out, it is to be replaced with an entire drive axle shaft assembly.

FIGURE 31–16 The fixed outer joint is required to move in all directions because the wheels must turn for steering as well as move up and down during suspension movement. The inner joint has to be able to not only move up and down but also plunge in and out as the suspension moves up and down. (Courtesy of Dana Corporation)

DRIVE AXLE SHAFTS Unequal-length **drive axle shafts** (also called **half shafts**) result in unequal drive axle shaft angles to the front drive wheels. ● **SEE FIGURE 31–17.** This unequal angle often results in a pull on the steering wheel during acceleration. This pulling to one side during acceleration due to unequal engine torque being applied to the front drive wheels is called torque steer. To help reduce the effect of torque steer, some vehicles are manufactured with an intermediate shaft that results in equal drive axle shaft angles. Both designs use fixed outer CV joints with plunge-type inner joints.

? FREQUENTLY ASKED QUESTION

What Is That Weight for on the Drive Axle Shaft?

Some drive axle shafts are equipped with what looks like a balance weight. ● SEE FIGURE 31–18. It is actually a dampener weight used to dampen out certain drive line vibrations. The weight is not used on all vehicles and may or may not appear on the same vehicle depending on engine, transmission, and other options. The service technician should always try to replace a defective or worn drive axle shaft with the exact replacement. When replacing an entire drive axle shaft, the technician should always follow the manufacturer's instructions regarding either transferring or not transferring the weight to the new shaft.

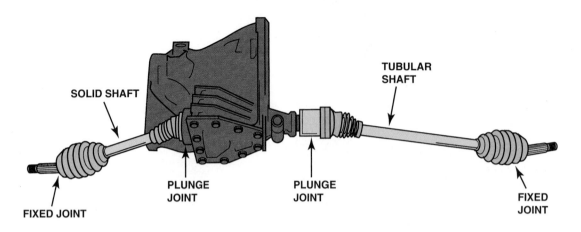

UNEQUAL LENGTH DRIVESHAFT

SOLID SHAFT

TUBULAR SHAFT

FIXED JOINT

PLUNGE JOINT

PLUNGE JOINT

FIXED JOINT

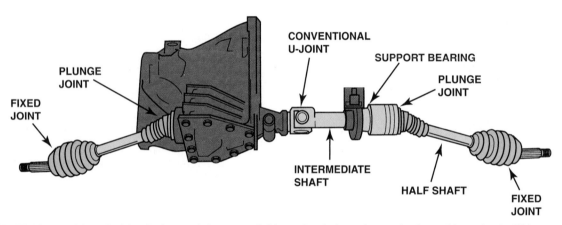

EQUAL LENGTH DRIVESHAFT

CONVENTIONAL U-JOINT

SUPPORT BEARING

PLUNGE JOINT

PLUNGE JOINT

FIXED JOINT

FIXED JOINT

INTERMEDIATE SHAFT

HALF SHAFT

FIGURE 31–17 Unequal-length driveshafts result in unequal drive axle shaft angles to the front drive wheels. This unequal angle side-to-side often results in a steering of the vehicle during acceleration called torque steer. By using an intermediate shaft, both drive axles are the same angle and the torque steer effect is reduced. *(Courtesy of Dana Corporation)*

FIGURE 31–18 A typical drive axle shaft with dampener weight.

CONSTANT VELOCITY JOINTS (CONTINUED)

Typical types of inner CV joints that are designed to move axially, or *plunge,* include the following:

1. Tripod. ● **SEE FIGURE 31–19.**
2. Cross groove. ● **SEE FIGURE 31–20.**
3. Double offset. ● **SEE FIGURE 31–21.**

CV joints are also used in rear-wheel-drive vehicles and in many four-wheel-drive vehicles.

CV JOINT BOOT MATERIALS The pliable boot surrounding the CV joint, or **CV joint boot**, must be able to remain

TRIPOD TYPE PLUNGE JOINT

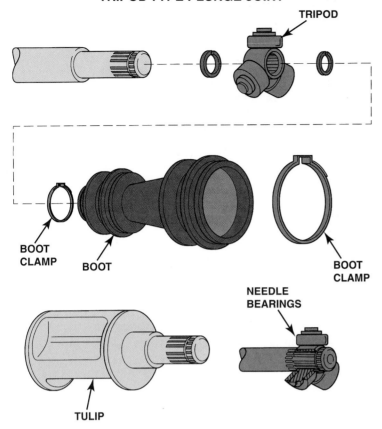

TRIPOD

BOOT CLAMP

BOOT

BOOT CLAMP

NEEDLE BEARINGS

TULIP

NOTE: CARE MUST BE TAKEN OR TRIPOD ROLLERS MAY COME OFF TRIPOD

FIGURE 31–19 A tripod joint is also called a tripot, tripode, or tulip design. *(Courtesy of Dana Corporation)*

CROSS-GROOVE PLUNGE JOINT

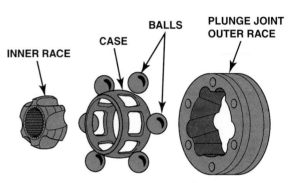

INNER RACE

CASE

BALLS

PLUNGE JOINT OUTER RACE

FIGURE 31–20 A cross-groove plunge joint is used on many German front-wheel-drive vehicles and as both inner and outer joints on the rear of vehicles that use an independent-type rear suspension. *(Courtesy of Dana Corporation)*

DOUBLE-OFFSET BALL-TYPE PLUNGE JOINT

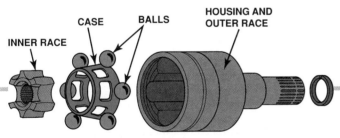

INNER RACE

CASE

BALLS

HOUSING AND OUTER RACE

FIGURE 31–21 Double-offset ball-type plunge joint. *(Courtesy of Dana Corporation)*

flexible under all weather conditions and still be strong enough to avoid being punctured by road debris. There are four basic types of boot materials used over CV joints:

1. *Natural rubber* (black) uses a bridge-type stainless steel clamp to retain.

2. *Silicone rubber* (gray) is a high-temperature-resistant material that is usually only used in places that need heat protection, such as the inner CV joint of a front-wheel-drive vehicle.

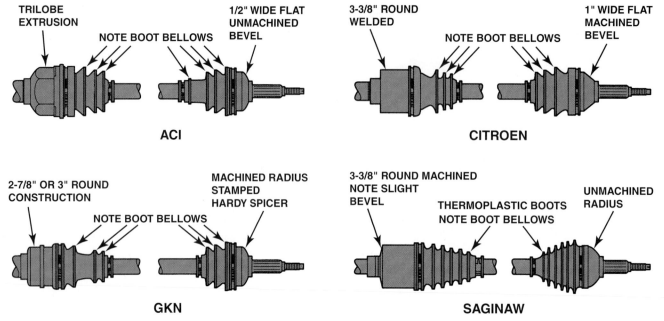

FIGURE 31–22 Getting the correct boot kit or parts from the parts store is more difficult on many Chrysler front-wheel-drive vehicles because Chrysler has used four different manufacturers for its axle shaft assemblies. *(Courtesy of Dana Corporation)*

CONSTANT VELOCITY JOINTS (CONTINUED)

3. *Hard thermoplastic* (black) is a hard plastic material requiring heavy-duty clamps and a lot of torque to tighten (about 100 lb-ft!).

4. *Urethane* (usually blue) is a type of boot material usually found in an aftermarket part. ● **SEE FIGURE 31–22** for examples of various types of CV joint boots depending on the manufacturer of the CV joints and shafts.

NOTE: Some aftermarket companies offer a split-style replacement CV joint boot. Being split means that the boot can be replaced without having to remove the drive axle shaft. Vehicle manufacturers usually do *not* recommend this type of replacement boot because the joint cannot be disassembled and properly cleaned with the drive axle still in the vehicle. The split boots must also be kept perfectly clean (a hard job to do with all the grease in the joint) in order to properly seal the seam on the split boot.

It is important that boot seals be inspected regularly and replaced if damaged. The inboard (plunging joint) can often pump water into the joint around the seals or through small holes in the boot material itself because the joint moves in and out. Seal retainers are used to provide a leakproof connection between the boot seal and the housing or axle shaft.

CV JOINT GREASE CV joints require special greases. Grease is an oil with thickening agents. Greases are named for the thickening agents used.

Most CV joint grease is molybdenum-disulfide-type grease, commonly referred to as *moly* grease. The exact composition of grease can vary depending on the CV joint manufacturer. *The grease supplied with a replacement CV joint or boot kit should be the only grease used.*

The exact mix of chemicals, viscosity (thickness), wear, and corrosion-resistant properties varies from one CV joint application to another. Some technicians mistakenly think that the *color* of the grease determines in which CV joint it is used. The color—such as black, blue, red, or tan—is used to identify the grease during manufacturing and packaging as well as to give the grease a consistent, even color (due to blending of various ingredients in the grease).

The exact grease to use depends on many factors, including the following:

1. The type (style) of CV joint. For example, outer (fixed) and inner (plunging) joints have different lubricating needs.

2. The location of the joint on the vehicle. For example, inner CV joints are usually exposed to the greatest amount of heat.

3. The type of boot. The grease has to be compatible with the boot material.

1. The driveshaft of a rear-wheel-drive vehicle transmits engine torque from the transmission to the differential.

2. Driveshaft length is usually limited to about 65 inches due to balancing considerations unless a two-piece or a composite material shaft is used.

3. Universal joints (U-joints) allow the driveshaft to transmit engine torque while the suspension and the rear axle assembly are moving up and down during normal driving conditions.

4. Acceptable working angles for a Cardan-type U-joint fall within 1/2 to 3 degrees. Some angle is necessary to cause the roller bearings to rotate; a working angle of greater than 3 degrees can lead to driveline vibrations.

5. Constant velocity (CV) joints are used on all front-wheel-drive vehicles and many four-wheel-drive vehicles to provide a smooth transmission of torque to the drive wheels regardless of angularity of the wheel or joint.

6. Outer or fixed CV joints commonly use a Rzeppa design, while inner CV joints are the plunging or tripod type.

REVIEW QUESTIONS

1. Explain why Cardan-type U-joints on a driveshaft must be within 1/2-degree working angles.

2. What makes a constant velocity joint able to transmit engine torque through an angle at a constant velocity?

3. What type of grease must be used in CV joints?

CHAPTER QUIZ

1. The name most often used to describe the universal joints on a conventional rear-wheel-drive vehicle driveshaft is _____.
   a. Trunnion
   b. Cardan
   c. CV
   d. Spider

2. A rear-wheel-drive vehicle shudders or vibrates when first accelerating from a stop. The vibration is less noticeable at higher speeds. The most likely cause is _____.
   a. Driveshaft unbalance
   b. Excessive U-joint working angles
   c. Unequal U-joint working angles
   d. Brinelling of the U-joint

3. All driveshafts are balanced.
   a. True
   b. False

4. The maximum difference between the front and rear working angle of a driveshaft is _____.
   a. 1/4 degree
   b. 1/2 degree
   c. 1 degree
   d. 3 degrees

5. Which series U-joint has the greatest torque capacity?
   a. 1260
   b. 1310
   c. 1350
   d. 1480

6. Two technicians are discussing torque steer on a front-wheel-drive vehicle. Technician A says that equal length drive axle shafts help reduce torque steer. Technician B says that equal drive axle shaft angles help reduce torque steer. Which technician is correct?
   a. Technician A only
   b. Technician B only
   c. Both Technicians A and B
   d. Neither Technician A nor B

7. The outer CV joints used on front-wheel-drive vehicles are _____.
   a. Fixed type
   b. Plunge type

8. The proper grease to use with a CV joint is _____.
   a. Black chassis grease
   b. Dark blue EP grease
   c. Red moly grease
   d. The grease that is supplied with the boot kit

9. Drive axle shafts are also called _____.
   a. Double-Cardan shafts
   b. Half shafts
   c. Driveshafts
   d. Propeller shafts

10. Two technicians are discussing a dented driveshaft. Technician A says that it should be repaired. Technician B says it should be replaced. Which technician is correct?
    a. Technician A only
    b. Technician B only
    c. Both Technicians A and B
    d. Neither Technician A nor B

DRIVE AXLE SHAFT AND CV JOINT SERVICE

OBJECTIVES

After studying Chapter 32, the reader will be able to:

1. Prepare for ASE Suspension and Steering (A4) certification test content area "C" (Related Suspension and Steering Service).

2. Explain how to perform a U-joint inspection.

3. List the steps necessary to replace a U-joint.

4. Explain how to perform a measurement of the working angles of a U-joint.

5. Describe the service procedures for replacing CV joints and boots.

6. Describe the routine maintenance service procedures required for drive axle shafts and universal CV joints.

KEY TERMS

Inclinometer 625
Pin bushings 624
Pinch bolt 627
Spline bind 629

Synthetic retainers 624
Torque prevailing nut 629
U-joints 621

FIGURE 32–1 Notice how the needle bearings have worn grooves into the bearing surface of the U-joint.

The driveshaft of a typical rear-wheel-drive (RWD) vehicle rotates about three times faster than the wheels. This is due to the gear reduction that occurs in the differential. The differential not only provides gear reduction but also allows for a difference in the speed of the rear wheels that is necessary whenever turning a corner.

The driveshaft rotates at the same speed as the engine if the transmission ratio is 1 to 1 (1:1). The engine speed, in revolutions per minute (RPM), is transmitted through the transmission at the same speed. In lower gears, the engine speed is many times faster than the output of the transmission. Most transmissions today, both manual and automatic, have an overdrive gear. This means that at highway speeds, the driveshaft is rotating faster than the engine (the engine speed is decreased or overdriven to help reduce engine speed and improve fuel economy).

The driveshaft must travel up and down as the vehicle moves over bumps and dips in the road while rotating and transmitting engine power to the drive wheels. The driveshaft and universal joints should be carefully inspected whenever any of the following problems or symptoms occur:

1. Vibration or harshness at highway speed
2. A clicking sound whenever the vehicle is moving either forward or in reverse
3. A clunking sound whenever changing gears, such as moving from Drive to Reverse

NOTE: A click-click-click sound while moving in reverse is usually the first indication of a defective U-joint. This clicking occurs in reverse because the needle bearings are being forced to rotate in a direction opposite the usual.

 REAL WORLD FIX

The Squeaking Pickup Truck

The owner of a pickup truck complained that a squeaking noise occurred while driving in reverse. The "eeeee-eeeee-eeee" sound increased in frequency as the truck increased in speed, yet the noise did not occur when driving forward.

Because there was no apparent looseness in the U-joints, the service technician at first thought that the problem was inside either the transmission or the rear end. When the driveshaft was removed to further investigate the problem, it became obvious where the noise was coming from. The U-joint needle bearing had worn the cross-shaft bearing surface of the U-joint. ● **SEE FIGURE 32–1.** The noise occurred only in reverse because the wear had occurred in the forward direction, and therefore only when the torque was applied in the opposite direction did the needle bearing become bound up and start to make noise. A replacement U-joint solved the squeaking noise in reverse.

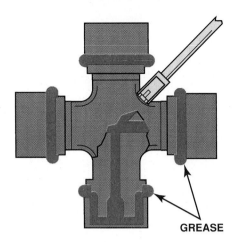

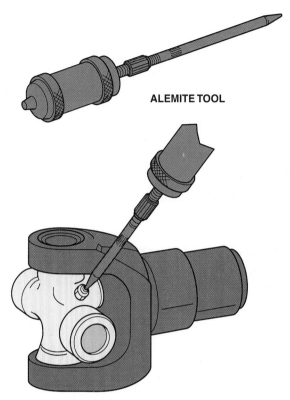

ALEMITE TOOL

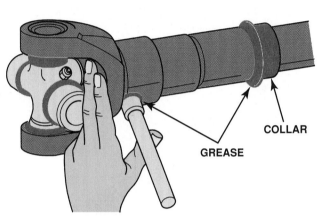

GREASE

COLLAR

GREASE

FIGURE 32–2 All U-joints and spline collars equipped with a grease fitting should be greased four times a year as part of a regular lubrication service. *(Courtesy of Dana Corporation)*

FIGURE 32–3 Many U-joints require a special grease gun tool to reach the grease fittings. *(Courtesy of Dana Corporation)*

DRIVESHAFT AND U-JOINT INSPECTION

The driveshaft should be inspected for the following:

1. Any dents or creases caused by incorrect hoisting of the vehicle or by road debris.

   CAUTION: A dented or creased driveshaft can collapse, especially when the vehicle is under load. This collapse of the driveshaft can cause severe damage to the vehicle and may cause an accident.

2. Undercoating, grease, or dirt buildup on the driveshaft can cause a vibration.

3. Undercoating should be removed using a suitable solvent and a rag. Always dispose of used rags properly.

The **U-joints** should be inspected every time the vehicle chassis is lubricated, or four times a year. Original equipment (OE) U-joints are permanently lubricated and have no provision for greasing. If there is a grease fitting, the U-joint should be lubricated by applying grease with a grease gun. ● **SEE FIGURES 32–2 AND 32–3.**

In addition to periodic lubrication, the driveshaft should be grabbed and moved to see if there is any movement of the U-joints. If *any* movement is noticed when the driveshaft is moved, the U-joint is worn and must be replaced.

NOTE: U-joints are not serviceable items and cannot be repaired. If worn or defective, they must be replaced.

FIGURE 32–4 Always mark the original location of U-joints before disassembly.

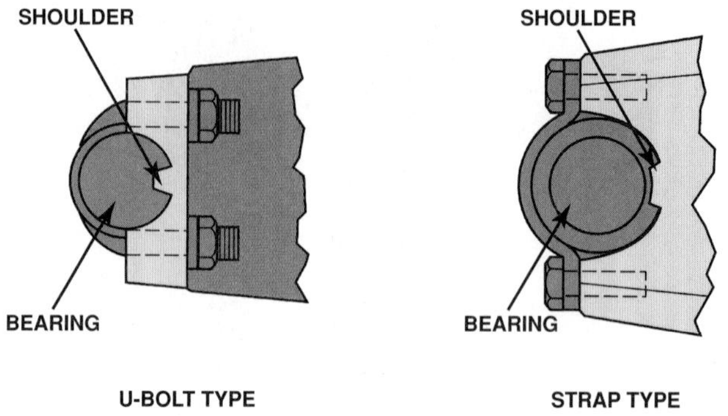

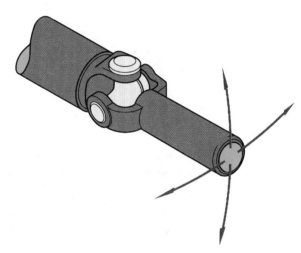

FIGURE 32–5 Two types of retaining methods that are commonly used at the rear U-joint at the differential. *(Courtesy of Dana Corporation)*

DRIVESHAFT AND U-JOINT INSPECTION (CONTINUED)

U-joints can be defective and still not show noticeable free movement. *A proper U-joint inspection can be performed only by removing the driveshaft from the vehicle.*

Before removing the driveshaft, always mark the position of all mating parts to ensure proper reassembly. White correction fluid, also known as "White Out" or "Liquid Paper," is an easy and fast-drying marking material. ● **SEE FIGURE 32–4.**

To remove the driveshaft from a rear-wheel-drive vehicle, remove the four fasteners at the rear U-joint at the differential. ● **SEE FIGURE 32–5.**

Push the driveshaft forward toward the transmission and then down and toward the rear of the vehicle. The driveshaft should slip out of the transmission spline and can be removed from underneath the vehicle.

NOTE: With the driveshaft removed, transmission lubricant can leak out of the rear extension housing. To prevent a mess, use an old spline the same size as the one being removed or place a plastic bag over the extension housing to hold any escaping lubricant. A rubber band can be used to hold the bag onto the extension housing.

To inspect U-joints, move each joint through its full travel, making sure it can move (articulate) freely and equally in all directions. ● **SEE FIGURE 32–6.**

FIGURE 32–6 The best way to check any U-joint is to remove the driveshaft from the vehicle and move each joint in all directions. A good U-joint should be free to move without binding. *(Courtesy of Dana Corporation)*

U-JOINT REPLACEMENT

All movement in a U-joint should occur between the trunnions and the needle bearings in the end caps. The end caps are press-fit to the yokes, which are welded to the driveshaft. Three types of retainers are used to keep the bearing caps on the U-joints: the outside snap ring (● **SEE FIGURE 32–7**), the inside retaining ring (● **SEE FIGURE 32–8**), and injected synthetic (usually nylon).

After removing the retainer, use a press or a vise to separate the U-joint from the yoke. ● **SEE FIGURE 32–9.**

FIGURE 32–7 Typical U-joint that uses an outside snap ring. This style of joint bolts directly to the companion flange that is attached to the pinion gear in the differential.

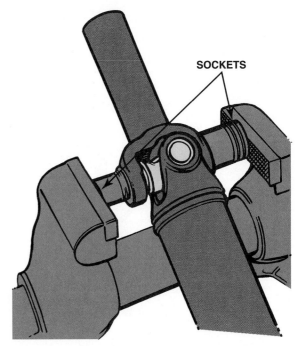

FIGURE 32–9 Use a vise and two sockets to replace a U-joint. One socket fits over the bearing cup and one fits on the bearing to press fit the cups from the crosspiece.

FIGURE 32–8 A U-joint that is held together by nylon and usually requires that heat be applied to remove from the yoke.

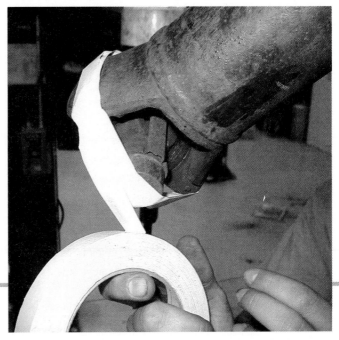

FIGURE 32–10 Taping the U-joint to prevent the caps from coming off.

 TECH TIP

Use Tape to Be Safe

When removing a driveshaft, use tape to prevent the rear U-joint caps from falling off. If the caps fall off the U-joint, all of the needle bearings will fall out and scatter over the floor. ● **SEE FIGURE 32–10.**

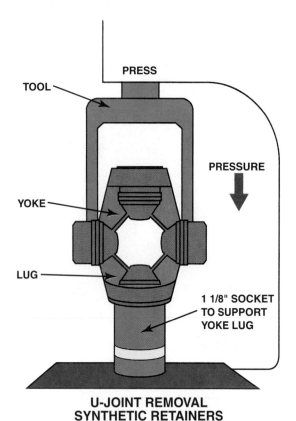

U-JOINT REMOVAL SYNTHETIC RETAINERS

FIGURE 32–11 A special tool being used to press apart a U-joint that is retained by injected plastic. Heat from a propane torch may be necessary to soften the plastic to avoid exerting too much force on the U-joint.

U-JOINT REPLACEMENT (CONTINUED)

U-joints that use **synthetic retainers** must be separated using a press and a special tool to press onto both sides of the joint in order to shear the plastic retainer, as shown in ● **FIGURE 32–11.**

Replacement U-joints use spring clips instead of injected plastic. Remove the old U-joint from the yoke, as shown in ● **FIGURE 32–12,** and replace with a new U-joint. Replacement U-joints should be *forged* (never cast) and use up to 32 needle bearings (also called **pin bushings**) instead of just 24 needle bearings, as used in lower-quality U-joints. Replacement U-joints usually have a grease fitting so that the new replacement U-joint can be properly lubricated. ● **SEE FIGURE 32–13.**

After removing any dirt or burrs from the yoke, press in a new U-joint. Rotate the new joint after installation to make sure it moves freely, without binding or stiffness. If a U-joint is stiff, it can cause a vibration.

FIGURE 32–12 Removing the worn cross from the yoke.

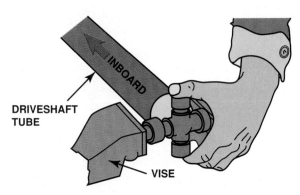

FIGURE 32–13 When installing a new U-joint, position the grease fitting on the inboard side (toward the driveshaft tube) and in alignment with the grease fitting of the U-joint at the other end.

NOTE: If a U-joint is slightly stiff after being installed, strike the U-joint using a brass punch and a light hammer. This often frees a stiff joint and is often called "relieving the joint." The shock aligns the needle bearings in the end caps.

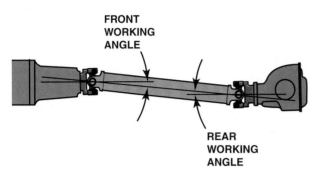

FIGURE 32-14 The working angle of most U-joints should be at least 1/2 degree (to permit the needle bearing to rotate in the U-joints) and should not exceed 3 degrees or a vibration can occur in the driveshaft, especially at higher speeds. The difference between the front and rear working angles should be within 1/2 degree of each other.

FIGURE 32-15 An inclinometer with a magnetic base is being used to measure the angle of the driveshaft at the rear U-joint.

U-JOINT WORKING ANGLES

Unequal or incorrect U-joint working angles can cause severe vibrations. Driveshaft and U-joint angles may change from the original factory setting due to one or more of the following:

1. Defective or collapsed engine or transmission mounts

2. Defective or sagging springs, especially the rear springs due to overloading or other causes

3. Accident damage or other changes to the chassis of the vehicle

4. Vehicle modification that raises or lowers the ride height

Replace any engine or transmission mount that is cracked or collapsed. When a mount collapses, the engine drops from its original location. Now the driveshaft angles are changed and a vibration may be felt.

Rear springs often sag after many years of service or after being overloaded. This is especially true of pickup trucks. Many people carry as much as the cargo bed can hold, often exceeding the factory-recommended carry capacity or gross vehicle weight (GVW) of the vehicle.

To measure U-joint and driveshaft angles, the vehicle must be hoisted using an axle contact or drive-on-type lift so as to maintain the same driveshaft angles as the vehicle has while being driven.

The working angles of the two U-joints on a driveshaft should be within 1/2 degree of each other in order to cancel out speed changes. ● **SEE FIGURE 32-14.**

To measure the working angle of a U-joint, follow these steps:

STEP 1 Place an **inclinometer** (a tool used to measure angles) on the rear U-joint bearing cap. Level the bubble and read the angle. ● **SEE FIGURE 32-15;** the pictured reading is 19.5 degrees.

STEP 2 Rotate the driveshaft 90 degrees and read the angle of the rear yoke. For example, this reading is 17 degrees.

STEP 3 Subtract the smaller reading from the larger reading to obtain the working angle of the joint. In this example, it is 2.5 degrees (19.5 degrees − 17 degrees = 2.5 degrees).

Repeat the same procedure for the front U-joint. The front and rear working angles should be within 0.5 degrees. If the two working angles are not within 0.5 degrees, shims can be added to bring the two angles closer together. The angle of the rear joint is changed by installing a tapered shim between the leaf spring and the axle, as shown in ● **FIGURE 32-16.**

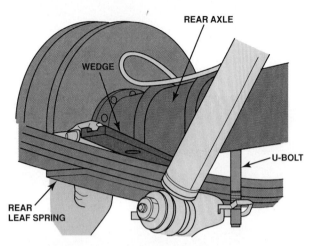

FIGURE 32–16 Placing a tapered metal wedge between the rear leaf spring and the rear axle pedestal to correct rear U-joint working angles.

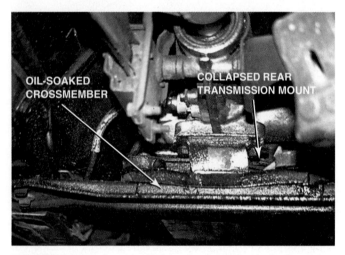

FIGURE 32–17 A transmission oil pan gasket leak allowed automatic transmission fluid (ATF) to saturate the rear transmission mount rubber, causing it to collapse. After replacing the defective mount, proper driveshaft angles were restored and the driveline vibration was corrected.

U-JOINT WORKING ANGLES (CONTINUED)

CAUTION: Use caution whenever using wedges between the differential and the rear leaf spring to restore the correct U-joint working angle. Even though wedges are made to raise the front of the differential, the tilt often prevents rear-end lubricant from reaching the pinion bearing, resulting in pinion bearing noise and eventual failure.

The angle of the front joint is changed by adding or removing shims from the mount under the transmission. ● **SEE FIGURE 32–17.**

CV JOINT DIAGNOSIS

When a CV joint wears or fails, the most common symptom is noise while driving. An outer fixed CV joint will most likely be heard when turning sharply and accelerating at the same time. This noise is usually a clicking sound. While inner joint failure is less common, a defective inner CV joint often creates a loud clunk while accelerating from rest. To help verify a defective joint, drive the vehicle in reverse while turning and accelerating. This almost always will reveal a defective outer joint.

🔧 **TECH TIP**

Quick and Easy Backlash Test

Whenever a driveline clunk is being diagnosed, one possible cause is excessive backlash (clearance) between the ring gear teeth and differential pinion teeth in the differential. Another common cause of excessive differential backlash is too much clearance between differential carrier pinion teeth and side gear teeth. A quick test to check backlash involves three easy steps:

STEP 1 Hoist the vehicle on a frame contact lift, allowing the drive wheels to be rotated.

STEP 2 Have an assistant hold one drive wheel and the driveshaft to keep them from turning.

STEP 3 Move the other drive wheel, observing how far the tire can rotate. This is the amount of backlash in the differential; it should be less than 1 in. (25 mm) of movement measured *at the tire.*

If the tire can move more than 1 in. (25 mm), then the differential should be inspected for wear and parts should be replaced as necessary. If the tire moves *less* than 1 in. (25 mm), then the backlash between the ring gear and pinion is probably *not* the cause of the noise.

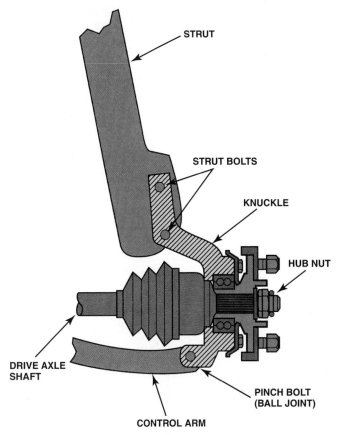

FIGURE 32–18 The hub nut must be removed before the hub bearing assembly or drive axle shaft can be removed from the vehicle.

REPLACEMENT SHAFT ASSEMBLIES

Front-wheel-drive vehicles were widely used in Europe and Japan long before they became popular in North America. The standard repair procedure used in these countries is the replacement of the entire drive assembly if there is a CV joint failure. Replacement boot kits are rarely seen in Europe because it is felt that even a slight amount of dirt or water inside a CV joint is unacceptable. Vehicle owners simply wait until the joint wear causes severe noise, and then the entire assembly is replaced.

The entire drive axle shaft assembly can easily be replaced and the defective unit can be sent to a company for remanufacturing. Even though cost to the customer is higher, the parts and repair shop does not have to inventory every type, size, and style of boot kit and CV joint. Service procedures and practices therefore vary according to location and the availability of parts. For example, some service technicians use replacement drive axle assemblies from salvage yards with good success.

NOTE: Some drive axle shafts have a weight attached between the inner and outer CV joints. This is a dampener weight. It is not a balance weight, and it need not be transferred to the replacement drive axle shaft (half shaft) unless instructed to do so in the directions that accompany the replacement shaft assembly.

CV JOINT SERVICE

The hub nut must be removed whenever servicing a CV joint or shaft assembly on a front-wheel-drive vehicle. Since these nuts are usually torqued to almost 200 lb-ft (260 N-m), keep the vehicle on the ground until the hub nut is loosened and then follow these steps (● **SEE FIGURE 32–18**):

STEP 1 Remove the front wheel and hub nut.

   NOTE: Most manufacturers warn against using an hair impact wrench to remove the hub nut. The impacting force can damage the hub bearing.

STEP 2 To allow the knuckle room to move outward enough to remove the drive axle shaft, some or all of the following will have to be disconnected:
   a. Lower ball joint or **pinch bolt** (● **SEE FIGURE 32–19**).
   b. Tie rod end (● **SEE FIGURE 32–20**).
   c. Stabilizer bar link.
   d. Front disc brake caliper.

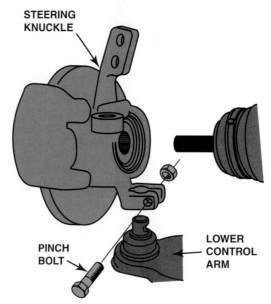

FIGURE 32–19 Many knuckles are attached to the ball joint on the lower control arm by a pinch bolt.

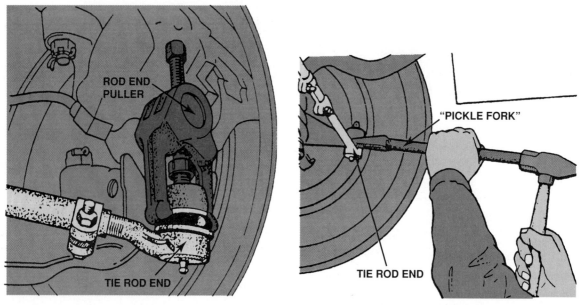

FIGURE 32–20 The preferred method for separating the tie rod end from the steering knuckle is to use a puller such as the one shown. A "pickle-fork"-type tool should be used only if the tie rod is going to be replaced. A pickle-fork-type tool can damage or tear the rubber grease boot. Striking the tie rod end with a hammer while holding another hammer behind the joint to shock and break the taper from the steering knuckle can also be used.

CV JOINT SERVICE (CONTINUED)

STEP 3 Remove the splined end of the axle from the hub bearing. Sometimes a special puller may be necessary, but in most cases the shaft can be tapped inward through the hub bearing with a light hammer and a brass punch can be used. To protect the threads of the drive axle shaft, install the hub nut temporarily. ● **SEE FIGURES 32–21 AND 32–22.**

STEP 4 Use a prybar or special tool with a slide hammer, as shown in ● **FIGURE 32–23,** and remove the inner joint from the transaxle.

STEP 5 Disassemble, clean, and inspect all components. ● **SEE FIGURES 32–24 THROUGH 32–30.**

Spline Bind Cure

Driveline "clunk" often occurs in rear-wheel-drive ve-hicles when shifting between drive and reverse or when accelerating from a stop. Often the cause of this noise is excessive clearance between the teeth of the ring and pinion in the differential. Another cause is called **spline bind,** where the changing rear pinion angle creates a binding in the spline when the rear springs change in height. For example, when a pickup truck stops, the weight transfers toward the front and unloads the rear springs. The front of the differential noses downward and forward as the rear springs unload. When the driver accelerates forward, the rear of the truck squats downward, causing the drive shaft to be pulled rearward when the front of the differential rotates upward. This upward movement on the spline often causes the spline to bind and make a loud clunk when the bind is finally released.

The method recommended by vehicle manufac-turers to eliminate this noise is to follow these steps:

1. Remove the driveshaft.
2. Clean the splines on both the driveshaft yoke and the transmission output shaft.
3. Remove any burrs on the splines with a small metal file (remove all filings).
4. Apply a high-temperature grease to the spline teeth of the yoke. Apply grease to each spline, but do not fill the splines. Synthetic chassis grease is preferred because of its high temperature resistance.
5. Reinstall the driveshaft.

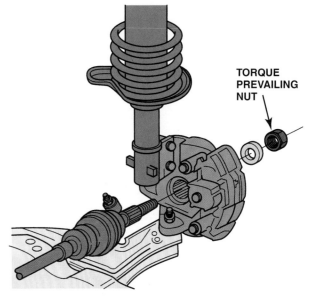

FIGURE 32–21 Many drive axles are retained by **torque prevailing nuts** that must not be reused. Torque prevailing nuts are slightly deformed or contain a plastic insert that holds the nut tight (retains the torque) to the shaft without loosening.

FIGURE 32–22 A special General Motors tool is being used to separate the drive axle shaft from the wheel hub bearing.

STEP 6 Replace the entire joint if there are *any* worn parts. Pack *all* the grease that is supplied into the assembly or joint. ● **SEE FIGURE 32–31.** Assemble the joint and position the boot in the same location as marked. Be-fore clamping the last seal on the boot, be sure to re-lease trapped air to prevent the boot from expanding when heated and collapsing when cold. This is some-times called *burping the boot.* Clamp the boot accord-ing to the manufacturer's specifications.

STEP 7 Reinstall the drive axle shaft in the reverse order of re-moval, and torque the drive axle nut to factory specifi-cations. ● **SEE FIGURE 32–32.**

FIGURE 32–25 If other service work requires that just one end of the drive axle shaft be disconnected from the vehicle, be sure that the free end is supported to prevent damage to the protective boots or allowing the joint to separate.

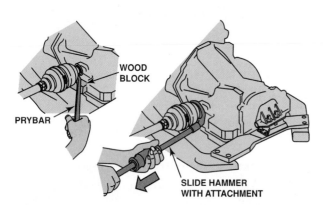

FIGURE 32–23 Most inner CV joints can be separated from the transaxle with a prybar.

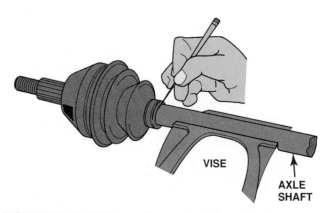

FIGURE 32–26 With a scribe, mark the location of the boots before removal. The replacement boots must be in the same location.

FIGURE 32–24 When removing a drive axle shaft assembly, use care to avoid pulling the plunge joint apart.

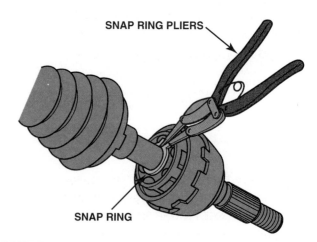

FIGURE 32–27 Most CV joints use a snap ring to retain the joint on the drive axle shaft.

FIGURE 32–28 After releasing the snap ring, most CV joints can be tapped off the shaft using a brass or shot-filled plastic (dead-blow) hammer.

FIGURE 32–30 The cage of this Rzeppa-type CV joint is rotated so that one ball at a time can be removed. Some joints require that the technician use a brass punch and a hammer to move the cage.

FIGURE 32–29 Typical outer CV joint after removing the boot and the joint from the drive axle shaft. This joint was removed from the vehicle because a torn boot was found. After disassembly and cleaning, this joint was found to be OK and was put back into service. Even though the grease looks terrible, there was enough grease in the joint to provide enough lubrication to prevent any wear from occurring.

FIGURE 32–31 Be sure to use *all* of the grease supplied with the replacement joint or boot kit. Use only the grease supplied and do not use substitute grease.

FIGURE 32–32 A screwdriver is shown, but a punch would be better, to keep the rotor from rotating while removing or installing the drive axle shaft spindle nut.

FIGURE 32–33 The engine had to be raised higher to get the new (noncollapsed) engine mount installed.

 REAL WORLD FIX

The Vibrating Buick

The owner of a front-wheel-drive Buick complained that it vibrated during acceleration only. The vehicle would also pull toward one side during acceleration. An inspection discovered a worn (cracked) engine mount. After replacing the mount, the CV joint angles were restored and both the vibration and the pulling to one side during acceleration were solved. ● **SEE FIGURE 32–33**.

1 Tools needed to replace a drive axle shaft on a General Motors vehicle include a drift, sockets, plus a prybar bearing/axle shaft special tool.

2 The drive axle shaft retaining nut can be loosened with the tire on the ground, or use a drift inserted into the rotor cooling fins before removing the nut.

3 Using a special tool to push the drive axle splines from the bearing assembly.

4 Remove the disc brake caliper and support it out of the way. Then, remove the disc brake rotor.

5 To allow for the removal of the drive axle shaft, the strut is removed from the steering knuckle assembly.

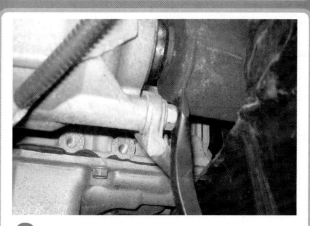

6 A prybar is used to separate the inner drive axle shaft joint from the transaxle.

CONTINUED ▶

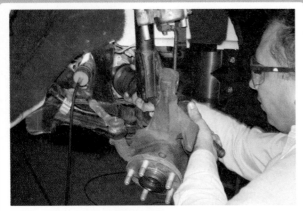

7 After the inner joint splines have been released from the transaxle, carefully remove the drive axle shaft assembly from the vehicle.

8 To install, reverse the disassembly procedure and be sure to install the washer under the retainer-nut, and always use a new prevailing torque nut.

9 Reinstall the disc brake rotor and caliper and then torque the drive axle shaft retaining nut to factory specifications.

SUMMARY

1. A defective U-joint often makes a *clicking* sound when the vehicle is driven in reverse. Severely defective U-joints can cause driveline vibrations or a *clunk* sound when the transmission is shifted from Reverse to Drive or from Drive to Reverse.

2. Incorrect driveshaft working angles can result from collapsed engine or transmission mounts.

3. Driveline clunk noise can often be corrected by applying high-temperature chassis grease to the splines of the front yoke on the driveshaft.

4. CV joints require careful cleaning, inspection, and lubrication with specific CV joint grease.

REVIEW QUESTIONS

1. List two items that should be checked when inspecting a driveshaft.

2. List the steps necessary to measure driveshaft U-joint working angles.

3. Describe how to replace a Cardan-type U-joint.

4. Explain the proper steps to perform when replacing a CV joint.

CHAPTER QUIZ

1. Two technicians are discussing U-joints. Technician A says that a defective U-joint could cause a loud clunk when the transmission is shifted between Drive and Reverse. Technician B says a worn U-joint can cause a clicking sound only when driving the vehicle in reverse. Which technician is correct?
   a. Technician A only
   b. Technician B only
   c. Both Technicians A and B
   d. Neither Technician A nor B

2. Incorrect or unequal U-joint working angles are most likely to be caused by _____.
   a. A bent driveshaft
   b. A collapsed engine or transmission mount
   c. A dry output shaft spline
   d. Defective or damaged U-joints

3. A defective outer CV joint will usually make a _____.
   a. Rumbling noise
   b. Growling noise
   c. Clicking noise
   d. Clunking noise

4. The last step after installing a replacement CV boot is to _____.
   a. "Burp the boot"
   b. Lubricate the CV joint with chassis grease
   c. Mark the location of the boot on the drive axle shaft
   d. Separate the CV joint before installation

5. A Cardan-type U-joint may require what tool(s) to replace?
   a. A special tool
   b. A torch
   c. A press or a vise
   d. May require any of the above

6. What needs to be removed to replace a drive axle shaft from a front-wheel-drive vehicle?
   a. Tie rod end
   b. Lower control arm or ball joint
   c. Hub nut
   d. All of the above

7. The splines of the driveshaft yoke should be lubricated to prevent _____.
   a. A vibration
   b. Spline bind
   c. Rust
   d. Transmission fluid leaking from the extension housing

8. It is recommended by many experts that an air impact wrench *not* be used to remove or install the drive axle shaft nut because the impacting force can damage the hub bearing.
   a. True
   b. False

9. Front and rear driveshaft U-joint working angles should be within _____ degrees of each other.
   a. 0.5
   b. 1.0
   c. 3.0
   d. 4.0

10. A defective (collapsed) engine mount on a front-wheel-drive vehicle can cause a vibration.
    a. True
    b. False

chapter 33
WHEEL ALIGNMENT PRINCIPLES

OBJECTIVES

After studying Chapter 33, the reader will be able to:

1. Prepare for ASE Suspension and Steering (A4) certification test content area "D" (Wheel Alignment Diagnosis, Adjustment, and Repair).

2. Discuss which vehicle handling problems can and cannot be corrected by an alignment.

3. Define camber, toe, caster, SAI, included angle, scrub radius, turning radius, setback, and thrust line.

4. Explain how camber, caster, and toe affect the handling and tire wear of the vehicle.

KEY TERMS

BJI 647
Camber 638
Camber roll 642
Caster 641
Dog tracking 653
Drift 637
Four-wheel alignment 654
Included angle 648
KPI 647
Lead 637
MSI 647
Pull 637

Returnability 642
Road crown 637
SAI 647
Scrub radius 649
Setback 652
Shimmy 638
Steering dampener 642
Steering offset 649
Thrust line 652
Toe 644
TOOT 651
Tramp 638
Wander 637

DEFINITION OF A WHEEL ALIGNMENT

A wheel alignment is the adjustment of the suspension and steering to ensure proper vehicle handling with minimum tire wear. When a vehicle is new, the alignment angles are set at the factory. After many miles and/or months of driving, the alignment angles can change slightly. The change in alignment angles may result from one or more of the following conditions:

1. Wear of the steering and the suspension components
2. Bent or damaged steering and suspension parts
3. Sagging springs, which can change the ride height of the vehicle and therefore the alignment angles

By adjusting the suspension and steering components, proper alignment angles can be restored. An alignment includes checking and adjusting, if necessary, both front and rear wheels.

PULL

FIGURE 33–1 A pull is usually defined as a tug on the steering wheel toward one side or the other.

ALIGNMENT-RELATED PROBLEMS

Most alignment diagnosis is symptom-based diagnosis. This means that the problem with the alignment is determined from symptoms such as excessive tire wear or a pull to one side of the road. The definitions of alignment symptom terms used in this book are discussed next.

PULL A **pull** is generally defined as a definite tug on the steering wheel toward the left or the right while driving straight on a level road. ● **SEE FIGURE 33–1.** Bent, damaged, or worn suspension and/or steering components can cause this problem, as well as a tire problem.

LEAD OR DRIFT A **lead** or **drift** is a mild pull that does not cause a force on the steering wheel that the driver must counteract. A lead or drift is observed by momentarily removing your hands from the steering wheel while driving on a straight, level road. When the vehicle moves toward one side or the other, this is called a lead or a drift.

CAUTION: When test-driving a vehicle for a lead or a drift, make sure that the road is free of traffic and that your hands remain close to the steering wheel. Your hands should be held away from the steering wheel for just a second or two—just long enough to check for a lead or drift condition.

ROAD CROWN EFFECTS Most roads are constructed with a slight angle to permit water to drain from the road surface. On a two-lane road, the center of the road is often higher than the berms, resulting in a **road crown**. ● **SEE FIGURE 33–2.**

On a four-lane expressway (freeway), the crown is often *between the two sets* of lanes. Because of this slight angle to the road, some vehicles may lead or drift away from the road crown. In other words, it may be perfectly normal for a vehicle to lead toward the right while being driven in the slow lane and toward the left while being driven in the fast (or inside) lane of a typical divided highway.

WANDER A **wander** is a condition where constant steering wheel corrections are necessary to maintain a straight-ahead direction on a straight, level road. ● **SEE FIGURE 33–3.**

Worn suspension and/or steering components are the most likely cause of this condition. Incorrect or unequal alignment angles such as caster and toe, as well as defective tire(s), can also cause this condition.

STIFF STEERING OR SLOW RETURN TO CENTER Hard-to-steer problems are commonly caused by leaks, either low tire pressure (due to the leak of air) and/or lack of proper power steering (due to the leak of power steering fluid). Other causes include excessive positive caster on the front wheels or binding steering linkage.

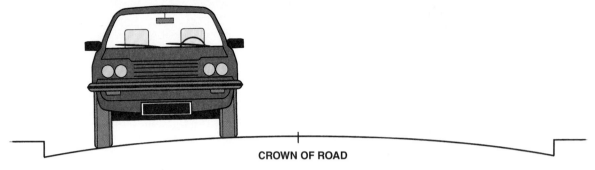

FIGURE 33–2 The crown of the road refers to the angle or slope of the roadway needed to drain water off the pavement. *(Courtesy of Hunter Engineering Company)*

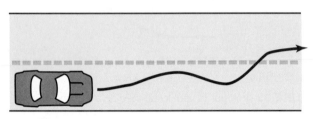

WANDER

FIGURE 33–3 Wander is an unstable condition requiring constant driver corrections.

ALIGNMENT-RELATED PROBLEMS (CONTINUED)

TRAMP OR SHIMMY VIBRATION **Tramp** is a vertical-type (up-and-down) vibration usually caused by out-of-balance or defective tires or wheels. **Shimmy** is a back-and-forth vibration that can be caused by an out-of-balance tire or defective wheel or by an alignment problem.

NOTE: Wheel alignment will not correct a tramp-type vibration.

CAMBER **Camber** *is the inward or outward tilt of the wheels from true vertical as viewed from the front or rear of the vehicle.*

1. If the top of the tire is tilted out, then camber is positive (+), as shown in ● **FIGURE 33–4.**

2. If the top of the tire is tilted in, then camber is negative (−), as shown in ● **FIGURE 33–5.**

3. Camber is zero (0 degrees) if the tilt of the wheel is true vertical, as shown in ● **FIGURE 33–6.**

4. Camber is measured in degrees or fractions of degrees.

5. *Camber can cause tire wear if not correct.*
   a. *Excessive positive camber* causes scuffing and wear on the outside edge of the tire, as shown in ● **FIGURE 33–7.**
   b. *Excessive negative camber* causes scuffing and wear on the inside edge of the tire, as shown in ● **FIGURE 33–8.**

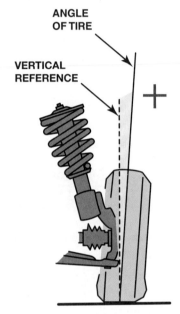

FIGURE 33–4 Positive camber. The solid vertical line represents true vertical, and the dotted line represents the angle of the tire.

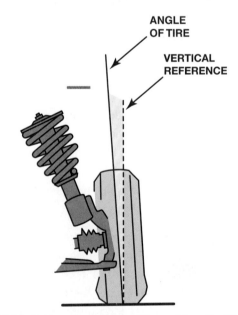

FIGURE 33–5 Negative camber. The solid vertical line represents true vertical, and the dotted line represents the angle of the tire.

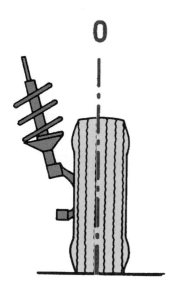

FIGURE 33–6 Zero camber. Note that the angle of the tire is true vertical.

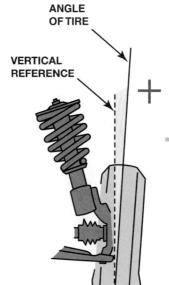

ANGLE OF TIRE

VERTICAL REFERENCE

FIGURE 33–7 Excessive positive camber and how the front tires would wear due to the excessive camber.

SCUFFING

OUTER SHOULDER WEAR

SCUFFING

INNER SHOULDER WEAR

ANGLE OF TIRE

VERTICAL REFERENCE

FIGURE 33–8 Excessive negative camber and how the front tires would wear due to the excessive camber.

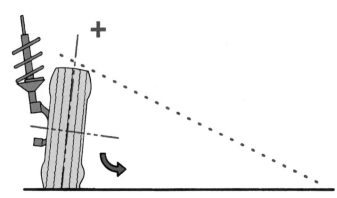

FIGURE 33–9 Positive camber tilts the tire and forms a cone shape that causes the wheel to roll away or pull outward toward the point of the cone.

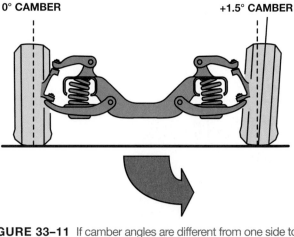

FIGURE 33–11 If camber angles are different from one side to the other, the vehicle will pull toward the side with the most camber.

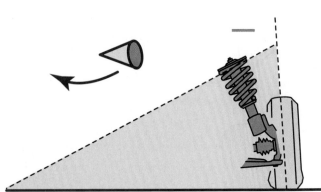

FIGURE 33–10 Negative camber creates a pulling force toward the center of the vehicle.

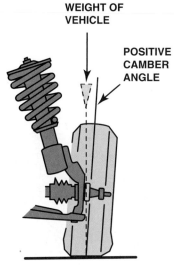

FIGURE 33–12 Positive camber applies the vehicle weight toward the larger inner wheel bearing. This is desirable because the larger inner bearing is designed to carry more vehicle weight than the smaller outer bearing.

ALIGNMENT-RELATED PROBLEMS (CONTINUED)

6. Camber can cause pull if it is unequal side-to-side. **The vehicle will pull toward the side with the most positive camber.** A difference of more than 1/2 degree from one side to the other will cause the vehicle to pull. ● **SEE FIGURES 33–9 THROUGH 33–11.**

7. Incorrect camber can cause excessive wear on wheel bearings, as shown in ● **FIGURES 33–12 AND 33–13.** Many vehicle manufacturers specify positive camber so that the vehicle's weight is applied to the larger inner wheel bearing and spindle. As the vehicle is loaded or when the springs sag, camber usually decreases. If camber is kept positive, then the running camber is kept near zero degrees for best tire life.

NOTE: Many front-wheel-drive vehicles that use sealed wheel bearings often specify negative camber.

8. Camber is *not* adjustable on many vehicles.

9. If camber is adjustable, the change is made by moving the upper or the lower control arm or strut assembly by means of one of the following methods:
   a. Shims
   b. Eccentric cams
   c. Slots

10. Camber should be equal on both sides; however, if camber cannot be adjusted exactly equal, make certain that there is more camber on the front of the left side to help compensate for the road crown (1/2 degree maximum difference).

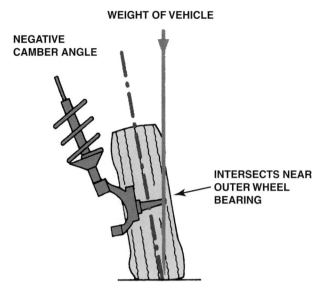

FIGURE 33–13 Negative camber applies the vehicle weight to the smaller outer wheel bearing. Excessive negative camber, therefore, may contribute to outer wheel bearing failure.

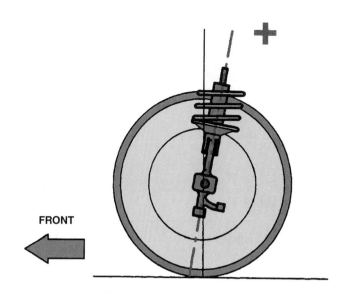

FIGURE 33–15 Positive (+) caster.

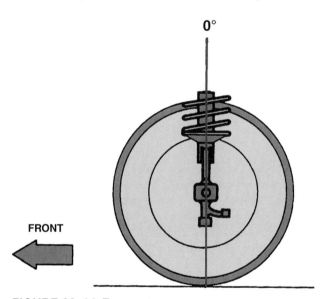

FIGURE 33–14 Zero caster.

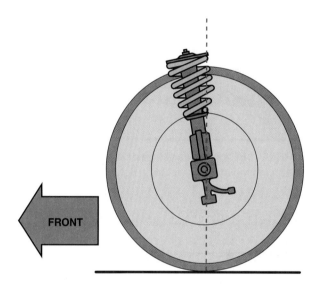

FIGURE 33–16 Negative (−) caster is seldom specified on today's vehicles because it tends to make the vehicle unstable at highway speeds. Negative caster was specified on some older vehicles not equipped with power steering to help reduce the steering effort.

CASTER

Caster *is the forward or rearward tilt of the steering axis in reference to a vertical line as viewed from the side of the vehicle.* The steering axis is defined as the line drawn through the upper and lower steering pivot points. On an SLA suspension system, the upper pivot is the upper ball joint and the lower pivot is the lower ball joint. On a MacPherson strut system, the upper pivot is the center of the upper bearing mount and the lower pivot point is the lower ball joint. Zero caster means that the steering axis is straight up and down, also called 0 degrees or perfectly vertical, as shown in ● **FIGURE 33–14.**

1. Positive (+) caster is present when the upper suspension pivot point is behind the lower pivot point (ball joint) as viewed from the side. ● **SEE FIGURE 33–15.**

2. Negative (−) caster is present when the upper suspension pivot point is ahead of the lower pivot point (ball joint) as viewed from the side. ● **SEE FIGURE 33–16.**

3. Caster is measured in degrees or fractions of degrees.

FIGURE 33–17 As the spindle rotates, it lifts the weight of the vehicle due to the angle of the steering axis. *(Courtesy of Hunter Engineering Company)*

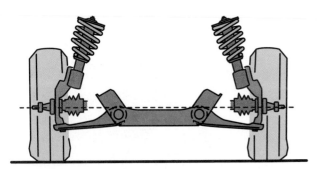

FIGURE 33–18 Vehicle weight tends to lower the spindle, which returns the steering to the straight-ahead position.

CASTER (CONTINUED)

4. Caster is not a tire-wearing angle, but positive caster does cause changes in camber during a turn. ● **SEE FIGURE 33–17.** This condition is called **camber roll** (see the Tech Tip titled "Caster Angle Tire Wear").

5. Caster is a stability angle.
   a. If caster is positive, the vehicle steering will be very stable (will tend to go straight with little steering wheel correction needed). This degree of caster helps with steering wheel **returnability** after a turn. ● **SEE FIGURE 33–18.**
   b. If the caster is positive, steering effort will increase with increasing positive caster. Greater road shocks will be felt by the driver when driving over rough road surfaces. ● **SEE FIGURE 33–19.** Vehicles with as many as 11 degrees positive caster, such as many Mercedes vehicles, usually use a steering dampener to control possible shimmy at high speeds and to dampen the snap-back of the spindle after a turn. ● **SEE FIGURE 33–20.**
   c. If caster is negative, or excessively unequal, the vehicle will not be as stable and will tend to wander (constant

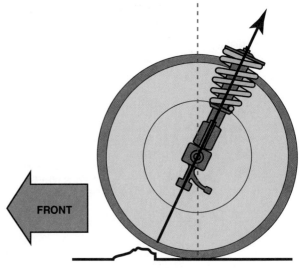

FIGURE 33–19 High caster provides a road shock path to the vehicle.

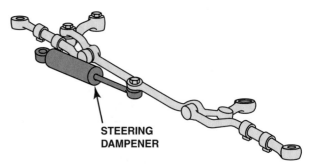

STEERING DAMPENER

FIGURE 33–20 A **steering dampener** is used on many pickup trucks, sport utility vehicles (SUVs), and many luxury vehicles designed with a high-positive-caster setting. The dampener helps prevent steering wheel kickback when the front tires hit a bump or hole in the road and also helps reduce steering wheel shimmy that may result from the high-caster setting.

steering wheel movement will be required to maintain straight-ahead direction). If a vehicle is heavily loaded in the rear, caster increases. ● **SEE FIGURE 33–21.**

6. Caster can cause pull if unequal; **the vehicle will pull toward the side with the least positive caster.** However, the pulling force of unequal caster is only about one-fourth the pulling force of camber. It would require a difference of caster of one full degree to equal the pulling force of only 1/4-degree difference of camber.

7. Caster is *not* adjustable on many vehicles.

8. If caster is adjustable, it is changed by moving either the lower or the upper pivot point forward or backward by means of the following:
   a. Shims
   b. Eccentric cams

FIGURE 33–21 As the load increases in the rear of a vehicle, the top steering axis pivot point moves rearward, increasing positive (+) caster.

 TECH TIP

Caster Angle Tire Wear

The caster angle is generally considered to be a *non-tire-wearing* angle. However, excessive or unequal caster can *indirectly* cause tire wear. When the front wheels are turned on a vehicle with a lot of positive caster, they become angled. This is called *camber roll*. (Caster angle is a measurement of the difference in camber angle from when the wheel is turned inward compared to when the wheel is turned outward.) Most vehicle manufacturers have positive caster designed into the suspension system. This positive caster increases the directional stability.

However, if the vehicle is used exclusively in city driving, positive caster can cause tire wear to the outside shoulders of both front tires. ● **SEE FIGURE 33–22.**

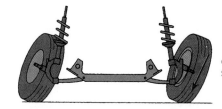

OUTSIDE TURN SPINDLE MOVES DOWN

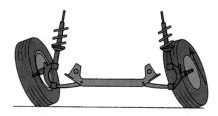

INSIDE TURN SPINDLE MOVES DOWN

FIGURE 33–22 Note how the front tire becomes tilted as the vehicle turns a corner with positive caster. The higher the caster angle, the more the front tires tilt, causing camber-type tire wear.

   c. Slots

   d. Strut rods

9. Caster should be equal on both sides; however, if caster cannot be adjusted to be exactly equal, make certain that there is more caster on the right side (maximum 1/2-degree difference) to help compensate for the crown of the road.

NOTE: Caster is only measured on the front turning wheels of the vehicle. While some caster is built into the rear suspension of many vehicles, rear caster is not measured as part of a four-wheel alignment.

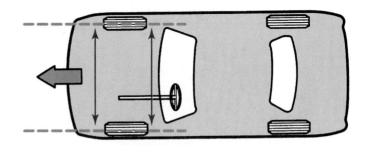

FIGURE 33-23 Zero toe. Note how both tires are parallel to each other as viewed from above the vehicle.

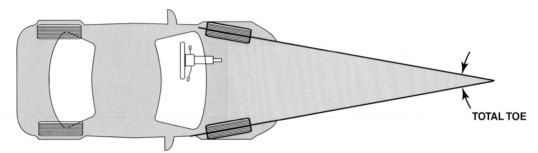

FIGURE 33-24 Total toe is often expressed as an angle. Because both front wheels are tied together through the tie rods and center link, the toe angle is always equally split between the two front wheels when the vehicle moves forward.

TOTAL TOE

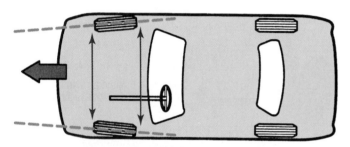

FIGURE 33-25 Toe-in, also called positive (+) toe.

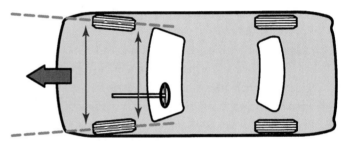

FIGURE 33-26 Toe-out, also called negative (−) toe. *(Courtesy of Hunter Engineering Company)*

TOE

Toe *is the difference in distance between the front and rear of the tires.* Toe is the most important of the alignment angles. As viewed from the top of the vehicle (a bird's eye view), zero toe means that both wheels on the same axle are parallel, as shown in ● **FIGURE 33-23.**

Toe is also described as a comparison of horizontal lines drawn through both wheels on the same axle, as shown in ● **FIGURE 33-24.**

If the front of the tires is closer than the rear of the same tires, then the toe is called *toe-in* or positive (+) toe. ● **SEE FIGURE 33-25.**

If the front of the tires is farther apart than the rear of the same tires, then the wheels are *toed-out,* or have negative (−) toe. ● **SEE FIGURE 33-26.**

The purpose of the correct toe setting is to provide maximum stability with a minimum of tire wear when the vehicle is being driven.

1. Toe is measured in fractions of degrees or in fractions of an inch (usually 1/16s), millimeters (mm), or decimals of an inch (such as 0.06 in.).

2. *Incorrect toe is the major cause of excessive tire wear!* ● **SEE FIGURE 33-27.**

NOTE: If the toe is improper by just 1/8 in. (3 mm), the resulting tire wear is equivalent to dragging a tire sideways 28 feet (8.5 m) for every mile traveled (1.6 km).

FIGURE 33–27 This tire is just one month old! It was new and installed on the front of a vehicle that had about 1/4 inch (6 mm) of toe-out. By the time the customer returned to the tire store for an alignment, the tire was completely bald on the inside. Note the almost new tread on the outside.

If not correct, toe causes camber-type wear on one side of the tire. ● **SEE FIGURES 33–28 AND 33–29.** Feather-edge wear is also common, especially if the vehicle is equipped with nonradial tires. ● **SEE FIGURE 33–30.**

3. *Incorrect front toe does not cause a pull condition.* Incorrect toe on the front wheels is split equally as the vehicle is driven because the forces acting on the tires are exerted through the tie rod and steering linkage to both wheels.

4. *Incorrect (or unequal) rear toe can cause tire wear.* ● **SEE FIGURES 33–31 THROUGH 33–33.** If the toe of the rear wheels is not equal, the steering wheel will not be straight and will pull toward the side with the most toe-in.

5. All vehicles can be adjusted for front toe.

6. Front toe adjustment must be made correctly by adjusting the tie rod sleeves. ● **SEE FIGURE 33–34** on page 647.

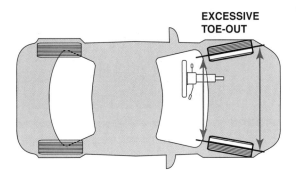

EXCESSIVE TOE-OUT

SCUFFING ON INSIDE SHOULDER

INNER SHOULDER WEAR

FIGURE 33–28 Excessive toe-out and the type of wear that can occur to the side of both front tires.

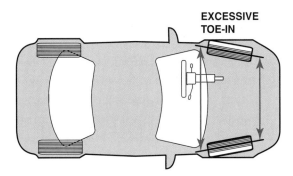

EXCESSIVE TOE-IN

FIGURE 33–29 Excessive toe-in and the type of wear that can occur to the outside of both front tires.

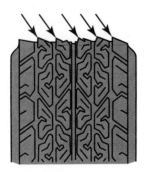

FIGURE 33–30 Feather-edge wear pattern caused by excessive toe-in or toe-out.

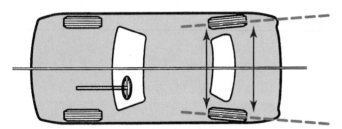

FIGURE 33–31 Rear toe-in (+). The rear toe (unlike the front toe) can be different for each wheel while the vehicle is moving forward because the rear wheels are not tied together as they are in the front. *(Courtesy of Hunter Engineering Company)*

TOE (CONTINUED)

7. Many vehicle manufacturers specify a slight amount of toe-in to compensate for the natural tendency of the front wheels to spread apart (become toed-out) due to centrifugal force of the rolling wheels acting on the steering linkage.

   NOTE: Some manufacturers of front-wheel-drive vehicles specify a toe-out setting to compensate for the toe-in forces created by the engine drive forces on the front wheels.

8. Normal wear to the tie rod ends and other steering linkage parts usually causes toe-out.

   Excessive front toe-out will cause wandering (lack of directional stability), especially during braking. Incorrectly set toe will cause an uncentered steering wheel. If toe is unequal in the *rear*, the vehicle will pull toward the side with the most toe-in.

FIGURE 33–32 Incorrect toe can cause the tire to run sideways as it rolls, resulting in a diagonal wipe.

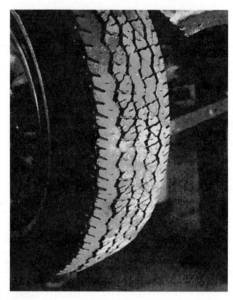

FIGURE 33–33 Diagonal wear such as shown here is usually caused by incorrect toe on the rear of a front-wheel-drive vehicle.

? FREQUENTLY ASKED QUESTION

Why Doesn't Unequal Front Toe on the Front Wheels Cause the Vehicle to Pull?

Each wheel could have individual toe, but as the vehicle is being driven, the forces on the tires tend to split the toe, causing the steering wheel to cock at an angle as the front wheels both track the same. If the toe is different on the rear of the vehicle, the rear will be "steered" similar to a rudder on a boat because the rear wheels are not tied together as are the front wheels.

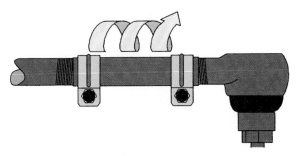

FIGURE 33–34 Toe on the front of most vehicles is adjusted by turning the tie rod sleeve as shown. *(Courtesy of John Bean Company)*

FEATHERED OR SAWTOOTH
TIRE WEAR PATTERN

SHARP EDGES POINT IN THE DIRECTION
OF THE TOE PROBLEM
(IN - TOE IN / OUT TOE OUT)

FIGURE 33–35 While the feathered or sawtooth tire tread wear pattern may not be noticeable to the eye, this wear can usually be felt by rubbing your hand across the tread of the tire. *(Courtesy of John Bean Company)*

 TECH TIP

Smooth In, Toed-In; Smooth Out, Toed-Out

Whenever the toe setting is not zero, a rubbing action occurs that causes a feather-edge-type wear. ● **SEE FIGURE 33–35.** A quick, easy method to determine if incorrect toe could be causing problems is simply to rub your hand across the tread of the tire. If it feels smoother moving your hand toward the center of the vehicle than when you move your hand toward the outside, then the cause is excessive toe-in. The opposite effect is caused by toe-out. This may be felt on all types of tires, including radial-ply tires where the wear may not be seen as feather edged. Just remember this simple saying: "Smooth in, toed-in; smooth out, toed-out."

STEERING AXIS INCLINATION (SAI)

The steering axis is the angle formed between true vertical and an imaginary line drawn between the upper and lower pivot points of the spindle. ● **SEE FIGURE 33–36. Steering axis inclination (SAI)** is the inward tilt of the steering axis. SAI is also known as **kingpin inclination (KPI)** and is the imaginary line drawn through the kingpin as viewed from the front. SAI is also called **ball joint inclination (BJI),** if SLA-type suspension is used, or **MacPherson strut inclination (MSI).**

The purpose of SAI is to provide an upper suspension pivot location that causes the spindle to travel in an arc when turning, which tends to raise the vehicle, as shown in ● **FIGURE 33–37.**

Vehicle weight tends to keep the front wheels in a straight-ahead position when driving, thereby increasing vehicle stability, directional control, and steering wheel returnability. The greater the SAI, the more stable the vehicle. It also helps center the steering wheel after making a turn and reduces the need for excessive positive caster. The SAI/KPI angle of all vehicles ranges between 2 and 16 degrees. Front-wheel-drive vehicles usually have greater than 9 degrees SAI (typically 12 to 16 degrees) for directional stability, whereas rear-wheel-drive vehicles usually have less than 8 degrees of SAI. The steering axis inclination angle and the camber angle together are called the *included angle*.

FIGURE 33–36 The left illustration shows that the steering axis inclination angle is determined by drawing a line through the center of the upper and lower ball joints. This represents the pivot points of the front wheels when the steering wheel is rotated during cornering. The right illustration shows that the steering axis inclination angle is determined by drawing a line through the axis of the upper strut bearing mount assembly and the lower ball joint.

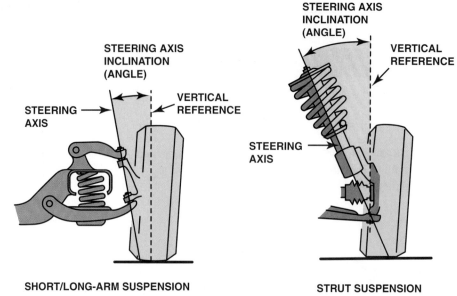

SHORT/LONG-ARM SUSPENSION

STRUT SUSPENSION

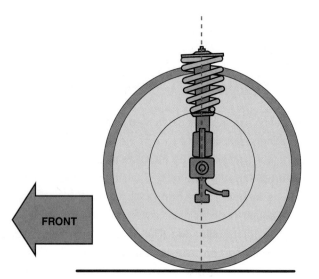

FIGURE 33–37 The SAI causes the spindle to travel in an arc when the wheels are turned. The weight of the vehicle is therefore used to help straighten the front tires after a turn and to help give directional stability.

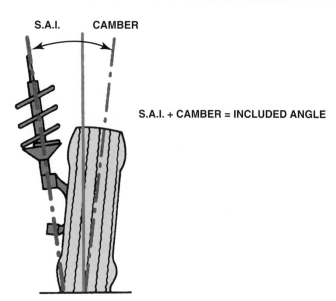

S.A.I. + CAMBER = INCLUDED ANGLE

FIGURE 33–38 Included angle on a MacPherson-strut-type suspension.

INCLUDED ANGLE

The **included angle** is the SAI added to the camber reading of the front wheels only. *The included angle is determined by the design of the steering knuckle, or strut construction.* ● **SEE FIGURES 33–38 AND 33–39.**

Included angle is an important angle to measure for diagnosis of vehicle handling or tire wear problems. For example, if the cradle is out of location due to previous service work or an accident, knowing SAI, camber, and the included angle can help

in determining what needs to be done to correct the problem. ● **SEE FIGURE 33–40.**

Figure 33–40 shows the included angle is equal on both sides but the camber and SAI are not equal. For best handling both the included angle and SAI should be within 1/2 degree of the other side of the vehicle.

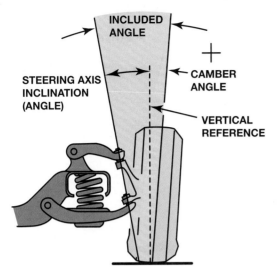

FIGURE 33–39 Included angle on an SLA-type suspension. The included angle is the SAI angle and the camber angle added together.

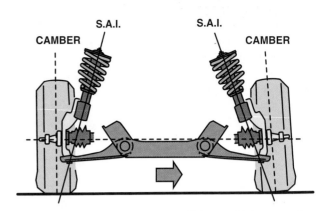

FIGURE 33–40 Cradle placement. If the cradle is not replaced in the exact position after removal for a transmission or clutch replacement, the SAI, camber, and included angle will not be equal side-to-side.

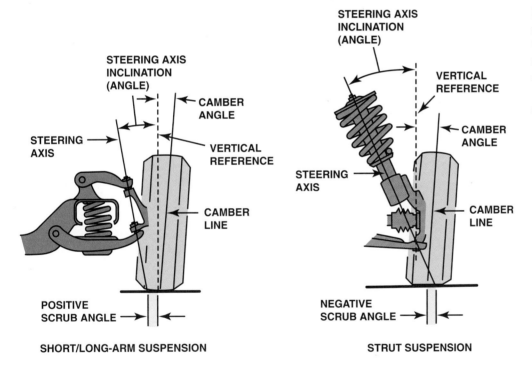

SHORT/LONG-ARM SUSPENSION

STRUT SUSPENSION

FIGURE 33–41 A positive scrub radius (angle) is usually built into most SLA front suspensions, and a negative scrub radius is usually built into most MacPherson-strut-type front suspensions.

SCRUB RADIUS

Scrub radius refers to the *distance* between the line through the steering axis and the centerline of the wheel at the contact point with the road surface. ● **SEE FIGURE 33–41.**

Scrub radius is *not* adjustable and cannot be measured. Scrub radius can be zero, positive, or negative. Zero scrub radius means that the line through the steering axis intersects the centerline of the tire at the road surface. Positive scrub radius means that the line intersects the centerline of the tire below the road surface. Negative scrub radius means that the line intersects the centerline of the tire above the road surface. Scrub radius is also called **steering offset** by some vehicle manufacturers. If a wheel is permitted to roll rather than pivot, then steering will be

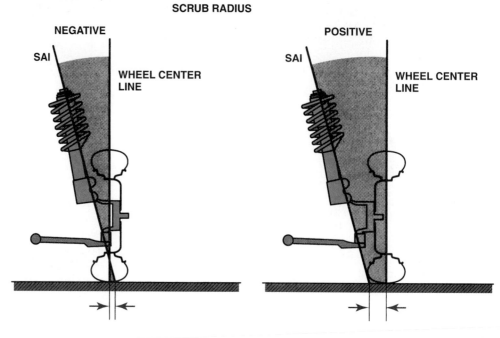

FIGURE 33–42 With negative scrub radius, the imaginary line through the steering axis inclination (SAI) intersects the road outside of the centerline of the tire. With positive scrub radius, the SAI line intersects the road inside the centerline of the tires.

SCRUB RADIUS

NEGATIVE

SAI

WHEEL CENTER LINE

POSITIVE

SAI

WHEEL CENTER LINE

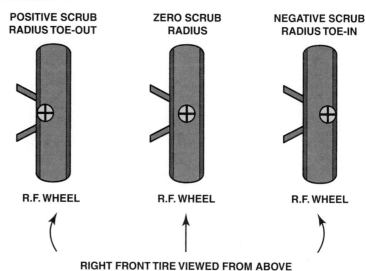

FIGURE 33–43 With a positive scrub radius, the pivot point, marked with a + mark, is inside the centerline of the tire and will cause the wheel to turn toward the outside, especially during braking. Zero scrub radius does not create any force on the tires and is not usually used on vehicles because it does not create an opposing force on the tires, which in turn makes the vehicle more susceptible to minor bumps and dips in the road. Negative scrub radius, as is used with most front-wheel-drive vehicles, generates an inward force on the tires.

POSITIVE SCRUB RADIUS TOE-OUT

ZERO SCRUB RADIUS

NEGATIVE SCRUB RADIUS TOE-IN

R.F. WHEEL

R.F. WHEEL

R.F. WHEEL

RIGHT FRONT TIRE VIEWED FROM ABOVE

SCRUB RADIUS (CONTINUED)

more difficult because a tire can pivot more easily than it can roll while turning the front wheels. If the point of intersection is inside the centerline of the tire and below the road surface, this creates a toe-out force on the front wheels. Negative scrub radius is required on front-wheel-drive vehicles to provide good steering stability during braking. ● **SEE FIGURES 33–42 AND 33–43.**

Scrub radius is designed into each vehicle to provide acceptable handling and steering control under most conditions. Scrub radius also causes resistance to rolling of the front wheels to exert force on the steering linkage. This tends to dampen the effect of minor movements of the front wheels. Negative scrub radius causes the tire to toe-in during acceleration, braking, or traveling over bumps.

NOTE: It is this tendency to toe-in caused by the negative scrub radius and engine torque that requires many front-wheel-drive vehicles to specify a toe-out setting for the front-drive wheels.

Zero scrub radius is acceptable; positive scrub radius is less desirable because it causes the wheel to toe-out during acceleration, braking, or traveling over bumps and causes instability. Positive scrub radius is commonly used on rear-wheel-drive vehicles and requires a toe-in setting to help compensate for the tendency to toe-out.

A bent spindle can cause a change in the scrub radius and could cause hard steering, wander, or pull.

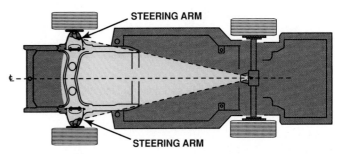

FIGURE 33–45 The proper toe-out on turns is achieved by angling the steering arms.

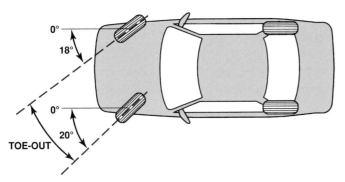

FIGURE 33–44 To provide handling, the inside wheel has to turn at a greater turning radius than the outside wheel.

Also, changing tire or wheel sizes can affect the centerline location of the wheel or the height of the tire assembly and will change the scrub radius, which can negatively affect the steering control. When larger-diameter tires and positive-offset wheels are installed, the scrub radius becomes positive and the wheels tend to toe-out, causing wander, poor handling, and tire wear.

TURNING RADIUS (TOE-OUT ON TURNS)

Whenever a vehicle turns a corner, the inside wheel has to turn at a sharper angle than the outside wheel because the inside wheel has a shorter distance to travel. ● **SEE FIGURE 33–44.**

Turning radius is also called **toe-out on turns**, abbreviated TOT or **TOOT,** and is determined by the angle of the steering knuckle arms. **Turning radius is a nonadjustable angle.** The turning radius can and should be measured as part of an alignment to check if the steering arms are bent or damaged. Symptoms of out-of-specification turning angle include the following:

1. Tire squeal noise during normal cornering, even at low speeds

2. Scuffed tire wear

The proper angle of the steering arms is where imaginary lines drawn from the steering arms should intersect exactly at the center of the rear axle. ● **SEE FIGURE 33–45.** This angle is called the Ackerman Effect (named for its promoter, an English publisher, Rudolph Ackerman, circa 1898).

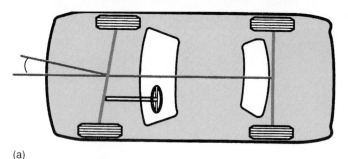

(a)

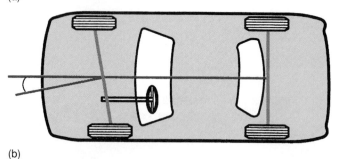

(b)

FIGURE 33–46 (a) Positive setback. (b) Negative setback.

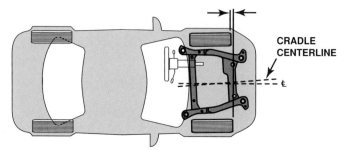

CRADLE
CENTERLINE

FIGURE 33–47 Cradle placement affects setback.

SETBACK

Setback is the angle formed by a line drawn perpendicular (at 90 degrees) to the front axles. ● **SEE FIGURE 33–46.**

Setback is a nonadjustable measurement, even though it may be corrected. Positive setback means the right front wheel is set back farther than the left; negative setback means the left front wheel is set back farther than the right.

Setback can be measured with a four-wheel alignment machine or can be determined by measuring the wheel base on both sides of the vehicle.

NOTE: The wheel base of any vehicle is the distance between the center of the front wheel and the center of the rear wheel on the same side. The wheel base should be within 1/8 in. (3 mm) side-to-side.

The causes of setback include the following:

1. Cradle placement not correct on a front-wheel-drive vehicle. This can be caused by incorrectly installing the cradle after a transmission, clutch, or engine replacement or service. ● **SEE FIGURE 33–47.**

2. An accident that affected the frame or cradle of the vehicle and was unnoticed or not repaired.

Most vehicle manufacturers do not specify a minimum setback specification. However, a reading of 0.50 degrees or 0.5 in. (13 mm) or less of setback is generally considered to be acceptable.

THRUST ANGLE

Thrust angle is the angle of the rear wheels as determined by the total rear toe. If both rear wheels have zero toe, then the thrust angle is the same as the geometric centerline of the vehicle. The total of the rear toe setting determines the **thrust line**, or the direction the rear wheels are pointed. ● **SEE FIGURE 33–48.**

On vehicles with an independent rear suspension, if both wheels do not have equal toe, the vehicle will pull in the direction of the side with the most toe-in.

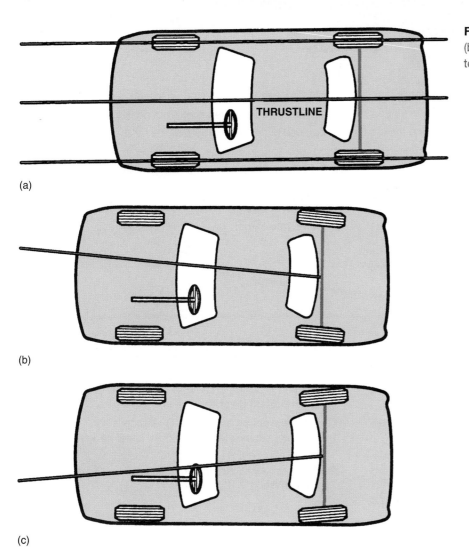

FIGURE 33–48 (a) Zero thrust angle. (b) Thrust line to the right. (c) Thrust line to the left.

(a)

(b)

(c)

THRUSTLINE

TRACKING

The rear wheels should track directly behind the front wheels. If the vehicle has been involved in an accident, it is possible that the frame or rear axle mounting could cause **dog tracking.**
● **SEE FIGURE 33–49.**

To check the frame for possible damage, two diagonal measurements of the frame and/or body are required. The diagonal measurements from known points at the front and the rear should be within 1/8 in. (3 mm) of each other.

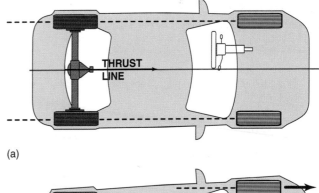

(a)

THRUST LINE

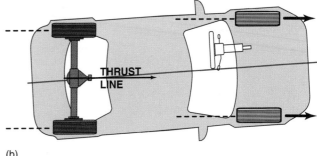

(b)

THRUST LINE

FIGURE 33–49 (a) Proper tracking. (b) Front wheels steering toward thrust line.

nment refers to the checking and/or adjust- wheels. Four-wheel alignment is important for ...g and tire wear, to check the camber and the toe wheels of front-wheel-drive vehicles. Some rear- e vehicles equipped with independent rear suspen- be adjusted for camber and toe. Rear-wheel caster be measured or adjusted because to measure caster, heels must be turned from straight ahead. Since rear

wheels are securely attached, a caster *sweep* (turning the wheels to take a caster reading) is not possible. While rear camber can cause tire wear problems, by far the greatest tire wear occurs due to toe settings. *Unequal* toe in the rear can cause the vehicle to pull or lead. The rear camber and toe are always adjusted first before adjusting the front caster, camber, and toe. This procedure ensures that the thrust line and centerline of the vehicle are the same.

SUMMARY

1. The need for a wheel alignment results from wear or damage to suspension and steering components.
2. Camber is both a pulling angle (if not equal side-to-side) as well as a tire wearing angle (if not set to specifications).
3. Incorrect camber can cause tire wear and pulling if camber is not within 1/2 degree from one side to the other.
4. Toe is the most important alignment angle because toe is usually the first requiring correction. When incorrect, toe causes severe tire wear.
5. Incorrect toe causes excessive tire wear and creates instability if not within specifications.
6. Caster is the basic stability angle, yet it does not cause tire wear (directly) if not correct or equal side-to-side.
7. SAI and included angle (SAI and camber added together) are important diagnostic tools.
8. If the toe-out on turns (TOOT) reading is not within specifications, a bent steering spindle (steering knuckle) is the most likely cause.
9. A four-wheel alignment includes aligning all four wheels of the vehicle.

REVIEW QUESTIONS

1. Explain the three basic alignment angles of camber, caster, and toe.
2. Describe what happens to tire wear and vehicle handling if toe, camber, and caster are out of specification or *not* equal side-to-side.
3. Explain how knowing SAI, TOOT, and included angle can help in the correct diagnosis of an alignment problem.
4. Explain what thrust angle means.

1. When performing an alignment, which angle is the most important for tire wear?
   a. Toe
   b. Camber
   c. Caster
   d. SAI (KPI)

2. Positive camber means _____.
   a. The top of the tire is tilted outward.
   b. The top of the tire is tilted inward.
   c. Either a or b
   d. Both a and b

3. Which alignment angle is adjustable on all vehicles?
   a. Camber
   b. Caster
   c. Toe
   d. SAI (KPI)

4. Positive (+) toe is _____.
   a. Toe-in
   b. Toe-out

5. If the top of the steering axis is tilted 2 degrees toward the rear of the vehicle, this is _____.
   a. Positive camber
   b. Negative camber
   c. Negative caster
   d. Positive caster

6. A steering dampener may be needed to reduce shimmy on vehicles that have high positive _____.
   a. Camber
   b. Caster
   c. Toe
   d. Included angle

7. If the turning radius (toe-out on turns, or TOOT) is out of specification, what part or component is defective?
   a. The strut is bent.
   b. The steering arm is bent.
   c. The spindle is bent.
   d. The control arm is bent.

8. Which angle determines the thrust angle?
   a. Front toe
   b. Rear toe
   c. Rear camber
   d. Front caster, SAI, and included angle

9. Included angle is _____.
   a. SAI + caster
   b. Camber + caster
   c. Camber + SAI
   d. Toe + camber

10. Two technicians are discussing scrub radius. Technician A says that scrub radius cannot be measured. Technician B says that scrub radius cannot be adjusted. Which technician is correct?
    a. Technician A only
    b. Technician B only
    c. Both Technicians A and B
    d. Neither Technician A nor B

chapter 34

ALIGNMENT DIAGNOSIS AND SERVICE

FIGURE 34–1 The owner of this Honda thought that all it needed was an alignment. Obviously, something more serious than an alignment caused this left rear wheel to angle inward at the top.

Proper wheel alignment of all four wheels is important for the safe handling of any vehicle. When all four wheels are traveling the same path and/or being kept nearly vertical, tire life and fuel economy are maximized and vehicle handling is sure and predictable. A complete wheel alignment is a complex process that includes many detailed steps and the skill of a highly trained technician.

PREALIGNMENT CORRECTION TECHNIQUES

There are four basic steps in the correction of any problem:

1. **Verify.** What, when, where, and to what extent does the problem occur?

2. **Isolate.** Eliminate known good parts and systems. Always start with the simple things first. For example, checking and correcting tire pressure and rotation of the tires should be one of the first things performed whenever trying to isolate the cause of an alignment-related problem.

3. **Repair the problem.** This step involves replacing any worn or damaged components and making sure that the alignment is within factory specifications. ● **SEE FIGURE 34–1.**

4. **Recheck.** *Always* test-drive the vehicle after making a repair. Never allow the customer to be the first to drive the vehicle after any service work.

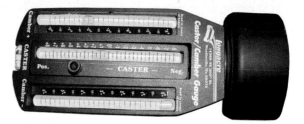

FIGURE 34–2 Magnetic bubble-type camber/caster gauge. To help it keep its strong magnetism, it is best to keep it stored stuck to a metal plate or metal tool box.

🔧 **TECH TIP**

Align and Replace at the Same Time

Magnetic bubble-type camber/caster gauges can be mounted directly on the hub or on an adapter attached to the wheel or spindle nut on front-wheel-drive vehicles. ● **SEE FIGURE 34–2.** Besides being used as an alignment setting tool, a magnetic alignment head is a great tool to use whenever replacing suspension components.

Any time a suspension component is replaced, the wheel alignment should be checked and corrected as necessary. An easy way to avoid having to make many adjustments is to use a magnetic alignment head on the front wheels to check camber with the vehicle hoisted in the air *before* replacing front components, such as new MacPherson struts. Then, before tightening all of the fasteners, check the front camber readings again to make sure they match the original setting. This is best done when the vehicle is still off the ground. For example, a typical front-wheel-drive vehicle with a MacPherson strut suspension may have a camber reading of +1/4 degree on the ground and +2 degrees while on the hoist with the wheels off the ground. After replacing the struts, simply return the camber reading to +2 degrees and it should return to the same +1/4 degree when lowered to the ground.

Though checking and adjusting camber before and after suspension service work does not guarantee a proper alignment, it does permit the vehicle to be moved around with the alignment fairly accurate until a final alignment can be performed.

A thorough inspection of the steering, suspension, and tires should be performed *before* the alignment of the vehicle is begun.

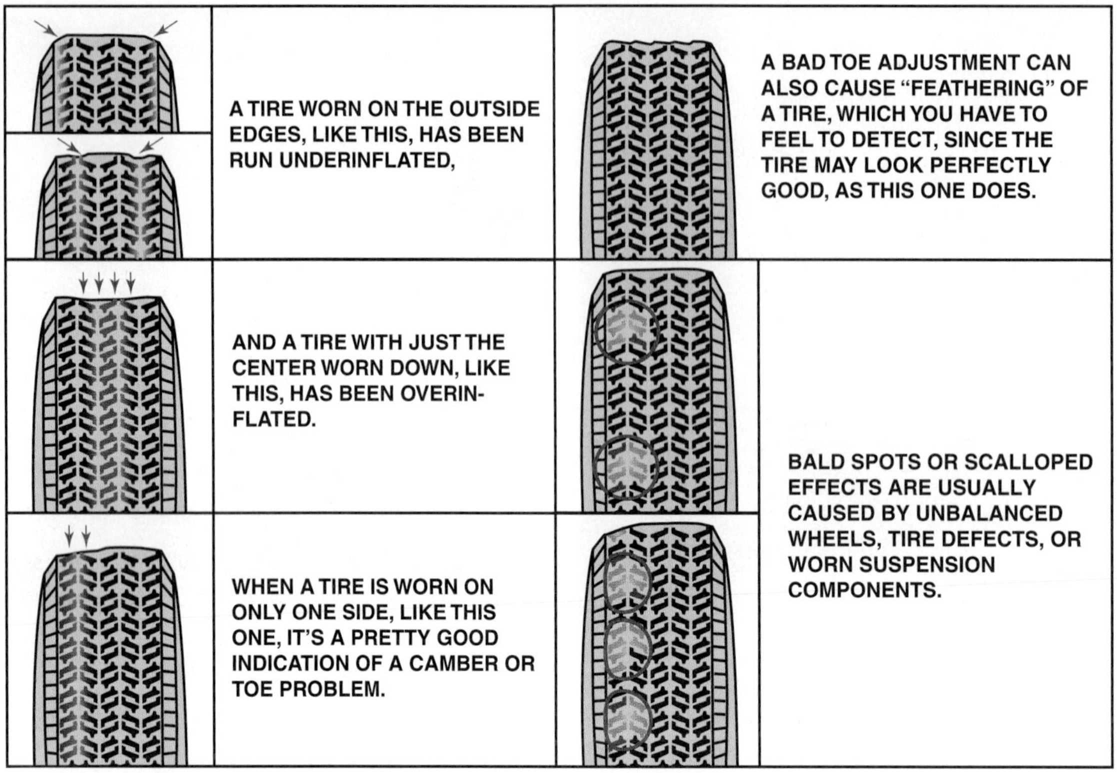

	A TIRE WORN ON THE OUTSIDE EDGES, LIKE THIS, HAS BEEN RUN UNDERINFLATED,		A BAD TOE ADJUSTMENT CAN ALSO CAUSE "FEATHERING" OF A TIRE, WHICH YOU HAVE TO FEEL TO DETECT, SINCE THE TIRE MAY LOOK PERFECTLY GOOD, AS THIS ONE DOES.
	AND A TIRE WITH JUST THE CENTER WORN DOWN, LIKE THIS, HAS BEEN OVERINFLATED.		BALD SPOTS OR SCALLOPED EFFECTS ARE USUALLY CAUSED BY UNBALANCED WHEELS, TIRE DEFECTS, OR WORN SUSPENSION COMPONENTS.
	WHEN A TIRE IS WORN ON ONLY ONE SIDE, LIKE THIS ONE, IT'S A PRETTY GOOD INDICATION OF A CAMBER OR TOE PROBLEM.		

FIGURE 34–3 Typical tire wear chart as found in a service manual. Abnormal tire wear usually indicates a fault in a steering or suspension component that should be corrected or replaced before an alignment is performed.

PREALIGNMENT CHECKS

Before checking or adjusting the front-end alignment, the following items should be checked and corrected, if necessary, as part of the **prealignment checks:**

1. Check all the tires for proper inflation pressures. Tires should be approximately the same size and tread depth, and the recommended size for the vehicle. ● **SEE FIGURE 34–3.**

   NOTE: Some alignment technicians think that the vehicle must have new tires installed before an accurate alignment can be performed. Excessively worn tires, especially if only one tire is worn, can cause the vehicle to lean slightly. It is this unequal ride height that is the important fact to consider. If, for example, all four tires are equally worn, then the vehicle *can* be properly aligned. (Obviously, excessively worn tires should be replaced, and it would be best to align the vehicle with the replacement tires installed to be assured of an accurate alignment.)

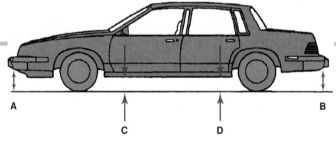

FIGURE 34–4 Measuring points for ride (trim) height vary by manufacturer. *(Courtesy of Hunter Engineering Company)*

2. Check the wheel bearings for proper adjustment.

3. Check for loose ball joints or torn ball joint boots.

4. Check the tie rod ends for damage or looseness.

5. Check the center link or rack bushings for play.

6. Check the pitman arm for any movement.

7. Check for runout of the wheels and the tires.

8. Check for vehicle ride height (should be level front to back as well as side-to-side). Make sure that the factory load-leveling system is functioning correctly, if the vehicle is so equipped. Check height according to the manufacturer's specifications. ● **SEE FIGURES 34–4 AND 34–5.**

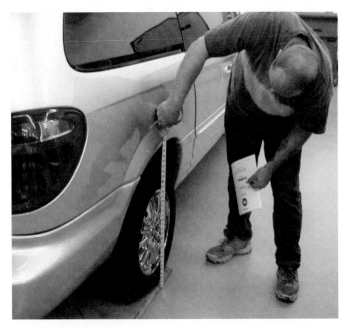

FIGURE 34–5 Measuring to be sure the left and right sides of the vehicle are of equal height. If this measurement is not equal side-to-side by as little as 1/8 in. (3 mm), it can affect the handling of the vehicle.

FIGURE 34–6 The bulge in this tire was not noticed until it was removed from the vehicle as part of a routine brake inspection. After replacing this tire, the vehicle stopped pulling and vibrating.

NOTE: Manufacturers often have replacement springs or spring spacers that can be installed between the coil spring and the spring seat to restore proper ride level.

9. Check for steering gear looseness at the frame.
10. Check for improperly operating shock absorbers.
11. Check for worn control arm bushings.
12. Check for loose or missing stabilizer bar attachments.
13. Check the trunk for excess loads.
14. Check for dragging brakes.

NOTE: Checking for dragging brakes is usually performed when installing alignment heads to the wheels prior to taking an alignment reading. A brake dragging can cause the vehicle to pull or lead toward the side with the dragging brake.

LEAD/PULL

DIAGNOSIS Many alignment requests come from customers attempting to have a lead or pull condition corrected. Before aligning the vehicle, verify the customer complaint first, then perform a careful inspection.

1. Inspect all tires for proper inflation. Both tires on the same axle (front and rear) should be the same size and brand. A lead/pull problem could be due to a defect or condition in one or more of the tires, as shown in ● **FIGURE 34–6.** Before attempting to correct the lead/pull condition by changing alignment angles, try rotating the tires front to back or side to side.

2. Road test the vehicle on a straight, level road away from traffic, if possible. Bring the vehicle to about 40 mph (65 km/h), shift into neutral, and feel for a pull in the steering, either to the left or to the right. A lead or drift is less severe than a pull, and may occur only if you momentarily remove your hands from the steering wheel while driving.

3. If the lead/pull problem is sometimes toward the left and other times toward the right, check for a **memory steer** condition. If the lead/pull problem occurs during acceleration and deceleration, check for a **torque steer** condition.

MEMORY STEER

DIAGNOSIS *Memory steer* is a term used to describe the lead or pull of a vehicle caused by faults in the steering or suspension system. Often a defective upper strut bearing or steering gear can cause a pulling condition in one direction after making a turn in the same direction. It is as if the vehicle had a memory and pulled in the same direction. To test for memory steer, follow these simple steps during a test drive:

1. With the vehicle stopped at an intersection or in a parking area, turn the steering wheel completely to the left stop and then straighten the wheel without going past the straight-ahead position.

2. Lightly accelerate the vehicle and note any tendency of the vehicle to lead or pull toward the left.

3. Repeat the procedure, turning the steering wheel to the right.

If the vehicle first pulls to the left, then pulls to the right, the vehicle has a memory steer condition.

CORRECTION A binding suspension or steering component is the most likely cause of memory steer. Disconnect each wheel from its tie rod end and check for free rotation of movement of each wheel. Each front wheel should rotate easily without binding or roughness. Repair or replace components as necessary to eliminate the binding condition.

NOTE: One of the most common causes of memory steer is the installation of steering or suspension components while the front wheels are turned. Most steering and suspension parts contain rubber, which has a memory if moved from its installed position. If the memory steer condition is only in one direction, then this is the most likely cause. The rubber component exerts a force on the suspension or steering that causes the vehicle to pull toward the side that the wheels were turned toward when the part was installed.

The Five-Wheel Alignment

The steering wheel should always be straight when driving on a straight, level road. If the steering wheel is not straight, the customer will often think that the wheel alignment is not correct. One such customer complained that the vehicle pulled to the right while driving on a straight road. The service manager test drove the vehicle and everything was perfect, except that the steering wheel was not perfectly straight, even though the toe setting was correct. Whenever driving on a straight road, the customer would "straighten the steering wheel" and, of course, the vehicle went to one side. After adjusting toe with the steering wheel straight, the customer and the service manager were both satisfied. The technician learned that regardless of how accurate the alignment, the steering wheel *must* be straight; it is the "fifth wheel" that the customer notices most. Therefore, a **five-wheel alignment** rule includes a check of the steering wheel.

NOTE: Many vehicle manufactures now include the maximum allowable steering wheel angle variation from straight. This specification is commonly ±3 degrees (plus or minus 3 degrees) or less.

TORQUE STEER

DIAGNOSIS Torque steer occurs in front-wheel-drive vehicles when engine torque causes a front wheel to change its angle from straight ahead. ● **SEE FIGURE 34–7.** This resulting pulling effect is most noticeable during rapid acceleration, especially whenever upshifting of the transmission creates a sudden change in torque being applied to the front wheels. When turning and accelerating at the same time, torque steer has a tendency to straighten the vehicle, so more steering effort may be required to make the turn. Then, if the accelerator is released, a reversing force is applied to the front wheels. Now the driver must take corrective steering motions to counteract the change in steering effect of engine torque.

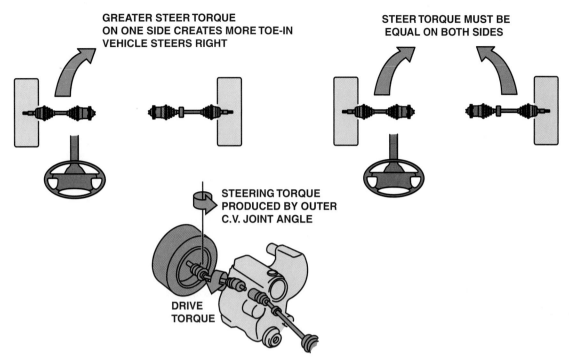

GREATER STEER TORQUE ON ONE SIDE CREATES MORE TOE-IN VEHICLE STEERS RIGHT

STEER TORQUE MUST BE EQUAL ON BOTH SIDES

STEERING TORQUE PRODUCED BY OUTER C.V. JOINT ANGLE

DRIVE TORQUE

FIGURE 34–7 Equal outer CV joint angles produce equal steer torque (toe-in). If one side receives more engine torque, that side creates more toe-in and the result is a pull toward one side, especially during acceleration.

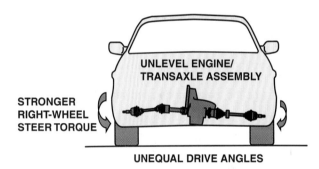

UNLEVEL ENGINE/ TRANSAXLE ASSEMBLY

STRONGER RIGHT-WHEEL STEER TORQUE

UNEQUAL DRIVE ANGLES

FIGURE 34–8 Broken or defective engine or transaxle mounts can cause the powertrain to sag, causing unequal drive axle shaft CV joint angles.

Torque steer sequence of events

Torque to wheel	a toe-in condition
More torque	more toe-in
Unequal torque	unequal toe-in
Unequal driveshaft angles	unequal torque to the wheels

Most manufacturers try to reduce torque steer in the design of their vehicles by keeping drive axle angles low and equal side-to-side. If the engine and transaxle are level and the drive axle shafts are kept level, then the torque from the engine will be divided equally between the front wheels.

CORRECTION The service technician cannot change the design of a vehicle, but the technician can, and should, check and correct problems that often cause torque steer. **Check to be sure that the condition is not normal.** It is normal for front-wheel-drive vehicles to exert a tug on the steering wheel and steer toward one side (usually to the right) during acceleration. This is especially noticeable when the transmission shifts from first to second gear under heavy acceleration. To determine how severe the problem is, place a strip of masking tape at the top of the steering wheel. Drive the vehicle and observe the amount of movement required to steer the vehicle straight during heavy acceleration. Repeat the test with a vehicle of similar make and model. If the torque steer is excessive, determine and correct the cause by carefully following the prealignment inspection steps and checking for a level powertrain.

A defective engine mount can cause the entire drivetrain to sag on one end. If the engine and transaxle of any front-wheel-drive vehicle is not level, the drive axle shaft angles will not be equal, as shown in ● **FIGURE 34–8.**

Hold a straightedge along the engine's supporting frame and measure up to points along the transaxle pan rail or the drive axle shaft. Side-to-side distances should be equal. Standard alignment shims can be used to shim the mounts and level the drivetrain.

If torque steer is still excessive, check all alignment angles, including SAI and included angle. Unequal alignment angles can cause a pull or a lead condition. SAI and included angle should be within 1/2 (0.5) degree side-to-side for best results. A vehicle will tend to pull toward the side with the least SAI.

ALIGNMENT SPECIFICATIONS

Before attempting any alignment, consider the following:

1. Determine the make, model, and year of the vehicle.

2. Determine if the vehicle is equipped with power steering or manual steering. (Some older models use lower caster specifications for manual steering to reduce steering effort.)

3. Check the trunk and with the customer to determine the normal load being carried. Sometimes customers take out heavy things they normally carry or have something in the vehicle now that they normally do not carry.

4. Determine the correct specifications (if possible, check the specifications from two different sources to ensure correct readings).

5. Compensate for the lack of a full gas tank by placing an equal amount of weight in the luggage compartment. (Gasoline weighs 6 lb per gallon [0.7 kg per l]—a 20-gallon gas tank, when full, weighs 120 lb [80 liters weighs 54 kg].)

6. Determine the correct specifications for the *exact* vehicle being checked.

NOTE: Some alignment specifications are published as guidelines for acceptable values for state or local vehicle inspections. Be sure to use the *service* or *set to* specifications.

TECH TIP

Keep the Doors Closed, but the Window Down

An experienced alignment technician became upset when a beginning technician opened the driver's door to lock the steering wheel in a straight-ahead position on the vehicle being aligned. The weight of the open door caused the vehicle to sag. This disturbed the level position of the vehicle and changed all the alignment angles.

The beginning technician learned an important lesson that day: Keep the window down on the driver's door so that the steering wheel and brakes can be locked without disturbing the vehicle weight balance by opening a door. The brake pedal must be locked with a pedal depressor to prevent the wheels from rolling as the wheels are turned during a caster sweep. The steering must be locked in the straight-ahead position when adjusting toe.

READING ALIGNMENT SPECIFICATIONS There are several methods used by vehicle manufacturers and alignment equipment manufacturers to specify alignment angles.

MAXIMUM/MINIMUM/PREFERRED METHOD. This method indicates the preferred setting for each alignment angle and the minimum and maximum allowable value for each. The alignment technician should always attempt to align the vehicle to the preferred setting.

PLUS OR MINUS METHOD. This method indicates the preferred setting with the lowest and highest allowable value indicated by a negative (−) and positive (+) sign, as in ● **FIGURE 34–9.** For example, if a camber reading is specified as +1/2 degree with a + and − value of 1/2 degree, it could be written as +1/2 degree ±1/2 degree. The minimum value would be 0 degree (1/2° − 1/2° = 0°) and the maximum value would be +1 degree (+1/2° + 1/2° = 1°). The range would be from 0 to 1 degree.

NOTE: The angle is assumed positive unless labeled with a negative (−) sign in front of the number.

WHEEL ALIGNMENT SPECIFICATIONS

	CASTER	CROSS CASTER (LH-RH)	CAMBER	CROSS CAMBER (LH-RH)	TOE (TOTAL IN) DEGREES	STEERING WHEEL ANGLE	THRUST ANGLE
FRONT	+3°±.5°	0°±.75°	+.2° ±.5°	0°±.75°	0°±.3°	0°±3°	– –
REAR	– –	– –	-.3° ±.5°	0°±.75°	+.1° ±.2°	– –	0°±.1°

FIGURE 34–9 This alignment chart indicates the preferred setting with a plus or minus tolerance.

DEGREES, MINUTES, AND FRACTIONS

Specifications are often published in **fractional** or decimal **degrees**, or in degrees and **minutes**. There are 60 minutes (written as 60') in 1 degree.

Fractions	Decimal Degrees	Minutes-Seconds
1/4°	0.25°	0°15'
1/2°	0.50°	0°30'
3/4°	0.75°	0°45'
1°	1.0°	1° or 60'

To help visualize the amount of these various units, think of decimal degrees as representing money or cents (100 cents = 1 dollar).

0.75 = 75 cents, or 3/4 of a dollar

Minutes can be visualized as minutes in an hour (60' = 1 hour).

45' = 3/4 of an hour

Now which is larger, 35 minutes or 0.40 degrees? The larger angle is 35 minutes because this is slightly greater than 1/2 degree, whereas 0.40 minutes is less than 1/2 degree.

FINDING THE MIDPOINT OF SPECIFICATIONS

Many manufacturers specify alignment angles within a range. If you are using equipment that requires a midpoint to be entered, use the following method to determine easily the midpoint of specifications.

Example 1:

Specification: 55' to 2° 25'

STEP 1 The first step is to determine the specification range or span, which is the total angle value from lowest to highest:

$$\begin{array}{r} 2°\ 25' \\ -55' \\ \hline 1°\ 30'\ \text{Specification range} \end{array}$$

STEP 2 Dividing the specification range by 2 will give the midpoint of the range:

$$\frac{1°\ 30'}{2} = \frac{90'}{2'} = 45'$$

STEP 3 To find the midpoint of the specifications, add the midpoint of the range to the smaller specification (or subtract from the larger specification):

$$\begin{array}{r} 45'\ \text{midpoint of range} \\ +55'\ \text{lowest specification} \\ \hline 1°40'\ \text{midpoint of specification} \end{array}$$

Example 2:

Specification: $-0.5°$ to $+0.80°$

STEP 1 The total range of the specification is determined by adding 0.5 (1/2) to 0.80, totaling $1.30°$.

NOTE: Since the lower specification is a negative number, we had to *add* the 0.5 degree to bring the lower range of the specification to zero. Then the total is simply the upper range specification added to the number required to bring the lower end of the range to zero.

STEP 2 Dividing the specification range by 2 gives the midpoint of the range:

$$\frac{1.30°}{2} = 0.65°$$

STEP 3 To find the midpoint of the specification, add the midpoint of the range to the smaller specification:

$$0.65 + (-0.50) = 0.15$$

ALIGNMENT SETUP PROCEDURES

After confirming that the tires and all steering and suspension components are serviceable, the vehicle is ready for an alignment. Setup procedures for the equipment being used must always be followed. Typical alignment procedures include the following:

STEP 1 Drive onto the alignment rack straight and adjust the ramps and/or turn plates so that they are centered under the tires of the vehicle. ● **SEE FIGURE 34–10.**

STEP 2 Use chocks for the wheels to keep the vehicle from rolling off the alignment rack.

STEP 3 Attach and calibrate the wheel sensors to each wheel as specified by the alignment equipment manufacturer. ● **SEE FIGURE 34–11.** The calibration procedure is required whenever the head of the machine is attached to the wheel of the vehicle. All alignment angles and measurements are taken from the readings of the wheel sensors.

FIGURE 34–10 Using the alignment rack hydraulic jacks, raise the tires off the rack so that they can be rotated as part of the compensating process.

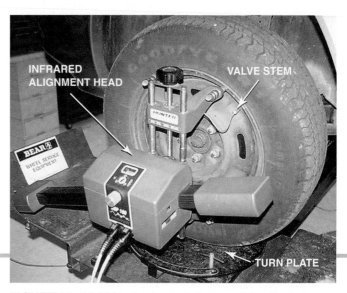

FIGURE 34–11 This wheel sensor has a safety wire that screws to the valve stem to keep the sensor from falling onto the ground if the clamps slip on the wheel lip.

Calibration of these wheel sensors is needed for two reasons:

a. *The wheel may be bent.*   If the wheel (rim) is bent, even slightly, this small amount of tilt would be read as an angle of the suspension.

NOTE: Compensating or calibrating the wheel sensor for a bent wheel does *not* correct (or repair) the bent wheel! The bent wheel is still present and can result in a shimmy-type vibration.

b. *The sensors may not be identically installed on the wheel.*   Most sensors use three or four wheel-mounting locations. It is not possible to install all wheel sensors perfectly at the same depth on the

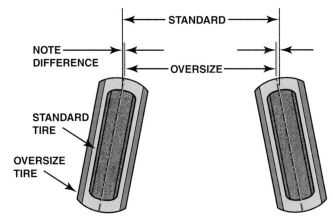

FIGURE 34–12 If toe for an oversize tire is set by distance, the toe angle will be too small. Toe angle is the same regardless of tire size.

wheel in all locations. If a sensor must be removed during the alignment process and reinstalled, it should be recalibrated. Always follow the manufacturer's recommended procedure for compensating the sensors.

STEP 4 Unlock all rack or turn plates.

STEP 5 Lower the vehicle and jounce the vehicle by pushing down on the front, then rear, bumper. This motion allows the suspension to become centered.

STEP 6 Following the procedures for the alignment equipment, determine all alignment angles.

MEASURING CAMBER, CASTER, SAI, TOE, AND TOOT

CAMBER Camber is measured with the wheels in the straight-ahead position on a level platform. Since camber is a vertical reference angle, alignment equipment reads camber directly.

CASTER Caster is measured by moving the front wheels through an arc inward, then outward, from straight ahead. This necessary movement of the front wheels to measure caster is called *caster sweep*. What the alignment measuring equipment is actually doing is measuring the camber at one wheel sweep and measuring the camber again at the other extreme of the caster sweep. *The caster angle itself is the difference between the two camber readings.*

SAI Steering axis inclination (SAI) is also measured by performing a caster sweep of the front wheels. While this angle can be read at the same time as caster on many alignment machines, most experts recommend that SAI be measured separately from the caster reading. When measuring SAI separately, the usual procedure involves raising the front wheels off the ground and leveling and locking the wheel sensors before performing a caster sweep. The reason for raising the front wheels is to allow the front suspension to extend to its full droop position. When the suspension is extended, the SAI is more accurately determined because the angle itself is expanded.

TOE Toe is determined by measuring the angle of both front and/or both rear wheels from the straight-ahead (0 degree) position. Most alignment equipment reads the toe angle for each wheel *and* the combined toe angle of both wheels on the same axle. This combined toe is called **total toe**. Toe angle is more accurate than the center-to-center distance, especially if oversize tires are installed on the vehicle. ● **SEE FIGURE 34–12.**

TOOT Toe-out on turns (TOOT) is a diagnostic angle and is normally not measured as part of a regular alignment, but it is recommended to be performed as part of a total alignment check. TOOT is measured by recording the angle of the front wheels as indicated on the alignment machine display or on the front turn plates. ● **SEE FIGURE 34–13.**

If, for example, the inside wheel is turned 20 degrees, then the outside wheel should indicate about 18 degrees on the turn plate. The exact angles are usually specified by the vehicle manufacturer. The turning angle should be checked only after the toe is

FIGURE 34–13 The protractor scale on the front turn plates allows the technician to test the turning radius by turning one wheel to an angle specified by the manufacturer and observing the angle of the other front wheel. Most newer alignment machines can display turning angle based on sensor readings, and therefore the protractor scale on the turn plate is not needed or used.

MEASURING CAMBER, CASTER, SAI, TOE, AND TOOT (CONTINUED)

correctly set. *The turning angle for the wheel on the outside of the turn should not vary more than 1 1/2 degrees from specifications.* For example, if the specification calls for the right wheel to be steered into the turn 20 degrees, the outside wheel should measure 18 degrees. This measurement should be within 1 1/2 degrees (16.5 to 19.5 degrees). If the TOOT is not correct, a bent steering arm is the usual cause. If TOOT is not correct, tire squealing noise is usually noticed while cornering and excessive tire wear may occur.

NOTE: Some front-wheel-drive vehicles use a nonsymmetrical (unequal) turning angle design. This design is found on various makes and models of vehicles to assist in controlling torque steer. The test procedure is the same except that the turning angle specifications include left-wheel and right-wheel angles when turned inward and outward and may be different readings without indicating a problem.

SPECIFICATIONS VERSUS ALIGNMENT READINGS

Secure both the alignment specifications from the manufacturer and the alignment readings and compare the two. Before starting an alignment, the smart technician checks the SAI, included angle, setback, and toe-out on turns to make sure that there is no hidden damage such as a bent spindle or strut that was not found during the prealignment inspection. *Setback is also a diagnostic angle and should be less than 0.5 in. (13 cm or 1/2 degree).* If setback is greater than 0.5 in. (13 cm or 1/2 degree), check the body, frame, and cradle for accident damage or improper alignment.

NOTE: If the SAI or included angle are unequal, suggesting a possible problem such as a bent strut, check the front and rear toe readings. Some alignment equipment cannot show accurate SAI readings if the front or rear toe readings are not within specifications. If the front and rear toe readings are OK and the alignment readings indicate a bent strut, go ahead with the diagnosis and correction as explained later in this chapter.

CHECKING FOR BENT STRUTS, SPINDLES, OR CONTROL ARMS

Even a minor bump against a curb can bend a spindle or a strut housing.

Before attempting to correct an alignment, check all the angles and use the appropriate diagnostic chart to check for hidden damage that a visual inspection may miss.

The chart in ● **FIGURE 34–14** can be used to determine what is wrong if the alignment angles are known. Simply use the chart that correctly identifies the type of suspension on the problem vehicle. The terms used regarding the specifications in Figure 34–14 include:

At spec	The alignment angle is within specifications.
Over spec	The alignment angle is greater or higher than specified by the manufacturer.
Under spec	The alignment angle is less than or lower than specified by the manufacturer.

DIAGNOSING SAI, CAMBER, AND INCLUDED ANGLE			
SLA AND STRUT/SLA SUSPENSIONS			
SAI	**CAMBER**	**INCLUDED ANGLE**	**DIAGNOSIS**
CORRECT	LESS THAN SPECS	LESS THAN SPECS	BENT STEERING KNUCKLE OR SPINDLE
LESS THAN SPECS	GREATER THAN SPECS	CORRECT	BENT LOWER CONTROL ARM
LESS THAN SPECS	GREATER THAN SPECS	GREATER THAN SPECS	BENT LOWER CONTROL ARM AND STEERING KNUCKLE OR SPINDLE
GREATER THAN SPECS	LESS THAN SPECS	CORRECT	BENT UPPER CONTROL ARM
STRUT SUSPENSIONS			
SAI	**CAMBER**	**INCLUDED ANGLE**	**DIAGNOSIS**
CORRECT	LESS THAN SPECS	LESS THAN SPECS	BENT SPINDLE AND/OR STRUT
CORRECT	GREATER THAN SPECS	GREATER THAN SPECS	BENT SPINDLE AND/OR STRUT
LESS THAN SPECS	GREATER THAN SPECS	CORRECT	BENT CONTROL ARM OR STRUT TOWER OUT AT TOP
LESS THAN SPECS	GREATER THAN SPECS	GREATER THAN SPECS	BENT CONTROL ARM OR STRUT TOWER OUT AT TOP, ALSO BENT SPINDLE AND/OR STRUT
LESS THAN SPECS	LESS THAN SPECS	LESS THAN SPECS	BENT CONTROL ARM OR STRUT TOWER OUT AT TOP, ALSO BENT SPINDLE AND/OR STRUT
GREATER THAN SPECS	LESS THAN SPECS	CORRECT	STRUT TOWER IN AT TOP
GREATER THAN SPECS	GREATER THAN SPECS	GREATER THAN SPECS	STRUT TOWER IN AT TOP AND BENT SPINDLE AND/OR BENT STRUT
KINGPIN TWIN I-BEAM SUSPENSION			
SAI (KPI)	**CAMBER**	**INCLUDED ANGLE**	**DIAGNOSIS**
CORRECT	GREATER THAN SPECS	GREATER THAN SPECS	BENT SPINDLE
LESS THAN SPECS	GREATER THAN SPECS	CORRECT	BENT I-BEAM
LESS THAN SPECS	GREATER THAN SPECS	GREATER THAN SPECS	BENT I-BEAM AND SPINDLE
GREATER THAN SPECS	LESS THAN SPECS	CORRECT	BENT I-BEAM

FIGURE 34–14 By checking the SAI, camber, and included angle, a damaged suspension component can be determined by using this chart.

CHECKING FRAME ALIGNMENT OF FRONT-WHEEL-DRIVE VEHICLES

Many front-wheel-drive vehicles mount the drive train (engine and transaxle) and lower suspension arms to a subframe or cradle. If the frame is shifted either left or right, this can cause differences in SAI, included angle, setback, and camber.

● **SEE FIGURES 34–15 AND 34–16.** Adjust the frame if SAI and camber angles are different left and right side, yet the included angles are equal.

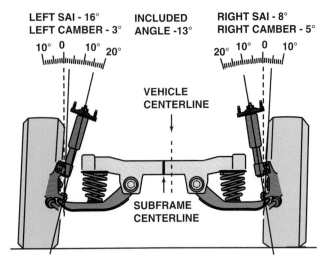

LEFT SAI - 16°
LEFT CAMBER - 3°
INCLUDED ANGLE -13°
RIGHT SAI - 8°
RIGHT CAMBER - 5°

VEHICLE CENTERLINE

SUBFRAME CENTERLINE

FIGURE 34–15 In this example, both SAI and camber are far from being equal side-to-side. However, both sides have the same included angle, indicating that the frame may be out of alignment. An attempt to align this vehicle by adjusting the camber on both sides with either factory or aftermarket kits would result in a totally incorrect alignment.

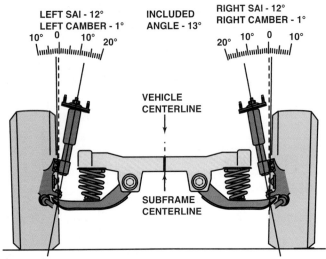

LEFT SAI - 12°
LEFT CAMBER - 1°
INCLUDED ANGLE - 13°
RIGHT SAI - 12°
RIGHT CAMBER - 1°

VEHICLE CENTERLINE

SUBFRAME CENTERLINE

FIGURE 34–16 This is the same vehicle as shown in Figure 34–15, except now the frame (cradle) has been shifted over and correctly positioned. Notice how both the SAI and camber become equal without any other adjustments necessary.

TECH TIP

Damage Analysis Tips

To check if a vehicle has been in a collision, technicians should look for the following:

1. Drive the vehicle through a water puddle to see if the tire marks are wider than the tires. If they are, then the front and rear wheels are not tracking correctly.

2. If the setback is out of specifications, then the front of the vehicle may be damaged.

3. If the thrust angle is out of specifications, then rear suspension damage is likely.

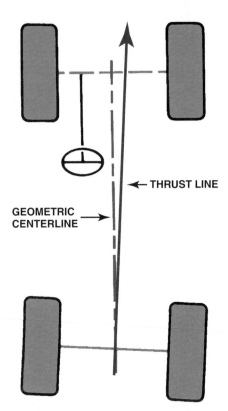

THRUST LINE

GEOMETRIC CENTERLINE

FIGURE 34–17 Geometric-centerline-type alignment sets the front toe readings based on the geometric centerline of the vehicle and does not consider the thrust line of the rear wheel toe angles. *(Courtesy of Hunter Engineering Company)*

TYPES OF ALIGNMENTS

There are three types of alignment: geometric centerline, thrust line, and four-wheel alignment.

GEOMETRIC CENTERLINE Until the 1980s, most wheel alignment concerned only the front wheels. Vehicles, such as sports cars, that had independent rear suspensions were often aligned by backing the vehicle onto the alignment rack and adjusting the rear camber and/or toe. This type of alignment is simply an alignment that uses the **geometric centerline** of the vehicle as the basis for all measurements of toe (front or rear). ● SEE FIGURE 34–17.

This method is now considered to be obsolete.

THRUST LINE A **thrust line** alignment uses the thrust angle of the rear wheels and sets the front wheels parallel to the thrust line. ● SEE FIGURE 34–18.

The thrust line is the bisector of rear total toe, or the actual direction in which the rear wheels are pointed. The rear wheels of any vehicle *should* be pointing parallel to the geometric centerline of the vehicle. However, if the rear toe angles of the rear wheels

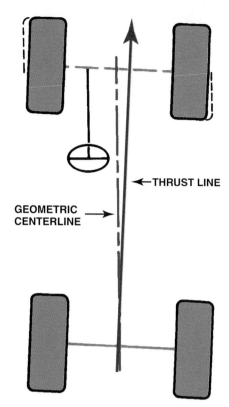

FIGURE 34–18 Thrust line alignment sets the front toe parallel with the rear-wheel toe. *(Courtesy of Hunter Engineering Company)*

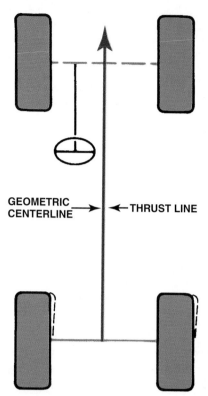

FIGURE 34–19 Four-wheel alignment corrects for any rear-wheel toe to make the thrust line and the geometric centerline of the vehicle both the same. *(Courtesy of Hunter Engineering Company)*

do not total exactly zero (perfectly in a line with the centerline of the vehicle), a thrust condition exists. The front wheels will automatically steer to become parallel to that condition. A crooked steering wheel may also result from an improper thrust condition.

NOTE: It has often been said that while the front wheels steer the vehicle, the rear wheels determine the direction in which the vehicle will travel. Think of the rear wheels as a rudder on a boat. If the rudder is turned, the direction of the boat changes due to the angle change at the rear of the boat.

Thrust line alignment is *required* for any vehicle with a non-adjustable rear suspension. If a vehicle has an adjustable rear suspension, then a four-wheel alignment is necessary to ensure proper tracking.

FOUR-WHEEL ALIGNMENT

A **four-wheel alignment** is the most accurate alignment method and is necessary to ensure maximum tire wear and vehicle handling. The biggest difference between a thrust-line alignment and a four-wheel alignment is

that the rear toe is adjusted to bring the thrust line to zero. In other words, the rear toe on both rear wheels is adjusted equally so that the actual direction in which the rear wheels are pointed is the same as the geometric centerline of the vehicle. ● **SEE FIGURE 34–19.**

The procedure for a four-wheel alignment includes these steps:

1. Adjust the rear camber (if applicable).
2. Adjust the rear toe (this should reduce the thrust angle to near zero).
3. Adjust the front camber and caster.
4. Adjust the front toe, being sure that the steering wheel is in the straight-ahead position.

TECH TIP

Ask Yourself These Three Questions

An older technician told a beginning technician that the key to success in doing a proper alignment is to ask yourself three questions about the alignment angles:

Question 1. **"Is it within specifications?"** For example, if the specification reads 1° ±1/2°, any reading between +1/2° and 1 1/2° is within specifications. All vehicles should be aligned within this range. Individual opinions and experience can assist the technician as to whether the actual setting should be at one extreme or the other or held to the center of the specification range.

Question 2. **"Is it within 1/2° of the other side of the vehicle?"** Not only should the alignment be within specifications, but it should also be as equal as possible from one side to the other. The difference between the camber from one side to the other side is called cross camber. Cross caster is the difference between the caster angle from one side to another. Some manufacturers and technicians recommend that this side-to-side difference be limited to just 1/4 degree!

Question 3. **"If the camber and caster cannot be exactly equal side-to-side in the front, is there more camber on the left and more caster on the right to help compensate for road crown?"** Seldom, if ever, are the alignment angles perfectly equal. Sometimes one side of the vehicle is more difficult to adjust than the other side. Regardless of the reasons, if there *has* to be a difference in front camber and/or caster angle, follow this advice to avoid a possible lead or drift problem even if the answers to the first two questions are "yes."

SAMPLE ALIGNMENT SPECIFICATIONS AND READINGS

The service technician must know not only all of the alignment angles but also the interrelationship that exists among the angles. As an aid toward understanding these relationships, two examples are presented: Example 1 gives the front wheel angles that are acceptable when compared with the specifications; Example 2 gives four-wheel alignment and readings of a vehicle that are not within specifications.

Example 1: Wheel Alignment

Alignment Specifications

	Left	Right
Camber =	+1/2° ± 1/2°	+1/2° ± 1/2°
Caster =	+1° ± 1/2°	+1° ± 1/2°
Toe (total) =	1/8 in. ± 1/16 in.	

Actual Reading

	Left	Right
Camber =	+1/4°	0°
Caster =	+1°	+1 1/4°
Toe (total) =	1/8 in.	

Answer:

Alignment is perfect:

a. No tire wear

b. No pulling

Explanation:

Camber is within specifications.

Camber is within 1/2-degree difference side-to-side.

Camber is not equal, but there is more camber on the left (1/4 degree) than on the right, thereby helping to compensate for the road crown.

Caster is within specifications.

Caster is within 1/2-degree difference side-to-side.

Caster is not equal, but there is more caster on the right (1/4 degree) than on the left, thereby helping (very slightly) to compensate for road crown.

Toe is within specifications.

Example 2: Four-Wheel Alignment

Specifications

	Left	Right
Front camber =	+1/4° ± 1/2°	0° ± 1/2°
Front caster =	+3° ± 1/2°	+1/2° ± 1/2°
Front toe (total) =	3/16 in. ± 1/16 in.	
Rear camber =	0° ± 1/4°	0° ± 1/4°
Rear toe =	0 in. ± 1/16 in.	

Actual Reading

	Left	Right
Front camber =	−1/2°	−1°
Front caster =	+2 3/4°	+2°
Front toe =	−1/8 in. (toe-out)	
Rear camber =	0°	+1/4°
Rear toe =	1 1/2° (toe-in)	

Answer:

Alignment is incorrect.

a. Left front tire will wear slightly on the inside edge.

b. Right front tire will wear on the inside edge.

c. Vehicle could tend to pull slightly to the left due to the camber difference (may not pull at all due to the pulling effect of the road crown).

d. Vehicle could tend to pull slightly to the right due to the caster difference (3/4 degree more caster on the left).

e. Overall pull could be slight toward the left because it requires four times the caster difference to have the same pulling forces as camber.

f. Tires could wear slightly on both the inside edges due to toe-out.

g. The negative camber of the present alignment puts a heavy load on the outer wheel bearing, if RWD, because the load is being carried by the smaller outer wheel bearing instead of the larger inner wheel bearing.

Conclusion:

The vehicle would wear the inside edges of both front tires.

The vehicle may or may not pull slightly to the left.

The vehicle would not act as stable while driving—possible wander.

 FREQUENTLY ASKED QUESTION

How does normal wear affect the alignment angles?

As a vehicle ages, the springs sag and steering and suspension components wear.

- When springs sag the ride height changes and the camber usually is reduced and often becomes negative compared to slightly positive when the vehicle was new in most cases.

- When tie rod ends and other steering components wear, the front wheels tend to toe out.

- Worn suspension components can cause excessive play making the vehicle unstable and cause the tires to wear abnormally.

Alignment alone cannot take the place of worn parts. All an alignment can do is try to compensate for the worn parts.

Toe is the most common angle that needs to be adjusted because any wear in the steering or suspension systems affect the toe.

ADJUSTING REAR CAMBER

Adjusting rear camber is the first step in the four-wheel alignment process. Rear camber is rarely made adjustable, but can be corrected by using aftermarket alignment kits or shims. If rear camber is not correct, vehicle handling and tire life are affected. Before attempting to adjust or correct rear camber, carefully check the body and/or frame of the vehicle for accident damage, including the following:

1. Weak springs, torsion bars, or overloading (check ride height)
2. Bowed rear axle, trailing arm, or rear control arm
3. Suspension mount or body dimension not in proper location
4. Incorrectly adjusted camber from a previous repair

The cause of the incorrect rear camber could be accident-related and the body or frame may have to be pulled into correct position. ● **SEE FIGURES 34–20 THROUGH 34–22** for examples of various methods used to adjust rear camber.

USING PLASTIC OR METAL ALIGNMENT SHIMS

Using plastic or metal alignment shims to correct angles in the rear of the vehicle is relatively simple and includes the following steps:

1. Take alignment readings and determine the change needed.
2. Select proper shims using the easy-to-read chart.
3. Using the template provided, mark and remove tabs to create a proper mounting bolt pattern.
4. Install shim.

ADJUSTING REAR TOE Many vehicle manufacturers provide adjustment for rear toe on vehicles that use an independent rear suspension. Rear toe adjusts the thrust angle. A thrust angle that exceeds 1/2 degree (0.5 degree) on a vehicle with a solid axle is an indication that a component may be damaged or out of place in the rear of the vehicle. Rear toe is often adjusted using an adjustable tie rod end or an eccentric cam on the lower control arm. Check a service manual for the exact method for the vehicle being aligned. Most solid rear axles do not have a method to adjust rear toe except for aftermarket shims or kits. ● **SEE FIGURES 34–24 THROUGH 34–26.**

NOTE: On vehicles equipped with four-wheel steering, refer to the service manual for the exact procedure to follow to lock or hold the rear wheels in position for a proper alignment check.

FIGURE 34–20 The rear camber is adjustable on this vehicle by rotating the eccentric cam and watching the alignment machine display.

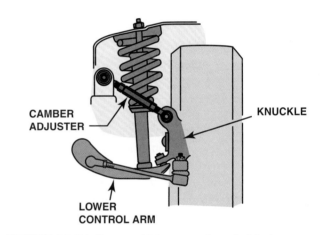

FIGURE 34–21 Some vehicles use a threaded fastener similar to a tie rod to adjust camber on the rear suspension.

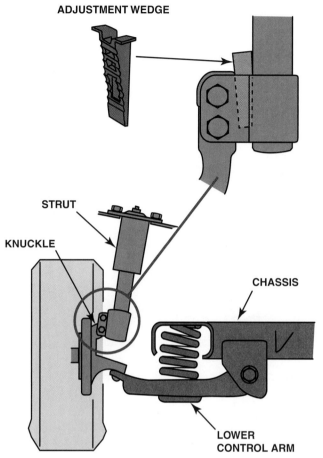

ADJUSTMENT WEDGE

STRUT

KNUCKLE

CHASSIS

LOWER
CONTROL ARM

FIGURE 34–22 Aftermarket alignment parts or kits are available to change the rear camber.

TECH TIP

The Gritty Solution

Many times it is difficult to loosen a Torx bolt, especially those used to hold the backing plate onto the rear axle on many GM vehicles. ● **SEE FIGURE 34–23.**

A technique that always seems to work is to place some valve grinding compound on the fastener. The gritty compound keeps the Torx socket from slipping up and out of the fastener, and more force can be exerted to break loose a tight bolt. Valve grinding compound can also be used on Phillips head screws as well as other types of bolts, nuts, and sockets.

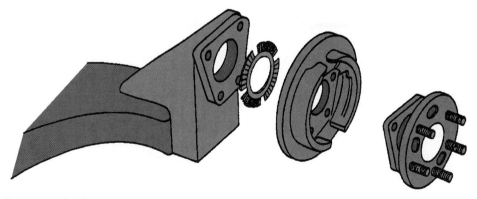

FIGURE 34–23 Full-contact plastic or metal shims can be placed between the axle housing and the brake backing plate to change rear camber, toe, or both. *(Courtesy of Northstar Manufacturing Company, Inc.)*

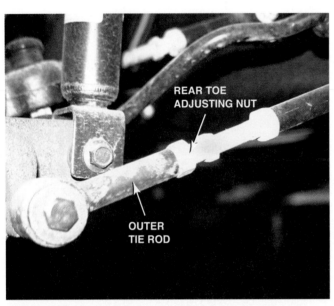

FIGURE 34–24 The rear toe was easily set on this vehicle. The adjusting nuts were easy to get to and turn. Adjusting rear toe is not this easy on every vehicle.

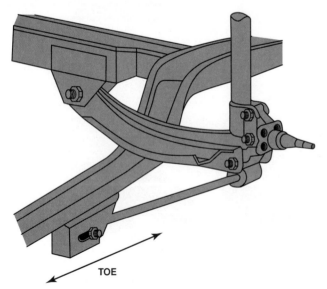

FIGURE 34–25 By moving various rear suspension members, the rear toe can be changed.

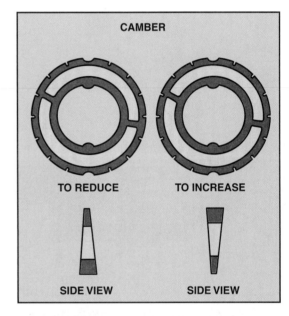

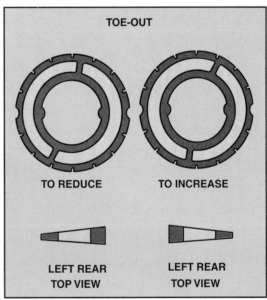

FIGURE 34–26 The use of these plastic or metal shims requires that the rear wheel as well as the hub assembly and/or backing plate be removed. Proper torque during reassembly is critical to avoid damage to the shims.

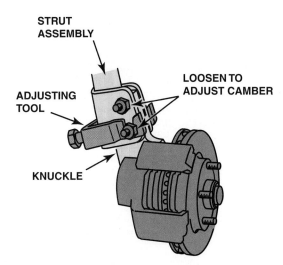

FIGURE 34–27 Many struts allow camber adjustment at the strut-to-knuckle fasteners. Here a special tool is being used to hold and move the strut into alignment with the fasteners loosened. Once the desired camber angle is achieved, the strut nuts are tightened and the tool is removed.

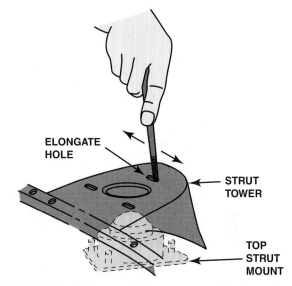

FIGURE 34–28 Some struts require modification of the upper mount for camber adjustment.

GUIDELINES FOR ADJUSTING FRONT CAMBER/SAI AND INCLUDED ANGLE

If the camber is adjusted at the base of the MacPherson strut, camber and included angle are changed and SAI remains the same. ● SEE FIGURE 34–27.

If camber is adjusted by moving the upper strut mounting location, included angle remains the same, but SAI and camber change. ● SEE FIGURE 34–28.

This is the reason to use the factory alignment methods before using an aftermarket alignment adjustment kit. SAI and included angle should be within 1/2 degree (0.5 degrees) side-to-side. If these angles differ, check the frame mount location before attempting to correct differences in camber. As the frame is changed, camber and SAI change, but the included angle remains the same. Cross camber/caster is the difference between the camber or caster on one side of the vehicle and the camber or caster on the other side of the vehicle.

Alignment Angle	Recommended Maximum Variation
SAI	Within 1/2° (0.5°) side-to-side
Included angle	Within 1/2° (0.5°) side-to-side
Cross camber	Within 1/2° (0.5°) side-to-side
Cross caster	Within 1/2° (0.5°) side-to-side

CAUTION: Do not attempt to correct a pull condition by increasing cross camber or cross caster beyond the amount specified by the vehicle manufacturer.

METHODS OF ADJUSTMENT

TOOLS AND ADJUSTMENT DEVICES MAY BE AVAILABLE FROM AFTERMARKET SUPPLIERS TO PERFORM ADJUSTMENTS IN CASES WHERE MANUFACTURERS DO NOT MAKE SUCH PROVISIONS.

CASTER & CAMBER ADJUSTMENT

SHIMS

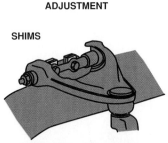

TO INCREASE CASTER, MOVE SHIMS REAR TO FRONT. CAMBER: CHANGE SHIM THICKNESS EQUALLY.

CASTER & CAMBER ADJUSTMENT

SHIMS

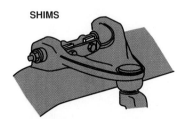

TO INCREASE CASTER, MOVE SHIMS FRONT TO REAR. CAMBER: CHANGE SHIM THICKNESS EQUALLY.

CASTER & CAMBER ADJUSTMENT

SLOTTED HOLES

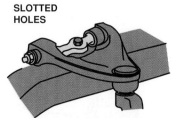

LOOSEN BOLTS, MOVE UPPER ARM SHAFT TO OBTAIN SPECIFIED READINGS. USE SPECIAL TOOL.

CASTER & CAMBER ADJUSTMENT

SHIMS

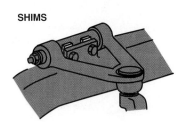

TO INCREASE CASTER, MOVE SHIMS FRONT TO REAR. CAMBER: CHANGE SHIM THICKNESS EQUALLY.

CASTER & CAMBER ADJUSTMENT

CAMS

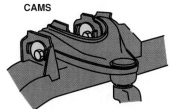

TO ADJUST, ROTATE CAM BOLTS. SET CAMBER FIRST, CHECK/ADJUST CASTER, RECHECK CAMBER.

CAMBER ADJUSTMENT

NUTS

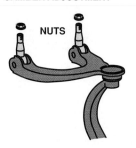

TO ADJUST CAMBER, LOOSEN TWO NUTS ON UPPER ARM AND MOVE WHEEL IN OR OUT.

FRONT CASTER OR REAR TOE ADJUSTMENT

THREADED ROD

TO INCREASE CASTER TO POSITIVE, LENGTHEN STRUT. INCREASE OR DECREASE TOE-IN BY LENGTHENING OR SHORTENING ROD.

CAMBER ADJUSTMENT

ECCENTRIC CAM

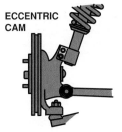

TO INCREASE OR DECREASE CAMBER SETTING, ROTATE CAM BOLT.

CAMBER ADJUSTMENT

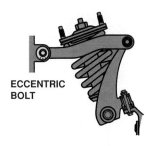

ECCENTRIC BOLT

LOOSEN NUT ON UPPER CONTROL ARM AND ROTATE BOLT TO SET CAMBER.

FIGURE 34–29 An example of the many methods that are commonly used to adjust front caster and camber.

FRONT CAMBER/CASTER ADJUSTMENT METHODS

Many vehicles are constructed with only limited camber/caster factory adjustment. ● **SEE FIGURE 34–29** for a summary of which adjustments are *generally* possible for various types of vehicles and suspension systems.

CAUTION: Most vehicle manufacturers warn technicians not to adjust camber by bending the strut assembly. Even though several equipment manufacturers make tools that are designed to bend the strut, most experts agree that it can cause harm to the strut itself.

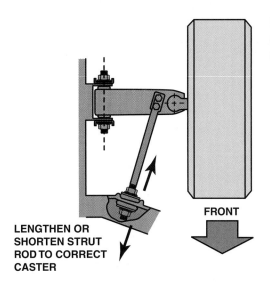

FIGURE 34–30 If there is a nut on both sides of the strut rod bushing, then the length of the rod can be adjusted to change caster.

LENGTHEN OR SHORTEN STRUT ROD TO CORRECT CASTER

FRONT

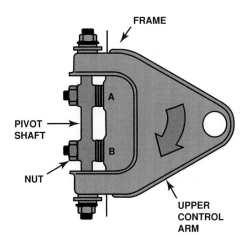

FRAME

PIVOT SHAFT

NUT

A

B

UPPER CONTROL ARM

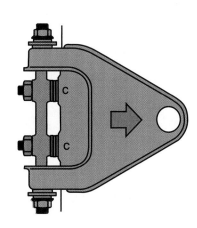

C

C

FIGURE 34–31 Placing shims between the frame and the upper control arm pivot shaft is a popular method of alignment for many SLA suspensions. Both camber and caster can be easily changed by adding or removing shims.

| A | SUBTRACT SHIMS TO INCREASE POSITIVE CASTER |

| B | ADD SHIMS TO INCREASE POSITIVE CASTER |

| C | SUBTRACT SHIMS EQUALLY TO INCREASE POSITIVE CAMBER OR ADD SHIMS EQUALLY TO REDUCE POSITIVE CAMBER |

ADJUSTING FRONT CAMBER/CASTER

Most SLA-type suspensions can be adjusted for caster and camber. Most manufacturers recommend adjusting caster, then camber, before adjusting the toe. As the caster is changed, such as when the strut rod is adjusted as shown in ● **FIGURE 34–30,** the camber and toe also change.

If the camber is then adjusted, the caster is unaffected. Many technicians adjust caster and camber at the same time using shims (● **FIGURES 34–31 AND 34–32**), slots (● **FIGURE 34–33**), or **eccentric cams** (● **FIGURE 34–34**).

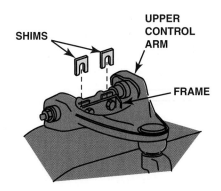

SHIMS

UPPER CONTROL ARM

FRAME

FIGURE 34–32 The general rule of thumb is that a 1/8-in. shim added or removed from both shim locations changes the camber angle about 1/2 degree. Adding or removing a 1/8-in. shim from one shim location changes the caster by about 1/4 degree.

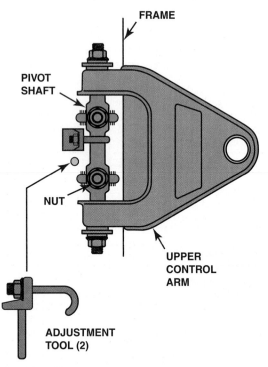

FRAME

PIVOT
SHAFT

NUT

ADJUSTMENT
TOOL (2)

UPPER
CONTROL
ARM

FIGURE 34–33 Some SLA-type suspensions use slotted holes for alignment angle adjustments. When the pivot shaft bolts are loosened, the pivot shaft is free to move unless held by special clamps as shown. By turning the threaded portion of the clamps, the camber and caster can be set and checked before tightening the pivot shaft bolts.

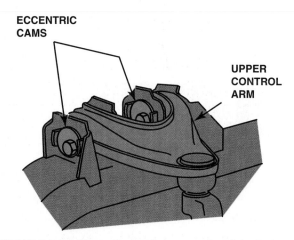

ECCENTRIC
CAMS

UPPER
CONTROL
ARM

FIGURE 34–34 When the nut is loosened and the bolt on the eccentric cam is rotated, the upper control arm moves in and out. By adjusting both eccentric cams, both camber and caster can be adjusted.

ADJUSTING FRONT CAMBER/CASTER (CONTINUED)

Always follow the manufacturer's recommended alignment procedure. For example, many manufacturers include a **shim chart** in their service manual that gives the thickness and location of the shim changes based on the alignment reading. Shim charts are used to set camber and caster at the same time. Shim charts are designed for each model of vehicle. ● **SEE FIGURE 34–35.**

Regardless of the methods or procedures used, toe is always adjusted after all the angles are set because caster and camber both affect the toe.

DEGREES CASTER

DEGREES CAMBER	BOLT	+4.9°	+4.7°	+4.5°	+4.3°	+4.1°	+3.9°	+3.7°	+3.5K	+3.3°	+3.1°	+2.9°	+2.7°	+2.5°	+2.3K	+2.1°
+2.2°	FRONT	+300	+211	+211	+210	+210	+201	+201	+201	+200	+200	+111	+111	+110	+110	+110
	REAR	+101	+101	+110	+110	+111	+200	+200	+201	+210	+210	+201	+211	+300	+301	+301
+2.0°	FRONT	+210	+210	+210	+201	+201	+200	+200	+111	+111	+110	+110	+110	+101	+101	+100
	REAR	+011	+100	+101	+101	+110	+110	+111	+200	+200	+201	+210	+210	+211	+300	+300
+1.8°	FRONT	+201	+201	+200	+200	+111	+111	+110	+110	+110	+101	+101	+100	+100	+100	+011
	REAR	+010	+011	+011	+100	+101	+101	+110	+110	+111	+200	+200	+201	+210	+210	+211
+1.6°	FRONT	+200	+200	+111	+111	+110	+110	+101	+101	+100	+100	+100	+011	+011	+010	+010
	REAR	+001	+001	+010	+011	+011	+100	+100	+101	+110	+110	+111	+200	+200	+201	+210
+1.4°	FRONT	+111	+110	+110	+101	+101	+100	+100	+100	+011	+011	+010	+010	+010	+001	+001
	REAR	+000	+000	+001	+001	+010	+011	+011	+100	+100	+101	+110	+110	+111	+200	+200
+1.2°	FRONT	+110	+101	+101	+100	+100	+011	+011	+010	+010	+010	+001	+001	+000	-000	-000
	REAR	-010	-001	+000	+000	+001	+001	+010	+011	+011	+100	+101	+101	+110	+111	+111
+1.0°	FRONT	+100	+109	+011	+011	+010	+010	+010	+001	+001	+000	-000	-000	-001	-001	-010
	REAR	-011	-010	-010	-001	-000	+000	+001	+001	+010	+011	+011	+100	+101	+101	+110
+0.8°	FRONT	+011	+011	+010	+010	+001	+001	+000	-000	-000	-001	-001	-010	-010	-010	-011
	REAR	-100	-100	-011	-010	-010	-001	-001	+000	+001	+001	+010	+011	+011	+100	+101
+0.6°	FRONT	+010	+001	+001	+001	+000	-000	-001	-001	-010	-010	-010	-011	-011	-100	-100
	REAR	-101	-101	-100	-100	-011	-010	-010	-001	-001	+000	+001	+001	+010	+011	+011
+0.4°	FRONT	+001	+000	+000	-001	-001	-010	-010	-010	-011	-011	-100	-100	-100	-101	-101
	REAR	-111	-110	-101	-101	-100	-100	-011	-010	-010	-001	-000	+000	+001	+010	+010
+0.2°	FRONT	-001	-001	-001	-010	-010	-011	-011	-100	-100	-101	-101	-101	-110	-110	-110
	REAR	-200	-111	-111	-110	-101	-101	-100	-100	-011	-010	-010	-001	-000	+000	+001
+0.0°	FRONT	-010	-010	-011	-011	-100	-100	-100	-101	-101	-110	-110	-111	-111	-111	-200
	REAR	-201	-201	-200	-111	-111	-110	-101	-101	-100	-100	-011	-010	-010	-001	-000
-0.2°	FRONT	-011	-011	-100	-100	-101	-101	-110	-110	-111	-111	-111	-200	-200	-201	-201
	REAR	-210	-210	-201	-201	-200	-111	-111	-110	-101	-101	-100	-100	-011	-010	-010
-0.4°	FRONT	-100	-101	-101	-110	-110	-110	-111	-111	-200	-200	-201	-201	-201	-210	-210
	REAR	-300	-211	-210	-210	-201	-201	-200	-111	-111	-110	-101	-101	-100	-011	-011

1. DETERMINE VEHICLE'S CURRENT CASTER AND CAMBER MEASUREMENTS.
2. USING THE CURRENT CASTER READING, READ DOWN THE APPROPRIATE COLUMN TO THE LINES CORRESPONDING TO THE CURRENT CAMBER READING.
3. CORRECTION VALUES WILL BE GIVEN FOR THE FRONT AND REAR BOLTS.
   EXAMPLE: CURRENT READING +1.6° CASTER +0.4° CAMBER. BY READING DOWN THE CHART FROM +1.6° CASTER TO +0.4° CAMBER YOU WILL FIND THAT THE FRONT BOLT REQUIRES AN ADJUSTMENT OF -101 AND THE REAR BOLT REQUIRES AN ADJUSTMENT OF +010.

FIGURE 34–35 Typical shim alignment chart. As noted, 1/8-in. (0.125) shims can be substituted for the 0.120-in. shims; 1/32-in. (0.0625) shims can be substituted for the 0.060-in. shims; and 1/32-in. (0.03125) shims can be substituted for the 0.030-in. shims.

SETTING TOE

Front toe is the last angle that should be adjusted and is the most likely to need correction. This has led to many sayings in the alignment field:

"Set the toe and let it go."

"Do a toe and go."

"Set the toe and collect the dough."

As wear occurs at each steering joint such as tie rod ends, the forces exerted on the linkage by the tire tend to cause a toe-out condition.

Front-wheel-drive (FWD) vehicles transmit engine power through the front wheels. Many manufacturers of FWD vehicles specify a toe-out setting. This toe-out setting helps compensate for the slight toe-in effect of the engine torque being transferred through the front wheels.

Most newer alignment equipment displays in degrees of toe instead of inches of toe. (See the toe unit conversion chart.) Just remember that positive (+) toe means toe-in and negative (−) toe means toe-out.

Toe Unit Conversions

Units	Conversions			
Fractional inches	1/16 in.	1/8 in.	3/16 in.	1/4 in.
Decimal inches	0.062 in.	0.125 in.	0.188 in.	0.250 in.
Millimeters	1.60 mm	3.18 mm	4.76 mm	6.35 mm
Decimal degrees	0.125°	0.25°	0.375°	0.5°
Degrees and minutes	0°8′	0°15′	0°23′	0°30′
Fractional degrees	1/8°	1/4°	3/8°	1/2°

To make sure the steering wheel is straight after setting toe, the steering wheel *must* be locked in the straight-ahead position while the toe is being adjusted. Another term used to describe steering wheel position is **spoke angle.** To lock the steering wheel, always use a steering wheel lock that presses against the seat and the outer rim of the steering wheel. *Do not* use the locking feature of the steering column to hold the steering wheel straight. Always unlock the steering column, straighten the steering wheel, and install the steering wheel lock. ● **SEE FIGURES 34–36 THROUGH 34–38.**

NOTE: The engine must be started and the steering wheel straightened with the engine running to be assured of a straight steering wheel. Lock the steering wheel with the steering lock tool before stopping the engine.

 **TECH TIP**

Race Vehicle Alignment

Vehicles used in autocrossing (individual timed runs through cones in a parking lot) or road racing usually perform best if the following alignment steps are followed:

1. **Increase caster** (+). Not only will the caster provide a good solid feel for the driver during high speed on a straight section of the course, but it will also provide some lean into the corners due to the camber change during cornering. A setting of 5 to 9 degrees positive caster is typical depending on the type of vehicle and the type of course.

2. **Adjust for 1 to 2 degrees of negative camber.** As a race vehicle corners, the body and chassis lean. As the chassis leans, the top of the tire also leans outward. By setting the camber to 1 to 2 degrees negative, the tires will be neutral while cornering, thereby having as much rubber contacting the road as possible.

NOTE: Though setting negative camber on a street-driven vehicle will decrease tire life, the negative setting on a race vehicle is used to increase cornering speeds, and tire life is not a primary consideration.

3. **Set toe to a slight toe-out position.** When the front toe is set negative (toe-out), the vehicle is more responsive to steering commands from the driver. With a slight toe-out setting, one wheel is already pointed in the direction of a corner or curve. Set the toe-out to −3/8 to −1/2 degree depending on the type of vehicle and the type of race course.

After straightening the steering wheel, turn the tie rod adjustment until the toe for both wheels is within specifications. ● **SEE FIGURE 34–39.**

Test drive the vehicle for proper handling and centerline steering. *Centerline steering* is a centered steering wheel with the vehicle traveling a straight course.

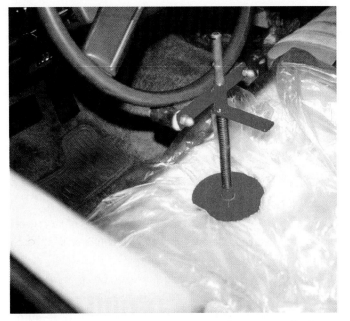

FIGURE 34–36 Many procedures for setting toe specify that the steering wheel be held in the straight-ahead position using a steering wheel lock, as shown. One method recommended by Hunter Engineering sets toe without using a steering wheel lock.

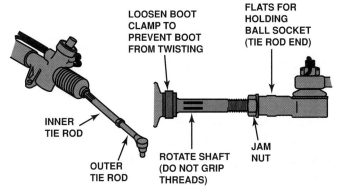

FIGURE 34–37 Adjusting toe by rotating the tie rod on a vehicle equipped with rack-and-pinion steering.

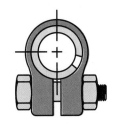

SLEEVE ROTATING TOOL

LEFT-HAND SLEEVE

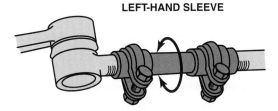

TURN DOWNWARD TO DECREASE ROD LENGTH

TURN UPWARD TO INCREASE ROD LENGTH

RIGHT-HAND SLEEVE

TURN DOWNWARD TO INCREASE ROD LENGTH

TURN UPWARD TO DECREASE ROD LENGTH

FIGURE 34–38 Toe is adjusted on a parallelogram-type steering linkage by turning adjustable tie rod sleeves. Special tie rod sleeve adjusting tools should be used that grip the slot in the sleeve and will not crush the sleeve while it is being rotated.

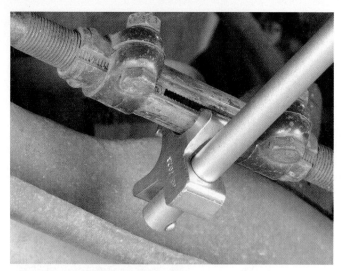

FIGURE 34-39 Special tie rod adjusting tools should be used to rotate the tie rod adjusting sleeves. The tool grips the slot in the sleeve and allows the service technician to rotate the sleeve without squeezing or damaging the sleeve.

CENTERING THE STEERING WHEEL

Centerline steering *should* be accomplished by adjusting the tie rod length on both sides of the vehicle while the toe is set.

CAUTION: Do not attempt to straighten the steering wheel by relocating the wheel on the steering column on a vehicle with two tie rod end adjusters. The steering wheel is positioned at the factory in the center of the steering gear, regardless of type. If the steering wheel is not in the center, then the variable ratio section of the gear will not be in the center as it is designed. Another possible problem with moving the steering wheel from its designed straight-ahead position is that the turning radius may be different for right- and left-hand turns.

STEERING WHEEL REMOVAL

If the steering wheel *must* be removed, first disconnect the airbag wire connector at the base of the steering column. This reduces the chance of personal injury and prevents accidental airbag deployment.

CAUTION: Always follow the manufacturer's recommended procedures whenever working on or around the steering column.

Remove the center section of the steering column by removing the retaining screws, including the inflator module on vehicles equipped with an airbag.

After removal of the airbag inflator module, remove the steering wheel retaining nut. Note the locating marks on the steering wheel and steering shaft. ● **SEE FIGURE 34-40** on page 683. These marks indicate the proper position of the steering wheel for centerline steering. This means that the steering wheel spoke angle is straight and in line with the centerline position of the steering gear or rack-and-pinion steering unit.

Most steering wheels are attached to the steering shaft with a spline and a taper. After removing the steering wheel nut, use a steering wheel puller to remove the steering wheel from the steering shaft. ● **SEE FIGURE 34-41.**

NOTE: Because of the taper, it is easier to remove a steering wheel if the steering wheel puller is struck with a dead-blow hammer. The shock often releases the taper and allows the easy removal of the steering wheel. Some technicians simply use their hands and pound the steering wheel from the taper without using a puller.

 **TECH TIP**

Locking Pliers to the Rescue

Many vehicles use a jam nut on the tie rod end. This jam nut must be loosened to adjust the toe. Because the end of the tie rod is attached to a tie rod end that is movable, loosening the nut is often difficult. Every time force is applied to the nut, the tie rod end socket moves and prevents the full force of the wrench from being applied to the nut. To prevent this movement, simply attach locking pliers (Vise Grips®) to hold the tie rod. Wedge the pliers against the control arm to prevent any movement of the tie rod. By preventing the tie rod from moving, full force can be put on a wrench to loosen the jam nut without doing any harm to the tie rod end.

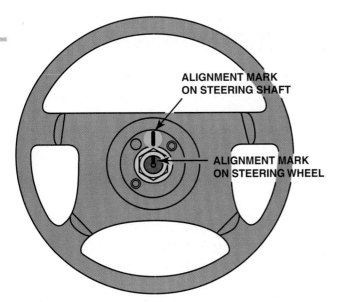

FIGURE 34–40 Most vehicles have alignment marks made at the factory on the steering shaft and steering wheel to help the service technician keep the steering wheel in the center position.

ALIGNMENT MARK ON STEERING SHAFT

ALIGNMENT MARK ON STEERING WHEEL

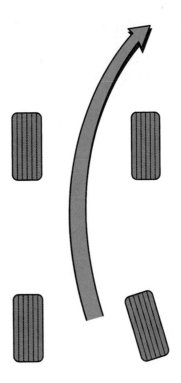

FIGURE 34–42 The toe-in on the right wheel creates a turning force toward the right.

FIGURE 34–41 A puller being used to remove a steering wheel after the steering wheel retaining nut has been removed.

To reinstall the steering wheel, align the steering wheel in the desired straight-ahead position and slip it down over the splines. Install and tighten the retaining nut to specifications.

 REAL WORLD FIX

Left Thrust Line, but a Pull to the Right!

A new four-door sport sedan had been aligned several times at the dealership in an attempt to solve a pull to the right. The car had front-wheel-drive and four-wheel independent suspension. The dealer rotated the tires, and it made no difference. The alignment angles of all four wheels were in the center of specifications. The dealer even switched all four tires from another car in an attempt to solve the problem.

In frustration, the owner took the car to an alignment shop. Almost immediately the alignment technician discovered that the right rear wheel was slightly toed-in. This caused a pull to the right.
● SEE FIGURE 34–42.

The alignment technician adjusted the toe on the right rear wheel and reset the front toe. The car drove beautifully.

The owner was puzzled about why the new car dealer was unable to correct the problem. It was later discovered that the alignment machine at the dealership was out of calibration by the exact amount that the right rear wheel was out of specification. The car pulled to the right because the independent suspension created a rear steering force toward the left that caused the front to pull to the right. Alignment equipment manufacturers recommend that alignment equipment be calibrated regularly.

TOLERANCE ADJUSTMENT PROCEDURE

Many vehicles are designed and built without a method to change caster or camber, or both. (All vehicles have an adjustment for toe.) Before trying an aftermarket alignment correction kit, many technicians first attempt to correct the problem by moving the suspension attachment points within the build tolerance. All vehicles are constructed with a slight amount of leeway or tolerance; slight corrections can be made because bolt holes are almost always slightly larger than the bolt diameter, allowing for slight movement. When several fasteners are involved, such as where the powertrain cradle (subframe) attaches to the body of the front-wheel-drive vehicle, a measurable amount of alignment change (often over 1/2 degree) can be accomplished without special tools or alignment kits. The steps for **tolerance adjustment** include the following:

STEP 1 Determine which way the suspension members have to be moved to accomplish the desired alignment—for example, the right front may require more positive camber to correct a pulling or tire wear problem.

STEP 2 Locate and loosen the cradle (subframe) bolts about four turns each. DO NOT REMOVE ANY OF THE BOLTS.

STEP 3 Using prybars, move the cradle in the direction that will result in an improvement of the alignment angles. Have an assistant tighten the bolts as pressure is maintained on the cradle.

STEP 4 Measure the alignment angles and repeat the procedure if necessary.

AFTERMARKET ALIGNMENT METHODS

Accurate alignments are still possible on vehicles without factory methods of adjustment by using alignment kits or parts. Aftermarket alignment kits are available for most vehicles. Even when there are factory alignment methods, sometimes the range of adjustment is not enough to compensate for sagging frame members or other normal or accident-related faults.
● **SEE FIGURES 34–43 AND 34–44.**

(a)

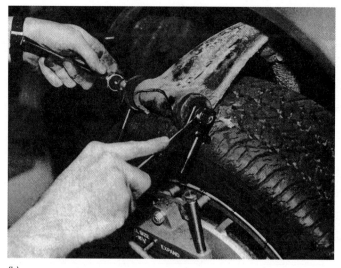
(b)

FIGURE 34–43 (a) Aftermarket camber kit designed to provide some camber adjustments for a vehicle that does not provide any adjustment. (b) Installation of this kit requires that the upper control arm shaft be removed. Note that the upper control arm was simply rotated out over the wheel pivoting on the upper ball joint.

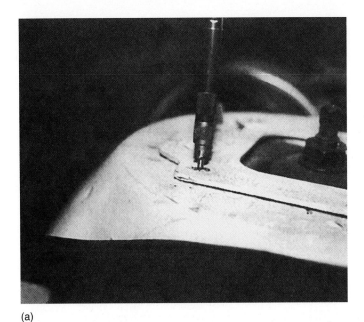

(a)

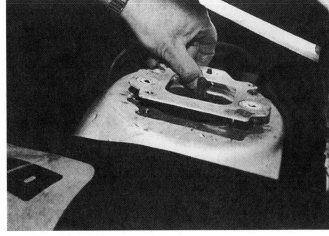

(b)

(c)

FIGURE 34–44 (a) The installation of some aftermarket alignment kits requires the use of special tools such as this cutter being used to drill out spot welds on the original alignment plate on a strut tower. (b) Original plate being removed. (c) Note the amount of movement the upper strut bearing mount has around the square openings in the strut tower. An aftermarket plate can now be installed to allow both camber and caster adjustment.

ALIGNING ELECTRONIC-SUSPENSION VEHICLES

When aligning a vehicle equipped with an electronic suspension, several additional steps may be required. Always check service information and read carefully all on-screen instructions on the alignment machine. Some examples of the steps that may be needed include:

■ Verify the exact type of electronic suspension. This step could include checking the regular production order (RPO) code.

■ Check that the ride height (suspension height) is within factory specifications.

■ The steering wheel angle, as well as the radar cruise control sensor, will often need to be recalibrated using a scan tool. This is needed because the steering wheel may be in a different position after the alignment, and the steering wheel position sensor needs to be reset because the rear toe setting was changed. The rear thrust line could also have been changed. The radar cruise control needs to be calibrated to the revised rear thrust angle using a scan tool.

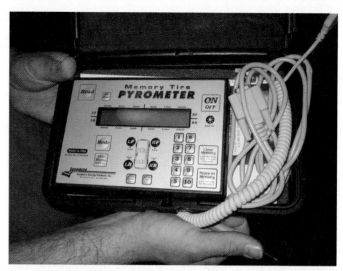

FIGURE 34–45 A typical tire temperature pyrometer. The probe used is a needle that penetrates about 1/4 inch (7 mm) into the tread of the tire for most accurate readings.

ALIGNING MODIFIED VEHICLES

If different springs were installed which in turn changes the suspension height, or if larger or smaller wheels and tires were installed, many alignment shops would reject doing an alignment. If a shop attempted to align a vehicle, handling and tire wear problems were common. Because the ride height is changed from stock factory setting, the following can occur:

1. The steering axis inclination (SAI) is now incorrect.

2. Because the steering linkage and the control arms are no longer parallel, bump steer can occur. Bump steer causes the vehicle to dart to one side when a wheel hits a bump.

3. Because the ride height changed, camber and toe also changed. The camber change is often enough to prevent it from being able to be adjusted to within specifications.

Alignment alone will not correct these concerns. To allow for proper handling, the following aftermarket kits and parts are available:

- **Camber kits** —These kits usually include a replacement control arm or offset cam, which provides additional camber adjustment.

- **Bump steer kits** —A bump steer kit can include a modified steering arm or rack-and-pinion steering gear repositioning components.

The kits available can be found listed on the alignment screen of many newer alignment machines, such as the Hunter Engineering Company's WinAlign Tuner Custom Alignment for Modified Vehicles. During part of this alignment, the technician has to select one of two options:

- Maximum tire wear
- Maximum handling

Therefore, the technician has to determine from the customer which of these two parameters are most important. After the alignment, the instructions often state that the vehicle should be driven and then the temperature of the tires measured and recorded. Using a tire pyrometer, be sure to measure the temperature of each tire at the following locations for each tire:

- Approximately 1.5 inches (38 mm) from the outside edge of the tire in the tread rubber
- In the middle of the tread
- Approximately 1.5 inches (38 mm) from the inside edge of the tire in the tread rubber

The temperatures are then typed into the alignment machine, and the program calculates the final alignment settings.
● **SEE FIGURE 34–45.**

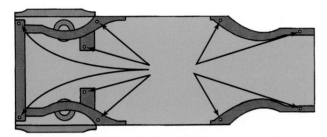

FIGURE 34–46 Jig holes used at the assembly plant to locate suspension and drivetrain components. Check service information for the exact place to measure and the specified dimensions when checking for body or frame damage.

HIDDEN STRUCTURAL DAMAGE DIAGNOSIS

Many accidents result in hidden structural damage that can cause alignment angles to be out of specification. If alignment angles are out of specification tolerances, then accident damage should be suspected. Look for evidence of newly replaced suspension parts, body work, or repainted areas of the body. While a body and/or frame of a vehicle can be straightened, it must be done by a knowledgeable person using body-measuring equipment.

The first thing that must be done is to determine a *datum plane*. *Datum* means a basis on which other measurements can be based. The datum plane is the horizontal plane.

However, most alignment technicians do not have access to body/frame alignment equipment. The service technician can use a common steel rule to measure several points of the vehicle to determine if the vehicle is or is not damaged or needs to be sent to a frame shop for repair.

FRAME/BODY DIAGONALS If the frame or body is perfectly square, then the diagonal measurements should be within 1/8 in. (3 mm) of each other. ● **SEE FIGURE 34–46**.

While there are specified measurement points indicated by the manufacturer, the diagonal measurements can be made from almost any point that is repeated exactly on the other side, such as the center of a bolt in the suspension mounting bracket.

ALIGNMENT GUIDE

The following chart lists common alignment problems and their probable causes.

Symptom-Based Alignment Guide

Problems	Probable Causes
Pull left/right	Uneven tire pressure, tire conicity, mismatched tires, unequal camber, unequal caster, brake drag, setback, suspension/frame sag, unbalanced power assist, bent spindle, bent strut, worn suspension components (front or rear), rear suspension misalignment.
Incorrect steering wheel position	Incorrect individual or total toe, rear wheel misalignment, excessive suspension or steering component play, worn rack-and-pinion attachment bushings, individual toe adjusters not provided.
Hard steering	Improper tire pressure, binding steering gear or steering linkage, low P/S fluid, excessive positive caster, lack of lubrication, upper strut mount(s), worn power steering pump, worn P/S belt.
Loose steering	Loose wheel bearings, worn steering or suspension components, loose steering gear mount, excessive steering gear play, loose or worn steering coupler.
Excessive road shock	Excessive positive caster, excessive negative camber, improper tire inflation, too wide wheel/tire combination for the vehicle, worn or loose shocks, worn springs.
Poor returnability	Incorrect camber or caster, bent spindle or strut, binding suspension or steering components, improper tire inflation.
Wander/instability	Incorrect alignment, defective or improperly inflated tires, worn steering or suspension parts, bent spindle or strut, worn or loose steering gear, loose wheel bearings.
Squeal/scuff on turns	Defective or improperly inflated tires, incorrect turning angle (TOOT), bent steering arms, excessive wheel setback, poor driving habits (too fast for conditions), worn suspension or steering parts.
Excessive body sway	Loose or broken stabilizer bar links or bushings, worn shocks or mountings, broken or sagging springs, uneven vehicle load, uneven or improper tire pressure.
Memory steer	Binding steering linkage, binding steering gear, binding upper strut mount, ball joint, or kingpin.
Bump steer	Misalignment of steering linkage, bent steering arm or frame, defective or sagged springs, uneven load, bent spindle or strut.
Torque steer	Bent spindle or strut, bent steering arm, misaligned frame, worn torque strut, defective engine or transaxle mounts, drive axle misalignment, mismatched or unequally inflated tires.

1 Begin the alignment procedure by first driving the vehicle onto the alignment rack as straight as possible.

2 Position the front tires in the center of the turn plates. These turn plates can be moved inward and outward to match a vehicle of any width.

3 Raise the vehicle and position the alignment rack following the rack manufacturer's instructions.

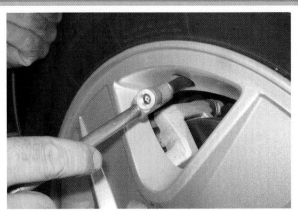

4 Check and adjust tire pressures and perform the pre-alignment checks necessary to be assured of proper alignment.

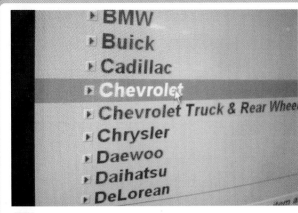

▸ BMW
▸ Buick
▸ Cadillac
▫ Chevrolet
▸ Chevrolet Truck & Rear Whee
▸ Chrysler
▸ Daewoo
▸ Daihatsu
▸ DeLorean

5 Select the exact vehicle on the alignment machine.

6 Securely mount the alignment heads or target wheels.

CONTINUED ▶

7 If mounting a transmitter-type alignment head, be sure to attach the retaining wire to the tire valve.

8 After installation of the heads, follow the specified procedure for compensation, which allows accurate alignment readings.

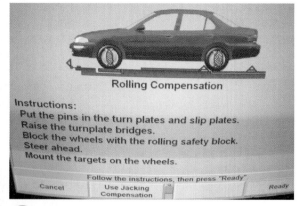

Rolling Compensation

Instructions:
Put the pins in the turn plates and slip plates.
Raise the turnplate bridges.
Block the wheels with the rolling safety block.
Steer ahead.
Mount the targets on the wheels.

Follow the instructions, then press "Ready".

Cancel | Use Jacking Compensation | Ready

9 Rolling compensation is used on machines that use lasers and wheel targets.

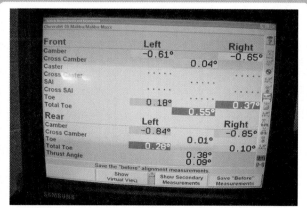

10 An alignment reading is displayed even though caster has not yet been measured. The readings marked in red indicate that they are not within specifications.

11 Before performing a caster sweep, install a brake pedal depressor to keep the front wheels from rotating when the steering wheel is turned.

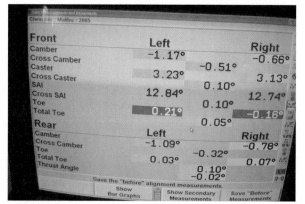

12 Perform the caster sweep by turning the front wheels inward, and then outward following the instructions on the screen.

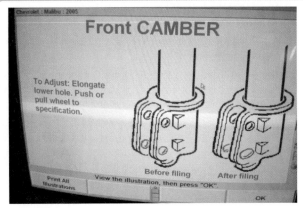

13 Most alignment machines will display where to make the alignment correction and will often include drawings and live-action videos that show the procedure.

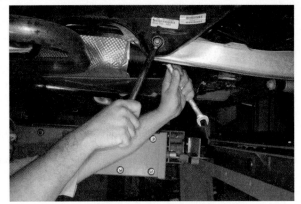

14 The rear toe is being adjusted by rotating the eccentric cam on the lower control arm while watching the display.

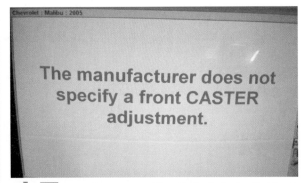

15 The alignment machine display indicates that front caster is not a factory-adjustable angle.

16 Adjusting the front toe on this vehicle involves loosening the jam nut (left wrench) and rotating the tie rod using the right wrench.

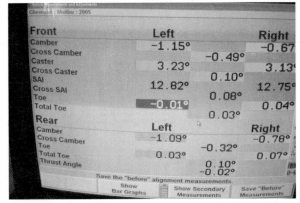

17 One last adjustment of the left front toe is needed to achieve a perfect alignment. The final alignment reading can be printed and attached to the work order.

18 After disconnecting all of the attachments, reinstalling the valve caps, and removing the steering wheel holder, the vehicle should be test driven to check for proper alignment before returning it to the customer.

SUMMARY

1. Before attempting to align any vehicle, it must be checked for proper ride height (trim height), tire conditions, and tire pressures. A thorough inspection of all steering and suspension components must also be made.

2. Memory steer is a condition that causes the vehicle to lead or pull to the same direction it was last steered. Binding steering or suspension components are the most frequent causes of memory steer.

3. Torque steer is the pull or lead caused by engine torque being applied to the front wheels unevenly on a front-wheel-drive vehicle. Out-of-level drivetrain, suspension components, or tires are the most common causes of excessive torque steer.

4. Lead/pull diagnosis involves a thorough road test and careful inspection of all tires.

5. There are three types of alignment: geometric centerline, thrust line, and four-wheel alignment. Only an a four-wheel alignment should be used on a vehicle with an adjustable rear suspension.

6. The proper sequence for a complete four-wheel alignment is rear camber, rear toe, front camber and caster, and front toe.

REVIEW QUESTIONS

1. List 10 prealignment checks that should be performed before the wheel alignment is checked and/or adjusted.

2. Describe the difference between a lead (drift) and a pull.

3. Explain the causes and possible corrections for torque steer.

4. Explain the causes and possible corrections for memory steer.

5. List the necessary steps to follow for a four-wheel alignment.

CHAPTER QUIZ

1. If the tie rod ends become worn, which angle is most affected?
   a. Camber   b. Caster   c. Toe   d. SAI

2. Technician A says that a vehicle will pull (or lead) to the side with the most camber (or least negative camber). Technician B says that a vehicle will pull (or lead) to the side with the most positive caster. Which technician is correct?
   a. Technician A only   c. Both Technicians A and B
   b. Technician B only   d. Neither Technician A nor B

3. Technician A says that the front toe determines the thrust angle. Technician B says that the rear toe angle determines the thrust angle. Which technician is correct?
   a. Technician A only   c. Both Technicians A and B
   b. Technician B only   d. Neither Technician A nor B

4. Strut rods, if they are adjustable, can be used to adjust which angle?
   a. Toe   c. Caster
   b. Camber   d. Toe-out on turns

5. If metal shims are used for alignment adjustment in the front, they adjust _____.
   a. Camber   b. Caster   c. Toe   d. Both a and b

6. Which angle is largest?
   a. 0.55 degrees   c. 45 minutes
   b. 1/4 degree   d. 1/2 degree

Use the following information to answer question 7:

Specifications:	Min.	Preferred	Max.
Camber (degree)	0	1.0	1.4
Caster (degree)	.8	1.5	2.1
Toe (inch)	−.10	.06	.15

Results:	L	R
Camber (degree)	−.1	.6
Caster (degree)	1.8	1.6
Toe (inch)	1.12	+.12

7. The vehicle above will _____.
   a. Pull toward the right and feather-edge both tires
   b. Pull toward the left
   c. Wear the outside of the left tire and the inside of the right tire
   d. None of the above

Use the following information to answer questions 8 and 9:

Specifications:	Min.	Preferred	Max.
Camber (degree)	−1/4	+1/2	1
Caster (degree)	0	+2	+4
Toe (inch)	−1/16	1/16	3/16

Results:	L	R
Camber (degree)	−0.3	−0.1
Caster (degree)	3.6	1.8
Toe (inch)	−1/16	+1/32

8. The vehicle above will _____.
   a. Pull toward the left
   b. Pull toward the right
   c. Wander
   d. Lead to the left slightly

9. The vehicle above will _____.
   a. Wander
   b. Wear tires, but will not pull
   c. Will pull, but not wear tires
   d. Pull toward the left and cause feather-edge tire wear

10. Which alignment angle is most likely to need correction and cause the most tire wear?
    a. Toe   c. Caster
    b. Camber   d. SAI/KPI

1. Vehicles equipped with electronic stability control (ESC) systems use a braking system that has how many wheel speed sensors?
   - **a.** 4
   - **b.** 3
   - **c.** 2
   - **d.** 1

2. To prevent getting air trapped in the ABS hydraulic unit, what should a technician do when replacing a caliper and opening the hydraulic system?
   - **a.** Use DOT 3 brake fluid and keep the brake fluid level above the minimum.
   - **b.** Torque the caliper retaining bolts to factory specifications.
   - **c.** Keep the bleed valve open.
   - **d.** Use a brake pedal depressor to depress the brake pedal to seal the master cylinder reservoir from the rest of the system.

3. A customer complains that the brake pedal pulsates and a clicking sound is heard and felt while cornering on a wet street. The vehicle is equipped with ABS and ESC. Technician A says that this is normal. Technician B says that the sound and vibration is caused by the ABS hydraulic unit pulsing the individual wheel brakes to help keep the vehicle under control. Which technician is correct?
   - **a.** Technician A only
   - **b.** Technician B only
   - **c.** Both Technicians A and B
   - **d.** Neither Technician A nor B

4. The type of test performed to determine if the ESC system is functioning is called _____.
   - **a.** Skid pad test
   - **b.** Sine with dwell test
   - **c.** 360-degree circle test
   - **d.** Avoidance test

5. Rear brakes tend to lock up during hard braking before front brakes because:
   - **a.** The rear brakes are larger
   - **b.** The vehicle weight transfers forward
   - **c.** The tires have less traction
   - **d.** Both b and c are correct

6. Most vehicle manufacturers recommend using _____ brake fluid.
   - **a.** DOT 2
   - **b.** DOT 3
   - **c.** DOT 4
   - **d.** DOT 5

7. Used brake fluid should be disposed of _____.
   - **a.** According to local, state, or federal regulations
   - **b.** As hazardous waste
   - **c.** By burning in an EPA certified facility
   - **d.** By recycling

8. The rubber used in most brake system components will swell if exposed to _____.
   - **a.** Engine oil or ATF
   - **b.** Moisture in the air
   - **c.** DOT 5 brake fluid
   - **d.** Water

9. The edge code lettering on the side of friction material tells the technician _____.
   - **a.** The coefficient of friction code
   - **b.** The quality of the friction material
   - **c.** The temperature resistance rating
   - **d.** All of the above

10. Technician A says that linings with asbestos can be identified by the dark gray color. Technician B says that all brake pads and linings should be treated as if they do contain asbestos. Which technician is correct?
    - **a.** Technician A only
    - **b.** Technician B only
    - **c.** Both Technicians A and B
    - **d.** Neither Technician A nor B

11. Technician A says brake fluid should be filled to the top of the reservoir to be assured of proper brake pressure when the brakes are applied. Technician B says that the brake fluid level should be filled only to the maximum level line to allow for expansion when the brake fluid gets hot during normal operation. Which technician is correct?
    - **a.** Technician A only
    - **b.** Technician B only
    - **c.** Both Technicians A and B
    - **d.** Neither Technician A nor B

12. Self apply of the brakes can occur if _____.
    - **a.** The master cylinder is overfilled
    - **b.** The vent port is clogged or covered
    - **c.** The replenishing port is clogged or covered
    - **d.** Both a and b

13. Technician A says that the brake pedal height should be checked as part of a thorough visual inspection of the brake system. Technician B says the pedal free play and pedal reserve should be checked. Which technician is correct?
    - **a.** Technician A only
    - **b.** Technician B only
    - **c.** Both Technicians A and B
    - **d.** Neither Technician A nor B

14. Two technicians are discussing overhauling master brake cylinders. Technician A says that the bore of an aluminum master cylinder cannot be honed because of the special anodized surface. Technician B says that many overhaul (OH) kits include replacement piston assemblies. Which technician is correct?
    a. Technician A only
    b. Technician B only
    c. Both Technicians A and B
    d. Neither Technician A nor B

15. Technician A says the red brake warning lamp on the dash will light if there is a hydraulic failure or low brake fluid level. Technician B says the red brake warning lamp on the dash will light if the parking brake is on. Which technician is correct?
    a. Technician A only
    b. Technician B only
    c. Both Technicians A and B
    d. Neither Technician A nor B

16. A vehicle tends to lock up the *front* wheels when being driven on slippery road surfaces. Technician A says that the metering valve may be defective. Technician B says the proportioning valve may be defective. Which technician is correct?
    a. Technician A only
    b. Technician B only
    c. Both Technicians A and B
    d. Neither Technician A nor B

17. A vehicle pulls to the left during braking. Technician A says that the metering valve may be defective. Technician B says the proportioning valve may be defective. Which technician is correct?
    a. Technician A only
    b. Technician B only
    c. Both Technicians A and B
    d. Neither Technician A nor B

18. A vehicle tends to lock up the rear wheels during hard braking. Technician A says that the metering valve may be defective. Technician B says the proportioning valve may be defective. Which technician is correct?
    a. Technician A only
    b. Technician B only
    c. Both Technicians A and B
    d. Neither Technician A nor B

19. Two technicians are discussing loosening a stuck bleeder valve. Technician A says to use a 6-point wrench and simply pull on the wrench until it loosens. Technician B says that a shock is usually necessary to loosen a stuck bleeder valve. Which technician is correct?
    a. Technician A only
    b. Technician B only
    c. Both Technicians A and B
    d. Neither Technician A nor B

20. The proper brake bleeding sequence for a front/rear split hydraulic system is _____.
    a. Right front, right rear, left front, left rear
    b. Right rear, left front, right front, left rear
    c. Left front, left rear, right front, right rear
    d. Right rear, left rear, right front, left front

21. Two technicians are discussing bleeding air from the brake hydraulic system. Technician A says to depress the brake pedal slowly and not to the floor to prevent possible seal damage inside the master cylinder. Technician B says to wait 15 seconds between strokes of the brake pedal. Which technician is correct?
    a. Technician A only
    b. Technician B only
    c. Both Technicians A and B
    d. Neither Technician A nor B

22. Two technicians are discussing wheel bearings. Technician A says that conventional tapered roller bearings as used on the front of most rear-wheel drive vehicles should be slightly loose when adjusted properly. Technician B says that the spindle nut should not be tightened more than finger tight as the final step. Which technician is correct?
    a. Technician A only
    b. Technician B only
    c. Both Technicians A and B
    d. Neither Technician A nor B

23. Wheel bearings are being packed with grease. Technician A says to use grease that is labeled "GC". Technician B says to use grease with a NLGI number of 2. Which technician is correct?
    a. Technician A only
    b. Technician B only
    c. Both Technicians A and B
    d. Neither Technician A nor B

24. Technician A says that brake drums should be labeled left and right before being removed from the vehicle so that they can be reinstalled in the same location. Technician B says that the hold-down pins may have to be cut off to remove a worn brake drum. Which technician is correct?
    a. Technician A only
    b. Technician B only
    c. Both Technicians A and B
    d. Neither Technician A nor B

25. Technician A says that the backing plate should be lubricated with chassis grease on the shoe pads. Technician B says that the brakes will squeak when applied if the shoe pads are not lubricated. Which technician is correct?
    a. Technician A only
    b. Technician B only
    c. Both Technicians A and B
    d. Neither Technician A nor B

26. Technician A says that most experts recommend replacing all drum brake hardware including the springs every time the brake linings are replaced. Technician B says that the star wheel adjuster must be cleaned and lubricated to assure proper operation. Which technician is correct?
    a. Technician A only
    b. Technician B only
    c. Both Technicians A and B
    d. Neither Technician A nor B

27. New brake shoes are being installed and they do not touch the anchor pin at the top. Technician A says the brake shoes are not the correct size. Technician B says the parking brake cable may need to be loosened. Which technician is correct?
   a. Technician A only
   b. Technician B only
   c. Both Technicians A and B
   d. Neither Technician A nor B

28. A star wheel adjuster is installed on the wrong side of the vehicle. Technician A says that the adjuster cannot operate at all if installed on the wrong side. Technician B says the adjuster would cause the clearance to increase rather than decrease when activated. Which technician is correct?
   a. Technician A only
   b. Technician B only
   c. Both Technicians A and B
   d. Neither Technician A nor B

29. Technician A says to use synthetic grease to lubricate the backing plate. Technician B says to use special lithium-based brake grease. Which technician is correct?
   a. Technician A only
   b. Technician B only
   c. Both Technicians A and B
   d. Neither Technician A nor B

30. One disc brake pad is worn more than the other. Technician A says that the caliper piston may be stuck in the caliper bore. Technician B says that the caliper slides may need to be cleaned and lubricated. Which technician is correct?
   a. Technician A only
   b. Technician B only
   c. Both Technicians A and B
   d. Neither Technician A nor B

31. Technician A says that all metal-to-metal contact areas of the disc brake system should be lubricated with special brake grease for proper operation. Technician B says that the lubrication helps reduce brake noise (squeal). Which technician is correct?
   a. Technician A only
   b. Technician B only
   c. Both Technicians A and B
   d. Neither Technician A nor B

32. After a disc brake pad replacement, the brake pedal went to the floor the first time the brake pedal was depressed. The most likely cause was _____.
   a. Air in the lines
   b. Improper disc brake pad installation
   c. Lack of proper lubrication of the caliper slides
   d. Normal operation

33. Technician A says the parking brake cable adjustment should be performed before adjusting the rear brakes. Technician B says the parking brake cable should allow for about 15 "clicks" before the parking brake holds. Which technician is correct?
   a. Technician A only
   b. Technician B only
   c. Both Technicians A and B
   d. Neither Technician A nor B

34. Technician A says that rotor thickness variation is a major cause of a pulsating brake pedal. Technician B says that at least 0.015 in. (0.4 mm) should be left on a rotor after machining to allow for wear. Which technician is correct?
   a. Technician A only
   b. Technician B only
   c. Both Technicians A and B
   d. Neither Technician A nor B

35. The brake pedal of a vehicle equipped with ABS pulsates rapidly during hard braking on a slippery road surface. Technician A says that the rotor may require machining. Technician B says the lateral runout of the disc brake rotors may be excessive. Which technician is correct?
   a. Technician A only
   b. Technician B only
   c. Both Technicians A and B
   d. Neither Technician A nor B

36. Two technicians are discussing hard spots in brake drums. Technician A says the drum should be replaced. Technician B says the hard spots are caused by using riveted rather than bonded brake shoes. Which technician is correct?
   a. Technician A only
   b. Technician B only
   c. Both Technicians A and B
   d. Neither Technician A nor B

37. Disc brake rotors should be machined if rusted.
   a. True
   b. False

38. A vehicle equipped with ABS is being checked as part of a visual inspection. How many places could there be to check brake fluid level and condition?
   a. 1
   b. 2
   c. 3
   d. Any of the above depending on the system

39. Technician A says that wheel speed sensors should be cleaned regularly as part of normal vehicle service. Technician B says that wheel speed sensors are magnetic and can attract metal particles. Which technician is correct?
   a. Technician A only
   b. Technician B only
   c. Both Technicians A and B
   d. Neither Technician A nor B

40. A vehicle equipped with ABS is being bled and the service information specifies that it be done using an automated bleed procedure. What tools or equipment are needed?
   a. Bleeder wrench
   b. Generic scan tool
   c. Factory level scan tool and bleeder wrench
   d. Special automated bleeder and tester unit

ANSWERS TO THE SAMPLE BRAKES (A5) ASE CERTIFICATION TEST

1. a	**11.** b	**21.** c	**31.** c
2. d	**12.** d	**22.** c	**32.** d
3. c	**13.** c	**23.** c	**33.** d
4. b	**14.** c	**24.** c	**34.** c
5. d	**15.** c	**25.** b	**35.** d
6. b	**16.** a	**26.** c	**36.** a
7. a	**17.** d	**27.** c	**37.** a
8. a	**18.** b	**28.** b	**38.** d
9. a	**19.** b	**29.** c	**39.** c
10. b	**20.** d	**30.** c	**40.** c

SAMPLE SUSPENSION AND STEERING (A4) ASE CERTIFICATION TEST

1. A customer complains that the steering lacks power assist all the time. Technician A says that the power steering pump drive belt could be slipping or loose. Technician B says that worn outer tie rod ends could be the cause. Which technician is correct?
   a. Technician A only
   b. Technician B only
   c. Both Technicians A and B
   d. Neither Technician A nor B

2. A front-wheel-drive vehicle pulls toward the right during hard acceleration. The most likely cause is _____.
   a. Worn or defective tires
   b. Leaking or defective shock absorbers
   c. Normal torque steer
   d. A defective power steering rack-and-pinion steering assembly

3. When replacing a rubber-bonded socket (RBS) tie rod end, the technician should be sure to _____.
   a. Remove the original using a special tool
   b. Install and tighten the replacement with the front wheels in the straight-ahead position
   c. Grease the joint before installing on the vehicle
   d. Install the replacement using a special clamp vise

4. Whenever installing a tire on a rim, do not exceed _____.
   a. 25 psi
   b. 30 psi
   c. 35 psi
   d. 40 psi

5. Two technicians are discussing mounting a tire on a wheel. Technician A says that for best balance, the tire should be match mounted. Technician B says that silicone spray should be used to lubricate the tire bend. Which technician is correct?
   a. Technician A only
   b. Technician B only
   c. Both Technicians A and B
   d. Neither Technician A nor B

6. Technician A says that radial tires should *only* be rotated front to rear, never side to side. Technician B says that vehicle manufacturers usually recommend that radial tires should be rotated using the modified X method. Which technician is correct?
   a. Technician A only
   b. Technician B only
   c. Both Technicians A and B
   d. Neither Technician A nor B

7. For a tire that has excessive radial runout, Technician A says that it should be broken down on a tire-changing machine and then rotated 180 degrees on the wheel and retested. Technician B says that the tire should be replaced. Which technician is correct?
   a. Technician A only
   b. Technician B only
   c. Both Technicians A and B
   d. Neither Technician A nor B

8. Technician A says that overloading a vehicle can cause damage to the wheel bearings. Technician B says that tapered roller bearings used on a nondrive wheel should be adjusted hand tight only after seating. Which technician is correct?
   a. Technician A only
   b. Technician B only
   c. Both Technicians A and B
   d. Neither Technician A nor B

9. Defective wheel bearings usually sound like _____.
   a. A growl
   b. A rumble
   c. Snow tires
   d. All of the above

10. Defective outer CV joints usually make a clicking noise _____.
    a. Only when backing
    b. While turning and moving
    c. While turning only
    d. During braking

11. The proper lubricant usually specified for use in a differential is _____.
    a. SAE 15-40 engine oil
    b. SAE 80W-90 GL-5
    c. STF
    d. SAE 80W-140 GL-1

12. A vehicle owner complained that a severe vibration was felt throughout the entire vehicle only during rapid acceleration from a stop and up to about 20 mph (32 km/h). The most likely cause is _____.
    a. Unequal drive shaft working angles
    b. A bent drive shaft
    c. Defective universal joints
    d. A bent rim or a defective tire

13. To remove a C-clip axle, what step does *not* need to be done?
    a. Remove the differential cover
    b. Remove the axle flange bolts/nuts
    c. Remove the pinion shaft
    d. Remove the pinion shaft lock bolt

14. Drive shaft working angles can be changed by _____.
    a. Replacing the U-joints
    b. Using shims or wedges under the transmission or rear axle
    c. Rotating the position of the drive shaft on the yoke
    d. Tightening the differential pinion nut

15. A driver complains that the vehicle darts, or moves first toward one side and then to the other side of the road. Technician A says that bump steer caused by an unlevel steering linkage could be the cause. Technician B says that a worn housing in the spool valve area of the power rack and pinion is the most likely cause. Which technician is correct?
    a. Technician A only
    b. Technician B only
    c. Both Technicians A and B
    d. Neither Technician A nor B

16. A vehicle equipped with power rack-and-pinion steering is hard to steer when cold only. After a couple of miles of driving, the steering power assist returns to normal. The most likely cause of this temporary loss of power assist when cold is _____.
    a. A worn power steering pump
    b. Worn grooves in the spool valve area of the rack-and-pinion steering unit
    c. A loose or defective power steering pump drive belt
    d. A defective power steering computer sensor

17. A dry park test is performed _____.
    a. On a frame-type lift with the wheels hanging free
    b. By pulling and pushing on the wheels with the vehicle supported by a frame-type lift
    c. On the ground or on a drive-on lift by moving the steering wheel while observing for looseness
    d. Driving in a figure 8 in a parking lot

18. On a parallelogram-type steering linkage, the part that usually needs replacement first is the _____.
    a. Pitman arm
    b. Outer tie rod end(s)
    c. Center link
    d. Idler arm

19. What parts need to be added to a "short" rack to make a "long" rack-and-pinion steering unit?
    a. Bellows and ball socket assemblies
    b. Bellows and outer tie rod ends
    c. Ball socket assemblies and outer tie rod ends
    d. Outer tie rod ends

20. The adjustment procedure for a typical integral power steering gear is _____.
    a. Overcenter adjustment, then worm thrust bearing preload
    b. Worm thrust bearing preload, then overcenter adjustment

21. A vehicle is sagging at the rear. Technician A says that standard replacement shock absorbers should restore proper ride (trim) height. Technician B says that replacement springs are needed to properly restore ride height. Which technician is correct?
    a. Technician A only
    b. Technician B only
    c. Both Technicians A and B
    d. Neither Technician A nor B

22. Technician A says that indicator ball joints should be loaded with the weight of the vehicle on the ground to observe the wear indicator. Technician B says that the non-indicator ball joints should be inspected *unloaded*. Which technician is correct?
    a. Technician A only
    b. Technician B only
    c. Both Technicians A and B
    d. Neither Technician A nor B

23. The maximum allowable axial play in a ball joint is usually _____.
    a. 0.001 in. (0.025 mm)
    b. 0.003 in. (0.076 mm)
    c. 0.030 in. (0.76 mm)
    d. 0.050 in. (1.27 mm)

24. The ball joint used on a MacPherson strut suspension is usually load carrying.
    a. True
    b. False

25. Technician A says that tapered parts, such as tie rod ends, should be tightened to specifications, then loosened 1/4 turn before installing the cotter key. Technician B says that the nut used to retain tapered parts should never be loosened after torquing, but rather tightened further, if necessary, to line up the cotter key hole. Which technician is correct?
    a. Technician A only
    b. Technician B only
    c. Both Technicians A and B
    d. Neither Technician A nor B

26. When should the strut rod (retainer) nut be removed?
    a. After compressing the coil spring
    b. Before removing the MacPherson strut from the vehicle
    c. After removing the cartridge gland nut
    d. Before removing the brake hose from the strut housing clip

27. "Dog tracking" is often caused by a broken or damaged _____.
    a. Stabilizer bar links
    b. Strut rod bushings
    c. Rear leaf springs
    d. Track (panhard) rod

28. A pull toward one side during braking is one symptom of (a) defective or worn _____.
    a. Stabilizer bar links
    b. Strut rod bushings
    c. Rear leaf springs
    d. Track (panhard) rod

29. Oil is added to the MacPherson strut housing before installing a replacement cartridge to _____.
    a. Lubricate the cartridge
    b. Transfer heat form the cartridge to the outside strut housing
    c. Act as a shock dampener
    d. Prevent unwanted vibrations

30. A vehicle will pull toward the side with the _____.
    a. Most camber
    b. Least camber

31. Excessive toe-out will wear the edges of both front tires, on the _____.
    a. Inside
    b. Outside

32. A vehicle will pull toward the side with the _____.
    a. Most caster
    b. Least caster

33. If the turning radius (TOOT) is out of specification, what should be replaced?
    a. The outer tie rod ends
    b. The inner tie rod ends
    c. The idler arm
    d. The steering knuckle

34. SAI and camber together form the _____.
    a. Included angle
    b. Turning radius angle
    c. Scrub radius angle
    d. Setback angle

35. The thrust angle is being corrected. The alignment technician should adjust which angle to reduce thrust angle?
    a. Rear camber
    b. Front SAI or included angle and camber
    c. Rear toe
    d. Rear caster

36. Strut rods adjust _____ if there is a nut on both sides of the frame bushings.
    a. Camber
    b. Caster
    c. SAI or included angle, depending on the exact vehicle
    d. Toe

Questions 37 through 40 will use the following specifications:

    front camber 0.5° ± 0.3°
    front caster 3.5° to 4.5°
    toe 0° ± 0.1°
    rear camber 0° ± 0.5°
    rear toe −0.1° to 0.1°
    alignment angles

    front camber left 0.5°
    front camber right −0.1°
    front caster left 3.8°
    front caster right 4.5°
    front toe left −0.2°
    front toe right +0.2°
    total toe 0.0°
    rear camber left 0.15°
    rear camber right −0.11°
    rear toe left 0.04°
    rear toe right 0.14°

37. The first angle corrected should be _____.
    a. Right front camber
    b. Right rear camber
    c. Right rear toe
    d. Left front camber

38. The present alignment will cause excessive tire wear to the inside of both front tires.
    a. True
    b. False

39. The present alignment will cause excessive tire wear to the rear tires.
    a. True
    b. False

40. With the present alignment, the vehicle will _____.
    a. Pull toward the right
    b. Go straight
    c. Pull toward the left

ANSWERS TO THE SAMPLE SUSPENSION AND STEERING (A4) ASE CERTIFICATION TEST

1. a	11. b	21. b	31. a
2. c	12. a	22. c	32. b
3. b	13. b	23. d	33. d
4. d	14. b	24. b	34. a
5. a	15. a	25. b	35. c
6. b	16. b	26. a	36. b
7. a	17. c	27. c	37. b
8. c	18. d	28. b	38. b
9. d	19. a	29. b	39. b
10. b	20. b	30. a	40. a

BRAKES (A5)

TASK	TEXTBOOK PAGE NO.
A. HYDRAULIC SYSTEM DIAGNOSIS AND REPAIR (14 QUESTIONS)	
1. Master Cylinder (non-ABS) (3 questions)	
1. Diagnose poor stopping or dragging caused by problems in the master cylinder; determine needed repairs.	81–90
2. Diagnose poor stopping, dragging, high or low pedal, or hard pedal caused by problems in the step bore master cylinder and internal valves (e.g., volume control devices, quick take-up valve, fast-fill valve, pressure regulating valve); determine needed repairs.	80–90
3. Measure and adjust master cylinder pushrod length.	300
4. Check master cylinder for defects by depressing brake pedal; determine needed repairs.	86–87
5. Diagnose the cause of master cylinder external fluid leakage.	89
6. Remove master cylinder from vehicle; install master cylinder; test operation of the hydraulic system.	89–92
7. Bench bleed (check for function and remove air) all non-ABS master cylinders.	92
2. Fluids, Lines, and Hoses (3 questions)	
1. Diagnose poor stopping, pulling, or dragging caused by problems in the brake fluid, lines, and hoses; determine needed repairs.	117–120
2. Inspect brake lines and fittings for leaks, dents, kinks, rust, cracks, or wear; tighten loose fittings and supports.	117–120
3. Inspect flexible brake hoses for leaks, kinks, cracks, bulging, or wear; tighten loose fittings and supports.	119–120
4. Fabricate and/or replace brake lines (double flare and ISO types), hoses, fittings, and supports.	114–118
5. Select, handle, store, and install proper brake fluids (including silicone fluids).	112
6. Inspect brake lines and hoses for proper routing.	117–119
3. Valves and Switches (non-ABS) (4 questions)	
1. Diagnose poor stopping, pulling, or dragging caused by problems in the hydraulic system valve(s); determine needed repairs.	98–104
2. Inspect, test, and replace metering, proportioning, pressure differential, and combination valves.	98–105
3. Inspect, test, replace, and adjust load or height sensing-type proportioning valve(s).	100–101
4. Inspect, test, and replace brake warning light, switch, and wiring.	105
4. Bleeding, Flushing, and Leak Testing (Non-ABS) (4 questions)	
1. Bleed (manual, pressure, vacuum, or surge method) and/or flush hydraulic system.	123–132
2. Pressure test brake hydraulic system.	101; 226

TASK	TEXTBOOK PAGE NO.
B. DRUM BRAKE DIAGNOSIS AND REPAIR (6 QUESTIONS)	
1. Diagnose poor stopping, pulling, or dragging caused by drum brake hydraulic problems; determine needed repairs.	181–183
2. Diagnose poor stopping, noise, pulling, grabbing, dragging, or pedal pulsation caused by drum brake mechanical problems; determine needed repairs.	176–181
3. Remove, clean, inspect, and measure brake drums; follow manufacturers' recommendations in determining need to machine or replace.	253–254
4. Machine drums according to manufacturers' procedures and specifications.	254–256; 271–276
5. Using proper safety procedures, remove, clean, and inspect brake shoes/linings, springs, pins, self-adjusters, levers, clips, brake backing (support) plates and other related brake hardware; determine needed repairs.	176–184
6. Lubricate brake shoe support pads on backing (support) plate, self-adjuster mechanisms, and other brake hardware.	179; 186
7. Install brake shoes and related hardware.	184–190
8. Pre-adjust brake shoes and parking brake before installing brake drums or drum/hub assemblies and wheel bearings.	184; 189
9. Reinstall wheel, torque lug nuts, and make final checks and adjustments.	229
C. DISC BRAKE DIAGNOSIS AND REPAIR (13 QUESTIONS)	
1. Diagnose poor stopping, pulling, or dragging caused by disc brake hydraulic problems; determine needed repairs.	214–218
2. Diagnose poor stopping, noise, pulling, grabbing, dragging, pedal pulsation, or pedal travel caused by disc brake mechanical problems; determine needed repairs.	218–222
3. Retract integral parking brake caliper piston(s) according to manufacturers' recommendations.	221
4. Remove caliper assembly from mountings; clean and inspect for leaks and damage to caliper housing.	217–220
5. Clean, inspect, and measure caliper mountings and slides for wear and damage.	220–221
6. Remove, clean, and inspect pads and retaining hardware; determine needed repairs, adjustments, and replacements.	212–214
7. Disassemble and clean caliper assembly; inspect parts for wear, rust, scoring, and damage; replace all seals, boots, and any damaged or worn parts.	214–217
8. Reassemble caliper.	217–220
9. Clean, inspect, and measure rotor with a dial indicator and a micrometer; follow manufacturers' recommendations in determining need to machine or replace.	259–263
10. Remove and replace rotor.	258–262
11. Machine rotor, using on-car or off-car method, according to manufacturers' procedures and specifications.	263–270; 277–289
12. Install pads, calipers, and related attaching hardware; bleed system.	227–229
13. Adjust calipers with integrated parking brakes according to manufacturers' recommendations.	240–244
14. Fill master cylinder to proper level with recommended fluid; inspect caliper for leaks.	97; 212–213
15. Reinstall wheel, torque lug nuts, and make final checks and adjustments.	229

TASK	TEXTBOOK PAGE NO.

D. POWER ASSIST UNITS DIAGNOSIS AND REPAIR (4 QUESTIONS)

1. Test pedal free travel with and without engine running to check power booster operation.	299–300
2. Check vacuum supply (manifold or auxiliary pump) to vacuum-type power booster.	295
3. Inspect the vacuum-type power booster unit for vacuum leaks and proper operation; inspect the check valve for proper operation; repair, adjust, or replace parts as necessary.	295–301
4. Inspect and test hydro-boost system and accumulator for leaks and proper operation; repair, adjust, or replace parts as necessary.	301–306

E. MISCELLANEOUS SYSTEMS (WHEEL BEARINGS, PARKING BRAKES, ELECTRICAL, ETC.) DIAGNOSIS AND REPAIR (7 QUESTIONS)

1. Diagnose wheel bearing noises, wheel shimmy and vibration problems; determine needed repairs.	140
2. Remove, clean, inspect, repack wheel bearings, or replace wheel bearings and races; replace seals; adjust wheel bearings according to manufacturers' specifications.	140–144
3. Check parking brake system; inspect cables and parts for wear, rusting, and corrosion; clean or replace parts as necessary; lubricate assembly.	236
4. Adjust parking brake assembly; check operation.	244–246
5. Test the service and parking brake indicator and warning light(s), switch(es), and wiring.	236
6. Test, adjust, repair or replace brake stop light switch, lamps, and related circuits.	105

F. ANTI-LOCK BRAKE SYSTEM (ABS) DIAGNOSIS AND REPAIR (11 QUESTIONS)

1. Follow accepted service and safety precautions when inspecting, testing, and servicing of ABS hydraulic, electrical, and mechanical components.	380
2. Diagnose poor stopping, wheel lock up, pedal feel and travel, pedal pulsation, and noise problems caused by the ABS; determined needed repairs.	381–387
3. Observe ABS warning light(s) at startup and during road test; determine if further diagnosis is needed.	379
4. Diagnose ABS electronic control(s), components, and circuits using self diagnosis and/or recommended test equipment; determine needed repairs.	381–387
5. Depressurize integral (high pressure) components of the ABS following manufacturers' recommended safety procedures.	391
6. Fill the ABS master cylinder with recommended fluid to proper level following manufacturers' procedures; inspect system for leaks.	391
7. Bleed the ABS hydraulic circuits following manufacturers' procedures.	391–392
8. Perform a fluid pressure (hydraulic boost) diagnosis on integral (high pressure) ABS; determine needed repairs.	391
9. Remove and install ABS components following manufacturers' procedures and specifications; observe proper placement of components and routing of wiring harness.	391
10. Diagnose, service, and adjust ABS speed sensors and circuits following manufacturers' recommended procedures (includes voltage output, resistance, shorts to voltage/ground, and frequency data).	388–390
11. Diagnose ABS braking problems caused by vehicle modifications (tire size, curb height, final drive ratio, etc.) and other vehicle mechanical and electrical/electronic modifications (communication, security, and radio, etc.).	390
12. Repair wiring harness and connectors following manufacturers' procedures.	390

AUTOMOTIVE SUSPENSION AND STEERING (A4)

ASE TASK LIST	TEXTBOOK PAGE NO.
A. STEERING SYSTEMS DIAGNOSIS AND REPAIR (10 QUESTIONS)	
1. Steering Columns (3 questions)	
1. Diagnose steering column noises and steering effort concerns (including manual and electronic tilt and telescoping mechanisms); determine needed repairs.	531–536
2. Inspect and replace steering column, steering shaft U-joint(s), flexible coupling(s), collapsible columns, steering wheels (includes steering wheels and columns equipped with airbags and/or other steering wheel/column mounted controls, sensors, and components).	530–532
3. Disarm, enable, and properly handle airbag system components during vehicle service following manufacturers' procedures.	530
2. STEERING UNITS (4 QUESTIONS)	
1. Diagnose steering gear (non-rack and pinion type) noises, binding, vibration, freeplay, steering effort, steering pull (lead) and leakage concerns; determine needed repairs.	537–539
2. Diagnose rack and pinion steering gear noises, binding, vibration, freeplay, steering effort, steering pull (lead), and leakage concerns; determine needed repairs.	543–545
3. Inspect power steering fluid level and condition; determine fluid type and adjust fluid level in accordance with vehicle manufacturers' recommendations.	593–594
4. Inspect, adjust, align, and replace power steering pump belts(s) and tensioners.	593
5. Diagnose power steering pump noises, vibration, and fluid leakage; determine needed repairs.	593
6. Remove and replace power steering pump; inspect pump mounting and attaching brackets; remove and replace power steering pump pulley.	594
7. Inspect and replace power steering pump seals, gaskets, reservoir, and valves.	598
8. Perform power steering system pressure and flow tests; determine needed repairs.	596–598
9. Inspect and replace power steering hoses, fittings, O-rings, coolers, and filters.	599
10. Remove and replace steering gear (non-rack and pinion type).	539
11. Remove and replace rack and pinion steering gear; inspect and replace mounting bushings and brackets.	543–545
12. Adjust steering gear (non-rack and pinion type) worm bearing preload and sector lash.	539–542
13. Inspect and replace steering gear (non-rack and pinion type) seals and gaskets.	539
14. Adjust rack and pinion steering gear.	546
15. Inspect and replace rack and pinion steering gear bellow/boots.	545
16. Flush, fill, and bleed power steering system.	596
17. Diagnose, inspect, repair, or replace components of variable-assist steering systems.	585

3. STEERING LINKAGE (3 QUESTIONS)

1. Inspect and adjust (where applicable) front and rear steering linkage geometry (including parallelism and vehicle ride height).	560
2. Inspect and replace pitman arm.	565
3. Inspect and replace center link (relay rod/drag link/intermediate rod).	561
4. Inspect, adjust (where applicable), and replace idler arm(s) and mountings.	562
5. Inspect, replace, and adjust tie rods, tie rod sleeves/adjusters, clamps, and tie rod ends (sockets/bushings).	562–564
6. Inspect and replace steering linkage damper(s).	551

B. SUSPENSION SYSTEMS DIAGNOSIS AND REPAIR (13 QUESTIONS)

1. Front Suspensions (6 questions)

1. Diagnose front suspension system noises, body sway/roll, and ride height concerns; determine needed repairs.	471
2. Inspect and replace upper and lower control arms, bushings, and shafts.	490
3. Inspect and replace rebound and jounce bumpers.	487
4. Inspect, adjust, and replace strut rods/radius arms (compression/tension), and bushings.	486
5. Inspect and replace upper and lower ball joints (with or without wear indicators).	474–479
6. Inspect non-independent front axle assembly for bending, warpage, and misalignment.	486
7. Inspect and replace front steering knuckle/spindle assemblies and steering arms.	488
8. Inspect and replace front suspension system coil springs and spring insulators (silencers).	486–488
9. Inspect and replace front suspension system leaf spring(s), leaf spring insulators (silencers), shackles, brackets, bushings, and mounts.	505
10. Inspect, replace, and adjust front suspension system torsion bars and mounts.	489
11. Inspect and replace front stabilizer bar (sway bar) bushings, brackets, and links.	485
12. Inspect and replace front strut cartridge or assembly.	482
13. Inspect and replace front strut bearing and mount.	484

2. REAR SUSPENSIONS (5 QUESTIONS)

1. Diagnose rear suspension system noises, body sway/roll, and ride height concerns; determine needed repairs.	504
2. Inspect and replace rear suspension system coil springs and spring insulators (silencers).	505
3. Inspect and replace rear suspension system lateral links/arms (track bars), control (trailing) arms, stabilizer bars (sway bars), bushings, and mounts.	504
4. Inspect and replace rear suspension system leaf spring(s), leaf spring insulators (silencers), shackles, brackets, bushings, and mounts.	506
5. Inspect and replace rear rebound and jounce bumpers.	505
6. Inspect and replace rear strut cartridge or assembly, and upper mount assembly.	482–484
7. Inspect non-independent rear axle assembly for bending, warpage, and misalignment.	504
8. Inspect and replace rear ball joints and tie rod/toe link assemblies.	506
9. Inspect and replace rear knuckle/spindle assembly.	506

C. RELATED SUSPENSION AND STEERING SERVICE (2 QUESTIONS)

1. Inspect and replace shock absorbers, mounts, and bushings.	481; 505
2. Diagnose and service front and/or rear wheel bearings.	139–143

3. Diagnose, inspect, adjust, repair, or replace components (including sensors, switches, and actuators) of electronically controlled suspension systems (including primary and supplemental air suspension and ride control systems). — 511–527

4. Inspect and repair front and/or rear cradle (crossmember/subframe) mountings, bushings, brackets, and bolts. — 471–472

5. Diagnose, inspect, adjust, repair, or replace components (including sensors, switches, and actuators) of electronically controlled steering systems; initialize system as required. — 588–591

6. Diagnose, inspect, repair, or replace components of power steering idle speed compensation systems. — 585

D. WHEEL ALIGNMENT DIAGNOSIS, ADJUSTMENT, AND REPAIR (12 QUESTIONS)

1. Diagnose vehicle wander, drift, pull, hard steering, bump steer (toe curve), memory steer, torque steer, and steering return concerns; determine needed repairs. — 659–662

2. Measure vehicle ride height; determine needed repairs. — 658–659

3. Measure front and rear wheel camber; determine needed repairs. — 665

4. Adjust front and/or rear wheel camber on suspension systems with a camber adjustment. — 677

5. Measure caster; determine needed repairs. — 677–678

6. Adjust caster on suspension systems with a caster adjustment. — 678–679

7. Measure and adjust front wheel toe. — 680

8. Center steering wheel. — 682

9. Measure toe-out-on-turns (turning radius/angle); determine needed repairs. — 665

10. Measure SAI/KPI (steering axis inclination/king pin inclination); determine needed repairs. — 667

11. Measure included angle; determine needed repairs. — 665

12. Measure rear wheel toe; determine needed repairs or adjustments. — 682

13. Measure thrust angle; determine needed repairs or adjustments. — 683

14. Measure front wheelbase setback/offset; determine needed repairs or adjustments. — 667

15. Check front and/or rear cradle (crossmember/subframe) alignment; determine needed repairs or adjustments. — 687

E. WHEEL AND TIRE DIAGNOSIS AND SERVICE (5 QUESTIONS)

1. Diagnose tire wear patterns; determine needed repairs. — 418

2. Inspect tire condition, size, and application (load and speed ratings). — 376–377

3. Measure and adjust tire air pressure. — 411

4. Diagnose wheel/tire vibration, shimmy, and noise concerns; determine needed repairs. — 418–422

5. Rotate tires/wheels and torque fasteners according to manufacturers' recommendations. — 416–417

6. Measure wheel, tire, axle flange, and hub runout (radial and lateral); determine needed repairs. — 418–420

7. Diagnose tire pull (lead) problems; determine corrective actions. — 659

8. Dismount and mount tire on wheel. — 413–414

9. Balance wheel and tire assembly. — 421

10. Test and diagnose tire pressure monitoring system; determine needed repairs. — 399–404

Brakes

For every task in Brakes, the following safety requirement must be strictly enforced:

Comply with personal and environmental safety practices associated with clothing; eye protection; hand tools; power equipment; proper ventilation; and the handling, storage, and disposal of chemicals/materials in accordance with local, state, and federal safety and environmental regulations.

TASK	TEXTBOOK PAGE NO.	WORKTEXT PAGE NO.
A. GENERAL BRAKE SYSTEMS DIAGNOSIS		
1. Complete work order to include customer information, vehicle identifying information, customer concern, related service history, cause, and correction. (P-1)	5	4
2. Identify and interpret brake system concern; determine necessary action. (P-1)	57–61	9
3. Research applicable vehicle and service information, such as brake system operation, vehicle service history, service precautions, and technical service bulletins. (P-1)	4	5, 6
4. Locate and interpret vehicle and major component identification numbers. (P-1)	3	7
B. HYDRAULIC SYSTEM DIAGNOSIS AND REPAIR		
1. Diagnose pressure concerns in the brake system using hydraulic principles (Pascal's Law). (P-1)	81–90	13
2. Measure brake pedal height, travel, and free play (as applicable); determine necessary action. (P-1)	89	14
3. Check master cylinder for internal/external leaks and proper operation; determine necessary action. (P-1)	89	15
4. Remove, bench bleed, and reinstall master cylinder. (P-1)	92	15
5. Diagnose poor stopping, pulling, or dragging concerns caused by malfunctions in the hydraulic system; determine necessary action. (P-2)	80–90	16
6. Inspect brake lines, flexible hoses, and fittings for leaks, dents, kinks, rust, cracks, bulging, or wear; tighten loose fittings and supports; determine necessary action. (P-1)	117–120	23
7. Replace brake lines, hoses, fittings, and supports. (P-2)	114–118	23
8. Fabricate brake lines using proper material and flaring procedures (double flare and ISO types). (P-2)	114–118	23
9. Select, handle, store, and fill brake fluids to proper level. (P-1)	112	24
10. Inspect, test, and/or replace metering (hold-off), proportioning (balance), pressure differential, and combination valves. (P-3)	98–105	17, 18, 19, 20
11. Inspect, test, and/or replace components of brake warning light system. (P-3)	105	21

TASK	TEXTBOOK PAGE NO.	WORKTEXT PAGE NO.
12. Bleed and/or flush brake system. (P-1)	123–132	25
13. Test brake fluid for contamination. (P-1)	110–111	24

C. DRUM BRAKE DIAGNOSIS AND REPAIR

TASK	TEXTBOOK PAGE NO.	WORKTEXT PAGE NO.
1. Diagnose poor stopping, noise, vibration, pulling, grabbing, dragging, or pedal pulsation concerns; determine necessary action. (P-1)	181–183	32
2. Remove, clean, inspect, and measure brake drums; determine necessary action. (P-1)	253–254	43
3. Refinish brake drum; measure final drum diameter. (P-1)	254–256; 271–276	43
4. Remove, clean, and inspect brake shoes, springs, pins, clips, levers, adjusters/self-adjusters, other related brake hardware, and backing support plates; lubricate and reassemble. (P-1)	176–184	33
5. Inspect and install wheel cylinders. (P-2)	181–183	33
6. Pre-adjust brake shoes and parking brake; install brake drums or drum/hub assemblies and wheel bearings. (P-2)	184; 189	33
7. Install wheel, torque lug nuts, and make final checks and adjustments. (P-1)	229	34

D. DISC BRAKE DIAGNOSIS AND REPAIR

TASK	TEXTBOOK PAGE NO.	WORKTEXT PAGE NO.
1. Diagnose poor stopping, noise, vibration, pulling, grabbing, dragging, or pulsation concerns; determine necessary action. (P-1)	214–218	36
2. Remove caliper assembly; inspect for leaks and damage to caliper housing; determine necessary action. (P-1)	217–220	36
3. Clean and inspect caliper mounting and slides/pins for operation, wear, and damage; determine necessary action. (P-1)	220–221	36
4. Remove, inspect, and replace pads and retaining hardware; determine necessary action. (P-1)	212–214	36
5. Disassemble and clean caliper assembly; inspect parts for wear, rust, scoring, and damage; replace seal, boot, and damaged or worn parts. (P-3)	214–217	36
6. Reassemble, lubricate, and reinstall caliper, pads, and related hardware; seat pads, and inspect for leaks. (P-1)	217–220	36
7. Clean, inspect, and measure rotor thickness, lateral runout, and thickness variation; determine necessary action. (P-1)	259–263	44
8. Remove and reinstall rotor. (P-1)	258–262	44
9. Refinish rotor on vehicle; measure final rotor thickness. (P-11)	269; 285–289	44
10. Refinish rotor off vehicle; measure final rotor thickness. (P-1)	263–270; 277–285	44
11. Retract caliper piston on an integrated parking brake system. (P-1)	221	39
12. Install wheel, torque lug nuts, and make final checks and adjustments. (P-1)	229	37
13. Check brake pad wear indicator system operation; determine necessary action. (P-2)	212	38

E. POWER ASSIST UNITS DIAGNOSIS AND REPAIR

TASK	TEXTBOOK PAGE NO.	WORKTEXT PAGE NO.
1. Test pedal free travel; check power assist operation. (P-2)	299–300	45
2. Check vacuum supply to vacuum-type power booster. (P-1)	295	46
3. Inspect the vacuum-type power booster unit for leaks; inspect the check valve for proper operation; determine necessary action. (P-1)	295–301	47

TASK	TEXTBOOK PAGE NO.	WORKTEXT PAGE NO.
4. Inspect and test hydraulically assisted power brake system for leaks and proper operation; determine necessary action. (P-3)	301–306	48
5. Measure and adjust master cylinder pushrod length. (P-3)	300	49

F. MISCELLANEOUS (WHEEL BEARINGS, PARKING BRAKES, ELECTRICAL, ETC.) DIAGNOSIS AND REPAIR

TASK	TEXTBOOK PAGE NO.	WORKTEXT PAGE NO.
1. Diagnose wheel bearing noises, wheel shimmy, and vibration concerns; determine necessary action. (P-1)	140	26
2. Remove, clean, inspect, repack, and install wheel bearings and replace seals; install hub and adjust bearings. (P-1)	140–144	27
3. Check parking brake cables and components for wear, binding, and corrosion; clean, lubricate, adjust, or replace as needed. (P-2)	236	40
4. Check parking brake and indicator light system operation; determine necessary action. (P-1)	236	41
5. Check operation of brake stop light system; determine necessary action. (P-1)	105	22; 42
6. Replace wheel bearing and race. (P-2)	140–144	28
7. Inspect and replace wheel studs. (P-1)	270	29
8. Remove and reinstall sealed wheel bearing assembly. (P-1)	144–145	30

G. ELECTRONIC BRAKE, TRACTION AND STABILITY CONTROL SYSTEMS DIAGNOSIS AND REPAIR

TASK	TEXTBOOK PAGE NO.	WORKTEXT PAGE NO.
1. Identify and inspect electronic brake control system components; determine necessary action. (P-1)	379	52
2. Diagnose poor stopping, wheel lock-up, abnormal pedal feel, unwanted application, and noise concerns associated with the electronic brake control system; determine necessary action. (P-2)	379–381	53
3. Diagnose electronic brake control system electronic control(s) and components by retrieving diagnostic trouble codes, and/or using recommended test equipment; determine necessary action. (P-1)	382–388	53
4. Depressurize high-pressure components of the electronic brake control system. (P-3)	391	54
5. Bleed the electronic brake control system hydraulic circuits. (P-1)	391	55
6. Remove and install electronic brake control system electrical/electronic and hydraulic components. (P-3)	391–393	56
7. Test, diagnose, and service electronic brake control system speed sensors (digital and analog), toothed ring (tone wheel), and circuits using a graphing multimeter (GMM)/digital storage oscilloscope (DSO) (includes output signal, resistance, shorts to voltage/ground, and frequency data). (P-1)	388–390	57
8. Diagnose electronic brake control system braking concerns caused by vehicle modifications (tire size, curb height, final drive ratio, etc.). (P-3)	390	58
9. Identify traction control/vehicle stability control system components. (P-3)	398–402	51
10. Describe the operation of a regenerative braking system. (P-3)	315–318	50

NATEF CORRELATION CHART

Suspension and Steering (A4)

For every task in Suspension and Steering, the following safety requirement must be strictly enforced: Comply with personal and environmental safety practices associated with clothing; eye protection; hand tools; power equipment; proper ventilation; and the handling, storage, and disposal of chemicals/materials in accordance with local, state, and federal safety and environmental regulations.

TASK	TEXTBOOK PAGE NO.	WORKTEXT PAGE NO.
A. GENERAL SUSPENSION AND STEERING SYSTEMS DIAGNOSIS		
1. Complete work order to include customer information, vehicle identifying information, customer concern, related service history, cause, and correction. (P-1)	5	4
2. Identify and interpret suspension and steering concern; determine necessary action. (P-1)	471; 537; 659	84
3. Research applicable vehicle and service information, such as suspension and steering system operation, vehicle service history, service precautions, and technical service bulletins. (P-1)	4	5; 6
4. Locate and interpret vehicle and major component identification numbers. (P-1)	3	7
B. STEERING SYSTEMS DIAGNOSIS AND REPAIR		
1. Disable and enable supplemental restraint system (SRS). (P-1)	530	80
2. Remove and replace steering wheel; center/time supplemental restraint system (SRS) coil (clock spring). (P-1)	530	80
3. Diagnose steering column noises, looseness, and binding concerns (including tilt mechanisms); determine necessary action. (P-2)	530–532	81
4. Diagnose power steering gear (non-rack and pinion) binding, uneven turning effort, looseness, hard steering, and noise concerns; determine necessary action. (P-2)	537–539	88
5. Diagnose power steering gear (rack and pinion) binding, uneven turning effort, looseness, hard steering, noise concerns; determine necessary action. (P-2)	543–545	88
6. Inspect steering shaft universal-joint(s), flexible coupling(s), collapsible column, lock cylinder mechanism, and steering wheel; perform necessary action. (P-2)	531–533	81
7. Adjust non-rack and pinion worm bearing preload and sector lash. (P-3)	539–542	82
8. Remove and replace rack and pinion steering gear; inspect mounting bushings and brackets. (P-2)	546	82
9. Inspect and replace rack and pinion steering gear inner tie rod ends (sockets) and bellows boots. (P-2)	545	85
10. Determine proper power steering fluid type; inspect fluid level and condition. (P-1)	596	89
11. Flush, fill, and bleed power steering system. (P-2)	596	89

TASK	TEXTBOOK PAGE NO.	WORKTEXT PAGE NO.
12. Diagnose power steering fluid leakage; determine necessary action. (P-2)	598	90
13. Remove, inspect, replace, and adjust power steering pump belt. (P-1)	593	91
14. Remove and reinstall power steering pump. (P-2)	593	91
15. Remove and reinstall press fit power steering pump pulley; check pulley and belt alignment. (P-2)	594	91
16. Inspect and replace power steering hoses and fittings. (P-2)	599	92
17. Inspect and replace pitman arm, relay (centerlink/intermediate) rod, idler arm and mountings, and steering linkage damper. (P-2)	560–565	86
18. Inspect, replace, and adjust tie rod ends (sockets), tie rod sleeves, and clamps. (P-1)	562–564	87
19. Test and diagnose components of electronically controlled steering systems using a scan tool; determine necessary action. (P-3)	585–588	88
20. Inspect and test electric-power assist steering. (P-3)	588–591	94
21. Identify hybrid vehicle power steering system electrical circuits, service, and safety precautions. (P-3)	591–593	95

C. SUSPENSION SYSTEMS DIAGNOSIS AND REPAIR

TASK	TEXTBOOK PAGE NO.	WORKTEXT PAGE NO.
1. Diagnose short and long arm suspension system noises, body sway, and uneven riding height concerns; determine necessary action. (P-1)	467–469	71
2. Diagnose strut suspension system noises, body sway, and uneven ride height concerns; determine necessary action. (P-1)	469–471	71
3. Remove, inspect, and install upper and lower control arms, bushings, shafts, and rebound bumpers. (P-2)	490	72
4. Remove, inspect, and install strut rods and bushings. (P-2)	486	73
5. Remove, inspect, and install upper and/or lower ball joints. (P-1)	474–479	72
6. Remove, inspect, and install steering knuckle assemblies. (P-2)	488	72
7. Remove, inspect, and install short and long arm suspension system coil springs and spring insulators. (P-3)	486–488	72
8. Remove, inspect, install, and adjust suspension system torsion bars; inspect mounts. (P-3)	489	74
9. Remove, inspect, and install stabilizer bar bushings, brackets, and links. (P-2)	485	73
10. Remove, inspect, and install strut cartridge or assembly, strut coil spring, insulators (silencers), and upper strut bearing mount. (P-1)	482	75; 78
11. Remove, inspect, and install leaf springs, leaf spring insulators (silencers), shackles, brackets, bushings, and mounts. (P-3)	506	77

D. RELATED SUSPENSION AND STEERING SERVICE

TASK	TEXTBOOK PAGE NO.	WORKTEXT PAGE NO.
1. Inspect, remove, and replace shock absorbers. (P-1)	481; 505	76; 78
2. Remove, inspect, and service or replace front and rear wheel bearings. (P-1)	139–143	26–30
3. Test and diagnose components of electronically controlled suspension systems using a scan tool; determine necessary action. (P-3)	511–527	79
4. Diagnose, inspect, adjust, repair, or replace components of electronically controlled steering systems (including sensors, switches, and actuators); initialize system as required. (P-3)	585	93
5. Describe the function of the idle speed compensation switch. (P-3)	585	93
6. Lubricate suspension and steering systems. (P-2)	558	83

TASK	TEXTBOOK PAGE NO.	WORKTEXT PAGE NO.
E. WHEEL ALIGNMENT DIAGNOSIS, ADJUSTMENT, AND REPAIR		
1. Diagnose vehicle wander, drift, pull, hard steering, bump steer, memory steer, torque steer, and steering return concerns; determine necessary action. (P-1)	659–662	98
2. Perform prealignment inspection and measure vehicle ride height; perform necessary action. (P-1)	658–659	100
3. Prepare vehicle for wheel alignment on the alignment machine; perform four-wheel alignment by checking and adjusting front and rear wheel caster, camber; and toe as required; center steering wheel. (P-1)	665	101; 102
4. Check toe-out-on-turns (turning radius); determine necessary action. (P-2)	665	103
5. Check SAI (steering axis inclination) and included angle; determine necessary action. (P-2)	667	103
6. Check rear wheel thrust angle; determine necessary action. (P-1)	682–683	104
7. Check for front wheel setback; determine necessary action. (P-2)	667	104
8. Check front and/or rear cradle (subframe) alignment; determine necessary action. (P-3)	687	104
F. WHEEL AND TIRE DIAGNOSIS AND REPAIR		
1. Inspect tire condition; identify tire wear patterns; check and adjust air pressure; determine necessary action. (P-1)	418	62
2. Diagnose wheel/tire vibration, shimmy, and noise; determine necessary action. (P-2)	418–422	63
3. Rotate tires according to manufacturer's recommendations. (P-1)	411	64
4. Measure wheel, tire, axle flange, and hub runout; determine necessary action. (P-2)	418–420	65
5. Diagnose tire pull (lead) problems; determine necessary action. (P-2)	659	63
6. Dismount, inspect, and remount tire on wheel; balance wheel and tire assembly (static and dynamic). (P-1)	421	67
7. Dismount, inspect, and remount tire on wheel equipped with tire pressure monitoring system sensor. (P-2)	413–414	67
8. Reinstall wheel; torque lug nuts. (P-1)	415	66
9. Inspect tire and wheel assembly for air loss; perform necessary action. (P-1)	411	62
10. Repair tire using internal patch. (P-1)	425–426	68
11. Inspect, diagnose, and calibrate tire pressure monitoring system. (P-2)	399–404	61

μ in. Microinches; a millionth of an inch.

Above ground storage tank (ABST) A storage tank that stores used oil and is located above ground.

Active mode The mode where a tire pressure sensor is transmitting tire inflation pressure information after the vehicle reaches 20 MPH or faster and at a rate of once every minute.

ABS See *Antilock braking system*.

Acceleration slip regulation (ASR) A name for a traction control system used on some General Motors vehicles.

Accumulator A temporary location for fluid under pressure.

Active sensor A type of wheel speed sensor that produces a digital output signal.

Actuator A mechanical device that operates something like a valve on a shock absorber.

Adjustable pedals Brake and accelerator pedals are mounted on a moveable support that allows them to be moved by the driver.

Adjustable wrench A wrench that has a moveable jaw to allow it to fit many sizes of fasteners.

AGST Abbreviation for above ground storage tank.

Air gap The distance between the wheel speed sensor and the reluctor wheel.

Air spring A type of spring that uses air pressure inside a rubber bag to support the weight of a vehicle.

Air suspension A type of suspension that uses air springs instead of metal or fiberglass springs.

Alert mode An operating mode of a tire pressure sensor that causes the dash warning lamp to flash in the event of a rapid decrease in tire inflation pressure.

Align To bring the parts of a unit into the correct position with respect to each other.

Amber ABS warning lamp The dash warning lamp that lights (amber color) if a fault in the antilock braking system (ABS) is detected.

Antifriction bearings Bearings that use steel balls or rollers to reduce friction.

Antilock braking system (ABS) A system that is capable of pulsing the wheel brakes if lockup is detected to help the driver maintain control of the vehicle.

Antiseize compound A type of lubricant that includes small glass beads which reduces friction between the two surfaces.

Asbestosis A health condition where asbestos causes scar tissue to form in the lungs causing shortness of breath.

ASR See *Acceleration slip regulation*.

Atmospheric pressure Pressure exerted by the atmosphere on all things. (14.7 pounds per square inch at sea level)

Axial load A force in line (same axis) as the centerline of the bearing or shaft.

Ball bearings An antifriction bearing that uses steel balls between the inner and outer race to reduce friction.

BCI (Battery Council International) A trade organization of battery manufacturers.

Bench grinder A type of electric motor driven grinder that mounts to a bench.

BOB Abbreviation for break out box.

Bolts Threaded fasteners that are threaded into a casting or use a nut to hold two parts together.

Breaker bar (flex handle) A long-handled socket drive tool.

Breakout box (BOB) A piece of test equipment that installs between an electrical/electronic component, such as a controller, and the wiring harness.

Brinelling A type of wheel bearing failure where dents are created in the races due to shock loading.

BTU (British Thermal Unit) A unit of heat measurement.

Bump cap A hat that is plastic and hard to protect the head from bumps.

CAA (Clean Air Act) A federal law passed in 1970 and updated in 1990.

CAB See *Controller antilock brake*.

Cage The support for rollers or ball bearings.

Calibration codes Codes used on many powertrain control modules.

Campaign A recall where vehicle owners are contacted to return a vehicle to a dealer for corrective action.

Cap screw A type of threaded fastener that is threaded into a casting. Often called *bolts*.

Casting number An identification code cast into an engine block or other large cast part of a vehicle.

Castle nut A nut with notches cut out around the top to allow the installation of a cotter key to keep the nut from loosening.

CFR (Code of Federal Regulations) A compilation of the general and permanent rules published in the federal register by the executive departments and agencies of the federal government.

Cheater bar A bar used on a wrench to increase the amount of torque that can be applied to a fastener. Not recommended.

Chisels A type of hand tool used with a hammer to cut or mark metal and other materials.

C-lock axle A type of rear differential that uses a C-lock to retain the axles.

Close end An end of a wrench that grips all sides of the fastener.

Cold placard inflation pressure The specified tire inflation pressure as found on a placard on the driver's side door or door post. The pressure is specified for a cold tire meaning that the vehicle has not been driven for a while to allow the tires to cool.

Combination wrench A type of wrench that has an open end at one end and a closed end at the other end of the wrench.

Cone The inner race of a wheel bearing. Also a tapered metal cone with a hole in the center used to center a hubless brake drum or rotor on a brake lathe.

Control module An electronic device used to control the operation of actuators.

Controller antilock brake (CAB) The term used by Chrysler for their ABS.

Crest The outside diameter of a bolt measured across the threads.

Cup Rubber seals that have a lip that forces outward when pressure is applied.

Delta pressure method A procedure to reset or relearn tire pressure monitoring systems (TPMS) by changing the air pressure in the tire until the controller senses the change.

Department of Transportation (DOT) United States Federal agency that regulates transportation-related products such as tires.

Drive size The size in fractions of an inch of the square drive for sockets.

Dynamic seals Seals used between two surfaces where there is movement.

EBCM (electronic brake control module) The name Cadillac uses to describe the control module used on the Bosch 3 ABS unit.

EBTCM (electronic brake traction control module) The term used to describe the valve body and control module of a Bosch 5 ABS unit.

EHCU (electrohydraulic control unit) General Motors ABS control module for four-wheel antilock braking systems.

Energy A term used to describe the capacity for performing work.

EPA (Environmental Protection Agency) A federal agency created by the Clean Air Act of 1970.

ESC An abbreviation for electronic stability control system.

Extension A socket wrench tool used between a ratchet or breaker bar and a socket.

Eye wash station A water fountain designed to rinse the eyes with a large volume of water.

Files A type of hand tool used to smooth metal and other materials.

Fire extinguisher classes The classification of fire extinguishers by the type of fires they are designed to handle.

Flare nut wrench A type of wrench used to remove brake lines. Also called *line wrench*, *fitting wrench*, and *tube-nut wrench*.

Flex handle A long-handled socket drive tool, also called a breaker bar.

FMVSS Federal Motor Vehicle Safety Standard.

Force Energy applied to an object.

Fractional Wrench sizes that use Tractions of an inch instead of millimeters.

Friction The resistance between two objects in contact with each other.

G force The force of gravity.

Garter spring A spring used around the lip of a seal.

GAWR Abbreviation for gross axle weight rating.

GC-LB A grease rating for GC is the highest rating for wheel bearing grease and LB is the highest rating for chassis grease. A GC-LB grease, therefore, can be used.

Grade The strength rating of a bolt.

Grease Oil with thickener.

Grease seal A rubber seal with a steel backing used to keep grease in a bearing assembly from leaking.

GVWR Abbreviation for gross vehicle weight rating.

Hacksaws A type of hand tool that is used to cut metal and other materials.

Hammers A type of hand tool used to force objects into position using a swinging motion.

Hand-wheel position sensor A sensor that detects the position as well as the direction and speed that the driver is rotating the steering wheel. Used as an input to the electronic suspension and electronic stability control system.

Hazardous waste material Chemicals or components that pose a danger to the environment or to people.

HEPA Abbreviation for High Efficiency Particulate Air filter.

HEPA vacuum High efficiency particulate air filter (HEPA) vacuum used to clean brake dust.

HEV Abbreviation for hybrid electric vehicles

In. Hg Abbreviation for inches of mercury—a unit of measure for vacuum.

Inches of Mercury A measurement of vacuum; pressure below atmospheric pressure.

Initialization A procedure that resets or relearns where each tire sensor is located after a tire rotation.

ISO Abbreviation for International Standard Organization.

Lateral acceleration sensor A type of sensor used to detect cornering forces and used as an input from electronic stability control systems.

LED Abbreviation for light emitting diode. A type of light used in trouble lights and in vehicle lighting systems.

Lithium-based grease A type of grease that uses lithium to thicken an oil to turn it into a grease.

LRR Abbreviation for low rolling resistance tires.

μ The Greek letter that represents the coefficient of friction.

Mass The weight of an object.

Mercury A heavy metal that is liquid at room temperature and is hazardous to health.

Mesothelioma A fatal type of cancer of the lining of the chest or abdominal cavity, which can be caused by asbestos inhalation.

Metric bolts Bolts manufactured and sized in the metric system of measurement.

Microinches (M in.) One-millionth of an inch; a unit of measure of surface finish. The lower the number, the smoother the surface.

Mm Hg Abbreviation for millimeters of mercury which is a metric measure of vacuum.

MSDS (Material Safety Data Sheets) A listing of all materials used in a building with a description and the hazards associated with it.

Needle rollers A type of bearing that use small rollers called needle rollers to reduce friction.

NLGI Abbreviation for National Lubricating Grease Institute.

Nuts The female part of a threaded fastener.

Open end The end of a wrench that is open to allow the wrench to be inserted onto a fastener from the side.

OSHA (Occupational Safety and Health Administration) An organization formed in 1970 to assist and encourage safe working conditions.

Oversteer A condition while cornering where the rear of the vehicle breaks traction before the front resulting in a spin out-of-control condition.

Pascal's law A law of hydraulics named for the person who developed it, Blaise Pascal (1632–1662).

Personal protective equipment (PPE) PPE are items worn or used by workers to protect them from hazards of the work place, including safety glasses, gloves, and eye protection.

Pinch weld seam   A strong section under a vehicle where two body panels are welded together.

Pitch   The number of threads per inch of a threaded fastener.

Platform   The basic structure of a vehicle, such as the axles, brakes and other structural parts.

Pliers   A type of hand tool that has two movable parts and are used to hold or rotate an object or fastener.

Positive slip   A condition where a driven tire loses traction during acceleration.

PPE   See *Personal protective equipment*.

Prevailing torque nut   A type of nut that holds torque; also called a lock nut.

PSCM   Abbreviation for Power steering control module.

Punches   A type of hand tool used with a hammer to drive pins or other similar uses.

PWM (pulse-width modulation)   PWM is the control of a solenoid or actuator using an electronic controller to pulse the unit on and off for various percentages of time which is used to control the output of a device.

Race   Inner and outer machined surface of a ball or roller bearing.

Radial load   The load applied to a bearing 90 degrees from the axis. The weight of the vehicle applies a radial load to the wheel bearing.

Ratchet   A hand tool used to drive a socket wrench that is capable of being changed to tighten or loosen a fastener.

RCRA   Resource Conservation and Recovery Act.

Recall   A notification to the owner of a vehicle that a safety issue needs to be corrected.

Relearn   A process where a tire pressure sensor is reset after a tire rotation.

Retainer plate-type rear axles   A type of rear axle that uses a retainer plate instead of C-clips to keep the axle retained to the axle housing.

Right-to-know laws   Laws that state that employees have a right to know when the materials they use at work are hazardous.

Roller bearings   Antifriction bearings that use hardened steel rollers between the inner and outer races.

SAE   Society of Automotive Engineers.

Screwdrivers   A type of hand tool designed to remove screws.

Shimmy   A type of tire vibration usually noticed as a rapid back and forth motion in the steering wheel. Usually caused by dynamic out-of-balance or a bent wheel.

Sine with dwell (SWD) test   A test used to determine if an aftermarket suspension-related part is able to still allow the electronic stability control system to control the vehicle.

Sleep mode   A mode of operation of a tire pressure monitoring sensor that occurs when the wheels are not rotating and is used to help extend battery life.

Snips   A type of hand tool used to cut sheet metal and other thin materials.

Socket   A type of tool that fits over the top and used to remove a threaded fastener.

Socket adapter   An adapter that allows the use of one size of driver (ratchet or breaker bar) to rotate another drive size of socket.

Solenoid valves   Valves that are opened and closed using an electromagnetic solenoid.

Solvent   Usually colorless liquids that are used to remove grease and oil.

Spalling   A type of bearing failure where metal from the surface flakes off due to metal fatigue.

Special service tools (SST)   Tools specified by the vehicle manufacturer to be used to remove/install or disassemble/assemble vehicle components.

Spider   A part of a simple universal joint where the two Y-shaped yokes are connected.

Spontaneous combustion   Ignition of oily rags without the use of an ignition source.

SST   Abbreviation for special service tools.

Stabilitrack   A brand name of the General Motors Corporation electronic stability control (ESC) system.

Static balance   The balance of a tire with even distribution of weight about its axis.

Static seal   A seal used between two surfaces that are not moving.

Steering wheel position sensor   A sensor that detects the position as well as the direction and speed that the driver is rotating the steering wheel. Used as an input to the electronic suspension and electronic stability control system.

Storage mode   A mode where a tire pressure monitoring system pressure sensor is in prior to being installed in a wheel. It does not become active until installed and air is applied.

Stud   A short rod with threads on both ends.

Tapered roller bearings   A type of antifriction bearing that uses tapered rollers between the inner and outer races.

TC   Abbreviation for traction control.

Technical service bulletins (TSB)   A written notification published by a vehicle manufacturer regarding the diagnosis and correction of a problem affecting certain year or models of vehicles.

Telltale light   A dash warning light.

Tensile strength   The maximum stress used under tension (lengthwise force) without causing failure.

Tire pressure monitoring system (TPMS)   A system of sensors or calculations used to detect a tire that has low tire pressure.

Tire slip   The difference between the actual speed and the rate at which the tire tread moves across the road surface.

Tone ring   A notched wheel used as a reluctor for the wheel speed sensor.

Torque   A twisting force that may or may not result in motion.

Torque wrench   A wrench that registers the amount of applied torque.

TPMS   Tire pressure monitoring system.

Traction   The friction (traction) between tires and the pavement.

Traction control (TC)   The electromechanical parts used to control wheel slip during acceleration.

Tramp   An up and down vibration of a tire/wheel assembly usually due to out-of-round tire or out-of-balance condition.

Transmitter ID   The identification on a TPMS sensor.

TREAD ACT   The act that created the requirement that all vehicles built after September 2007 be equipped with a direct reading tire pressure monitoring system.

Trouble light   A light used to help a service technician see while performing service work on a vehicle.

Trunnions A simple universal joint can be made from two yokes connected by a crossmember called a cross. The four arms of the cross are called **trunnions.**

TSB See *Technical service bulletin*.

Twin I-Beam A type of front suspension used on some Ford pickup trucks and vans.

UGST Abbreviation for underground storage tank.

UNC (Unified National Coarse) A standard for coarse threads used on fractional sized fasteners.

Underground storage tank (UST) A tank that is located underground and used to store used oil.

Understeer A condition when cornering where the vehicle tends to keep going straight when the driver is turning the steering wheel.

UNF (Unified National Fine) A standard for fine threads used on fractional sized fasteners.

Unit-body A type of vehicle construction that uses the body itself to support the suspension and drive train components instead of using a separate body and frame.

Universal joint (U-joint) A joint in a steering or drive shaft that allows torque to be transmitted at an angle.

Unsprung weight Weight of a vehicle that is not supported by the suspension such as the wheels and tires.

Used oil Any petroleum-based or synthetic oil that has been used.

UTQGS The abbreviation for the Uniform Tire Quality and Grading System.

Variable ratio a steering gear that provides a variable ratio that changes depending on how far from straight ahead the steering wheel is rotated.

VECI (vehicle emission control information) This underhood label shows settings and emission hose routing information and other emission control information.

Vehicle Identification Number (VIN) A unique 17 character string of numbers and letters that identify most major systems of the vehicle, as well as the serial number.

Vehicle speed (VS) sensor A sensor that detects vehicle speed and is used for many functions including electronic suspension systems and electronic stability control systems.

VES Abbreviation for variable-effort steering

Vibration order A term used to define how often a vibration occurs.

VIN See *Vehicle identification number*.

VSES (Vehicle Stability Enhancement System) A General Motors term used to describe one type of electronic stability control system.

VSS (vehicle speed sensor) This sensor, usually located at the extension housing of the transmission/transaxle is used by the electronic control module for vehicle speed.

Wander A term used to describe when a vehicle has tendency to require constant steering corrections to maintain a straight heading.

Warning light A light on the instrument panel to alert the driver when one half of a split hydraulic system fails as determined by the pressure-differential switch.

Washers A hardware item usually a thin metal round piece of metal with a hole in the center used to spread the force of a threaded fastener or to prevent the fastener from loosening.

Watts link An element used in the rear suspension of some vehicles to keep the rear axle centered under the body.

Wear bars An area in the tread of a tire that is not molded as deeply as the rest and shows as a bald strip when the tire wears to the depth of the bars.

Wheel mounting torque The torque applied to the lug nuts to keep the wheels attached to the hubs.

Wheel rate The ratio between wheel travel and spring travel.

Wheel speed sensors (WSS) Sensors used to detect the speed of the wheels. Used by an electronic controller for antilock brakes and/or traction control.

WHMIS Workplace Hazardous Materials Information Systems.

Witness mark A mark showing where two objects have made contact.

Work The transfer of energy from one physical system to another. Actually moving an object is work.

Worm gear A type of gear used in a conventional steering gear assembly.

Wrench A hand tool used to grasp and rotate a threaded fastener.

Yaw rate sensor A sensor that detects when the center of a vehicle is rotating around a vertical axis. Used as an input sensor for the electronic stability control system.

Zerk fitting A name for a chassis grease fitting, also known as an alemite fitting (named for Oscar U. Zerk).

µ in.   Microinches; Una millonésima parte de una pulgada.

Above ground storage tank (ABST)   Un tanque de almacenamiento que almacena aceite usado y está localizado por encima de tierra.

Active Mode   El modo donde un sensor de presión de los neumáticos transmite información de presión de inflación de la llanta después del vehículo alcanza 20 MILLAS POR HORA o el ayunador y en una tasa de una vez cada minuto.

ABS   See Antilock *frenando sistema*.

Actuator   Un dispositivo mecánico que opera algo así como una válvula en un amortiguador.

Acceleration slip regulation (ASR)   Un nombre para un controlador de tracción usado en algunos vehículos Generales de Motores.

Accumulator   Una posición temporal para fluido a presión.

Active sensor   Un Tipo de sensor de velocidad de la rueda que produce una señal digital de salida.

Adjustable pedals   el Freno y los pedales aceleradores son en los que se encaramó en un soporte movible que los deja ser movidos por el conductor.

Adjustable wrench   Una torcedura que tiene una mandíbula movible para permitir que eso equipe muchos dimensiona de sujetadores.

AGST   la Abreviación para arriba tanque molido de almacenamiento.

Air gap   La distancia entre el sensor de velocidad de la rueda y el reluctor giran.

Air Spring   Un Tipo de primavera que los usos aireen presión dentro de un bolso cauchero para soportar el peso de un vehículo.

Air Suspension   Un Tipo de suspensión que los usos exteriorizan brota en lugar de las primaveras de metal o de fibra de vidrio.

Alert Mode   modo que opera **Mode-An** de un sensor de presión de los neumáticos que causa que la lámpara de advertencia de arranque brille intermitentemente en el caso de una disminución rápida en la presión de inflación de la llanta.

Align   Para meter las partes de una unidad en la posición correcta con relación a cada otro.

Amber ABS warning lamp   La lámpara de advertencia del guión que ilumina (el color ámbar) si una falla en el sistema de frenado del anticerrojo (el sistema de frenos ABS) es detectada.

Antifriction bearings   las Composturas que acostumbran acera las pelotas o los rodillos para reducir fricción.

Antilock braking system (ABS)   Un sistema que es capaz de pulsar la rueda frena si La prisión es detectada para ayudar al conductor mantiene control del vehículo.

Antiseize compound   Un Tipo de lubricante que incluye cuentas de cristal pequeñas que reduce fricción entre las dos superficies.

Asbestosis   Una condición de salud donde las causas de asbesto dejen una cicatriz en tejido fino para formar en los pulmones dando lugar a que La dificultad para respirar.

ASR   *la regulación de desliz de Aceleración* de la Sede.

Atmospheric pressure   la Presión ejercida por la atmósfera en todas las cosas. (14.7 libras por cuadrado avanzan lentamente a nivel del mar)

Axial load   Una fuerza en posición (el mismo eje) como la línea divisoria central de la carretera de la compostura o el eje.

Ball bearings   Una antifricción soportando eso acero de usos se apelotona como bola entre la carrera interior y exterior para reducir fricción.

BCI (Battery Council International)   Una organización de comercio de fabricantes de la batería.

Bench grinder   Un Tipo de trituradora conducida motora eléctrica que se acumula para un banco.

BOB   la Abreviación para la suspensión fuera de caja.

Bolts   los sujetadores Roscados que se ensartó en una fundición o uso una nuez para mantener unidas dos partes.

Breaker bar (flex handle)   Una herramienta de paseo en coche del conector bastante maniobrado.

Breakout box (BOB)   Un pedazo de equipo experimental que instala entre un componente / electrónico eléctrico, como un controlador, y el arnés del cableado.

Brinelling   Un Tipo de fracaso de compostura de la rueda donde las abolladuras son creadas en las carreras debido a la sacudida cargando.

BTU (British Thermal Unit)   Una medida de unidad de calor.

Bump cap   Un sombrero que es plástico y duro para proteger la cabeza de golpes.

CAA (Clean Air Act)   Una ley federal pasó en 1970 y actualizado en 1990.

CAB   *el freno del anticerrojo* de la Sede *Controller*.

Cage   El soporte para rodillos o cojinetes de bolas.

Calibration codes   Codes acostumbró en muchos módulos de control del powertrain.

Campaign   Una retentiva donde los dueños del vehículo son contactados para devolverle un vehículo a un distribuidor para la acción correctiva.

Cap screw   Un Tipo de sujetador roscado que se ensartó en una fundición. A menudo *los pernos* designados.

Casting number   Un código de la identificación emitido en un bloque del motor u otro molde grande divide de un vehículo.

Castle nut   Una nuez con muescas deja de alrededor de la parte superior para dejar la instalación de una llave de la chaveta prevenirle la nuez de aflojarse.

CFR (Code of Federal Regulations)   Una recopilación de las reglas de la permanente generales y publicadas en el registro federal por las agencias y departamentos ejecutivos del gobierno federal.

Cheater bar   Una barra usada en una llave mecánica para aumentar la cantidad de fuerza de torsión que puede ser aplicada a un sujetador. No recomendable.

Chisels   Un Tipo de herramienta de la mano usada con un martillo a cortar o marcar metal y otros materiales.

C-lock axle   Un Tipo de diferencial trasero que usa una C-Lock para retener los ejes.

Close end   Un fin de una llave mecánica que se agarra todos los lados del sujetador.

Cold placard inflation pressure   La presión especificada de inflación de la llanta tan encontrado en una pancarta en la puerta lateral del conductor o la puerta viaja de prisa. La presión es especificada para una llanta fría queriendo decir que el vehículo no ha sido conducido para mientras para dejar las llantas enfriarse.

Combination wrench   Un Tipo de llave mecánica que tiene un fin del claro en un extremo y un fin cerrado en el otro extremo de la llave mecánica.

Cone La carrera interior de una rueda aguantando. También un cono terminado en filo de metal con un hueco en medio usado para centrar unos hubless frenan el tambor o el rotor en un torno del freno.

Control module Un dispositivo electrónico acostumbró controlar la operación de accionadores.

Controller antilock brake (CAB) El término usado por Chrysler para su sistema de frenos ABS.

Crest El diámetro exterior de un perno medido a través de los hilos.

Cup los sellos de Caucho que tienen un labio que fuerzas hacia afuera cuando la presión es aplicada.

Delta pressure method Un método a poner a cero o reaprender presión de los neumáticos monitoreando sistemas (TPMS) por ahí cambiando la presión atmosférica en la llanta hasta el controlador siente el cambio.

Department of Transportation (DOT) la agencia de Estados Unidos Federal que regula productos relacionados en transporte como llantas.

Drive size El tamaño en fracciones de una pulgada del paseo en coche cuadrado para conectores.

Dynamic seals los Sellos usados entre dos superficies donde hay movimiento.

EBCM (electronic brake control module) El Cadillac de nombre acostumbra describir el módulo de control usó en el Bosch 3 unidad del sistema de frenos ABS.

EBTCM (electronic brake traction control module) El término acostumbró describir el cuerpo humano de la válvula y controlar módulo de un Bosch 5 unidad del sistema de frenos ABS.

EHCU (electrohydraulic control unit) el módulo General de control del sistema de frenos ABS de Motores para sistemas que frenan anticerrojo de cuatro ruedas.

Energy Un término acostumbró describir la aptitud para realizar trabajo.

EPA (Environmental Protection Agency) Una agencia federal creada por el Acto Limpio de Aire de 1970.

ESC una abreviación para controlador electrónico de estabilidad.

Extension Una herramienta de la llave de tubo usada entre un trinquete o el interruptor atranca y un conector.

Eye wash station Una fuente de agua diseñada para enjuagar los ojos con un volumen grande de agua.

Files Un Tipo de herramienta de la mano acostumbró alisar metal y otros materiales.

Fire extinguisher classes La clasificación de extintores de fuego por el tipo de fuegos que son Diseñado para manipular.

Flare nut wrench Un Tipo de llave mecánica acostumbró quitar líneas del freno. También *la llave mecánica* designada *de la línea*, *Equipando llave mecánica*, y *llave mecánica de la nuez de tubo*.

Flex handle Una herramienta de paseo en coche del conector bastante maniobrada, también designado una barra del interruptor.

FMVSS Federal Transporte por Vehículo Estándar de Seguridad del Vehículo.

Force la Energía se aplicó a un objeto.

Fractional Tuerza tamaños que usan tracciones de una pulgada en lugar de los milímetros.

Friction La resistencia entre dos objetos en el contacto con cada otro.

G force La fuerza de gravedad.

Garter spring Una primavera usada alrededor del labio de un sello.

GAWR la Abreviación para la valuación vulgar del peso del eje.

GC-LB Una valuación grasa para GC es la valuación de más alto para grasa de compostura de la rueda y LB lo es lo La valuación más alta para grasa del chasis. Una grasa GC-LB, por consiguiente, puede ser usada.

Grade La valuación de fuerza de un perno.

Grease el Aceite con espesante.

Grease seal Una foca cauchera con un apoyo de acero solió mantener grasa en una asamblea de compostura de filtrándose.

GVWR la Abreviación para la valuación vulgar del peso del vehículo.

Hacksaws Un Tipo de herramienta de la mano que se usa para cortar metal y otros materiales.

Hammers Un Tipo de herramienta de la mano usada para forzarle objeta en posición correcta usando un movimiento mecedor.

Hand-wheel position sensor Un sensor que detecta la posición así como también la dirección y la velocidad que el conductor alterna el timón. Usado como un aporte para la suspensión electrónica y la estabilidad electrónica controlen sistema.

Hazardous waste material los Productos Químicos o los componentes que implican un peligro para el ambiente o personas.

HEPA la Abreviación para filtro Alto Efficiency Particulate Air.

HEPA vacuum el vacío Alto del filtro de aire del particulate de eficiencia (HEPA) acostumbró por completo frenar polvo.

HEV la Abreviación para vehículos eléctricos híbridos.

In. Hg la Abreviación para las pulgadas de mercurio—una unidad de medida para vacío.

Inches of Mercury Una medida de vacío; Ejerza presión sobre debajo de la presión atmosférica.

Initialization Un método que vuelve a arrancar o reaprende dónde cada sensor de la llanta es halló aftete una rotación de la llanta.

LRR la Abreviación para la resistencia baja del rodamiento cansa.

ISO la Abreviación para la Organización Estándar Internacional.

Lateral acceleration sensor Un Tipo de sensor acostumbró detectar poner en una esquina a las Fuerzas Armadas y acostumbró como un aporte de controladores electrónicos de estabilidad.

LED la Abreviación para diodo ligero que emite. Un tipo de luz usada en luces de emergencia y en los sistemas del alumbrado del vehículo.

Lithium-based grease Un Tipo de grasa que usa litio para espesar un aceite para convertirlo en una grasa.

μ La carta del greco que representa el coeficiente de fricción.

Mass El peso de un objeto.

Mercury Un metal pesado que es temperatura líquida del cuarto de la t y es arriesgado para la salud.

Mesothelioma Un tipo fatal de cáncer del forro del pecho o la cavidad abdominal, que puede deberse a la inhalación de asbesto.

Metric bolts los Pernos manufacturados y dimensionado en el sistema métrico de medida.

Microinches (M in.) Una millonésima parte de una pulgada; Una unidad de medida de final de la superficie. Mientras inferior el número, más suave la superficie.

Mm Hg la Abreviación para los milímetros de mercurio que es una medida métrica de vacío.

MSDS (Material Safety Data Sheets) Un listado de todos los materiales usaron en un edificio con una descripción y que los peligros asociaron con eso.

Needle rollers Un Tipo de compostura que los rodillos de la parte pequeña de uso llamaron rodillos de la aguja a reducir fricción.

NLGI la Abreviación para Instituto Nacional de Grasa Lubricating.

Nuts La parte propia de las mujeres de un sujetador roscado.

Open end El cabo de una llave mecánica que está abierto para dejar la llave mecánica estar inserto encima de un sujetador de lado.

OSHA (Occupational Safety and Health Administration) Una organización establecida en 1970 a ayudar y caja fuerte que alentar trabaja condiciones.

Oversteer Una condición al poner en una esquina donde la parte posterior del vehículo quebranta tracción antes del frente dando como resultado un giro fuera de condición de control.

Pascal's law Una ley de hidráulica nombró para la persona que lo desarrolló a eso, Pascal Blaise (1632–1662).

Personal protective equipment (PPE) PPE son artículos usados o usados por trabajadores para protegerlos de peligros del lugar de trabajo, incluyendo vidrios de seguridad, los guantes, y atisbar protección.

Pinch weld seam Una sección fuerte bajo un vehículo donde dos paneles del cuerpo humano son soldados juntos.

Pitch El número de hilos por la pulgada de un sujetador roscado.

Pliers Un Tipo de herramienta de la mano que tiene dos partes móviles y se usa para sujetar o rotar un objeto o un sujetador.

Platform La estructura básica de un vehículo, como los ejes, los frenos y otras partes estructurales.

Positive slip Una condición donde una llanta conducida desate tracción durante la aceleración.

PPE Vea *equipo protector Personal.*

Prevailing torque nut Un Tipo de nuez que mantiene fuerza de torsión; También designado una nuez del cerrojo.

PSCM la Abreviación para el Poder timoneando módulo de control.

Punches Un Tipo de herramienta de la mano usada con un martillo para conducir alfileres u otros usos similares.

PWM (pulse-width modulation) PWM es el control de un solenoide o un accionador utilizando a un controlador electrónico para pulsar la unidad de vez en cuando para los porcentajes diversos de tiempo que se usa para controlar la salida de un dispositivo.

Race la superficie Interior y exterior y labrada a máquina de una pelota o el rodín.

Radial load La carga se aplicó a una compostura 90 grados del eje. El peso del vehículo le aplica una carga radial a la rueda enrumbando.

Ratchet Una herramienta de la mano acostumbró conducir una llave de tubo que es capaz de estar cambiada para apretarse o aflojar un sujetador.

RCRA Recurso Conservation y Recovery Actúan.

Recall Una notificación para el dueño de un vehículo que un asunto de seguridad necesita a corregirse.

Relearn Un proceso donde un sensor de presión de los neumáticos sea vuelto a arrancar después de una rotación de la llanta.

Retainer plate-type rear axles Un Tipo de eje trasero que usa un plato del retenedor en lugar de una C-Clip para mantener el eje retenido para la vivienda del eje.

Right-to-know laws las Leyes que manifiestan que los empleados tienen derecho a saber cuándo los materiales que acostumbran en el trabajo es arriesgado.

Roller bearings las composturas de la Antifricción que usan rodillos acerados endurecidos entre las carreras interiores y exteriores.

SAE la Sociedad de Ingenieros Automotores.

Screwdrivers Un Tipo de herramienta de la mano diseñada para cambiar de dirección atornilla.

Shimmy Un Tipo de vibración de la llanta usualmente advertida como un movimiento de vaivén rápido en la dirección La rueda. Usualmente causado por el balance apagado dinámico o una rueda de inclinación.

Sine with dwell (SWD) test Una prueba usado determinar si un aftermarket relacionado en suspensión parte puede todavía dejar el controlador electrónico de estabilidad controlar el vehículo.

Sleep mode Una modalidad de operación de un sensor de monitoreo de presión de la llanta que ocurre cuando las ruedas no giran y se usa para ayudar a prolongar vida de la batería.

Snips Un Tipo de herramienta de la mano acostumbró cortar metal en chapa y otros materiales delgados.

Socket Un Tipo de herramienta que calza sobre la parte superior y usado para quitar un sujetador roscado.

Socket adapter Un adaptador que permite el uso de un tamaño de conductor (el trinquete o el interruptor atranca) para Rote otro tamaño de paseo en coche de conector.

Solenoid valves Valves que es abierto y cerrado usando un solenoide electromagnético.

Solvent los líquidos Usualmente incoloros que se usan para quitar engrasan y aceitan.

Spalling Un Tipo de fracaso de compostura donde la forma de metal que la superficie se descasque debido a la fatiga de metal.

Special service tools (SST) las Herramientas especificaron por el fabricante del vehículo usarse para cambiar de dirección/instale o desensamble/ensamblan componentes del vehículo.

Spider Una Parte de un acoplamiento universal simple donde las dos yuntas conformadas a Y están conectadas.

Spontaneous combustion la Ignición de harapos aceitosos sin el uso de una fuente de ignición.

SST la Abreviación para herramientas de servicio discrecional.

Stabilitrack Un nombre de marca de la General Motors el sistema electrónico de control de estabilidad (ESC).

Static balance el balance de una llanta con aun distribución de peso acerca de su eje.

Static seal Un sello usado entre dos superficies que no se mueven.

Steering wheel position sensor Un sensor que detecta la posición así como también la dirección y la velocidad que el conductor alterna el timón. Usado como un aporte para la suspensión electrónica y la estabilidad electrónica controlen sistema.

Storage mode El modo de la A **de modo de almacenamiento** donde un sensor de presión de sistema de la llanta de presión monitor esté dentro antes de ser instalado en una rueda. No se activa hasta instalado y el aire es aplicado.

Stud Una barra pequeña con hilos en ambos fenece.

Tapered roller bearings Un Tipo de antifricción cargando eso usa rodillos terminados en filo entre las carreras interiores y exteriores.

Telltale light Una luz de advertencia del guión.

TC la Abreviación para el control de tracción.

Technical service bulletins (TSB) Una notificación escrita publicada por un fabricante del vehículo estimando el diagnóstico y la corrección de un problema haciendo mella cierto año o los modelos de vehículos.

Tensile strength   El máximo estrés usado bajo la tensión (la fuerza colocada a lo largo) sin causar fracaso.

Tire pressure monitoring system (TPMS)   Un sistema de sensores o los cálculos acostumbró detectar una llanta que tiene presión de los neumáticos baja.

Tire slip   La diferencia entre la velocidad real y la tasa en la cual la banda de rodamiento se mueve a través de la superficie de la carretera.

Tone ring   Una rueda mellada usada como un reluctor para el sensor de velocidad de la rueda.

Torque   Una fuerza serpenteante que puede o no puede resultar en marcha.

Torque wrench   Una llave mecánica que registra la cantidad de fuerza de torsión aplicada.

TPMS   Tire ejerza presión sobre sistema monitor.

Traction   La fricción (la tracción) de en medio se cansa y el pavimento.

Traction control (TC)   Las partes electromecánicas usadas para controlar rotan boleto durante la aceleración.

Tramp   Una vibración levantada y detenida de una asamblea de la llanta/rueda usualmente debido a fuera de llanta redonda o Fuera de condición de balance.

Transmitter ID   La identificación en un sensor TPMS.

TREAD ACT   El acto que creó el requisito que todos los vehículos construyó después de septiembre del 2007 sea equipado con un sistema directo de monitoreo de presión de los neumáticos de lectura.

Trouble light   Una luz acostumbró ayudar un técnico de servicio a ver mientras realizando trabajo de servicio en un vehículo.

Trunnions   Un acoplamiento universal simple puede hacerse de dos yuntas conectadas por un crossmember designado una cruz. Los cuatro brazos de la cruz son llamados **muñones.**

TSB   Vea *boletín Técnico de servicio.*

Twin I-Beam   Un tipo de suspensión delantera usada en algunas furgonetas y camionetas Ford.

UGST   la Abreviación para tanque subterráneo de almacenamiento.

UNC (Unified National Coarse)   Un estándar para hilos gruesos usados en sujetadores dimensionados fraccionados.

Underground storage tank (UST)   un tanque que está localizado clandestinamente y está acostumbrado a la tienda usó aceite.

Understeer   La condición de **Understeer-A** al poner en una esquina donde el vehículo tiene tendencia a continuar directamente cuando el conductor revuelve el timón.

UNF (Unified National Fine)   Un estándar para hilos finos usados en sujetadores dimensionados fraccionados.

Unit-body   un tipo de construcción del vehículo que usa el cuerpo humano mismo para soportar la suspensión y paseo en coche entrenan componentes en lugar de usar un marco y cuerpo humano separado.

Universal joint (U-joint)   Una juntura en una dirección o el árbol propulsor que deja a fuerza de torsión serle transmitidas en ángulo.

Unsprung weight   Peso de un vehículo que se soportó por la suspensión como las ruedas y las llantas.

Used oil   Cualquier aceite basado en petróleos o sintético que ha sido usado.

UTQGS   La abreviación de **UTQGS-THE** para la Calidad Uniforme de la Llanta y el Sistema de Graduación.

Variable ratio   un engranaje de la dirección que provee una proporción variable que cambia a merced de hasta dónde de directamente el timón es rotado.

VECI (vehicle emission control information)   Esta etiqueta de la poco capucha sale a la vista que trasfondos y la manguera de la emisión encaminando información y otra emisión controlan información.

Vehicle Identification Number (VIN)   Una la cadena de caracteres 17 única de números y las cartas que identifican la mayoría de sistemas principales del vehículo, así como también el número de serie.

Vehicle speed (VS) sensor   un sensor que detecta vehículo acelerar y sirve para sistemas de suspensión electrónicas de muchos funciones de inclusivo y electrónico estabilidad controlador.

VES   para dirección de esfuerzo variable.

Vibration order   El término de la A **de orden de vibración** acostumbró definir cada cuánto ocurre una vibración.

VIN   *el número de la identificación del Vehículo de la Sede.*

VSES (Vehicle Stability Enhancement System)   Un término General de Motores acostumbró describir un tipo de controlador electrónico de estabilidad.

VSS (vehicle speed sensor)   Este sensor, usualmente localizado en la vivienda de la extensión del transeje de transmisión es usado por el módulo electrónico de control para la velocidad del vehículo.

Wander   un término acostumbró describir cuándo tiene un vehículo tendencia para requerir que la constante timoneando correcciones mantenga un encabezamiento derecho.

Warning light   Una luz en el panel de instrumentos para alertar al conductor cuando la mitad de una hendidura El sistema hidráulico fracasa tan decidido por el interruptor diferencial en la presión.

Washers   Un artículo del hardware que usualmente un trozo de metal delgado de la ronda de metal con un hueco en medio usó para esparcir la fuerza de un sujetador roscado o para impedir el sujetador de dejar suelto.

Watts link   Un elemento usado en la suspensión trasera de algunos vehículos para mantener el eje trasero puesto en el centro bajo el cuerpo humano.

Wear bars   Un área en el paso de una llanta que no se moldea como profundamente como el resto y funciones como una tira calva cuando la llanta lleva puesta para la profundidad de las barras.

Wheel mounting torque   que La fuerza de torsión le aplicó a las tuercas de la rueda para mantener las ruedas le correspondieron a los centros.

Wheel rate   que La proporción entre el viaje de la rueda y la primavera viaje.

Wheel speed sensors (WSS)   Sensors solieron detectar la velocidad de las ruedas. Usado por un controlador electrónico para frenos del anticerrojo y / o el control de tracción.

WHMIS   los Sistemas de Información de Materiales del Lugar de Trabajo Hazardous.

Witness mark   La marca de la A **de marca del testigo** saliendo a la vista donde dos objetos han establecido contacto.

Work   El reembarque de energía de un sistema físico para otro. Realmente moviendo un objeto es trabajo.

Worm gear   El tipo de la A **de engranaje del gusano** de engranaje usado en una asamblea convencional del mecanismo de dirección.

Wrench   Una herramienta de la mano acostumbró agarre y rotáceo uno sujetador roscado.

Yaw rate sensor   Un sensor que detecta cuándo el centro de un vehículo gira alrededor de un eje vertical. Usado como un sensor de aporte para el controlador electrónico de estabilidad.

Zerk fitting   Un nombre para una grasa del chasis calzando, también conocido como un alemite calzando (denominado para Oscar U. Zerk).

Index